Elements of Econometrics

Jan Kmenta

PROFESSOR OF ECONOMICS AND STATISTICS
UNIVERSITY OF MICHIGAN

Elements of Econometrics

SECOND EDITION

Macmillan Publishing Company
NEW YORK
Collier Macmillan Publishers
LONDON

Printed in the United States of America

MACMILLAN PUBLISHING COMPANY
866 Third Avenue, New York, New York 10022

Collier Macmillan Canada, Inc.

Library of Congress Cataloging in Publication Data

Kmenta, Jan.
Elements of econometrics.

Includes index.
1. Econometrics. 2. Statistics. I. Title.
HB139.K56 1986 330'.028 86-2740
ISBN 0-02-365070-2

Printing: 8 Year: 0 1 2 3 4 5

ISBN 0-02-365070-2

Preface

Since the publication of the first edition of this book, the subject of econometrics has expanded considerably and has undergone some marked changes in emphasis. The expansion has involved development of new results in established areas as well as extension of the scope of the subject to new areas. Changes in emphasis have been stimulated by the appearance of new data sources, by the rapid development of computer technology, and by shifts of interest and methodological approaches. This edition represents an effort to incorporate all important new results in the established areas of econometrics, to present most of the new models and methods introduced since 1971, and to reflect the changes in emphasis that have taken place. In addition, rewriting the book has offered a welcome opportunity to simplify some expositions and, I hope, to make them clearer and more succinct.

The motto of my undergraduate alma mater, the University of Sydney in Australia, *sidere mens eadem mutato* ("the same spirit under a different sky"), has also applied in producing this edition. The basic philosophy of making everything as simple and clear as possible, which underlay the first edition, has been maintained. All methods are still explained and discussed within the simplest framework, and generalizations are presented as logical extensions of the simple cases. And while every attempt has been made to preserve a relatively high degree of rigor, every conflict between rigor and clarity of exposition has been resolved in favor of the latter. Finally, in every case the emphasis is on understanding rather than a cookbook type of learning. The consequence of all this is that the organization and style of the second edition are the same as those of the first edition, although much has been added.

The second edition differs from the first in two ways. First, simplifications of exposition and introduction of new topics have been incorporated in the existing sections of the first edition. The largest changes with respect to content concern heteroskedasticity and autocorrelated disturbances in Chapter 8, errors of measurement and grouped data in Chapter 9, multicollinearity and specification errors in Chapter 10, restricted coefficients, nonlinear models, and distributed lags in Chapter 11, pooling of cross-section and time-series data in Chapter 12, and special topics in Chapter 13. Second, new material has been introduced — or old material considerably expanded — by the inclusion of new sections. There is a new section on Bayes theorem in Chapter 3 and on Bayesian inference in Chapter 6 to acquaint the students with the basic ideas of the Bayesian approach to inference. Chapter 8 has a new section on nonnormality and nonzero means of the disturbance, which includes robust estimation. Major additions appear in Chapter 11, which has new sections on models involving qualitative or limited dependent variables, varying coefficients, unobservable variables, disequilibrium models, and model choice. In the Appendix, the section on computational design for least squares estimation has been replaced by a section on asymptotic distributions in regression models with stochastic explanatory variables written by E. P. Howrey and S. H. Hymans.

The incorporation of new results and the inclusion of new sections in the second edition cover most important innovations in econometrics since 1971. There is, however, no section on time-series analysis, even though time-series models do appear in the econometric literature, because these models have no economic content and their use for modeling exogenous variables is not theoretically justified. As pointed out in the text, time-series analysis may be useful for modeling the behavior of the disturbances and thus enriching the dynamic specification of econometric models, but this is a matter for specialists. The fact that time-series models may produce better short-run forecasts than econometric models simply points to the need for improving econometric models rather than replacing them by the ad hoc models of time-series analysis. The only other major omission involves topics usually put under the heading of "longitudinal analysis of labor market data," including duration analysis, intervention analysis, analysis of survey samples of life histories, and others. These topics represent a new and exciting branch of econometrics, but are too specialized to be included in a general textbook. The most important changes in emphasis in econometrics involve increased concern with hypothesis testing as compared to estimation, a burgeoning interest in microeconometrics and less interest in macromodels, the development of specification error tests and tests for model choice to replace more informal procedures, and a shift toward rational expectation models and away from other distributed lag schemes. All of these are — to varying degrees — taken into account in the discussion of different topics.

The changes incorporated in the second edition have not affected the level of difficulty at which the discussion is set, except perhaps for allowing for a natural growth of sophistication on the part of students of economics. The book is still intended for economists rather than for econometric specialists, and it is expected to be used as a text in first-year graduate or advanced undergraduate economics programs or as a reference book for research workers in economics, business, and other social sciences. The prerequisites are the same as for the first edition, namely, a knowledge of basic economic theory, college algebra, basic calculus, and some descriptive statistics. Chapters 10 – 13 also use matrix algebra, which can be learned from Appendix B. However, the prospective reader should be warned that the book represents a serious and reasonably thorough approach to the subject and is not suitable for audiences desiring only superficial acquaintance with econometric methods.

The first edition contains acknowledgments and expressions of gratitude to my former teachers, colleagues, and students who influenced my thinking and helped me in various ways. Unfortunately, a slip in communication resulted in the omission of my undergraduate professor of statistics, R. S. G. Rutherford of the University of Sydney, who first introduced me to econometrics and who provided me with guidance and support well beyond the call of duty.

Preparation of this revision has greatly benefitted from comments, corrections, and suggestions of colleagues and students too numerous to mention. Those whose input has been particularly extensive and who deserve special credit are D. Asher, E. Berndt, A. Buse, A. Havenner, A. Maeshiro, H.-J. Mittag, A. and M. Nakamura, B. Rafailzadeh, E. Rost, H. Roth, E. Sowey, and V. M. Rao Tummala. Further, I owe a great deal of gratitude to Gerry Musgrave, who helped me with advice and with many calculations presented in the book, to Terry Seaks and Jeff Pliskin, who have gone thoroughly through the entire book and caught many errors and made many useful suggestions, and to Bijan Rafailzadeh, who has carefully read and corrected most of the chapters and worked out the answers to the exercises. (A separate Solutions Manual is available on request from the publisher.) The book has certainly been improved because of their selfless contributions. The suggestions and criticisms concerning the first six chapters offered by reviewers engaged by the publisher—Richard E. Bennett, John F. Chizmar, J. Malcolm Dowlin, Nicholas M. Kiefer, Craig Swan, and David J. Weinschrott—have also been very helpful. The last two chapters were written at the University of Saarland in Germany, whose support is gratefully acknowledged. My thanks go also to Mrs. Morag Nairn for her expert help with managing the manuscript and typing, and to Mrs. Elisabeth Belfer of Macmillan for her assistance in the final stages of the production of the book. The largest thanks, of course, belong to my wife, who has been invaluable in helping to produce the manuscript and who has patiently put up with all the inconveniences that she was subjected to during the lengthy process. Finally, I am indebted to the Literary Executor of the late Sir Ronald A. Fisher, F.R.S., and to Oliver & Boyd Ltd, Edinburgh, for their permission to reprint Table D-3 from their book *Statistical Methods for Research Workers.*

J. K.

Contents

PART ONE Basic Statistical Theory

PART ONE
Basic Statistical Theory

1 Introduction to Statistical Inference

Until the early part of the nineteenth century, statistics was understood to be concerned with characteristics of the state, particularly those related to political and military institutions. Descriptions of these characteristics were at first mainly in verbal terms, but they gradually became more and more numerical. The change to an increasingly more quantitative character was accompanied by an extension to fields other than those concerned with the affairs of the state. Later advances in the theory of probability led to the development of the theory of statistics that permits scientific generalization from incomplete information — in other words, statistical inference.

As a result of this historical development, the subject known as "statistics" consists of two parts: descriptive statistics and statistical inference. Descriptive statistics deals with the collection, organization, and presentation of data, while statistical inference deals with generalizations from a part to the whole. Statistical inference, like any other science, is concerned with the development of methods (statistical theory) as well as with their use (statistical application).

In econometrics we are mainly concerned with statistical inference. Descriptive statistics is relevant only to the extent that measures developed by descriptive statisticians for the purpose of summarizing various characteristics of the data — averages, measures of dispersion, etc. — are also used in statistical inference. But while in the field of descriptive statistics these measures represent ends in themselves, in statistical inference they are only means in the process of inquiry.

1-1 Basic Concepts of Statistical Inference

Before explaining the nature of statistical inference more specifically, we must introduce a few basic concepts. The most crucial concepts in traditional or classical statistics are those of a population and of a sample.

A *population* can be defined as the totality of all possible observations on measurements or outcomes. Examples are incomes of all people in a certain country in a specific period of time, national income of a country over a number of periods of time, and all outcomes of a given experiment such as repeatedly tossing a coin. A population may be either finite or infinite. A *finite population* is one in which the number of all possible observations is less than infinity. However, the distinction between finite and infinite populations is more subtle than may at first appear. For instance, a series of national income figures for the United States for a number of years, e.g., 1948–1977, represents a finite collection of thirty observations and thus might seem to be a finite population. But this would be a very narrow interpretation of historical events, since it would imply that the thirty measurements of national income were the only possible ones, i.e., that there is only one course that history might have taken. Now there are obviously not many people who would take such an extremely fatalistic view of the world; most people would admit that it was not impossible for some other, even if only slightly different, values of national income to have occurred. This latter view underlies virtually all policy-oriented research in economics and econometrics and will be used throughout this book. Thus a population of national incomes in a given time interval includes not only the actual history represented by the values that were in fact observed but also the potential history consisting of all the values that might have occurred but did not. The population so defined is obviously an infinite one. Similarly, the population of all possible outcomes of coin tosses is also infinite, since the tossing process can generate an infinite number of outcomes, in this case "heads" and "tails." Most of the populations with which we deal in econometrics are infinite.

Related to the concept of a population is the concept of a *sample,* which is a set of measurements or outcomes selected from the population. The selection can be done by the investigator, in which case we can speak of a sampling experiment, or it may happen independently either by design of others or by nature. In the latter case, the investigator is a mere observer, and this situation is particularly frequent in econometrics. While samples from infinite populations can themselves be infinite, the relevance of such samples is at best only a theoretical one. In practice we deal only with finite samples and, regrettably, quite often only with very small ones. Since samples are obtained by a selection from a given population, the principle of selection clearly plays an important part in determining the composition of the sample. In econometrics our attention is confined to samples drawn in accordance with some specified chance mechanism. Such samples are called *probability samples.* An important type of probability sample is the *random sample.* In finite populations, the principle of selecting a random sample is that of giving every individual in the population an equal chance of being chosen. In the case of infinite populations, a sample is random if each observation (of a measurement or an outcome) is independent of every other observation. The meaning of *independence* will be given in a rigorous way later; at present it is sufficient to note that two events (which can be either measured or counted) are independent if the occurrence of one in no way influences the occurrence of the other.

Both populations and samples can be described by stating their characteristics. Numerical characteristics of a population are called *parameters;* the characteristics of a sample, given in the form of some summary measure, are called *statistics* (a plural of the word "statistic"). Such characteristics may be, for instance, central tendency of measurements (e.g., the mean or the mode), their dispersion (e.g., standard deviation), or, in the case of qualitative phenomena, the proportion of observations of a given kind. Obviously, the parameters of an infinite population are never observed; the parameters of a finite population could be observed in theory but may be impossible to observe in practice.

From our discussion so far it should be clear that statistics deals with phenomena that can be either measured or counted. With respect to a phenomenon that can be measured, we speak of a *variable,* meaning a homogeneous quantity that can assume different values at different points of observation. If a phenomenon can only be counted but not measured (each observation representing one count), we speak of an *attribute.* Thus an attribute is the presence or absence of a given characteristic. An outcome of an event such as the birth of a child leads to an observation of an attribute of sex (i.e., "male" or "not male"); an outcome of a toss of a die may be classified as a presence or an absence of "1," of "2," and so on. In a way the concept of attribute is redundant because we can, and often do, simply assign the value of 1 to the presence, and 0 to the absence, of a given characteristic. In this case we equate "attribute" with the concept of a *qualitative* or *binary variable.* Another and more colorful name, "dummy variable," is also widely used.

The definition of a *variable,* and indeed the name itself, stresses the possibility of variation at different points of observation. On the other hand, a quantity that cannot vary from one observation to another is called a *constant.* If the quantity in question is a variable and not a constant, one may wish to ask about the general source of variation. In particular, it is important to distinguish between those variations that can and those that cannot be fully controlled or predicted. In the case of a variation that cannot be fully controlled or predicted, its existence is due to chance. An obvious example of an uncontrolled variation would be the outcomes of tossing a coin (in the absence of cheating, of course), but many other less obvious instances exist. In fact, as we shall elaborate at length in the rest of this book, most economic variables are always to some extent determined by chance. The variables whose values cannot be fully controlled or determined prior to observation are called *random* or *stochastic variables;* their chief characteristic is that they assume different values (or fall into different value intervals) with some probability other than one. In contrast, a *nonrandom* or *nonstochastic* or *fixed variable* is one that is fully controllable or at least fully predictable. A constant may be regarded as a special case of a fixed variable.

Another important classification of variables is that which distinguishes between continuous and discrete variables. A *continuous variable* is a variable that can assume any value on the numerical axis or a part of it. Typical examples are time and temperature, but income, expenditure, and similar variables can all be classified as continuous. In fact, most economic variables are continuous or at least approximately so. The last qualification is added to take care of such possible objections as those pointing out that money values of less than a dollar (or possibly a cent) are, in fact, not observable. In contrast to a continuous variable, a *discrete variable* is one that can assume only some specific values on the numerical axis.

These values are usually (but not always) separated by intervals of equal length. Examples are a number of children in a family, a number of dots on a die after a toss, or any binary variable.

The final concept to be introduced at this stage is that of a *distribution.* In the case of a sample we have a frequency distribution, while in the case of a population we speak of a probability distribution. A *frequency distribution* represents an organization of data so as to give the number of observations for each value of the variable (in the case of a discrete variable) or for each interval of values of the variable (in the case of a continuous variable). The number of observations in each class (represented by a point in the case of a discrete variable or by an interval in the case of a continuous variable) is called *absolute frequency.* This can be distinguished from *relative frequency,* which gives the proportion of observations rather than their number for each class. As an example, consider a sample of 64 families being observed with respect to the number of children. The results might be those given in Table 1-1. Another example, this time related to a continuous variable, is given by

Table 1-1

Number of children (=variable)	Number of families (=absolute frequency)	Proportion of families (=relative frequency)
0	4	0.0625
1	12	0.1875
2	20	0.3125
3	16	0.2500
4	8	0.1250
5 and over	4	0.0625
Totals	64	1.0000

family income distribution in the United States in 1978 (Table 1-2). Here, absolute frequencies are not shown, and the relative frequencies are stated in percentages rather than in simple proportions. Sample data in the form of a time series, such as national income figures for a number of years, could also be presented in the form of a frequency distribution, although this is usually not done. The fact that different observations are made at different points of time is relevant only to the extent that the population from which the sample was drawn may have changed through time.

In a population the concept corresponding to a sample frequency distribution is known as a *probability distribution.* Consider, for instance, the population of United States families classified by income received in 1978 as shown in Table 1-2. It is fairly clear that to state that 8.2% of all families received an income of less than \$5000 is equivalent to stating that the probability of selecting (at random) a family with an income of less than \$5000 is 0.082. If the population is infinite, the probabilities can be represented by *limits* of relative frequencies (this will be explained more rigorously in Chapter 3). Picturing, then, the probability distribution of one variable as a population counterpart of the frequency distribution in a sample, we

Table 1-2

Income (=variable)	Percent of families (=relative frequency)
Under $5000	8.2
$5000 to $9999	15.8
$10,000 to $14,999	16.7
$15,000 to $24,999	31.4
$25,000 to $49,999	24.3
$50,000 and over	3.6
Total	100.0

Source: *Statistical Abstract of the United States,* 1980, p. 451.

can see that it is possible to deal with more than one variable at a time. For example, a distribution giving the probability of death at various ages confines itself to one variable—it is an *univariate distribution.* If, however, we tabulate these probabilities separately for each sex, we are considering two variables and have a *bivariate distribution.* A further classification by other characteristics could produce a *multivariate distribution.*

There also exists another kind of probability distribution for which the probabilities are not relative frequencies but are simply results of a personal judgment. Such probability distributions are particularly relevant in situations where it is impossible to determine probabilitics by repeated observations and counting. For instance, in considering the prospects of one's score in a golf game, one can typically form a set of probabilities assigned to various scores. Probability distributions of this kind are called *subjective* or *prior* probability distributions. They play a crucial role in the so-called Bayesian approach to statistical inference, which differs from the traditional sampling theory approach and which will be explained later. (The Reverend Thomas Bayes was an English mathematician who lived in the 18th century.)

1-2 The Nature of Statistical Inference

Having introduced, however briefly, some of the most important concepts of statistical theory, we are now in a position to describe the nature of statistical inference. As indicated earlier, statistical inference is concerned with generalizations about the population on the basis of information provided by a sample. Such a procedure is, of course, frequent in everyday life: we make generalizations about the temperature of our soup on the basis of the first spoonful, or about the life expectancy of a pair of tennis shoes on the basis of past experience. This is precisely what is done in statistical inference, except that we go about it in a somewhat more scientific way. What makes the application of statistical inference scientific is that we take into account the way in which the sample was selected, and that we express our generalization in specific probability terms. For example, instead of saying that tennis shoes last five years, we specify a range and state the level of probability associated with it.

To sum up, we use a sample to make a judgment about the population from which the sample comes. If the population is infinite, then it can never be observed as a whole and any judgment about it can only come from a sample. But even if the population is a finite one, there may be a good reason for observing only a sample since making observations (as in the case of tasting soup or measuring the lifetime of light bulbs) is destructive or, at best, expensive. Now, in general we are not interested in knowing everything about a population but are concerned with only *some* of its characteristics, which, it may be recalled, we call parameters. The purpose of sampling, and the business of statistical inference, is to make judgments about population parameters on the basis of sample statistics. These judgments are, in fact, guesses endowed with a specific degree of reliability, and they can be of two types, one concerned with estimation of a parameter and the other with testing some hypothesis about it. Estimation is done with the help of an *estimator,* which is a formula describing a procedure of guessing the value of a given population parameter; a specific value of an estimator is called an *estimate.* Judgments in the form of *hypothesis testing* involve an a priori assumption about the value of a parameter. If the sample information provides evidence against the hypothesis, we reject it; otherwise, we keep it. The evidence provided by the observations in the sample is, for the purpose of hypothesis testing, summarized in the form of a *test statistic;* this is then used in arriving at a verdict concerning the hypothesis.

A sample provides evidence about the population from which it was drawn. This evidence can be summarized in the form of an estimator when the problem is one of estimation, or in the form of a test statistic when the problem is one of hypothesis testing. In either case we follow some formula into which we substitute the values observed in our sample. The values thus obtained for an estimator and for a test statistic are closely related, as they ought to be, since they draw upon the same source of information, i.e., the sample. In any case, the value of an estimator or of a test statistic represents a guess concerning the relevant population parameter. Now it is obvious that different samples would lead to different guesses. Some will be closer to the truth (e.g., to the true value of the parameter) than others. In reality we have, of course, usually just one sample and therefore only one guess. The basic contention of the classical sampling theory approach to statistics is that it is important for us to know what the guesses might have been had we had different samples. If all possible samples lead to guesses that are always near the truth, any single guess is obviously quite reliable. On the other hand, if all possible samples lead to widely differing guesses, only some of the guesses can be near the truth and no single guess can be trusted much. (The third extreme case is one where all possible guesses are similar to each other but far from the true value of the parameter.)

A different view of statistical inference is taken by the Bayesian statisticians who regard all probability statements essentially as statements of *rational belief.* The information provided by the sample is just one ingredient in the judgment about the characteristics of a population. A description of the basic difference between the classical and the Bayesian approaches to statistical inference is provided at the end of the following section.

1-3 Sampling Distributions

The preceding discussion suggests that the way to know the reliability of a guess is by knowing the behavior of all guesses that could be made on the basis of all possible samples. We can envision drawing one sample after another, from each sample calculating the value of our guess (say, an estimate of a certain population parameter), and arranging these guesses in the form of a distribution. If we had an infinite number of such samples, the resulting distribution would be called a *sampling distribution.* Consider, for example, the problem of estimating the mean family income in the United States in a given year on the basis of a sample of, say, 100 families. One possibility is to calculate the mean family income in our sample and use it as our estimate of the population mean. Of course, we could use the mode, or the median, or some other measure as our estimator. Suppose we estimate the population mean by using the sample mean. Then we wish to know how reliable this estimator is. One way to find this out would be by drawing an infinite number of such samples, calculating the value of the sample mean from each sample, and arranging these values in the form of a distribution. Note that although the population of all families in the United States is a finite one, the number of samples that we can draw from this population is infinite as long as we allow each family to be included in any sample. Such sampling is called *sampling with replacement.* By studying the resulting sampling distribution, we would know all about the possible behavior of our guess. If we, in fact, knew the characteristics of the population beforehand, then this exercise would serve the function of extending our knowledge about the relationship between the sample and the population mean; this knowledge could then be used in other cases when we are limited to only one sample.

If each family contained in the sample is selected at random, we do not know beforehand what its income is going to be. Thus, in this case family income is a random variable. Furthermore, the *mean* income observed in a sample is also a random variable. This means that the sampling distribution of sample mean (based on an infinite number of samples) is really a probability distribution. This distribution could be either discrete or continuous depending upon whether the population variable is a discrete or a continuous; in our example the sampling distribution is continuous since income is a continuous variable. Of course, the idea is quite general: *a sampling distribution is a probability distribution of an estimator or of a test statistic.*

It is quite obvious that samples of different sizes give different amounts of information about the population from which they are drawn. Therefore, estimators that use all information contained in a sample and are based on samples of different sizes will display different degrees of reliability. To avoid the effects of changed sample size upon the quality of an estimator, any given sampling distribution always refers to samples of the same size. The effects of changing the sample size are best studied by comparing different sampling distributions.

Suppose we are dealing with a population of all possible values of a variable X (e.g., family incomes in a given year) and are interested in estimating a parameter θ (e.g., the mean family income). To estimate this parameter, we use a sample statistic $\hat{\theta}$. In usual terminology, $\hat{\theta}$ is an estimator of θ, while a specific value of $\hat{\theta}$ (obtained from a specific sample) is called an estimate of θ. Incidentally, a common notation is to use plain Greek letters to describe population parameters and to use Greek letters with hats, tildes, etc., to describe estimators. Then if X is a continuous variable (as in the case of family income), the sampling distribution of $\hat{\theta}$ may look something like the distribution in Figure 1-1. As pointed out earlier, this is really a probability distribution; since we do not intend to define and describe probability distributions until Chapter 3, we are not in a position to discuss sampling distributions with any degree of rigor. However, we may gain a better understanding of the concept of a sampling distribution if we view it for the time being simply as a relative frequency distribution compiled from an infinite number of observations, i.e., samples in this case. In Figure 1-1 the relative frequencies of $\hat{\theta}$ are measured along the $f(\hat{\theta})$ axis.

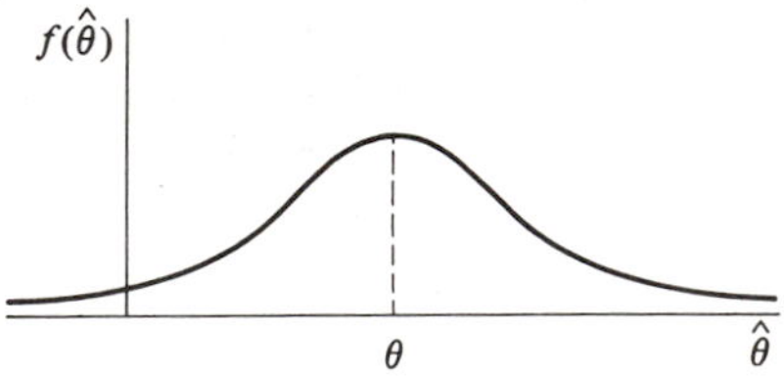

Figure 1-1

A reasonable and generally useful way of judging the quality of a guess, at least according to the classical statisticians, is to evaluate the quality of the procedure that produced the guess. Suppose, for example, that a man, who has spent a lot of time learning about horse racing, goes to a race track with his wife, who is completely ignorant of such matters, and in the first race the wife wins her bet whereas the man does not. Then we do not necessarily conclude that the wife's guesses are better in general and that we should bet on the same horse that she does in the next race. Such a conclusion could be reached only after more evidence (i.e., more observations) was gathered and the wife's "system" led to bigger gains (or smaller losses) than that of her husband. Of course, if only one bet—that on the first race, say—was allowed, then there is no question that the wife's guess was better, since it led to a win while her husband lost, but this is obviously a special case of little general interest. In general, the result of any specific act of guessing is considered of little relevance; what is relevant is how often a guessing procedure leads to bad results and how often it leads to good ones. In other words, we need to know about the results of a large number of guesses, each based on the same guessing procedure. This is precisely the information conveyed by a sampling distribution. To compare the quality of guesses we compare the results of the guessing procedures from which these guesses were derived, which means that we compare their sampling distributions.

It may be noted that the concept of a sampling distribution based on an infinite number of samples is regarded as irrelevant by Bayesian statisticians. They point out that in reality we usually have only *one* sample to go by. In the Bayesian approach to statistical inference the observed sample is taken as given, and it is used for the purpose of modifying one's subjective probabilities about the characteristics of the population from which the sample was drawn. The classical statisticians, on the other hand, are concerned about the probabilities of observing different samples from a population with given characteristics. Thus the basic difference between the two approaches lies in the fact that classical statisticians study the probabilities of different results (samples) of a given cause (a population with given characteristics), whereas Bayesian statisticians try to figure out the probabilities of different causes (populations with different characteristics) of a given result (observed sample).

The difference between the classical and the Bayesian approach to statistical inference may be somewhat illuminated by the following example. Let us consider a population of all adult males in the United States in which a certain (unknown) proportion, say, π, can be classified as beer drinkers. Let us also suppose that a random sample of adult males reveals 7 beer-drinkers and 3 nonbeer-drinkers. A classical statistician might then use the sample information to estimate the proportion of drinkers in the population (i.e., the value of π) and to determine the reliability of the estimate. Or he or she might want to test the claim that the value of π is some given number and use the appropriate sampling distribution to determine the probability of observing 7 beer-drinkers and 3 nonbeer-drinkers for that value of π. A Bayesian statistician, on the other hand, would start with assigning prior probabilities to various values of π. These prior probabilities would represent his or her personal judgment derived from introspection, casual observation, knowledge of the results of an earlier sample, or similar sources. The prior probabilities would then be appropriately modified by the information provided by the sample at hand and a new judgment about the value of π would be formed. Thus in this example the classical statistician would regard the proportion of beer-drinkers in the population as fixed and the proportion of beer-drinkers in the sample as a random variable, whereas the Bayesian statistician would take just the opposite view.

In this book we will treat statistical inference and econometrics mainly from the classical sampling theory viewpoint, partly because this is the prevailing view, and partly because the knowledge of classical statistics is indispensable even for those who prefer the Bayesian approach. Bayesian inference will be discussed in connection with conditional probabilities in Chapter 3 and will be explained in greater detail at the end of Chapter 6.

1-4 Properties of Sampling Distributions

When estimating the value of a population parameter, we want to know the specific features of a sampling distribution that enable us to pass a judgment on a particular estimator. We shall deal with this question quite thoroughly in Chapter 6, but some observations can be made right now. We may start with the simplest case, which is that of a perfect estimator. A perfect estimator is one that is never wrong, i.e., one whose sampling distribution is concentrated entirely in one point, the point that happens to be the true value of the parameter to be estimated. Needless to say, perfect estimators are very rare. One situation in which we can have a perfect estimator is that of no variation in the population. In our example of sampling the temperature of a bowl of soup by a spoonful, our guessing would be perfect if the temperature were the same everywhere in the bowl and we used the temperature of the spoonful as an estimate. Normally this would be achieved by a thorough mixing before tasting. In the example of family income, we would have a perfect estimator if all families had the same income and we used the mean of a sample as an estimate of the population mean. Another situation that may produce perfect estimation is when the sample is of infinite size.

Almost invariably estimators are not perfect but are such that only a small proportion of an estimator's values is at or near the true value of the parameter. This means that we have to be satisfied by lesser achievements; these can be summarized by stating some properties of an estimator that are commonly considered desirable. At this stage we shall only mention the basic idea behind three of these properties; an elaborate and extended discussion will be left for another chapter. Perhaps the best-known desirable property of an estimator is that of *unbiasedness.* An unbiased estimator is one that has a sampling distribution with a mean equal to the parameter to be estimated. A perfect estimator gives a perfect guess every time; an unbiased estimator gives a perfect result only on the average. An unbiased estimator will lead to estimates that are sometimes higher and sometimes lower than the true value of the parameter, but the amount of overstating and understating "averages out" when an infinite number of estimates is made. If the sampling distribution is symmetric, then the fact that an estimator is unbiased implies that half of all possible estimates are higher and half are lower than the value of the parameter. Such a situation (in the case of a continuous estimator) is depicted by Figure 1-1. It should be emphasized that unbiasedness tells us nothing about the distance between the estimates and the value of the parameter, only that all the (positive and negative) distances add up to zero. It is quite possible that an unbiased estimator will never produce an estimate that is, in fact, equal to the value of the parameter. Consider our example of estimating the mean family income by using the mean of a sample. Let us accept the proposition—which we shall prove later—that the sample mean is an unbiased estimator of the population mean. Suppose the population mean family income is $20,901.46; obviously, the probability that a sample mean would be *precisely* the same figure is negligible.

A further important desirable property of an estimator is *efficiency,* a property concerned with the distances of the values of an estimator from the value of the parameter. Unfortunately, there appear to be some differences in the definition of efficiency among statisticians. There is, however, a generally accepted definition if we restrict our consideration to unbiased estimators only; in this case, an efficient estimator is one that has the smallest dispersion, i.e., one whose sampling distribution has the smallest variance. In Figure 1-2 we depict two estimators, $\hat{\theta}_1$ with

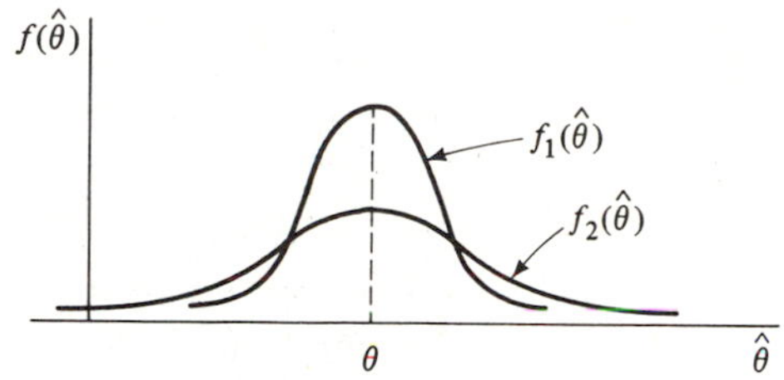

Figure 1-2

sampling distribution $f_1(\hat{\theta})$ and $\hat{\theta}_2$ with sampling distribution $f_2(\hat{\theta})$. Both estimators are unbiased, but $\hat{\theta}_2$ is obviously more dispersed than $\hat{\theta}_1$ and is, therefore, less efficient. If we could find no other unbiased estimator that would have a smaller variance than $\hat{\theta}_1$, then $\hat{\theta}_1$ would be an efficient estimator among the family of all unbiased estimators. If we do not wish to be restricted only to unbiased estimators, then we have to consider the trade-off between bias and variance. Figure 1-3 demonstrates a case in point: the estimator $\hat{\theta}_1$ is unbiased but has a large variance,

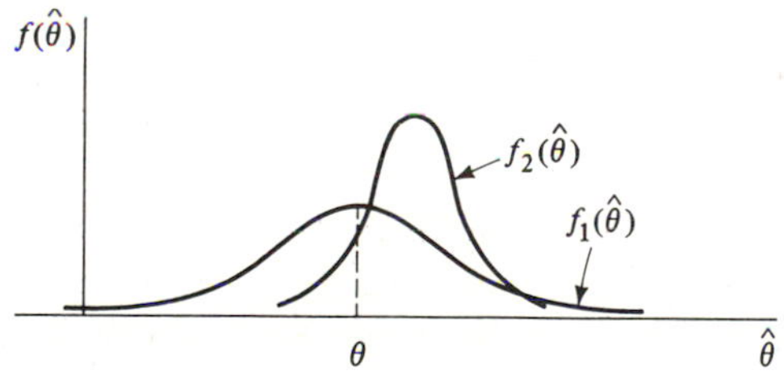

Figure 1-3

whereas $\hat{\theta}_2$ is biased but has a small variance. We cannot say which of the two estimators is preferable unless we assign relative weights (i.e., prices) to bias and to variance. It is worth noting, though, that minimum variance by itself is not a desirable property; if it were, we could simply use some constant (which has, by definition, zero variance) regardless of sample evidence. The sampling distribution of such an "estimator" would be concentrated entirely in one point, and yet obviously the estimator would be useless.

Another desirable property is *consistency*. This property relates to changes in the sampling distribution as sample sizes are increased. An estimator is said to be consistent if its sampling distribution tends to become concentrated on the true

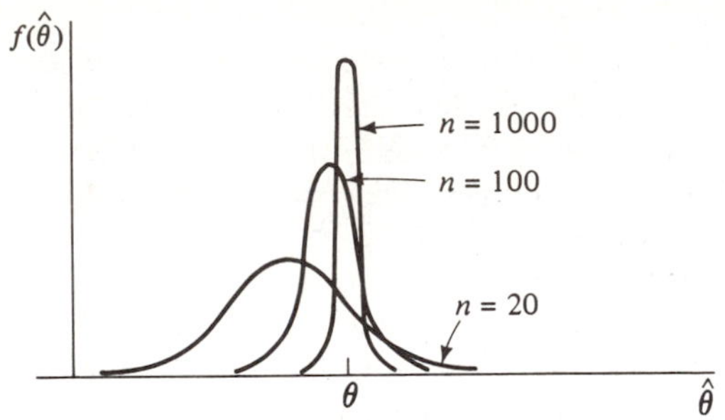

Figure 1-4

value of the parameter as sample size increases to infinity. Figure 1-4 shows the sampling distributions of a consistent estimator for different sample sizes. As we move from a smaller sample size to a larger one, two things happen: (a) the bias becomes smaller, and (b) the estimates become less dispersed. Consistency is an important property because it guarantees that our estimates improve with sample size. If it is at all possible to increase sample size, then we can buy greater reliability by spending more on sampling. Even observations from national income accounts can be made more numerous by having data for shorter periods of time.

Estimating a parameter from a sample can be compared to our shooting at a target with a rifle. In this parallel, the bull's-eye represents the true value of the parameter, each shot represents a particular estimate (sample), the rifle is our estimator (i.e., estimation formula), and the distance from the target reflects our sample size. In reality we normally have only one sample and thus can make only one estimate; that is—in our parallel—we are allowed only one shot. However, the quality of any shot before it is made clearly depends on the quality of the rifle. The rifle can be judged either by its actual performance—i.e., by making a large number of shots—or by examining its construction, the type of material used, etc. The former corresponds to empirical and the latter to theoretical derivation of properties of an estimator. An unbiased rifle is one that produces shots that are randomly scattered around the bull's-eye. If we compare all unbiased rifles, then the one whose shots are most heavily concentrated around the bull's-eye can be considered efficient. Finally, a rifle may be considered consistent if the probability of a shot falling within some (small) distance from the bull's-eye increases when the distance between the shooter and the target is decreased. Note that the quality of a rifle is judged by its repeated performance (actual or expected) and not by a single shot. Given just one shot, it may happen that an inaccurate rifle may hit the bull's-eye while an obviously superior and highly accurate rifle may not. Obviously, this would not affect our judgment of the respective qualities of the two rifles unless it tended to happen repeatedly.

So far we have not considered the question of constructing an estimator. As pointed out earlier, an estimator is a formula for generating estimates. Consider, for instance, sample mean as an estimator of population mean. Here the formula requires that we take all values of the variable observed in our sample, add them up, and divide them by the number of observations. A specific sample will lead to a specific estimate. In this case we have chosen the sample mean for an estimator of population mean more or less because it appears intuitively plausible. This, indeed, is one way of obtaining estimators — namely, by invoking some plausible idea and trying it out — which, in this context, means finding the properties of such estimators. Another way is to construct an estimator by design, to develop a formula so as to satisfy certain conditions that ensure at least some of the desirable properties. Or, finally, we may use some principles that, although not directly guaranteeing desirable properties, nevertheless appear promising on some other grounds. We shall discuss this in detail in Section 6-2.

1-5 Derivation of Sampling Distributions

The main purpose of the preceding discussion was to explain the crucial importance of sampling distributions in statistical inference. The next problem is to derive the sampling distributions of given estimators. In general, this can be done either experimentally or theoretically. The *experimental derivation* is based upon simulation: we create a specific population (which is, therefore, completely known to us) and actually draw from it a large number of random samples. These samples enable us to construct an approximate sampling distribution of the estimator we are examining. While the result is only specific in the sense that it applies solely to the specific population (characterized by specific parameters) with which we are experimenting, we usually hope to be able to generalize our results at least within a certain range. Such generalizations can be tested by further experiments on populations with different parameter values. The *theoretical derivation* of sampling distributions uses probability theory; instead of physically drawing a large number of samples as in the experimental approach, we can find what would happen without actually doing it. Thus, theory may save us a lot of work, which is a great advantage. Another advantage is that theory is more precise: while in experiments we can never produce an infinite number of samples, in theory the concept of infinity may be handled quite easily. And last but not least, in contrast to the experimental method, the results of theoretical derivation are quite general, at least within some well-defined boundaries. Theoretical derivation of sampling distribution is thus clearly superior to the experimental derivation. Its only drawback is that we may not always be able to manage it. The problem is sometimes so complicated that our knowledge is simply insufficient to deal with it. This has been particularly the case with estimation problems in modern econometrics, as will be demonstrated in the discussion of simultaneous economic relations.

The concept of a sampling distribution is the basic element of classical statistical inference since it enables us to assess the quality of our generalizations about a population on the basis of a sample. The rest of the first part of the book will be almost entirely devoted to the derivation and use of sampling distributions. The process of deriving sampling distributions will be demonstrated experimentally in Chapter 2; then, after presenting some basic probability theory in Chapter 3, we will derive sampling distributions theoretically in Chapter 4. Chapters 5 and 6 deal with the use of sampling distributions for hypothesis testing and estimation. Bayesian inference, which does not involve sampling distributions, will be explained in the last part of Chapter 6.

EXERCISES

In our exposition we assume that the reader is familiar with the basic concepts of descriptive statistics. The exercises below provide practice in this respect. (Note than an outline of basic algebra of summations is given in Appendix A.)

1-1. The sum of ten numbers $x_1, x_2, \ldots, x_{10}$ is 60, and the sum of their squares is 396. Find the following.

a. The arithmetic mean $\bar{x}$.

b. The standard deviation of x, say, SD (using 10 as the denominator).

c. $\sum_{i=1}^{10} (x_i - \bar{x})/SD$. **d.** $\sum_{i=1}^{10} 2(x_i - 5)$.

e. The arithmetic mean of z_i, where $z_i = x_i - (x_i - \bar{x})/SD$.

1-2. Draw a rough sketch of each of the frequency distributions characterized as follows.

a. The frequency is the same for all values of the variables.

b. The variable assumes the same value at each observation.

c. The distance between the upper quartile and the median is twice as long as the distance between the lower quartile and the median.

d. The value of the standard deviation is zero.

e. The value of the arithmetic mean is smaller than that of the mode.

1-3. Suppose we wish to determine the mean age in a specified population of individuals. Suppose further that in the census one quarter of the individuals underestimate their ages by one year, one half give their correct ages, and one quarter overestimate their ages by two years. Determine the relationship between the true mean age and the mean age obtained from the census.

1-4. The annual unemployment rate in a certain locality is determined by averaging the monthly unemployment rates for the year. Let the monthly unemployment rates be X_1, $X_2, \ldots X_{12}$ so that the annual rate is

$$\bar{X} = \frac{1}{12} \sum_{i=1}^{12} X_i.$$

Suppose now that we are given the average for the first eleven months,

$$\bar{X}_{11} = \frac{1}{11} \sum_{i=1}^{11} X_i.$$

a. What would the value of X_{12} have to be if **(i)** $\bar{X} = \bar{X}_{11}$? **(ii)** $\bar{X} = \frac{11}{12}\bar{X}_{11}$? **(iii)** $\bar{X} = X_{12}$?

b. Consider the standard deviation of the unemployment rate for the first eleven months, SD_{11}, and the standard deviation for the whole year, SD_{12}. Suppose it turns out that $X_{12} = \bar{X}_{11}$. Which of the following is then true?

$$SD_{12} < SD_{11}, \quad SD_{12} > SD_{11}, \quad \text{or} \quad SD_{12} = SD_{11}.$$

Give a reason for your answer.

[NOTE: $SD^2 = \Sigma_{i=1}^n (X_i - \bar{X})^2/n = (\Sigma_{i=1}^n X_i^2 - n\bar{X}^2)/n$.]

1-5. Consider a set of n positive numbers $X_1, X_2, \ldots, X_n$ characterized by a specific value of the mean ($\bar{X}$), of the standard deviation (SD), and of the α_3 measure of skewness. State how each of these would be affected by changes listed below. Prove the correctness of your answers.

a. Each number is increased by the same amount.

b. Each number is doubled.

c. Each number is increased or decreased to make it equal to $\bar{X}$.

d. Each number is divided by $\bar{X}$.

e. Each number is decreased by the value of $\bar{X}$.

f. Each number is decreased by the value of $\bar{X}$ and then divided by SD.

[NOTE: $\alpha_3 = [\Sigma_{i=1}^n (X_i - \bar{X})^3/n]/SD^3$.]

1-6. A sample of 10 readings of temperature in Fahrenheit degrees has a mean of 50 and a standard deviation of 6. Determine the mean and the standard deviation for these readings in terms of Celsius degrees. [NOTE: 32°F = 0°C and 212°F = 100°C.]

1-7. A hotel has 100 rooms, each of an exact square shape. (Not all the rooms are the same size, though.) The mean length of a room is 16 feet with a standard deviation of 2 feet.

a. What is the average area of a room? If all rooms were to be provided with wall-to-wall carpeting, how many square feet of carpeting would be needed for all the 100 rooms?

b. Suppose the person who measured the rooms had a business interest in the firm supplying the carpeting for the hotel, and that he added 1 foot to the length of each room when reporting the measurements. Determine the correct mean length and the correct standard deviation of the length of the rooms.

1-8. According to the National Bureau of Economic Research, a poor family is one whose income falls below one-half of the median family income. Using this definition of poverty, answer the following questions.

a. How, if at all, would the proportion of poor families be affected if **(i)** The income distribution changed from a positively skewed one to a symmetric one, leaving the median income unchanged? **(ii)** Every income was increased by 20%?

b. Draw a rough sketch of an income distribution, indicating the position of the median and of the half-median income on the horizontal axis, if **(i)** 25% of all families are poor; **(ii)** 50% of all families are poor; **(iii)** there are no poor families at all.

1-9. The arithmetic mean score in Statistics 405 last semester was 65. The teaching assistant determined that the mean score of the male students was 62 and that of the female students was 80. What was the proportion of female students in the class?

2 Experimental Derivation of Sampling Distributions

Since sampling distributions play such an important role in classical statistics, their derivation is of considerable interest. As pointed out in Section 1-5, sampling distributions can be derived either experimentally or theoretically. Experiments designed for the purpose of deriving sampling distributions are frequently called *Monte Carlo experiments* because of their resemblance to games of chance. In this chapter we use the *experimental* approach to derive the sampling distributions of two common estimators. Doing this should help to clarify the concept of a sampling distribution. The *theoretical* derivation of the sampling distributions of the two estimators—and a comparison of the results of the experimental and theoretical approaches—will be presented in Chapter 4.

Sampling distribution of an estimator can be viewed as a relative frequency distribution of the values of the estimator obtained from an infinite number of random samples, each sample being of the same size and drawn from the same population. We can do this experimentally as follows. First we create our own population with certain given characteristics, i.e., parameters. Next we choose the parameter to be estimated and the formula for its estimation from the information provided by the sample. Then we draw a large number of random samples of equal size and from each sample calculate the value of the estimator. Finally, we analyze the results in the form of a relative frequency distribution. This will be an approximation of the sampling distribution of the given estimator. We say "an approximation" because we have only a finite, although large, number of samples, while a proper sampling distribution is based upon an infinite number of samples.

The problem of creating or simulating a population is generally a very simple one. For one thing, some populations do not need to exist physically before we start drawing samples. An example would be the population of all possible outcomes of some chance mechanism such as the population of all outcomes of a toss of a coin. Suppose we wish to estimate the probability of getting a head and use as an estimator the proportion of heads in, say, 30 tosses. Then we may take a coin with known probability of getting a head (e.g., an unbiased coin for which the probability of getting a head is one half), toss it 30 times, and record the result. By repeating this a large number of times we should be able to construct a reasonable approximation of the sampling distribution of the proportion of heads in samples of size 30. In the case of other populations, it may be necessary to have a physical representation of each unit before drawing samples. Thus, for instance, the population of United States families may be represented by cards bearing relevant information, one card for each family. A random sample of families would then be given by a random sample of cards.

In this chapter we consider experimental derivation of sampling distributions in two simple cases. In case A we consider sampling of attributes. In particular, we would like to estimate the proportion of people (objects, outcomes, etc.) possessing a certain attribute and to use the proportion found in the sample as our estimator. Then our task is to derive the sampling distribution of this estimator. To make the case more concrete, we may envision it as a problem of estimating the proportion of coffee-drinkers in a given population. In case B we shall be concerned with sampling of a (nonbinary) variable. Here we will wish to derive the sampling distribution of sample mean as an estimator of population mean. As an illustrative interpretation, we may think of a variable describing the number of dental appointments for each adult per year, and consider the problem of estimating the mean number of dental appointments per person in the population.

The mechanical aspects of the sampling experiment to be carried out are the same in both cases. We have a container with a large number of differently marked marbles representing units of the population. The container is shaken, and a number of marbles equal to the desired sample size are drawn at random, one by one. After each marble has been drawn and its number (or color) recorded, it is returned to the box and the box is thoroughly shaken. In this way the number of possible drawings—and therefore the size of the population—is infinite. Randomness is achieved by virtue of the fact that each marble has an equal chance of being included in the sample.

It should be noted that simulating a population by using marbles, or any other objects, to represent units of population is possible only if the variable is not continuous. If the population consisted of all possible values within a certain interval, we could not represent it by a collection of discrete objects. For such cases we would have to use some other ways of simulation. A device that would go a long way toward achieving a reasonable simulation for variables with a finite range of values is a dial with a needle freely rotating around its center. Other methods, particularly those relying on electronic computers, are also available. In the cases discussed here this problem does not arise since we do not use a continuous variable.

2-1 Sampling Distribution of Sample Proportion of Successes

Let us consider the proportion of successes (e.g., coffee-drinkers) in the sample as an estimator of the proportion of successes in the population. We wish to derive the sampling distribution of this estimator by repeated sampling. Our population is a container with a large number of marbles that are identical in every respect except for color. In this particular population, 70% of all marbles are red and 30% are white. We may envision that the red balls represent successes (coffee-drinkers) and the white ones failures. We conduct two experiments with this population. In the first experiment we draw 100 samples of size 4, and in the second experiment 100 samples of size 16. (The difference between the *number of samples* and *sample size* should be carefully noted; it is as important as that between the number of shoes and shoe size!) Since in each experiment we use 100 samples as our approximation of an infinite number of samples, our results will contain errors of approximation. These errors could be decreased by making the number of samples larger if one should so desire. For our purposes the degree of approximation given by 100 samples is sufficient. In describing the results we shall use the following notation.

π = proportion of successes in the population;

$\hat{\pi}$ = proportion of successes in the sample (an estimator of π);

f = relative frequency;

n = size of sample.

In our experiments, $\hat{\pi}$ will assume 100 values, one for each sample. Note that in our population $\pi = 0.7$.

Experiment A.1. 100 samples of size 4. Here $n = 4$, so that each sample may give only 1 of 5 possible results (no success, one success, etc.). These results are described in Table 2-1 and Figure 2-1. The last column of Table 2-1 gives the frequencies that

Table 2-1

Successes		Frequency	
Number	Proportion: $\hat{\pi}$	Absolute	Relative: f
0	0.00	1	0.01
1	0.25	6	0.06
2	0.50	28	0.28
3	0.75	42	0.42
4	1.00	23	0.23
		100	1.00

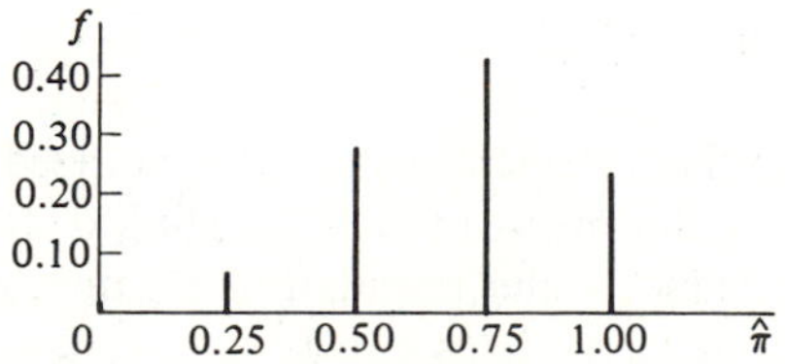

Figure 2-1

approximate the sampling distribution in question. The main characteristics of this sampling distribution are

$$\text{Mean} = \sum_{i=0}^{4} f_i \hat{\pi}_i$$
$$= 0.01 \times 0 + 0.06 \times 0.25 + 0.28 \times 0.50$$
$$+ 0.42 \times 0.75 + 0.23 \times 1.00$$
$$= 0.700.$$

$$\text{Standard deviation} = \sqrt{\sum_{i=0}^{4} f_i(\hat{\pi}_i - 0.7)^2} = 0.2233.$$

(Note that here $\hat{\pi}_0 = 0$, $\hat{\pi}_1 = 0.25$, $\hat{\pi}_2 = 0.50$, etc., and f_0, f_1, f_2, etc., are the corresponding relative frequencies. The formulas for the mean and for the standard deviation of $\hat{\pi}$ are the same as those for any variable X as presented in all elementary statistical texts.)

An examination of the derived sampling distribution shows that had we used the sample proportion of successes from sample size 4 as our estimate of the proportion of successes in the population (which, as we know, is equal to 0.7), we would have made a serious underestimate 35% of the time ($0.01 + 0.06 + 0.28 = 0.35$) and a serious overestimate 23% of the time, and we would have been quite close to the true value 42% of the time. These percentages are, of course, only approximate since our experiment is limited to 100 samples.

Experiment A.2. 100 samples of size 16. Here $n = 16$, so that there are 17 different possible results. These are presented in Table 2-2 and Figure 2-2. The main characteristics of the sampling distribution in this case are

$$\text{Mean} = \sum_{i=0}^{16} f_i \hat{\pi}_i = 0.7006.$$

$$\text{Standard deviation} = \sqrt{\sum_{i=0}^{16} f_i(\hat{\pi}_i - 0.7006)^2} = 0.1191.$$

(Note that here $\hat{\pi}_0 = 0$, $\hat{\pi}_1 = 1/16$, $\hat{\pi}_2 = 2/16$, etc., and f_0, f_1, f_2, etc., are the corresponding relative frequencies.) The derived sampling distribution shows a fair concentration of estimates around the true value: 95% of all estimates lie in the interval 0.5 to 0.9, and a high percentage is in the near vicinity of the population parameter. In contrast to the previous experiment, the sample evidence never suggests that the population consists entirely of successes or of failures.

The main results of our experiments can be summarized in the following points: (i) in both experiments the mean of the sampling distribution is found to be virtually equal to the value of the population parameter; (ii) the dispersion of the sampling distribution for samples size 16 is less than that for samples size 4, the standard deviation of the former being about one half of that of the latter; and

Table 2-2

Successes		Frequency	
Number	Proportion: $\hat{\pi}$	Absolute	Relative: f
0	0.0000	0	0.00
1	0.0625	0	0.00
2	0.1250	0	0.00
3	0.1875	0	0.00
4	0.2500	0	0.00
5	0.3125	1	0.01
6	0.3750	0	0.00
7	0.4375	1	0.01
8	0.5000	5	0.05
9	0.5625	10	0.10
10	0.6250	17	0.17
11	0.6875	21	0.21
12	0.7500	20	0.20
13	0.8125	15	0.15
14	0.8750	7	0.07
15	0.9375	3	0.03
16	1.0000	0	0.00
		100	1.00

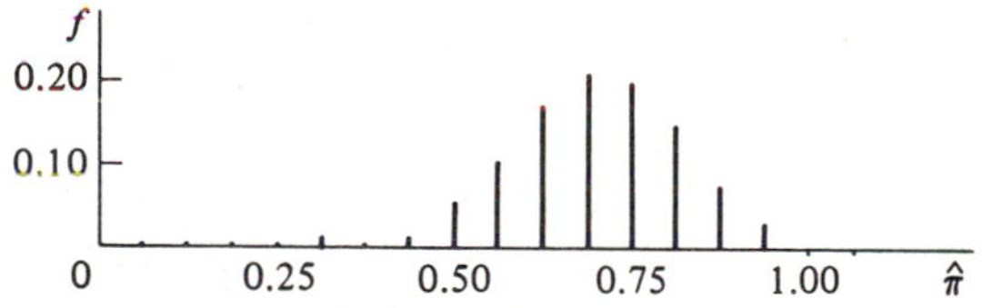

Figure 2-2

(iii) the sampling distribution for samples size 16 is considerably more symmetric than that for samples size 4.

These results have been obtained by repeated sampling from a dichotomous population (i.e., a population containing only two types of individuals) with a proportion of successes equal to 0.7. Only two sampling distributions, those corresponding to samples size 4 and size 16, have been derived. But even given this specific character of our experiments, the results clearly inspire certain generalizations about the sampling distribution of the proportion of successes observed in a sample ($\hat{\pi}$) as an estimator of the proportion of successes in the population (π). These generalizations are

1. $\hat{\pi}$ is an *unbiased estimator* of π (i.e., the mean of the sampling distribution of $\hat{\pi}$ is equal to the population parameter π).

2. As sample size increases, the sampling distribution of $\hat{\pi}$ becomes increasingly more concentrated around π. This implies that $\hat{\pi}$ is a *consistent estimator* of π.
3. Sampling distribution of $\hat{\pi}$ based on larger samples tends to be more symmetric than that based on small samples.

The fourth generalization is less obvious and involves a greater degree of uncertainty than the first three. It arises in connection with generalization 2; since dispersion (or, conversely, concentration) is measured by standard deviation, we would expect some relationship between the change in sample size and the change in the standard deviation. Noting that as sample size is increased fourfold, the standard deviation is halved, we may suspect that the proposition given below also holds.

4. The standard deviation of the sampling distribution of $\hat{\pi}$ changes in inverse proportion to the square root of the sample size.

This final generalization appears to be more risky than the previous three. For one thing, the standard deviation for samples size 16 is only roughly equal to one half of that for sample size 4; for another thing, we only have two sample sizes (i.e., one ratio) from which we generalize. The first difficulty could be remedied by using more than 100 samples and thus sharpening the accuracy, the second by conducting further experiments.

It may have been noticed that our sampling experiment does not allow any generalizations about the efficiency of $\hat{\pi}$. While it would certainly be interesting to see whether any other unbiased estimator has a smaller variance than $\hat{\pi}$, the answer cannot be extracted from our experiments since we considered only one estimator and thus are not able to make comparisons. But even if we did consider several alternative estimators rather than just one, sampling experiments would at best settle the question of efficiency within the small class of estimators actually considered and not with respect to all (unbiased) estimators as desired.

We hope the foregoing generalizations hold for all values of the population parameter π and all sample sizes n. Whether they do or do not will be found when we derive the sampling distribution theoretically in Chapter 4.

2-2 Sampling Distribution of Sample Mean

Let us now consider the problem of deriving the sampling distribution of sample mean as an estimator of the population mean. The population we are simulating is that of, say, all adults in a given geographical region, each being characterized by the number of dental appointments in a given year. Our variable X then represents the number of dental appointments by an adult in a year. To simplify the construction of the population we will postulate that X can only assume the values 0, 1, 2, . . . , 9, and that each of these values can be observed with equal probability. Such a distribution of values is called a *discrete uniform distribution.* This population is simulated by a container with a large number of marbles that are identical in every respect except for a numeral embossed in the surface. The numerals are 0, 1, 2, . . . , 9, and the container includes an equal number of marbles of each denomination. A more elaborate description of the population is given in Table 2-3. (In our notation capital letters represent variables and lowercase letters represent the *values* of the variables.)

Table 2-3

Value of X: x	Relative frequency in the population
0	0.1
1	0.1
2	0.1
3	0.1
4	0.1
5	0.1
6	0.1
7	0.1
8	0.1
9	0.1
	1.0

Population mean: $\mu = \Sigma f_i x_i$
$= 4.5.$

Population standard deviation:
$\sigma = \sqrt{\Sigma f_i (x_i - \mu)^2}$
$= 2.8723.$

As in case A, we will again conduct two sampling experiments. In the first experiment, we will draw 100 samples of size 5 and derive the sampling distribution of sample mean. To get some idea about its efficiency we will also derive the sampling distribution of an alternative estimator, namely sample median. Thus each sample will be used for producing two estimates of the population mean. In the second experiment, we will draw 100 samples of size 10 and derive the distribution of sample mean. As in the experiments in connection with case A, we will again be satisfied with approximating infinity by a mere 100 samples. In describing the results, the following notation will be used.

μ = population mean;

σ = population standard deviation;

$\bar{X}$ = sample mean;

$\tilde{X}$ = sample median;

f = relative frequency;

n = size of sample.

Experiment B.1. 100 samples of size 5. Let us first consider the sampling distribution of sample mean, which is the focal point of our interest. Obviously, even though the variable (and thus individual observations) can assume only integer values 0 to 9, sample means will, in general, not be intergers. Thus the sampling distribution will be a frequency distribution with classes defined by intervals and not by points. We may, of course, choose a single value such as the center of each interval to represent each class. The distribution obtained as a result of our experi-

Table 2-4

Value of sample mean: $\bar{x}$		Frequency	
Interval	Midpoint	Absolute	Relative: f
0.5 to 1.499	1	1	0.01
1.5 to 2.499	2	5	0.05
2.5 to 3.499	3	12	0.12
3.5 to 4.499	4	31	0.31
4.5 to 5.499	5	28	0.28
5.5 to 6.499	6	15	0.15
6.5 to 7.499	7	5	0.05
7.5 to 8.499	8	3	0.03
8.5 to 9.499	9	0	0.00
		100	1.00

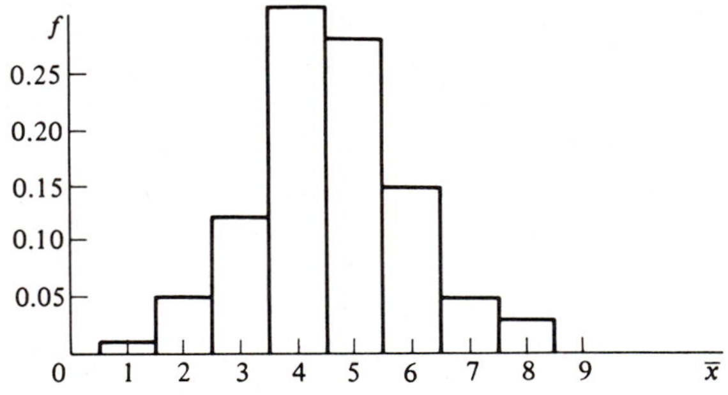

Figure 2-3

ment is shown in Table 2-4 and illustrated by Figure 2-3. The main characteristics of this distribution are

$$\text{Mean} = \sum_{i=1}^{9} f_i \bar{x}_i = 4.60.$$

$$\text{Standard deviation} = \sqrt{\sum_{i=1}^{9} f_i(\bar{x}_i - 4.60)^2} = 1.3638.$$

The results indicate that 59% of the estimated values $(0.31 + 0.28 = 0.59)$ fall within ± 1 of the true value of 4.5, while 86% of the estimates lie within ± 2 of 4.5.

Next we present the derived sampling distribution of sample median. Since the sample size is an odd number and all values of X are integers, sample median will

Table 2-5

Value of sample median: $\tilde{x}$	Frequency: Absolute	Frequency: Relative: f
0	1	0.01
1	4	0.04
2	4	0.04
3	19	0.19
4	23	0.23
5	14	0.14
6	17	0.17
7	11	0.11
8	5	0.05
9	2	0.02
	100	1.00

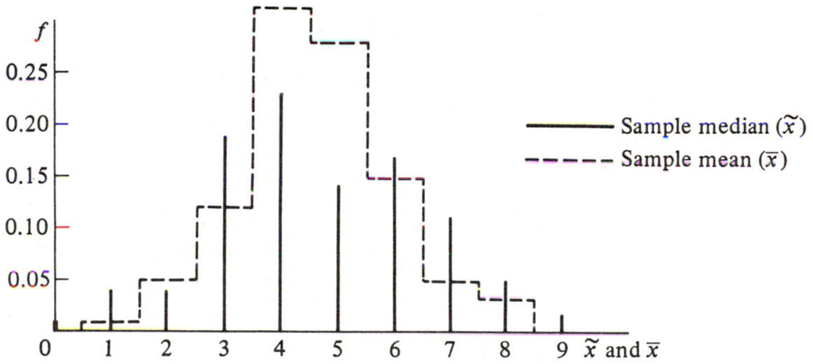

Figure 2-4

always be an integer. The distribution is given in Table 2-5. The main characteristics of this distribution are

$$\text{Mean} = \sum_{i=0}^{9} f_i \tilde{x}_i = 4.68.$$

$$\text{Standard deviation} = \sqrt{\sum_{i=0}^{9} f_i(\tilde{x}_i - 4.68)^2} = 1.8755.$$

The distribution is shown graphically in Figure 2-4. To facilitate a comparison with the sampling distribution of sample mean, we reproduce the distribution of Figure 2-3 on the same diagram with dotted lines. It is obvious at first sight that the two distributions are quite different, that of $\tilde{X}$ being much less regular and considerably more dispersed than that of $\bar{X}$.

Experiment B.2. 100 samples of size 10. The results of this experiment are summarized in Table 2-6 and Figure 2-5. The main characteristics of this distribution

Table 2-6

Value of sample mean: $\bar{x}$		Frequency	
Interval	Midpoint	Absolute	Relative: f
0.5 to 1.499	1	0	0.00
1.5 to 2.499	2	1	0.01
2.5 to 3.499	3	14	0.14
3.5 to 4.499	4	34	0.34
4.5 to 5.499	5	32	0.32
5.5 to 6.499	6	16	0.16
6.5 to 7.499	7	3	0.03
7.5 to 8.499	8	0	0.00
8.5 to 9.499	9	0	0.00
		100	1.00

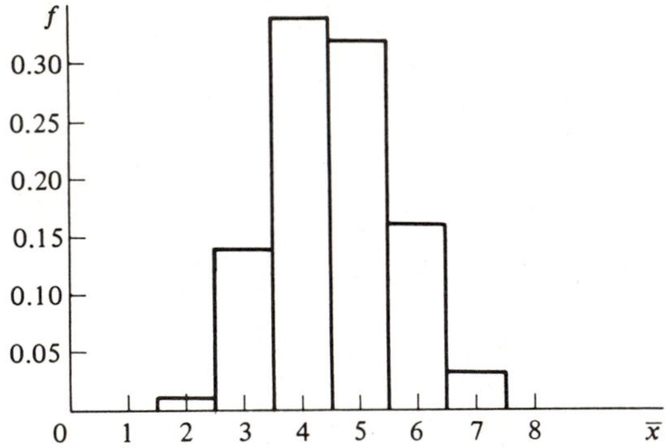

Figure 2-5

are

$$\text{Mean} = \sum_{i=2}^{7} f_i \bar{x}_i = 4.57.$$

$$\text{Standard deviation} = \sqrt{\sum_{i=2}^{7} f_i(\bar{x}_i - 4.57)^2} = 1.0416.$$

The results of our sampling experiments in case B can be summarized as follows: (i) the mean of the sampling distribution of sample mean is approximately equal to the population mean for both sample sizes examined; (ii) the dispersion of the sampling distribution of sample mean for samples size 10 is less than that for samples size 5, the variance of the latter (1.3638^2) being almost twice as large as that of the former (1.0416^2); and (iii) the mean of the sampling distribution of sample median is also approximately equal to the population mean, but its variation is greater than that of the sample mean in samples of equal size.

These results, although based on a specific case, obviously inspire some generalizations.

1. Sample mean $\overline{X}$ is an *unbiased estimator* of the population mean μ.
2. As sample size increases, the sampling distribution of $\overline{X}$ becomes increasingly more concentrated around the population mean; thus $\overline{X}$ is a *consistent estimator* of μ.
3. Sample median $\tilde{X}$ is an unbiased estimator of μ, but its variance is greater than that of $\overline{X}$; thus $\tilde{X}$ is an inefficient estimator of μ.

These generalizations follow quite obviously from the main findings of our experiments. The next generalization is less obvious and somewhat more risky.

4. The standard deviation of the sampling distribution of $\overline{X}$ changes in inverse proportion to the square root of sample size.

Generalization 4 is borne out by our experiment only very roughly; it means that we consider $1.3638 \div 1.0416 = 1.3093$ as "approximately equal" to $\sqrt{2} = 1.4142$.

These four generalizations will be considered again when we discuss theoretical derivations of sampling distributions. For the time being we will hold them only tentatively and hope to be able to confirm or refute them later. Before we do that, we have to master the basic tools of probability theory, and this is the subject of Chapter 3.

EXERCISES

2-1. Using 100 samples, construct experimental sampling distributions of the proportion of heads for samples of 4 and of 16 tosses of a coin. Calculate the mean and the standard deviation of both distributions, and relate the results to those presented under case A of this chapter.

2-2. Consider a population consisting of equal proportions of numbers 1, 2, and 3.

a. Construct all possible samples of size 3, noting that the relative frequency of each sample is the same. Describe the resulting distribution of sample mean and of sample median. Calculate the means and the standard deviations of the two distributions. [HINT: There are 27 different samples of size 3 that can be drawn from this population.]

b. Do the same for samples of size 4. Compare the ratio of the standard deviation of the mean to the standard deviation of the median with the corresponding ratio obtained in **a** above.

2-3. Call getting two heads and a tail in tossing three coins of equal denominations a "success." Make 10 such tosses and record the number of successes. Repeat this 100 times, each time making 10 tosses and recording the number of successes.

a. Present the resulting sampling distribution.

b. Calculate the mean and the standard deviation of the proportion of successes.

2-4. Using a computer program that generates random normal deviates, construct an empirical sampling distribution of sample mean for samples of size 5 drawn from a normal population.

2-5. Consider an infinite population consisting of the numbers 1 and 3, each present in equal proportion.

a. Describe all possible *different* samples of size 2 that can be drawn from this population, noting that the relative frequency (probability) of each of these samples is the same.

b. The mean of the population is, of course, 2. Suppose we are interested in estimating the *square* of the mean, whose true value is 4. Two estimators have been proposed for this purpose. The first (say, $\hat{\alpha}_1$) is obtained by squaring the sample mean, i.e.,

$$\hat{\alpha}_1 = \bar{X}^2,$$

whereas the second (say, $\hat{\alpha}_2$) is obtained by averaging the squared values observed in the sample, i.e.,

$$\hat{\alpha}_2 = \frac{X_1^2 + X_2^2 + \cdots + X_n^2}{n}.$$

Present the sampling distribution of the two estimators using sample size $n = 2$.

c. Is either of the two estimators unbiased? Can anything be said about the efficiency of either estimator?

2-6. Suppose a very large population consists of families whose distribution according to the number of children is as follows.

Number of children	Proportion of families
0	0.25
1	0.50
2	0.25
	1.00

We wish to estimate the median number of children in a family (which is, of course, 1 child) by using two estimators—the sample median ($\tilde{X}$) and the sample mean ($\bar{X}$), both based on a sample of 3 randomly selected families. The sampling distributions of these estimators are given below.

$\tilde{x}$	Proportion of samples
0	10/64
1	44/64
2	10/64
	1

$\bar{x}$	Proportion of samples
0	1/64
1/3	6/64
2/3	15/64
1	20/64
4/3	15/64
5/3	6/64
2	1/64
	1

a. Which of the two estimators is or is not unbiased?

b. What is the probability that our estimate based on 3 sample observations will be *perfect* if we use **(i)** the sample median? **(ii)** the sample mean?

c. What is the probability that we *overstate* the median number of children in a family if we use **(i)** the sample median? **(ii)** the sample mean?

d. Which of the two estimators of the population median would you consider to be the better one? Give reasons.

3 | Probability and Probability Distributions

The laborious way of deriving sampling distributions by experimental simulation and the imprecision and limited validity of the results were amply demonstrated in the preceding chapter. One of the purposes of that chapter was to provide sufficient motivation for the student to learn enough probability theory to avoid having to use such a "brute force" approach. By using the laws of probability to determine what would happen if one were to draw a large (infinite) number of random samples, one avoids the need for doing the actual drawing. On the other hand, without the experience of constructing a sampling distribution experimentally as shown in Chapter 2, the role of probability presented in this chapter might appear mystifying. Mastering the basic tools of probability theory will enable us to proceed to the theoretical derivation of sampling distributions in Chapter 4 and to the Bayesian approach to inference in the last part of Chapter 6.

In spite of the fact that probability is a concept which is frequently used in many branches of science as well as in everyday life, the term itself is very difficult to define and is surrounded by controversy. We will mention the main points of view and illustrate the nature of the difficulties. According to the so-called *classical* view, the probability of a favorable outcome is given by the ratio f/n where n is the number of all possible mutually exclusive and equally likely outcomes and f is the number of those outcomes which are taken as favorable. Two outcomes are mutually exclusive if the occurrence of one rules out the occurrence of the other; for example, the appearance of a head when tossing a coin rules out the appearance of a tail in the same toss. Furthermore, outcomes are "equally likely" if it is expected a priori that each outcome would occur with equal frequency in the long run. Thus the probability of getting a 3 when tossing a fair six-sided die is 1/6 since there are six possible outcomes and, assuming that the die is fair, they are all equally likely. As another example, consider the probability of getting two heads as a result of tossing two unbiased coins. The possible outcomes are

1st coin	2nd coin
H	H
H	T
T	H
T	T

Thus there are four (not three!) possible and equally likely outcomes, and the probability of getting two heads is then 1/4. Note that this definition of probability may easily be adapted to continuous cases as well. Consider, for example, a clock dial without the clock and with only one freely rotating hand. Here there is an infinite number of points at which the hand may stop after being rotated. Since a point has no dimension and, in particular, no length, the probability that the hand stops at any specific point is zero. However, an interval (unlike a point) has a nonzero length, and thus the probability that the hand will stop within any interval is positive and can be determined. The probability definition given above can be rephrased in terms of length (volume, etc.) instead of numbers; for example, in our illustration the probability that the hand stops between the 10th and the 12th minute is 1/30.

There are two major difficulties associated with the use of the classical definition of probability. The first arises from the crucial dependence of the definition on the assumption that all outcomes are equally likely. If we were asked what is the probability of throwing a head when the coin is biased in an unspecified way, we would not be able to answer. The second difficulty is similar. There exist some events for which it is impossible—with our present knowledge—to derive prior probabilities. Examples are given by mortality tables, labor force participation rates, income changes, and many others. Both of these difficulties are due to the fact that the classical definition relies on prior analysis. In fact, probabilities determined by using the classical definition are sometimes called "prior probabilities" to emphasize their theoretical nature.

The difficulties associated with the classical view of probability are avoided if we adopt the *objectivistic* or *frequency* concept of probability. This view of probability represents a newer development in probability theory; it defines probabilities as the limits of relative frequencies as the number of observations approaches infinity. The relative frequencies in a large number of trials can be used as approximations of probabilities. Thus, if we were to toss an unbiased coin a large number of times, we would notice that the proportion (i.e., relative frequency) of heads tends to become stable and close to 1/2. In this objectivistic view, probabilities are considered as empirically determined; thus they are sometimes labeled "positive probabilities." The difficulty with this view is its dependence on observations; since infinity can never be observed, empirically determined probabilities are necessarily only approximations of the limiting values. Another difficulty is that in some cases the relative frequency may not approach a limiting value.

A third approach to defining probability is the Bayesian approach, which considers probability as the *degree of rational belief.* This definition covers frequently made or implied probability statements which cannot be justified by the use of either classical or frequency definitions of probability. We are here referring to cases in which it is impossible to count (or measure) favorable and/or all possible outcomes. Examples are such statements as "I am almost certain that I will fail the examination tomorrow" or "It is quite probable that we will never know the full truth about the death of President Kennedy." In none of these examples is it possible to use well-defined theory for the development of prior probabilities or to conceive of natural repetitions to obtain probabilities *a posteriori.*

The diversity of views on probability may appear somewhat bewildering, but fortunately it causes relatively little difficulty in practice. In part, this is because quite often the specific probability given to an event is the same from all viewpoints. For example, if a respectable person produces a normal-looking coin, the probability of getting a head would be considered as 1/2 regardless of which definition of probability one uses. Further, the laws of probability apply quite generally without regard to the definition of probability.

3-1 Sets and Sample Spaces

The elements of probability theory can be developed rather conveniently with the help of simple *set theory.* This seems desirable also because the language of set theory has acquired great popularity in modern statistics and to some extent in economics as well. A *set* is a collection of definite and well-distinguished objects (members, elements). For example, a set may be three numbers 1, 2, and 3; then we write

$$S = \{1, 2, 3\}.$$

But note that a set for five numbers 1, 2, 2, 3, 3 is also

$$S = \{1, 2, 3\}$$

since only three of the five numbers are well distinguished. Also note that the order in which the elements are listed does not matter. A set can be specified either by listing all its elements, or by giving a rule which would enable us to decide whether any given object does or does not belong to it. Thus we can conceive of a rule to define a set of all families in the United States at a given time instead of having a full list. A *null,* or an *empty set,* is one with no elements in it; we write

$$S = \varnothing.$$

If element a belongs to the set S, we write

$$a \in S;$$

if it does not, then

$$a \notin S.$$

If every element in S_1 is an element of S, then S_1 is a *subset* of S. This is expressed by

$$S_1 \subseteq S.$$

For example, if $S_1 = \{1\}$ and $S = \{1, 2, 3\}$, then $S_1 \subseteq S$. S_1 is a *proper subset* of S if S contains at least one element not in S_1; this can be written as

$$S_1 \subset S.$$

If $S_1 = \{1\}$ and $S = \{1, 2, 3\}$, then S_1 is a proper subset of S. As an example of the logic and set construction consider the statement

$$\varnothing \subseteq S.$$

This must be true because if it were not true then $\varnothing$ would have at least one element not in S; but $\varnothing$ has no elements, thus the statement must hold. Further, if $S \neq \varnothing$, then S contains at least one element not in $\varnothing$, so $\varnothing$ must be a proper subset of S, i.e., $\varnothing \subset S$.

Let us now define two concepts that are of particular relevance to probability theory. The first of these is the *union of sets*. The union of two sets S_1 and S_2 is defined as the set of elements that belong either to S_1 or to S_2, or to both. If we denote by S the set that is the union of S_1 and S_2, then we can write

$$S = S_1 \cup S_2.$$

For example, if $S_1 = \{a, b, c, 2\}$ and $S_2 = \{1, 2, 3\}$, then $S = S_1 \cup S_2 = \{a, b, c, 1, 2, 3\}$. A diagrammatic representation of the concept is given in Figure 3-1. The other concept of importance in probability theory is that of *intersection of*

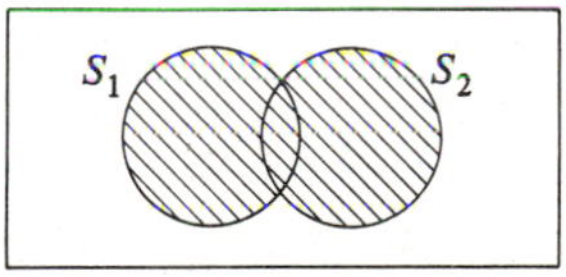

Figure 3-1

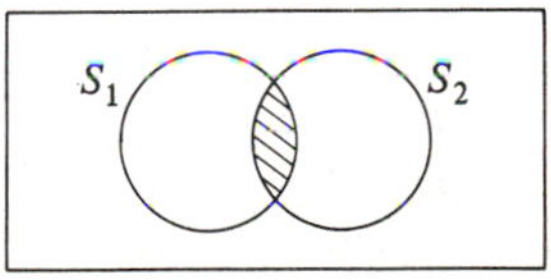

Figure 3-2

sets. The intersection of two sets S_1 and S_2 is the set of elements that belong to both S_1 and S_2. If such a set is denoted by S, then we have

$$S = S_1 \cap S_2.$$

For example, if $S_1 = \{a, b, c, 2\}$ and $S_2 = \{1, 2, 3\}$, then $S = S_1 \cap S_2 = \{2\}$. Figure 3-2 illustrates this concept diagrammatically.

The algebra of sets is based upon a few basic postulates or laws. These postulates include, among others, the so-called *commutative* and *associative laws*. Consider the sets $S_1, S_2, S_3, \ldots$, all of which are subsets of some set S. Then the commutative law states

$$S_1 \cup S_2 = S_2 \cup S_1.$$

$$S_1 \cap S_2 = S_2 \cap S_1.$$

The associative law gives the following.

$$(S_1 \cup S_2) \cup S_3 = S_1 \cup (S_2 \cup S_3),$$

$$(S_1 \cap S_2) \cap S_3 = S_1 \cap (S_2 \cap S_3).$$

These laws allow us to extend the definitions of the union and of the intersection of sets to cover more than two sets.

The most important set in probability and sampling theory is called *sample space.* This is a set whose elements represent all possible well-distinguished outcomes of an experiment (where the experiment may either have been conducted by design or have happened naturally). Thus the sample space corresponding to the experiment of tossing a coin consists of two elements, viz. $\{H, T\}$; the sample space corresponding to the experiment of tossing a die consists of six elements, viz. $\{1, 2, 3, 4, 5, 6\}$; and so on. A sample space that consists of a finite number of elements (or an infinite number but with elements that can be counted) is called a *discrete sample space.* A space that contains a continuum of points is called a *continuous* one. It should be noted that the sample space corresponding to an experiment need not be unique. That is, two or more different sample spaces may refer to the same experiment. Suppose, for example, that the experiment consists of tossing two coins. One sample space corresponding to this experiment is

{no head, one head, two heads},

and another is

{head on both coins, tail on both coins, head on first coin and tail on second coin, tail on first coin and head on second coin}.

The difference between the first and the second sample space is that one element of the first sample space (one head) is further subdivided into two elements in the second set. In general, it is desirable to use sample spaces whose elements cannot be further subdivided. Finally, note that an *event* is simply a subset of the sample space.

3-2 Permutations and Combinations

A discrete sample space can be defined, and its elements counted, by making out a complete list. Alternatively, we may develop counting formulas that will simplify this task, particularly where there is a larger number of elements involved. These counting formulas refer to the number of *permutations* and *combinations* of various outcomes; they will be of particular use in the theoretical derivation of sampling distributions when we deal with attributes.

Let us consider permutations first. By a *permutation* we mean an arrangement of objects in a definite order. We are concerned with finding the number of permutations that can be formed using the elements of a given set. Consider, for example, the set $\{A, B, C\}$. In this set there are three types of permutations possible: those consisting of one element, those consisting of two elements, and those consisting of three elements. The complete enumeration is as follows.

1. Possible permutations of *one* element: *A, B, C* (i.e., three in number).
2. Possible permutations of *two* elements: *AB, BA, AC, CA, BC, CB* (i.e., six in number).
3. Possible permutations of *three* elements: *ABC, BAC, ACB, CAB, BCA, CBA* (i.e., six in number).

Next consider the general case of a set with n elements $\{A, B, \ldots, Z\}$.

1. Possible permutations of *one* element: *A, B, . . . , Z*. There are obviously n of these.
2. Possible permutations of *two* elements: *AB, BA, AC, CA, . . . , AZ, ZA, BC, CB, . . . ,YZ, ZY*. The construction of these two-element permutations can be shown explicitly as follows.

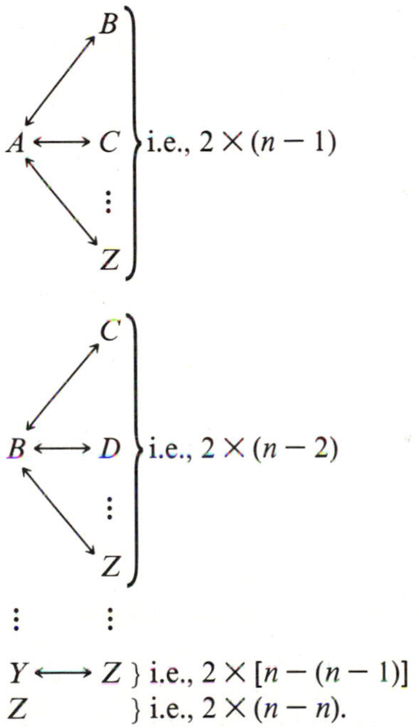

(The two-way arrows indicate that the associations go both ways; e.g., $A \leftrightarrow B$ stands for *AB as well as BA*.) The sum total of these permutations is

$$2[(n-1)+(n-2)+\cdots+2+1]=2\left[\left(\frac{n-1}{2}\right)n\right]=n(n-1).$$

This result could also be obtained by noting that in the case of two-element permutations each of the n elements gets associated with the remaining $(n-1)$ elements. Since there are altogether n elements, the total must be $n(n-1)$.

3. Possible permutations of *three* elements: *ABC, BAC, ADC, DAC, . . . , AZX, ZAX, BCA, CBA, . . . ,YZX, ZYX*. That is, each of the $n(n-1)$ permutations obtained in 2 gets associated with the remaining $(n-2)$ elements of the set. The sum total is, therefore, $n(n-1)(n-2)$.

This could be continued but the answers should be quite obvious by now. They are summarized in Table 3-1. Let us denote by ${}_nP_r$ the number of permutations of r

Table 3-1

Number of elements	Number of permutations
1	n
2	$n(n-1)$
3	$n(n-1)(n-2)$
⋮	⋮
r	$n(n-1)(n-2) \cdots (n-r+1)$
⋮	⋮
$(n-1)$	$n(n-1)(n-2) \cdots 2$
n	$n(n-1)(n-2) \cdots 2 \times 1$

distinct elements selected from a set of n elements. Then from the formula for permutations of r elements, listed in Table 3-1, we have

$$ {}_nP_r = n(n-1)(n-2) \cdots (n-r+1). $$

This expression can be simplified by using the so-called factorial notation. A *factorial* of a number n is denoted by $n!$ and defined as

$$ n! = n(n-1)(n-2) \cdots 3 \times 2 \times 1, $$

where n can be any positive integer. We also define

$$ 0! = 1. $$

When we use these symbols, the formula for the number of permutations becomes

$$ {}_nP_r = \frac{n!}{(n-r)!}. \tag{3.1} $$

The following points are worth noting.

1. ${}_nP_0 = 1$, i.e., there is only one way in which an empty set can be arranged.
2. Suppose we have n objects of which k objects are exactly the same. Then

   $$ {}_nP_n^{(k)} = \frac{n!}{k!}. \tag{3.2} $$

For example, consider the number of permutations of the four letters in the word POOH.

POOH	HPOO	OPHO	
POHO	HOPO	OPOH	
PHOO	HOOP	OHPO	Total = 12.
		OHOP	
		OOHP	
		OOPH	

$$_4P_4^{(2)} = \frac{4!}{2!} = \frac{4 \times 3 \times 2 \times 1}{2 \times 1} = 12.$$

This result can be extended to the case of n objects of which k are of one kind (and all are exactly the same), l are of another kind, etc. Then

(3.3) $$_nP_n^{(k,l,\ldots)} = \frac{n!}{k!\, l! \cdots}.$$

3. If one set of objects can be arranged in m_1 ways and another set of objects in m_2 ways, then the total number of permutations is $m_1 \times m_2$. This is sometimes known as the *multiplication principle.*

As an example of the multiplication principle, consider the number of permutations given by the outcomes of tossing two coins. Here m_1 is the number of permutations given by the possible outcomes of tossing the first coin (H and T) and is equal to 2, and m_2 refers to the outcomes of tossing the second coin and is also equal to 2. Thus, the total number of permutations is $2 \times 2 = 4$. This can be easily verified: the possible outcomes of tossing two coins are HH, HT, TH, TT, i.e., four in number. As another example, consider the number of permutations given by the outcomes of tossing two six-sided dice. In this case, $m_1 = 6$ and $m_2 = 6$, so that the total number is 36.

All permutations that involve the same elements represent a given combination. More precisely, a *combination* is a subset of r elements selected, without regard to their order, from a set of n different elements. It is assumed that $n \geq r$. Consider the set $\{A, B, C\}$. From the elements of this set we can form combinations of one, two, or three elements. These are as follows.

1. Combinations of *one* element: $\{A\}$, $\{B\}$, $\{C\}$ (i.e., three in number).
2. Combinations of *two* elements: $\{A, B\}$, $\{A, C\}$, $\{B, C\}$ (i.e., three in number).
3. Combinations of *three* elements: $\{A, B, C\}$ (i.e., *one* in number).

Next consider the general case of n elements $\{A, B, C, \ldots, Z\}$.

1. Combinations of *one* element: $\{A\}$, $\{B\}$, . . . , $\{Z\}$. These are n in number.
2. Combinations of *two* elements: $\{A, B\}$, $\{A, C\}$, . . . , $\{X, Z\}$. These can be depicted as follows.

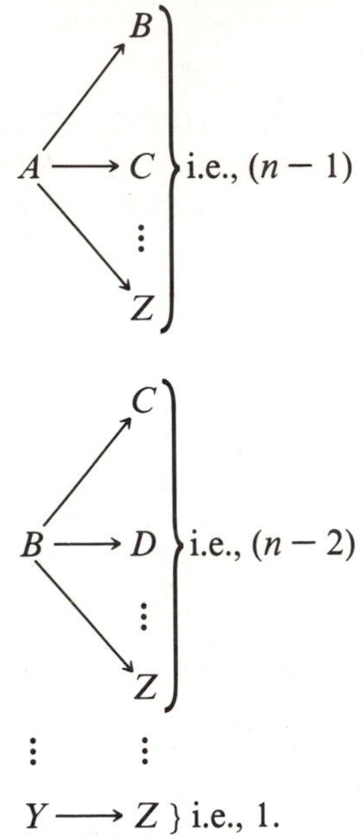

The total is

$$(n-1)+(n-2)+\cdots+1=\frac{1}{2}n(n-1)=\frac{1}{2}\,{}_nP_2.$$

This result could also be obtained by noting that any two-letter combination leads to two permutations. Thus all we have to do to get the total number of two-letter combinations is to divide the total number of two-letter permutations by two.

3. Combinations of *three* elements: $\{A, B, C\}, \{A, B, D\}, \ldots, \{X, Y, Z\}$. Since any three-letter combination leads to $3! = 6$ permutations, the total number of three-letter combinations is

$$\frac{1}{6}\,{}_nP_3=\frac{n(n-1)(n-2)}{3!}.$$

This could be continued for any number of elements; the results are summarized in Table 3-2. The number of combinations of r distinct elements selected without regard to order from a set of n elements is usually denoted by $\binom{n}{r}$. From Table 3-2 we obviously have

$$\binom{n}{r}=\frac{n!}{(n-r)!r!}. \tag{3.4}$$

Table 3-2

Number of elements	Number of combinations
1	n
2	$\dfrac{n(n-1)}{2}$
3	$\dfrac{n(n-1)(n-2)}{3!}$
$\vdots$	
r	$\dfrac{n(n-1)\cdots(n-r+1)}{r!}$
$\vdots$	$\vdots$
$(n-1)$	n
n	1

Note that

$$\binom{n}{0} = 1,$$

$$\binom{n}{n} = 1,$$

$$\binom{n}{r} = \binom{n}{n-r}.$$

A well-known use of the formula for the number of combinations is the determination of *binomial coefficients.* Consider the following algebraic expansions.

$$(a+b)^0 = 1,$$

$$(a+b)^1 = a+b,$$

$$(a+b)^2 = a^2 + 2ab + b^2,$$

$$(a+b)^3 = a^3 + 3a^2b + 3ab^2 + b^3,$$

$$(a+b)^4 = a^4 + 4a^3b + 6a^2b^2 + 4ab^3 + b^4,$$

and so on.

The numerical coefficients in the foregoing expansions are known as the binomial coefficients. Note that they are, in fact, given by the formula for the number of combinations, since the expansions could equivalently be written as

$$(a+b)^0 = 1,$$

$$(a+b)^1 = \binom{1}{0} a + \binom{1}{1} b,$$

$$(a+b)^2 = \binom{2}{0} a^2 + \binom{2}{1} ab + \binom{2}{2} b^2,$$

$$(a+b)^3 = \binom{3}{0} a^3 + \binom{3}{1} a^2b + \binom{3}{2} ab^2 + \binom{3}{3} b^3,$$

$$(a+b)^4 = \binom{4}{0} a^4 + \binom{4}{1} a^3b + \binom{4}{2} a^2b^2 + \binom{4}{3} ab^3 + \binom{4}{4} b^4,$$

and so on.

Generalizing we have

$$(3.5) \qquad (a+b)^n = \binom{n}{0} a^n + \binom{n}{1} a^{n-1}b + \binom{n}{2} a^{n-2}b^2 + \cdots + \binom{n}{n} b^n$$

$$= \sum_{r=0}^{n} \binom{n}{r} a^{n-r}b^r.$$

An easy way of calculating the binomial coefficients is by using what is known as the *Pascal triangle* (Figure 3-3). Each row begins and ends with a 1; each other number is a sum of the two neighboring numbers in the row immediately above.

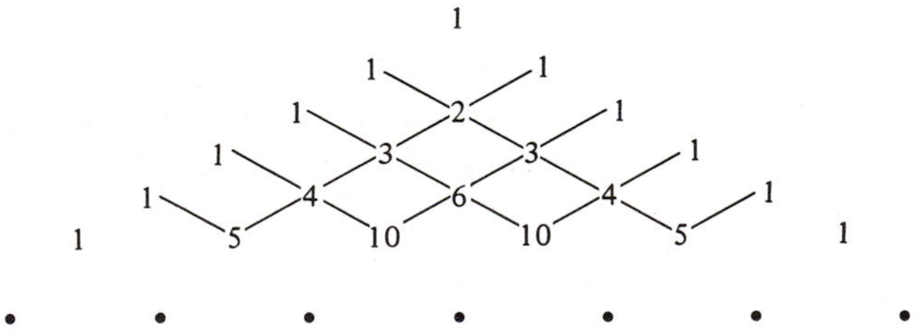

Figure 3-3

The binomial formula (3.5) facilitates the determination of the total number of subsets that can be formed from a set of n distinct elements. The first subset is the null set, then there are n subsets of one element each, $n(n-1)/2$ subsets of two elements, and so on. The total number is given by the sum

$$\binom{n}{0} + \binom{n}{1} + \binom{n}{2} + \cdots + \binom{n}{n}.$$

These are the binomial coefficients for the expansion with $a = 1$ and $b = 1$, i.e.,

$$(1+1)^n = \binom{n}{0} + \binom{n}{1} + \binom{n}{2} + \cdots + \binom{n}{n}.$$

But, obviously,

$$(1+1)^n = 2^n.$$

Thus we have found that *a set of n elements has 2^n subsets.*

3-3 Basic Theorems of Probability Theory

While there exists a considerable uncertainty about the definition of probability, there is complete agreement among statisticians about the rules (axioms) that every measure of probability must satisfy. These rules can be stated as follows.

Let $A, B, C, \ldots$ be events represented by subsets of a discrete sample space S and let $P(A), P(B), P(C), \ldots$ be their respective probabilities. We postulate that

1. $0 \leq P(S_i) \leq 1$ for each subset S_i of S;
2. $P(S) = 1$;
3. if $A, B, C, \ldots, Z$ are mutually exclusive, then

$$P(A \cup B \cup C \cdots \cup Z) = P(A) + P(B) + P(C) + \cdots + P(Z).$$

Let us now consider the basic theorems of probability theory.

Theorem 1 *If $\bar{A}$ is an event "not A," then $P(\bar{A}) = 1 - P(A)$.*

This, we hope, needs no elaboration. If the probability that it will rain is 0.40, then it is quite obvious that the probability that it will not rain is 0.60. Theorem 1 is represented by Figure 3-4.

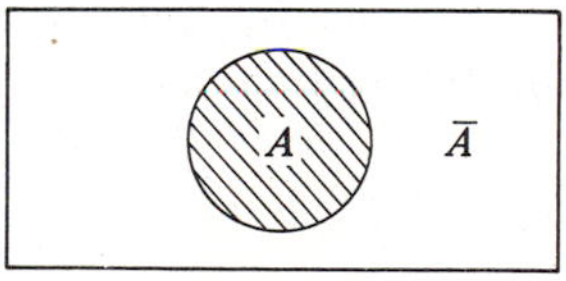

Figure 3-4

Before we proceed any further, we ought to digress in order to clarify the meaning of conditional statements of the form "if . . . , then . . ." and similar, which are frequently used in the language of theorems and proofs. Such a clarification requires that we distinguish between different types of conditions; in particular, we have to distinguish between a "necessary," a "sufficient," and a "necessary and sufficient" condition. This distinction will be illustrated by reference to two non-identical propositions P_1 and P_2. First, take a *sufficient* condition: if P_1 is true, then P_2 is true. This is sometimes expressed as "P_1 implies P_2." Here P_1 is a sufficient condition for P_2. For instance, P_1 may be "being a mother" and P_2 "being a woman," since motherhood is obviously a sufficient condition for womanhood. Or, as another example, P_1 may be a statement "today is Tuesday" and P_2 a statement "tomorrow is Wednesday." Next, consider a *necessary* condition: if P_1 is not true, then P_2 is not true, or alternatively, P_2 is true *only if* P_1 is true. Here P_1 is a necessary condition for P_2. For instance, "being a woman" is a necessary condition for "being a mother." Note that a sufficient condition may or may not be a necessary one; similarly, a necessary condition may or may not be sufficient. An example of a sufficient but not necessary condition is "being a mother" as a condition for "being a woman," since it is possible to be a woman without being a mother. If we reverse these propositions and put "being a woman" as a condition of "being a mother," we have an example of a necessary but not sufficient condition since being a woman is not enough for being a mother. The last example illustrates a universal property of a sufficiency relation: *if P_1 is sufficient for P_2, then P_2 is necessary for P_1.* Finally, we have the case of a *necessary and sufficient condition:* if P_1, then P_2, and if P_2, then P_1. This condition is described by an "if and only if" statement. For example, "if and only if today is Tuesday, then tomorrow is Wednesday." That is, the truth of "today is Tuesday" is not only sufficient but also necessary for the truth of "tomorrow is Wednesday." In our discussion the most frequently used conditional statement will be "if P_1, then P_2." This means that P_1 is a sufficient, but may or may not be a necessary, condition for P_2. With this remark we finish our digression and return to the discussion of basic theorems in probability.

Theorem 2 *(Addition Theorem)* $P(A \cup B) = P(A) + P(B) - P(A \cap B)$.

This theorem states that the probability of either A or B or of both is equal to the probability of A *plus* the probability of B *minus* the probability of both A and B occurring simultaneously. It is illustrated by Figure 3-5. Because A and B overlap, the term $P(A \cap B)$ has to be deducted from the sum $P(A) + P(B)$; otherwise it would be counted twice.

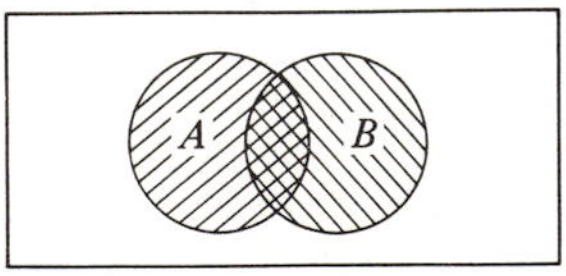

Figure 3-5

EXAMPLE 1 Consider the probability that a card drawn at random from a pack of 52 cards is either a spade or a face card. Let A = spade and B = face card. Note that

$$P(A) = \frac{13}{52} \quad \text{(since there are 13 spades in a pack),}$$

$$P(B) = \frac{12}{52} \quad \text{(since there are 12 face cards in a pack),}$$

$$P(A \cap B) = \frac{3}{52} \quad \text{(since there are 3 face cards in a suit of spades).}$$

Then

$$P(A \cup B) = \frac{13}{52} + \frac{12}{52} - \frac{3}{52} = \frac{22}{52}.$$

EXAMPLE 2 What is the probability that a toss of a six-sided die will result in a "1" or "2"?

$$\begin{aligned} P(\text{"1"} \cup \text{"2"}) &= P(\text{"1"}) + P(\text{"2"}) - P(\text{"1"} \cap \text{"2"}) \\ &= \frac{1}{6} + \frac{1}{6} - 0 \\ &= \frac{1}{3}. \end{aligned}$$

The second example brings us to the theorem that deals with the probability of mutually exclusive events already mentioned in connection with the classical definition of probability. In the language of set theory, events (i.e., subsets of the sample space) are mutually exclusive if and only if their intersection is an empty set. The theorem is

Theorem 3 *If A and B are mutually exclusive, then* $P(A \cap B) = 0$.

This theorem is illustrated by Figure 3-6. It can be extended to any number of mutually exclusive events. In particular, if $A, B, C, \ldots, Z$ are all mutually exclusive, then

$$P(A \cap B \cap C \cap \cdots \cap Z) = 0.$$

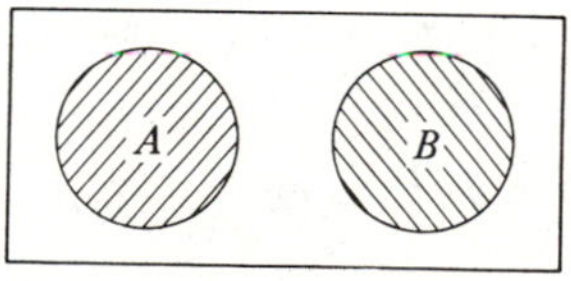

Figure 3-6

Let us now examine events that are not mutually exclusive. Consider, for example, the situation where we randomly select a person from a certain population and record two characteristics, smoking habit (S or $\bar{S}$) and sex (M or F). The two characteristics are obviously not mutually exclusive, at least not in a modern society. The sample space for this experiment is $\{(MS), (FS), (M\bar{S}), (F\bar{S})\}$, where MS represents "male smoker," etc. If the population is a finite one, the distribution may be described by absolute frequencies as follows:

		Smoking habit S	$\bar{S}$	Totals
Sex	M	a	b	$a+b$
	F	c	d	$c+d$
Totals		$a+c$	$b+d$	N

where $N = a + b + c + d$ is the population total. In terms of probabilities this distribution would be

		Smoking habit S	$\bar{S}$	
Sex	M	$P(M \cap S)$	$P(M \cap \bar{S})$	$P(M)$
	F	$P(F \cap S)$	$P(F \cap \bar{S})$	$P(F)$
		$P(S)$	$P(\bar{S})$	1

The probabilities in the body of the table, pertaining to intersections of sets, are called *joint probabilities*. For example, $P(M \cap S)$ is the probability that a person selected at random will be both a male and a smoker, i.e., has the two joint characteristics. The probabilities that appear in the last row and in the last column of the table are known as *marginal probabilities*. Thus, $P(M)$ gives the probability of drawing a male regardless of his smoking habits, $P(S)$ gives the probability of selecting a smoker regardless of sex, and so on. It is important to note that *marginal probabilities are equal to the sum of the corresponding joint probabilities*, i.e., that

$$P(M) = P(M \cap S) + P(M \cap \bar{S}),$$

since the events $M \cap S$ and $M \cap \bar{S}$ are mutually exclusive. Similarly,

$$P(S) = P(M \cap S) + P(F \cap S),$$

and so on. Let us now see how the addition theorem given earlier works in our example.

$$P(M \cup S) = P(M) + P(S) - P(M \cap S) = \frac{a+b}{N} + \frac{a+c}{N} - \frac{a}{N}$$

$$= \frac{a+b+c}{N} = 1 - \frac{d}{N} = 1 - P(F \cap \bar{S}).$$

That is, the probability of drawing either a male or a smoker or both is simply equal to 1 *minus* the probability of drawing a female nonsmoker (the only category not covered by $M \cup S$). Similarly,

$$P(M \cup \bar{S}) = 1 - P(F \cap S),$$

$$P(F \cup S) = 1 - P(M \cap \bar{S}),$$

$$P(F \cup \bar{S}) = 1 - P(M \cap S).$$

Suppose now that we wish to know the probability that a person of *given* sex is a smoker (nonsmoker), or that a person of *given* smoking habits is a male (female). Such probabilities are known as *conditional probabilities,* and we write them as $P(S|M)$, which we read "probability of S given M," etc. For instance, $P(S|M)$ means that we have a male and want to know the probability that he is a smoker. This probability, in a finite population, is obviously given by the total number of male smokers divided by the total number of males. Thus we have

$$P(S|M) = \frac{a}{a+b},$$

$$P(M|S) = \frac{a}{a+c},$$

and so on.

Note that

$$P(S|M) + P(\bar{S}|M) = 1,$$

$$P(S|F) + P(\bar{S}|F) = 1,$$

and so on.

In terms of probabilities we can write

$$P(S|M) = \frac{P(S \cap M)}{P(M)},$$

$$P(\bar{S}|M) = \frac{P(\bar{S} \cap M)}{P(M)},$$

and so on.

Note that the conditional probability that a male is a smoker, i.e., $P(S|M)$, is simply given by the proportion of smokers among males; the conditional probability that a smoker is a male, i.e., $P(M|S)$, is given by the proportion of males among smokers, and so on.

This discussion leads to an important theorem.

Theorem 4 *(Conditional Probability) If A and B are subsets of a discrete sample space and $P(B) \neq 0$, then $P(A|B) = P(A \cap B)/P(B)$.*

That is, the conditional probability of A given B is equal to the joint probability of A and B divided by the (nonzero) marginal probability of B.

The following points should be noted in connection with this theorem on conditional probability.

1. $A|B$ is *not* a set.
2. $P(A|B)$ and $P(B|A)$ are not necessarily the same. In fact, they are equal to each other if and only if $P(A) = P(B) \neq 0$.
3. By writing $P(A|B)$ we do not necessarily imply any temporal ordering between A and B. It does not matter whether B occurred prior to, simultaneously with, or after A.

EXAMPLE 1

$$P(\text{face card}|\text{spade}) = \frac{3/52}{13/52} = \frac{3}{13}$$

and

$$P(\text{spade}|\text{face card}) = \frac{3/52}{12/52} = \frac{3}{12}.$$

EXAMPLE 2 Suppose we toss an unbiased coin twice. What is the probability that the outcome of the second toss is a head, given that the outcome of the first toss was a head? Let H_i stand for "head in the ith toss." Then

$$P(H_2|H_1) = \frac{P(H_1 \cap H_2)}{P(H_1)} = \frac{1/4}{1/2} = \frac{1}{2}.$$

Let us consider the second example more closely. The results show that the probability of getting a head in the second toss, given that we obtained a head in the first toss, is 1/2. But 1/2 is precisely the probability of getting a head in *any* toss, regardless of what happened in the first toss. Indeed, we should be very surprised if we got any other answer since the coin obviously has no memory. Therefore, what happened to it in the first toss is irrelevant for determining what is going to happen to it in the second toss. Such events for which the occurrence of one event in no way affects the probability of occurrence of the other event are called *independent events.* Thus, if A is independent of B, we must have

$$P(A|B) = P(A). \tag{3.6}$$

That is, the conditional probability of A given B is equal to the marginal probability of A. By using the development of $P(A|B)$ given by Theorem 4 (under the assumption that $P(B) \neq 0$, we obtain

$$\frac{P(A \cap B)}{P(B)} = P(A). \tag{3.7}$$

If we now also assume that $P(A) \neq 0$, we can rewrite (3.7) as

$$\frac{P(A \cap B)}{P(A)} = P(B). \tag{3.8}$$

But the left-hand side of (3.8) is nothing else than $P(B|A)$, so that we have

$$P(B|A) = P(B). \tag{3.9}$$

That is, if A is independent of B, then B is independent of A. Equations (3.7) and (3.8) lead to the following important theorem.

Theorem 5 *(Independence) If $P(A) \neq 0$ and $P(B) \neq 0$, then A and B are independent if and only if $P(A \cap B) = P(A) \times P(B)$.*

In other words, A and B are independent if and only if their joint probability is equal to the product of their respective marginal probabilities. The theorem can be extended to any number of events. In particular, $A, B, C, \ldots, Z$, each occurring with nonzero probability, are independent if and only if

$$P(A \cap B \cap C \cdots \cap Z) = P(A) \times P(B) \times P(C) \times \cdots \times P(Z).$$

EXAMPLE 1 Suppose we toss a six-sided die twice. What is the probability that the first toss will show an even number and the second an odd number? Let E = even number and O = odd number. Then $P(E) = 1/2$, $P(O) = 1/2$. $P(E \cap O) = 1/2 \times 1/2 = 1/4$.

EXAMPLE 2 What is the probability of getting three heads in three tosses of an unbiased coin?

$$P(H_1 \cap H_2 \cap H_3) = P(H_1) \times P(H_2) \times P(H_3) = \frac{1}{2} \times \frac{1}{2} \times \frac{1}{2} = \frac{1}{8}.$$

EXAMPLE 3 Suppose smoking habits are independent of sex, i.e., $P(M \cap S) = P(M) \times P(S)$. Does this necessarily imply that $P(F \cap \bar{S}) = P(F) \times P(\bar{S})$? We have

	S	$\bar{S}$	
M	$P(M)P(S)$	$P(M \cap \bar{S})$	$P(M)$
F	$P(F \cap S)$	$P(F \cap \bar{S})$	$P(F)$
	$P(S)$	$P(\bar{S})$	1

Now,

$$P(F \cap S) = P(S) - P(M)P(S) = P(S)[1 - P(M)] = P(S)P(F)$$

and

$$\begin{aligned} P(F \cap \bar{S}) &= P(F) - P(F \cap S) = P(F) - P(F)P(S) \\ &= P(F)[1 - P(S)] = P(F)P(\bar{S}). \end{aligned}$$

The answer, then, is yes.

Those not well versed in probability theory often tend to confuse the applicability of the addition theorem for mutually exclusive events with the applicability of the multiplication theorem for independent events. The confusion is due to the failure of distinguishing $P(A \cup B)$ (i.e., probability that *either A or B or both A and B* will

Figure 3-7

occur) from $P(A \cap B)$ (i.e., probability that *both A* and *B* will occur) (see Figure 3-7). Now if A and B are mutually exclusive, then

$$P(A \cap B) = 0, \tag{3.10}$$

as implied by Theorem 3 and illustrated by Figure 3-6. For A and B to be independent we require that

$$P(A \cap B) = P(A) \times P(B) \tag{3.11}$$

But equations (3.10) and (3.11) can hold simultaneously only if either $P(A)$ or $P(B)$ (or both) is equal to zero, which is ruled out by our Theorem 5. Thus, mutually exclusive events cannot be independent at the same time, as should be obvious even by much less formal reasoning. If A and B are mutually exclusive, then the occurrence of one prevents the occurrence of the other, i.e., the occurrence of A makes the probability of occurrence of B zero. However, we described independent events as those for which the occurrence of one in *no way* affects the probability of the other, and this is clearly not the case when two events are mutually exclusive. By the same reasoning it is also quite clear that independent events cannot be mutually exclusive.

3-4 Bayes Theorem

Let us consider a special theorem that was first introduced by Reverend Thomas Bayes in the 18th century and that has recently given rise to a whole school of followers known as Bayesian statisticians. From the expression for the conditional probability of A given B,

$$P(A|B) = \frac{P(A \cap B)}{P(B)},$$

we have

$$P(A \cap B) = P(B)P(A|B). \tag{3.12}$$

Further, the conditional probability of B given A is

$$P(B|A) = \frac{P(A \cap B)}{P(A)}. \tag{3.13}$$

A substitution for $P(A \cap B)$ from (3.12) into (3.13) then leads to the following theorem.

Theorem 6 *(Bayes Theorem) If* $P(A) \neq 0$ *and* $P(B) \neq 0$, *then*

$$P(B|A) = \frac{P(B)P(A|B)}{P(A)}.$$

The theorem follows in a straightforward way from (3.12) and (3.13) and is seemingly quite innocuous, but its interpretation and use have led to a serious controversy among statisticians. The point at issue arises when event B occurs before A, or when B is the cause of A. In these situations we normally wish to find the probability of A given that B has occurred or that B is the cause of A. For instance, we may wish to find the probability of an increase in the stock market prices today given that there was a decline in prices yesterday; or we may wish to determine the probability of getting 3 heads in 3 tosses of a coin, given that the coin is unbiased. Thus we normally assume the existence of a given state of nature (e.g., yesterday's price behavior or the unbiasedness of a coin) and then determine the probability that some event will occur. Bayes theorem, on the other hand, leads us in the opposite direction. Having observed an event, the theorem enables us to impute a probability to a given state of nature. Thus having observed an increase in the stock market prices today (after returning from a camping trip in the wilderness), we may use Bayes theorem to determine the probability that there was a price decline yesterday. Or having observed 3 heads in 3 tosses of a coin, we may use the Bayes theorem to assign a probability to the claim that the coin is unbiased.

In the context of statistical inference, the states of nature are represented by populations, and the events are represented by sample observations. Bayes theorem has accordingly been used to assign probabilities to populations on the basis of sample observations, rather than the other way around. This has led to the description of Bayesian probabilities as *inverse probabilities,* and of Bayes theorem as *Bayes rule for the probability of causes.*

To elaborate a little further, let us consider an experiment that involves drawing a sample from one of m hypothesized populations $H_1, H_2, \ldots, H_m$. The observed sample data are designated D. This situation is illustrated by Figure 3-8 where $m = 4$ and where the circled area corresponds to D. The probability that the sample was drawn from, say, population H_4, given that we observe D, is

$$P(H_4|D) = \frac{P(H_4)P(D|H_4)}{P(D)}.$$

This is represented in Figure 3-8 by the ratio of the area common to D and H_4 to the total area of the circle D. In classical, non-Bayesian inference we would take one of

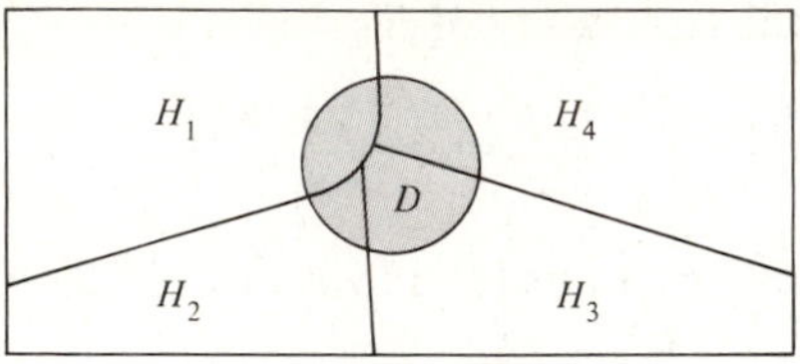

Figure 3-8

the populations, say, H_4, as given and then inquire about the probability of observing D. This probability would be represented in Figure 3-8 by the ratio of the area common to D and H_4 to the total area under H_4. The difficulty with implementing the Bayes formula is that we have to assign a probability to the state of nature H_4. This is done by falling back on our prior knowledge and/or beliefs. Accordingly, probabilities such as $P(H_4)$ are called *prior probabilities.* The resulting conditional probabilities such as $P(H_4|D)$ are then called *posterior probabilities.*

The above discussion suggests that we may use Bayes theorem as a convenient framework for adjusting our beliefs in light of newly observed sample evidence. We can start with our prior judgment about the various states of nature, observe the available sample evidence, and finish with a revised judgment. In the Bayesian framework both the prior and the posterior (revised) probabilities are subjective and reflect the degree of our belief about the various states of nature in the absence of our absolute knowledge of those states.

EXAMPLE Let us consider the question of unbiasedness of a given coin. Suppose we believe strongly that the coin is unbiased but have some minor doubts about the quality control of the U.S. mint so that our prior probabilities may look something like the following.

	Probability of getting a head	Prior probability (degree of belief)
H_1	0.40	0.05
H_2	0.50 (unbiased coin)	0.90
H_3	0.60	0.05

Thus our prior probability that the coin is unbiased is 0.90. What is our posterior probability of unbiasedness after observing 3 heads in 3 tosses? Here

$$\begin{aligned}
P(H_2) &= 0.90,\\
P(D|H_2) &= 0.5^3\\
&= 0.125,\\
P(D) &= P(D \cap H_1) + P(D \cap H_2) + P(D \cap H_3)\\
&= P(H_1)P(D|H_1) + P(H_2)P(D|H_2) + P(H_3)P(D|H_3)\\
&= 0.40^3 \times 0.05 + 0.50^3 \times 0.90 + 0.60^3 \times 0.05\\
&= 0.1265.
\end{aligned}$$

Therefore,

$$P(H_2|D) = \frac{P(H_2)P(D|H_2)}{P(D)}$$

$$= \frac{0.90 \times 0.125}{0.1265}$$

$$= 0.8893.$$

Thus the observed evidence leads to a reduction of the prior probability of unbiasedness from 0.90 to 0.8893.

3-5 Discrete Random Variables and Probability Functions

Suppose we carry out an experiment that consists of tossing two coins. The sample space associated with this experiment can be described by $S = \{TT, TH, HT, HH\}$. Each element of this sample space is associated with a given number of heads (or tails). Thus we have

Elements of sample space	Number of heads
TT	0
TH	1
HT	1
HH	2

Alternatively, we could present this association as follows.

Number of heads	Elements of sample space
0	TT
1	TH, HT
2	HH

The principle of associating the elements of a sample space with some numerical characteristic can obviously be applied quite generally to any sample space. This numerical characteristic is called a *discrete random* (or *stochastic*) *variable.* Thus a discrete random variable is a variable whose values are associated with the elements of a sample space. A common notation is to denote a random variable by a capital letter (e.g., X) and its values by small letters (e.g., x); if the values follow some ordering (e.g., a sequence of observations), the order is indicated by a subscript (e.g., x_1, x_2, etc.). In our example we associated the number of heads with the elements of the sample space, but we could have equally well chosen the proportion, rather than the number, of heads as the numerical characteristic. Obviously, either the number or the proportion of heads is a random variable.

Since a sample space consists of elements that refer to outcomes of an experiment, each element can be associated with a certain probability value. In addition, since each value of a discrete random variable is associated with (one or more) elements of the sample space, it follows that each value can be associated with a certain probability. That is, a discrete random variable can be described as a variable that assumes different values with given probabilities. In our example of tossing two coins, each element of the sample space consists of two independent events. If the coins are unbiased, we have

$$P(T \cap T) = P(T)P(T) = \frac{1}{4},$$

$$P(T \cap H) = P(T)P(H) = \frac{1}{4},$$

$$P(H \cap T) = P(H)P(T) = \frac{1}{4},$$

$$P(H \cap H) = P(H)P(H) = \frac{1}{4}.$$

Let x be the number of heads and $f(x)$ the probability of getting that number. Then we can write

Elements of sample space	Number of heads: x	Probability of x: $f(x)$
TT	0	1/4
TH	1	1/4
HT	1	1/4
HH	2	1/4
		1

An alternative way of presenting the above information is simply

x	$f(x)$
0	1/4
1	1/2
2	1/4
	1

The above distribution is known as a probability function. The idea can easily be generalized to give the following definition.

If X is a discrete random variable with values $x_1, x_2, \ldots, x_m$ and with associated probabilities $f(x_1), f(x_2), \ldots, f(x_m)$, then the set of pairs,

$$\begin{array}{ll} x_1 & f(x_1) \\ x_2 & f(x_2) \\ \vdots & \\ x_m & f(x_m) \end{array}$$

is called the probability function (or distribution) of X. Since X is discrete, the distribution of probabilities is also discrete.

As an example, consider the experiment of tossing two six-sided dice. Let the random variable in this case be the total number of dots observed. Its values then are 2, 3, . . . , 12. The sample space corresponding to this experiment can be considered to consist of all possible permutations of the two sets of numbers from 1 to 6. By the multiplication principle there will be $6 \times 6 = 36$ such permutations, each occurring with equal probability (assuming that the dice are not loaded). The resulting probability distribution for the total number of dots observed is given in Table 3-3.

Table 3-3

x	Elements of sample space	$f(x)$
2	11	1/36
3	12, 21	2/36
4	13, 31, 22	3/36
5	14, 41, 23, 32	4/36
6	15, 51, 24, 42, 33	5/36
7	16, 61, 25, 52, 34, 43	6/36
8	26, 62, 35, 53, 44	5/36
9	36, 63, 45, 54	4/36
10	46, 64, 55	3/36
11	56, 65	2/36
12	66	1/36
		1

When X assumes any given value, say, x_i, this represents an event, and $f(x_i)$ represents the probability of this event. Since X can assume only one value at a time, the probability that the value of X is x_i *or* x_j $(x_i \neq x_j)$ is the probability of two mutually exclusive events; by Theorem 3 this is equal to $f(x_i) + f(x_j)$. For example, the probability that the total number of dots obtained by a toss of two dice is either 4 or 8 is equal to $3/36 + 5/36 = 2/9$. And, of course, the probability that X will assume any value *other than* x_i is equal to $1 - f(x_i)$ by Theorem 1.

For some problems, we need to find the probability that X will assume a value *less than or equal to* a given number. Such probabilities are called *cumulative probabilities* and are usually denoted by $F(x)$. If $x_1, x_2, \ldots, x_m$ are values of X given in increasing order of magnitude, that is, if $x_1 < x_2 < \cdots < x_m$, then the cumulative probability of x_k is given by

$$F(x_k) = f(x_1) + f(x_2) + \cdots + f(x_k) = \sum_{i=1}^{k} f(x_i). \tag{3.14}$$

Since the values outside the range of X (i.e., values smaller than x_1 or larger than x_m)

occur only with probability equal to zero, we may equally well write

$$F(x_k) = \sum_{i=-\infty}^{k} f(x_i). \tag{3.15}$$

A distribution that gives the cumulative probabilities $F(x)$ for every value of X is known as the *cumulative distribution* of X. For the experiment of tossing two six-sided dice the cumulative distribution is given in Table 3-4. The probability

Table 3-4

x	$F(x)$
2	1/36
3	3/36
4	6/36
5	10/36
6	15/36
7	21/36
8	26/36
9	30/36
10	33/36
11	35/36
12	1

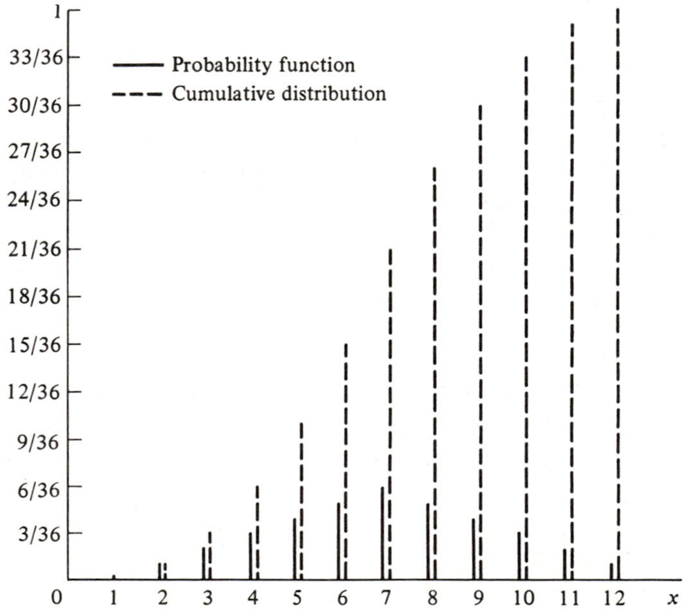

Figure 3-9

function and the cumulative distribution for this experiment are illustrated diagrammatically by Figure 3-9. The following points related to the cumulative probabilities should be noted.

1. If x_m is the largest value of X, then $F(x_m) = 1$.
2. $F(-\infty) = 0$, $F(\infty) = 1$.
3. $F(x_i) - F(x_{i-1}) = f(x_i) \qquad (x_i > x_{i-1} > x_{i-2} > \cdots)$.

So far we have concerned ourselves with only one random variable and its probability distribution. Such distributions may be termed *univariate* distributions. To extend our scope, we can consider a sample space which involves more than one random variable at a time. The corresponding probability distribution is then called a *multivariate* distribution; the case involving only two random variables is a special case known as the *bivariate* distribution. As an example, we might consider the experiment of drawing a card from a pack of 52 cards. Each card is distinguished by two characteristics, denomination and suit. Let X be the denomination with values 1 (for ace), 2, 3, . . . 10, 11 (for Jack), 12 (for Queen), and 13 (for King), and let Y be the suit with values 1 (for Hearts), 2 (for Diamonds), 3 (for Spades), and 4 (for Clubs). The bivariate probability distribution corresponding to this experiment is as follows.

		Values of X						
		1	2	3	⋯	12	13	$f(y)$
Values of Y	1	1/52	1/52	1/52	⋯	1/52	1/52	13/52
	2	1/52	1/52	1/52	⋯	1/52	1/52	13/52
	3	1/52	1/52	1/52	⋯	1/52	1/52	13/52
	4	1/52	1/52	1/52	⋯	1/52	1/52	13/52
	$f(x)$	4/52	4/52	4/52	⋯	4/52	4/52	1

The probability that X assumes a given value x and Y assumes a given value y is called the *joint probability* of x and y and is written as $f(x, y)$. For instance, the probability of drawing a Queen of Hearts is $f(12, 1) = 1/52$. The probability that X will assume a given value x *whatever the value of* Y is called the *marginal probability* of x; the distribution of these probabilities is called the *marginal distribution of* X and, in our example, is given in the bottom row. Similarly, the *marginal distribution of* Y consists of probabilities of different values of Y regardless of the values assumed by X; in our example this distribution is shown in the last right-hand column. Thus, for example, the probability of drawing a Queen (whatever suit) is 4/52, and the probability of drawing a Heart (whatever denomination) is 13/52. Marginal probability distributions are, in fact, univariate distributions and are denoted in the same way, that is, $f(x)$, $f(y)$, etc. Note that the probabilities of the marginal distribution of one variable are given by adding up the corresponding probabilities over *all* values of the other variable. Thus in the bivariate case we can write

$$f(x_i) = \sum_{j=1}^{\infty} f(x_i, y_j) = f(x_i, y_1) + f(x_i, y_2) + \cdots \tag{3.16}$$

and

$$f(y_i) = \sum_{j=1}^{\infty} f(x_j, y_i) = f(x_1, y_i) + f(x_2, y_i) + \cdots. \tag{3.17}$$

Finally, the probability that X is equal to x, *given* that Y is equal to y, is known as the *conditional probability of x given y* and is denoted by $f(x|y)$. Similarly, the *conditional probability of y given x* is denoted $f(y|x)$. By applying Theorem 4 we get

$$f(x|y) = \frac{f(x, y)}{f(y)}. \tag{3.18}$$

Using our example of drawing a card from a pack, we see that the probability of drawing, say, a Queen, *given* that the card is a Heart, is

$$f(x=12|y=1) = \frac{1/52}{13/52} = \frac{1}{13}$$

and the probability that the card is a Heart, *given* that its denomination is Queen, is

$$f(x-1|y=12) = \frac{1/52}{4/52} = \frac{1}{4}.$$

When we consider multivariate distributions, the question of dependence or independence becomes relevant. Earlier we defined independence as the condition under which the conditional probability of an event is equal to its marginal probability. Thus X and Y are independent if and only if, for all values of X and Y,

$$f(x|y) = f(x), \qquad f(y) \neq 0,$$

and

$$f(y|x) = f(y), \qquad f(x) \neq 0.$$

This means that for each variable the conditional and the marginal distributions are precisely the same. A further implication given by Theorem 5 is that X and Y are independent if and only if

$$f(x, y) = f(x)f(y) \tag{3.19}$$

for all values of X and Y. This can be generalized to any number of random variables. In particular, discrete random variables $X, Y, Z, \ldots$ are considered to be *independent* if and only if

$$f(x, y, z, \ldots) = f(x)f(y)f(z) \cdots \tag{3.20}$$

for all values of $X, Y, Z, \ldots$.

Consider, for example, the experiment of tossing two six-sided dice *twice*. Let X be the variable with values given by the number of dots in the first toss, and Y the variable with values given by the number of dots in the second toss. Obviously, the probabilities of various outcomes of the second toss are completely unaffected by the outcome of the first toss, and vice versa, so that X and Y are independent. Note that the (marginal) distribution of X is precisely the same as that of Y and can be found in Table 3-3. From this we find that the probability of throwing 7 twice is

$(6/36) \times (6/36) = 1/36$, the probability of throwing 4 followed by 8 is $(3/36) \times (5/36) = 5/432$, and so on.

With the exception of the various examples, our discussion of probability functions in this section has been quite general. It is obvious that different experimental situations may lead to different probability distributions. When describing these distributions, it is not always necessary to write out the whole distribution as we have done in our examples; frequently we may find an algebraic formula for $f(x)$ (or even for the multivariate case) that will provide a complete description of the distribution in question. Some of the distributions are very common in the sense that they describe the probabilities of many experimental situations encountered in practice. One of the most common discrete probability distributions, and the simplest one, is the so-called *discrete uniform distribution.* In this distribution the probability that X will assume any of a number of specific values is the same; i.e., $f(x)$ is a constant for all values of X. This distribution describes the probabilities of various outcomes of a toss of a die, of pulling a card of a given suit from a pack, of winning in a lottery, and many others. Another extremely common discrete distribution is the so-called *binomial distribution,* which is especially important in statistical inference and will be discussed in detail in Section 4-1.

3-6 Continuous Random Variables and Probability Functions

In the discrete case the elements of sample space are represented by points that are separated by finite distances. To each point we can ascribe a numerical value and to each value we can ascribe a given probability. However, there are many experiments for which the sample space does not consist of countable points but covers an entire interval (or collection of intervals). The random variable associated with the outcomes of such experiments is called a *continuous random variable.* An example of such an experiment is that of observing a freely rotating hand on a clock dial. The random variable in this case may be the time (say, in hours) indicated by the hand when stopped at random. There is obviously an infinite number of points between 0 and 12 at which the hand may stop, so that the probability that the hand stops at any particular *point* is zero. On the other hand, the probability that the hand stops within an *interval* around any particular point is nonzero and can be found.

The probabilities associated with the clock-dial experiment for all intervals are shown graphically by Figure 3-10. The probabilities that the value of X will fall

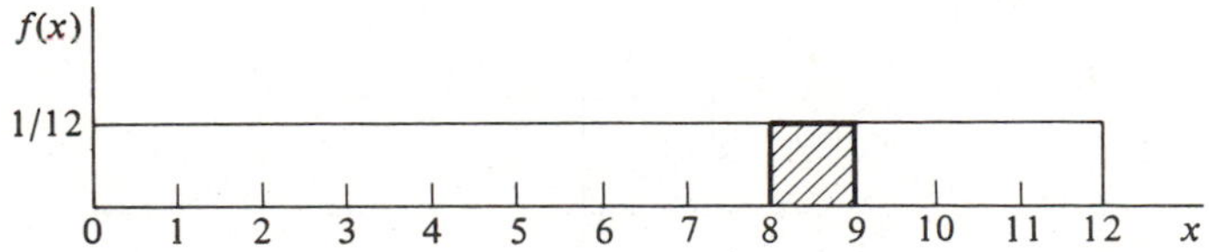

Figure 3-10

within any interval are given by the corresponding area under the curve (in this case a straight line). For example, the shaded area in Figure 3-10 gives the probability that x will fall between 8 and 9, which is 1/12. This idea can be generalized to apply to other experiments involving continuous variables. Thus the *probability distribution for a continuous variable X (called the probability density function) is represented by a curve, and the probability that X assumes a value in the interval from a to b (a < b) is given by the area under this curve bounded by a and b.* Most probability distributions that we will encounter will be continuous.

To develop the idea of the probability density function further, we can contrast it with the probability function of a discrete variable. Suppose we have a discrete random variable that can assume values $x_1, x_2, \ldots, x_n$, and the values are in ascending order of magnitude. Suppose that the probability function of this variable is given by Figure 3-11. Now the probability that, e.g., X will assume a value greater than x_3 but smaller than or equal to x_{10} is

$$P(x_3 < x \leq x_{10}) = f(x_4) + f(x_5) + \cdots + f(x_{10}) = \sum_{i=4}^{10} f(x_i).$$

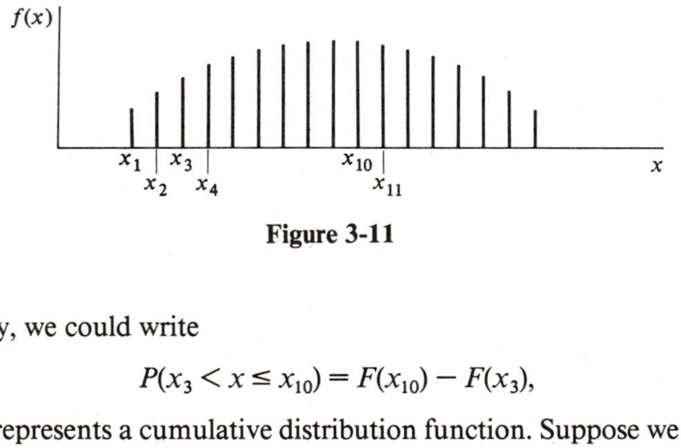

Figure 3-11

Alternatively, we could write

$$P(x_3 < x \leq x_{10}) = F(x_{10}) - F(x_3),$$

where $F(x)$ represents a cumulative distribution function. Suppose we now have a continuous random variable with probability density given by Figure 3-12. Then the probability that X will assume a value in the interval from x_3 to x_{10} is given by the shaded area under the curve. Now, areas under a curve are determined by integrals so that, given that the algebraic formula describing the density function in

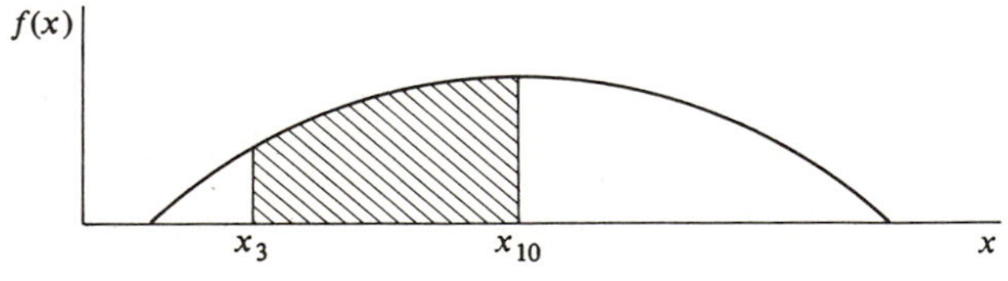

Figure 3-12

Figure 3-12 is $f(x)$, the area under the curve between x_3 and x_{10} is given by the appropriate integral. Thus we have

$$P(x_3 < x < x_{10}) = \int_{x_3}^{x_{10}} f(x)dx.$$

(Since the probability that $x = x_{10}$ is zero, $P(x_3 < x < x_{10})$ and $P(x_3 < x \leq x_{10})$ are equivalent.) The integration from x_3 to x_{10} in the case of the continuous variable is analogous to the summation of probabilities in the discrete case. In general, *if X is a continuous random variable, then the probability that it assumes a value in the interval from a to b is determined by*

$$P(a < x < b) = \int_a^b f(x)dx, \tag{3.21}$$

where f(x) is the relevant probability density function. As it turns out, we will have very little need for actual enumeration of integrals, but they do provide a convenient conceptual framework for considering probability densities.

Since the probability that X will assume *any* value is 1 (i.e., it is a certainty),

$$P(-\infty < x < +\infty) = \int_{-\infty}^{+\infty} f(x)dx = 1. \tag{3.22}$$

Furthermore, the probability that X will assume any value less than or equal to some specific x is

$$F(x) = \int_{-\infty}^{x} f(x)dx. \tag{3.23}$$

As in the discrete case, $F(x)$ is called the *cumulative probability of x*. Note that

1. $F(-\infty) = 0$ and $F(+\infty) = 1$.
2. For $a < b$,

$$F(b) - F(a) = \int_{-\infty}^{b} f(x)dx - \int_{-\infty}^{a} f(x)dx = \int_a^b f(x)dx = P(a < x < b).$$

(In other words, the difference between two cumulative probabilities is equal to simple probability.)

A diagrammatic representation of cumulative probability is given in Figure 3-13.

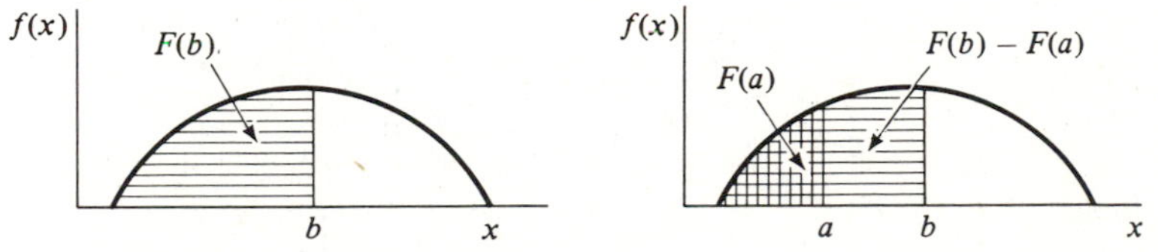

Figure 3-13

As in the case of discrete variables, continuous sample spaces may involve more than one variable at a time. The corresponding probability distribution is called *multivariate probability density function.* It gives the *joint probability* that each of the variables involved will fall within specified intervals; if the variables are, e.g., X, Y, Z, then the *joint probability density function* would be $f(x, y, z)$. In an analogy with the discrete case, we define *marginal density function* of X as the probability density function of X whatever the values of the remaining variables. Note that the marginal density function of one variable is given by integrating the joint distribution function over all values of the other variable, namely,

$$f(x) = \int_{-\infty}^{+\infty} f(x, y)dy \qquad \text{and} \qquad f(y) = \int_{-\infty}^{+\infty} f(x, y)dx.$$

Also, as in the discrete case, the continuous random variables $X, Y, Z, \ldots$ are *independent* if and only if

$$f(x, y, z, \ldots) = f(x)f(y)f(z) \ldots . \tag{3.24}$$

Some continuous distributions are of special importance because they are frequently encountered in practice. The *continuous uniform distribution,* used in connection with our clock-dial example and depicted by Figure 3-10, is one such distribution. Another one is the so-called *normal distribution,* which is extremely common and will be discussed at length in Section 4-2. Other distributions will be introduced as the occasion arises.

3-7 Mathematical Expectation

Probability distributions, like ordinary frequency distributions, display various characteristics. These characteristics, of which the best known are the mean and the variance, are defined in terms of so-called *expected values* or *mathematical expectations.* An explanation of these terms can best be carried out by analogy to an ordinary frequency distribution. Suppose, for instance, that we have a sample of 64 families classified by the number of children as shown in Table 3-5. Here n represents

Table 3-5

Number of children: x	Number of families: n	Proportion of families: f
0	4	0.06250
1	12	0.18750
2	20	0.31250
3	16	0.25000
4	8	0.12500
5	2	0.03125
6	2	0.03125
	64	1.00000

sents absolute frequencies and f represents relative frequencies. There are seven different values of X, $x_1 = 0$, $x_2 = 1$, . . . , $x_7 = 6$, associated with various frequencies. Let us now determine the average number of children per family. Although several different types of averages exist, most people would in this case probably choose the arithmetic mean—the total number of children in the sample divided by the total number of families. This is given by

$$\bar{x} = \frac{\sum_{i=1}^{7} n_i x_i}{\sum_{i=1}^{7} n_i} = \frac{1}{64}(4 \times 0 + 12 \times 1 + \cdots + 2 \times 6) = 2.40625.$$

The same result would be obtained by using relative frequencies.

$$\bar{x} = \sum_{i=1}^{7} f_i x_i = (0.06250 \times 0 + 0.18750 \times 1 + \cdots + 0.03125 \times 6)$$
$$= 2.40625.$$

That is, the arithmetic mean of a frequency distribution is, in fact, a weighted mean of the different values of the variable with weights given by the respective relative frequencies. Consider now a *discrete random variable* X with the following probability function.

x	$f(x)$
x_1	$f(x_1)$
x_2	$f(x_2)$
$\vdots$	$\vdots$
x_m	$f(x_m)$

where m is some integer. Then the *expected value* or the *mathematical expectation* of X is

(3.25) $$E(X) = \sum_{i=1}^{m} x_i f(x_i).$$

We can see that $E(X)$ is nothing else but a weighted average of the different values of X with weights given by the respective probabilities. This is the reason why $E(X)$ is identified with the population mean μ; that is,

(3.26) $$\mu = E(X).$$

The analogy between the mean of an ordinary frequency distribution and the expected value of a discrete random variable X should be clear from our exposition.

The term *expected value* is used to emphasize the relation between the population mean and one's anticipation about the outcome of an experiment. Suppose, for instance, that we are asked to toss a six-sided die and are told that we will receive as many dollars as the number of dots shown. The question is how much do we expect to receive before actually throwing the die. If our expectation is formed in accordance with the rule given by (3.25), the answer is

$$E(X) = 1 \times \frac{1}{6} + 2 \times \frac{1}{6} + \cdots + 6 \times \frac{1}{6} = 3.5.$$

While we cannot actually get (and therefore do not "expect" in the colloquial sense of the word) \$3.50, this figure represents a summary of the possible results. If the tosses were repeated an infinite number of times, the average return per toss would be precisely \$3.50.

The *expected value of a continuous variable* is defined in a very similar fashion. As we mentioned earlier, we may view a continuous variable as a limiting case of a discrete variable, where the values that the variable can assume get more and more numerous and closer and closer to each other. Therefore, if X is a continuous random variable with probability density $f(x)$, its expected value (or mathematical expectation) is

$$E(X) = \int_{-\infty}^{+\infty} xf(x)dx. \tag{3.27}$$

The integration is carried out from $-\infty$ to $+\infty$ to make sure that all possible values of X are covered.

It should be noted that there are some probability distributions for which the *expected value of the variable does not exist;* that is, $E(X)$ might be equal to infinity. A classical example is given by the following probability function.

x	$f(x)$
2	1/2
4	1/4
8	1/8
16	1/16
⋮	⋮

This is a perfectly legitimate probability function since $f(x) \geq 0$ for every x and

$$\sum_{i=1}^{\infty} f(x_i) = \frac{1}{2} + \frac{1}{4} + \frac{1}{8} + \cdots = 1.$$

In fact, $f(x)$ can be interpreted as representing the probability of getting 1 head in 1 toss of an unbiased coin, 2 heads in 2 tosses, 3 heads in 3 tosses, and so on in an ascending order. The expected value of X is[1]

$$E(X) = 2 \times \frac{1}{2} + 4 \times \frac{1}{4} + 8 \times \frac{1}{8} + \cdots = 1 + 1 + 1 + \cdots = \infty.$$

[1] This case is known as the *St. Petersburg paradox.* Suppose somebody asks us to toss a coin and offers to pay us $\$2^x$ when, in a series of flips of a coin, the first head appears on the xth flip. How much is the value of this game to us? According to our calculations, the expected value (i.e., the expected gain in this case) is infinity, but it is unlikely that anybody would be willing to pay that amount (or even, say, a mere million dollars) for the privilege of playing this game. This is the paradoxical aspect of the situation.

Fortunately, distributions of this sort are not very frequent. In what follows we shall assume that we are dealing with distributions for which expected values exist. When this is not the case, we shall make the point of emphasizing it.

The concept of mathematical expectation can easily be extended to apply to problems other than simple determination of the mean value of X. In particular, if X is a random variable and $g(X)$ is a single-valued function of this variable, then,

$$(3.28) \qquad Eg(X) = \begin{cases} \sum_{i=1}^{\infty} g(x_i)f(x_i) & (X \text{ discrete}) \\ \int_{-\infty}^{+\infty} g(x)f(x)dx & (X \text{ continuous}). \end{cases}$$

As an example, we shall prove the following theorem.

Theorem 7 *If X is a random variable and a and b are constants, then*

$$E(aX + b) = aE(X) + b.$$

Proof: (a) X is discrete.

$$\begin{aligned} E(aX + b) &= \sum_{i=1}^{m} (ax_i + b)f(x_i) \\ &= \sum_i ax_i f(x_i) + \sum_i bf(x_i) \\ &= a \sum_i x_i f(x_i) + b \sum_i f(x_i) \\ &= aE(X) + b. \end{aligned}$$

(b) X is continuous.

$$\begin{aligned} E(aX + B) &= \int_{-\infty}^{+\infty} (ax + b)f(x)dx \\ &= \int axf(x)dx + \int bf(x)dx \\ &= aE(X) + b. \end{aligned}$$

A direct application of (3.28) enables us to determine special characteristics of a probability distribution called *moments.* These represent a family of parameters which characterize a distribution. Two kinds of moments can be distinguished: moments about the origin (i.e., zero) and moments about the mean (i.e., μ). *Moments about the origin* are defined by

$$(3.29) \qquad \mu_r' = E(X^r) = \begin{cases} \sum_i x_i^r f(x_i) & (X \text{ discrete}) \\ \int_{-\infty}^{+\infty} x^r f(x)dx & (X \text{ continuous}) \end{cases}$$

for $r = 0, 1, 2, \ldots$. That is, substitution of different values for r will lead to moments of different order. In particular,

$$\mu'_0 = 1,$$

$$\mu'_1 = E(X) = \mu.$$

Thus the *mean is the first moment about the origin.* Moments about the origin of order higher than one are less commonly used and have no special names. *Moments about the mean* are defined by

(3.30) $$\mu_r = E[(X - \mu)^r] = \begin{cases} \sum_i (x_i - \mu)^r f(x_i) & (X \text{ discrete}) \\ \int_{-\infty}^{+\infty} (x - \mu)^r f(x)dx & (X \text{ continuous}) \end{cases}$$

for $r = 0, 1, 2, \ldots$. Note that

$$\mu_0 = 1,$$

$$\mu_1 = E(X - \mu) = E(X) - \mu = 0,$$

$$\mu_2 = E(X - \mu)^2 = \text{Var}(X).$$

Thus the *variance is the second moment about the mean.* Its square root is called the *standard deviation* of the distribution.

The most important characteristics of a distribution are noted below.

1. The *mean* $\mu = E(X)$ is a measure of central tendency of a distribution. Its chief distinction is the fact that in the population the deviations of all the values of X from μ average out to zero. This is true whether the variable is discrete or continuous. In particular, we see that in the discrete case we have

$$\sum_i (x_i - \mu) f(x_i) = \sum_i x_i f(x_i) - \mu = E(X) - \mu = 0.$$

If the distribution is symmetric, then the mean lies in its center.

2. The *variance* σ^2 or Var(X), frequently presented as

(3.31) $$\text{Var}(X) = E[X - E(X)]^2,$$

is a measure of the spread or dispersion of a distribution. It is, in fact, the mean of the squared deviations of X from μ since, by the definition of mathematical expectation,

$$\sigma^2 = \begin{cases} \sum_i (x_i - \mu)^2 f(x_i) & (X \text{ discrete}) \\ \int_{-\infty}^{+\infty} (x - \mu)^2 f(x)dx & (X \text{ continuous}). \end{cases}$$

Variance, of course, can never be negative. If all values of X are highly concentrated, the point of concentration must be the mean (or at least its neighborhood) and the variance will be very small. In the extreme case where all values of X are the same (i.e., X is a constant), the variance will be equal to zero. Note that an alternative way of determining the variance can be developed as follows:

(3.32)
$$\sigma^2 = E(X-\mu)^2 = E(X^2 - 2\mu X + \mu^2)$$
$$= E(X^2) - 2\mu E(X) + \mu^2 = E(X^2) - \mu^2,$$

since μ is a constant. Further, we have an important theorem.

Theorem 8 *If X is a random variable and a and b are constants, then*

$$Var(aX+b) = a^2 Var(X).$$

Proof:

$$\text{Var}(aX+b) = E[(aX+b) - E(aX+b)]^2$$

by the definition of a variance. Now,

$$E(aX+b) = aE(X) + b$$

by Theorem 7, where $E(X) = \mu$ by definition. Therefore,

$$\text{Var}(aX+b) = E[aX + b - (a\mu + b)]^2 = E[aX - a\mu]^2$$
$$= E[a^2(X-\mu)^2] = a^2 E[(X-\mu)^2] = a^2\text{Var}(X).$$

Sometimes it is more convenient to use the *standard deviation* of X, which is simply

$$\sigma = \sqrt{\text{Var}(X)}.$$

3. A *measure of skewness* (departure from symmetry) is given by

(3.33)
$$\mu_3 = E(X-\mu)^3.$$

If the distribution is symmetric, μ_3 will be equal to zero. If the distribution is skewed to the left (i.e., its left tail is elongated), μ_3 will be negative, and if the distribution is skewed to the right, μ_3 will be positive. In Figure 3-14, the first distribution, $f_1(x)$, is skewed to the left, the second $f_2(x)$, is symmetric, and the third, $f_3(x)$, is skewed to the right. For many purposes it is preferable to use a slightly different measure of skewness, called α_3, which is defined as

(3.34)
$$\alpha_3 = \frac{\mu_3}{\sigma^3}.$$

The denominator in this expression functions as a scale factor so that comparisons

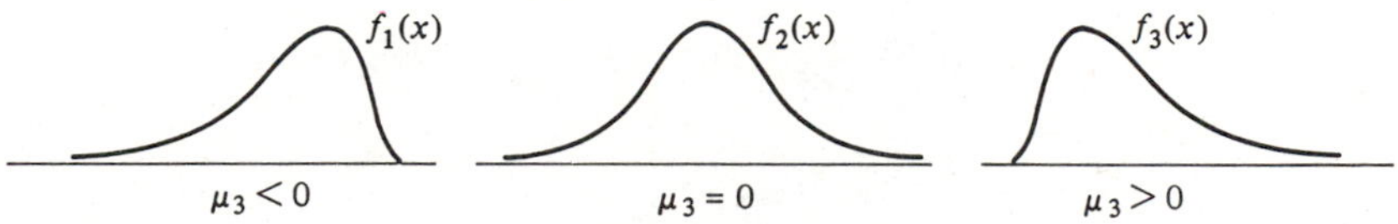

Figure 3-14

of different distributions with respect to skewness are not distorted by the differences in dispersion. Since $\sigma^3 = [\text{Var}(X)]^{3/2}$ is always positive, the sign of α_3 is fully determined by the sign of μ_3.

So far we have considered only univariate probability distributions, but there is no difficulty in extending the concept of mathematical expectation to distributions involving more than one random variable. Suppose we have two random variables X and Y with a joint distribution $f(x, y)$. We wish to determine the expected value of some single-valued function of X and Y, say, $g(X, Y)$. Then,

$$(3.35)\quad E[g(X, Y)] = \begin{cases} \sum_{i=1}^{\infty} \sum_{j=1}^{\infty} g(x_i, y_j) f(x_i, y_j) & (X \text{ and } Y \text{ discrete}) \\ \int_{-\infty}^{+\infty} \int_{-\infty}^{+\infty} g(x, y) f(x, y) dx dy & (X \text{ and } Y \text{ continuous}). \end{cases}$$

This can be generalized for any number of random variables. Some functions of random variables are of special interest; these are given in the following theorems, which are very important in econometric theory. We shall prove them for two discrete random variables, but the extension to other cases is quite straightforward.

Theorem 9 *The expected value of a sum of random variables is equal to the sum of their expected values, i.e.,* $E(X + Y + Z + \cdots) = E(X) + E(Y) + E(Z) + \cdots$.

Proof:

$$\begin{aligned} E(X + Y) &= \sum_i \sum_j (x_i + y_j) f(x_i y_j) = \sum_i \sum_j x_i f(x_i, y_j) + \sum_i \sum_j y_j f(x_i, y_j) \\ &= \sum_i x_i \sum_j f(x_i, y_j) + \sum_j y_j \sum_i f(x_i, y_j) = \sum_i x_i f(x_i) + \sum_j y_j f(y_j) \\ &= E(X) + E(Y). \end{aligned}$$

Theorem 10 *The expected value of a linear combination of random variables is equal to the linear combination of their expected values, i.e.,*

$$E(aX + bY + cZ + \cdots) = aE(X) + bE(Y) + cE(Z) + \cdots,$$

where a, b, c, . . . are any constants.

Proof:

$$\begin{aligned} E(aX + bY) &= \sum_i \sum_j (ax_i + by_j) f(x_i, y_j) \\ &= \sum_i \sum_j ax_i f(x_i, y_j) + \sum_i \sum_j by_j f(x_i, y_j) \\ &= a \sum_i x_i \sum_j f(x_i, y_j) + b \sum_j y_j \sum_i f(x_i, y_j) \\ &= aE(X) + bE(Y). \end{aligned}$$

Theorem 11 *If X and Y are two independent random variables, then the expected value of their product is equal to the product of their expected values, i.e.,* $E(XY) = E(X)E(Y)$.

Proof:

$$E(XY) = \sum_i \sum_j x_i y_j f(x_i, y_j).$$

But if X and Y are independent,

$$f(x_i, y_j) = f(x_i)f(y_j).$$

Therefore,

$$E(XY) = \sum_i \sum_j x_i y_j f(x_i)f(y_j) = \sum_i x_i f(x_i) \sum_j y_j f(y_j) = E(X)E(Y).$$

It is important to note the difference in the expected value of a sum and the expected value of a product. The expected value of a sum is *always* equal to the sum of expected values, whereas the expected value of a product is equal to the product of the expected values *only* if the variables are uncorrelated.

The next theorem on expected values that we intend to present requires the definition of a *covariance* between two random variables, say X and Y. This is usually denoted by $\text{Cov}(X, Y)$ (or sometimes σ_{XY}) and is defined as

(3.36) $$\text{Cov}(X, Y) = E[X - E(X)][Y - E(Y)].$$

The sign of the covariance depends on the direction of association between X and Y. If there is a positive association—that is, if small values of X tend to be associated with small values of Y and large values of X with large values of Y—then the covariance will be *positive*. If, on the other hand, there is a negative association—that is, if small values of X tend to be associated with large values of Y and large values of X with small values of Y—the covariance will be *negative*. (Here by "small" we mean values less than the mean and by "large," values greater than the mean.) That is, if there is a positive association, then $[x - E(X)]$ and $[y - E(Y)]$ will tend to be of the same sign; therefore, their product will tend to be positive and this will make for a positive covariance. But if there is a negative association, $[x - E(X)]$ and $[y - E(Y)]$ will tend to be of opposite signs; therefore, their product will tend to be negative, and this will be reflected in the sign of the covariance. An illustration is given by Figure 3-15.

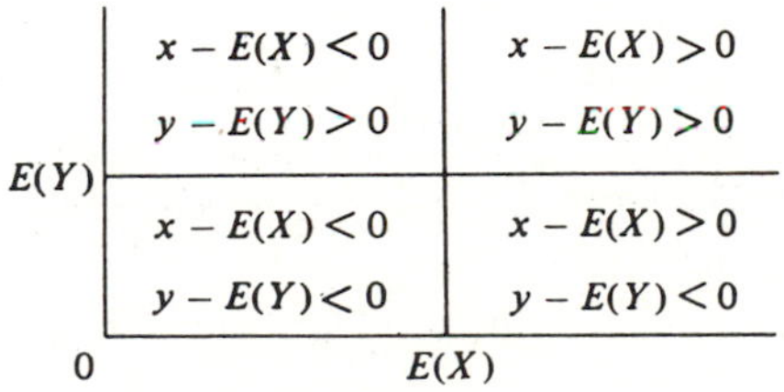

Figure 3-15

With this introduction we can now present the following theorem.

Theorem 12 *If X and Y are two independent random variables, then*

$$Cov(X, Y) = 0.$$

Proof:

$$\begin{aligned} \text{Cov}(X, Y) &= E[X - E(X)][Y - E(Y)] \\ &= E[XY - YE(X) - XE(Y) + E(X)E(Y)] \\ &= E(XY) - E(X)E(Y). \end{aligned}$$

But if X and Y are independent, then, by Theorem 11,

$$E(XY) = E(X)E(Y);$$

therefore

$$\text{Cov}(X, Y) = E(X)E(Y) - E(X)E(Y) = 0.$$

It is important to note that while independence necessarily implies zero covariance, the *converse is not true.* It is not very difficult to find cases for which $\text{Cov}(X, Y) = 0$ and yet X and Y are not independent. As an example consider the following distribution.

		Values of Y 0	1	$f(x)$
Values of X	1	0	1/3	1/3
	2	1/3	0	1/3
	3	0	1/3	1/3
	$f(y)$	1/3	2/3	1

X and Y are obviously not independent since the conditional and the marginal distributions are quite different. Now,

$$\text{Cov}(X, Y) = E[X - E(X)][Y - E(Y)] = E(XY) - E(X)E(Y).$$

But

$$E(XY) = \sum_i \sum_j x_i y_j f(x_i, y_j) = 1 \times 1 \times \frac{1}{3} + 2 \times 0 \times \frac{1}{3} + 3 \times 1 \times \frac{1}{3} = \frac{4}{3}.$$

Further,

$$E(X) = 1 \times \frac{1}{3} + 2 \times \frac{1}{3} + 3 \times \frac{1}{3} = 2$$

and

$$E(Y) = 0 \times \frac{1}{3} + 1 \times \frac{2}{3} = \frac{2}{3}.$$

Therefore,

$$\text{Cov}(X, Y) = \frac{4}{3} - 2 \times \frac{2}{3} = 0.$$

The variables that have zero covariance are called *uncorrelated.* The point of the preceding discussion was to show that independence is a sufficient but not necessary condition for zero covariance. In a broad sense, the difference between independence and noncorrelation lies in the fact that independence rules out any kind of relationship, whereas noncorrelation rules out only *linear* relations between variables.

Theorem 13 *If X and Y are two random variables, then*

$$Var(X + Y) = Var(X) + Var(Y) + 2\ Cov(X, Y)$$

and

$$Var(X - Y) = Var(X) + Var(Y) - 2\ Cov(X, Y)$$

Proof:

$$\begin{aligned}\text{Var}(X + Y) &= E[(X + Y) - E(X + Y)]^2 \\ &= E[X - E(X) + Y - E(Y)]^2 \\ &= E[X - E(X)]^2 + E[Y - E(Y)]^2 + 2\ E[X - E(X)][Y - E(Y)]\end{aligned}$$

and similarly for $\text{Var}(X - Y)$.

If X and Y are independent, their covariance is zero, and the preceding theorem leads to a very important corollary: *the variance of a sum of independent variables is equal to the sum of their variances.*

As a final point we note that, in analogy to the concept of conditional probability, we have *conditional expectation* of, say, Y given X, which is defined as

$$E(Y|X) = \begin{cases} \sum\limits_i y_i f(y_i|x_i) & (Y \text{ discrete}) \\ \int_{-\infty}^{+\infty} y f(y|x) dy & (Y \text{ continuous}). \end{cases} \tag{3.37}$$

That is, the conditional expectation of Y given X is equal to the mean of the conditional distribution of Y given X. In terms of the example just given, the conditional expectation of Y given that the value of X is 1 is

$$E(Y|x = 1) = 0 \times \frac{0}{1/3} + 1 \times \frac{1/3}{1/3} = 1.$$

Also

$$E(Y|x = 2) = 0 \times \frac{1/3}{1/3} + 1 \times \frac{0}{1/3} = 0$$

and $$E(Y|x=3) = 0 \times \frac{0}{1/3} + 1 \times \frac{1/3}{1/3} = 1,$$

while the unconditional mean of Y is

$$E(Y) = 0 \times \frac{1}{3} + 1 \times \frac{2}{3} = \frac{2}{3}.$$

The concept of the conditional expectation can be generalized to any single-valued function of Y, say $g(Y)$. Then, we have

$$E[g(Y)|X] = \begin{cases} \sum_i g(y_i) f(y_i|x_i) & (Y \text{ discrete}) \\ \int_{-\infty}^{+\infty} g(y) f(y|x) dy & (Y \text{ continuous}) \end{cases} \tag{3.38}$$

There is one important difference between an unconditional and a conditional expectation: while $E[g(Y)]$ is always a constant, $E[g(Y)|X]$ is not necessarily a constant but may be a function of X.

In the rest of this book, operations involving expected values will be quite frequent. This is because we are very much concerned with the derivation of the properties of sampling distributions, and, as pointed out earlier, sampling distributions are nothing but probability distributions of estimators or test statistics. Expected values are very convenient means of describing the characteristics of these distributions.

EXERCISES

3-1. List the elements of the sample spaces corresponding to the following experiments.

a. Drawing (with replacement) two balls from an urn containing 7 white and 3 red balls.

b. Flipping a coin and, providing a head appears, rolling a six-sided die (if a tail appears, the experiment is stopped).

c. Drawing cards from a pack of 52 cards until a face card is obtained.

3-2. Consider a set of equally likely outcomes,

$$S = \{1, 2, \ldots, n\},$$

where n is a multiple of six. Let

$$S_1 = \{1, 3, \ldots, (n-1)\},$$
$$S_2 = \{2, 4, \ldots, n\},$$
$$S_3 = \{3, 6, \ldots, n\}.$$

Find the following probabilities.

a. $P(n)$, $P(S_1)$, $P(S_2)$, and $P(S_3)$. **b.** $P(S_1 \cap S_3)$.

c. $P(S_2 \cap S_3)$. **d.** $P(S_1 \cup S_2)$.

e. $P(S_1 \cup S_3)$. **f.** $P(S_2 \cup S_3)$.

g. $P[S_1 \cup (S_2 \cap S_3)]$.

3-3. Let S_1 and S_2 be subsets of the sample space S. Given $P(S_1)$, $P(S_2)$, and $P(S_1 \cap S_2)$, find

a. $P(\bar{S}_1 \cup \bar{S}_2)$. **b.** $P(\bar{S}_1 \cap \bar{S}_2)$.

c. $P(\bar{S}_1 \cap S_2)$. **d.** $P(\bar{S}_1 \cup S_2)$.

3-4. Given $P(A) = 0.4$, $P(B) = 0.5$, and $P(A \cap B) = 0.3$, find

a. $P(A \cup B)$. **b.** $P(A \cap \bar{B})$.

c. $P(\bar{A} \cap B)$. **d.** $P(\bar{A} \cap \bar{B})$.

3-5. a. If A and B are mutually exclusive and $P(A) = 0.25$ and $P(B) = 0.40$, find (i) $P(A \cup B)$; (ii) $P(\bar{A} \cap \bar{B})$.

b. If A and B are independent, and $P(A) = 0.20$ and $P(B) = 0.45$, find (i) $P(A|B)$; (ii) $P(A \cup B)$; (iii) $P(\bar{A} \cap \bar{B})$.

3-6. The joint probability function of X, Y, and Z is given below.

x	y	z	$f(x, y, z)$
0	0	0	0.125
0	0	1	0.125
0	1	0	0.100
1	0	0	0.080
0	1	1	0.150
1	0	1	0.120
1	1	0	0.090
1	1	1	0.210

a. Write out the joint probability distribution of X and Y.

b. Write out the marginal probability distributions of X, Y, and Z.

c. Find the value of the mean and of the variance of X.

d. Write out the conditional probability distribution of X given that $Z = 0$, and compute the mean of this distribution.

e. Define $W = X + Y + Z$. Write out the probability distribution of W.

f. Define $V = XY$. Write out the probability distribution of V and compute the mean of V.

3-7. At a school carnival a booth offers a chance to throw a dart at balloons. If you break a balloon, you get a prize equal to the amount hidden behind the balloon. Suppose that each balloon is equally likely to be hit and that the chances of hitting any balloon is 0.5. The prizes are distributed as follows:

40% of the balloons pay 5¢;

30% of the balloons pay 10¢;

20% of the balloons pay 25¢;

10% of the balloons pay $1.

If the charge for one throw is 25¢, what is the booth's expected profit on 400 throws?

3-8. The random variable X is continuous with the distribution given by the accompanying diagram.

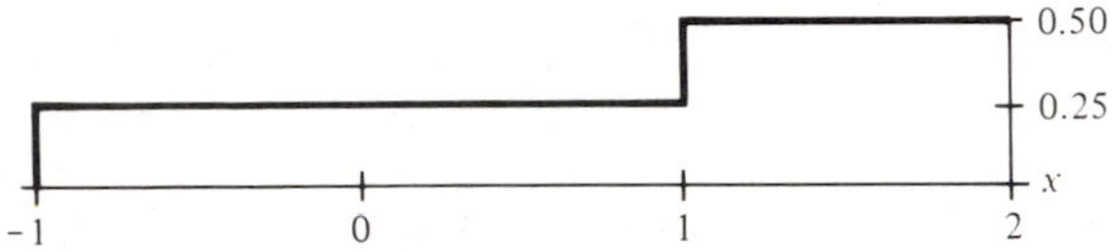

Determine each of the following.

a. $P(x < 1)$. **b.** $P(x < -0.50)$.

c. $P(0 < x < 1)$. **d.** $P(x < 0 \quad \text{or} \quad x > 1)$.

e. $P(|x| < 0.50)$. **f.** $P(|x - 1| < 0.5)$.

g. $P(x = 1)$. **h.** The median and the mean of X.

3-9. There are equal numbers of male and female students at Podunk State University, and 1/5 of the male students and 1/20 of the female students are economics majors. Calculate the following probabilities.

a. That a student selected at random will be an economics major.

b. That a student selected at random will be a male economics major.

c. That an economics major selected at random will be male.

3-10. Consider three fair tosses of a coin, and let

$X =$ number of heads,

$Y =$ number of changes in the sequence of toss results (e.g., *HHH* has no change of sequence, *HTH* has two changes of sequence, etc.).

a. Construct the sample space of all outcomes of this experiment and tabulate the marginal probability distributions of X and Y.

b. Tabulate the joint probability distribution of X and Y in the form of a two-way table.

c. Find the values of $E(X)$, $\text{Var}(X)$, $E(Y)$, $\text{Var}(Y)$, and $\text{Cov}(X, Y)$.

3-11. The records for a certain large city show the following distribution of applicants for unskilled jobs by the duration of their unemployment.

Duration of unemployment (weeks)	0	1	2	3	4	5	6	7	8	9–12
Proportion of applicants	0.25	0.20	0.15	0.10	0.10	0.05	0.04	0.03	0.02	0.06

a. What is the expected duration of unemployment of an applicant?

b. Calculate the value of the standard deviation and of the α_3-measure of skewness of this distribution.

3-12. If X is a random variable with mean μ and variance σ^2, and if Z is defined as $Z = X - (X - \mu)/\sigma$, find $E(Z)$ and $\text{Var}(Z)$.

3-13. If X is a random variable with mean μ and b is a constant different from μ, prove that $E(X-\mu)^2 < E(X-b)^2$.

3-14. If X and Y are two random variables and a and b are constants, prove that

a. $\text{Var}(X + a) = \text{Var}(X)$.

b. $\text{Var}(Y + b) = \text{Var}(Y)$.

c. $\text{Cov}[(X + a), (Y + b)] = \text{Cov}(X, Y)$.

3-15. Consider a sample of identically and independently distributed variables X_1, $X_2, \ldots, X_n$, each having a mean μ and variance σ^2. Find, for $i = 1, 2, \ldots, n$ and $i \neq j$,

a. $E(X_i^2)$.

b. $E(X_i \bar{X})$.

c. $E(\bar{X}^2)$.

d. $E[X_i(X_i - \bar{X})]$.

e. $E[\bar{X}(X_i - \bar{X})]$.

f. $E[X_i(X_j - \bar{X})]$.

g. $\text{Cov}(X_i, \bar{X})$.

h. $\text{Var}(X_i - \bar{X})$.

i. $\text{Cov}[(X_i - \bar{X}), \bar{X}]$.

j. $\text{Cov}[(X_i - \bar{X}), (X_j - \bar{X})]$.

3-16. The joint distribution of X and Y is as follows.

		X				
		−2	−1	0	1	2
Y	10	.09	.15	.27	.25	.04
	20	.01	.05	.08	.05	.01

a. Find the marginal distributions of X and Y.

b. Find the conditional distribution of X given $y = 20$.

c. Are X and Y uncorrelated?

d. Are X and Y independent?

3-17. Mr. Slick makes the following offer to you. You can toss four coins (furnished by him), and he will pay you an amount equal to the square of the number of heads showing (e.g., if you get three heads, he will pay you \$9). In order to play this game you must pay \$4 for each four-coin toss. On the naive assumption that the coins are fair, what is your expected gain?

3-18. A company has to decide between two investment projects. Project A will yield a \$20,000 profit if it is successful or a loss of \$2000 if it is unsuccessful, whereas Project B will yield a \$25,000 profit if it is successful or a \$5000 loss if it is not. The probability of success is thought to be the same for both projects. Find this probability given that, on the basis of expected profit, the two projects were judged to be equivalent.

4 Theoretical Derivation of Sampling Distributions

The purpose of the discussion on probability and probability distributions in Chapter 3 was to provide tools for theoretical derivation of the sampling distributions of estimators and test statistics, and also to facilitate our understanding of the process and results of estimation or hypotheses testing. In this chapter we come to the point where we shall *use* probability theory to derive various sampling distributions. As explained in Section 1-5, sampling distributions can be derived either experimentally or theoretically. In the experimental approach we construct our population from which we draw a large number of samples. Each sample then provides us with one value of the estimator or test statistic with which we are concerned. The resulting frequency distribution is our approximation of the probability distribution that we would have obtained had the number of samples been not just large but infinite. The experimental approach has two major disadvantages. The first is that we have to be satisfied with approximations of sampling distributions instead of their exact forms, and the second is that the results are, strictly speaking, applicable only to the specific population underlying the experiment. Theoretically derived sampling distributions are free from both of these difficulties and are, therefore, clearly superior to those that are experimentally derived. The one drawback in using the theoretical approach is that it may not always work — in the sense that our mathematical knowledge and skill may not be sufficient to lead to results. This happens particularly frequently with respect to estimators of a system of economic relations, as we shall see later.

In this chapter we shall limit ourselves to the derivation of the sampling distribution of sample proportion of successes and of sample mean. Both of these distributions were already derived experimentally for specific populations in Chapter 2, and can be derived mathematically for any population without much difficulty. Other sampling distributions will be discussed later as the occasion arises.

4-1 Sampling Distribution of Sample Proportion of Successes: Binomial Distribution

Consider a population in which every unit can be classified as either possessing or not possessing a given attribute. This population may or may not be infinite. If it is not infinite, then we assume that, when we draw a sample, every unit drawn is replaced before another unit is drawn (i.e., we have sampling with replacement). This means that there is no limit to sample size. A unit that possesses the given attribute will be called a *success;* that which does not, a *failure.* As a concrete example, we may envision that we are dealing with the adult population of the United States at a given point of time and that the attribute of interest is whether a person is a coffee-drinker or a noncoffee-drinker. Drawing a coffee-drinker is considered a success, a noncoffee-drinker a failure. In accordance with Section 2-1 let us use the following notation.

π = proportion (or limit of relative frequency) of successes in the population;

ρ = proportion (or limit of relative frequency) of failures in the population;

n = size of sample;

$\hat{\pi}$ = proportion of successes in the sample;

X = number of successes in the sample.

Note that if we make a single random drawing, the probability of success is π and of failure ρ. (Such a drawing is known as a *Bernoulli trial.*) Let S stand for "success," and F for "failure." Then we have

$$P(S) = \pi$$

and $$P(F) = \rho \qquad \text{or} \qquad P(F) = 1 - \pi,$$

since F is "not S."

Let us now derive the sampling distributions of X and $\hat{\pi}$ for samples of various sizes. Since there is a one-to-one correspondence between X and $\hat{\pi}$ given by the fact that

$$\hat{\pi} = \frac{X}{n} \qquad \text{or} \qquad X = n\hat{\pi},$$

knowledge of the distribution of X gives a complete knowledge of the distribution of $\hat{\pi}$, and vice versa. We will give a full description of sampling distributions for each sample size, using X as the random variable; however, we will determine the main distributional characteristics for both X and $\hat{\pi}$. In presenting each distribution, we will determine the values of X, their probability, and the quantities $xf(x)$ and $x^2f(x)$, which are needed for calculating the mean and the variance.

Sampling distribution for sample size 1

Number of successes: x	Probability: $f(x)$	$xf(x)$	$x^2f(x)$
0	$P(F) = \rho$	0	0
1	$P(S) = \pi$	π	π
Sum	$\rho + \pi = 1$	π	π

Mean and variance of X:

$$E(X) = \sum_i x_i f(x_i) = \pi,$$

$$\text{Var}(X) = E(X^2) - [E(X)]^2 = \sum_i x_i^2 f(x_i) - [\sum_i x_i f(x_i)]^2$$

$$= \pi - \pi^2 = \pi(1 - \pi) = \pi\rho,$$

Mean and variance of $\hat{\pi}$:

$$E(\hat{\pi}) = E\left(\frac{X}{n}\right) = E(X) = \pi,$$

$$\text{Var}(\hat{\pi}) = \text{Var}\left(\frac{X}{n}\right) = \text{Var}(X) = \pi\rho.$$

Sampling distribution for sample size 2

Number of successes: x	Probability: $f(x)$	$xf(x)$	$x^2f(x)$
0	$P(F)P(F) = \rho^2$	0	0
1	$P(S)P(F) + P(F)P(S) = 2\pi\rho$	$2\pi\rho$	$2\pi\rho$
2	$P(S)P(S) = \pi^2$	$2\pi^2$	$4\pi^2$
Sum	$(\rho + \pi)^2 = 1$	$2\pi(\rho + \pi)$	$2\pi(\rho + 2\pi)$

Note that the "no success" can be obtained only if both the first and second observations are failures. Since drawings are random, the outcomes of the first and the second drawings are independent, therefore the probability of two failures is equal to the product $P(F)P(F)$. The same applies to the probability of two successes. However, "one success and one failure" can be obtained in two ways, either success followed by failure or failure followed by success. The two are mutually exclusive so that the probability of one failure and one success is $P(S)P(F) + P(F)P(S)$, as shown.

Mean and variance of X:

$$E(X) = 2\pi(\rho + \pi) = 2\pi,$$

$$\text{Var}(X) = 2\pi(\rho + 2\pi) - (2\pi)^2 = 2\pi\rho + 4\pi^2 - 4\pi^2 = 2\pi\rho.$$

Mean and variance of $\hat{\pi}$:

$$E(\hat{\pi}) = E\left(\frac{X}{2}\right) = \pi \qquad \text{(by Theorem 7),}$$

$$\text{Var}(\hat{\pi}) = \text{Var}\left(\frac{X}{2}\right) = \frac{1}{4}\,\text{Var}(X) \qquad \text{(by Theorem 8)}$$

$$= \frac{\pi\rho}{2}.$$

Sampling distribution for sample size 3

Number of successes: x	Probability: $f(x)$	$xf(x)$	$x^2f(x)$
0	$P(F)P(F)P(F) = \rho^3$	0	0
1	$P(S)P(F)P(F) + P(F)P(S)P(F) + P(F)P(F)P(S) = 3\pi\rho^2$	$3\rho^2\pi$	$3\rho^2\pi$
2	$P(S)P(S)P(F) + P(S)P(F)P(S) + P(F)P(S)P(S) = 3\pi^2\rho$	$6\rho\pi^2$	$12\rho\pi^2$
3	$P(S)P(S)P(S) = \pi^3$	$3\pi^3$	$9\pi^3$
	Sum $\quad (\rho + \pi)^3 = 1$		

Mean and variance of X:

$$E(X) = 3\rho^2\pi + 6\rho\pi^2 + 3\pi^3 = 3\pi(\rho^2 + 2\rho\pi + \pi^2) = 3\pi(\rho + \pi)^2 = 3\pi.$$

$$\text{Var}(X) = 3\rho^2\pi + 12\rho\pi^2 + 9\pi^3 - (3\pi)^2 = 3\rho^2\pi + 12\rho\pi^2 + 9\pi^2(\pi - 1)$$

$$= 3\rho^2\pi + 12\rho\pi^2 - 9\rho\pi^2 = 3\rho\pi(\rho + 4\pi - 3\pi) = 3\rho\pi.$$

Mean and variance of $\hat{\pi}$:

$$E(\hat{\pi}) = E\left(\frac{X}{3}\right) = \pi,$$

$$\text{Var}(\hat{\pi}) = \text{Var}\left(\frac{X}{3}\right) = \frac{1}{9}\,\text{Var}(X) = \frac{\pi\rho}{3}.$$

We could continue this for larger and larger sample sizes, but the results are already obvious: the probabilities of drawing 0, 1, 2, . . . , n successes in a sample size n are given by the respective terms of $(\rho + \pi)^n$, the so-called *binomial expansion.* Table 4-1 summarizes the distributions of X for various sample sizes. Note that the first element in the last column could also be written as

$$\rho^n = \binom{n}{0}\rho^n\pi^0,$$

and the last element in the same column as

$$\pi^n = \binom{n}{n}\rho^0\pi^n.$$

Table 4-1

	$f(x)$					
x	Size 1	Size 2	Size 3	Size 4	. . .	Size n
0	ρ	ρ^2	ρ^3	ρ^4		ρ^n
1	π	$2\rho\pi$	$3\rho^2\pi$	$4\rho^3\pi$		$\binom{n}{1}\rho^{n-1}\pi$
2		π^2	$3\rho\pi^2$	$6\rho^2\pi^2$		$\binom{n}{2}\rho^{n-2}\pi^2$
3			π^3	$4\rho\pi^3$		$\binom{n}{3}\rho^{n-3}\pi^3$
4				π^4		$\binom{n}{4}\rho^{n-4}\pi^4$
⋮						⋮
$n-1$						$\binom{n}{n-1}\rho\pi^{n-1}$
n						π^n

Thus the probability of getting x successes in a sample size n is

(4.1) $$f(x) = \binom{n}{x}\rho^{n-x}\pi^x.$$

Similarly, the probability of obtaining $\hat{\pi}$ proportion of successes in a sample size n is

(4.2) $$f(\hat{\pi}) = \binom{n}{n\hat{\pi}}\rho^{n(1-\hat{\pi})}\pi^{n\hat{\pi}}.$$

These probabilities can be interpreted as limits of relative frequencies, i.e., the frequencies that would be obtained if an infinite number of samples of each size were taken. The distributions defined by these probabilities are, therefore, the true and exact sampling distributions: (4.1) defines the sampling distribution of the number of successes, and (4.2) the sampling distribution of the proportion of successes.

The calculation of the individual probabilities of the binomial distribution becomes quite laborious unless the sample size is very small. Some work can be saved by using the *Pascal triangle* (Figure 3-3), which gives the values of

$$\binom{n}{0},\ \binom{n}{1},\ \binom{n}{2},\quad \text{and so on,}$$

for any n. But we can save ourselves all the calculating work involved if we use the tables of *binomial probabilities,* which give the probabilities for different values of n

and π.[1] For large values of n, the binomial distribution can be reasonably well approximated by the so-called *normal distribution* (unless π is very small and $n\pi$ remains constant as $n \to \infty$). This will be discussed in detail in Section 4-2.

Let us now derive the basic characteristics of the sampling distribution of X and of $\hat{\pi}$. (Recall that $\hat{\pi} = X/n$.) In particular, we are interested in the mean, the variance, and the skewness of these distributions. The mean and the variance for samples size 1, 2, and 3 are summarized in Table 4-2. The generalization to sample

Table 4-2

	Mean		Variance	
Sample size	Number of successes: x	Proportion of successes: $\hat{\pi}$	Number of successes: x	Proportion of successes: $\hat{\pi}$
1	π	π	$\pi\rho$	$\pi\rho$
2	2π	π	$2\pi\rho$	$\pi\rho/2$
3	3π	π	$3\pi\rho$	$\pi\rho/3$
$\vdots$	$\vdots$	$\vdots$	$\vdots$	$\vdots$
n	$n\pi$	π	$n\pi\rho$	$\pi\rho/n$

size n is quite straightforward. Its validity could be proved without much difficulty, but the proof would involve a fair amount of tedious algebra and therefore will not be given here. As for the measure of skewness, we can use α_3 given as

$$\alpha_3 = \frac{\mu_3}{(\mu_2)^{3/2}},$$

where μ_2 is the variance and μ_3 is the third moment around the mean. Then it can be shown that, for the distribution of X as well as for that of $\hat{\pi}$, the expression for α_3 is

$$\alpha_3 = \frac{2\rho - 1}{\sqrt{n\pi\rho}}. \tag{4.3}$$

The basic characteristics of the two sampling distributions are summarized in Table 4-3.

Table 4-3

Characteristic	Distribution of X	Distribution of $\hat{\pi}$
Mean	$n\pi$	π
Variance	$n\pi\rho$	$\pi\rho/n$
α_3 (skewness)	$(2\rho - 1)/\sqrt{n\pi\rho}$	$(2\rho - 1)/\sqrt{n\pi\rho}$

[1] These are available in quite a few statistical texts or handbooks, including John E. Freund and Ronald E. Walpole, *Mathematical Statistics*, 3rd ed. (Englewood Cliffs, NJ: Prentice-Hall, 1980).

Since now we have a complete knowledge of the sampling distribution of $\hat{\pi}$ for *any* specific population parameter π and for *any* sample size n, we can draw definite conclusions about the *properties* of $\hat{\pi}$ (proportion of successes in the sample) as an estimator of π (proportion of successes or the probability of success in the population). The main conclusions are

1. The mean of the sampling distribution of $\hat{\pi}$ is equal to the population parameter π. That is, *$\hat{\pi}$ is an unbiased estimator of π.*
2. Since the standard deviation of the sampling distribution of $\hat{\pi}$ is

   (4.4) $$\sigma_{\hat{\pi}} = \sqrt{\frac{\pi\rho}{n}},$$

   the distribution becomes more and more concentrated as the sample size is increased. This, together with conclusion 1, implies that *$\hat{\pi}$ is a consistent estimator of π.*
3. Given the formula for $\sigma_{\hat{\pi}}$ it follows that *the dispersion of the sampling distribution of $\hat{\pi}$* (as measured by its standard deviation) *decreases in inverse proportion to the square root of sample size.* This can be seen as follows. Consider two samples, the first of size n and the second of size $2n$. Then using the appropriate formula of Table 4-3, we have

   $$\frac{\sigma_{\hat{\pi}}\text{ (2nd sample)}}{\sigma_{\hat{\pi}}\text{ (1st sample)}} = \frac{\sqrt{\pi\rho/2n}}{\sqrt{\pi\rho/n}} = \frac{1}{\sqrt{2}};$$

   i.e., $$\sigma_{\hat{\pi}}\text{ (2nd sample)} = \frac{\sigma_{\hat{\pi}}\text{ (1st sample)}}{\sqrt{2}}.$$

   In other words, as the sample size is increased k times, the standard deviation of the sampling distribution decreases $\sqrt{k}$ times.
4. For any given sample size, the sampling distribution of $\hat{\pi}$ is *most dispersed* when the population parameter π is equal to 1/2, and is *least dispersed* when π is 0 or 1. This follows from the fact that $0 \leq \pi \leq 1$ and

   $$\sigma_{\hat{\pi}} = \sqrt{\frac{\pi\rho}{n}} = \sqrt{\frac{\pi(1-\pi)}{n}}$$

   is at maximum when $\pi = 1/2$ and at minimum when $\pi = 0$ or 1. In fact, the largest value which $\sigma_{\hat{\pi}}$ can have is $1/(2\sqrt{n})$ and the smallest is 0.
5. *The skewness (asymmetry) of the sampling distribution of $\hat{\pi}$* decreases in inverse proportion to the square root of sample size. This clearly follows from (4.3) above.
6. For any *given* sample size, the sampling distribution of $\hat{\pi}$ is *least skewed* when π is equal to 1/2, and *is most skewed* when π is 0 or 1. This can be seen from (4.3) again: α_3 is zero when $\pi = 1/2$ and its departure from zero is greatest when π is either 0 or 1.

These conclusions have been reached with the help of probability theory and apply quite universally. In Section 2-1 we tried to derive the sampling distribution of $\hat{\pi}$ from a sampling experiment related to a population with $\pi = 0.70$. The experiment consisted of drawing 100 samples of size 4 and 100 samples of size 16. It enabled us to construct frequency distributions (one for each sample size), which were supposed to approximate the true sampling distributions. The results led to generalizations about the sampling distribution of $\hat{\pi}$ for any π and any sample size. Now we are in a position, first, to check the results to see how well the experimentally derived distributions fit the theoretical ones and, second, to verify or refute the validity of the generalizations.

Let us first compare the experiment and the theoretical distributions and their characteristics.

Sampling distribution for sample size 4 (Table 4-4). The results for the experimentally determined probabilities are the relative frequencies of Table 2-1. The

Table 4-4

Proportion of successes: $\hat{\pi}$	Experimental $f(\hat{\pi})$	Theoretical $f(\hat{\pi})$
0.00	0.01	0.01
0.25	0.06	0.07
0.50	0.28	0.26
0.75	0.42	0.41
1.00	0.23	0.24
Mean	0.7	0.7
Standard deviation	0.2233	0.2291

theoretical probabilities were derived from Freund and Walpole,[2] rounded off to two decimal places. They could be calculated as follows.

$$f(0) = \left(\frac{4!}{4!0!}\right)(0.3)^4(0.7)^0 = (0.3)^4 = 0.0081 \cong 0.01,$$

$$f\left(\frac{1}{4}\right) = \left(\frac{4!}{3!1!}\right)(0.3)^3(0.7)^1 = 4 \times (0.3)^3 \times (0.7) = 0.0756 \cong 0.07,$$

and so on.

Sampling distribution for sample size 16 (Table 4-5). The results for the experimentally determined probabilities have been taken from Table 2-2. The theoretical probabilities are from the same source as those for Table 4-4, again rounded off to two decimal places.

It is clear that the experimental results describe the sampling distributions quite closely; the errors are quite small and are unlikely to be of practical importance.

[2] *Ibid.*, Table 1.

Table 4-5

Proportion of successes: $\hat{\pi}$	Experimental $f(\hat{\pi})$	Theoretical $f(\hat{\pi})$
0	0	0
1/16	0	0.00
2/16	0	0.00
3/16	0	0.00
4/16	0	0.00
5/16	0.01	0.00
6/16	0	0.01
7/16	0.01	0.02
8/16	0.05	0.05
9/16	0.10	0.10
10/16	0.17	0.17
11/16	0.21	0.21
12/16	0.20	0.20
13/16	0.15	0.15
14/16	0.07	0.07
15/16	0.03	0.02
1	0	0.00
Mean	0.7006	0.7
Standard deviation	0.1191	0.1146

Thus, in this case, distributions based on 100 samples come quite close to those that would result from an infinite number of samples. Furthermore, the generalizations made on the basis of experimental results—namely unbiasedness, consistency, relative change in the standard deviation, and decrease in skewness—all proved to be correct. However, the experimental results compare unfavorably with the theoretical ones in two respects. In the first place, the experimental results fail to give us any formulas for variance, measure of skewness, and, of course, the individual probabilities. In the second place, and this is much more important, there is no guarantee at all that the generalizations deduced from the experimental distributions are, in fact, valid. The conclusions are not proved, only suggested by the results of isolated experiments.

4-2 Normal Distribution as the Limiting Case of Binomial Distribution

One of the findings of Section 4-1 was that the binomial distribution tends to be increasingly more symmetric as n (size of sample) increases, regardless of the value of π. Even the distributions with π close to zero (or to unity), which for small n are very skewed, tend to become symmetric when n is somewhat larger. This point is demonstrated by Figure 4-1 which shows the binomial probabilities for $\pi = 0.10$ for

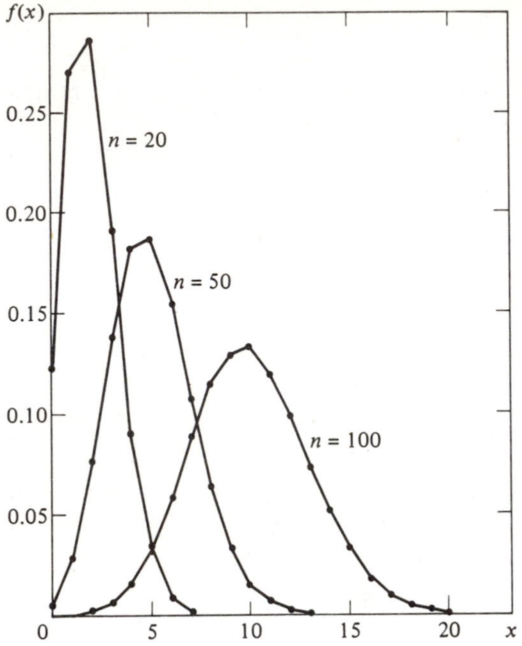

Figure 4-1

various values of n. Note also that as n increases, the points become more numerous and the connecting lines become smoother.

In this section, we shall carry the previous point still farther by asserting that *as n approaches infinity, the binomial distribution approaches the so-called normal distribution.*[3] Normal distribution is a continuous distribution with probability density

$$f(x) = \frac{1}{\sqrt{2\pi\sigma^2}} e^{-(1/2)[(x-\mu)/\sigma]^2}, \tag{4.5}$$

where σ = standard deviation of X,

μ = mean of X,

$\pi = 3.14159\ldots$ (not to be confused with π, the population parameter),

$e = 2.71828\ldots$

Graphical representation of a normal distribution is given in Figure 4-2. This shows that the distribution is symmetric around its mean μ, and that it extends from $-\infty$ to $+\infty$. Other properties are discussed on pages 89–90.

The fact that the binomial distribution approaches normal as $n \rightarrow \infty$ means, in effect, that for a large n we can use normal distribution as an approximation to the

[3] The proof can be found in many statistical texts. A relatively simple proof is presented in *ibid.*, pp. 212–214.

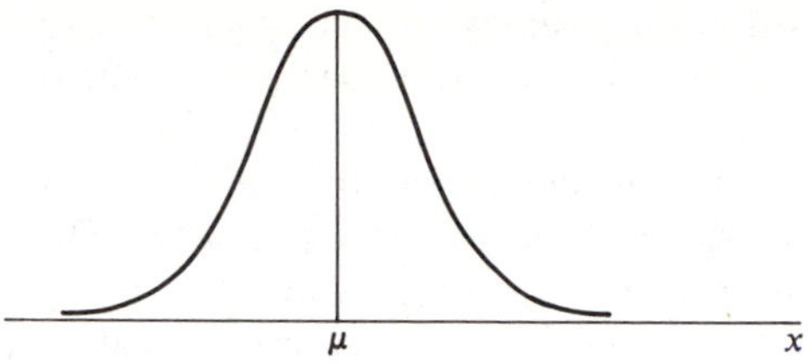

Figure 4-2

binomial distribution. Thus, if X is the number of successes in the sample and if n is large, we can write.

(4.6)
$$f(x) = \frac{1}{\sqrt{2\pi}} \frac{1}{\sqrt{n\pi\rho}} e^{-(1/2)[(x - n\pi)/\sqrt{n\pi\rho}]^2}$$

since the mean of X is $n\pi$ and the variance is $n\pi\rho$. Similarly, when n is large the probability function of the proportion of successes in the sample ($\hat{\pi}$) can be represented by

(4.7)
$$f(\hat{\pi}) = \frac{1}{\sqrt{2\pi}} \frac{\sqrt{n}}{\sqrt{\pi\rho}} e^{-(1/2)[(\hat{\pi} - \pi)\sqrt{n}/\sqrt{\pi\rho}]^2},$$

since the mean of $\hat{\pi}$ is π and its variance is $\pi\rho/n$. How good these approximations are depends on n and π. If π is not too far from 1/2, the correspondence between the binomial and the normal curve is surprisingly close even for low values of n. In general, in most practical situations one can use the normal distribution as a reasonable approximation of the binomial distribution without much hesitation as long as $n \geq 30$.

When using the normal distribution formula to approximate a binomial distribution, we must take into account the fact that we are trying to approximate a *discrete* distribution by a *continuous* one. This can be done by representing the point values of the discrete variable by neighboring intervals. For example, if $n = 20$ the points and the corresponding intervals would be as shown in Table 4-6.

Table 4-6

x (discrete)	x (continuous approximation)	$\hat{\pi}$ (discrete)	$\hat{\pi}$ (continuous approximation)
0	$-\frac{1}{2}$ to $\frac{1}{2}$	0	$-1/40$ to $1/40$
1	$\frac{1}{2}$ to $1\frac{1}{2}$	1/20	1/40 to 3/40
2	$1\frac{1}{2}$ to $2\frac{1}{2}$	2/20	3/40 to 5/40
3	$2\frac{1}{2}$ to $3\frac{1}{2}$	3/20	5/40 to 7/40
⋮	⋮	⋮	⋮
20	$19\frac{1}{2}$ to $20\frac{1}{2}$	1	39/40 to 41/40

Since the normal distribution extends, in fact, from $-\infty$ to $+\infty$, we may start the first intervals at $-\infty$ and end the last intervals at $+\infty$ instead of the lower and upper limits shown.

The reconciliation between the discrete binomial and the continuous normal distribution becomes easier as the sample size gets larger. This can be seen particularly clearly with respect to the distribution of $\hat{\pi}$. As n gets larger, the intervals corresponding to each value of $\hat{\pi}$ become shorter. As an example, consider the intervals corresponding to the point $\hat{\pi} = 0.1$ for various sample sizes.

n	Interval
10	0.05 to 0.15
20	0.075 to 0.125
50	0.090 to 0.110
100	0.095 to 0.105
1000	0.0995 to 0.1005
	etc.

Note that, e.g., for $n = 1000$, we replace the probability of $\hat{\pi}$ being equal to 0.1 by the probability that $\hat{\pi}$ is within 0.1 ± 0.0005, which is certainly not too rough. If we represent the binomial probabilities of $\hat{\pi}$ by rectangles with base equal to the appropriate interval and heights equal to $nf(\hat{\pi})$ (to make the total *area* equal to unity), we can see how the broken curve gets smoother as n gets larger. This is illustrated by Figure 4-3 for π equal to 0.1.

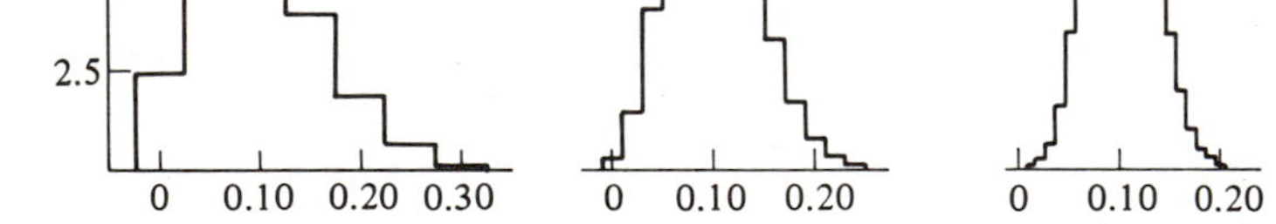

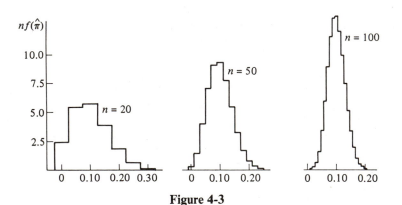

Figure 4-3

In asserting that binomial distribution converges to normal as n approaches infinity, we took it for granted that the population parameter π (and therefore ρ) is fixed, and that it is different from 0 or 1. If π is *not* fixed but decreases as $n \rightarrow \infty$ (so that $n\pi$ remains constant), the limiting form of the binomial distribution is not normal but becomes what is known as the *Poisson distribution.* This distribution became famous because it fitted extremely well the frequency of deaths from the kick of a horse in the Prussian army corps in the last quarter of the nineteenth century. As it is, the Poisson distribution has little relevance to us since our attention is confined to populations with a fixed proportion (probability) of successes. It can be used, though, for approximating the binomial probabilities when π is close to 0 or 1 (say, $\pi \leq 0.05$ or $\pi \geq 0.95$) and n is large (say, $n \geq 20$). In this case the calculation of the binomial probabilities can be based on the following formula for the Poisson distribution,

$$f(x) = \frac{\lambda^x e^{-\lambda}}{x!}$$

where the parameter λ is set to equal $n\pi$ when π is close to 0, or equal to $n(1 - \pi)$ when π is close to 1.

Normal distribution is extremely important in econometrics, not only because it represents the limiting form of the binomial distribution, but because it applies to many other situations as well. This will become apparent in the subsequent section and in further discussions throughout the book. For that reason, it will be useful to consider the normal distribution in greater detail. First, let us describe its *main features.*

1. The distribution is *continuous* and *symmetric* around its mean μ. This has the following implications: (a) the mean, the median, and the mode are all equal; and (b) the mean divides the area under the normal curve into exact halves.
2. The range of the distribution extends from $-\infty$ to $+\infty$, i.e., the distribution is *unbounded.*
3. The maximum height of the normal curve is attained at the point $x = \mu$, and the points of inflection (i.e., the points where the distribution starts flattening out) occur at $x = \mu \pm \sigma$. This means that the standard deviation measures the distance from the center of the distribution to a point of inflection, as illustrated in Figure 4-4.

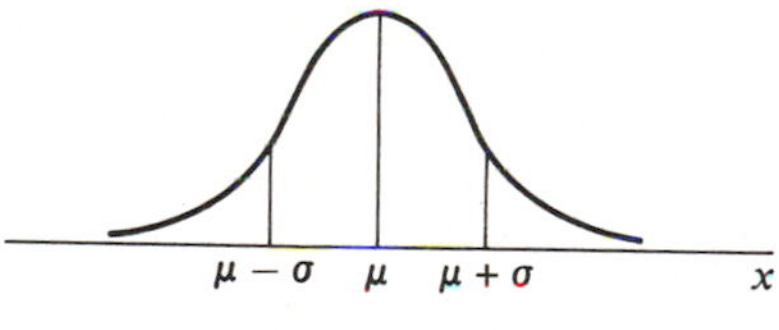

Figure 4-4

4. Normal distribution is *fully specified by two parameters, mean and variance.* This means that if we know μ and σ^2 of a normal distribution, we know all there is to know about it. Note that the binomial distribution is also fully specified by only two parameters, π and n. Figure 4-5 shows various comparisons of two normal distributions. Case (a) represents two normal distributions with different means but equal var-

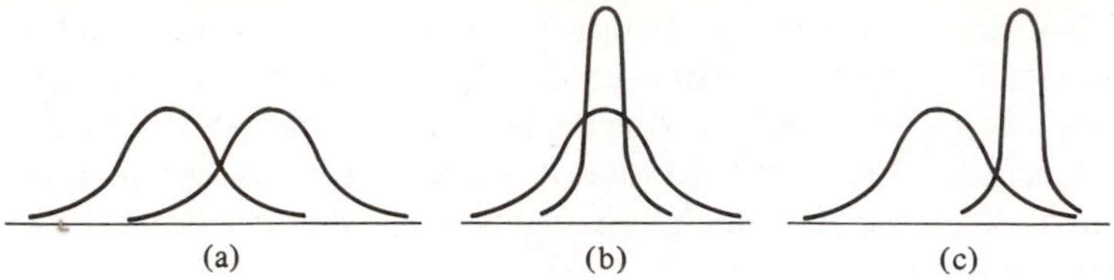

Figure 4-5

iances. In case (b) the means are equal but the variances are different, and in (c) both means and variances differ.

5. The last feature to be mentioned will be found particularly useful in later work. We present it here in the form of a theorem.

Theorem 14 *If $X, Y, \ldots, Z$ are normally and independently distributed random variables and $a, b, \ldots, c$ are constants, then the linear combination $aX + bY + \cdots + cZ$ is also normally distributed.*

The proof of this theorem can be found in many texts on mathematical statistics.[4]

Having stated the main properties of the normal distribution, we still have to face the problem of how to operate with it. In particular, we would like to be able to calculate different probabilities for a variable which is normally distributed. This was, at least in principle, no problem in the case of the binomial distribution since the terms of binomial expansion are determined by a straightforward formula. In the case of a normal distribution, however, the probability density formula is quite formidable. Fortunately, we do not have to use the formula; the probabilities, given by the corresponding areas under the curve, can be obtained from tabulated results. Of course, different normal distributions lead to different probabilities but since the differences can only be due to differences in means and variances, this presents no difficulty. If we know the areas under one specific normal curve, we can derive the areas under any other normal curve simply by allowing for the difference in the mean and the variance. The one specific distribution for which areas (corresponding to relatively narrow intervals) have been tabulated is a normal distribution with mean $\mu = 0$ and variance $\sigma^2 = 1$, called *standard normal distribution* (sometimes also called *unit normal distribution*).

The problem of determining the probabilities for a normally distributed variable X can be then stated as follows: given that we know (a) μ and σ^2 of X, and (b) the areas under the standard normal curve, how do we determine the probability that x will lie within some interval bordered by, say, x_1 and x_2?

To develop the solution, let us introduce the following notation.

Z = a normally distributed variable with mean zero and variance equal to unity (i.e., a "standard normal variable");

$P(x_1 < x < x_2)$ = probability that X will lie between x_1 and x_2 $(x_1 < x_2)$;

$P(z_1 < z < z_2)$ = probability that Z will lie between z_1 and z_2 $(z_1 < z_2)$.

[4] See, e.g., Morris H. DeGroot, *Probability and Statistics* (Reading, MA: Addison-Wesley, 1975), p. 223.

We will proceed in two steps: first we determine the relationship between X and Z, and then we examine the relationship between corresponding areas under the two curves.

Since X is normally distributed, a linear function of X will also be normal (see Theorem 14). Such a linear function can be represented generally as

$$aX + b,$$

where a and b are some constants. If we find a and b such that they would make the mean of $(aX + b)$ zero and its variance unity, we will have a standard normal variable. That is, we require that

$$E(aX + b) = 0 \qquad \text{and} \qquad \text{Var}(aX + b) = 1.$$

This can be written as

$$a\mu + b = 0 \qquad \text{(by Theorem 7)}$$

and

$$a^2\sigma^2 = 1 \qquad \text{(by Theorem 8).}$$

Solving for a and b we obtain

$$a = \frac{1}{\sigma} \qquad \text{and} \qquad b = -\frac{\mu}{\sigma}.$$

Thus we have

$$aX + b = \frac{X - \mu}{\sigma}.$$

Since $(X - \mu)/\sigma$ has mean zero and variance equal to one, it is a standard normal variable, i.e.,

$$\frac{X - \mu}{\sigma} = Z. \tag{4.8}$$

Thus any normal variable with mean μ and variance σ^2 can be transformed into a standard normal variable by expressing it in terms of deviations from its mean, each deviation being divided by σ.

Let us consider $P(x_1 < x < x_2)$, where $x_1 < x_2$, which is a probability statement about X. We wish to find an exactly equivalent probability statement about Z. Now

$$\frac{X - \mu}{\sigma} = Z \quad \text{implies} \quad X = \sigma Z + \mu.$$

Therefore, we can write

$$x_1 = \sigma z_1 + \mu \qquad \text{and} \qquad x_2 = \sigma z_2 + \mu$$

Consequently, by substitution we have

$$P(x_1 < x < x_2) = P(\sigma z_1 + \mu < \sigma z + \mu < \sigma z_2 + \mu).$$

After canceling out all the common positive terms in the right-hand-side inequality, this becomes

(4.9) $$P(x_1 < x < x_2) = P(z_1 < z < z_2),$$

where $$z_1 = \frac{x_1 - \mu}{\sigma} \quad \text{and} \quad z_2 = \frac{x_2 - \mu}{\sigma}.$$

Thus we have found that the probability that x lies between x_1 and x_2 is equal to the probability that a standard normal variable lies between $(x_1 - \mu)/\sigma$ and $(x_2 - \mu)/\sigma$.

As an example, consider a normally distributed variable X which has a mean of 5 and standard deviation of 2. The problem is to find the probability $P(2 < x < 3)$. To do that we have to find an equivalent probability statement in terms of the standard normal variable Z. Here the lower limit $x_1 = 2$ and the upper limit $x_2 = 3$. Since

$$z_1 = \frac{x_1 - \mu}{\sigma},$$

we have

$$z_1 = \frac{2 - 5}{2} = -\frac{3}{2}.$$

Similarly,

$$z_2 = \frac{x_2 - \mu}{\sigma} = \frac{3 - 5}{2} = -1.$$

Therefore, $P(2 < x < 3) = P(-3/2 < z < -1)$. This is shown graphically in Figure 4-6. The two shaded areas under the two curves are exactly the same.

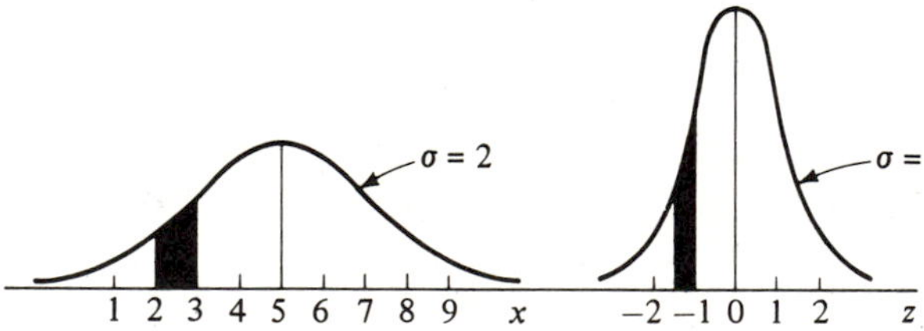

Figure 4-6

After these preliminaries, all that is left to do is to learn how to use the table of areas under the standard normal distributions. Such a table can be found in practically every text on introductory statistics. The most common tabular presentation is that of giving the probabilities that Z will lie between 0 and a positive number z_0 (rounded off to two decimal places) as shown in Figure 4-7. Table D-1 in Appendix D of this book is of that form. The probabilities shown refer to only one half of the distribution. Since the distribution is perfectly symmetric this is, of course, sufficient. The largest probability (area) shown could then be 0.5 at the point where $z = +\infty$. However, since the tail of the distribution tapers off fairly rapidly, the

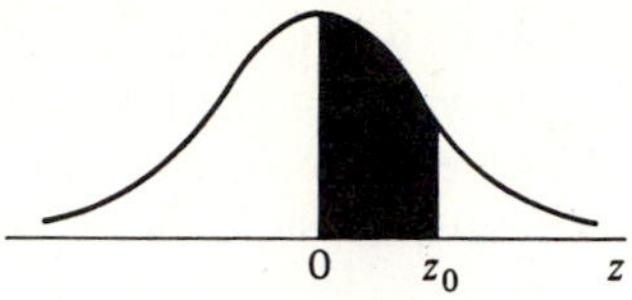

Figure 4-7

probability that z lies between 0 and 3 is already very close to 0.5 (in fact, it is 0.4987); therefore, most tables stop there. (Some tables give probabilities that z lies between $-\infty$ and a positive number. In these tables the *lowest* probability shown is 0.5 and the highest is close to 1.) The use of the table for solving various problems is indicated in Figure 4-8. Note that $z_0 > 0$ and $z_1 > z_0$.

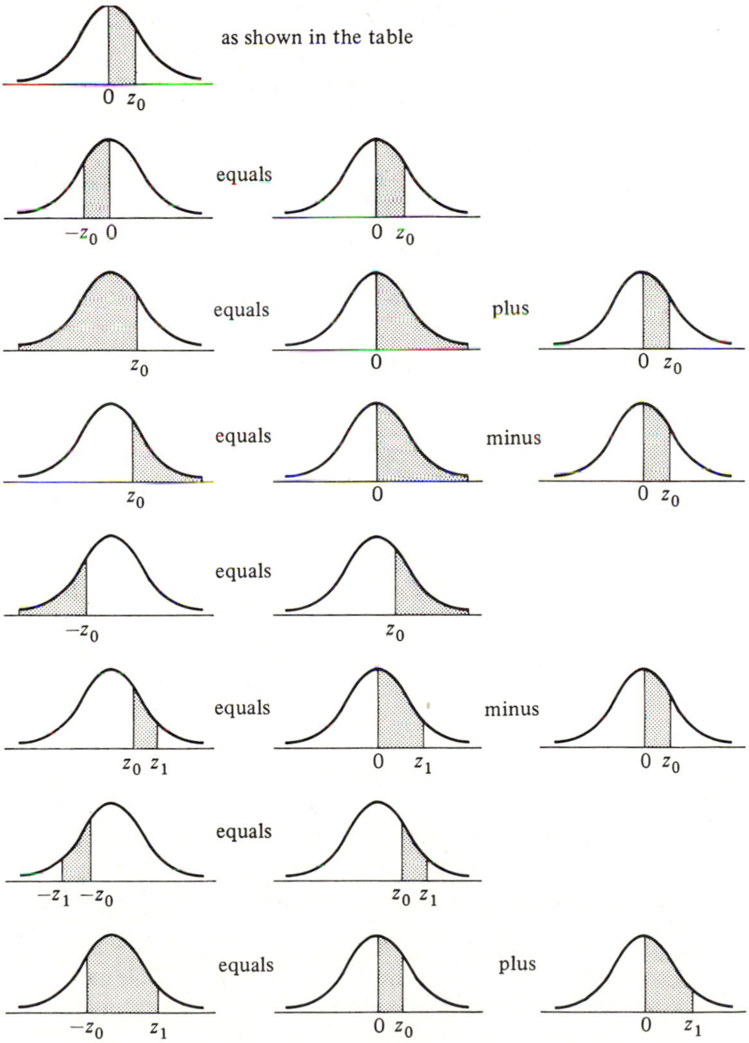

Figure 4-8

Let us now consider two examples on the use of the table areas under the standard normal curve. The first example will provide us with information that will prove useful in later work. The second example is concerned with the relationship between the binomial and the normal distribution in a specific case which is of interest to us.

EXAMPLE 1 If X is a random normal variable with mean μ and variance σ^2, find the following.

(a) $P(\mu - \sigma < x < \mu + \sigma)$.
(b) $P(\mu - 2\sigma < x < \mu + 2\sigma)$.
(c) $P(\mu - 3\sigma < x < \mu + 3\sigma)$.
(d) The two values of X that cut off the central 95% of the area under the curve.
(e) The two values of X that cut off the central 99% of the area under the curve.

The answers are found as follows.

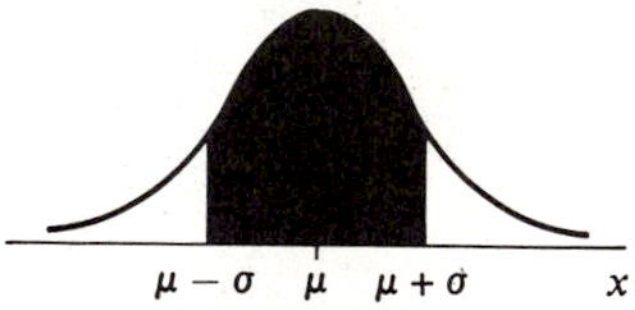

Figure 4-9

For (a): We wish to determine the area shown in Figure 4-9. The corresponding lower and upper limits in terms of the standard normal variable are

$$z_1 = \frac{x_1 - \mu}{\sigma} = \frac{(\mu - \sigma) - \mu}{\sigma} = -1$$

and

$$z_2 = \frac{x_2 - \mu}{\sigma} = \frac{(\mu + \sigma) - \mu}{\sigma} = +1.$$

Then

$$P(-1 < z < +1) = P(0 < z < +1) + P(0 < z < +1) = 0.3413 + 0.3413 = 0.6826.$$

That is, *the probability that x lies within one standard deviation in either direction from its mean is* 68.26%.

For (b):

$$P(\mu - 2\sigma < x < \mu + 2\sigma) = P\left(\left[\frac{(\mu - 2\sigma) - \mu}{\sigma}\right] < z < \left[\frac{(\mu + 2\sigma) - \mu}{\sigma}\right]\right)$$
$$= P(-2 < z < +2) = 0.4772 + 0.4772 = 0.9544.$$

That is, *the probability that x lies within two standard deviations in either direction from its mean is* 95.44%.

For (*c*):

$$P(\mu - 3\sigma < x < \mu + 3\sigma) = P\left(\left[\frac{(\mu - 3\sigma) - \mu}{\sigma}\right] < z < \left[\frac{(\mu + 3\sigma) - \mu}{\sigma}\right]\right)$$

$$= P(-3 < z < +3) = 0.4987 + 0.4987 = 0.9974.$$

That is, *the probability that x lies within three standard deviations in either direction from its mean is* 99.74%. In other words, practically all values of X are confined to an interval of six standard derivations; the midpoint of this interval is, of course, the mean.

The previous problems were all cases in which we knew the values of X and determined the areas under the curve bounded by these values. The two problems that follow are of just the opposite kind: this time we know the area and want to find the boundary values of X.

For (*d*): Here we have $P(x_1 < x < x_2) = 0.95$, and the interval x_1 to x_2 is centered around the mean. Our problem is to find x_1 and x_2. We solve it by first finding the corresponding boundaries of the standard normal distribution. Given the probability statement for X, the corresponding probability statement for the standard normal variable Z is $P(z_1 < z < z_2) = 0.95$, and the interval z_1 to z_2 is centered around 0 (Figure 4-10). Because of the centering

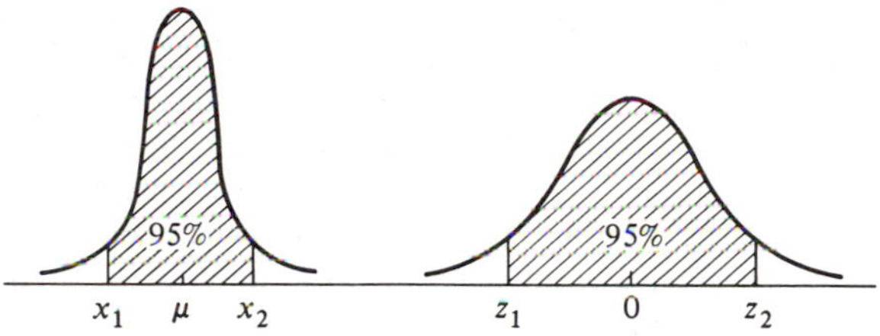

Figure 4-10

around zero we have

$$P(0 < z < z_2) = P(z_1 < z < 0) = \frac{0.95}{2} = 0.475.$$

Searching the body of the table of areas of standard normal distribution, we find that the value of Z which corresponds to the area of 0.475 is 1.96. Thus,

$$z_2 = 1.96,$$

$$z_1 = -1.96.$$

Therefore

$$\frac{x_2 - \mu}{\sigma} = 1.96,$$

$$\frac{x_1 - \mu}{\sigma} = -1.96.$$

This gives

$$x_2 = \mu + 1.96\sigma$$

and

$$x_1 = \mu - 1.96\sigma.$$

That is, *the interval* $\mu \pm 1.96\sigma$ *contains the central* 95% *of all values of* X.

For (*e*):

$$P(x_1 < x < x_2) = 0.99,$$

$$P(z_1 < z < z_2) = 0.99,$$

$$P(0 < z < z_2) = 0.495.$$

The value of Z corresponding to the area of 0.495 is 2.57. Thus,

$$z_2 = 2.57,$$

$$z_1 = -2.57,$$

and therefore

$$x_2 = \mu + 2.57\sigma$$

and

$$x_1 = \mu - 2.57\sigma.$$

That is, *the interval* $\mu \pm 2.57\sigma$ *contains the central* 99% *of all values of* X.

EXAMPLE 2 Consider the distribution of sample proportion $\hat{\pi}$ for samples of size 16 coming from a population with a proportion of successes $\pi = 0.7$. This is the binomial distribution which was derived earlier; it is given in the last column of Table 4-5 (and reproduced in the last column of Table 4-7). We are supposed to find a normal approximation of this distribution. The solution is as follows. First, we have to replace the points $\hat{\pi}$ of the discrete binomial distribution by intervals that would pertain to the corresponding normal distribution. This was explained and described at the beginning of this section. The next step is to obtain the normal probabilities corresponding to each interval. Since in this case the binomial distribution of $\hat{\pi}$ has a mean of 0.7 and standard deviation of 0.114564, the approximating normal distribution must be characterized by these parametric values. To find the probabilities we have to make a transformation to the standard normal variable given by

$$z = \frac{\hat{\pi} - 0.7}{0.114564} = 8.728742\hat{\pi} - 6.11012.$$

This will enable us to state the intervals in terms of z rather than $\hat{\pi}$, and to find the corresponding probabilities from the table of areas of the standard normal distribution. The results are presented in Table 4-7. It is obvious that the normal approximation to the binomial distribution is extremely close in spite of the fact the size of the sample is only 16.

In our discussion about the normal distribution, we started with the assertion that normal distribution is the limiting form of binomial distribution. It should be pointed out that this is only one way in which the normal distribution may be deduced and that there are other lines of reasoning which would lead to it.[5] Of these the most important one is that in which the derivation is based on the behavior of random errors. For instance, consider the problem of measuring the length of an object. Under ordinary circumstances each measurement may be subject to an error. Now let us suppose that any error is the result of some infinitely large number of small causes, each producing a small deviation. If we then assume that all of these

[5] For a compact survey, see J. K. Patel and C. B. Read, *Handbook of the Normal Distribution* (New York: Marcel Dekker, 1980), Ch. 1.

Table 4-7

$\hat{\pi}$ (discrete values)	$\hat{\pi}$ (intervals)	z (intervals)	$F(\hat{\pi})$ (cumulative normal approximation)[a]	$f(\hat{\pi})$ (normal approximation)[b]	$f(\hat{\pi})$ (binomial distribution)
0	−1/32 to 1/32	−∞ to −5.84	0.0000	0.0000 (0.00)	0.00
1/16	1/32 to 3/32	−5.84 to −5.29	0.0000	0.0000 (0.00)	0.00
2/16	3/32 to 5/32	−5.29 to −4.75	0.0000	0.0000 (0.00)	0.00
3/16	5/32 to 7/32	−4.75 to −4.20	0.0000	0.0000 (0.00)	0.00
4/16	7/32 to 9/32	−4.20 to −3.66	0.0000	0.0000 (0.00)	0.00
5/16	9/32 to 11/32	−3.66 to −3.11	0.0009	0.0009 (0.00)	0.00
6/16	11/32 to 13/32	−3.11 to −2.57	0.0050	0.0041 (0.00)	0.01
7/16	13/32 to 15/32	−2.57 to −2.02	0.0217	0.0167 (0.02)	0.02
8/16	15/32 to 17/32	−2.02 to −1.48	0.0694	0.0477 (0.05)	0.05
9/16	17/32 to 19/32	−1.48 to −0.93	0.1762	0.1068 (0.11)	0.10
10/16	19/32 to 21/32	−0.93 to −0.38	0.3520	0.1758 (0.17)	0.17
11/16	21/32 to 23/32	−0.38 to 0.16	0.5636	0.2116 (0.21)	0.21
12/16	23/32 to 25/32	0.16 to 0.71	0.7611	0.1975 (0.20)	0.20
13/16	25/32 to 27/32	0.71 to 1.25	0.8944	0.1333 (0.13)	0.15
14/16	27/32 to 29/32	1.25 to 1.80	0.9641	0.0697 (0.07)	0.07
15/16	29/32 to 31/32	1.80 to 2.34	0.9904	0.0263 (0.03)	0.02
1	31/32 to 33/32	2.34 to +∞	1.0000	0.0096 (0.01)	0.00

[a] $F(\hat{\pi})$ is represented by the area from $-\infty$ to the upper limit of each interval.
[b] $f(\hat{\pi})$ is given by the area corresponding to each interval. The figures in parentheses are the probabilities rounded off to two decimal places.

small deviations are equal and that positive deviations are just as likely as negative deviations, then it can be shown that the *errors are normally distributed* about zero, i.e., that the measurements are normally distributed about the "true" value. The basis of this derivation can, of course, be interpreted quite generally. In particular, the term "error" can be taken to mean any deviation from some systematic behavior, and this is the interpretation which underlies most theoretical developments in modern econometrics. This will become obvious as soon as we start discussing regression models. For now we ought to mention that the extensive use of the normal distribution has led to the following abbreviated notation:

$X \sim N(\mu, \sigma^2)$ *means that X is a normally distributed random variable with mean* μ *and variance* σ^2. *Therefore,* $X \sim N(0, 1)$ *stands for standard normal variable.* This notation will be followed hereafter.

4-3 Sampling Distribution of Sample Mean

In the case of the sampling distribution of sample proportion discussed in Section 4-1, we dealt with sampling from a dichotomous population. Every observation was classified as a failure or a success, and we considered the proportion of successes in the sample as an estimator of the probability of success in the population. As mentioned earlier, the labeling of observations as failure or success could be replaced by numerical values, namely 0 for failure and 1 for success. Thus instead of dealing with attributes we would be dealing with a *binary variable.* Suppose we call this variable Y and observe the following values in a sample of six observations.

$$y_1 = 0,$$
$$y_2 = 1,$$
$$y_3 = 0,$$
$$y_4 = 0,$$
$$y_5 = 1,$$
$$y_6 = 0.$$

Then the observed proportion of successes is

$$\hat{\pi} = \frac{0+1+0+0+1+0}{6} = \frac{2}{6} = \frac{1}{n}\sum_{i=1}^{6} y_i = \bar{y}.$$

That is, the proportion of successes in the sample is nothing else but the sample mean of Y. Further, we know that the probability of success in the population is the limit of the relative frequency of successes as the number of observations approaches infinity. Since the limit of relative frequency of y is the probability of y—which we labeled $f(y)$—and since observing a success means that $y = 1$, it follows that

$$\pi = P(\text{success}) = P(y = 1) = f(1),$$

or

$$\pi = 1 \times f(1).$$

This may as well be written as

$$\pi = 0 \times f(0) + 1 \times f(1),$$

since zero times any number is zero. But writing the expression for π in this form shows that π is, in fact, equal to the weighted average of the different values of Y (i.e., 0 and 1) with the weights given by the respective probabilities. This is precisely the definition of the mathematical expectation of Y as stated in (3.23). Therefore, we have

$$\pi = E(Y) = \mu_Y.$$

In other words, the probability of success in the population is the population mean of Y. Therefore, the sampling distribution of sample proportion (as an estimator of the probability of success) can be viewed as a sampling distribution of sample mean (as an estimator of population mean) when the variable is a binary one.

At this stage we are interested in the problem of deriving the sampling distribution of sample mean in cases in which the variable can assume more than two values and have any kind of distribution. In general, we expect that different distributions of the variable in the population (i.e., "parent" distributions) lead to different forms of sampling distributions of sample mean. For example, there is no apparent reason why the distribution of sample mean for samples drawn from a highly skewed population should have the same form as that for samples drawn from a symmetric population. However, we cannot and do not want to discuss every conceivable form of parent distribution individually. For our purpose, it is sufficient if we limit ourselves to a detailed discussion of only two distributions—a discrete uniform and a normal distribution—and consider all the other distributions in general terms. The discrete uniform distribution is of special interest to us because it was used as the basis of our sampling experiment in Section 2-2; it also provides a convenient background for illustrating a way of deriving theoretical sampling distributions. The normal distribution will be discussed because many inference statements in econometrics depend heavily on the assumption of normality in the parent population.

First, we take up the problem of deriving the sampling distribution of sample mean when the variable of interest (say, X) has a *discrete uniform distribution.* This means that X can assume a finite number of different values, each with equal probability. The case of a binary variable represents a special case; we already know that this case leads to a binomial distribution of sample mean (see Section 4-1). Here our concern is with a more general problem. We will start by specifying the parent distribution as that which was used in our sampling experiment in Section 2-2. There, it may be recalled, we let X take on values 0, 1, 2, . . . , 9, each with probability of 1/10. As worked out earlier, the main characteristics of this distribution are

Mean: $E(X) = 4.5$

Variance: $\text{Var}(X) = 2.8723^2 = 8.25.$

Let us then derive the sampling distribution of $\bar{X}$ as an estimator of $\mu = 4.5$. In this we will follow the procedure of Section 4-1 by "building up" the probabilities of individual values of the estimator and by calculating the main characteristics of the resulting distribution. As before, we will do this for different sample sizes and try to discover the pattern that would allow us to develop a general formula to apply to any sample size.

Sampling distribution of $\bar{X}$ for sample size 1. In this case $\bar{X}$ can assume 10 different values: 0, 1, 2, . . . , 9, the same as the variable X. The probability of each of these values is 1/10, as shown in Table 4-8 and Figure 4-11.

Mean and variance of $\bar{X}$:

$$E(\bar{X}) = \sum_i \bar{x}_i f(\bar{x}_i) = 4.5,$$

$$\text{Var}(\bar{X}) = E(\bar{X}^2) - [E(\bar{X})]^2 = \sum_i \bar{x}_i^2 f(\bar{x}_i) - [\sum_i \bar{x}_i f(\bar{x}_i)]^2 = 28.5 - 4.5^2 = 8.25.$$

Table 4-8

$\bar{x}$	$f(\bar{x})$	$\bar{x}f(\bar{x})$	$\bar{x}^2f(\bar{x})$
0	$P(0) = 1/10$	0	0
1	$P(1) = 1/10$	1/10	1/10
2	$P(2) = 1/10$	2/10	4/10
3	$P(3) = 1/10$	3/10	9/10
4	$P(4) = 1/10$	4/10	16/10
5	$P(5) = 1/10$	5/10	25/10
6	$P(6) = 1/10$	6/10	36/10
7	$P(7) = 1/10$	7/10	49/10
8	$P(8) = 1/10$	8/10	64/10
9	$P(9) = 1/10$	9/10	81/10
	Sum 1	45/10	285/10

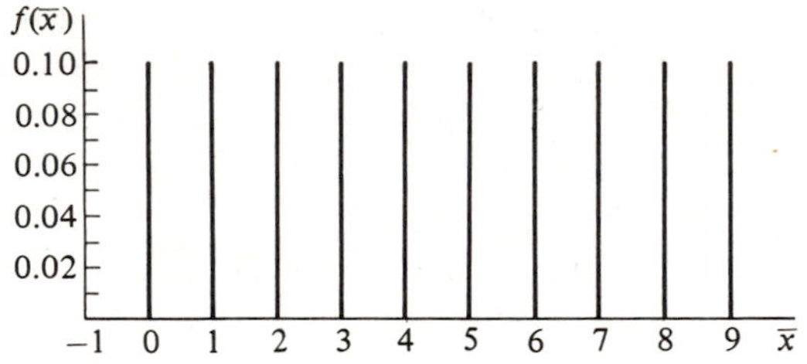

Figure 4-11

The mean and variance of $\bar{X}$ in this case are, of course, the same as those of X in the population.

Sampling distribution of $\bar{X}$ for sample size 2. Here the possible values of $\bar{X}$ are 0, 1/2, 2/2, . . . , 18/2. That is, there are 19 different values that $\bar{X}$ can assume. The probability distribution is given in Table 4-9.

Mean and variance of $\bar{X}$:

$$E(\bar{X}) = 4.5,$$

$$\text{Var}(\bar{X}) = 24.375 - 4.5^2 = 24.375 - 20.25 = 4.125.$$

The resulting distribution has a "triangular" form, as shown in Figure 4-12.

Sampling distribution of $\bar{X}$ for sample size 3. The possible values of $\bar{X}$ in this case are 0, 1/3, 2/3, . . . , 27/3. The corresponding probabilities and the values of the mean and of the variance can be determined in the same way as for sample size 2. The derivation, which is left to the reader, leads to the following results.

Mean and variance of $\bar{X}$: $E(\bar{X}) = 4.5,$

$$\text{Var}(\bar{X}) = 2.75.$$

Table 4-9

$\bar{x}$	$f(\bar{x})$		$\bar{x}f(\bar{x})$	$\bar{x}^2 f(\bar{x})$
0	$P(0, 0)$	$= 1/10^2$	0.00	0.000
1/2	$P(0, 1) + P(1, 0)$	$= 2/10^2$	0.01	0.005
2/2	$P(0, 2) + P(2, 0) + P(1, 1)$	$= 3/10^2$	0.03	0.030
3/2	$P(0, 3) + P(3, 0) + P(1, 2) + P(2, 1)$	$= 4/10^2$	0.06	0.090
4/2	. . .	$= 5/10^2$	0.10	0.200
5/2	. . .	$= 6/10^2$	0.15	0.375
6/2	. . .	$= 7/10^2$	0.21	0.630
7/2	. . .	$= 8/10^2$	0.28	0.980
8/2	. . .	$= 9/10^2$	0.36	1.440
9/2	$P(0, 9) + P(9, 0) + P(1, 8) + P(8, 1) + P(2, 7) + P(7, 2) + P(3, 6) + P(6, 3) + P(4, 5) + P(5, 4)$	$= 10/10^2$	0.45	2.025
10/2	$P(1, 9) + P(9, 1) + P(2, 8) + P(8, 2) + P(3, 7) + P(7, 3) + P(4, 6) + P(6, 4) + P(5, 5)$	$= 9/10^2$	0.45	2.250
⋮	⋮	⋮	⋮	⋮
17/2	$P(8, 9) + P(9, 8)$	$= 2/10^2$	0.17	1.445
18/2	$P(9, 9)$	$= 1/10^2$	0.09	0.810
	Sum	1	4.50	24.375

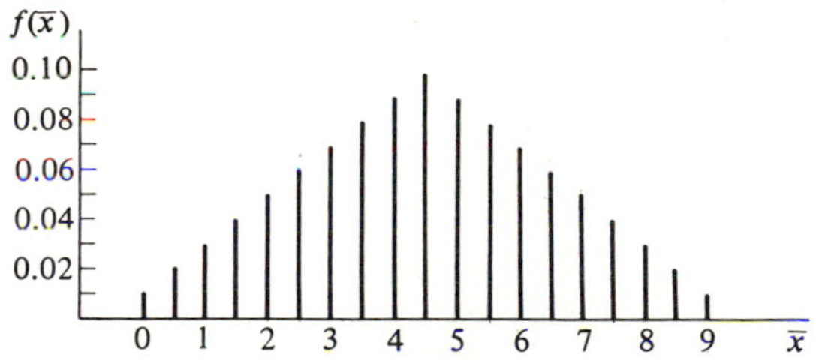

Figure 4-12

The distribution is perfectly symmetric around the point 4.5. Its graphical representation is given in Figure 4-13.

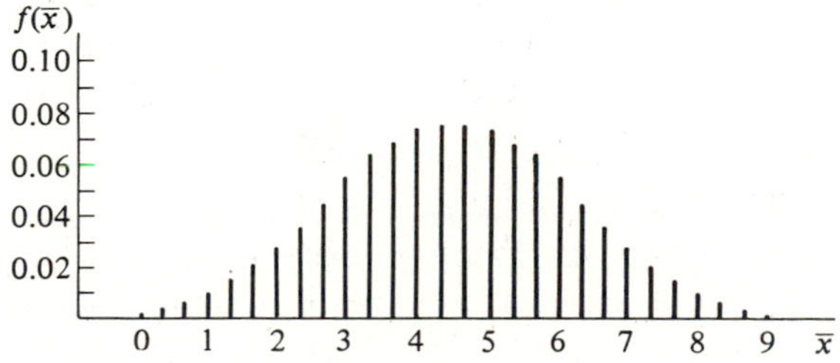

Figure 4-13

By now it should be clear how to go about constructing the sampling distributions, and there is no need for us to continue in detail. A comparison of Figure 4-13 with Figure 4-10 makes it quite clear that the distribution of $\bar{X}$ based on samples of size 3 or larger can be well approximated by the normal distribution. As for the mean and the variance of $\bar{X}$, a summary of the results is presented in Table 4-10.

Table 4-10

Sample size	Mean	Variance
1	4.5	8.25
2	4.5	4.125
3	4.5	2.75

The most obvious feature of Table 4-10 is the fact that the value of the mean is equal to the population mean for all sample sizes examined. As far as the variance is concerned, note that its value for sample size 1 is exactly equal to the population variance and that the remaining values decrease in proportion to sample size, i.e., that

$$4.125 = \frac{8.25}{2} \quad \text{and} \quad 2.75 = \frac{8.25}{3}.$$

Finally, since we found all the sampling distributions to be exactly symmetric, the third moment μ_3 (and, therefore, also α_3) must be equal to zero. These results can easily be generalized to apply to any sample size n. Then we have

$$E(\bar{X}) = \mu,$$

$$\sigma_{\bar{x}}^2 = \frac{\sigma_x^2}{n},$$

$$\alpha_3 = 0,$$

where $\sigma_{\bar{x}}^2 = \mathrm{Var}(\bar{X})$ and $\sigma_x^2 = \mathrm{Var}(X)$.

It can be shown that these generalizations are perfectly valid. (The proof concerning the mean and the variance will be given toward the end of this section; the proof concerning α_3 is left to the reader.)

Now we are in a position to make definite statements about the properties of sample mean as an estimator of the population mean for samples from a *discrete uniform population* with equally spaced values of X. The following conclusions can be made.

1. *$\bar{X}$ is an unbiased estimator of μ.*
2. *The variance of $\bar{X}$ is equal to the variance of X divided by sample size.* Thus, as the sample size increases, the distribution of $\bar{X}$ becomes more and more concentrated.
3. Conclusions 1 and 2 together imply that *$\bar{X}$ is a consistent estimator of μ.*

4. *The distribution of $\bar{X}$ is perfectly symmetric.*
5. *The distribution of $\bar{X}$ based on samples of size 3 or larger is approximately normal.*

These properties of $\bar{X}$ have been deduced from the theoretically derived sampling distribution. In Section 2-2 we tried to find these properties by conducting a sampling experiment on a discrete uniform population with values of X equal to 0, 1, 2, . . . , 9. The experiment consisted of drawing 100 samples of size 5 and 100 samples of size 10. For sample size 5, we constructed frequency distributions of sample mean and of sample median, and for sample size 10 of sample mean alone. The frequency distributions obtained in this way were assumed to approximate the true sampling distributions of these estimators. The results enabled us to make some tentative conclusions concerning the properties of these estimators. With respect to sample mean we are now in a position to check the experimental results by comparing them with the theoretically derived ones. The comparisons are presented in Tables 4-11 and 4-12. The experimental results are reproduced from

Table 4-11

	Sample size 5	
Interval: $\bar{x}$	Experimental $f(\bar{x})$	Theoretical $f(\bar{x})$
0.5 to 1.499	0.01	0.01
1.5 to 2.499	0.05	0.05
2.5 to 3.499	0.12	0.16
3.5 to 4.499	0.31	0.28
4.5 to 5.499	0.28	0.28
5.5 to 6.499	0.15	0.16
6.5 to 7.499	0.05	0.05
7.5 to 8.499	0.03	0.01
8.5 to 9.499	0.00	0.00
Mean	4.60	4.5
Standard deviation	1.3638	1.2845

Tables 2-4 and 2-6. The theoretical results were obtained by using the normal approximation and the derived expressions for $E(\bar{X})$ and $\sigma_{\bar{x}}$.

Tables 4-11 and 4-12 show that the experimentally derived frequency distributions give a reasonable approximation of the true sampling distributions. The tentative conclusions about $\bar{X}$ as an estimator of the population mean—namely unbiasedness, consistency, and reduction of variance proportional to sample size—all proved to be correct. However, the experimental results did not give us any formulas for the variance and were not clear enough to suggest symmetry. The theoretical results are not only more accurate, but they are also considerably more explicit and more general.

Table 4-12

Interval: $\bar{x}$	Sample size 10: Experimental $f(\bar{x})$	Theoretical $f(\bar{x})$
0.5 to 1.499	0.00	0.00
1.5 to 2.499	0.01	0.02
2.5 to 3.499	0.14	0.12
3.5 to 4.499	0.34	0.36
4.5 to 5.499	0.32	0.36
5.5 to 6.499	0.16	0.12
6.5 to 7.499	0.03	0.02
7.5 to 8.499	0.00	0.00
8.5 to 9.499	0.00	0.00
Mean	4.57	4.5
Standard deviation	1.0416	0.9083

So far we have dealt with sampling from a discrete uniform population. Let us now turn to sampling from *normal populations.* In particular, our task now is to find the sampling distribution of sample mean given that the variable X, whose values make up the sample, is distributed normally with mean μ and variance σ^2, i.e., given that $X \sim N(\mu, \sigma^2)$. Note that we made a slight change in notation: instead of σ_x^2 we use σ^2 to describe the population variance. Now we know that

$$\bar{X} = \frac{1}{n}\sum_{i=1}^{n} X_i = \frac{1}{n}(X_1 + X_2 + \cdots + X_n) = \frac{1}{n}X_1 + \frac{1}{n}X_2 + \cdots + \frac{1}{n}X_n.$$

The n elements $X_1, X_2, \ldots, X_n$ can be viewed as n variables, each having the same distribution, mean, and variance as X. That is, X_1 stands for all possible values of X that can be obtained when drawing the first observation, X_2 for all possible values of X that can be obtained when drawing the second observation, and so on. This way of looking at the sample to be drawn as a set of n *identically and independently distributed (i.i.d.)* variables makes the subsequent analysis simpler and neater. Since n (and therefore $1/n$) is a constant for a given sample size, it follows that $\bar{X}$ can be regarded as a linear combination of n independent normal variables X_1, $X_2, \ldots, X_n$. But we know, by Theorem 14 of this chapter, that a linear combination of normally distributed independent random variables is also normally distributed. This saves us all the work of deriving the form of the sampling distribution of $\bar{X}$ because the theorem clearly implies that *if X (and therefore $X_1, X_2, \ldots, X_n$) is normal, then $\bar{X}$ is also normal, whatever the sample size.*

Having obtained this result, our task is reduced to determining the mean and the variance of the sampling distribution of $\bar{X}$. As emphasized in Section 4-2, the knowledge of the mean and the variance of a normal distribution is sufficient for its complete identification. Fortunately, the derivation of these two parameters turns out to be relatively simple. Let us start with the mean.

$$E(\bar{X}) = E\frac{1}{n}\sum_{i=1}^{n} X_i.$$

Since $1/n$ is a constant, we can, according to Theorem 6, write this as

$$E(\bar{X}) = \frac{1}{n} E \sum_i X_i.$$

But, by Theorem 9 of Section 3-7, the expectation of a sum is equal to the sum of expectations so that

$$E(\bar{X}) = \frac{1}{n}\sum_i E(X_i) = \frac{1}{n}[E(X_1) + E(X_2) + \cdots + E(X_n)].$$

Now each of $X_1, X_2, \ldots, X_n$ has the same mean as X, i.e., μ. Therefore,

$$E(\bar{X}) = \frac{1}{n}[\mu + \mu + \cdots + \mu] = \frac{n\mu}{n} = \mu.$$

That is, the mean of the sampling distribution of $\bar{X}$ is equal to the population mean μ. Next we derive the variance of $\bar{X}$ denoted by $\sigma_{\bar{x}}^2$. We have

$$\sigma_{\bar{x}}^2 = \mathrm{Var}(\bar{X}) = \mathrm{Var}\left[\frac{1}{n}\sum_{i=1}^{n} X_i\right] = \frac{1}{n^2}\mathrm{Var}\left[\sum_i X_i\right] \qquad \text{(by Theorem 8).}$$

But since the variables are independent of each other, their covariances are all equal to zero and we have, by Theorem 13 of Section 3-7,

$$\mathrm{Var}(\sum_{i=1}^{n} X_i) = \sum_{i=1}^{n} \mathrm{Var}(X_i).$$

Thus for the variance of $\bar{X}$ we can write

$$\sigma_{\bar{x}}^2 = \frac{1}{n^2}[\mathrm{Var}(X_1) + \mathrm{Var}(X_2) + \cdots + \mathrm{Var}(X_n)].$$

Now each of $X_1, X_2, \ldots, X_n$ has the same variance as X, i.e., σ^2. Therefore,

$$\sigma_{\bar{x}}^2 = \frac{1}{n^2}[\sigma^2 + \sigma^2 + \cdots + \sigma^2] = \frac{\sigma^2}{n}.$$

That is, the variance of the sampling distribution of $\bar{X}$ is equal to the population variance divided by sample size. These results can be summarized as follows.

If $X \sim N(\mu, \sigma^2)$, then $\bar{X} \sim N(\mu, \sigma^2/n)$.

This result is very important and will be used frequently throughout the rest of the book.

The preceding result implies certain properties of $\bar{X}$ as an estimator of the mean (μ) of a normal population.

1. Since $E(\bar{X}) = \mu$, *$\bar{X}$ is an unbiased estimator of μ.*
2. Since $\sigma_{\bar{x}}^2 = \sigma^2/n$, the distribution of $\bar{X}$ becomes more and more concentrated as the sample size n increases.

3. The preceding two properties imply that $\bar{X}$ *is a consistent estimator of* μ.
4. Since the distribution of $\bar{X}$ is normal, it is perfectly symmetric.

These properties are the same as those of $\bar{X}$ as an estimator of the mean of a discrete uniform population.

Another interesting implication of the result concerns the relationship between the variance of the sampling distribution of $\bar{X}$ and the variance of X in the population. Note that the dispersion of $\bar{X}$ depends only on two things, the size of the sample and the dispersion of the variable X in the population. For a given sample size, the smaller the population variance happens to be, the less dispersed (that is, the more reliable) are our guesses about the population mean. We use the term "happens to be" to emphasize the fact that the size of the population variance, unlike that of the sample, is not under our control—not even in theory. Thus, if we were to estimate the mean of some normally distributed variable such as, e.g., annual family expenditure of families in a given income bracket, we would obtain a more reliable estimate from a population with similar tastes, values, etc., than from a less conformist population. (The relationship between the variance of $\bar{X}$ and that of X was found to be the same in the case of a discrete uniform parent population as in the case of a normal parent. However, the former case is less interesting in practice, and thus we made no comment about it at the time.)

We have now completed a detailed derivation of the sampling distribution of sample mean for two parent populations—a discrete uniform population and a normal population. The latter is of considerable practical importance but, even so, cases of sampling from nonnormal populations (and from nonuniform populations) arise quite often in econometric work. However, we cannot conceivably pay individual attention to all remaining distributions, nor do we have any useful criterion for singling out some in preference to others. Therefore, we shall deal with the rest of the distributions only in a summary form, while trying to come to as many conclusions of general applicability as possible. Fortunately, we can go quite some way in this direction by establishing results which are independent of the form of the parent distribution of X.

One feature of the sampling distribution of $\bar{X}$, which in no way depends on the form of the distribution of X in the population, has already been obtained in connection with sampling from a normal population. This concerns the mean and the variance of $\bar{X}$. Suppose that the variable X has *any* distribution with mean μ and variance σ^2, and that $X_1, X_2, \ldots, X_n$ are regarded as n identically and independently distributed variables, each having exactly the same mean and variance as X. Then the mean of $\bar{X}$ is given by

$$E(\bar{X}) = E\frac{1}{n}(X_1 + X_2 + \cdots + X_n) = \mu,$$

and the variance of $\bar{X}$ is

$$\mathrm{Var}(\bar{X}) = \mathrm{Var}\left[\frac{1}{n}(X_1 + X_2 + \cdots + X_n)\right] = \frac{\sigma^2}{n}.$$

These results are summarized in the following theorem.

Theorem 15 *If X is a variable with mean μ and variance σ^2 then, whatever the distribution of X, the sampling distribution of $\bar{X}$ has the same mean μ and variance equal to σ^2/n.*

Another feature of the sampling distribution of $\bar{X}$ which is independent of the distribution of X is described in the next theorem. This theorem, generally referred to as the *central limit theorem,* is one of the most important propositions in the theory of statistics. Its proof can be found in many texts on mathematical statistics and will not be developed here.[6]

Theorem 16 *(Central Limit Theorem). If X has any distribution with mean μ and variance σ^2, then the distribution of $(\bar{X} - \mu)/\sigma_{\bar{x}}$ approaches the standard normal distribution as sample size n increases. Therefore the distribution of $\bar{X}$ in large samples is approximately normal with mean μ and variance σ^2/n.*

This is quite a remarkable result. It means that, in large samples, the distribution of $\bar{X}$ can be approximated by a normal distribution whatever the parent distribution of X. This is what gives the central limit theorem its practical importance. The degree of closeness of the normal approximation depends not only on sample size but also on the shape of the parent distribution. If the parent distribution is symmetric or is close to being symmetric, the normal approximation will work well even for relatively small sample sizes. In cases where the parent distribution is highly skewed, it would take a large sample size before one could feel reasonably satisfied with using normal distribution for $\bar{X}$. And this, in fact, is all that one can legitimately expect from the central limit theorem.

Our discussion on sampling distribution of sample mean may best be closed by highlighting the most important results. We started by deriving the sampling distribution of $\bar{X}$ for samples drawn from a *discrete uniform population.* The resulting distribution of $\bar{X}$ turned out to be perfectly symmetric and capable of being closely approximated by a normal distribution, whatever sample size. Next, we found that the distribution of $\bar{X}$ for samples from a *normal population* is itself exactly normal for every sample size. Finally, by invoking the central limit theorem, we concluded that the distribution of $\bar{X}$ of a large sample will be approximately normal whatever the parent population. All these results bring out the importance of a normal distribution in statistical inference. In dealing with large samples we can *always* rely on normal distribution to describe the sampling distribution of $\bar{X}$. (Strictly speaking, the central limit theorem does not hold in the case in which the population variance is not finite. The statement in the text is based on the assumption that such cases are excluded from our discussion. Also, note the qualifying footnote.[6]) If the parent population is not normal, the description will be approximate; if it is normal,

[6] It ought to be emphasized, though, that the validity of the theorem is restricted by the assumption that the variables X_i are mutually independent and are drawn from the same population with constant parameters.

the description will be exact. In dealing with small samples, normal distribution will give a perfect description of the distribution of $\bar{X}$ if the parent population is normal, and an approximate description if the parent population is nonnormal but symmetric. Only in the case of small samples and a skewed parent population would it be inadvisable to approximate the distribution of $\bar{X}$ by a normal distribution. Finally, concerning the properties of the sample mean as an estimator of the population mean, we found that, whatever the parent population, the distribution of $\bar{X}$ has a mean equal to the population mean and variance equal to the population variance divided by sample size. Thus $\bar{X}$ is an unbiased and consistent estimator of the population mean.

EXERCISES

4-1. In a certain city, 20% of all consumers are users of brand D soap. What are the probabilities that in an elevator containing 10 people there will be 0, 1, 2, . . . , 10 users of brand D soap?

4-2. How many times would we have to toss a coin in order that the probability will be at least 0.95 that the proportion of heads will lie between 0.40 and 0.60?

4-3. Given that the mean number of successes in n trials is 8 with standard deviation equal to 2, find n and π.

4-4. Consider a continuous uniform population with $0 < x < 1$. What is the probability that the mean of 20 observations will lie between 0.4 and 0.6?

4-5. A population consists of 10 balls of which 5 are white and 5 are red. Construct the sampling distribution of the proportion of white balls in a sample of 3 balls that are drawn *without replacement*.

4-6. A company operating in a certain city has been charged with making excessive profits. As evidence, it has been stated that the company's rate of profit last year was 22% while the national average for the industry was 16%. In defense, the officials of the company claimed that the profits in their industry are highly variable and that substantial deviations from the average are not infrequent. They pointed out that, while the mean rate of profit for the industry was 16%, the standard deviation was as large as 4%. Assuming that profits are normally distributed, what is the probability of making a profit of 22% or higher by pure chance?

4-7. If $X \sim N(8, 16)$, find each of the following.

a. $P(6 < X < 10)$. **b.** $P(10 < X < 12)$. **c.** $P(X < 0)$. **d.** $P(X > 20)$.

e. The two values of X that cut off the central 50% of the area under the curve.

4-8. The quantitative SAT scores of incoming home-state freshmen (X) and out-of-state freshmen (Y) at the University of Michigan are approximately normally distributed. In the last academic year the mean quantitative SAT score for home-state freshmen was 590 (with a standard deviation of 80) and the mean quantitative score for out-of-state freshmen was 620 (with a standard deviation of 60).

a. Suppose we select at random one home-state and one out-of-state freshman. What is the probability that the home-state student has a higher quantitative SAT score than the out-of-state student?

b. If two home-state freshmen are selected at random, what is the probability that their quantitative SAT scores will differ by more than 50 points?

c. A home-state freshman is selected at random and you are invited to guess his or her quantitative score. You pay a certain fee and if your guess is correct within ± 20 points, you will get \$10. If your guess is outside this range, you get nothing. What is the maximum amount that you should be willing to pay as a fee?

d. Suppose we draw two independent random samples, one consisting of 25 home-state freshmen and the other of 25 out-of-state freshmen. What is the probability that the sample mean quantitative SAT score of the home-state freshmen ($\bar{X}$) exceeds that of the out-of-state freshmen ($\bar{Y}$)?

4-9. Let $Y =$ income and $X = \log Y$. A frequently made claim is that the distribution of X is approximately normal. Check this claim by fitting a normal curve to the distribution of X obtained from the data in Table 4-13.

Table 4-13 Income of Families and Unattached Individuals, United States, 1978

Income	Frequency (%)
Under \$ 5,000	8.2
\$ 5,000 to \$ 6,999	6.1
\$ 7,000 to \$ 9,999	9.7
\$10,000 to \$11,999	6.8
\$12,000 to \$14,999	9.9
\$15,000 to \$24,999	31.4
\$25,000 to \$49,999	24.3
\$50,000 and over	3.6

Source: *Statistical Abstract of the United States, 1980* (U.S. Department of Commerce), p. 451.

4-10. A particular elevator is designed to carry a maximum of 10 persons. If its capacity load limit of 1800 pounds is exceeded, the elevator will not move. The weights of the people using the elevator are normally distributed with a mean of 162.5 pounds and a standard deviation of 22 pounds.

a. What is the probability that a random group of 10 people will exceed the capacity load limit of the elevator?

b. What are the expected weight and the standard deviation of a load of 10 people?

5 Tests of Hypotheses

At the beginning of this text we stated that there are essentially two kinds of statistical inference in classical statistics: estimation and tests of hypotheses. Both are concerned with making judgments about some unknown aspect of a given population on the basis of sample information. The unknown aspect may be the value of one or more of the population parameters or, less frequently, the functional form of the parent distribution. Whether a problem is one of estimation or one of hypothesis testing is determined by the type of question that is being asked. In the case of estimation, we ask a question about the value of a particular parameter. In hypothesis testing the question is preceded by a statement concerning the population; the question then is whether this statement is true or false. In other respects the two cases are quite similar. In either case we arrive at an answer by combining our prior knowledge and assumptions about the population with the evidence provided by the sample. In either case we make considerable use of the concept of a sampling distribution developed in the previous sections. Finally, whatever the type of question, the answer is always tentative. However, there are some differences in approach which warrant separate discussion. Accordingly, we shall devote this chapter to the problem of testing hypotheses and the next to that of estimation.

5-1 Design and Evaluation of Tests

A hypothesis is defined as an assumption about the population. Typically, we make more than one such assumption, but not all of them are to be tested. Those assumptions that are not intended to be exposed to a test are called the *maintained hypothesis.* They consist of all the assumptions that we are willing to make and to believe in. Of course, we are never absolutely certain that these assumptions are valid; if we were, they would cease to be assumptions and would become facts. The usual situation in this respect is one in which we believe that the assumptions in question very likely hold at least approximately so that the maintained hypothesis is very nearly correct. The remaining assumptions that are to be tested are called the *testable hypothesis.* Usually the testable hypothesis consists of a statement that a certain population parameter is equal to a given value—or that it does not exceed or does not fall below a certain value. In statistical theory this hypothesis is called the *null hypothesis* since it implies that there is no difference between the *true* value of the population parameter and that which is being hypothesized.

As an example, consider the statement that "economists and psychologists spend an equal average amount on tipping during their annual conventions." This can be interpreted as a testable hypothesis stating that the population means of the two professional groups are equal. One would normally test this by drawing a random sample of economists and a random sample of psychologists and comparing the respective sample means (in a manner to be discussed presently). The maintained hypothesis in this case might consist of the following assumptions.

1. If there is a difference in average tipping behavior, it is because of the profession of the tipper, and the two professional groups do not differ with respect to other possibly relevant factors, such as income, sex, and age.
2. In each group the amount spent on tipping is normally distributed with the same variance.
3. There is no definite prior presumption that either of the two population means is greater than the other.

The first of these assumptions implies that no factors other than difference in profession have to be taken into account when the test is carried out. The second assumption is needed in order to determine the sampling distribution of the test statistic. The final assumption determines the alternative to the null hypothesis. In this case the alternative hypothesis is that the means are *not* the same. The specification of the alternative hypothesis is needed when setting up the test.

The idea of an alternative hypothesis is quite important and requires elaboration. Since the null hypothesis is a testable proposition, there must exist a counterproposition to it, otherwise there would be no need for a test. The counterproposition is called the *alternative hypothesis.* Suppose the null hypothesis states that the population mean μ is equal to some value, say, μ_0. Usually we denote the null hypothesis by H_0 and the alternative by H_A. Then the alternative hypothesis may be, for instance, the proposition that μ is equal to some *other* value, say, μ_A. That is, we would have

$$H_0: \quad \mu = \mu_0,$$

$$H_A: \quad \mu = \mu_A.$$

If this is the case, the implication is that μ can be equal to either μ_0 or μ_A, but nothing else. Obviously such a case is very rare since it means that we really know quite a lot about the population mean a priori; the only thing that we are not certain about is which of the two values it has. More frequently, our prior knowledge concerning the population mean (or any other population parameter) is much less. If we know absolutely nothing about μ, then the alternative hypothesis would be that μ is *not* equal to μ_0, as described by

$$H_0: \quad \mu = \mu_0,$$

$$H_A: \quad \mu \neq \mu_0.$$

Sometimes the counterproposition is that μ is greater (or smaller) than μ_0. Then we would have

$$H_0: \quad \mu \leq \mu_0,$$

$$H_A: \quad \mu > \mu_0.$$

Hypotheses of a general form such as $\mu \neq \mu_0$, are called *composite hypotheses,* whereas specific claims such as $\mu = \mu_0$ are called *simple hypotheses.*

Since specific claims are easier to disprove than vague claims, it is desirable—and it has been the common practice—to formulate problems of hypotheses testing so that the null hypothesis is stated as specifically as possible. Thus, if—as frequently is the case—we have two rival hypotheses, one simple and one composite, we choose the simple one as the null hypothesis to be tested. (If both the null and the alternative hypotheses are composite, it is common practice to choose as the null hypothesis that claim which more nearly represents the status quo.) This means that we often introduce the null hypothesis as that proposition which we actually wish to disprove. A good example of this is a test of a new drug. There is an obvious presumption that the new drug will do better, say in terms of mean percentage of recoveries, than the old drug or therapy used, otherwise there would be no point in testing. Yet the null hypothesis for this case will be the proposition that the new drug leads to the same (or smaller) mean percentage of recoveries as the old drug; the alternative hypothesis will be that the mean percentage is higher for the new drug.

The decision as to which of the two rival hypotheses is to be regarded as the null hypothesis has some implications which ought to be taken into account. According to established methodology, a null hypothesis is a proposition which is considered valid unless evidence throws serious doubt on it. In this respect a statistical test is like a trial in a court of law. A man on trial is considered innocent unless the evidence suggests *beyond reasonable doubt* that he is guilty. Similarly, a null hypothesis is regarded as valid unless the evidence suggests—also beyond reasonable doubt—that it is not true. (However, while in court the definition of "reasonable doubt" is presumably the same from case to case, in statistical tests it may vary depending upon the cost of making an incorrect verdict.) Furthermore, just as in court it is up to the prosecution to prove the accused guilty, so in statistical testing it is up to the statistician to prove the null hypothesis incorrect. Of course, in neither case is the word "prove" to be taken in an absolute sense since a "shadow" of a doubt always exists; only God knows whether a man is really guilty or a null hypothesis is really incorrect. Finally, there is also a similarity in procedure. In court all evidence and other information relevant to the case are produced and weighed in accordance with the rules set by law, and a verdict of "guilty" or "not guilty" is reached. Similarly, when a statistical test is conducted, all evidence and prior information are used in accordance with predetermined rules, and a conclusion of "reject" or "do not reject" the null hypothesis is obtained. Interestingly enough, just as a court pronounces a verdict as "not guilty" rather than "innocent," so the conclusion of a statistical test is "do not reject" rather than "accept." (However, the term "acceptance" is sometimes used instead of the awkward term "nonrejection.")

The parallel between a trial in a court and a statistical test stops abruptly when it comes to the application of the Fifth Amendment of the United States Constitution. Unlike a man on trial who is not to "be subject for the same offense to be twice put in jeopardy of life or limb," a null hypothesis is *always* open to a test. In fact, while a null hypothesis is viewed as valid unless there is serious evidence against it, such a view is always held only tentatively. In this respect, a null hypothesis is like a titleholder who is forever open to challenge. In fact, one can visualize the course of science as a process of establishing hypotheses and then busily collecting evidence to bring about their downfall. Only the sturdiest hypotheses withstand the repeated attacks and become worthy of our faith, at least until the next attack comes along.

So far we have not mentioned the question concerning the source of hypotheses. In principle, this question has a simple answer: economic hypotheses are drawn from economic theory. In practice, however, the matter is much less simple. In the first place, economic theory is rarely sufficiently precise and detailed to lead to hypotheses suitable for application of statistical tests. For instance, one would be hard put to find in economic literature a theoretical development that would lead to a proposition specifying a definite value of the government expenditure multiplier as well as spelling out all the assumptions that would be embraced by the maintained hypothesis. Economic theory typically specifies only the interrelationships between different economic variables, usually described in quite general terms. The econometrician, then, must specify the mathematical form of those relationships and spell out the maintained hypothesis more completely and in greater detail. The null hypothesis usually states that the postulated relationship does *not* exist, which normally means that the value of one or more of the parameters is equal to zero, while the alternative hypothesis states that the relationship does exist. The second difficulty with economic theory as a source of hypotheses is that frequently the variables involved are difficult to define, or to measure, or both. This, unfortunately, applies not only to such notoriously difficult concepts as capital, but also to less obviously troublesome concepts such as income or consumption. Finally, there are many problems for which economic theory is not at all well developed, and thus it offers little help in leading to relevant hypotheses. In these situations the researcher usually resorts to ad hoc theorizing, that is, to setting up maintained and testable hypotheses by using his common sense and whatever inspiration he can get from theory. Most of the applied econometric work that has been done so far is of this kind, or at least predominantly so. All these difficulties in setting up economic hypotheses to some extent account for the greater concentration on problems of estimation rather than on problems of hypothesis testing in a good deal of econometric research.

One source of testable hypotheses that is definitely *inadmissible* is the sample itself. Using the sample observations for both formulating *and* testing the null hypothesis would clearly defeat the entire purpose of carrying out the test. For instance, it would make no sense to draw a sample of households, calculate the average household income, e.g., \$25,000, and then set up a hypothesis to be tested that the population mean income is \$25,000. Although this represents an extreme case, more subtle violations of the rule that hypotheses should originate from sources other than the sample itself are frequently encountered in practice. A related and extremely important point to remember is that testable hypotheses are statements about population parameters, *never* about sample statistics.

Setting up the null hypothesis and its alternative represents the first step in dealing with a problem involving hypothesis testing. The next step consists of devising a criterion that would enable us to decide whether the null hypothesis is or is not to be rejected on the basis of evidence. This criterion or rule is in principle the same regardless of the problem: it defines a test statistic and a boundary for dividing the sample space into a region of rejection and a region of nonrejection. The test statistic is simply a formula telling us how to confront the null hypothesis with the evidence. It is a random variable whose value varies from sample to sample. The *region of rejection,* sometimes called the *critical region,* is a subset of the sample space such that if the value of the test statistic falls in it, the null hypothesis is rejected. Similarly, the *region of nonrejection,* usually called the *acceptance region,* is a subset of the sample space such that if the value of the test statistic falls in it, the null hypothesis is not rejected. The boundary between the rejection and the acceptance regions (called the *critical value*) is determined by prior information concerning the distribution of the test statistic, by the specification of the alternative hypothesis, and by considerations of the costs of arriving at an incorrect conclusion. An important feature of the boundary is the fact that it does not depend on sample information; in fact, its determination comes logically prior to drawing the sample.

Test Criterion

The procedure of devising a criterion for rejecting the null hypothesis can be conveniently explained with reference to a standard textbook problem of hypothesis testing. Consider a null hypothesis which states that the mean of some variable X is equal to μ_0. Suppose that our maintained hypothesis consists of the following assumptions: (1) X is normally distributed; (2) the variance of X is σ^2 and is *known.* Since the maintained hypothesis tells us nothing about μ (for instance, that μ is restricted to positive values or some such information), the alternative hypothesis is then simply that μ is not equal to μ_0. Thus we can write

$$H_0: \quad \mu = \mu_0,$$

$$H_A: \quad \mu \neq \mu_0.$$

Let us now develop a suitable test statistic. The information that we will receive from the sample will obviously tell us *something* about the population mean; the question is how this information should be used. Our discussion in Section 4-3 indicated that sample mean has some desirable properties as an estimator of the population mean. This suggests that we may use the sample mean to summarize the sample evidence about the population mean. Then an obvious criterion for rejecting or not rejecting the null hypothesis will be as follows: if the value of $\bar{X}$ is very different from μ_0, reject the null hypothesis; if it is not very different, do not reject it.

The foregoing criterion is clearly useless for defining the critical and the acceptance region unless we state precisely which values of $\bar{X}$ are to be regarded as "very different" from μ_0 and which are not. To decide that, we have to consider the sampling distribution of $\bar{X}$. If X is normal and has, in fact, mean μ_0 and variance σ^2, then $\bar{X}$ will be normal with mean μ_0 and variance σ^2/n (where n is the sample size). Of course, since the normal distribution extends from $-\infty$ to $+\infty$, *any* value of $\bar{X}$ can be observed whatever the population mean. However, if the true mean is μ_0, then the values of $\bar{X}$ in intervals close to μ_0 will occur with greater probability than those in intervals (of the same length) farther away from μ_0. It is natural then to regard as "very different from μ_0" those values of $\bar{X}$ which—if μ_0 were the true mean—would occur by chance only very rarely. By "very rarely" we mean, at least for the time being, "with probability 0.01."

At this stage we have to introduce the alternative hypothesis which states that $\mu \neq \mu_0$. This, in fact, means that if the null hypothesis does not hold, the true mean may be on either side of μ_0. Therefore, values of $\bar{X}$ that are very much larger than μ_0 *as well as* values that are very much smaller would constitute evidence against the null hypothesis. (If the alternative hypothesis were, for example, that $\mu > \mu_0$, then only those values of $\bar{X}$ that are very much *larger* than μ_0 would represent evidence against the null hypothesis.) That is, the boundaries between the critical and the acceptance regions must be such that we would reject the null hypothesis if the value of $\bar{X}$ turned out to be *either* so low *or* so high compared to μ_0 that its occurrence by chance would be very unlikely. Since we decided to call an event very unlikely (i.e., very rare) if it occurs with probability of only 0.01, this probability must be "shared" equally by excessively low and excessively high values of $\bar{X}$. In other words, the boundaries are to be set in such a way that the probability of $\bar{x}$ being that excessively low is 0.005 and the probability of $\bar{x}$ being that excessively high is also 0.005. Then, by the Addition Theorem (Theorem 2 in Section 3-3), the probability that $\bar{x}$ will be either excessively high or excessively low compared to μ_0 will be $0.005 + 0.005 = 0.01$, as required.

Let us denote that value below which $\bar{x}$ would be considered excessively low by μ_L, and that value above which $\bar{x}$ would be considered excessively high by μ_H. These points are marked off on the sampling distribution of $\bar{X}$ shown in Figure 5-1.

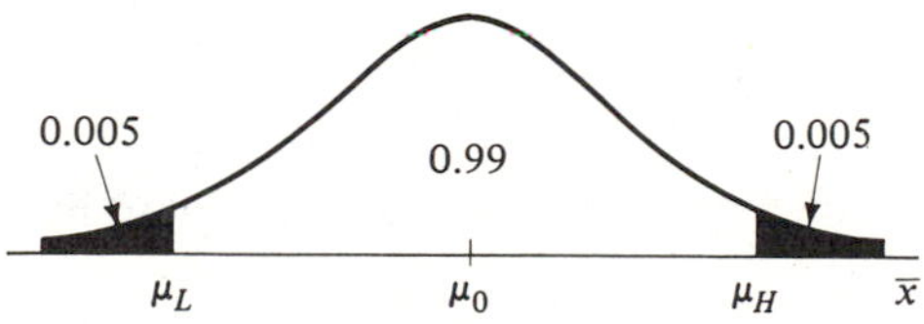

Figure 5-1

We have

$$P(\bar{x} < \mu_L) = 0.005,$$

$$P(\bar{x} > \mu_H) = 0.005;$$

therefore

$$P(\mu_L \leq \bar{x} \leq \mu_H) = 0.99.$$

We could actually consider $\bar{X}$ as an appropriate test statistic and the interval from μ_L to μ_H as the acceptance region, but this is not very practical since we do not know the location of μ_L and μ_H. We can, however, very easily determine the location of their counterparts in a standard normal distribution for which probabilities are tabulated. How this can be done was described in detail in Section 4-2.

Given that $\bar{X} \sim N(\mu_0, \sigma^2/n)$, the corresponding standard normal variable will be

$$Z = \frac{\bar{X} - \mu_0}{\sqrt{\sigma^2/n}} = \frac{(\bar{X} - \mu_0)\sqrt{n}}{\sigma}. \tag{5.1}$$

This will be our *test statistic.*

Now we wish to find those values on the z scale which correspond to μ_L and μ_H on the $\bar{x}$ scale. These values of Z, which we will call z_L and z_H, can be found by noting that they have to cut off on each end 0.005 of the area under the curve, as shown in Figure 5-2. That is, we have to find from the normal probability tables the value of

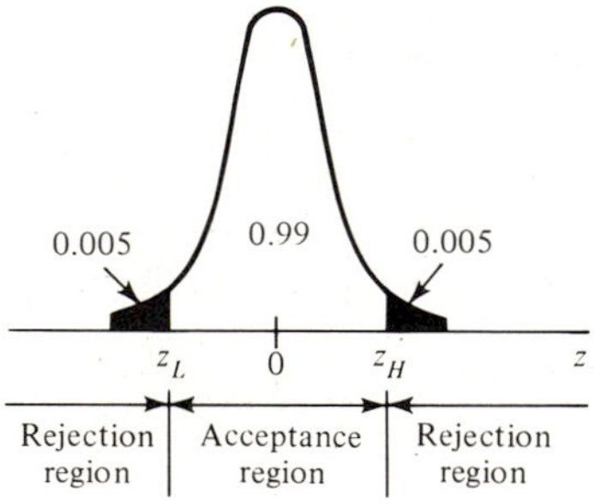

Figure 5-2

z_L such that

$$P(z < z_L) = 0.005,$$

or

$$P(z \geq z_L) = 0.995,$$

which amounts to exactly the same. Similarly, we have to find z_H such that

$$P(z > z_H) = 0.005,$$

or, equivalently,

$$P(z \leq z_H) = 0.995.$$

By consulting the normal probability tables we get

$$z_L = -2.575,$$

$$z_H = +2.575.$$

This completes our task. The interval from -2.575 to $+2.575$ represents the acceptance region, and the intervals from $-\infty$ to -2.575 and from $+2.575$ to $+\infty$ our rejection region. (Since the probability of getting a value of Z equal to z_L or z_H is zero, it is of little practical importance whether the acceptance region does or does not include the boundary values.) The criterion for rejecting or not rejecting the null hypothesis is then

$$\textit{reject } H_0 \textit{ if } \quad \frac{(\bar{x} - \mu_0)\sqrt{n}}{\sigma} < -2.575 \quad \textit{or if } \quad \frac{(\bar{x} - \mu_0)\sqrt{n}}{\sigma} > +2.575;$$

$$\textit{do not reject } H_0 \textit{ if } \quad -2.575 \leq \frac{(\bar{x} - \mu_0)\sqrt{n}}{\sigma} \leq +2.575.$$

This division between the rejection and the acceptance regions is contingent upon our decision to consider as "very different" from μ_0 only those values of $\bar{X}$ which would occur by chance with probability of 0.01. In other words, if we drew an infinite number of samples from the population with mean μ_0, only 1% of the time would we get a value of $\bar{X}$ that would lead to an incorrect rejection of the null hypothesis. This probability is known as the *significance level* of the test. Of course, there is nothing sacrosanct about the figure of 1% which we chose; in absence of any information, some other figure may just as well have been chosen. Had we chosen a higher percentage, the acceptance region would have been narrower and the rejection region wider. As it happens, 1% is one of the "popular" levels of significance but that is all that can be said for it at this stage. We shall discuss the possibility for a more rational choice of the level of significance before the end of the present section, but first let us consider a numerical example of the test procedure that we have just developed.

EXAMPLE Psychological studies indicate that in the population at large intelligence—as measured by IQ—is normally distributed with mean of 100 and standard deviation of 16. Suppose we want to test whether a given subpopulation—for instance, all people who are left-handed—is characterized by a different mean. As our maintained hypothesis, we assume that intelligence among the left-handed is normally distributed with the same standard deviation as that of the population at large, i.e., 16. Let us call the mean IQ among left-handed persons μ. The null and the alternative hypotheses will be

$$H_0: \quad \mu = 100,$$

$$H_A: \quad \mu \neq 100.$$

Our test statistic will then be

$$\frac{(\bar{X} - 100)\sqrt{n}}{16}.$$

As the appropriate level of significance we choose 5%, which happens to be the other "popular" level. That is, if the value of $\bar{X}$ should be so different from the hypothesized mean of 100 that it would occur by pure chance only 5% of the time, we will consider the null hypothesis as unlikely and reject it. Now, to find the boundaries of the acceptance region, we have to locate those values of the standard normal variable which cut off 2.5% of total area at each end of the

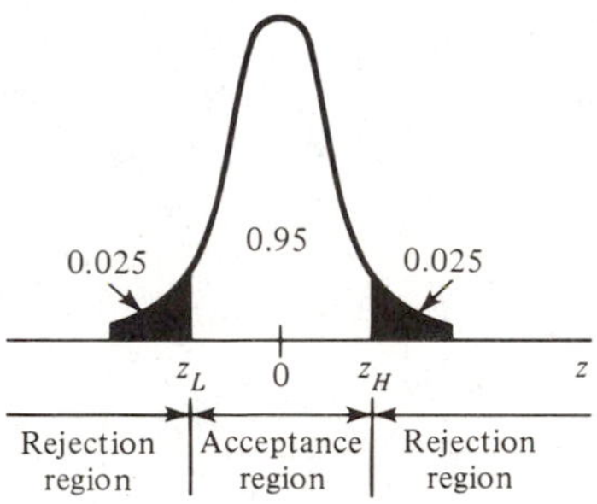

Figure 5-3

distribution, as shown in Figure 5-3. From the normal probability tables we find

$$z_L = -1.96,$$
$$z_H = +1.96.$$

Therefore our criterion is

$$\textit{do not reject } H_0 \textit{ if} \quad -1.96 \leq \frac{(\bar{x} - 100)\sqrt{n}}{16} \leq +1.96;$$

otherwise reject it.

At this stage we can draw a sample and calculate the value of $\bar{X}$ and of the test statistic. Suppose the sample consists of 400 observations of left-handed persons, and the mean IQ is 99. Then the value of our test statistic will be

$$\frac{(99 - 100)\sqrt{400}}{16} = -1.25.$$

This obviously falls into the acceptance region so that the sample gives no evidence against the null hypothesis. In other words, there is no evidence that the mean IQ of left-handed persons is any different from that of the population at large. This completes the answer to the problem.

Thus far we have made no assumptions that would help us in formulating the alternative hypothesis. Therefore the alternative hypothesis had to be of the form $\mu \neq \mu_0$. Consequently, the rejection region covered both tail ends of the distribution of the test statistic. A test with this kind of rejection region is called a *two-tail test.*

However, sometimes we are able to make assumptions that permit a somewhat less general specification of the alternative hypothesis. In particular, sometimes the null hypothesis is that $\mu \leq \mu_0$ with the alternative hypothesis being that $\mu > \mu_0$, or vice versa. For instance, it has been claimed that the marginal propensity to save (MPS) of "profit makers" is higher than that of the labor force at large. In this case the null hypothesis would be that the MPS of the profit makers is no higher than that of the labor force at large, and the alternative hypothesis would be the claim that it is higher. In such cases the values of $\bar{X}$ (and therefore of the test statistic) that would be regarded as evidence against the null hypothesis would all be concentrated at just one end of the distribution. A test of this kind is called a *one-tail test.*

To illustrate the point, consider again a variable $X \sim N(\mu, \sigma^2)$ where σ^2 is known. Suppose the null and the alternative hypotheses are given as follows:

$$H_0: \quad \mu \leq \mu_0,$$

$$H_A: \quad \mu > \mu_0.$$

As our test statistic we use

$$Z = \frac{(\bar{X} - \mu_0)\sqrt{n}}{\sigma},$$

as given by (5.1). Suppose now that we wish to carry out the test at 1% level of significance. That is, we will reject the null hypothesis if the value of $\bar{X}$ is so much greater than μ_0 that it would occur by chance with probability of only 0.01 if H_0 were true and the value of μ were as close to the alternative as possible. In this case the acceptance and the rejection regions will be shown in Figure 5-4. The value of z_H,

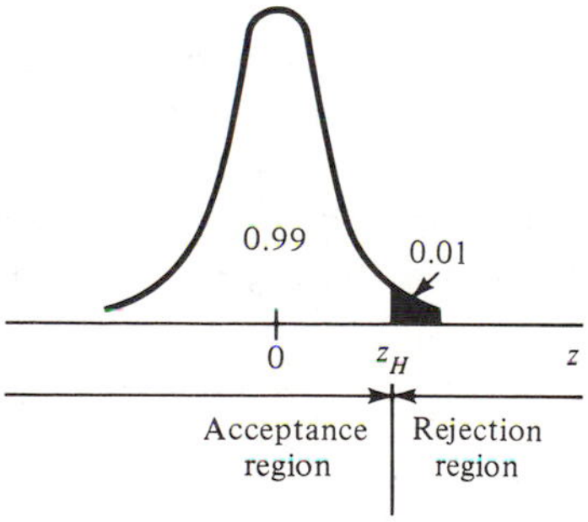

Figure 5-4

which can be looked up in the normal probability tables, is 2.327. Therefore, the criterion for rejecting H_0 in this case is

$$\textit{reject } H_0 \textit{ if } \quad \frac{(\bar{x} - \mu_0)\sqrt{n}}{\sigma} > 2.327;$$

do not reject otherwise.

If the chosen level of significance were 5% instead of 1%, the criterion would be

$$\textit{reject } H_0 \textit{ if } \quad \frac{(\bar{x}-\mu_0)\sqrt{n}}{\sigma} > 1.645;$$

do not reject otherwise.

The procedure for testing hypotheses involving population means is the same for all hypothesis testing. It can be succinctly described in the following steps.

Preamble. State the maintained hypothesis. [E.g., X is normally distributed with σ^2 equal to . . . .]

Step 1. State the null hypothesis and the alternative hypothesis. [E.g., $H_0: \mu = \mu_0$ and $H_A: \mu \neq \mu_0$.]

Step 2. Select the test statistic. [E.g., $\bar{X}$ based on sample size $n =$ . . . .]

Step 3. Determine the distribution of the test statistic under the null hypothesis. [E.g., $(\bar{X} - \mu_0)\sqrt{n}/\sigma \sim N(0, 1)$.]

Step 4. Choose the level of significance and determine the acceptance and the rejection regions. [E.g., *"do not reject* H_0 *if* $-1.96 \leq (\bar{X} - \mu_0)\sqrt{n}/\sigma \leq +1.96$; *otherwise reject it."*]

Step 5. Draw a sample and evaluate the results. [E.g., *"the value of* $\bar{X}$ *is . . . , which lies inside (outside) the acceptance region."*]

Step 6. Reach a conclusion. [E.g., *"the sample does (does not) provide evidence against the null hypothesis."*] To distinguish between 5% and 1% levels of significance we may add the word *strong* before *evidence* when using the 1% level.

According to the above scheme, the planning of the test and the decision strategy are set *before* the actual drawing of the sample observations, which does not occur until step 5. This prevents prejudging the verdict to suit the investigator's wishes. Preserving the recommended order of the test procedure also eliminates the possibility of using sample observations both for formulating the null hypothesis *and* for testing it.

Types of Error

The criterion for rejecting or not rejecting the null hypothesis on the basis of sample evidence is not a guarantee of arriving at a correct conclusion. Let us now consider in detail the kinds of errors that could be made. Suppose we have a problem of testing a hypothesis about the population mean, as in the preceding discussion. The solution of the problem consists essentially of two basic steps: setting up the boundaries between the acceptance and the critical regions and obtaining the sample value of the test statistic. Two outcomes are possible: either the value of the test statistic falls in the acceptance region or it does not. Let us take the second outcome first. In this case the value of the test statistic is such that, if the null hypothesis were in fact true, the probability of this happening by chance would be very small, e.g., 5% or 1%. This means that if the test were repeated an infinite number of times and if the null hypothesis were in fact true, we would *incorrectly reject* the null hypothesis 5% or 1% (or whatever the level of significance) of the time. Such an error is called *Error Type I.* Earlier we compared statistical testing to a trial in a court of law where the innocence of the accused (our null hypothesis) is challenged by the claim of guilt by the prosecution (our alternative hypothesis). Using this parallel, the Error Type I would be represented by the error of convicting an innocent man. In statistical testing the probability of committing this error is given precisely by the chosen level of significance. Consider now the second possible outcome of the test, that is, the case where the value of the test statistic falls inside the acceptance region. In this case we do not reject the null hypothesis, i.e., we keep on believing it to be true. However, the possibility that we came to an incorrect conclusion, namely that the null hypothesis is in fact false, cannot be ruled out. An error of this sort is called *Error Type II.* In terms of the parallel with the court trial, the Error Type II would mean letting a guilty man go. In statistical testing the exact probability of this kind of error is usually unknown. The two types of errors are represented schematically in Table 5-1.

Table 5-1 Errors in Hypothesis Testing

	State of the world	
Verdict	H_0 is true	H_A is true
Reject H_0	Type I error	Correct decision
Do not reject H_0	Correct decision	Type II error

The general idea behind the two types of error can be clearly illustrated by the—unfortunately not very common—case of testing a simple null hypothesis against a *simple* alternative. Suppose the hypotheses are

$$H_0: \quad \mu = \mu_0,$$

$$H_A: \quad \mu = \mu_A,$$

where μ_0 and μ_A are given numbers and $\mu_A > \mu_0$. As before, we assume X to be normal with a known variance σ^2. Thus the two hypotheses can be identified with two competing populations, both normal with the same variance σ^2 but distinguished by their means. Each population generates—for a given sample size n—its own sampling distribution of $\bar{X}$. To carry out the test we have to establish the boundary between the critical and the acceptance region. This will depend, as we have seen, on the chosen level of significance and on the alternative hypothesis. The level of significance, equal to the probability of Error Type I, can be chosen a priori as, say, 5%. Since the alternative hypothesis is that $\mu = \mu_A$ and since $\mu_A > \mu_0$, only high values of $\bar{X}$ relative to μ_0 would constitute evidence against H_0. That is, the appropriate test is a one-tail test with the rejection region concentrated at the right-hand tail of the distribution. With these considerations in mind, we can determine the boundary between the acceptance and the rejection region for the distribution of the test statistic

$$Z = \frac{(\bar{X} - \mu_0)\sqrt{n}}{\sigma}.$$

For the 5% level of significance with the rejection region concentrated at the right tail of the distribution, the boundary value z_H is equal to 1.645. Therefore the acceptance region will be

$$z \leq 1.645.$$

If the true mean is μ_0, then the probability that a value of $\bar{X}$ falls inside the acceptance region is 0.95. To determine the probability of Error Type II, we have to find the probability that a value of $\bar{X}$ falls inside the acceptance region if the true mean is *not* μ_0 but μ_A. This can be found as follows. First we note that

$$P(z > 1.645) = 0.05$$

can be written as

$$P\left[\frac{(\bar{x} - \mu_0)\sqrt{n}}{\sigma} > 1.645\right] = 0.05.$$

Consider the inequality inside the square bracket. By multiplying both sides by $\sigma/\sqrt{n}$ and adding μ_0 to both sides, we get

$$\bar{x} > \mu_0 + 1.645\left(\frac{\sigma}{\sqrt{n}}\right).$$

Thus we can write

$$P\left[\bar{x} > \mu_0 + 1.645\left(\frac{\sigma}{\sqrt{n}}\right)\right] = 0.05,$$

which is a probability statement about $\bar{X}$ rather than Z. Thus the boundary between the acceptance and the rejection region on the $\bar{x}$ axis is given by $[\mu_0 + 1.645(\sigma/\sqrt{n})]$.

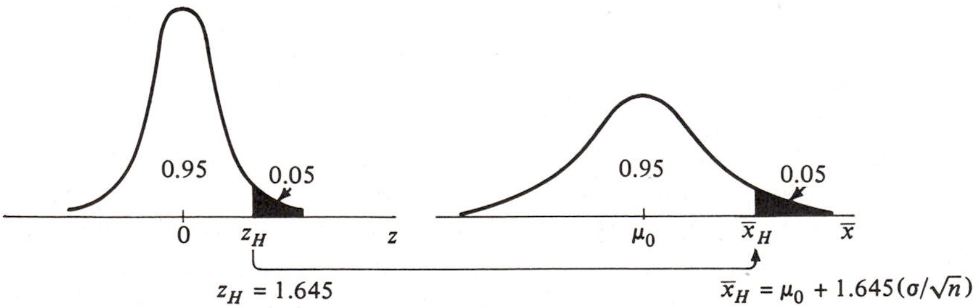

Figure 5-5

Since μ_0, σ, and n are known, the boundary will be a known number. Figure 5-5 shows the two distributions with the boundaries marked off.

Now let us consider the sampling distribution of $\bar{X}$ for samples from the population with mean μ_A. This distribution will be normal with mean equal to the population mean (i.e., μ_A) and variance σ^2/n. Thus the only way in which this distribution differs from the distribution of $\bar{X}$ from the population with mean μ_0 is with respect to the mean. The two distributions of $\bar{X}$ are compared in Figure 5-6, which shows

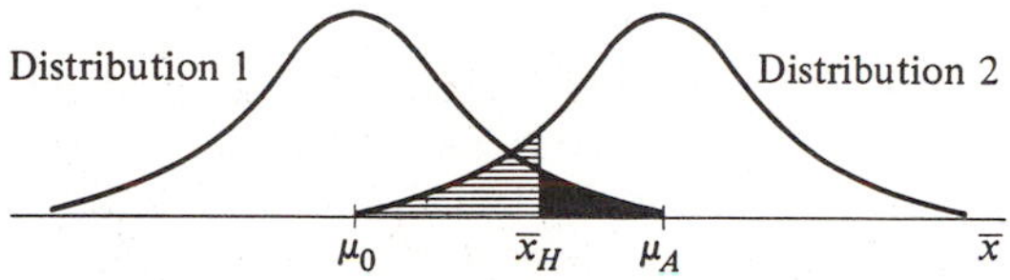

Figure 5-6

clearly the probabilities of the two types of error involved in hypothesis testing. Recall that Error Type I is committed any time we reject H_0 when it is, in fact, the correct hypothesis. This happens whenever $\bar{x}$ falls to the right of the boundary point $\bar{x}_H$. Note that if H_0 is correct, then $\bar{X}$ follows distribution 1 in Figure 5-6. Therefore the probability of Error Type I is given by the chosen level of significance (0.05) and corresponds to the blackened area. The Error Type II occurs whenever we do not reject H_0 when it is in fact false. This happens whenever $\bar{x}$ falls to the left of $\bar{x}_H$. In the present case if H_0 should be false, i.e., if μ_0 were not the true mean, then the only other possibility is that the true mean is μ_A. But if μ_A should be the true mean, the sample mean $\bar{X}$ would follow distribution 2, and the probability of making Error Type II is given by the striped area in Figure 5-6. In reality we do not know which is the true mean and therefore do not know which is the true distribution of $\bar{X}$. If the true distribution of $\bar{X}$ is "1," then our test will lead to an incorrect conclusion 5% (or whatever the chosen level of significance) of the time. If the true distribution of $\bar{X}$ is "2," then our test will produce incorrect results with a probability given by the striped area to the left of $\bar{x}_H$.

The preceding discussion, although restricted to the case of a simple alternative hypothesis, brings out an important facet of hypothesis testing which remains equally relevant in tests involving composite alternatives. This is the fact that *by decreasing the probability of one type of error we increase the probability of the other type of error.* For instance, we can make the probability of Error Type I (rejecting H_0 when in fact it is true) as small as we like by setting a very low level of significance. In terms of Figure 5-6, this amounts to shifting the boundary point $\bar{x}_H$ farther to the right. But by doing this we would obviously increase the striped area, which represents the probability of Error Type II (not rejecting H_0 when in fact it is false). Similarly, we can reduce the probability of Error Type II by increasing the level of significance, i.e., by shifting $\bar{x}_H$ to the left, but this would increase the probability of Error Type I. By reference to our comparison of statistical testing with trials before a court of law, we could obviously diminish the probability of convicting an innocent man by letting almost everybody go, but this would clearly increase the probability of not convicting a guilty man. Similarly, we could reduce the probability of letting a guilty man go free by requiring less stringent evidence for conviction, but this would increase the probability of convicting an innocent man. In statistical testing, the only way in which we could reduce the probabilities of both kinds of error at the same time is by increasing the sample size (assuming that the test statistic used is the best that can be devised).

EXAMPLE A manufacturer produces two types of tires, one type with a life expectancy of 25,000 miles and the other with a life expectancy of 30,000 miles. The variation in durability around the expected lifetime is the same for both types of tires, the standard deviation being 3000 miles. The distribution can be assumed to be normal. The two types of tires are indistinguishable except for markings. At the time of inventory taking, it is discovered that there is a forgotten case with 100 tires that do not have any markings. The examining engineer thinks that the tires are of the less durable kind but recommends a test. The test is to be performed on a sample of 4 tires. What should be the appropriate test criterion?

First, we specify the null and the alternative hypotheses as

$$H_0:\quad \mu = 25{,}000,$$

$$H_A:\quad \mu = 30{,}000.$$

Next, we set up the boundary between the acceptance and the rejection regions. This will depend on the chosen level of significance. We shall consider 1%, 5%, and 10% levels of significance and determine the corresponding probabilities of Error Type II. Because μ_0 $(=25{,}000) < \mu_A$ $(=30{,}000)$, we shall use the upper-tail rejection region in every case.

1. If the level of significance is 1%, the boundary point on the z scale (for the standard normal distribution) will be the point which cuts off the top 1% of the area. From the normal probability tables, we find that this is given by

$$z_H = 2.327.$$

To determine the probability of Error Type II we have to find the corresponding point on the $\bar{x}$ scale, $\bar{x}_H$. From the previous discussion, we know that

$$\bar{x}_H = \mu_0 + 2.327\,\frac{\sigma}{\sqrt{n}}.$$

Substituting, we get

$$\bar{x}_H = 25{,}000 + 2.327\left(\frac{3000}{\sqrt{4}}\right) = 28{,}490.5.$$

Now we have to determine the probability that $\bar{x} < 28{,}490.5$ *given* that the mean of $\bar{X}$, $E(\bar{X})$, is 30,000. To do that we have to make the appropriate transformation to standard normal variable. We can write

$$P[\bar{x} < 28{,}490.5 | E(\bar{X}) = 30{,}000] = P\left[z < \frac{(28{,}490.5 - 30{,}000)\sqrt{4}}{3000}\right]$$

$$= P(z < -1.0063).$$

But from the normal probability tables we find

$$P(z < -1.0063) = 0.1571.$$

This is the probability of making Error Type II.

2. If the chosen level of significance is 5%, then

$$z_H = 1.645,$$

and

$$\bar{x}_H = 25{,}000 + 1.645\left(\frac{3000}{\sqrt{4}}\right) = 27{,}467.5.$$

The probability that $\bar{x} < 27{,}467.5$ *given* that the mean of $\bar{X}$ is 30,000 is

$$P[\bar{x} < 27{,}467.5 | E(\bar{X}) = 30{,}000] = P\left[z < \frac{(27{,}476.5 - 30{,}000)\sqrt{4}}{3000}\right]$$

$$= P(z < -1.6883) = 0.0457.$$

3. Finally, if the level of significance is 10%, then

$$z_H = 1.280,$$

and

$$\bar{x}_H = 25{,}000 + 1.280\left(\frac{3000}{\sqrt{4}}\right) = 26{,}920.$$

Consequently

$$P[\bar{x} < 26{,}920 | E(\bar{X}) = 30{,}000] = P\left[z < \frac{(26{,}920 - 30{,}000)\sqrt{4}}{3000}\right]$$

$$= P(z < -2.0533) = 0.0200.$$

In summary, the results are

Boundary		Probability of	
z scale	$\bar{x}$ scale	Error Type I	Error Type II
2.327	28,490.5	0.0100	0.1571
1.645	27,467.5	0.0500	0.0457
1.280	26,920.0	0.1000	0.0200

These results show that, as expected, the two probabilities are inversely related. The question then is which pair of probabilities should be considered as the optimal choice. The answer depends on the cost of making each of the two kinds of error. If the error of rejecting the null hypothesis that is in fact true (Error Type I) is costly relative to the error of not rejecting the null hypothesis that is in fact false (Error Type II), it will be rational to set the probability of the first kind of error low. If, on the other hand, the cost of making Error Type I is low relative to the cost of making Error Type II, it will pay to make the probability of the first kind of error high (thus making the probability of the second type of error low).

A concrete illustration of this point can be given by extending the information in the given example. Suppose the manufacturer sells the less durable tires for \$10 and the more durable ones for \$12. Suppose further that the more durable tires carries a "money-back" guarantee if the tire should wear out before 25,000 miles, and that there is no guarantee attached to the less durable tire. Given this information, we can estimate the cost of either type of error.

Cost of Error Type I If the hypothesis that $\mu = 25{,}000$ is rejected, the manufacturer will sell the tires for the higher price (assuming that the demand in this price range is inelastic). This will represent a gain of $100 \times (\$12 - \$10) = \$200$. On the other hand, if the true mean actually is 25,000 miles, one half of all tires (in the population) will have a lifetime of less than that. Thus in a shipment of 100 tires the expected number of returns will be 50, and the corresponding outlay will be $50 \times \$12 = \$600$. Therefore, the total cost of making Error Type I is $\$600 - \$200 = \$400$.

Cost of Error Type II If the hypothesis that the mean is 25,000 miles is *not* rejected while, in fact, the mean is 30,000 miles, the tires will be sold for \$1000 instead of \$1200. The latter figure, however, has to be adjusted downward because the guarantee does represent a de facto reduction in price. If the mean is 30,000 miles, then 4.78% of the tires will not last for 25,000 miles. This is the result of the fact that

$$P\left(z < \frac{25{,}000 - 30{,}000}{3000}\right) = 0.0478.$$

Therefore in a shipment of 100 tires of the more durable kind the expected number of returns will be 4.78. The cost of the guarantee is then $4.78 \times \$12 = \$57.36$. Thus the expected revenue from selling 100 better quality tires is $\$1200 - \$57.36 = \$1142.36$. The total net cost of making Error Type II then is $\$1142.36 - \$1000 = \$142.36$.

With the additional information on the problem on hand, we find that Error Type I is costlier than Error Type II. Thus it will be rational to set the probability of Error Type I lower than that of Error Type II. Just how much lower can be determined by comparing the expected losses for each level of significance. "Expected loss" is defined as the amount of loss multiplied by the probability of its occurrence. For example, if the loss is \$400 and the probability of its occurrence is 0.01, the expected loss is \$4.00. The calculations of the expected losses in our example are

Error Type I		Error Type II	
Probability	Expected loss	Probability	Expected loss
0.01	\$4.00	0.1571	\$22.36
0.05	\$20.00	0.0457	\$6.51
0.10	\$40.00	0.0200	\$2.85

Assuming that the manufacturer gets no utility from gambling as such, the rational choice will be one which gives equal expected loss for each type of error. From the above figures it appears that this would be realized somewhere between the 1% and 5% levels of significance. Carrying out the calculations for levels in this interval leads to the following.

Error Type I		Error Type II	
Probability	Expected loss	Probability	Expected loss
0.02	\$8.00	0.1006	\$14.32
0.03	\$12.00	0.0732	\$10.42
0.04	\$16.00	0.0567	\$8.07

It appears, then, that the optimum of significance lies between 2% and 3%. If the level of significance is set at 2.75%, then the expected loss from Error Type I will be approximately the same as that from Error Type II (about \$11.00). This then would be optimal level of significance in our example.

The preceding example illustrates the relevance of considering the cost implications of different decisions in setting up statistical tests. Modern statistical theory puts a great emphasis on this and develops a formal apparatus for incorporating loss and risk functions in the determination of a proper test criterion. Unfortunately very little of this is of use or relevance in econometric research since prior (or even posterior) ideas about losses due to incorrect conclusions are either completely nonexistent or are so vague that they offer no guidance at all. For instance, consider the question whether liquid assets do or do not affect consumption expenditure. The econometrician will specify the relevant maintained and testable hypothesis and calculate the value of the appropriate test statistic, but he has absolutely no idea as to what is the cost—to him, to the profession, to the society—of drawing an incorrect conclusion. Consequently, it has been a standard practice in econometrics to use the traditional approach of classical statistics, namely, to fix the level of significance at 1% or 5% and to use a test statistic that would make the probability of Error Type II as small as possible. If the value of the test statistic is such that it falls in the rejection region given by the 5% significance level, it is said to be *significant;* if the value of the test statistic falls in the rejection region given by the 1% significance level, it is said to be *highly significant.* However, there is nothing superior about these two significance levels other than that they are widely used. And it is only this popularity which stifles the competition from other levels of significance.

When the test procedure is carried out in the sequence outlined earlier, and when the acceptance and rejection regions are specified *before* the sample results are known, all investigators faced with the same set of sample observations will arrive at the same conclusion. However, if the sample results are known before the decision criterion is set up, then different investigators may select different levels of significance and may arrive at different conclusions. To avoid this arbitrariness in setting the significance level, some statisticians advocate reporting the *smallest* significance level at which the null hypothesis would be rejected and leave the decision whether to reject or not to reject the null hypothesis up to the reader. The smallest level of significance at which the given sample observations would lead us to reject the null hypothesis is called the p value. The main virtue of the p value is that it is a very clear indicator of the degree of agreement between the null hypothesis and the sample data: the less the p value, the smaller the agreement. The main disadvantage of the p value is its inconclusiveness, which unfortunately cannot be avoided in many cases.

EXAMPLE In the earlier example concerning the IQ of left-handed persons, the IQs were assumed to be normally distributed with $\sigma = 16$. The null and the alternative hypotheses were $H_0: \mu = 100$ and $H_A: \mu \neq 100$. The test statistic was the mean of a sample of 400 left-handed persons, which was found to be 99. From the normal probability tables we find that

$$P\left[\bar{x} \leq \frac{(99 - 100)\sqrt{400}}{16}\right] = 0.1056.$$

Since the alternative hypothesis leads us to use a two-tail test, the above probability has to be doubled. So in this case the p value equals 0.2112, indicating no strong disagreement between the null hypothesis and the sample data.

Another difficulty with classical hypothesis testing is that we frequently state the null hypothesis much more precisely than we are in fact willing to accept. For instance, in the preceding example we would be willing to consider that left-handed individuals have, on the average, the same intelligence as the population at large even if their mean IQ were 99.99 rather than 100. But if H_0 states that $\mu = 100$ when the true mean is 99.99, with large enough samples the null hypothesis will nearly always be rejected at a given (fixed) level of significance. Thus whether a test rejects a null hypothesis or not becomes a question of the sample size: the larger the sample size, the more likely we are to reject the null hypothesis *as stated.* (This is true for both one-sided tests as well as two-sided ones.) The fundamental problem lies in the poor formulation of the null hypothesis. One ad hoc remedy used by practitioners is to change the level of significance with the sample size, making it harder to reject the null hypothesis for large samples than for small ones.

Power of a Test

The classification of errors into the two types was explained with reference to the case of a simple null hypotheses and a simple alternative. The idea can easily be extended to the more common case of testing a null hypothesis against a composite alternative. Suppose we have

$$H_0: \quad \mu = \mu_0,$$

$$H_A: \quad \mu \neq \mu_0.$$

As before, the probability of Error Type I (rejecting H_0 when it is true) is given by the level of significance. However, the probability of Error Type II (not rejecting H_0 when it is false) is now no longer a single number for a given level of significance but depends on the value of μ. For values of μ close to μ_0 the probability of Error Type II will be high compared to the probability of this error for values of μ farther away from μ_0. If, for example, the null hypothesis states that the mean is equal to 10, then the probability of *not* rejecting H_0 is obviously greater if the true mean is 15 than if it is 20. This is illustrated by Figure 5-7, where the probability of Error Type II is shown by the striped area.

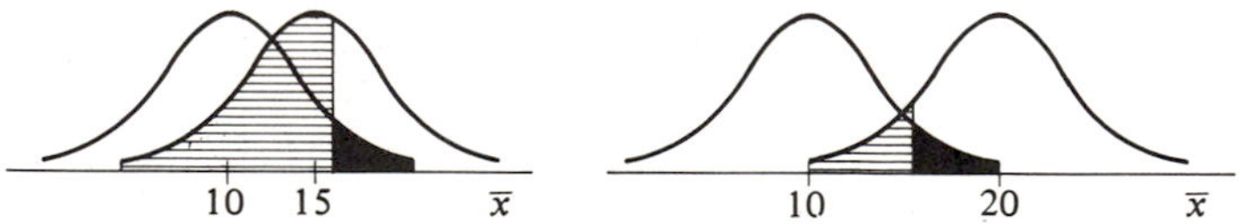

Figure 5-7

Obviously, we can determine the probability of Error Type II for any value of μ. The smaller this probability, the better is the test in discriminating between true and false hypotheses. In the illustration given in Figure 5-7, the test will discriminate more clearly between the null hypothesis and the alternative hypothesis if the alternative mean is 20 than if it is 15. In the common terminology of statistics, the lower the probability of not rejecting H_0 when it is false, the more *powerful* is the test. That is, the *power of a test* is measured by the *probability of rejecting H_0 when it is false.* Since the probability of Error Type II is the probability of *not* rejecting H_0 when it is false, the power of a test is equal to

$$1 - P(\text{Error Type II}).$$

Furthermore, since for composite alternatives the probability of Error Type II depends on the value of μ, the power of a test is likewise dependent on μ. If we plot the probabilities of rejecting H_0 when it is false on the vertical axis against the values of μ on the horizontal axis, we get what is known as the *power function* of a test.

EXAMPLE Consider the following statement of hypotheses concerning the mean of a variable $X \sim N(\mu, 81)$.

$$H_0: \quad \mu = 10,$$

$$H_A: \quad \mu \neq 10.$$

Suppose the test statistic is based on sample size 9 and the chosen level of significance is 5%. The appropriate test is then a two-tail one with the acceptance region given by

$$-1.96 \leq \frac{(\bar{x} - 10)\sqrt{9}}{\sqrt{81}} \leq 1.96$$

or

$$-1.96 \leq \frac{\bar{x} - 10}{3} \leq 1.96.$$

On the $\bar{x}$ scale, the equivalent acceptance region is

$$4.12 \leq \bar{x} \leq 15.88.$$

To find the power function we have to calculate $[1 - P(\text{Error Type II})]$ for the acceptance region for various values of μ. Let us start with some very small value of μ, say, -10. Then

$$\begin{aligned} P(\text{Error Type II}) &= P(4.12 \leq \bar{x} \leq 15.88 | \mu = -10) \\ &= P\left[\frac{4.12 - (-10)}{3} \leq z \leq \frac{15.88 - (-10)}{3}\right] \\ &= P(4.707 \leq z \leq 8.627) = 0.0000, \end{aligned}$$

where, as before, z is the value of a standard normal variable. The value of the power function therefore is $1 - 0.0000 = 1.0000$. Carrying out these calculations for other values of μ leads to the following results.

μ	Power	μ	Power
−10	1.0000	10	0.0500
−5	0.9988	12	0.1022
0	0.9152	14	0.2659
2	0.7602	16	0.5159
4	0.5159	18	0.7602
6	0.2659	20	0.9152
8	0.1022	25	0.9988

A graphical representation of this power function is shown in Figure 5-8. The graph confirms our previous contention that the power of a test increases as μ gets farther away from μ_0 in the direction (or directions) specified by the alternative hypothesis. In our case we see that if the true value of μ were -5 or $+25$, we would correctly reject the false hypothesis virtually every time. If the true value of μ were equal to 0 or $+20$, we would correctly reject the false hypothesis 91.5% of the time. Note that if the true mean were almost equal to $+10$, we would correctly reject the false hypothesis only about 5% of the time.

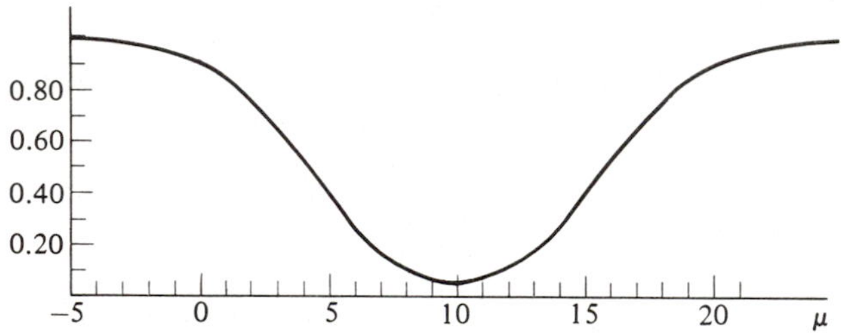

Figure 5-8

The power function in Figure 5-8 has a shape which is typical for symmetric two-tail tests concerning the mean of a normal population. A one-tail test leads to a different curve, which we shall not present here. The interested reader can do the calculations and plotting or consult almost any standard test on statistical inference. We only wish to point out that the power function is another way of demonstrating some weaknesses of statistical testing. An ideal power function—which, needless to say, does not exist—would be one that would show a value of 1 for all values of μ (or whatever the relevant parameter) specified by the alternative hypothesis, and a value of 0 for the value of μ specified by the null hypothesis.

Quality of a Test

What is the best test we can design, given the size of the sample and given all the prior information that is available? We can answer this question by noting the choices that are open to us when we are setting up the test criterion. In general, there are three areas of choice that are relevant.

1. Choice of the level of significance.

2. Choice of the location of the acceptance region.
3. Choice of test statistic.

We have already found that a rational choice can be made in the first area *providing* we have a way of assessing the losses due to an incorrect conclusion. Otherwise—and this is normally the case in econometric research—we have no firm basis for the choice of the level of significance other than tradition.

The second area of choice concerns the location of the acceptance region on the z or the $\bar{x}$ axis. Suppose the problem involves the hypotheses

$$H_0: \quad \mu = \mu_0,$$

$$H_A: \quad \mu \neq \mu_0,$$

and the chosen level of significance is 5%. Previously, in a problem of this kind, we chose a two-tail test and located the acceptance region symmetrically around 0 on the z axis or, equivalently, around μ_0 on the $\bar{x}$ axis. The acceptance region then covered the central 95% of the area, leaving 2.5% of the area at each tail to be taken up by the critical region. Obviously, we could have the same 5% level of significance—and therefore the same probability of Error Type I—with the acceptance region located in a different position. For instance, we could locate the acceptance region in such a way that it would cut off 1% of the area at the lower tail and 4% of the area at the upper tail. The number of possibilities is clearly infinite. Previously we justified our choice of the symmetric acceptance region largely on intuitive grounds; now we are in a position to make a stronger case for such a choice. Since any acceptance region that preserves the same level of significance automatically preserves the same probability of Error Type I, the argument in favor of the symmetric acceptance region can only run in terms of probabilities of Error Type II. But because the problem involves a composite alternative hypothesis, different values of μ embraced by the alternative hypothesis will be associated with different probabilities of Error Type II. Therefore, we have to compare the *power functions* of tests based on differently located acceptance regions, not just individual probability values. Suppose we compare the power function of a test with a symmetric acceptance region with the power function of a test with an assymetric acceptance region, such as one which cuts off 1% of the area at the lower tail and 4% of the area at the upper tail. Then, as can be easily confirmed by carrying out the necessary calculations, the symmetric test turns out to be more powerful for values of μ larger than μ_0. Since the power function measures the capability of a test to discriminate between a true and a false hypothesis, the comparison shows that the symmetric test discriminates better than the asymmetric test (with a smaller lower and a larger upper tail) when $\mu > \mu_0$ and worse when $\mu < \mu_0$. If there is no reason why we should want to be able to discriminate between hypotheses more effectively when μ is on one side of μ_0 than when it is on the other, then a symmetric test is clearly more appropriate than an asymmetric one. If there *is* a reason, it must be included in the prior information relevant to testing and the acceptance region would be then located accordingly. Normally the choice of a symmetric acceptance region (when H_A is $\mu \neq \mu_0$) is the most reasonable one that can be specified. Incidentally, it is interesting to note that this acceptance region is shorter than any other one based on the same test statistic and the same level of significance. By similar reasoning we can also establish that, for problems involving alternative hypothesis of the kind $\mu > \mu_0$ or $\mu < \mu_0$, the most reasonable test is a one-tail test as previously described.

This leaves only the third area of choice, that involving the test statistic. For the problem of testing a hypothesis concerning the population mean of a normal population—the only problem specifically considered in this section—we used as the test statistic the standard normal variable Z constructed as

$$Z = \frac{\bar{X} - \mu_0}{\sigma_{\bar{x}}},$$

where μ_0 is the population mean postulated by the null hypothesis and $\sigma_{\bar{x}} = \sigma/\sqrt{n}$. The use of $\bar{X}$ was justified on the grounds that it is an unbiased and consistent estimate of μ and thus represents a reasonable summary of the sample evidence about the population mean. For, say, a two-tail test with 5% level of significance, the acceptance region for the Z statistic is

$$-1.96 \leq z \leq 1.96;$$

and for $\bar{X}$,

$$\mu_0 - 1.96\sigma_{\bar{x}} \leq \bar{x} \leq \mu_0 + 1.96\sigma_{\bar{x}}.$$

Let us now demonstrate why the desirable properties of an estimator (unbiasedness, etc.) may also be desirable when it comes to hypothesis testing. Consider a test statistic similar to Z but one in which instead of $\bar{X}$ we use an unspecified estimator of μ to be called $\hat{\mu}$. The variance of this estimator, which is also unspecified, is $\sigma^2_{\hat{\mu}}$. The only restriction that we place on $\hat{\mu}$ is that it should be normally distributed (at least approximately) so that we can make the transformation to the standard normal variable. The latter will then be given by

$$Z^* = \frac{\hat{\mu} - E(\hat{\mu})}{\sigma_{\hat{\mu}}}.$$

Now in the form in which it is given, Z^* does not involve μ_0 and therefore does not fulfill the basic function of a test statistic, namely confronting the null hypothesis with sample evidence. However, we can introduce μ_0 into the formula quite easily by writing

$$Z^* = \frac{\hat{\mu} - E(\hat{\mu})}{\sigma_{\hat{\mu}}} + \frac{\mu_0}{\sigma_{\hat{\mu}}} - \frac{\mu_0}{\sigma_{\hat{\mu}}} = \frac{(\hat{\mu} - \mu_0) - [E(\hat{\mu}) - \mu_0]}{\sigma_{\hat{\mu}}}.$$

If the null hypothesis is valid and μ_0 is the true mean, $[E(\hat{\mu}) - \mu_0]$ represents the bias and will be equal to zero only if $\hat{\mu}$ is an unbiased estimator of μ. The acceptance region for a two-tail test with 5% level of significance will be

$$-1.96 \leq \frac{(\hat{\mu} - \mu_0) - [E(\hat{\mu}) - \mu_0]}{\sigma_{\hat{\mu}}} \leq 1.96.$$

The equivalent acceptance region on the $\hat{\mu}$ axis will be

$$\mu_0 - 1.96\sigma_{\hat{\mu}} + [E(\hat{\mu}) - \mu_0] \leq \hat{\mu} \leq \mu_0 + 1.96\sigma_{\hat{\mu}} + [E(\hat{\mu}) - \mu_0].$$

The first property of $\hat{\mu}$ which we shall consider is *unbiasedness.* Suppose $\hat{\mu}$ is a biased estimator of μ. The obvious consequence of this is the fact that the above acceptance region is not symmetric around μ_0. For instance, if $\mu_0 = 10$, $E(\hat{\mu}) = 5$, and $\sigma_{\hat{\mu}} = 3$, the acceptance region will be

$$10 - 1.96 \times 3 + (5 - 10) \leq \hat{\mu} \leq 10 + 1.96 \times 3 + (5 - 10),$$

that is,

$$-0.88 \leq \hat{\mu} \leq 10.88,$$

which is clearly not symmetric around 10. If such an asymmetric acceptance region were to be used, then the power function of the test would be shifted so that its lowest value would be at the point $E(\hat{\mu})$ and not at μ_0. Unless there is a special reason why we would wish to have the capacity for discriminating between true and false hypotheses so unevenly distributed, a test like this is hardly appropriate. Of course, if the extent of the bias of $\hat{\mu}$ is not known, then we cannot specify the boundary between the acceptance and the rejection region as we did above and thus cannot carry out the test. But even more troublesome is the situation when the estimator *is* biased but we are not aware of it. Then we would clearly be using an acceptance region which is incorrect for the chosen level of significance, and our conclusion would be correspondingly distorted. All this applies equally to one-tail tests and points to the desirability of using an unbiased estimator of μ in constructing the test statistic.

Next let us consider *consistency.* Earlier we described an estimator as consistent if its distribution tends to become more and more concentrated around the true value of the parameter as sample size increases. Except for some special cases (i.e., estimators which do not have a finite mean or variance or both), this means that as sample size increases both the bias (if any) and the variance of the distribution will decrease and, in the limit, will approach zero. Therefore, the larger the sample size, the narrower is the acceptance region on the $\hat{\mu}$ scale, and the more powerful is the test. This is illustrated in Figure 5-9. Here μ_0 is the value of the mean postulated by the null hypothesis, and μ^* is one of the values of the mean postulated by the alternative hypothesis. The blackened area represents the probability of Error Type I and the striped area the probability of Error Type II. The diagram illustrates how, for the same level of significance, the increase in sample size reduces the probability of Error Type II or, equivalently, increases the power of the test. If the variance of the distribution did not decrease with an increase in sample size—i.e., if the estimator were not consistent—then an increase in sample size would not reduce the probability of Error Type II. This would be obviously undesirable since it would mean that the additional cost involved in increasing the size of the sample would result in no additional information about the population mean.

The last property that we shall mention in this context is *efficiency.* If we have two

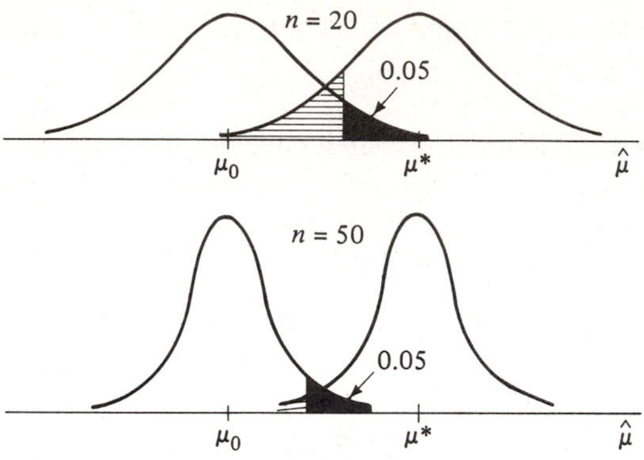

Figure 5-9

estimators of the population mean, both unbiased and normally distributed but characterized by different variances, then the estimator with the larger variance is not efficient. The acceptance region of this estimator—measured on the $\hat{\mu}$ axis—will be wider than that of the other estimator and the corresponding power of the test will be lower. A demonstration is given in Figure 5-10. In the diagram, $\hat{\mu}_{\mathrm{I}}$ is

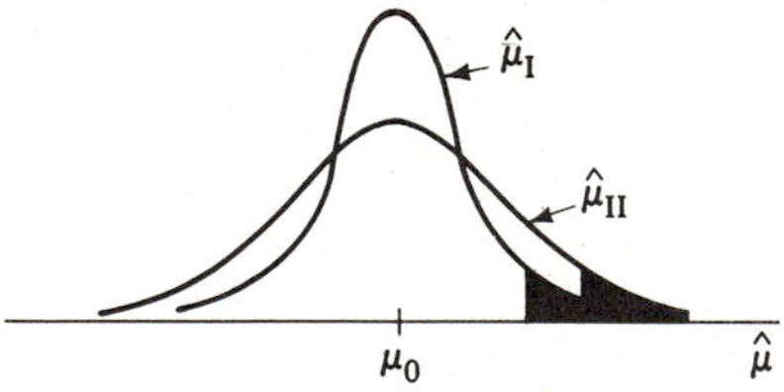

Figure 5-10

more efficient compared with $\hat{\mu}_{\mathrm{II}}$. If we were to compare the power functions of the two tests corresponding to these two estimators, we would find that the values of the power function related to μ_{I} are always higher than those of the power function related to μ_{II}. Thus, efficiency is obviously a highly desirable feature in setting up a statistic. It should be noted, though, that this conclusion is based on the assumption that each of the two estimators has the same variance under the null hypothesis as under the alternative hypothesis.

The preceding discussion about an optimal design of a test indicates that, for most problems in econometrics, the only way of getting the best design is by using the best estimator in constructing the appropriate test statistic. Normally, we have no information that would allow us to make a rational choice of the level of significance or of the location of the acceptance region. Thus, for given prior information and for a given sample size, the only avenue of search is that for the best estimator. As we shall see, for some problems the search is already completed; that is, the best estimator has already been found.[1] Unfortunately, this is true only for simple problems—such as estimating the mean of a normal population—but for many problems in econometrics the search still goes on. This, at least in part, is the reason for the heavy concentration of pure econometric research on problems of estimation.

Concluding Remarks

This brings us to the end of the section on design and evaluation of statistical tests. The reader may recall that the discussion started with the division of hypotheses into maintained hypotheses on one hand and testable hypotheses on the other. There is a question about this division that has never been asked, namely, why *any* hypothesis should be considered as maintained, that is, beyond challenge. It would appear more reasonable to test all the assumptions involved rather than just some. This certainly would be safer than relying upon our prior beliefs that make up the maintained hypothesis. The difficulty with doing this, however, lies in the fact that our *factual* knowledge of the population is very meager, so that without assumptions the only source of information would be the sample. As a result, the scope for making errors would be greater and, thus, the power of the test would be weakened. Consider, for instance, the problem of testing a hypothesis about the mean of a normal population with known variance—a problem considered throughout this section. A part of the maintained hypothesis is the assumption that the population variance is known. If this assumption is not made, the variance of the distribution of sample mean is not known and we cannot construct the test statistic given by (5.1). We can, of course, estimate the population variance from sample data. But using an estimate rather than the actual value of the variance increases the degree of uncertainty concerning the population and, predictably, results in a wider acceptance region. We still can choose whatever level of significance we desire but, with a wider acceptance region, the power of the test will be diminished (a detailed explanation of this test is given in Section 5-2). Thus, by replacing an assumption with a sample estimate, we lose some information and pay for it by having a less powerful test. Of course, if we have *no idea* about the value of the population variance, then we have no choice. On the other hand, by relying on the assumptions contained in the maintained hypothesis, we get results that are strictly conditional on these assumptions and do not hold without them. This elementary fact seems to be frequently forgotten in applied econometric research.

5-2 Distribution of Selected Test Statistics

In Section 5-1 we illustrated the ideas underlying the test of statistical hypotheses by considering the problem of testing a hypothesis about the mean of a normal

[1] There is, however, also the question of whether we use *all* prior information as effectively as possible. Some prior knowledge (e.g., the numerical results of previous estimations) is typically not used at all unless one adopts the Bayesian approach to statistical inference.

population with known variance σ^2. As the test statistic we suggested

$$Z = \frac{(\bar{X} - \mu_0)}{\sigma_{\bar{x}}},$$

where μ_0 is the mean postulated by the null hypothesis, and $\sigma_{\bar{x}}$ is the standard deviation of the distribution of $\bar{X}$ given by $\sigma/\sqrt{n}$. If $\bar{X}$ is the best estimator of the population mean that can be found, then Z is the best test statistic that can be devised. As we shall see in Chapter 6, $\bar{X}$ is—except for special circumstances—the best estimator of the population mean so that we cannot, in general, improve on Z.

Test for the Equality of Two Means

A test procedure similar to the one just described can be employed in the problem involving *two independent random samples* from two normal populations with *known variances.* The question may arise whether there is any difference between the two population means. Suppose the mean of the first population is μ_1 and the mean of the second population is μ_2. Then the null hypothesis is

$$H_0: \quad \mu_1 = \mu_2,$$

and the alternative hypothesis is

$$H_A: \quad \mu_1 \neq \mu_2 \qquad (\text{or } \mu_1 > \mu_2).$$

As the sample summary of evidence about the population means, we can use the respective sample means, say $\bar{X}_1$ and $\bar{X}_2$. If the null hypothesis is true, then $(\mu_1 - \mu_2) = 0$; therefore, the value of $(\bar{X}_1 - \bar{X}_2)$ would seldom be very different from zero. Consequently, sample values of $(\bar{X}_1 - \bar{X}_2)$ which *are* very different from zero could be considered as evidence against the null hypothesis. If we determine the distribution of $(\bar{X}_1 - \bar{X}_2)$, we can specify the appropriate acceptance and rejection region. Now, since both $\bar{X}_1$ and $\bar{X}_2$ come from normal populations, their difference must also be normally distributed. The mean of this distribution is

$$E(\bar{X}_1 - \bar{X}_2) = E(\bar{X}_1) - E(\bar{X}_2) = \mu_1 - \mu_2,$$

which, if the null hypothesis is true, is equal to zero. Thus the only thing to determine is the variance. Since $\bar{X}_1$ and $\bar{X}_2$ are means of two independent samples, their covariance is zero and we have

$$\text{Var}(\bar{X}_1 - \bar{X}_2) = \text{Var}(\bar{X}_1) + \text{Var}(\bar{X}_2) = \frac{\sigma_1^2}{n_1} + \frac{\sigma_2^2}{n_2},$$

where σ_1^2 and σ_2^2 are the variances of the two normal populations from which the samples were drawn, and n_1 and n_2 are the respective sample sizes. When the two population means are the same as postulated by the null hypothesis,

$$(\bar{X}_1 - \bar{X}_2) \sim N\left(0, \frac{\sigma_1^2}{n_1} + \frac{\sigma_2^2}{n_2}\right).$$

The corresponding standard normal variable then is

$$(5.2) \qquad Z_{\bar{x}_1-\bar{x}_2} = \frac{\bar{X}_1 - \bar{X}_2}{\sigma_{\bar{x}_1-\bar{x}_2}} = \frac{\bar{X}_1 - \bar{X}_2}{\sqrt{(\sigma_1^2/n_1) + (\sigma_2^2/n_2)}}.$$

This is the appropriate test statistic for which we can define the acceptance and the rejection regions with the help of normal probability tables. (The case of unknown variances is considered under the heading of t distribution.)

Estimation of σ^2

In both tests considered so far, we have assumed that the population variance is always known. Usually this is not the case and the variance has to be estimated from the sample. But if we use an *estimate* of the population variance rather than its actual value, the tests concerning the population mean have to be modified. Before developing the necessary modification, we shall discuss the problem of estimating the population variance of $X \sim N(\mu, \sigma^2)$. As a possible candidate we may consider the sample variance, which we shall call $\hat{\sigma}^2$, that is defined as

$$(5.3) \qquad \hat{\sigma}^2 = \frac{1}{n} \sum_{i=1}^{n} (X_i - \bar{X})^2.$$

Different samples will, of course, lead to different values of $\hat{\sigma}^2$. We are interested to know whether $\hat{\sigma}^2$ has any desirable properties and what its distribution is.

We may start by examining $\hat{\sigma}^2$ for biasedness. This we can do by taking the mathematical expectation of $\hat{\sigma}^2$ and by checking whether it is equal to σ^2 or not. If it is, then $\hat{\sigma}^2$ is unbiased. We have

$$E(\hat{\sigma}^2) = E\frac{1}{n} \sum_i (X_i - \bar{X})^2 = \frac{1}{n} \sum_i E(X_i - \bar{X})^2.$$

As it is, we do not know $E(X_i - \bar{X})^2$. However, we know that

$$E(X_i - \mu)^2 = \mathrm{Var}(X_i) = \sigma^2,$$

since X_i has exactly the same distribution as X and, therefore, the same variance. Also, we know that

$$E(\bar{X} - \mu)^2 = \mathrm{Var}(\bar{X}) = \frac{\sigma^2}{n}$$

by Theorem 15 (Section 4-3). Therefore, we will rewrite the expression for $E(\hat{\sigma}^2)$ by simultaneously adding and deducting μ.

$$E(\hat{\sigma}^2) = \frac{1}{n}\sum_i E[(X_i - \mu) - (\bar{X} - \mu)]^2$$

$$= \frac{1}{n}\sum_i [E(X_i - \mu)^2 + E(\bar{X} - \mu)^2 - 2E(X_i - \mu)(\bar{X} - \mu)]$$

$$= \frac{1}{n}\sum_i E(X_i - \mu)^2 + \frac{1}{n}\sum_i E(\bar{X} - \mu)^2 - \frac{2}{n}\sum_i E(X_i - \mu)(\bar{X} - \mu)$$

$$= \frac{1}{n}\sum_i \sigma^2 + \frac{1}{n}\sum_i \frac{\sigma^2}{n} - 2E(\bar{X} - \mu)\frac{1}{n}\sum_i (X_i - \mu)$$

$$= \sigma^2 + \frac{\sigma^2}{n} - 2E(\bar{X} - \mu)^2 = \sigma^2 + \frac{\sigma^2}{n} - 2\frac{\sigma^2}{n}.$$

That is,

$$E(\hat{\sigma}^2) = \left(\frac{n-1}{n}\right)\sigma^2, \tag{5.4}$$

which is not equal to σ^2. This means that $\hat{\sigma}^2$ is a *biased* estimator of σ^2.

This result, although negative, is nevertheless helpful since it suggests an easy way of finding an unbiased estimator of $\hat{\sigma}^2$. By multiplying both sides of (5.4) by $n/(n-1)$ we obtain

$$\left(\frac{n}{n-1}\right)E(\hat{\sigma}^2) = \sigma^2,$$

which can be written as

$$E\left(\frac{n}{n-1}\right)\hat{\sigma}^2 = \sigma^2$$

or

$$E\left(\frac{n}{n-1}\right)\frac{1}{n}\sum_i (X_i - \bar{X})^2 = \sigma^2;$$

that is,

$$E\frac{1}{n-1}\sum_i (X_i - \bar{X})^2 = \sigma^2, \tag{5.5}$$

so that an estimator of σ^2, which we shall call s^2, defined as

$$s^2 = \frac{1}{n-1}\sum_i (X_i - \bar{X})^2, \tag{5.6}$$

is an *unbiased* estimator of σ^2.

Because of the property of unbiasedness, we shall use s^2 as our preferred estimator of σ^2. Its distribution, which we shall not derive or present here, is a special case of the so-called gamma distribution.[2] The exact shape of the distribution of s^2 depends on two parameters, the population variance σ^2 and the sample size n. The distribution is always skewed to the right for small sample sizes and becomes more and more symmetric as the sample size increases. The mean of the distribution is, as shown, equal to σ^2 and its variance is given[3] by

$$\text{Var}(s^2) = \frac{2\sigma^4}{n-1}. \tag{5.7}$$

Since s^2 is unbiased and since its variance approaches zero as $n \to \infty$, s^2 is a *consistent* estimator of σ^2. Another feature of s^2 that is worth a passing reference is the fact that s^2 is independent of $\bar{X}$ in the sense that the joint distribution of s^2 and $\bar{X}$ is equal to the product of their respective marginal distributions. That is,

$$f(s^2, \bar{x}) = f(s^2)f(\bar{x}).$$

The Chi-Square Distribution

To determine the probability that s^2 lies within any specific interval, we would have to find the areas under the corresponding gamma curve. This curve would be different for each different combination of σ^2 and n, and the determination of the appropriate area would be quite complicated. This problem has already been encountered in connection with the normal distribution, which also differs from one combination of parameter values—in this case μ and σ^2—to another, and for which the mathematical formula is also highly complicated. In the case of the normal distribution, the problem was solved by transforming a normal variable to one with mean 0 and variance 1 (a "standard normal variable") for which the probabilities are tabulated. In the case of s^2, the solution is similar. The transformation in this case is to a variable called *chi-square*, which is defined as

$$\chi^2 = \frac{(n-1)s^2}{\sigma^2}, \tag{5.8}$$

and for which probabilities are calculated. However, unlike the standard normal distribution, the distribution of χ^2 changes its shape with sample size. For small samples the distribution is skewed to the right, but it becomes more and more symmetric as the sample size increases. No value of χ^2 is, of course, negative. Because of the dependence of the chi-square distribution on sample size, we usually use an identifying subscript. For instance, (5.8) would normally be written as

$$\chi^2_{n-1} = \frac{(n-1)s^2}{\sigma^2}. \tag{5.8a}$$

[2] See, e.g., John E. Freund and Ronald E. Walpole, *Mathematical Statistics*, 3rd ed. (Englewood Cliffs, NJ: Prentice-Hall, 1980), pp. 196–197. For the special case of s^2 we have, in their notation, $\alpha = (n-1)/2$ and $\beta = 2\sigma^2/(n-1)$.

[3] *Ibid.*, p. 199. Note that the mean of s^2 is equal to σ^2 regardless of the form of the parent distribution of X, but the variance formula (5.7) hinges on the assumption of normality of X.

An equivalent way of writing (5.8a) is

$$\chi^2_{n-1} = \frac{\sum_{i=1}^{n} (X_i - \bar{X})^2}{\sigma^2}. \tag{5.8b}$$

The subscript of χ^2, which is equal to the sample size reduced by 1, is called the number of *degrees of freedom* and is often designated by ν instead of $(n - 1)$. The terms "degrees of freedom" refers to the number of independent squares in the numerator of the chi-square statistics, i.e., in

$$\sum_{i=1}^{n} (X_i - \bar{X})^2.$$

The total number of squares in this expression is n, but only $(n - 1)$ of them are independent since after calculating any first $(n - 1)$ squares, the value of the nth square will be automatically determined. The reason for this is the presence of $\bar{X}$ and one of the well-known features of $\bar{X}$ is that

$$\sum_i (X_i - \bar{X}) = 0.$$

This represents a restriction that must be fulfilled. For example, suppose we have three squares of which the values of the first two are

$$(x_1 - \bar{x})^2 = 2^2,$$
$$(x_2 - \bar{x})^2 = 4^2.$$

If the third square were independent of the first two, its value could be any number, say 5^2. But that cannot be because in that case we would have

$$\sum_i (x_i - \bar{x}) = 2 + 4 + 5,$$

which adds up to 11 and not to 0 as required. In fact, with the first two squares being 2^2 and 4^2, the third square can only be equal to $(-6)^2 = 36$ because only then we get $2 + 4 - 6 = 0$. This explanation of the determination of the number of degrees of freedom in the present context is relatively straightforward; in other cases the issue is more clouded. For that reason most basic statistical texts do not dwell too much upon the subject and suggest that the reader may think of the degrees of freedom as simply a name given to a parameter.

From the knowledge of the probability distribution of χ^2 we can determine the probabilities for the sampling distribution of s^2. This can be seen as follows. If a and b are any constants such that $0 \leq a \leq b$, then

$$P(a \leq \chi^2_{n-1} \leq b) = P\left[a \leq \frac{(n-1)s^2}{\sigma^2} \leq b\right]$$
$$= P\left[a\left(\frac{\sigma^2}{n-1}\right) \leq s^2 \leq b\left(\frac{\sigma^2}{n-1}\right)\right],$$

so that a probability statement about χ^2 can readily be translated into an equivalent probability statement about s^2. It can be shown that the mean and the variance of the chi-square distribution are

$$E(\chi^2_{n-1}) = n - 1$$

and

$$\text{Var}(\chi^2_{n-1}) = 2(n-1),$$

and its modal value is $(n-3)$. Finally, note that the distribution χ^2_1 is the distribution of the *square* of a standard normal variable, and that χ^2_m is the distribution of the *sum of squares of m independent standard normal variables.* The table of the chi-square probabilities (see Appendix D) is described below in connection with testing hypotheses concerning σ^2. A graph of the chi-square distribution for various degrees of freedom ν is given in Figure 5-11.

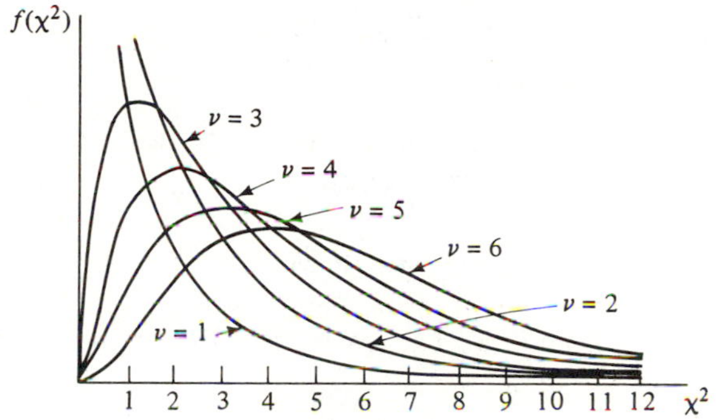

Figure 5-11

The nature of the chi-square distribution can be made clearer by comparing it with the normal distribution. The normal distribution appears in statistics for two principal reasons. First, it is a distribution of some importance on its own right, in the sense that it provides a description of many parent populations. It is not very difficult to find variables which refer to natural or social phenomena and which are—or can be assumed to be—normally distributed. Examples are intelligence, physical height of persons, errors of measurement or behavior, and many others. The second reason for the use of the normal distribution is the fact that it describes some important sampling distributions, in particular that of sample mean. Thus the normal distribution can serve as a description of a parent population or of a sampling distribution. The chi-square distribution, on the other hand, serves only as a description of certain sampling distributions, one of which is the distribution of the statistic (5.8).[4] There are no noted parent populations whose distributions could be described by the chi-square distribution.

[4] Apart from describing the distribution of (5.8), the chi-square distribution also describes, among others, the distribution of a certain statistic used in testing for independence in contingency tables and for "goodness of fit" of frequency distributions.

The *t* Distribution

Having settled the problem of estimating the population variance, we may return to the original problem of testing a hypothesis about the population mean of a normally distributed variable with unknown variance. To recapitulate, we know that if

$$X \sim N(\mu, \sigma^2),$$

then

$$\bar{X} \sim N\left(\mu, \frac{\sigma^2}{n}\right).$$

Further, if the null hypothesis is given as

$$H_0: \quad \mu = \mu_0,$$

then the appropriate test statistic is

$$\frac{(\bar{X} - \mu_0)\sqrt{n}}{\sigma} \sim N(0, 1),$$

providing σ is known. When, as presently supposed, the value of σ is not known, we may replace it by its estimate obtained from

$$s = \sqrt{\frac{1}{n-1} \sum_i (X_i - \bar{X})^2},$$

which follows directly from (5.6). The test statistic then would be

$$\frac{(\bar{X} - \mu_0)\sqrt{n}}{s}.$$

The problem is to find its distribution. Note that by dividing the numerator and the denominator by σ and rearranging the result we get

$$\frac{(\bar{X} - \mu_0)\sqrt{n}/\sigma}{\sqrt{(n-1)s^2/(n-1)\sigma^2}}.$$

The numerator is the standard normal variable Z, and in the denominator $(n-1)s^2/\sigma^2 = \chi^2_{n-1}$, as we saw from (5.8a). That is, we have

$$\frac{N(0, 1)}{\sqrt{\chi^2_{n-1}/(n-1)}}.$$

This variable has a distribution known as the *t distribution*. Because of the presence of the chi-square variable in the denominator, the shape of this distribution depends on the size of the sample. Therefore, we usually use an identifying subscript and write

$$\frac{(\bar{X} - \mu_0)\sqrt{n}}{s} \sim t_{n-1}. \tag{5.9}$$

Here $(n-1)$ is referred to as the number of the degrees of freedom. The number of the degrees of freedom is, of course, derived from the chi-square variable in the denominator. But unlike the chi-square distribution, the t distribution is *always* symmetric; its mean is equal to zero and its variance is $(n-1)/(n-3)$, provided that n is greater than 3. This variance will be close to unity when n is large. As the sample size increases, the t distribution approaches the standard normal distribution. The probabilities for different sample sizes are available in tabulated form (see Appendix D). For $n > 30$ we use the normal distribution.

To carry out a test of a hypothesis that the population mean is equal to a given value, we have to specify the boundary between the acceptance and the rejection region for the test statistic (5.9). This will depend on the form of the alternative hypothesis, on the desired level of significance, and on the number of degrees of freedom. Suppose we wish to test

$$H_0: \quad \mu = \mu_0$$

$$H_A: \quad \mu \neq \mu_0.$$

The desired level of significance is some number α. Then the acceptance region is defined as

$$-t_{n-1,\,\alpha/2} \leq \frac{(\bar{X}-\mu_0)\sqrt{n}}{s} \leq t_{n-1,\,\alpha/2}.$$

Here $t_{n-1,\,\alpha/2}$ stands for the value of the t statistic with $(n-1)$ degrees of freedom, which cuts off $\alpha/2$ of the area of the distribution at each tail end. This value can be looked up in the table of probabilities of the t distribution. The table is arranged in such a way that each row corresponds to a different number of the degrees of freedom, and each column corresponds to a different area at the tail end of the distribution. For instance, in the row labeled "14" and column "0.05," the value shown is 1.761. This means that a value of the t statistic—calculated from a sample of size 15—that would exceed 1.761 (or, alternatively, one that would be less than -1.761) would occur with a probability of 0.05. That is, the values of the test statistic are shown in the main body of the table, and the probabilities are given on the margin. This is a different arrangement from that of the normal probability tables where the order is just the reverse. The table of the t values gives, in fact, a description of many different distributions (as many as there are rows) and is therefore much less detailed than the normal probability table.

Consider now the two-tail test mentioned above. If the desired level of significance is 5%, then $\alpha/2$ is 0.025, and the appropriate column in the t table would be headed by this number. Which is the appropriate row would depend on the size of the sample. Some selected values are

Sample size: n	Degrees of freedom: ν	Value of $t_{n-1,\,0.025}$
5	4	2.776
10	9	2.262
20	19	2.093
30	29	2.045
∞		1.960

Note that the values of t get smaller as n gets larger, and that they approach 1.960, the value that would be assumed by a standard normal variable at the same level of significance. In comparison to the tests in which the population variance is known and therefore does not have to be estimated, the acceptance region based on the t distribution is always wider. This can be seen by noting that in each column of the t table all values are larger than the value in the bottom row which corresponds to standard normal variable. The consequence of having a wider acceptance region is a higher probability of Error Type II and, therefore, a less powerful test.

The test outlined above is a two-tail test. The procedure in the case of a one-tail test is very similar. Instead of giving a general description, we shall illustrate it by a numerical example.

EXAMPLE A worker handling a certain product takes, on the average, 7 minutes to complete his task. An efficiency expert suggests a slightly different way of handling the product and decides to take a sample to see if there is any saving of time. The null and the alternative hypotheses then are

$$H_0:\quad \mu \geq 7 \text{ min} \quad (\text{or } 420 \text{ sec}),$$

$$H_A:\quad \mu < 7 \text{ min.}$$

The level of significance is to be the traditional 5% and the size of the sample 16. Assuming that the parent population is normal, the appropriate test statistic is t of (5.9) with 15 degrees of freedom. The boundary on the t distribution can be looked up in the t table in row "15" and column "0.05." The resulting test criterion is

$$\textit{do not reject } H_0 \textit{ if } \quad \frac{(\bar{x} - 420)\sqrt{16}}{s} \geq -1.753;$$

reject otherwise.

Note that $\bar{x}$ and s are to be measured in seconds. The recorded observations are

6 min 26 sec	6 min 0 sec	7 min 30 sec	6 min 4 sec
6 min 38 sec	7 min 0 sec	7 min 8 sec	6 min 42 sec
6 min 48 sec	7 min 12 sec	7 min 20 sec	7 min 6 sec
6 min 58 sec	6 min 46 sec	6 min 22 sec	6 min 48 sec

The following results are obtained.

$$\bar{x} = 6528/16 = 408 \quad (\text{i.e., 6 min 48 sec}),$$

$$s = \sqrt{9872/15} = 25.65.$$

Therefore, the value of the test statistic is

$$\frac{(408 - 420)\sqrt{16}}{25.65} = -1.871.$$

This falls outside the acceptance region and thus the "7 minute" hypothesis has to be rejected at the 5% level of significance. The p value, obtained from the t distribution table by interpolation, is in this case equal to 0.0422.

The preceding discussion involved a test concerning the mean of a normally distributed variable with unknown variance. A similar procedure can be devised to deal with a problem involving the difference between two means of two normally distributed variables, each variable being characterized by the same unknown variance σ^2. By appropriate substitution, the test statistic Z in (5.2) then becomes

$$Z_{\bar{x}_1-\bar{x}_2} = \frac{\bar{X}_1 - \bar{X}_2}{\sigma\sqrt{(1/n_1) + (1/n_2)}}.$$

Since σ is unknown, we replace it by s defined as

$$s = \sqrt{\frac{(n_1 - 1)s_1^2 + (n_2 - 1)s_2^2}{n_1 + n_2 - 2}},$$

where s_1^2 and s_2^2 are unbiased estimators of σ^2 obtained from sample 1 and 2. It is easy to show that s^2 is also an unbiased estimator of σ^2. The resulting test statistic then is

$$\frac{\bar{X}_1 - \bar{X}_2}{s\sqrt{(1/n_1) + (1/n_2)}} \sim t_{n_1+n_2-2}. \tag{5.10}$$

If the two hypothesized populations have different variances, the problem of testing for equality of the means becomes very difficult. This problem is commonly referred to as the *Behrens–Fisher problem* by statisticians. (This is a small sample problem. When the samples are large, we can use the test statistic in (5.2) with σ_1^2 replaced by s_1^2 and σ_2^2 replaced by s_2^2. This test statistic will be approximately distributed as a standard normal variable.)

Tests Concerning the Mean of a Nonnormal Population

Next we will consider a test concerning the value of the mean of a variable which is *not necessarily normally distributed* (but has a finite variance). *If the sample is large,* we can invoke the central limit theorem (our Theorem 16 in Section 4-3), which states that whatever the distribution of X, the distribution of $\bar{X}$ in large samples will be approximately normal. Given this, and given the fact that for large n the t distribution is approximately normal, it follows that

$$\frac{(\bar{X} - \mu_0)\sqrt{n}}{s} \qquad (n \geq 30)$$

has a distribution which can be approximated by the standard normal distribution. Therefore, in this situation we can use the test described in Section 5-1. If the sample size is small and the parent distribution is not known, we can resort to so-called *distribution-free* or *nonparametric* tests, which are described in many texts.

Tests Concerning σ^2

Let us now consider some tests concerning the population variance. Suppose we wish to test the null hypothesis that the variance of a normal population has a specified value against the alternative claim that it has a different value. That is,

$$H_0: \quad \sigma^2 = \sigma_0^2,$$

$$H_A: \quad \sigma^2 \neq \sigma_0^2.$$

This hypothesis can be tested by taking a sample estimate of σ^2 as defined by (5.6), namely,

$$s^2 = \frac{1}{n-1} \sum_{i=1}^{n} (X_i - \bar{X})^2,$$

and by setting up the acceptance and the rejection region for the distribution of s^2. We use, as our test statistic, a transformation of s^2 given as

$$\chi^2_{n-1} = \frac{(n-1)s^2}{\sigma_0^2},$$

where $(n - 1)$ is the number of *degrees of freedom.* The properties of this distribution were discussed earlier. If the chosen level of significance is α, then the acceptance region for a two-tail test is

$$\chi^2_{n-1,\,1-\alpha/2} \leq \frac{(n-1)s^2}{\sigma_0^2} \leq \chi^2_{n-1,\,\alpha/2},$$

where the subscripts $(1 - \alpha/2)$ and $(\alpha/2)$ refer to the area to the *right* of the particular boundary value of χ^2. The table of the chi-square probabilities is arranged in the same way as the table of the t distribution. The rows refer to different degrees of freedom, the columns to different probabilities, and the entries in the main body of the table are the corresponding values of χ^2. For instance, in the row labeled "4" and the column "0.975" the value shown is 0.484. The row refers to the chi-square distribution for samples of size 5, and the value 0.484 is that value of the chi-square variable which would be exceeded with a probability of 0.975. In other words, 0.484 is the lower limit of an interval that extends to $+\infty$, and 0.975 is the probability that a value of χ^2_4 would fall in that interval. Some selected values of χ^2 for a two-tailed test with 5% level of significance are given below.

Sample size: n	Degrees of freedom: ν	Value of $\chi^2_{n-1,\,0.975}$	Value of $\chi^2_{n-1,\,0.025}$
5	4	0.484	11.143
10	9	2.700	19.023
20	19	8.907	32.852
30	29	16.047	45.722
1001	1000	914	1090

For large n we can determine the chi-square probabilities by using the fact that $[\sqrt{2\chi^2_{n-1}} - \sqrt{2(n-1)}]$ has a distribution which can be approximated by the standard normal distribution. For instance, when $(n-1) = 1000$, then

$$\sqrt{2 \times 914} - \sqrt{2 \times 1000} = -1.966$$

and

$$\sqrt{2 \times 1090} - \sqrt{2 \times 1000} = +1.969$$

which is almost the same as the corresponding values -1.960 and $+1.960$ of a standard normal variable. Our explanation of the above test procedure referred to a two-tail test but can be easily adapted to a one-tail test for $H_A: \sigma^2 > \sigma_0^2$ or $\sigma^2 < \sigma_0^2$; this will be left to the reader.

EXAMPLE Consider the previous example dealing with the time taken by a worker to perform a certain task. Suppose the variance of this variable, which is assumed to be normally distributed, is claimed to be 30^2 seconds. The efficiency expert contends that the new method of handling the product which he suggested will also change the previous variation in the time. The null and the alternative hypotheses will then be

$$H_0: \quad \sigma^2 = 900,$$

$$H_A: \quad \sigma^2 \neq 900.$$

The null hypothesis is to be tested at the 5% level of significance by using the 16 observations given in the previous example. The acceptance region is defined as

$$6.262 \leq \frac{(n-1)s^2}{900} \leq 27.488,$$

where the boundary values are taken from the chi-square table. From the observations the value of the test statistic is

$$\frac{9872}{900} = 10.97,$$

which falls inside the acceptance region. Thus the sample provides no evidence against the null hypothesis.

The *F* Distribution

Another test concerns the variances of two normal populations. The null and the alternative hypotheses to be tested are[5]

$$H_0: \quad \sigma_1^2 \leq \sigma_2^2,$$

$$H_A: \quad \sigma_1^2 > \sigma_2^2,$$

where we regard as the *first* population the one which may, according to H_A, have the larger variance. The null hypothesis can be tested by drawing a sample from each of the two populations and calculating the estimates s_1^2 and s_2^2 of the respective variances. The samples are assumed to be independently drawn and to be of size n_1 and n_2, respectively. As the appropriate test statistic, we may consider the ratio

[5] A two-sided test could, of course, also be considered, but it happens to be much less common so it is usually not presented.

s_1^2/s_2^2. If the null hypothesis is true, this ratio would exceed unity only because the sample estimates differ from the respective parameters. In any case, we would expect s_1^2/s_2^2 to approach unity (or a number between 0 and 1) as both sample sizes get larger unless the null hypothesis were false.

To carry out the test we have to set up the boundary between the acceptance and the rejection regions, and for that we have to know the sampling distribution of s_1^2/s_2^2. Let us divide the numerator by σ_1^2 and the denominator by σ_2^2; if the null hypothesis is true, the ratio will be unaffected. Thus we can write

$$\frac{s_1^2/\sigma_1^2}{s_2^2/\sigma_2^2},$$

which is equivalent to

$$\frac{(n_1-1)s_1^2/(n_1-1)\sigma_1^2}{(n_2-1)s_2^2/(n_2-1)\sigma_2^2} = \frac{\chi^2_{n_1-1}/(n_1-1)}{\chi^2_{n_2-1}/(n_2-1)}$$

by (5.8a). Since the two samples are independent of each other, the numerator and the denominator of the preceding expression are likewise independent. We mention this because the distribution of a ratio of two independent chi-square variables, each divided by its respective number of degrees of freedom, is the well-known *F distribution.* This distribution is asymmetric and depends on two parameters, the number of the degrees of freedom in the numerator and the number of degrees of freedom in the denominator. These two numbers are usually given as subscripts of F to ensure proper identification. Thus we write

$$\text{(5.11)} \qquad \frac{s_1^2}{s_2^2} \sim F_{n_1-1,\, n_2-1}.$$

The values for the F distribution are available in tabulated form. Usually there are two tables, one for 5% and one for 1% level of significance. Each table gives the boundary value of F for a one-tail test when the two population variances are equal. The rows in each table refer to the number of degrees of freedom in the denominator and the columns to the number of degrees of freedom in the numerator. For example, in the table for the 5% level of significance, the entry in the row labeled "10" and the column labeled "15" is 2.85. This means that when we have two independent samples, one of size 16 and the other of size 11, the probability that the ratio (s_1^2/s_2^2) would exceed 2.85 is 0.05. That is, the value 2.85 stands for the lower limit of an interval which extends to $+\infty$, and the probability that a value of (s_1^2/s_2^2) would fall within this interval is 0.05.

These tests concerning population variances are strictly true only for normal parent populations. There are some indications, however, that the results apply to a large extent also to other types of parent populations, providing they do not differ from the normal population too markedly.[6] But if there are good reasons to suspect that the parent population is highly skewed or U-shaped, then the tests cannot be applied with much confidence.

[6] For a discussion on this topic see, e.g., G. Udny Yule and M. G. Kendall, *An Introduction to the Theory of Statistics* (London: Griffin, 1950), p. 486.

Goodness-of-Fit Test

The *goodness-of-fit* test is applicable to problems of deciding whether a sample frequency distribution is compatible with some given theoretical distribution. It would be used, for instance, to test the assumption that some variable is normally distributed. In general, the null hypothesis is the proposition that a certain variable has a specified probability distribution, while the alternative hypothesis states that the proposition is not true. To test the null hypothesis, we use the frequency distribution obtained in the sample as the evidence concerning the form of the distribution in the population. The test statistic commonly used in this case is

$$\sum_{i=1} \frac{(f_i - e_i)^2}{e_i},$$

where f_i is the sample frequency in the ith interval, e_i is the frequency expected in the theoretical (hypothesized) distribution, and m is the number of intervals. It can be shown that this test statistic has a distribution which for *large samples* can be approximated by the *chi-square distribution.* In particular, if the sample is large, then

$$\sum_{i} \frac{(f_i - e_i)^2}{e_i} \sim \chi^2_{m-k-1}, \tag{5.12}$$

where the subscript $(m - k - 1)$ refers to the number of degrees of freedom. The sample frequencies f_i are observed, and the theoretical frequencies e_i can be calculated by using the distribution formula specified by the null hypothesis. This formula may involve some unknown parameters which have to be replaced by their respective sample estimates. For instance, if the null hypothesis specifies that the population distribution is normal, it will be necessary to estimate the mean and the variance of this distribution from the sample. (Actually, if (5.12) is to hold, the estimates must be of a certain kind. Specifically, the estimates should be of "maximum likelihood" type—a term that will be explained in Section 6-2. At this stage it is sufficient to note that $\bar{X}$ *is* a maximum likelihood estimate, and s^2 is approximately so in large samples.) The number of the degrees of freedom is determined as follows.

m = number of intervals;

k = number of parameters that had to be replaced by sample estimates.

For the test to be reasonably satisfactory, it is required that $m \geq 5$ and $e_i \geq 5$ for each i.

If the null hypothesis is true, f_i can be considered as a sample estimate of e_i, and the expression in (5.12) will differ from zero only because we observe a sample rather than the entire population. Therefore, if we observe a sample for which the value of the test statistic (5.12) is large, we consider it as evidence against the null hypothesis. To carry out the test we have to determine the boundary between the acceptance and the rejection regions. This depends on the number of degrees of freedom and the chosen level of significance and can be looked up in the chi-square table. Note that since the statistic (5.12) cannot be negative, evidence against the null hypothesis can only take the form of very large values (and not very small ones) so that the appropriate test is a *one-tail* test. (Of course, if one admits the possibility of "cooked data," then too close an agreement of the observed frequencies with the expected ones may well be suspicious.)

EXAMPLE Suppose we wish to test the unbiasedness of a die against the claim that the die is loaded, using 5% level of significance. The result of 120 tosses leads to the following frequency distribution.

Number of dots	1	2	3	4	5	6
Frequency	13	17	30	30	21	9

The expected frequency for any side of an unbiased die is 20 out of 120. The null hypothesis of unbiasedness will be rejected if the calculated value of the goodness-of-fit test statistic exceeds the tabulated value of $\chi^2_{5,\,0.05}$ equal to 11.07. (Note that here $m = 6$ and $k = 0$.) In fact, we have

$$\sum_{i=1}^{6} \frac{(f_i - e_i)^2}{e_i} = \frac{(13-20)^2}{20} + \frac{(17-20)^2}{20} + \cdots + \frac{(9-20)^2}{20}$$

$$= 19,$$

which exceeds the tabulated value of chi-square and leads to the rejection of the hypothesis. (Note that the p value in this case is less than 0.005 according to the chi-square table.)

Conclusion

This brings us to the end of the present section containing the description of several basic tests. There was a twofold purpose to it. First, we wanted to illustrate the development of test procedures in general so that the reader could see in concrete terms the kind of problems involved and the method of handling them. Actually, the specific problems and related tests given in this section are *not* very frequently encountered in enconometrics. This is because the statistical models used are too simple to satisfy the usual demands of economic theory. In particular, the concentration on one variable to the exclusion of all other factors does not do justice to the complexity of economic relations. There is, however, one common feature between the simple tests discussed in this section and the tests applicable to more complex situations. This common feature is the use of distributions described on the preceding pages: the normal, the chi-square, the t and the F distributions. This was the second and the more important purpose of this section. The discussion of the simple tests enabled us to introduce these distributions in a natural way, and gave us an opportunity to highlight their main characteristics and to relate them to each other. An extended summary of the main features of these distributions is presented in Table 5-2.[7]

[7] A considerably more detailed discussion of these and other distributions can be found in, e.g., N. L. Johnson and S. Kotz, *Continuous Univariate Distributions,* Vols. 1 and 2 (Boston: Houghton Mifflin, 1970).

Table 5-2

Variable	Distribution	Mean	Variance	Mode	Coefficient of skewness	Relation to other distributions
X	Normal	μ	σ^2	μ	0	
Z	Standard normal	0	1	0	0	$Z = (X - \mu)/\sigma$
χ^2_ν	Chi-square	ν	2ν	$\nu - 2$	$\sqrt{8/\nu}$	(a) $\chi^2_1 = Z^2$
						(b) $\chi^2_\nu = \sum_{i=1}^{\nu} Z_i^2$ (Zs independent)
						(c) $\chi^2_\nu = \nu F_{\nu,\infty}$
t_ν	t distribution	0	$\dfrac{\nu}{\nu - 2}$ $(\nu > 2)$	0	0	(a) $t_\nu = \dfrac{Z}{\sqrt{\chi^2_\nu/\nu}}$
						(b) Approximation for $\nu > 30$: $t_\nu = Z$
F_{ν_1,ν_2}	F distribution	$\dfrac{\nu_2}{\nu_2 - 2}$ $(\nu_2 > 2)$	$\dfrac{2\nu_2^2(\nu_1 + \nu_2 - 2)}{\nu_1(\nu_2 - 2)^2(\nu_2 - 4)}$ $(\nu_2 > 4)$	$\dfrac{\nu_2(\nu_1 - 1)}{\nu_1(\nu_2 + 2)}$	$\dfrac{(2\nu_1 + \nu_2 - 2)[8(\nu_2 - 4)]^{1/2}}{(\nu_2 - 6)(\nu_1 + \nu_2 - 2)^{1/2}}$ $(\nu_2 > 6)$	(a) $F_{\nu_1,\nu_2} = \dfrac{\chi^2_{\nu_1}/\nu_1}{\chi^2_{\nu_2}/\nu_2}$
						(b) $F_{\nu_1,\infty} = \dfrac{\chi^2_{\nu_1}}{\nu_1}$
						(c) $P(\sqrt{F_{1,\nu_2}} = a) = \frac{1}{2}P(t_{\nu_2} = a)$ $P(F^{1/2}_{1,\nu_2} = a) = \frac{1}{2}P(t_{\nu_2} = a)$

EXERCISES

5-1. Let $X \sim N(\mu, 81)$. The null and the alternative hypotheses are

$$H_0: \quad \mu = 10,$$

$$H_A: \quad \mu > 10.$$

The test statistic is to be based on a sample of size 9, and the chosen level of significance is to be 5%. Draw a diagram of the power function for this test.

5-2. In conducting a survey of food prices, two samples of prices of a given food item were collected. Sample I came from a congested city area, and Sample II was obtained in the suburbs. The results were

	Sample I	Sample II
n	14	18
$\sum_{i=1}^{n} p_i$	12.60	14.96
$\frac{1}{n}\sum_{i=1}^{n} p_i^2$	1.68	1.96

where p_i = price recorded in the ith store.

a. Test the hypothesis that there is no difference between the mean price of the particular food item in the two areas.

b. Test the hypothesis that the dispersion of prices in the suburbs is no greater than in the city.

5-3. Two competing pizza makers claim that more than 75% of their customers are very satisfied with their product. To test this claim, a market research organization has drawn a random sample of pizza customers and obtained the number of very satisfied customers for each of the two pizza makers. Consider now the following.

a. Of 30 customers of "pizza A," 20 were found to be very satisfied. Test the hypothesis that in the population of all customers of "pizza A" the proportion of very satisfied customers is *no less* than 75%. (Use the normal approximation to the binomial distribution and a 5% level of significance.)

b. Of 5 customers of "pizza B," 2 were found to be very satisfied. Test the hypothesis that in the population of all customers of "pizza B" the proportion of very satisfied customers is *no less* than 75%. (Use the binomial distribution and a level of significance not exceeding 5%.)

5-4. A claim is made that the cyclical fluctuations in the demand for teenage workers are greater than those in the demand for married males. Test this claim by reference to the data in Table 5-3.

Table 5-3 Unemployment in the United States (Rate in Percent)

	Married men	Teenagers 14–19 years
1949	3.4	12.2
1950	4.6	11.3
1951	1.5	7.7
1952	1.4	8.0
1953	1.7	7.1
1954	4.0	11.4
1955	2.6	10.2
1956	2.3	10.4
1957	2.8	10.8
1958	5.1	14.4
1959	3.6	13.2
1960	3.7	13.6
1961	4.6	15.2

Source: *Economic Report of the President, 1965* (Washington, DC: U.S. Government Printing Office, 1965), p. 217.

5-5. A tire manufacturer claims that his new steel-belted tire has a mean life expectancy of 40,000 miles and that the standard deviation is only 2000 miles. A consumer association decides to test these claims against the alternatives that the mean life expectancy is *less* than 40,000 miles and that the standard deviation is *more* than 2000 miles. A 5% level of significance is to be used for each of the tests. Three tires are selected at random and tested. The claims are not rejected at the 5% level, but in each case the value of the test statistic is very close to the borderline. What are the values of the sample mean and of the sample standard deviation?

5-6. Shipments of peaches from farmer A include 5% defective peaches, while those from farmer B contain 10% defective fruit. An unmarked shipment arrives at the wholesaler's warehouse and has to be identified from a sample of 100 peaches. Suppose the cost of claiming that the peaches come from farmer A, when they in fact come from farmer B, is \$1000; the cost of making the opposite mistake is \$800. If H_0: $\pi = 0.05$ and H_A: $\pi = 0{,}10$, find the critical value of $\hat{\pi}$ (i.e., the boundary between the acceptance and the rejection regions) *and* the probabilities of Error Type I and of Error Type II for which the expected loss is minimized.

5-7. A probability distribution of a continuous random variable X is given as

$$f(x) = \frac{1}{k} \quad \text{for } 0 \leq x \leq k,$$
$$= 0 \quad \text{otherwise.}$$

Suppose you are testing the hypothesis

$$H_0: \quad k = 1$$

against

$$H_A: \quad k = 2$$

by means of a single observed value of X. What would be the probabilities of Error Type I and of Error Type II if you choose your rejection region as

(a) $\frac{1}{2} \leq x$? **(b)** $1 \leq x \leq 2$?

5-8. Suppose we have a coin that we suspect is "rigged" to produce three times as many heads as tails in a large number of tosses. We wish to test the fairness of the coin. We decide to accept the null hypothesis that the coin is unbiased if we get less than 3 heads in 3 tosses and to accept the alternative hypothesis that the coin is biased if we get 3 heads in 3 tosses. What are the probabilities of Error Type I and of Error Type II for this decision criterion?

5-9. It is argued that the proportion of male college students who drink beer is no different from that of noncollege males in the same age group. Test this claim (at the 5% level of significance) against the alternative that the proportion of the beer-drinking college males is higher, given that in random samples 60 out of 100 college males and 120 out of 260 noncollege males were beer-drinkers.

6 Estimation

In the introductory chapter we described briefly the traditional division of the problems of statistical inference in classical statistics into problems of hypothesis testing and problems of estimation. The similarity between the two types of problems lies in the fact that they are both concerned with questions concerning the value of some unknown population parameter or parameters. The difference is that in estimation, unlike in hypothesis testing, we make no prior claims whose credibility would be disputed. In hypothesis testing, the initial ingredients are prior information (in the form of a maintained hypothesis) and a claim concerning the value of the parameter in question. In estimation we also start with prior information (in the form of a model), but we have an open mind as to the value of the parameter. (Prior specification about the possible *range* of the parameter—e.g., a specification that the parameter must be positive—is considered to be a part of the model.) As mentioned earlier, estimation problems have received more attention by the econometricians than problems of hypothesis testing. Thus estimation theory for various types of economic models is quite well developed, although, of course, many difficulties still remain.

The theory of estimation can be divided into two parts, point estimation and interval estimation. In *point estimation* the aim is to use the prior and the sample information for the purpose of calculating a value that would be, in some sense, our best guess as to the actual value of the parameter of interest. In *interval estimation* the same information is used for the purpose of producing an interval that would contain the true value of the parameter with some given level of probability. Since an interval is fully characterized by its limits, estimating an interval is equivalent to estimating its limits. The interval itself is usually called a *confidence interval.* Confidence intervals can also be viewed as possible measures of the precision of a point estimator. This view will be adopted in our discussion of confidence intervals in Section 6-3.

The problem of point estimation is that of producing an estimate that would represent our best guess about the value of the parameter. To solve this problem we have to do two things: first, we have to specify what we mean by "best guess" and, second, we have to devise estimators that would meet this criterion or at least come close. In other words, we have to specify what we want, and provide a formula that would tell us how to get it or at least how to come close to getting it. The first part of the problem—the definition of the best guess—amounts to specifying various properties of an estimator that can be considered desirable. Since an estimator is a random variable whose value varies from sample to sample, its properties are, in fact, the properties of its sampling distribution. These properties will be discussed in Section 6-1. The second part of the problem involves devising estimators that would have at least some of the desirable properties. This will be the subject of Section 6-2. Section 6-3 will be devoted to a discussion of confidence intervals. The last section deals with Bayesian inference.

6-1 Properties of Estimators

Let us consider some random variable X whose distribution is characterized, among others, by some parameter θ that we would like to estimate. Thus the parent population consists of all possible values of X, and θ is one of the parametric characteristics of this population. X may be continuous or discrete, or even an attribute (i.e., a binary variable). An example would be family income—which is a continuous variable—and its mean. This specification constitutes a relatively simple estimation problem; a more complicated problem would involve a joint estimation of several parameters related to several variables. As it is, the simple estimation problem is perfectly sufficient for the purpose of describing various properties of estimators and for outlining the basic estimation methods. The more complicated estimation problems, which are typical in econometrics, will be considered in the following chapters.

To estimate a population parameter we combine the prior information that we may have with the information provided by the sample. The prior information is really nothing else but what, in the context of hypothesis testing, was called the "maintained hypothesis." In the context of estimation we usually use the term *model,* but the term *maintained hypothesis* is also perfectly acceptable. Such prior information concerns the population of X; it may consist of assumptions about the form of the distribution, the value of some parameters other than θ, or some specification (e.g., range) concerning θ itself. The information provided by the sample is given by the sample observations $X_1, X_2, \ldots, X_n$. The way of utilizing the information to obtain an estimate of θ is prescribed by the estimation formula called the *estimator.* There may be, and generally is, more than one such formula to choose from. In this chapter we will, for the most part, consider only problems with a minimum of prior information. Problems involving more elaborate models will be discussed in the rest of the book.

An estimator of parameter θ, which is one of the characteristics of the distribution of X, may be called $\hat{\theta}$. Since $\hat{\theta}$ is constructed by substituting sample observations on X into a formula, we may write

$$\hat{\theta} = \hat{\theta}(x_1, x_2, \ldots, x_n),$$

which is read "$\hat{\theta}$ is a function of $x_1, x_2, \ldots, x_n$." (If not *all* sample observations are to be used, the expression will be modified accordingly.) This function can be of any form *except* for the restriction that it must not involve any unknown parameters including, of course, θ itself. The basic characteristics of the distribution of $\hat{\theta}$ are its mean $E(\hat{\theta})$ and the variance,

$$\text{Var}(\hat{\theta}) = E[\hat{\theta} - E(\hat{\theta})]^2 = E(\hat{\theta}^2) - [E(\hat{\theta})]^2.$$

The standard deviation of $\hat{\theta}$, defined as $\sqrt{\text{Var}(\hat{\theta})}$, is known as the *standard error* of $\hat{\theta}$. Of special importance are also the following concepts.

$$\text{Sampling error} = \hat{\theta} - \theta,$$

$$\text{Bias} = E(\hat{\theta}) - \theta,$$

$$\text{Mean square error} = E(\hat{\theta} - \theta)^2.$$

Sampling error is simply the difference between the value of the estimator and the true value of the parameter to be estimated. The extent of the sampling error does, of course, vary from sample to sample. *Bias* is the difference between the mean of the sampling distribution of a given estimator and the true value of the parameter. This value is, for any given estimator, a fixed value which may or may not be equal to zero. Finally, the *mean square error* is a concept related to the dispersion of the distribution of an estimator, and, thus, is similar to the concept of the variance. The difference between the variance of an estimator and its mean square error is that while the variance measures the dispersion of the distribution *around the mean,* the mean square error measures the dispersion *around the true value of the parameter.* If the mean of the distribution coincides with the true value of the parameter, then the variance and the mean square error are identical, otherwise they differ.

The relationship between the mean square error (MSE) and the variance can be shown explicitly as follows.

$$\begin{aligned}\text{MSE}(\hat{\theta}) &= E(\hat{\theta} - \theta)^2 = E[\hat{\theta} - E(\hat{\theta}) + E(\hat{\theta}) - \theta]^2\\ &= E\{[\hat{\theta} - E(\hat{\theta})] + [E(\hat{\theta}) - \theta]\}^2\\ &= E[\hat{\theta} - E(\hat{\theta})]^2 + E[E(\hat{\theta}) - \theta]^2 + 2E[\hat{\theta} - E(\hat{\theta})][E(\hat{\theta}) - \theta].\end{aligned}$$

Consider the last term

$$2E[\hat{\theta} - E(\hat{\theta})][E(\hat{\theta}) - \theta] = 2\{[E(\hat{\theta})]^2 - [E(\hat{\theta})]^2 - \theta E(\hat{\theta}) + \theta E(\hat{\theta})\} = 0.$$

Taking this into account and noting that the expected value of a constant is simply the constant itself, we can write

$$\text{MSE}(\hat{\theta}) = E[\hat{\theta} - E(\hat{\theta})]^2 + [E(\hat{\theta}) - \theta]^2 = \text{variance } \textit{plus} \text{ square bias.}$$

That is, the value of the mean square error can never be smaller than that of the variance, and the difference between the two is precisely equal to the squared bias.

Let us now turn to the description of some of the properties of estimators commonly considered to be desirable. These can be divided into two groups depending upon the size of sample. *Finite sample* or *small sample properties* refer to the properties of the sampling distribution of an estimator based on any fixed sample size. Finite sample properties characterize estimates calculated from any number of observations; they are frequently called small sample properties because they may apply *even* if the samples are small. On the other hand, *asymptotic* or *large sample properties* are restricted to sampling distributions based on samples whose size approaches infinity. These properties, when they apply, are assumed to hold only approximately when the sample size is large, and possibly not at all when the samples are small. This will be discussed more fully when we come to the actual description of various asymptotic properties, but first we shall concern ourselves with finite samples.

Small Sample Properties

The first property that we shall mention is *unbiasedness.* This property of an estimator is more widely known among empirical research workers than any other. We already explained the meaning of unbiasedness in Section 1-4, where we stated than an unbiased estimator is one whose mean is equal to the value of the population parameter to be estimated. Now, after having discussed the meaning and terminology of mathematical expectation, we can define unbiasedness in a precise and technical way as follows.

(6.1) *$\hat{\theta}$ is an unbiased estimator of θ if $E(\hat{\theta}) = \theta$.*

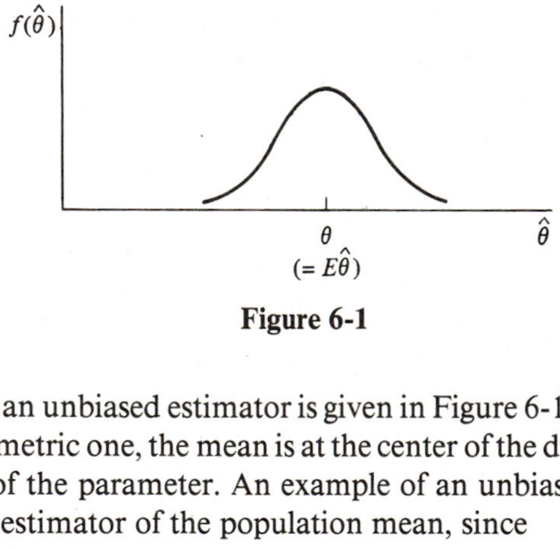

Figure 6-1

An illustration of an unbiased estimator is given in Figure 6-1; since the distribution shown is a symmetric one, the mean is at the center of the distribution, and it is equal to the value of the parameter. An example of an unbiased estimator is the sample mean as an estimator of the population mean, since

$$E(\bar{X}) = E\frac{1}{n}\sum_{i=1}^{n} X_i = \frac{1}{n}\sum E(X_i) = \mu.$$

(Note that $E(X_i)$ is the mean of X_i, which is μ.)

It should be emphasized that unbiasedness by itself is not a very comforting property since it implies nothing about the *dispersion* of the distribution of the estimator. An estimator that is unbiased but has a large variance will frequently lead to estimates that are quite far off the mark. On the other hand, an estimator that has a very small variance but is biased—and the extent of the bias is not known—is even less useful. This can be seen by taking the extreme case of an estimator with zero variance. Such an estimator is not hard to construct since any constant, which has zero variance by definition, qualifies. Thus if we decide that our estimate of θ will always be the number 5, then the sampling distribution of this "estimator" will be entirely concentrated at the point $\hat{\theta} = 5$. Such an estimator makes obviously very little sense since it pays no attention to the evidence provided by the sample and thus disregards all the information from this source. In light of this argument, it would seem desirable that an estimator should minimize the mean square error. Indeed, it can be shown that such an estimator would be an optimal one in the case where the loss of using an estimate in place of the true value of the parameter increases with the squared distance of $\hat{\theta}$ from θ. Unfortunately, in practice the formula for an estimator that would give the minimum value of mean square error very frequently includes the true value of the parameter to be estimated. This obviously makes the formula quite useless; it would be like a recipe for a cake that starts with "take a cake . . . ." Our definition of an estimator specifically excluded such formulas as not being worthy of the name "estimator."

The preceding discussion provides a background to the introduction of the concept of *efficiency* in estimation. As mentioned in Section 1-4, there is a lack of general agreement as to the most appropriate definition of this concept in statistical literature. Some authors equate efficiency with minimum mean square error in spite of the difficulty just mentioned; others define efficiency only in the context of asymptotic rather than finite sample properties, and others consider an estimator to be efficient if (and only if) it is unbiased and at the same time has a minimum variance. This last view of efficiency is becoming quite common among the econometricians and we will adopt it here. Accordingly, we make the formal definition of efficiency as follows.

(6.2) *$\hat{\theta}$ is an efficient estimator of θ if the following conditions are satisfied.*

(a) *$\hat{\theta}$ is unbiased.*
(b) *$Var(\hat{\theta}) \leq Var(\tilde{\theta})$, where $\tilde{\theta}$ is any other unbiased estimator of θ.*

An efficient estimator thus defined is also sometimes called "minimum variance unbiased estimator" (MVUE) or "best unbiased estimator." Note that, by our definition, an even slightly biased estimator cannot be called efficient no matter how small its variance is. A diagrammatic illustration of efficiency is given in Figure 6-2. Here are shown the distributions of three estimators of θ, namely, $\hat{\theta}_a$, $\hat{\theta}_b$, and

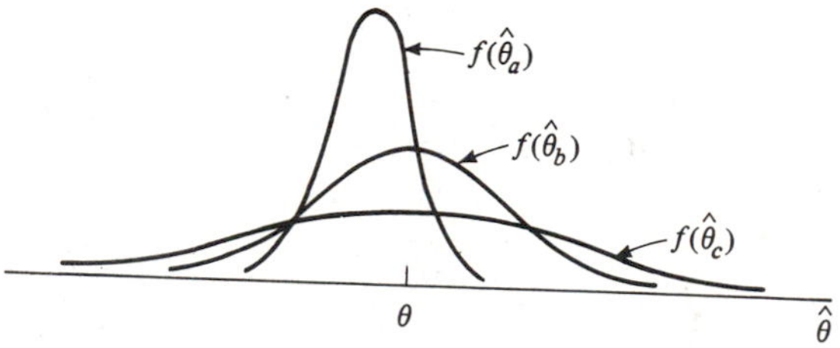

Figure 6-2

$\hat{\theta}_c$. Of these, $\hat{\theta}_a$ has the smallest variance but is not efficient because it is biased. Furthermore, $\hat{\theta}_b$ and $\hat{\theta}_c$ are both unbiased, but $\hat{\theta}_c$ has a larger variance than $\hat{\theta}_b$ so that $\hat{\theta}_c$ is also not efficient. That leaves $\hat{\theta}_b$, which is efficient *providing* there is no other unbiased estimator that would have a smaller variance than $\hat{\theta}_b$.

The last remark brings us to considering one practical aspect of efficiency, and that is the problem of ascertaining whether a given estimator is or is not efficient. We have not worried about this kind of a problem in connection with unbiasedness since there the problem is, at least in principle, quite trivial. All we have to do to check whether an estimator is or is not unbiased is to determine its mathematical expectation, i.e., the mean of its sampling distribution. In connection with efficiency, and in particular with the condition of minimum variance, the problem is potentially very complex. Since we have to make a statement about the variance of *all* unbiased estimators, of which there may be an infinite number, it may be hard to claim that a particular estimator is efficient. One way of avoiding this difficulty is by lowering our standards and, instead of proclaiming a given unbiased estimator as better—in the sense of having a smaller variance—or at least as good as any other unbiased estimator, we may be satisfied with the claim that the estimator in question is better than some other unbiased estimator. Thus, in comparing two unbiased estimators, we could concern ourselves merely with their *relative efficiency* and declare the estimator that has a smaller variance more efficient than the other estimator. A case in point is the comparison of sample mean and sample median as estimators of population mean. As we saw in Section 2-2, both estimators are unbiased, but the variance of sample mean is smaller than the variance of sample median. Then we can say that sample mean is a more efficient estimator of the population mean relative to sample median.

Fortunately, in quite a few cases there is no need for us to confine ourselves to comparing the variances of a small number of estimators, since we can make a definite statement concerning efficiency in an absolute sense. The reason is the existence of the following theorem, which is known as the *Cramer–Rao inequality*.

Theorem 17 *Let X be a random variable with a probability distribution f(x) characterized by parameters* $\theta_1, \theta_2, \ldots, \theta_k$. *Let* $\hat{\theta}_i$ *be any unbiased estimator of* θ_i *derived from a sample* $X_1, X_2, \ldots, X_n$. *Define* $L = \log f(x_1, x_2, \ldots, x_n)$; *L is known as the logarithmic likelihood function of a given sample. Form the following matrix:*

$$\begin{bmatrix} -E\left[\dfrac{\partial^2 L}{\partial\theta_1^2}\right] & -E\left[\dfrac{\partial^2 L}{\partial\theta_1\partial\theta_2}\right] & \cdots & -E\left[\dfrac{\partial^2 L}{\partial\theta_1\partial\theta_k}\right] \\ -E\left[\dfrac{\partial^2 L}{\partial\theta_2\partial\theta_2}\right] & -E\left[\dfrac{\partial^2 L}{\partial\theta_1^2}\right] & \cdots & -E\left[\dfrac{\partial^2 L}{\partial\theta_2\partial\theta_k}\right] \\ \vdots & \vdots & & \vdots \\ -E\left[\dfrac{\partial^2 L}{\partial\theta_k\partial\theta_1}\right] & -E\left[\dfrac{\partial^2 L}{\partial\theta_k\partial\theta_2}\right] & \cdots & -E\left[\dfrac{\partial^2 L}{\partial\theta_k^2}\right] \end{bmatrix}$$

The matrix is called the information matrix. Consider now the inverse of the information matrix, and call the element in the ith row and the ith column of this inverse matrix I^{ii}. Then the Cramer–Rao inequality is

$$\mathrm{Var}(\hat{\theta}_i) \geq I^{ii}.$$

This theorem enables us to construct a lower limit (greater than zero) for the variance of *any* unbiased estimator providing we can specify the functional form of the parent distribution.[1] The lower limit specified in the theorem is called the *Cramer–Rao lower bound.* If we can find an unbiased estimator whose variance is equal to the Cramer–Rao lower bound, then we know that no other unbiased estimator can have a smaller variance and the estimator under consideration is efficient. For example, we know that the variance of sample mean $\bar{X}$ is equal to (σ^2/n). Now if the parent population is normal, then it can be shown that (σ^2/n) is, in fact, equal to the Cramer–Rao lower bound for unbiased estimators of the population mean. Therefore $\bar{X}$ is an efficient estimator of the mean of a normal population. It should be noted, though, that the use of the Cramer–Rao inequality need not always work to our satisfaction, because the lower bound need not be *attainable* by any unbiased estimator. For instance, in the case of estimating the variance of a normal population the Cramer–Rao lower bound for an unbiased estimator is $(2\sigma^4/n)$, but there is *no* unbiased estimator of σ^2 that would have a variance as low as that.[2]

The preceding discussion indicates that determining efficiency is not without difficulties. At best we have to be able to specify the form of the parent distribution and hope that there is an unbiased estimator with variance equal to the Cramer–Rao lower bound. If we do not know the form of the parent distribution, then we have little hope of establishing that a given estimator is or is not efficient. For this reason we may be willing to abandon the idea of looking for an estimator with minimum variance among *all* unbiased estimators and may confine our attention to a smaller class of unbiased estimators. In fact, it turns out that the problem of finding an unbiased estimator with minimum variance may be quite simple if we confine ourselves to the estimators that are *linear* functions of the sample observations. This has led to the definition of a more specialized concept of efficiency as described below.

(6.3) *$\hat{\theta}$ is a best linear unbiased estimator (or BLUE) of θ if the following three conditions are satisfied.*

(a) *$\hat{\theta}$ is a linear function of the sample observations.*
(b) *$\hat{\theta}$ is unbiased.*
(c) *$Var(\hat{\theta}) \leq Var(\tilde{\theta})$, where $\hat{\theta}$ is any other linear unbiased estimator of θ.*

[1] This inequality holds under very general conditions. Full details are given in, e.g., C. R. Rao, *Linear Statistical Inference and Its Applications,* 2nd ed. (New York: Wiley, 1973).

[2] *Ibid.*

The condition of linearity means that, for a sample $X_1, X_2, \ldots, X_n$, the estimator has to be of the form $a_1X_1 + a_2X_2 + \cdots + a_nX_n$, where $a_1, a_2, \ldots, a_n$ are some constants. Thus, for instance, $\bar{X}$ is a linear estimator since

$$\bar{X} = \frac{1}{n}\sum_{i=1}^{n} X_i = \frac{1}{n}X_1 + \frac{1}{n}X_2 + \cdots + \frac{1}{n}X_n.$$

Concerning the relationship between best linear unbiasedness and efficiency, one of the following situations may prevail.

1. The efficient estimator is itself linear in the sample observations. In this case the BLUE and the efficient estimator are identical. Thus, for example, since $\bar{X}$ is an efficient estimator of the mean of a normal population, μ, and since $\bar{X}$ is linear in the sample observations, $\bar{X}$ is also the BLUE of μ.
2. The efficient estimator is *approximately* linear. In this case the BLUE is not efficient, but its variance is likely to be close to that of the efficient estimator.
3. The efficient estimator is highly nonlinear. In this case the variance of the efficient estimator may be quite considerably smaller than that of BLUE.

It should be noted that the linearity condition may be appropriate for estimating means but would be quite inappropriate for estimating higher order moments such as variances. An appropriate property for estimating the variance would be *best quadratic unbiasedness* (BQU).

Another finite sample property of an estimator which is sometimes mentioned is *sufficiency.* An estimator is said to be sufficient if it utilizes all the information about the parameter that is contained in the sample. Since the value of every observation tells us something about the population, an estimator, to be sufficient, must be based on the values of all sample observations. Thus, for instance, sample median is not a sufficient estimator since it uses only the ranking and not the values of sample observations. Note that there is nothing desirable about sufficiency as such; we obviously do not care whether an estimation formula does or does not utilize all the sample observations as long as it produces good estimates of the parameter in question. The real relevance of sufficiency lies in the fact that sufficiency is a necessary condition for efficiency.[3] That is, an estimator cannot be efficient—as defined in (6.2)—unless it makes use of all the sample information. It has also been shown that unbiasedness and sufficiency imply efficiency. (This is known as the *Blackwell-Rao theorem.*)

The three properties—unbiasedness, efficiency, and best linear unbiasedness—represent all the desirable small sample properties of estimators that are important and commonly mentioned in econometric work. They are all defined in terms of means and variances and thus cannot be determined for those estimators whose means or variances do not exist. For instance, let us consider unbiasedness. If $\hat{\theta}$ is an

[3] See, e.g., B. W. Lindgren, *Statistical Theory,* 3rd ed. (New York: Macmillan, 1976), p. 264.

estimator of θ whose distribution is continuous and described by $f(\hat{\theta})$, then, for $\hat{\theta}$ to be unbiased, we would require that

$$E(\hat{\theta}) = \theta.$$

But, by definition,

$$E(\hat{\theta}) = \int_{-\infty}^{+\infty} \hat{\theta} f(\hat{\theta}) d\hat{\theta}.$$

Now, the above integral represents nothing else but the area under the curve $\hat{\theta} f(\hat{\theta})$ measured from $-\infty$ to $+\infty$, and one cannot exclude the possibility that this area is infinite. If this happens, we say that the integral is *divergent* and that the mean of the distribution *does not exist.* We mention this since we will come across estimators whose mean or variance may not exist, and the reader should be clear as to what it means.

Asymptotic Properties

Let us now turn to the asymptotic properties of estimators. As mentioned earlier, these properties relate to the distribution of an estimator when the sample size is large and approaches infinity. In general, the distribution of a given estimator based on one sample size is different from the distribution of this estimator based on a different sample size. The distributions may differ not only with respect to the mean or variance but even with respect to the mathematical form. Take, for example, the distribution of the mean of samples from a discrete uniform population discussed at the beginning of Section 4-3. We found that for samples of size 1, the distribution was uniform, i.e., rectangular in shape; for samples of size 2, the distribution was triangular (see Figure 4-12); and for larger sample sizes, the distribution was close to being normal. The process of change in the distribution of sample mean for samples from *any* population is described by the Central Limit Theorem (i.e., Theorem 16 in Section 4-3). This theorem states, in essence, that as the sample size increases, the distribution of sample mean approaches the normal distribution. Then we say that normal distribution is the *asymptotic* (or *limiting*) *distribution* of sample mean. In general, if the distribution of an estimator tends to become more and more similar in form to some specific distribution as the sample size increases, then such a specific distribution is called the *asymptotic distribution* of the estimator in question.

The use of the term "asymptotic" should not lead the reader to think that the asymptotic distribution is necessarily the final form that the distribution of an estimator takes as the sample size approaches infinity. In fact, what typically happens to the distribution of an estimator as the sample size approaches infinity is that it collapses on one point—hopefully that representing the true value of the parameter. (A distribution that is entirely concentrated at one point is called a *degenerate* distribution.) Again take the distribution of sample mean as an example. We know (by Theorem 15 of Section 4-3) that for *every* sample size the mean of this distribution is equal to the population mean and its variance is equal to (σ^2/n), where σ^2 is the population variance and n is the sample size. Now, clearly, as the sample size approaches infinity, (σ^2/n) approaches zero, and the distribution will collapse on the population mean. A graphical representation of such a distribution would show a straight vertical line of height equal to 1. This is obviously *not* the normal distribution that, as we know by the Central Limit Theorem, represents the asymptotic distribution of sample mean. What is meant by the asymptotic distribution is not the ultimate form of the distribution, which may be degenerate, but the form that the distribution tends to put on in the last part of its journey to the final collapse (if this occurs). As for the distribution of sample mean, as the sample size increases, the distribution will have a smaller and smaller variance, but it also will look more and more like a normal distribution. Just before the distribution collapses, it will be indistinguishable from a normal distribution, although one with an extremely small variance.

Having discussed the meaning of "asymptotic distribution," we can now turn to the problem of how to determine its existence and its form. In many cases this is relatively simple. First, some estimators have a distribution which is of the same form regardless of the sample size, and this form is known. If that is the case, then the estimators will also have that form when the sample size is large and approaches infinity. The asymptotic distribution of these estimators is therefore the same as the finite sample distribution. An example is sample mean as an estimator of the mean of a *normal* population. The distribution of sample mean in this case is normal for *every* sample size, with mean equal to the population mean and variance equal to σ^2/n. Therefore, the asymptotic distribution of sample mean is also normal with mean μ and variance σ^2/n. Second, some estimators have a distribution which, although not necessarily always of the same form, is known for every sample size. The asymptotic distribution of these estimators is the distribution based on a sample size that tends to infinity. This case is exemplified by the distribution of sample proportion of successes. As we found in Section 4-2, this distribution is binomial but converges to a normal distribution as n approaches infinity. Thus the asymptotic distribution of sample proportion of successes is normal. Third, for some estimators the distribution is not necessarily known for every sample size, but it is known for $n \to \infty$. An example of such an estimator is sample mean as an estimator of the mean of a nonnormal population. We know, by the Central Limit Theorem, that this distribution tends to become normal as $n \to \infty$. The three categories of estimators just enumerated cover most of the estimation problems encountered in economics. Furthermore, in practice many asymptotic distributions are normal, which is convenient since the normal distribution is so well known.

Asymptotic distributions, like other distributions, may be characterized by their moments. Of these the most important are the mean, known as the *asymptotic mean,* and the variance, known as the *asymptotic variance.* The asymptotic mean may be found by determining the limiting value (as $n \to \infty$) of the finite sample mean. Consider an estimator $\hat{\theta}$. By definition, the mean of this estimator is equal to its mathematical expectation, i.e., $E(\hat{\theta})$. Its *asymptotic mean* is equal to $\lim_{n\to\infty} E(\hat{\theta})$ providing, of course, that the mean of $\hat{\theta}$ exists. The asymptotic variance, however, is *not* equal to $\lim_{n\to\infty} \text{Var}(\hat{\theta})$. The reason is that in the case of estimators whose variance decreases with an increase in n, the variance will approach zero as $n \to \infty$. This will happen when the distribution collapses on a point. But, as we explained, the asymptotic distribution is *not* the same as the collapsed (degenerate) distribution, and its variance is *not* zero. For example, consider the distribution of sample mean. The asymptotic distribution of sample mean is normal and its variance is σ^2/n. But $\lim_{n\to\infty}(\sigma^2/n) = 0$, which is not the variance of a normal distribution. The term "asymptotic variance" is thus somewhat misleading; it is, strictly speaking, just an abbreviation for the term "variance of the asymptotic distribution." The following formula for asymptotic variance may often by used[4]

$$\text{Asympt. Var}(\hat{\theta}) = \frac{1}{n} \lim_{n\to\infty} E[\sqrt{n}(\hat{\theta} - \theta)]^2,$$

assuming that $\lim_{n\to\infty} E(\hat{\theta}) = \theta$. To avoid the awkwardness of premultiplying a limit as n goes to infinity by the reciprocal of n, many statisticians prefer to work with $\sqrt{n}(\hat{\theta} - \theta)$ rather than with $\hat{\theta}$ itself. This leads to the following "cleaner" definition.

$$\text{Asympt. Var}[\sqrt{n}(\hat{\theta} - \theta)] = \lim_{n\to\infty} E[\sqrt{n}(\hat{\theta} - \theta)]^2.$$

In what follows we shall describe three so-called asymptotic properties of an estimator which are considered desirable: asymptotic unbiasedness, consistency, and asymptotic efficiency. Two of these, asymptotic unbiasedness and asymptotic efficiency, are defined in terms of specific features of the asymptotic distribution of an estimator as just described, while the remaining property, consistency, is defined as a feature of the "collapsed" (i.e., degenerate) distribution given when $n \to \infty$.

Let us begin with the *asymptotic unbiasedness.*

(6.4) *$\hat{\theta}$ is an asymptotically unbiased estimator of θ if $\lim_{n\to\infty} E(\hat{\theta}) = \theta$.*

This definition simply states that an estimator is asymptotically unbiased if it becomes unbiased as the sample size approaches infinity. Note that if an estimator is unbiased, it is also asymptotically unbiased, but the reverse is not necessarily true. Unbiasedness implies asymptotic unbiasedness, because if an estimator is unbiased, its expectation is equal to the true value of the parameter for *every* sample size, including one close to infinity. A common example of a biased but asymptotically unbiased estimator is the sample variance

$$\hat{\sigma}^2 = \frac{1}{n} \sum_{i=1}^{n} (X_i - \bar{X})^2$$

and, by (5.4),

$$\lim_{n\to\infty} E(\hat{\sigma}^2) = \lim_{n\to\infty} \left(\frac{n-1}{n}\right)\sigma^2 = \sigma^2,$$

since $(n-1)/n$ approaches unity as $n \to \infty$.

[4] See A. S. Goldberger, *Econometric Theory* (New York: Wiley, 1964), p. 116.

The next desirable property to consider is *consistency.* As mentioned above, this property is defined in reference to the "collapsed" distribution of an estimator when $n \rightarrow \infty$. The point on which the distribution of an estimator, say, $\hat{\theta}$, collapses is called the *probability limit of* $\hat{\theta}$, frequently abbreviated as plim $\hat{\theta}$. More formally, let θ^* be some point which may or may not be equal to θ. Then the statement

$$\text{plim } \hat{\theta} = \theta^*$$

is equivalent to the statement

$$\lim_{n \rightarrow \infty} P(\theta^* - \varepsilon \leq \hat{\theta} \leq \theta^* + \varepsilon) = 1,$$

where ε is any arbitrarily small positive number. We say then that $\hat{\theta}$ *converges in probability* to θ^*. Now, an estimator is considered to be consistent if it collapses on the point of the true value of the parameter. Specifically,

(6.5) *$\hat{\theta}$ is a consistent estimator of θ if plim $\hat{\theta} = \theta$.*

A way of finding whether an estimator is consistent is to trace the behavior of the bias and of the variance of an estimator as the sample size approaches infinity. If the increase in sample size is accompanied by a reduction in bias (if there is one) as well as in variance, and if this continues until both the bias and the variance approach zero when $n \rightarrow \infty$, then the estimator in question is consistent. This is depicted in Figure 1-4. Since the sum of squared bias and variance is equal to the mean square error, the disappearance of the bias and the variance as $n \rightarrow \infty$ is equivalent to the disappearance of the mean square error. Thus we can state the following.

(6.6) *If $\hat{\theta}$ is an estimator of θ and if $\lim_{n\rightarrow\infty} MSE(\hat{\theta}) = 0$, then $\hat{\theta}$ is a consistent estimator of θ.*

The condition described by (6.6) is, in general, a sufficient but not necessary condition for consistency. That is, it is possible to find estimators whose mean square error does *not* approach zero when $n \rightarrow \infty$, and yet they are consistent. Such a situation may arise when the asymptotic distribution of an estimator is such that its mean or variance does not exist. This complicates the problem of determinng whether an estimator is consistent or not. Fortunately, estimators with nonexisting asymptotic means or variances are not frequent.

EXAMPLE Following is an example[5] of a consistent estimator whose mean square error does not approach zero when $n \rightarrow \infty$. Let $\hat{\alpha}$ be an estimator of α, and let the probability distribution of $\hat{\alpha}$ be

$\hat{\alpha}$	$f(\hat{\alpha})$
α	$1 - \frac{1}{n}$
n	$\frac{1}{n}$

[5] This example was suggested by Phoebus Dhrymes.

That is, $\hat{\alpha}$ can assume only two different values, α and n. Clearly, $\hat{\alpha}$ is consistent since as $n \rightarrow \infty$, the probability that $\hat{\alpha}$ is equal to α will approach unity. But

$$\lim_{n\rightarrow\infty} \text{MSE}(\hat{\alpha}) = \lim_{n\rightarrow\infty} E(\hat{\alpha} - \alpha)^2$$

$$= \lim_{n\rightarrow\infty} \left[(\alpha - \alpha)^2 \left(1 - \frac{1}{n}\right) + (n - \alpha)^2 \left(\frac{1}{n}\right)\right] = \infty.$$

If we expressly exclude such estimators from consideration and confine ourselves to estimators with finite asymptotic means and variances, then condition (6.6) represents a necessary, as well as a sufficient, condition for consistency. Some authors refer to this somewhat more limited concept as the *square-error consistency.*[6] Since the fact that the mean square error of an estimator approaches zero as $n \rightarrow \infty$ implies that bias also goes to zero, an estimator which is square-error consistent is necessarily asymptotically unbiased. The reverse is not true, since asymptotic unbiasedness *alone* is not sufficient for square-error consistency.

An important feature of consistent estimators is the fact that any continuous function of a consistent estimator is itself a consistent estimator. This is established by the following theorem.

Theorem 18 *(Slutsky Theorem) If plim $\hat{\theta} = \theta$ and $g(\hat{\theta})$ is a continuous function of $\hat{\theta}$, then plim $g(\hat{\theta}) = g(\theta)$.*

The proof of this theorem is given elsewhere.[7] This property of consistent estimators, sometimes also described as "consistency carries over," is very convenient, and we shall make good use of it later on. It means, for instance, that if $\hat{\theta}$ is a consistent estimator of θ, then $(1/\hat{\theta})$ is a consistent estimator of $(1/\theta)$, $\log \hat{\theta}$ is a consistent estimator of $\log \theta$, etc. Note carefully that the same does not, in general, apply to unbiasedness. That is, unlike consistency, unbiasedness *does not* "carry over," at least not to nonlinear functions. In particular, the fact that $\hat{\theta}$ is an unbiased estimator of θ does not imply that $(1/\hat{\theta})$ is an unbiased estimator of $(1/\theta)$, or that $\log \hat{\theta}$ is an unbiased estimator of $\log \theta$, and so on.

The last desirable property that we shall mention is *asymptotic efficiency,* which is related to the dispersion of the asymptotic distribution of an estimator. Asymptotic efficiency is defined only for those estimators whose asymptotic mean and variance exist (i.e., are equal to some finite numbers). In fact, it is a property that gives us a criterion of choice within the family of estimators that are square error consistent (and therefore asymptotically unbiased). Given that the distribution of consistent estimators collapses on the true value of the parameter when $n \rightarrow \infty$, preference should be given to those estimators that approach this point in the fastest possible way. These will be the estimators whose asymptotic distributions have the smallest variance. This is because asymptotic distribution represents the last stage

[6] See, e.g., A. M. Mood and F. A. Graybill, *Introduction to the Theory of Statistics* (New York: McGraw-Hill, 1963), p. 176.

[7] See S. S. Wilks, *Mathematical Statistics* (New York: Wiley, 1962), pp. 102–103.

before the distribution completely collapses, and estimators with the smallest variance are closer to collapsing than other consistent estimators.

The above considerations lead to the following definition of asymptotic efficiency.

(6.7) *$\hat{\theta}$ is an asymptotically efficient estimator of θ if all of the following conditions are satisfied.*

(a) *$\hat{\theta}$ has an asymptotic distribution with finite mean and finite variance.*
(b) *$\hat{\theta}$ is consistent.*
(c) *No other consistent estimator of θ has a smaller asymptotic variance than $\hat{\theta}$.*

The first two conditions taken together state that an estimator must be square-error consistent to qualify for asymptotic efficiency. Whether this is or is not satisfied can be established simply by determining the limiting value (as $n \to \infty$) of the mean square error. The estimator in question is or is not square-error consistent depending upon whether the limiting value of its mean square error is or is not equal to zero. To establish whether a consistent estimator satisfies the third condition of asymptotic efficiency is more difficult, very much like the problem of establishing efficiency in the finite sample case. As in the case of finite sample efficiency, the question of the smallest asymptotic variance can be settled only for those estimators for which we know the distributional form of the parent population. For such estimators we can establish asymptotic efficiency by comparing their asymptotic variance with the Cramer-Rao lower bound (as defined in Theorem 17); if the two are equal, then the estimator in question is asymptotically efficient. Thus both efficiency and asymptotic efficiency are established by reference to the Cramer-Rao lower bound—in the case of efficiency by comparing it with ordinary (finite sample) variance and in the case of asymptotic efficiency by comparing it with asymptotic variance. Since an efficient estimator is efficient for *any* sample size no matter how large, it follows that efficiency implies asymptotic efficiency. The reverse, however, is not true.

Concluding Remarks

This brings us toward the end of our discussion of desirable properties of an estimator. These properties can be listed as follows.

Finite (small) sample properties	Asymptotic (large) sample properties
Unbiasedness	Asymptotic unbiasedness
Efficiency	Consistency
BLUE	Asymptotic efficiency

In our early discussion of estimation in Section 1-4, we compared estimation of a parameter to shooting at a target with a rifle. The bull's-eye can be taken to represent the true value of the parameter, the rifle the estimator, and each shot a particular estimate (calculated from a particular sample). The distance from the target is inversely related to the size of sample. In this parallel desirable properties of an estimator are described in terms of various qualities of a rifle. An unbiased rifle is one whose shots are scattered around the bull's-eye as the center, whereas the shots from a biased rifle are centered around some other point. If we compare all unbiased rifles, then that rifle whose shots are, on the whole, closest to the bull's-eye is regarded as efficient. If we know what kind of bullet is being used, we can determine the minimum possible scatter of the shots; this corresponds to the Cramer–Rao lower bound. With respect to the BLUE property, the comparison is restricted to rifles of a particular and relatively simple construction. A BLUE rifle is unbiased and produces shots closer to the bull's-eye than the shots from any other unbiased rifle of the same construction. Coming now to the asymptotic properties, we must consider the effect of decreasing the distance from the target. Asymptotic unbiasedness means that the shots tend to become centered around the bull's-eye as the distance from the target decreases. Consistency means that the probability of hitting the bull's-eye, or being within some small distance from it, increases with a decrease in distance. Square-error consistency (which implies consistency) can be viewed as the tendency for the shots to become centered around the bull's-eye and to be less and less scattered as the distance is decreased. Finally, a rifle can be considered asymptotically efficient if it is square-error consistent, and if its shots are closer to the bull's eye than those from other consistent rifles when the distance from the target is nearly negligible.

The discussion about desirable properties of estimators presented in this section is quite crucial since it provides a basis for much of the work in econometrics. We shall close it by giving an example of the determination of various properties of three estimators of the mean of a normal population.

EXAMPLE Let X be a normally distributed variable with mean μ and variance σ^2. Consider the problem of estimating μ from a random sample of observations on $X_1, X_2, \ldots, X_n$. Three estimators are proposed.

$$\bar{X} = \frac{1}{n}\sum_{i=1}^{n} X_i,$$

$$\hat{\mu} = \frac{1}{n+1}\sum_{i=1}^{n} X_i,$$

$$\tilde{\mu} = \frac{1}{2}X_1 + \frac{1}{2n}\sum_{i=2}^{n} X_i.$$

What are the desirable properties (if any) of each of these estimators?

1. *Unbiasedness*

$$E(\bar{X}) = E\left(\frac{1}{n}\sum_{i=1}^{n} X_i\right) = \frac{1}{n}\sum_{i=1}^{n} E(X_i) = \mu;$$

i.e., $\bar{X}$ is unbiased.

$$E(\hat{\mu}) = E\left(\frac{1}{n+1}\sum_{i=1}^{n} X_i\right) = \left(\frac{n}{n+1}\right)\mu;$$

i.e., $\hat{\mu}$ is biased.

$$E(\tilde{\mu}) = E\left(\frac{1}{2}X_1 + \frac{1}{2n}\sum_{i=2}^{n} X_i\right) = \frac{1}{2}E(X_1) + \frac{1}{2n}\sum_{i=2}^{n} E(X_i)$$

$$= \frac{1}{2}\mu + \left(\frac{n-1}{2n}\right)\mu = \left(\frac{2n-1}{2n}\right)\mu;$$

i.e., $\tilde{\mu}$ is biased.

2. *Efficiency*. Since $\hat{\mu}$ and $\tilde{\mu}$ are biased, only $\bar{X}$ qualifies as a candidate for efficiency. We know that the variance of $\bar{X}$ is (σ^2/n). We know further that the sample comes from a normal population. Therefore we can determine the Cramer–Rao lower bound for the variance of an unbiased estimator of μ. It can be shown that this is also equal to (σ^2/n), from which it follows that $\bar{X}$ is an efficient estimator of μ.

3. *BLUE*. Here again only $\bar{X}$ qualifies as a candidate, since the other two estimators are biased. $\bar{X}$ also satisfies the condition of linearity since

$$\bar{X} = \frac{1}{n}\sum_{i=1}^{n} X_i = \frac{1}{n}X_1 + \frac{1}{n}X_2 + \cdots + \frac{1}{n}X_n.$$

Finally, since $\bar{X}$ is efficient, it has the smallest variance among *all* unbiased estimators. Therefore $\bar{X}$ must also have the smallest variance among those unbiased estimators which are linear in observations. Consequently $\bar{X}$ is BLUE. (A full derivation of the BLUE property of $\bar{X}$ independent of the form of the parent distribution is given in Section 6-2.)

4. *Asymptotic unbiasedness*

$$\lim_{n\to\infty} E(\bar{X}) = \lim_{n\to\infty} \mu = \mu;$$

i.e., $\bar{X}$ is asymptotically unbiased.

$$\lim_{n\to\infty} E(\hat{\mu}) = \lim_{n\to\infty} \left(\frac{n}{n+1}\right)\mu = \mu;$$

i.e., $\hat{\mu}$ is asymptotically unbiased.

$$\lim_{i\to\infty} E(\tilde{\mu}) = \lim_{n\to\infty} \left(\frac{2n-1}{2n}\right)\mu = \mu;$$

i.e., $\tilde{\mu}$ is asymptotically unbiased.

5. *Consistency*

$$\text{MSE}(\bar{X}) = \text{Var}(\bar{X}) = \frac{\sigma^2}{n},$$

$$\lim_{n\to\infty} \text{MSE}(\bar{X}) = 0;$$

i.e., $\bar{X}$ is consistent.

$$\text{MSE}(\hat{\mu}) = \text{Var}(\hat{\mu}) + (\text{Bias of } \hat{\mu})^2 = \text{Var}\left(\frac{1}{n+1}\sum_{i=1}^{n} X_i\right) + \left[\left(\frac{n}{n+1}\right)\mu - \mu\right]^2$$

$$= \left(\frac{1}{n+1}\right)^2 \sum_{i=1}^{n} \text{Var}(X_i) + \left(\frac{-1}{n+1}\right)^2 \mu^2 = \frac{n\sigma^2 + \mu^2}{(n+1)^2},$$

$$\lim_{n\to\infty} \text{MSE}(\hat{\mu}) = 0;$$

i.e., $\hat{\mu}$ is consistent.

$$\begin{aligned}\text{MSE}(\tilde{\mu}) &= \text{Var}(\tilde{\mu}) + (\text{Bias of } \tilde{\mu})^2 \\ &= \text{Var}\left(\frac{1}{2}X_1 + \frac{1}{2n}\sum_{i=2}^{n} X_i\right) + \left[\left(\frac{2n-1}{2n}\right)\mu - \mu\right]^2 \\ &= \frac{1}{4}\text{Var}(X_1) + \left(\frac{1}{2n}\right)^2 \sum_{i=2}^{n} \text{Var}(X_i) + \left(\frac{-1}{2n}\right)^2 \mu^2 \\ &= \frac{(n^2+n-1)\sigma^2 + \mu^2}{4n^2},\end{aligned}$$

$$\lim_{n\to\infty} \text{MSE}(\tilde{\mu}) = \frac{\sigma^2}{4}.$$

Since $\lim_{n\to\infty} \text{MSE}(\tilde{\mu})$ is not equal to zero, $\tilde{\mu}$ is not square-error consistent. In fact, it can be shown that $\tilde{\mu}$ is not consistent in the general sense either.

6. *Asymptotic efficiency.* $\bar{X}$ and $\hat{\mu}$ satisfy the condition of square-error consistency and thus qualify as candidates for asymptotic efficiency; $\tilde{\mu}$ does not qualify. Now, since $\bar{X}$ is efficient for *any* sample size, it is also efficient when the sample size increases toward infinity. Thus $\bar{X}$ is asymptotically efficient as well. Note that since $\text{Var}(\bar{X}) = (\sigma^2/n)$ for any n, (σ^2/n) is also the asymptotic variance of $\bar{X}$. Concerning $\hat{\mu}$, we have

$$\text{Var}(\hat{\mu}) = \frac{n\sigma^2}{(n+1)^2} = \left(\frac{n}{n+1}\right)^2 \frac{\sigma^2}{n}.$$

In large samples $n/(n+1)$ will be close to unity so that the asymptotic variance of $\hat{\mu}$ will be (σ^2/n). Since this is the same as the asymptotic variance of $\bar{X}$, and since $\bar{X}$ is asymptotically efficient, it follows that $\hat{\mu}$ is also asymptotically efficient.

The above results are summarized in Table 6-1. The general conclusion then is that $\bar{X}$ is the superior estimator in small samples, but in large samples $\bar{X}$ and $\hat{\mu}$ are equally good. The third estimator, $\tilde{\mu}$, has none of the desirable properties except for asymptotic unbiasedness.

Table 6-1

	Estimator		
Properties	$\bar{X}$	$\hat{\mu}$	$\tilde{\mu}$
Finite sample			
Unbiasedness	Yes	No	No
Efficiency	Yes	No	No
BLUE	Yes	No	No
Asymptotic properties			
Unbiasedness	Yes	Yes	Yes
Consistency	Yes	Yes	No
Efficiency	Yes	Yes	No

The disadvantage of using various desirable properties to choose an estimator is that we have no basis for assigning weights to different properties to reflect their importance. This can be avoided if we can specify the loss incurred in having only an estimate of θ rather than knowing its true value. Such a loss could be described by a loss function whose value would, in general, depend on the value of our estimator ($\hat{\theta}$) and the value of the parameter. One of the most common loss functions in use is the so-called quadratic loss function for which the loss incurred is proportional to the squared difference between $\hat{\theta}$ and θ, i.e.,

$$L(\hat{\theta}, \theta) = \lambda(\hat{\theta} - \theta)^2,$$

where λ is a proportionality factor. Since $L(\hat{\theta}, \theta)$ is a random variable, a reasonable criterion of optimality of $\hat{\theta}$ would be to minimize the *expected* loss given as

$$E[L(\hat{\theta}, \theta)] = \lambda E(\hat{\theta} - \theta)^2.$$

Thus the optimum estimator is that which minimizes the mean square error. An estimator $\hat{\theta}$ is called *inadmissible* if there exists another estimator $\tilde{\theta}$ such that

$$\text{MSE}(\tilde{\theta}) \leq \text{MSE}(\hat{\theta})$$

for every value of θ, and there is strict inequality for at least one value of θ. If that is the case, then we say that $\tilde{\theta}$ *dominates* $\hat{\theta}$. An estimator is admissible if it is not dominated by any other estimator. The use of the loss functions is advocated in the decision theoretic approach to estimation in the context of Bayesian inference. The difficulties of determining expected loss when θ is not known are overcome by the use of a prior distribution of θ. In the context of classical statistics, these difficulties are, as a rule, insurmountable.

6-2 Methods of Estimation

Having defined the desirable properties of estimators, we come to the problem of devising estimation formulas that would generate estimates with all or at least some of these desirable properties. At the outset of Section 6-1, we defined an estimator as an estimation formula which does not involve any unknown parameters. Estimators can originate in several ways. One possible way is to invoke some more or less intuitively plausible principle, use this principle to derive a formula, and then check whether the resulting estimator possesses any of the desirable properties. The estimators are given names that indicate the nature of the principle used in deriving the formula. The *method of moments,* the *least squares method,* and the *maximum likelihood method,* all lead to estimators of this kind. Another way of devising estimators is to construct an estimation formula in such a way that the desirable properties are built into it in the process of construction. The *BLUE method,* which leads to best linear unbiased estimators, is the most notable representative of this category.

Method of Moments

The *method of moments* is probably the oldest estimation method known in statistics. It is based on a very simple principle which states that one should estimate a moment of the population distribution by the corresponding moment of the sample. Thus the population mean is to be estimated by the sample mean, the population variance by the sample variance, and so on. As for the properties of the moments estimators, it can be shown that, under very general conditions, these estimators are square-error consistent (and therefore generally consistent) and asymptotically normal.[8] They may, of course, have other desirable properties as well, but this need not be so. For instance, the sample mean as an estimator of the population mean has other desirable properties in addition to consistency. The method of moments is not applicable when the population moments do not exist, and may be difficult to apply when dealing with more complicated problems of estimation.

Least Squares Estimation

Another method of estimation that has long been used is the *method of least squares*. This method is suitable for estimating moments about zero of a population distribution. The underlying principle is somewhat more involved than in the case of the method of moments. Consider a random variable X and its rth moment about zero,

$$E(X^r) = \mu_r',$$

where $r = 0, 1, 2, \ldots$. The sample to be used is given by $X_1, X_2, \ldots, X_n$. To derive the least squares estimator of μ_r' we form the sum

$$\sum_{i=1}^{n} [X_i^r - \mu_r']^2.$$

As the least squares estimator we select that value of μ_r' which makes the above sum as small as possible. For instance, to find the least squares estimator of the population mean μ $(=\mu_1')$, we find that value of μ that minimizes the sum

$$\sum_{i=1}^{n} [X_i - \mu]^2.$$

Note that since X_i^r is the ith observation on X^r and $E(X_i^r) = \mu_r'$ is the mean of X_i^r, the expression to be minimized is, in fact, equal to the sum of squared deviations of the observed values from their mean. The least squares estimator of this mean is that value which makes the sum as small as possible.

To derive the least squares estimation formula we have to solve the problem of minimizing a function with respect to a given "variable"—in our case with respect to μ_r'. It is well known from elementary calculus that a necessary condition for the occurrence of a minimum (or a maximum) is that the first derivative of the function to be minimized by equal to zero. That is, we have to differentiate the sum of squares with respect to μ_r', set this derivative equal to zero, and solve the resulting equation for μ_r'. The solution then satisfies the necessary condition for the occur-

[8] See, e.g., Lindgren, *op. cit.*, p. 268.

rence of a minimum or a maximum. However, it can be easily shown that what we are getting is really a minimum and not a maximum so that the solution does, in fact, represent the least squares estimator of μ'_r.

We may illustrate the derivation of the least squares estimation formula by considering the problem of estimating population mean. Here the sum to be minimized is

$$\sum_{i=1}^{n} (X_i - \mu)^2.$$

Differentiating with respect to μ we get

$$\frac{d\sum_i (X_i - \mu)^2}{d\mu} = \sum_i \left[\frac{d(X_i - \mu)^2}{d\mu}\right] = \sum_i 2(X_i - \mu)(-1) = -2\sum_i (X_i - \mu).$$

Equating this to zero and putting a "hat" on μ to indicate that it is only the estimator of μ (rather than its true value) that satisfies this equation, we obtain

$$-2\sum_i (X_i - \hat{\mu}) = 0,$$

$$\left(\sum_i X_i\right) - n\hat{\mu} = 0,$$

$$\hat{\mu} = \frac{1}{n}\sum_i X_i = \bar{X}.$$

Thus we find that the least squares estimator of the population mean is given by the sample mean, i.e., is equal to the moments estimator. As another example, let us derive the least squares estimator of $E(X^2) = \mu'_2$. In this case we minimize the sum

$$\sum_{i=1}^{n} (X_i^2 - \mu'_2)^2.$$

Differentiating with respect to μ'_2 gives

$$\frac{d\sum_i (X_i^2 - \mu'_2)^2}{d(\mu'_2)} = -2\sum_i (X_i^2 - \mu'_2).$$

Equating this to zero, we have

$$-2\sum_i (X_i^2 - \hat{\mu}'_2) = 0,$$

$$\left(\sum_i X_i^2\right) - n\hat{\mu}'_2 = 0,$$

$$\hat{\mu}'_2 = \frac{1}{n}\sum_i X_i^2,$$

which is the same as the moments estimator of μ'_2.

The properties of least squares estimators have to be established in each case. In the two examples given in the preceding paragraph, least squares estimators were the same as moments estimators and, therefore, we are justified in claiming that they are consistent. This need not be the case with more complicated models. Indeed, a large part of modern econometrics owes its existence to the discovery that in many economic models least squares estimators are, in fact, inconsistent estimators of the parameters of interest.

Maximum Likelihood Estimation

The third method of estimation is the *maximum likelihood method.* This method is based on the relatively simple idea that different populations generate different samples, and that any given sample is more likely to have come from some populations than from others. To illustrate this idea, let us consider the case of normal populations and a given sample of n observations. The sample observations are points on the numerical axis scattered around their mean. Suppose the observed sample mean is equal to 5. The question is: To which population does this sample most likely belong? In general, any normal population is a candidate. Since normal populations are fully characterized by a mean and a variance, they differ only with repect to these two parameters. Let us, for the time being, consider populations with the same variance. Of these the one with mean 5 will, of course, generate samples with mean equal to or near 5 more frequently than a population with mean 6, a population with mean 6 will generate such samples more frequently than a population with mean 7, and so on. Similar statements could be made by considering populations with means less than 5.

The foregoing argument is shown graphically in Figure 6-3. The points x_1,

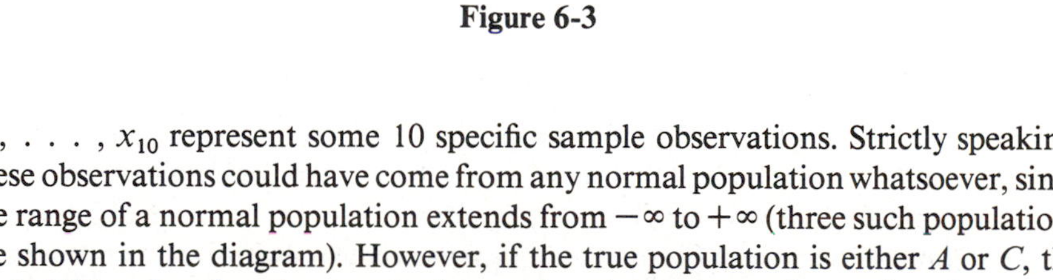

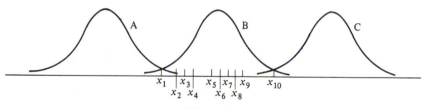

Figure 6-3

$x_2, \ldots, x_{10}$ represent some 10 specific sample observations. Strictly speaking, these observations could have come from any normal population whatsoever, since the range of a normal population extends from $-\infty$ to $+\infty$ (three such populations are shown in the diagram). However, if the true population is either A or C, the probability of getting the sample observations in the range shown (i.e., from x_1 to x_{10}) is very small. On the other hand, if the true population is B, then the probability of drawing observations in this range is very high. Thus we conclude that the particular sample is more likely to have come from population B than from population A or C.

In the example just given we have not considered populations that would differ with respect to the variance as well as the mean. Such an extension makes the explanation of the likelihood principle somewhat more complicated but leads to the same conclusion. A given sample may have come from a population characterized by *any* mean and *any* variance, but some populations would generate such a sample more frequently than others. Just as a sample with mean 5 is more likely to have come from a population with mean 5 than from a population with the same variance but with mean 6 or 7, so a sample with a large variance is more likely to have come from a population with a large variance than from a population with a small variance. All that is required is that we consider combinations of specific mean and variance in the population in relation to combinations of specific mean and variance in the sample.

With these introductory remarks in mind, we may now define *maximum likelihood estimators.*

> *If a random variable X has a probability distribution $f(x)$ characterized by parameters $\theta_1, \theta_2, \ldots, \theta_k$ and if we observe a sample $x_1, x_2, \ldots, x_n$, then the maximum likelihood estimators of $\theta_1, \theta_2, \ldots, \theta_k$ are those values of these parameters that would generate the observed sample most often.*

In other words, the maximum likelihood estimators of $\theta_1, \theta_2, \ldots, \theta_k$ are those values for which the probability (or probability density) of the given set of sample values is at maximum. That is, to find the maximum likelihood estimators of $\theta_1, \theta_2, \ldots, \theta_k$ we have to find those values which maximize $f(x_1, x_2, \ldots, x_n)$.

Let us take a simple example to illustrate the concept of the maximum likelihood estimator (MLE). Suppose X is a binary variable which assumes a value of 1 with probability π and a value of 0 with probability $(1 - \pi)$. That is,

$$f(0) = 1 - \pi,$$

$$f(1) = \pi.$$

This means that the distribution of X is characterized by a single parameter π, which can be viewed as the proportion of successes (or a probability of success) in the population. Suppose a random sample—drawn by sampling with replacement—consists of the three observations

$$\{1, 1, 0\}.$$

Our problem is to find the MLE of π. From the description of the population, it is obvious that π cannot be less than 0 or more than 1. To find which population would generate the given sample $\{1, 1, 0\}$ most often, we can simply consider various values of π between 0 and 1, and for these values determine the probability of drawing our sample. Let us start with $\pi = 0$. If this is the case, there are no "successes" in the population, and it would be impossible to observe two 1's. Thus for $\pi = 0$, the probability of drawing our sample is 0. Consider now $\pi = 1/10$. In this case the probability of drawing a 1 is 1/10 and the probability of drawing a 0 is

9/10. Therefore, the probability of drawing our sample in this case is

$$f(1, 1, 0) = f(1)f(1)f(0) = \frac{1}{10} \times \frac{1}{10} \times \frac{9}{10} = \frac{9}{1000},$$

since the sample observations are independent. (Recall that in the case of independence the joint probability is equal to the product of simple—i.e., marginal—probabilities.) Thus for $\pi = 1/10$ the probability of observing our sample is 9/1000. Similarly, we can calculate the probability of drawing {1, 1, 0} for other values of π. The results are

π	$f(1, 1, 0)$
0	0
1/10	0.009
2/10	0.032
3/10	0.063
4/10	0.096
5/10	0.125
6/10	0.144
7/10	0.147
8/10	0.128
9/10	0.081
1	0.000

The function $f(1, 1, 0)$ is the *likelihood function* for the sample {1, 1, 0}. In our calculations we selected values of π at intervals of one tenth. Obviously, we could have selected shorter intervals since the likelihood function is continuous. Figure 6-4, which is based on the preceding calculations, reveals that the likelihood function for our sample is maximized when π is about 0.7. That is, a population with

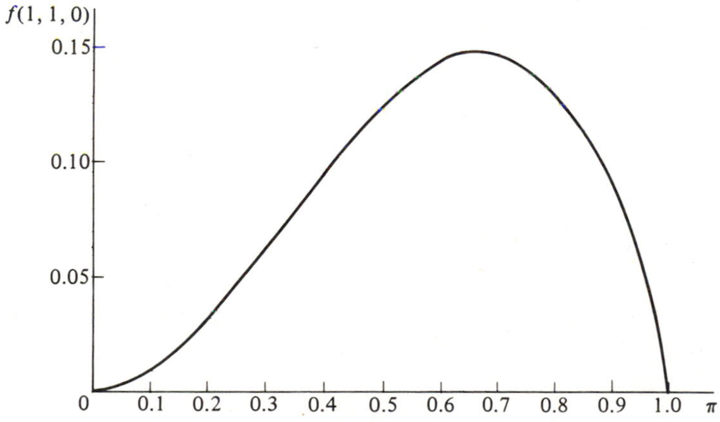

Figure 6-4

$\pi = 0.7$ would generate samples $\{1, 1, 0\}$ more frequently than any other population. Thus the MLE of π is 0.7 (see also Example 1 on page 180).

The concept of a *likelihood function* is crucial for the derivation of maximum likelihood estimates and thus deserves a more general explanation. A likelihood function, usually denoted by ℓ, is a name given to the formula of the joint probability distribution of the sample. The reader may recall our discussion in Sections 3-4 and 3-5 of a joint probability distribution of random variables $X, Y, Z, \ldots,$ described as $f(x, y, z, \ldots)$. It was stated that if $X, Y, Z,$ are independent, then we have

$$f(x, y, z, \ldots) = f(x)f(y)f(z) \ldots.$$

Now consider a random variable X with probability distribution $f(x)$ characterized by some parameters $\theta_1, \theta_2, \ldots, \theta_k$. A random sample $X_1, X_2, \ldots, X_n$ represents a set of n independent random variables, each having exactly the same probability distribution as X. Then the likelihood function ℓ is defined by the formula of the joint probability distribution of the sample, i.e.,

$$\ell = f(x_1, x_2, \ldots, x_n). \tag{6.8a}$$

Since the sample observations are independent, we can also write

$$\ell = f(x_1)f(x_2) \ldots f(x_n). \tag{6.8b}$$

While the formula for the joint probability distribution of the sample is exactly the same as that for the likelihood function, the interpretation of the formula is different. In the case of the joint probability distribution the parameters $\theta_1, \theta_2, \ldots, \theta_k$ are considered as fixed and the X's (representing the sample observations) as variable. In the case of the likelihood function the values of the parameters can vary but the X's are fixed numbers as observed in a particular sample. The maximum likelihood estimates are found by maximizing the likelihood function with respect to the parameters.

Obtaining the maximum likelihood estimators involves specifying the likelihood function and finding those values of the parameters that give this function its maximum value. As mentioned in connection with the least squares method, a necessary condition for a function to be at a maximum (or a minimum) is that at this point its first derivative is equal to zero. If there is only one unknown parameter in the likelihood function, then there is only one first derivative for which this applies. In general, however, the number of the unknown parameters in the likelihood function is more than one and we have to resort to partial derivatives. In this case it is required that the partial derivative of ℓ with respect to *each* of the unknown parameters is to be equal to zero. That is, if the unknown parameters are $\theta_1, \theta_2, \ldots, \theta_k$, the equations given by the necessary conditions for the occurrence of a maximum (or a minimum) are

$$\frac{\partial \ell}{\partial \theta_1} = 0, \quad \frac{\partial \ell}{\partial \theta_2} = 0, \quad \ldots, \quad \frac{\partial \ell}{\partial \theta_k} = 0. \tag{6.9a}$$

Thus we have k equations to solve for the values of the k unknown parameters.

These equations are sometimes referred to as the first-order conditions for the occurrence of a maximum (or a minimum). These conditions guarantee that, for the values of $\theta_1, \theta_2, \ldots, \theta_k$ obtained by solving the above equations, we may obtain a maximum *or* a minimum value of ℓ. To be sure that the solution of (6.9a) gives, in fact, a maximum value of ℓ, certain second-order conditions have to be fulfilled. A description of these conditions is beyond the scope of our discussion, but it is not very difficult to show that they are fulfilled in the cases with which we shall be dealing.[9] However, an easy way of ascertaining that we do *not* have a minimum (rather than a maximum) is by calculating the value of ℓ corresponding to the solution of (6.9a) and then calculating the value of ℓ for slightly different values of $\theta_1, \theta_2, \ldots, \theta_k$. If the second result gives a smaller number than the first, the first result obviously could *not* have been a minimum.

A final point to be made in connection with the maximization procedure concerns the form of the first-order conditions. In practice these conditions are usually stated somewhat differently than as given in (6.9a). The development of the alternative formulation is based on the fact that the *logarithm* of ℓ is a "monotonic transformation" of ℓ. This means that whenever ℓ is increasing, its logarithm is also increasing, and whenever ℓ is falling, its logarithm is also falling. Therefore, the point corresponding to the maximum of ℓ is also the point which corresponds to the maximum of the logarithm of ℓ. Since ℓ, being a formula for a joint probability distribution, can never be negative, there is no problem about obtaining its logarithm. A sketch illustrating the monotonicity of the logarithmic transformation in the case of one unknown parameter (θ) is given in Figure 6-5. The point $\hat{\theta}$ clearly

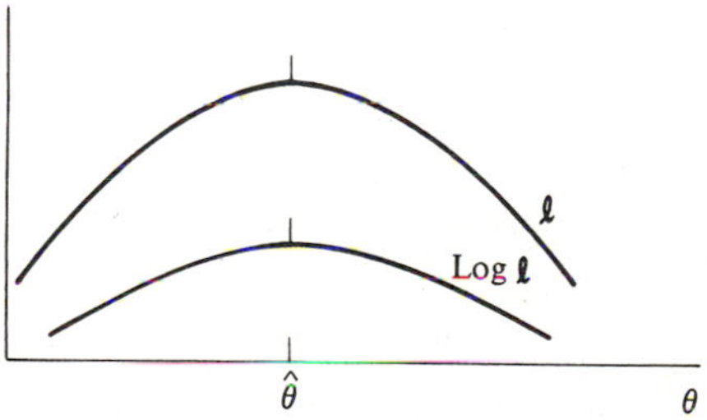

Figure 6-5

corresponds to a maximum on both the ℓ function as well as the log ℓ function. Therefore, it does not matter whether we maximize ℓ or log ℓ. Since in practice the solution of the first-order conditions turns out to be easier when working with log ℓ than with ℓ, we put

$$L = \log_e \ell$$

[9] A simple description of the second-order conditions can be found in, e.g., A. C. Chiang, *Fundamental Methods of Mathematical Economics,* 3rd ed. (New York: McGraw-Hill, 1984), pp. 315–318.

and restate the first-order conditions as

$$\text{(6.9b)} \qquad \frac{\partial L}{\partial \theta_1} = 0, \quad \frac{\partial L}{\partial \theta_2} = 0, \quad \ldots, \quad \frac{\partial L}{\partial \theta_k} = 0.$$

We shall illustrate the derivation of MLEs by presenting two examples. The first of these relates to the problem of estimating the proportion of "successes" in the population and provides a theoretical generalization of the graphical solution given in Figure 6-4. The second example deals with the standard problem of deriving the MLE of the mean of a normal population.

EXAMPLE 1 Suppose X is a binary variable which assumes a value of 1 with probability π and a value of 0 with probability $(1 - \pi)$. Observing a "1" can be considered a "success," and observing a "0" a "failure." Thus we have

$$f(0) = 1 - \pi,$$
$$f(1) = \pi.$$

Note that the probability distribution of X can be described by

$$f(x) = (1 - \pi)^{1-x}\pi^x.$$

We can check the appropriateness of this by substituting the values 0 and 1 for x. We get

$$f(0) = (1-\pi)^{1-0}\pi^0 = (1-\pi)^1 = 1 - \pi$$

and

$$f(1) = (1-\pi)^{1-1}\pi^1 = \pi^1 = \pi,$$

which agrees with the earlier specification. Also note that

$$E(X) = 0 \times (1 - \pi) + 1 \times \pi = \pi,$$

so that π can be interpreted as the mean of X. Now suppose we draw a random sample of n values $\{x_1, x_2, \ldots, x_n\}$. Our problem is to find the MLE of π. To this end we first derive the likelihood function.

$$\begin{aligned}
\ell &= f(x_1)f(x_2) \cdots f(x_n) \\
&= [(1-\pi)^{1-x_1}\pi^{x_1}][(1-\pi)^{1-x_2}\pi^{x_2}] \cdots [(1-\pi)^{1-x_n}\pi^{x_n}] \\
&= (1-\pi)^{(1-x_1)+(1-x_2)+\cdots+(1-x_n)}\pi^{x_1+x_2+\cdots+x_n} \\
&= (1-\pi)^{n-\Sigma x_i}\pi^{\Sigma x_i}.
\end{aligned}$$

The logarithm of this function is

$$L = \left(n - \sum x_i\right)\log(1-\pi) + \left(\sum x_i\right)\log \pi.$$

The only unknown parameter involved in L is π. Differentiating L with respect to π gives

$$\frac{dL}{d\pi} = \left(n - \sum x_i\right)\left(\frac{1}{1-\pi}\right)(-1) + \left(\sum x_i\right)\left(\frac{1}{\pi}\right).$$

Equating this to zero and putting a "triangle" on π to indicate that we are solving for an estimator of π and not for π itself, we obtain

$$\frac{\left(\sum x_i\right) - n}{1 - \hat{\pi}} + \frac{\sum x_i}{\hat{\pi}} = 0.$$

For a $\hat{\pi}$ not equal to 0 or 1 we can multiply both sides of the equation by $\hat{\pi}(1 - \hat{\pi})$ to get

$$\left[\left(\sum x_i\right) - n\right]\hat{\pi} + \left(\sum x_i\right)(1 - \hat{\pi}) = 0,$$

which gives

$$\hat{\pi} = \frac{1}{n} \sum x_i.$$

Since Σx_i is the number of "successes" and n is the number of all observations in the sample, the MLE of π is simply the proportion of successes found in the sample. In the specific case considered earlier, in which the sample was $\{1, 1, 0\}$, the MLE of π is

$$\hat{\pi} = \frac{2}{3} \cong 0.7.$$

EXAMPLE 2 Consider a normally distributed random variable X with mean μ and variance σ^2, i.e., $X \sim N(\mu, \sigma^2)$. We observe a random sample $\{x_1, x_2, \ldots, x_n\}$. Find the MLE of μ. Now the normal density function is defined as

$$f(x) = (2\pi\sigma^2)^{-1/2} e^{-(1/2)[(x-\mu)/\sigma]^2}$$

where $\pi = 3.14159$. Its logarithm is

$$\log f(x) = -\frac{1}{2}\log(2\pi\sigma^2) - \frac{1}{2}\left(\frac{x-\mu}{\sigma}\right)^2,$$

since $\log_e e = 1$. The likelihood function is

$$\ell = f(x_1) f(x_2) \cdots f(x_n),$$

and its logarithm is

$$L = \sum_{i=1}^{n} \log f(x_i).$$

Substituting for $\log f(x_i)$ gives

$$L = \sum_i \left[-\frac{1}{2}\log(2\pi\sigma^2) - \frac{1}{2}\left(\frac{x_i - \mu}{\sigma}\right)^2\right] = -\frac{n}{2}\log(2\pi\sigma^2) - \frac{1}{2\sigma^2}\sum_i (x_i - \mu)^2.$$

There are two unknown parameters involved in L: μ and σ^2. Differentiating with respect to each of them gives

$$\frac{\partial L}{\partial \mu} = -\frac{1}{2\sigma^2}\sum_i 2(x_i - \mu)(-1),$$

$$\frac{\partial L}{\partial(\sigma^2)} = -\frac{n}{2}\frac{1}{\sigma^2} + \frac{1}{2\sigma^4}\sum_i (x_i - \mu)^2.$$

Equating these to zero, we get

(6.10a) $$\frac{1}{\hat{\sigma}^2}\sum_i (x_i - \hat{\mu}) = 0,$$

(6.10b) $$-\frac{n}{2}\frac{1}{\hat{\sigma}^2} + \frac{1}{2\hat{\sigma}^4}\sum_i (x_i - \hat{\mu})^2 = 0.$$

For $\hat{\sigma}^2$ different from zero the first equation reduces to

$$\sum_i (x_i - \hat{\mu}) = 0,$$

giving

$$\hat{\mu} = \frac{1}{n}\sum_i x_i.$$

Thus the maximum likelihood estimator of the mean of a normal population is equal to the sample mean. It should be noted that the two equations (6.10a) and (6.10b) can also be solved for $\hat{\sigma}^2$, which is the MLE of σ^2. Multiplying the second equation by $2\hat{\sigma}^4$ leads to

$$-n\hat{\sigma}^2 + \sum_i (x_i - \hat{\mu})^2 = 0.$$

Substituting $\bar{x}$ for $\hat{\mu}$ and solving for $\hat{\sigma}^2$ gives

$$\hat{\sigma}^2 = \frac{1}{n}\sum_i (x_i - \bar{x})^2.$$

That is, the maximum likelihood estimator of the variance of a normal population is simply equal to the sample variance. As shown earlier, the sample variance is a *biased* estimator of the population variance. In fact, by equation (5.4) we see that

$$E(\hat{\sigma}^2) = \left(\frac{n-1}{n}\right)\sigma^2.$$

We mention this to illustrate the fact that a maximum likelihood estimator need not always be unbiased.

Knowledge of the likelihood function enables us to determine not only the MLEs of μ and σ^2 but also the Cramer–Rao lower bounds for the variances of the unbiased estimators of μ and σ^2. These are obtained by substituting into the formula for the information matrix given in Theorem 17 (Section 6-1) as follows.

$$\begin{bmatrix} -E\dfrac{\partial^2 L}{\partial \mu^2} & -E\dfrac{\partial^2 L}{\partial\mu\partial(\sigma^2)} \\ -E\dfrac{\partial^2 L}{\partial\mu\partial(\sigma^2)} & -E\dfrac{\partial^2 L}{\partial(\sigma^2)^2} \end{bmatrix}^{-1} = \begin{bmatrix} \dfrac{n}{\sigma^2} & 0 \\ 0 & \dfrac{n}{2\sigma^4} \end{bmatrix}^{-1} = \begin{bmatrix} \dfrac{\sigma^2}{n} & 0 \\ 0 & \dfrac{2\sigma^4}{n} \end{bmatrix}$$

The Cramer–Rao lower bound for an unbiased estimator of the mean of a normal population is given by the element in the upper left corner of the last matrix, i.e., it is equal to (σ^2/n). Note that since the off-diagonal term is zero, it follows that $\bar{X}$ and s^2 are asymptotically uncorrelated.

The maximum likelihood principle is based on the intuitively appealing idea of choosing those parameters from which the actually observed sample is most likely to have come. However, this intuitive appeal by itself is of little value unless the resulting estimators have some desirable properties. This, in fact, is the case. It can be shown[10] that, under quite general conditions, maximum likelihood estimators are

1. Square-error consistent.
2. Asymptotically efficient.

Another convenient feature of the MLEs is that their asymptotic distribution is normal, and that a formula for determining their asymptotic variances is readily available. In particular, the asymptotic variances of the MLEs are given by the diagonal elements of the inverse of the information matrix; that is, they are equal to the Cramer–Rao lower bounds. In finite samples we use as estimates of the asymptotic variances the diagonal elements of

$$\begin{bmatrix} -\dfrac{\partial^2 L}{\partial \theta_1^2} & -\dfrac{\partial^2 L}{\partial \theta_1 \partial \theta_2} & \cdots & -\dfrac{\partial^2 L}{\partial \theta_1 \partial \theta_k} \\ -\dfrac{\partial^2 L}{\partial \theta_2 \partial \theta_1} & -\dfrac{\partial^2 L}{\partial \theta_2^2} & \cdots & -\dfrac{\partial^2 L}{\partial \theta_2 \partial \theta_k} \\ \vdots & & & \\ -\dfrac{\partial^2 L}{\partial \theta_k \partial \theta_1} & -\dfrac{\partial^2 L}{\partial \theta_k \partial \theta_2} & \cdots & -\dfrac{\partial^2 L}{\partial \theta_k^2} \end{bmatrix}^{-1}$$

evaluated at θ_i = MLE of θ_i $(i = 1, 2, \ldots, k)$. While all these properties are only asymptotic, in many situations this is frequently all that we can hope for.

Best Linear Unbiased Estimation

The last method of estimation to be discussed at this stage is the *best linear unbiased estimation method.* This method, unlike the preceding ones, leads to an estimation formula which guarantees certain desirable properties by definition. Let $\tilde{\theta}$ be a best linear unbiased estimator (BLUE) of some parameter θ. Then the formula for $\tilde{\theta}$ must satisfy the following conditions.

1. $\tilde{\theta}$ is a linear function of the sample observations.
2. $E(\tilde{\theta}) = \theta$.
3. $\mathrm{Var}(\tilde{\theta}) \leq \mathrm{Var}(\theta^*)$, where θ^* is any other linear unbiased estimator of θ.

In addition, the formula for $\tilde{\theta}$ must not involve θ or any other unknown parameter, otherwise $\tilde{\theta}$ would not qualify as an estimator. To devise a best linear unbiased

[10] See, e.g., Wilks, *op. cit.*, pp. 358–365. The general conditions under which the MLEs have the stated properties are not very restrictive. The one condition which may sometimes cause problems and which is frequently neglected is the requirement that the number of parameters in the likelihood function be finite as $n \rightarrow \infty$.

estimator, we have to find that linear function of the sample observations which satisfies conditions 2 and 3. We shall show how to go about finding such a function by deriving the BLUE of the population mean.

Suppose a random variable X comes from a population with mean μ and variance σ^2. The sample observations are $X_1, X_2, \ldots, X_n$. We wish to find the BLUE of μ, say, $\tilde{\mu}$. To do that we consider each of the three conditions in turn.

1. *Linearity.* Since $\tilde{\mu}$ is to be a linear combination of the sample observations, we can write

$$\tilde{\mu} = \sum_{i=1}^{n} a_i X_i, \tag{6.11}$$

where $a_1, a_2, \ldots, a_n$ are constants to be determined. Thus the whole problem of finding the BLUE of μ is really a problem of specifying $a_1, a_2, \ldots, a_n$ in such a way that the conditions 2 and 3 are satisfied.

2. *Unbiasedness.* For $\tilde{\mu}$ to be unbiased we require that

$$E(\tilde{\mu}) = \mu.$$

Now

$$E(\tilde{\mu}) = E\left[\sum_i a_i X_i\right] = \sum_i a_i E(X_i) = \sum_i a_i \mu = \mu \sum_i a_i.$$

That is, for $E(\tilde{\mu})$ to be equal to μ we require that $\Sigma_i\, a_i = 1$. The condition then is that the constants $a_1, a_2, \ldots, a_n$ add up to unity.

3. *Minimum variance.* Finally, we require that, among all estimators of μ that satisfy the above conditions, $\tilde{\mu}$ is the one with the smallest variance. Using Theorem 13 of Section 3-7, we have

$$\text{Var}(\tilde{\mu}) = \text{Var}\left(\sum_i a_i X_i\right) = \sum_i a_i^2 \text{Var}(X_i) = \sigma^2 \sum_i a_i^2 \tag{6.12}$$

This means that we have to find $a_1, a_2, \ldots, a_n$ such that $\Sigma\, a_i = 1$ (by condition 2) and at the same time $\sigma^2\, \Sigma\, a_i^2$ is as small as possible. That is, our problem is to minimize $\sigma^2\, \Sigma\, a_i^2$ subject to the condition that $\Sigma\, a_i = 1$. This is a problem of minimizing a function subject to a constraint, and it can be solved with the help of the *Lagrange multiplier method.*[11]

Very briefly, the Lagrange multiplier method works as follows. Suppose we wish to find those values of $z_1, z_2, \ldots, z_m$ which would minimize (maximize) a function $F(z_1, z_2, \ldots, z_m)$ subject to the condition that $G(z_1, z_2. \ldots, z_m) = 0$. The function G is the constraint expressed in such a way that all terms are transferred to the left-hand side of the equation. Then we form a new function, say H, defined as

$$H = F(z_1, z_2, \ldots, z_m) - \lambda G(z_1, z_2, \ldots, z_m). \tag{6.13}$$

Here λ is the Lagrange multiplier. Its value is to be determined, along with the values of $z_1, z_2, \ldots, z_m$ that minimize (maximize) F subject to the condition G.

[11] See, e.g., Chiang, *op. cit.,* pp. 372–386.

To obtain the required solution we differentiate H with respect to $z_1, z_2, \ldots, z_m$ and λ and put each of the derivatives equal to zero. This gives us $(m+1)$ equations to be solved for the $(m+1)$ unknowns. The solution represents the first-order (necessary) conditions; the second-order conditions, which determine whether the solution is a minimum or a maximum, are given elsewhere.[12] A well-known application of the Lagrange multiplier method in economics arises in connection with the problem of utility maximization subject to the budget constraint.[13]

Let us turn now to the specific problem of minimizing $\sigma^2 \Sigma a_i^2$ subject to $\Sigma a_i = 1$. In this problem the function F to be minimized is

$$F(a_1, a_2, \ldots, a_n) = \sigma^2 \sum_i a_i^2,$$

and the constraint G is

$$G(a_1, a_2, \ldots, a_n) = \sum_i a_i - 1.$$

Following the Lagrange multiplier method, we form

$$H = \sigma^2 \sum_i a_i^2 - \lambda \left(\sum_i a_i - 1 \right).$$

The first-order conditions are

$$\text{(6.14a)} \qquad \frac{\partial H}{\partial a_1} = 0, \quad \frac{\partial H}{\partial a_2} = 0, \quad \ldots, \quad \frac{\partial H}{\partial a_n} = 0, \quad \frac{\partial H}{\partial \lambda} = 0,$$

or, explicitly,

$$\text{(6.14b)} \qquad \begin{aligned} 2a_1\sigma^2 - \lambda &= 0, \\ 2a_2\sigma^2 - \lambda &= 0, \\ &\vdots \\ 2a_n\sigma^2 - \lambda &= 0, \\ -\left(\sum_i a_i - 1 \right) &= 0. \end{aligned}$$

This gives us $(n+1)$ equations to be solved for the unknowns $a_1, a_2, \ldots, a_n$ and λ. From the first n equations we get

$$a_1 = \frac{\lambda}{2\sigma^2}, \quad a_2 = \frac{\lambda}{2\sigma^2}, \quad \ldots, \quad a_n = \frac{\lambda}{2\sigma^2}.$$

Substitution into the last equation gives

$$-\left(\frac{n\lambda}{2\sigma^2} - 1 \right) = 0,$$

[12] *Ibid.*

[13] See, e.g., *ibid.*, pp. 400–408.

or

$$\lambda = \frac{2\sigma^2}{n}.$$

Therefore,

$$a_1 = \frac{1}{n}, \quad a_2 = \frac{1}{n}, \quad \ldots, \quad a_n = \frac{1}{n}.$$

These are then the constants that make $\tilde{\mu}$ unbiased and minimize its variance. Substituting for $a_1, a_2, \ldots, a_n$ into the formula for $\tilde{\mu}$ given by (6.11) leads to

$$\tilde{\mu} = \sum_i \frac{1}{n} X_i = \frac{1}{n} \sum_i X_i = \bar{X}.$$

In other words, the BLUE of the population mean is given by the sample mean. The result is frequently called the *Gauss–Markov theorem.* Further, substituting for a_i into the formula for the variance of $\tilde{\mu}$ given by (6.12), we get

$$\text{Var}(\tilde{\mu}) = \sigma^2 \sum_i \left(\frac{1}{n}\right)^2 = \sigma^2 n \left(\frac{1}{n}\right)^2 = \frac{\sigma^2}{n},$$

which is a well-known expression for the variance of the sample mean.

Consider an estimator

$$\mu^* = \sum_i a_i X_i,$$

where the constants $a_1, a_2, \ldots, a_n$ are to be determined so as to minimize

$$\text{Var}(\mu^*) + (\text{Bias of } \mu^*)^2.$$

That is, we wish to minimize the *mean square error* of μ^*. The resulting formula is

$$\mu^* = \left(\frac{n\mu^2}{n\mu^2 + \sigma^2}\right) \bar{X},$$

which clearly indicates that μ^* does not qualify as an estimator since μ^2 and σ^2 are unknown. However, since for any value of μ^2 and σ^2 other than zero

$$\frac{n\mu^2}{n\mu^2 + \sigma^2} < 1,$$

the absolute value of the linear-minimum-mean-square-error estimator of μ is less than that of $\bar{X}$, though of course we do not know how much less.

The preceding result, though not operative, suggests that unbiased estimators need not be the best ones for achieving a small mean square error. In fact, when estimating the means of several independent normal random variables, Stein proposed the following biased estimator of the jth mean ($\hat{\mu}_j$).

$$\hat{\mu}_j = \left[1 - \frac{(p-2)\sigma^2}{\sum_{i=1}^{\mu} \bar{x}_i^2}\right] \bar{x}_j \qquad (j = 1, 2, \ldots, p).$$

When $p \geq 3$, the sum of the MSEs of the above estimators is less than that of the unbiased sample means.[14] It has been shown that the result holds when σ^2 is replaced by its unbiased estimator s^2.[15] These results have bestowed some respectability on biased estimators and created a good deal of excitement in the statistical profession.

Conclusion

This brings us to the end of our present discussion on methods of estimation. We have confined our attention to four basic methods; additional methods will be developed in the following chapters. The methods discussed do, however, provide the backbone of most if not all of the other estimation methods. The usefulness of the four methods has been illustrated by applying them to the problem of estimating the population mean. By each of the four methods we have obtained exactly the same estimator, namely, the sample mean. This result is rather reassuring, since we know from Section 6-1 that the sample mean as an estimator of the population mean has all the optimal properties.

6-3 Confidence Intervals

Now we take up the question of the precision of an estimator. Suppose we are interested in a population parameter θ for which there is an estimator $\hat{\theta}$. Suppose further that $\hat{\theta}$ possesses all the optimal properties of an estimator and incorporates all our knowledge concerning the relevant population. Since this knowledge is not complete, we shall be making an error by using $\hat{\theta}$ in place of the true parameter θ. The question then arises as to the size of this error. It is in this context that we speak of the precision of an estimator. That is, having obtained the best estimator that can be constructed given our limited knowledge, we may want to ask how well we can expect this estimator to perform.

The answer is obviously connected with the dispersion of the sampling distribution of the estimator. If this dispersion is small, a large proportion of estimates will lie within a close range from the true value of the parameter; if the dispersion is large, the same proportion of estimates will lie within a wider range. Thus the degree of precision of an estimator could be measured by the standard deviation of its sampling distribution, i.e., by its standard error. In most cases in practice this is not known but can be estimated from the sample along with the value of the estimator itself. Indeed, it is becoming a standard practice in econometrics to present not only the value of the estimator but also the calculated standard error. The latter is usually

[14] A simple and effective explanation of Stein estimation may be found in B. Efron and C. Morris, "Stein's Paradox in Statistics," *Scientific American,* 236 (May 1977), pp. 119–127.

[15] See B. Efron and C. Morris, "Families of Minimax Estimators of the Mean of a Multivariate Normal Distribution," *Annals of Statistics,* 4 (1976), pp. 11–21.

presented in parentheses below the value of the estimator, i.e.,

$$\underset{(s_{\hat{\theta}})}{\hat{\theta}}$$

A more systematic and explicit method of indicating the precision of an estimator exists in the case in which we know the form of the sampling distribution of the estimator. We are then able to construct so-called *confidence intervals* for the population parameter. The idea of confidence intervals can best be explained by reference to our discussion on hypothesis testing in Section 5-1, using as an illustration the problem of estimating the mean of a normal population. In this case we use as an estimator the sample mean $\bar{X}$, which has all the optimal properties. We know that if the normal population in question has mean μ and variance σ^2, the distribution of the sample mean will be normal with mean μ and variance σ^2/n, i.e., $\bar{X} \sim N(\mu, \sigma^2/n)$. Therefore,

$$\frac{\bar{X}-\mu}{\sqrt{\sigma^2/n}} \sim N(0, 1),$$

where $N(0, 1)$ is the standard normal distribution whose areas have been calculated and tabulated (see Appendix D). With this knowledge we are able to make certain probability statements that, in turn, lead to the construction of confidence intervals for μ.

The reader may recall that in the case of a variable with standard normal distribution, 95% of all values fall within -1.96 and $+1.96$. That is, we can write

$$P\left(-1.96 \leq \frac{\bar{X}-\mu}{\sqrt{\sigma^2/n}} \leq +1.96\right) = 0.95. \tag{6.15}$$

This statement implies that 95% of all samples drawn from a normal population with mean μ and variance σ^2 will have $\bar{X}$ such that

$$-1.96 \leq \frac{\bar{X}-\mu}{\sqrt{\sigma^2/n}} \leq +1.96 \tag{6.16}$$

will be true. Multiplying this inequality by $\sqrt{\sigma^2/n}$ throughout, we get

$$-1.96\sqrt{\sigma^2/n} \leq (\bar{X}-\mu) \leq +1.96\sqrt{\sigma^2/n}.$$

Deducting $\bar{X}$ from all sides gives

$$-1.96\sqrt{\sigma^2/n} - \bar{X} \leq (-\mu) \leq +1.96\sqrt{\sigma^2/n} - \bar{X}.$$

Finally, multiplying throughout by -1 and switching the sides around leads to

$$\bar{X} - 1.96\sqrt{\sigma^2/n} \leq \mu \leq \bar{X} + 1.96\sqrt{\sigma^2/n}. \tag{6.17}$$

The expression in (6.17) is called the *95% confidence interval* for the population mean μ. The probability that this interval covers the true mean μ is equal to 0.95.

This means that if we drew an infinite number of samples from the specified population, and if, for each sample, we computed the interval according to (6.17), then 95% of those intervals would contain the true mean μ. The measure "95%" represents the degree of our confidence that the interval—constructed on the basis of a given sample—will contain the true population mean. Note that we cannot say that "the probability that μ will lie within the stated interval is 0.95" because μ is a fixed number, not a random variable. The only probability statement that can be made about μ is that μ will assume its true value with probability 1 and all other values with probability 0. However, the end points of the interval—and therefore the interval itself—are random. It may also be noted that, for a given value of $\bar{X}$, the interval in (6.17) represents all values of μ that would be accepted at a 5% level against a two-sided alternative.

In setting up a confidence interval we can, of course, choose any level of confidence we like. However, we should realize that the higher the level of confidence, the wider the corresponding confidence interval and, therefore, the less useful is the information about the precision of the estimator. This can be seen by taking an extreme case, namely, that in which the confidence level is 100%. In this case the corresponding confidence interval, derived from a normally distributed estimator, is from $-\infty$ to $+\infty$, which obviously conveys no information about the precision of the estimator. On the other hand, narrower confidence intervals will be associated with lower levels of confidence. The problem here is very much like that of the level of significance in the context of hypothesis testing. A common solution in both cases is to use those levels which are most frequently used by others. In connection with hypothesis testing, we pointed out that there are two customarily employed levels of significance, 5% and 1%. Similarly, in connection with confidence intervals the two customary levels of confidence are 95% and 99%. For the mean of a normal population—with $\bar{X}$ as an estimator—the 95% confidence interval was given in (6.17); the 99% confidence interval is

$$\bar{X} - 2.57\sqrt{\sigma^2/n} \leq \mu \leq \bar{X} + 2.57\sqrt{\sigma^2/n}. \tag{6.18}$$

In constructing this interval we have made use of the fact that in the case of the standard normal distribution 99% of all values fall within -2.57 and $+2.57$.

The confidence interval (6.17) has been derived from a probability statement about the standard normal distribution. In particular, we have used the boundary points -1.96 and $+1.96$ that contain 95% of the total area. These boundary points are not unique since we can find other boundaries that also contain 95% of the area, for instance, -2.10 and $+1.85$, or -2.20 and $+1.80$, among others. The difference is that the interval from -1.96 to $+1.96$ contains the *central* portion of the area since it cuts off 2.5% of the area at each end of the distribution, whereas all the other intervals are asymmetric. The fact that the interval from -1.96 to $+1.96$ is symmetric implies that it is the *shortest* of all intervals that contain 95% of the area. This, in turn, means that the resulting 95% confidence interval is shorter than any other interval of the same level of confidence. The same conclusion can be drawn with respect to the 99% confidence interval (6.18). Obviously, given the level of confidence, a shorter interval is more desirable than a longer one.

EXAMPLE As a numerical example consider the following problem. Suppose we wish to construct a 95% confidence interval for the mean of $X \sim N(\mu, 16)$, having drawn a sample of 400 observations and obtained $\bar{x} = 99$. Then the 95% confidence interval is

$$99 - 1.96\sqrt{16/400} \leq \mu \leq 99 + 1.96\sqrt{16/400}$$

or

$$98.61 \leq \mu \leq 99.39.$$

Note that the 99% confidence interval in this case is

$$99 - 2.57\sqrt{16/400} \leq \mu \leq 99 + 2.57\sqrt{16/400}$$

or

$$98.486 \leq \mu \leq 99.514.$$

The reader has probably noticed the similarity between confidence intervals for the population mean and acceptance regions of a test about the population mean. Let us consider this in explicit terms. Suppose, for instance, that we are dealing with a variable $X \sim N(\mu, \sigma^2)$ and that we wish to test the null hypothesis

$$H_0: \quad \mu = \mu_0$$

against the alternative

$$H_A: \quad \mu \neq \mu_0.$$

Then the acceptance region corresponding to a 5% level of significance is

$$-1.96 \leq \frac{\bar{X} - \mu_0}{\sqrt{\sigma^2/n}} \leq +1.96.$$

This can be rewritten as

$$\bar{X} - 1.96\sqrt{\sigma^2/n} \leq \mu_0 \leq \bar{X} + 1.96\sqrt{\sigma^2/n}.$$

Now compare this with the 95% confidence interval for the population mean μ given by (6.17).

$$\bar{X} - 1.96\sqrt{\sigma^2/n} \leq \mu \leq \bar{X} + 1.96\sqrt{\sigma^2/n}.$$

The implication is that the 95% confidence interval is simply an interval that contains all those hypotheses about the population mean (i.e., all μ_0's) that would be accepted in a two-tail test at the 5% level of significance. A similar case could be made out for a 99% confidence interval and a two-tail test at the 1% level of significance. The difference between the acceptance regions and the confidence intervals is implied by the difference between hypothesis testing and estimation: in one case we make statements abut the population and check whether or not they are contradicted by sample evidence; in the other case we regard the population as a blank that is to be filled by the sample.

So far we have assumed that the confidence intervals involves estimators with optimal properties. In discussing confidence intervals for the mean of a normal population, the estimator was represented by the sample mean that satisfies this condition. Now we shall concern ourselves with the desirability of these optimal properties in confidence interval construction. First, if the estimator in question should be biased and the extent of the bias were not known, then the stated level of confidence would be incorrect. This can be easily demonstrated by replacing $\bar{X}$ in (6.17) or (6.18) by $(\bar{X} + B)$, where B is the bias and the value of B is not known. It is obvious that the interval involving $(\bar{X} + B)$ is associated with a different probability statement than the interval involving only $\bar{X}$ (unless, of course, $B = 0$), and thus the two intervals are characterized by different levels of confidence. Second, if the estimator is unbiased but not efficient, then the confidence interval is wider than otherwise. This follows from the fact that the variance of an inefficient estimator is larger than that of the efficient one and this "pushes" the end points of a confidence interval farther apart. Finally, square-error consistency guarantees that as the sample size increases, the confidence interval narrows and, at the limit, completely collapses at the point of the true value of the parameter.

In our discussion about confidence intervals, we have used as an illustration the problem of constructing confidence intervals for the mean of a normal population with *known* variance. In practical applications we rarely know the population variance but rather have to estimate it from the sample. An unbiased estimator of σ^2 was derived earlier and presented by (5.6) as

$$s^2 = \frac{1}{n-1} \sum_{i=1}^{n} (X_i - \bar{X})^2.$$

Furthermore, we know by (5.9) that if

$$\frac{\bar{X} - \mu}{\sqrt{\sigma^2/n}} \sim N(0, 1),$$

then

$$\frac{\bar{X} - \mu}{\sqrt{s^2/n}} \sim t_{n-1},$$

where t_{n-1} represents the t distribution with $(n-1)$ degrees of freedom. This enables us to make the following probability statement:

$$P\left(-t_{n-1,\,\alpha/2} \leq \frac{\bar{X} - \mu}{\sqrt{s^2/n}} \leq +t_{n-1,\,\alpha/2}\right) = 1 - \alpha, \tag{6.19}$$

where $t_{n-1,\,\alpha/2}$ stands for the value of the t statistic with $(n-1)$ degrees of freedom that cuts off $\alpha/2$ of the area of the t distribution at each tail end. The term $(1-\alpha)$ represents the area between the points $-t_{n-1,\,\alpha/2}$ and $+t_{n-1,\,\alpha/2}$. From (6.19) we can construct a confidence interval for μ at any level of confidence. For instance, the 95% confidence interval for μ is

$$\bar{X} - t_{n-1,\,0.0025}\sqrt{s^2/n} \leq \mu \leq \bar{X} + t_{n-1,\,0.025}\sqrt{s^2/n}. \tag{6.20}$$

EXAMPLE As a numerical example, consider the problem of constructing the 95% confidence interval for the mean μ of $X \sim N(\mu, \sigma^2)$, given that $\bar{X} = 20$, $s^2 = 100$, and $n = 25$. In this case the value of $t_{24,\,0.025}$ is 2.064 so that the 95% confidence interval for μ is

$$20 - 2.064\sqrt{100/25} \leq \mu \leq 20 + 2.064\sqrt{100/25}$$

or

$$15.872 \leq \mu \leq 24.128.$$

In a similar way we could construct intervals corresponding to 99% level of confidence, or any other level we might desire.

The idea of a confidence interval, developed above with respect to the mean of a normal population, can be used quite generally in connection with any parameter for which we have an estimator with known sampling distribution. For instance, we could construct a confidence interval for the variance of a normal population since we know that $[(n-1)s^2/\sigma^2]$ has the chi-square distribution with $(n-1)$ degrees of freedom. In our discussion we have viewed confidence intervals as a certain means of formally measuring the precision of an estimator. An alternative and more traditional view is to regard confidence intervals as more or less a separate subject treated under the heading of "interval estimation," to be distinguished from "point estimation," which is the subject of Sections 6-1 and 6-2. We do not follow this traditional view since the connection between "point estimation" and "interval estimation" is so intimate as to make the separation rather artificial.

6-4 Bayesian Inference

The approach to statistical inference described in Chapter 5 and in the preceding sections of Chapter 6 is known as the *classical* or *sampling theory* approach. It is based on the presumption of a given population of all potential observations from which one can—at least in theory—draw an infinite number of samples and construct a sampling distribution of a test statistic or of an estimator. This approach focuses on the probabilities of various outcomes (samples) resulting from a given state of nature (population). An alternative approach is that of viewing an observed outcome (sample) as given, and of considering the probabilities of various states of nature (populations) from which the sample might have come. The latter approach to inference relies crucially on the use of Bayes theorem (Theorem 6 of Section 3-4) and is accordingly known as *Bayesian inference.*

The salient aspect of the Bayesian approach to inference is the role played by the prior information in drawing conclusions about the states of nature. The investigator starts with *prior* (subjective) probabilities concerning various states of nature, combines them with the information contained in the sample, and obtains *posterior* probabilities of various states of nature. The mechanism of doing this is provided by Bayes theorem. Since various states of nature are typically characterized by parameters, specifying prior probabilities of various states of nature amounts to specifying prior probabilities of different parameter values. This means that, from the Bayesian viewpoint, parameters are treated as random variables and, therefore, are associated with probability distributions. Sample observations, on the other hand, are considered as given in the sense that posterior probabilities are *conditional* on observed sample values.

Another difference between the classical and the Bayesian approach concerns the inferential process itself. The classical approach to inference involves either hypothesis testing or estimation. In testing hypotheses, one starts with a null and an alternative hypothesis and uses the sampling distribution of a selected test statistic to determine the regions of acceptance and of rejection. In classical estimation, one selects an estimator and uses its sampling distribution to determine its properties and reliability. In the Bayesian approach the inferential process revolves around the posterior probabilities. These probabilities are represented by a posterior distribution that embodies all there is to know about the parameter of interest. The posterior distribution may be used to assign probabilities to various hypotheses, or to pick a specific characteristic of the posterior distribution (such as its mean) as an estimator. Estimation is frequently carried out in terms of decision theory involving the cost of not knowing the true state of nature.

The concept underlying a posterior distribution is that it represents a revision of one's prior judgment in light of sample evidence. This concept has a few interesting implications. First, a posterior distribution can—in the absence of any further information—serve as a prior distribution for the next revision based on the next available set of sample observations, and so on. In this way there is a cumulation of knowledge which has no clear counterpart in the classical setting. Second, if the sample is very large, it will dominate whatever prior information we have; thus the posterior distribution will be based predominantly on the sample information. In this case the results of Bayesian and classical estimations tend to coincide. This also happens when we have absolutely no prior information or belief about the parameter of interest, although some Bayesians claim that this can never be the case.

Derivation of the posterior distribution is based upon Bayes theorem. In its simplest form, this theorem involves two events, A and B, such that $P(A) \neq 0$ and $P(B) \neq 0$. The theorem then states that

$$P(B|A) = \frac{P(B)P(A|B)}{P(A)}.$$

With the interpretation that B is a specific value of the parameter of interest, say, θ, and that A stands for the sample observations, which we will call "data," we have

$$P(\theta|\text{data}) = \frac{P(\theta)P(\text{data}|\theta)}{P(\text{data})}. \tag{6.21}$$

(Here we suppose that θ and the data are discrete; otherwise we could not speak of the probabilities of specific values.) Now, for any value of θ, $P(\theta|\text{data})$ represents the revised, *posterior* probability of that value of θ, and $P(\theta)$ is the *prior* probability. Further, $P(\text{data}|\theta)$ is the probability of observing the sample *given* θ, which can be readily identified as the likelihood function (6.8a) presented in connection with the maximum likelihood estimation. This function summarizes the information about θ provided by the sample. Finally, $P(\text{data})$ represents the probability of observing the given sample *whatever* the value of θ. It is the marginal probability of sample observations obtained by adding probabilities over *all* values of θ. This quantity thus does not vary with θ; its role on the right-hand side of (6.21) is that of a *normalizing constant,* which ensures that the probabilities $P(\theta|\text{data})$ of all possible values of θ add up to unity. For this reason, $P(\text{data})$ is frequently ignored and (6.21) is written as

$$P(\theta|\text{data}) \propto P(\theta)P(\text{data}|\theta), \tag{6.21a}$$

where $\propto$ means "is proportional to."

The results in (6.21) and (6.21a) refer to specific probabilities and require that θ and the data be discrete. These results can be equally well applied to probability distributions and to continuous θ and data. Then we write

$$f(\theta|\text{data}) \propto g(\theta)\ell(\text{data}|\theta), \tag{6.22}$$

where f refers to the posterior distribution, g to the prior distribution, and ℓ to the likelihood function. To make it easier to remember, (6.22) can be expressed as

(6.22a) posterior distribution $\propto$ prior distribution $\times$ likelihood function.

To construct a posterior distribution we need to form the likelihood function and the prior distribution. The formation of the likelihood function has already been discussed in Section 6-2 in the context of classical estimation, and it presents no difficulties as long as the form of the parent distribution is known. The formation of the prior distribution $g(\theta)$ is unique to the Bayesian approach and requires some explanation. If this distribution is provided by the investigator in the form of a formula, and if this formula combined with the likelihood function leads to the same functional form as $g(\theta)$, it is called a *conjugate prior.* Such prior distributions are highly desirable since they are relatively easy to work with.

Sometimes the investigator does not have any prior notion about θ, the parameter of interest. Such a lack of prior knowledge or belief may be interpreted as implying that any value of θ is just as likely as any other value as far as the investigator is concerned. Thus prior ignorance may be represented by a uniform distribution as follows.

$$g(\theta) \propto \text{constant}. \tag{6.23}$$

If it is known that θ cannot be negative, as when θ stands for variance, and if nothing else is known, the prior distribution of θ can be represented as

$$g(\log\theta) \propto \text{constant}, \tag{6.24}$$

because logarithms of negative numbers do not exist. It can be shown (with the help of a "change of variable" rule that will be presented in Chapter 7) that (6.24) is equivalent to

$$g(\theta) \propto \frac{1}{\theta}. \tag{6.24a}$$

Prior distributions of the form (6.23) or (6.24) are called *diffuse* or *noninformative.* They are also called "improper" because the integral of $g(\theta)$ from $-\infty$ to $+\infty$ (or from 0 to $+\infty$) is not equal to 1, as is required if $g(\theta)$ were to be a proper probability distribution.

Let us now demonstrate the derivation of posterior distributions by examples. Two examples will be considered: one concerns the posterior distribution of the proportion of successes in the population (π), and the other concerns the posterior distribution of the mean (μ) of a normal population. In each example we will use noninformative as well as conjugate prior distributions.

EXAMPLE 1 Suppose X is a binary variable that assumes a value of 1 with probability π and a value of 0 with probability $(1 - \pi)$. Observing a 1 can be considered a success, and observing a 0 a failure. A random sample consists of n values $x_1, x_2, \ldots, x_n$. The total number of successes is Σx_i, which we denote by m. The likelihood function for a specific sample is

$$\ell = (1 - \pi)^{n-m}\pi^m.$$

If the prior distribution of π is noninformative, i.e., if

$$g(\pi) \propto \text{constant} \qquad (0 \leq \pi \leq 1),$$

then the posterior distribution of π is simply

$$f(\pi|\text{data}) \propto (1 - \pi)^{n-m}\pi^m.$$

On the other hand, if our prior information about π takes the form

$$g(\pi) \propto (1 - \pi)^{\alpha}\pi^{\beta},$$

where α and β are some given numbers, then the posterior distribution becomes

$$f(\pi|\text{data}) \propto (1 - \pi)^{n-m+\alpha}\pi^{m+\beta}.$$

Clearly, for this prior distribution the functional form of $f(\pi|\text{data})$ is the same as that of $g(\pi)$. Therefore $g(\pi)$ qualifies as a conjugate prior distribution. Note that if $\alpha < \beta$, the prior information favors values of π greater than 0.5; if $\alpha > \beta$, the prior information favors values of π less than 0.5; and if $\alpha = \beta$, the prior distribution of π is symmetric around 0.5.

EXAMPLE 2 Consider a normally distributed variable X with mean μ and variance σ^2, i.e., $X \sim N(\mu, \sigma^2)$. The value of σ^2 is assumed to be known. A random sample consists of n values $x_1, x_2, \ldots, x_n$. In this case the likelihood function is given as

$$\ell = (2\pi\sigma^2)^{-n/2} \exp\left\{-\frac{1}{2}\Sigma\left(\frac{x_i - \mu}{\sigma}\right)^2\right\}$$

or

$$\ell \propto \exp\left\{-\frac{1}{2}\Sigma\left(\frac{x_i - \mu}{\sigma}\right)^2\right\}$$

where exp and the expression in braces represent e with its exponent equal to that expression.

If the prior distribution of μ is noninformative, i.e., if

$$g(\mu) \propto \text{constant},$$

then the posterior distribution of μ is

$$f(\mu|\text{data}) \propto \exp\left\{-\frac{1}{2}\sum\left(\frac{x_i-\mu}{\sigma}\right)^2\right\}.$$

Now, we wish to rearrange the right-hand side of the above expression so that it is in the form indicating that μ is a normally distributed *variable.* That is, we wish the exponent to be of the form

$$-\frac{1}{2}\left(\frac{\mu-a}{b}\right)^2,$$

where a is the mean and b the standard deviation of μ. This can be accomplished by noting that

$$\frac{1}{2}\sum\left(\frac{x_i-\mu}{\sigma}\right)^2=\frac{1}{2}\sum\left[\frac{(x_i-\bar{x})-(\mu-\bar{x})}{\sigma}\right]^2$$
$$=\frac{1}{2}\sum\left(\frac{x_i-\bar{x}}{\sigma}\right)^2+\frac{1}{2}\left(\frac{\mu-\bar{x}}{\sigma/\sqrt{n}}\right)^2.$$

Since the first term on the right-hand side above does not involve μ, it can be absorbed in the factor of proportionality. Thus the posterior distribution of μ becomes

$$f(\mu|\text{data}) \propto \exp\left\{-\frac{1}{2}\left(\frac{\mu-\bar{x}}{\sigma/\sqrt{n}}\right)^2\right\},$$

which shows that the posterior distribution of μ is normal with mean $\bar{x}$ and standard deviation $\sigma/\sqrt{n}$, i.e., posterior $\mu \sim N(\bar{x}, \sigma^2/n)$.

Suppose now that the prior distribution is informative and takes the form

$$g(\mu) \sim N(\mu_0, \sigma_0^2),$$

where μ_0 and σ_0^2 are some given numbers. Then we can write

$$g(\mu) \propto \exp\left\{-\frac{1}{2}\left(\frac{\mu-\mu_0}{\sigma_0}\right)^2\right\},$$

and the posterior distribution of μ becomes

$$f(\mu|\text{data}) \propto \exp\left\{-\frac{1}{2}\left[\sum\left(\frac{x_i-\mu}{\sigma}\right)^2+\left(\frac{\mu-\mu_0}{\sigma_0}\right)^2\right]\right\}.$$

Using the reformulation presented in the earlier context of noninformative prior, we can write

$$f(\mu|\text{data}) \propto \exp\left\{-\frac{n(\mu-\bar{x})^2}{2\sigma^2}-\frac{(\mu-\mu_0)^2}{2\sigma_0^2}\right\}$$
$$\propto \exp\left\{-\frac{n(\mu-\bar{x})^2+n_0(\mu-\mu_0)^2}{2\sigma^2}\right\},$$

where $n_0 = \sigma^2/\sigma_0^2$. Now

$$n(\mu - \bar{x})^2 + n_0(\mu - \mu_0)^2 = (n + n_0)\mu^2 - 2\mu(n\bar{x} + n_0\mu_0) + n\bar{x}^2 + n_0\mu_0^2$$

$$= (n + n_0)\left[\mu^2 - 2\mu\left(\frac{n\bar{x} + n_0\mu_0}{n + n_0}\right) + \left(\frac{n\bar{x} + n_0\mu_0}{n + n_0}\right)^2\right]$$

$$+ \text{ terms not involving } \mu.$$

Therefore,

$$f(\mu|\text{data}) \propto \left\{-\frac{[\mu - (n\bar{x} + n_0\mu_0)/(n + n_0)]^2}{2\sigma^2/(n + n_0)}\right\}.$$

Thus the posterior distribution of μ is normal with mean $(n\bar{x} + n_0\mu_0)/(n + n_0)$ and standard deviation $\sigma/\sqrt{n + n_0}$, i.e.,

$$\text{posterior } \mu \sim N\left(\frac{n\bar{x} + n_0\mu_0}{n + n_0}, \frac{\sigma^2}{n + n_0}\right).$$

Note that the posterior mean of μ is a weighted average of the sample mean and the mean of the prior distribution, with weights given by the sample size n and the ratio $n_0 = \sigma^2/\sigma_0^2$. If the prior information is very vague, that is, if σ_0^2 is large and thus n_0 is small, the weight given to the prior mean μ_0 will be relatively light. Also, a small n_0 will not decrease the posterior variance in a marked way. On the other hand, if $\sigma_0^2 \to 0$, then $n_0 \to \infty$ and the posterior mean will be equal to the prior mean μ_0, with variance approaching zero.

The most common use of the posterior distribution is to obtain a Bayes estimator of the parameter of interest. In the Bayesian framework, the selection of an estimator is based on the cost to the investigator of using an estimate instead of the true value of the parameter. Such a cost is measured by the quantity $L(\theta, \hat{\theta})$, where θ is the true value of the parameter and $\hat{\theta}$ is the estimate of θ. This quantity, evaluated for different values of θ, is called a *loss function*. If θ is known to lie in the interval (a, b) and if $f(\theta|\text{data})$ is the posterior distribution of θ, then the expected loss will be

$$E\, L(\theta, \hat{\theta}) = \int_a^b L(\theta, \hat{\theta}) f(\theta|\text{data}) d\theta. \tag{6.25}$$

A *Bayes estimator* is then defined as that value of θ for which the expected loss is minimum.

By far the most popular loss function is the *square-error loss function*. This is defined as

$$L(\theta, \hat{\theta}) = k(\theta - \hat{\theta})^2, \tag{6.26}$$

where k is a constant. It is well known that $E(\theta - \hat{\theta})^2$ will be minimized when $\hat{\theta}$ is set to be equal to the mean of the distribution of θ.[16] Thus the Bayes estimator of θ in this case will be the *mean* of the posterior distribution of θ. If, on the other hand, the

[16] See, e.g., DeGroot, *op. cit.*, pp. 275–279.

applicable loss function is the *absolute-error loss function,* defined as

$$L(\theta, \hat{\theta}) = k|\theta - \hat{\theta}|, \tag{6.27}$$

then the minimizing value of $\hat{\theta}$ will be the *median* of the posterior distribution of θ. One could also formulate a loss function for which the Bayes estimator would be the mode of the posterior distribution of θ. Other loss functions can be devised to apply to situations in which it might be more costly to underestimate the true value of θ than to overestimate it, and to other cases.

The Bayesian approach to inference has a distinct advantage over the classical approach, because it forces the investigator to use *all* the information at his or her disposal, not just the sample observations. Although prior information could also be built into the process of classical inference, the mechanism for doing so is not always well developed and the interpretation of the results can become questionable.

The disadvantage of the Bayesian approach is that the prior information has to be in the form of a probability distribution, which sometimes may be hard to accomplish. There is clearly a danger of misrepresenting prior information or prior belief by forcing it into the form of a conjugate prior distribution. Further, in order to form a likelihood function, one has to know the functional form of the parent distribution, and this is not always available. Last but not least, the posterior distributions are frequently very complicated, even when conjugate priors are used. This is particularly the case when the number of unknown parameters involved is not very small. In fact, the mean of the posterior distribution frequently has to be determined by numerical integration because the analytical solution is intractable. It is a consolation that, at least in general, the difference between the classical and the Bayesian results tend to disappear when the sample is large.

EXERCISES

6-1. Let $X \sim N(\mu, \sigma^2)$. Consider two independent random samples of observations on X. The samples are of size n_1 and n_2 with means $\bar{X}_1$ and $\bar{X}_2$, respectively. Two estimators of the population mean are proposed.

$$\hat{\mu} = \frac{1}{2}(\bar{X}_1 + \bar{X}_2),$$

$$\tilde{\mu} = \frac{n_1\bar{X}_1 + n_2\bar{X}_2}{n_1 + n_2}.$$

Compare the properties of these estimators.

6-2. Let the sample proportion of successes, $\hat{\pi}$, be an estimator of the population proportion of successes, π. It is known that $\text{Var}(\hat{\pi}) = \pi(1 - \pi)/n$. Find an unbiased estimator of $\text{Var}(\hat{\pi})$.

6-3. Let X be the number of successes in a sample of size n. The observations are assumed to be independent. Two estimators of the population proportion of successes, π, are

$$\hat{\pi} = \frac{X}{n},$$

$$\tilde{\pi} = \frac{(X+1)}{(n+2)}.$$

a. Examine the properties of these estimators.

b. Compare the mean square errors of these estimators.

6-4. A k-sided die has sides marked 1, 2, . . . , k. The die is tossed, and the uppermost number shown is 9. On the basis of this observation, obtain the maximum likelihood estimate of k and draw the likelihood function.

6-5. Let X be a random variable with mean μ and variance σ^2. Find a linear estimator of μ, say, $\mathring{\mu}$, such that

$$\frac{\text{Var}(\mathring{\mu})}{\sigma^2} + \frac{(\text{Bias of } \mathring{\mu})^2}{\mu^2}$$

is at minimum.

6-6. Let $X \sim N(\mu, \sigma^2)$. Consider the following two estimators of σ^2.

$$\hat{\sigma}^2 = \frac{1}{n} \sum_{i=1}^{n} (X_i - \bar{X})^2,$$

$$s^2 = \frac{1}{n-1} \sum_{i=1}^{n} (X_i - \bar{X})^2.$$

Show that

a. $\text{Var}(\hat{\sigma}^2) < \text{Var}(s^2)$.

b. $\text{MSE}(\hat{\sigma}^2) < \text{MSE}(s^2)$.

c. Both estimators are consistent.

d. Both estimators are asymptotically efficient.

[HINT: $\text{Var}(\hat{\sigma}^2) = 2\sigma^4(n-1)/n^2$.]

6-7. Let X represent the earnings of a commercial bank such that $X \sim N(\mu, \sigma^2)$. A random sample of earnings of n banks is denoted $X_1, X_2, \ldots, X_n$. However, because of disclosure laws, individual bank earnings are not disclosed and only the following average values are made available to the investigator: $(X_1 + X_2)/2, (X_3 + X_4)/2, \ldots, (X_{n-1} + X_n)/2$, where n is an even number.

a. Devise an unbiased estimator of μ given the available information. What is the variance of the proposed estimator of μ?

b. Devise an unbiased estimator of σ^2 given the available information. What is the variance of the proposed estimator of σ^2?

6-8. Consider a population of all married graduate students at U.S universities. (If both husband and wife are graduate students, only one of them is counted.) Let π_0, π_1, and π_2 be the proportion of married graduate students with no children, one child, and two children, respectively. No married graduate student has more than two children. Further, it is known that $\pi_1 = 3\pi_2$. A random sample of four married graduate students, listed in the order in which they were interviewed, yields 1, 2, 0, 1 children. Find the maximum likelihood estimates of π_0, π_1, and π_2.

6-9. A physicist has a cube whose *volume* he wishes to estimate, and he intends to take n measurements of the *length* of one side of the cube. It is assumed that the measurements are normally and independently distributed with mean μ (the true length of the side of the cube) and variance σ^2. The physicist then considers the following two estimators of the true volume of the cube (μ^3).

$$\hat{\mu}_1^3 = \frac{1}{n}\sum X_i^3 \quad \text{and} \quad \hat{\mu}_2^3 = \bar{X}^3.$$

a. Using the criterion of lesser bias, which of the two estimators—if any—is to be preferred?

b. Devise an unbiased estimator of μ^3.

[HINTS: (1) $E(X-\mu)^3 = E(X^3) - 3\mu E(X^2) + 3\mu^2 E(X) - \mu^3$. (2) If X is normally distributed, then $E(X-\mu)^3 = 0$, and $\bar{X}$ and s^2 are independent.]

6-10. Following are 20 observations drawn at random from a normal population:

0.464	0.137	2.455	−0.323
0.060	−2.526	−0.531	−0.194
1.486	−0.354	−0.634	0.697
1.022	−0.472	1.279	3.521
1.394	−0.555	0.046	0.321

a. Find the 95% confidence interval for the population mean.

b. Find the 95% confidence interval for the population standard deviation.

c. Plot the likelihood function for the population mean and locate the ML estimate of μ.

[NOTE: Since the ML estimate of μ does not depend on σ^2, for the purpose of graphing we can set its value to be some convenient number, e.g., unity.]

6-11. A soft drink machine is regulated so that the amount of drink dispensed is approximately normally distributed with the value of the standard deviation equal to 0.1 ounce. How many drinks do we have to sample if we wish the length of the 95% confidence interval for the population mean to be 0.1 ounce?

6-12. Let π be the proportion of successes in the population. Suppose that in a random sample of 5 observations we find 3 successes. Calculate the mean and the variance of the posterior distribution of π if

a. The prior distribution of π is diffuse.

b. The prior distribution of π is given as $g(\pi) \propto \pi(1-\pi)$.

6-13. The heights of adult males in a certain population are normaly distributed with mean μ and variance of 4 inches. The prior distribution of male heights is also normal with variance of 1 inch. What is the smallest sample size to yield a posterior distribution of μ with variance equal to 0.01?

PART TWO
Basic Econometric Theory

7 Simple Regression

Economic theory is mainly concerned with relations among variables. Demand and supply relations, cost functions, production functions, and many others are familiar to every student who has taken a course in economics. In fact, the entire body of economic theory can be regarded as a collection of relations among variables.[1] As pointed out in Chapter 1, econometrics is concerned with testing the theoretical propositions embodied in these relations, and with estimating the parameters involved. In the chapters of Part Two we will discuss various methods that can be used in performing this task and the problems encountered in the process. In the present chapter we will discuss the simplest case of a linear relation involving only two measurable variables; the subsequent chapters will contain increasingly more complicated cases.

7-1 Relations Between Variables

An appropriate way to start our discussion is by defining the new concepts with which we will be working. We define a *relation* between variables X and Y as a set of all values of X and Y that are characterized by a given equation. For example, if the characterizing equation is given by

$$y = \alpha + \beta x,$$

where α and β are some constants, then the relation between X and Y is the set $\{x, y\}$ consisting of all possible values of X and Y that satisfy the equation. Typically, the form of the characterizing equation gives the name to the corresponding relation: a linear equation describes a linear relation, an exponential equation describes an exponential relation, and so on. The concept of a relation is closely associated with the concepts of a domain and of a range. If a relation between X and Y is character-

[1] See, e.g., Paul A. Samuelson, *Foundations of Economic Analysis* (Cambridge, Mass.: Harvard University Press, 1947).

ized by an equation $y = f(x)$, then the *domain* of this relation is the set of all possible values of X, and the *range* is the set of all possible corresponding values of Y. In practice, relations are usually described simply by stating the appropriate characterizing equation, while the domain and the range are implied but unstated.

All relations can be classified as either deterministic or stochastic. A relation between X and Y is *deterministic* if each element of the domain is paired off with *just one* element of the range. That is, a relationship between X and Y characterized as $y = f(x)$ is a deterministic relation if for each value of X there is only one corresponding value of Y. However, the *variables* X and Y may both be nonstochastic (i.e., they may assume values that are fully controllable or predictable), or they may both be stochastic. This means that a relation may be deterministic (i.e., nonstochastic) even if both variables involved are stochastic; however, if both variables are stochastic while the relation is deterministic, the conditional distribution of Y given X is degenerate. On the other hand, a relation between X and Y is said to be *stochastic* if for each value of X there is a whole probability distribution of values of Y. Thus, for any given value of X the variable Y may, in this case, assume some specific value—or fall within some specific interval—with a probability smaller than one and greater than zero.

To illustrate the distinction between a deterministic and a stochastic relation, suppose we conduct a series of experiments in class to determine the demand for Mackintosh apples at different prices. Let q_t = quantity of apples sold at time t, and let p_t = price in cents. The apples are offered for sale at a given price every time the class meets during the term. The results at the end of the term may be as follows.

p_t	q_t
25	1
20	3
15	5
10	7
5	9
0	11

These results can be summarized in the form of a "demand equation" as

$$q_t = 11 - 0.4p_t.$$

The relation between price and quantity then is such that *any time* the apples were offered at 25 cents apiece, only one apple was sold. Any time the price was 20 cents, three apples were sold, and so on. This is a deterministic relation, since for each price there is always only one corresponding quantity of apples sold. Now consider a different set of results (Table 7-1). The "demand equation" must now be rewritten as

$$q_t = 11 - 0.4p_t + \varepsilon_t,$$

Table 7-1

p_t	q_t
25	0 apples 25% of the time 1 apple 50% of the time 2 apples 25% of the time
20	2 apples 25% of the time 3 apples 50% of the time 4 apples 25% of the time
⋮	⋮
0	10 apples 25% of the time 11 apples 50% of the time 12 apples 25% of the time

where ε_t is a random variable having the following probability distribution, whatever the specified price.

ε_t	$f(\varepsilon_t)$
-1	0.25
0	0.50
$+1$	0.25
	1.00

This variable is commonly called a *random disturbance* since it "disturbs" an otherwise deterministic relation (an alternative expression for ε_t is "a random error term"). The last relation is a stochastic one since, because of the presence of the disturbance, there are several quantities demanded for each price, each quantity occurring with a given probability. A diagrammatic representation of the two relations is shown in Figure 7-1.

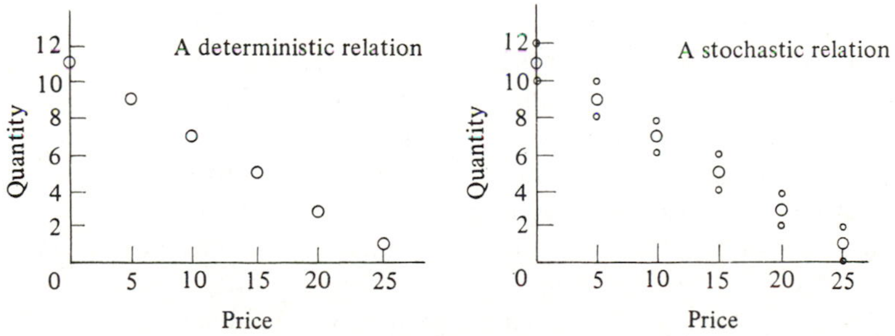

Figure 7-1

Let us now consider the question of dependence between two variables involved in a relation. First, consider a deterministic relation characterized by

$$y = f(x).$$

Then, if $f(x)$ is not constant over all values of X (that is, if $f(x)$ is not constant over all elements of the domain), we say that *Y is dependent on X in the functional sense.* In other words, Y is considered to depend on X if, at least for some values of X, a change in X implies a change in Y. If, in a two-dimensional diagram, the values of Y are measured along the vertical and those of X along the horizontal axis, then Y is dependent on X if all points do not lie on a straight horizontal line. With respect to a *stochastic relation,* we say that *Y is dependent on X in the functional sense* if the probability distribution of Y is not the same for all values of X. A typical case of dependence of Y on X arises when the mean of Y changes as X assumes different values. However, Y would be considered as dependent on X even if the mean of Y remained constant for all values of X, as long as some other characteristic of the distribution of Y would change with X. For instance, if the variance of Y were to increase with increases in X, this alone would make Y dependent on X according to our definition.

It is interesting to note that, in the numerical example on the stochastic demand curve given above, the mean quantity demanded changes with price while the variance remains unchanged. In particular, we have

p_t	$E(q_t)$	$\mathrm{Var}(q_t)$
25	1	0.5
20	3	0.5
15	5	0.5
10	7	0.5
5	9	0.5
0	11	0.5

In a more general case of dependence both the mean and the variance of Y may change in response to changes in X.

In economic theory all relations are, as a rule, stated in a deterministic form. This is not because economists would believe in a complete absence of chance when it comes to economic relations, but because they consider the stochastic disturbances to be of less importance than the systematic influences. The introduction of stochastic disturbances into the economic relations would greatly complicate the task of the theorist. However, the stress on the need for *testing* economic theories, which is frequently encountered in economic writings, implies a belief in the existence of stochastic factors. If the theoretical relations were, in fact, deterministic, the question of statistical testing would not arise; all that we would have to do to determine the values of the unknown parameters would be to carry out precise measurements rather than tests. To illustrate this, we may consider a theory that Y is linearly dependent on X. If the relation between Y and X were, in fact, deterministic, we would simply measure two pairs of values of X and Y. If the line connecting these two points were horizontal, the theory would be rejected; in all other cases the theory would be verified. The intercept and the slope of the line could be simply read off the graph. If, however, the relation between X and Y were stochastic, our observations of the values of the two variables would have to be considered a sample. The sample would then be used to test a proposition about the population, and the slope and the intercept would have to be estimated.

7-2 The Regression Model

In econometrics we deal exclusively with stochastic relations. The simplest form of stochastic relation between two variables X and Y is called a *simple linear regression model.* This model is formally described as

$$Y_i = \alpha + \beta X_i + \varepsilon_i, \tag{7.1}$$

where Y is called the "dependent variable," X the "explanatory variable," and ε the "stochastic disturbance," and α and β are the "regression parameters," which are unknown. The subscript i refers to the ith observation. The values of the variables X and Y are observable, but those of ε are not. Observations on X and Y can be made over time, in which case we speak of "time-series data," or they can be made over individuals, groups of individuals, objects, or geographical areas, in which case we speak of "cross-section data." Thus the subscript i may refer to the ith point or period of time, or to the ith individual, object, etc. Of course, data of both kinds can be combined to obtain "pooled time-series and cross-section data"; for example, we may have data on consumption expenditure and income of N individual households for T periods of time. In this case it would be convenient to use a double subscript. Typically, aggregate relations such as aggregate consumption functions, market demand relations, or aggregate production functions are estimated from time-series data, while microrelations such as household expenditure functions or firm production functions are estimated from cross-section data obtained from sample surveys. The origin of the data is not explicitly taken into account in the development of estimators of the regression parameters. But, as we shall see, the properties of these estimators depend on certain assumptions concerning the observations, and some of these assumptions are more likely to be violated when the data are of one kind than another.

The stochastic nature of the regression model implies that for every value of X there is a whole probability distribution of values of Y. This means that the value of Y can never be forecast exactly. The uncertainty concerning Y arises because of the presence of the stochastic disturbance ε which, being random, imparts randomness to Y. Consider, for example, a production function of a firm. Suppose that output depends in some specified way on the quantity of labor input in accordance with the engineer's blueprint. Such a production function may apply in the short run when the quantities of other inputs are fixed. But, in general, the same quantity of labor will lead to different quantities of output because of variations in weather, human performance, frequency of machine breakdowns, and many other factors. Output, which is the dependent variable in this case, will depend not only on the quantity of labor input, which is the explanatory variable, but also on a large number of random causes, which we summarize in the form of the stochastic disturbance. Individually these causes are too insignificant to note, but their collective influence may be quite perceptible. The probability distribution of Y and its characteristics are then determined by the values of X and by the probability distribution of ε. If the "blueprint" relation between output and labor were completely and correctly specified, then we could measure the value of ε from the observations on X and Y after each production run. In reality this is almost never the case. In fact, we consider ourselves lucky when we know even the mathematical form of the relation without knowing the parameters.

It should be clear now that the full specification of the regression model includes not only the form of the regression equation given in (7.1) but also a specification of the probability distribution of the disturbance and a determination of the values of the explanatory variable. This information is given by what we shall call the *basic assumptions.* These assumptions are

(7.2) *Normality:* ε_i is normally distributed.

(7.3) *Zero mean:* $E(\varepsilon_i) = 0$.

(7.4) *Homoskedasticity:* $\mathrm{Var}(\varepsilon_i) = \sigma^2$.

(7.5) *Nonautocorrelation:* $\mathrm{Cov}(\varepsilon_i, \varepsilon_j) = 0 \quad (i \neq j)$.

(7.6) *Nonstochastic X:* X is a nonstochastic variable with values fixed in repeated samples and such that, for any sample size n,

$$\frac{1}{n}\sum_{i=1}^{n}(X_i - \bar{X})^2$$

is different from 0, and its limit, as $n \to \infty$, is a finite number.

The full specification of the simple linear regression model then consists of the regression equation (7.1) and the five basic assumptions (7.2) through (7.6).[2] This represents the so-called "classical normal linear regression model," which provides a point of departure for most of the work in econometric theory.

Let us now examine the meaning of the various assumptions. The first two assumptions state that, for each value of X, the disturbance is normally distributed around zero. The implications are that ε_i is continuous and ranges from $-\infty$ to $+\infty$, that it is symmetrically distributed around its mean, and that its distribution is fully determined by two parameters, the mean and the variance. The rationalization of normality relies on the same argument as that which applies to the behavior of random errors of measurement and which was mentioned at the end of Section 4-2. In particular, we may consider each value of the stochastic disturbance as the result of a large number of small causes, each cause producing a small deviation of the

[2] Strictly speaking, there is one further assumption, which is made only implicitly, namely, that there exists no further information about the regression parameters other than that provided by the sample.

dependent variable from what it would be if the relation were deterministic. Under these circumstances the analogy with the behavior of errors of measurement may be valid and the assumptions of normality and zero mean appropriate. The third assumption concerning homoskedasticity means that every disturbance has the same variance σ^2 whose value is unknown. This assumption rules out, for example, the possibility that the dispersion of the disturbances would be greater for higher than for lower values of X. In terms of our production functions example, the assumption of homoskedasticity implies that the variation in output is the same whether the quantity of labor is 20, 100, or any other number of units. The fourth assumption requires that the disturbances be uncorrelated. Under this assumption the fact that, say, output is higher than expected today should not lead to a higher (or lower) than expected output tomorrow. Note that assumptions (7.2) and (7.5) together imply that the disturbances are independent in the probability sense.[3] Thus $\varepsilon_1, \varepsilon_2, \ldots, \varepsilon_n$ can be viewed as a set of n identically and independently distributed variables. Note that since $E(\varepsilon_i) = 0$, it follows that $\text{Var}(\varepsilon_i) = E(\varepsilon_i^2)$ and $\text{Cov}(\varepsilon_i, \varepsilon_j) = E(\varepsilon_i \ \varepsilon_j)$. The final assumption, which states that the explanatory variable is to be nonstochastic, is quite straightforward. This assumption confines us to considering those situations in which the values of X are either controllable or fully predictable. An important implication of this assumption is that $E(\varepsilon_i X_j) = X_j E(\varepsilon_i) = 0$ for all i, j. The statement that the values of X are "fixed in repeated samples" indicates that the set of values of X is taken to be the same from sample to sample. Finally, the requirement that $(1/n)\ \Sigma(X_i - \bar{X})^2$ be a finite number different from zero means that the values of X in the sample must not all be equal to the same number, and that they cannot grow or decline without limit as the sample size increases.

Note that the basic assumptions (7.2) through (7.5) imply—and are implied by—the interpretation of the disturbance as accounting for a large number of individually insignificant and independent factors usually called *chance.* This interpretation rules out the frequently made assertion that the disturbance includes all *systematic* explanatory variables that have been omitted from the deterministic part of the regression equation because of nonmeasurability, ignorance, or convenience. In practice, of course, we do not insist on absolute adherence to the basic assumptions but are satisfied when these assumptions hold only approximately.

The assumptions underlying the classical normal linear regression model are used in deriving estimators of the regression parameters. Since the disturbance is assumed to be normally distributed with a mean equal to zero, the only thing that is not known about this distribution is its variance σ^2. Thus the model described by (7.1) through (7.6) involves altogether three unknown parameters, the regression parameters α and β and the variance of the disturbance σ^2. It should be emphasized, however, that we do not ignore the possibility that any one or more of the basic assumptions may not be fulfilled. In fact, Chapter 8 is devoted to precisely this question. There we shall examine what happens to the properties of the estimators developed in the present chapter when various assumptions are violated. We shall

[3] For normally distributed random variables, uncorrelatedness implies independence. See, e.g., A. S. Goldberger, *Econometric Theory* (New York: Wiley, 1964), pp. 107–108.

also try to develop alternative estimators appropriate to the situation on hand whenever necessary and describe suitable test procedures.

Having made a complete specification of the regression model as described by the regression equation and the five basic assumptions, we may take a closer look at some of its basic features. In particular, let us turn to the probability distribution of the dependent variable Y. First, the mean of Y_i can be obtained by taking the mathematical expectation of both sides of equation (7.1). We get

$$E(Y_i) = E(\alpha + \beta X_i + \varepsilon_i) = \alpha + \beta X_i. \tag{7.7}$$

This follows from the specification that α and β are parameters, X_i is nonstochastic (i.e., some given number), and the mean of ε_i is 0 by (7.3). Furthermore, the variance of Y_i is

$$\begin{aligned} \text{Var}(Y_i) &= E[Y_i - E(Y_i)]^2 = E[(\alpha + \beta X_i + \varepsilon_i) - (\alpha + \beta X_i)]^2 \\ &= E(\varepsilon_i^2) = \sigma^2. \end{aligned} \tag{7.8}$$

In this derivation we first used the general definition of a variance, then substituted for Y_i from (7.1) and for $E(Y_i)$ from (7.7), and finally made use of the assumption of homoskedasticity given by (7.4). Concerning the distribution of Y_i, we can see from equation (7.1) that Y_i is merely a linear function of ε_i. Since ε_i is normally distributed, it follows by Theorem 14 of Section 4-2 that Y_i is also normally distributed. Therefore, we can assert that Y_i is a normally distributed variable with mean $(\alpha + \beta X_i)$ and variance σ^2, i.e., that $Y_i \sim N(\alpha + \beta X_i, \sigma^2)$. This is illustrated graphically by Figure 7-2. Note that the means of the distributions all lie on a straight line, and that each distribution has exactly the same variance.

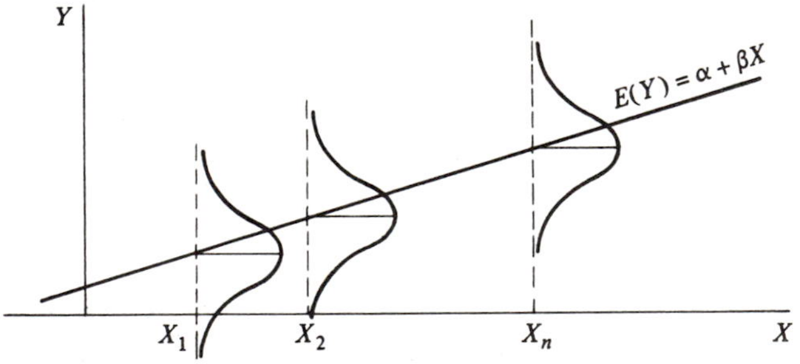

Figure 7-2

Further, since for $i \neq j$,

$$\begin{aligned} \text{Cov}(Y_i, Y_j) &= E[Y_i - E(Y_i)][Y_j - E(Y_j)] \\ &= E(\varepsilon_i \varepsilon_j) \\ &= 0 \qquad \text{[by (7.3) and (7.5)]}, \end{aligned}$$

we can view $Y_1, Y_2, \ldots, Y_n$ as a set of n normally and independently distributed variables. However, these variables are not *identically* distributed because they have different means.

Equation (7.7), which gives the mean value of Y for each value of X, is known as the *population regression line.* The intercept of this line, α, measures the mean value of Y corresponding to zero value of X. The slope of the line, β, measures the change in the mean value of Y corresponding to a unit change in the value of X. If, for instance, Y represents aggregate consumption and X aggregate income, then α measures the level of consumption at zero income and β represents the marginal propensity to consume. Since the values of these parameters are not known, the population regression line is not known. When the values of α and β are estimated, we obtain a *sample regression line* that serves as an estimate of the population regression line. If α and β are estimated by $\hat{\alpha}$ and $\hat{\beta}$, respectively, then the sample regression line is given by

$$\hat{Y}_i = \hat{\alpha} + \hat{\beta}X_i, \tag{7.9}$$

where $\hat{Y}_i$ is the fitted value of Y_i. Most, if not all, of the observed values of Y will not lie exactly on the sample regression line so that the values of Y_i and $\hat{Y}_i$ will differ. This difference is called a *residual* and is designated by e_i. Thus we have to distinguish the following.

$$Y_i = \alpha + \beta X_i + \varepsilon_i \quad \text{(population);}$$

$$Y_i = \hat{\alpha} + \hat{\beta}X_i + e_i \quad \text{(sample).}$$

Note that, in general, e_i is different from ε_i because $\hat{\alpha}$ and $\hat{\beta}$ differ from the true values of α and β. In fact, one can view the residuals e_i as "estimates" of the disturbances ε_i. (Alternatively, we might say that the distribution of e_i is used to approximate the distribution of ε_i.) This is illustrated in Figure 7-3. In Section 7-3 we will develop a procedure for estimating the regression parameters and, therefore, the population regression line.

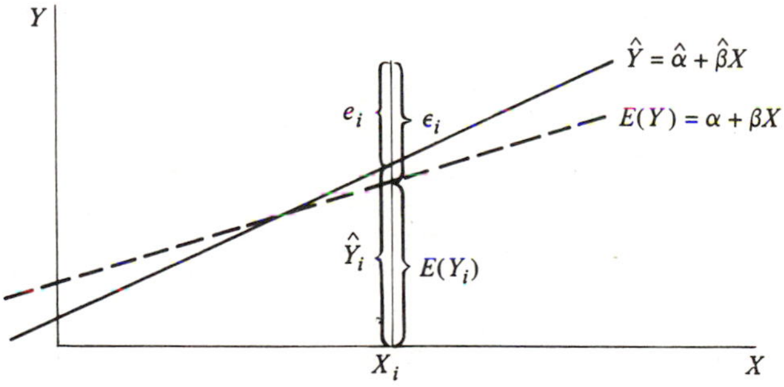

Figure 7-3

7-3 Estimation of the Regression Parameters

The problem of estimating the parameters of the regression model can be viewed as one of estimating the parameters of the probability distribution of the dependent variable Y. As we have shown, under the assumptions of the model, Y_i is normally distributed with the mean $E(Y_i) = \alpha + \beta X_i$ and variance $\text{Var}(Y_i) = \sigma^2$. The problem of estimating the regression parameters α and β is thus equivalent to the problem of estimating the mean of Y_i. This can be solved by a number of different estimation methods as described in Section 6-2. We shall try three such methods—least squares, best linear unbiased estimation, and maximum likelihood—and compare the resulting estimators and their properties. The object is to obtain an estimator that will have as many desirable properties as possible. Such an estimator can then be used to test hypotheses about the regression model and to make predictions.

Least Squares Estimation

Let us begin with the derivation of the *least square estimators* (LSE, or frequently OLS for *ordinary least squares*) of α and β. The principle of least squares estimation involves minimizing the sum of squared deviations of the observed values from their mean. That is, we have to find the value of the mean that makes the required sum as small as possible. In our case we have to minimize the sum S given by

$$S = \sum_{i=1}^{n} [Y_i - E(Y_i)]^2,$$

or

$$S = \sum_{i=1}^{n} (Y_i - \alpha - \beta X_i)^2.$$

To find the values of α and β that minimize this sum we have to differentiate S with respect to α and β. This gives

$$\frac{\partial S}{\partial \alpha} = \sum_i \frac{\partial(Y_i - \alpha - \beta X_i)^2}{\partial \alpha} = \sum_i 2(Y_i - \alpha - \beta X_i)(-1)$$

$$= -2 \sum_i (Y_i - \alpha - \beta X_i),$$

and

$$\frac{\partial S}{\partial \beta} = \sum_i \frac{\partial(Y_i - \alpha - \beta X_i)^2}{\partial \beta} = \sum_i 2(Y_i - \alpha - \beta X_i)(-X_i)$$

$$= -2 \sum_i X_i(Y_i - \alpha\, \beta X_i).$$

Equating each of these derivatives to zero and putting a "hat" on α and β to indicate that the resulting equations are satisfied by the least squares estimators of α and β, not by their true values, we obtain

$$-2 \sum_i (Y_i - \hat{\alpha} - \hat{\beta} X_i) = 0,$$

$$-2 \sum_i X_i(Y_i - \hat{\alpha} - \hat{\beta} X_i) = 0,$$

or, equivalently,

(7.10) $$\sum Y_i = \hat{\alpha} n + \hat{\beta}\left(\sum X_i\right),$$

(7.11) $$\sum X_i Y_i = \hat{\alpha}\left(\sum X_i\right) + \hat{\beta}\left(\sum X_i^2\right).$$

These equations are generally known as the "least squares normal equations."[4] Since we can write

$$Y_i = \hat{\alpha} + \hat{\beta} X_i + e_i,$$

where e_i represents the "least squares residuals," the least squares normal equations can be presented more simply as

(7.10a) $$\sum e_i = 0,$$

(7.11a) $$\sum X_i e_i = 0.$$

Equations (7.10) and (7.11) can be solved for $\hat{\alpha}$ and $\hat{\beta}$. The solution for $\hat{\beta}$ is

(7.12) $$\hat{\beta} = \frac{n\left(\sum X_i Y_i\right) - \left(\sum X_i\right)\left(\sum Y_i\right)}{n\left(\sum X_i^2\right) - \left(\sum X_i\right)^2}.$$

This expression can be written in a somewhat different way. Note that

(7.13) $$\begin{aligned} n \sum (X_i - \bar{X})(Y_i - \bar{Y}) &= n\left(\sum X_i Y_i\right) - n\bar{X}\left(\sum Y_i\right) - n\bar{Y}\left(\sum X_i\right) + n^2 \bar{X}\bar{Y} \\ &= n\left(\sum X_i Y_i\right) - \left(\sum X_i\right)\left(\sum Y_i\right) - \left(\sum X_i\right)\left(\sum Y_i\right) \\ &\quad + \left(\sum X_i\right)\left(\sum Y_i\right) \\ &= n\left(\sum X_i Y_i\right) - \left(\sum X_i\right)\left(\sum Y_i\right), \end{aligned}$$

[4] The following rule may be found useful in obtaining the least squares normal equation. In the regression equation, $Y_i = \alpha + \beta X_i + \varepsilon_i$, the multiplier of α is 1 and the multiplier of β is X_i. The first least squares normal equation is obtained by multiplying both sides of the regression equation by 1, adding all observations, and omitting the last term involving ε_i. The second equation is obtained by multiplying both sides of the regression equation by X_i, adding all observations, and omitting the last term involving ε_i. This rule can be extended to regression equations with any number of explanatory variables.

which is the numerator of the expression for $\hat{\beta}$. Also

$$n \sum (X_i - \bar{X})^2 = n(\sum X_i^2) - 2n\bar{X}(\sum X_i) + n^2\bar{X}^2 \tag{7.14}$$

$$= n(\sum X_i^2) - 2(\sum X_i)^2 + (\sum X_i)^2$$

$$= n(\sum X_i^2) - (\sum X_i)^2,$$

which is the denominator of the expression for $\hat{\beta}$. Therefore, we can write

$$\hat{\beta} = \frac{\sum (X_i - \bar{X})(Y_i - \bar{Y})}{\sum (X_i - \bar{X})^2},$$

since the n in the numerator and the denominator cancel out. A further simplification can be achieved by introducing new notation for the deviations of X_i and Y_i from their respective sample means. In particular, let

$$x_i' = X_i - \bar{X} \quad \text{and} \quad y_i' = Y_i - \bar{Y}.$$

Of course, this implies that $\Sigma x_i' = 0$ and $\Sigma y_i' = 0$. The expression for the least squares estimator of $\hat{\beta}$ then simplifies to

$$\hat{\beta} = \frac{\sum x_i' y_i'}{\sum x_i'^2}. \tag{7.12a}$$

Note that

$$\sum (X_i - \bar{X})(Y_i - \bar{Y}) = \sum X_i(Y_i - \bar{Y}) - \bar{X} \sum (Y_i - \bar{Y})$$
$$= \sum X_i(Y_i - \bar{Y}),$$

and also that

$$\sum (X_i - \bar{X})(Y_i - \bar{Y}) = \sum (X_i - \bar{X})Y_i - \bar{Y} \sum (X_i - \bar{X})$$
$$= \sum (X_i - \bar{X})Y_i,$$

so that only *one* of the variables in the cross product has to be measured in terms of deviations from the mean.

Once $\hat{\beta}$ is determined, the solution for $\hat{\alpha}$ can be obtained quite easily from equation (7.10). This leads to

$$\hat{\alpha} = \frac{1}{n}(\sum Y_i) - \hat{\beta}\frac{1}{n}(\sum X_i) = \bar{Y} - \hat{\beta}\bar{X}, \tag{7.15}$$

which means that the sample regression line

$$\hat{Y}_i = \hat{\alpha} + \hat{\beta}X_i$$

passes through the point $(\bar{X}, \bar{Y})$. The value of $\hat{\alpha}$ measures the intercept, and the value of $\hat{\beta}$ the slope of the sample regression line. The sampling properties of these estimators will be discussed at the end of this section. The process of obtaining least squares estimates of α and β is often referred to as "regressing Y on X" or "running a regression of Y on X."

EXAMPLE As a numerical example, consider the data in Table 7-2 on prices and quantities of oranges sold in a supermarket on twelve consecutive days. Let X_i be the price charged

Table 7-2

Price: ¢/lb	Quantity: lb
100	55
90	70
80	90
70	100
70	90
70	105
70	80
65	110
60	125
60	115
55	130
50	130

and Y_i the quantity sold on the ith day. Let us further postulate that the demand function is of the form

$$Y_i = \alpha + \beta X_i + \varepsilon_i$$

and such that the basic assumptions of the classical normal regression model are satisfied. We wish to obtain the least squares estimate of α and β. Carrying out the appropriate calculations we get

$$\bar{X} = 70, \qquad \sum x_i' y_i' = -3550,$$

$$\bar{Y} = 100, \qquad \sum x_i'^2 = 2250.$$

(We also note for future reference that $\Sigma y_i'^2 = 6300$.) The least squares estimates then are

$$\hat{\beta} = \frac{-3550}{2250} = -1.578,$$

$$\hat{\alpha} = 100 - (-1.578) \times 70 = 210.460,$$

so that the estimated sample regression line is

$$\hat{Y}_i = 210.460 - 1.578X_i.$$

This is our estimated demand curve. Since the function is linear, the price elasticity of demand is different at different prices. At the point of average price (i.e., when $X_i = 70$), the price elasticity η is estimated as

$$\hat{\eta}_{X_i=\bar{X}} = (-1.578) \times \frac{70}{100} = -1.105,$$

indicating that the demand is estimated to be slightly elastic at this point.

Best Linear Unbiased Estimation

Let us now turn to the derivation of the *best linear unbiased estimators* (BLUE) of α and β. The BLU estimation method requires that the estimator be a linear combination of sample observations, that it be unbiased, and that its variance be smaller than that of any other linear unbiased estimator. We shall use this method to derive the BLUE of β, say, $\tilde{\beta}$, first. By the condition of linearity we have

$$\tilde{\beta} = \sum_i a_i Y_i, \tag{7.16}$$

where a_i ($i = 1, 2, \ldots, n$) are some constants to be determined. Now

$$E(\tilde{\beta}) = E\left(\sum a_i Y_i\right) = \sum a_i E(Y_i) = \sum a_i(\alpha + \beta X_i) = \alpha\left(\sum a_i\right) + \beta\left(\sum a_i X_i\right).$$

This means that for $\tilde{\beta}$ to be unbiased we require that

$$\sum a_i = 0 \qquad \text{and} \qquad \sum a_i X_i = 1.$$

Finally, we require that $\tilde{\beta}$ have a smaller variance than any other estimator that satisfies the above conditions. The variance of $\tilde{\beta}$ is given as

$$\begin{aligned} \text{Var}(\tilde{\beta}) &= \text{Var}\left(\sum a_i Y_i\right) = \sum a_i^2 \,\text{Var}(Y_i) \\ &= \sum a_i^2 \sigma^2 = \sigma^2 \sum a_i^2, \end{aligned} \tag{7.17}$$

since the Ys are independent and each has the same variance σ^2, and the as are nonstochastic.

The problem now is to find $a_1, a_2, \ldots, a_n$ such that $\Sigma a_i = 0$, $\Sigma_i a_i X_i = 1$, and, at the same time, $\sigma^2 \Sigma a_i^2$ is as small as possible. That is, we have to minimize

$$\sigma^2 \sum a_i^2$$

subject to the conditions

$$\sum a_i = 0 \qquad \text{and} \qquad \left(\sum a_i X_i\right) - 1 = 0.$$

This is a problem of constrained minimization, which can be solved with the help of *Lagrange multiplier method.* The method for the case of one constraint was outlined earlier in describing the derivation of best linear unbiased estimators (Section 6-2). An extension to the case of two or more constraints can be made by simple analogy.[5] In the problem at hand we form a new function

$$H = \sigma^2 \sum_i a_i^2 - \lambda_1 \left(\sum_i a_i \right) - \lambda_2 \left[\left(\sum_i a_i X_i \right) - 1 \right],$$

which consists of the function to be minimized, the two constraints imposed, and two Lagrange multipliers, λ_1 and λ_2. To obtain the required solution we differentiate H with respect to $a_1, a_2, \ldots, a_n, \lambda_1$, and λ_2, and put each of the derivatives equal to zero. That is,

$$\text{(7.18a)} \qquad \frac{\partial H}{\partial a_1} = 0 \quad \frac{\partial H}{\partial a_2} = 0, \quad \ldots, \quad \frac{\partial H}{\partial a_n} = 0, \quad \frac{\partial H}{\partial \lambda_1} = 0, \quad \frac{\partial H}{\partial \lambda_2} = 0,$$

or, explicitly,

$$\text{(7.18b)} \qquad \begin{aligned} 2a_1\sigma^2 - \lambda_1 - \lambda_2 X_1 &= 0, \\ 2a_2\sigma^2 - \lambda_1 - \lambda_2 X_2 &= 0, \\ &\vdots \\ 2a_n\sigma^2 - \lambda_1 - \lambda_2 X_n &= 0, \\ -\sum_i a_i &= 0, \\ -\left(\sum_i a_i X_i\right) + 1 &= 0. \end{aligned}$$

This gives us $(n + 2)$ equations to be solved for the unknown $a_1, a_2, \ldots, a_n, \lambda_1$, and λ_2. The first n equations can be rewritten as

$$\text{(7.19)} \qquad \begin{aligned} a_1 &= \frac{1}{2\sigma^2}(\lambda_1 + \lambda_2 X_1) \\ a_2 &= \frac{1}{2\sigma^2}(\lambda_1 + \lambda_2 X_2) \\ &\vdots \\ a_n &= \frac{1}{2\sigma^2}(\lambda_1 + \lambda_2 X_n). \end{aligned}$$

By summing up these equations we get

$$\text{(7.20)} \qquad \sum_i a_i = \frac{1}{2\sigma^2}\left(\lambda_1 n + \lambda_2 \sum_i X_i\right).$$

Furthermore, multiplying the first equation of (7.19) by X_1, the second by X_2, the

[5] See, e.g., A. C. Chiang, *Fundamental Methods of Mathematical Economics,* 3rd ed. (New York: McGraw-Hill, 1984), pp. 372–386.

third by X_3, and so on, and then summing up over all n equations leads to

$$\sum_i a_i X_i = \frac{1}{2\sigma^2} [\lambda_1 (\sum_i X_i) + \lambda_2 (\sum_i X_i^2)]. \tag{7.21}$$

Substituting for Σa_i and $\Sigma a_i X_i$ from (7.20) and (7.21) into the last two equations of (7.18b) then gives

$$-\frac{1}{2\sigma^2}(\lambda_1 n + \lambda_2 \sum_i X_i) = 0,$$

$$-\frac{1}{2\sigma^2}[\lambda_1 (\sum_i X_i) + \lambda_2 (\sum_i X_i^2)] = -1.$$

Thus we have obtained two equations in two unknowns, λ_1 and λ_2. The reader can easily verify that the solution is

$$\lambda_1 = \frac{-2\sigma^2 \sum X_i}{n(\sum X_i^2) - (\sum X_i)^2},$$

$$\lambda_2 = \frac{2n\sigma^2}{n(\sum X_i^2) - (\sum X_i)^2}.$$

These expressions for λ_1 and λ_2 can be substituted into (7.19) to obtain the solution for $a_1, a_2, \ldots, a_n$. This is

$$a_i = \frac{-(\sum X_i) + nX_i}{n(\sum X_i^2) - (\sum X_i)^2} = \frac{(X_i - \bar{X})}{\sum (X_i - \bar{X})^2} = \frac{x_i'}{\sum x_i'^2} \qquad (i = 1, 2, \ldots, n). \tag{7.22}$$

These are then the constants that make $\hat{\beta}$ an unbiased estimator and minimize its variance.[6] Substituting for a_i into the formula for $\tilde{\beta}$ given by (7.16) leads to

$$\tilde{\beta} = \sum a_i Y_i = \frac{\sum x_i' Y_i}{\sum x_i'^2} = \frac{\sum x_i' y_i'}{\sum x_i'^2}.$$

This is precisely the same result as that obtained for the least squares estimator of β.

The application of the BLUE principle leads not only to the derivation of the formula for the estimator in question, but also to the determination of its variance. The formula for the variance of $\tilde{\beta}$ given by (7.17) is

$$\text{Var}(\tilde{\beta}) = \sigma^2 \sum a_i^2.$$

[6] It can be shown that the second-order conditions for the existence of a minimum are also fulfilled. For an elaboration see *ibid.*

To evaluate the term Σa_i^2 we use the result given in (7.22). Multiplying both sides of (7.22) by a_i and summing over all observations we get

$$\sum a_i^2 = \frac{-(\sum X_i)(\sum a_i) + n(\sum a_i X_i)}{n(\sum X_i^2) - (\sum X_i)^2}.$$

But from the last two equations in (7.18b) we know that

$$\sum a_i = 0 \qquad \text{and} \qquad \sum a_i X_i = 1.$$

This means that, in fact,

$$\sum a_i^2 = \frac{n}{n(\sum X_i^2) - (\sum X_i)^2} = \frac{1}{\sum x_i'^2}$$

so that

$$\text{(7.23)} \qquad \text{Var}(\tilde{\beta}) = \frac{\sigma^2}{\sum x_i'^2},$$

This, then, is the variance of the BLUE (and, equivalently, of the LSE) of β.[7]

Having obtained the BLUE of β we are left with the task of finding the BLUE of α, the intercept of the regression line. The derivation of this estimator—to be called $\tilde{\alpha}$—proceeds in exactly the same steps as the derivation of $\tilde{\beta}$ and, therefore, will not be presented here. As in the case of $\tilde{\beta}$, the process of determining the BLUE of α leads not only to the formula for the estimator itself, but also to the formula for its variance. The results are as follows.

$$\text{(7.24)} \qquad \tilde{\alpha} = \bar{Y} - \tilde{\beta}\bar{X},$$

$$\text{(7.25)} \quad \text{Var}(\tilde{\alpha}) = \frac{\sigma^2(\sum X_i^2)}{n(\sum x_i'^2)} = \frac{\sigma^2(\sum x_i'^2 + n\bar{X}^2)}{n(\sum x_i'^2)} = \sigma^2\left(\frac{1}{n} + \frac{\bar{X}^2}{\sum x_i'^2}\right).$$

By noting that $\tilde{\beta}$ and $\hat{\beta}$ are the same, and by comparing (7.24) with (7.15), we can see

[7] It should be noted that $\tilde{\beta}$ is not, in general, a linear estimator of β with the minimum mean square error. The formula for the linear combination of sample observations that gives the minimum MSE is

$$\left(\frac{\beta^2}{(\sigma^2/\sum x_i'^2) + \beta^2}\right)\hat{\beta}.$$

While this expression does not qualify as an estimator (since it involves unknown parameters), it shows that—for β and σ^2 different from zero—the value of the linear minimum MSE estimator of β is less than $\hat{\beta}$ in absolute value by some unknown amount.

that the BLUE of α is the same as the least squares estimator of α. This result—and that for the BLUE of β—is known as the *Gauss–Markov theorem.*

Maximum Likelihood Estimation

The last method to be applied is the *maximum likelihood method.* As explained in Section 6-2, the maximum likelihood estimators (MLE) of the parameters of a given population are considered to be those values of the parameters that would generate the observed sample most often. To find these estimators, we have to determine the likelihood function for the observations in the sample and then maximize it with respect to the unknown parameters. In the case of our regression model, the sample consists of observations on the n variables $Y_1, Y_2, \ldots Y_n$. These variables are normally distributed with means $(\alpha + \beta X_1)$, $(\alpha + \beta X_2)$, . . . , $(\alpha + \beta X_n)$ and with a common variance equal to σ^2. Let us denote these observations by $y_1, y_2, \ldots, y_n$. The relationship between the probability distribution of Y_i and that of ε_i can be established with the help of the following theorem.

Theorem 19 *(Change of Variable). If a random variable X has a probability density $f(x)$, and if a variable Z is a function of X such that there is a one-to-one correspondence between X and Z, then the probability density of Z is $f(z) = |dx/dz| f(x)$, $dx/dz \neq 0$.*

Here $|dx/dz|$ stands for the absolute value of the derivative of x with respect to z. The proof of this theorem can be found elsewhere.[8] Its importance lies in the fact that, under general conditions, it enables us to determine the distribution of one variable from the knowledge of the distribution of a related variable. In the context of our regression model the known distribution is that of ε_i, and the distribution to be determined is that of Y_i. Since we have

$$Y_i = \alpha + \beta X_i + \varepsilon_i,$$

there is obviously a one-to-one correspondence between Y_i and ε_i. Therefore, we can write

$$f(y_i) = \left|\frac{d\varepsilon_i}{dY_i}\right| f(\varepsilon_i).$$

But

$$\varepsilon_i = Y_i - \alpha - \beta X_i,$$

so that

$$\frac{d\varepsilon_i}{dY_i} = 1.$$

[8] See, e.g., John E. Freund and Ronald E. Walpole, *Mathematical Statistics,* 3rd ed. (Englewood Cliffs, NJ: Prentice-Hall, 1980), pp. 232–233.

Consequently, we have

$$f(y_i) = f(\varepsilon_i).$$

Now, as noted earlier, since the Ys are normal and uncorrelated, they are independent. Armed with this result, we can present the likelihood function as

$$\ell = f(y_1)f(y_2) \cdots f(y_n).$$

Since the values of the parameters that maximize ℓ are the same as those that maximize its logarithm, we can operate with $L = \log \ell$ instead of operating with ℓ itself. Thus we wish to maximize

$$L = \sum_{i=1}^{n} \log f(y_i).$$

Now, since Y_i is normally distributed with mean $(\alpha + \beta X_i)$ and variance σ^2 we have, from the formula for normal distribution,

$$\log f(y_i) = -\frac{1}{2}\log(2\pi\sigma^2) - \frac{1}{2}\left(\frac{Y_i - \alpha - \beta X_i}{\sigma}\right)^2,$$

where $\pi = 3.14159. \ldots$ (In writing out the formula, we use a capital letter for the values of the variables Y_i and X_i in order to conform to the notation customarily used in a simple regression model in other texts.) Therefore,

$$L = -\frac{n}{2}\log(2\pi) - \frac{n}{2}\log\sigma^2 - \frac{1}{2\sigma^2}\sum_i (Y_i - \alpha - \beta X_i)^2. \tag{7.26}$$

There are three unknown parameters in L, namely, α, β, and σ^2. Differentiating with respect to each of them, we obtain

$$\frac{\partial L}{\partial \alpha} = -\frac{1}{2\sigma^2}\sum 2(Y_i - \alpha - \beta X_i)(-1),$$

$$\frac{\partial L}{\partial \beta} = -\frac{1}{2\sigma^2}\sum_i 2(Y_i - \alpha - \beta X_i)(-X_i),$$

$$\frac{\partial L}{\partial \sigma^2} = -\frac{n}{2\sigma^2} + \frac{1}{2\sigma^4}\sum_i (Y_i - \alpha - \beta X_i)^2.$$

Equating these to zero and putting a "triangle" on the parameters to be estimated leads to

$$\frac{1}{2\hat{\sigma}^2}\sum_i (Y_i - \hat{\alpha} - \hat{\beta}X_i) = 0,$$

$$\frac{1}{2\hat{\sigma}^2}\sum_i X_i(Y_i - \hat{\alpha} - \hat{\beta}X_i) = 0,$$

$$-\frac{n}{2\hat{\sigma}^2} + \frac{1}{2\hat{\sigma}^4}\sum (Y_i - \hat{\alpha} - \hat{\beta}X_i)^2 = 0.$$

A simple manipulation of the first two equations gives

$$\sum Y_i = -\hat{\alpha}n + \hat{\beta}(\sum X_i),$$

$$\sum X_iY_i = \hat{\alpha}(\sum X_i) + \hat{\beta}(\sum X_i^2).$$

These equations are precisely the same as the least squares normal equations given by (7.10) and (7.11) above. This means that *the maximum likelihood estimators of α and β are the same as the least squares estimators.* The third equation gives the maximum likelihood estimator of σ^2, which is

$$\hat{\sigma}^2 = \frac{1}{n}\sum_i (Y_i - \hat{\alpha} - \hat{\beta}X_i)^2; \tag{7.27}$$

or, since $\hat{\alpha}$ and $\hat{\beta}$ are equal to the least squares estimators,

$$\hat{\sigma}^2 = \frac{1}{n}\sum_i e_i^2, \tag{7.27a}$$

where, in accordance with the earlier notation, the terms e_i represent least squares residuals. Since $\Sigma e_i = 0$, it follows from (7.27a) that the MLE of the variance of the disturbances is equal to the (unadjusted) sample variance of the least squares residuals.

It may be interesting to note that the results of of maximum likelihood estimation are exactly the same as those obtained by the method of moments, which is based on the principle of estimating the moments of a population by the corresponding moments of a sample. In the case of the regression model we can implement this moments principle by imposing the assumptions made about the disturbance (ε) on the sample residuals (e). First, we note that the assumption of *normality* (7.2) together with the assumption of *nonautocorrelation* (7.5) implies independence, which means random sampling. These two assumptions provide no specific information about the regression parameters. Next, the assumptions of *zero mean* (7.3) and of *homoskedasticity* (7.4) lead to the requirements that

$$\frac{1}{n}\sum e_i = 0,$$

$$\frac{1}{n}\sum e_i^2 = \hat{\sigma}^2,$$

where $\hat{\sigma}^2$ is the moments estimator of σ^2. Finally, the assumption of a *nonstochastic explanatory variable* implies that ε and X are uncorrelated, which yields the condition

$$\frac{1}{n}\sum e_iX_i = 0.$$

Solving the above three equations for the estimated α, β, and σ^2, we obtain the same results as those given by MLE.

Properties of the Least Squares Estimators

In summary, we find then that each of the estimation methods considered leads to the same estimates of the regression parameters. In other words, under the assumption of the classical normal linear regression model, the least squares estimators of the regression parameters are equivalent to the best linear unbiased and the maximum likelihood estimators. However, while the least squares method provided us only with the formulas for the estimators of α and β, the BLU estimation method supplied us also with the formulas for their variances, and the ML estimation method gave us a formula for an estimator of σ^2. Both of these subsidiary results are very useful.

Let us now consider the properties of the least squares estimators of α and β. Beginning with the finite sample properties, we see immediately that the least squares estimators are *unbiased* because they are BLUE. We can also show that they are *efficient*. The Cramer–Rao lower bounds for unbiased estimators of α and β are given by the first two diagonal elements of the following information matrix.

$$\begin{bmatrix} -E\left(\frac{\partial^2 L}{\partial\alpha^2}\right) & -E\left(\frac{\partial^2 L}{\partial\alpha\partial\beta}\right) & -E\left(\frac{\partial^2 L}{\partial\alpha\partial\sigma^2}\right) \\ -E\left(\frac{\partial^2 L}{\partial\beta\partial\alpha}\right) & -E\left(\frac{\partial^2 L}{\partial\beta^2}\right) & -E\left(\frac{\partial^2 L}{\partial\beta\partial\sigma^2}\right) \\ -E\left(\frac{\partial^2 L}{\partial\sigma^2\partial\alpha}\right) & -E\left(\frac{\partial^2 L}{\partial\sigma^2\partial\beta}\right) & -E\left(\frac{\partial^2 L}{\partial(\sigma^2)^2}\right) \end{bmatrix}^{-1} = \begin{bmatrix} \frac{n}{\sigma^2} & \frac{\sum X_i}{\sigma^2} & 0 \\ \frac{\sum X_i}{\sigma^2} & \frac{\sum X_i^2}{\sigma^2} & 0 \\ 0 & 0 & \frac{n}{2\sigma^4} \end{bmatrix}^{-1}$$

$$= \begin{bmatrix} \frac{\sigma^2 \sum X_i^2}{n(\sum x_i'^2)} & \frac{-\bar{X}\sigma^2}{\sum x_i'^2} & 0 \\ \frac{-\bar{X}\sigma^2}{\sum x_i'^2} & \frac{\sigma^2}{\sum x_i'^2} & 0 \\ 0 & 0 & \frac{2\sigma^4}{n} \end{bmatrix}.$$

Comparison of the first two diagonal elements with the formulas (7.25) and (7.23) of the text shows that these elements are, indeed, equal to the variances of the regression parameters.

Finally, the least squares estimators have all the desirable asymptotic properties since they are the same as the maximum likelihood estimators, and the latter are known to be *asymptotically unbiased, consistent,* and *asymptotically efficient.* Therefore, the least squares estimators of the regression parameters of the classical normal linear regression model have all the desirable finite sample *and* asymptotic properties. It can also be shown that the LSE of α and β are *minimax* in the sense that among all linear (not necessarily unbiased) estimators of α and β the maximum possible value of

$$\text{MSE}(\alpha^*) + \text{MSE}(\beta^*)$$

for all values of α and β is smallest when α^* and β^* are the least squares estimates.[9]

In conclusion we recall the role that the various assumptions (7.2) through (7.6) played in demonstrating the properties of the least squares estimators. First we note that in order to prove unbiasedness we only needed the assumptions of zero mean and a nonstochastic X. For best linear unbiasedness we needed all of the basic assumptions except normality. The normality assumption, along with the other four assumptions, was needed for the proof of efficiency by means of the Cramer–Rao lower bound, and also for the proof that LSE are MLE, which guaranteed the desirable asymptotic properties of the LS estimators. However, the assumption of normality is not needed for consistency, as shown in (8.1) below. It is utilized, though, for establishing confidence intervals and for the tests of significance introduced in the next section.

7-4 Further Results of Statistical Inference

In Section 7-3 we derived the least squares estimators of the regression parameters and established their desirable properties. We shall now consider other features of these estimators and show how the regression model can be used for testing hypotheses about the regression parameters and for prediction.

Distribution of $\hat{\alpha}$ and $\hat{\beta}$

The distribution of the least squares estimators $\hat{\alpha}$ and $\hat{\beta}$ is easy to deduce from the results so far obtained. First, since these estimators are unbiased, their means are equal to the true values of α and β, respectively. Second, from the derivation of the BLUE properties we know what their variances are. Finally, since both $\hat{\alpha}$ and $\hat{\beta}$ are linear combinations of independent normal variables $Y_1, Y_2, \ldots, Y_n$, they must themselves be normally distributed (see Theorem 14 of Section 4-2). That is, we can write

$$\text{(7.28)} \qquad \hat{\alpha} \sim N\left[\alpha, \sigma^2\left(\frac{1}{n} + \frac{\bar{X}^2}{\sum x_i'^2}\right)\right]$$

$$\hat{\beta} \sim N\left[\beta, \frac{\sigma^2}{\sum x_i'^2}\right],$$

using the variance formulas (7.23) and (7.25).

Let us now consider the variances of $\hat{\alpha}$ and $\hat{\beta}$ in greater detail. By examining the formulas we can observe the following.

[9] See E. Greenberg and C. E. Webster, Jr., *Advanced Econometrics* (New York: Wiley, 1983), pp. 165–166.

1. The larger the variance of the disturbance (σ^2), the larger the variances of $\hat{\alpha}$ and $\hat{\beta}$.
2. The more dispersed the values of the explanatory variable X, the smaller the variances of $\hat{\alpha}$ and $\hat{\beta}$.
3. If all the values of X were the same, i.e., if $X_1 = X_2 = \cdots = X_n$, both variances would be infinitely large.
4. The variance of $\hat{\alpha}$ is smallest when $\bar{X} = 0$ ($\Sigma x_i'^2 \neq 0$).

The first point is obvious; it means that the greater the dipersion of the disturbance around the population regression line, the greater the dispersion of our "guesses" concerning the value of the regression parameters. If all disturbances were completely concentrated at their means—that is, if all disturbances were equal to zero—our "guesses" as to the values of the regression parameters would always be perfect (as long as we observed at least two different valus of the dependent variable, of course). The second point is based on the fact that the larger the dispersion of the Xs, the larger $\Sigma x_i'^2$. In fact, if we have an absolutely free choice of selecting a given number of values of X within some interval—say, from a to b ($0 < a < b$)—then *the optimal choice would be to choose one half of the Xs equal to* a *and the other half equal to* b. Such a choice would maximize $\Sigma x_i'^2$. The third point follows from the fact that if all values of the explanatory variable were the same, the value of $\Sigma x_i'^2$ would be zero, and any finite number divided by zero is equal to infinity. Another way of making the same point is to state that if all observed values of Y were to lie along a vertical line (as they would do if they all corresponded to the same value of X), we could not make any inference about either the slope or the intercept of the regression line. The final point is somewhat less important in practice since it refers only to the variance of $\hat{\alpha}$. If the values of X can be negative as well as positive, Var($\hat{\alpha}$) would be smallest if the values of X were selected so as to make $\bar{X}$ equal to zero. In this case Var($\hat{\alpha}$) would be equal to σ^2/n, which is its lowest attainable value.

EXAMPLE To illustrate the gain in efficiency that can be achieved by a judicious choice of the values of the explanatory variable, we use the example given in Section 7-3, which involved estimating the demand for oranges. The values of X (= price of oranges) were given as follows: 100, 90, 80, 70, 70, 70, 70, 65, 60, 60, 55, and 50. For these twelve values we found that $\bar{X} = 70$ and $\Sigma x_i'^2 = 2250$. The variances of the least squares estimators in this case are

$$\mathrm{Var}(\hat{\alpha}) = \sigma^2\left(\frac{1}{n} + \frac{\bar{X}^2}{\sum x_i'^2}\right) = \sigma^2\left(\frac{1}{12} + \frac{70^2}{2250}\right) = 2.261111\sigma^2,$$

$$\mathrm{Var}(\hat{\beta}) = \frac{\sigma^2}{\sum x_i'^2} = \frac{\sigma^2}{2250} = 0.000444\sigma^2.$$

Suppose now that instead of the above values we had $X_1 = X_2 = \cdots = X_6 = 100$ and $X_6 = X_7 = \cdots = X_{12} = 50$. Then we would have $\bar{X} = 75$ and $\Sigma x_i'^2 = 7500$. The resulting variances would then be

$$\mathrm{Var}(\hat{\alpha}) = \sigma^2 \left(\frac{1}{12} + \frac{75^2}{7500} \right) = 0.833333\sigma^2,$$

$$\mathrm{Var}(\hat{\beta}) = \frac{\sigma^2}{7500} = 0.000133\sigma^2.$$

Comparing the variances for these two cases we get

$$\frac{\mathrm{Var}(\hat{\alpha})_{\text{case I}}}{\mathrm{Var}(\hat{\alpha})_{\text{case II}}} = \frac{2.261111\sigma^2}{0.833333\sigma^2} = 2.713,$$

$$\frac{\mathrm{Var}(\hat{\beta})_{\text{case I}}}{\mathrm{Var}(\hat{\beta})_{\text{case II}}} = \frac{0.000444\sigma^2}{0.000133\sigma^2} = 3.338.$$

That is, the variance of $\hat{\alpha}$ in the first case is more than $2\frac{1}{2}$ times, and that of $\hat{\beta}$ $3\frac{1}{3}$ times, as large as the corresponding variance in the second case.

It is clear that the gain in efficiency resulting from an optimal choice of the values of X can be quite considerable. In practice the difficulty is, of course, that the econometrician usually has no choice in the matter because the sampling has been done by somebody else and the econometrician gets only the completed sample results.[10]

Covariance of $\hat{\alpha}$ and $\hat{\beta}$

A question that is of some interest concerns the relationship between $\hat{\alpha}$ and $\hat{\beta}$. By using $\hat{\alpha}$ instead of α and $\hat{\beta}$ instead of β, we are committing sampling errors, and it is of some relevance to know whether these two sampling errors can be expected to be of the same sign or not. That is, we wish to find the sign of

$$E(\hat{\alpha} - \alpha)(\hat{\beta} - \beta),$$

which is, by definition, the covariance of $\hat{\alpha}$ and $\hat{\beta}$. Now, by (7.15) we have

$$\hat{\alpha} = \bar{Y} - \hat{\beta}\bar{X}.$$

The regression model is, as stated earlier,

$$Y_i = \alpha + \beta X_i + \varepsilon_i.$$

Adding all sample observations and dividing by n we get

$$\bar{Y} = \alpha + \beta\bar{X} + \bar{\varepsilon} \quad \text{or} \quad \alpha = \bar{Y} - \beta\bar{X} - \bar{\varepsilon}, \tag{7.29}$$

so that

$$\hat{\alpha} - \alpha = (\bar{Y} - \hat{\beta}\bar{X}) - (\bar{Y} - \beta\bar{X} - \bar{\varepsilon}) = -(\hat{\beta} - \beta)\bar{X} + \bar{\varepsilon}. \tag{7.30}$$

[10] It is to be noted, though, that the optimality of the sampling design which "piles up" the values of X at each end of the interval is crucially dependent on the linearity of the model. Such a sampling design would be poor for models in which linearity were not to be assumed but to be tested for.

Further, by (7.12a) we have

$$\hat{\beta} = \frac{\sum x_i' y_i'}{\sum x_i'^2};$$

but by deducting (7.29) from (7.1), we get

$$(7.31) \qquad (Y_i - \bar{Y}) = \beta(X_i - \bar{X}) + (\varepsilon_i - \bar{\varepsilon}),$$

or, using the abbreviated notation for deviations from sample means,

$$(7.31a) \qquad y_i' = \beta x_i' + \varepsilon_i'.$$

Substituting this into the formula for $\hat{\beta}$ gives

$$\hat{\beta} = \frac{\sum x_i' (\beta x_i' + \varepsilon_i')}{\sum x_i'^2} = \beta + \frac{\sum x_i' \varepsilon_i'}{\sum x_i'^2},$$

so that

$$(7.32) \qquad \hat{\beta} - \beta = \frac{\sum x_i' \varepsilon_i'}{\sum x_i'^2} = \frac{\sum x_i' (\varepsilon_i - \bar{\varepsilon})}{\sum x_i'^2} = \frac{\sum x_i' \varepsilon_i - \bar{\varepsilon} \sum x_i'}{\sum x_i'^2} = \frac{\sum x_i' \varepsilon_i}{\sum x_i'^2},$$

which is the sampling error of $\hat{\beta}$. Thus, combining (7.30) and (7.32), we obtain

$$E(\hat{\alpha} - \alpha)(\hat{\beta} - \beta) = E[-(\hat{\beta} - \beta)\bar{X} + \bar{\varepsilon}](\hat{\beta} - \beta) = -\bar{X}E(\hat{\beta} - \beta)^2 + E\bar{\varepsilon}\left(\frac{\sum x_i' \varepsilon_i}{\sum x_i'^2}\right).$$

Let us consider the last term:

$$E\bar{\varepsilon}\left(\frac{\sum x_i' \varepsilon_i}{\sum x_i'^2}\right) = E\left(\frac{\sum x_i' \varepsilon_i \bar{\varepsilon}}{\sum x_i'^2}\right)$$

$$= \frac{\sum x_i' E\varepsilon_i (1/n)(\varepsilon_1 + \varepsilon_2 + \cdots + \varepsilon_i + \cdots + \varepsilon_n)}{\sum x_i'^2}$$

$$= \frac{(1/n) \sum x_i' (E\varepsilon_i\varepsilon_1 + E\varepsilon_i\varepsilon_2 + \cdots + E\varepsilon_i^2 + \cdots + E\varepsilon_i\varepsilon_n)}{\sum x_i'^2}$$

$$= \frac{(1/n) \sum x_i' (0 + 0 + \cdots + \sigma^2 + \cdots + 0)}{\sum x_i'^2} = \frac{(1/n)\sigma^2 \sum x_i'}{\sum x_i'^2} = 0$$

because $\Sigma x_i' = 0$. Therefore,

$$(7.33) \qquad E(\hat{\alpha} - \alpha)(\hat{\beta} - \beta) = -\bar{X}E(\hat{\beta} - \beta)^2 = -\bar{X}\operatorname{Var}(\hat{\beta}) = -\bar{X}\left(\frac{\sigma^2}{\sum x_i'^2}\right),$$

by (7.23). This, then, is the covariance of $\hat{\alpha}$ and $\hat{\beta}$. From this result we can see that, *as long as* $\bar{X}$ *is positive,* the sampling errors of $\hat{\alpha}$ and $\hat{\beta}$ can be expected to be of opposite sign. In this case an overstatement of the true value of α can be expected to be associated with an understatement of the true value of β, and vice versa.

Estimation of σ^2 and of Var($\hat{\alpha}$) and Var($\hat{\beta}$)

Under the assumptions of the classical normal linear regression model, the least squares estimators of α and β have all the desirable properties of an estimator. But whether or not they are really useful depends on the size of their variances. If their variances were to be very large, the fact that no other unbiased estimator can have a smaller variance is of little consolation. With large variances our guesses about the true values of the parameters are likely to be far off the mark. In Section 7-3 we developed formulas for the variances of $\hat{\alpha}$ and $\hat{\beta}$, but these formulas involve an unknown parameter σ^2 so that their evaluation is impossible. However, σ^2 can be estimated; in fact, we have already derived an estimation formula for it in connection with the maximum likelihood estimators in Section 7-3 above. The estimator of σ^2 was a "by-product" of getting the maximum likelihood estimators of α and β. The formula, given by (7.27), is

$$\hat{\sigma}^2 = \frac{1}{n} \sum_i (Y_i - \hat{\alpha} - \hat{\beta}X_i)^2.$$

Since this is a maximum likelihood estimator of σ^2, it has all the desirable asymptotic properties, but its small sample properties remain to be established. In particular, we may want to check whether $\hat{\sigma}^2$ is or is not an unbiased estimator of σ^2. To do this we rewrite the expression for $\hat{\sigma}^2$ in a somewhat different form. First, substituting for Y_i gives

$$\hat{\sigma}^2 = \frac{1}{n} \sum (\alpha + \beta X_i + \varepsilon_i - \hat{\alpha} - \hat{\beta}X_i)^2 = \frac{1}{n} \sum [-(\hat{\alpha} - \alpha) - (\hat{\beta} - \beta)X_i + \varepsilon_i]^2.$$

Next, substituting for $(\hat{\alpha} - \alpha)$ from (7.30) we get

$$\begin{aligned}
\hat{\sigma}^2 &= \frac{1}{n} \sum [(\hat{\beta} - \beta)\bar{X} - \bar{\varepsilon} - (\hat{\beta} - \beta)X_i + \varepsilon_i]^2 \\
&= \frac{1}{n} \sum [-(\hat{\beta} - \beta)x_i' + \varepsilon_i']^2 \\
&= \frac{1}{n} \sum [(\hat{\beta} - \beta)^2 x_i'^2 + \varepsilon_i'^2 - 2(\hat{\beta} - \beta)\, \varepsilon_i' x_i'] \\
&= \frac{1}{n} (\hat{\beta} - \beta)^2 \sum x_i'^2 + \frac{1}{n} \sum \varepsilon_i'^2 - \frac{2}{n} (\hat{\beta} - \beta) \sum \varepsilon_i' x_i'.
\end{aligned}$$

But from (7.32) we have

$$\sum x_i'\varepsilon_i' = (\hat{\beta} - \beta) \sum x_i'^2,$$

so that we can write

$$\hat{\hat{\sigma}}^2 = -\frac{1}{n}(\hat{\beta}-\beta)^2 \sum x_i'^2 + \frac{1}{n}\sum \varepsilon_i'^2.$$

Taking mathematical expectation on both sides, we obtain

$$E(\hat{\hat{\sigma}}^2) = -\frac{1}{n}\sum x_i'^2 E(\hat{\beta}-\beta)^2 + \frac{1}{n}\sum E(\varepsilon_i'^2).$$

Now

$$E(\hat{\beta}-\beta)^2 = \text{Var}(\hat{\beta}) = \frac{\sigma^2}{\sum x_i'^2},$$

and

$$E\frac{1}{n}\sum(\varepsilon_i'^2) = E\frac{1}{n}\sum(\varepsilon_i-\bar{\varepsilon})^2 = E\left(\frac{1}{n}\sum \varepsilon_i^2 - \bar{\varepsilon}^2\right)$$

$$= \sigma^2 - \frac{\sigma^2}{n}$$

$$= \left(\frac{n-1}{n}\right)\sigma^2.$$

We use these results to get

(7.34)
$$E(\hat{\hat{\sigma}}^2) = -\frac{1}{n}\left(\sum x_i'^2\right)\left(\frac{\sigma^2}{\sum x_i'^2}\right) + \left(\frac{n-1}{n}\right)\sigma^2$$

$$= -\frac{\sigma^2}{n} + \left(\frac{n-1}{n}\right)\sigma^2 = \left(\frac{n-2}{n}\right)\sigma^2.$$

That is, $\hat{\hat{\sigma}}^2$ is a *biased* estimator of σ^2. However, given the result in (7.34) it is easy to devise an unbiased estimator of σ^2. Multiplying both sides of (7.34) by $n/(n-2)$ gives

$$\left(\frac{n}{n-2}\right)E(\hat{\hat{\sigma}}^2) = \sigma^2,$$

or

$$E\left(\frac{n}{n-2}\right)\frac{1}{n}\sum(Y_i-\hat{\alpha}-\hat{\beta}X_i)^2 = \sigma^2,$$

which reduces to

$$E\left(\frac{1}{n-2}\right)\sum(Y_i-\hat{\alpha}-\hat{\beta}X_i)^2 = \sigma^2.$$

Thus an unbiased estimator of σ^2, say, s^2, is given by

(7.35)
$$s^2 = \frac{1}{n-2}\sum(Y_i-\hat{\alpha}-\hat{\beta}X_i)^2 = \frac{1}{n-2}\sum e_i^2.$$

It can also be shown that s^2 is a best quadratic unbiased estimator (BQUE) of σ^2, that is, that among all quadratic unbiased estimators of σ^2 the estimator s^2 has the smallest variance.[11] Since asymptotically there is no difference between $1/(n-2)$ and $1/n$, s^2 is asymptotically equal to $\hat{\hat{\sigma}}^2$ and, therefore, has the same optimal asymptotic properties.

An interesting property of s^2 is that it is independent of $\hat{\alpha}$ and $\hat{\beta}$. To show this we first note that s^2 is, by definition, just a function of the least squares residuals, so that it is sufficient to show that $\hat{\alpha}$ and $\hat{\beta}$ are independent of $e_1, e_2, \ldots, e_n$. Further, since each of these quantities is normally distributed, it is sufficient to show that $\hat{\alpha}$ and $\hat{\beta}$ are uncorrelated with $e_1, e_2, \ldots, e_n$. Considering $\hat{\beta}$ first, we have, for any $j = 1, 2, \ldots, n$,

$$\begin{aligned} E(\hat{\beta}-\beta)e_j &= E(\hat{\beta}-\beta)[-(\hat{\beta}-\beta)x_j' + \varepsilon_j'] \\ &= -x_j' E(\hat{\beta}-\beta)^2 + E(\hat{\beta}-\beta)\,\varepsilon_j' \\ &= -\frac{\sigma^2 x_j'}{\sum x_i'^2} + E\left(\frac{\varepsilon_j' \sum x_i'\varepsilon_i}{\sum x_i'^2}\right). \end{aligned}$$

But

$$\begin{aligned} E\left(\varepsilon_j' \sum x_i'\varepsilon_i\right) &= E(\varepsilon_j - \bar{\varepsilon})(x_1'\varepsilon_1 + x_2'\varepsilon_2 + \cdots + x_n'\varepsilon_n) \\ &= \sigma^2 x_j' - E\left(\bar{\varepsilon} \sum x_i'\varepsilon_i\right) \\ &= \sigma^2 x_j' - \frac{\sigma^2}{n} \sum x_i' \\ &= \sigma^2 x_j', \end{aligned}$$

so that

$$\begin{aligned} E(\hat{\beta}-\beta)e_j &= -\frac{\sigma^2 x_j'}{\sum x_i'^2} + \frac{\sigma^2 x_j'}{\sum x_i'^2} \\ &= 0. \end{aligned}$$

Similarly, it could also be shown that

$$E(\hat{\alpha}-\alpha)e_j = 0.$$

Thus there is no relationship between the size of the least squares regression coefficients and that of the estimate of σ^2.

For the purpose of computing the value of s^2, the formula (7.35) can be simplified so that we avoid the need for calculating individual es, the deviations of the ob-

[11] See Henri Theil, *Principles of Econometrics* (New York: Wiley, 1971), p. 128.

served values from the sample regression line. By substituting for $\hat{\alpha}$ we obtain

$$s^2 = \frac{1}{n-2}\sum [Y_i - (\overline{Y} - \hat{\beta}\overline{X}) - \hat{\beta}X_i]^2 = \frac{1}{n-2}\sum (y_i' - \hat{\beta}x_i')^2$$

$$= \frac{1}{n-2}\left(\sum y_i'^2 + \hat{\beta}^2 \sum x_i'^2 - 2\hat{\beta}\sum x_i'y_i'\right);$$

but from (7.12a) we have

$$\hat{\beta}\sum x_i'^2 = \sum x_i'y_i',$$

so that

$$\hat{\beta}^2\sum x_i'^2 = \hat{\beta}\sum x_i'y_i'.$$

Using this result leads to

$$s^2 = \frac{1}{n-2}\left(\sum y_i'^2 - \hat{\beta}\sum x_i'y_i'\right), \tag{7.36}$$

which is much easier to compute than the result given by (7.35). (In some of the earlier texts and in some computer printouts s is called the *standard error of estimate.*)

By using s^2 as the estimator of σ^2, we can obtain estimators of $\text{Var}(\hat{\alpha})$ and $\text{Var}(\hat{\beta})$; these estimators will be unbiased and will have optimal asymptotic properties. Following the customary notation, we denote the estimator of $\text{Var}(\hat{\alpha})$ by $s^2_{\hat{\alpha}}$ and the estimator of $\text{Var}(\hat{\beta})$ by $s^2_{\hat{\beta}}$. The appropriate formulas are

$$s^2_{\hat{\alpha}} = s^2\left(\frac{1}{n} + \frac{\overline{X}^2}{\sum x_i'^2}\right) \tag{7.37}$$

$$s^2_{\hat{\beta}} = \frac{s^2}{\sum x_i'^2}.$$

The square roots of these estimators, $s_{\hat{\alpha}}$ and $s_{\hat{\beta}}$, represent the estimated standard errors of $\hat{\alpha}$ and $\hat{\beta}$. They are used extensively as measures of precision of $\hat{\alpha}$ and $\hat{\beta}$. (In referring to $s_{\hat{\alpha}}$ and $s_{\hat{\beta}}$ research workers frequently use the term "standard errors" instead of "estimated standard errors." Since the true standard errors are hardly ever known, the omission of the word "estimated" usually creates no confusion.)

Confidence Intervals for α, β, and σ^2

A more formal indication of the precision of $\hat{\alpha}$, $\hat{\beta}$, and s^2 can be achieved by constructing confidence intervals. Let us begin with $\hat{\beta}$. Since

$$\hat{\beta} \sim N(\beta, \sigma^2_{\hat{\beta}}),$$

where $\sigma^2_{\hat{\beta}} = \text{Var}(\hat{\beta})$, it follows that

$$\frac{\hat{\beta} - \beta}{\sigma_{\hat{\beta}}} \sim N(0, 1).$$

Furthermore, we know from (5.8b) that

$$\frac{\sum (Y_i - \hat{\alpha} - \hat{\beta}X_i)^2}{\sigma^2} \sim \chi^2_{n-2}.$$

In this case the number of the degrees of freedom of the chi-square distribution is $(n - 2)$, since two degrees of freedom got "used up" for calculating $\hat{\alpha}$ and $\hat{\beta}$. Note that we can write

$$\frac{\sum (Y_i - \hat{\alpha} - \hat{\beta}X_i)^2}{\sigma^2} = \frac{(n-2)s^2}{\sigma^2} = \frac{(n-2)s^2/(\sum x_i'^2)}{\sigma^2/(\sum x_i'^2)} = \frac{(n-2)s^2_{\hat{\beta}}}{\sigma^2_{\hat{\beta}}}.$$

Thus we have

$$\frac{(n-2)\, s^2_{\hat{\beta}}}{\sigma^2_{\hat{\beta}}} \sim \chi^2_{\hat{\beta}-2}.$$

Therefore,

$$\frac{(\hat{\beta} - \beta)/\sigma_{\hat{\beta}}}{\sqrt{(n-2)s^2_{\hat{\beta}}/(n-2)\sigma^2_{\hat{\beta}}}} = \frac{\hat{\beta} - \beta}{s_{\hat{\beta}}}$$

is a ratio in which the numerator is a standard normal variable and the denominator an independent $[\chi^2_{n-2}/(n-2)]^{1/2}$ variable. As explained in Section 5-2, such a ratio has a t distribution with $(n - 2)$ degrees of freedom. That is,

$$\text{(7.38)} \qquad \frac{\hat{\beta} - \beta}{s_{\hat{\beta}}} \sim t_{n-2}.$$

By a similar deduction we also get

$$\text{(7.39)} \qquad \frac{\hat{\alpha} - \alpha}{s_{\hat{\alpha}}} \sim t_{n-2}.$$

These results enable us to make the following probability statements.

$$P\left(-t_{n-2,\lambda/2} \le \frac{\hat{\alpha} - \alpha}{s_{\hat{\alpha}}} \le +t_{n-2,\lambda/2}\right) = 1 - \lambda,$$

$$P\left(-t_{n-2,\lambda/2} \le \frac{\hat{\beta} - \beta}{s_{\hat{\beta}}} \le +t_{n-2,\lambda/2}\right) = 1 - \lambda,$$

where $t_{n-2,\lambda/2}$ stands for the value of the t statistic with $(n - 2)$ degrees of freedom, which cuts off $\lambda/2$ of the area of the t distribution at each tail end. This value can be looked up in the t table for whatever λ we desire. The term $(1 - \lambda)$ represents the area of the distribution between the points $-t_{n-2,\lambda/2}$ and $+t_{n-2,\lambda/2}$. From these probability statements we can construct the confidence intervals for α and β as

(7.40)
$$\hat{\alpha} - t_{n-2,\lambda/2}s_{\hat{\alpha}} \leq \alpha \leq \hat{\alpha} + t_{n-2,\lambda/2}s_{\hat{\alpha}},$$
$$\hat{\beta} - t_{n-2,\lambda/2}s_{\hat{\beta}} \leq \beta \leq \hat{\beta} + t_{n-2,\lambda/2}s_{\hat{\beta}}.$$

The probability that the specified confidence interval covers the true value of the regression parameter is $(1 - \lambda)$. This is referred to as the "level of confidence." As mentioned in Section 6-3, the most commonly used levels are 95% and 99%.

It can also be shown that

$$P\left(\frac{\sum (\hat{Y}_i - E\hat{Y}_i)^2}{2s^2} \leq F_{2,n-2,\lambda}\right) = 1 - \lambda,$$

where $F_{2,n-2,\lambda}$ is the value of the F statistic with 2 and $(n - 2)$ degrees of freedom that would be exceeded with λ probability and that can be looked up in the F table. Since

$$\sum (\hat{Y}_i - E\hat{Y}_i)^2 = \sum [(\hat{\alpha} - \alpha) + (\hat{\beta} - \beta)X_i]^2,$$

we use the preceding probability statement to form the following inequality:

(7.40a)
$$n(\hat{\alpha} - \alpha)^2 + 2n\bar{X}(\hat{\alpha} - \alpha)(\hat{\beta} - \beta) + (\hat{\beta} - \beta)^2 \sum X_i^2 \leq 2s^2 F_{2,n-2,\lambda}.$$

Given the sample values of $\hat{\alpha}$, $\hat{\beta}$, $\bar{X}$, and ΣX_i^2, and given a value of λ and therefore F, the boundaries of the inequality in (7.40a) will be represented by an ellipse in the plane whose coordinates are α and β. This ellipse represents a *joint confidence region* for α and β at the chosen level of confidence.

A confidence interval for σ^2 can be constructed by noting that

$$\frac{(n-2)s^2}{\sigma^2} \sim \chi^2_{n-2}.$$

If the chosen level of the confidence interval is $(1 - \lambda)$, then we have

$$P\left[\chi^2_{n-2,1-\lambda/2} \leq \frac{(n-2)s^2}{\sigma^2} \leq \chi^2_{n-2,\lambda/2}\right] = 1 - \lambda.$$

The limits of the desired confidence interval can then be determined readily by looking up the appropriate critical values of χ^2_{n-2} in the χ^2 table and then restating the bracketed inequality above in the form $a \leq \sigma^2 \leq b$. Incidentally, since we know from Section 5-2 that

$$\text{Var}(\chi^2_m) = 2m,$$

where m is the appropriate number of degrees of freedom, we have

$$\text{Var}\left[\frac{(n-2)s^2}{\sigma^2}\right] = 2(n-2)$$

or

$$\frac{(n-2)^2}{\sigma^2}\text{Var}(s^2) = 2(n-2),$$

so that

$$\text{Var}(s^2) = \frac{2\,\sigma^2}{n-2}. \tag{7.41}$$

EXAMPLE As a numerical example, let us construct the 95% confidence intervals for α and β for the function describing the demand for oranges from the data given in Section 7-3. To do that we have to calculate the estimates of the standard errors of $\hat{\alpha}$ and $\hat{\beta}$ using the formulas (7.36) and (7.37). From the data given for this example, we already calculated

$$\bar{X} = 70,$$

$$\bar{Y} = 100,$$

$$\sum x_i' y_i' = -3550,$$

$$\sum x_i'^2 = 2250,$$

which led to

$$\hat{\alpha} = 210.460,$$

$$\hat{\beta} = -1.578.$$

In addition we have

$$\sum y_i'^2 = 6300.$$

Substituting into (7.36) gives

$$s^2 = \frac{1}{12-2}[6300 - (-1.578)(-3550)] = 69.8.$$

Further substitution into (7.37) leads to

$$s_{\hat{\alpha}}^2 = 69.8\left(\frac{1}{12} + \frac{70^2}{2250}\right) = 157.825555$$

and

$$s_{\hat{\beta}}^2 = \frac{69.8}{2250} = 0.031022.$$

The resulting estimates of the standard errors of $\hat{\alpha}$ and $\hat{\beta}$ are

$$s_{\hat{\alpha}} = 12.563,$$

$$s_{\hat{\beta}} = 0.176.$$

The last piece of information needed for the construction of the confidence intervals is the appropriate t value. Since we had 12 observations, we have 10 degrees of freedom. Furthermore, since the desired level of confidence is 95%, we want to find the value of t that cuts off 0.025 of the area at the tail end of the distribution. Thus we look up the row labeled "10" and the column labeled "0.025" in the t table. The corresponding entry is 2.228. Therefore, the 95% confidence intervals for α and β are

$$210.460 - 2.228 \times 12.563 \leq \alpha \leq 210.460 + 2.228 \times 12.563$$

$$182.470 \leq \alpha \leq 238.450,$$

and
$$-1.578 - 2.228 \times 0.176 \leq \beta \leq -1.578 + 2.228 \times 0.176$$
$$-1.970 \leq \beta \leq -1.186.$$

We may also construct the 95% confidence interval for σ^2 by reference to the χ^2 table in Appendix D table, which leads to the inequality

$$34.08 \leq \sigma^2 \leq 214.97.$$

This is the desired 95% confidence interval for σ^2.

Confidence Interval for $E(Y_i)$

We may extend the use of confidence intervals and consider the precision of the entire sample regression line as a representation of the population regression line. The population regression line is given by $E(Y_i) = \alpha + \beta X_i$ and is defined for *any* value of X_i within some range. Its estimator is the sample regression line $\hat{Y}_i = \hat{\alpha} + \hat{\beta}X_i$. Since $E(\hat{Y}_i) = \alpha + \beta X_i$, $\hat{Y}_i$ is an unbiased estimator of $E(Y_i)$. Other desirable properties of $\hat{Y}_i$ as an estimator of $E(Y_i)$ can also be established; heuristically, we may argue that since $\hat{\alpha}$ and $\hat{\beta}$ are the best estimators of α and β we can devise, $(\hat{\alpha} + \hat{\beta}X_i)$ is the best estimator of $(\alpha + \beta X_i)$. To determine the confidence interval for any given point on the population regression line $E(Y_i)$, we have to find the variance of its estimator $\hat{Y}_i$. Let us call this variance $\sigma^2_{\hat{Y}_i}$. It can be determined as follows.

$$\begin{aligned}
\sigma^2_{\hat{Y}_i} = E[\hat{Y}_i - E(\hat{Y}_i)]^2 &= E[(\hat{\alpha} + \hat{\beta}X_i) - (\alpha + \beta X_i)]^2 \\
&= E[(\hat{\alpha} - \alpha) + (\hat{\beta} - \beta)X_i]^2 \\
&= E(\hat{\alpha} - \alpha)^2 + E(\hat{\beta} - \beta)^2 X_i^2 + 2E(\hat{\alpha} - \alpha)(\hat{\beta} - \beta)X_i \\
&= \text{Var}(\hat{\alpha}) + X_i^2 \text{Var}(\hat{\beta}) + 2X_i \text{Cov}(\hat{\alpha}, \hat{\beta}) \\
&= \sigma^2 \left(\frac{1}{n} + \frac{\bar{X}^2}{\sum x_i'^2} \right) + X_i^2 \left(\frac{\sigma^2}{\sum x_i'^2} \right) - 2X_i\bar{X} \left(\frac{\sigma^2}{\sum x_i'^2} \right).
\end{aligned}$$

The last result has been obtained by substitution from (7.23), (7.25), and (7.33). Further manipulation gives

$$\text{(7.42)} \qquad \begin{aligned}
\sigma^2_{\hat{Y}_i} &= \frac{\sigma^2}{\sum x_i'^2} \left(\frac{\sum x_i'^2}{n} + \bar{X}^2 + X_i^2 - 2X_i\bar{X} \right) \\
&= \frac{\sigma^2}{\sum x_i'^2} \left[\frac{\sum x_i'^2}{n} + (X_i - \bar{X})^2 \right] = \sigma^2 \left[\frac{1}{n} + \frac{(X_i - \bar{X})^2}{\sum x_i'^2} \right].
\end{aligned}$$

Having determined the mean and the variance of $\hat{Y}_i$, we should consider its distribution. This turns out to be quite simple: since $(\hat{\alpha} + \hat{\beta}X_i)$ is a linear combination of normally and independently distributed random variables $\varepsilon_1, \varepsilon_2, \ldots, \varepsilon_n$, it will also be normally distributed. Thus we have

$$\hat{Y}_i \sim N\left[\alpha + \beta X_i,\ \sigma^2\left(\frac{1}{n} + \frac{(X_i - \bar{X})^2}{\sum x_i'^2}\right)\right];$$

and, therefore,

$$\frac{\hat{Y}_i - (\alpha + \beta X_i)}{\sigma_{\hat{Y}_i}} \sim N(0,\ 1).$$

In general, the expression for $\sigma^2_{\hat{Y}_i}$ given by (7.42) cannot be evaluated because it involves an unknown parameter σ^2. However, we can replace σ^2 by its unbiased, consistent, and asymptotically efficient estimator s^2 given by formula (7.35). This will lead to an estimator of $\sigma^2_{\hat{Y}_i}$, say $s^2_{\hat{Y}_i}$, which has the same desirable properties and which is defined as

$$s^2_{\hat{Y}_i} = s^2\left[\frac{1}{n} + \frac{(X_i - \bar{X})^2}{\sum x_i'^2}\right]. \tag{7.43}$$

Then we have

$$\frac{\hat{Y}_i - (\alpha + \beta X_i)}{s_{\hat{Y}_i}} \sim t_{n-2},$$

and the confidence interval for $(\alpha + \beta X_i)$ will be

$$\hat{Y}_i - t_{n-2,\lambda/2}s_{\hat{Y}_i} \leq (\alpha + \beta X_i) \leq \hat{Y}_i + t_{n-2,\lambda/2}s_{\hat{Y}_i},$$

where $(1 - \lambda)$ is the chosen level of confidence. Since this confidence interval can be calculated for any value X_i within the applicable domain, we can construct confidence intervals for *any* point on the population regression line.

EXAMPLE For an illustration we can use the example of Section 7-3 on the demand for oranges. We will construct the 95% confidence intervals for the points on the population demand curve. We note that the estimated sample regression line was

$$\hat{Y}_i = 210.460 - 1.578X_i.$$

The estimate of the variance of $\hat{Y}_i$ is

$$s^2_{\hat{Y}_i} = 69.8\left[\frac{1}{12} + \frac{(X_i - 70)^2}{2250}\right],$$

and the value of the t statistic is 2.228 as before. These are all the necessary ingredients for the calculation of the confidence intervals. Table 7-3 shows the results of these calculations. The last two columns represent the intervals that, we expect, will contain the corresponding population values. Note that the narrowest interval is the one that corresponds to $X_i = 70$, i.e., to $\bar{X}$. The intervals get wider as we move farther away from $\bar{X}$. By connecting the appropriate points we get the lower and the upper boundaries of the confidence band for the population regression line, as illustrated in Figure 7-4.

Table 7-3

X_i	$\hat{Y}_i$	$s_{\hat{Y}_i}$	$2.228 s_{\hat{Y}_i}$	95% confidence interval Lower limit	Upper limit
0	210.46	12.57	28.01	182.45	238.47
10	194.66	10.84	24.15	170.51	218.81
20	178.88	9.14	20.36	158.52	199.24
30	163.10	7.45	16.60	146.50	179.70
40	147.32	5.81	12.94	134.38	160.26
50	131.54	4.27	9.51	122.03	141.05
60	115.76	2.98	6.64	109.12	122.40
70	99.98	2.41	5.37	94.61	105.35
80	84.20	2.98	6.64	77.56	90.84
90	68.42	4.27	9.51	58.91	77.93
100	52.64	5.81	12.94	39.70	65.58
110	36.86	7.45	16.60	20.26	53.46
120	21.08	9.14	20.36	0.72	41.44

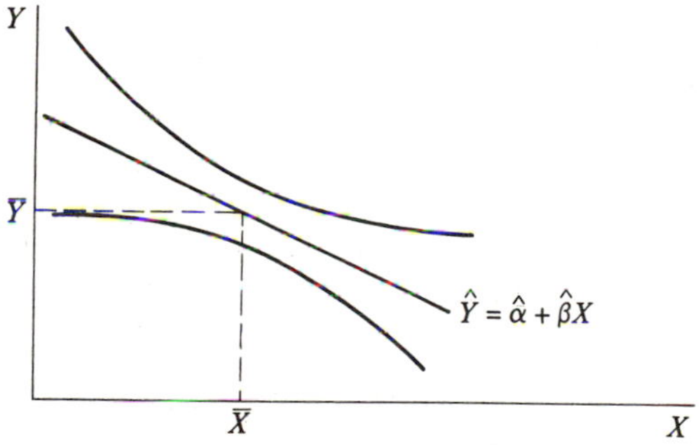

Figure 7-4

Decomposition of the Sample Variation of Y

Certain concepts connected with the problem of decomposing the sample variation of the values of the dependent variable[12] can be used to supplement the estimation results we have derived. As an illustration, consider the variation of Y as shown in Figure 7-5. Here the values of Y observed in a given sample have been plotted against the corresponding values of X. Such a graph is generally known as a "scatter

[12] By "variation of the dependent variable" we mean the changes in Y from one sample observation to another. This is to be distinguished from the "variance of Y_i," which refers to the dispersion of the values of Y_i corresponding to one fixed value of X, say X_i. In the case of the sample variation of Y, the values of X may change from observation to observation.

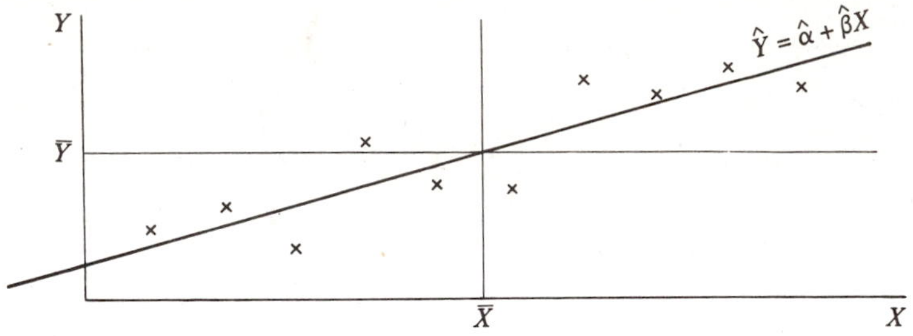

Figure 7-5

diagram." In Figure 7-5 we give 10 observations on Y corresponding to 10 different values of X. The question that now arises is why the values of Y differ from observation to observation. The answer, in accordance with the hypothesized regression model, is that the variation in Y is partly due to changes in X—which lead to changes in the expected value of Y—and partly due to the effect of the random disturbance. The next question, then, is how much of the observed variation in Y can be attributed to the variation in X and how much to the random effect of the disturbance. This question can be answered with the help of certain measures that we develop below.

First of all, let us define the term "sample variation of Y." If there were no variation, all the values of Y, when plotted against X, would lie on a horizontal line. Since if all values of Y were the same, they would all be equal to their sample mean, the horizontal line would be the one corresponding to $\bar{Y}$ in Figure 7-5. Now, in reality, the observed values of Y will be scattered around this line so that the variation of Y could be measured by the distances of the observed values of Y from $\bar{Y}$. A convenient summary measure of these distances is the sum of their squared values, usually called the "total sum of squares," abbreviated SST. That is, we define

$$\text{SST} = \sum_i (Y_i - \bar{Y})^2 = \sum_i y_i'^2.$$

Our aim is to decompose this sum of squares into two parts, one designed to account for the variations of Y that can be ascribed to the variations of X, and the other presumed to account for the variations in Y that can be ascribed to random causes.

Let us now return to Figure 7-5 and the sample observations shown therein. Suppose a sample regression line has been obtained by the method of least squares and drawn in the scatter diagram as shown. Since, as the name of the estimation method implies, the line is such that the sum of squares of deviations from it is a minimum, it is sometimes called the "line of the best fit." Consider now a specific observation, say Y_i, which corresponds to the value of X equal to X_i. We are interested in the vertical distance of (X_i, Y_i) from $\bar{Y}$. From Figure 7-6, we can see that this distance can be divided into two parts, one represented by the distance of the observed point from the sample regression line, and the other by the distance of

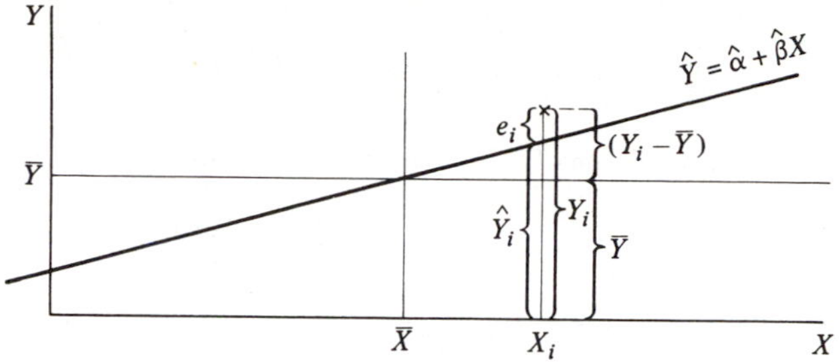

Figure 7-6

the sample regression line from $\bar{Y}$. That is, we have

$$Y_i = \hat{Y}_i + e_i,$$

where $\hat{Y}_i$ is the point on the sample regression line corresponding to X_i. Deducting $\bar{Y}$ from both sides we obtain

$$\underset{\substack{\text{Total}\\ \text{distance}\\ \text{from } \bar{Y}}}{(Y_i - \bar{Y})} = \underset{\substack{\text{Distance}\\ \text{of the}\\ \text{regression}\\ \text{line from}\\ \bar{Y}}}{(\hat{Y}_i - \bar{Y})} + \underset{\text{Residual}}{e_i}.$$

This analysis applies to a single observation. Since we want a summary measure for *all* sample observations, we square both sides of this equality and sum over all sample observations. This gives

$$\begin{aligned}\sum_i (Y_i - \bar{Y})^2 &= \sum_i [(\hat{Y}_i - \bar{Y}) + e_i]^2 \\ &= \sum_i (\hat{Y}_i - \bar{Y})^2 + \sum_i e_i^2 + 2\sum_i (\hat{Y}_i - \bar{Y})e_i.\end{aligned}$$

Consider the last term on the right-hand side. Substituting for $\hat{Y}_i$ we get

$$\begin{aligned}\sum_i (\hat{Y}_i - \bar{Y})e_i &= \sum_i (\hat{\alpha} + \hat{\beta}X_i - \bar{Y})e_i \\ &= \hat{\alpha}\sum_i e_i + \hat{\beta}\sum_i X_i e_i - \bar{Y}\sum_i e_i.\end{aligned}$$

But by (7.10a) and (7.11a) we know that $\Sigma_i\, e_i = 0$ and $\Sigma_i\, X_i e_i = 0$, so we conclude that

$$\sum_i (\hat{Y}_i - \bar{Y})e_i = 0.$$

Therefore,

(7.44)
$$\sum_i (Y_i - \bar{Y})^2 = \sum_i (\hat{Y}_i - \bar{Y})^2 + \sum_i e_i^2.$$

Total sum of squares (SST)	Regression sum of squares (SSR)	Error sum of squares (SSE)

The term SSR can be further developed as follows.

(7.45)
$$\begin{aligned}\text{SSR} &= \sum (\hat{Y}_i - \bar{Y})^2 = \sum (\hat{\alpha} + \hat{\beta}X_i - \bar{Y})^2 \\ &= \sum [(\bar{Y} - \hat{\beta}\bar{X}) + \hat{\beta}X_i - \bar{Y}]^2 \\ &= \sum [\hat{\beta}(X_i - \bar{X})]^2 \\ &= \hat{\beta}^2 \sum (X_i - \bar{X})^2 = \hat{\beta}^2 \sum x_i'^2.\end{aligned}$$

Thus we have found that the sample variation of Y (SST) can be decomposed into two parts, one describing the variation of the fitted values of Y and the other describing the variation of the regression residuals. That is, SSR represents the estimated effect of X on the variation of Y, and SSE the estimated effect of the random disturbance.

The decomposition of the sample variation of Y leads to a measure of the "goodness of fit," which is known as the *coefficient of determination* and denoted by R^2. This is simply the proportion of the variation of Y that can be attributed to the variation of X. Since

$$\text{SST} = \text{SSR} + \text{SSE},$$

dividing through by SST gives

$$1 = \frac{\text{SSR}}{\text{SST}} + \frac{\text{SSE}}{\text{SST}}.$$

The coefficient of determination is defined as

(7.46)
$$R^2 = \frac{\text{SSR}}{\text{SST}} = \frac{\hat{\beta}^2 \sum x_i'^2}{\sum y_i'^2},$$

or

(7.46a)
$$R^2 = 1 - \frac{\text{SSE}}{\text{SST}} = 1 - \frac{\sum e_i^2}{\sum y_i'^2}.$$

R^2 is a measure commonly used to describe how well the sample regression line fits the observed data. Note that R^2 cannot be negative or greater than one, i.e.,

$$0 \leq R^2 \leq 1.$$

A zero value of R^2 indicates the poorest, and a unit value the best fit that can be attained. In fact, it is easy to show that R^2 as defined in (7.46) is equal to the squared coefficient of correlation between the actual and the fitted values of Y, i.e., that

$$(7.46b) \qquad R^2 = \frac{\sum (Y_i - \bar{Y})(\hat{Y}_i - \bar{Y})^2}{\sum (Y_i - \bar{Y})^2 \sum (\hat{Y}_i - \bar{Y})^2},$$

noting that $\bar{\hat{Y}} = \bar{Y}$.

A necessary but not sufficient condition for R^2 to be zero is that the sample regression line be horizontal—that is, that $\hat{\beta}$ be equal to zero. Note that the sample regression line can be horizontal for several diferent reasons. This is illustrated in Figure 7-7. In case *(a)* the observations are scattered randomly around $\bar{Y}$. In case *(b)*

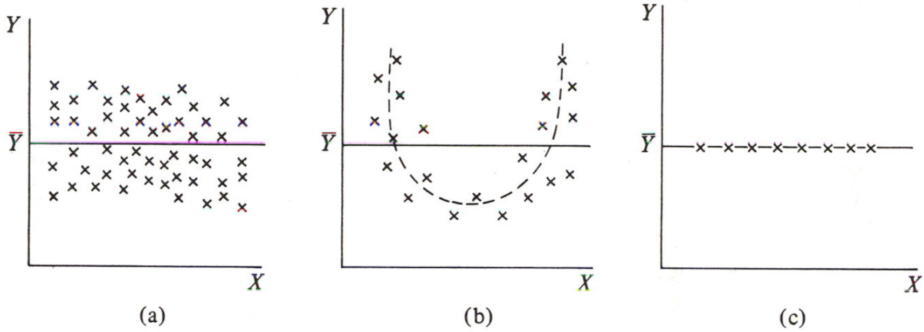

Figure 7-7

the observations are scattered around a curve such that the best-fitting straight line is a horizontal one. In this case there *is* a relationship between X and Y, but the relationship is highly nonlinear so that a straight line gives a very poor fit. Finally, in case *(c)* all observed values of Y are the same regardless of X. This is an exceptional case. With all values of Y being constant there is *no* variation to be explained, and thus the question of decomposition of variation is irrelevant. The value of R^2 in this case is indeterminate.

Three final points about decomposing the sample variation of Y should be noted. First, nowhere in the discussion have we alluded to problems of statistical inference. This omission was deliberate since our purpose was only to provide certain information about the sample. As the sample size increases, R^2 converges to

$$\text{plim } R^2 = \frac{\beta^2 \sigma_x^2}{\beta^2 \sigma_x^2 + \sigma^2}$$

where $\sigma_x^2 = \lim_{n \to \infty} \Sigma x_i'^2 / n$. This result follows directly from (7.45), and plim R^2 is sometimes referred to as the "population R^2." As an estimator of plim R^2, the finite sample R^2 is biased.[13] Second, the decomposition of SST as developed above is crucially dependent on the use of the method of least squares to obtain the sample regression line. If we used an estimation method that would lead to a different

[13] See A. P. Barten, "Note on Unbiased Estimation of the Squared Multiple Correlation Coefficient," *Statistica Neerlandica,* 16 (1962), pp. 151–163.

sample regression line, the decomposition of SST into SSR and SSE would not have been possible. As for R^2, however, we can generalize the formula (7.46a) to apply to *any* estimation method by defining R^2 as

$$(7.47) \qquad R^2 = 1 - \frac{\text{sum of squares of residuals}}{\text{SST}}.$$

Here the residuals are represented by the deviation from the sample regression line regardless of the method of estimation used. (Specialized definitions of R^2 are available for some specific estimation methods as noted.) But if the sample regression line is different from the one that would be obtained by the least squares method, R^2 can no longer be interpreted as a measure of the proportion of variation of Y attributable to sample regression. In this case R^2 would be used purely as a measure of the goodness of fit. Finally, it should be noted that R^2 is crucially dependent on the way in which the dependent variable is measured. Thus, for example, a comparison of the values of R^2 for two competing models, one explaining variations in Y and the other explaining variations in log Y, is inappropriate.

If R^2 is regarded as a descriptive statistic, we might ask about the value of the information that it conveys. Suppose, in particular, that we find a very low value of R^2 for a given sample. This means that the sample regression line fits the observations rather poorly. One possible explanation is that X is a poor explanatory variable in the sense that variation in X leaves Y unaffected. This is a proposition about the population regression line—a proposition that states that the population regression line is horizontal—and consequently can be tested by reference to the sample. We shall explain how this can be done presently. The validity of the test depends on the validity of the maintained hypothesis—that is, on the correct specification of the regression equation and on the validity of the basic assumptions. In particular, correct specification of the regression equation implies that no other explanatory variable enters into the model and that the effect of X_i on $E(Y_i)$ is a linear one. If we do not reject the hypothesis that the population regression line is horizontal, we are, in fact, claiming that Y is influenced *only* by the random disturbance ε. Another possible explanation of a low value of R^2 is that while X is the relevant explanatory variable, its influence on Y is weak compared to the influence of the random disturbance. This, indeed, seems to be the case for relationships describing household behavior that have been estimated from cross-section data. For example, a typical value of R^2 for various household behavior functions from the University of Michigan's Survey Research Center data is close to 0.20. This would indicate that 80% of the sample behavioral variation from household to household can be accounted for by factors other than the explanatory variable or variables. A third possible explanation of a low value of R^2 is that the regression equation is misspecified. In practice, this is frequently the conclusion that the research worker reaches in this case. The value of R^2 tends to be taken as an indicator of the "correctness" of the specification of the model. This is obviously a purely operational criterion that has no foundation in statistical inference. We shall say more about it when we come to the discussion of specification errors. In any case, it is customary to state the value of R^2 along with the results of the estimation procedure when presenting the regression results.

EXAMPLE The decomposition of SST and the calculation of R^2 can be illustrated with the example of demand for oranges introduced in Section 7-3. From the previous calculations we have

$$\sum y_i'^2 = 6300,$$
$$\sum x_i'^2 = 2250,$$
$$\hat{\beta} = -1.578.$$

Thus,

$$\text{SST} = \sum y_i'^2 = 6300,$$
$$\text{SSR} = \hat{\beta}^2 \sum x_i'^2 = 5602,$$
$$\text{SSE} = \text{SST} - \text{SSR} = 698.$$

That is,

$$\underset{(\text{SST})}{6300} = \underset{(\text{SSR})}{5602} + \underset{(\text{SSE})}{698}.$$

The coefficient of determination is

$$R^2 = \frac{\text{SSR}}{\text{SST}} = \frac{5602}{6300} = 0.889.$$

This means that 88.9% of the sample variation of Y can be attributed to the variation of the fitted values of Y, i.e., to $\hat{Y}$. The value of R^2 indicates that the sample regression line fits the observations quite well. This is shown graphically in Figure 7-8.

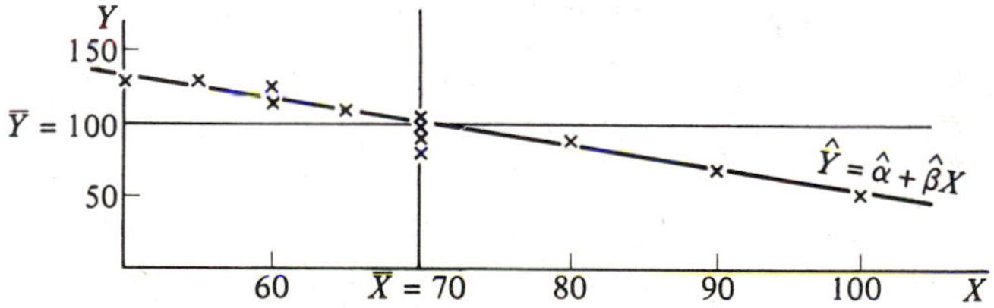

Figure 7-8

Tests of Hypotheses

Let us now turn to the problem of using the regression model for the purpose of *testing hypotheses.* The most common type of hypothesis tested with the help of the regression model is that there is no relationship between the explanatory variable X and the dependent variable Y. This hypothesis can be given a more precise interpretation if we first specify the ingredients of the associated maintained hypothesis; that is, if we state all the assumptions about the population that we are willing to make. These assumptions are all those underlying the classical normal linear regression model as specified by statements (7.1) through (7.6). Under this maintained hypothesis the relationship between X and Y is given by the linear dependence of the mean value of Y_i on X_i, i.e., by $E(Y_i) = \alpha + \beta X_i$. Thus the statement that "there is no relationship between X and Y" is to be interpreted as meaning that the mean value of Y_i is *not* linearly dependent on X_i—that is, that the population regression line is horizontal. But this is simply another way of saying that β is equal to zero. Therefore, the *null hypothesis* of no relationship between X and Y is

$$H_0: \quad \beta = 0.$$

If we have no prior knowledge about the values of the regression parameters, the alternative hypothesis would be

$$H_A: \quad \beta \neq 0.$$

If we know a priori that β cannot be positive or negative, the alternative hypothesis would be modified accordingly. To test H_0 we have to develop a test statistic and determine the acceptance and the critical regions. The test statistic can be derived from the least squares estimator of β, which has all the optimal properties under the given assumptions. We can simply utilize the fact that

$$\frac{\hat{\beta} - \beta}{s_{\hat{\beta}}} \sim t_{n-2},$$

as given by (7.38). Under the null hypothesis, β equals zero and thus the appropriate test statistic is

$$\frac{\hat{\beta}}{s_{\hat{\beta}}},$$

which has a t distribution with $(n-2)$ degrees of freedom. The boundary between the acceptance and the critical region can be determined from the table of the t distribution for any given level of significance and for any number of degrees of freedom. For a two-tail test with λ level of significance and $(n-2)$ degrees of freedom the acceptance region is defined by

$$-t_{n-2,\lambda/2} \leq \frac{\hat{\beta}}{s_{\hat{\beta}}} \leq +t_{n-2,\lambda/2}. \tag{7.48}$$

EXAMPLE As an example, consider the demand for oranges estimated by a linear regression model from the data given in Section 7-3. The null hypothesis of no relationship between X (price) and Y (quantity demanded) is tantamount to the claim that the demand for oranges is not influenced by price. We have

$$H_0: \quad \beta = 0.$$

For the alternative hypothesis, we take

$$H_A: \quad \beta \neq 0.$$

We wish to test H_0 at 1% level of significance. Since the t distribution extends from $-\infty$ to $+\infty$, *any* value of $\hat{\beta}/s_{\hat{\beta}}$ is consistent with the null hypothesis. But if H_0 is true, values of $\hat{\beta}/s_{\hat{\beta}}$ that are "far" from zero are not very likely. Our decision to use 1% level of significance means that if the deviation of $\hat{\beta}/s_{\hat{\beta}}$ from zero is so great as to occur by chance only 1% of the time, we shall reject H_0. Since we have 12 observations, the appropriate value of the t statistic for a two-tail test is the value corresponding to $t_{10,0.005}$. From the table of the t distribution, we find that this is equal to 3.169. The acceptance region for our test then is

$$-3.169 \leq \frac{\hat{\beta}}{s_{\hat{\beta}}} \leq +3.169.$$

From the previous calculations we have

$$\hat{\beta} = -1.578 \qquad \text{and} \qquad s_{\hat{\beta}} = 0.176,$$

so that

$$\frac{\hat{\beta}}{s_{\hat{\beta}}} = -8.965,$$

which clearly lies outside the acceptance region. Therefore, the hypothesis of no relationship between X and Y is to be rejected. Actually, in a case like this we would probably want to use a one-sided alternative hypothesis since positive values of β (that is, an upward-sloping demand curve) can be ruled out on theoretical grounds. Thus a "sharper" test would be one with the alternative hypothesis stated as

$$H_A: \ \beta < 0,$$

and the acceptance region given by

$$-t_{n-2,\lambda} \leq \frac{\hat{\beta}}{s_{\hat{\beta}}},$$

or

$$-2.764 \leq \frac{\hat{\beta}}{s_{\hat{\beta}}}.$$

Since -8.965 lies outside this region, the verdict of rejecting H_0 is unchanged.

It should be noted that the hypothesis of no relationship between X and Y can also be tested by using a different (but equivalent) test than the t test. If the null hypothesis is true, then the variation of Y from observation to observation will not be affected by changes in X but must be explained by the random disturbance alone. Thus we might consider a test based on the relationship between the "sum of squares due to regression" (SSR) and the "error sum of squares" (SSE). Since

$$\begin{aligned} E(\text{SSR}) &= E(\hat{\beta}^2 \sum x_i'^2) \\ &= E[(\hat{\beta} - \beta) + \beta]^2 \sum x_i'^2 \\ &= E(\hat{\beta} - \beta)^2 \sum x_i'^2 + \beta^2 \sum x_i'^2 \\ &= \sigma^2 + \beta^2 \sum x_i'^2, \end{aligned}$$

it follows that under the null hypothesis $\beta = 0$ we have

$$E(\text{SSR}) = \sigma^2.$$

Further

$$E\left(\frac{\text{SSE}}{n-2}\right) = E(s^2) = \sigma^2.$$

Therefore we would expect that the ratio

$$\frac{\text{SSR}}{\text{SSE}/(n-2)}$$

would converge to unity as $n \to \infty$, whereas under the alternative hypothesis that $\beta \neq 0$ this ratio would exceed 1. To determine the distribution of this ratio, we note that

$$\frac{\text{SSR}}{\sigma^2} = \frac{\hat{\beta}^2 \sum x_i'^2}{\sigma^2}$$

$$= \frac{\hat{\beta}^2}{\sigma_{\hat{\beta}}^2}.$$

Now, under the null hypothesis $\hat{\beta} \sim N(0, \sigma_{\hat{\beta}}^2)$ and $\hat{\beta}/\sigma_{\hat{\beta}} \sim N(0, 1)$, so that $\hat{\beta}^2/\sigma_{\hat{\beta}}^2$ is a square of a standard normal variable, which is known to have a chi-square distribution with 1 degree of freedom. Further,

$$\frac{\text{SSE}}{\sigma^2} = \frac{(n-2)s^2}{\sigma^2}$$

has a χ^2 distribution with $(n-2)$ degrees of freedom. We have also noted that $\hat{\beta}$ and s^2 are independent. Thus

$$\frac{\text{SSR}/1}{\text{SSE}/(n-2)}$$

is a ratio of two independent chi-square variables, each divided by its respective number of degrees of freedom. This means that this ratio has an F distribution (see Section 5-2), i.e., that

$$\frac{\text{SSR}/1}{\text{SSE}/(n-2)} \sim F_{1,n-2}. \tag{7.49}$$

The acceptance region for the null hypothesis of no relationship between X and Y would then be

$$\frac{\text{SSR}/1}{\text{SSE}/(n-2)} \leq F_{1,n-2}^{(\lambda)}, \tag{7.50}$$

where $F_{1,n-2}^{(\lambda)}$ is the value of the F statistic with 1 and $(n-2)$ degrees of freedom that corresponds to a level of significance λ. The test (7.50) is equivalent to the two-tail t test (7.48) in the sense that both tests give the same answer as long as the level of significance and the sample data are the same. In fact, since

$$\frac{\text{SSR}}{\text{SSE}/(n-2)} = \frac{\hat{\beta}^2 \sum x_i'^2}{s^2} = \frac{\hat{\beta}^2}{s_{\hat{\beta}}^2},$$

we see that

$$F_{1,n-2}^{(\lambda)} = t_{n-2,\lambda/2}^2.$$

The difference, as we shall see, is that the F test can be readily generalized to apply to a regression model with more than one explanatory variable, whereas the t test can only be applied to a single regression coefficient.

The calculations needed for carrying out the preceding F test of the null hypothesis that there is no relationship between Y and X (i.e., H_0: $\beta = 0$ against H_A: $\beta \neq 0$) are frequently presented in what is called an "analysis of variance (ANOVA)" table, such as Table 7-4.

Table 7-4

Source of variation	Sum of squares	Degrees of freedom	Mean square	F value
Regression	$SSR = \hat{\beta}^2 \sum x_i'^2$	1	SSR	$\dfrac{SSR}{SSE/(n-2)}$
Error	$SSE = SST - SSR$	$n - 2$	$\dfrac{SSE}{n-2}$	
Total	$SST = \sum y_i'^2$	$n - 1$		

EXAMPLE For the numerical example given in the preceding paragraph we have

$$SSR = 5602,$$

$$SSE = 698,$$

so that

$$\frac{SSR/1}{SSE/(n-2)} = \frac{5602}{698/10} = 80.26.$$

A tabular ANOVA representation of these results would be

Source of variation	Sum of squares	Degrees of freedom	Mean square	F value
Regression	5602	1	5602	80.26
Error	698	10	69.8	
Total	6300	11		

Since the value of the F statistic with 1 and 10 degrees of freedom at 1% level of significance is 10.0, the null hypothesis is obviously to be rejected.

In addition to testing a hypothesis about the existence of a relationship between X and Y, we can carry out tests for any specific values of the regression coefficients. For example, a hypothesis that α is equal to zero is, in fact, a hypothesis that the population regression line passes through the origin. The appropriate test statistic would be

$$\frac{\hat{\alpha}}{s_{\hat{\alpha}}},$$

which has a t distribution with $(n - 2)$ degrees of freedom. Or we may wish to test the hypothesis that the regression slope β is equal to some value β_0. In this case the test statistic would be

$$\frac{\hat{\beta} - \beta_0}{s_{\hat{\beta}}} \sim t_{n-2}.$$

Sometimes instead of dealing with a single hypothesis about α or β we may face a joint hypothesis involving α and β simultaneously. For instance, the hypothesis that common stock values move with consumer prices could be tested by using the simple regression model in which Y represents the rate of change in stock values and X represents the rate of change of consumer prices. The hypothesis to be tested would then be

$$H_0: \quad \alpha = 0 \qquad \text{and} \qquad \beta = 1,$$

$$H_A: \quad H_0 \text{ is not true.}$$

The test statistic in this case (or in any other case involving a joint hypothesis) is

$$\text{(7.51)} \qquad \frac{(\text{SSE}_\text{R} - \text{SSE}_\text{U})/r}{\text{SSE}_\text{U}/(n - K)} \sim F_{r,n-K},$$

where SSE_R is the "restricted error sum of squares"—i.e., the error sum of squares when the null hypothesis is imposed; SSE_U is the "unrestricted error sum of squares"—the usual error sum of squares defined in (7.44); r is the number of restrictions imposed by H_0; and K is the number of regressors (including the constant term). In our example $r = 2$, since there are two coefficients involved in H_0, and $K = 2$, since there are altogether two coefficients (α and β) in the simple regression model of this chapter. In the case of stock values and consumer prices we have

$$\text{SSE}_\text{R} = \sum (Y_i - 0 - 1X_i)^2 = \sum (Y_i - X_i)^2.$$

The test in (7.51) is very useful on many occasions.

Prediction

Apart from estimation and hypotheses testing, the regression model can also be used for prediction. In particular, we are frequently interested in *"forecasting"* the value of Y for a given value of X. For example, the manager of a supermarket may be interested to know what quantity of oranges he can expect to sell when he sets the price at a certain level. To be specific, suppose the given value of the explanatory variable is X_0 so that our task is to predict the value of Y_0. Since Y_0 is a *random* variable with values scattered around the point on the population regression line corresponding to X_0, we will never know its value prior to the experiment, not even if we knew all the population parameters. If the population parameters *were known*, our predictor of Y_0 would be its mean,

$$E(Y_0) = \alpha + \beta X_0,$$

which defines a point on the population regression line. This is the best predictor of Y_0 in the sense that the variance of Y_0 around $E(Y_0)$ is smaller than around any other point. The values of Y_0 will be normally distributed with variance equal to σ^2. This follows from the presence of the random disturbance ε in the regression equation. In reality, $E(Y_0)$ is not known and has to be estimated. The estimator is the corresponding point on the sample regression line,

$$\hat{Y}_0 = \hat{\alpha} + \hat{\beta} X_0,$$

since $\hat{\alpha}$ and $\hat{\beta}$ are the best estimators of α and β that we can devise under given assumptions. Now, the actual value of Y_0 will differ from the predicted value $\hat{Y}_0$ for the following two reasons.

1. The value of Y_0 will not be equal to $E(Y_0)$—i.e., will not lie on the population regression line—because of the random disturbance ε_0.
2. The sample regression will not be the same as the population regression line because of the sampling error.

Formally, we may write

$$Y_0 - \hat{Y}_0 = [Y_0 - E(Y_0)] + [E(Y_0) - \hat{Y}_0].$$

The first type of error is inherent in the mechanism by which the values of the dependent variable are generated, and there is nothing that we can do to diminish it. However, the second type of error would be reduced if we increased the precision of estimating the population regression line by increasing the sample size.

The difference between the actual value of Y_0 and the predicted value Y_0 is known as the *forecast error.* We note that

$$Y_0 - \hat{Y}_0 = (\alpha + \beta X_0 + \varepsilon_0) - (\hat{\alpha} + \hat{\beta} X_0)$$

is a linear combination of normally and independently distributed random variables $\varepsilon_0, \varepsilon_1, \varepsilon_2, \ldots, \varepsilon_n$. Therefore, the forecast error is also a normally distributed random variable. Thus its distribution is fully determined by its mean and its variance. The mean can be simply determined as follows.

$$\begin{aligned} E(Y_0 - \hat{Y}_0) &= E(\alpha + \beta X_0 + \varepsilon_0 - \hat{\alpha} - \hat{\beta} X_0) \\ &= \alpha + \beta X_0 + E(\varepsilon_0) - E(\hat{\alpha}) - E(\hat{\beta}) X_0 = 0. \end{aligned}$$

The variance of the forecast error is

$$\begin{aligned} E[(Y_0 - \hat{Y}_0) - E(Y_0 - \hat{Y}_0)]^2 &= E(Y_0 - \hat{Y}_0)^2 \\ &= E\{[Y_0 - E(Y_0)] + [E(Y_0) - \hat{Y}_0]\}^2 \\ &= E[Y_0 - E(Y_0)]^2 + E[E(Y_0) - \hat{Y}_0]^2 \\ &\quad + 2E[Y_0 - E(Y_0)][E(Y_0) - \hat{Y}_0]. \end{aligned}$$

Taking the last term on the right-hand side,

$$\begin{aligned}2E[Y_0 - E(Y_0)][E(Y_0) - \hat{Y}_0] &= 2E(\varepsilon_0)[E(Y_0) - \hat{Y}_0] \\ &= 2E(\varepsilon_0)(\alpha + \beta X_0 - \hat{\alpha} - \hat{\beta} X_0) \\ &= 2E(\varepsilon_0)[-(\hat{\alpha} - \alpha) - (\hat{\beta} - \beta) X_0] \\ &= 0,\end{aligned}$$

since $(\hat{\alpha} - \alpha)$ and $(\hat{\beta} - \beta)$ each depend only on the sample disturbances ε_1, $\varepsilon_2, \ldots, \varepsilon_n$, and these are independent of ε_0. Thus

$$E(Y_0 - \hat{Y}_0)^2 = E[Y_0 - E(Y_0)]^2 + E[E(Y_0) - \hat{Y}_0]^2$$

Total variance of the forecast error (σ_F^2)	Variance due to random disturbance (σ^2)	Variance due to sampling error ($\sigma_{\hat{Y}}^2$)

or

$$\sigma_F^2 = \sigma^2 + \sigma_{\hat{Y}_0}^2.$$

That is, the variance of the forecast error consists of two parts, one equal to the variance of the disturbance and the other to the variance of the predictor $\hat{Y}_0$ around its mean $E(Y_0)$. The variance of the disturbance is beyond our control, but the variance of the predictor can be diminished by increasing the size of the sample used for estimating the population regression line.

By using the expression for $\sigma_{\hat{Y}_0}^2$ given by (7.42) above, we obtain the following formula for the variance of the forecast error.

$$\sigma_F^2 = \sigma^2 + \sigma^2 \left[\frac{1}{n} + \frac{(X_0 - \bar{X})^2}{\sum x_i'^2}\right] = \sigma^2 \left[1 + \frac{1}{n} + \frac{(X_0 - \bar{X})^2}{\sum x_i'^2}\right]. \tag{7.52}$$

This means that the variance of the forecast error will be the smaller:

1. The larger the sample size n.
2. The greater the dispersion of the explanatory variable in the sample (i.e., the larger $\Sigma x_i'^2$).
3. The smaller the distance between X_0 and the sample mean $\bar{X}$.

The first two conclusions are quite straightforward; they reflect the fact that the better the estimate of the population regression line, the smaller the variance of the forecast error. The third conclusion is more interesting; it means that our forecast will be better for values of X which are close to $\bar{X}$ than for those which lie farther away from $\bar{X}$. This is consistent with the intuitively plausible contention that we are better able to forecast within our range of experience than outside of it. In this case the range of our "experience" is represented by the sample values of the explanatory variable X, and the central point of this range is $\bar{X}$. The farther away we venture with our forecasting, the less reliable the forecast.

In general, the expression for σ_F^2 given by (7.52) will not be known and must be estimated. This can be done simply by replacing σ^2 by its estimator s^2, which will give an unbiased, consistent, and asymptotically efficient estimator of σ_F^2, say, s_F^2, defined as

$$s_F^2 = s^2\left[1 + \frac{1}{n} + \frac{(X_0 - \overline{X})^2}{\sum x_i'^2}\right]. \tag{7.53}$$

In summary, we have found that the forecast error $(Y_0 - \hat{Y}_0)$ is normally distributed, has zero mean, and its variance is σ_F^2. That is,

$$(Y_0 - \hat{Y}_0) \sim N(0, \sigma_F^2);$$

and, therefore

$$\frac{Y_0 - \hat{Y}_0}{\sigma_F} \sim N(0, 1).$$

Replacing σ_F with s_F gives

$$\frac{Y_0 - \hat{Y}_0}{s_F} \sim t_{n-2}.$$

The last result enables us to make definite probability statements about our forecast. In particular, we can set up an interval that will contain the actual value of Y_0 with a given probability. Let this level of probability be $(1 - \lambda)$, where λ is any given number between 0 and 1 that we care to choose. Then we can write

$$P\left(-t_{n-2,\lambda/2} \leq \frac{Y_0 - \hat{Y}_0}{s_F} \leq +t_{n-2,\lambda/2}\right) = 1 - \lambda.$$

The corresponding prediction interval for Y_0 is

$$\hat{Y}_0 - t_{n-2,\lambda/2}s_F \leq Y_0 \leq \hat{Y}_0 + t_{n-2,\lambda/2}s_F.$$

This interval is symmetric around the predictor $\hat{Y}_0$, and can be expected to contain the actual value of Y_0 with a probability $(1 - \lambda)$. If the eventually observed value of Y_0 falls outside the prediction interval, we have reason to doubt the validity of the model. If we wish to predict more than one future value of Y simultaneously, we have to construct a *joint* prediction interval, which is more complicated than the preceding analysis.

EXAMPLE Suppose we wish to predict the demand for oranges at a price of 110¢ per pound, using the previously estimated demand curve. The predicted quantity demanded will be

$$\hat{Y}_0 = 210.460 - 1.578 \times 110 = 36.88,$$

with standard error

$$s_F = \sqrt{69.8\left[1 + \frac{1}{12} + \frac{(110 - 70)^2}{2250}\right]} = 11.20.$$

The 95% confidence interval for Y_0 is $36.88 \pm 2.228 \times 11.20$ or from 12 to 62 pounds.

Presentation of Regression Results

One last note to be added concerns the presentation of the results of the regression analysis. Whatever the purpose, operating on sample data will involve estimating the regression coefficients and the standard errors of these estimators. These results are usually supplemented by R^2, the coefficient of determination, which indicates how well the sample regression line fits the observations. It has become customary to present all these results by writing out the estimated regression equation with the estimated standard errors in parentheses under the respective coefficients. This is followed by the value of R^2. That is, we write

$$\hat{Y}_i = \underset{(s_{\hat{\alpha}})}{\hat{\alpha}} + \underset{(s_{\hat{\beta}})}{\hat{\beta}} X_i, \qquad R^2 = \cdots .$$

In the case of our example on the demand for oranges, we have

$$\hat{Y}_i = \underset{(12.563)}{210.460} - \underset{(0.176)}{1.578} X_i, \qquad R^2 = 0.889.$$

The "hat" on $\hat{Y}_i$ indicates that the equation holds only for the fitted values of the dependent variable, not for the actually observed values. Alternatively, we can write

$$Y_i = \underset{(s_{\hat{\alpha}})}{\hat{\alpha}} + \underset{(s_{\hat{\beta}})}{\hat{\beta}} X_i + e_i, \qquad R^2 = \cdots ,$$

where e_i represents the least squares residuals. But note that writing $Y_i = \hat{\alpha} + \hat{\beta}X_i$ is incorrect. Some researchers present the ratios of the estimated coefficients to their estimated standard errors in place of the estimated standard errors themselves, which is an acceptable alternative. These so-called t ratios are typically shown on the computer printout of a regression output, along with the p values for each of the coefficients and the ANOVA table.

Selected Applications

Most economic relationships involve more than one explanatory variable, and applications of the simple regression model discussed in this chapter are not as common as applications of the multiple regression model of Chapter 10. However, some important applications of this model do exist. A very brief description of three such applications is presented below.

One of the best known relations in economics is the relation between output and inputs known as a *production function.* An early effort at specifying this function led to the introduction of the Cobb–Douglas production function, defined as

$$Q_i = \mu L_i^{\lambda} K_i^{1-\lambda},$$

where Q = quantity of output, L = quantity of labor input, K = quantity of capital input, and μ and λ are parameters. It is easy to see that if L and K are doubled, Q will also be doubled. This property is known as *constant returns to scale.* The above production function can be simplified by dividing both sides of the equality by L to get

$$\frac{Q_i}{L_i} = \mu \left(\frac{K_i}{L_i}\right)^{1-\lambda}.$$

Taking logarithms of both sides and adding a stochastic disturbance term to account for random increases or decreases in output, we get

$$\log \frac{Q_i}{L_i} = \log \mu + (1 - \lambda)\log \frac{K_i}{L_i} + \varepsilon_i,$$

or, in an obvious change of notation,

$$Y_i = \alpha + \beta X_i + \varepsilon_i.$$

This equation has been estimated with data for different industries, different countries, and different time periods. For instance, the results for the U.S. manufacturing sector for the period 1899–1922 resulted in $\hat{\beta} = 0.24$ with an estimated standard error of 0.04.[14] The interpretation of this result is that a 1% increase in capital per worker led to a 0.24% increase in output per worker, which is an interesting finding.

A more recent study of production functions dealt with the question of substituting capital for labor. It was found that one property of the Cobb–Douglas production function is that substitutability is assumed to be the same for every industry and, when measured by the so-called "marginal rate of substitution," equal to 1. To avoid the need for such an assumption, a new production function, called a *CES production function,* was introducted.[15] This function is specified as

$$Q = \gamma[\delta K^{-\rho} + (1 - \delta)L^{-\rho}]^{-1/\rho}.$$

When combined with the condition of profit maximization, the above production function leads to the following *marginal productivity condition:*

$$\log \frac{P_i Q_i}{L_i} = \text{constant} + \frac{1}{1-\rho} \log W_i,$$

where P_i = price of output and W_i = wage rate. With an obvious change in notation and allowing for a random disturbance, we obtain again

$$Y_i = \alpha + \beta X_i + \varepsilon_i.$$

It turns out that the coefficient $\beta[= 1/(1 - \rho)]$ is precisely the marginal rate of substitution mentioned earlier. Empirical studies based on cross-section data for 19 countries resulted in estimates of β being in the range from 0.7 to 1.0, but typically less than 1.

[14] See P. H. Douglas, "Are There Laws of Production?" *American Economic Review,* 38 (March 1948), pp. 1–41.

[15] See K. J. Arrow et al., "Capital–Labor Substitution and Economic Efficiency," *Review of Economics and Statistics,* 43 (August 1961), pp. 225–250.

A different type of relationship links household consumption of a specific commodity with household income. When such a relationship is estimated from survey data at a specific point or period of time, all households face the same prices and thus prices can be treated as constant. Such a relationship between household consumption and household income is called an *Engel curve* and is frequently specified as

$$\log C_i = \alpha + \beta \log Y_i + \varepsilon_i,$$

where C = household consumption of a specific commodity and Y = household income. The coefficient β measures the income elasticity of demand. An extensive study of British households, for instance, yielded an estimate of β for butter as 0.35 (with $s_{\hat{\beta}} = 0.04$) and for tea as 0.68 (with $s_{\hat{\beta}} = 0.08$).[16] In fact, all food items turned out to be income inelastic except for coffee, for which the estimated income elasticity was 1.42 (with $s_{\hat{\beta}} = 0.20$).

Bayesian Analysis

In Section 6-4 we explained the Bayesian approach to statistical inference and derived the posterior distribution of the mean of a normally distributed variable. Since the simple regression model discussed in this chapter relates to a normally distributed variable Y_i with a mean of $(\alpha + \beta X_i)$ and variance of σ^2, we can apply a similar analysis here. Starting with the case where there is no prior information about α and β and the value of σ is known, we specify the joint prior distributon of α and β as

$$g(\alpha, \beta) \propto \text{constant}.$$

The likelihood function for the sample data on Y is given as

$$\ell = (2\pi\sigma^2)^{-n/2} \exp\left\{\frac{-\sum (Y_i - \alpha - \beta X_i)^2}{2\sigma^2}\right\},$$

where exp and the expression in braces represent e with its exponent equal to that expression. Combining the prior distribution with the likelihood function, we obtain the following posterior distribution.

$$f(\alpha, \beta \mid \text{data}) \propto \exp\left\{\frac{-\sum (Y_i - \alpha - \beta X_i)^2}{2\sigma^2}\right\}$$

$$\propto \exp\left\{\frac{-\sum [(Y_i - \hat{\alpha} - \hat{\beta} X_i) - (\alpha - \hat{\alpha}) - (\beta - \hat{\beta})X_i]^2}{2\sigma^2}\right\}$$

$$\propto \exp\left\{\frac{-[\, n(\alpha - \hat{\alpha})^2 + (\beta - \hat{\beta})^2 \sum X_i^2 + 2(\alpha - \hat{\alpha})(\beta - \hat{\beta}) \sum X_i \,]}{2\sigma^2}\right\}$$

[16] See S. J. Prais and H. S. Houthakker, *Analysis of Family Budgets* (Cambridge, England: The University Press, 1955).

where $\hat{\alpha}$ and $\hat{\beta}$ are the LS estimates of α and β. The term $\Sigma(Y_i - \hat{\alpha} - \hat{\beta}X_i)^2$ has been absorbed in the constant term since it does not involve either α or β. This posterior distribution can be identified as a bivariate normal distribution.[17] The marginal posterior distribution of β can be obtained by integrating $f(\alpha, \beta \mid \text{data})$ over α. This gives

$$\beta \sim N\left(\hat{\beta}, \frac{\sigma^2}{\sum x_i'^2}\right).$$

Similarly, the marginal posterior distribution of α, obtained by integrating $f(\alpha, \beta \mid \text{data})$ over β, is given as

$$\alpha \sim N\left(\hat{\alpha}, \frac{\sigma^2 \sum X_i^2}{n \sum x_i'^2}\right).$$

This means that if we take as Bayes estimators of α and β the means of their posterior distributions, we finish with $\hat{\alpha}$ and $\hat{\beta}$ as in the classical case. When σ is not known and the prior distribution is specified as

$$g(\alpha, \beta, \sigma) \propto 1/\sigma,$$

then the posterior distributions of α and β can be expressed as[18]

$$\frac{\beta - \hat{\beta}}{s/(\sum x_i'^2)^{1/2}} \sim t_{n-2}$$

and

$$\frac{\alpha - \hat{\alpha}}{s[(\sum X_i^2/n)(\sum x_i'^2)]^{1/2}} \sim t_{n-2},$$

where

$$s^2 = \frac{\sum (Y_i - \hat{\alpha} - \hat{\beta}X_i)^2}{n-2}.$$

Suppose now that we have prior information about α and β in the form of a normal distribution, and that σ is known. Then we may specify the prior distribution as

$$g(\alpha, \beta) \propto \exp\left\{-\frac{(\alpha - \alpha_0)^2}{2\sigma_\alpha} - \frac{(\beta - \beta_0)^2}{2\sigma_\beta}\right\},$$

assuming that α and β are independently distributed. Combining this information

[17] See A. Zellner, *An Introduction to Bayesian Inference to Econometrics* (New York: Wiley, 1971), pp. 60–61.

[18] *Ibid.*

with the likelihood function, we obtain the following marginal posterior distribution of β:

$$(7.54)\qquad \beta \sim N\left(\frac{\hat{\beta}\sum x_i'^2 + \beta_0 m}{\sum x_i'^2 + m};\ \frac{\sigma^2}{\sum x_i'^2 + m}\right),$$

where $m = \sigma^2/\sigma_\beta^2$. Thus we can see that the mean of the posterior distribution of β is a weighted average of $\hat{\beta}$ and β_0. A similar result could be obtained for α. Finally, if the condition that σ is known is dropped and the prior distribution $g(\alpha, \beta, \sigma)$ is a conjugate prior distribution of the so-called normal-gamma type, then the marginal posterior distributions of α and of β will be of the t-distribution type.[19]

EXAMPLE Consider again the example on the demand for oranges given in Section 7-3. From the data in Table 7-2 we calculated $\hat{\beta} = -1.578$, $s^2 = 69.8$, $\Sigma x_i'^2 = 2250$, and $s_{\hat{\beta}}^2 = 0.031022$. Suppose the prior distribution is specified as

$$\beta \sim N(-1, 0.25).$$

Assuming that σ^2 can be represented by the sample value 69.8, we obtain the following mean of the posterior distribution of β:

$$\frac{-1.578 \times 2250 - 69.8/0.25}{2250 + 69.8/0.25} = -1.514.$$

The variance of the posterior distribution of β is

$$\frac{69.8}{2250 + 69.8/0.25} = 0.027598.$$

This variance is smaller than the sample variance 0.031022 because of the effect of prior information.

EXERCISES

All problems in this set of exercises refer to a simple linear regression model,

$$Y_i = \alpha + \beta X_i + \varepsilon_i,$$

for which assumptions (7.2) through (7.6) are all satisfied.

7-1. Derive the best linear unbiased estimator of α and its variance.

7-2. Consider any two regression disturbances ε_t and ε_s $(t \neq s)$. By our assumptions, these disturbances have the same variance and are mutually independent. Can the same be asserted about the respective least squares residuals e_t and e_s?

[19] See G. G. Judge et al., *Introduction to the Theory and Practice of Econometrics* (New York: Wiley, 1981), p. 229.

7-3. One alternative to the least squares method of estimation is the *method of semi-averages*. This method calls for arranging the observations so that the values of X proceed in order of magnitude, dividing them into two equal (or approximately equal) parts, and calculating the average values of X and Y for each part separately. This gives us two points, one for each part. The estimated regression line is the line passing through these two points. For simplicity, we assume that the number of observations is even. Let $\bar{X}_A$ and $\bar{Y}_A$ be the sample means of the first $n/2$ values of X and Y, and $\bar{X}_B$ and $\bar{Y}_B$ the sample means of the last $n/2$ values of X and Y. Further, let a and b be the "semi-average" estimators of α and β, respectively. Then a and b can be calculated from

$$\bar{Y}_A = a + b\bar{X}_A,$$

$$\bar{Y}_B = a + b\bar{X}_B,$$

since the estimated regression line is required to pass through the points $(\bar{X}_A, \bar{Y}_A)$ and $(\bar{X}_B, \bar{Y}_B)$.

a. Prove that a and b are unbiased estimators of α and β.

b. Derive $\text{Var}(b)$ and show that $\text{Var}(b) \geq \text{Var}(\hat{\beta})$, where $\hat{\beta}$ is a LS estimator of β.

c. Using the data and the model for the demand for oranges (Table 7-2), show that $\text{Var}(b)/\text{Var}(\hat{\beta}) = 1.875$.

7-4. Consider the following regression model with zero intercept, $Y_i = \beta X_i + \varepsilon_i$, for which all classical assumptions hold and $i = 1, 2, \ldots, n$.

a. Find the best linear unbiased estimator of β, say, $\tilde{\beta}$, and its variance.

b. The best linear unbiased predictor of Y when $X = X_0$ is $\tilde{Y}_0 = \tilde{\beta}X_0$. Find an unbiased predictor of Y_0^2.

7-5. Suppose Y_i = log value of production per worker, X_i = log wage rate, and the subscript i refers to the ith firm. The parameter β may be interpreted as a measure of the elasticity of substitution between labor and capital. The least squares results for industry A are

$$Y_i = \underset{}{-0.4} + \underset{(0.1)}{1.0}X_i + e_i \qquad (n = 52).$$

Show that $R_A^2 = 2/3$.

7-6. Two research workers, working independently of each other, considered the same regression model,

$$Y_i = \alpha + \beta X_i + \varepsilon_i,$$

with all classical assumptions satisfied. Some of the results for their two random samples (which were independently drawn) were as follows.

Sample I	Sample II
$n = 20$	$n = 20$
$\Sigma X_i = 100$	$\Sigma X_i = 200$
$\Sigma X_i^2 = 600$	$\Sigma X_i^2 = 2{,}400$
$\Sigma Y_i = 500$	$\Sigma Y_i = 700$
$\hat{\beta}_{\text{I}} = 2$	$\hat{\beta}_{\text{II}} = 2.5$

When the two research workers found out about each other's work, they decided to collaborate and present one joint estimate of β. Researcher I suggested the use of

$$\tilde{\beta} = \frac{1}{2}(\hat{\beta}_{\text{I}} + \hat{\beta}_{\text{II}}).$$

Researcher II, however, claimed that $\tilde{\beta}$ is inefficient and that he can provide an unbiased estimator of β with a considerably smaller variance than that of $\tilde{\beta}$. Present the estimate proposed by researcher II and determine the percentage reduction in variance relative to $\tilde{\beta}$.

7-7. Suppose the explanatory variable X can only assume the values 0 and 1. The sample consists of n_1 observations for which $X = 0$, and n_2 observations for which $X = 1$. Let $\bar{Y}_1$ be the mean value of Y for the n_1 observations for which $X = 0$, and $\bar{Y}_2$ be the mean value of Y for the n_2 observations for which $X = 1$. Find $\hat{\alpha}$, $\hat{\beta}$, Var($\hat{\alpha}$), and Var($\hat{\beta}$).

7-8. A regression model is specified as

$$Y_i = \beta X_i + \varepsilon_i,$$

where ε and X satisfy all the basic assumptions. Three estimators of β have been proposed.

$$\hat{\beta}_1 = \frac{\bar{Y}}{\bar{X}},$$

$$\hat{\beta}_2 = \frac{\sum X_i Y_i}{\sum X_i^2},$$

$$\hat{\beta}_3 = \frac{\sum (X_i - \bar{X})(Y_i - \bar{Y})}{\sum (X_i - \bar{X})^2}.$$

a. Show that all three estimators are unbiased.

b. Derive the variance of each of the three estimators and determine which one (if any) has the smallest variance.

7-9. The least squares regression equation estimated from 22 observations is

$$Y_i = 10 + 5X_i + e_i, \qquad R^2 = 0.8.$$

Carry out the test for the existence of a relationship between X and Y by using (**a**) the t test; (**b**) the F test.

7-10. The relationship between the yield of a crop and the quantity of fertilizer is given as

$$Y_i = \alpha + \beta X_i + \varepsilon_i,$$

where all basic assumptions are satisfied. Suppose two research workers estimated this relationship by the method of least squares from the same set of n observations. How, if at all, would the values of (1) the estimated regression coefficient $\hat{\beta}$, (2) the t statistic given as $\hat{\beta}/s_{\hat{\beta}}$, and (3) R^2 of the two researchers differ if

a. Researcher A measured both X and Y in kilograms, whereas researcher B measured both of these variables in metric tons (1 ton = 1000 kg)?

b. Researcher A measured both X and Y in kilograms, whereas researcher B measured Y in metric tons and X in kilograms?

7-11. One test for the existence of a relationship between X and Y is carried out by constructing a t statistic $\hat{\beta}/s_{\hat{\beta}}$. Show that this is exactly equal to

$$[R^2(n-2)/(1-R^2)]^{1/2}.$$

7-12. The true relationship between X and Y in the population is given by

$$Y_i = 2 + 3X_i + \varepsilon_i.$$

Suppose the values of X in the sample of 10 observations are 1, 2, . . . , 10. The values of the disturbances are drawn at random from a normal population with zero mean and unit variance.

$\varepsilon_1 = 0.464$	$\varepsilon_6 = 0.296$
$\varepsilon_2 = 0.137$	$\varepsilon_7 = -0.288$
$\varepsilon_3 = 2.455$	$\varepsilon_8 = 1.298$
$\varepsilon_4 = -0.323$	$\varepsilon_9 = 0.241$
$\varepsilon_5 = -0.068$	$\varepsilon_{10} = -0.957$

a. Present the 10 observed values of X and Y.

b. Use the least squares formulas to estimate the regression coefficients and their standard errors, and compare the results with the true values.

c. Carry out a test for the existence of a relationship between X and Y.

d. Obtain the predicted value of Y—and its 95% confidence limits—for $X = 12$.

7-13. Consider the model $Y_i = \beta X_i + \varepsilon_i$ for which all the basic assumptions hold. Suppose the value of σ^2 is known. Derive the posterior distribution of β given that

a. There is no prior information about β.

b. The prior distribution of β is normal with mean β_0 and variance σ_0^2.

8 Violations of Basic Assumptions

In Chapter 7 we have developed a so-called classical normal linear regression model and showed how this model can be used for estimation, hypothesis testing, and prediction. In deriving the results we have made use of certain assumptions, which we termed *basic assumptions,* concerning the stochastic disturbance ε_i and the explanatory variable X_i. The first four assumptions involving the stochastic disturbance are normality, zero mean, homoskedasticity, and nonautocorrelation. The fifth assumption concerns the explanatory variable, which is assumed to be nonstochastic and such that its sample variance is a finite number, whatever the sample size. Given these assumptions, we have been able to show that the least squares estimators of the regression parameters have all the desirable properties. The main objective of the present chapter is to find how the properties of the least squares estimators are affected when any one of the basic assumptions is violated. Furthermore, if and when we find that the consequences of such a violation are serious, we shall try to develop alternative methods of estimation that would give more satisfactory results.

A violation of one or more of the basic assumptions can sometimes be deduced from theoretical considerations or from the way in which the data are measured. For example, when the regression model under consideration is a production function relating *maximum* output to a given input (or inputs), the disturbances may be only negative (or zero) and thus not have a normal distribution and zero mean. Or, in the case where the specified regression model satisfies all basic assumptions but the variables involved are measured as averages of various groups, the disturbance will also represent a group average and, in general, will not have a constant variance. In other situations, violations of basic assumptions can be expected on purely empirical grounds. Thus regression equations estimated from time series data are frequently characterized by autocorrelated disturbances, particularly when the period of observation is short. On the other hand, regression equations estimated from survey data have often been found to be heteroskedastic.

To discover the presence of a violation of one or more of the basic assumptions, research workers in disciplines other than econometrics frequently plot the least squares residuals against the sample values of the explanatory variable (X), or against the fitted values of the dependent variable ($\hat{Y}$), or against time if applicable. A plot of the residuals on the so-called "normal probability paper" is also used. If no violation exists, the residual plots should show no distinct pattern of variation. However, the interpretation of the plots is based on a subjective judgment and requires "skill and experience."[1] Econometricians appear to prefer formal statistical tests such as those described and explained at the end of each of the following sections. When a test indicates a violation, a common practice is to reestimate the regression coefficients by an estimation method that takes the violation into account. However, when this is done, the conventional significance levels or confidence intervals do not have the same meaning as when no preliminary test is involved since the stated probabilities are *conditional* on the outcome of the preliminary test. The presumed properties and the distribution of the resulting estimators can also be affected. In statistical literature this is known as a "pretest bias."[2] No such problem exists when the violation is presumed and taken into account from the start of the investigation.

Perhaps we should start with a warning. While all the results pertaining to the classical normal linear regression model discussed in the preceding chapter are well established, the problems arising in situations in which the basic assumptions do not hold have not been always satisfactorily resolved. In fact, it is the preoccupation with these problems that distinguishes an econometrician from a statistician. The main reason for this is that some of the basic assumptions are likely to be violated because of the particular nature of economic relationships or economic data. The resulting problems of estimation and hypotheses testing are thus of special relevance to economics. Many of the results to be presented here are relatively new. Some of the unresolved problems are still the subject of current research and may be solved in the near future; others may stay unresolved for a long time.

8-1 Nonnormality and Nonzero Mean

The first basic assumption of the classical regression model

$$Y_i = \alpha + \beta X_i + \varepsilon_i$$

is that the stochastic disturbance ε_i is normally distributed. As mentioned in Section 7-2, this assumption is based on the argument that ε_i represents the sum or average of a large number of independent effects which are as likely to be positive as negative and none of which has dominating variability. At the end of Section 7-3 we considered the role of this assumption in demonstrating the desirable properties of the least squares estimators. We noted that the assumption of normality was needed

[1] See D. C. Montgomery and E. A. Peck, *Introduction to Linear Regression Analysis* (New York: Wiley, 1982), p. 70.

[2] See, e.g., George G. Judge et al., *The Theory and Practice of Econometrics*, 2nd ed. (New York: Wiley, 1985), p. 72.

for the proof of efficiency of the least squares estimators of the regression coefficients by means of the Cramer–Rao lower bound, and for establishing confidence intervals and the tests of significance presented in Section 7-4. But as long as the remaining basic assumptions hold (and as long as the variance ε_i is finite), the least squares estimators (LSE) of the regression coefficients are best linear unbiased estimators (BLUE) regardless of the form of the distribution of ε_i.

With respect to other desirable properties, it is clear that the LSE of α and β are asymptotically unbiased since they are unbiased for any sample size. Their consistency can be proved as follows:

$$\lim_{n\to\infty} \text{MSE}(\hat{\beta}) = \lim_{n\to\infty} \text{Var}(\hat{\beta}) \tag{8.1}$$

$$= \lim_{n\to\infty} \frac{\sigma^2}{\sum x_i'^2} \qquad \text{[using (7.23)]}$$

$$= \lim_{n\to\infty} \frac{\sigma^2/n}{\sum x_i'^2/n}$$

$$= 0 \qquad \text{[using (7.6)]}$$

where, as before, $\hat{\beta}$ denotes the LSE of β and $x_i' = X_i - \overline{X}$. The fact that MSE($\hat{\beta}$), the mean square error of $\hat{\beta}$, approaches zero as the sample size approaches infinity implies that $\hat{\beta}$ is consistent. The same proof could be applied to show the consistency of $\hat{\alpha}$, the LSE of α. Thus when the disturbance is not normally distributed (but has a finite variance σ^2), the LSEs of α and β are still BLUE and consistent, but not necessarily efficient or asymptotically efficient. Further, the formulas for the variances of $\hat{\alpha}$ and $\hat{\beta}$ given by (7.23) and (7.25) and derived without using the assumption of normality remain valid. The estimator of σ^2, labeled s^2 and presented in (7.35) is also unbiased under nonnormality, and can be shown to be consistent.[3] Finally, with the use of a version of the central limit theorem it can be determined that $\hat{\alpha}$ and $\hat{\beta}$ are asymptotically normal, and that the usual confidence intervals and tests of significance involving α and β are asymptotically valid even if the disturbances are not normal, as long as the remaining basic assumptions hold and σ^2 is finite.[4] This means that the results concerning confidence intervals and tests of significance of the regression coefficients established in Section 7-4 under the assumption of normality do, in general, hold at least approximately in large samples even without this assumption.

Estimation Under Nonnormality

The violation of the assumption of normality does not appear to have very serious consequences for least squares estimation. Some critics, however, point out that the LSEs, being based on *squared* deviations from the regression line, tend to be

[3] See P. Schmidt, *Econometrics* (New York: Marcel Dekker, 1976), p. 9.

[4] *Ibid.*, pp. 56–64.

unduly influenced by extreme deviations occurring with a low probability. Such extreme deviations may be caused by highly abnormal weather conditions, strikes, gross errors, political events or rumors, and similar events. It is claimed that the disturbances may perhaps be better modeled by a distribution with fatter tails and with a larger variance (possibly an infinite one) than by the normal distribution. In that case the LSEs of the regression coefficients might have considerably larger variance than the maximum likelihood estimators. (If the distribution of the disturbance has an infinite variance, then the variance of the LSEs is also infinite.)

To illustrate the inefficiency of the LSEs under nonnormality, let us consider the so-called *Laplace* (or *double exponential*) distribution of ε_i defined as

$$f(\varepsilon_i) = \frac{1}{2\phi} e^{-|\varepsilon_i/\phi|} \qquad (\phi > 0). \tag{8.2}$$

The main difference between the Laplace distribution and the normal distribution is that the Laplace distribution involves absolute values of ε_i, whereas the normal distribution involves the squares of ε_i. The Laplace distribution of ε_i is symmetric with mean zero and variance $2\phi^2$, and its tails are fatter than those of the corresponding normal distribution.[5] A diagrammatic representation of this distribution is shown in Figure 8-1.

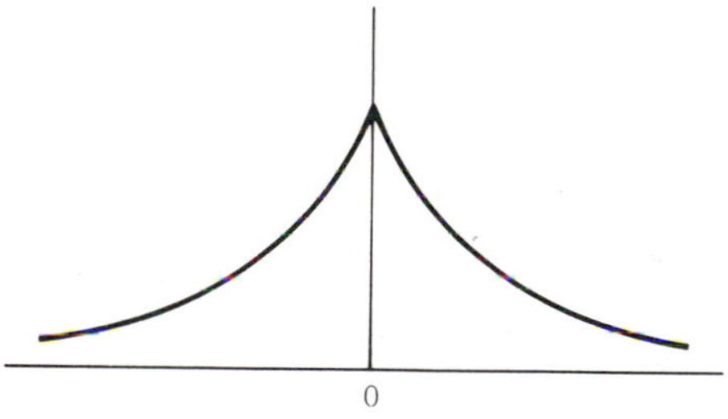

Figure 8-1

The maximum likelihood estimation of the regression coefficients is equivalent to minimizing the sum of absolute values of the residuals

$$\sum_i |Y_i - \alpha - \beta X_i|$$

with respect to α and β. Such a minimization is a problem in linear programming and can be solved using a standard computer program. The solution involves selecting two of the n available sample observations and letting the estimating regression line pass through these two points.[6] The resulting estimator of β, say, $\overset{\Delta}{\beta}$, is

[5] See A. C. Harvey, *The Econometric Analysis of Time Series* (New York: Wiley, 1981), pp. 114–115.

[6] See L. D. Taylor, "Estimation by Minimizing the Sum of Absolute Errors" in P. Zarembka, *Frontiers in Econometrics* (New York: Academic Press, 1974). In the case of a multiple regression model with K coefficients, the estimated regression would pass through K sample points.

asymptotically efficient, with its asymptotic variance given as

$$\text{(8.3)} \qquad \text{Asympt. Var}(\overset{\triangle}{\beta}) = \frac{\phi^2}{\sum x_i'^2}.$$

The asymptotic variance of the LSE of β for the Laplace distribution is

$$\text{(8.4)} \qquad \text{Asympt. Var}(\hat{\beta}) = \frac{2\phi^2}{\sum x_i'^2},$$

which is twice as large as that of $\overset{\triangle}{\beta}$.[7]

The estimator of the regression coefficients obtained by minimizing the sum of absolute deviations (frequently abbreviated as MAD) is a natural analog of the sample median as an estimator of the population mean or median. Since this estimator is less influenced by extreme deviations than is the LSE, it has been suggested that it be used in *all* cases when a fat-tailed distribution of the disturbance cannot be ruled out. It has been shown that the MAD estimator of a regression coefficient is asymptotically unbiased and normally distributed, and its asymptotic variance is smaller than that of the LSE for a large class of fat-tailed distributions.[8] Of course, when the distribution of ε_i is normal the MAD estimator is inefficient, its asymptotic variance being about 57% larger than that of the LSE.

Since the LSEs perform very well when the disturbance is normally distributed but may perform very poorly when it is not, attempts have been made to construct estimators that would perform considerably better than LSE when the distribution of the disturbance is fat-tailed, and that would perform nearly as well as LSE when the distribution is normal. Estimators of this sort are called *robust estimators.* The best known of these are the so-called M estimators (for "maximum likelihood type" estimators). Whereas the LSEs are obtained by minimizing

$$\sum_i (Y_i - \alpha - \beta X_i)^2$$

with respect to α and β, the idea behind the M estimators is to minimize

$$\sum_i f(Y_i - \alpha - \beta X_i),$$

where $f(Y_i - \alpha - \beta X_i)$ is some function of $(Y_i - \alpha - \beta X_i)$ that would yield estimators with the desired property of robustness mentioned above. One such function suggested by Huber and frequently mentioned in the statistical literature involves using LS estimation for all deviations smaller (in absolute value) than or equal to a preassigned value, and using MAD estimation for all deviations larger than that.[9]

[7] A. C. Harvey, *op. cit.*, pp. 114–115. The maximum likelihood estimator of ϕ is $\Sigma |Y_i - \overset{\triangle}{\alpha} - \overset{\triangle}{\beta} X_i|/n$.

[8] See G. Bassett, Jr., and R. Koenker, "Asymptotic Theory of Least Absolute Error Regression," *Journal of the American Statistical Association,* 73 (September 1978), pp. 618–622. A formula for the asymptotic variance is also given in this article.

[9] See P. J. Huber, *Robust Statistics* (New York: Wiley, 1981).

When the preassigned number is infinity, this method reduces to LS estimation; when the number is zero, we have pure MAD estimation. For other values we have a mixture of the two. Another suggestion has been simply to discard all observations corresponding to large deviations and to apply LS estimation to the remaining observations. This is known as "trimmed" estimation.

The difficulty with robust estimation is the arbitrariness in selecting the preassigned constant in the case of the estimator proposed by Huber, or in deciding which observations to discard in the case of the trimmed estimator. Further, and perhaps more importantly, dealing with extreme deviations by fudging their influence is much less satisfactory than explaining their presence. If extreme deviations are caused by unusual events such as abnormal weather conditions, strikes, etc., then a preferable procedure would be to include these events as qualitative (or so-called "dummy") explanatory variables in the regression equation (see Section 11-1). For these reasons robust estimation has not been very popular in econometrics, although this may change.

Testing for Normality

A reasonable and practical approach to estimation when the normality of the disturbance is in doubt is to compute both LS and MAD estimates of the regression coefficients. If the two sets of estimates are not too far apart, we may have no cause for concern. If, however, there is a substantial difference between them, we may try to identify those observations that correspond to extreme deviations and to check their cause, including the possibility of gross error of measurement or recording.

EXAMPLE The preceding point may be illustrated by reference to the regression model of the demand for oranges used in Section 7-3. Using the data for 12 observations presented in Table 7-2, we obtained the LS estimates

$$Y_i = 210.460 - 1.578X_i + e_i.$$

The MAD estimates, which in this case can be obtained even without a computer program, are

$$Y_i = 205 - 1.5X_i + \tilde{e}_i.$$

Clearly, the two sets of estimates are quite similar. (It may be worth noting that $\Sigma_i|\tilde{e}_i| = 60$, whereas $\Sigma_i|e_i| = 64.68$.)

A more formal way of checking for a departure from normality involves a proper statistical testing procedure. Several procedures for testing the hypothesis that a set of random sample observations comes from a normal population are available in the literature. Their application to the case of regression disturbances, however, is complicated by the fact that these disturbances are unobservable and all that we have to go by are the calculated residuals. When the estimation method is that of least squares, the residuals (denoted by e) can be expressed as follows:[10]

$$e_j = \varepsilon_j - \sum_{i=1}^{n} h_{ij}\varepsilon_i \qquad (j = 1, 2, \ldots, n) \tag{8.5}$$

where
$$h_{ij} = \frac{1}{n} + \frac{x_i' x_j'}{\sum x_i'^2}.$$

Thus each residual is a linear combination of all n disturbances in the sample and, therefore, the residuals are correlated. However, since the expression

$$\sum_{i=1}^{n} h_{ij}\varepsilon_i = \sum_{i=1}^{n} \left(\frac{\varepsilon_i}{n} + \frac{x_j' x_i' \varepsilon_i / n}{\sum x_i'^2 / n} \right) \tag{8.6}$$

$$= \bar{\varepsilon} + \left(x_j' \frac{\sum x_i' \varepsilon_i / n}{\sum x_i'^2 / n} \right)$$

approaches zero as n approaches infinity, e_j approaches ε_j as sample size increases. This means that the usual tests for normality hold only asymptotically when applied to least squares residuals.

Since distributions are characterized by their moments, a natural way to test for a particular shape of a distribution is to test for the values of the moments corresponding to the shape of the distribution in question. In the case of the normal distribution, the moments of special relevance are those relating to symmetry (the third moment, μ_3) and to "peakedness" or "kurtosis" (the fourth moment, μ_4). The standard measures of symmetry and kurtosis are

$$\sqrt{\beta_1} = \frac{\mu_3}{\mu_2^{3/2}} \qquad \text{and} \qquad \beta_2 = \frac{\mu_4}{\mu_2^2} \tag{8.7}$$

where μ_r $(r = 2, 3, 4)$ is the rth moment about the mean. For the normal distribution $\beta_1 = 0$ (since the distribution is symmetric) and $\beta_2 = 3$. The estimates of β_1 and β_2, say, b_1 and b_2, are obtained by replacing the μ's by their sample estimates defined as

$$\hat{\mu}_r = \frac{1}{n} \sum_i e_i^r \qquad (r = 2, 3, 4). \tag{8.8}$$

A test for normality is then a test of the null hypothesis

$$H_0\colon \quad \beta_1 = 0 \qquad \text{and} \qquad \beta_2 = 3$$

against an appropriate alternative. A simple way of testing H_0 exists when the alternative hypothesis is that H_0 is not true *and* the distribution of the disturbance belongs to a large class of distributions known as the "Pearson family." In this case

[10] See D. A. Belsley, E. Kuh, and R. E. Welsch, *Regression Diagnostics* (New York: Wiley, 1980), pp. 16–18.

we may use the following test statistic which, under the null hypothesis, has a chi-square distribution with two degrees of freedom.[11]

$$n\left[\frac{b_1}{6}+\frac{(b_2-3)^2}{24}\right]\sim\chi_2^2 \qquad (8.9)$$

The test performed well in a simulation study even when applied to small samples.[12]

EXAMPLE Continuing with the example on the demand for oranges involving the data presented in Table 7-2, we obtain the following measurements for the calculation of the value of the test statistic (8.9):

$$\hat{\mu}_2 = 58.2407, \qquad \hat{\mu}_3 = -635.1749, \qquad \hat{\mu}_4 = 15053.607$$

$$b_1 = 2.0422, \qquad b_2 = 4.43779.$$

The value of the test statistic (8.9) in this case is 5.118, whereas the tabulated value of χ_2^2 at 5% level of significance is 5.991. If we were willing to use the asymptotic test procedure even though our sample is quite small, we would not reject the hypothesis of normality at the 5% level.

Nonzero Mean

The second assumption—zero mean of the regression disturbance—is made in accordance with the specification that the population regression line is

$$E(Y_i) = \alpha + \beta X_i.$$

If the mean of the disturbance is not zero but, say, μ_i, we have

$$E(Y_i) = \alpha + \beta X_i + \mu_i.$$

The implications of this depend on the nature of μ_i. In particular, we have to distinguish between the case where μ_i has the same value for all observations and the case where μ_i may vary. In the first case we can write $\mu_i = \mu$, and the true population regression line is

$$E(Y_i) = \alpha + \mu + \beta X_i$$

or

$$E(Y_i) = \alpha^* + \beta X_i$$

or

$$Y_i = \alpha^* + \beta X_i + \varepsilon_i^*,$$

where $\alpha^* = \alpha + \mu$, $\varepsilon_i^* = \varepsilon_i - \mu$, and the mean of ε_i^* is zero. It is clear, then, that

[11] This test as a test for normality of observations was proposed in K. O. Bowman and L. R. Shenton, "Omnibus Contours for Departures from Normality Based on $\sqrt{b_1}$ and b_2," *Biometrika*, 62 (1975), pp. 243–250. It was proposed as a test for normality of regression disturbances in C. M. Jarque and A. K. Bera, "An Efficient Large-Sample Test for Normality of Observations and Regression Residuals," manuscript, Australian National University, Canberra, 1981.

[12] Jarque and Bera, *op cit.* The test is designated a "Lagrange multiplier (LM) test" by the authors.

while the least squares estimator of β is unaffected, the least squares formula for estimating the intercept gives an estimate of α^* and not of α. As long as ε_i is normally distributed, there is no way in which we can estimate α and μ separately and get consistent estimates.

EXAMPLE A good example of a situation in which the mean of ε_i is nonzero is the case of the so-called *frontier production function.* In its simplest version this function can be represented as

$$Y_i = \alpha + \beta X_i + \varepsilon_i \qquad (\varepsilon_i \leq 0),$$

where Y = logarithmic quantity of output, X = logarithmic quantity of input, and i refers to the ith firm. If, in the absence of a disturbance, the production function refers to the *maximum* quantity of output for a given quantity of input, then the presence of the disturbance cannot have a *positive* effect on the dependent variable, only negative or zero. The obvious implication of this is that the mean of ε_i is negative. This mean is assumed to be the same for each firm, and it can be interpreted as measuring the average inefficiency of the industry. Since the disturbance is bounded from above, it cannot be normally distributed. However, as long as the remaining three basic assumptions are satisfied, the LSE of β will have all desirable asymptotic properties. A consistent estimate of α and of the mean of ε_i can be obtained only under certain distributional assumptions about ε_i.[13] Of course, if the deterministic part of the production function is considered to refer to the *average* (rather than absolute) maximum output, then the assumption of zero mean and of normality may be quite reasonable.

In the case where μ_i is not a constant, the intercept becomes $(\alpha + \mu_i)$; that is, it may vary from observation to observation. This means that the mean value of the dependent variable, $E(Y_i)$, changes not only because of changes in X_i but also for other reasons; in other words, the relationship between X_i and Y_i has not been correctly specified. This might occur when $E(Y_i)$ is affected not only by X_i but also by another nonstochastic variable Z_i that we have left out of the regression equation. That is, the true model is

$$Y_i = \alpha + \beta X_i + \gamma Z_i + \varepsilon_i^*,$$

where ε_i^* satisfies all basic assumptions, but we estimate

$$Y_i = \alpha + \beta X_i + \varepsilon_i,$$

in which case

$$\mu_i = \gamma Z_i.$$

Or suppose the true model is nonlinear of the form

$$Y_i = \alpha + \beta X_i + \gamma X_i^2 + \varepsilon_i^*$$

[13] See F. R. Forsund, C. A. K. Lovell, and P. Schmidt, "A Survey of Frontier Production Functions and of Their Relationship to Efficiency Measurement," *Journal of Econometrics,* 13 (May 1980), pp. 5–25.

so that for our estimating equation we have

$$\mu_i = \gamma X_i^2,$$

which is the same as the omitted variable case with $Z_i = X_i^2$. The consequence of such misspecification for least squares estimation can be found, using (7.32), as follows:

$$E(\hat{\beta}) = \beta + E\left(\frac{\sum x_i' \varepsilon_i}{\sum x_i'^2}\right) \tag{8.10}$$

$$= \beta + \frac{\sum x_i' \mu_i}{\sum x_i'^2}$$

$$= \beta + \gamma \left(\frac{\sum x_i' Z_i}{\sum x_i'^2}\right).$$

This means that $\hat{\beta}$ is biased unless $Sx'_i Z_i$ $(= Sx'_i z'_i) = 0$, that is, unless X and Z are uncorrelated. If the bias does not disappear as the sample size approaches infinity, $\hat{\beta}$ is also inconsistent. Similar analysis can be carried out for $\hat{\alpha}$. Further discussion of specification errors is presented in Section 10-4.

8-2 Heteroskedasticity

By the assumption (7.4) of the classical normal linear regression model, we have

$$\text{Var}(\varepsilon_i) = \sigma^2 \quad \text{for all } i.$$

Since the mean of ε_i is assumed to be zero, we can write

$$E(\varepsilon_i^2) = \sigma^2.$$

This feature of the regression disturbance is known as homoskedasticity. It implies that the variance of the disturbance is constant for all observations. This assumption has not been considered to be too troublesome for models involving observations on aggregates over time, since the values of the explanatory variable are typically of a similar order of magnitude at all points of observation, and the same is true of the values of the dependent variable. For example, in an aggregate consumption function the level of consumption in recent years is of a similar order of magnitude as the level of consumption twenty years ago, and the same is true of income. Unless there are some special circumstances or the time period covered is very long, the assumption of homoskedasticity in aggregate models seems plausible. However, when we are dealing with microeconomic data, the observations may involve substantial differences in magnitude as, for example, in the case of data on income and expenditure of individual families. Here the assumption of homoskedasticity is not very plausible on a priori grounds since we would expect less variation in consumption for low-income families than for high-income families. At low levels of income the average level of consumption is low, and variation around this level is restricted: consumption cannot fall too far below the average level because this might mean starvation, and it cannot rise too far above the average because the asset and the credit position does not allow it. These constraints are likely to be less binding at higher income levels. Empirical evidence suggests that these prior considerations are in accord with actual behavior.[14] The appropriate model in this and other similar cases may then be one with *heteroskedastic* disturbances.

Properties of Least Squares Estimators

If the regression disturbance is heteroskedastic, we have

$$E(\varepsilon_i^2) = \sigma_i^2.$$

This implies that the variance of the disturbance may vary from observation to observation, and we want to know how this behavior of the variance affects the properties of the least squares estimators of the regression coefficients. First, we consider the property of unbiasedness. The least squares estimator of β is

$$\hat{\beta} = \frac{\sum x_i' y_i'}{\sum x_i'^2} = \beta + \frac{\sum x_i' \varepsilon_i}{\sum x_i'^2},$$

as given by (7.32). Then

$$E(\hat{\beta}) = \beta + E\left(\frac{\sum x_i'\varepsilon_i}{\sum x_i'^2}\right) = \beta.$$

Similarly,

$$\hat{\alpha} = \bar{Y} - \hat{\beta}\bar{X} = (\alpha + \beta\bar{X} + \bar{\varepsilon}) - \hat{\beta}\bar{X},$$

and

$$E(\hat{\alpha}) = \alpha + \beta\bar{X} + E(\bar{\varepsilon}) - E(\hat{\beta})\bar{X} = \alpha.$$

That is, the least squares estimators are *unbiased* even under the conditions of heteroskedasticity.

Next, let us see whether the least squares estimators are still best linear unbiased estimators (BLUE). We can check this by deriving the BLUE formulas for the heteroskedastic case and by comparing them with the least squares formulas. If there is a difference, the least squares estimators are not BLUE. The simplest way of deriving the BLUE of the regression coefficients is by transforming the regression equation

$$Y_i = \alpha + \beta X_i + \varepsilon_i$$

with a heteroskedastic disturbance into an equivalent equation in which the transformed disturbance is homoskedastic. This can be done by dividing both sides of

[14] See S. J. Prais and H. S. Houthakker, *The Analysis of Family Budgets* (Cambridge, England: The University Press, 1955).

the original regression equation by σ_i to get

(8.11) $$\frac{Y_i}{\sigma_i} = \alpha\left(\frac{1}{\sigma_i}\right) + \beta\left(\frac{X_i}{\sigma_i}\right) + \frac{\varepsilon_i}{\sigma_i}$$

or

(8.11a) $$Y_i^* = \alpha W_i^* + \beta X_i^* + \varepsilon_i^*,$$

where $Y_i^* = (Y_i/\sigma_i)$, $W_i^* = (1/\sigma_i)$, $X_i^* = (X_i/\sigma_i)$, and $\varepsilon_i^* = (\varepsilon_i/\sigma_i)$. In the transformed regression equation (8.11a) there are two nonstochastic explanatory variables W^* and X^*, and there is no intercept term. (Of course, the values of these explanatory variables and of the dependent variable in the transformed equation cannot be measured if the values of σ_i are not known.) Now clearly

$$E(\varepsilon_i^*) = \frac{E(\varepsilon_i)}{\sigma_i} = 0,$$

$$\mathrm{Cov}(\varepsilon_i^*, \varepsilon_j^*) = \frac{E(\varepsilon_i\varepsilon_j)}{\sigma_i\sigma_j} = 0,$$

and

$$\mathrm{Var}(\varepsilon_i^*) = \mathrm{Var}\left(\frac{\varepsilon_i}{\sigma_i}\right) = \frac{\mathrm{Var}(\varepsilon_i)}{\sigma_i^2} = 1.$$

Since in (8.11a) the explanatory variables are nonstochastic and the disturbance has zero mean, is nonautocorrelated, and has a constant variance, all preconditions for the equality of the least squares estimators (LSE) and best linear unbiased estimators (BLUE) of α and β are met. By applying the least squares principles, we obtain the following "least squares normal equations" (see fn. 4, page 213).

(8.12) $$\sum W_i^* Y_i^* = \tilde{\alpha} \sum W_i^{*2} + \tilde{\beta} \sum W_i^* X_i^*,$$
$$\sum X_i^* Y_i^* = \tilde{\alpha} \sum W_i^* X_i^* + \tilde{\beta} \sum X_i^{*2}.$$

Reverting to the notation in (8.11) we have

(8.12a) $$\sum \frac{Y_i}{\sigma_i^2} = \tilde{\alpha} \sum \frac{1}{\sigma_i^2} + \tilde{\beta} \sum \frac{X_i}{\sigma_i^2},$$
$$\sum \frac{X_i Y_i}{\sigma_i^2} = \tilde{\alpha} \sum \frac{X_i}{\sigma_i^2} + \tilde{\beta} \sum \frac{X_i^2}{\sigma_i^2}.$$

Let us now introduce a more convenient notation by writing

$$\frac{1}{\sigma_i^2} = w_i$$

so that (8.12a) becomes

(8.12b) $$\sum w_i Y_i = \tilde{\alpha} \sum w_i + \tilde{\beta} \sum w_i X_i,$$
$$\sum w_i X_i Y_i = \tilde{\alpha} \sum w_i X_i + \tilde{\beta} \sum w_i X_i^2.$$

Solving these equations we obtain

$$\tilde{\beta} = \frac{(\sum w_i)(\sum w_i X_i Y_i) - (\sum w_i X_i)(\sum w_i Y_i)}{(\sum w_i)(\sum w_i X_i^2) - (\sum w_i X_i)^2} \tag{8.13}$$

$$= \frac{\sum w_i (X_i - \tilde{X})(Y_i - \tilde{Y})}{\sum W_i (X_i - \tilde{X})^2}$$

and

$$\tilde{\alpha} = \tilde{Y} - \tilde{\beta}\tilde{X}, \tag{8.14}$$

where $\tilde{X} = (\Sigma w_i X_i)/(\Sigma w_i)$ and $\tilde{Y} = (\Sigma w_i Y_i)/(\Sigma w_i)$. These formulas for the best linear unbiased estimators of α and β are obviously different from those for the least squares estimators. Thus we have to conclude that the least squares estimators of the regression coefficients are not BLUE when the assumption of homoskedasticity does not hold. From this conclusion it also follows that the least squares estimators do not have the smallest variance among all unbiased estimators and, therefore, are not *efficient*.

The inefficiency of the least squares estimators of the regression coefficients can be intuitively explained as follows. The standard least squares principle involves minimizing

$$S = \sum (Y_i - \alpha - \beta X_i)^2,$$

which means that each squared disturbance is given equal weight. This is justifiable when each disturbance comes from the same distribution. Under heteroskedasticity, however, different disturbances come from distributions with different variances. Clearly, those disturbances that come from distributions with a smaller variance give more precise information about the regression line than those coming from distributions with a larger variance. To use sample information efficiently, one should give more weight to the observations with less dispersed disturbances than to those with more dispersed disturbances. This is exactly reflected in formulas (8.13) and (8.14) where the weights w_i are equal to the reciprocals of the respective variances. It is also interesting to note that the same formulas could have been obtained by minimizing

$$S^* = \sum w_i (Y_i - \alpha - \beta X_i)^2 \tag{8.15}$$

with respect to α and β. For this reason $\tilde{\alpha}$ and $\tilde{\beta}$ are sometimes called "weighted least squares estimators" of α and β. Note that if the variance of the disturbance is constant, i.e., if $\sigma_i^2 = \sigma^2$ and $w_i = w$ for all i, then $\tilde{X} = \bar{X}$, $\tilde{Y} = \bar{Y}$, and formulas (8.13) and (8.14) will reduce to the simple least squares formulas (7.12) and (7.15).

Turning to the asymptotic properties, we can check if the least squares estimators of the regression coefficients are consistent under heteroskedasticity by examining the limit of their mean square error as the sample size goes to infinity. If this limit is zero, then the estimators are consistent. Let us first consider $\hat{\beta}$, the least squares estimator of β. Since $\hat{\beta}$ is unbiased, it follows that $\text{MSE}(\hat{\beta}) = \text{Var}(\hat{\beta})$. Further, using

(7.32) we have

$$\mathrm{Var}(\hat{\beta}) = E(\hat{\beta} - \beta)^2 = E\left(\frac{\sum x_i'\varepsilon_i}{\sum x_i'^2}\right)^2$$

which, since $E(\varepsilon_i^2) = \sigma_i^2$ and $E(\varepsilon_i\varepsilon_j) = 0$, becomes

$$\mathrm{Var}(\hat{\beta}) = \frac{\sum x_i'^2\sigma_i^2}{(\sum x_i'^2)^2}. \tag{8.16}$$

Note that when $\sigma_i^2 = \sigma^2$ for all i, the above formula reduces to the classical formula given in (7.23). Now let us write $\theta_i' = \sigma_i^2 - \bar{\sigma}^2$ where $\bar{\sigma}^2 = \Sigma\sigma_i^2/n$ so that $\Sigma\theta_i' = 0$. Then

$$\begin{aligned}\mathrm{Var}(\hat{\beta}) &= \frac{\sum x_i'^2(\bar{\sigma}^2 + \theta_i')}{(\sum x_i'^2)^2} = \frac{\bar{\sigma}^2}{\sum x_i'^2} + \frac{\sum x_i'^2\theta_i'}{(\sum x_i'^2)^2} \\ &= \frac{\bar{\sigma}^2/n}{\sum x_i'^2/n} + \frac{(\sum x_i'^2\theta_i'/n)(1/n)}{(\sum x_i'^2/n)^2},\end{aligned} \tag{8.16a}$$

where $\Sigma x_i'^2\,\theta_i'/n$ is the sample covariance of $x_i'^2$ and σ_i^2, which we can safely assume to be finite as $n \to \infty$ as long as $\sigma_i^2 < \infty$ for all i. Since $\lim_{n\to\infty} \Sigma x_i'^2/n$ is a finite number by the assumption (7.6), and since $\lim_{n\to\infty} (\bar{\sigma}^2/n) = 0$, we have

$$\lim_{n\to\infty} \mathrm{Var}(\hat{\beta}) = 0.$$

Therefore $\hat{\beta}$ is consistent even if the disturbance is heteroskedastic. The same result could be obtained for $\hat{\alpha}$.

To find whether the least squares estimators are asymptotically efficient under the condition of heteroskedasticity, we derive the appropriate maximum likelihood estimators that are known to be asymptotically efficient. Then we will check whether the variances of the maximum likelihood estimators are asymptotically equivalent to those of the least squares estimators. If they are not, the least squares estimators are not asymptotically efficient. Setting up the log-likelihood function as in (7.26) but allowing for heteroskedasticity, we get

$$L = -\frac{n}{2}\log(2\pi) - \frac{1}{2}\sum_{i=1}^{n}\log\sigma_i^2 - \frac{1}{2}\sum_{i=1}^{n}\left(\frac{Y_i - \alpha - \beta X_i}{\sigma_i}\right)^2. \tag{8.17}$$

The first derivatives of L with respect to α and β are

$$\frac{\partial L}{\partial\alpha} = \sum_i\left(\frac{Y_i - \alpha - \beta X_i}{\sigma_i^2}\right),$$

$$\frac{\partial L}{\partial\beta} = \sum_i\left[\frac{X_i(Y_i - \alpha - \beta X_i)}{\sigma_i^2}\right].$$

Putting these derivatives equal to zero and solving for the estimators of α and β leads to the formulas (8.13) and (8.14) for the best linear unbiased estimators.

Since the maximum likelihood estimators of α and β are the same as BLUE, their variances must also be the same. The formulas for these variances can be derived as follows. Given that

$$Y_i = \alpha + \beta X_i + \varepsilon_i$$

and

$$\tilde{Y} = \alpha + \beta\tilde{X} + \tilde{\varepsilon},$$

where $\tilde{\varepsilon} = \Sigma w_i \varepsilon_i / \Sigma w_i$, we have

$$\tilde{\beta} = \frac{\sum w_i(X_i - \tilde{X})(Y_i - \tilde{Y})}{\sum w_i(X_i - \tilde{X})^2} = \frac{\sum w_i(X_i - \tilde{X})[\beta(X_i - \tilde{X}) + (\varepsilon_i - \tilde{\varepsilon})]}{\sum w_i(X_i - \tilde{X})^2}$$

$$= \beta + \frac{\sum w_i(X_i - \tilde{X})(\varepsilon_i - \tilde{\varepsilon})}{\sum w_i(X_i - \tilde{X})^2} = \beta + \frac{\sum w_i(X_i - \tilde{X})\varepsilon_i}{\sum w_i(X_i - \tilde{X})^2}.$$

Therefore

$$(8.18) \qquad \mathrm{Var}(\tilde{\beta}) = E(\tilde{\beta} - \beta)^2 = E\left(\frac{\sum w_i(X_i - \tilde{X})\varepsilon_i}{\sum w_i(X_i - \tilde{X})^2}\right)^2$$

$$= \frac{\sum w_i^2(X_i - \tilde{X})^2\sigma_i^2}{[\sum w_i(X_i - \tilde{X})^2]^2} = \frac{\sum w_i(X_i - \tilde{X})^2}{[\sum w_i(X_i - \tilde{X})^2]^2}$$

$$= \frac{\sum w_i}{(\sum w_i)(\sum w_i X_i^2) - (\sum w_i X_i)^2}$$

$$= \frac{1}{\sum w_i(X_i - \tilde{X})^2}.$$

A similar derivation yields the following formula for the variance of the BLUE of α under heteroskedasticity.

$$(8.19) \qquad \mathrm{Var}(\tilde{\alpha}) = \frac{\sum w_i X_i^2}{\sum w_i \sum w_i X_i^2 - (\sum w_i X_i)^2}$$

$$= \frac{1}{\sum w_i} + \frac{\tilde{X}^2}{\sum w_i(X_i - \tilde{X})^2}.$$

Note that if $w_i = w = 1/\sigma^2$ for all i, then the expressions in (8.18) and (8.19) are the same as those given in (7.23) and (7.25) for the classical model.

The question of asymptotic efficiency of the least squares estimators of α and β under heteroskedasticity can be settled by comparing their asymptotic variances with those of the maximum likelihood estimators. Clearly, the variance of the least estimator of β given in (8.16) is different from that of the maximum likelihood estimator given in (8.18), *whatever the sample size.* A similar conclusion can be reached with respect to the variance of the least squares estimator of α. Therefore, since the variances of the least squares estimators are not asymptotically equivalent to the variances of the maximum likelihood estimators, the least squares estimators are *not* asymptotically efficient when the disturbance is not homoskedastic.

To sum up, when the regression disturbance is heteroskedastic, the least squares estimators of the regression coefficients are unbiased and consistent, but they are *not* BLUE, efficient, or asymptotically efficient. The loss of efficiency of the least squares estimators can be determined (if σ_i are known) by comparing their variances with those of the *weighted* least squares estimators, which are BLUE and efficient. The extent of the loss clearly depends on the sample values of the explanatory variable and of the variances of the disturbance.

EXAMPLE The extent of the loss of efficiency under heteroskedasticity of the simple least squares as compared with the weighted least squares estimation can be illustrated as follows. Let $X_i = 1, 2, \ldots, 20$ and $\sigma_i^2 = 2X_i^2$ (i.e., $w_i = 1/2X_i^2$). Then

$$\sum x_i'^2\sigma_i^2 = 2\sum (X_i - \bar{X})^2 X_i^2 = 2\left[\sum X_i^4 - 2\bar{X}\sum X_i^3 + \bar{X}^2\sum X_i^2\right]$$
$$= 225{,}967$$

and

$$\sum x_i'^2 = \sum X_i^2 - 20\bar{X}^2 = 665,$$

so that

$$\mathrm{Var}(\hat{\beta}) = \frac{\sum x_i'^2\sigma_i^2}{(\sum x_i'^2)^2} = 0.510977.$$

Further,

$$\tilde{X} = \frac{\sum w_i X_i}{\sum w_i} = \frac{\sum (1/X_i)}{\sum (1/X_i^2)}$$
$$= 2.253994$$

and

$$\sum w_i(X_i - \tilde{X})^2 = \frac{1}{2}(20) - \tilde{X}\sum\left(\frac{1}{X_i}\right) + \frac{1}{2}\tilde{X}^2\sum\left(\frac{1}{X_i^2}\right)$$
$$= 5.945399,$$

so that

$$\mathrm{Var}(\tilde{\beta}) = \frac{1}{\sum w_i(X_i - \tilde{X})^2}$$
$$= 0.168198$$

and

$$\frac{\text{Var}(\hat{\beta})}{\text{Var}(\tilde{\beta})} = 3.038.$$

Thus the variance of the least squares estimator of β is more than three times as large as that of the BLUE of β.

Properties of the Estimated Variances of the Least Squares Estimators

We have found that under heteroskedasticity the least squares estimators of the regression coefficients are unbiased and consistent but not efficient or asymptotically efficient. Thus, if the disturbance is heteroskedastic and we do not know it (or know it but disregard it) and use the least squares formulas, the resulting estimators will still have some desirable properties. But when we come to using these estimators for testing hypotheses or constructing confidence intervals, we require not only that the estimators themselves be unbiased, but also that their estimated variances by unbiased. Otherwise, the tests are invalid and the constructed confidence intervals incorrect. Therefore, the next question concerns the biasedness or unbiasedness of the estimated variances obtained from the conventional formulas for the least squares estimators. For the least squares estimator of the regression slope, $\hat{\beta}$, the conventional formula for calculating the variance is given by (7.37) as

$$s_{\hat{\beta}}^2 = \frac{s^2}{\sum x_i'^2},$$

where $s^2 = [\Sigma(Y_i - \hat{\alpha} - \hat{\beta}X_i)^2]/(n-2)$. Under homoskedasticity, this is an unbiased estimator of the variance of $\hat{\beta}$. We wish to know whether the property of unbiasedness of $s_{\hat{\beta}}^2$ is preserved when the assumption of homoskedasticity does not hold. To answer this we have to find the mathematical expectation of s^2. We have

$$E(s^2) = E\left(\frac{1}{n-2}\right) \sum_i [\alpha + \beta X_i + \varepsilon_i - \hat{\alpha} - \hat{\beta}X_i]^2$$

$$= \frac{1}{n-2} \sum_i E[-(\hat{\alpha} - \alpha) - (\hat{\beta} - \beta)X_i + \varepsilon_i]^2.$$

Substituting for $(\hat{\alpha} - \alpha)$ from (7.30) we get

$$E(s^2) = \frac{1}{n-2} \sum_i E[-(\hat{\beta} - \beta)x_i' + \varepsilon_i']^2$$

$$= \frac{1}{n-2}\left(E(\hat{\beta} - \beta)^2 \sum_i x_i'^2 + E \sum_i \varepsilon_i'^2 - 2E(\hat{\beta} - \beta) \sum x_i'\varepsilon_i'\right).$$

Now

$$E(\hat{\beta} - \beta)^2 \sum x_i'^2 = \left(\sum x_i'^2\right)\text{Var}(\hat{\beta})$$

and, by (7.32),

$$E(\hat{\beta}-\beta)\sum x_i'\varepsilon_i' = E\left(\frac{\sum x_i'\varepsilon_i'}{\sum x_i'^2}\right)\sum x_i'\varepsilon_i'$$

$$= E\left(\frac{\sum x_i'\varepsilon_i'}{\sum x_i'^2}\right)^2 \sum x_i'^2$$

$$= (\sum x_i'^2)\operatorname{Var}(\hat{\beta}).$$

Finally

$$E(\sum \varepsilon_i'^2) = E(\sum \varepsilon_i^2) + nE(\bar{\varepsilon}^2) - 2E(\bar{\varepsilon}\sum \varepsilon_i)$$

$$= E(\sum \varepsilon_i^2) - nE(\bar{\varepsilon}^2) = \sum \sigma_i^2 - \frac{1}{n}E(\sum \varepsilon_i^2).$$

$$= \sum \sigma_i^2 - \frac{1}{n}\sum \sigma_i^2 = \left(\frac{n-1}{n}\right)\sum \sigma_i^2.$$

Substituting these results into the expression for $E(s^2)$ and recalling the formula for $\operatorname{Var}(\hat{\beta})$ from (8.16), we obtain

$$(8.20) \qquad E(s^2) = \frac{1}{n-2}\left[-(\sum x_i'^2)\operatorname{Var}(\hat{\beta}) + E(\sum \varepsilon_i'^2)\right]$$

$$= \frac{1}{n-2}\left[-\frac{\sum x_i'^2\sigma_i^2}{\sum x_i'^2} + \frac{(n-1)\sum \sigma_i^2}{n}\right].$$

Now, if we use the notation $\sigma_i^2 = \bar{\sigma}^2 + \theta_i'$ and $\Sigma\, \theta_i' = 0$ as in (8.16a), $E(s^2)$ becomes

$$(8.20a) \qquad E(s^2) = \frac{1}{n-2}\left[-\frac{\bar{\sigma}^2\sum x_i'^2 + \sum x_i'^2\theta'}{\sum x_i'^2} + \frac{(n-1)n\bar{\sigma}^2}{n}\right]$$

$$= \frac{1}{n-2}\left[(n-2)\bar{\sigma}^2 - \frac{\sum x_i'^2\theta_i'}{\sum x_i'^2}\right]$$

$$= \bar{\sigma}^2 - \frac{\sum x_i'^2\theta_i'}{(n-2)\sum x_i'^2}.$$

Therefore,

$$(8.21) \qquad E(s_{\hat{\beta}}^2) = E\left(\frac{s^2}{\sum x_i'^2}\right)$$

$$= \frac{\bar{\sigma}^2}{\sum x_i'^2} - \frac{\sum x_i'^2\theta_i'}{(n-2)\left(\sum x_i'^2\right)^2}.$$

But, from (8.16) we have

$$\mathrm{Var}(\hat{\beta}) = \frac{\sum x_i'^2 \sigma_i^2}{(\sum x_i'^2)^2}$$

$$= \frac{\bar{\sigma}^2}{\sum x_i'^2} + \frac{\sum x_i'^2 \theta_i'}{(\sum x_i'^2)^2},$$

and, therefore,

$$E(s_{\hat{\beta}}^2) \neq \mathrm{Var}(\hat{\beta}),$$

unless $\Sigma x_i'^2 \theta_i' = 0$. Thus we have to conclude that the conventionally calculated variance of $\hat{\beta}$ is, in general, biased when the disturbance is heteroskedastic. A similar conclusion can be reached with respect to $\hat{\alpha}$.

The consequence of the preceding result is that if we use the least squares estimators of the regression coefficients when the assumption of homoskedasticity is not satisfied, the confidence limits and the tests of significance developed in Chapter 7 *do not apply.* This means that if we proceed with our regression analysis under the false belief that the disturbance is homoskedastic, our inferences about the population coefficients are incorrect—that is, the calculated confidence intervals and acceptance regions will be wrong. It would be interesting to know the direction of error in this case because then we would be able to say whether the incorrect confidence intervals and acceptance regions are likely to be wider or narrower than the correct ones. We can find the answer by determining the direction of the bias of the calculated variance. If the bias is positive, the incorrect intervals and acceptance regions will be wider than the correct ones; if the bias is negative, they will be narrower. The bias is given by

$$(8.22) \qquad E(s_{\hat{\beta}}^2) - \mathrm{Var}(\hat{\beta}) = -\frac{\sum x_i'^2 \theta_i'}{(n-2)(\sum x_i'^2)^2} - \frac{\sum x_i'^2 \theta_i'}{(\sum x_i'^2)^2}$$

$$= \frac{(n-1) \sum x_i'^2 \theta_i'}{(n-2)(\sum x_i'^2)^2}.$$

Thus for $n > 2$ the direction of the bias depends on the sign of $\Sigma x_i'^2 \theta_i'$. Since $(\Sigma x_i'^2 \theta_i'/n)$ is the sample covariance of $x_i'^2$ and σ_i^2, it follows that when $x_i'^2$ and σ_i^2 are *positively* associated, the bias is *negative.* In cases like this, a reliance on the conventionally calculated standard errors will tend to lead to confidence intervals and acceptance regions that are narrower than the correct ones. This means that the estimators will then be presented as having a greater precision than is justified by the chosen level of confidence, and that the probability of rejecting the null hypothesis will be higher than indicated by the stated level of significance. In the special case when there is no association between $x_i'^2$ and σ_i^2 in the sample, no bias will occur.

EXAMPLE Let us continue with the preceding example with $X_i = 1, 2, \ldots, 20$ and $\sigma_i^2 = 2X_i^2$. For this example we found that $\Sigma x_i'^2 = 665$, $\Sigma x'^2\sigma_i^2 = 225{,}967$, and $\text{Var}(\hat{\beta}) = 0.510977$. Further, $\Sigma\sigma_i^2 = 2\Sigma X_i^2 = 5740$. Therefore, by (8.20),

$$E(s_{\hat{\beta}}^2) = \frac{1}{18(665)}\left[-\frac{225{,}967}{665} + \frac{19(5740)}{20}\right]$$
$$= 0.427168.$$

In this case the bias amounts to 0.083 809 or about 16.4% of the true variance of $\hat{\beta}$.

Our conclusion then is that the consequences of heteroskedasticity for statistical inference based on least squares estimation are twofold.

1. The least squares estimators of the regression coefficients are unbiased and consistent but have no other desirable properties.
2. The estimated variances of the least squares estimators are, in general, biased and the conventionally calculated confidence intervals and tests of significance are invalid.

Under these circumstances it appears advisable to find an estimation method that would perform better under heteroskedasticity than the least squares method and that would yield valid confidence intervals and tests of significance. The one method that we have already developed, namely the weighted least squares method (or BLUE) presented in (8.13) and (8.14), fulfills this purpose perfectly. The difficulty with it, though, is the requirement that the values of σ_i^2, whose reciprocals serve as weights, be known. The weights are known when heteroskedasticity is caused by grouping observations (see Section 9-2) and perhaps in some other special situations, but in most cases they will not be known and the weighted least squares method will not be feasible. This difficulty can frequently be overcome by making certain assumptions about σ_i^2 or by estimating σ_i^2 from the sample. We will deal with each of these approaches in turn.

Assumptions Concerning σ_i^2

When formulating a regression model we are sometimes able to bring in additional information about σ_i^2. The information is frequently in the form of an assumption stating that σ_i^2 is associated with some variable, say, Z_i. For instance, in the case of the microconsumption function the variance of the disturbance is often assumed to be positively associated with the level of income. In this case the place of Z_i would be taken by the explanatory variable of the regression equation, X_i (income). An alternative, though similar, assumption would be that the variance of the disturbance is positively associated with the mean level of consumption, in which case the place of Z_i would be taken by $E(Y_i)$. Or the changes in the variance of the disturbance may be thought to be associated with changes in some "outside" variable, for instance the size of the family. Using Z_i just gives us a way of formulating the assumption about σ_i^2 in a fairly general manner. However, to make the assumption operational, we have to specify the form of the association.

Two forms of association have been proposed in the literature and applied in practice, one representing *multiplicative heteroskedasticity* and the other *additive heteroskedasticity.* Multiplicative heteroskedasticity, which is more common, takes the form

$$\sigma_i^2 = \sigma^2 Z_i^\delta, \tag{8.23}$$

which involves two parameters, σ^2 and δ. Of particular importance is the parameter δ, which measures the strength of heteroskedasticity: the lower its magnitude, the smaller the differences between individual variances. When $\delta = 0$, the model is homoskedastic.[15]

The two parameters in (8.23) may both be unknown, in which case they have to be estimated along with the regression coefficients α and β, or the value of at least one of them may be specified a priori. For example, the value of δ is sometimes assumed to be 2 since this makes the standard deviation of the disturbance proportional to Z_i. We shall first discuss the estimation problem in general, and then consider some special cases. The complete regression model for this kind of heteroskedastic condition then is

$$\begin{aligned} &Y_i = \alpha + \beta X_i + \varepsilon_i, \\ &\varepsilon_i \sim N(0, \sigma_i^2), \\ &\sigma_i^2 = \sigma^2 Z_i^\delta \qquad (\sigma > 0;\ Z_i > 0). \end{aligned}$$

The disturbance ε_i is, of course, assumed to be nonautocorrelated, and X_i and Z_i are considered to be nonstochastic. Then we can obtain the maximum likelihood estimators of α, β, σ^2, and δ by a simple substitution for σ_i^2 in the log-likelihood function (8.17), which then becomes

$$L = -\frac{n}{2}\log 2\pi - \frac{1}{2}\sum_{i=1}^{n}(\log \sigma^2 + \delta \log Z_i) - \frac{1}{2}\sum_{i=1}^{n}\left[\frac{Y_i - \alpha - \beta X_i}{\sigma Z_i^{\delta/2}}\right]^2. \tag{8.24}$$

The first derivatives of L are

$$\begin{aligned} \frac{\partial L}{\partial \alpha} &= \frac{1}{\sigma^2}\sum_i \left[\frac{Y_i - \alpha - \beta X_i}{Z_i^\delta}\right] \\ \frac{\partial L}{\partial \beta} &= \frac{1}{\sigma^2}\sum_i \left[\frac{(Y_i - \alpha - \beta X_i)X_i}{Z_i^\delta}\right] \end{aligned} \tag{8.25}$$

[15] A general representation of multiplicative heteroskedasticity is of the form $\log \sigma_i^2 = \log \sigma^2 + \delta_1 \log Z_{i1} + \delta_2 \log Z_{i2} + \cdots + \delta_p \log Z_{ip}$, indicating a dependence of σ_i^2 on p variables. This representation may be appropriate for a multiple regression model in which Zs may just be the explanatory variables of the regression model. Note that this specification applies only when all Zs are positive.

$$\frac{\partial L}{\partial \sigma^2} = -\frac{n}{2\sigma^2} + \frac{1}{2\sigma^4}\sum_i \left[\frac{Y_i - \alpha - \beta X_i}{Z_i^{\delta/2}}\right]^2$$

$$\frac{\partial L}{\partial \delta} = -\frac{1}{2}\sum_i \log Z_i + \frac{1}{2\sigma^2}\sum_i \left[\frac{(Y_i - \alpha - \beta X_i)^2 \log Z_i}{Z_i^\delta}\right].$$

By putting each of these derivatives equal to zero, we obtain four equations to be solved for the four unknown values of α, β, σ^2, and δ. These equations are highly nonlinear because of the presence of δ. A relatively simple way of obtaining a solution is as follows. By putting each of the first three derivatives of (8.25) equal to zero and rearranging terms we obtain the following three equations.

(8.26)
$$\sum_i \left(\frac{Y_i}{Z_i^\delta}\right) = \hat{\alpha}\sum_i \left(\frac{1}{Z_i^\delta}\right) + \hat{\beta}\sum_i \left(\frac{X_i}{Z_i^\delta}\right),$$

$$\sum_i \left(\frac{X_iY_i}{Z_i^\delta}\right) = \hat{\alpha}\sum_i \left(\frac{X_i}{Z_i^\delta}\right) + \hat{\beta}\sum_i \left(\frac{X_i^2}{Z_i^\delta}\right),$$

$$\hat{\sigma}^2 = \frac{1}{n}\left(\sum_i \frac{Y_i}{Z_i^\delta} - \hat{\alpha}\sum_i \frac{1}{Z_i^\delta} - \hat{\beta}\sum_i \frac{X_i}{Z_i^\delta}\right)^2.$$

If δ were known, the equations in (8.26) could be solved for $\hat{\alpha}$, $\hat{\beta}$, and $\hat{\sigma}^2$. Now we almost always have some prior information about δ. Frequently we know its sign (i.e., we know whether the values of σ_i^2 are increasing or decreasing with increasing values of Z_i), and we can determine its range, which should include zero to allow for possible homoskedasticity. In most economic models it is most unlikely that δ would lie outside of the range from 0 to 3 or 4. We can obtain estimates of α, β, and σ^2 for $\delta = 0$, $\delta = 0.1$, $\delta = 0.2$, and so on until we come to 3.0 or 4.0. For each value of δ—and the corresponding values of α, β, and σ^2—we also calculate the value of L as given by (8.24). Then, out of all the solutions we select the one that gives the largest value of L. This solution will maximize the likelihood function as desired. If the precision of one decimal place for the estimate of δ is not sufficient, we can choose finer intervals for the successive values of δ in the vicinity of the solution. This method of calculating maximum likelihood estimates is called a *search method.* Other computational methods are also available, but the advantage of the search method is that it is conceptually simple and that it minimizes the risk of obtaining a solution at a local rather than global maximum of the likelihood function.[16]

The asymptotic variances and covariances of the maximum likelihood estima-

[16] See A. C. Harvey, "Estimating Regression Models with Multiplicative Heteroskedasticity," *Econometrica,* 44 (May 1976), pp. 461–465. A general description of various methods of nonlinear optimization can be found in G. S. Maddala, *Econometrics* (New York: McGraw-Hill, 1977), pp. 171–174.

tors can be determined by reference to the inverse of the information matrix (see Theorem 17 of Section 7-3).

$$
(8.27)\quad
\begin{bmatrix}
-E\left(\frac{\partial^2 L}{\partial \alpha^2}\right) & -E\left(\frac{\partial^2 L}{\partial \alpha \partial \beta}\right) & -E\left(\frac{\partial^2 L}{\partial \alpha \partial \delta}\right) & -E\left(\frac{\partial^2 L}{\partial \alpha \partial \sigma^2}\right) \\
-E\left(\frac{\partial^2 L}{\partial \beta \partial \alpha}\right) & -E\left(\frac{\partial^2 L}{\partial \beta^2}\right) & -E\left(\frac{\partial^2 L}{\partial \beta \partial \delta}\right) & -E\left(\frac{\partial^2 L}{\partial \beta \partial \sigma^2}\right) \\
-E\left(\frac{\partial^2 L}{\partial \delta \partial \alpha}\right) & -E\left(\frac{\partial^2 L}{\partial \delta \partial \beta}\right) & -E\left(\frac{\partial^2 L}{\partial \delta^2}\right) & -E\left(\frac{\partial^2 L}{\partial \delta \partial \sigma^2}\right) \\
-E\left(\frac{\partial^2 L}{\partial \sigma^2 \partial \alpha}\right) & -E\left(\frac{\partial^2 L}{\partial \sigma^2 \partial \beta}\right) & -E\left(\frac{\partial^2 L}{\partial \sigma^2 \partial \delta}\right) & -E\left(\frac{\partial^2 L}{\partial (\sigma^2)^2}\right)
\end{bmatrix}^{-1}
$$

$$
= \begin{bmatrix}
\sum w_i & \sum w_i X_i & 0 & 0 \\
\sum w_i X_i & \sum w_i X_i^2 & 0 & 0 \\
0 & 0 & \frac{1}{2}\sum (\log Z_i)^2 & \frac{1}{2\sigma^2}\sum \log Z_i \\
0 & 0 & \frac{1}{2\sigma^2}\sum \log Z_i & \frac{n}{2\sigma^4}
\end{bmatrix}^{-1},
$$

where $w_i = 1/\sigma^2 Z_i^\delta$ and $\log Z_i$ denotes natural logarithm of Z_i. Consistent estimates of the variances and covariances are obtained by replacing w_i by $1/\hat{\sigma}^2 Z_i^{\hat{\delta}}$. The maximum likelihood estimators of α, β, δ, and σ^2 have all desirable *asymptotic properties;* their respective asymptotic variances are displayed on the diagonal of the inverse of the information matrix (8.27). Further, all relevant confidence intervals and tests of significance are at least approximately valid in large samples.

From the practical point of view the greatest problem is likely to be that of selecting Z. Usually it is not likely that an investigator would know of a further variable related to the variance of the disturbance that has not already been included in the regression equation. Thus the usual choice of Z is likely to be the explanatory variable X. Of course, situations do exist when Z can be determined outside of the regression equation. For example, in a household consumption function Z can represent the length of time that the household has been in existence, on the assumption that people learn to manage their affairs better and their errors of behavior become smaller as time goes on. However, such situations are not likely to be very common.

EXAMPLE Lahiri and Egy[17] present two applications of multiplicative heteroskedasticity with $\sigma_i^2 = \sigma^2 X_i^\delta$. In the first application the authors relate radio sales in various states of the USA in 1963 to incomes. With $n = 49$ they find that $\hat{\delta} = 1.56$ and $s_{\hat{\delta}} = 0.189$, indicating

[17] K. Lahiri and D. Egy, "Joint Estimation and Testing for Functional Form and Heteroskedasticity," *Journal of Econometrics,* 15 (February 1981), pp. 299–307.

substantial heteroskedasticity. In the second application the dependent variable is the stopping distance of automobiles and there are two explanatory variables (with no intercept)—speed and speed squared. With 63 experimental observations the authors find $\hat{\delta} = 2.17$ and $s_{\hat{\delta}} = 0.135$, again indicating substantial heteroskedasticity.

A special case of multiplicative heteroskedasticity commonly used in applied work arises when $Z_i = X_i$ and the value of δ is set to equal to 2, i.e., when

$$\sigma_i^2 = \sigma^2 X_i^2. \tag{8.28}$$

Here the standard deviation of the regression disturbance is assumed to be proportional to the value of the explanatory variable, which sometimes may be a reasonable assumption. The regression equation can then easily be made homoskedastic by dividing both sides by X_i to give

$$\frac{Y_i}{X_i} = \alpha\left(\frac{1}{X_i}\right) + \beta + \frac{\varepsilon_i}{X_i} \tag{8.29}$$

or

$$Y_i^* = \beta + \alpha X_i^* + \varepsilon_i^*, \tag{8.29a}$$

where $Y_i^* = Y_i/X_i$, $X_i^* = 1/X_i$, and ε_i^* satisfies all relevant basic assumptions of the classical model with $\text{Var}(\varepsilon_i^*) = \sigma^2$. The regression equation (8.29a) can thus be handled in exactly the same way as the classical model, except that the roles of α and β are reversed. If the specification of heteroskedasticity is correct, the least squares estimators of β and α will have all desirable properties, and all relevant confidence intervals and tests of significance will be valid for all sample sizes. The advantage of this specification of heteroskedasticity is its simplicity, which accounts for its popularity. Its disadvantage is its rigidity since this specification excludes the possibility that the disturbance is homoskedastic or that it is heteroskedastic to a degree different from that corresponding to $\delta = 2$.

EXAMPLE Consider the following sample data on annual expenditures for clothing and on income, collected from a sample of 20 families.

Income, $	Number of families	Clothing expenditures, $
2000	8	160, 160, 180, 200, 210, 220, 230, 250
4000	7	200, 220, 230, 300, 310, 340, 350
6000	5	300, 300, 400, 450, 540

These observations are shown graphically in Figure 8-2. The relationship between expenditure on clothing and income is hypothesized to be

$$Y_i = \alpha + \beta X_i + \varepsilon_i,$$

where Y = expenditure on clothing, X = income, ε = random disturbance, and the subscript i refers to the ith family. The explanatory variable X_i is considered to be nonstochastic, and

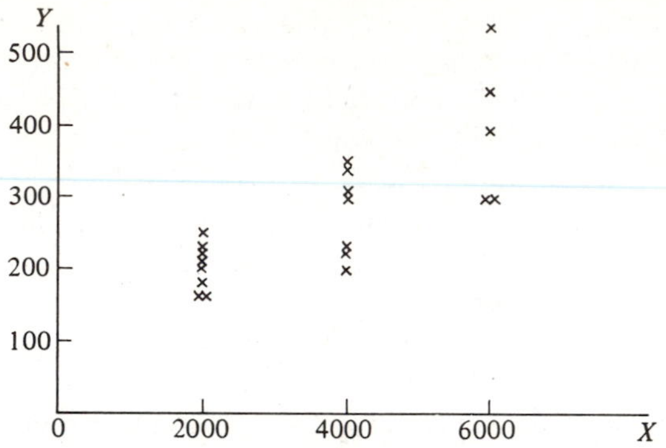

Figure 8-2

the disturbance ε_i is assumed to be a normally distributed, nonautocorrelated random variable with zero mean and variance σ_i^2. The ordinary least squares estimators of the regression coefficients are

$$\hat{\beta} = \frac{\sum y_i' x_i'}{\sum x_i'^2} = \frac{2{,}425{,}000}{50{,}200{,}000} = 0.0483,$$

$$\hat{\alpha} = \bar{Y} - \hat{\beta}\bar{X} = 277.5 - 0.0483 \times 3700 = 98.79,$$

and the coefficient of determination is

$$R^2 = \frac{\hat{\beta} \sum x_i' y_i'}{\sum x_i'^2} = \frac{0.0483 \times 2{,}425{,}000}{190{,}975} = 0.6134.$$

Given that the model is a heteroskedastic one, the least squares estimators are unbiased but not efficient or asymptotically efficient. Their conventionally calculated standard errors are biased and, therefore, are not presented. Note that the above value of R^2 is the maximum value for the given sample since the least squares regression line gives the best fit of any line by definition.

Now, if we assume that

$$\sigma_i^2 = \sigma^2 X_i^2,$$

we can obtain efficient estimators of α and β by applying the least squares method to (8.29). The results are

$$\underset{}{\frac{Y_i}{X_i}} = \underset{(0.0089)}{0.0450} + \underset{(24.82)}{110.00}\frac{1}{X_i} + e_i.$$

Reverting to the original regression equation, we get

$$Y_i = \underset{(24.82)}{110.00} + \underset{(0.0089)}{0.0450}\; X_i + e_i^*.$$

To compare the value of R^2 for the weighted least squares with that for the ordinary least squares regression, we use formula (7.47) to obtain

$$R^2 = 1 - \frac{\sum (Y_i - \hat{\alpha} - \hat{\beta} X_i)^2}{\sum y_i'^2} = 0.6106.$$

As expected, the value of R^2 is lower than that for the least squares regression, but the difference is very small. Note that the implied estimate of the elasticity of demand is

$$\hat{\eta} = \hat{\beta} \frac{X_i}{\hat{Y}_i}$$

$$= 0.045 \frac{X_i}{\hat{Y}_i}$$

so that

$$\hat{\eta}_{x=2000} = 0.450,$$

$$\hat{\eta}_{x=4000} = 0.621,$$

$$\hat{\eta}_{x=6000} = 0.711,$$

which suggests that for the incomes observed in the sample the demand for clothing is income inelastic.

Another form of heteroskedasticity is that of *additive heteroskedasticity.* This form can be represented as[18]

(8.30) $$\sigma_i^2 = a + bX_i + cX_i^2,$$

where a, b, and c are constants to be estimated or assigned assumed values. When b and c are equal to zero, the model is homoskedastic. On the other hand, when a and b are zero, we have a special case of multiplicative heteroskedasticity presented in (8.28). Thus the form (8.30) allows for homoskedasticity as well as for two different kinds of heteroskedasticity, which is considerably less restrictive than the form (8.28).

To obtain asymptotically efficient estimators of the regression coefficients under heteroskedasticity of the form presented in (8.30), we can set up a likelihood function analogous to that in (8.24) and maximize it with respect to the unknown parameters.[19] An alternative and asymptotically equivalent estimation method proceeds as follows.[20]

1. Apply the least squares method to

(8.31) $$e_i^2 = a + bX_i + cX_i^2 + v_i,$$

[18] See S. M. Goldfeld and R. E. Quandt, *Nonlinear Methods of Econometrics* (Amsterdam: North-Holland, 1972), Ch. 3. A more general representation of additive heteroskedasticity is $\sigma_i^2 = a_0 + a_1 Z_{i1} + a_2 Z_{i2} + \cdots + a_p Z_{ip}$. The representation given by (8.30) can be obtained by letting $p = 2$, $Z_{i1} = X_i$, and $Z_{i2} = X_i^2$.

[19] A relatively simple iterative procedure for obtaining MLE of α, β, a, b, and c is described in A. Buse, "Tests for Additive Heteroskedasticity: Goldfeld and Quandt Revisited," *Empirical Economics,* 9 (1984), pp. 199–216.

[20] See T. Amemiya, "A Note on a Heteroskedastic Model," *Journal of Econometrics,* 6 (November 1977), pp. 365–370; see also "Corrigenda," *Journal of Econometrics,* 8 (October 1978), p. 265.

where the es are the least squares residuals from the regression of Y on X, and $v_i = e_i^2 - \sigma_i^2$. In this way we obtain "first-round" estimators of a, b, and c, say, $\hat{a}$, $\hat{b}$, and $\hat{c}$. The corresponding first-round estimator of σ_i^2 then is

$$\hat{\sigma}_i^2 = \hat{a} + \hat{b}X_i + \hat{c}X_i^2. \tag{8.32}$$

2. The first-round estimators of a, b, and c are not asymptotically efficient because v_i is heteroskedastic. Therefore we obtain "second-round" estimators of a, b, and c by applying the least squares method to

$$\frac{e_i^2}{\hat{\sigma}_i^2} = a\frac{1}{\hat{\sigma}_i^2} + b\frac{X_i}{\hat{\sigma}_i^2} + c\frac{X_i^2}{\hat{\sigma}_i^2} + v_i^*. \tag{8.33}$$

   These estimators, to be called $\tilde{a}$, $\tilde{b}$, and $\tilde{c}$, can be shown to be asymptotically efficient. The corresponding second-round estimator of σ_i^2 then is

$$\tilde{\sigma}_i^2 = \tilde{a} + \tilde{b}X_i + \tilde{c}X_i^2. \tag{8.34}$$

3. Apply the least squares method to

$$\frac{Y_i}{\tilde{\sigma}_i} = \alpha\frac{1}{\tilde{\sigma}_i} + \beta\frac{X_i}{\tilde{\sigma}_i} + \varepsilon_i^*. \tag{8.35}$$

It can be shown that the resulting estimators of α and β have the same asymptotic properties as the maximum likelihood estimators.[21] Consistent estimators of their variances can be obtained by substituting $1/\tilde{\sigma}_i^2$ for w_i in (8.18) and (8.19).

EXAMPLE In the preceding example we referred to two regression models, one relating radio sales to income and the other relating stopping distance of automobiles to speed and speed squared. Each of the two models was assumed to be characterized by multiplicative heteroskedasticity and estimates of the "heteroskedasticity parameter" δ were presented. The same two models were considered earlier by Rutemiller and Bowers[22] to demonstrate *additive* heteroskedasticity specified as

$$\sigma_i = \gamma_0 + \gamma_1 X_i$$

or

$$\sigma_i^2 = \gamma_0^2 + 2\gamma_0\gamma_1 X_i + \gamma_1^2 X_i^2.$$

The estimates for the radio sales model were

$$\hat{\sigma}_i = \underset{(1.282)}{2.673} + \underset{(0.001)}{0.004}\,X_i$$

[21] *Ibid.*

[22] H. C. Rutemiller and D. A. Bowers, "Estimation in a Heteroskedastic Regression Model," *Journal of the American Statistical Association,* 63 (June 1968), pp. 552–557.

and those for the stopping distance model were

$$\hat{\sigma}_i = \underset{(0.729)}{-0.301} + \underset{(0.069)}{0.464}\, X_i .$$

In both models the presence of heteroskedasticity is again indicated.

A special case of additive heteroskedasticity, which is sometimes proposed in applied work[23] and called *dependent variable heteroskedasticity,* involves the assumption that the variance of the disturbance is proportional to the squared mean of Y_i. That is, we assume that

(8.36) $$\sigma_i^2 = \sigma^2[E(Y_i)]^2 = \sigma^2(\alpha + \beta X_i)^2.$$

The log-likelihood function in this case becomes

(8.37) $$L = -\frac{n}{2}\log(2\pi) - \frac{n}{2}\log \sigma^2 - \sum_i \log(\alpha + \beta X_i) - \frac{1}{2\sigma^2}\sum_i \left[\frac{Y_i - \alpha - \beta X_i}{(\alpha + \beta X_i)}\right]^2.$$

This function involves only three unknown parameters, α, β, and σ^2.

Obtaining the maximizing values of these parameters is feasible though not simple.[24] The computational problem can be considerably simplified by resorting to weighted least squares estimation, i.e., by applying the ordinary least squares method to

(8.38) $$\frac{Y_i}{\hat{Y}_i} = \alpha\frac{1}{\hat{Y}_i} + \beta\frac{X_i}{\hat{Y}_i} + \varepsilon_i^*,$$

where $\hat{Y}_i$ represents the fitted values of Y from the least squares regression of Y on X. This procedure is motivated by the fact that $\hat{Y}_i$ is an unbiased and consistent estimator of $E(Y_i)$. Unfortunately, in this case when the regression disturbance is normally distributed, the weighted least squares estimators of the regression coefficients have larger asymptotic variances than the maximum likelihood estimators.[25]

The types of heteroskedasticity so far discussed have all been traditionally considered in the context of cross-sectional observations. In the context of time-series observation, heteroskedasticity, when it exists, may perhaps be better modeled by the so-called *autoregressive conditional heteroskedasticity,* abbreviated ARCH.[26]

[23] See, e.g., Prais and Houthhakker, *op. cit.,* pp. 55–56.

[24] See, e.g., Maddala, *op. cit.,* pp. 171–174.

[25] See T. Amemiya, "Regression Analysis When the Variance of the Dependent Variable Is Proportional to the Square of Its Expectation," *Journal of the American Statistical Association,* 68 (December 1973), pp. 928–934; see also A. C. Harvey, *The Econometric Analysis of Time Series* (New York: Wiley, 1981), pp. 97–98.

[26] See R. F. Engle, "Autoregressive Conditional Heteroscedasticity with Estimates of the Variance of United Kingdom Inflations," *Econometrica,* 50 (July 1982), pp. 987–1007.

The motivation for this model of heteroskedasticity was provided by the fact that some econometric forecasters have found that their ability to predict varies from one period to another, and that there is clustering of large and of small prediction errors. If it can be assumed that the behavior of the prediction errors is caused by the behavior of the regression disturbance, then the magnitude of the disturbance of the preceding period provides information about the variance of the current disturbance. A simple way of representing such a pattern of disturbance behavior is to postulate that

$$\varepsilon_t = u_t(\lambda_0 + \lambda_1 \varepsilon_{t-1}^2)^{1/2} \qquad (\lambda_0 > 0, 0 \leq \lambda_1 < 1), \tag{8.39}$$

where $u_t \sim N(0, 1)$, $E(u_t u_s) = 0$ for $t \neq s$, and $E(u_t \varepsilon_s) = 0$ for all $t > s$. In this case the *unconditional* variance of ε_t is

$$\begin{aligned} \text{Var}(\varepsilon_t) &= E(\varepsilon_t^2) \\ &= E(u_t^2)E(\lambda_0 + \lambda_1 \varepsilon_{t-1}^2) \\ &= \lambda_0 + \lambda_1 E(\varepsilon_{t-1}^2) \\ &= \lambda_0 + \lambda_1 \lambda_0 + \lambda_1 E(\varepsilon_{t-2}^2) \\ &\vdots \\ &= \lambda_0(1 + \lambda_1 + \lambda_1^2 + \cdots) \\ &= \frac{\lambda_0}{1 - \lambda_1}, \end{aligned} \tag{8.40}$$

so that the unconditional variance is still constant and the regression model is unconditionally homoskedastic. However, the *conditional* variance of ε_t *given* ε_{t-1} is

$$\begin{aligned} \text{Var}(\varepsilon_t | \varepsilon_{t-1}) &= E(u_t^2 | \varepsilon_{t-1}) E(\lambda_0 + \lambda_1 \varepsilon_{t-1}^2 | \varepsilon_{t-1}) \\ &= \lambda_0 + \lambda_1 \varepsilon_{t-1}^2. \end{aligned} \tag{8.41}$$

It is, of course, possible to generalize this model by allowing for more than one lag on the right-hand side of (8.41).

The consequences of the ARCH type of heteroskedasticity are that the least squares estimators of the regression coefficients are still *best linear unbiased,* since the regression disturbances are unconditionally homoskedastic and, as can easily be shown, nonautocorrelated (but not independent). However, they are not the same as the maximum likelihood estimators, which can be derived as follows. To correct for the conditional heteroskedasticity and, therefore, for the lack of independence of the regression disturbances, we divide both sides of the regression equation by $(\lambda_0 + \lambda_1 \varepsilon_{t-1}^2)^{1/2}$ to get

$$Y_t(\lambda_0 + \lambda_1 \varepsilon_{t-1}^2)^{-1/2} = \alpha(\lambda_0 + \lambda_1 \varepsilon_{t-1}^2)^{-1/2} + \beta X_t(\lambda_0 + \lambda_1 \varepsilon_{t-1}^2)^{-1/2} + u_t.$$

Then, in accordance with Theorem 19 (Change of Variable) of Section 7-3, we have

$$f(y_t) = \left|\frac{du_t}{dY_t}\right| f(u_t)$$
$$= (\lambda_0 + \lambda_1 \varepsilon_{t-1}^2)^{-1/2} f(u_t)$$

and

$$\log f(y_i, \ldots, y_n) = -\frac{1}{2} \sum_t \log(\lambda_0 + \lambda_1 \varepsilon_{t-1}^2) + \log f(u_1, \ldots, u_n),$$

so that the log-likelihood function becomes

$$(8.42) \qquad L = -\frac{1}{2} \sum_t \log[\lambda_0 + \lambda_1 (Y_{t-1} - \alpha - \beta X_{t-1})^2]$$
$$- \frac{n}{2} \log(2\pi) - \frac{1}{2} \sum_t \left\{ \frac{(Y_t - \alpha - \beta X_t)}{\lambda_0 + \lambda_1 (Y_{t-1} - \alpha - \beta X_{t-1})^2} \right\},$$

noting that $\mathrm{Var}(u_t) = 1$. The "initial" disturbance, ε_0, is of no asymptotic importance and its value is usually set equal to zero. Maximization of L with respect to α, β, λ_0, and λ_1 leads to estimators with asymptotic variances smaller than those of the least squares estimators. The asymptotic standard errors of the maximum likelihood estimators may be determined by reference to the information matrix.[27] Unlike the least squares estimators, the maximum likelihood estimators are clearly nonlinear.

Estimation of σ_i^2

When no assumptions about the nature of heteroskedasticity are made, we have to rely entirely on the sample information and estimate the variances of the disturbance from the data. Since for each specific value of X the value of the variance of the disturbance may be different, we need several observations on the dependent variable for each X_i. Suppose that there are m different values of X in the sample, and that for each X_i we have n_i observations on the dependent variable. Then the regression equation can be written as

$$Y_{ij} = \alpha + \beta X_i + \varepsilon_{ij} \qquad (i = 1, 2, \ldots, m; j = 1, 2, \ldots, n_i),$$
$$n = \sum_{i=1}^{m} n_i$$
$$X_i \neq X_j \qquad (i \neq j).$$

To illustrate the new subscript notation, we use the data on family expenditure on

[27] For a description of simplified calculations see Judge, *op. cit.*, pp. 442–444.

clothing and income on page 283. There we have

$$m = 3,$$
$$n_1 = 8,$$
$$n_2 = 7,$$
$$n_3 = 5,$$
$$n = 20.$$

Also, for example, $Y_{25} = 310$ is the value of the dependent variable for the fifth family in the \$4000 income bracket. In general, there are $(m + 2)$ parameters to be estimated: $\alpha, \beta, \sigma_1^2, \sigma_2^2, \ldots, \sigma_m^2$. The appropriate log-likelihood function is given by

$$(8.43) \qquad L = -\frac{n}{2}\log(2\pi) - \frac{1}{2}\sum_{i=1}^{m} n_i \log \sigma_i^2 - \frac{1}{2}\sum_{i=1}^{m}\sum_{j=1}^{n_i}\left(\frac{Y_{ij} - \alpha - \beta X_i}{\sigma_i}\right)^2.$$

By differentiating L with respect to the unknown parameters, and by putting the resulting derivatives equal to zero, we would obtain $(m + 2)$ equations that could be solved for the $(m + 2)$ values of the parameters. The solution can be obtained by the following iterative procedure.

1. Obtain ordinary least squares estimates of α and β, to be called $\hat{\alpha}$ and $\hat{\beta}$. Use these to get "first-round" estimates of σ_i^2, say, $\hat{\sigma}_i^2$, given as
$$\hat{\sigma}_i^2 = \frac{1}{n_i}\sum_{j=1}^{n_i}(Y_{ij} - \hat{\alpha} - \hat{\beta}X_i)^2.$$
2. In formulas (8.13) and (8.14), replace w_i with $1/\hat{\sigma}_i^2$, and obtain new estimates of α and β, say $\hat{\hat{\alpha}}$ and $\hat{\hat{\beta}}$. Use these to obtain "second-round" estimates of σ_i^2, say, $\hat{\hat{\sigma}}_i^2$, given as
$$\hat{\hat{\sigma}}_i^2 = \frac{1}{n_i}\sum_{j=1}^{n_i}(Y_{ij} - \hat{\hat{\alpha}} - \hat{\hat{\beta}}X_i)^2.$$
3. In formulas (8.13) and (8.14), replace w_i by $1/\hat{\hat{\sigma}}_i^2$, and obtain a new set of estimates of α and β. Use these estimates to obtain "third-round" estimates of σ_i^2.

This procedure is to be continued until the values of the estimates converge, that is, until the differences between successive sets of estimates are negligible.[28] The standard errors of the estimated regression coefficients can be estimated by putting $w_i = 1/\tilde{\sigma}_i^2$ (where $\tilde{\sigma}_i^2$ is the "final-round" estimate of σ_i^2) in formulas (8.18) and (8.19).

[28] The proof that the "final-round" estimates are the solution to the first-order conditions for maximizing the likelihood function is given in W. Oberhofer and J. Kmenta, "A General Procedure for Obtaining Maximum Likelihood Estimates in Generalized Regression Models," *Econometrica*, 42 (May 1974), pp. 579–590.

This iterative procedure is obviously quite laborious. A simple alternative is to estimate σ_i^2 by

$$s_i^2 = \sum_{j=1}^{n_i} \frac{(Y_{ij} - \overline{Y}_i)^2}{(n_i - 1)}, \tag{8.44}$$

where

$$\overline{Y}_i = \frac{1}{n_i} \sum_{j=1}^{n_i} Y_{ij}.$$

It is easy to show that s_i^2 is a consistent estimator of σ_i^2. By replacing w_i with $1/s_i^2$ in (8.13) and (8.14), we obtain estimates of the regression coefficients; and by making the same substitution in (8.18) and (8.19), we obtain their estimated standard errors. The resulting estimators have the same asymptotic properties as the maximum likelihood estimators.

EXAMPLE Returning to the data on family expenditure on clothing and income (page 283), we can consider estimating the variances of the disturbance from the data rather than making any assumptions about them. Using (8.44) we obtain

$$s_1^2 = 1069.64,$$

$$s_2^2 = 3714.29,$$

$$s_3^2 = 10520.00.$$

Weighted least squares estimates of α and β can then be obtained by applying the least squares method to

$$\frac{Y_{ij}}{s_i} = \alpha\left[\frac{1}{s_i}\right] + \beta\left[\frac{X_i}{s_i}\right] + \varepsilon_i^*,$$

or by using the weighted least squares formulas (8.13), (8.14), (8.18), and (8.19), with w_i replaced by $(1/s_i^2)$. The results are

$$\underset{}{Y_{ij}} = \underset{(25.70)}{111.10} + \underset{(0.0092)}{0.0444}X_i + e_{ij}, \qquad R^2 = 0.6094.$$

These results are similar to those obtained earlier under the assumption that $\sigma_i^2 = \sigma^2 X_i^2$. (The value of R^2 has been calculated according to the formula $R^2 = 1 - \text{SSE/SST}$.)

Since the variances σ_i^2 are not known but have to be estimated, the maximum likelihood (or weighted least squares) estimators are only known to possess all desirable *asymptotic* properties. As for their small sample properties, recent theoretical results indicate that these estimators are unbiased, and that the loss of efficiency from having to estimate the unknown variances is likely to be relatively small as long as $n_i > 5$ for all i.[29]

The approach to heteroskedasticity outlined so far has been confined to weighted least squares (or maximum likelihood) estimation, with weights determined either

[29] See W. E. Taylor, "The Heteroscedastic Linear Model: Exact Finite Sample Results," *Econometrica,* 46 (May 1978), pp. 663–675.

by assumption or by estimation. The former requires prior knowledge of the form of heteroskedasticity, while the latter is feasible only when there are replicated observations on Y for each different value of X. When there is no basis for making assumptions about σ_i^2 and there are no replicated data available, we can still use the ordinary least squares method, which yields unbiased and consistent estimators of the regression coefficients. To avoid—at least asymptotically—the problem of biased estimation of the *variances* of the least squares regression coefficients, we can use the following estimator:

$$\text{(8.45)} \qquad \text{Est. Var}(\hat{\beta}) = \frac{\sum x_i'^2 e_i^2}{(\sum x_i'^2)^2},$$

where, as before, e_i represents the values of the least squares residuals. This estimator, obtained by replacing σ_i^2 by e_i^2 in (8.16), is under fairly general conditions consistent.[30] There is some evidence, though, that in small and moderate size samples this estimator has a downward bias.[31]

EXAMPLE Using the data on family income and on family clothing expenditure in the preceding example, we found the least squares estimate of β was 0.0483. The conventionally calculated estimate of its standard error based on the assumption of homoskedasticity and defined as $s/\sqrt{\Sigma x_i'^2}$ is 0.00904. On the other hand, the estimate based on the assumption of heteroskedasticity given by the square root of (8.45) turns out to be 0.00995, i.e., somewhat larger.

Tests for Homoskedasticity

Up to this point, our discussion has been concerned with the implications of heteroskedasticity in a linear regression model. We have examined the effects of heteroskedasticity on the properties of ordinary least squares estimators and their conventionally calculated standard errors, and we have discussed alternative estimators designed for heteroskedastic models. However, if we do not know whether the model under investigation is or is not homoskedastic, we may wish to resort to the information provided by the sample and carry out a test. Specifically, we may want to test the null hypothesis,

$$H_0: \quad \sigma_1^2 = \sigma_2^2 = \cdots = \sigma_m^2 \qquad (m \leq n),$$

where m is the number of different values of the variance, against the alternative hypothesis that H_0 is not true.

A variety of tests for homoskedasticity is available in the literature. One of the earliest tests, which is quite simple and frequently useful, is the *Goldfeld–Quandt*

[30] See H. White, "A Heteroskedasticity-Consistent Covariance Matrix Estimator and a Direct Test for Heteroskedasticity," *Econometrica*, 48 (May 1980), pp. 817–838.

[31] J. G. Cragg, "More Efficient Estimation in the Presence of Heteroscedasticity of Unknown Form," *Econometrica*, 51 (May 1983), pp. 751–763.

test. This test is based on the idea that if the sample observations have been generated under the conditions of homoskedasticity (i.e., if H_0 is true), then the variance of the disturbances of one part of the sample observations is the same as the variance of the disturbances of another part of the observations. The respective *sample* variances will then differ only because of sampling fluctuations. Thus a test for homoskedasticity becomes simply a test for equality of two variances. Such a test can conveniently be based on the ratio of the two sample variances. Since under H_0 each sample variance has a chi-square distribution divided by the number of degrees of freedom, their ratio has an F distribution, provided the two sample variances are independent (see Section 5-2 above). The requirement that the two sample variances be independent means that one has to estimate two separate regression equations, one for each part of the sample observations. The Goldfeld–Quandt test statistic then is

$$\frac{s_2^2}{s_1^2} \sim F_{n_2-2,\, n_1-2}, \tag{8.46}$$

where

$$s_1^2 = \frac{\sum (Y_i - \hat{\alpha}_1 - \hat{\beta}_1 X_i)^2}{n_1 - 2} \qquad (i = 1, 2, \ldots, n_1),$$

$$s_2^2 = \frac{\sum (Y_i - \hat{\alpha}_2 - \hat{\beta}_2 X_i)^2}{n_2 - 2} \qquad (i = n_1 + p + 1, n_1 + p + 2, \ldots, n_1 + p + n_2).$$

Note that n_1 is the number of observations in the first part of the sample, n_2 the number of observations in the second part, and p the number of middle observations not included in any part. The Goldfeld–Quandt test is exact but it is not very powerful (i.e., it has a high probability of accepting H_0 when it is false) when the disturbances are heteroskedastic but their "average" variance in the first part of the sample is not too different from that in the second part. For this reason the Goldfeld–Quandt test is recommended mainly for use in situations in which the observations can be arranged in order of increasing variance of the disturbances. This is simple when, for instance, we know that the variance is related to the value of the explanatory variable X. Further, if the observations are ordered and divided into two equal or approximately equal parts, the variances of the last several disturbances in the first half are likely to be similar to those of the first several disturbances in the second half even under heteroskedasticity. Thus it is frequently considered desirable to drop the middle p observations altogether. The number of observations to be dropped is not clear, because while the power of the test is increased by increasing the difference between the "average" variances under heteroskedasticity, it is at the same time decreased due to reduction in the number of observations used. Experimental results indicate that dropping about one-sixth of the middle observations may be reasonable. The arbitrariness in choosing the number of observations (p) to be discarded represents a rather unsatisfactory aspect of the test, because it opens the door to the possibility of tailoring the results to suit one's wishes by a judicious choice of p.

EXAMPLE We can apply the Goldfeld–Quandt test to the data on family income and on family expenditure on clothing (page 283). Since it is reasonable to assume that the variances increase with income, we leave the observations in the order in which they are presented. Also, given the nature of the observations and the small size of the sample, we will not discard any observations and will use 10 observations in each of the two subsamples. The numerical results are as follows.

SAMPLE 1

$$\hat{\beta}_1 = 0.004375,$$
$$\text{SSR}_1 = 122.5,$$
$$\text{SST}_1 = 7810,$$
$$s_1^2 = \text{SSE}/8 = 960.9375.$$

SAMPLE 2

$$\hat{\beta}_2 = 0.046,$$
$$\text{SSR}_2 = 21160,$$
$$\text{SST}_2 = 72160,$$
$$s_2^2 = \text{SSE}/8 = 6375.$$

Therefore, $s_2^2/s_1^2 = 6.634$. From the table of the F distribution we find that the critical value of $F_{8,8}$ is 3.44 at the 5% level of significance and 6.03 at the 1% level. Thus we are led to reject the null hypothesis of homoskedasticity.

A different test for homoskedasticity, known as the *Breusch–Pagan test,* is based on the idea that if the hypothesis of homoskedasticity is true, the ordinary least squares estimates of the regression coefficients should not differ significantly from the maximum likelihood estimates that allow for possible heteroskedasticity.[32] Specifically, if L is the log-likelihood function that allows for heteroskedasticity as in (8.17), then the first derivatives of L should be equal to zero when the unknown parameters are replaced by their respective maximum likelihood estimates. If, instead, the unknown parameters are replaced by the ordinary least squares estimates, and if the disturbances are in fact homoskedastic, then the first derivatives of L should not differ significantly from zero. (The generic name of this type of test is the *Lagrange multiplier test.*) In the Breusch–Pagan formulation of the test, the hypothesis of homoskedasticity is being tested against the alternative hypothesis

$$H_A\colon \quad \sigma_i^2 = g(\gamma_0 + \gamma_1 Z_{i1} + \gamma_2 Z_{i2} + \cdots + \gamma_p Z_{ip}) \qquad (i = 1, 2, \ldots, n),$$

where g is a continuous function with continuous first derivatives. The Z are some known nonstochastic variables; typically they will be the same as the explanatory variables of the regression equation or some known functions of them. The function g is sufficiently general that it includes multiplicative as well as additive heteroskedasticity as special cases (and need not be further specified).

[32] T. S. Breusch and A. R. Pagan, "A Simple Test for Heteroskedasticity and Random Coefficient Variation," *Econometrica,* 47 (September 1979), pp. 1287–1294; the same test, but with H_A confined to multiplicative heteroskedasticity, was also independently proposed in L. G. Godfrey, "Testing for Multiplicative Heteroskedasticity," *Journal of Econometrics,* 8 (October 1978), pp. 227–236.

The test statistic for the Breusch–Pagan test involves applying the least squares method to

$$\frac{e_i^2}{\hat{\sigma}^2} = \gamma_0 + \gamma_1 Z_{i1} + \gamma_2 Z_{i2} + \cdots + \gamma_p Z_{ip} + v_i, \tag{8.47}$$

where e_i are the residuals from the least squares regression of Y on X and $\hat{\sigma}^2 = \Sigma e_i^2/n$. Let SSR_{BP} be the "regression sum of squares" from (8.47). Then, given that the regression disturbances are normally distributed, it can be shown that under the null hypothesis we have, asymptotically,

$$\frac{\text{SSR}_{\text{BP}}}{2} \sim \chi_p^2. \tag{8.48}$$

This appears to be a reasonably powerful test when heteroskedasticity is present, but in small samples the stated level of significance is only a rough indication of the true level.

EXAMPLE If we apply the Breusch–Pagan test to the data on family income and on family clothing expenditure and if we specify the g function as depending only on X, we obtain the following results:

$$\hat{\sigma}^2 = 3{,}691.55,$$

$$\frac{e_i^2}{\hat{\sigma}^2} = -0.83 + 0.0004946X_i + \hat{v}_i,$$

$$\frac{\text{SSR}_{\text{BP}}}{2} = 6.141.$$

The tabulated critical value of the chi-square with 1 degree of freedom is 3.841 at the 5% level of significance and 6.635 at the 1% level. Thus the null hypothesis would be rejected at the 5% level but not rejected at the 1% level. When this outcome is compared with that for the Goldfeld–Quandt test in the preceding example, the inaccuracy of the Breusch–Pagan test in small samples is apparent.

The Breusch–Pagan test has been criticized on the grounds that it is very sensitive to minor violations of the assumption of normality of the regression disturbance. This dependence on normality can be removed by a slight modification of the test statistic. It turns out, though, that with this modification and an appropriate specification of the Zs, the Breusch–Pagan test becomes equivalent to the test subsequently proposed by H. White.[33] The *White test* is based on the comparison of the sample variance of the least squares estimators under homoskedasticity and

[33] See White, *op. cit.* The modification of the Breusch–Pagan test to remove its dependence on normality was proposed in R. Koenker, "A Note on Studentizing a Test for Heteroskedasticity," *Journal of Econometrics,* 17 (September 1981), pp. 107–112. The equivalence of the modified Breusch–Pagan and the White test is elegantly demonstrated in D. M. Waldman, "A Note on Algebraic Equivalence of White's Test and a Variation of the Godfrey/Breusch–Pagan Test for Heteroskedasticity," *Economics Letters* 13 (1983), pp. 197–200.

under heteroskedasticity. When the null hypothesis is true, the two estimated variances should, in large samples, differ only because of sampling fluctuations. The test involves applying the least squares method to

$$e_i^2 = \delta_0 + \delta_1 Z_{i1} + \delta_2 Z_{i2} + \cdots + \delta_p Z_{ip} + u_i \tag{8.49}$$

and calculating the coefficient of determination to be called R_W^2. Asymptotically, under the null hypothesis of homoskedosticity,

$$nR_W^2 \sim \chi_p^2, \tag{8.50}$$

where, as before, n is the number of observations. For the simple regression model with one explanatory variable, White sets $p = 2$, $Z_{i1} = X_i$, and $Z_{i2} = X_i^2$. For a multiple regression model with two explanatory variables, X_{i1} and X_{i2}, the specification is $p = 3$, $Z_{i1} = X_{i1}$, $Z_{i2} = X_{i2}$, $Z_{i3} = X_{i1}X_{i2}$, $Z_{i4} = X_{i1}^2$, and $Z_{i5} = X_{i2}^2$. (For models with more than two explanatory variables the Zs would be determined in analogous fashion.) As in the Breusch–Pagan test, the White test does not require a specification of the form of heteroskedasticity.

EXAMPLE Suppose we apply the White test to the data on family income and family expenditure on clothing. The results of the relevant calculations are

$$e_i^2 = 1324.13 - 0.863634X_i + 0.000343387X_i^2 + \hat{u}_i,$$

$$\text{SSR}_\text{W} = 175.799 \times 10^6,$$

$$\text{SST}_\text{W} = 534.2156 \times 10^6,$$

$$R_\text{W}^2 = 0.329,$$

$$20\text{R}_\text{W}^2 = 6.580.$$

The tabulated value of χ^2 with 2 degrees of freedom is 5.991 at the 5% level of significance and 9.210 at the 1% level. This means that the null hypothesis would be rejected at the 5% level but not at the 1% level. The outcome of the White test is thus the same as that of the Breusch–Pagan test in the preceding example.

When dealing with time-series observations, we may wish to test the hypothesis of homoskedasticity against the alternative of autoregressive conditional heteroskedasticity (ARCH). In this case we may use a simple test developed by Engle.[34] This test involves using squared least squares residuals and applying the least squares method to

$$e_t^2 = \lambda_0 + \lambda_1 e_{t-1}^2 + \lambda_2 e_{t-2}^2 + \cdots + \lambda_p e_{t-p}^2 + u_t, \tag{8.51}$$

where p is the chosen length of the longest lag. (In our earlier discussion of the ARCH model we used $p = 1$.) Then under the null hypothesis we have, asymptotically,

$$nR_\text{E}^2 \sim \chi_p^2, \tag{8.52}$$

[34] See Engle, *op. cit.*

where $R_{\hat{E}}^2$ is the coefficient of determination calculated for the relation in (8.51) above. This test is closely related to the Breusch–Pagan test and to the White test.

A test of the homoskedasticity hypothesis with no specification of the nature of heteroskedasticity as the alternative hypothesis is most straightforward when there are several observations on the dependent variable for each different value of the explanatory variable. In this case we can use the so-called *Bartlett test.* This test is based on the idea that if the null hypothesis is true, the value of the maximized likelihood function obtained under the assumption of homoskedasticity should not differ significantly from that obtained under the assumption of possible heteroskedasticity. (The generic name of this type of test is the *likelihood ratio test.*) For n sample observations with m different values of X $(m < n)$, the null hypothesis and the alternative hypotheses are

$$H_0:\quad \sigma_1^2 = \sigma_2^2 = \cdots = \sigma_m^2 = \sigma^2,$$

$$H_A:\quad H_0 \text{ is not true.}$$

The test statistic, modified to be suitable for samples of moderate size, is[35]

$$\frac{-4.60517 \log M}{1 + N} \sim \chi_{m-1}^2, \tag{8.53}$$

where

$$\log M = \frac{\sum (n_i - 1)}{2} \log s_i^2 - \frac{n - m}{2} \log \frac{\sum (n_i - 1) s_i^2}{n - m},$$

$$N = \frac{\sum (1/n_i) - (1/n)}{3(m - 1)},$$

and

$$s_i^2 = \frac{\sum (Y_{ij} - \bar{Y}_i)^2}{n_i - 1} \qquad (i = 1, 2, \ldots, m;\, j = 1, 2, \ldots, n_i).$$

Note that in (8.53) we use *common* logarithms.

EXAMPLE In our example on family income and family clothing expenditure we have three different values of X so that the test statistic in (8.53) will have a χ^2 distribution with 2 degrees of freedom. By substitution from sample data we obtain

$$\log M = \frac{7}{2} \log 1069.64 + \frac{6}{2} \log 3714.29 + \frac{4}{2} \log 10520 - \frac{17}{2} \log 4226.66$$

$$= -1.464988,$$

$$N = \frac{1/8 + 1/7 + 1/5 - 1/20}{3 \times 2}$$

$$= 0.069643,$$

[35] See Paul G. Hoel, *Introduction to Mathemtical Statistics,* 2nd ed. (New York: Wiley, 1954), p. 195.

so that

$$\frac{-4.60517 \log M}{1+N} = 6.307.$$

The critical value of χ^2 with 2 degrees of freedom is 5.991 at the 5% level of significance and 9.210 at the 1% level. Thus the null hypothesis again is rejected at the 5% level but not at the 1% level.

The approach to heteroskedasticity by transforming the regression equation so that the transformed disturbance becomes homoskedastic leads to a nonlinear form of the transformed regression equation. The question then arises whether the problem is really one of heteroskedasticity or one of nonlinearity of the regression equation. We noted earlier that heteroskedasticity is typically encountered when dealing with microeconomic data but not when dealing with aggregates observed over time unless the time period covered is very long. This could be explained by the fact that microdata cover a relatively longer range of values than the aggregate time series, and that linear approximation works better over a short range of values than over a long range. This point might be kept in mind when interpreting the preceding tests for homoskedasticity since they could also be possibly regarded as tests of the linearity of the regression line.

8-3 Autocorrelated Disturbances

By the assumption (7.5) of the classical normal linear regression model we have

$$\text{Cov}(\varepsilon_i, \varepsilon_j) = E[\varepsilon_i - E(\varepsilon_i)][\varepsilon_j - E(\varepsilon_j)] = 0 \qquad (\text{for all } i \neq j).$$

Since the mean of ε_i and of ε_j is assumed to be zero, this means that

$$E(\varepsilon_i \varepsilon_j) = 0.$$

Combined with the assumption of normality, the zero covariance of ε_i and ε_j also means that ε_i and ε_j are independent. This feature of the regression disturbances is known as nonautocorrelation; some authors refer to it as nonautoregression or as the absence of serial correlation. It implies that the disturbance occurring at one point of observation is not correlated with any other disturbance. This means that when observations are made over time, the effect of the disturbance occurring at one period does not carry over into another period. For instance, in a study of the relationship between output and inputs of a firm or industry from monthly observations, nonautocorrelation of the disturbance implies that the effect of machine breakdown is strictly temporary in the sense that only the current month's output is affected. In the case of cross-sectional observations such as those on income and expenditure of different families, the assumption of nonautocorrelation means that if the expenditure behavior of one family is "disturbed"—for example, by the visit of a relative—this does not affect the expenditure behavior of any other family.

Our present task is to consider the plausibility of the assumption of nonautocorrelation, to examine the consequences of its violation on the properties of the least squares estimators, and to develop alternative methods of estimation if needed. In Section 8-2 we argued that the assumption of homoskedasticity is frequently reasonable in the case of models describing the behavior of aggregates over time, but that its plausibility is questionable when microeconomic relations are estimated from cross-sectional data. Here, in connection with the assumption of nonautocorrelation, the argument is just the reverse. The usual contention is that the assumption of nonautocorrelation is more frequently violated in the case of relations estimated from time series data than in the case of relations estimated from cross-sectional data. This contention relies largely on the interpretation of the disturbance as a summary of a large number of random and independent factors that enter into the relationship under study, but that are not measurable. Then, one might suspect that the effect of these factors operating in one period would, in part, carry over to the following periods. This seems more likely than that the effect would carry over from one family, firm, or other similar unit to another.

Autocorrelation of the disturbances can be compared with the sound effect of tapping a musical string: while the sound is loudest at the time of impact, it does not stop immediately but lingers on for a time until it finally dies off. This may also be the characteristic of the disturbance, since its effect may linger for some time after its occurrence. But while the effect of one disturbance lingers on, other disturbances take place, as if the musical string were tapped over and over, sometimes harder than at other times. The shorter the time between the tappings, the greater the likelihood that the preceding sound can still be heard. Similarly, the shorter the periods of individual observations, the greater the likelihood of encountering autocorrelated disturbances. Thus we would be more suspicious of the presence of autocorrelation when dealing with monthly or quarterly observations than when the data are given at annual intervals.

The presumption that relationships estimated from observations over time involve autocorrelated disturbances is so common that, in any discussion of autocorrelation in the literature, the variables are given a subscript t (for "time") rather than the subscript i that is used in the general case. We shall follow this custom in our discussion. Thus, if the disturbances are autocorrelated, we have

$$E(\varepsilon_t \varepsilon_{t-s}) \neq 0 \qquad (t > s).$$

This expression implies that the disturbance occurring at time t is related to the disturbance occurring at time $(t - s)$. The consequences of autocorrelation for estimation can best be traced if we specify the nature of autocorrelation more precisely. Most of the work in this context has been done on the assumption that the regression disturbance follows a *first-order autoregressive scheme,* abbreviated as AR(1) and described in detail below. From the subsequent analysis it is clear, though, that the general results concerning the properties of the least squares estimators and of the estimated variances are applicable to other kinds of autocorrelation as well.

First-Order Autoregressive Disturbances

In the case where all the basic assumptions hold, each disturbance represents an independent drawing from a normal population with mean zero and variance σ^2. When the disturbances are first-order autoregressive, the drawings are no longer independent but are generated according to the following scheme:

(8.54) $$\varepsilon_t = \rho\varepsilon_{t-1} + u_t \qquad \text{(for all } t\text{)},$$

where ρ is a parameter whose absolute value is less than one, and u_t is a normally and *independently* distributed random variable with mean zero and variance σ_u^2 that is independent of ε_{t-1}. That is

$$u_t \sim N(0, \sigma_u^2) \qquad \text{(for all } t\text{)},$$

$$E(u_t u_s) = 0 \qquad \text{(for all } t \neq s\text{)},$$

$$E(u_t \varepsilon_{t-1}) = 0 \qquad \text{(for all } t\text{)}.$$

In the language of time-series analysis, u_t is known as a *pure white noise.*

A relationship such as (8.54) implies that each current disturbance is equal to a "portion" of the preceding disturbance *plus* a random effect represented by u_t. By a successive substitution for $\varepsilon_{t-1}, \varepsilon_{t-2}, \ldots, \varepsilon_1$, we obtain

$$\begin{aligned}
\varepsilon_t &= \rho\varepsilon_{t-1} + u_t \\
&= \rho(\rho\varepsilon_{t-2} + u_{t-1}) + u_t \\
&= \rho^2\varepsilon_{t-2} + \rho u_{t-1} + u_t \\
&= \rho^2(\rho\varepsilon_{t-3} + u_{t-2}) + \rho u_{t-1} + u_t \\
&= \rho^3\varepsilon_{t-3} + \rho^2 u_{t-2} + \rho u_{t-1} + u_t \\
&\ \ \vdots \\
&= \rho^s\varepsilon_{t-s} + \rho^{s-1}u_{t-s+1} + \rho^{s-2}u_{t-s+2} + \cdots + \rho u_{t-1} + u_t.
\end{aligned}$$

Since $\rho^s \rightarrow 0$ as $s \rightarrow \infty$, we can write

(8.55) $$\varepsilon_t = \sum_{s=0}^{\infty} \rho^s u_{t-s}.$$

The expression for ε_t in (8.55) is called the *moving average representation* of ε_t corresponding to AR(1). Since $|\rho| < 1$, ρ^2 will be smaller in absolute value than ρ, ρ^3 will be smaller than ρ^2, and so on. That means that the effect of lagged u's diminishes the further back we go, and eventually it dies off completely. The fact that under the first-order autoregressive scheme the effect of the past disturbances wears off gradually and—for a positive ρ—smoothly, as we would frequently expect in reality, has undoubtedly contributed to the popularity of this scheme in econometrics.

The expression for ε_t in (8.55) is convenient for working out the variances and covariances of the ε's. Specifically, from (8.55) and the independence of the *u*s it follows directly that

$$\text{(8.56)}\qquad \begin{aligned}\mathrm{Var}(\varepsilon_t) &= \mathrm{Var}(u_t) + \rho^2\mathrm{Var}(u_{t-1}) + \rho^4\mathrm{Var}(u_{t-2}) + \cdots \\ &= \sigma_u^2(1 + \rho^2 + \rho^4 + \cdots),\end{aligned}$$

or

$$\text{(8.56a)}\qquad \sigma^2 = \frac{\sigma_u^2}{1-\rho^2},$$

where $\sigma^2 = \mathrm{Var}(\varepsilon_t)$ as before. Further,

$$\text{(8.57)}\qquad \begin{aligned}\mathrm{Cov}(\varepsilon_t, \varepsilon_{t-1}) &= E(u_t + \rho u_{t-1} + \rho^2 u_{t-2} + \cdots) \\ &\qquad \times (u_{t-1} + \rho u_{t-2} + \rho^2 u_{t-3} + \cdots) \\ &= \rho\sigma_u^2 + \rho^3\sigma_u^2 + \rho^5\sigma_u^2 + \cdots \\ &= \frac{\rho\sigma_u^2}{1-\rho^2} \\ &= \rho\sigma^2 \qquad \text{by (8.56a).}\end{aligned}$$

Similarly,

$$\mathrm{Cov}(\varepsilon_t, \varepsilon_{t-2}) = \rho^2\sigma^2,$$

$$\mathrm{Cov}(\varepsilon_t, \varepsilon_{t-3}) = \rho^3\sigma^2,$$

and, in general,

$$\text{(8.58)}\qquad \mathrm{Cov}(\varepsilon_t, \varepsilon_{t-s}) = \rho^s\sigma^2.$$

The preceding remarks make it clear that the relationships between disturbances are crucially dependent on the value of the parameter ρ. This dependence is particularly emphasized by the following interpretation of ρ. In (8.57), the covariance between any two successive disturbances, say, ε_t and ε_{t-1}, is given by

$$\mathrm{Cov}(\varepsilon_t, \varepsilon_{t-1}) = \rho\sigma^2.$$

Therefore,

$$\rho = \frac{\mathrm{Cov}(\varepsilon_t, \varepsilon_{t-1})}{\sigma^2},$$

which, since $\sigma^2 = \mathrm{Var}(\varepsilon_t) = \mathrm{Var}(\varepsilon_{t-1})$, can be written as

$$\rho = \frac{\mathrm{Cov}(\varepsilon_t, \varepsilon_{t-1})}{\sqrt{\mathrm{Var}(\varepsilon_t)}\sqrt{\mathrm{Var}(\varepsilon_{t-1})}}.$$

Now, an expression in which the covariance of two variables is divided by the product of the standard deviations of these variables is known as the *coefficient of correlation* between the two variables. This coefficient measures the degree of the relationship between two random variables and its values range from -1 to $+1$. Positive values of the coefficient reflect the existence of a positive relationship, and negative values the presence of a negative relationship. The coefficient of correlation whose value is close to +1 or to −1 indicates a high degree of relationship between the variables, and the coefficient whose value is close to zero indicates a low degree of relationship. This means that ρ is, in fact, the coefficient of correlation between ε_t and ε_{t-1}, ρ^2 is the coefficient of correlation between ε_t and ε_{t-2}, ρ^3 is the coefficient of correlation between ε_t and ε_{t-3}, and so on. Note that $\rho = +1$ or $\rho = -1$ is ruled out by the maintained hypothesis specified in connection with (8.54). *When ρ is equal to zero,* we have

$$\varepsilon_t = u_t,$$

$$\mathrm{Var}(\varepsilon_t) = \sigma_u^2;$$

and since u_t is a normally and independently distributed variable with zero mean and constant variance, *all* the basic assumptions concerning ε hold.

If we consider the coefficients of correlation between ε_t and ε_{t-1}, ε_t and ε_{t-2}, and so on, as a function of the lag involved, we have what is known as an *autocorrelation function.* The graph of this function is called a *correlogram.* In the case of the first-order autoregressive process, the autocorrelation function is geometrically declining when ρ is positive and is characterized by damped oscillations when ρ is negative. Processes such as this, for which neither the variance of ε_t nor the autocorrelation between ε_t and ε_{t-s} depend on t, are called *stationary.*

Before proceeding any further, we afford ourselves a certain simplification. The representation of ε_t in (8.55) involves the presumption that the process of generating ε_t started at $t = -\infty$, but our sample starts with the first observation at $t = 1$. A convenient way of taking the effect of the pre-sample disturbances into account is to specify the first sample disturbance as

$$\varepsilon_1 = \frac{u_1}{\sqrt{1-\rho^2}}, \tag{8.59}$$

while leaving the remaining sample disturbances to be generated according to (8.54). Note that

$$E(\varepsilon_1) = 0,$$

$$\mathrm{Var}(\varepsilon_1) = \frac{\sigma_u^2}{1-\rho,^2} = \sigma^2,$$

$$\mathrm{Cov}(\varepsilon_1, \varepsilon_2) = E[\varepsilon_1(\rho\varepsilon_1 + u_2)] = \rho\sigma^2,$$

$$\mathrm{Cov}(\varepsilon_1\ \varepsilon_3) = E[\varepsilon_1(\rho^2\varepsilon_1 + \rho u_2 + u_1)] = \rho^2\sigma^2,$$

and so on. Thus all the characteristics of $\varepsilon_1, \varepsilon_2, \ldots, \varepsilon_n$ as previously specified as preserved. In this way a sample of n observations on Y can be expressed as a function of exactly n disturbances.

Properties of the Least Squares Estimators

Let us now examine the properties of the least squares estimators of α and β in

$$Y_t = \alpha + \beta X_t + \varepsilon_t,$$

when the disturbance ε_t is autoregressive. The least squares estimator of β is

$$\hat{\beta} = \frac{\sum x_t' y_t}{\sum x_t'^2} = \beta + \frac{\sum x_t' \varepsilon_t}{\sum x_t'^2},$$

as given by (7.32). Then,

$$E(\hat{\beta}) = \beta + \frac{\sum x_t' E(\varepsilon_t)}{\sum x_t'^2} = \beta.$$

The least squares estimator of α is

$$\hat{\alpha} = \overline{Y} - \hat{\beta}\overline{X} = (\alpha + \beta\overline{X} + \bar{\varepsilon}) - \hat{\beta}\overline{X},$$

and

$$E(\hat{\alpha}) = \alpha + \beta\overline{X} + E(\bar{\varepsilon}) - E(\hat{\beta})\overline{X} = \alpha.$$

This means that the least squares estimators are *unbiased* even when the disturbances are autoregressive.

Next, we determine whether the least squares estimators are still best linear unbiased estimators (BLUE) by deriving the BLUE formulas for the autoregressive case and by comparing them with the least squares formulas. If the two sets of formulas differ, then the least squares estimators are not BLUE. As in the case of heteroskedasticity in the preceding section, the simplest way of deriving the BLUE of the regression coefficients is by transforming the original regression equation with autoregressive disturbances into an equivalent equation in which the disturbances are independent. This can be done as follows. The original equation

$$Y_t = \alpha + \beta X_t + \varepsilon_t$$

can be multiplied by ρ and lagged by one period to obtain

$$\rho Y_{t-1} = \alpha\rho + \beta\rho X_{t-1} + \rho\varepsilon_{t-1}.$$

If we now substract the second equation from the first, we obtain

$$Y_t - \rho Y_{t-1} = \alpha(1 - \rho) + \beta(X_t - \rho X_{t-1}) + \varepsilon_t - \rho\varepsilon_{t-1}.$$

But since $\varepsilon_t - \rho\varepsilon_{t-1} = u_t$ by (8.54), we can write

$$(8.60) \quad Y_t - \rho Y_{t-1} = \alpha(1 - \rho) + \beta(X_t - \rho X_{t-1}) + u_t \qquad (t = 2, 3, \ldots, n).$$

In this way we replaced the autoregressive disturbance ε_t by the "classical" disturbance u_t. This transformation is known in econometrics as the "Cochrane-Orcutt transformation." Its only drawback is that in the process we lost one observation pertaining to u_1. To bring u_1 back in, we consider

$$Y_1 = \alpha + \beta X_1 + \varepsilon_1,$$

or, in accordance with (8.59),

$$Y_1 = \alpha + \beta X_1 + \frac{u_1}{\sqrt{1 - \rho^2}}.$$

Clearly, we can isolate u_1 by multiplying both sides of the equation by $\sqrt{1-\rho^2}$ to get

$$Y_1\sqrt{1-\rho^2} = \alpha\sqrt{1-\rho^2} + \beta X_1\sqrt{1-\rho^2} + u_1.$$

The complete transformation of the original regression equation can then be represented as

$$(8.61) \qquad Y_t^* = \alpha W_t^* + \beta X_t^* + u_t \qquad (t = 1, 2, \ldots, n),$$

where, for $t = 1$,

$$Y_t^* = Y_t\sqrt{1-\rho^2}, \qquad W_t^* = \sqrt{1-\rho^2}, \qquad X_t^* = X_t\sqrt{1-\rho^2},$$

and, for $t = 2, 3, \ldots, n$,

$$Y_t^* = Y_t - \rho Y_{t-1}, \qquad W_t^* = 1-\rho, \qquad X_t^* = X_t - \rho X_{t-1}.$$

In the transformed equation (8.61) there are two nonstochastic explanatory variables W^* and X^*, and there is no intercept term. (Of course, the values of these explanatory variables and of the dependent variable in the transformed equation cannot be measured unless the value of ρ is known.) Note that W^* has the same value for all observations except the first one. The transformation (8.61) is known as the "Prais–Winsten transformation."

Since the explanatory variables in (8.61) are nonstochastic and since u_t satisfies all basic assumptions, all preconditions for the equality of the least squares estimators (LSE) and best linear unbiased estimators (BLUE) of α and β are met. By applying the least squares method to (8.61), we obtain the following "least squares normal equations":

$$(8.62) \qquad \begin{aligned} \sum W_t^*Y_t^* &= \tilde{\alpha}\sum W_t^{*2} + \tilde{\beta}\sum W_t^*X_t^*, \\ \sum X_t^*Y_t^* &= \tilde{\alpha}\sum W_t^*X_t^* + \tilde{\beta}\sum X_t^{*2}, \end{aligned}$$

where

$$\sum_{t=1}^{n} W_t^*Y_t^* = (1-\rho^2)Y_1 + (1-\rho)\sum_{t=2}^{n}(Y_t - \rho Y_{t-1}),$$

$$\sum_{t=1}^{n} W_t^{*2} = (1-\rho^2) + (n-1)(1-\rho)^2,$$

$$\sum_{t=1}^{n} W_t^*X_t^* = (1-\rho^2)X_1 + (1-\rho)\sum_{t=2}^{n}(X_t - \rho X_{t-1}),$$

$$\sum_{t=1}^{n} X_t^*Y_t^* = (1-\rho^2)X_1Y_1 + \sum_{t=2}^{n}(X_t - \rho X_{t-1})(Y_t - \rho Y_{t-1}),$$

$$\sum_{t=2}^{n} X_t^{*2} = (1-\rho^2)X_1^2 + \sum_{t=2}^{n}(X_t - \rho X_{t-1})^2.$$

The two equations in (8.62) can be solved for $\tilde{\alpha}$ and $\tilde{\beta}$, the BLUE of α and β. The formulas for $\tilde{\alpha}$ and $\tilde{\beta}$ are somewhat complicated, but they will clearly involve the parameter ρ. Since the ordinary least squares estimators do not involve ρ, they are not BLUE when the disturbance is autoregressive. From this conclusion it also follows that the least squares estimators do not have the smallest variance among all unbiased estimators and, therefore, are not *efficient.* If ρ were equal to zero, the solution of (8.62) would yield the usual least squares estimators.

The inefficiency of the least squares estimators of the regression coefficients can be intuitively explained as follows. Since under autoregression each disturbance depends upon the preceding disturbance, each observation contains some information about the following observation. The extent of this information is given by the value of the autoregressive parameter ρ. The ordinary least squares method does not take this link between observations into account and thus does not fully utilize all the information about the regression coefficients in the sample.

Let us now turn to the asymptotic properties of the least squares estimators of the regression coefficients under autoregression in the disturbances. With respect to consistency, we may check whether the variances of these estimators approach zero as the sample size grows to infinity. Since the least squares estimators are unbiased, this is a sufficient condition for consistency. Starting with the variance of $\hat{\beta}$, the least squares estimator of β, we have

(8.63)

$$\operatorname{Var}(\hat{\beta}) = E(\hat{\beta}-\beta)^2 = E\left[\frac{\sum x_t'\varepsilon_t}{\sum x_t'^2}\right]^2$$

$$= \frac{1}{(\sum x_t'^2)^2} E\Big[\sum_i x_i'^2\varepsilon_t^2 + 2\sum_{s<t} x_t'\varepsilon_t x_{t-s}'\varepsilon_{t-s}\Big]$$

$$= \frac{\sigma^2}{(\sum x_t'^2)^2}\Big[\sum_t x_t'^2 + 2\sum_{s<t} x_t' x_{t-s}'\rho^s\Big]$$

$$= \frac{\sigma^2}{\sum x_t'^2} + \frac{2\sigma^2}{(\sum x_t'^2)^2}\Big[\rho\sum_{t=2}^{n} x_t'x_{t-1}' + \rho^2\sum_{t=3}^{n} x_t'x_{t-2}' + \cdots\Big].$$

To simplify notation, we introduce the coefficient of correlation between X_t and X_{t-s}, say, r_s, which we define as

$$r_s = \frac{(1/n)\sum x_t'x_{t-s}'}{\sqrt{(1/n)\sum x_t'^2}\sqrt{(1/n)\sum x_{t-s}'^2}} = \frac{\sum x_t'x_{t-s}'}{\sqrt{\sum x_t'^2}\sqrt{\sum x_{t-s}'^2}},$$

where $s = 1, 2, \ldots, n-1$; $t = s+1, s+2, \ldots, n$; and $s < t$. It can easily be shown that the maximum value of r_s^2 (like that of any squared coefficient of correlation) is unity. Then we can write $\mathrm{Var}(\hat{\beta})$ as

$$(8.63a)\quad \mathrm{Var}(\hat{\beta}) = \frac{\sigma^2}{\sum x_t'^2} + \frac{2\sigma^2}{(\sum x_t'^2)^2}\Big[\rho r_1 \sqrt{\sum x_t'^2}\sqrt{\sum x_{t-1}'^2}$$

$$+ \rho^2 r_2 \sqrt{\sum x_t'^2}\sqrt{\sum x_{t-2}'^2} + \cdots\Big]$$

$$= \frac{(\sigma^2/n)}{(1/n)\sum x_t'^2} + \frac{2(\sigma^2/n)}{[(1/n)\sum x_t'^2]^2}\Big[\rho r_1 \sqrt{\frac{1}{n}\sum x_t'^2}\sqrt{\frac{1}{n}\sum x_{t-1}'^2}$$

$$+ \rho^2 r_2 \sqrt{\frac{1}{n}\sum x_t'^2}\sqrt{\frac{1}{n}\sum x_{t-2}'^2} + \cdots\Big].$$

As n approaches infinity, the terms

$$\frac{1}{n}\sum x_t'^2,\quad \frac{1}{n}\sum x_{t-1}'^2,\quad \frac{1}{n}\sum x_{t-2}'^2,\quad \ldots,$$

will all approach the same finite positive number, say, m_{xx}, and the terms r_1, r_2, r_3, . . . , will approach some numbers with an absolute value less than or equal to one, say, r_1^*, r_2^*, r_3^*, ... Therefore, we have

$$\lim_{n\to\infty} \mathrm{Var}(\hat{\beta}) = \frac{\lim(\sigma^2/n)}{m_{xx}} + \frac{2\lim(\sigma^2/n)}{m_{xx}}[\rho r_1^* + \rho^2 r_2^* + \cdots]$$

$$= \frac{\lim(\sigma^2/n)}{m_{xx}}[1 + 2\rho r_1^* + 2\rho^2 r_2^* + \cdots].$$

Now, since ρ lies between -1 and $+1$ and r_1^*, r_2^*, . . . , are each less than one in absolute value, the sum of the infinite series

$$[1 + 2\rho r_1^* + 2\rho^2 r_2^* + \cdots]$$

will be a finite number. Thus, since $\lim_{n\to\infty}(\sigma^2/n) = 0$,

$$\lim_{n\to\infty} \mathrm{Var}(\hat{\beta}) = 0.$$

By using a similar argument we can also show that

$$\lim_{n\to\infty} \mathrm{Var}(\hat{\alpha}) = 0.$$

This means that the least squares estimators of the regression coefficients are *consistent* even when the regression disturbances are autoregressive.

The last property that is of interest to us is asymptotic efficiency. This can be examined by comparing the asymptotic variances of the least squares estimators with the asymptotic variances of the best linear unbiased estimators. Using the formula for the asymptotic variance of an estimator given in Section 6-1, we can determine the asymptotic variance of the least squares estimator of β as follows.

$$\text{Asympt. Var}(\hat{\beta}) = \frac{1}{n}\lim_{n\to\infty} En\left[\frac{\sum x_t'\varepsilon_t}{\sum x_t'^2}\right]^2$$

$$= \frac{1}{n}\lim_{n\to\infty}\frac{n}{(\sum x_t'^2)^2}[\sigma^2\sum_t x_t'^2 + 2\sigma^2\sum_{s<t} x_t'x_{t-s}'\rho^s]$$

$$= \frac{\sigma^2}{n}\left[\frac{m_{xx} + 2\rho r_1^* m_{xx} + 2\rho^2 r_2^* m_{xx} + \cdots}{m_{xx}^2}\right]$$

$$= \frac{\sigma^2}{nm_{xx}}[1 + 2\rho r_1^* + 2\rho^2 r_2^* + \cdots].$$

The asymptotic variance of the BLUE of β could be derived from the formula for $\tilde{\beta}$ obtained from (8.62). This formula is based on the transformation defined in (8.61), with the transformation of the first observation being out of line with the transformation of the remaining $(n-1)$ observations. If we discard the first observation and use the Cochrane–Orcutt transformation given in (8.60), we obtain the following estimator of β, say, $\tilde{\tilde{\beta}}$:

$$\text{(8.64)} \qquad \tilde{\tilde{\beta}} = \frac{\sum (x_t' - \rho x_{t-1}')(y_t' - \rho y_{t-1}')}{\sum (x_t' - \rho x_{t-1}')} \qquad (t = 2, 3, \ldots, n),$$

where $x_t' = X_t - \bar{X}$, $x_{t-1}' = X_{t-1} - \bar{X}_{-1}$, $\bar{X} = \frac{1}{n-1}\Sigma_{t=2}^n X_t$, $\bar{X}_{-1} = \frac{1}{n-1}\Sigma_{t=2}^n X_{t-1}$, etc. The variance of $\tilde{\tilde{\beta}}$ is

$$\text{(8.65)} \qquad \text{Var}(\tilde{\tilde{\beta}}) = \frac{\sigma_u^2}{\sum (x_r' - \rho x_{t-1}')^2} = \frac{\sigma^2(1-\rho^2)}{\sum (x_t' - \rho x_{t-1}')^2}.$$

The asymptotic variance of $\tilde{\tilde{\beta}}$ then is

$$\text{Asympt. Var}(\tilde{\tilde{\beta}}) = \frac{1}{n}\lim_{n\to\infty} n\left[\frac{\sigma^2(1-\rho^2)}{\sum (x_t' - \rho x_{t-1}')^2}\right]$$

$$= \frac{1}{n}\left[\frac{\sigma^2(1-\rho^2)}{m_{xx} - 2\rho r_1^* m_{xx} + \rho^2 m_{xx}}\right]$$

$$= \frac{\sigma^2}{nm_{xx}}\left[\frac{1-\rho^2}{1 - 2\rho r_1^* + \rho^2}\right].$$

The asymptotic variances of $\hat{\beta}$ and $\tilde{\tilde{\beta}}$ can be compared by forming the ratio

$$\frac{\text{Asympt. Var}(\hat{\beta})}{\text{Asympt. Var}(\tilde{\tilde{\beta}})} = \frac{(\sigma^2/nm_{xx})[1 + 2\rho r_1^* + 2\rho^2 r_2^* + \cdots]}{(\sigma^2/nm_{xx})[(1-\rho^2)/(1 - 2\rho r_1^* + \rho^2)]}$$

$$= \frac{1 + 2\rho r_1^* + 2\rho^2 r_2^* + \cdots}{[(1-\rho^2)/(1 - 2\rho r_1^* + \rho^2)]}.$$

If this ratio is greater than one, then $\hat{\beta}$ cannot be considered to be asymptotically efficient. (Strictly speaking, this statement is true only if ρ is known or can be consistently estimated; otherwise $\tilde{\tilde{\beta}}$ would not qualify as an estimator. The problem of developing a consistent estimator of ρ will be discussed in the latter part of the present section.) Suppose we evaluate the above ratio for $1 > \rho > 0$ and $r_2^* = r_1^{*2}$, $r_3^* = r_1^{*3}$, ... That is, we consider a situation in which the disturbances are positively autocorrelated, and the coefficients of correlation between X_t and X_{t-1}, X_t and X_{t-2}, etc., follow a geometric progression. Such situations are thought to be quite common with economic time series.[36] With this specification we obtain

$$\frac{\text{Asympt. Var}(\hat{\beta})}{\text{Var}(\tilde{\tilde{\beta}})} = \frac{1 + 2\rho r_1^* + 2\rho^2 r_1^{*2} + \cdots}{[(1-\rho^2)/(1 - 2\rho r_1^* + \rho^2)]}$$

$$= \frac{1 - \rho r_1^* - 2\rho^2 r_1^{*2} + \rho^2 + \rho^3 r_1^*}{1 - \rho r_1^* - \rho^2 + \rho^3 r_1^*}.$$

This expression will be greater than or equal to one if

$$1 - \rho r_1^* - 2\rho^2 r_1^{*2} + \rho^2 + \rho^3 r_1^* \geq 1 - \rho r_1^* - \rho^2 + \rho^3 r_1^*$$

or

$$-2\rho^2 r_1^{*2} + \rho^2 \geq -\rho^2;$$

that is, if

$$2\rho^2(1 - r_1^{*2}) \geq 0.$$

This condition will always be satisfied. For example, when $\rho = 0.6$ and $r_1^* = 0.8$, $r_2^* = 0.64$, $r_3^* = 0.512$, etc., the ratio of the two asymptotic variances is equal to 1.78, i.e., the asymptotic variance of $\hat{\beta}$ is 78 percent larger than that of $\tilde{\tilde{\beta}}$. A similar result can be obtained with respect to $\hat{\alpha}$. Thus we have to conclude that the least squares estimators of the regression coefficients are *not asymptotically efficient* when the disturbances are autoregressive.

To sum up, when the regression disturbance is autoregressive, the least squares estimators of the regression coefficients are unbiased and consistent, but they are *not* BLUE, efficient, or asymptotically efficient. This means that the consequences of autoregression for the properties of the least squares estimators are the same as the consequences of heteroskedasticity. The extent of the loss of efficiency because of autoregression can be determined by a comparison of the variances of the least squares estimators with those of the best linear unbiased estimators. We will do this when we come to the discussion of best linear unbiased estimation.

Properties of the Estimated Variances of the Least Squares Estimators

The preceding results show that when the regression disturbance is autoregressive, the least squares estimators of the regression coefficients still have some desir-

[36] See E. Ames and S. Reiter, "Distributions of Correlation Coefficients in Economic Time Series," *Journal of the American Statistical Association,* 56 (September 1961), pp. 637–656. The authors consider 100 annual series of 25 observations selected at random from the abstract of statistics of the United States. They find that, on the average, the first five autocorrelation coefficients were 0.84, 0.71, 0.60, 0.53 and 0.45.

able properties. However, if we want to use these estimators for the purpose of testing hypotheses or constructing confidence intervals, we require unbiasedness not only of the estimators themselves, but also of their estimated variances. The question then is whether the conventional formulas for estimating the variances of the least squares estimators do, in fact, guarantee unbiasedness even under autoregression in the disturbances. We note that the conventional least squares formula for estimating the variance of $\hat{\beta}$ is

$$s_{\hat{\beta}}^2 = \frac{s^2}{\sum x_t'^2},$$

where s^2 is an estimator of σ^2 defined as the sum of squares of the least squares residuals divided by $(n-2)$. Since $\Sigma x_t'^2$ is nonstochastic, we only have to concern ourselves with s^2. For that, we have

$$\begin{aligned} s^2 &= \frac{1}{n-2}\sum_t (y_t' - \hat{\beta}x_t')^2 = \frac{1}{n-2}\sum_t (\beta x_t' + \varepsilon_t' - \hat{\beta}x_t')^2 \\ &= \frac{1}{n-2}\sum_t [-(\hat{\beta}-\beta)x_t' + \varepsilon_t']^2 \\ &= \frac{1}{n-2}[(\hat{\beta}-\beta)^2\sum_t x_t'^2 + \sum_t \varepsilon_t'^2 - 2(\hat{\beta}-\beta)\sum_t x_t'\varepsilon_t'] \\ &= \frac{1}{n-2}[\sum_t \varepsilon_t'^2 - (\hat{\beta}-\beta)^2\sum_t x_t'^2] \end{aligned}$$

and

$$E(s^2) = \frac{1}{n-2}[E(\sum_t \varepsilon_t'^2) - (\sum x_t'^2)\,\mathrm{Var}(\hat{\beta})].$$

Now

$$\begin{aligned} E(\sum \varepsilon_t'^2) &= E[\sum (\varepsilon_t - \bar{\varepsilon})^2] = E[(\sum \varepsilon_t^2) - n\bar{\varepsilon}^2] \\ &= n\sigma^2 - nE(\bar{\varepsilon}^2). \end{aligned}$$

Unfortunately, to develop the exact expression for $E(\bar{\varepsilon}^2)$ when the εs are autoregressive is rather complicated. It can be shown, though, that *asymptotically* $nE(\bar{\varepsilon}^2) = \sigma_u^2/(1-\rho)^2 = \sigma^2(1+\rho)/(1-\rho)$. Thus when n is large, we have

$$\begin{aligned} E(s^2) &\cong \frac{1}{n}\left[n\sigma^2 - \frac{\sigma^2(1+\rho)}{1-\rho} - (\sum x_t'^2)\mathrm{Var}(\hat{\beta})\right] \\ &\cong \sigma^2 - \frac{(\sum x_t'^2)\mathrm{Var}(\hat{\beta})}{n} - \frac{\sigma^2(1+\rho)}{n(1-\rho)} \\ &\cong \sigma^2 - \left(\frac{1}{n}\sum x_t'^2\right)\mathrm{Var}(\hat{\beta}). \end{aligned}$$

From this it follows that

$$(8.66)\qquad E(s_{\hat{\beta}}^2) = E\left(\frac{s^2}{\sum x_t'^2}\right) \cong \frac{\sigma^2}{\sum x_t'^2}.$$

Since the expression for $E(s_{\hat{\beta}}^2)$ differs from that for $\mathrm{Var}(\hat{\beta})$ given by (8.63), we conclude that the conventionally calculated estimator of the variance of $\hat{\beta}$ is *biased* when the disturbances are autoregressive. This bias will be, to the degree of approximation that we work with,

$$(8.67)\qquad E(s_{\hat{\beta}}^2) - \mathrm{Var}(\hat{\beta}) \cong \frac{\sigma^2}{\sum x_t'^2} - \mathrm{Var}(\hat{\beta}).$$

But from (8.63) we can see that

$$\frac{\sigma^2}{\sum x_t'^2} - \mathrm{Var}(\hat{\beta}) = -2\sigma^2\left[\frac{\rho\sum x_t'x_{t-1}' + \rho^2\sum x_t'x_{t-2}' + \cdots}{(\sum x_t'^2)^2}\right].$$

Therefore when $\rho > 0$ and X_t is positively correlated with $X_{t-1}, X_{t-2}, \ldots$, the bias is *negative*. As pointed out earlier, such a situation is fairly common with economic time series. Thus, if the disturbances are autoregressive and we persist in using the conventional least squares formulas, the calculated acceptance regions or confidence intervals will be often *narrower* than they should be for the specified level of significance or confidence.

EXAMPLE To obtain an idea about the extent of the bias in using $s^2/\Sigma x_t'^2$ to estimate $\mathrm{Var}(\hat{\beta})$, we consider a situation where X follows a simple linear trend of the form $X_t = 1, 2, \ldots, n$, and where the sample size $n = 20$ and $\rho = 0.6$. For the determination of the value of $\mathrm{Var}(\hat{\beta})$ we need the following calculations:

$$\sum_{t=1}^{20} x_t'^2 = \sum t^2 - (\sum t)^2/20 = 665,$$

$$\sum_{t=2}^{20} x_t'x_{t-1}' = \sum t(t-1) - 10.5\,[\sum t + \sum (t-1)] + 19(10.5)^2 = 565.25,$$

etc. These calculations lead to

$$\mathrm{Var}(\hat{\beta}) = 0.004389\sigma^2.$$

From (8.67) we obtain

$$\frac{E(s_{\hat{\beta}}^2)}{\mathrm{Var}(\hat{\beta})} \cong \frac{\sigma^2/665}{0.004389\sigma^2} \cong 0.34.$$

Thus the expected value of the conventionally calculated estimator would be only about one-third of the true value of the variance of $\hat{\beta}$ in this case.

Our conclusion then is that the consequences of autoregression for statistical inference based on least squares estimation are, as in the case of heteroskedasticity, twofold.

1. The least squares estimators of the regression coefficients are unbiased and consistent but have no other desirable properties.
2. The estimated variances of the least squares estimators are biased and the conventionally calculated confidence intervals and tests of significance are not valid.

Given this conclusion it appears advisable to find an estimation method or methods that would be efficient, at least asymptotically, and that would yield valid confidence intervals and tests of significance. The best linear unbiased estimators introduced in (8.62) would serve this purpose very well except for the presumption of a known value of ρ. Since the value of ρ is rarely known, we have to develop other methods of estimation that are less demanding. The best linear unbiased estimation will be considered again, but mainly for the purpose of comparison with other methods.

Best Linear Unbiased Estimation

The best linear unbiased estimators of the regression coefficients, also known as *generalized least squares estimators,* can be obtained in the case of first-order autoregression by solving the equations in (8.62) for $\tilde{\alpha}$ and $\tilde{\beta}$. These equations have been obtained by minimizing Σu_t^2 $(t = 1, 2, \ldots, n)$ with respect to α and β. This approach can be compared with the maximum likelihood approach as follows. Since the u's are normally and independently distributed, their joint density function can easily be determined. From the density function of the u's we can determine the density function of the observed values of the Y's, which is the likelihood function that we want. By an extension of Theorem 19 (the "change-of-variable" theorem in Section 7-3) we have

$$f(y_1, y_2, \ldots, y_n) = \left|\frac{\partial u}{\partial Y}\right| f(u_1, u_2, \ldots, u_n),$$

where $|\partial u/\partial Y|$ is the absolute value of the determinant

$$\begin{vmatrix} \dfrac{\partial u_1}{\partial Y_1} & \dfrac{\partial u_1}{\partial Y_2} & \cdots & \dfrac{\partial u_1}{\partial Y_n} \\ \dfrac{\partial u_2}{\partial Y_1} & \dfrac{\partial u_2}{\partial Y_2} & \cdots & \dfrac{\partial u_2}{\partial Y_n} \\ \vdots & \vdots & & \\ \dfrac{\partial u_n}{\partial Y_1} & \dfrac{\partial u_n}{\partial Y_2} & \cdots & \dfrac{\partial u_n}{\partial Y_n} \end{vmatrix}.$$

This determinant is known as the *Jacobian* of the transformation from

$u_1, u_2, \ldots, u_n$ to $Y_1, Y_2, \ldots, Y_n$. Now since by (8.61) we have

$$u_1 = Y_1\sqrt{1-\rho^2} - \alpha\sqrt{1-\rho^2} - \beta X_1\sqrt{1-\rho^2}$$
$$u_2 = (Y_2 - \rho Y_1) - \alpha(1-\rho) - \beta(X_2 - \rho X_1)$$
$$\vdots$$
$$u_n = (Y_n - \rho Y_{n-1}) - \alpha(1-\rho) - \beta(X_n - \rho X_{n-1}),$$

it follows that

$$\frac{\partial u_1}{\partial Y_1} = \sqrt{1-\rho^2},$$
$$\frac{\partial u_t}{\partial Y_t} = 1 \qquad (\text{for } t = 2, 3, \ldots, n),$$
$$\frac{\partial u_t}{\partial Y_s} = 0 \qquad (\text{for all } t < s).$$

Thus

$$\left|\frac{\partial u}{\partial Y}\right| = +\sqrt{1-\rho^2}.$$

The log-likelihood function is then given as

$$(8.68)\quad L = \log f(y_1, y_2, \ldots, y_n)$$
$$= \frac{1}{2}\log(1-\rho^2) - \frac{n}{2}\log(2\pi\sigma_u^2) - \frac{1}{2\sigma_u^2}\sum u_t^2 \qquad (t = 1, 2, \ldots, n).$$

When ρ is known, maximizing L with respect to α and β is equivalent to minimizing Σu_t^2 with respect to the same parameters. Thus, *when ρ is known,* the BLUE and the MLE of α and β are the same.

The solution of (8.62) for the BLUE of β gives

$$(8.69)\quad \tilde{\beta} = \frac{(\sum W_t^{*2})(\sum Y_t^* X_t^*) - (\sum X_t^* Y_t^*)(\sum W_t^* X_t^*)}{(\sum W_t^{*2})(\sum X_t^{*2}) - (\sum W_t^* X_t^*)^2}$$
$$(t = 1, 2, \ldots, n),$$

where W_t^*, X_t^*, and Y_t^* are defined as in (8.62). Substitution for Y_t^* from (8.61) into (8.62) yields

$$(8.69a)\qquad \tilde{\beta} = \beta + \frac{(\sum W_t^{*2})(\sum X_t^* u_t) - (\sum W_t^* X_t^*)(\sum W_t^* u_t)}{\Delta},$$

where $\Delta = (\Sigma W_t^{*2})(\Sigma X_t^{*2}) - (\Sigma W_t^* X_t^*)^2$. Therefore,

$$\text{(8.70)} \qquad \operatorname{Var}(\tilde{\beta}) = E(\tilde{\beta} - \beta)^2 = \frac{\sigma_u^2(\sum W_t^{*2})}{\Delta},$$

where

$$\sum W_t^{*2} = (1-\rho^2) + (n-1)(1-\rho)^2,$$

and

$$\Delta = [(1-\rho^2) + (n-1)(1-\rho)^2][(1-\rho^2)X_1^2 + \sum (X_t - \rho X_{t-1})^2] - [(1-\rho^2)X_1 + (1-\rho)\sum (X_t - \rho X_{t-1})]^2.$$

The loss of efficiency of the LSE of β because of autoregression can be determined by comparing $\operatorname{Var}(\hat{\beta})$ with $\operatorname{Var}(\tilde{\beta})$. It may also be instructive to compare $\operatorname{Var}(\hat{\beta})$ with $\operatorname{Var}(\tilde{\tilde{\beta}})$ given in (8.65), which is based on the Cochrane–Orcutt estimator of β obtained by dropping the first observation. Such comparisons are made in the example below.

EXAMPLE Let us consider again the situation described in the preceding example, where X follows a simple linear trend of the form $X_t = 1, 2, \ldots, n$ and where $n = 20$ and $\rho = 0.6$. In this case we determined that

$$\operatorname{Var}(\hat{\beta}) = 0.004389\sigma^2.$$

For calculating the value of $\operatorname{Var}(\tilde{\beta})$ we need

$$\begin{aligned}
\sigma_u^2 \sum W_t^{*2} &= [0.64 + 19(0.16)]\sigma_u^2 \\
&= [0.64 + 19(0.16)]0.64\sigma^2 \\
&= 2.3552\sigma^2,
\end{aligned}$$

$$\sum_{t=2} (X_t - 0.6X_{t-1}) = 209 - (0.6)\,190 = 95,$$

$$\sum_{t=2} (X_t - 0.6X_{t-1})^2 = 2869 - (1.2)2660 + (0.36)2470 = 566.2,$$

$$\begin{aligned}
\Delta &= [0.64 + 19(0.16)][0.64 + 566.2] - [0.64 + (0.4)95]^2 \\
&= 592.9216.
\end{aligned}$$

Therefore,

$$\operatorname{Var}(\tilde{\beta}) = \frac{2.3552\sigma^2}{592.916} = 0.001686\sigma^2.$$

Finally, for the variance of the Cochrane-Orcutt estimator in (8.59) we need

$$\sum_{t=2} (x_t' - \rho x_{t-1}')^2 = 570 - (1.2)570 + (0.36)570$$
$$= 91.2.$$

Then

$$\text{Var}(\tilde{\tilde{\beta}}) = 0.007017\sigma^2.$$

Collecting the results we get

BLUE:	$\text{Var}(\tilde{\beta}) = 0.001686\sigma^2$,
LSE:	$\text{Var}(\hat{\beta}) = 0.004389\sigma^2$,
Cochrane-Orcutt:	$\text{Var}(\tilde{\tilde{\beta}}) = 0.007017\sigma^2$.

The preceding example brings out an interesting facet of estimation with autoregressive transformations. In the case that we considered, the variance of the Cochrane-Orcutt estimator, which is the same as the BLUE except for dropping the first observation, is in fact considerably larger than the variance of the LSE, which is based on ignoring autoregression altogether. This occurs because the explanatory variable in our example follows a trend. In such cases the Cochrane-Orcutt transformation reduces the sample variation in the transformed explanatory variable as compared with the untransformed variable. As we noted at the outset of Section 7-4, a reduction in the dispersion of the explanatory variable increases the variance of least squares estimators. Thus the gain in efficiency from using the Cochrane-Orcutt transformation is more than offset by the loss of efficiency resulting from the smaller dispersion of the transformed explanatory variable. The dispersion of the explanatory variable in the case of BLU estimation is not adversely affected by the transformation because of the retention of the first transformed observation. This observation, which by definition is out of line with the remaining observations, becomes very influential when the explanatory variable follows a trend.[37]

Cochrane-Orcutt Two-Step and Iterative Estimation

The Cochrane-Orcutt (C-O) estimation procedure described above must be modified when the value of the autoregressive parameter ρ is not known but has to be estimated. A simple way of estimating ρ is to replace the εs in

$$\varepsilon_t = \rho\varepsilon_{t-1} + u_t$$

by the corresponding least squares residuals. The least squares estimator of ρ from

$$e_t = \rho e_{t-1} + u_t$$

[37] This point was first raised by A. Maeshiro in "Autoregressive Transformation, Trended Independent Variables and Autocorrelated Disturbance Terms," *Review of Economics and Statistics,* 58 (1976), pp. 497-500.

is given as

$$(8.71)\qquad \hat{\rho} = \frac{\sum e_t e_{t-1}}{\sum e_{t-1}^2} \qquad (t = 2, 3, \ldots, n).$$

It can be shown that $\hat{\rho}$ is a consistent estimator of ρ.[38] The *two-step C–O estimators* of α and β and their estimated standard errors are then obtained by applying the least squares method to

$$(Y_t - \hat{\rho}Y_{t-1}) = \alpha^* + \beta(X_t - \hat{\rho}X_{t-1}) + u_t^* \qquad (t = 2, 3, \ldots, n),$$

where $\alpha^* = \alpha(1 - \hat{\rho})$.

The above estimators are called two-step estimators because they require two successive applications of the least squares method: the first to obtain $\hat{\rho}$ and the second to obtain estimates of α and β and their estimated standard errors. The *iterative C–O estimators* of α and β are obtained by a repeated application of these two steps until convergence is reached. Specifically, let the two-step C–O estimates be called $\overline{\alpha}$ and $\overline{\beta}$. These can be used to obtain a new set of residuals, say, $\hat{e}_t$, given as

$$\hat{e}_t = Y_t - \overline{\alpha} - \overline{\beta}X_t,$$

and a new estimate of ρ, say $\tilde{\hat{\rho}}$, given as

$$\tilde{\hat{\rho}} = \frac{\sum \hat{e}_t \hat{e}_{t-1}}{\sum \hat{e}_{t-1}^2}.$$

The new estimate of ρ can then be used in applying the least squares method to

$$(Y_t - \tilde{\hat{\rho}}Y_{t-1}) = \alpha^{**} + \beta(X_t - \tilde{\hat{\rho}}X_{t-1}) + u_t^{**} \qquad (t = 2, 3, \ldots, n),$$

and the procedure can be followed until the values of the estimated α and β converge.

The iterative C–O estimates could also be obtained by the following approach known as the *Hildreth–Lu method,*[39] abbreviated as H–L. This method involves repeatedly applying the least squares estimation method to

$$(Y_t - \rho Y_{t-1}) = \alpha(1 - \rho) + \beta(X_t - \rho X_{t-1}) + u_t \qquad (t = 2, 3, \ldots, n)$$

using different values of ρ between -1 and 1, say, $\rho = -0.95, -0.90, -0.85, \ldots, 0.85, 0.90, 0.95$. From all these results one selects the one that yields the smallest sum of squared residuals. This "search" procedure leads to exactly the same estimates of α and β as the iterative C–O method. These estimates could also be interpreted as *conditional maximum likelihood estimates* since minimizing the sum of squared residuals from the preceding equation is the same as maximizing

[38] See P. J. Dhrymes, *Introductory Econometrics* (New York: Springer-Verlag, 1978), p. 122.

[39] See C. Hildreth and J. Y. Lu, "Demand Relations with Autocorrelated Disturbances," *Technical Bulletin* 276, Michigan State University Agricultural Experiment Station, November 1960.

the likelihood function in (8.68) *after* dropping the first observation. This amounts to treating Y_1 as a constant so that the results are *conditional* in Y_1.[40]

The two-step and iterative C–O estimators have, under fairly general conditions, all desirable asymptotic properties.[41] Both estimators have been very popular in applied work because of their computational simplicity. However, as we noted earlier, these estimators cannot be recommended when the explanatory variable follows a trend because of the importance of the first observation in samples other than very large samples.

EXAMPLE Friedman and Meiselman[42] estimated an equation representing a simple form of the quantity theory of money,

$$C_t = \alpha + \beta M_t + \varepsilon_t,$$

where C = consumer expenditure and M = stock of money, both measured in billions of current dollars. We shall re-estimate this relation using the quarterly data in Table 8-1 and assuming that the disturbance follows a first-order autoregressive scheme.

The results for the ordinary least squares estimation are

$$\underset{(19.85)}{Y_t = -154.72} + \underset{(0.1146)}{2.3004X_t} + e_t, \qquad R^2 = 0.9573.$$

Note that the estimated standard errors are biased, presumably downward. The first-round estimate of ρ is

$$\hat{\rho} = 0.8745.$$

Using $\hat{\rho}$ we obtain the following two-step C–O estimates.

$$(Y_t - \hat{\rho}Y_{t-1}) = \underset{(111.949)}{-244.233}(1-\hat{\rho}) + \underset{(0.6113)}{2.7956}(X_t - \hat{\rho}X_{t-1}) + \hat{u}_t, \qquad R^2 = 0.5516,$$

where the value of R^2 refers to the transformed equation.

The iterative C–O estimation leads to the following final-round estimate of ρ, say, $\bar{\bar{\rho}}$:

$$\bar{\bar{\rho}} = 0.8241,$$

[40] The exact equivalence of the iterative C–O and the H–L method follows from the main theorem in Oberhofer and Kmenta, *op. cit.* The convergence to the global rather than local maximum of the (conditional) likelihood function is guaranteed by the fact that the first-round estimators of α, β, and ρ are consistent and that maximizing likelihood equations have at most one consistent solution.

[41] See, e.g., Schmidt, *op. cit.*, p. 71.

[42] Milton Friedman and David Meiselman, "The Relative Stability of Monetary Velocity and the Investment Multiplier in the United States, 1897–1958," in Commission on Money and Credit, *Stabilization Policies* (Englewood Cliffs, NJ: Prentice-Hall, 1963).

Table 8-1

Year and quarter	Consumer expenditure[a]	Money stock[a]	Year and quarter	Consumer expenditure[a]	Money stock[a]
1952 I	214.6	159.3	1954 III	238.7	173.9
II	217.7	161.2	IV	243.2	176.1
III	219.6	162.8			
IV	227.2	164.6	1955 I	249.4	178.0
			II	254.3	179.1
1953 I	230.9	165.9	III	260.9	180.2
II	233.3	167.9	IV	263.3	181.2
III	234.1	168.3			
IV	232.3	169.7	1956 I	265.6	181.6
			II	268.2	182.5
1954 I	233.7	170.5	III	270.4	183.3
II	236.5	171.6	IV	275.6	184.3

Source: Milton Friedman and David Meiselman, "The Relative Stability of Monetary Velocity and the Investment Multiplier in the United States, 1897–1958," in Commission on Money and Credit, *Stabilization Policies* (Englewood Cliffs, NJ: Prentice-Hall, 1963), p. 266.

[a] In billions of dollars.

and the following final-round estimates of the regression coefficients:

$$(Y_t - \bar{\bar{\rho}} Y_{t-1}) = \underset{(78.356)}{-235.458}(1 - \bar{\bar{\rho}}) + \underset{(0.4367)}{2.7532}(X_t - \bar{\bar{\rho}} X_{t-1}) + \hat{u}_t^*, \qquad R^2 = 0.7004,$$

where again the value of R^2 refers to the transformed equation.

The H–L search procedure yields

Value of ρ	Sum of squared residuals
−0.9	857.158
−0.8	773.451
⋮	⋮
0.7	90.696
0.8	85.072
0.822	84.815
0.823	84.814
0.824	84.813
0.825	84.813
0.826	84.815
0.9	87.873

The minimizing value of ρ lies between 0.824 and 0.825, which is precisely where the iterative C–O estimate lies.

Durbin Two-Step Method

A different suggestion for estimating ρ made by Durbin[43] is based on the equation (8.60) rewritten as

$$Y_t = \alpha(1-\rho) + \beta X_t - \beta\rho X_{t-1} + \rho Y_{t-1} + u_t \qquad (t = 2, 3, \ldots, n)$$

or

$$Y_t = \delta + \beta X_t + \gamma X_{t-1} + \rho Y_{t-1} + u_t.$$

This expression can be treated as a regression equation with three explanatory variables, X_t, X_{t-1}, and Y_{t-1}, and estimated by the ordinary least squares method. The estimated coefficient of Y_{t-1}, say, $\tilde{\rho}$, can then be used to construct new variables $(Y_t - \tilde{\rho}Y_{t-1})$ and $X_t - \tilde{\rho}X_{t-1})$. The second step of the procedure involves applying the least squares method to

$$(Y_t - \tilde{\rho}Y_{t-1}) = \alpha^* + \beta(X_t - \tilde{\rho}X_{t-1}) + u_t^* \qquad (t = 2, 3, \ldots, n),$$

where $\alpha^* = \alpha(1-\tilde{\rho})$. The resulting estimators of α and β have the same asymptotic properties as the C–O two-step or iterative estimators. As in the case of the preceding two methods, the omission of the first transformed observation makes this method unsuitable for situations in which the explanatory variable follows a trend.

EXAMPLE We can use the "quantity theory" relation and the data of the preceding example to illustrate the Durbin procedure. In the first round we obtain

$$\underset{(23.03)}{Y_t = -34.72} + \underset{(1.0965)}{1.2167}\, X_t - \underset{(1.2416)}{0.7996}\, X_{t-1} + \underset{(0.1535)}{0.8527}\, Y_{t-1} + \hat{u}_t, \qquad R^2 = 0.9880.$$

The second round yields

$$(Y_t - \tilde{\rho}Y_{t-1}) = \underset{(94.908)}{-242.664}(1-\tilde{\rho}) + \underset{(0.5227)}{2.7901}(X_t - \tilde{\rho}X_{t-1}) + \hat{u}_t^*, \qquad R^2 = 0.6263,$$

where $\tilde{\rho} = 0.8527$. These results are fairly similar to those for the C–O two-step estimation presented earlier.

Prais–Winsten Two-Step and Iterative Procedure

The first attempt to incorporate the first transformed observation into the estimation process was made by Prais and Winsten.[44] At the outset these authors noted that the C–O estimator of ρ can be obtained by minimizing

[43] J. Durbin, "Estimation of Parameters in Time-Series Regression Models," *Journal of the Royal Statistical Society,* Series B, 22 (January 1960), pp. 139–153.

[44] S. J. Prais and C. B. Winsten, "Trend Estimators and Serial Correlation," Cowles Commission Discussion Paper No. 383, Chicago, 1954.

$$S = \sum_{t=2}^{n} (e_t - \rho e_{t-1})^2$$

with respect to ρ (with e_t and e_{t-1} denoting ordinary least squares residuals as before). Then if the first observation is taken into account, ρ can be estimated by minimizing

$$S^* = (1-\rho^2)\, e_1^2 + \sum_{t=2}^{n} (e_t - \rho e_{t-1})^2,$$

which yields

$$\hat{\rho}_{PW} = \frac{\sum_{t=2}^{n} e_t e_{t-1}}{\sum_{t=3}^{n} e_{t-1}^2}. \tag{8.72}$$

The *Prais–Winsten (P–W) two-step method* then consists of applying the ordinary least squares method to equation (8.61), after replacing ρ by $\hat{\rho}_{PW}$. If the two-step procedure is repeated until convergence, the resulting estimators of α and β are known as the *P–W iterative estimators.* Exactly the same estimators could also be obtained by minimizing

$$\sum_{t=1}^{n} (Y_t^* - \alpha W_t^* - \beta X_t^*)^2$$

with respect to α, β, and ρ. This minimization can be accomplished by "searching" over different values of ρ between -1 and $+1$ as in the case of the Hildreth–Lu procedure. For this reason the P–W iterative estimators are also referred to as *nonlinear least squares estimators.* Both the two-step and the iterative P–W estimators have the same asymptotic properties as the BLU estimators.

EXAMPLE Continuing with the "quantity theory" example, the results for the P–W two-step procedure are

$$\hat{\rho}_{PW} = 0.9050,$$

$$Y_t^* = \underset{(45.21)}{-153.42}W_t^* + \underset{(0.2613)}{2.3059}X_t^* + \hat{u}_t, \qquad R^2 = 0.7674,$$

and for the P–W iterative procedure,

$$\hat{\rho}_{PW}^* = 0.8938,$$

$$Y_t^* = \underset{(43.70)}{-154.24}W_t^* + \underset{(0.2526)}{2.3098}X_t^* + \hat{u}_t, \qquad R^2 = 0.7584.$$

The nonlinear least squares search procedure yields

Values of ρ	Sum of squared residuals
−0.9	858.79
−0.8	776.59
⋮	⋮
0.7	99.70
0.8	92.16
0.893	89.744
0.8937	89.743587
0.8938	89.743583
0.8939	89.743585
0.8940	89.73592

Thus we see that the results of the search procedure are exactly the same as those of the iterative method. It is interesting that the P–W estimates are much closer to the ordinary least squares estimates than either the Cochrane–Orcutt or the Durbin estimates.

Full Maximum Likelihood Estimation

In discussing the BLU estimation we introduced the likelihood function for the n observations of Y and pointed out that *when ρ is known,* the BLUE and the MLE of α and β are the same. When ρ is not known but has to be estimated along with α and β, the MLE of these parameters are obtained by maximizing the log-likelihood function (8.68) given as

$$L = \frac{1}{2}\log(1-\rho^2) - \frac{n}{2}\log(2\pi\sigma_u^2) - \frac{\sum u_t^2}{2\,\sigma_u^2} \qquad (t = 1, 2, \ldots, n)$$

with respect to α, β, ρ, and σ_u^2. Maximizing L is not the same as minimizing Σu_t^2—which yields the iterative P–W estimators—because of the presence of the Jacobian term $\frac{1}{2}\log(1-\rho^2)$ in L. Maximization of L can be accomplished by "searching" over different values of ρ. The resulting estimators are labeled *full maximum likelihood estimators* to distinguish them from the *conditional* maximum likelihood estimators discussed in connection with the iterative C–O method. The presence of the Jacobian term in L guarantees that the estimated value of ρ lies in the interval from -1 to $+1$, but asymptotically this term has no effect on the value of the estimators of α and β. The full MLE of α and β have all desirable asymptotic properties; their asymptotic variances can be determined from the information matrix.[45] Using the information matrix it is possible to show that the MLE of ρ is asymptotically independent of the MLE of α, β, and σ_u^2, and that its asymptotic variance is $(1-\rho^2)/n$.

[45] See J. R. Magnus, "Maximum Likelihood Estimation of the GLS Model with Unknown Parameters in the Disturbance Covariance Matrix," *Journal of Econometrics,* 7 (June 1978), pp. 305–306.

EXAMPLE Let us consider the full MLE of the coefficients of the "quantity relation." The results of maximizing L are

Value of ρ	Value of L
−0.90	−66.807105
⋮	⋮
0.84	−44.092116
0.844	−44.091061
0.845	−44.090993
0.8453	−44.0909876
0.8454	−44.0909875
0.8455	−44.0909882
0.85	−44.091845
⋮	⋮

Thus the maximum likelihood value of ρ is 0.8454. The MLE estimates of the regression coefficients are

$$Y_t^* = -\underset{(38.24)}{156.54}\, W_t^* + \underset{(0.2210)}{2.3203}\, X_t^* + \hat{u}_t, \qquad R^2 = 0.9834.$$

The Use of First Differences

In earlier applied studies, research workers frequently attempted to deal with the problem of autoregression in disturbances by using the *method of first differences.* This method calls for transforming the original data on Y and X into first differences $(Y_t - Y_{t-1})$ and $(X_t - X_{t-1})$, and for setting up the regression equation as

$$(8.73) \qquad (Y_t - Y_{t-1}) = \alpha^{**} + \beta(X_t - X_{t-1}) + v_t.$$

α^{**} and β are then estimated by the method of least squares. Note that since

$$Y_t = \alpha + \beta X_t + \varepsilon_t$$

and

$$Y_{t-1} = \alpha + \beta X_{t-1} + \varepsilon_{t-1},$$

it follows that $\alpha^{**} = 0$ and $v_t = \varepsilon_t - \varepsilon_{t-1}$. The rationale of the method of first differences is the belief that the true value of ρ is close to unity. Since $\alpha^{**} = 0$, one does not expect that its estimate in (8.73) would be significantly different from zero. The implication is that α cannot be estimated by this method. We note in passing that a result giving the estimate of α^{**} as significantly different from zero has often been rationalized by the claim that the original model had been misspecified and that, in addition to X_t, it should have included a trend as an explanatory variable. If that were the case and the trend were measured by the "time variable" t, we would have

$$Y_t = \alpha + \beta X_t + \delta t + \varepsilon_t,$$

$$Y_{t-1} = \alpha + \beta X_{t-1} + \delta (t-1) + \varepsilon_{t-1},$$

and

$$Y_t - Y_{t-1} = \beta(X_t - X_{t-1}) + \delta + (\varepsilon_t - \varepsilon_{t-1}),$$

so that the intercept in (8.73) would measure the coefficient of the trend variable.

Let us consider the properties of the estimator of β when using the method of first differences. We assume, as before, that ε_t follows a first-order autoregressive scheme. Now the disturbance in (8.73) is

$$v_t = \varepsilon_t - \varepsilon_{t-1},$$

so that

$$E(v_t) = 0,$$

$$E(v_t^2) = E(\varepsilon_t^2 + \varepsilon_{t-1}^2 - 2\varepsilon_t\varepsilon_{t-1}) = \sigma^2 + \sigma^2 - 2\rho\sigma^2 = 2\sigma^2(1-\rho)$$

$$= \frac{2\sigma_u^2(1-\rho)}{1-\rho^2} = \frac{2\sigma_u^2}{1+\rho},$$

$$E(v_t v_{t-1}) = E(\varepsilon_t - \varepsilon_{t-1})(\varepsilon_{t-1} - \varepsilon_{t-2})$$

$$= E(\varepsilon_t\varepsilon_{t-1} - \varepsilon_{t-1}^2 - \varepsilon_t\varepsilon_{t-2} + \varepsilon_{t-1}\varepsilon_{t-2}) = \rho\sigma^2 - \sigma^2 - \rho^2\sigma^2 + \rho\sigma^2$$

$$= -\sigma^2(1-\rho)^2 = \frac{-\sigma_u^2(1-\rho)}{1+\rho}.$$

It follows, then, that the new disturbance v has zero mean and a constant variance but is still autoregressive, although, of course, the extent of autoregression would be small if ρ were close to unity.

The least squares estimators of β based on first differences, say, $\bar{\beta}$, is

$$\bar{\beta} = \frac{\sum (y_t' - y_{t-1}')(x_t' - x_{t-1}')}{\sum (x_t' - x_{t-1}')^2} \tag{8.74}$$

$$= \beta + \frac{\sum z_t'(\varepsilon_t - \varepsilon_{t-1})}{\sum z_t'^2} \qquad (t = 2, 3, \ldots, n),$$

where

$$z_t' = x_t' - x_{t-1}'.$$

Now

$$E(\bar{\beta}) = \beta,$$

so that $\bar{\beta}$ is unbiased. However, the *estimator* of the variance of $\bar{\beta}$, like that of the variance of $\hat{\beta}$, is biased. Therefore, the use of $\bar{\beta}$ for testing hypotheses or constructing confidence intervals is inappropriate. For this reason, the use of the method of first differences is not recommended unless it is really believed that ρ is very close to unity.

Small Sample Properties of Alternative Estimators

The small sample properties of the alternative estimators of the regression coefficients in models with autoregressive disturbances are generally unknown, because the determination of the sampling distributions of these estimators is very complicated. Nevertheless, we can get some idea about the small-sample behavior of these estimators by deriving their sampling distributions *experimentally.* This can, of course, be done only for specific models and specific populations of the disturbances. The experimental derivation of sampling distributions for the case of discrete variables was discussed in Section 2-2. In the case of normally distributed disturbances the variables are continuous, but the principle of experimental sampling remains the same. Sampling experiments of this sort have become known as *Monte Carlo experiments* because of their similarity to games of chance.

The results of several extensive Monte Carlo experiments have been reported in the literature.[46] Although there are some discrepancies in the experimental design and in the results, the following consensus seems to be emerging.

1. Unless the value of $|\rho|$ is quite small (say, less than 0.3), the Prais–Winsten or the maximum likelihood estimators perform better than the ordinary least squares estimators.
2. The estimators that omit the first transformed observation are generally inferior to those that do not. (In particular, the Cochrane–Orcutt estimators are generally inferior to the full maximum likelihood estimators.)
3. Iteration frequently helps in improving the performance of the estimators.
4. The tests of significance, even when performed with transformed data, may be unreliable.

These results are helpful in choosing a method of estimation, but less helpful with respect to carrying out statistical tests or setting up confidence intervals.

Prediction with AR(1) Disturbances

Suppose we have a set of sample observations for $t = 1, 2, \ldots, n$ and wish to predict the value of Y for $t = n + 1$ for a given value of X_{n+1}. Let the predicted value of Y be $\hat{Y}_{n+1}$. If the disturbance follows a first-order autoregressive scheme, we can use the transformed regression equation (8.61) and apply the results for the classical model obtained in Section 7-4. The optimal predictor of Y^*_{n+1}, say, $\hat{Y}^*_{n+1}$, will then be

$$\hat{Y}^*_{n+1} = \tilde{\alpha} W^*_{n+1} + \tilde{\beta} X^*_{n+1},$$

where $\tilde{\alpha}$ and $\tilde{\beta}$ are the BLUE of α and β as before. Since for $t \geq 2$ we have $Y^*_t = Y_t - \rho Y_{t-1}$, $W^*_t = 1 - \rho$, and $X^*_t = X_t - \rho X_{t-1}$, and since Y_n is already known and need not be predicted, we can write

$$\hat{Y}_{n+1} - \rho Y_n = \tilde{\alpha}(1 - \rho) + \tilde{\beta}(X_{n+1} - \rho X_n)$$

[46] See, e.g., R. E. Park and B. M. Mitchell, "Estimating the Autocorrelated Error Model with Trended Data," *Journal of Econometrics,* 13 (June 1980), pp. 185–201; J. J. Spitzer, "Small Sample Properties of Nonlinear Least Squares and Maximum Likelihood Estimators in the Context of Autocorrelated Errors," *Journal of the American Statistical Association,* 74 (March 1979), pp. 41–47; or C. M. Beach and J. G. MacKinnon, "A Maximum Likelihood Procedure for Regression with Autocorrelated Errors," *Econometrica,* 46 (January 1978), pp. 51–58.

or

(8.75)
$$\hat{Y}_{n+1} = \tilde{\alpha} + \tilde{\beta}X_{n+1} + \rho(Y_n - \tilde{\alpha} - \tilde{\beta}X_n)$$
$$= \tilde{\alpha} + \tilde{\beta}X_{n+1} + \rho\tilde{e}_n,$$

where $\tilde{e}_n$ is the BLU residual for $t = n$. The last term in the prediction formula (8.75) reflects the fact that since the εs are autoregressive, each disturbance contains some information about the disturbance in the following period. The same applies to the BLUE residuals, which are the best approximations of the εs that we can get.

The prediction error using $\hat{Y}_{n+1}$ is equal to $Y_{n+1} - \hat{Y}_{n+1}$. Its mean is zero, and its variance can be determined from the transformed equation as in the classical model, but allowing for the fact that in (8.62) there is no intercept. In particular,

$$\begin{aligned}\sigma_F^{*2} &= E(Y_{n+1}^* - \hat{Y}_{n+1})^2 \\ &= E[(Y_{n+1} - \rho Y_n) - (\hat{Y}_{n+1} - \rho Y_n)]^2 \\ &= E(Y_{n+1} - \hat{Y}_{n+1})^2 \\ &= \sigma_F^2,\end{aligned}$$

and

(8.76)
$$\sigma_F^2 = \sigma_u^2\left[1 + \frac{(1-\rho)^2(\sum X_t^{*2}) + X_{n+1}^2(\sum W_t^{*2}) - 2(1-\rho)X_{n+1}(\sum W_t^* X_t^*)}{(\sum W_t^{*2})(\sum X_t^{*2}) - (\sum W_t^* X_t^*)^2}\right],$$

where, as before,

$$\begin{aligned}\sum W_t^{*2} &= (1-\rho^2) + (n+1)(1-\rho)^2, \\ \sum X_t^{*2} &= (1-\rho^2)X_1^2 + \sum_{t=2} (X_t - \rho X_{t-1})^2, \\ \sum W_t^* X_t^* &= (1-\rho^2)X_1 + (1-\rho)\sum (X_t - \rho X_{t-1}).\end{aligned}$$

Suppose now that we wish to predict the value of Y for $t = n + 2$. Then from (8.61) we have

$$\hat{Y}_{n+2} = \tilde{\alpha}(1-\rho) + \tilde{\beta}(X_{n+2} - \rho X_{n+1}) + \rho\hat{Y}_{n+1}.$$

Substituting for $\hat{Y}_{n+1}$ from (8.75), we obtain

(8.77)
$$\hat{Y}_{n+2} = \tilde{\alpha} + \tilde{\beta}X_{n+2} + \rho^2(Y_n - \tilde{\alpha} - \tilde{\beta}X_n)$$
$$= \tilde{\alpha} + \tilde{\beta}X_{n+2} + \rho^2\tilde{e}_n.$$

An obvious generalization of (8.77) to the prediction of the value Y for *any* period in the future is

(8.78)
$$\hat{Y}_{n+s} = \tilde{\alpha} + \tilde{\beta}X_{n+s} + \rho^s\tilde{e}_n \qquad (s \geq 1).$$

Thus the further in the future we predict, the less the influence of autoregression will be.

So far we have developed the prediction formulas on the assumption that the value of ρ is known. When, as usual, the value of ρ is not known, it has to be replaced by a consistent estimator. In this case the optimal properties of the predictor (8.78) will hold only asymptotically. The available Monte Carlo evidence indicates that in small samples the predictor (8.78), with ρ replaced by its consistent estimator, will entail a small loss of efficiency compared to the ordinary least squares predictor when ρ is close to zero, but it can produce a substantial gain in efficiency when ρ is not close to zero.

Autoregression in Quarterly Data

Wallis[47] suggested that when observations pertaining to a regression model are made at quarterly intervals, the current disturbance may be correlated with the disturbance of four quarters ago rather than with the disturbance of the immediately preceding quarter. This would be the case if autocorrelation were caused by season-specific disturbances (for instance, an excess purchase of winter clothing this year will not affect the demand for clothing until next winter) or by improper deseasonalization of the observations. In this case the appropriate autoregressive scheme would be

$$\varepsilon_t = \rho_4 \varepsilon_{t-4} + u_t \qquad \text{(for all } t\text{)}, \tag{8.79}$$

where u_t again satisfies all classical assumptions and is independent of ε_{t-4}. To take the effect of the pre-sample disturbances into account, we specify

$$\varepsilon_t = \frac{u_t}{\sqrt{1-\rho_4^2}} \qquad (t = 1, 2, 3, \text{ and } 4). \tag{8.80}$$

The remaining disturbances for $t = 5, 6, \ldots, n$ are generated according to (8.79). Then we have

$$\begin{aligned}
E(\varepsilon_t) &= 0, \\
\text{Var}(\varepsilon_t) &= \frac{\sigma_u^2}{1-\rho_4^2} && \text{(for all } t\text{)} \\
\text{Cov}(\varepsilon_t \varepsilon_{t-s}) &= \sigma^2 \rho_4^{s/4} && \text{(if } s \text{ is a multiple of 4)}, \\
&= 0 && \text{(otherwise)}.
\end{aligned}$$

To replace the fourth-order autoregressive disturbance ε_t by the "classical" disturbance u_t, we use the tranformation

$$Y_t^* = \alpha W_t^* + \beta X_t^* + u_t, \tag{8.81}$$

[47] K. F. Wallis, "Testing for Fourth-Order Autocorrelation in Quarterly Regression Equations," *Econometrica,* 40 (July 1972), pp. 617–636.

where for $t = 1, 2, 3$, and 4,

$$Y_t^* = \sqrt{1-\rho_4^2}Y_t, \qquad W_t^* = \sqrt{1-\rho_4^2} \qquad X_t^* = \sqrt{1-\rho_4^2}X_t,$$

and for $t = 5, 6, \ldots, n$,

$$Y_t^* = Y_t - \rho_4 Y_{t-4}, \qquad W_t^* = (1-\rho_4), \qquad X_t^* = X_t - \rho_4 X_{t-4}.$$

If ρ_4 were known, the parameters in the transformed equation (8.81) could be estimated by the ordinary least squares method. Since ρ_4 is usually unknown, we can estimate α, β, and ρ_4 by the *nonlinear least squares* (NLS) method, which involves minimizing

$$S = \sum (Y_t^* - \alpha W_t^* - \beta X_t^*)^2$$

with respect to α, β, and ρ_4. Alternatively, we can use the full maximum likelihood estimation method, which involves maximizing the log-likelihood function

$$L = \frac{1}{2}\log(1-\rho_4^2)^4 - \frac{n}{2}\log(2\pi\sigma_u^2) - \frac{\sum u_t^2}{2\sigma_u^2},$$

or, equivalently, minimizing

$$S^* = \frac{S}{(1-\rho_4^2)^{4/n}}.$$

In the case of either method we can "search" over different values of ρ_4 in the interval from -1 to $+1$. Both methods are asymptotically equivalent to BLUE.

EXAMPLE We can try Wallis's model using the "quantity relation" of the preceding example and the data presented in Table 8-1. Searching over different values of ρ_4, we find that the NLS estimate of ρ_4 is -0.012 and the ML estimate is -0.010. Thus there is no evidence that the fourth-order autoregressive scheme is appropriate for this model and data.

First-Order Moving Average Disturbances

In certain situations the regression disturbance is more appropriately modeled by what is called a *moving average* process than by an autoregressive process. The simplest form of the moving average process is that of a first-order, abbreviated MA(1). This is represented as

$$\varepsilon_t = u_t + \theta u_{t-1} \qquad \text{(for all } t\text{)}, \tag{8.82}$$

where u_t again satisfies all classical assumptions. The process is characterized by the following moments:

$$E(\varepsilon_t) = 0,$$

$$\text{Var}(\varepsilon_t) = \frac{\sigma_u^2}{1+\theta^2},$$

$$\begin{aligned}\text{Cov}(\varepsilon_t, \varepsilon_{t-s}) &= \theta \qquad &&\text{(for } s = 1\text{)}\\ &= 0 &&\text{(otherwise).}\end{aligned}$$

Since

$$u_t = \varepsilon_t - \theta u_{t-1},$$

by a successive substitution for $u_{t-1}, u_{t-2}, \ldots$, we obtain

(8.83) $$u_t = \sum_{s=0}^{\infty} (-\theta)^s \varepsilon_{t-s}^s.$$

The expression for u_t in (8.83) is called the *autoregressive representation* of u_t corresponding to MA(1). Finally, we note that since the coefficient of correlation between ε_t and ε_{t-1}, say, ρ, is

$$\rho = \frac{\theta}{1+\theta^2},$$

the moving average parameter θ can be expressed as

$$\theta = \frac{1 \pm \sqrt{1-4\rho^2}}{2\rho},$$

so that it is required that $(1 - 4\rho^2) \geq 0$ or, equivalently, that $|\rho| \leq \frac{1}{2}$.

Moving average processes have not often been postulated in econometrics, but they do apply to situations in which the data are aggregated over different periods than those measured (for instance, when the financial and the calendar years do not coincide) or when we deal with models of adaptive expectations (see Section 12-4).[48]

The estimation of the regression coefficients of a model with MA(1) disturbances is based on (8.83), expressed as

(8.83a) $$u_t = \varepsilon_t - \theta\varepsilon_{t-1} + \cdots + (-\theta)^{t-1}\varepsilon_1 + (-\theta)^t u_0.$$

This is used to transform the regression equation so that the moving average disturbance ε_t is replaced by the "classical" disturbance u_t. One approach known as *approximate maximum likelihood estimation* involves the assumption that u_0 equals zero. This leads to the following transformed equation.

(8.84) $$Y_t^* = \alpha W_t^* + \beta X_t^* + u_t \qquad (t = 1, 2, \ldots, n)$$

where

$$Y_t^* = Y_t - \theta Y_{t-1} + \cdots + (-\theta)^{t-1}Y_1,$$

$$W_t^* = 1 - \theta + \cdots + (-\theta)^{t-1},$$

$$X_t^* = X_t - \theta X_{t-1} + \cdots + (-\theta)^{t-1}X_1,$$

or, equivalently,

$$Y_t^* = Y_t - \theta Y_{t-1}^* \qquad (Y_0^* = 0),$$

$$W_t^* = W_t - \theta W_{t-1}^* \qquad (W_0^* = 0),$$

$$X_t^* = X_t - \theta X_{t-1}^* \qquad (X_0^* = 0).$$

[48] For arguments in favor of using MA processes see, e.g., D. F. Nicholls, A. R. Pagan, and R. D. Terrell, "The Estimation and Use of Models with Moving Average Disturbance Terms: A Survey," *International Economic Review*, 16 (February 1975), pp. 113–134.

Maximizing the likelihood function on the assumption that $u_0 = 0$ is equivalent to minimizing

$$S = \sum (Y_t^* - \alpha W_t^* - \beta X_t^*)^2$$

with respect to α, β, and ρ.

A more complicated approach called *full maximum likelihood estimation* does not involve the assumption that $u_0 = 0$. Instead, the transformation is specified in such a way that the effect of the presample disturbances is taken fully into account.[49]

EXAMPLE Formulating the "quantity relation" model as one with MA(1) disturbances and searching over different values of θ leads to an estimate of θ equal to 0.87. The corresponding estimates of α and β are

$$\underset{}{Y_t^*} = \underset{(22.26)}{153.97 W_t^*} + \underset{(0.1285)}{2.2973 X_t^*} + u_t.$$

These estimates are very close to those obtained for the first-order autoregressive model using the iterative method of Prais–Winsten.

A formulation of the disturbance generating process over time that allows for both autoregressive and moving average scheme is known as a *mixed autoregressive moving average* process. When the autoregression is of order p and the moving average of order q, the process is abbreviated ARMA (p, q). Its representation is

$$\varepsilon_t = \rho_t \varepsilon_{t-1} + \rho_2 \varepsilon_{t-2} + \cdots + \rho_p \varepsilon_{t-p} + u_t + \theta_1 u_{t-1} + \theta_2 u_{t-2} + \cdots + \theta q u_{t-q}.$$

This process has not been very popular in econometrics since it is difficult to justify theoretically and to deal with analytically. In practice p and q are typically unspecified and are determined, along with the ρs and θs, by applying the so-called Box–Jenkins method to least squares residuals.[50]

Tests for the Absence of Autocorrelation

Thus far in this section we have been concerned with the implications of the presence of autocorrelated disturbances in a linear regression model. We have examined the properties of the ordinary least squares estimators of the regression coefficients and, having uncovered their shortcomings, we discussed various alternative estimation methods. However, if we do not know—or are not willing to assume—that the regression disturbance is not autocorrelated, we may have to turn to the sample for information. In the context of first-order autoregression, we

[49] See P. Balestra, "A Note on the Exact Transformation Associated with the First-Order Moving Average Process," *Journal of Econometrics,* 14 (December 1980), pp. 381–394.

[50] See, e.g., E. Greenberg and C. E. Webster, Jr., *Advanced Econometrics* (New York: Wiley, 1983), pp. 95–97 and 105–126.

may want to test the hypothesis of no autoregression,

$$H_0: \quad \rho = 0,$$

against a one-sided or a two-sided alternative. The usual alternative hypothesis in economic relations is that of positive autoregression, i.e.,

$$H_A: \quad \rho > 0.$$

The most widely used test of the above hypothesis is known as the *Durbin–Watson test.* To apply this test we calculate the value of a statistic d given by

$$d = \frac{\sum_{t=2}^{n} (e_t - e_{t-1})^2}{\sum_{t=1}^{n} e_t^2},$$

where the e's represent the ordinary least squares residuals. If the alternative hypothesis is that of positive autoregression, the decision rules are

1. Reject if $d < d_L$.
2. Do not reject if $d > d_U$.
3. The test is inconclusive if $d_L \leq d \leq d_U$.

The values of d_L (for "lower limit") and d_U (for "upper limit") are given in the table provided by Durbin and Watson and reproduced in Appendix D. These values vary with the number of observations and the number of explanatory variables in the regression equation. If the alternative hypothesis is a two-sided one, the decision rules for the Durbin–Watson test are

1. Reject if $d < d_L$, or if $d > 4 - d_L$.
2. Do not reject if $d_U < d < 4 - d_U$.
3. The test is inconclusive if $d_L \leq d \leq d_U$, or if $4 - d_U \leq d \leq 4 - d_L$.

Since

$$d = \frac{\sum_{t=2}^{n} e_t^2}{\sum_{t=1}^{n} e_t^2} + \frac{\sum_{t=2}^{n} e_{t-1}^2}{\sum_{t=1}^{n} e_t^2} - 2\frac{\sum_{t=2}^{n} e_t e_{t-1}}{\sum_{t=1}^{n} e_t^2},$$

it follows, by reference to (8.71), that

$$\text{plim } d = 2(1 - \rho).$$

Therefore values of d close to 2 will lead to the acceptance of the null hypothesis, whereas those close to zero (or close to 4) will lead to its rejection. A diagrammatic representation of the test is shown in Figure 8-3. Incidentally, it should be noted that the Durbin–Watson test is not applicable to regression equations in which the place of the explanatory variable is taken by the lagged value of the dependent

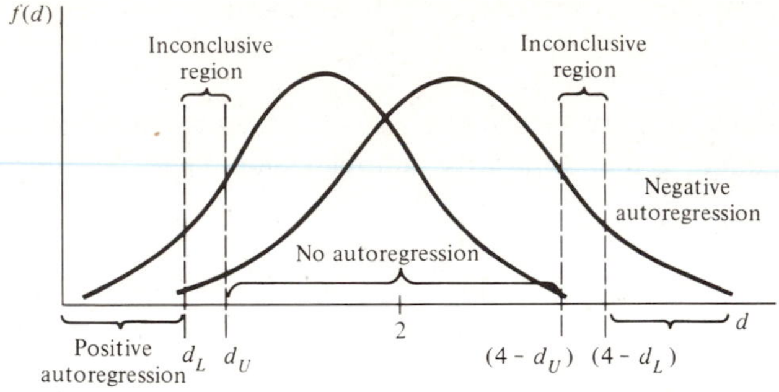

Figure 8-3

variable or in which there is no constant term. (In the latter case one should *include* the constant term before using the test.)

EXAMPLE Consider again estimation of the "quantity theory" equation. Suppose we wish to test the hypothesis

$$H_0: \quad \rho = 0$$

against

$$H_A: \quad \rho > 0$$

at the 5% level of significance, using the Durbin–Watson test. From the table, the appropriate values of d_L and d_U for twenty observations and one explanatory variable are

$$d_L = 1.20 \qquad \text{and} \qquad d_U = 1.41.$$

This means that we will reject H_0 if $d < 1.20$, and not reject H_0 if $d > 1.41$. The calculated value of the d statistic is

$$d = 0.328,$$

so that the hypothesis of no autoregression ($\rho = 0$) has to be rejected.

As mentioned earlier, the Durbin–Watson test has been widely used in econometric applications. In fact, in most studies concerned with estimating regression equations from time-series data, the value of the d statistic is presented along with the other estimates. A troublesome aspect of the test is the inconclusive region. This arises because the exact distribution of d depends on the sample values of the explanatory variable (or variables) and, therefore, changes from application to application. One possibility of dealing with the inconclusive region is to recalculate the relevant part of the distribution for each new set of values of the explanatory variables. A computer program for doing this is now a part of several econometric software packages. Another possibility is to use some kind of an approximation to the distribution of d. Several such approximations have been proposed in the literature.[51] Some authors have advocated that when one is in doubt, one should always reject the null hypothesis.[52] These authors reason that proceeding on the assumption that the disturbances are independent when they are not is considerably more harmful than allowing for autoregression when none exists.

While the Durbin–Watson test is a test of the hypothesis of nonautoregression against the hypothesis of autoregression of the first order, there is some evidence that this test is also reasonably powerful against higher order autoregression and against the MA(1) process.[53] Further, the Durbin–Watson test is reasonably robust with respect to nonnormality or heteroskedasticity of the disturbances, and appears to perform better in small samples than any competing test that has been suggested so far.[54]

In line with the argument that quarterly models may have disturbances characterized by a fourth-order rather than a first-order autoregressive process, Wallis[55] adapted the Durbin–Watson test to the model

$$\varepsilon_t = \rho_4 \varepsilon_{t-4} + u_t .$$

The hypotheses in this case are

$$H_0: \quad \rho_4 = 0$$

$$H_A: \quad \rho_4 > 0.$$

The appropriate test statistic then is

$$d_4 = \frac{\sum_{t=5}^{n} (e_t - e_{t-4})^2}{\sum_{t=1}^{n} e_t^2} .$$

The critical values of d_{4L} and d_{4U} are tabulated in the same way as in the Durbin–

[51] Of the available approximations, perhaps the most successful and straightforward one has been proposed by J. Durbin and G. S. Watson in "Testing for Serial Correlation in Least Squares Regression III," *Biometrika,* 58 (1971), pp. 1–42. For a simplified exposition see G. G. Judge et al., *Introduction to the Theory and Practice of Econometrics* (New York: Wiley, 1982).

[52] See, e.g., R. Bartels and J. Goodhew, "The Robustness of the Durbin–Watson Test," *Review of Economics and Statistics,* 63 (February 1981), pp. 136–139, or A. Nakamura and M. Nakamura, "On the Impact of the Tests for Serial Correlation upon the Test of Significance for the Regression Coefficient," *Journal of Econometrics,* 7 (April 1978), pp. 199–210.

[53] See R. C. Blattberg, "Evaluation of the Power of the Durbin–Watson Statistic for Non-First Order Serial Correlation Alternatives," *Review of Economics and Statistics,* 55 (August 1973), pp. 508–515.

[54] See Bartels and Goodhew, *op. cit.;* T. W. Epps and M. L. Epps, "The Robustness of Some Standard Tests for Autocorrelation and Heteroskedasticity When Both Problems Are Present," *Econometrica,* 45 (April 1977), pp. 745–753; P. Schmidt and D. K. Guilkey, "Some Further Evidence on the Power of the Durbin–Watson and Geary Tests," *Review of Economics and Statistics,* 57 (August 1975), pp. 379–382.

[55] Wallis, *op. cit.*

Watson tables (see Appendix D), and the decision rules are also the same as those for the Durbin–Watson d statistic.

EXAMPLE Referring again to the "quantity theory" equation, we calculate the value of d_4 as 1.694. From the tables of critical values of d_4 we find the value of d_{4U} at the 5% level of significance to be 1.102, and at the 1% level to be 1.428. On the basis of this result the null hypothesis cannot be rejected.

The fact that the Durbin–Watson test is designed to test the hypothesis of no autocorrelation against a specific alternative has spurred efforts to develop a test against a general alternative of any kind of autocorrelation. One such test, which is rather popular in time-series analysis, is the so-called *portmanteau test,* sometimes also referred to as the *Q-test.*[56] The test statistic for this test is

$$Q = n \sum_{k=1}^{m} \hat{r}_k^2,$$

where

$$\hat{r}_k = \frac{\sum_{t=k+1}^{n} e_t e_{t-k}}{\sum_{t=1}^{n} e_t^2},$$

and m is to be chosen as the highest presumed order of autoregression or moving average. Under the null hypothesis of no autocorrelation, the asymptotic distribution of Q is chi-square with m degrees of freedom. A modified version of the test, designed to improve its small sample performance, is based on the test statistic

$$Q^* = n(n+2) \sum_{k=1}^{m} \frac{\hat{r}_k^2}{n-k},$$

whose asymptotic distribution is also chi-square with m degrees of freedom when H_0 is true.

An obvious difficulty with these tests concerns the choice of m, which is rather arbitrary. The temptation to choose a large m in order to capture autocorrelations of higher orders has to be tempered by the resulting loss of power. The test is, therefore, considered as mainly diagnostic and its results are to be regarded with caution.

[56] The original version of the test is presented in G. E. P. Box and D. A. Pierce, "Distribution of Residual Autocorrelations in Autoregressive-Integrated Moving Average Time Series Models," *Journal of the American Statistical Association,* 65 (December 1970), pp. 1509–1526. A modified version of the test appears in G. M. Ljung and G. E. P. Box, "On a Measure of Lack of Fit in Time Series Models," *Biometrika,* 65 (1978), pp. 297–303.

Testing for the Absence of Autoregression in the Presence of a Lagged Dependent Variable

As mentioned earlier, the Durbin–Watson test is not applicable when the explanatory variable—or one of the explanatory variables—is a lagged dependent variable. For this situation Durbin developed two asymptotic (and asymptotically equivalent) tests, the *h test* and the *m test*.[57] These tests can be most easily described in the context of the following regression model:

$$Y_t = \alpha + \beta X_t + \gamma Y_{t-1} + \varepsilon_t \qquad (t = 2, 3, \ldots, n),$$

$$\varepsilon_t = \rho\varepsilon_{t-1} + u_t.$$

The null hypothesis that $\rho = 0$ is to be tested against a one-sided or a two-sided alternative. The h test is based on the test statistic

$$h = \left(1 - \frac{d}{2}\right)\sqrt{\frac{n}{1 - ns_{\hat{\gamma}}^2}},$$

where d is the usual Durbin–Watson test statistic and $s_{\hat{\gamma}}^2$ is the estimated variance of the least squares estimate of γ. Under the null hypothesis h is distributed as $N(0, 1)$. This test cannot be used when $ns_{\hat{\gamma}}^2 > 1$.

The m test, also proposed by Durbin, consists of calculating the least squares residuals and applying the least squares method to

$$e_t = \beta_1 + \beta_2 X_t + \beta_3 Y_{t-1} + \beta_4 e_{t-1} + \text{error}, \tag{8.85}$$

and testing the significance of the estimated coefficient of e_{t-1} by the standard t test. The m test is intuitively plausible and does not suffer from the indeterminacy that may be encountered in using the h test. Its further advantage lies in the fact that the test can easily be extended to involve autoregression of an order higher than one by including further lagged residuals in (8.85). Specifically, if we wish to test the null hypothesis of no autocorrelation against AR(p), we apply the least squares method to

$$e_t = \beta_1 + \beta_2 X_t + \beta_3 Y_{t-1} + \beta_4 e_{t-1} + \beta_5 e_{t-2} + \cdots + \beta_{p+3} e_{t-p} + \text{error} \tag{8.86}$$

and test the hypothesis that $\beta_4 = \beta_5 = \cdots = \beta_{p+3} = 0$ as explained in Section 10-2.

Concerning the small sample properties of these two tests, one Monte Carlo experiment indicated that there is not much difference in their performance, while another experiment appears to favor the m test.[58] All things considered, the m test is to be preferred to the h test.

[57] J. Durbin, "Testing for Serial Correlation in Least-Squares Regression When Some of the Regressors Are Lagged Dependent Variables," *Econometrica,* 38 (May 1970), pp. 410–421.

[58] No substantial difference between the two tests is reported in G. S. Maddala and A. S. Rao, "Tests for Serial Correlation in Regression Models with Lagged Dependent Variables and Serially Correlated Errors," *Econometrica,* 41 (July 1973), pp. 761–774. Evidence in favor of the m test is presented in B. G. Spencer, "The Small Sample Bias of Durbin's Tests for Serial Correlation When One of the Regressors is the Lagged Dependent Variable and the Null Hypothesis is True," *Journal of Econometrics,* 3 (August 1975), pp. 249–254.

EXAMPLE Let us reformulate the "quantity theory" relation as follows.

$$Y_t = \alpha + \beta X_t + \gamma Y_{t-1} + \varepsilon_t \qquad (t = 2, 3, \ldots, n).$$

Using the data of Table 8-1, we obtain the following least squares estimates:

$$\underset{(21.63)}{Y_t = -39.02} + \underset{(0.2764)}{0.5342 X_t} + \underset{(0.1173)}{0.7906 Y_{t-1}} + e_t$$

and $h = 1.225$. Since the critical value of the standard normal variable for a positive alternative at the 5% level is 1.645, the null hypothesis cannot be rejected on the basis of this test. As for the m test, the least squares estimates of (8.85) are

$$e_t = \underset{(24.13)}{-17.52} + \underset{(0.3010)}{0.2100 X_t} - \underset{(0.1249)}{0.0786 Y_{t-1}} + \underset{(0.2783)}{0.4280 e_{t-1}} + \text{error}.$$

Since $0.4280/0.2783 = 1.538$ and the critical value of t_{15} at the 5% level is 1.753, the null hypothesis cannot be rejected by this test either. All results are presented on the assumption that small sample values are reasonable approximations of asymptotic values.

After carrying out a test for the absence of autocorrelation, we have to decide what action, if any, is to be taken in response to a particular outcome of the test. If no autoregression is indicated, we can retain the least squares estimates without fearing a loss of efficiency and a bias of the estimated standard errors. However, if the test indicates autoregression, then we have some reason to be concerned. One response is to re-estimate the equation, using one of the estimation methods designed for this situation (e.g., maximum likelihood). This response would involve a transformation of the regression equation so that the autocorrelated disturbances ε_t are replaced by the "classical" disturbances u_t. The transformed regression equation involves new variables X_{t-1} and Y_{t-1}. The question then arises whether the problem is one of autocorrelation or one of incorrect specification of the regression equation in the first place. A possible way of checking this would be by testing the restrictions of the coefficients of the transformed equation implied by the transformation. (Tests of this kind will be discussed in Section 11-2.) This point should be kept in mind since a test for the absence of autocorrelation may also be interpreted as a test for the exclusion of X_{t-1} and Y_{t-1} from the regression equation.

8-4 Stochastic Explanatory Variable

Assumption (7.6) of the classical normal linear regression model consists of

1. X is nonstochastic.
2. Values of X are fixed in repeated samples.
3. $(1/n) \Sigma_i (X_i - \bar{X})^2$ is equal to a finite, nonzero number for any sample size.

In this section we shall be concerned mainly with 1; 2 and 3 deserve only a brief mention. To start with, the requirement that the values of X are fixed in repeated samples is only of theoretical interest since, in reality, we rarely draw or observe more than one sample for a given set of values of X. The purpose of this requirement is to set the framework for the sampling distributions of the various estimators that we discuss. It really amounts to saying that *if* we drew an infinite number of samples of one size (i.e., an infinite number of sets of values of $Y_1, Y_2, \ldots, Y_n$) for a fixed set of values of X (i.e., *one* set of values of $X_1, X_2, \ldots, X_n$), then the sampling distributions and properties of the estimators would be as we asserted. Thus we avoid the complications that would arise if the values of X were to change from sample to sample. Note that the values of X can be considered to be held fixed from sample to sample even if X is a stochastic variable (as long as holding X fixed does not make Y fixed as well).

By the assumption that for any sample size $\Sigma_i(X_i - \bar{X})^2/n$ is a finite number different from zero, it is required that the values of X in the sample are not all the same, and that they do not grow or decline without limit. The first requirement—that not all values of X are the same—is crucial, since otherwise the determination of the least squares regression coefficients would become impossible, as pointed out in Section 7-4. If the values of X are not all the same but the differences between them are very small, $\Sigma(X_i - \bar{X})^2$ will be small, and the variances of the estimators are likely to be very large. This, in turn, implies that in the tests of significance the probability of Error Type II (accepting H_0 when it is false) is high, and that the confidence intervals for the population parameters are wide. As to the second requirement, the restriction that $\Sigma(X_i - \bar{X})/n$ be a finite number for any n is less crucial. It is utilized mainly in proving the desirable asymptotic properties of the least squares estimators.

The foregoing discussion leaves only the requirement of a nonstochastic explanatory variable to be considered. Let us now deal with the problem of estimating the coefficients of a regression equation when this is violated, i.e., when X is a stochastic variable. In this case the values of X are not fixed; instead, different values of X—or intervals of values of X—occur with certain probabilities. Regressions with stochastic explanatory variables are common, if not predominant, in econometrics. In many economic relations the values of the explanatory variable are determined, along with those of the dependent variable, as a result of some probability mechanism rather than being controlled by the experimenter or other persons or institutions. If X is stochastic, the important thing is whether it is or is not independent of the disturbance ε, and if dependent, what is the nature of the dependence. We shall distinguish among three possibilities.

1. X and ε are independent.
2. X and ε are contemporaneously uncorrelated.
3. X and ε are *not* independent *or* contemporaneously uncorrelated.

In each case we shall be concerned with the properties of the least squares estimators of the regression coefficients, given that all the basic assumptions about the disturbance term hold. We shall also make the assumption that the variance of X is a finite number different from zero.

Let us start with the case where X and ε are *independent*. As an example, consider the relationship

$$Y_i = \alpha + \beta X_i + \varepsilon_i,$$

with X_i and Y_i defined as

$$Y_i = \log\left(\frac{V}{PL}\right)_i \quad \text{and} \quad X_i = \log\left(\frac{W}{P}\right)_i,$$

where V = value added in production, L = labor input, P = price of product, W = money wage rate, and subscript i refers to the ith region. The observations are made for a particular industry and a given period of time. The coefficient β represents the elasticity of substitution between labor and capital.[59] Here X is a stochastic variable that can be assumed to be independent of ε. The least squares estimator of β is

$$\hat{\beta} = \beta + \frac{\sum x_i'\varepsilon_i}{\sum x_i'^2}$$

and

$$E(\hat{\beta}) = \beta + \sum_i E\left(\frac{x_i'}{\sum_j x_j'^2}\right) E(\varepsilon_i) = \beta.$$

This result follows from the assumption that X and ε are independent (i.e., that X_i and ε_j are independent for all i and j), and from the assumption that $E(\varepsilon_i) = 0$. Similarly,

$$\begin{aligned} E(\hat{\alpha}) &= E(\bar{Y} - \hat{\beta}\bar{X}) = E(\alpha + \beta\bar{X} + \bar{\varepsilon} - \hat{\beta}\bar{X}) \\ &= \alpha + \beta E(\bar{X}) + E(\bar{\varepsilon}) - E\left(\beta + \frac{\sum x_i'\varepsilon_i}{\sum x_i'^2}\right)\bar{X} = \alpha, \end{aligned}$$

so that $\hat{\alpha}$ and $\hat{\beta}$ retain their property of unbiasedness.

Since X is a stochastic variable, $\hat{\alpha}$ and $\hat{\beta}$ are no longer linear functions of $Y_1, Y_2, \ldots, Y_n$; that is, they can no longer be described as equal to $\Sigma_i a_i Y_i$ where $a_1, a_2, \ldots, a_n$ are *constants*. Therefore, in the strictest sense, $\hat{\alpha}$ and $\hat{\beta}$ cannot be considered as best-*linear*-unbiased estimators. However, it is not difficult to see that $\hat{\alpha}$ and $\hat{\beta}$ are efficient if we consider their variances as being conditional on a given set of values of $X_1, X_2, \ldots, X_n$. We may think of the population of all pairs of values of X and Y as an enormous card file with each card representing a specific pair. Then we can specify one set of values of $X_1, X_2, \ldots, X_n$ and have the sorting machine pull out all the cards with these values of X. This subset of cards represents a population from which samples can be drawn. Each such sample can be used to estimate the regression coefficients. If we drew an infinite number of these samples, we could construct sampling distributions for these estimators and determine their properties. Obviously, the properties of the estimators determined in this way would be conditional on the chosen values $X_1, X_2, \ldots, X_n$. This means that these values can be treated *as if* they were fixed numbers, which in fact they are *after* we

[59] See K. J. Arrow et al., "Capital-Labor Substitution and Economic Efficiency," *Review of Economics and Statistics,* 43 (August 1961), p. 238, eq. (8a).

pull out all the appropriate cards from the original file. Now we know that for a fixed set of values $X_1, X_2, \ldots, X_n$, the least squares estimators of the regression coefficients are efficient. We also know that this is true for *any* fixed set of values of X. Therefore, since the least squares estimators of the regression coefficients are unconditionally unbiased, and since for *each* set of values of $X_1, X_2, \ldots, X_n$ they are efficient, it follows that they are *efficient* unconditionally, too. The distribution of the least squares estimators of the regression coefficients will be conditionally normal, but unconditionally this distribution will depend on the distribution of X. However, since the probability statements made in connection with testing hypotheses or constructing confidence intervals are valid for *any* fixed set of values of X, they are valid unconditionally as well as conditionally.[60]

With respect to the asymptotic properties, we can show, using the maximum likelihood principle, that the least squares estimators retain all their desirable properties when X is stochastic but independent of ε. Given the joint density function of the sample observations

$$f(x_1, x_2, \ldots, x_n, \varepsilon_1, \varepsilon_2, \ldots, \varepsilon_n),$$

the log-likelihood function becomes

$$\begin{aligned} L &= \log f(x_1, x_2, \ldots, x_n) + \log f(\varepsilon_1, \varepsilon_2, \ldots, \varepsilon_n) \\ &= \log f(x_1, x_2, \ldots, x_n) - \frac{n}{2}\log(2\pi\sigma^2) - \frac{1}{2\sigma^2}\sum (Y_i - \alpha - \beta X_i)^2. \end{aligned}$$

As long as the distribution of X does not involve any of the parameters α, β, or σ^2, maximizing the likelihood function with respect to these parameters will not be affected by the presence of the first term. The resulting estimators of α and β will then be the same as the least squares estimators. Thus, the least squares estimators of the regression coefficients are consistent, asymptotically efficient, and asymptotically normal whether X is nonstochastic or stochastic, provided X and ε are independent and the remaining basic assumptions concerning ε hold. (If the assumption of normality of the regression disturbances is dropped, the least squares estimators of the regression coefficients will still be *asymptotically* normal, as shown in Appendix C.)

As a final point, consider the variances of the least squares estimators of α and β. For $\hat{\beta}$ we have

$$\operatorname{Var}(\hat{\beta}) = E\left(\frac{\sum x_i'\varepsilon_i}{\sum x_i'^2}\right)^2 = E\left[\frac{\sum x_i'^2\varepsilon_i^2}{(\sum x_i'^2)^2}\right]$$

$$+ 2E\left[\frac{\sum_{i<j} x_i'x_j'\varepsilon_i\varepsilon_j}{(\sum x_i'^2)^2}\right] = \sigma^2 E\left(\frac{1}{\sum x_i'^2}\right).$$

[60] See J. Johnston, *Econometric Methods,* 3rd ed. (New York: McGraw-Hill, 1984), pp. 281–285, or T. B. Fomby, R. C. Hill, and S. R. Johnson, *Advanced Econometric Methods* (New York: Springer Verlag, 1984), p. 76.

Similarly, we can show that

$$\text{Var}(\hat{\alpha}) = \sigma^2 E\left(\frac{1}{n} + \frac{\overline{X}^2}{\sum x_i'^2}\right).$$

That is, the variances of $\hat{\alpha}$ and $\hat{\beta}$ are the same as when X is nonstochastic, *except* that the terms involving X are replaced by their mathematical expectations. The formulas for unbiased estimators of $\text{Var}(\hat{\alpha})$ and $\text{Var}(\hat{\beta})$ are given by (7.37). Also, the classical procedures for interval estimation and hypothesis testing developed in Chapter 7 remain valid when X is stochastic but independent of ε. Thus, *relaxing the assumption that X is nonstochastic and replacing it by the assumption that X is stochastic but independent of* ε *does not change the desirable properties and feasibility of least squares estimation.*

Now we come to the second possibility concerning the explanatory variable, namely, the case where X and ε are *contemporaneously uncorrelated.* That is, we assume that

$$\text{Cov}(X_1, \varepsilon_1) = \text{Cov}(X_2, \varepsilon_2) = \cdots = \text{Cov}(X_n, \varepsilon_n) = 0.$$

Note that we do not assume that X and ε are contemporaneously independent, which would be a stronger requirement. As an example, consider the following highly simplified model of income determination.

$$C_t = \gamma_0 + \gamma_1 Y_t + \varepsilon_{1t} \qquad \text{(consumption function)},$$

$$I_t = \delta_0 + \delta_1 Y_{t-1} + \varepsilon_{2t} \qquad \text{(invest nent function)},$$

$$Y_t = C_t + I_t \qquad \text{(income identity)},$$

where C = consumption, Y = income, I = investment, and ε_{1t} and ε_{2t} are random disturbances that satisfy the basic assumptions. The three-equation model can be reduced to one equation by solving for Y_t to get

$$Y_t = (\gamma_0 + \gamma_1 Y_t + \varepsilon_{1t}) + (\delta_0 + \delta_1 Y_{t-1} + \varepsilon_{2t}).$$

This can be written as

$$Y_t = \alpha + \beta Y_{t-1} + \varepsilon_t, \tag{8.87}$$

where $\alpha = \dfrac{\gamma_0 + \delta_0}{1 - \gamma_1}$, $\beta = \dfrac{\delta_1}{1 - \gamma_1}$, and $\varepsilon_t = \dfrac{\varepsilon_{1t} + \varepsilon_{2t}}{1 - \gamma_1}$.

In (8.87) the explanatory variable is represented by the lagged value of the dependent variable. A model of this kind is generally known as a "model autoregressive in variables." In our case, we shall confine it to the situations where $-1 < \beta < 1$. By carrying out successive substitutions we can express Y_t as

$$Y_t = \alpha(1 + \beta + \beta^2 + \cdots + \beta^{t-1}) + \beta^t Y_0$$
$$+ \varepsilon_t + \beta\varepsilon_{t-1} + \beta^2\varepsilon_{t-2} + \cdots + \beta^{t-1}\varepsilon_1.$$

As $t \rightarrow \infty$, Y_t becomes

$$Y_t = \frac{\alpha}{1-\beta} + \varepsilon_t + \beta\varepsilon_{t-1} + \beta^2\varepsilon_{t-2} + \cdots;$$

that is, in the long run Y_t "settles down" to random fluctuations around a fixed level. Note that in (8.87) the explanatory variable Y_{t-1} is *not* correlated with the current disturbance ε_t since Y_{t-1} depends on $Y_0, \varepsilon_1, \varepsilon_2, \ldots, \varepsilon_{t-1}$ but not on ε_t.

Consider now the least squares estimator of β in (8.87). We have

$$\hat{\beta} = \beta + \frac{\sum y'_{t-1}\varepsilon_t}{\sum y'^2_{t-1}}.$$

Now y'_{t-1} and ε_t are not independent since

$$y'_{t-1} = Y_{t-1} - \frac{1}{n}(Y_0 + Y_1 + \cdots + Y_t + \cdots + Y_{n-1});$$

that is, y'_{t-1} involves Y_t, which is *not* independent of ε_t. Further, ε_t is also not independent of $\Sigma y'^2_{t-1}$ in the denominator. This means that we cannot separate out ε_t when taking mathematical expectation of $\hat{\beta}$ as we could in case of independence. Thus $\hat{\beta}$ cannot be said to be unbiased. However, the probability limit of $\hat{\beta}$ is

$$\text{plim } \hat{\beta} = \beta + \frac{\text{plim } (\sum y'_{t-1}\varepsilon_t/n)}{\text{plim } (\sum y'^2_{t-1}/n)} = \beta,$$

since $(\Sigma y'_{t-1}\varepsilon_t)/n$ is a consistent estimator of the population covariance of Y_{t-1} and ε_t, which is zero, and $(\Sigma y'^2_{t-1})/n$ is a consistent estimator of the variance of Y_{t-1}, which is a finite number different from zero. Thus $\hat{\beta}$ is a consistent estimator of β. Similarly, $\hat{\alpha}$ can be shown to be a consistent estimator of α. Asymptotic efficiency and asymptotic normality of the least squares estimators of α and β are more difficult to prove, but they also have been established.[61] The conclusion then is that *when the explanatory variable and the disturbance are contemporaneously uncorrelated (as in the model which is autoregressive in variables), the classical results of least squares estimation established in Chapter 7 hold only asymptotically.*

The last possibility concerning the explanatory variable is the case where X and ε are *neither independent nor contemporaneously uncorrelated.* In this case,

$$\text{plim } \hat{\beta} = \beta + \frac{\text{plim } (\sum x'_t\varepsilon_t/n)}{\text{plim } (\sum x'^2_t/n)} \neq \beta$$

[61] For details see E. Malinvaud, *Statistical Methods of Econometrics,* 3rd ed. (Amsterdam: North-Holland, 1980), pp. 535–539. Asymptotic normality of the least squares estimators of the regression coefficients *without* the assumption of normality of the disturbances is derived in Appendix C.

and $$\text{plim}\ \hat{\alpha} \neq \alpha,$$

so that the least squares estimators of the regression coefficients are not even consistent. An intuitive explanation for this is that the least squares estimation method is designed in such a way that the total variation of Y (SST) can always be divided into two parts, one representing the variation due to the explanatory variable (SSR) and the other representing the variation due to other factors. But when the explanatory variable and the disturbance are correlated, such a division is not valid since it does not allow for the *joint* effect of X and ε on Y.

EXAMPLE As an example of a situation in which the explanatory variable and the disturbance are contemporaneously correlated, consider a market demand equation given by

$$Q_t = \alpha + \beta P_t + \varepsilon_t \qquad (\alpha > 0, \beta < 0),$$

where Q = quantity and P = price of a given commodity. If the market is in a competitive equilibrium, the quantity of the commodity sold in the market and the equilibrium price are determined by the intersection of the demand and the supply functions. Suppose the supply function is

$$Q_t = \gamma + \delta P_t + \eta_t \qquad (\gamma > \alpha, \delta > 0),$$

where $\eta_t \sim N(0, \sigma_\eta^2)$ is a stochastic disturbance which is nonautoregressive and independent of ε_t. The demand and the supply equations can be solved for the equilibrium quantity and price to give

$$Q_t = \frac{\alpha\delta - \beta\gamma}{\delta - \beta} + \frac{\delta\varepsilon_t - \beta\eta_t}{\delta - \beta},$$

$$P_t = \frac{\alpha - \gamma}{\delta - \beta} + \frac{\varepsilon_t - \eta_t}{\delta - \beta}.$$

From the last result we can see that P_t and ε_t are correlated; in particular,

$$\text{Cov}(P_t, \varepsilon_t) = E[P_t - E(P_t)][\varepsilon_t - E(\varepsilon_t)] = E\left(\frac{\varepsilon_t - \eta_t}{\delta - \beta}\right)\varepsilon_t = \frac{\sigma^2}{\delta - \beta}.$$

To show that the least squares estimator of the slope of the demand equation is inconsistent, note that

$$\hat{\beta} = \beta + \frac{\sum p_t'\varepsilon_t'}{\sum p_t'^2},$$

where $$p_t' = P_t - \bar{P} = \frac{\varepsilon_t' - \eta_t'}{\delta - \beta}.$$

Substitution for p_t' into $\hat{\beta}$ gives

$$\hat{\beta} = \beta + \frac{[1/(\delta - \beta)] \sum \varepsilon_t'(\varepsilon_t' - \eta_t')}{[1/(\delta - \beta)]^2 \sum (\varepsilon_t' - \eta_t')^2}$$

$$= \beta + \frac{(\delta - \beta)[(1/n) \sum \varepsilon_t'^2 - (1/n) \sum \varepsilon_t'\eta_t']}{(1/n) \sum \varepsilon_t'^2 + (1/n) \sum \eta_t'^2 - (2/n) \sum \varepsilon_t'\eta_t'}.$$

Therefore,

$$\operatorname{plim} \hat{\beta} = \beta + \frac{\operatorname{Cov}(P_t, \varepsilon_t)}{\operatorname{Var}(P_t)}$$

$$= \beta + \frac{(\delta - \beta)\sigma^2}{\sigma^2 + \sigma_\eta^2},$$

which proves that the least squares estimator of β is inconsistent. This example illustrates the so-called "simultaneous equation problem" that occurs when estimating certain economic relationships.

Regression equations in which the explanatory variable and the disturbance are correlated are rather common in econometrics, most notoriously in the area of simultaneous equation models as illustrated by the preceding example. However, the problem arises also in connection with some single equation models, such as the "distributed lag" model or the "errors-in-variables" model, which will be discussed in the following chapters. In each case the breakdown of the least squares estimation method has led to development of alternative methods of estimation that provide us with consistent estimates. These methods will be discussed in connection with the models for which they were developed or to which they were found to be applicable.

EXERCISES

8-1. A random sample of observations on income and saving of households obtained from a sample survey conducted in 1963 and 1964 is reproduced in Table 8-2. Let us assume that

$$Y_i = \alpha + \beta X_i + \varepsilon_i$$

where Y = household annual saving (in dollars), and X = household annual income (in dollars).

a. Obtain MAD estimates of α and β and compare them with the respective least squares estimates.

b. Carry out a test of the hypothesis that the regression disturbance is normally distributed.

8-2. Consider a simple regression model for which all of the basic assumptions are satisfied except that $E(\varepsilon_i) = \gamma Z_i$, where Z_i is nonstochastic and such that $\Sigma(X_i - \bar{X})(Z_i - \bar{Z}) = 0$. Determine the bias (if any) in estimating the intercept α by the method of least squares.

8-3. Consider the model

$$Y_i = \alpha + \varepsilon_i,$$

where $\varepsilon_i \sim N(0, \sigma^2 X_i)$, $E(\varepsilon_i \varepsilon_j) = 0$ $(i \neq j)$, and X is nonstochastic. Find the best linear unbiased estimator of α and its variance.

Table 8-2

Household no.	Income	Saving
1	1,920	30
2	12,403	874
3	6,396	370
4	7,005	1,200
5	6,990	275
6	6,500	1,400
7	26,007	31,599
8	15,343	1,766
9	14,999	3,984
10	9,185	1,017
11	10,600	1,004
12	12,089	687
13	6,254	−34
14	9,010	−1,389
15	6,217	1,000
16	5,912	1,831
17	4,800	613
18	2,340	50
19	7,832	13
20	9,543	1,389

Source: T. W. Mirer, *Economic Statistics and Econometrics* (New York: Macmillan, 1983), pp. 15–22.

8-4. Using the data in Table 8-3 on income (X) and expenditure (Y) of a sample of households, estimate the regression equation

$$Y_i = \alpha + \beta X_i + \varepsilon_i$$

for the following heteroskedastic models.

a. $\text{Var}(\varepsilon_i) = \sigma^2 X_i^2$. **b.** $\text{Var}(\varepsilon_i) = \sigma^2[E(Y_i)]^2$. **c.** $\text{Var}(\varepsilon_i) = \sigma_i^2$.

Table 8-3

	Y										
X	14	19	21	23	25	27	29	31	33	35	Total
18	74	13	7	1							95
23	6	4	2	7	4						23
25	2	3	2	2	4						13
27	1	1	2	3	3	2					12
29	2		1	3	2		6				14
31	2		2	1			1	2	1		9
33				2			1	1	3		7
35		1		1					2		4
37					1	1		1		1	4

8-5. Using the regression equation of Exercise 8-4 and the data presented in Table 8-3, and assuming that σ_i^2 depends on X_i, carry out the following tests for homoskedasticity.

a. The Goldfeld–Quandt test.

b. The Breusch–Pagan test.

c. The White test.

d. The Bartlett test.

8-6. Consider the model

$$Y_i = \beta X_i + \varepsilon_i$$

for which all of the basic assumptions hold except that

$$\text{Var}(\varepsilon_i) = \sigma^2 X_i^2 \qquad (X_i > 0).$$

Derive the best linear unbiased estimator of β and its variance, given a sample of n observations.

8-7. Let

$$Y_t = \alpha + \varepsilon_t$$

and

$$\varepsilon_t = \rho\varepsilon_{t-1} + u_t \qquad (0 \le \rho^2 < 1),$$

where the u's are normally and independently distributed with mean zero, and u_t and ε_{t-1} are independent. The value of ρ is *known*. Describe the best estimation procedure for α that you can devise and state the desirable properties of your estimator, given that

a. $\text{Var}(\varepsilon_t) = \sigma^2$.

b. $\text{Var}(\varepsilon_t) = \sigma^2 X_t^2$, where X_t is positive, nonstochastic, and measurable.

8-8. Let

$$Y_t = \alpha + \varepsilon_t$$

and

$$\varepsilon_t = \rho\varepsilon_{t-1} + u_t \qquad (0 \le \rho^2 < 1),$$

where the u's are normally and independently distributed with mean zero and a constant variance, and u_t and ε_{t-1} are independent. The value of ρ is *not known*. Given the observations $Y_1 = 1$, $Y_2 = 4$, $Y_3 = 6$, $Y_4 = 5$, and $Y_5 = 9$, obtain the best estimate of α that you can get. State all the desirable properties of the estimator used.

8-9. Consider the model

$$Y_t = \beta X_t + \varepsilon_t$$

for which all of the basic assumptions are satisfied except that

$$\varepsilon_t = \rho\varepsilon_{t-1} + u_t \qquad (0 \le \rho^2 < 1),$$

with u_t and ε_{t-1} mutually independent. Derive the best linear unbiased estimator of β and its variance.

8-10. A model for estimating the elasticity of substitution between labor and capital has been proposed as follows.

$$Y_t = \alpha + \beta X_t + \varepsilon_t,$$

where Y = log production per worker and X = log wage rate. Data for U.S. manufacturing for

1947–1982 are presented in Table 8-4. Assume that Y_t can be measured by $\log(P_t/L_t)$ and that X_t can be measured by $\log W_t$.

Table 8-4

Year	Mfg. production index: P_t	Thousands of workers in mfg.: L_t	Average weekly earnings: W_t
1947	39.4	15,545	\$ 49.13
1948	40.9	15,582	53.08
1949	38.7	14,441	53.80
1950	45.0	15,241	58.28
1951	48.6	16,393	63.34
1952	50.6	16,632	66.75
1953	55.2	17,549	70.47
1954	51.5	16,314	70.49
1955	58.2	16,882	75.30
1956	60.5	17,243	78.78
1957	61.2	17,174	81.19
1958	57.0	15,945	82.32
1959	64.2	16,675	88.26
1960	65.4	16,796	89.72
1961	65.6	16,326	92.34
1962	71.5	16,853	96.56
1963	75.8	16,995	99.23
1964	81.0	17,274	102.97
1965	89.7	18,062	107.53
1966	97.9	19,214	112.19
1967	100.0	19,447	114.49
1968	106.4	19,781	122.51
1969	111.0	20,167	129.51
1970	106.4	19,367	133.33
1971	108.2	18,623	142.44
1972	118.9	19,151	154.71
1973	129.8	20,154	166.46
1974	129.4	20,077	176.80
1975	116.3	18,323	190.79
1976	130.3	18,997	209.32
1977	138.4	19,682	228.90
1978	146.8	20,505	249.27
1979	153.6	21,040	269.34
1980	146.7	20,285	288.62
1981	150.4	20,173	318.00
1982	137.6	18,849	330.65

Source: *Economic Report of the President,* February 1983, Tables B-37, B-39, and B-42.

a. Obtain least squares estimates of α and β and their estimated standard errors.

b. Test for the absence of autocorrelation using the Durbin–Watson test.

c. Test for the absence of autocorrelation using the portmanteau Q test.

8-11. Consider the model specified in Exercise 8-7a above. Show that for this model the ordinary least squares estimator of α is asymptotically efficient.

8-12. Show that the variance of the prediction error $Y^*_{n+1} - \hat{Y}^*_{n+1}$ for the model

$$Y^*_t = \alpha W^*_t + \beta X^*_t + u_t$$

is

$$\sigma_F^{*2} = \sigma_u^2\left[1 + \frac{1}{\Delta}(W^{*2}_{n+1} \sum X^{*2}_t + X^{*2}_{n+1} \sum W^{*2}_t - 2W^*_{n+1}X^*_{n+1} \sum W^*_t X^*_t)\right],$$

where

$$\Delta = \sum W^{*2}_t \sum X^{*2}_t - (\sum W^*_t X^*_t)^2.$$

Note that since $W^*_{n+1} = (1-\rho)$, this result yields equation (8.76) in the text.

8-13. Consider the model

$$Y_i = \beta X_i + \varepsilon_i,$$

where X_i is stochastic but independent of ε_i, and ε_i satisfies all basic assumptions. Suppose that a researcher mistakenly applies the least squares method to

$$X_i = \delta Y_i + u_i$$

and then uses $1/\hat{\delta}$ as an estimator of β. Check the consistency of this estimator.

8-14. A market for an agricultural commodity is frequently described by the relations

$$P_t = \alpha + \beta Q_t + u_t \qquad \text{(demand)},$$

$$Q_t = \gamma + \delta P_{t-1} + v_t \qquad \text{(supply)},$$

where P = price, Q = quantity, and u and v are stochastic disturbances. It is assumed that each of the disturbances satisfies the basic assumptions, and that the two disturbances are mutually independent. Check the consistency of the least squares estimator of β.

9 Estimation with Deficient Data

In Chapter 8 we dealt with the problem of estimating the coefficients of a linear regression equation when one of the basic assumptions of the classical normal linear regression model does not hold. The discussion in the present chapter deals with the estimation problem in situations where the sample data are in some respect deficient. The particular deficiencies that we discuss are

1. Errors of measurement.
2. Grouped data.
3. Missing observations.

These deficiencies, which are likely to be encountered in empirical work, give rise to estimation problems that deserve our special attention.

9-1 Errors of Measurement

Up to this point, we have always taken for granted that the values of the variables in the regression model are measured without error. This presumption has been implicit in our entire discussion, and all of our formulas are based on it. Here we are investigating what happens to the estimators of the regression coefficients when this is not true and what can be done to cope with such a situation. In doing so, we restrict ourselves to cases in which the errors of measurement can be assumed to be random and to have specific probability characteristics. This fairly standard way of treating errors of measurement in the statistical and econometric literature corresponds to a wide variety of situations encountered in real life. Further, our discussion is confined to errors of measurement caused by imperfection of the measuring techniques. With improved techniques the errors of measurement could, at least in principle, be eliminated. The problem of dealing with variables that are intrinsically unobservable (e.g., "intelligence" or "permanent income") and that are represented in practice by "proxy" variables or "indicators" is treated in Section 11-8.

Let us start by considering the problem of errors of measurement in the context of the classical normal linear regression model of Chapter 7. As in (7.1), the regression equation is

$$Y_i = \alpha + \beta X_i + \varepsilon_i .$$

We also retain all the basic assumptions (7.2) through (7.6). The assumption (7.6) stating that X is *nonstochastic* is particularly relevant. In the context of measurement errors, a regression model characterized by this assumption is known in the statistical literature as a *functional form* model.

Suppose now that our observations on Y and X contain errors, so that instead of Y_i and X_i we observe Y_i^* and X_i^*, which are given as

$$Y_i^* = Y_i + v_i,$$

$$X_i^* = X_i + w_i,$$

where v_i and w_i represent the errors in measuring the ith value of Y and of X. The behavioral characteristics of the errors are assumed to be

$$(9.1) \qquad v_i \sim N(0, \sigma_v^2),$$

$$w_i \sim N(0, \sigma_w^2);$$

$$(9.2) \qquad E(v_i v_j) = 0 \qquad (i \neq j),$$

$$E(w_i w_j) = 0 \qquad (i \neq j);$$

$$(9.3) \qquad E(v_i w_i) = 0,$$

$$E(v_i \varepsilon_i) = 0,$$

$$E(w_i \varepsilon_i) = 0.$$

Assumption (9.1) states that each error is a random normal variable with zero mean and a constant variance. Assumption (9.2) rules out situations in which the errors are autocorrelated; together with (9.1), this assumption implies that errors made at one point of observation are independent of errors made at other points of observation. Assumption (9.3) states how the errors are related—or, rather, unrelated—to each other. Assumptions (9.1) through (9.3) and the basic assumptions about the disturbance ε jointly imply that the errors of measurement are independent of each other and of the disturbance in the regression equation.

Let us now consider the problem of estimating the regression coefficients from data on Y^* and X^*. Since

$$Y_i = Y_i^* - v_i$$

and

$$X_i = X_i^* - w_i,$$

the regression equation can be rewritten as

$$(Y_i^* - v_i) = \alpha + \beta(X_i^* - w_i) + \varepsilon_i$$

or

$$Y_i^* = \alpha + \beta X_i^* + \varepsilon_i^*,$$

where

$$\varepsilon_i^* = \varepsilon_i + v_i - \beta w_i.$$

At this stage we note that the error in measuring the dependent variable plays quite a different role from the error in measuring the explanatory variable. This can be seen as follows. If we substitute $(Y^* - v)$ for Y in the regression equation (7.1), we obtain

$$Y_i^* = \alpha + \beta X_i + \varepsilon_i + v_i.$$

Now clearly ε and v can be merged into one "generalized" disturbance $(\varepsilon + v)$, which, under the stated assumptions, behaves in exactly the same way as the simple disturbance ε itself. In particular the regression with the "generalized" disturbance replacing the simple disturbance satisfies all of the basic assumptions and thus could be treated in exactly the same way as the classical model of Chapter 7, provided the values of X were correctly measured. About the only difference between ε and $(\varepsilon + v)$ is that since the methods of measuring economic variables have been improving over the last several decades, the variance of v—and therefore the variance of $(\varepsilon + v)$—may have been diminishing over time. Thus in models based on time-series observations the presence of measurement errors in the dependent variable may cause heteroskedasticity. In the following analysis we shall not consider the possibility of this complication, and we shall ignore the measurement errors in the dependent variable since they are otherwise inconsequential. Our subsequent discussion will, therefore, proceed *as if*

$$v_i = 0 \qquad (\text{for all } i = 1, 2, \ldots, n)$$

in order to simplify the notation.

The situation concerning errors in measuring the explanatory variable is quite different. After substituting $(X^* - w)$ for X in the regression equation (7.1), we obtain

$$(9.4) \qquad \begin{aligned} Y_i^* &= \alpha + \beta(X_i^* - w_i) + \varepsilon_i \\ &= \alpha + \beta X_i^* + \varepsilon_i^*, \end{aligned}$$

where

$$\varepsilon_i^* = \varepsilon_i - \beta w_i \qquad \text{and} \qquad Y_i^* = Y_i.$$

When the regression model is written in the form (9.4) where the dependent and the explanatory variables are observable, the explanatory variable X^* is now stochastic and correlated with the new disturbance term ε^*. The correlation of X^* and ε^* follows from the fact that

$$\begin{aligned} \text{Cov}(X_i^* \varepsilon_i^*) &= E[X_i^* - E(X_i^*)][\varepsilon_i^* - E(\varepsilon_i^*)] = E[w_i(\varepsilon_i - \beta w_i)] \\ &= -\beta\sigma_w^2. \end{aligned}$$

As we have seen in Section 8-4, this violation of the basic assumption results in inconsistency of the least squares estimators of the regression coefficients.

The model represented by (9.4) is frequently referred to as an *errors-in-variables* model. The extent of the inconsistency of the least squares estimator of β can be determined as follows:

$$\hat{\beta} = \frac{\sum (Y_i^* - \bar{Y}^*)(X_i^* - \bar{X}^*)}{\sum (X_i^* - \bar{X}^*)^2} = \frac{\sum y_i^{*\prime} x_i^{*\prime}}{\sum x_i^{*\prime 2}}$$

$$= \frac{\sum (\beta x_i^{*\prime} + \varepsilon_i^{*\prime}) x_i^{*\prime}}{\sum x_i^{*\prime 2}} = \beta + \frac{\sum x_i^{*\prime} \varepsilon_i^{*\prime}}{\sum x_i^{*\prime 2}}$$

$$= \beta + \frac{\sum (x_i' + w_i')(\varepsilon_i' - \beta w_i')/n}{\sum (x_i' + w_i')^2/n}.$$

It follows that

$$\text{(9.5)} \qquad \text{plim } \hat{\beta} = \beta - \frac{\beta \sigma_w^2}{\sigma_x^2 + \sigma_w^2} = \frac{\beta \sigma^2{}_x}{\sigma_x^2 + \sigma_w^2},$$

where the term σ_x^2 is used to designate $\lim(\Sigma x_i'^2/n)$ as $n \to \infty$. In deriving (9.5) we have made use of the assumption of independence between w and ε and of the nonstochastic nature of X, which makes X and w uncorrelated.

Except for the special case of $\beta = 0$, $\hat{\beta}$ would be consistent only if either σ_w^2 were zero or σ_x^2 were infinity. The former would occur if X were measured without error, and the latter if X were to follow an unbounded upward or downward trend. In any other case $\hat{\beta}$ is *asymptotically biased toward zero.* We also note that

$$\text{(9.6)} \qquad \begin{aligned} \text{plim } \hat{\alpha} &= \text{plim}(\bar{Y}^* - \hat{\beta}\bar{X}^*) \\ &= \text{plim}(\alpha + \beta\bar{X}^* + \bar{\varepsilon}^* - \hat{\beta}\bar{X}^*) \\ &= \alpha - \mu_x \text{ plim}(\hat{\beta} - \beta), \end{aligned}$$

where the term μ_x is used to designate plim $\bar{X}^*$. Thus when $\mu_x > 0$, $\hat{\alpha}$ is asymptotically biased in the direction opposite to that of the asymptotic bias of $\hat{\beta}$.

The derivation of the small sample properties of the least squares estimators is difficult and beyond the scope of this book. It has been provided by Richardson and Wu[1] who found the exact mean of $\hat{\beta}$ and its approximation that differs from the exact expression only with respect to terms of order $(1/n^2)$ in the degree of smallness. The latter is given as

$$\text{(9.7)} \qquad E(\hat{\beta}) \cong \beta - \frac{\beta \sigma_w^2}{\hat{\sigma}_x^2 + \sigma_w^2} \left\{ 1 - \frac{2}{n} \left[\frac{\hat{\sigma}_x^2}{\hat{\sigma}_x^2 + \sigma_w^2} \right]^2 \right\},$$

where the term $\hat{\sigma}_x^2$ is used to designate $\Sigma x_i'^2/(n-1)$. Thus $\hat{\beta}$ is clearly biased unless $\sigma_w^2 = 0$ or $\beta = 0$. As expected, the expression for $\hat{\beta}$ in (9.7) does reduce to the expression for plim $\hat{\beta}$ in (9.5) as $n \to \infty$. An unexpected and easily demonstrable

[1] D. H. Richardson and De-Min Wu, "Least Squares and Grouping Method Estimators in the Errors in Variables Model," *Journal of the American Statistical Association,* 65 (June 1970), pp. 724–748.

result is that the absolute size of the bias *increases* with sample size until it reaches its maximum as $n \rightarrow \infty$.

Apart from deriving $E(\hat{\beta})$, Richardson and Wu also determined the distribution of $\hat{\beta}$ and its variance. It turns out that when n is large *and* $\beta = 0$, $\hat{\beta}$ is approximately normal with mean 0 and variance $(\sigma^2/n)/\text{plim}(\Sigma x_i^{*\prime 2}/n)$. Therefore if the null hypothesis *is* that $\beta = 0$ and the sample size is large, we can use the standard least squares regression results to test this hypothesis even when the explanatory variable is measured with error.

Given the biasedness and inconsistency of the least squares estimator in the errors-in-variables model when $\beta \neq 0$, the least squares results cannot be used to determine confidence intervals or test hypotheses about the regression coefficients. As for prediction, since the measured values of X are stochastic and the true values of X are unknown, a meaningful prediction can only be conditional on the measured values of X. For instance, if the explanatory variable is household income and the dependent variable is household expenditure on transportation, and if household income is measured with error, we may wish to predict the value of Y^*, say, Y_0^*, for a household with measured income equal to X_0^*. The least squares predictor, say, $\hat{Y}_0^*$, then is

$$\hat{Y}_0^* = \hat{\alpha} + \hat{\beta} X_0^*$$

and

$$\text{plim } \hat{Y}_0^* = \alpha + \beta \left(\frac{\sigma_w^2}{\sigma_x^2 + \sigma_w^2} \right) \mu_x + \beta \left(\frac{\sigma_x^2}{\sigma_x^2 + \sigma_w^2} \right) X_0^*. \tag{9.8}$$

However,

$$E(Y_0^* | X_0^*) = \alpha + \beta X_0^*.$$

Clearly, plim $\hat{Y}_0^*$ is not equal to $E(Y_0^* | X_0^*)$ unless $X_0^* = \mu_x$. Therefore the least squares predictor is, in general, inconsistent.

The preceding analysis presupposes the validity of the regression model (7.1) as stated at the outset of this section. If the situation were such that the appropriate explanatory variable represented the *measured* rather than the true values of X (implying that $\varepsilon^* = \varepsilon$), then the errors of measurement would be irrelevant and the least squares estimator would be consistent and have other desirable properties. Such a situation could arise if, for example, economic agents were reacting to measured prices regardless of possible errors of measurement.

Large Sample Bounds for the Regression Coefficients

According to (9.5), the least squares estimator of β is asymptotically biased toward zero. Thus

$$|\text{plim } \hat{\beta}| \leq |\beta|$$

and $|\hat{\beta}|$ provides an approximate lower bound for $|\beta|$ in large samples. It turns out that it is possible to establish a large-sample *upper* bound for $|\beta|$ as well. Since in the equation (9.4)

$$Y_i^* = \alpha + \beta X_i^* + \varepsilon_i^*,$$

both Y^* and X^* are stochastic, their roles can be interchanged (unless $\beta = 0$) and the equation can be equivalently written as

$$X_i^* = -\frac{\alpha}{\beta} + \frac{1}{\beta} Y_i^* + \varepsilon_i^{**}, \tag{9.9}$$

where

$$\varepsilon_i^{**} = -\frac{\varepsilon_i^*}{\beta}.$$

From (9.9) we can obtain the least squares estimator of $1/\beta$, say, $1/\hat{\hat{\beta}}$, as

$$\frac{1}{\hat{\hat{\beta}}} = \frac{\sum x_i^{*\prime} y_i^{*\prime}}{\sum y_i^{*\prime 2}},$$

which yields the so-called "inverse least squares estimator"

$$\hat{\hat{\beta}} = \frac{\sum y_i^{*\prime 2}}{\sum x_i^{*\prime} y_i^{*\prime}}. \tag{9.10}$$

The difference between $\hat{\beta}$ and $\hat{\hat{\beta}}$ is that $\hat{\beta}$ has been obtained by minimizing the sum of the squared *vertical* distances of the observed Y^* from the regression line, whereas $\hat{\hat{\beta}}$ is the result of minimizing the sum of squared *horizontal* distances of the observed Y^* from the regression line.

Substituting from (9.4) into (9.10), we obtain

$$\hat{\hat{\beta}} = \frac{\sum (\beta x_i^{*\prime} + \varepsilon_i^{*\prime})^2}{\sum (\beta x_i^{*\prime} + \varepsilon_i^{*\prime}) x_i^{*\prime}} = \frac{\sum (\beta x_i' + \varepsilon_i')^2/n}{\sum (\beta x_i' + \varepsilon_i')(x_i' + w_i')/n},$$

where we have made use of the fact that $(\beta x_i^{*\prime} + \varepsilon_i^{*\prime}) = \beta(x_i' + w_i') + (\varepsilon_i' - \beta w_i')$. Therefore

$$\text{plim } \hat{\hat{\beta}} = \frac{\beta^2 \sigma_x^2 + \sigma^2}{\beta \sigma_x^2} = \beta + \frac{\sigma^2}{\beta \sigma_x^2}, \tag{9.11}$$

where $\sigma^2 = \text{Var}(\varepsilon_i)$ as before. Since $\sigma^2/\sigma_x^2 \geq 0$, it follows that

$$|\beta| \leq |\text{plim } \hat{\hat{\beta}}|$$

and $|\hat{\hat{\beta}}|$ provides an approximate upper bound for $|\beta|$ in large samples. Therefore we have

$$|\text{plim } \hat{\beta}| \leq |\beta| \leq |\text{plim } \hat{\hat{\beta}}|. \tag{9.12}$$

A similar result can be obtained when the regression equation contains additional explanatory variables measured without errors.[2] It can also easily be shown that, provided $\beta > 0$ and $\mu_x > 0$,

$$|\text{plim } \hat{\hat{\alpha}}| \leq |\alpha| \leq |\text{plim } \hat{\alpha}|, \tag{9.13}$$

where

$$\hat{\hat{\alpha}} = \bar{Y}^* - \hat{\hat{\beta}}\bar{X}^*.$$

The practical significance of the preceding results is that in large samples the interval provided by the two kinds of least squares estimators gives an indication of the seriousness of the presence of errors of measurement in the explanatory variable. If this interval is narrow, the effect is muted and the standard least squares results need not be unduly biased. A wide interval, on the other hand, would give us cause to worry.

Adjusted Least Squares and Weighted Regression Estimation

Since the least squares estimation of the regression parameters is unsatisfactory, alternative methods of estimation have to be considered. Given the normality of the regression disturbance and of the error of measurement, an obvious method to try would seem to be that of maximum likelihood estimation. The log-likelihood function for the observations on $(Y_1^*, X_1^*), (Y_2^*, X_2^*), \ldots, (Y_n^*, X_n^*)$ is given as

$$\begin{aligned} L &= \log f(y_1^*, y_2^*, \ldots, y_n^*) f(x_1^*, x_2^*, \ldots, x_n^*) \\ &= -\frac{n}{2}\log(2\pi\sigma^2) - \frac{1}{2\sigma^2}\sum (Y_i^* - \alpha - \beta X_i)^2 \\ &\quad - \frac{n}{2}\log(2\pi\sigma_w^2) - \frac{1}{2\sigma_w^2}\sum (X_i^* - X_i)^2. \end{aligned} \tag{9.14}$$

The unknowns are the parameters α, β, σ^2, σ_w^2, and the quantities $X_1, X_2, \ldots, X_n$. In the context of the functional form of the errors-in-variables model, the X's have to be treated as unknown parameters to be estimated along with α, β, σ^2, and σ_w^2. However, this means that each observation brings in one new unknown parameter so that the number of parameters increases with the number of observations. Therefore the additional information represented by each new observation is exactly offset by the addition of an unknown parameter to be estimated. Under these circumstances the maximum likelihood estimators no longer possess their usual desirable asymptotic properties. More precisely, the general conditions under which the MLE's are guaranteed to have the stated desirable asymptotic properties are not fulfilled for the likelihood function (9.14). Indeed, there is no way of obtaining consistent estimators of the regression coefficients without further prior information or further assumptions.

In order to find out what kind of prior information we need (short of the knowledge of the values of the measurement errors themselves), we turn back to our proof of inconsistency of the LSE of β leading to (9.5), which shows that

$$\text{plim } \hat{\beta} = \frac{\beta\sigma_x^2}{\sigma_x^2 + \sigma_w^2}.$$

[2] See M. D. Levi, "Errors in the Variables Bias in the Presence of Correctly Measured Variables," *Econometrica,* 41 (September 1973), pp. 985–986.

This result indicates that the source of inconsistency of $\hat{\beta}$ is the presence of the term σ_w^2 in the denominator. If that term were not there, σ_x^2 in the numerator would cancel against the σ_x^2 in the denominator and the estimator would be consistent. A consistent estimator of β would enable us to construct a consistent estimator of α. Thus a knowledge of σ_w^2 would make it possible to adjust the standard least squares formulas for inconsistency.

While situations in which the variance of the measurement error (σ_w^2) is known are not common, there are cases where the researcher may have a good idea what its value may be, or have a close estimate for it. For instance, official statistical data on economic variables frequently come in preliminary versions before the final figures are published. Assuming that the final figures represent the true values, the variance of the difference between the preliminary and the final figures might provide a reasonable estimate of σ_w^2. Or in some instances it may be known that the error of measurement is very unlikely to exceed a certain percentage of the measured value, or a similar type of information may be available. For the cases when σ_w^2 is known, the *adjusted least squares estimator* of the regression coefficients can be developed as follows. Since

$$\sigma_x^2 = \text{plim} \frac{\sum x_i^{*\prime 2}}{n} - \sigma_w^2,$$

an adjusted least squares estimator of β, say, $\hat{\beta}_A$, will be

$$\hat{\beta}_A = \frac{\sum x_i^{*\prime} y_i^{*\prime}/n}{\left(\sum x_i^{*\prime 2}/n\right) - \sigma_w^2}. \tag{9.15}$$

The asymptotic variance of this estimator has been derived by Schneeweiss.[3] Given $\hat{\beta}_A$, the corresponding estimator of α, say, $\hat{\alpha}_A$, is [4]

$$\hat{\alpha}_A = \bar{Y}^* - \hat{\beta}_A \bar{X}^*. \tag{9.16}$$

Another way to obtain consistent estimators of the regression coefficients is available if we can make a prior assumption about the ratio of the variance of the measurement error in X to the variance of the regression disturbance (which includes the error in measuring Y), i.e., about σ_w^2/σ^2. Let

$$\frac{\sigma_w^2}{\sigma^2} = \lambda$$

and let us assume that λ is *known*. For example, at times we may reasonably expect that the errors in measuring X have about the same dispersion as those in measuring Y, and that the variation in ε is largely due to errors in measuring Y, i.e., that $\varepsilon_i \cong v_i$.

[3] H. Schneeweiss, "Consistent Estimation of a Regression with Errors in the Variables," *Metrika,* 23 (1976), pp. 101–115. See also H. Schneeweiss and H.-J. Mittag, *Lineare Modelle mit Fehlerbehafteten Daten* (Würzburg, Germany: Physica-Verlag, in press).

[4] The results in (9.15) and (9.16) can easily be extended to the multiple regression model by reference to the "least squares normal equations" with all variables measured in terms of observations from their respective means and with $\Sigma x_i^{*\prime 2}$ replaced by $(\Sigma x_i^{*\prime 2} - n\sigma_w^2)$.

In such a case we may be willing to assume that λ is equal to one (or a little less than one). Using prior information about the value of λ, we can develop consistent estimators of the regression coefficients known as *weighted regression estimators*. Referring to (9.15) we note that, for any consistent estimator of σ_w^2 (denoted by $\tilde{\sigma}_w^2$), $\tilde{\beta}$ given as

$$\tilde{\beta} = \frac{\sum x_i^{*\prime} y_i^{*\prime}/n}{(\sum x_i^{*\prime 2}/n) - \tilde{\sigma}_w^2} \tag{9.17}$$

is a consistent estimator of β. The problem then is to find a consistent estimator of σ_w^2 given the information that $\sigma_w^2 = \lambda\sigma^2$ with λ known.

Let us start by noting that if X were measurable, a consistent estimator of σ^2— and, therefore, of σ_w^2/λ—would be given as

$$\begin{aligned}\tilde{\sigma}^2 &= \frac{\sum (y_i^{*\prime} - \tilde{\beta}x_i')^2}{n}\\ &= \frac{\sum y_i^{*\prime 2}}{n} + \tilde{\beta}^2\left(\frac{\sum x_i'^2}{n}\right) - 2\tilde{\beta}\left(\frac{\sum y_i^{*\prime}x_i'}{n}\right).\end{aligned}$$

Substituting $(x_i^{*\prime} - w_i')$ for x_i' and noting that $\Sigma w_i'^2/n = \tilde{\sigma}_w^2$ and that $\Sigma w_i' y_i^{*\prime}/n$ is asymptotically equal to zero, we obtain

$$\tilde{\sigma}^2 = \frac{\sum y_i^{*\prime 2}}{n} + \tilde{\beta}^2\left(\frac{\sum x_i^{*\prime 2}}{n}\right) - \tilde{\beta}^2\tilde{\sigma}_w^2 - 2\tilde{\beta}\left(\frac{\sum x_i^{*\prime}y_i^{*\prime}}{n}\right).$$

At this stage we introduce the following simplifying notation.

$$\frac{\sum y_i^{*\prime 2}}{n} = m_{yy}^*,$$

$$\frac{\sum x_i^{*\prime 2}}{n} = m_{xx}^*,$$

$$\frac{\sum x_i^{*\prime}y_i^{*\prime}}{n} = m_{xy}^*.$$

Using this notation, we get

$$\begin{aligned}\tilde{\sigma}_w^2 &= \lambda\tilde{\sigma}^2\\ &= \lambda m_{yy}^* + \tilde{\beta}^2\lambda m_{xx}^* - \tilde{\beta}^2\lambda\tilde{\sigma}_w^2 - 2\tilde{\beta}\lambda m_{xy}^*\end{aligned}$$

or

$$\tilde{\sigma}_w^2 = \frac{\lambda m_{yy}^* + \tilde{\beta}^2\lambda m_{xx}^* - 2\tilde{\beta}\lambda m_{xy}^*}{1 + \tilde{\beta}^2\lambda}. \tag{9.18}$$

Now from (9.17) we have

$$\tilde{\beta} = \frac{m^*_{xy}}{m^*_{xx} - \tilde{\sigma}^2_w}$$

or

$$\tilde{\beta} m^*_{xx} - \tilde{\beta}\tilde{\sigma}^2_w - m^*_{xy} = 0. \tag{9.19}$$

Substituting for $\tilde{\sigma}^2_w$ from (9.18) into (9.19) and rearranging the terms, we obtain the following quadratic equation to be solved for the weighted regression estimator of β:

$$\tilde{\beta}^2 \lambda m^*_{xy} + \tilde{\beta}(m^*_{xx} - \lambda m^*_{yy}) - m^*_{xy} = 0. \tag{9.20}$$

The solution leads to two values for $\tilde{\beta}$, one positive and one negative. The choice between the two is determined by the value of the "error sum of squares,"

$$\sum (y^{*\prime}_i - \tilde{\beta} x^{*\prime}_i)^2 = n(m^*_{yy} - 2\tilde{\beta} m^*_{xy} + \tilde{\beta}^2 m^*_{xx}).$$

Since we want this to be as small as possible, we chose that value of $\tilde{\beta}$ which has the same sign as m^*_{xy}.

We can gain some insight into the principle of weighted regression estimation—and explain the basis for the name—by considering the value of the weighted regression estimator $\tilde{\beta}$ for different values of λ. Suppose first that X is observed without error so that all w's are zero and, therefore, $\sigma^2_w = 0$. Recalling that $\sigma^2_w = \lambda\sigma^2$, this implies that $\lambda = 0$. Substituting zero for λ in (9.20) leads to

$$\tilde{\beta} = \frac{m^*_{xy}}{m^*_{xx}},$$

which is the formula for the ordinary least squares estimator of β. As we noted in connection with establishing the asymptotic boundaries for β, this estimator is based on minimizing the sum of the squared *vertical* distances of the observed Y^* from the regression line. At the other extreme, suppose that there are no errors in measuring Y and that there are no regression disturbances so that all ε's are zero and, therefore, $\sigma^2 = 0$. This then implies that $\lambda \to \infty$. After dividing both sides of (9.20) by λ and letting $\lambda \to \infty$, the expression for $\tilde{\beta}$ becomes

$$\tilde{\beta} = \frac{m^*_{yy}}{m^*_{xy}},$$

which is the same as $\hat{\hat{\beta}}$ of (9.10). As we noted, this estimator is based on minimizing the sum of the squared *horizontal* distances of the observed Y^* from the regression line. We could also establish that in the case when $\lambda = 1$ the resulting estimator $\tilde{\beta}$ (called in this case the "orthogonal regression estimator") is based on minimizing the sum of squared *perpendicular* distances of the observed Y^* from the regression line. These results show that the size of λ determines the direction of the minimization of the squared deviations toward that variable which is more contaminated by errors. Thus λ serves as a weighting factor in allocating the direction of minimization between X and Y. From this it also follows that

$$\hat{\beta} \leq \tilde{\beta} \leq \hat{\hat{\beta}}.$$

The asymptotic variance of the weighted regression estimator has been derived by Schneeweiss.[5] To complete the discussion of weighted regression estimation we present the weighted regression estimator of α as

$$\tilde{\alpha} = \bar{Y}^* - \tilde{\beta}\bar{X}^*. \tag{9.21}$$

EXAMPLE In a well-known paper on capital–labor substitution,[6] the authors estimate the relationship

$$Y_i = \alpha + \beta X_i + \varepsilon_i$$

with X and Y defined as

$$X = \log \frac{W}{P},$$

$$Y = \log \frac{V}{PL},$$

where W = money wage rate, P = price of product, V = value added in production, L = labor input, and the subscript i refers to the ith country. The observations are made for a particular industry and a given year. The authors used ordinary least squares to estimate the regression coefficients. The results for the *furniture manufacturing industry* based on the data presented in Table 9-1 are

$$m^*_{xx} = 0.1669,$$

$$m^*_{yy} = 0.1194,$$

$$m^*_{xy} = 0.1401.$$

The ordinary least squares estimates corresponding to $\lambda = 0$ (i.e., no errors in measuring X) are

$$Y^*_i = \underset{(0.0966)}{-2.2879} + \underset{(0.0331)}{0.8402}\, X_i + e_i, \qquad R^2 = 0.986.$$

If we assume that $\lambda \to \infty$, that is, that the *only* source of error in the equation are errors in measuring X, the resulting estimates are

$$Y_i = -2.32273 + 0.8519\, X^*_i + e_i.$$

Assuming that $\lambda = 1$, that is, that $\sigma^2_w = \sigma^2$, we obtain

$$Y^*_i = -2.3023 + 0.8452\, X^*_i + e_i.$$

We note that the weighted regression estimates of α and β for $\lambda = 1$ lie between those for $\lambda = 0$ and those for $\lambda \to \infty$, as they should. Since the estimates are numerically close for $\lambda = 0$ and $\lambda \to \infty$, the errors of measuring X do not appear to cause great problems, given the stated assumptions.

[5] H. Schneeweiss, "Modelle mit Fehlern in den Variablen," *Methods of Operations Research,* 37 (1981), pp. 41–77.

[6] K. J. Arrow et al., "Capital–Labor Substitution and Economic Efficiency," *Review of Economics and Statistics,* 43 (August 1961), pp. 225–250. All logarithms are to base 10.

Table 9-1

	Furniture manufacturing industry				
Country	L/V	P	W, \$	$\log(V/PL)$ $=Y^*$	$\log(W/P)$ $=X^*$
United States	0.1706	1.0000	3515	0.7680	3.5459
Canada	0.2385	1.5470	2668	0.4330	3.2367
New Zealand	0.3678	0.9482	1834	0.4575	3.2865
Australia	0.3857	0.8195	1713	0.5002	3.3202
Denmark	0.5040	0.8941	1288	0.3462	3.1585
Norway	0.5228	0.9437	1342	0.3068	3.1529
United Kingdom	0.6291	0.6646	1078	0.3787	3.2101
Colombia	0.7200	1.8260	738	−0.1188	2.6066
Brazil	0.9415	1.4590	448	−0.1379	2.4872
Mexico	0.9017	1.7580	471	−0.2001	2.4280
Argentina	1.0863	2.2300	464	−0.3843	2.3182

	Knitting mill products		
Country	P	W, \$	$\log(W/P)$ $=Z^*$
United States	1.0000	2698	3.4310
Canada	1.4891	2260	3.1812
New Zealand	1.0346	1548	3.1750
Australia	0.7358	1487	3.3055
Denmark	0.7713	1169	3.1806
Norway	0.8990	1021	3.0553
United Kingdom	0.6030	802	3.1238
Colombia	2.2570	845	2.5733
Brazil	0.9720	364	2.5734
Mexico	1.2458	546	2.6417
Argentina	1.3901	523	2.5755

Instrumental Variable Estimation

At the beginning of our discussion on the adjusted least squares and weighted regression methods, we pointed out that consistent estimation of the regression coefficients of the errors-in-variables model requires additional information (or assumptions). So far we have considered information about the variance of the errors in measuring X (σ_w^2) or about the ratio of the error variances (σ_w^2/σ^2). Another and entirely different type of information underlies the so-called *method of instrumental variables.* This method is available whenever we can find a new variable Z such that

1. $\text{plim}(\Sigma z_i' \varepsilon_i^{*\prime})/n = 0.$
2. $\text{plim}(\Sigma z_i' x_i^{*\prime})/n$ is a finite number different from zero.

Here, in accordance with the previously adopted notation, we define

$$z'_i = Z_i - \bar{Z},$$

$$x_i^{*\prime} = X_i^* - \bar{X}^*.$$

The first condition will be satisfied if Z is asymptotically uncorrelated with ε and w. The second condition will be satisfied if Z and X^* are asymptotically correlated with each other. An additional condition, which is not necessary for consistency but helps to reduce the asymptotic variance of the instrumental variables estimator, is that the $\text{plim}(\Sigma z'_i x_i^{*\prime})/n$ is as large as possible—that is, that the degree of correlation between Z and X^* is high. The variable Z is called an "instrumental variable." It does not matter whether Z is or is not measured without error as long as the specified conditions are satisfied with respect to the observable values of Z. The conditions 1 and 2 that make Z an appropriate instrumental variable for X^* are implied by the existence of a relation of the form

$$X_i^* = \gamma + \delta Z_i + u_i \qquad (\delta \neq 0), \tag{9.22}$$

where Z is correlated with X^* but asymptotically uncorrelated with ε and with w, and u is an error term that is uncorrelated with Z. In this case

$$\text{plim} \frac{\sum z'_i \varepsilon_i^{*\prime}}{n} = \text{plim} \frac{\sum z'_i(\varepsilon'_i - \beta w'_i)}{n}$$

$$= 0,$$

and

$$\text{plim} \frac{\sum z'_i x_i^{*\prime}}{n} = \text{plim} \frac{\sum z'_i(\delta z'_i + u'_i)}{n}$$

$$= \delta \,\text{plim} \frac{\sum z_i'^2}{n}$$

$$\neq 0,$$

as required. The additional information, therefore, takes the form of expanding the original single-equation regression model by the addition of another relationship such as (9.22).

Given that a suitable instrumental variable has been determined and its values measured, the estimators of α and β, say, $\alpha^\dagger$ and $\beta^\dagger$, are then defined as follows.

$$\beta^\dagger = \frac{\sum y_i^{*\prime} z'_i}{\sum x_i^{*\prime} z'_i}, \tag{9.23}$$

$$\alpha^\dagger = \bar{Y}^* - \beta^\dagger \bar{X}^*, \tag{9.24}$$

where

$$y_i^{*\prime} = Y_i^* - \bar{Y}^*.$$

The idea behind the method of instrumental variables can be explained by reference to the least squares "normal equations" given by (7.10) and (7.11). For the regression equation (9.4) the least squares normal equations are

$$\sum Y_i^* = \hat{\alpha}n + \hat{\beta} \sum X_i^*,$$
$$\sum Y_i^* X_i^* = \hat{\alpha} \sum X_i^* + \hat{\beta} \sum X_i^{*2}.$$

A rule for obtaining these equations is as follows. To obtain the first normal equation, multiply both sides of (9.4) by the multiplier of α (which is 1), add all observations, and omit the last term involving the disturbance. To obtain the second normal equation, multiply both sides of (9.4) by the multiplier of β (which is X_i^*), add all observations, and omit the last term involving the disturbance. In obtaining the normal equations for the instrumental variables estimators, we proceed in a similar way. The first normal equation is obtained in exactly the same way as the first normal equation in the least squares method. The second normal equation is obtained by multiplying both sides of (9.4) by Z_i instead of X_i^* as in the case of least squares. The result is

$$\sum Y_i^* = \alpha^\dagger n + \beta^\dagger \sum X_i^*,$$
$$\sum Y_i^* Z_i = \alpha^\dagger \sum Z_i + \beta^\dagger \sum X_i^* Z_i.$$

This leads to the formulas for instrumental variables estimators as given by (9.23) and (9.24).

Note that in the case of a regression equation in which the explanatory variable X is independent of the disturbance ε, a suitable instrumental variable would be X itself since, in this case, X is uncorrelated with ε and at the same time is (perfectly) correlated with itself; therefore, conditions 1 and 2 are satisfied. Thus, an ordinary least squares estimator may be thought of as an instrumental variables estimator with $Z = X$.

A common error in implementing the instrumental variables estimation procedure is to regard the instrumental variable Z as a *replacement* for X^* and to apply the least squares method to a regression of Y^* on Z. This is incorrect and will yield inconsistent estimates of α and β. The intended role of Z is one of an *instrumental variable* for X^* and *not* of a *proxy variable.* (The use of the latter will be discussed in Section 11-8.)

Let us now demonstrate that the instrumental variables estimators are consistent. With respect to $\beta^\dagger$, we have

$$\beta^\dagger = \frac{\sum y_i^{*\prime} z_i'}{\sum x_i^{*\prime} z_i'} = \beta + \frac{\sum \varepsilon_i^{*\prime} z_i'}{\sum x_i^{*\prime} z_i'},$$

and

$$\text{plim } \beta^\dagger = \beta + \frac{\text{plim } (\sum \varepsilon_i^{*\prime} z_i')/n}{\text{plim } (\sum x_i^{*\prime} z_i')/n} = \beta$$

by making use of the conditions that Z is supposed to satisfy. Similarly,

$$\text{plim } \alpha^\dagger = \text{plim}(\overline{Y}^* - \beta^\dagger \overline{X}^*) = \text{plim}(\alpha + \beta \overline{X}^* + \bar{\varepsilon}^* - \beta^\dagger \overline{X}^*) = \alpha.$$

This shows that $\alpha^\dagger$ and $\beta^\dagger$ are consistent.

The asymptotic variances of the instrumental variables estimators can be derived from the appropriate formulas.[7] The results are

$$\text{(9.25a)} \qquad \text{Asympt. Var}\,\sqrt{n}(\beta^\dagger - \beta) = \frac{\sigma_{\varepsilon*}^2 \,\text{plim}(\sum z_i'^2/n)}{\text{plim}(\sum x_i^{*\prime} z_i'/n)^2},$$

$$\text{(9.25b)} \qquad \text{Asympt. Var}\,\sqrt{n}(\alpha^\dagger - \alpha) = \sigma_{\varepsilon*}^2 \left[1 + \frac{\bar{X}^{*2}\,\text{plim}(\sum z_i'^2/n)}{\text{plim}(\sum x_i^{*\prime} z_i'/n)^2}\right],$$

where $\sigma_{\varepsilon*}^2 = \text{Var}(\varepsilon_i^*)$. Using (9.22) it is not difficult to show that the higher the asymptotic correlation between Z and X^*, the smaller the asymptotic variances of $\alpha^\dagger$ and $\beta^\dagger$. To obtain consistent estimators of $\text{Var}(\beta^\dagger)$ and $\text{Var}(\alpha^\dagger)$, we use

$$\text{(9.26a)} \qquad \text{Est. Var}(\beta^\dagger) = \frac{s_{\varepsilon*}^2 \sum z_i'^2}{(\sum x_i^{*\prime} z_i')^2},$$

$$\text{(9.26b)} \qquad \text{Est. Var}(\alpha^\dagger) = s_{\varepsilon*}^2 \left[\frac{1}{n} + \frac{\bar{X}^{*2} \sum z_i'^2}{(\sum x_i^{*\prime} z_i')^2}\right],$$

where

$$s_{\varepsilon*}^2 = \frac{\sum (Y_i^* - \alpha^\dagger - \beta^\dagger X_i^*)^2}{n-2}.$$

The choice of an instrumental variable is determined by its supposed relationship with X. However, there may be more than one variable correlated with X and uncorrelated with ε^*; that is, there may be more than one relationship such as (9.22), or more than one regressor appearing in (9.22). If these variables are known and measurable, we may choose the one that is most highly correlated with X, or we may use a linear combination of some or all of the qualifying variables. Unfortunately, the theory that enables us to postulate relationships such as (9.22) is frequently lacking and, in practice, is frequently replaced by hoc reasoning. The resulting arbitrariness in the choice of an instrumental variable and the difficulty of checking that the chosen variable is indeed uncorrelated with ε^* make this method somewhat unattractive.

EXAMPLE Continuing with the example on the relationship between $\log(V/PL)$ and $\log(W/P)$ in the furniture manufacturing industry and using the data in Table 9-1, let us

[7] See J. Johnston, *Econometric Methods*, 3rd ed. (New York: McGraw-Hill, 1984), pp. 363–366.

calculate the instrumental variables estimates of the regression coefficients. Assuming that wages of workers in several industries are determined in the same labor market, we may postulate the following relationship analogous to (9.22),

$$\log\left(\frac{W}{P}\right)^*_F = \gamma + \delta \log\left(\frac{W}{P}\right)^*_{KM} + u,$$

where the subscripts F and KM refer to the furniture and the knitting mills industry, respectively, and the asterisks indicate that the respective variables may be measured with error. The coefficients γ and δ measure the differences in the labor skill mix of the two industries, and u represents factors that are omitted from the equation. The variable $\log(W/P)^*_{KM}$ can be assumed to be uncorrelated with ε^* and, therefore, is a suitable instrumental variable for $\log(W/P)^*_F$. The instrumental variables estimates of the relationship between logarithmic output per worker (Y^*) and logarithmic wage rate (X^*) in the furniture industry then are

$$\underset{}{Y_i^*} = \underset{(0.1025)}{-2.2978} + \underset{(0.0342)}{0.8435}\, X_i^* + e_i, \qquad R^2 = 0.985,$$

where R^2 was calculated as $1 - (SSE/SST)$. The results obtained by the method of instrumental variables are very similar to those obtained earlier by the least squares and the weighted regression methods.

Method of Group Averages

An alternative way of estimating (9.4) is by the *method of group averages* which, in its simplest form, requires ordering the observed pairs (X_i^*, Y_i^*) by the magnitude of the X^*s so that

$$X_1^* \leq X_2^* \leq \cdots \leq X_n^*.$$

The pairs are then divided into three groups of approximately equal size. The group-averages estimators of the regression coefficients are

$$\beta^{\dagger\dagger} = \frac{\bar{Y}_3^* - \bar{Y}_1^*}{\bar{X}_3^* - \bar{X}_1^*}, \tag{9.27a}$$

$$\alpha^{\dagger\dagger} = \bar{Y}^* - \beta^{\dagger\dagger}\bar{X}^*, \tag{9.27b}$$

where $\bar{Y}_1^*$ and $\bar{Y}_3^*$ are the calculated means of Y^* of the first and the third group, respectively, and $\bar{X}_1^*$ and $\bar{X}_3^*$ are the corresponding means of X^*. The group-averages estimators are consistent providing the grouping is such that, had we grouped the data by the unobserved Xs rather than by the observed X^*s, no pairs in the first group would have to be re-allocated to the third group and vice versa. It is interesting to note that the method of group averages can be viewed as a special case of the method of instrumental variables. If the three groups of observations are of equal size, and if the values of the instrumental variable Z_i are such that

$$\begin{aligned} Z_i &= -1 \quad \text{if } i \text{ belongs to the 1st group,} \\ &= \ \ 0 \quad \text{if } i \text{ belongs to the 2nd group,} \\ &= \ \ 1 \quad \text{if } i \text{ belongs to the 3rd group,} \end{aligned}$$

we find that (9.23) and (9.24) are equivalent to (9.27a) and (9.27b), respectively. We can then utilize formulas (9.25a) and (9.25b) to estimate the variances of $\alpha^{\dagger\dagger}$ and $\beta^{\dagger\dagger}$.

EXAMPLE Let us calculate the group-averages estimates for the relationship between $\log(V/PL)$ and $\log(W/P)$ discussed in the previous example. From the data in Table 9-1, we see that there are eleven observations; we shall use four observations for the first and third groups, leaving three observations unused. The calculations are

$$\bar{X}_1^* = \frac{1}{4}(2.3182 + 2.4280 + 2.4872 + 2.6066) = 2.4600,$$

$$\bar{X}_3^* = \frac{1}{4}(3.2367 + 3.2865 + 3.3202 + 3.5459) = 3.3473,$$

$$\bar{Y}_1^* = \frac{1}{4}(-0.3845 - 0.2001 - 0.1379 - 0.1188) = -0.2103,$$

$$\bar{Y}_3^* = \frac{1}{4}(0.4330 + 0.4575 + 0.5002 + 0.7680) = 0.5397.$$

Then,

$$\beta^{\dagger\dagger} = \frac{0.5397 - (-0.2103)}{3.3473 - 2.4600} = 0.8453$$

$$\alpha^{\dagger\dagger} = \frac{1}{11}(2.3491 - 0.8453 \times 32.7508) = -2.3031.$$

The estimated relationship would then be

$$Y_i^* = -2.3031 + 0.8453X_i^* + \xi_i,$$

which is numerically quite similar to the result obtained previously.

Structural Form of the Errors-in-Variables Model

So far we have considered only the standard regression model for which the correctly measured explanatory variable is nonstochastic—the so-called *functional form* model. When the correctly measured explanatory variable is stochastic, the resulting errors-in-variables model is known in the statistical literature as a *structural form* model. Let us consider the case where X is normally and independently distributed with mean μ_x and variance σ_x^2. It is also assumed that X is independent of the measurement error w and of the regression disturbance ε. Retaining all other earlier assumptions about w and ε we find that the measured variables X^* and Y^* have a bivariate normal distribution whose joint probability density function is given in logarithmic form by

$$\begin{aligned}\log f(x^*,y^*) = &-\log(2\pi\sigma_x^*\sigma_y^*\sqrt{1-\rho^2}) \\ &- \frac{1}{2(1-\rho^2)}\left[\left(\frac{X^*-\mu_x^*}{\sigma_x^*}\right)^2\right. \\ &\left.- 2\rho\left(\frac{X^*-\mu_x^*}{\sigma_x^*}\right)\left(\frac{Y^*-\mu_y^*}{\sigma_y^*}\right) + \left(\frac{Y^*-\mu_y^*}{\sigma_y^*}\right)^2\right]\end{aligned}$$

where $\mu_x^* = E(X^*)$, $\mu_y^* = E(Y^*)$, $\sigma_x^{*2} = \text{Var}(X^*)$, $\sigma_y^{*2} = \text{Var}(Y^*)$, $\rho = \sigma_{xy}^*/\sigma_x^*\sigma_y^*$, and $\sigma_{xy}^* = \text{Cov}(X^*, Y^*)$. The means, the variances, and the covariance of X^* and Y^* can be expressed as follows.

(9.28) $$\begin{aligned}\mu_x^* &= E(X + w) = \mu_x,\\ \mu_y^* &= E(\alpha + \beta X + \varepsilon) = \alpha + \beta\mu_x,\\ \sigma_x^{*2} &= E[(X + w) - E(X + w)]^2 = \sigma_x^2 + \sigma_w^2,\\ \sigma_y^{*2} &= E[(\alpha + \beta X + \varepsilon) - E(\alpha + \beta X + \varepsilon)]^2, = \beta^2\sigma_x^2 + \sigma^2,\\ \sigma_{xy}^* &= E[(X + w) - E(X + w)][(\alpha + \beta X + \varepsilon) - E(\alpha + \beta X + \varepsilon)] = \beta\sigma_x^2.\end{aligned}$$

It is not difficult—although it is tedious—to show that in general obtaining the maximum likelihood estimators of the unknown parameters is equivalent to replacing the means, the variances, and the covariance of X^* and Y^* by their respective sample counterparts and solving for the unknowns. Specifically, the set of equations to be solved is

(9.29) $$\begin{aligned}\bar{X}^* &= \hat{\mu}_x,\\ \bar{Y}^* &= \hat{\alpha} + \hat{\beta}\hat{\mu}_x,\\ \frac{\sum (X_i^* - \bar{X}^*)^2}{n} &= \hat{\sigma}_x^2 + \hat{\sigma}_w^2,\\ \frac{\sum (Y_i^* - \bar{Y}^*)^2}{n} &= \hat{\beta}^2\hat{\sigma}_x^2 + \hat{\sigma}^2,\\ \frac{\sum (X_i^* - \bar{X})(Y_i^* - \bar{Y}^*)}{n} &= \hat{\beta}\hat{\sigma}_x^2.\end{aligned}$$

Thus we have a set of five equations to be solved for the six unknowns, $\hat{\alpha}$, $\hat{\beta}$, $\hat{\mu}_x$, $\hat{\sigma}_x^2$, $\hat{\sigma}_w^2$, and $\hat{\sigma}^2$. We can solve for $\hat{\mu}_x$, but that still leaves four equations with five unknowns. Such a situation is known as *underidentification* and implies that consistent estimation is impossible without further prior information.

Let us consider various types of prior information that might help in solving (9.29). The simplest one is when it is known that the population regression line passes through the origin, that is, when $\alpha = 0$. In this case

$$\hat{\beta} = \frac{\bar{Y}^*}{\bar{X}^*},$$

and the values of the remaining maximum likelihood estimators can also be determined. When the prior information is represented by a knowledge of σ_w^2, the MLE's of α and β are exactly the same as the adjusted LSE's presented in (9.15) and (9.16). Similarly, when the ratio of error variances, σ_w^2/σ^2, is known, the MLEs of α and β are equal to the weighted regression estimators given by (9.20) and (9.21).

Identification can also be accomplished by the availability of an instrumental variable Z, implied by the relationship presented in (9.22) as

$$X_i^* = \gamma + \delta Z_i + u_i.$$

If, as presupposed, Z is correlated with X^* but uncorrelated with w and ε, the five equations in (9.28) can be extended by the following.

$$\begin{aligned}(9.30)\qquad \sigma^*_{zx} &= E[\gamma + \delta Z + u - E(\gamma + \delta Z + u)][Z - E(Z)] \\ &= \delta\sigma_z^2,\end{aligned}$$

$$\begin{aligned}(9.31)\qquad \sigma^*_{zy} &= E[Z - E(Z)][\alpha + \beta X + \varepsilon - E(\alpha + \beta X + \varepsilon)] \\ &= \beta E[Z - E(Z)][X - E(X)] \\ &= \beta\delta\sigma_z^2.\end{aligned}$$

Clearly, $\beta = \sigma^*_{zy}/\sigma^*_{zx}$, and if we replace σ^*_{zx} and σ^*_{zy} by the respective sample covariances, we obtain the instrumental variable estimator of β presented in (9.23).[8]

With respect to prediction when the correctly measured explanatory variable is normally and independently distributed, the least squares predictor of Y_0^* given X_0^* is

$$\begin{aligned}\hat{Y}_0^* &= \hat{\alpha} + \hat{\beta}X_0^* \\ &= \bar{Y}^* + \hat{\beta}(X_0^* - \bar{X}^*)\end{aligned}$$

and
$$\text{plim } \hat{Y}_0^* = \mu_y^* + \frac{\sigma^*_{xy}}{\sigma_x^{*2}}(X_0^* - \mu_x^*),$$

since plim $\Sigma x_i^{*\prime} y_i^{*\prime}/n = \sigma^*_{xy}$ and plim $\Sigma x^{*\prime 2}/n = \sigma_x^{*2}$. Now since

$$Y_0^* = \alpha + \beta X_0 + \varepsilon_0$$

the conditional mean of Y_0^* given X_0^* is

$$E(Y_0^*|X_0^*) = \alpha + \beta E(X_0|X_0^*).$$

But from the properties of normal distributions[9] we have

$$(9.32)\qquad E(X_0|X_0^*) = \lambda\mu_x + (1 - \lambda)X_0^*,$$

where $\lambda = \sigma_w^2/\sigma_x^{*2}$. This leads to

$$\begin{aligned}(9.33)\qquad E(Y_0^*|X_0^*) &= \mu_y - \beta\mu_x + \beta\lambda\mu_x + \beta(1 - \lambda)X_0^* \\ &= \mu_y + \left(\frac{\sigma_{xy}}{\sigma_x^2}\right)\left(\frac{\sigma_x^2}{\sigma_x^{*2}}\right)(X_0^* - \mu_x) \\ &= \mu_y^* + \left(\frac{\sigma^*_{xy}}{\sigma_x^{*2}}\right)(X_0^* - \mu_x^*),\end{aligned}$$

where we have made use of the fact that $\alpha = \mu_y - \beta\mu_x$, $\beta = \sigma_{xy}/\sigma_x^2$, $\mu_y^* = \mu_y$, $\mu_x^* = \mu_x$, $\sigma_x^{*2} = \sigma_x^2 + \sigma_w$, and $\sigma^*_{xy} = \sigma_{xy}$. Thus in this case the least squares predictor is consistent in spite of the presence of errors of measurement.

[8] Another way of achieving identification may be possible when the distribution of X is not normal and the set of equations in (9.28) can be extended by bringing in equations for higher moments of X^*. See Schneeweiss and Mittag, *op. cit.*

[9] See, e.g., J. Johnston, *Econometric Methods,* 2nd ed. (New York: McGraw-Hill, 1972), p. 291.

Testing for the Absence of Errors of Measurement

One way of assessing the seriousness of the presence of measurement errors in the explanatory variable in large samples is to estimate the bounds for the true regression coefficients as given in (9.12). This involves obtaining least squares estimates by regressing Y^* on X^* and, conversely, by regressing X^* on Y^*. The width of the interval given by the two sets of estimates gives an indication of the seriousness of the presence of measurement errors for estimation. A somewhat more formal approach may be adopted when it is possible to use instrumental variable estimation. In this case the instrumental variable estimates and their estimated standard errors may be used to construct confidence intervals for the true regression coefficients. If the ordinary least squares estimates fall outside of the respective intervals, the effects of errors of measurement on estimation are likely to be serious.[10]

A formal test for the absence of measurement errors in the explanatory variable when the sample is large has been proposed by Hausman.[11] This test can be used whenever we can implement an instrumental variables estimation procedure. To develop the test, let us recall the basic errors-in-variables regression equation given in (9.4) as

$$Y_i^* = \alpha + \beta X_i^* + \varepsilon_i^*,$$

where, as before, Y^* represents the measured values of Y, X^* represents the measured values of X, and $\varepsilon^* = \varepsilon - \beta w$, with ε representing the regression disturbance (plus possible errors in measuring the dependent variable), and w representing errors in measuring X. The availability of an instrumental variable for X^* can be expressed in the form of a relationship between an instrumental variable Z and the explanatory variable X^* as

$$X_i^* = \gamma + \delta Z_i + u_i, \tag{9.34}$$

or as

$$\begin{aligned} X_i^* &= \hat{\gamma} + \hat{\delta} Z_i + \hat{u}_i \\ &= \hat{X}_i^* + \hat{u}_i, \end{aligned} \tag{9.34a}$$

where $\hat{\gamma}$ and $\hat{\delta}$ represent ordinary least squares estimators of λ and δ, and $\hat{u}$'s are least squares residuals that are uncorrelated with the fitted values of $\hat{X}^*$.

The null hypothesis of no errors of measurement in the explanatory variable and its alternative may be stated as

$$H_0: \quad \sigma_w^2 = 0,$$

$$H_A: \quad \sigma_w^2 \neq 0.$$

To develop Hausman's test procedure, substitute for X^* from (9.34a) into (9.4) to

[10] See J. D. Sargan, "The Estimation of Economic Relationships Using Instrumental Variables," *Econometrica,* 26 (July 1958), pp. 393–415.

[11] J. A. Hausman, "Specification Tests in Econometrics," *Econometrica,* 46 (November 1978), pp. 1251–1271. The test can easily be extended to multiple regression.

get

$$Y_i^* = \alpha + \beta\hat{X}_i^* + \beta\hat{u}_i + \varepsilon_i^*. \tag{9.35}$$

Now $\text{plim}(\Sigma\hat{x}_i^{*\prime}\varepsilon_i^{*\prime}/n) = \text{plim}[\hat{\delta}\Sigma z_i'(\varepsilon_i' - \beta w_i')/n]$, which is equal to zero *whether the null hypothesis is true or not.* Thus the LSE of the coefficient of $\hat{X}^*$ in (9.35) is consistent under both H_0 and H_A. However, $\text{plim}(\Sigma\hat{u}_i'\varepsilon_i^{*\prime}/n) = \text{plim}[\Sigma(x_i^{*\prime} - \hat{\delta}z_i')(\varepsilon_i - \beta w_i)/n] = -\beta\sigma_w^2$, which is equal to zero only if the null hypothesis is true but not otherwise. Thus the LSE of the coefficient of $\hat{u}$ in (9.35) is consistent (and, therefore, its probability limit equals β) if H_0 is true but not if H_A is true. In order to make this distinction, we rename the coefficient of $\hat{u}$ as θ and rewrite equation (9.35) as

$$Y_i^* = \alpha + \beta\hat{X}_i^* + \theta\hat{u}_i + \varepsilon_i^*. \tag{9.35a}$$

The null and the alternative hypothesis can then be restated as

$$H_0\colon\quad \theta = \beta,$$

$$H_A\colon\quad \theta \neq \beta.$$

Since $\hat{X}^* = X^* - \hat{u}$, equation (9.35a) can be expressed more conveniently as

$$Y_i^* = \alpha + \beta X_i^* + (\theta - \beta)\hat{u}_i + \varepsilon_i^*, \tag{9.35b}$$

and the test of the null hypothesis becomes simply a standard test of significance of the least squares estimate of the coefficient of $\hat{u}$, whose probability limit under the null hypothesis is zero.[12] Since we are dealing with probability limits, the validity of the test is only asymptotic, which in practice means that the test is a large sample test.

9-2 Estimation from Grouped Data

Survey data are frequently presented in the form of a table summarizing the values for individual observations. Such tabular information has often been used for estimating the coefficients of a regression equation. One reason for this is the fact that tabular results are likely to be readily accessible, whereas the retrieval of the individual observations may be time-consuming and costly. Another reason for using condensed summaries of the sample observations is often the desire to avoid large-scale computations that may otherwise be necessary. In this section we shall inquire how the use of condensed sample information affects the properties of the estimators of the regression coefficients in a simple regression model. We shall consider two types of condensed tabular information, one consisting of group means for all variables involved, and the other consisting of intervals within which

[12] This test (a t test) is described in Section 10-2. In a multiple regression setting with several explanatory variables potentially contaminated by measurement errors and with each explanatory variable having its own instrumental variable, the appropriate test is an F test.

the values of the variables fall. In both cases the number of sample observation in each group or interval is assumed to be given.

Estimation Based on Group Means

Consider a simple linear regression model as described by (7.1) through (7.6). As will be recalled, this means that the explanatory variable X is nonstochastic and that the regression disturbance ε has zero mean and is normal, homoskedastic, and nonautoregressive. (The conclusions of this section, however, also apply to the case where X is stochastic but independent of ε.) Suppose the n sample observations are divided into G groups. Let n_1 be the number of observations in the first group, n_2 the number of observations in the second group, and so on. Since there are altogether n observations, we must have

$$\sum_{g=1}^{G} n_g = n.$$

Let us denote the ith observation in the gth group by the double subscript ig, so that the regression equation can be written as

$$Y_{ig} = \alpha + \beta X_{ig} + \varepsilon_{ig} \qquad (i = 1, 2, \ldots, n_g;\ g = 1, 2, \ldots, G). \tag{9.36}$$

Suppose now that instead of being given a complete enumeration of all observations in each group, we are only given their number and the mean values (or totals) of X and Y, presented as

Group	Number of Observations	Mean of X	Mean of Y
1	n_1	$\bar{X}_1$	$\bar{Y}_1$
2	n_2	$\bar{X}_2$	$\bar{Y}_2$
$\vdots$	$\vdots$	$\vdots$	$\vdots$
G	n_g	$\bar{X}_G$	$\bar{Y}_G$

where

$$\bar{X}_g = \frac{1}{n_g}\sum_{i=1}^{n_g} X_{ig} \quad \text{and} \quad \bar{Y}_g = \frac{1}{n_g}\sum_{i=1}^{n_g} Y_{ig} \qquad (g = 1, 2, \ldots, G).$$

The problem now is to derive estimation formulas for the regression coefficients using the group means, and to determine how the properties of the resulting estimators compare with the properties of the ordinary least squares estimators based on individual observations. Let us take the regression equation (9.36) and "condense" it by averaging over all observations within each group. In this way we obtain

$$\bar{Y}_g = \alpha + \beta \bar{X}_g + \bar{\varepsilon}_g \qquad (g = 1, 2, \ldots, G). \tag{9.37}$$

That is, we are replacing the original n observations with a smaller number of G groups means. Now, if X_{ig} is nonstochastic, $\bar{X}_g$ will also be nonstochastic so that we have to worry only about $\bar{\varepsilon}_g$. First, we note that

$$E(\bar{\varepsilon}_g) = E\frac{1}{n_g}(\varepsilon_{1g} + \varepsilon_{2g} + \cdots + \varepsilon_{n_g g}) = 0,$$

which means that ordinary least squares estimators of α and β based on group means are unbiased. Next, for $g \neq h$,

$$E(\bar{\varepsilon}_g\bar{\varepsilon}_h) = E\left[\frac{1}{n_g}(\varepsilon_{1g} + \varepsilon_{2g} + \cdots + \varepsilon_{n_g g})\right]\left[\frac{1}{n_h}(\varepsilon_{1h} + \varepsilon_{2h} + \cdots + \varepsilon_{n_h h})\right] = 0,$$

which means that $\bar{\varepsilon}_g$ is nonautoregressive. Finally,

$$\text{Var}(\bar{\varepsilon}_g) = \frac{1}{n_g^2}(\sigma^2 + \sigma^2 + \cdots + \sigma^2) = \frac{n_g\sigma^2}{n_g^2} = \frac{\sigma^2}{n_g},$$

which means that, unless the number of observations is the same in every group, the disturbance in (9.37) is *heteroskedastic.*

The heteroskedastic nature of $\bar{\varepsilon}_g$ implies that ordinary least squares estimators of α and β using group means as "observations" are not efficient. To make efficient use of the group means, we have to use the estimation formulas designed for heteroskedastic regressions. These formulas were developed in Section 8-2 and are given by (8.13), (8.14), (8.18), and (8.19). With respect to $\bar{\varepsilon}_g$, we are in a fortunate position of knowing exactly how its variance changes from "observation" to "observation," i.e., from group to group, because n_g is known. To adapt the formulas in Section 8-2 to the use of group means, we replace the subscipt i by g, put "bars" over the Xs and Ys, and replace w_i by n_g/σ^2. The resulting estimators of α and β, say, $\tilde{\alpha}$ and $\tilde{\beta}$, are

$$\text{(9.38)} \qquad \tilde{\beta} = \frac{[(\sum n_g)(\sum n_g\bar{X}_g\bar{Y}_g) - (\sum n_g\bar{X}_g)(\sum n_g\bar{Y}_g)]/\sigma^4}{[(\sum n_g)(\sum n_g\bar{X}_g^2) - (\sum n_g\bar{X}_g)^2]/\sigma^4}$$

$$= \frac{\sum n_g\bar{X}_g\bar{Y}_g - n\bar{X}\bar{Y}}{\sum n_g\bar{X}_g^2 - n\bar{X}^2}$$

$$= \frac{\sum n_g(\bar{X}_g - \bar{X})(\bar{Y}_g - \bar{Y})}{\sum n_g(\bar{X}_g - \bar{X})^2}$$

and

$$\text{(9.39)} \qquad \tilde{\alpha} = \frac{(\sum n_g\bar{Y}_g)/\sigma^2}{(\sum n_g)/\sigma^2} - \tilde{\beta}\frac{(\sum n_g\bar{X}_g)/\sigma^2}{(\sum n_g)/\sigma^2} = \bar{Y} - \tilde{\beta}\bar{X},$$

where $\overline{X}$ is the overall sample mean of X and $\overline{Y}$ the overall sample mean of Y. In simplifying the expressions for $\tilde{\alpha}$ and $\tilde{\beta}$ we have made use of the following equalities:

$$\sum_g n_g = n_1 + n_2 + \cdots + n_G = n,$$

$$\sum_g n_g \overline{X}_g = n_1 \overline{X}_1 + n_2 \overline{X}_2 + \cdots + n_G \overline{X}_G = \sum_i X_{i1} + \sum_i X_{i2} + \cdots + \sum_i X_{iG}$$

$$= \sum_i \sum_g X_{ig} = n\overline{X},$$

$$\sum_g n_g \overline{Y}_g = n_1 \overline{Y}_1 + n_2 \overline{Y}_2 + \cdots + n_G \overline{Y}_G = n\overline{Y}.$$

The variances of $\tilde{\alpha}$ and $\tilde{\beta}$ are

(9.40) $$\mathrm{Var}(\tilde{\beta}) = \frac{(\sum n_g)/\sigma^2}{[(\sum n_g)(\sum n_g \overline{X}_g^2) - (\sum n_g \overline{X}_g)^2]/\sigma^4}$$

$$= \frac{\sigma^2}{\sum n_g(\overline{X}_g - \overline{X})^2}$$

and

(9.41) $$\mathrm{Var}(\tilde{\alpha}) = \frac{(\sum n_g \overline{X}_g^2)/\sigma^2}{[(\sum n_g)(\sum n_g \overline{X}_g^2) - (\sum n_g \overline{X}_g)^2]/\sigma^4}$$

$$= \sigma^2 \left[\frac{1}{n} + \frac{\overline{X}^2}{\sum n_g(\overline{X}_g - \overline{X})^2} \right].$$

A question of particular interest to us is how the variances of $\tilde{\alpha}$ and $\tilde{\beta}$ compare with the variances of the ordinary least squares estimators based on ungrouped observations. We know that by grouping the observations and estimating the regression coefficients from group means rather than from the individual observations, we are losing some information contained in the sample, namely, the information about the variation of the observations *within* each group. Therefore, we would expect that we would lose some efficiency in going from estimation based on all individual observations to estimation based on group means. We shall see whether, and to what extent, this is true by evaluating the ratio of $\mathrm{Var}(\tilde{\beta})$ to $\mathrm{Var}(\hat{\beta})$, where $\hat{\beta}$ denotes the least squares estimator of β based on individual observations.

Now, from (7.23) the variance of $\hat{\beta}$ is

$$\mathrm{Var}(\hat{\beta}) = \frac{\sigma^2}{\sum_i \sum_g (X_{ig} - \bar{X})^2}.$$

Note that the denominator on the right-hand side of this expression can be written as

$$\begin{aligned}\sum_i \sum_g (X_{ig} - \bar{X})^2 &= \sum_i \sum_g [(X_{ig} - \bar{X}_g) + (\bar{X}_g - \bar{X})]^2 \\ &= \sum_i \sum_g (X_{ig} - \bar{X}_g)^2 + \sum_i \sum_g (\bar{X}_g - \bar{X})^2 \\ &\quad + 2 \sum_i \sum_g (X_{ig} - \bar{X}_g)(\bar{X}_g - \bar{X}) \\ &= \sum_i \sum_g (X_{ig} - \bar{X}_g)^2 + \sum_g n_g(\bar{X}_g - \bar{X})^2.\end{aligned}$$

The ratio of the two variances then is

$$\text{(9.42)} \qquad \frac{\mathrm{Var}(\tilde{\beta})}{\mathrm{Var}(\hat{\beta})} = \frac{\sigma^2 / \sum_g n_g(\bar{X}_g - \bar{X})^2}{\sigma^2 / [\sum_i \sum_g (X_{ig} - \bar{X}_g)^2 + \sum_g n_g(\bar{X}_g - \bar{X})^2]}$$

$$= 1 + \frac{\sum_i \sum_g (X_{ig} - \bar{X}_g)^2}{\sum_g n_g(\bar{X}_g - \bar{X})^2}.$$

This ratio is always greater than, or at best equal to, unity. The last term on the right-hand side measures the loss of efficiency resulting from the use of grouped data instead of individual observations. Note that the size of the numerator reflects the variation of the values of X *within* each group around the group mean, while the size of the denominator reflects the variation of the group means of X around the overall sample mean. Thus we will lose no efficiency by grouping if there is no variation of the values of X within each group, and the loss of efficiency will be small if this variation is small compared with the variation of the group means of X around the overall mean. In other words, there will always be some loss of efficiency by going from individual observations to groups unless the X's within each group are all equal. *This conclusion holds whether the groups contain the same number of observations or not.* Having groups of equal size would make $\bar{\varepsilon}_g$ homoskedastic but would not prevent a loss of efficiency as a result of grouping.

When estimating the regression coefficients from grouped data, we can use formulas (9.38) and (9.39) since they can be readily evaluated, but the expressions for the variances of these estimators involve an unknown parameter σ^2. To find an unbiased estimator of σ^2, we note that the formulas for $\tilde{\beta}$ and $\tilde{\alpha}$ given in (9.38) and (9.39) are the same as those obtained by the application of the ordinary least squares method to

$$\overline{Y}_g\sqrt{n_g} = \alpha\sqrt{n_g} + \beta\overline{X}_g\sqrt{n_g} + \bar{\varepsilon}\sqrt{n_g}.$$

This follows from the fact that the transformed disturbance $\bar{\varepsilon}\sqrt{n_g}$ satisfies all classical assumptions and that, in particular, $\text{Var}(\bar{\varepsilon}\sqrt{n_g}) = \sigma^2$. Thus an unbiased estimator of σ^2, say, $\tilde{s}^2$, is

$$\text{(9.43)} \qquad \tilde{s}^2 = \frac{1}{G-2}\sum_g n_g(\overline{Y}_g - \tilde{\alpha} - \tilde{\beta}\overline{X}_g)^2.$$

For the purpose of calculation, this expression may be simplified as follows.

$$\text{(9.43a)} \qquad \tilde{s}^2 = \frac{1}{G-2}\sum_g n_g[\overline{Y}_g - (\overline{Y} - \tilde{\beta}\overline{X}) - \tilde{\beta}\overline{X}_g]^2$$

$$= \frac{1}{G-2}\left[\sum_g n_g(\overline{Y}_g - \overline{Y})^2 - \tilde{\beta}^2\sum_g n_g(\overline{X}_g - \overline{X})^2\right].$$

By using $\tilde{s}^2$ as the estimator of σ^2 in (9.40) and (9.41), we obtain estimators of the variances of $\tilde{\alpha}$ and $\tilde{\beta}$. These are

$$\text{(9.44)} \qquad \tilde{s}^2_{\tilde{\beta}} = \frac{\tilde{s}^2}{\sum n_g(\overline{X}_g - \overline{X})^2},$$

$$\text{(9.45)} \qquad \tilde{s}^2_{\tilde{\alpha}} = \tilde{s}^2\left[\frac{1}{n} + \frac{\overline{X}^2}{\sum n_g(\overline{X}_g - \overline{X})^2}\right].$$

These estimators are unbiased, consistent, and asymptotically efficient among the class of all estimators that are based on the same information.

A final point of interest in connection with estimation based on group means concerns the behavior of the coefficient of determination (R^2). When the estimation is done on the basis of individual observations, the value of R^2 is calculated as

$$\text{(9.46)} \qquad R^2 = \frac{\hat{\beta}^2\sum_i\sum_g(X_{ig} - \overline{X})^2}{\sum_i\sum_g(Y_{ig} - \overline{Y})^2},$$

where $\hat{\beta}$ is an ordinary least squares estimator of β based on individual observations. On the other hand, when we estimate the regression coefficients by using group means, the value of R^2 is calculated as

$$\text{(9.47)} \qquad R^2 = 1 - \frac{\sum_g(\overline{Y}_g - \tilde{\alpha} - \tilde{\beta}\overline{X}_g)^2}{\sum_g(\overline{Y}_g - \overline{\overline{Y}})^2},$$

where

$$\sum_g (\overline{Y}_g - \tilde{\alpha} - \tilde{\beta}\overline{X}_g)^2 = \sum_g [\overline{Y}_g - (\overline{Y} - \tilde{\beta}\overline{X}) - \tilde{\beta}\overline{X}_g]^2$$
$$= \sum_g (\overline{Y}_g - \overline{Y})^2 - 2\tilde{\beta} \sum_g (\overline{Y}_g - \overline{Y})(\overline{X}_g - \overline{X})$$
$$+ \tilde{\beta}^2 \sum_g (\overline{X}_g - \overline{X})^2$$

and

$$\sum_g (\overline{Y}_g - \overline{\overline{Y}})^2 = \sum_g \overline{Y}_g^2 - \frac{1}{G}\left(\sum_g \overline{Y}_g\right)^2.$$

It has been shown that the value of R^2 calculated by (9.47) tends to be higher than that calculated by (9.46).[13] That is, as we go from individual observations to group means, the value of R^2 tends to increase. Since the underlying sample is the same whether we use individual observations or group means, the increase in the value of R^2 is entirely due to grouping and should be interpreted as such. It simply reflects the fact that the group means tend to be less dispersed around the fitted regression line than the individual observations.

EXAMPLE A sample survey of immigrants in Australia conducted in 1959 by the Department of Demography of the Australian National University contained information on weekly income and consumption expenditure of immigrant families. The results for the 181 British immigrants included in the sample survey are given in Table 9-2.

Table 9-2

Income class	Number of observations: n_g	Mean income:[a] $\overline{X}_g$	Mean consumption expenditure:[a] $\overline{Y}_g$
Under 18	51	15.5	13.900
18 and under 20	22	19.0	15.291
20 and under 22	22	21.0	18.195
22 and under 24	23	23.0	20.104
24 and under 26	13	25.0	20.985
26 and under 28	12	27.0	22.742
28 and under 30	14	29.0	24.414
30 and under 32	9	31.0	24.089
32 and under 34	7	33.0	29.286
34 and under 36	4	35.0	27.000
36 and over	4	37.0	29.500

Data made available by Dr. J. Zubrzycki of the Australian National University.
[a] In Australian pounds per week.

[13] See J. S. Cramer, "Efficient Grouping, Regression and Correlation in Engel Curve Analysis," *Journal of the American Statistical Association,* 59 (March 1964), pp. 233–250.

Suppose we wish to estimate the coefficients of a linear consumption function,

$$Y = \alpha + \beta X + \varepsilon,$$

from this information. The results of the basic calculations are

$$\bar{X} = \frac{1}{181} \sum_g n_g \bar{X}_g = 22.390,$$

$$\bar{Y} = \frac{1}{181} \sum_g n_g \bar{Y}_g = 19.024,$$

$$\bar{\bar{Y}} = \frac{1}{11} \sum_g \bar{Y}_g = 22.319,$$

$$\sum_g n_g(\bar{X}_g - \bar{X})(\bar{Y}_g - \bar{Y}) = \sum_g n_g \bar{X}_g \bar{Y}_g - 181(\bar{X}\bar{Y}) = 82{,}153.2 - 77{,}096.5$$

$$= 5056.7,$$

$$\sum_g n_g(\bar{X}_g - \bar{X})^2 = \sum_g n_g \bar{X}_g^2 - 181(\bar{X}^2) = 97{,}358.8 - 90{,}735.5 = 6623.3,$$

$$\sum_g n_g(\bar{Y}_g - \bar{Y})^2 = \sum_g n_g \bar{Y}_g^2 - 181(\bar{Y}^2) = 69{,}475.8 - 65{,}506.2 = 3969.6,$$

$$\sum_g (\bar{Y}_g - \bar{\bar{Y}})^2 = 273.7,$$

$$\sum_g (\bar{Y}_g - \tilde{\alpha} - \tilde{\beta}\bar{X}_g)^2 = 12.069.$$

Therefore

$$\tilde{\beta} = \frac{5056.7}{6623.3} = 0.763,$$

$$\tilde{\alpha} = 19.024 - 0.763 \times 22.390 = 1.940,$$

$$\tilde{s}^2 = \frac{113.7201}{9} = 12.6356,$$

$$s_{\tilde{\alpha}}^2 = 12.6356 \left[\frac{1}{181} + \frac{22.390^2}{6623.3} \right] = 1.026188,$$

$$s_{\tilde{\beta}}^2 = \frac{12.6356}{6623.3} = 0.001908,$$

$$R^2 = 1 - \frac{12.069}{273.7} = 0.956.$$

The estimated regression equation then is

$$\underset{}{\bar{Y}_g} = \underset{(1.012)}{1.940} + \underset{(0.044)}{0.763}\,\bar{X}_g + e_g, \qquad R^2 = 0.956.$$

Estimation with Categorized Data

In many cases of reported statistical data, the information provided for various continuous variables is given in a categorical form. For instance, in a survey of firms, employment may be recorded as the number of firms with less than 100 employees, with 100 and less than 500 employees, etc. Such categorized variables may be dependent or explanatory or both.

Let us start with the situation in which the categorized variable is the dependent variable in a classical regression model. For example, when considering the relationship between household expenditure on a given commodity and household income, a household respondent taking part in a survey may be asked to check off an appropriate expediture category, but household income may be recorded as a continuous variable obtained from the household income tax records. In this case the standard approach is to treat the *midpoint* of each category (interval) as if it were the observed value of the dependent variable. Let us consider the consequences of this. The true relationship between Y and X is represented as

$$(9.48) \qquad Y_{ig} = \alpha + \beta X_{ig} + \varepsilon_{ig}, \qquad (i = 1, 2, \ldots, n_g, \; g = 1, 2, \ldots, G),$$

$$\sum_{g=1}^{G} n_g = n,$$

where the double subscript ig refers to the ith observation in the gth category (interval). In the case under consideration the values of X are available but the values of Y are represented by intervals, and we use the midpoint of each interval, say, M_g, for each value of Y in the gth interval. (In the case of open-ended intervals, an arbitrary lower and/or upper limit has to be set.) That is, if the lower and the upper limits of the gth interval are L_{g-1} and L_g, respectively, then $M_g = (L_{g-1} + L_g)/2$, and we may write

$$Y_{ig} = M_g + v_{ig},$$

where v is the "error" resulting from using the midpoint values rather than the actual values of Y. The estimates of the regression coefficients are obtained by applying the least squares method to

$$(9.49) \qquad M_g = \alpha + \beta X_{ig} + u_{ig},$$

where $u = \varepsilon - v$. The resulting formulas are

$$(9.50a) \qquad \hat{\beta} = \frac{\sum_i \sum_g m'_g x'_{ig}}{\sum_i \sum_g x'^2_{ig}},$$

$$(9.50b) \qquad \hat{\alpha} = \overline{M} - \hat{\beta}\overline{X},$$

where

$$m'_g = M_g - \overline{M}, \quad \overline{M} = \frac{1}{n}\sum_i \sum_g M_g = \frac{1}{n}\sum_g n_g M_g, \quad x'_{ig} = X_{ig} - \overline{X},$$

and $\quad \overline{X} = \frac{1}{n}\sum_i \sum_g X_{ig}.$

Let us consider the properties of $\hat{\beta}$. First we note that in the formula for $\hat{\beta}$ in (9.50a) the quantities m'_g and x'_g are nonstochastic by assumption, and that the only stochastic element in the formula is n_g, the number of values of Y that fall within the gth interval. Therefore the determination of the mathematical expectation of $\hat{\beta}$ is rather complicated.[14] However, we can get an idea about the potential bias of $\hat{\beta}$ by examining the expected difference between $\hat{\beta}$ and the (unavailable) least squares estimator that would be used if all values of Y were properly observed, to be denoted by $\tilde{\beta}$. Since the latter is known to be unbiased, then $E(\tilde{\beta} - \hat{\beta})$ gives the extent of the bias of $\hat{\beta}$. Specifically,

$$(9.51) \qquad E(\tilde{\beta} - \hat{\beta}) = E\left[\frac{\sum_i \sum_g x'_{ig} y'_{ig}}{\sum_i \sum_g x'^2_{ig}} - \frac{\sum_i \sum_g x'_{ig} m'_g}{\sum_i \sum_g x'^2_{ig}}\right]$$

$$= E\left[\frac{\sum_i \sum_g x'_{ig}(Y_{ig} - M_g)}{\sum_i \sum_g x'^2_{ig}}\right]$$

$$= E\left[\frac{\sum_i \sum_g x'_{ig} v'_{ig}}{\sum_i \sum_g x'^2_{ig}}\right].$$

Thus $\hat{\beta}$ is, in general, biased unless the values of X are uncorrelated with the errors that result from using the midpoints to represent the values of Y. If the behavior of v approximates that of a standard error of measurement, the bias of $\hat{\beta}$ may be small.[15]

Let us suppose now that, in contrast to the preceding situation, the dependent variable is measured exactly but the explanatory variable is categorized and its values are represented by the midpoints of the respective intervals, to be denoted by M^*. The least squares method is then applied to

$$(9.52) \qquad Y_{ig} = \alpha + \beta M^*_g + \varepsilon^*_{ig},$$

where

$$\varepsilon^*_{ig} = \varepsilon_{ig} + \beta(X_{ig} - M^*_g).$$

The results are

$$(9.53a) \qquad \hat{\beta} = \frac{\sum_i \sum_g y'_{ig} m^{*\prime}_g}{\sum_i \sum_g m^{*\prime 2}_g},$$

$$(9.53b) \qquad \hat{\alpha} = \bar{Y} - \hat{\beta}\bar{M}^*,$$

[14] See M. B. Stewart, "On Least Squares Estimation When the Dependent Variable Is Grouped," *Review of Economic Studies,* 50 (1983), pp. 737–753.

[15] For an extensive treatment of this and similar problems, see Y. Haitovsky, *Regression Estimation from Grouped Observations* (New York: Hafner, 1973).

where

$$y'_{ig} = Y_{ig} - \overline{Y}, \quad \overline{Y} = \frac{1}{n}\sum_i \sum_g Y_{ig}, \quad m_g^{*\prime} = M_g^* - \overline{M}^*, \quad \text{and} \quad \overline{M}^* = \frac{1}{n}\sum_g n_g M_g^*.$$

Then

$$(9.54) \qquad E(\hat{\beta}) = \beta + E\left[\frac{\sum_i \sum_g m_g^{*\prime}\varepsilon_{ig}^{*\prime}}{\sum_g n_g m_g^{*\prime 2}}\right]$$

$$= \beta + \beta\left[\frac{\sum_i \sum_g (x'_{ig} - m_g^{*\prime})m_g^{*\prime}}{\sum_g n_g m_g^{*\prime 2}}\right].$$

Thus the LSE of β is biased unless the midpoints are uncorrelated with the deviations of the values of X from their respective midpoints. The latter would be the case if the values of X were uniformly distributed over the range of X from the lower limit of the first interval to the upper limit of the last interval; in that case the positive and the negative deviations of X from M^* would cancel out within each interval.

An alternative way of dealing with a categorized explanatory variable is to represent each interval of X by a binary ("dummy") variable that takes on the value of 1 for each observation that falls in the particular interval, and the value of 0 for all other observations.[16] If the values of X are classified into G mutually exclusive intervals, then the values of X can be represented by G binary variable Z_1, $Z_2, \ldots, Z_G$ as follows.

$$
\begin{aligned}
Z_{i1} &= 1 \quad \text{if the value of } X \text{ belongs to the 1st interval,}\\
&= 0 \quad \text{otherwise,}\\
Z_{i2} &= 1 \quad \text{if the value of } X \text{ belongs to the 2nd interval,}\\
&= 0 \quad \text{otherwise,}\\
&\vdots\\
Z_{iG} &= 1 \quad \text{if the value of } X \text{ belongs to the } G\text{th interval,}\\
&= 0 \quad \text{otherwise.}
\end{aligned}
$$

The regression equation is then respecified as

$$(9.55) \qquad Y_{ig} = \gamma_1 Z_{i1} + \gamma_2 Z_{i2} + \cdots + \gamma_G Z_{iG} + u_{ig},$$

where $\quad u_{ig} = \alpha + \beta X_{ig} + \varepsilon_{ig} - \sum_g \gamma_g Z_{ig}.$

[16] See D. J. Aigner, A. S. Goldberger, and G. Kalton, "On the Explanatory Power of Dummy Variable Regressions," *International Economic Review,* 16 (June 1975), pp. 503–510.

For appropriately arranged observations the values of the Z variables are

$$Z_{i1}:\ 1, 1, \ldots, 1, 0, 0, \ldots, 0, 0, \ldots, 0, 0, 0, \ldots, 0$$
$$Z_{i2}:\ 0, 0, \ldots, 0, 1, 1, \ldots, 1, 0, \ldots, 0, 0, 0, \ldots, 0$$
$$\vdots$$
$$Z_{iG}:\ 0, 0, \ldots, 0, 0, 0, \ldots, 0, 0, \ldots, 0, 1, 1, \ldots, 1,$$

where the first n_1 values of Z_1, the following n_2 values of Z_2, . . . , and the last n_g values of Z_G are 1's, and the remaining values are zeros.

Equation (9.55) is a multiple regression equation (without an intercept) whose least squares estimation is discussed in Chapter 10. Here we simply state the results that can easily be checked by the reader after mastering the techniques explained in Chapter 10. Specifically, the least squares estimators of the regression coefficients in (9.55) are

(9.56)
$$\hat{\gamma}_1 = \frac{\sum_{i=1}^{n_1} Y_{i1}}{n_1} = \bar{Y}_1,$$
$$\hat{\gamma}_2 = \frac{\sum_{i=1}^{n_2} Y_{i2}}{n_2} = \bar{Y}_2,$$
$$\vdots$$
$$\hat{\gamma}_G = \frac{\sum_{i=1}^{n_G} Y_{iG}}{n_G} = \bar{Y}_G.$$

Since the γ coefficients are not easily related to the original regression coefficients, there is no obvious or natural way of deriving estimates of α and β from the estimates of the γ's. However, a statement that the γ coefficients are all equal—which means that moving from one category of the values of X into another leaves the mean value of Y unaffected—is equivalent to the statement that $\beta = 0$. Thus the test of the hypothesis

$$H_0:\ \beta = 0,$$
$$H_A:\ \beta \neq 0,$$

can be accomplished by testing the hypothesis

$$H_0:\ \gamma_1 = \gamma_2 = \cdots = \gamma_G,$$
$$H_A:\ H_0 \text{ is not true.}$$

Under H_0 the disturbance in (9.55) becomes

$$Y_{ig} = \alpha - \gamma \sum_g Z_{ig} + \varepsilon_{ig} = \varepsilon_{ig},$$

since for each observation one of the Z's is equal to 1 and the others are equal to 0.

To test H_0 we can use the test statistic given in (7.51) as

$$\frac{(SSE_R - SSE_U)/r}{SSE_U/(n-K)} \sim F_{r,n-K},$$

where SSE_R is the error sum of squares obtained when the restrictions imposed by H_0 are taken into account in estimation, SSE_U is the unrestricted error sum of squares, r is the number of restrictions involved in H_0, and K is the number of regressors in the (unrestricted) regression equation. In the case under consideration there are $(G-1)$ restrictions on the γ's in H_0, and the number of regressors is G. When H_0 is true, all the γ's are equal and (9.55) becomes

$$\begin{aligned} Y_{ig} &= (Z_{i1} + Z_{i2} + \cdots + Z_{iG})\gamma + u_{ig} \\ &= \gamma + u_{ig}, \end{aligned}$$

and the least squares estimator of γ is $\bar{Y}\,(=\Sigma_i \Sigma_g Y_{ig}/n)$. Therefore

$$\begin{aligned} SSE_R &= \sum_i \sum_g (Y_{ig} - \bar{Y})^2 \\ &= \sum_i \sum_g (Y_{ig} - \bar{Y}_g)^2 + \sum_g n_g(\bar{Y}_g - \bar{Y})^2, \end{aligned}$$

where $\bar{Y}_g = \Sigma_i Y_{ig}/n_g$. When the equality of the γ's is not imposed and the estimators presented in (9.56) are used, the unrestricted error sum of squares is

$$\begin{aligned} SSE_U &= \sum_i \sum_g (Y_{ig} - \bar{Y}_1 Z_{i1} - \bar{Y}_2 Z_{i2} - \cdots - \bar{Y}_G Z_{iG})^2 \\ &= \sum_i (Y_{i1} - \bar{Y}_1)^2 + \sum_i (Y_{i2} - \bar{Y}_2)^2 + \cdots + \sum_i (Y_{iG} - \bar{Y}_G)^2 \\ &= \sum_i \sum_g (Y_{ig} - \bar{Y}_g)^2. \end{aligned}$$

Therefore

$$SSE_R - SSE_U = \sum_g n_g(\bar{Y}_g - \bar{Y})^2,$$

and the statistic is

$$\text{(9.57)} \qquad \frac{\Sigma_g n_g(\bar{Y}_g - \bar{Y})^2/(G-1)}{\Sigma_i \Sigma_g (Y_{ig} - \bar{Y}_g)^2/(n-G)} \sim F_{G-1,\,n-G}.$$

Thus it is possible to test for the existence of a relationship between Y and X as stated in (9.48) without having continuous measurements on X and using only a classification of the values of X by intervals.[17]

[17] The test statistic in (9.57) is the same as that used in the "analysis of variance" models for testing the equality of several group means. This is discussed in Section 11-1.

9-3 Estimation When Some Observations Are Missing

We shall consider now the question of estimating the parameters of the regression equation

$$Y_i = \alpha + \beta X_i + \varepsilon_i$$

when some of the sample values are missing. That is, we shall be concerned with the situation where some of the pairs of observations $(X_1, Y_1), (X_2, Y_2), \ldots, (X_n, Y_n)$ are incomplete in the sense that *one* of the values is missing. Missing observations are sometimes encountered in the case of cross-section or time-series data. For instance, when estimating a family consumption function from survey data, one finds that some families may have failed to report their income, while others may have omitted to state their consumption expenditure. Or, in the case of time series, the values of either variable may not be given for certain periods of time because of a change in the recording procedure, or for a number of other reasons. The question then is whether, when estimating the regression coefficients, we should discard the incomplete pairs of observations or whether the partial information contained in them could be put to some use.

In discussing the problem of using the information contained in the incomplete pairs of observations, we shall confine ourselves to situations where all the basic assumptions about the disturbance term—that is, assumption (7.2) through (7.5)—are valid. However, we shall distinguish between the case where X is nonstochastic and the case where X is stochastic but independent of the disturbance. If we use only the complete pairs of observations, then the least squares estimators of α and β are

$$\hat{\beta}_c = \frac{\sum_c (X_i - \bar{X}_c)(Y_i - \bar{Y}_c)}{\sum_c (X_i - \bar{X}_c)^2}, \tag{9.58}$$

and

$$\hat{\alpha}_c = \bar{Y}_c - \hat{\beta}_c \bar{X}_c, \tag{9.59}$$

where $\bar{X}_c$ and $\bar{Y}_c$ are the sample means of X and of Y calculated from the complete pairs, and Σ_c denotes the summation over all such pairs. The estimators $\hat{\alpha}_c$ and $\hat{\beta}_c$ are unbiased and efficient in the class of all estimators of α and β that use the same information.

Nonstochastic Explanatory Variable

In the case where X is nonstochastic, the values of X are under the control either of the investigator or of the original "experimenter." Of course, this is to be interpreted in a broad sense—for instance, viewing the government as conducting an "experiment" whenever it incurs some expenditure. The implication of this is that those pairs of observations for which the values of Y are not shown give no information about the outcome of the "experiment" and should not be counted as a part of the sample at all. Thus the only interesting case in this context is that where some of the X's are missing while all the values of Y are available. The incomplete pairs give us information about Y, i.e., about the outcome of the "experiment," but not about the conditioning variable X. We will first determine the loss of efficiency that results from using only the complete pairs instead of all of the pairs *if* they were all complete. Then we will try to use the incomplete pairs in an effort to make the loss of efficiency smaller. In the process, and throughout this section, we will use the following notation, in addition to the symbols already used in (9.58) and (9.59).

$\sum_{x}$	the summation over all pairs for which X is observed
$\sum_{y}$	the summation over all pairs for which Y is observed
$\sum_{0x}$	the summation over all pairs for which X is not observed
$\sum_{0y}$	the summation over all pairs for which Y is not observed
n_c	number of complete pairs
n_x	number of pairs for which X is observed
n_y	number of pairs for which Y is observed
m_x	number of pairs for which X is not observed
m_y	number of pairs for which Y is not observed

$$\bar{X}_x = \frac{1}{n_x} \sum_{x} X_i, \text{ etc.}$$

Note that

$$n_c + m_x + m_y = n,$$

$$n_c + m_y = n_x,$$

$$n_c + m_x = n_y.$$

In the present context, where all of the values of Y are available, we have

$$n_x = n_c,$$

$$n_y = n,$$

$$m_y = 0,$$

$$\bar{X}_x = \bar{X}_c.$$

If we use only the complete pairs of observations, the variance of the least squares estimator of β is

(9.60)
$$\operatorname{Var}(\hat{\beta}_c) = \frac{\sigma^2}{\sum_x (X_i - \bar{X}_x)^2}.$$

If *all* pairs were complete, the variance of the least squares estimator of β, say, $\hat{\beta}_y$, would be

(9.61)
$$\operatorname{Var}(\hat{\beta}_y) = \frac{\sigma^2}{\sum_y (X_i - \bar{X}_y)^2}.$$

The loss of efficiency due to the fact that some pairs of observations do not show a value for X (and we use only the complete pairs) can be measured by the ratio $\operatorname{Var}(\hat{\beta}_c)$ to $\operatorname{Var}(\hat{\beta}_y)$, i.e., by

(9.62)
$$\frac{\operatorname{Var}(\hat{\beta}_c)}{\operatorname{Var}(\hat{\beta}_y)} = \frac{\sum_y (X_i - \bar{X}_y)^2}{\sum_x (X_i - \bar{X}_x)^2}.$$

Now,

$$\begin{aligned}
\sum_y (X_i - \bar{X}_y)^2 &= \sum_x (X_i - \bar{X}_y)^2 + \sum_{0x} (X_i - \bar{X}_y)^2 \\
&= \sum_x [(X_i - \bar{X}_x) + (\bar{X}_x - \bar{X}_y)]^2 \\
&\quad + \sum_{0x} [(X_i - \bar{X}_{0x}) + (\bar{X}_{0x} - \bar{X}_y)]^2 \\
&= \sum_x (X_i - \bar{X}_x)^2 + n_x(\bar{X}_x - \bar{X}_y)^2 + \sum_{0x} (X_i - \bar{X}_{0x})^2 \\
&\quad + m_x(\bar{X}_{0x} - \bar{X}_y)^2.
\end{aligned}$$

By using the fact that

$$\bar{X}_y = \frac{1}{n}(n_x\bar{X}_x + m_x\bar{X}_{0x}),$$

we can write

$$n_x(\bar{X}_x - \bar{X}_y)^2 = n_x\left[\bar{X}_x - \frac{1}{n}(n_x\bar{X}_x + m_x\bar{X}_{0x})\right]^2 = \frac{n_x m_x^2}{n^2}(\bar{X}_x - \bar{X}_{0x})^2,$$

and

$$m_x(\bar{X}_{0x} - \bar{X}_y)^2 = m_x\left[\bar{X}_{0x} - \frac{1}{n}(n_x\bar{X}_x + m_x\bar{X}_{0x})\right]^2 = \frac{n_x^2 m_x}{n^2}(\bar{X}_x - \bar{X}_{0x})^2.$$

Therefore

$$\text{(9.62a)} \qquad \frac{\operatorname{Var}(\hat{\beta}_c)}{\operatorname{Var}(\hat{\beta}_y)} = 1 + \frac{\sum_{0x}(X_i - \bar{X}_{0x})^2 + (n_x m_x/n)(\bar{X}_x - \bar{X}_{0x})^2}{\sum_x (X_i - \bar{X}_x)^2}.$$

This result shows that the loss of efficiency will be small if the missing values of X have a small dispersion and, at the same time, the mean of the missing values of X is close to the mean of the available values of X. There will be no loss of efficiency involved (in finite samples) if and only if each one of the missing values of X is equal to the mean of the available values of X. Of course, since the missing values of X are not known, the ratio (9.62a) cannot be evaluated, but it can be estimated from the available sample information as shown below.

Let us try now to utilize the information contained in the pairs of observations for which the values of X are missing. These missing values can be viewed as unknown parameters that can be estimated along with the regression coefficients and σ^2. We will denote the missing value of X by ξ_i; according to our notation, their number will be m_x. The log-likelihood function for $(Y_1, Y_2, \ldots, Y_n)$ then is

$$L = -\frac{n}{2}\log 2\pi - \frac{n}{2}\log\sigma^2 - \frac{1}{2\sigma^2}\sum_x (Y_i - \alpha - \beta X_i)^2 - \frac{1}{2\sigma^2}\sum_{0x}(Y_i - \alpha - \beta\xi_i)^2.$$

By differentiating L with respect to α, β, σ^2, and each of the ξ_i's, putting each of the derivatives equal to zero, and solving for the values of the unknown parameters, we obtain the respective maximum likelihood estimators. It is a matter of simple algebra to show that the maximum likelihood estimators of α and β are exactly the same as the least squares estimators (9.58) and (9.59), that the estimator of σ^2 is based on complete pairs only, and that the estimators of ξ_i are

$$\text{(9.63)} \qquad \overset{\triangle}{\xi}_i = \frac{Y_i - \hat{\alpha}_c}{\hat{\beta}_c}.$$

This means that the maximum likelihood estimation method applied to all observations for which Y is observed provides estimates of the missing values of X but leaves the estimates of α, β, and σ^2 as they are when estimated only from the complete pairs. This is somewhat disappointing. Nevertheless, we are a little ahead because we can at least use the estimates of the missing values of X to get some idea about the loss of efficiency resulting from the presence of incomplete pairs of observations. This can be done by substituting $\overset{\triangle}{\xi}_i$ for the missing values of X in (9.62a). The result is

$$\text{(9.64)} \qquad \text{Est.}\left[\frac{\operatorname{Var}(\hat{\beta}_c)}{\operatorname{Var}(\hat{\beta}_y)}\right] = 1 + \frac{\sum_{0x}(\overset{\triangle}{\xi}_i - \bar{\overset{\triangle}{\xi}})^2 + (n_x m_x/n)(\bar{X}_x - \bar{\overset{\triangle}{\xi}})^2}{\sum_x (X_i - \bar{X}_x)^2}.$$

The estimator $\overset{\triangle}{\xi}_i$ has the desirable asymptotic properties possessed by other maximum likelihood estimators, provided the number of missing values of X does not grow with sample size.

EXAMPLE In the example in Section 7-3, we were concerned with estimating the coefficients of a linear relation between price (X) and quantity or oranges sold (Y) in a given supermarket over twelve consecutive days. The observations were

X:	100	90	80	70	70	70	70	65	60	60	55	50
Y:	55	70	90	100	90	105	80	110	125	115	130	130

The results of the relevant calculations were

$$\bar{X} = 70,$$

$$\sum (X_i - \bar{X})^2 = 2250,$$

$$\hat{\alpha} = 210.460,$$

$$\hat{\beta} = -1.578.$$

Suppose now that, in addition to the 12 pairs of observations, we also had the information that the quantity sold on the thirteenth day was 37 pounds but that no price has been reported. That is, $Y_{13} = 37$. This observation has been discarded. We wish to know how much efficiency we would have gained in estimating β if X_{13} had been known. First, we use (9.63) to estimate X_{13} as

$$\hat{\xi}_{13} = \frac{Y_{13} - \hat{\alpha}}{\hat{\beta}} = \frac{37 - 210.460}{-1.578} = 110.$$

Then, the estimated ratio of $\text{Var}(\hat{\beta}_c)$ to $\text{Var}(\hat{\beta}_y)$ is

$$1 + \frac{0 + [(12 \times 1)/13](70 - 110)^2}{2250} = 1.6564,$$

which means that the loss of efficiency is estimated to be 65.64%.

An alternative way of using the information contained in the incomplete pairs of observations is to fill in the gaps by using some approximations of the missing values of X. This approach is probably fairly common in practice. The approximations are obtained by, e.g., interpolation from the observed values of X, or by reference to some other variable Z that is correlated with X. However, if we replace the missing values of X with some approximations, we introduce errors of measurement into the values of the explanatory variable and, as a consequence, obtain inconsistent estimates of the regression coefficients. This was explained in detail in Section 9-1. How serious this inconsistency will be depends, of course, on the extent of the errors of approximation. In fact, what is being done in this case is giving up consistency in the hope of reducing the variance of the estimator. If we are reasonably certain that the errors of approximation are small while the gain in efficiency is potentially large, this may be a rational procedure. Otherwise, the trade may result in a loss.

Stochastic Explanatory Variable

Let us now turn to the case where X is a stochastic variable that is distributed independently of the disturbance. The formulas for the least squares estimators of the regression coefficients based on complete pairs of observations remain unchanged, and so do the formulas for their variances—except that the latter have to be interpreted as conditional upon the given set of available values of X. Each pair of the observed values of X and Y now comes from a bivariate probability distribution. Our problem is to estimate the regression coefficients when some of the pairs of observations are incomplete. Other than disregarding the incomplete pairs, we may try to fill in the gaps and *then* apply the least squares estimation. One way of filling the gaps is to ask which value of X, or of Y, would one expect to observe *before* making the observation. Commonly, this would be the mathematical expectation of X or of Y, i.e., their means. Since the means are unknown, we can use the available sample means as estimators. That is, we may complete the missing observations in the incomplete pairs by using the available sample means of the respective variables. The least squares estimators of α and β obtained from the sample completed in this way are called *zero-order regression estimators.*[18] They are defined as follows:

$$(9.65)\quad \hat{\beta}_0 = \frac{\sum_c (X_i - \bar{X}_x)(Y_i - \bar{Y}_y) + \sum_{0x} (\bar{X}_x - \bar{X}_x)(Y_i - \bar{Y}_y)}{\sum_c (X_i - \bar{X}_x)^2 + \sum_{0x} (\bar{X}_x - \bar{X}_x)^2 + \sum_{0y} (X_i - \bar{X}_x)^2}$$

$$+ \frac{\sum_{0y} (X_i - \bar{X}_x)(\bar{Y}_y - \bar{Y}_y)}{\sum_c (X_i - \bar{X}_x)^2 + \sum_{0x} (\bar{X}_x - \bar{X}_x)^2 + \sum_{0y} (X_i - \bar{X}_x)^2}$$

$$= \frac{\sum_c (X_i - \bar{X}_x)(Y_i - \bar{Y}_y)}{\sum_x (X_i - \bar{X}_x)^2},$$

and

$$(9.66)\quad \hat{\alpha}_0 = \bar{Y}_y - \hat{\beta}_0 \bar{X}_x.$$

In order to see whether these estimators are unbiased, we substitute

$$Y_i - \bar{Y}_y = \beta(X_i - \bar{X}_y) + (\varepsilon_i - \bar{\varepsilon}_y)$$

into (9.65) to get

$$\hat{\beta}_0 = \frac{\sum\limits_c (X_i - \bar{X}_x)[\beta(X_i - \bar{X}_y) + (\varepsilon_i - \bar{\varepsilon}_y)]}{\sum\limits_x (X_i - \bar{X}_x)^2}.$$

[18] See A. A. Afifi and R. M. Elashoff, "Missing Observations in Multivariate Statistics II. Point Estimation in Simple Linear Regression," *Journal of the American Statistical Association,* 62 (March 1967), pp. 10–29.

The mathematical expectation of $\hat{\beta}_0$, conditional upon the observed values of X, is

$$E(\hat{\beta}_0) = \frac{\beta \sum_c (X_i - \overline{X}_c + \overline{X}_c - \overline{X}_x)[X_i - \overline{X}_c + \overline{X}_c - E(\overline{X}_y)]}{\sum_x (X_i - \overline{X}_x)^2}$$

$$= \frac{\beta \sum_c (X_i - \overline{X}_c)^2 + \beta n_c(\overline{X}_c - \overline{X}_x)[\overline{X}_c - E(\overline{X}_y)]}{\sum_x (X_i - \overline{X}_x)^2}.$$

But

$$E(\overline{X}_y) = E\left[\frac{1}{n_y}\left(\sum_c X_i + \sum_{0x} X_i\right)\right] = \frac{1}{n_y}(n_c\overline{X}_c + m_x\mu_x),$$

where μ_x, which is the population mean of X, is used to replace $E(\overline{X}_{0x})$ since $\overline{X}_{0x}$ is not observed. Therefore

$$E(\hat{\beta}_0) = \frac{\beta\,[\sum_c (X_i - X_c)^2 + (n_c m_x/n_y)(\overline{X}_c - \overline{X}_x)(\overline{X}_c - \mu_x)]}{\sum_x (X_i - \overline{X}_x)^2} \neq \beta.$$

The conclusion, then, is that the zero-order regression estimator of β is, in general, *biased.* The same is true of the zero-order regression estimator of α.

Before we leave the zero-order regression method, let us consider some special cases. First, suppose that the values of X are all available and only some of the Y's are missing. In this case,

$$n_x = n,$$

$$n_y = n_c,$$

$$m_x = 0,$$

$$\overline{X}_{0x} = 0.$$

Then

$$E(\hat{\beta}_0) = \beta \frac{\sum_c (X_i - \overline{X}_c)^2}{\sum_x (X_i - \overline{X}_x)^2},$$

so that, unless $\overline{X}_c = \overline{X}_x$, $\hat{\beta}_0$ is still biased. Alternatively, suppose that the values of Y

are all available but some of the X's are missing. Then

$$n_x = n_c,$$

$$n_y = n,$$

$$m_y = 0,$$

$$\bar{X}_x = \bar{X}_c,$$

and

$$E(\hat{\beta}_0) = \frac{\beta \sum_c (X_i - \bar{X}_c)^2}{\sum_c (X_i - \bar{X}_c)^2} = \beta,$$

so that in this case the zero-order regression estimator of β is unbiased. However, the variance of $\hat{\beta}_0$, conditional upon the observed X's, in this case is

$$\text{Var}(\hat{\beta}_0) = E(\hat{\beta}_0 - \beta)^2 = E\left[\frac{\sum_x (X_i - \bar{X}_x)(\varepsilon_i - \bar{\varepsilon}_y)}{\sum_x (X_i - \bar{X}_x)^2}\right]^2 = \frac{\sigma^2}{\sum_x (X_i - \bar{X}_x)^2},$$

which is the same as the expression for $\text{Var}(\hat{\beta}_c)$ given by (9.60). This means that we have nothing to gain in the way of efficiency by using $\hat{\beta}_0$ instead of $\hat{\beta}_c$.

The zero-order regression method of estimation is based on the idea of replacing each of the missing values of X by $\bar{X}_x$, and each of the missing values of Y by $\bar{Y}_y$. An alternative idea is to replace the missing values of X by a parameter ξ, and the missing values of Y by a parameter η. Since each of the missing values of X is replaced by the same parameter ξ and each of the missing values of Y is replaced by the same parameter η, this procedure brings in only two additional unknown parameters, regardless of sample size and the number of missing values. The regression coefficients α and β can then be estimated simultaneously with ξ and η. This can be done by minimizing

$$\sum_c (Y_i - \alpha - \beta X_i)^2 + \sum_{0x} (Y_i - \alpha - \beta\xi)^2 + \sum_{0y} (\eta - \alpha - \beta X_i)^2$$

with respect to α, β, ξ, and η. The resulting estimators, known as *modified zero-order regression estimators,*[19] are

(9.67)
$$\hat{\beta}_m = \frac{\sum_c (X_i - \bar{X}_c)(Y_i - \bar{Y}_c)}{\sum_c (X_i - \bar{X}_c)^2 + \sum_{0y} (X_i - \bar{X}_{0y})^2}$$

and

(9.68)
$$\hat{\alpha}_m = \bar{Y}_c - \hat{\beta}_m \bar{X}_c.$$

The estimators of ξ and η, which are of only incidental interest, are

$$\hat{\xi} = \frac{\bar{Y}_{0x} - \hat{\alpha}_m}{\hat{\beta}_m} \quad \text{and} \quad \hat{\eta} = \hat{\alpha}_m + \hat{\beta}_m \bar{X}_{0y}.$$

[19] *Ibid.*

Let us examine $\hat{\alpha}_m$ and $\hat{\beta}_m$ for unbiasedness. For $\hat{\beta}_m$ we have

$$(9.67a) \qquad \hat{\beta}_m = \frac{\beta \sum_c (X_i - \overline{X}_c)^2 + \sum_c (X_i - \overline{X}_c)(\varepsilon_i - \varepsilon_c)}{\sum_c (X_i - \overline{X}_c)^2 + \sum_{0y} (X_i - \overline{X}_{0y})^2},$$

and the mathematical expectation of $\hat{\beta}_m$, conditional upon the observed X's, is

$$E(\hat{\beta}_m) = \frac{\beta \sum_c (X_i - \overline{X}_c)^2}{\sum_c (X_i - \overline{X}_c)^2 + \sum_{0y} (X_i - \overline{X}_y)^2} \neq \beta.$$

This means that the modified zero-order regression estimator of β is, in general, *biased.* The same is true of the modified zero-order regression estimator of α.

Again, let us examine some special cases. First, suppose that all of the values of X are available and only some of the Y's are missing. In this case it is easy to show that formulas (9.67) and (9.68) remain the same, which means that we do not get any further ahead. Suppose, on the other hand, that all of the values of Y are available and only some of the X's are missing. In this case formulas (9.67) and (9.68) become the same as (9.58) and (9.59). This means that the estimators $\hat{\alpha}_m$ and $\hat{\beta}_m$ are exactly equal to the ordinary least squares estimators based on complete pairs of observations only.

Missing Observations and Autocorrelated Disturbances

An associated problem when some observations are missing is that of testing for the absence of autoregression of the disturbances. With some observations missing, the traditional Durbin–Watson test is no longer strictly applicable. However, the available research results indicate that if the D–W test is applied by treating all observations as if they were a full sample of successive observations, the distortion is relatively mild. Also, it appears that this test may be preferable to its modifications that allow for missing observations.[20] The application of the Durbin h or m test, designed for situations when one of the explanatory variables is a lagged dependent variable and described in (8.84) and (8.85), is not affected by the presence of a gap in observations.

Summary and Concluding Remarks

To sum up, when we deal with samples in which some pairs of observations are incomplete, the information contained in the incomplete pairs is of relatively little

[20] See N. E. Savin and K. J. White, "Testing for Autocorrelation with Missing Observations," *Econometrica,* 46 (January 1978), pp. 59–67.

use when estimating the regression coefficients. When X is nonstochastic, the information contained in the pairs for which only the Y's are given enables us to get an estimate of the loss of efficiency due to the fact that some of the X's are missing. If this loss is substantial, it may be worthwhile to go to the trouble of attempting to recover the missing values of X, or to find some good approximations for them. When X is stochastic and we use either the zero order regression method or its modified version, we get estimators that are generally biased. If only values of X are missing, both methods will lead to unbiased estimates of β, but these will be no more efficient than the ordinary least squares estimates based on complete pairs only. One redeeming feature of the estimators of the regression coefficients obtained by the zero order regression method or its modified version is the fact that when the correlation between X and Y is low, the mean square error of these estimators is less than that of the ordinary least squares estimators based on complete pairs.[21] Thus, under certain circumstances, either one of the former methods may be preferable to estimation from complete pairs only.

The results in this section have all been derived in the context of a simple regression model but they also hold for models with more than one explanatory variable.[22] In dealing with the problem of missing data in this context, most authors have proposed to fill the missing values of explanatory variables by invoking ad hoc the existence of an auxiliary relation between the explanatory variable for which some values are missing and other explanatory variables for which all values are available. This ad hoc relation is then to be used to predict the missing values. The problem with this is that for the predictions to work, the auxiliary relation should also hold in previously unobserved situations, which means that there should be a reason for it. Such a reason would be provided by theory. Without any justification for the postulated auxiliary relation other than that provided by the correlations observed in the sample, its presumption is inappropriate. In the case where there is some theoretical justification for the auxiliary relation, this should be made explicit —whether some measurements are missing or not. In such a case the researchers would be dealing with a system of equations rather than with a single regression equation.

EXERCISES

9-1. Assuming the "errors-in-variables" model, estimate the relationship between $\log(V/PL)$ and $\log(W/P)$ from the data for the furniture industry given in Table 9-1. Use the weighted regression method with $\lambda = 2$.

9-2. Suppose the income classes given in Table 9-2 in the text are combined as follows.

[21] For a proof and an elaboration of this statement, see Afifi and Elashoff, *op. cit.*

[22] See J. Kmenta, "On the Problem of Missing Measurements in the Estimation of Economic Relationships," in E. G. Charatsis (ed.), *Proceedings of the Econometric Society European Meeting 1979* (Amsterdam: North-Holland Publishing, 1981).

Income class	Number of observations: n_g
Under 18	51
18 and under 22	44
22 and under 26	36
26 and under 30	26
30 and under 34	16
34 and over	8

Calculate the appropriate values of $\bar{X}_g$ and $\bar{Y}_g$, and use these to estimate the coefficients of

$$\bar{Y} = \alpha + \beta \bar{X} + \bar{\varepsilon}$$

and their standard errors. Compare your results with those based on the information as originally given in Table 9-2.

9-3. Provide a derivation of formula (9.63).

9-4. Consider the following observations on X(price of oranges) and Y(quantity of oranges sold).

X	Y
100	55
90	70
80	90
70	100
70	90
70	105
70	80
65	110
60	125
60	115
55	130
50	130
—	130
—	140

Estimate the loss of efficiency in estimating β as a result of disregarding the last two incomplete observations.

9-5. Given the sample moments of the observed values of X and Y, the weighted regression estimator of β—as defined by (9.20)—becomes a function of λ. For the example presented in the text we found

$$m_{*xx} = 20.1834/121,$$

$$m_{*yy} = 14.4456/121,$$

$$m_{*xy} = 16.9577/121.$$

Calculate the values of $\hat{\beta}$ for different values of λ and plot the results in a diagram.

9-6. Using the instrumental variable relation (9.22), show that the stronger the relation between X^* and Z (as indicated by the magnitude of the variance of u), the smaller the asymptotic variances of the instrumental variables estimators of α and β.

9-7. Consider the quadratic equation for the determination of the weighted regression estimator of β, say, $\tilde{\beta}$,

$$\tilde{\beta}^2 \lambda m^*_{xy} + \tilde{\beta}(m^*_{xx} - \lambda m^*_{yy}) - m^*_{xy} = 0.$$

Prove the consistency of $\tilde{\beta}$ by taking probability limits of both sides of the equation. Further, using the log-likelihood function (9.14) with $\lambda = \sigma_w^2/\sigma^2$, show that $\tilde{\beta}$ is a maximum likelihood estimator of β.

9-8. Consider a simple regression model for which all assumptions hold. Suppose, however, that we do not observe X but only X^* where $X^* = X + w$ and w is a normally and independently distributed measurement error with mean zero and variance σ_i^{*2}. If it is known that $\sigma_i^{*2} = X_i^2/10$, derive the formula for a consistent estimator of the regression slope β.

9-9. Consider the model of household saving as a function of household income presented in Exercise 8-1 and estimated from the data in Table 8-2. Obtain the least squares estimates of the regression coefficients using the midpoints of intervals given that the data in Table 8-2 have been modified as described below.

a. All the data on income (X) are available but the data on saving (Y) are grouped as follows.

Saving	No. of households
Less than 0	2
0 and less than 500	5
500 and less than 1000	3
1000 and less than 1500	6
1500 and less than 2000	2
Over 2000	2
	20

b. All the data on saving (Y) are available, but the data on income (X) are grouped as follows.

Income	No. of households
Under 5000	3
5000 and less than 10,000	11
10,000 and less than 15,000	4
15,000 and less than 20,000	1
20,000 and less than 25,000	0
25,000 and less than 30,000	1
	20

c. Using the grouping of (**b**) above and a dummy variable representation of the categories of X, carry out a test of the hypothesis that $\beta = 0$ against the hypothesis that $\beta \neq 0$.

9-10. Consider a regression model $Y_i = \alpha + \beta X_i + \varepsilon_i$ for which all basic assumptions are satisfied except that X is stochastic but independent of ε. The values of X are generated by the relation $X_i = \gamma + \delta Z_i + u_i$ for which *all* basic assumptions hold. Further, the disturbances u and ε are independently distributed. Suppose now that for the n observations on Y and Z only n_x ($<n$) observations on X are available, the remaining m_x values of X being missing. In this case there are at least three sensible ways of estimating β.

1. Apply the least squares method to the n_x complete observations on X and Y only.
2. Use the n_x complete observations on X and Z to obtain least squares estimates of γ and δ. Replace the missing values of X by $\hat{X} = \hat{\gamma} + \hat{\delta} Z$ and apply the least squares method to the n values of X (or $\hat{X}$) and Y.
3. Since we can write

$$Y_i = \alpha + \beta(\gamma + \delta Z_i + u_i) + \varepsilon_i$$
$$= \gamma^* + \mu Z_i + \varepsilon_i^*,$$

   where $\mu = \beta\delta$, we can estimate μ by applying the least squares method the n values of Y and Z. Then β can be estimated by dividing $\hat{\mu}$ by $\hat{\delta}$, the latter having been obtained by regressing X on Z.

Show that of the three above estimators only the first is unbiased, but that all are consistent.

10 Multiple Regression

The regression model introduced in Chapter 7 is applicable to relationships that include only one explanatory variable. When the model is extended to include more than one explanatory variable, we speak of a *multiple regression* model. Relationships that can be described by a multiple regression model are very common in economics. For example, in production functions, output is typically a function of several inputs; in consumption functions, the dependent variable may be influenced by income as well as other factors; and in demand functions, the traditional explanatory variables are the price of the product, the prices of substitutes, and income.

The multiple regression model designed to describe these relationships is a natural extension of the simple regression model. In fact, most of the results derived for the simple regression model can easily be generalized so that they apply to the multiple regression case. The basic results concerning estimation are presented in Section 10-1; hypothesis testing and prediction are discussed in Section 10-2. The subject of Section 10-3 is multicollinearity—a feature that characterizes regression models with two or more explanatory variables. Finally, in Section 10-4 we examine the validity of the results of the preceding sections when the regression equation is not correctly specified.

10-1 Estimation of Regression Parameters

A common type of theoretical proposition in economics states that changes in one variable can be explained by reference to changes in *several* other variables. Such a relationship is described in a simple way by a multiple linear regression equation of the form

$$Y_i = \beta_1 + \beta_2 X_{i2} + \beta_3 X_{i3} + \cdots + \beta_K X_{iK} + \varepsilon_i, \tag{10.1}$$

where Y denotes the dependent variable, the X's denote the explanatory variables, and ε is a stochastic disturbance. The subscript i refers to the ith observation; the second subscript used in describing the explanatory variables identifies the variable in question. The number of the explanatory variables is $K-1$, so that for $K=2$ equation (10.1) reduces to a simple regression equation. An alternative way of writing (10.1) is

$$Y_i = \beta_1 X_{i1} + \beta_2 X_{i2} + \cdots + \beta_K X_{iK} + \varepsilon_i, \tag{10.1a}$$

where $X_{i1} = 1$ for all $i = 1, 2, \ldots, n$. Writing X_{i1} for 1 as the multiplication factor of β_1 makes the regression equation look symmetric without bringing about any real change. To complete the specification of the regression model, we add the following *basic assumptions:*

(10.2) ε_i is normally distributed.

(10.3) $E(\varepsilon_i) = 0$.

(10.4) $\text{Var}(\varepsilon_i) = \sigma^2$.

(10.5) $\text{Cov}(\varepsilon_i, \varepsilon_j) = 0 \qquad (i \neq j)$.

(10.6) Each of the explanatory variables is nonstochastic with values fixed in repeated samples and such that, for any sample size, $\sum_{i=1}^{n} (X_{ik} - \bar{X}_k)^2/n$ is different from zero and its limit, as $n \rightarrow \infty$, is a finite number for every $k = 2, 3, \ldots, K$.

(10.7) The number of observations exceeds the number of coefficients to be estimated.

(10.8) No exact linear relation exists between any of the explanatory variables.

These assumptions are taken to apply to all observations. The full specification of the model given by (10.1) through (10.8) describes the so-called "classical normal linear regression model" in the context of multiple regression. Assumptions (10.2) through (10.5) involve the disturbance term and are exactly the same as assumptions (7.2) through (7.5) of the simple regression model. The last three assumptions refer to the explanatory variables. Assumption (10.6) is the same as assumption (7.6) except that it is extended to a larger number of explanatory variables. Assumptions (10.7) and (10.8) are new. Assumption (10.7) makes a provision for a sufficient number of "degrees of freedom" in estimation. Assumption (10.8) states that none of the explanatory variables is to be perfectly correlated with any other explanatory variable or with any linear combination of other explanatory variables. This assumption is also necessary for estimation, as will soon become clear.

Given the above specification of the multiple regression model, the distribution of Y_i is normal, as in the case of the simple regression model.

The mean of Y_i is

$$E(Y_i) = \beta_1 + \beta_2 X_{i2} + \beta_3 X_{i3} + \cdots + \beta_k X_{iK}, \tag{10.9}$$

and its variance is

$$\text{Var}(Y_i) = E[Y_i - E(Y_i)]^2 = \sigma^2. \tag{10.10}$$

Note that by using (10.9) we can interpret the regression coefficients as follows.

β_1 = the mean of Y_i when each of the explanatory variables is equal to zero;

β_k = the change in $E(Y_i)$ corresponding to a unit change in the kth explanatory variable, holding the remaining explanatory variables constant

$$= \frac{\partial E(Y_i)}{\partial X_{ik}} \qquad (k = 2, 3, \ldots, K).$$

β_1 is sometimes called the *intercept* (or the *regression constant*), and $\beta_2, \beta_3, \ldots, \beta_K$ are referred to as the *regression slopes* (or the *partial regression coefficients*).

This interpretation of the regression coefficients has an important implication for their estimation. Consider, for instance, the problem of estimating β_K. Given that β_K measures the effect of X_{iK} on $E(Y_i)$ while $X_{i2}, X_{i3}, \ldots, X_{i,K-1}$ are being held constant, an obvious way of estimating β_K would be by using observations made when all the explanatory variables other than X_{iK} are, in fact, constant. That is, the observations would be obtained from a controlled experiment in which all explanatory variables other than X_{iK} were kept at fixed and unchanged levels. Let us see what would happen to the estimation problem in such a case. In particular, let the level of X_{i2} be kept at ξ_2, that of X_{i3} at ξ_3, and so on, and let X_{iK} vary. Then the regression equation (10.1) can be written as

$$Y_i = \beta_1 + \beta_2\xi_2 + \beta_3\xi_3 + \cdots + \beta_{K-1}\xi_{K-1} + \beta_K X_{iK} + \varepsilon_i$$

or

$$Y_i = \alpha + \beta_K X_{iK} + \varepsilon_i,$$

which clearly shows that in this case we are back in the realm of simple regression. This is precisely what the laboratories conducting experiments in natural sciences are frequently trying to do. It follows then that if we want to keep the assumption of nonstochastic explanatory variables and at the same time have a justification for the existence of a multiple regression model, we have to exclude the possibility that the values of the explanatory variables are controllable by the investigator. Thus we consider only those situations in which the "experiment" has been conducted by somebody other than the econometrician, and for a purpose other than estimating the regression coefficients or testing hypotheses about them. Of course, this is a common way in which economic data are acquired. The "laboratory" is the society and the econometrican is, by and large, a mere onlooker.

The description of the classical normal linear regression model is commonly presented in *matrix notation.* First, equation (10.1a) can be written as

$$\text{(10.1b)} \qquad \mathbf{y} = \mathbf{X}\boldsymbol{\beta} + \boldsymbol{\varepsilon},$$

where

$$\mathbf{y} = \begin{bmatrix} Y_1 \\ Y_2 \\ \vdots \\ Y_n \end{bmatrix}, \quad \mathbf{X} = \begin{bmatrix} X_{11} & X_{12} & \ldots & X_{1K} \\ X_{21} & X_{22} & \ldots & X_{2K} \\ \vdots & \vdots & & \vdots \\ X_{n1} & X_{n2} & \ldots & X_{nK} \end{bmatrix}, \quad \boldsymbol{\beta} = \begin{bmatrix} \beta_1 \\ \beta_2 \\ \vdots \\ \beta_K \end{bmatrix}, \quad \boldsymbol{\varepsilon} = \begin{bmatrix} \varepsilon_1 \\ \varepsilon_2 \\ \vdots \\ \varepsilon_n \end{bmatrix}.$$

This means that the dimensions of the matrices and vectors involved are $\mathbf{y} \rightarrow (n \times 1)$, $\mathbf{X} \rightarrow (n \times K)$, $\boldsymbol{\beta} \rightarrow (K \times 1)$, and $\boldsymbol{\varepsilon} \rightarrow (n \times 1)$. Note in particular that each row in the $\mathbf{X}$ matrix represents a set of values of the explanatory variables pertaining to one observation, while each column represents a set of values for one explanatory variable over the n sample observations. The first column of $\mathbf{X}$ consists entirely of 1's. The assumptions (10.2) through (10.5) can be stated in matrix notation as

(10.2a–3a) $\boldsymbol{\varepsilon} \sim N(\mathbf{0}, \boldsymbol{\Sigma})$, where $\mathbf{0}$ is a column vector of zeros and $\boldsymbol{\Sigma} = E(\boldsymbol{\varepsilon}\boldsymbol{\varepsilon}') \rightarrow (n \times n)$,

(10.4a–5a) $\boldsymbol{\Sigma} = \sigma^2 \mathbf{I}_n$, where $\mathbf{I}_n$ is an identity matrix of order $(n \times n)$, with units in the principal diagonal and zeros everywhere else.

The statement in (10.4a–5a) combines the assumptions of homoskedasticity and nonautocorrelation; the disturbances that satisfy both of these assumptions are called "spherical." Finally, assumptions (10.6) through (10.8) concerning the explanatory variables can be transcribed as

(10.6a–8a) The elements of the matrix $\mathbf{X}$ are nonstochastic with values fixed in repeated samples, and the matrix $(1/n)(\mathbf{X}'\mathbf{X})$ is nonsingular and its elements are finite as $n \rightarrow \infty$.

Least Squares Estimation

Consider now the derivation of the *least squares estimators* of the regression coefficients. The sum of squares to be minimized is

$$S = \sum_{i=1}^{n} (Y_i - \beta_1 - \beta_2 X_{i2} - \beta_3 X_{i3} - \cdots - \beta_K X_{iK})^2.$$

Differentiating S with respect to $\beta_1, \beta_2, \ldots, \beta_K$, we get

$$\frac{\partial S}{\partial \beta_1} = -2 \sum_i (Y_i - \beta_1 - \beta_2 X_{i2} - \beta_3 X_{i3} - \cdots - \beta_K X_{iK}),$$

$$\frac{\partial S}{\partial \beta_2} = -2 \sum_i X_{i2}(Y_i - \beta_1 - \beta_2 X_{i2} - \beta_3 X_{i3} - \cdots - \beta_K X_{iK}),$$

$$\vdots$$

$$\frac{\partial S}{\partial \beta_K} = - \sum_i X_{iK}(Y_i - \beta_1 - \beta_2 X_{i2} - \beta_3 X_{i3} - \cdots - \beta_K X_{iK}).$$

Equating each derivative to zero and rearranging terms gives us the following least squares normal equations:

$$\sum_i Y_i = \hat{\beta}_1 n + \hat{\beta}_2 \sum_i X_{i2} + \hat{\beta}_3 \sum_i X_{i3} + \cdots + \hat{\beta}_K \sum_i X_{iK},$$

$$\sum_i X_{i2}Y_i = \hat{\beta}_1 \sum_i X_{i2} + \hat{\beta}_2 \sum_i X_{i2}^2 + \hat{\beta}_3 \sum_i X_{i2}X_{i3} + \cdots + \hat{\beta}_K \sum_i X_{i2}X_{iK},$$

$$\vdots$$

$$\sum_i X_{iK}Y_i = \hat{\beta}_1 \sum_i X_{iK} + \hat{\beta}_2 \sum_i X_{i2}X_{iK} + \hat{\beta}_3 \sum_i X_{i3}X_{iK} + \cdots + \hat{\beta}_K \sum_i X_{iK}^2.$$

These equations represent a simple generalization of (7.10) and (7.11). (A simple rule for the formation of the least squares normal equations is given in footnote 4 on page 213.) Note that this system of normal equations could not be solved for the unknown $\hat{\beta}$'s if either (1) the number of explanatory variables *plus* one exceeded the number of observations or (2) any one of the explanatory variables represented an exact linear combination of other explanatory variables. In the former case, the number of equations would be less than the number of unknowns; in the latter case, the equations would not be independent.

To solve the least squares normal equations, we note that the first equation can be written as

$$\hat{\beta}_1 = \bar{Y} - \hat{\beta}_2\bar{X}_2 - \hat{\beta}_3\bar{X}_3 - \cdots - \hat{\beta}_K\bar{X}_K, \tag{10.11}$$

where $\bar{Y} = \frac{1}{n}\sum_i Y_i$ and $\bar{X}_k = \frac{1}{n}\sum_i X_{ik}$ $(k = 2, 3, \ldots, K)$.

Substitution of (10.11) into the remaining normal equations gives, after some simplifications,

$$m_{Y2} = m_{22}\hat{\beta}_2 + m_{23}\hat{\beta}_3 + \cdots + m_{2K}\hat{\beta}_K,$$

$$m_{Y3} = m_{23}\hat{\beta}_2 + m_{33}\hat{\beta}_3 + \cdots + m_{3K}\hat{\beta}_K,$$

$$\vdots$$

$$m_{YK} = m_{2K}\hat{\beta}_2 + m_{3K}\hat{\beta}_3 + \cdots + m_{KK}\hat{\beta}_K,$$

where $m_{Yk} = \sum_i (Y_i - \bar{Y})(X_{ik} - \bar{X}_k)$

and $m_{jk} = \sum_i (X_{ij} - \bar{X}_j)(X_{ik} - \bar{X}_k)$ $(j, k = 2, 3, \ldots, K)$.

These equations can be solved for $\hat{\beta}_2, \hat{\beta}_3, \ldots, \hat{\beta}_K$. The solution is quite straightforward but somewhat laborious. For the case of two explanatory variables (i.e., $K = 3$), we have

$$\hat{\beta}_2 = \frac{\begin{vmatrix} m_{Y2} & m_{23} \\ m_{Y3} & m_{33} \end{vmatrix}}{\begin{vmatrix} m_{22} & m_{23} \\ m_{23} & m_{33} \end{vmatrix}} = \frac{m_{Y2}m_{33} - m_{Y3}m_{23}}{m_{22}m_{33} - m_{23}^2}, \tag{10.12}$$

(10.13)
$$\hat{\beta}_3 = \frac{\begin{vmatrix} m_{22} & m_{Y2} \\ m_{23} & m_{Y3} \end{vmatrix}}{\begin{vmatrix} m_{22} & m_{23} \\ m_{23} & m_{33} \end{vmatrix}} = \frac{m_{Y3}m_{22} - m_{Y2}m_{23}}{m_{22}m_{33} - m_{23}^2}.$$

The least squares normal equations can be presented in matrix notation as

$$(\mathbf{X}'\mathbf{y}) = (\mathbf{X}'\mathbf{X})\hat{\boldsymbol{\beta}},$$

where

$$(\mathbf{X}'\mathbf{y}) = \begin{bmatrix} \Sigma Y_i \\ \Sigma X_{i2}Y_i \\ \vdots \\ \Sigma X_{iK}Y_i \end{bmatrix}, \qquad (\mathbf{X}'\mathbf{X}) = \begin{bmatrix} n & \Sigma X_{i2} & \dots & \Sigma X_{iK} \\ \Sigma X_{i2} & \Sigma X_{i2}^2 & \dots & \Sigma X_{i2}X_{iK} \\ \vdots & \vdots & & \vdots \\ \Sigma X_{iK} & \Sigma X_{i2}X_{iK} & \dots & \Sigma X_{iK}^2 \end{bmatrix},$$

$$\hat{\boldsymbol{\beta}} = \begin{bmatrix} \hat{\beta}_1 \\ \hat{\beta}_2 \\ \vdots \\ \hat{\beta}_K \end{bmatrix}.$$

The solution for $\hat{\boldsymbol{\beta}}$ then simply becomes

(10.14)
$$\hat{\boldsymbol{\beta}} = (\mathbf{X}'\mathbf{X})^{-1}(\mathbf{X}'\mathbf{y}).$$

Alternatively, we can eliminate $\hat{\beta}_1$ by substitution from (10.11), and then solve the reduced system of equations to get

(10.15)
$$\underline{\hat{\boldsymbol{\beta}}} = (\underline{\mathbf{X}}'\underline{\mathbf{X}})^{-1}(\underline{\mathbf{X}}'\underline{\mathbf{y}}).$$

where

$$\underline{\hat{\boldsymbol{\beta}}} = \begin{bmatrix} \hat{\beta}_2 \\ \hat{\beta}_3 \\ \vdots \\ \hat{\beta}_K \end{bmatrix}, \qquad (\underline{\mathbf{X}}'\underline{\mathbf{X}}) = \begin{bmatrix} m_{22} & m_{23} & \dots & m_{2K} \\ m_{23} & m_{33} & \dots & m_{3K} \\ \vdots & \vdots & & \vdots \\ m_{2K} & m_{3K} & \dots & m_{KK} \end{bmatrix}, \qquad (\underline{\mathbf{X}}'\underline{\mathbf{y}}) = \begin{bmatrix} m_{Y2} \\ m_{Y3} \\ \vdots \\ m_{YK} \end{bmatrix}.$$

Another way of expressing $\underline{\hat{\boldsymbol{\beta}}}$ is the following. Let the $(n \times K)$ matrix $\mathbf{X}$, the first column of which consists entirely of 1's, be partitioned as

$$\mathbf{X} = [\boldsymbol{\iota} \quad \mathbf{Z}]$$

where $\boldsymbol{\iota} \rightarrow (n \times 1)$ is a vector of 1's, and $\mathbf{Z} \rightarrow n \times (K-1)$ is a matrix of the values of the $(K-1)$ explanatory variables involved. The matrix $\mathbf{Z}$ can be transformed into

$\underline{\mathbf{X}}$, the matrix of the values of the $(K-1)$ explanatory variables measured in terms of deviations from their respective means, as follows:

$$\underline{\mathbf{X}} = \left(\mathbf{I} - \frac{\boldsymbol{\iota}\boldsymbol{\iota}'}{n}\right)\mathbf{Z},$$

where $\mathbf{I}$ is a $(n \times n)$ identity matrix and $\boldsymbol{\iota}\boldsymbol{\iota}'$ is a $(n \times n)$ matrix with every element equal to 1. The transformation matrix $(\mathbf{I} - \boldsymbol{\iota}\boldsymbol{\iota}'/n)$ is symmetric and idempotent, i.e., $(\mathbf{I} - \boldsymbol{\iota}\boldsymbol{\iota}'/n) = (\mathbf{I} - \boldsymbol{\iota}\boldsymbol{\iota}'/n)'$ and $(\mathbf{I} - \boldsymbol{\iota}\boldsymbol{\iota}'/n)(\mathbf{I} - \boldsymbol{\iota}\boldsymbol{\iota}'/n) = (\mathbf{I} - \boldsymbol{\iota}\boldsymbol{\iota}'/n)$. Therefore the formula for $\hat{\underline{\boldsymbol{\beta}}}$ in (10.15) can be equivalently written as

$$\hat{\underline{\boldsymbol{\beta}}} = \left[\mathbf{Z}'\left(\mathbf{I} - \frac{\boldsymbol{\iota}\boldsymbol{\iota}'}{n}\right)\mathbf{Z}\right]^{-1}\left[\mathbf{Z}'\left(\mathbf{I} - \frac{\boldsymbol{\iota}\boldsymbol{\iota}'}{n}\right)\mathbf{y}\right]. \tag{10.15a}$$

The partitioning of $\mathbf{X}$ as $\mathbf{X} = [\boldsymbol{\iota} \ \ \mathbf{Z}]$ is a special case of a general partitioning

$$\mathbf{X} = [\mathbf{X}_1 \ \ \mathbf{X}_2],$$

where $\mathbf{X}_1 \rightarrow (n \times K_1)$, $\mathbf{X}_2 \rightarrow (n \times K_2)$, and $K_1 + K_2 = K$. The corresponding partitioning of $\boldsymbol{\beta}$ is

$$\boldsymbol{\beta} = \begin{bmatrix} \boldsymbol{\beta}_1 \\ \boldsymbol{\beta}_2 \end{bmatrix},$$

where $\boldsymbol{\beta}_1 \rightarrow (K_1 \times 1)$ and $\boldsymbol{\beta}_2 \rightarrow (K_2 \times 1)$. The regression equation can then be conformably written as

$$\mathbf{y} = \mathbf{X}_1\boldsymbol{\beta}_1 + \mathbf{X}_2\boldsymbol{\beta}_2 + \boldsymbol{\varepsilon}. \tag{10.16}$$

Using (10.14) and the formulas for the inversion of partitioned matrices given in Appendix B, the formulas for the least squares estimators of $\boldsymbol{\beta}_1$ and $\boldsymbol{\beta}_2$ are

$$\hat{\boldsymbol{\beta}}_1 = (\mathbf{X}_1'\mathbf{M}_2\mathbf{X}_1)^{-1}(\mathbf{X}_1'\mathbf{M}_2\mathbf{y}) \tag{10.17a}$$

$$\hat{\boldsymbol{\beta}}_2 = (\mathbf{X}_2'\mathbf{M}_1\mathbf{X}_2)^{-1}(\mathbf{X}_2'\mathbf{M}_1\mathbf{y}), \tag{10.17b}$$

where $\mathbf{M}_r$ $(r = 1, 2)$ is a $(n \times n)$ symmetric and idempotent matrix defined as $\mathbf{M}_r = \mathbf{I} - \mathbf{X}_r(\mathbf{X}_r'\mathbf{X}_r)^{-1}\mathbf{X}_r'$. Note that if $\mathbf{X}_1 = \boldsymbol{\iota}$, then the formula for $\hat{\boldsymbol{\beta}}_2$ in (10.17b) becomes identical to the formula for $\hat{\underline{\boldsymbol{\beta}}}$ in (10.15a).

EXAMPLE In Section 7-3, we illustrated the method of least squares in the simple regression context by estimating the relationship between price and quantity of oranges sold in a supermarket on twelve consecutive days. Let us modify this example by postulating that the quantity sold depends not only on price but also on the amount spent on advertising the product. That is, let

$$Y_i = \beta_1 + \beta_2 X_{i2} + \beta_3 X_{i3} + \varepsilon_i,$$

where Y = quantity (pounds) of oranges sold, X_2 = price in cents per pound, and X_3 = advertising expenditure in dollars. The data are given in Table 10-1. The results of the basic

Table 10-1

Quantity, lb	Price, ¢/lb	Advertising expenditure, $
55	100	5.50
70	90	6.30
90	80	7.20
100	70	7.00
90	70	6.30
105	70	7.35
80	70	5.60
110	65	7.15
125	60	7.50
115	60	6.90
130	55	7.15
130	50	6.50

calculations are

$$\bar{Y} = 100, \qquad m_{22} = 2250, \qquad m_{Y2} = -3550,$$
$$\bar{X}_2 = 70, \qquad m_{33} = 4.857, \qquad m_{Y3} = 125.25,$$
$$\bar{X}_3 = 6.7, \qquad m_{23} = -54, \qquad m_{YY} = 6300.$$

(The quantity $m_{YY} = \Sigma_i (Y_i - \bar{Y})^2$ will be used in later examples.) The estimates of the regression coefficients are

$$\hat{\beta}_2 = \frac{-3550 \times 4.857 - (-54) \times 125.25}{2250 \times 4.857 - (-54)^2} = \frac{-10{,}480.065}{8012.925} = -1.308,$$

$$\hat{\beta}_3 = \frac{2250 \times 125.25 - (-54) \times (-3550)}{8012.925} = 11.246,$$

and $\hat{\beta}_1 = 100 - (-1.308) \times 70 - 11.247 \times 6.7 = 116.16.$

Therefore, the estimated regression equation is

$$Y_i = 116.16 - 1.308 X_{i2} + 11.246 X_{i3} + e_i.$$

This implies that we estimate that a 10¢ reduction in the price of oranges, with advertising expenditure unchanged, would increase sales by about 13 pounds, while a $1 increase in advertising expenditure, with price unchanged, would increase sales by about 11 pounds.

Best Linear Unbiased Estimation

Let us now derive the *best linear unbiased estimators* (BLUE) for the multiple regression model. For simplicity, we shall use a model with two explanatory variables; an extension to the general case only requires more involved algebraic expressions. Suppose, then, that we wish to derive the BLUE of, say, β_2, of the model

$$Y_i = \beta_1 + \beta_2 X_{i2} + \beta_3 X_{i3} + \varepsilon_i.$$

By the condition of linearity, we have

$$\tilde{\beta}_2 = \sum_i a_i Y_i,$$

where a_i ($i = 1, 2, \ldots, n$) are some constants to be determined. The mathematical expectation of $\tilde{\beta}_2$ is

$$E(\tilde{\beta}_2) = E \sum_i a_i Y_i = E \sum_i a_i(\beta_1 + \beta_2 X_{i2} + \beta_3 X_{i3} + \varepsilon_i)$$

$$= \beta_1 \sum_i a_i + \beta_2 \sum_i a_i X_{i2} + \beta_3 \sum_i a_i X_{i3},$$

so that, for $\tilde{\beta}_2$ to be unbiased, we require

$$\sum_i a_i = 0,$$

$$\sum_i a_i X_{i2} = 1,$$

$$\sum_i a_i X_{i3} = 0.$$

The variance of $\tilde{\beta}_2$ is

$$\text{Var}(\tilde{\beta}_2) = \sum_i a_i^2 \, \text{Var}(Y_i) = \sigma^2 \sum_i a_i^2 .$$

That is, we have to find those values of a_i that would minimize $\sigma^2 \Sigma_i a_i^2$, subject to the conditions that $\Sigma_i a_i = 0$, $\Sigma_i a_i X_{i2} = 1$, and $\Sigma_i a_i X_{i3} = 0$. Using the Lagrange multiplier method, we form

$$H = \sigma^2 \sum_i a_i^2 - \lambda_1\Big(\sum_i a_i\Big) - \lambda_2\Big(\sum_i a_i X_{i2} - 1\Big) - \lambda_3\Big(\sum_i a_i X_{i3}\Big).$$

Differentiating H with respect to $a_1, a_2, \ldots, a_n, \lambda_1, \lambda_2$, and λ_3 and putting each derivative equal to zero, we obtain

(10.18) $$2a_i\sigma^2 - \lambda_1 - \lambda_2 X_{i2} - \lambda_3 X_{i3} = 0 \qquad (i = 1, 2, \ldots, n),$$

(10.19) $$-\Big(\sum_i a_i\Big) = 0,$$

(10.20) $$-\Big(\sum_i a_i X_{i2}\Big) + 1 = 0,$$

(10.21) $$-\Big(\sum_i a_i X_{i3}\Big) = 0.$$

This gives us $(n + 3)$ equations to be solved for the unknown $a_1, a_2, \ldots, a_n$ and λ_1, λ_2, and λ_3. We start by adding the n equations of (10.18). This leads to

(10.22) $$2\sigma^2 \sum_i a_i - n\lambda_1 - \lambda_2 \sum_i X_{i2} - \lambda_3 \sum_i X_{i3} = 0.$$

Next, we multiply both sides of (10.18) by X_{i2} and add the resulting equations to get

(10.23) $$2\sigma^2 \sum_i a_i X_{i2} - \lambda_1 \sum_i X_{i2} - \lambda_2 \sum_i X_{i2}^2 - \lambda_3 \sum_i X_{i2}X_{i3} = 0.$$

Finally, we multiply both sides of (10.18) by X_{i3} and add again to get

(10.24) $$2\sigma^2 \sum_i a_i X_{i3} - \lambda_1 \sum_i X_{i3} - \lambda_2 \sum_i X_{i2}X_{i3} - \lambda_3 \sum_i X_{i3}^2 = 0,$$

Substitution for $\Sigma_i a_i$, $\Sigma_i a_i X_{i2}$, and $\Sigma_i a_i X_{i3}$ from (10.19), (10.20), and (10.21) into (10.22), (10.23), and (10.24) then leads to

(10.22a) $$-n\lambda_1 - \lambda_2 \sum_i X_{i2} - \lambda_3 \sum_i X_{i3} = 0,$$

(10.23a) $$-\lambda_1 \sum_i X_{i2} - \lambda_2 \sum_i X_{i2}^2 - \lambda_3 \sum_i X_{i2}X_{i3} = -2\sigma^2,$$

(10.24a) $$-\lambda_1 \sum_i X_{i3} - \lambda_2 \sum_i X_{i2}X_{i3} - \lambda_3 \sum_i X_{i3}^2 = 0.$$

Now from (10.22a) we get

$$\lambda_1 = -\lambda_2 \bar{X}_2 - \lambda_3 \bar{X}_3.$$

We can then substitute this expression for λ_1 into (10.23a) and (10.24a), which yields

$$\lambda_2 m_{22} + \lambda_3 m_{23} = 2\sigma^2,$$
$$\lambda_2 m_{23} + \lambda_3 m_{33} = 0.$$

Therefore,

$$\lambda_2 = \frac{2\sigma^2 m_{33}}{m_{22}m_{33} - m_{23}^2} \quad \text{and} \quad \lambda_3 = \frac{-2\sigma^2 m_{23}}{m_{22}m_{33} - m_{23}^2},$$

which implies that

$$\lambda_1 = \frac{2\sigma^2(-\bar{X}_2 m_{33} + \bar{X}_3 m_{23})}{m_{22}m_{33} - m_{23}^2}.$$

In this way, we have obtained the solution for λ_1, λ_2, and λ_3. Now from (10.18), we have

$$a_i = \frac{1}{2\sigma^2}(\lambda_1 + \lambda_2 X_{i2} + \lambda_3 X_{i3}),$$

which, after substituting for the λ's, becomes

(10.25) $$a_i = \frac{-\bar{X}_2 m_{33} + \bar{X}_3 m_{23} + m_{33}X_{i2} - m_{23}X_{i3}}{m_{22}m_{33} - m_{23}^2}.$$

Therefore

$$\tilde{\beta}_2 = \sum_i a_i Y_i = \frac{-n\bar{Y}\bar{X}_2 m_{33} + n\bar{Y}\bar{X}_3 m_{23} + m_{33}\sum X_{i2}Y_i - m_{23}\sum X_{i3}Y_i}{m_{22}m_{33} - m_{23}^2}$$

$$= \frac{m_{33}m_{Y2} - m_{23}m_{Y3}}{m_{22}m_{33} - m_{23}^2},$$

which is precisely the same formula as that for the least squares estimator of β_2 given by (10.12). Similarly, we could show that $\tilde{\beta}_3 = \hat{\beta}_3$ and $\tilde{\beta}_1 = \hat{\beta}_1$. Therefore, *least squares estimators of the regression coefficients are* BLUE. This conclusion applies to regression models with any number of explanatory variables.

The BLUE method provides us not only with a formula for $\tilde{\beta}_2$ but also one for the variance of $\tilde{\beta}_2$. In particular,

$$\text{Var}(\tilde{\beta}_2) = \sigma^2 \sum_i a_i^2.$$

Now, by multiplying both sides of (10.25) by a_i, adding over all observations, and substituting for Σa_i, $\Sigma a_i X_{i2}$, and $\Sigma a_i X_{i3}$, we obtain

$$\sum_i a_i^2 = \frac{m_{33}}{m_{22}m_{33} - m_{23}^2}.$$

This means that

$$\text{Var}(\tilde{\beta}_2) = \frac{\sigma^2 m_{33}}{m_{22}m_{33} - m_{23}^2}. \tag{10.26}$$

The result for the variance of $\tilde{\beta}_3$, which will not be derived here, is

$$\text{Var}(\tilde{\beta}_3) = \frac{\sigma^2 m_{22}}{m_{22}m_{33} - m_{23}^2}. \tag{10.27}$$

Maximum Likelihood Estimation

Next we come to the derivation of the *maximum likelihood estimators* of the parameters of a multiple normal linear regression model. This represents a direct extension of the procedure developed in connection with the simple regression model. When we set up the log-likelihood function as in (7.26) but allow for more than one explanatory variable, we get

$$L = -\frac{n}{2}\log(2\pi) - \frac{n}{2}\log\sigma^2 - \frac{1}{2\sigma^2}\sum_i (Y_i - \beta_1 - \beta_2 X_{i2} - \beta_3 X_{i3} - \cdots - \beta_K X_{iK})^2$$

$$= -\frac{n}{2}\log(2\pi) - \frac{n}{2}\log\sigma^2 - \frac{1}{2\sigma^2}(\mathbf{y} - \mathbf{X}\boldsymbol{\beta})'(\mathbf{y} - \mathbf{X}\boldsymbol{\beta}).$$

The maximum likelihood estimators are obtained by differentiating L with respect to $\beta_1, \beta_2, \ldots, \beta_K$, and σ^2, and by putting each of these derivatives equal to zero. It is easy to see that the first K of these equations, which can be solved for the values of the βs, are exactly the same as the least squares normal equations. This means that the *maximum likelihood estimators of the regression coefficients are equivalent to the least squares estimators.* The maximum likelihood estimator of σ^2 is

$$\hat{\sigma}^2 = \frac{1}{n}\sum_i (Y_i - \hat{\beta}_1 - \hat{\beta}_2 X_{i2} - \hat{\beta}_3 X_{i3} - \cdots - \hat{\beta}_K X_{iK})^2 \tag{10.28}$$

$$= \frac{1}{n}(\mathbf{y} - \mathbf{X}\hat{\boldsymbol{\beta}})'(\mathbf{y} - \mathbf{X}\hat{\boldsymbol{\beta}})$$

or

$$\hat{\sigma}^2 = \frac{1}{n}\sum_i e_i^2, \tag{10.28a}$$

where the terms e_i represent the least squares residuals.

10-2 Further Results of Statistical Inference

From the preceding discussion on estimation of the coefficients of a multiple regression model, we conclude that, as in the case of the simple regression model, each of the three estimation methods considered leads to exactly the same formulas. The implication is that the least squares estimators of the regression coefficients have all the desirable properties. We shall now describe some other features of these estimators and discuss their use for testing hypotheses and for prediction.

Variances and Covariances of the Least Squares Estimators

The formulas for the variances of the estimated regression coefficients of a model with two explanatory variables are presented in (10.26) and (10.27). Generalization of these formulas to models with a larger number of explanatory variables is quite straightforward. Substituting for $\mathbf{y}$ from (10.1b) into the formula for $\hat{\boldsymbol{\beta}}$ in (10.14), we obtain

$$\hat{\boldsymbol{\beta}} = (\mathbf{X}'\mathbf{X})^{-1}\mathbf{X}'(\mathbf{X}\boldsymbol{\beta} + \boldsymbol{\varepsilon}) = \boldsymbol{\beta} + (\mathbf{X}'\mathbf{X})^{-1}\mathbf{X}'\boldsymbol{\varepsilon}. \tag{10.29}$$

The $(K \times K)$ matrix of the variances and covariances of the least squares regression coefficients then is

$$\begin{aligned} E(\hat{\boldsymbol{\beta}} - \boldsymbol{\beta})(\hat{\boldsymbol{\beta}} - \boldsymbol{\beta})' &= E(\mathbf{X}'\mathbf{X})^{-1}\mathbf{X}'\boldsymbol{\varepsilon}\boldsymbol{\varepsilon}'\mathbf{X}(\mathbf{X}'\mathbf{X})^{-1} \\ &= (\mathbf{X}'\mathbf{X})^{-1}\mathbf{X}'E(\boldsymbol{\varepsilon}\boldsymbol{\varepsilon}')\mathbf{X}(\mathbf{X}'\mathbf{X})^{-1} \\ &= \sigma^2(\mathbf{X}'\mathbf{X})^{-1}, \end{aligned} \tag{10.30}$$

or, explicitly,

$$(10.30\text{a})\quad \begin{bmatrix} \text{Var}(\hat{\beta}_1) & \text{Cov}(\hat{\beta}_1, \hat{\beta}_2) & \dots & \text{Cov}(\hat{\beta}_1, \hat{\beta}_K) \\ \text{Cov}(\hat{\beta}_1, \hat{\beta}_2) & \text{Var}(\hat{\beta}_2) & \dots & \text{Cov}(\hat{\beta}_2, \hat{\beta}_K) \\ \vdots & \vdots & & \vdots \\ \text{Cov}(\hat{\beta}_1, \hat{\beta}_K) & \text{Cov}(\hat{\beta}_2, \hat{\beta}_K) & \dots & \text{Var}(\hat{\beta}_K) \end{bmatrix}$$

$$= \sigma^2 \begin{bmatrix} n & \Sigma X_{i2} & \dots & \Sigma X_{iK} \\ \Sigma X_{i2} & \Sigma X_{i2}^2 & \dots & \Sigma X_{i2} X_{iK} \\ \vdots & \vdots & & \vdots \\ \Sigma X_{iK} & \Sigma X_{i2} X_{iK} & \dots & \Sigma X_{iK}^2 \end{bmatrix}^{-1}.$$

The matrix $[\sigma^2(\mathbf{X}'\mathbf{X})^{-1}]$, whose dimension is $K \times K$, represents the *variance–covariance matrix* of the least squares estimators of the regression coefficients, including the intercept. In this matrix the variances of the estimators are displayed along the main diagonal, while the covariances of the estimators are given by the off-diagonal terms.

Using an alternative approach, we may consider the regression intercept and the regression slopes separately. Concerning the estimated slopes, their variance–covariance matrix can be derived by reference to (10.15) and by analogy with (10.29) and (10.30). The result is

$$(10.31)\quad E(\hat{\underline{\beta}} - \underline{\beta})(\hat{\underline{\beta}} - \underline{\beta})' = \sigma^2(\underline{\mathbf{X}}'\underline{\mathbf{X}})^{-1},$$

or, explicitly,

$$(10.31\text{a})\quad \begin{bmatrix} \text{Var}(\hat{\beta}_2) & \text{Cov}(\hat{\beta}_2, \hat{\beta}_3) & \dots & \text{Cov}(\hat{\beta}_2, \hat{\beta}_K) \\ \text{Cov}(\hat{\beta}_2, \hat{\beta}_3) & \text{Var}(\hat{\beta}_3) & \dots & \text{Cov}(\hat{\beta}_3, \hat{\beta}_K) \\ \vdots & \vdots & & \vdots \\ \text{Cov}(\hat{\beta}_2, \hat{\beta}_K) & \text{Cov}(\hat{\beta}_3, \hat{\beta}_K) & \dots & \text{Var}(\hat{\beta}_K) \end{bmatrix}$$

$$= \sigma^2 \begin{bmatrix} m_{22} & m_{23} & \dots & m_{2K} \\ m_{23} & m_{33} & \dots & m_{3K} \\ \vdots & \vdots & & \vdots \\ m_{2K} & m_{3K} & \dots & m_{KK} \end{bmatrix}^{-1}.$$

When the regression equation is written in the partitioned way as

$$\mathbf{y} = \mathbf{X}_1\boldsymbol{\beta}_1 + \mathbf{X}_2\boldsymbol{\beta}_2 + \boldsymbol{\varepsilon},$$

the LSE's of $\boldsymbol{\beta}_1$ and $\boldsymbol{\beta}_2$ are given in (10.17a) and (10.17b). The respective variance–covariance matrices are

$$(10.32\text{a})\quad E(\hat{\boldsymbol{\beta}}_1 - \boldsymbol{\beta}_1)(\hat{\boldsymbol{\beta}}_1 - \boldsymbol{\beta}_1') = \sigma^2(\mathbf{X}_1'\mathbf{M}_2\mathbf{X}_1)^{-1},$$

(10.32b) $$E(\hat{\beta}_2 - \beta_2)(\hat{\beta}_2 - \beta_2) = \sigma^2(\mathbf{X}_2'\mathbf{M}_1\mathbf{X}_2)^{-1},$$

where $$\mathbf{M}_r = \mathbf{I} - \mathbf{X}_r(\mathbf{X}_r'\mathbf{X}_r)^{-1}\mathbf{X}_r' \qquad (r = 1, 2).$$

When β_1 is the intercept and, consequently $\mathbf{X}_1$ is a vector with every element equal to unity, we have

$$\text{Var}(\hat{\beta}_1) = \frac{\sigma^2}{n} + \sum_k \bar{X}_k \text{ Var}(\hat{\beta}_K) + 2 \sum_{j<k} \bar{X}_j\bar{X}_k\text{Cov}(\hat{\beta}_j, \hat{\beta}_k)$$
$$(j, k = 2, 3, \ldots, K; j < k).$$

Properties of the Least Squares Estimators

Since by (10.29)

$$\hat{\boldsymbol{\beta}} = \boldsymbol{\beta} + (\mathbf{X}'\mathbf{X})^{-1}\mathbf{X}'\boldsymbol{\varepsilon},$$

the least squares estimators of $\boldsymbol{\beta}$ are linear combinations of the εs and, therefore, under the stated assumptions are normally distributed with mean vector $\boldsymbol{\beta}$ and variance-covariance matrix $\sigma^2(\mathbf{X}'\mathbf{X})^{-1}$; that is,

$$\hat{\boldsymbol{\beta}} \sim N[\boldsymbol{\beta}, \sigma^2(\mathbf{X}'\mathbf{X})^{-1}].$$

These estimators have been shown to be best linear unbiased. Their efficiency can be proved by reference to the Cramer-Rao lower bound derived from the log-likelihood function. The consistency of $\hat{\boldsymbol{\beta}}$ follows from the fact that

$$\lim_{n\to\infty} \sigma^2(\mathbf{X}'\mathbf{X})^{-1} = \lim_{n\to\infty} \frac{\sigma^2}{n}\left(\frac{\mathbf{X}'\mathbf{X}}{n}\right)^{-1} = 0,$$

since $\lim_{n\to\infty} \sigma^2/n = 0$, and $\lim_{n\to\infty} (\mathbf{X}'\mathbf{X}/n)^{-1}$ is finite by assumptions (10.6a–10.8a).

When the assumption of normality of the regression disturbance is dropped, the LSEs of $\boldsymbol{\beta}$ are still best linear unbiased and the formulas for their variances remain valid, but they are not efficient. Their asymptotic normality can be established by the use of a version of the central limit theorem.[1] When the explanatory variables are stochastic, the LSEs of $\boldsymbol{\beta}$ will still be asymptotically normal under certain conditions (see Appendix C).

Estimation of σ^2

The variances and covariances of the least squares estimators of the regression coefficients involve the parameter σ^2, the value of which has to be estimated. To find an unbiased estimator of σ^2, we first determine the mathematical expectation of the sum of squares of the least squares residuals. Let the $(n \times 1)$ vector of the least

[1] See P. Schmidt, *Econometrics* (New York: Marcel Dekker, 1976), pp. 56–64.

square residuals be

$$\begin{aligned}\mathbf{e} &= (\mathbf{y} - \mathbf{X}\hat{\boldsymbol{\beta}}) \\ &= \mathbf{y} - \mathbf{X}(\mathbf{X}'\mathbf{X})^{-1}\mathbf{X}'\mathbf{y} \\ &= \mathbf{M}\mathbf{y},\end{aligned}$$

where $\mathbf{M} = \mathbf{I} - \mathbf{X}(\mathbf{X}'\mathbf{X})^{-1}\mathbf{X}'$. We note that $\mathbf{M}$ is symmetric and idempotent, and that $\mathbf{M}\mathbf{X} = \mathbf{X} - \mathbf{X}(\mathbf{X}'\mathbf{X})^{-1}\mathbf{X}'\mathbf{X} = \mathbf{0}$. Therefore,

$$\begin{aligned}\mathbf{e} &= \mathbf{M}\mathbf{y} \\ &= \mathbf{M}(\mathbf{X}\boldsymbol{\beta} + \boldsymbol{\varepsilon}) \\ &= \mathbf{M}\boldsymbol{\varepsilon}.\end{aligned} \tag{10.33}$$

The sum of squares of the least squares residuals is

$$\begin{aligned}\sum e_i^2 &= \mathbf{e}'\mathbf{e} \\ &= \boldsymbol{\varepsilon}'\mathbf{M}'\mathbf{M}\boldsymbol{\varepsilon} \\ &= \boldsymbol{\varepsilon}'\mathbf{M}\boldsymbol{\varepsilon}.\end{aligned} \tag{10.34}$$

The expression $\boldsymbol{\varepsilon}'\mathbf{M}\boldsymbol{\varepsilon}$ is called a *quadratic form*. It is a scalar that can be evaluated by noting that

$$\begin{aligned}\boldsymbol{\varepsilon}'\mathbf{M}\boldsymbol{\varepsilon} &= [\varepsilon_1\ \varepsilon_2 \cdots \varepsilon_n]\begin{bmatrix} M_{11} & M_{12} & \cdots & M_{1n} \\ M_{21} & M_{22} & \cdots & M_{2n} \\ \vdots & \vdots & & \vdots \\ M_{n1} & M_{n2} & \cdots & M_{nn}\end{bmatrix}\begin{bmatrix}\varepsilon_1 \\ \varepsilon_2 \\ \vdots \\ \varepsilon_n\end{bmatrix} \\ &= \sum_{i=1}^{n}\sum_{j=1}^{n} \varepsilon_i\varepsilon_j M_{ij}.\end{aligned}$$

Now,

$$\begin{aligned}E(\mathbf{e}'\mathbf{e}) &= E\left(\sum_i\sum_j \varepsilon_i\varepsilon_j M_{ij}\right) \\ &= \sigma^2 \sum_i M_{ii},\end{aligned}$$

since $E(\varepsilon_i^2) = \sigma^2$ and $E(\varepsilon_i\varepsilon_j) = 0$ by assumption. But ΣM_{ii} is the sum of the diagonal elements of the matrix $\mathbf{M}$, which is called a *trace* and designated by $\mathrm{tr}(\mathbf{M})$. Two useful properties of traces are

1. For any two squares matrices $\mathbf{A}$ and $\mathbf{B}$ of the same order m, $\mathrm{tr}(\mathbf{A} + \mathbf{B}) = \mathrm{tr}(\mathbf{A}) + \mathrm{tr}(\mathbf{B})$.
2. For any two matrices $\mathbf{A}$ and $\mathbf{B}$ of order $m \times n$ and $n \times m$, respectively, $\mathrm{tr}(\mathbf{AB}) = \mathrm{tr}(\mathbf{BA})$.

We make use of these properties as follows:

$$(10.35)\qquad \begin{aligned} E(\mathbf{e}'\mathbf{e}) &= \sigma^2\mathrm{tr}(\mathbf{M}) \\ &= \sigma^2\mathrm{tr}[\mathbf{I} - \mathbf{X}(\mathbf{X}'\mathbf{X})^{-1}\mathbf{X}'] \\ &= \sigma^2\{\mathrm{tr}(\mathbf{I}) - \mathrm{tr}[\mathbf{X}(\mathbf{X}'\mathbf{X})^{-1}\mathbf{X}']\} \\ &= \sigma^2[n - \mathrm{tr}(\mathbf{X}'\mathbf{X})(\mathbf{X}'\mathbf{X})^{-1}] \\ &= \sigma^2(n-K), \end{aligned}$$

since $(\mathbf{X}'\mathbf{X}) \rightarrow K \times K$. Thus an unbiased estimator of σ^2 is

$$(10.36)\qquad \begin{aligned} s^2 &= \frac{\mathbf{e}'\mathbf{e}}{n-K} \\ &= \frac{1}{n-K}\sum_i (Y_i - \hat{\beta}_1 - \hat{\beta}_2X_{i2} - \hat{\beta}_3X_{i3} - \cdots - \hat{\beta}_KX_{iK})^2 \\ &= \frac{1}{n-k}(\mathbf{y} - \mathbf{X}\hat{\boldsymbol{\beta}})'(\mathbf{y} - \mathbf{X}\hat{\boldsymbol{\beta}}). \end{aligned}$$

Since asymptotically s^2 is equivalent to $\hat{\hat{\sigma}}^2$, the maximum likelihood estimator of σ^2, it follows that s^2 has the same optimal asymptotic properties as $\hat{\hat{\sigma}}^2$.

For computing the value of s^2, formula (10.36) can be simplified to avoid the calculation of individual residuals. Let us begin with the case of two explanatory variables,

$$\begin{aligned} s^2 &= \frac{1}{n-3}\sum_i [(Y_i - \bar{Y}) - \hat{\beta}_2(X_{i2} - \bar{X}_2) - \hat{\beta}_3(X_{i3} - \bar{X}_3)]^2 \\ &= \frac{1}{n-3}(m_{YY} + \hat{\beta}_2^2m_{22} + \hat{\beta}_3^2m_{33} - 2\hat{\beta}_2m_{Y2} - 2\hat{\beta}_3m_{Y3} + 2\hat{\beta}_2\hat{\beta}_3m_{23}). \end{aligned}$$

But from the least squares normal equations, we have

$$\begin{aligned} m_{Y2} &= \hat{\beta}_2m_{22} + \hat{\beta}_3m_{23}, \\ m_{Y3} &= \hat{\beta}_2m_{23} + \hat{\beta}_3m_{33}. \end{aligned}$$

Therefore,

$$\begin{aligned} \hat{\beta}_2^2m_{22} + \hat{\beta}_2\hat{\beta}_3m_{23} - \hat{\beta}_2m_{Y2} &= 0, \\ \hat{\beta}_2\hat{\beta}_3m_{23} + \hat{\beta}_3^2m_{33} - \hat{\beta}_3m_{Y3} &= 0. \end{aligned}$$

Thus s^2 becomes

$$s^2 = \frac{1}{n-3}(m_{YY} - \hat{\beta}_2m_{Y2} - \hat{\beta}_3m_{Y3}).$$

This can be generalized to the case of $(K-1)$ explanatory variables so that (10.36) becomes

(10.36a) $$s^2 = \frac{1}{n-K}(m_{YY} - \hat{\beta}_2 m_{Y2} - \hat{\beta}_3 m_{Y3} - \cdots - \hat{\beta}_K m_{YK})$$
$$= \frac{1}{n-K}(\underline{\mathbf{y}}'\underline{\mathbf{y}} - \underline{\mathbf{y}}'\underline{\mathbf{X}}\underline{\hat{\boldsymbol{\beta}}}).$$

This formula is computationally more convenient than (10.36). By using s^2 in place of σ^2 in (10.30), we obtain unbiased estimators of the variances and covariances of the least squares estimators of the regression coefficients. The *confidence intervals* for the regression coefficients can be constructed by noting that

$$\frac{\hat{\beta}_k - \beta_k}{s_{\hat{\beta}_k}} \sim t_{n-K} \qquad (k = 1, 2, \ldots, K),$$

where $s_{\hat{\beta}_k}$ represents the estimated standard error of $\hat{\beta}_k$.

EXAMPLE To illustrate the use of the preceding formulas, let us construct the 95% confidence intervals for the coefficients of the regression model described in the preceding example. Substituting the numerical results into the formula for s^2, we get

$$s^2 = \frac{1}{12-3}[6300 - (-1.308) \times (-3550) - 11.246 \times 125.25]$$
$$= \frac{248.393}{9} = 27.5993.$$

This result, combined with (10.31), gives

$$s^2_{\hat{\beta}_2} = \frac{27.5993 \times 4.857}{2250 \times 4.856 - (-54)^2} = 0.016730,$$

$$s^2_{\hat{\beta}_3} = \frac{27.5993 \times 2250}{2250 \times 4.857 - (-54)^2} = 7.749782,$$

and

$$s^2_{\hat{\beta}_1} = 27.5993 \left[\frac{1}{12} + \frac{70^2 \times 4.857 + 6.7^2 \times 2250 - 2 \times 70 \times 6.7 \times (-54)}{2250 \times 4.857 - (-54)^2}\right]$$
$$= 607.6225.$$

Therefore, the estimated standard errors of $\hat{\beta}_1$, $\hat{\beta}_2$, and $\hat{\beta}_3$ are

$$s_{\hat{\beta}_1} = 24.65, \quad s_{\hat{\beta}_2} = 0.129, \quad \text{and} \quad s_{\hat{\beta}_3} = 2.784.$$

The tabulated t value for $12 - 3 = 9$ degrees of freedom and 0.025 two-tail probability is 2.262. Therefore, the 95% confidence intervals for the regression coefficients are

$$60.40 \leq \beta_1 \leq 171.92,$$
$$-1.60 \leq \beta_2 \leq -1.02,$$
$$4.95 \leq \beta_3 \leq 17.54.$$

Confidence Interval for $E(Y_i)$

The confidence intervals that we have described indicate the precision of the estimators of each of the regression coefficients considered separately. The precision of the estimated regression equation as a whole is indicated by a *confidence band.* This can be derived as a confidence interval for $E(Y_i)$, using the fitted value $\hat{Y}_i$ as its estimator. We note that $\hat{Y}_i$ is normally distributed with mean equal to $E(Y_i)$. Its variance, in the case of two explanatory variables, is

$$\begin{aligned}\sigma^2_{\hat{Y}_i} &= E[\hat{Y}_i - E(\hat{Y}_i)]^2 = E[\hat{Y}_i - E(Y_i)]^2\\ &= E[(\hat{\beta}_1 - \beta_1) + (\hat{\beta}_2 - \beta_2)X_{i2} + (\hat{\beta}_3 - \beta_3)X_{i3}]^2.\end{aligned}$$

But

$$\hat{\beta}_1 - \beta_1 = -(\hat{\beta}_2 - \beta_2)\overline{X}_2 - (\hat{\beta}_3 - \beta_3)\overline{X}_3 + \bar{\varepsilon},$$

which gives

$$\begin{aligned}(10.37)\qquad \sigma^2_{\hat{Y}_i} &= E[(\hat{\beta}_2 - \beta_2)(X_{i2} - \overline{X}_2) + (\hat{\beta}_3 - \beta_3)(X_{i3} - \overline{X}_3) + \bar{\varepsilon}\,]^2\\ &= (X_{i2} - \overline{X}_2)^2\text{Var}(\hat{\beta}_2) + (X_{i3} - \overline{X}_3)^2\text{Var}(\hat{\beta}_3)\\ &\quad + 2(X_{i2} - \overline{X}_2)(X_{i3} - \overline{X}_3)\text{Cov}(\hat{\beta}_2, \hat{\beta}_3) + \frac{\sigma^2}{n}.\end{aligned}$$

For a model with $(K - 1)$ explanatory variables, we have

$$\begin{aligned}(10.38)\qquad \sigma^2_{\hat{Y}_i} &= \sum_k (X_{ik} - \overline{X}_k)^2\text{Var}(\hat{\beta}_k)\\ &\quad + 2\sum_{j<k} (X_{ij} - \overline{X}_j)(X_{ik} - \overline{X}_k)\text{Cov}(\hat{\beta}_j, \hat{\beta}_k) + \frac{\sigma^2}{n}\\ &\quad (j, k = 2, 3, \ldots, K;\quad j < k).\end{aligned}$$

The expression for $\sigma^2_{\hat{Y}_i}$ involves the parameter σ^2 whose value is not known. If we replace σ^2 by its unbiased estimator s^2, we obtain an unbiased estimator of $\sigma^2_{\hat{Y}_i}$, say $s^2_{\hat{Y}_i}$. The confidence band for $E(Y_i)$ can then be constructed by noting that

$$\frac{\hat{Y}_i - E(Y_i)}{s_{\hat{Y}_i}} \sim t_{n-K}.$$

From this, we can determine the confidence interval for $E(Y_i)$ for *any* set of values of the explanatory variables. Note that this interval will be narrowest when the value of each explanatory variable is equal to its sample mean (in which case $s_{\hat{Y}_i}$ will be equal to $s/\sqrt{n}$) and that the interval will get wider and wider as we move away from the sample means of the X's in either direction.

Decomposition of the Sample Variation of Y

Defining, as in the case of simple regression, the sample variation of Y by $\Sigma(Y_i - \overline{Y})^2$, we have

$$\sum_i (Y_i - \overline{Y})^2 = \sum_i [(\hat{Y}_i + e_i) - \overline{Y}]^2$$
$$= \sum_i (\hat{Y}_i - \overline{Y})^2 + \sum_i e_i^2 + 2\sum_i (\hat{Y}_i - \overline{Y})e_i,$$

where, as before, the terms e_i represent the least squares residuals. Now, from the least squares normal equations we find that

$$\sum_i (\hat{Y}_i - \overline{Y})e_i = \sum_i (\hat{\beta}_1 + \hat{\beta}_2 X_{i2} + \hat{\beta}_3 X_{i3} + \cdots + \hat{\beta}_K X_{iK})e_i - \overline{Y}\sum_i e_i = 0.$$

Thus

$$\underbrace{\sum_i (Y_i - \overline{Y})^2}_{\text{SST}} = \underbrace{\sum_i (\hat{Y}_i - \overline{Y})^2}_{\text{SSR}} + \underbrace{\sum_i e_i^2}_{\text{SSE}}.$$

Now, for the case of two explanatory variables we decompose SSR as follows.

$$\text{SSR} = \sum_i (\hat{\beta}_1 + \hat{\beta}_2 X_{i2} + \hat{\beta}_3 X_{i3} - \overline{Y})^2 \tag{10.39}$$
$$= \sum_i [(\overline{Y} - \hat{\beta}_2 \overline{X}_2 - \hat{\beta}_3 \overline{X}_3) + \hat{\beta}_2 X_{i2} + \hat{\beta}_3 X_{i3} - \overline{Y}]^2$$
$$= \hat{\beta}_2^2 m_{22} + \hat{\beta}_3^2 m_{33} + 2\hat{\beta}_2\hat{\beta}_3 m_{23}.$$

In this case SSR, which represents the estimated regression effect on Y, consists of three terms. The first term corresponds to the effect of X_2, the second to the effect of X_3, and the third to the combined effect of both variables. The combined effect of X_2 and X_3 reflects the fact that X_2 and X_3 may vary together to some extent. This joint variation of X_2 and X_3 accounts for a part of the variation of Y. The individual contributions of X_2 and X_3 to the variation of Y cannot be separated completely unless X_2 and X_3 are uncorrelated, that is, unless m_{23} is equal to zero. The decomposition of SSR given in (10.39) can be generalized to the case of $(K - 1)$ explanatory variables,

$$\text{SSR} = \sum_k \hat{\beta}_k^2 m_{kk} + 2\sum_{j<k} \hat{\beta}_j \hat{\beta}_k m_{jk} \qquad (j, k = 2, 3, \ldots, K; j < k), \tag{10.40}$$

or, in matrix notation,

$$\text{SSR} = \underline{\hat{\beta}}'(\underline{X}'\underline{X})\underline{\hat{\beta}}. \tag{10.40a}$$

If we are interested only in the total value of SSR and not in its components then we can obtain a computationally more convenient formula from (10.40) by a substitution from the least squares normal equations. This is

$$\text{SSR} = \sum_{k=2}^{K} \hat{\beta}_k m_{Yk}, \tag{10.41}$$

or, in matrix notation,

$$\text{SSR} = \underline{\hat{\beta}}'(\underline{X}'\underline{y}). \tag{10.41a}$$

The previous results are also utilized in calculating the value of the *coefficient of determination.* This is defined, as in (7.46), by

$$R^2 = \frac{\text{SSR}}{\text{SST}} = 1 - \frac{\text{SSE}}{\text{SST}}.$$

Some research workers prefer to measure the "goodness of fit" in the case of multiple regression by a somewhat different formula known as the *"adjusted coefficient of determination."* This is usually denoted by $\bar{R}^2$ and defined by

$$\bar{R}^2 = 1 - \frac{\text{SSE}/(n-k)}{\text{SST}/(n-1)}. \tag{10.42}$$

This measure takes into account the number of explanatory variables in relation to the number of observations. The purpose of $\bar{R}^2$ is to facilitate comparisons of the "goodness of fit" of several regression equations that may vary with respect to the number of explanatory variables and the number of observations. Note that

$$\bar{R}^2 \leq R^2,$$

With $\bar{R}^2$ being equal to R^2 in finite samples only if R^2 is equal to unity. Asymptotically the two measures are, of course, equal. Also note that, unlike R^2, $\bar{R}^2$ may have negative values. For instance, if $n = 10$, $K = 2$, and $R^2 = 0.1$, then $\bar{R}^2 = -0.0125$.

EXAMPLE From the data of the previous example, we can decompose the sample variation of Y as follows.

Source	Formula	Value	
X_2	$\hat{\beta}_2^2 m_{22}$	$(-1.308)^2 \times 2250$	$= 3849$
X_3	$\hat{\beta}_3^2 m_{33}$	$(11.245)^2 \times 4.857$	$= 614$
X_2 and X_3	$2\hat{\beta}_2\hat{\beta}_3 m_{23}$	$2 \times (-1.308) \times 11.246 \times (-54)$	$= 1588$
SSR	$\hat{\beta}_2 m_{22} + \hat{\beta}_3 m_{33} + 2\hat{\beta}_2\hat{\beta}_3 m_{23}$		$= 6051$
SSE	$m_{yy} - \text{SSR}$		$= 249$
SST	m_{yy}		$= 6300$

The value of the coefficient of determination is

$$R^2 = \frac{6051}{6300} = 0.960,$$

which indicates that 96% of the sample variation of the quantity of oranges sold can be attributed to the estimated effect of price variation and variation in advertising expenditure.

Concerning the use of the coefficient of determination, a couple of notes of caution may be in order. First, when the values of R^2 or $\bar{R}^2$ are used for comparing the goodness-of-fit of different regression equations, the comparison is purely descriptive and no formal statistical inference procedure is implied. Second, the formula for R^2 is based on the presumption of least squares estimation applied to a regression equation with a constant term. When a method of estimation other than least squares is used and *no other measure of goodness-of-fit is available,* the usual procedure is to use R^2 defined as

$$R^2 = 1 - \frac{\text{SSE}}{\text{SST}}.$$

When there is no constant term, some authors suggest using

$$R^2 = 1 - \frac{\sum e_i^2}{\sum Y_i^2}$$

to avoid negative values.[2]

Testing Hypotheses

With respect to *testing hypotheses,* the multiple regression model offers more opportunities than the simple regression model. First of all, there is the test of the hypothesis that the value of, say, β_k, is equal to some specific number. That is,

$$H_0: \quad \beta_k = \gamma_k,$$

which is to be tested against a two-sided or a one-sided alternative. The statistic that we can use to test H_0 is

$$\text{(10.43)} \qquad \frac{\hat{\beta}_k - \gamma_k}{s_{\hat{\beta}_k}} \sim t_{n-K} \qquad (k = 2, 3, \ldots, K).$$

Most frequently we are interested in testing the hypothesis that β_k is equal to zero. When $k = 1$, such a hypothesis implies that the intercept is equal to zero, namely, that the regression plane passes through the origin. When $k = 2, 3, \ldots, K$, the hypothesis that $\beta_k = 0$ means that the variable X_k has no influence on the mean of Y; if the hypothesis is not rejected, we conclude that X_k is not a relevant variable in the regression equation.

A more extensive hypothesis is that *none* of the explanatory variables has an influence on the mean of Y. In this case we test

$$H_0: \quad \beta_2 = \beta_3 = \cdots = \beta_K = 0$$

against the alternative that H_0 is not true, i.e., that at least one of the regression slopes is different from zero. If H_0 is true, then the variation of Y from observation to observation is not affected by changes in any one of the explanatory variables, but is purely random. By analogy with (7.49), the appropriate test statistic is

$$\text{(10.44)} \qquad \frac{\text{SSR}/(K-1)}{\text{SSE}/(n-K)} \sim F_{K-1, n-K},$$

[2] See, e.g., P. J. Dhrymes, *Introductory Econometrics* (New York: Springer-Verlag, 1978), p. 24.

where $F_{K-1,n-K}$ represents the F distribution with $(K-1)$ and $(n-K)$ degrees of freedom. If the value of the expression in (10.44) is not significantly different from one, the sample offers no evidence that the explanatory variables have any effect on the mean of Y. Incidentally, the value of the F statistic in (10.44) can be calculated by using R^2 since

$$\frac{\text{SSR}/(K-1)}{\text{SSE}/(n-K)} = \left[\frac{n-K}{K-1}\right]\left[\frac{\text{SSR/SST}}{1-(\text{SST/SST})}\right] = \left[\frac{n-K}{K-1}\right]\left[\frac{R^2}{1-R^2}\right].$$

The relationship between the values of the individual t statistics in the test of

$$H_0\colon \quad \beta_k = 0 \qquad (k = 2, 3, \ldots, K)$$

and the value of the F statistic in the test of

$$H_0\colon \quad \beta_2 = \beta_3 = \cdots = \beta_K$$

can be examined by expressing the F statistic in terms of the t statistics. We shall do this for the case of two explanatory variables. From (10.39) we have

$$\text{SSR} = \hat{\beta}_2^2 m_{22} + \hat{\beta}_3^2 m_{33} + 2\hat{\beta}_3\hat{\beta}_3 m_{23},$$

and from (10.36) we know that

$$\frac{\text{SSE}}{n-3} = s^2.$$

Therefore,

$$F_{2,n-3} = \frac{\text{SSR}/2}{\text{SSE}/(n-3)} = \frac{\hat{\beta}_2^2 m_{22} + \hat{\beta}_3^2 m_{33} + 2\hat{\beta}_2\hat{\beta}_3 m_{23}}{2s^2}. \tag{10.45}$$

Now let us denote the values of the t statistics for β_2 and β_3 by t_2 and t_3, respectively. Then

$$t_2 = \frac{\hat{\beta}_2}{s_{\hat{\beta}_2}} \quad \text{and} \quad t_3 = \frac{\hat{\beta}_3}{s_{\hat{\beta}_3}}.$$

By reference to (10.26) and (10.27) we can write

$$t_2^2 = \frac{\hat{\beta}_2^2(m_{22}m_{33} - m_{23}^2)}{s^2 m_{33}}.$$

$$t_3^2 = \frac{\hat{\beta}_3^2(m_{22}m_{33} - m_{23}^2)}{s^2 m_{22}},$$

or

$$\hat{\beta}_2^2 = \frac{t_2^2 s^2 m_{33}}{m_{22}m_{33} - m_{23}^2},$$

$$\hat{\beta}_3^2 = \frac{t_3^2 s^2 m_{22}}{m_{22}m_{33} - m_{23}^2},$$

and also

$$\hat{\beta}_2\hat{\beta}_3 = \frac{t_2 t_3 s^2 \sqrt{m_{22}}\sqrt{m_{33}}}{m_{22}m_{33} - m_{23}^2}.$$

Substitution into (10.45) then gives

(10.45a) $$F_{2,n-3} = \frac{t_2^2 s^2 m_{22} m_{33} + t_3^2 s^2 m_{22} m_{33} + 2t_2 t_3 s^2 (\sqrt{m_{22}}\sqrt{m_{33}}) m_{23}}{2s^2(m_{22}m_{33} - m_{23}^2)}.$$

If we use the symbol r_{23} to represent the sample coefficient of correlation between X_2 and X_3, that is, if we define

$$r_{23} = \frac{m_{23}}{\sqrt{m_{22}}\sqrt{m_{33}}},$$

then (10.45a) simplifies to

(10.45b) $$F_{2,n-3} = \frac{t_2^2 + t_3^2 + 2t_2 t_3 r_{23}}{2(1 - r_{23}^2)}.$$

This shows quite clearly that if r_{23}^2 is not far from unity, the value of $F_{2,n-3}$ will be quite large even if both t_2 and t_3 are small. Thus neither $\hat{\beta}_2$ nor $\hat{\beta}_3$ may be significantly different from zero and yet the value of $F_{2,n-3}$ may be highly significant. By the same token, it is also possible to find that either $\hat{\beta}_2$ or $\hat{\beta}_3$ or both are different from zero and yet the value of the F statistic need not be significant at the same level. The explanation lies in the fact that the two kinds of test—the F test and the t tests—are really not comparable since they are based on different presumptions. The t test concerning, say, β_2 is carried out without *any* presumption about β_3, whereas the F test is based on a joint statement about both β_2 *and* β_3. A geometric representation of the two kinds of tests is given in Figure 10-1. The ellipse represents

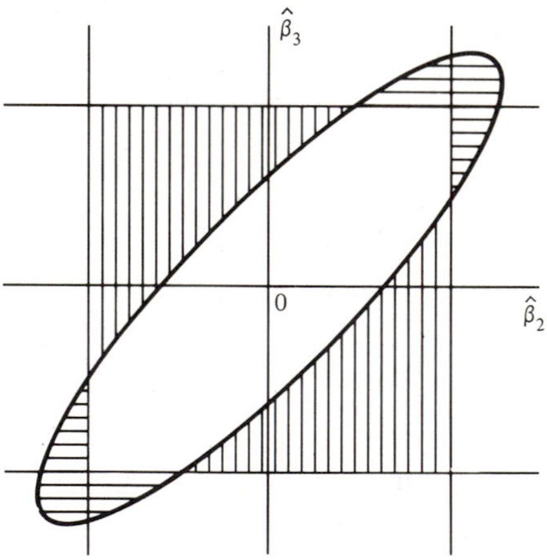

Figure 10-1

the acceptance region for the null hypothesis that $\beta_2 = \beta_3 = 0$ based on an F test, while the square represents the intersection of the acceptance regions of the hypotheses that $\beta_2 = 0$ and that $\beta_3 = 0$ based on two separate t tests. The vertically shaded area represents the situation where the t test leads to acceptance, whereas the F test leads to rejection of the respective hypotheses. This is a frequently encountered outcome. Since, as can be shown, the width of the ellipse is inversely related to the degree of correlation between the two regressors, the higher the correlation the more likely one would be to reject the null hypothesis by the F test but not by the t tests. The horizontally shaded area represents the opposite case where the F test leads to acceptance but either one or both of the t tests reject the null hypothesis.

EXAMPLE Consider a regression model

$$Y_i = \beta_1 + \beta_2 X_{i2} + \beta_3 X_{i3} + \varepsilon_i .$$

Suppose $n = 20$, and the calculated sample moments are

$$m_{YY} = 100, \qquad m_{22} = 100,$$
$$m_{Y2} = 90, \qquad m_{33} = 100,$$
$$m_{Y3} = 90, \qquad m_{23} = 95.$$

Then

$$\hat{\beta}_2 = \frac{90 \times 100 - 90 \times 95}{100 \times 100 - 95^2} = 0.461,$$

and

$$\hat{\beta}_3 = \frac{90 \times 100 - 90 \times 95}{100 \times 100 - 95^2} = 0.461.$$

Further,

$$\text{SSR} = 0.461^2 \times 100 + 0.461^2 \times 100 + 2 \times 0.461 \times 0.461 \times 95 = 83,$$
$$\text{SST} = 100,$$
$$\text{SSE} = 17.$$

Therefore,

$$s^2 = \frac{17}{17} = 1,$$

and

$$s^2_{\hat{\beta}_2} = \frac{1 \times 100}{100 \times 100 - 95^2} = 0.102564,$$

$$s^2_{\hat{\beta}_3} = \frac{1 \times 100}{100 \times 100 - 95^2} = 0.102564.$$

Consequently,

$$t_2 = \frac{0.461}{\sqrt{0.102564}} = 1.444,$$

$$t_3 = \frac{0.461}{\sqrt{0.102564}} = 1.444.$$

Since the tabulated t value for 17 degrees of freedom at the 5% level of significance (i.e., $t_{17, 0.025}$) is 2.110, which exceeds 1.444, neither $\hat{\beta}_2$ nor $\hat{\beta}_3$ is significantly different from zero at the 5% level of significance. On the other hand, the value

$$F = \frac{83/2}{1} = 41.5$$

is very much higher than the tabulated value of $F_{2,17}$ at the 5% level of significance, which is 3.59. Thus, by the t test we cannot reject the hypothesis that $\beta_2 = 0$ or the hypothesis that $\beta_3 = 0$, and yet by the F test we reject the hypothesis that $\beta_2 = \beta_3 = 0$. The reason is the fact that the separate contributions of X_2 and X_3 to the explanation of the variation of Y are weak, whereas their joint contribution, which cannot be decomposed, is quite strong. In fact,

$$\begin{aligned} \hat{\beta}_2^2 m_{22} &= 21.3 \\ \hat{\beta}_3^2 m_{33} &= 21.3 \\ \underline{2\hat{\beta}_2\hat{\beta}_3 m_{23}} &= \underline{40.4} \\ \text{SSR} &= 83.0, \end{aligned}$$

which shows that the joint contribution of X_2 and X_3 to SSR is almost twice as large as the separate contribution of either X_2 or X_3. Note that in this example $r_{23} = 0.95$, indicating a high degree of sample correlation between X_2 and X_3.

A somewhat different test concerns the influence of additional explanatory variables on the mean of Y. In particular, consider two theories, one stating that the regression equation is

$$Y_i = \beta_1 + \beta_2 X_{i2} + \beta_3 X_{i3} + \cdots + \beta_K X_{iK} + \varepsilon_i,$$

while the competing theory states that Y depends not only on $X_2, X_3, \ldots, X_K$ but also on additional explanatory variables $X_{K+1}, X_{K+2}, \ldots, X_Q$ $(Q > K)$, that is,

$$Y_i = \beta_1 + \beta_2 X_{i2} + \beta_3 X_{i3} + \cdots + \beta_K X_{iK} + \beta_{K+1} X_{i,K+1} + \cdots + \beta_Q X_{iQ} + \varepsilon_i.$$

In this case, the second theory can be tested by testing the hypothesis

$$H_0\text{:} \quad \beta_{K+1} = \beta_{K+2} = \cdots = \beta_Q = 0$$

against the alternative that H_0 is not true. To formulate the appropriate test, we introduce a new notation, using the subscript K to denote the values pertaining to the original set of explanatory variables, and the subscript Q to denote the values to the extended set of explanatory variables. Values with no subscript apply to either set. We can write

$$\text{SST} = \text{SSR}_K + \text{SSE}_K$$

and also

$$\text{SST} = \text{SSR}_Q + \text{SSE}_Q.$$

If the additional explanatory variables are not relevant in explaining the variation of Y, then, in the population, SSR_K and SSR_Q would be the same and the observed difference between them would be entirely due to sampling error. If the null hypothesis is true, then

$$\text{(10.46)} \qquad \frac{(\text{SSR}_Q - \text{SSR}_K)/(Q-K)}{\text{SSE}_Q/(n-Q)} \sim F_{Q-K,\, n-Q}.$$

This can be used to test H_0 at a specified level of significance. It is not difficult to show that

$$\text{SSR}_Q \geq \text{SSR}_K$$

so that the expression in (10.46) can never be negative. An implication of this is that

$$\frac{\text{SSR}_Q}{\text{SST}} \geq \frac{\text{SSR}_K}{\text{SST}};$$

that is,

$$R_Q^2 \geq R_K^2.$$

This means that adding new explanatory variables into a regression equation can never result in a reduction in the value of the coefficient of determination. However, this is not necessarily true of $\bar{R}^2$.

EXAMPLE In a paper on the short-run consumption function for the United States,[3] two of the proposed functions were

$$C_t = \beta_1 + \beta_2 Y_t + \varepsilon_t$$

and

$$C_t = \beta_1 + \beta_2 Y_t + \beta_3 C_{t-1} + \beta_4 L_{t-1} + \varepsilon_t,$$

where C = consumption, Y = income, and L = liquid assets. Let us test the hypothesis

$$H_0\colon \quad \beta_3 = \beta_4 = 0$$

against the alternative that H_0 is not true at, say, the 1% level of significance. To use the F test of (10.46), we have to calculate

$$F = \left[\frac{\text{SSR}_Q - \text{SSR}_K}{\text{SSE}_Q}\right]\left[\frac{n-Q}{Q-K}\right].$$

We have $n = 31$, $Q = 4$, $K = 2$. The values of SSR and SSE are not given in the paper but can be determined from the values of $\bar{R}^2$s, which are

$$\bar{R}_Q^2 = 0.984 \qquad \text{and} \qquad \bar{R}_K^2 = 0.944.$$

First, we find the values of "unadjusted" R^2s. Since

$$\bar{R}_K^2 = R_K^2 - \frac{K-1}{n-K}(1 - R_K^2),$$

we can solve for R_K^2 to get

$$R_K^2 = \frac{(n-K)\bar{R}_K^2 + (K-1)}{n-1} = 0.946,$$

[3] Arnold Zellner, "The Short-Run Consumption Function," *Econometrica*, 25 (October 1957), pp. 552–567.

and, similarly,

$$R_Q^2 = 0.986.$$

The value of the appropriate F statistic then is

$$F = \frac{(\text{SSR}_Q/\text{SST}) - (\text{SSR}_K/\text{SST})}{1 - (\text{SSR}_Q/\text{SST})}\left[\frac{n-Q}{Q-K}\right] = \left[\frac{R_Q^2 - R_K^2}{1 - R_Q^2}\right]\left[\frac{n-Q}{Q-K}\right] = 38.57.$$

Since the tabulated value of $F_{2,27}$ at the 1% level of significance is 5.49, the null hypothesis has to be rejected. That is, the evidence strongly suggests that the addition of lagged consumption and lagged liquid assets contributes to the explanation of variations in current consumption.

The preceding two tests—the test for the existence of a relationship presented in (10.44) and the test for relevance of additional explanatory variables presented in (10.46)—are really special cases of the general test of linear restrictions imposed by the null hypothesis introduced in (7.51) as

$$\frac{(\text{SSE}_R - \text{SSE}_U)/r}{\text{SSE}_U/(n-K)} \sim F_{r,n-K},$$

where SSE_R is the "restricted error sum of squares" (i.e., the error sum of squares when the null hypothesis is imposed), SSE_U is the "unrestricted error sum of squares," r is the number of restrictions imposed by the null hypothesis, and K is the number of regressors (including the constant term). In the case of testing for the existence of a relationship we have, under H_0,

$$Y_i = \beta_1 + 0 \times X_{i2} + 0 \times X_{i3} + \cdots + 0 \times X_{iK} + \varepsilon_i,$$

so that the restricted least squares estimator of β_1 is $\bar{Y}$ and

$$\begin{aligned} \text{SSE}_R &= \sum (Y_i - \bar{Y})^2 \\ &= \text{SST}. \end{aligned}$$

Further, $\text{SSE}_U = \text{SSE}$ and $r = K - 1$, so that the test statistic becomes

$$\frac{(\text{SST} - \text{SSE})/(K-1)}{\text{SSE}/(n-K)} = \frac{\text{SSR}/(K-1)}{\text{SSE}/(n-K)},$$

which is the same expression as that in (10.44). In the case of testing for the relevance of additional explanatory variables we have, under H_0,

$$\text{SSE}_R = \text{SSE}_K,$$
$$\text{SSE}_U = \text{SSE}_Q,$$

and

$$r = Q - K.$$

Then

$$\begin{aligned}\text{SSE}_R - \text{SSE}_U &= \text{SSE}_K - \text{SSE}_Q \\ &= (\text{SST} - \text{SSR}_K) - (\text{SST} - \text{SSR}_Q) \\ &= \text{SSR}_Q - \text{SSR}_K,\end{aligned}$$

and the result in (10.46) follows.

Another hypothesis that is sometimes of interest is

$$H_0\colon \quad \beta_j = \beta_k \qquad (j \neq k),$$

which can be tested against a one-sided or a two-sided alternative. For instance, one form of the aggregate consumption function proposed in the literature is

$$C_t = \beta_1 + \beta_2 W_t + \beta_3 P_t + \beta_4 C_{t-1} + \varepsilon_t,$$

where C = consumption, W = wage income, and P = nonwage income. An interesting hypothesis is that the marginal propensity to consume of the wage earners is equal to that of the nonwage earners, i.e., that $\beta_2 = \beta_3$. To test the hypothesis that two regression coefficients are equal, we consider the distribution of the difference of the corresponding least squares estimators. In general we have

$$E(\hat{\beta}_j - \hat{\beta}_k) = \beta_j - \beta_k$$

and

$$\text{Var}(\hat{\beta}_j - \hat{\beta}_k) = \text{Var}(\hat{\beta}_j) + \text{Var}(\hat{\beta}_k) - 2\,\text{Cov}(\hat{\beta}_j, \hat{\beta}_k).$$

Thus, if the null hypothesis is true,

$$(\hat{\beta}_j - \hat{\beta}_k) \sim N(0, \sigma^2_{\hat{\beta}_j - \hat{\beta}_k}).$$

An unbiased estimator of $\sigma^2_{\hat{\beta}_j - \hat{\beta}_k}$, say, $s^2_{\hat{\beta}_j - \hat{\beta}_k}$, can be obtained by using s^2 as an estimator of σ^2. It then follows that

$$\frac{\hat{\beta}_j - \hat{\beta}_k}{s_{\hat{\beta}_j - \hat{\beta}_k}} \sim t_{n-K}. \tag{10.47}$$

If the value of this statistic is significantly different from zero, the hypothesis that the two regression coefficients are equal is to be rejected.

For a test of equality of more than two regression coefficients, we can again use the F test presented in (7.51), which involves restricted and unrestricted residual sums of squares. Consider, for instance, the null hypothesis

$$H_0\colon \quad \beta_2 = \beta_3 = \beta_4,$$

which yields the following restrictions on the regression coefficients,

$$Y_i = \beta_1 + \beta_2(X_{i2} + X_{i3} + X_{i4}) + \beta_5 X_{i5} + \cdots + \beta_K X_{iK} + \varepsilon_i$$

or

$$Y_i = \beta_1 + \beta_2 X^*_{i2} + \beta_5 X_{i5} + \cdots + \beta_K X_{iK} + \varepsilon_i,$$

where $X_{i2}^{*} = (X_{i2} + X_{i3} + X_{i4})$. This leads to a straightforward application of the formula (7.51) with r (the number of restrictions) equal to 2.

A hypothesis that is sometimes interesting is the proposition that the sum of two regression coefficients is equal to a given number. For instance, in the Cobb–Douglas production function

$$Y_i = \beta_1 + \beta_2 X_{i2} + \beta_3 X_{i3} + \varepsilon_i,$$

where Y_i = log output, X_{i2} = log labor input, and X_{i3} = log capital input, the hypothesis of constant returns to scale is equivalent to the hypothesis

$$H_0: \quad \beta_2 + \beta_3 = 1.$$

In general, the hypothesis

$$H_0: \quad \beta_j + \beta_k = a$$

can be tested by noting that

$$\frac{\hat{\beta}_j + \hat{\beta}_k - a}{s_{\hat{\beta}_j + \hat{\beta}_k}} \sim t_{n-k}, \tag{10.48}$$

where $s_{\hat{\beta}_j + \hat{\beta}_k} = \sqrt{s_{\hat{\beta}_j}^2 + s_{\hat{\beta}}^2 + 2 \text{ Est. Cov}(\hat{\beta}_j, \hat{\beta}_k)}.$

This test can easily be extended to a sum of more than two regression coefficients.

The final test concerns the equality of two regression equations. In particular, consider a regression equation

$$Y_i = \beta_1 + \beta_2 X_{i2} + \beta_3 X_{i3} + \cdots + \beta_K X_{iK} + \varepsilon_i,$$

which has been estimated from a sample of n observations. Suppose now that we obtain m ($>K$) additional observations and wish to test the hypothesis that the additional observations come from the same population as the first n observations. For example, data on the aggregate consumption function frequently cover the prewar as well as the postwar period. If we concede the possibility that the parameters of the postwar consumption function may be different from those of the prewar consumption function, we would test the null hypothesis that the parameters of the consumption function have *not* changed. In particular, we may write

$$Y_i = \beta_1 + \beta_2 X_{i2} + \beta_3 X_{i3} + \cdots + \beta_K X_{iK} + \varepsilon_i \qquad (i = 1, 2, \ldots, n)$$

and

$$Y_i = \gamma_1 + \gamma_2 X_{i2} + \gamma_3 X_{i3} + \cdots + \gamma_K X_{iK} + \varepsilon_i \qquad (i = n+1, n+2, \ldots, n+m).$$

The null hypothesis then would be

$$H_0: \quad \beta_1 = \gamma_1, \quad \beta_2 = \gamma_2, \quad \ldots, \quad \beta_K = \gamma_K.$$

This is to be tested against the hypothesis that H_0 is not true, assuming that the variances of the disturbances in the two equations are the same. Here again we can use the F test presented in (7.51). The restrictions imposed by H_0 are

$$Y_i = \beta_1 + \beta_2 X_{i2} + \cdots + \beta_K X_{iK} + \varepsilon_i$$

for *all* $i = 1, 2, \ldots, n, n+1, \ldots, n+m$. Let the sum of squares of least squares residuals from this equation be called SSE_R as usual. When the restrictions imposed by H_0 are ignored, the least squares method is applied to each group of observations separately, thus allowing for different coefficient estimates. The resulting unrestricted error sum of squares then will be

$$\text{SSE}_U = \text{SSE}_1 + \text{SSE}_2,$$

where SSE_1 is the sum of squares of least squares residuals for the first n observations and SSE_2 is the sum of squares of least squares residuals for the next m observations. The number of restrictions imposed by H_0 is equal to the number of restricted coefficients, i.e., K, while the number of degrees of freedom for the unrestricted estimation is $n + m - 2K$ (since there are two sets of K coefficients involved). By reference to (7.51) the appropriate test statistic then becomes

$$\text{(10.49)} \qquad \frac{(\text{SSE}_R - \text{SSE}_1 - \text{SSE}_2)/K}{(\text{SSE}_1 + \text{SSE}_2)/(n + m - 2K)} \sim F_{K, n+m-2K}.$$

This test is known in econometrics as the "Chow test" after its main popularizer.[4]

A relatively simple way of carrying out the Chow test is by collapsing the two separate regressions based on two separate groups of observations into one equation as follows:

$$\text{(10.50)} \quad Y_i = \alpha_1 + \beta_2 X_{i2} + \cdots + \beta_K X_{iK} + \lambda_1 Z_i + \lambda_2 Z_i X_{i2} + \cdots + \lambda_K Z_i X_{iK} + \varepsilon_i,$$

where

$$\begin{aligned} Z_i &= 1 \quad \text{if } i > n, \\ &= 0 \quad \text{otherwise.} \end{aligned}$$

Thus in (10.50) the regression coefficients for the first n observations are β_1, $\beta_2, \ldots, \beta_K$, and for the following m observations they are $(\beta_1 + \lambda_1)$, $(\beta_2 + \lambda_2), \ldots, (\beta_K + \lambda_K)$. Clearly, the null hypothesis of equality of coefficients is

$$H_0\colon \quad \lambda_1 = \lambda_2 = \cdots = \lambda_K = 0,$$

so that the appropriate test for (10.50) is the test for relevance of additional explanatory variables. This is exactly equivalent to the test in (10.49). The advantage of using (10.50) is that it is easily adaptable to a test of equality of only some and not necessarily all regression coefficients.

Although the Chow test has been designed for testing the equality of regression coefficients of *two* equations, its extension to more than two equations (and more than two groups of corresponding observations), utilizing either (7.51) or (10.50), is quite straightforward. Further, if the variances of the regression disturbance of the two (or more) equations differ, the ensuing heteroskedasticity can easily be corrected by weighting the observations corresponding to different equations by the inverse of their respective estimated variances. However, since only estimates of the variances and not their true values are used, the validity of the Chow test in this case

[4] G. C. Chow, "Tests of Equality Between Sets of Coefficients in Two Linear Regressions," *Econometrica*, 28 (July 1960), pp. 591–605.

is only asymptotic. Finally, the test statistic in (10.49) is applicable only if the number of additional observations exceeds the number of explanatory variables *plus* one, i.e., if $m > K$. If $m \leqq K$, Chow proposed the test statistic

$$(10.51) \qquad \frac{(\text{SSE}_R - \text{SSE}_1)/m}{\text{SSE}_1/(n-K)} \sim F_{m,n-K}.$$

This test is known as "Chow predictive test" because it can be derived from the magnitude of the "prediction errors" involving observations beyond the nth one.

In discussing the problem of choosing an appropriate significance level in Section 5-1, we mentioned that whether a test rejects the null hypothesis or not is frequently a question of sample size. In general, the larger the sample size, the more likely we are to reject the null hypothesis *as stated.* To overcome this difficulty, Leamer suggested changing the level of significance with sample size.[5] In particular, the researcher should conclude that the sample evidence favors the alternative hypothesis if

$$F > \frac{n-K}{r}(n^{r/n} - 1),$$

where F is the calculated value of the F statistics, r is the number of restrictions, and $(n-K)$ is the number of degrees of freedom corresponding to the "unrestricted error sum of squares."

Beta Coefficients

The coefficients of a regression model—but not the tests or R^2—are affected by the units in which the variables are measured. For this reason a comparison of the magnitudes of individual regression coefficients is not very revealing. To overcome this problem, applied statisticians have at times been using a transformation of the regression coefficients resulting in "standardized" or "beta" coefficients, which yield values whose comparison is supposed to be more meaningful. The idea behind the transformation is to measure all variables in terms of their respective sample standard deviations. The resulting "beta" coefficients then measure the change in the dependent variable corresponding to a unit change in the respective explanatory variable, holding other explanatory variables constant and measuring all changes in standard deviation units. This amounts to replacing the original estimated coefficients $\hat{\beta}_k$ $(k = 2, 3, \ldots, K)$ by the "beta" coefficients $\hat{\beta}_k^*$ defined as

$$(10.52) \qquad \hat{\beta}_k^* = \hat{\beta}_k \left(\frac{\sqrt{(m_{kk}/n)}}{\sqrt{m_{yy}/n}} \right) \qquad (k = 2, 3, \ldots, K).$$

When $K = 2$, $\hat{\beta}_2^*$ is equal to the coefficient of correlation between the dependent and the explanatory variable, but for $K > 2$ the "beta" coefficients cannot be interpreted as any kind of simple correlation coefficients. Since the "beta" coefficients do not solve the main problem of separating the effects of each explanatory variable

[5] See E. E. Leamer, *Specification Searches* (New York: Wiley, 1978), pp. 114–115.

on the dependent variable any better than the usual regression coefficients, their use in econometrics has been rather rare.

Recursive Estimation

The formulas for the least squares estimators of the regression parameters that have been presented earlier in this chapter involve a once-and-for-all calculation and lead to a final set of estimates. However, in some situations we may wish to calculate the estimates sequentially as new observations become available. There is a considerable computational advantage—and possibly some insights—to be gained by using new data to update previous estimates. This approach, which is common in the engineering and optimal control literature has been pioneered by Kalman.[6] Let us consider the situation in which our estimates of the regression parameters, based on n observations, are to be updated by incorporating a new observation labeled $(n+1)$. Let $\mathbf{X_n} \rightarrow n \times K$, $\mathbf{Y_n} \rightarrow n \times 1$, and

$$\hat{\boldsymbol{\beta}}_{\mathbf{n}} = (\mathbf{X}'_{\mathbf{n}}\mathbf{X}_{\mathbf{n}})^{-1}\mathbf{X}'_{\mathbf{n}}\mathbf{Y}_{\mathbf{n}}.$$

With the addition of a new observation, the new data set consists of

$$\mathbf{X}_{\mathbf{n+1}} = \begin{bmatrix} \mathbf{X}_{\mathbf{n}} \\ \mathbf{x}_{\mathbf{n+1}} \end{bmatrix}, \qquad \mathbf{Y}_{\mathbf{n+1}} = \begin{bmatrix} \mathbf{Y}_{\mathbf{n}} \\ \mathbf{y}_{\mathbf{n+1}} \end{bmatrix},$$

where $\mathbf{x}_{\mathbf{n+1}} \rightarrow 1 \times K$ and $\mathbf{y}_{\mathbf{n+1}} \rightarrow 1 \times 1$. The "off-line" or "nonrecursive" least squares estimator of $\boldsymbol{\beta}$ is

$$\hat{\boldsymbol{\beta}}_{\mathbf{n+1}} = (\mathbf{X}'_{\mathbf{n+1}}\mathbf{X}_{\mathbf{n+1}})^{-1}\mathbf{X}'_{\mathbf{n+1}}\mathbf{Y}_{\mathbf{n+1}}.$$

The equivalent "recursive" or "on-line" estimator is[7]

$$\hat{\boldsymbol{\beta}}_{\mathbf{n+1}} = \hat{\boldsymbol{\beta}}_{\mathbf{n}} + \frac{(\mathbf{X}'_{\mathbf{n}}\mathbf{X}_{\mathbf{n}})^{-1}\mathbf{x}'_{\mathbf{n+1}}}{1 + \mathbf{x}_{\mathbf{n+1}}(\mathbf{X}'_{\mathbf{n}}\mathbf{X}_{\mathbf{n}})^{-1}\mathbf{x}'_{\mathbf{n+1}}}(\mathbf{y}_{\mathbf{n+1}} - \mathbf{x}_{\mathbf{n+1}}\hat{\boldsymbol{\beta}}_{\mathbf{n}}). \tag{10.53}$$

The formula (10.53) shows that the updated estimator $\hat{\boldsymbol{\beta}}_{\mathbf{n+1}}$ is equal to the previous estimator $\hat{\boldsymbol{\beta}}_{\mathbf{n}}$ *plus* an "adjustment factor," which is proportional to the prediction error $(\mathbf{y}_{\mathbf{n+1}} - \mathbf{x}_{\mathbf{n+1}}\hat{\boldsymbol{\beta}}_{\mathbf{n}})$. The prediction error is also known as an "innovation." The vector of proportionality is often called the "smoothing vector" in engineering literature. Further, let us define the error sum of squares based on n observations as

$$\text{SSE}_n = (\mathbf{Y}_{\mathbf{n}} - \mathbf{X}_{\mathbf{n}}\hat{\boldsymbol{\beta}}_{\mathbf{n}})'(\mathbf{Y}_{\mathbf{n}} - \mathbf{X}_{\mathbf{n}}\hat{\boldsymbol{\beta}}_{\mathbf{n}}).$$

[6] R. E. Kalman, "A New Approach to Linear Filtering and Prediction Problems," *Journal of Basic Engineering,* 83D (1961), pp. 95–108. We confine ourselves to models with time-invariant parameters here.

[7] For elucidation and extensions see A. Havenner and R. Craine, "Estimation Analogies in Control," *Journal of the Americal Statistical Association,* 76 (December 1981), pp. 850–859.

Then the updated error sum of squares can be shown to be

$$\text{SSE}_{n+1} = \text{SSE}_n + \frac{(\mathbf{y_{n+1}} - \mathbf{x_{n+1}}\hat{\boldsymbol{\beta}}_\mathbf{n})}{1 + \mathbf{x_{n+1}}(\mathbf{X'_n X_n})^{-1}\mathbf{x'_{n+1}}}. \tag{10.54}$$

The recursive estimation formulas (10.53) and (10.54) are useful not only because of computational convenience but also because they provide a convenient way of monitoring the stability of the model as new observations become available.

Detection of Influential Observations

In carrying out an empirical investigation and estimating regression parameters, we may be interested to know which observations have been particularly influential in producing the estimates that have been obtained. Such observations may then be especially carefully checked for errors since they shoulder a large burden of responsibility for the results. Given

$$\mathbf{y} = \mathbf{X}\boldsymbol{\beta} + \boldsymbol{\varepsilon},$$

we have

$$\begin{aligned}\hat{\mathbf{y}} &= \mathbf{X}\hat{\boldsymbol{\beta}}\\ &= \mathbf{X}(\mathbf{X'X})^{-1}\mathbf{X'y}\\ &= \mathbf{Hy},\end{aligned}$$

where $\mathbf{H} = \mathbf{X}(\mathbf{X'X})^{-1}\mathbf{X'}$ (called a "hat matrix") is a matrix that projects the observed values of $\mathbf{y}$ into the fitted values of $\hat{\mathbf{y}}$.[8] Let $\mathbf{x_i}$ be the ith row of $\mathbf{X}$. Then the ith diagonal element of $\mathbf{H}$ is

$$h_{ii} = \mathbf{x_i}(\mathbf{X'X})^{-1}\mathbf{x'_i}. \tag{10.55}$$

It can be shown that $0 \leq h_{ii} \leq 1$. The values of h_{ii} for some simple models are as follows.

Model	h_{ii}
$Y_i = \alpha + \varepsilon_i$	$\frac{1}{n}$
$Y_i = \beta X_i + \varepsilon_i$	$\frac{X_i^2}{\sum X_i^2}$
$Y_i = \alpha + \beta X_i + \varepsilon_i$	$\frac{1}{n} + \frac{(X_i - \bar{X})^2}{\sum (X_i - \bar{X})^2}$

The significance of h_{ii} lies in its influence on the estimated regression coefficients and on the fitted (or predicted) value of the dependent variable. Let $\hat{\boldsymbol{\beta}}$ be a least

[8] Our discussion on the topic of influential observations is largely based on D. Belsley, E. Kuh, and R. E. Welsch, *Regression Diagnostics* (New York: Wiley, 1980).

squares estimator of $\boldsymbol{\beta}$ based on *all* n observations, and let $\hat{\boldsymbol{\beta}}(\mathbf{i})$ be the corresponding estimator based on all observations *except* for the ith one. Further, let $\hat{y}_i = \mathbf{x_i}\hat{\boldsymbol{\beta}}$ and $\hat{y}_i(i) = \mathbf{x_i}\hat{\boldsymbol{\beta}}(\mathbf{i})$. Then

$$\text{(10.56a)} \qquad \hat{\boldsymbol{\beta}} - \hat{\boldsymbol{\beta}}(\mathbf{i}) = \frac{(\mathbf{X}'\mathbf{X})^{-1}\mathbf{x}_\mathbf{i}'e_i}{1 - h_{ii}},$$

$$\text{(10.56b)} \qquad \hat{y}_i - \hat{y}_i(i) = \frac{h_{ii}e_i}{1 - h_{ii}},$$

where e_i is the ith least squares residual. It is clear, then, that the closer the value of h_{ii} comes to unity, the greater the change in coefficient estimates and in prediction as a result of including the ith observation. In fact, when $h_{ii} = 1$, the ith observation is so influential that without it $\mathbf{X(i)'X(i)}$ is singular and the least squares estimator of $\boldsymbol{\beta}$ is indeterminate.

The obvious question concerns the value of h_{ii} which makes the ith observation "influential." Since

$$\begin{aligned}\text{tr}(\mathbf{H}) &= \text{tr}[\mathbf{X}(\mathbf{X}'\mathbf{X})^{-1}\mathbf{X}'] \\ &= \text{tr}[(\mathbf{X}'\mathbf{X})(\mathbf{X}'\mathbf{X})^{-1}] \\ &= K,\end{aligned}$$

it follows that $\Sigma_i h_{ii} = K$ and the average value of h_{ii} is K/n. By convention, a value of h_{ii} that exceeds twice its average is considered to indicate an influential observation. Such a value is sometimes called a "leverage point." Thus if

$$h_{ii} > \frac{2K}{n},$$

the ith observation may deserve closer scrutiny.

Apart from the influence on the value of the estimated regression coefficients, an observation may also be influential through its effect on the efficiency of the coefficient estimators. This can be ascertained by examining the effect of the ith observation on the variance of the least squares estimators. A suggested measure of this influence is the so-called "covariance ratio," defined as

$$\text{(10.57)} \qquad \text{Covratio} = \frac{\text{Det}\{s^2(i)[\mathbf{X(i)'X(i)}]^{-1}\}}{\text{Det}\{s^2(\mathbf{X}'\mathbf{X})^{-1}\}},$$

where "Det" stands for "determinant" and

$$s^2 = \frac{(\mathbf{y} - \mathbf{X}\hat{\boldsymbol{\beta}})'(\mathbf{y} - \mathbf{X}\hat{\boldsymbol{\beta}})}{n - K},$$

$$s^2(i) = \frac{[\mathbf{y(i)} - \mathbf{X(i)}\hat{\boldsymbol{\beta}}\mathbf{(i)}]'[\mathbf{y(i)} - \mathbf{X(i)}\hat{\boldsymbol{\beta}}\mathbf{(i)}]}{n - K - 1}.$$

A value of "covratio" in excess of $[1 + 3K/n]$ is considered significant.

The detection of influential observations leads to the identification of data points that tend to drive the results, and it ought to alert the researcher to the presence of potential errors. However, eliminating the influential observations (unless they are found to be in error) is not advisable since they are a valuable source of information.

It is interesting to note that the preceding analysis has not involved an examination of residuals, although this appears to have been a standard procedure on the part of some applied researchers. The reason is that a data point may be—and frequently is—highly influential even if its associated residual is very small. A good example is a situation in which all observations but one are clustered near each other while the solitary odd observation lies a way out. Clearly, the outlying observation is highly influential with respect to estimation and prediction, even though the value of its corresponding residual is likely to be quite small.

Prediction

Let us now turn our attention to the problem of *forecasting* the value of the dependent variable for a given set of values of the explanatory variables. More formally, let the given values of the explanatory variables be $X_{02}, X_{03}, \ldots, X_{0K}$, and let the corresponding value of the dependent variable be Y_0. We are interested in forecasting Y_0. As pointed out in connection with the simple regression model, the best predictor of Y_0 is $E(Y_0)$ because the variance of Y_0 around $E(Y_0)$ is smaller than around any other point. Since $E(Y_0)$ is not known, we use $\hat{Y}_0$, the least squares fitted value of Y_0, in its place. Since

$$\hat{Y}_0 = \hat{\beta}_1 + \hat{\beta}_2 X_{02} + \hat{\beta}_3 X_{03} + \cdots + \hat{\beta}_K X_{0K},$$

it follows that $\hat{Y}_0$ is normally distributed with mean

$$E(\hat{Y}_0) = \beta_1 + \beta_2 X_{02} + \beta_3 X_{03} + \cdots + \beta_K X_{0K}.$$

The variance of $\hat{Y}_0$ is, according to (10.38),

$$\begin{aligned}\operatorname{Var}(\hat{Y}_0) &= \sigma^2_{\hat{Y}_0} \\ &= \sum_k (X_{0k} - \bar{X}_k)^2 \operatorname{Var}(\hat{\beta}_k) \\ &\quad + 2 \sum_{j<k} (X_{0j} - \bar{X}_j)(X_{0k} - \bar{X}_k) \operatorname{Cov}(\hat{\beta}_j, \hat{\beta}_k) + \frac{\sigma^2}{n} \\ &\quad (j, k = 2, 3, \ldots, K; j < k),\end{aligned}$$

or, in matrix notation,

$$\operatorname{Var}(\hat{Y}_0) = \sigma^2 \left[\underline{\mathbf{X}}_0'(\underline{\mathbf{X}}'\underline{\mathbf{X}})^{-1}\underline{\mathbf{X}}_0 + \frac{1}{n} \right],$$

where

$$\underline{\mathbf{X}}_0 = \begin{bmatrix} X_{02} - \bar{X}_2 \\ X_{03} - \bar{X}_3 \\ \vdots \\ X_{0K} - \bar{X}_K \end{bmatrix}.$$

We are, of course, primarily interested in the *forecast error*, that is, in $(Y_0 - \hat{Y}_0)$. This random variable is normally distributed with mean

$$E(Y_0 - \hat{Y}_0) = 0$$

and variance

$$\sigma_F^2 = \text{Var}(Y_0 - \hat{Y}_0) = \text{Var}(Y_0) + \text{Var}(\hat{Y}_0) - 2\,\text{Cov}(Y_0, \hat{Y}_0).$$

Now

$$\text{Var}(Y_0) = \sigma^2,$$
$$\text{Var}(\hat{Y}_0) = \sigma_{\hat{Y}_0}^2,$$

and

$$-2\,\text{Cov}(Y_0, \hat{Y}_0) = -2E[Y_0 - E(Y_0)][\hat{Y}_0 - E(\hat{Y}_0)]$$
$$= -2E\varepsilon_0[\hat{Y}_0 - E(Y_0)] = 0.$$

Therefore,

(10.58) $$\sigma_F^2 = \sigma^2 + \frac{\sigma^2}{n} + \sum_k (X_{0k} - \bar{X}_k)^2\,\text{Var}(\hat{\beta}_k) + 2\sum_{j<k}(X_{0j} - \bar{X}_j)(X_{0k} - \bar{X}_k)\,\text{Cov}(\hat{\beta}_j, \hat{\beta}_k),$$

or, in matrix notation,

(10.58a) $$\sigma_F^2 = \sigma^2\left[1 + \frac{1}{n} + \underline{\mathbf{X}}_0'(\underline{\mathbf{X}}'\underline{\mathbf{X}})^{-1}\underline{\mathbf{X}}_0\right].$$

As with the simple regression model, the shorter the distance between the given values of the explanatory variables and their respective sample means, the smaller the variance of the forecast error. An unbiased estimator of σ_F^2 can be obtained by replacing σ^2 by s^2. If we denote the resulting estimator by s_F^2, then

(10.59) $$\frac{Y_0 - \hat{Y}_0}{s_F} \sim t_{n-K}.$$

From this result, we can construct a forecast interval that will contain the actual value of Y_0 with whatever probability we choose. Designating one *minus* the chosen probability level by λ $(0 < \lambda < 1)$, we have

$$\hat{Y}_0 - t_{n-K,\,\lambda/2}s_F \leq Y_0 \leq \hat{Y}_0 + t_{n-K,\,\lambda/2}s_F.$$

The expression in (10.59) can also be used to test the hypothesis that a new observation, say, $(n+1)$th, comes from the same population as the n observations that were used for estimating the regression parameters.

EXAMPLE In the first example of this section, we estimated a regression equation describing the demand for oranges. The sample consisted of twelve observations on the quantity of oranges sold, their price, and the amount spent on advertising (see Table 10-1). The estimated regression equation is

$$\hat{Y}_i = 116.16 - 1.308X_{i2} + 11.246X_{i3},$$

where Y = quantity of oranges sold, X_2 = price, and X_3 = advertising expenditure. Now suppose that no oranges are sold until a new shipment arrives, which is several weeks later. Then, the record for the first day of trading shows

$$Y_0 = 100, \quad X_{02} = 80, \quad \text{and} \quad X_{03} = 7.$$

The problem is to decide whether the demand function has changed since the time of the previous shipment of oranges. Here, we have

$$\hat{Y}_0 = 116.16 - 1.308 \times 80 + 11.246 \times 7 = 90.242.$$

This is the "forecast" value of Y. The estimated variance of the forecast error is

$$s_F^2 = \left[s^2 + \frac{s^2}{n} + (X_{02} - \bar{X}_2)^2 s_{\hat{\beta}_2}^2 + (X_{03} - \bar{X}_3)^2 s_{\hat{\beta}_3}^2 + 2(X_{02} - \bar{X}_2)(X_{03} - \bar{X}_3)\text{Est. Cov}(\hat{\beta}_2, \hat{\beta}_3) \right].$$

Now, from previous calculations we have

$$s = 27.5993, \qquad s_{\hat{\beta}_2}^2 = 0.016730,$$

$$\bar{X}_2 = 70, \qquad s_{\hat{\beta}_3}^2 = 7.749782,$$

$$\bar{X}_3 = 6.7, \qquad \text{Est. Cov}(\hat{\beta}_2, \hat{\beta}_3) = \frac{-27.5993 \times (-54)}{2250 \times 4.857 - (-54)^2} = 0.185995.$$

Therefore,

$$s_F^2 = 27.5993\left(1 + \frac{1}{12}\right) + (80 - 70)^2 \times 0.016730 + (7 - 6.7)^2 \times 7.749782 + 2 \times (80 - 70)(7 - 6.7) \times 0.185995 = 34.96728,$$

$$s_F = 5.913.$$

The 95% confidence interval for Y_0 can be constructed by noting that the tabulated value of $t_{9,0.025}$ is 2.262. Therefore we have

$$90.242 - 2.262 \times 5.913 \leq Y_0 \leq 90.242 + 2.262 \times 5.913$$

or

$$76.867 \leq Y_0 \leq 103.617.$$

This interval covers the observed value $Y_0 = 100$.

So far we have considered predicting only one observation ahead of the sample observations. A generalization to several out-of-sample observations is quite straightforward. Let $\mathbf{X}_0$ be a $(m \times K)$ matrix of m future observations on $\mathbf{X}$, and $\mathbf{y}_0$ a $(m \times 1)$ vector of m future values of $\mathbf{y}$, and $\boldsymbol{\varepsilon}_0$ a $(m \times 1)$ vector of future disturbances. The vector of the m prediction errors then is

$$\mathbf{y}_0 - \hat{\mathbf{y}}_0 = \mathbf{X}_0\boldsymbol{\beta} + \boldsymbol{\varepsilon}_0 - \mathbf{X}_0\hat{\boldsymbol{\beta}}$$
$$= \mathbf{X}_0(\hat{\boldsymbol{\beta}} - \boldsymbol{\beta}) + \boldsymbol{\varepsilon}_0,$$

whose expected value is, of course, zero. The variance-covariance matrix of the prediction errors is

$$(10.60)\qquad E(\mathbf{y}_0 - \hat{\mathbf{y}}_0)(\mathbf{y}_0 - \hat{\mathbf{y}}_0)' = E[-\mathbf{X}_0(\hat{\boldsymbol{\beta}} - \boldsymbol{\beta}) + \boldsymbol{\varepsilon}_0][-\mathbf{X}_0(\hat{\boldsymbol{\beta}} - \boldsymbol{\beta}) + \boldsymbol{\varepsilon}_0]'$$
$$= \sigma^2[\mathbf{I} + \mathbf{X}_0(\mathbf{X}'\mathbf{X})^{-1}\mathbf{X}_0'].$$

An equivalent formula is

$$(10.60a)\qquad E(\mathbf{y}_0 - \hat{\mathbf{y}}_0)(\mathbf{y}_0 - \hat{\mathbf{y}}_0)' = \sigma^2\left[\mathbf{I} + \frac{\boldsymbol{\iota}\boldsymbol{\iota}'}{n} + \underline{\mathbf{X}}_0(\underline{\mathbf{X}}'\underline{\mathbf{X}})^{-1}\underline{\mathbf{X}}_0'\right],$$

where $\boldsymbol{\iota}$ is a $(m \times 1)$ vector of ones and $\underline{\mathbf{X}}_0$ is a $m \times (K-1)$ matrix of the future values of the explanatory variables measured in terms of deviations from their respective sample means.

The calculation of the predicted values of $\mathbf{y}$ and of the estimated variances of the prediction errors can be considerably simplified by using a method suggested by Salkever.[9] The method involves applying least squares estimation to an extended model—and an extended set of "observations"—given as

$$(10.61)\qquad \begin{bmatrix} \mathbf{y} \\ \overline{Y}\boldsymbol{\iota} \end{bmatrix} = \begin{bmatrix} \mathbf{X} & \mathbf{0} \\ \mathbf{X}_0 & \mathbf{I} \end{bmatrix} \begin{bmatrix} \boldsymbol{\beta} \\ \boldsymbol{\gamma} \end{bmatrix} + \begin{bmatrix} \boldsymbol{\varepsilon} \\ \boldsymbol{\eta} \end{bmatrix},$$

where $\overline{Y}\boldsymbol{\iota}$ is a $(m \times 1)$ vector whose every element is the sample mean $\overline{Y}$, $\mathbf{I}$ is a $(m \times m)$ identity matrix, $\boldsymbol{\gamma}$ is a $(m \times 1)$ vector of additional coefficients, and $\boldsymbol{\eta}$ is a $(m \times 1)$ vector of artificial disturbances. By applying the least squares estimation to (10.61), we obtain

1. The estimates of $\boldsymbol{\beta}$ are the same as those obtained for the original regression equation based on n sample observations.
2. The estimates of $\boldsymbol{\gamma}$ give

   $$\hat{\gamma}_j = \overline{Y} + \hat{Y}_{0j} \qquad (j = 1, 2, \ldots, m),$$

   where $\hat{Y}_{0j}$ is the predicted value of Y for the jth prediction period.
3. The estimated standard errors of the $\hat{\gamma}$s are equal to the estimated standard deviations of the respective prediction errors.
4. The value of R^2 is the same as that for the original regression equation with n observations.

In certain situations the prediction provided by a regression model may be supplemented by the prediction from some outside source. For instance, a predictor of

[9] D. S. Salkever, "The Use of Dummy Variables to Compute Predictions, Prediction Errors, and Confidence Intervals," *Journal of Econometrics*, 4 (November 1976), pp. 393–397.

consumer expenditures in the current quarter based on a regression model may be supplemented by an official preliminary estimate based on actual expenditure for the first month of the quarter. Let $\hat{Y}_0$ be the predictor based on a regression model with variance $\hat{\sigma}^2$, and let $\tilde{Y}_0$ be the predictor from an outside source whose variance is $\tilde{\sigma}^2$. Then we can construct a combined predictor, say $\bar{\bar{Y}}_0$ as a weighted average of the two available predictors, i.e.,

$$\bar{\bar{Y}}_0 = w\hat{Y}_0 + (1 - w)\tilde{Y}_0, \tag{10.62}$$

where w represents the chosen weight. If the two predictors are independent, the variance of $\bar{\bar{Y}}_0$ will be

$$\mathrm{Var}(\bar{\bar{Y}}_0) = w^2\hat{\sigma}^2 + (1 - w)^2\tilde{\sigma}^2. \tag{10.63}$$

The value of w that minimizes $\mathrm{Var}(\bar{\bar{Y}}_0)$ is

$$w = \frac{\tilde{\sigma}^2}{\hat{\sigma}^2 + \tilde{\sigma}^2},$$

so that the optimal combined linear predictor is

$$\bar{\bar{Y}}_0 = \left(\frac{\tilde{\sigma}^2}{\hat{\sigma}^2 + \tilde{\sigma}^2}\right)\hat{Y}_0 + \left(\frac{\hat{\sigma}^2}{\hat{\sigma}^2 + \tilde{\sigma}^2}\right)\tilde{Y}_0. \tag{10.62a}$$

The weight given to each of the two original predictors is thus inversely related to their respective variances.

A Note on Basic Assumptions and Data

In Chapter 8 we discussed the consequences of violating the basic assumptions of the classical normal linear regression model in the context of simple regression. The conclusions reached there hold either completely or only with simple and obvious modifications in the context of multiple regression. In particular, the remarks concerning the assumption of normal distribution and of zero mean of ε apply equally to the multiple regression model. With respect to heteroskedasticity, the discussion and the findings of Section 8-2 can be extended to the multiple regression case simply by allowing for more than one explanatory variable. The same is true of the results for models with autocorrelated disturbances (Section 8-3) and for models with stochastic regressors (Section 8-4).

The problems of data deficiency studied in Chapter 9 also arise in multiple regression models. The derivations and the statements made in the context of simple regression models can, for the most part, be extended to multiple regression without much difficulty.

10-3 Multicollinearity

By assumption (10.8) of the classical normal linear regression model we require that none of the explanatory variables be perfectly correlated with any other explanatory variable *or* with any linear combination of other explanatory variables. When this assumption is violated, we speak of *perfect multicollinearity.* On the other hand, whenever all explanatory variables are uncorrelated with each other, we speak of *absence of multicollinearity.* The cases in between are then described by various degrees of multicollinearity. Of particular interest are cases of a *high degree of multicollinearity,* which arise whenever one explanatory variable is highly correlated with another explanatory variable *or* with a linear combination of other explanatory variables.

Before discussing multicollinearity in detail, two points should be made clear.

1. Multicollinearity is a question of degree and not of kind. The meaningful distinction is not between the presence and the absence of multicollinearity, but between its various degrees.
2. Since multicollinearity refers to the condition of the explanatory variables that are assumed to be nonstochastic, it is a *feature of the sample* and not of the population.[10]

Therefore, we do not "test for multicollinearity" but can, if we wish, measure its degree in any particular sample. In the discussion that follows, we will be concerned with the implication of various degrees of multicollinearity for estimation of the regression coefficients.

Absence of Multicollinearity

Let us start with the case of *no multicollinearity,* when the explanatory variables are uncorrelated with each other. In this case the matrix ($\underline{\mathbf{X}}'\underline{\mathbf{X}}$) is diagonal. In a regression model with two explanatory variables

$$Y_i = \beta_1 + \beta_2 X_{i2} + \beta_3 X_{i3} + \varepsilon_i,$$

where $m_{23} = 0$, the least squares normal equations for $\hat{\beta}_2$ and $\hat{\beta}_3$ become

$$m_{Y2} = \hat{\beta}_2 m_{22}, \qquad m_{Y3} = \hat{\beta}_3 m_{33}.$$

Therefore,

$$\hat{\beta}_2 = \frac{m_{Y2}}{m_{22}}, \qquad \hat{\beta}_3 = \frac{m_{Y3}}{m_{33}}.$$

These formulas are exactly the same as those for the *simple* regression of Y on X_2, and of Y on X_3.

The preceding result seems to suggest that, when X_2 and X_3 are uncorrelated, we might abandon the multiple regression model with two explanatory variables and replace it by two simple regression models

$$Y_i = \alpha_2 + \beta_2 X_{i2} + \varepsilon_{i2}.$$

and

$$Y_i = \alpha_3 + \beta_3 X_{i3} + \varepsilon_{i3}.$$

[10] If the explanatory variables are stochastic and there is an underlying relation among them in the population, such a relation should be specified as a part of the model. If such a relation does not exist in the population, we still may (and generally will) find *some* relation between the explanatory variables in the sample. Once again, multicollinearity is a feature of the sample, not of the population.

However, this would create difficulties. In the first place, neither one of the simple regressions will enable us to get an estimator of the regression constant β_1, although this is not so important since the least squares estimator of β_1 is simply

$$\hat{\beta}_1 = \bar{Y} - \hat{\beta}_2\bar{X}_2 - \hat{\beta}_3\bar{X}_3.$$

More important is that using the simple regressions for estimating the variances of $\hat{\beta}_2$ and $\hat{\beta}_3$ results in *biased* estimates. This can be seen as follows. From (10.26) we know that the variance of $\hat{\beta}_2$ is

$$\mathrm{Var}(\hat{\beta}_2) = \frac{\sigma^2 m_{33}}{m_{22}m_{33} - m_{23}^2},$$

which, for $m_{23} = 0$, becomes

$$\mathrm{Var}(\hat{\beta}_2) = \frac{\sigma^2}{m_{22}}.$$

Now the estimator of $\mathrm{Var}(\hat{\beta}_2)$ based on the simple regression is

$$s_{\hat{\beta}_2}^2 = \frac{s_2^2}{m_{22}},$$

where $$s_2^2 = \frac{1}{n-2}\sum_i [(Y_i - \bar{Y}) - \hat{\beta}_2(X_{i2} - \bar{X}_2)]^2.$$

Taking the mathematical expectation of s_2^2, we get

$$\begin{aligned} E(s_2^2) &= \frac{1}{n-2} E\sum_i [\beta_2(X_{i2} - \bar{X}_2) + \beta_3(X_{i3} - \bar{X}_3) \\ &\qquad + (\varepsilon_i - \bar{\varepsilon}) - \hat{\beta}_2(X_{i2} - \bar{X}_2)]^2 \\ &= \frac{1}{n-2}[m_{22}\mathrm{Var}(\hat{\beta}_2) + \beta_3^2 m_{33} - 2m_{22}\mathrm{Var}(\hat{\beta}_2) + (n-1)\sigma^2] \\ &= \frac{1}{n-2}[(n-2)\sigma^2 + \beta_3^2 m_{33}], \end{aligned}$$

so that

$$E(s_{\hat{\beta}_2}^2) = \mathrm{Var}(\hat{\beta}_2) + \frac{\beta_3^2 m_{33}}{m_{22}(n-2)}.$$

Similarly,

$$E(s_{\hat{\beta}_3}^2) = \mathrm{Var}(\hat{\beta}_3) + \frac{\beta_2^2 m_{22}}{m_{33}(n-2)}.$$

This means that the simple regression estimators of the variances of $\hat{\beta}_2$ and $\hat{\beta}_3$ have an upward bias. This result can be generalized to regression models with any number of mutually uncorrelated explanatory variables.

Perfect Multicollinearity

Next we turn our attention to the case of *perfect multicollinearity.* For the multiple regression model with two explanatory variables, perfect multicollinearity means that we can write

(10.63) $$X_{i2} = a + bX_{i3},$$

where a and b are some fixed numbers and $b \neq 0$. In this case there is perfect correlation between the two explanatory variables in the sample. Consider now the least squares estimators of the regression coefficients. The least squares normal equations for the model with two explanatory variables are

$$m_{Y2} = \hat{\beta}_2 m_{22} + \hat{\beta}_3 m_{23},$$
$$m_{Y3} = \hat{\beta}_2 m_{23} + \hat{\beta}_3 m_{33}.$$

But by (10.63) we have

$$m_{Y2} = bm_{Y3},$$
$$m_{22} = b^2 m_{33},$$
$$m_{23} = bm_{33}.$$

Therefore, the least squares normal equations become

$$bm_{Y3} = b(\hat{\beta}_2 bm_{33} + \hat{\beta}_3 m_{33}),$$
$$m_{Y3} = \hat{\beta}_2 bm_{33} + \hat{\beta}_3 m_{33}.$$

This shows that the first normal equation is exactly equal to the second normal equation multiplied by b. Therefore, the two equations are not independent, and the solution for $\hat{\beta}_2$ and $\hat{\beta}_3$ is indeterminate.

Let us now consider the case of three explanatory variables to illustrate a special feature of multicollinearity that does not show up in the two-variable case. In this case the presence of perfect multicollinearity means that we can write

(10.64) $$X_{i2} = a + b_3 X_{i3} + b_4 X_{i4},$$

where a, b_3, and b_4 are some fixed numbers. Suppose both b_3 and b_4 are different from zero. The sample coefficient of correlation between X_2 and X_3 is

$$r_{23} = \frac{m_{23}}{\sqrt{m_{22}}\sqrt{m_{33}}},$$
$$= \frac{b_3 m_{33} + b_4 m_{34}}{\sqrt{b_3^2 m_{33} + b_4^2 m_{44} + 2b_3 b_4 m_{34}}\sqrt{m_{33}}},$$
$$= \frac{b_3\sqrt{m_{33}} + b_4 r_{34}\sqrt{m_{44}}}{\sqrt{(b_3\sqrt{m_{33}} + b_4 r_{34}\sqrt{m_{44}})^2 + b_4^2 m_{44}(1 - r_{34}^2)}},$$

where r_{34} is the sample coefficient of correlation between X_3 and X_4. Similarly, the sample coefficient of correlation between X_2 and X_4 is

$$r_{24} = \frac{b_3 r_{34}\sqrt{m_{33}} + b_4\sqrt{m_{44}}}{\sqrt{(b_3 r_{34}\sqrt{m_{33}} + b_4\sqrt{m_{44}})^2 + b_3^2 m_{33}(1 - r_{34}^2)}}.$$

These results clearly show that the presence of perfect multicollinearity does *not* necessarily mean that the correlation between any two explanatory variables must be perfect, or even particularly high, when the total number of explanatory variables is greater than two. For example, when

$$X_{i2} = X_{i3} + X_{i4}, \quad m_{33} = m_{44}, \quad \text{and} \quad r_{34} = -0.5,$$

then

$$r_{23} = \frac{1 - 0.5}{\sqrt{(1 - 0.5)^2 + (1 - 0.5^2)}} = 0.5$$

and

$$r_{24} = \frac{-0.5 + 1}{\sqrt{(-0.5 + 1)^2 + (1 - 0.5^2)}} = 0.5.$$

In this case we have perfect multicollinearity, and yet none of the correlation coefficients is greater than one half in absolute value. This is important because it means that when there are more than two explanatory variables, we cannot simply look at the coefficients of correlation and conclude that the sample is *not* perfectly (or highly) multicollinear. On the other hand, if the correlation between any one pair of explanatory variables is perfect, then there *is* perfect multicollinearity present in the sample. For perfect correlation between, say, X_2 and X_3, implies that X_2 is an exact linear function of X_3 so that we can write

$$X_{i2} = a + b_3 X_{i3} \qquad (b_3 \neq 0),$$

which is equivalent to (10.64) with $b_4 = 0$. Thus, *perfect correlation between two explanatory variables is a sufficient but not necessary condition for the presence of perfect multicollinearity* in the sample when the number of explanatory variables exceeds two.

Now let us see what happens to the least squares estimators of the regression coefficients under conditions of perfect multicollinearity when the regression model contains three explanatory variables. The least squares normal equations are

$$m_{Y2} = \hat{\beta}_2 m_{22} + \hat{\beta}_3 m_{23} + \hat{\beta}_4 m_{24},$$
$$m_{Y3} = \hat{\beta}_2 m_{23} + \hat{\beta}_3 m_{33} + \hat{\beta}_4 m_{34},$$
$$m_{Y4} = \hat{\beta}_2 m_{24} + \hat{\beta}_3 m_{34} + \hat{\beta}_4 m_{44}.$$

But from (10.64) we have

$$m_{Y2} = b_3 m_{Y3} + b_4 m_{Y4},$$
$$m_{22} = b_3^2 m_{33} + b_4^2 m_{44} + 2b_3 b_4 m_{34},$$
$$m_{23} = b_3 m_{33} + b_4 m_{34},$$
$$m_{24} = b_3 m_{34} + b_4 m_{44}.$$

Substitution of these expressions into the least squares normal equations leads to

$$b_3 m_{Y3} + b_4 m_{Y4} = \hat{\beta}_2(b_3^2 m_{33} + b_4^2 m_{44} + 2b_3 b_4 m_{34}) + \hat{\beta}_3(b_3 m_{33} + b_4 m_{34}) + \hat{\beta}_4(b_3 m_{34} + b_4 m_{44}),$$

$$m_{Y3} = \hat{\beta}_2(b_3 m_{33} + b_4 m_{34}) + \hat{\beta}_3 m_{33} + \hat{\beta}_4 m_{34},$$

$$m_{Y4} = \hat{\beta}_2(b_3 m_{34} + b_4 m_{44}) + \hat{\beta}_3 m_{34} + \hat{\beta}_4 m_{44}.$$

Thus the first normal equation is simply equal to the second normal equation multiplied by b_3 *plus* the third normal equation multiplied by b_4. Therefore, under perfect multicollinearity, the three normal equations are not independent and cannot be solved for $\hat{\beta}_2$, $\hat{\beta}_3$, and $\hat{\beta}_4$. This result can be extended to regression models with any number of explanatory variables. Since by (10.14) the vector of the least squares estimators of the regression coefficients is

$$\hat{\boldsymbol{\beta}} = (\mathbf{X'X})^{-1}(\mathbf{X'y}),$$

the existence of an exact linear relation between the explanatory variables means that one of the columns of $(\mathbf{X'X})$ is an exact linear function of another one or more columns. Thus $(\mathbf{X'X})$ is a singular matrix and its inverse does not exist.

Given that the least squares estimators of the regression coefficients are indeterminate, the traditional suggestion has been to use information about the regression coefficients from sources other than the sample on hand. For instance, if in the model

$$Y_i = \beta_1 + \beta_2 X_{i2} + \beta_3 X_{i3} + \varepsilon_i,$$

the two explanatory variables are perfectly correlated but we know—or are willing to assume—that

$$\frac{\beta_3}{\beta_2} = k,$$

where k is a known fixed number, then estimation of the regression coefficients becomes possible. By substituting $\beta_3 = k\beta_2$ into the regression model, we obtain

$$Y_i = \beta_1 + \beta_2 X_{i2} + k\beta_2 X_{i3} + \varepsilon_i$$

or

$$Y_i = \beta_1 + \beta_2 Z_i + \varepsilon_i,$$

where Z_i is measured by $(X_{i2} + kX_{i3})$. In this case, we can obtain a least squares estimator of β_1 and β_2, and infer an estimator of β_3. These estimators can be viewed as conditional upon the given value of k. If there are several values of k that appear as likely candidates, we may obtain a set of different estimators, each conditional upon a different value of k.[11]

Cases in which we know the ratio of, or have some other exact information about, two regression coefficients are relatively rare. More frequently, we may have an

[11] In a case like this the Bayesian approach to estimation may appear particularly attractive. See A. Zellner, *An Introduction to Bayesian Inference in Econometrics* (New York: Wiley, 1971), pp. 75–81.

estimate of one or more of the regression coefficients from a different sample. For instance, we may have a sample of time-series observations to estimate a regression model, together with an unbiased estimate of one of the regression coefficients from cross-section data. This might be the case in the estimation of a demand function for a particular commodity as a function of price and income. If the observations are made over time, an estimate of the income coefficient is frequently available from a sample of cross-section data. Suppose the regression model to be estimated is

$$Y_t = \beta_1 + \beta_2 X_{t2} + \beta_3 X_{t3} + \varepsilon_t,$$

and we have an unbiased estimator of β_3, say $\hat{\hat{\beta}}_3$, from an independent sample of cross-section data. Then, the regression model can be rewritten as

$$(Y_t - \hat{\hat{\beta}}_3 X_{t3}) = \beta_1 + \beta_2 X_{t2} - (\hat{\hat{\beta}}_3 - \beta_3)X_{t3} + \varepsilon_t$$

or

$$Y_t^* = \beta_1 + \beta_2 X_{t2} + u_t.$$

The least squares estimator of β_2 becomes

$$(10.65) \qquad \hat{\beta}_2 = \frac{\sum (Y_t^* - \overline{Y}^*)(X_{t2} - \overline{X}_2)}{\sum (X_{t2} - \overline{X}_2)^2}$$

$$= \frac{\sum (Y_t - \hat{\hat{\beta}}_3 X_{t3} - \overline{Y} + \hat{\hat{\beta}}_3 \overline{X}_3)(X_{t2} - \overline{X}_2)}{\sum (X_{t2} - X_2)^2}$$

$$= \frac{m_{Y2} - \hat{\hat{\beta}}_3 m_{23}}{m_{22}}.$$

The mean and the variance of $\hat{\beta}_2$ are

$$(10.66) \qquad E(\hat{\beta}_2) = \frac{1}{m_{22}} E[\beta_2 m_{22} + \beta_3 m_{23} + \sum_t (X_{t2} - \overline{X}_2)\varepsilon_t - \hat{\hat{\beta}}_3 m_{23}] = \beta_2,$$

$$(10.67) \qquad \mathrm{Var}(\hat{\beta}_2) = E(\hat{\beta}_2 - \beta_2)^2$$

$$= \frac{1}{m_{22}^2} E[-(\hat{\hat{\beta}}_3 - \beta_3)m_{23} + \sum_t (X_{t2} - \overline{X}_2)\varepsilon_t]^2$$

$$= \frac{1}{m_{22}^2}[m_{23}^2 \mathrm{Var}(\hat{\hat{\beta}}_3) + \sigma^2 m_{22}]$$

$$= \frac{\sigma^2}{m_{22}} + \frac{m_{23}^2 \mathrm{Var}(\hat{\hat{\beta}}_3)}{m_{22}^2}.$$

In empirical applications the formula for the variance of $\hat{\beta}_2$ has often been simplified by being viewed as conditional upon the given value of $\hat{\hat{\beta}}_3$, which amounts to treating $\hat{\hat{\beta}}_3$ as a fixed number.

An objection to dealing with the multicollinearity problem by obtaining information from sources other than the sample on hand is that it calls for something that should be done in any case. Normally, we suppose that in specifying the regression model and the estimation procedure we use *all* of the available information about the population. There is no reason for us to wait for the presence of perfect multicollinearity before we search for all the relevant information, except when the search is very costly. Had we exhausted all sources of information by the time we came to estimation, the proposed remedy for the multicollinearity problem would not apply. Furthermore, with respect to the use of an estimate from another sample, we might also question the wisdom of using only this information from such a sample and disregarding the rest. An alternative and increasingly more popular approach to the problem of multicollinearity involves biased estimation, since the introduction of a small bias may result in a substantial reduction in variance. This approach is discussed at the end of this section.

High Degree of Multicollinearity

So far we have considered the two extreme cases of multicollinearity, the case of no multicollinearity and the case of perfect multicollinearity. Neither extreme is very frequent in practical applications, but most data exhibit some—though not perfect—multicollinearity. In this case we can always obtain a determinate solution for the least squares estimators of the regression coefficients, unless we run into the problem of rounding errors.

Let us now examine the connection between the degree of multicollinearity and the properties of the least squares estimators of the regression coefficients. Under the basic assumptions of the classical normal linear regression model, the least squares estimators of the regression coefficients have all the desirable properties. But, as pointed out in Section 7-4, knowing that the least squares estimators have these properties is only cold comfort to us if their variances are such that the resulting estimates are highly unreliable. That is, knowing that our estimators have the smallest possible variance (among all unbiased estimators) is not very helpful if, at the same time, this variance happens to be very large. And this is how multicollinearity comes in. Consider a regression model with two explanatory variables. According to (10.26) and (10.27) the variances of $\hat{\beta}_2$ and $\hat{\beta}_3$ are

$$\text{(10.68a)} \qquad \text{Var}(\hat{\beta}_2) = \frac{\sigma^2 m_{33}}{m_{22}m_{33} - m_{23}^2} = \frac{\sigma^2}{m_{22}(1 - r_{23}^2)},$$

$$\text{(10.68b)} \qquad \text{Var}(\hat{\beta}_3) = \frac{\sigma^2 m_{22}}{m_{22}m_{33} - m_{23}^2} = \frac{\sigma^2}{m_{33}(1 - r_{23}^2)},$$

and by (10.31) their covariance is

$$\text{(10.68c)} \qquad \text{Cov}(\hat{\beta}_2, \hat{\beta}_3) = \frac{-\sigma^2 m_{23}}{m_{22}m_{33} - m_{23}^2} = \frac{-\sigma^2 r_{23}}{\sqrt{m_{22}}\sqrt{m_{33}}(1 - r_{23}^2)},$$

This shows clearly that when r_{23}^2 is close to unity, the variances and the covariance of $\hat{\beta}_2$ and $\hat{\beta}_3$ are very large. (In the case when $r_{23}^2 = 1$, they would be infinite.) Since in the case of two explanatory variables the value of r_{23}^2 measures the degree of multicollinearity, the preceding result implies that the higher the degree of multicollinearity, the larger the variances and the covariance of $\hat{\beta}_2$ and $\hat{\beta}_3$. When there are more than two explanatory variables, the above formulas for the variances of the least squares coefficients generalize to

$$(10.69) \qquad \operatorname{Var}(\hat{\beta}_k) = \frac{\sigma^2}{m_{kk}(1 - R_k^2)} = \frac{\sigma^2}{\text{SSE}_k} \qquad (k = 2, 3, \ldots, K),$$

where R_k^2 is the coefficient of determination in the least squares regression with the kth explanatory variable as the "dependent" variable and all the remaining explanatory variables as regressors (SSE_k represents the error sum of squares for this regression). The quantity $1/(1 - R_k^2)$ is called the "variance inflation factor" or VIF in the literature.

We thus conclude that a high degree of multicollinearity is harmful in the sense that the estimates of the regression coefficients are highly imprecise. The imprecision arises because of the large variances of the least squares estimators. However, it should be noted that large variances of the estimated regression coefficients may exist even if there is no multicollinearity at all, either because the explanatory variables have a small dispersion or because σ^2 itself is large. If we want to put the blame on multicollinearity, we ought to be able to measure its degree. In the case of models with two explanatory variables, we can use the value of r_{23}^2 for this purpose, but when there are more than two explanatory variables, measurement of the degree of multicollinearity becomes more complicated. This is because, as we demonstrated earlier, the presence of a high degree of multicollinearity, or even of perfect multicollinearity, does not generally imply that the correlation between any two explanatory variables must be particularly high.

Measures of Multicollinearity

The problem of measuring multicollinearity in models with more than two explanatory variables has been attacked in a number of ways. Some research workers have used the value of the determinant of $(\mathbf{X'X})$ since this is low when the degree of multicollinearity is high, and it is zero when multicollinearity is perfect. This measure has the disadvantage of not being bounded and of being affected by the dispersion of the explanatory variables in addition to their interrelation. For instance, if we used this measure for the model with two explanatory variables, we would get

$$\operatorname{Det}\begin{bmatrix} n & \sum X_{i2} & \sum X_{i3} \\ \sum X_{i2} & \sum X_{i2}^2 & \sum X_{i2}X_{i3} \\ \sum X_{i3} & \sum X_{i2}X_{i3} & \sum X_{i3}^2 \end{bmatrix} = n(m_{22}m_{33} - m_{23}^2) = nm_{22}m_{33}(1 - r_{23}^2).$$

Thus two sets of sample data with the same number of observations and the *same value of* r_{23}^2 would give different values of the determinant if the product of m_{22} and m_{33} were not the same in the two samples. Most of the difficulties with using the determinant of $(\mathbf{X'X})$ can be avoided if, instead, we use the determinant of the matrix of the sample correlation coefficients. For a regression model with two explanatory variables this gives $(1 - r_{23}^2)$. The value of this determinant always lies between 0 and 1.

A relatively simple measure of the degree of multicollinearity is suggested by the fact that a high degree of multicollinearity simply means that at least one of the explanatory variables can be represented as a linear function of one or more of the remaining explanatory variables *plus* a small residual. If we "regress" each of the explanatory variables on all the remaining explanatory variables, we can obtain a measure of the "goodness of fit" by calculating the value of R^2 in each case. If any one of these R^2s is close to unity, the degree of multicollinearity is high. Or, in general, the highest of these R^2s can be taken as a measure of the degree of multicollinearity present in the sample.

Since a high degree of multicollinearity is accompanied by a small value of the determinant of $(\mathbf{X}'\mathbf{X})$, which in turn implies that at least one of the characteristic roots of $(\mathbf{X}'\mathbf{X})$ is very small, some authors suggest using the ratio of the largest to the smallest characteristic root as a suitable measure of multicollinearity. Such a measure is called a "condition number"; if its value exceeds 30, multicollinearity is thought to be harmful.[12] Another sign of harmful multicollinearity often considered in practice is finding that at, say, the 5% level of significance, the value of the F statistic is significantly different from zero but none of the t statistics for the regression coefficients (other than the regression constant) is. In this case we would *reject* the hypothesis that there is no relationship between Y on one side and $X_2, X_3, \ldots, X_K$ on the other side, but we would *not reject* the hypothesis that any one of the explanatory variables is irrelevant in influencing Y. Such a situation indicates that the separate influence of each of the explanatory variables is weak relative to their joint influence on Y. This is symptomatic of a high degree of multicollinearity, which prevents us from disentangling the separate influences of the explanatory variables. The disadvantage of this criterion is that it is too strong in the sense that multicollinearity is considered as harmful only when all of the influences of the explanatory variables on Y cannot be disentangled.

Suggested Remedies

Since multicollinearity is a reflection of a low informational content in the sample, a natural remedy for it would be to increase the pool of information. One possible way of doing this is to increase the sample size. For instance, consider the variances of $\hat{\beta}_2$ and $\hat{\beta}_3$ in a model with two explanatory variables. These are

$$\mathrm{Var}(\hat{\beta}_2) = \frac{\sigma^2}{m_{22}(1 - r_{23}^2)},$$

$$\mathrm{Var}(\hat{\beta}_3) = \frac{\sigma^2}{m_{33}(1 - r_{23}^2)}.$$

An increase in sample size may increase m_{22} and m_{33}, or reduce r_{23}^2, or do both at

[12] Belsley, Kuh, and Welsch, *op. cit.*

the same time. The increase in m_{22} and m_{33} will occur in all cases in which the additional values of X_2 and X_3 are different from $\bar{X}_2$ and $\bar{X}_3$, as they are quite likely to be. On the other hand, it is difficult to foresee what will happen to r_{23}^2 as n increases, given that the X's are nonstochastic and not under our control.

An entirely different approach to the problem of multicollinearity involves trading a little bias for a large reduction in variance. The leading method of this kind is the so-called "ridge regression" method of Hoerl and Kennard.[13] The simplest and most common version of the method is called "ordinary ridge regression" (ORR). The ORR estimator of β is defined as

$$(10.70) \qquad \begin{aligned} \tilde{\boldsymbol{\beta}} &= (\mathbf{X}'\mathbf{X} + k\mathbf{I})^{-1}\mathbf{X}'\mathbf{y} \\ &= (\mathbf{X}'\mathbf{X} + k\mathbf{I})^{-1}\mathbf{X}'\mathbf{X}\hat{\boldsymbol{\beta}} \\ &= [\mathbf{I} + k(\mathbf{X}'\mathbf{X})^{-1}]^{-1}\hat{\boldsymbol{\beta}}, \end{aligned}$$

where $\hat{\boldsymbol{\beta}}$ is the least squares estimator of $\boldsymbol{\beta}$ and k is a positive number, for now considered to be given. Since

$$E(\tilde{\boldsymbol{\beta}}) = (\mathbf{X}'\mathbf{X} + k\mathbf{I})^{-1}\mathbf{X}'\mathbf{X}\boldsymbol{\beta}$$

and

$$\begin{aligned} E(\tilde{\boldsymbol{\beta}} - \boldsymbol{\beta})(\tilde{\boldsymbol{\beta}} - \boldsymbol{\beta})' &= E(\mathbf{X}'\mathbf{X} + k\mathbf{I})^{-1}\mathbf{X}'\boldsymbol{\varepsilon}\boldsymbol{\varepsilon}'\mathbf{X}(\mathbf{X}'\mathbf{X} + k\mathbf{I})^{-1} \\ &= \sigma^2(\mathbf{X}'\mathbf{X} + k\mathbf{I})^{-1}\mathbf{X}'\mathbf{X}(\mathbf{X}'\mathbf{X} + k\mathbf{I})^{-1}, \end{aligned}$$

the trade-off between bias and variance hinges on the value of k: the larger the value of k, the larger the bias but the smaller the variance. The crucial aspect of ORR, demonstrated by Hoerl and Kennard, is that there exists a $k > 0$ such that

$$\text{tr MSE }(\tilde{\boldsymbol{\beta}}) \leq \text{tr MSE }(\hat{\boldsymbol{\beta}}).$$

This is sometimes referred to as the domination of ORR over LSE. The range of this dominance was established by Theobald[14] as that for which $0 < k < 2\sigma^2/\Sigma_k\beta_k^2 m_{kk}$. Unfortunately, the upper limit of the interval depends on unknown parameters.

An interesting feature of ORR is given by the easily established fact that

$$\tilde{\boldsymbol{\beta}}'\tilde{\boldsymbol{\beta}} < \hat{\boldsymbol{\beta}}'\hat{\boldsymbol{\beta}}.$$

For this reason, ORR is said to belong to the class of "shrinkage estimators," because it "pulls" the least squares estimator toward zero. The relationship between the ORR and the LS estimator is further illuminated by noting that while the LSE is obtained by unconstrained minimization of $(\mathbf{y} - \mathbf{X}\boldsymbol{\beta})'(\mathbf{y} - \mathbf{X}\boldsymbol{\beta})$, the ORR estimator is obtained by minimizing $(\mathbf{y} - \mathbf{X}\boldsymbol{\beta})'(\mathbf{y} - \mathbf{X}\boldsymbol{\beta})$, subject to the constraint that $\boldsymbol{\beta}'\boldsymbol{\beta} = r$, where r is given a number inversely related to k. ORR can also be interpreted as a Bayesian estimator incorporating the prior "information" that $\boldsymbol{\beta} = 0$.

[13] A. E. Hoerl and R. W. Kennard, "Ridge Regression: Biased Estimation for Non-Orthogonal Problems," *Technometrics,* 12 (February 1970), pp. 55–67.

[14] C. M. Theobald, "Generalizations of Mean Square Error Applied to Ridge Regression," *Journal of the Royal Statistical Society,* Series B, 36 (1974), pp. 103–106.

The major difficulty with the ORR estimator that has tended to restrain its popularity in econometrics is that k is rarely given and is typically deduced in some fairly arbitrary way from the data. (The resulting estimator is termed an "adaptive ORR estimator.") Another difficulty arises from the unsuitability of the ORR estimator for use in testing hypotheses, although this need not be too serious when k is small. On the other hand, the ORR frequently leads to drastic reductions in the mean square error as compared with the LS estimator, so it seems unwise to rule out its use.[15]

EXAMPLE Suppose we have a model

$$Y_t = \beta_1 + \beta_2 X_{t2} + \beta_3 X_{t3} + \varepsilon_t$$

for which all classical assumptions are satisfied. The sample data for 22 observations are

$$m_{22} = 10.01, \qquad m_{y2} = 10,$$
$$m_{33} = 90.01, \qquad m_{y3} = 30,$$
$$m_{23} = 30.00, \qquad m_{yy} = 12.$$

It is easy to see that here we have a very high degree of multicollinearity. Let us calculate the ORR estimate of β_2 and β_3 (disregarding β_1) for different values of k. The results are

k	$\tilde{\beta}_2$	$\tilde{\beta}_3$
0.00	0.1000	0.3000
0.01	0.1000	0.2999
0.10	0.0999	0.2997
0.20	0.0998	0.2994
⋮		
0.70	0.0993	0.2979
⋮		
1.00	0.0990	0.2970

Clearly, the value of the $\tilde{\beta}$'s change very little when k changes from 0 to 1.

In the preceding example all variables were expressed in terms of their original units. In practice variables are typically transformed by dividing the values of each variable by its respective sample standard deviation before the ORR method is applied. In this way all variables are measured in the same units, and the effect of changing the values of k on the estimated regression coefficients is not influenced by differences in the units of measurement. Empirical results with *variables measured in terms of their respective standard deviations* indicate that the largest gain in the

[15] See, e.g., K. Lin and J. Kmenta, "Ridge Regression under Alternative Loss Criteria," *Review of Economics and Statistics*, 64 (August 1982), pp. 488–494.

trade-off between precision and bias occurs for very small values of k. Thus a reasonable alternative to the adaptive ORR estimator is to assign k some small value such as 0.05. There are two advantages to this: first, a small value of k is likely to satisfy the dominance condition of Theobald; second, the resulting coefficients are likely to be only mildly biased so that the standard tests and confidence intervals are not apt to be too distorted.

Concluding Remarks

The problem of encountering a high degree of multicollinearity in the sample is frequently surrounded by a confusion in the applied literature. There is a tendency on the part of some applied research workers to point to the high degree of multicollinearity in the sample as the reason why the estimated regression coefficients are not significantly different from zero. The reader is led to believe that if the degree of multicollinearity were lower, the estimated regression coefficients would turn out to be significant. This may be so, but it certainly does not follow from the presented results. For this reason it is important to realize that a high degree of multicollinearity is simply a feature of the sample that contributes to the unreliability of the estimated coefficients, but has no relevance for the conclusions drawn as a *result* of this unreliability. If the estimated regression coefficients are highly unreliable—that is, if they have large variances—the acceptance region for the hypothesis that a given regression coefficient is zero will be wide. In turn, this means that the power of the test is weak. Thus the test, although correct, is not very helpful in discriminating between true and false hypotheses. This is all that can be said regardless of the reason for the large variances in the first place.

10-4 Specification Errors

The specification of a regression model consists of a formulation of the regression equation and of statements or assumptions concerning the regressors and the disturbance term. A "specification error," in the broad sense of the term, occurs whenever the formulation of the regression equation or one of the underlying assumptions is incorrect. In a narrower sense of the term, *specification error* refers only to the errors in formulating the appropriate regression equation, and this is the interpretation adopted here. Several kinds of such errors will be considered, in particular those resulting from

1. Omission of a relevant explanatory variable.
2. Inclusion of an irrelevant explanatory variable.
3. Incorrect mathematical form of the regression equation.
4. Incorrect specification of the way in which the disturbance enters the regression equation.

Although we shall consider only the cases in which the explanatory variables are nonstochastic, the conclusions would remain essentially unchanged even if the explanatory variables were stochastic, providing they were independent of the regression disturbance. Our main concern will be with determining the consequences of each type of specification error for the least squares estimators of the regression coefficients and their standard errors.

Omission of a Relevant Explanatory Variable

Let us consider a specification error due to *omitting a relevant explanatory variable* from the regression equation. In particular, suppose the correct specification of the regression equation is

$$Y_i = \beta_1 + \beta_2 X_{i2} + \beta_3 X_{i3} + \varepsilon_i, \tag{10.71}$$

but we estimate

$$Y_i = \beta_1 + \beta_2 X_{i2} + \varepsilon_i^*. \tag{10.72}$$

Such an error may be committed when no observations on X_3 are available, or when the researcher is not aware of the fact that X_3 should be included in the regression equation if the maintained hypothesis is to be correctly specified. Now if (10.72) were correct, the least squares estimators of β_1 and β_2 would be unbiased and efficient for all sample sizes. Let us see what happens to these estimators given that (10.71) rather than (10.72) is the correct formulation. For $\hat{\beta}_2$ we have

$$E(\hat{\beta}_2) = E\left[\frac{\sum (X_{i2} - \overline{X}_2)(Y_i - \overline{Y})}{\sum (X_{i2} - \overline{X}_2)^2}\right].$$

But from (10.71) we know that

$$(Y_i - \overline{Y}) = \beta_2(X_{i2} - \overline{X}_2) + \beta_3(X_{i3} - \overline{X}_3) + (\varepsilon_i - \bar{\varepsilon}),$$

so that

$$E(\hat{\beta}_2) = \beta_2 + \beta_3 d_{32},$$

where

$$d_{32} = \frac{\sum (X_{i2} - \overline{X}_2)(X_{i3} - \overline{X}_3)}{\sum (X_{i2} - \overline{X}_2)^2}.$$

Similarly, for $\hat{\beta}_1$ we have

$$E(\hat{\beta}_1) = E(\overline{Y} - \hat{\beta}_2 \overline{X}_2) = \beta_1 + \beta_2 \overline{X}_2 + \beta_3 \overline{X}_3 - (\beta_2 + \beta_3 d_{32})\overline{X}_2$$
$$= \beta_1 + \beta_3 d_{31},$$

where

$$d_{31} = \overline{X}_3 - d_{32}\overline{X}_2.$$

Note that the expressions for d_{31} and d_{32} are, in fact, the formulas for the least squares coefficients of the equation

$$X_{i3} = d_{31} + d_{32} X_{i2} + \text{residual}. \tag{10.73}$$

Since X_2 and X_3 are nonstochastic, equation (10.73) can be viewed only as a purely descriptive regression equation. In this equation the "dependent" variable is represented by the omitted variable X_3, and the "explanatory" variable by the included variable X_2. Given that β_3 is different from zero, the least squares estimator of β_2 based on (10.72) will be *biased* unless d_{32} equals zero, i.e., unless X_2 and X_3 are uncorrelated. If β_3 and d_{32} are both of the same sign, the bias of $\hat{\beta}_2$ will be positive; otherwise it will be negative. This means that the direction of the bias of $\hat{\beta}_2$ depends on

1. The sign of β_3.
2. The direction of the correlation between the omitted and the included explanatory variable.

If the correlation between X_2 and X_3 does not disappear as the sample size increases, i.e., if

$$\lim_{n\to\infty} d_{32} \neq 0,$$

$\hat{\beta}_2$ will also be inconsistent. Furthermore, the least squares estimator of β_1 based on (10.72) will be biased as long as

$$\bar{X}_3 - d_{32}\bar{X}_2 \neq 0,$$

and it will be inconsistent as long as

$$\lim_{n\to\infty} (\bar{X}_3 - d_{32}\bar{X}_2) \neq 0.$$

The foregoing seems to suggest that if the omitted explanatory variable is *uncorrelated* with the included explanatory variable, its omission may not lead to serious consequences for least squares estimation. Let us examine this point in detail. Suppose that X_2 and X_3 are uncorrelated; that is, suppose $d_{32} = 0$. Then $\hat{\beta}_2$ based on (10.72) is unbiased, and its variance is

$$\mathrm{Var}(\hat{\beta}_2) = E(\hat{\beta}_2 - \beta_2)^2 = \frac{\sigma^2}{\sum (X_{i2} - \bar{X}_2)^2}.$$

The estimator of $\mathrm{Var}(\hat{\beta}_2)$ based on (10.72) is

$$s^2_{\hat{\beta}_2} = \frac{s^2}{\sum (X_{i2} - \bar{X}_2)^2} = \frac{\sum [(Y_i - \bar{Y}) - \hat{\beta}_2(X_{i2} - \bar{X}_2)]^2/(n-2)}{\sum (X_{i2} - \bar{X}_2)^2}$$
$$= \frac{\sum [-(\hat{\beta}_2 - \beta_2)(X_{i2} - \bar{X}_2) + \beta_3(X_{i3} - \bar{X}_3) + (\varepsilon_i - \bar{\varepsilon})]^2}{(n-2)\sum (X_{i2} - \bar{X}_2)^2}.$$

The mathematical expectation of $s^2_{\hat{\beta}_2}$ is then given by

$$E(s^2_{\hat{\beta}_2}) = \frac{m_{22}\mathrm{Var}(\hat{\beta}_2) + \beta_3^2 m_{33} - 2m_{22}\mathrm{Var}(\hat{\beta}_2) + (n-1)\sigma^2}{(n-2)m_{22}}$$
$$= \mathrm{Var}(\hat{\beta}_2) + \frac{\beta_3^2 m_{33}}{(n-2)m_{22}}.$$

This implies that in this case the estimator of $\mathrm{Var}(\hat{\beta}_2)$ is positively biased. Therefore, the usual tests of significance concerning β_2 are not valid, since they will tend to accept the null hypothesis more frequently than is justified by the given level of significance. Further, the mathematical expectation of the least squares estimator of β_1 based on (10.72) is

$$E(\hat{\beta}_1) = E(\overline{Y} - \hat{\beta}_2\overline{X}_2) = \beta_1 + \beta_2\overline{X}_2 + \beta_3\overline{X}_3 - \beta_2\overline{X}_2 = \beta_1 + \beta_3\overline{X}_3,$$

which means that $\hat{\beta}_1$ is biased unless $\overline{X}_3 = 0$.

Our results concerning the least squares estimation of β_1 and β_2 on the basis of (10.72), given that (10.71) is the correct specification, can be summarized as follows: if the omitted explanatory variable is correlated with the included explanatory variable, the estimators of β_1 and β_2 will be biased and inconsistent. If the omitted explanatory variable is *not* correlated with the included variable, the estimator of β_1 will still be biased and inconsistent, at least in general, but the estimator of $\hat{\beta}_2$ will be unbiased. However, the estimator of the *variance* of $\hat{\beta}_2$ will contain an upward bias, so that the usual tests of significance and confidence intervals for β_2 will tend to lead to unduly conservative conclusions.

The preceding analysis can easily be extended to the case involving a larger number of explanatory variables. Suppose the correct specification of the regression equation is

$$Y_i = \beta_1 + \beta_2 X_{i2} + \beta_3 X_{i3} + \beta_4 X_{i4} + \varepsilon_i, \tag{10.74}$$

but we estimate

$$Y_i = \beta_1 + \beta_2 X_{i2} + \beta_3 X_{i3} + \varepsilon_i^*. \tag{10.75}$$

The least squares estimator of β_2 based on (10.75) is

$$\hat{\beta}_2 = \frac{m_{Y2}m_{33} - m_{Y3}m_{23}}{m_{22}m_{33} - m_{23}^2}.$$

Now,

$$E(m_{Y2}) = \beta_2 m_{22} + \beta_3 m_{23} + \beta_4 m_{24},$$

$$E(m_{Y3}) = \beta_2 m_{23} + \beta_3 m_{33} + \beta_4 m_{34},$$

so that

$$E(m_{Y2}m_{33} - m_{Y3}m_{23}) = \beta_2(m_{22}m_{33} - m_{23}^2) + \beta_4(m_{24}m_{33} - m_{34}m_{23}).$$

Therefore

$$E(\hat{\beta}_2) = \beta_2 + \beta_4 d_{42},$$

where
$$d_{42} = \frac{m_{42}m_{33} - m_{43}m_{23}}{m_{22}m_{33} - m_{23}^2}.$$

Note that the expression for d_{42} is exactly the same as the formula of the least squares coefficient of X_{i2} in the equation

$$X_{i4} = d_{41} + d_{42}X_{i2} + d_{43}X_{i3} + \text{residual}. \tag{10.76}$$

In (10.76) the omitted explanatory variable X_4 is "regressed" on the two included explanatory variables X_2 and X_3. Similarly,

$$E(\hat{\beta}_3) = \beta_3 + \beta_4 d_{43} \qquad \text{and} \qquad E(\hat{\beta}_1) = \beta_1 + \beta_4 d_{41}.$$

Thus the conclusion in this case is the same as when a smaller number of explanatory variables is involved.

EXAMPLE In a study of production functions for Indian industry, Murti and Sastry[16] use data on outputs and inputs for a sample of 320 firms, and obtain the following estimates of the Cobb–Douglas production function:

$$\log x_i = \log 0.68 + 0.53 \log n_i + 0.50 \log k_i + e_i,$$

where x = net value of output, n = wages and salaries, k = value of net assets, and the subscript i refers to the ith firm. If the "management" input varies systematically from firm to firm so that it cannot be regarded as a part of the random disturbance, the above equation is misspecified. If the management input—which, of course, is very difficult to measure—were brought into the production function in the same way as n_i and k_i, the sign of its coefficient clearly would be positive. The descriptive least squares regression linking the "management" input m with the two included explanatory variables n and k is

$$\log m_i = d_{41} + d_{42} \log n_i + d_{43} \log k_i + \text{residual}.$$

We can then speculate about the signs of d_{42} and d_{43}. If the firms with a high level of capital input possess a superior management input compared to the firms that are more labor-intensive, d_{42} would be negative and d_{43} positive. Under those circumstances—and in the absence of other violations of the assumptions of the classical normal linear regression model—the estimate of the coefficient of $\log n_i$ would be biased downward and that of the coefficient of $\log k_i$ would be biased upward.

Inclusion of an Irrelevant Explanatory Variable

Another type of specification error occurs when the set of relevant explanatory variables is enlarged by the inclusion of one or more *irrelevant variables.* (Regression equations that are formulated by including all conceivable candidates in the set of explanatory variables without much attention to the underlying theory are, for obvious reasons, sometimes called "kitchen sink models.") For instance, suppose the correctly specified regression equation is

$$Y_i = \beta_1 + \beta_2 X_{i2} + \varepsilon_i, \tag{10.77}$$

but we estimate

$$Y_i = \beta_1 + \beta_2 X_{i2} + \beta_3 X_{i3} + \varepsilon_i^*. \tag{10.78}$$

[16] V. N. Murti and V. K. Sastry, "Production Functions for Indian Industry," *Econometrica* 25 (April 1957), pp. 205–221.

The specification error involved in using (10.78) rather than (10.77) occurs because we ignore the restriction that $\beta_3 = 0$ in formulating our maintained hypothesis. Let us see what happens to the least squares estimators of the regression coefficients if we base our estimation on (10.78). First the mathematical expectation of $\hat{\beta}_3$ is

$$E(\hat{\beta}_3) = E\left[\frac{m_{Y3}m_{22} - m_{Y2}m_{23}}{m_{22}m_{33} - m_{23}^2}\right].$$

But from (10.77) we know that

$$E(m_{Y2}) = \beta_2 m_{22} \qquad \text{and} \qquad E(m_{Y3}) = \beta_2 m_{23},$$

so that

$$E(\hat{\beta}_3) = \frac{\beta_2 m_{22}m_{23} - \beta_2 m_{22}m_{23}}{m_{22}m_{33} - m_{23}^2} = 0.$$

That is, the mean of $\hat{\beta}_3$ is equal to the true value of β_3, which is zero. The probability that in any given sample we observe a value of $\hat{\beta}_3$ that is significantly different from zero is then equal to the chosen level of significance. Next, the mathematical expectation of $\hat{\beta}_2$ is

$$E(\hat{\beta}_2) = E\left[\frac{m_{Y2}m_{33} - m_{Y3}m_{23}}{m_{22}m_{33} - m_{23}^2}\right] = \beta_2.$$

Also,

$$E(\hat{\beta}_1) = E(\overline{Y} - \hat{\beta}_2\overline{X}_2 - \hat{\beta}_3\overline{X}_3) = (\beta_1 + \beta_2\overline{X}_2) - \beta_2\overline{X}_2 = \beta_1.$$

These results show that the estimators of the coefficients of (10.78) are all unbiased. As for their variances, we have

$$\text{Var}(\hat{\beta}_2) = \frac{\sigma^2 m_{33}}{m_{22}m_{33} - m_{23}^2} = \frac{\sigma^2}{m_{22}(1 - r_{23}^2)},$$

where r_{23} is the coefficient of correlation between X_{i2} and X_{i3}. Now, if β_2 were estimated on the basis of the correctly specified regression equation (10.77), its variance, say, $\text{Var}(\hat{\beta}_2^*)$, would be equal to

$$\text{Var}(\hat{\beta}_2^*) = \frac{\sigma^2}{m_{22}}.$$

The ratio of the two variances is

$$\frac{\text{Var}(\hat{\beta}_2)}{\text{Var}(\hat{\beta}_2^*)} = \frac{1}{1 - r_{23}^2}.$$

Since $0 \leq r_{23}^2 \leq 1$, it follows that

$$\frac{\text{Var}(\hat{\beta}_2)}{\text{Var}(\hat{\beta}_2^*)} \geq 1,$$

where the equality holds only for $r_{23} = 0$, i.e., only if X_2 and X_3 are uncorrelated.

The implication of this result is that $\hat{\beta}_2$ is generally *not efficient*. Similarly, by working through the formulas for $\text{Var}(\hat{\beta}_1)$ and $\text{Var}(\hat{\beta}_1^*)$—where $\hat{\beta}_1$ and $\hat{\beta}_1^*$ refer to the least squares estimators of β_1 from (10.78) and (10.77), respectively—we could show that $\hat{\beta}_1$ is also not efficient unless

$$(\bar{X}_3\sqrt{m_{22}} - \bar{X}_2 r_{23}\sqrt{m_{33}}) = 0.$$

Consider now the estimated variances of the least squares coefficients of (10.78). The formulas for $\text{Var}(\hat{\beta}_1)$, $\text{Var}(\hat{\beta}_2)$, and $\text{Var}(\hat{\beta}_3)$ involve only one unknown parameter, σ^2, which is estimated by

$$\begin{aligned} s^2 &= \frac{1}{n-3}\sum_i [(Y_i - \bar{Y}) - \hat{\beta}_2(X_{i2} - \bar{X}_2) - \hat{\beta}_3(X_{i3} - \bar{X}_3)]^2 \\ &= \frac{1}{n-3}\sum_i [\beta_2(X_{i2} - \bar{X}_2) + (\varepsilon_i - \bar{\varepsilon}) - \hat{\beta}_2(X_{i2} - \bar{X}_2) - \hat{\beta}_3(X_{i3} - \bar{X}_3)]^2 \\ &= \frac{1}{n-3}\sum_i [-(\hat{\beta}_2 - \beta_2)(X_{i2} - \bar{X}_2) - \hat{\beta}_3(X_{i3} - \bar{X}_3) + (\varepsilon_i - \bar{\varepsilon})]^2. \end{aligned}$$

The mathematical expectation of s^2 is

$$\begin{aligned} E(s^2) = \frac{1}{n-3}[&m_{22}\,\text{Var}(\hat{\beta}_2) + m_{33}\,\text{Var}(\hat{\beta}_3) + (n-1)\sigma^2 + 2m_{23}\text{Cov}(\hat{\beta}_2, \hat{\beta}_3) \\ &- 2E(\hat{\beta}_2 - \beta_2)\sum_i (X_{i2} - \bar{X}_2)\varepsilon_i - 2E\hat{\beta}_3 \sum_i (X_{i3} - \bar{X}_3)\varepsilon_i]. \end{aligned}$$

But

$$\begin{aligned} &-2E(\hat{\beta}_2 - \beta_2)\sum_i (X_{i2} - \bar{X}_2)\varepsilon_i \\ &\quad = -2E\left[\frac{m_{33}\sum (X_{i2} - \bar{X}_2)\varepsilon_i - m_{23}\sum (X_{i3} - \bar{X}_3)\varepsilon_i}{m_{22}m_{33} - m_{23}^2}\right]\sum (X_{i2} - \bar{X}_2)\varepsilon_i \\ &\quad = -2\sigma^2, \end{aligned}$$

$$\begin{aligned} &-2E\hat{\beta}_3 \sum_i (X_{i3} - \bar{X}_3)\varepsilon_i \\ &\quad = -2E\left[\frac{m_{22}\sum (X_{i3} - \bar{X}_3)\varepsilon_i - m_{23}\sum (X_{i2} - \bar{X}_2)\varepsilon_i}{m_{22}m_{33} - m_{23}^2}\right]\sum (X_{i3} - \bar{X}_3)\varepsilon_i \\ &\quad = -2\sigma^2, \end{aligned}$$

so that

$$\begin{aligned} E(s^2) &= \frac{1}{n-3}\left[\frac{\sigma^2(m_{22}m_{33} + m_{33}m_{22} - 2m_{23}^2)}{m_{22}m_{33} - m_{23}^2} + (n-1)\sigma^2 - 4\sigma^2\right] \\ &= \sigma^2. \end{aligned}$$

This means that the estimator of σ^2 based on (10.78) is unbiased. Therefore, the estimators of $\text{Var}(\hat{\beta}_1)$, $\text{Var}(\hat{\beta}_2)$, and $\text{Var}(\hat{\beta}_3)$ are also unbiased. This result holds whether X_2 and X_3 are correlated or not. The conclusion, then, is that if the specification error consists of including some irrelevant explanatory variables in the regression equation, the least squares estimators of the regression coefficients are unbiased but not efficient. The estimators of their variances are also unbiased, so that, in the absence of other complications, the usual tests of significance and confidence intervals for the regression parameters are valid. These results have been derived for a simple regression model, but it is not difficult to show that they apply to models with a larger number of explanatory variables as well.

Nonlinearity

Another specification error arises in the case where the correctly specified regression equation is *nonlinear* but we estimate what may be viewed as its linear approximation. Since linear relations are widely used in applied econometric research, this kind of error is likely to be committed quite often. Suppose that the correctly specified regression equation is given by

(10.79)
$$Y_i = f(X_i) + \varepsilon_i,$$

where $f(X_i)$ is some function of X_i. We assume that this function is continuous and possesses a continuous pth derivative, p being some positive integer. Then, with the use of the Taylor theorem,[17] we can expand $f(X_i)$ around, say, $\bar{X}$, and write (10.79) as

(10.79a)
$$Y_i = f(\bar{X}) + (X_i - \bar{X})f'(\bar{X}) + \frac{(X_i - \bar{X})^2}{2!}f''(\bar{X}) + \cdots + \frac{(X_i - \bar{X})^p}{p!}f^{(p)}(\bar{X}) + R_{p+1} + \varepsilon_i,$$

where
$$f(\bar{X}) = f(X_i)\Big|_{X_i=\bar{X}},$$
$$f'(\bar{X}) = \frac{df(X_i)}{dX_i}\Big|_{X_i=\bar{X}},$$
$$f''(\bar{X}) = \frac{d^2f(X_i)}{dX_i^2}\Big|_{X_i=\bar{X}},$$
$$\vdots$$
$$R_{p+1} = \text{remainder}.$$

By rearranging the terms on the right-hand side of (10.79a), we end up with

(10.79b)
$$Y_i = \beta_1 + \beta_2 X_i + \beta_3 X_i^2 + \cdots + \varepsilon_i,$$

[17] See, e.g., A. C. Chiang, *Fundamental Methods of Mathematical Economics,* 3rd ed. (New York: McGraw-Hill, 1984), p. 258.

where
$$\beta_1 = f(\bar{X}) - \bar{X}f'(\bar{X}) + \frac{\bar{X}^2}{2!}f''(\bar{X}) - \cdots,$$
$$\beta_2 = f'(\bar{X}) - \bar{X}f''(\bar{X}) + \frac{\bar{X}^2}{2!}f'''(\bar{X}) - \cdots,$$

and so on. That is, the β's are expressions in terms of $\bar{X}$ and the parameters of $f(X_i)$ and can be regarded as parametric regression coefficients. If we then estimate a linear approximation of (10.79), i.e.,

(10.80)
$$Y_i = \beta_1 + \beta_2 X_i + \varepsilon_i^*,$$

we are, in fact, omitting the relevant "explanatory variables" from the regression equation. The consequences of such an error were discussed in the early part of this section.

The preceding finding can be illustrated as follows. Suppose the correctly specified regression equation is represented by a parabolic function

(10.81)
$$Y_i = \beta_1 + \beta_2 X_i + \beta_3 X_i^2 + \varepsilon_i.$$

If we then approximate (10.81) by (10.80) and use the least squares estimation method, we can determine the properties of the resulting estimators in the same way as with (10.71) and (10.72). The specification error involved in estimating (10.80) in place of (10.81) is simply the omission of X^2 from the regression equation. Therefore, we have

$$E(\hat{\beta}_2) = \beta_2 + \beta_3 d_{32} \quad \text{and} \quad E(\hat{\beta}_1) = \beta_1 + \beta_3 d_{31},$$

where d_{31} and d_{32} represent the least squares coefficients of

(10.82)
$$X_i^2 = d_{31} + d_{32} X_i + \text{residual}.$$

In general, d_{32} will be different from zero, so that the estimator of β_2 (and of β_1) will be biased and inconsistent. The magnitude of the bias will depend on the size of β_3, which determines the curvature of the correctly specified regression equation, and on the values of X in the sample.

Incorrect Specification of the Disturbance Term

For another type of misspecification, consider the situation in which the *stochastic disturbance is brought into the regression equation in an incorrect way.* In particular, let the correctly specified regression equation be

(10.83)
$$Y_i = f(X_i)\varepsilon_i,$$

where ε_i follows a log-normal distribution with mean zero and variance σ^2, i.e.,

$$\log_e \varepsilon_i \sim N(0, \sigma^2).$$

Note that here we have[18]

$$E(\varepsilon_i) = e^{\sigma^2/2},$$

$$\text{Var}(\varepsilon_i) = e^{\sigma^2}(e^{\sigma^2} - 1).$$

Suppose now that instead of (10.83) we assume

(10.84) $$Y_i = f(X_i) + \varepsilon_i^*.$$

Then we have

$$\varepsilon_i^* = Y_i - f(X_i) = f(X_i)\varepsilon_i - f(X_i) = f(X_i)(\varepsilon_i - 1).$$

Consequently,

$$E(\varepsilon_i^*) = f(X_i)(e^{\sigma^2/2} - 1)$$

and $$\text{Var}(\varepsilon_i^*) = [f(X_i)]^2[e^{\sigma^2}(e^{\sigma^2} - 1)].$$

This means that ε_i^* does not satisfy the assumptions of zero mean and of homoskedasticity. Also, if ε_i is log-normal, ε_i^* cannot be normally distributed. The implications for the properties of the estimators of the parameters of (10.83) can be determined in detail when the mathematical form of $f(X_i)$ is spelled out. For example, let the correctly specified regression equation be

(10.85) $$Y_i = \gamma X_i \varepsilon_i,$$

with $\log_e \varepsilon_i$ satisfying all the assumptions of the classical normal regression model. Suppose that instead of (10.85), we postulate

(10.86) $$Y_i = \gamma X_i + \varepsilon_i^*.$$

Then the least squares estimator of γ based on (10.86) is

$$\hat{\gamma} = \frac{\sum Y_i X_i}{\sum X_i^2} = \frac{\gamma \sum X_i^2 \varepsilon_i}{\sum X_i^2}.$$

The mathematical expectation of $\hat{\gamma}$ is

$$E(\hat{\gamma}) = \gamma e^{\sigma^2/2},$$

which means that $\hat{\gamma}$ is *biased*. Also,

$$\text{plim}\ \hat{\gamma} = \frac{\gamma\ \text{plim}\ (\sum X_i^2 \varepsilon_i)/n}{\text{plim}\ (\sum X_i^2)/n} = \gamma e^{\sigma^2/2},$$

which means that $\hat{\gamma}$ is inconsistent.

[18] See A. Goldberger, *Econometric Theory* (New York: Wiley, 1964), p. 215.

Specification Error Tests

The above examination of the consequences of committing different types of specification errors has shown that, with the exception of the case of including irrelevant explanatory variables in the regression equation, all the specification errors that we have considered lead to biasedness and inconsistency of the least squares estimators. In the case of including irrelevant explanatory variables, the least squares estimators are unbiased and consistent but not efficient. Thus it is important that we try to avoid specification errors as much as possible or, if they are unavoidable, that we at least become aware of their presence. We have mentioned two possible reasons for committing a specification error. One is that the regression equation cannot be estimated in its correctly specified form because of data limitations. In such a case the preceding analysis, adapted to the problem at hand, may enable us to get at least some idea about the seriousness of the bias and its direction. The second reason for committing a specification error is our lack of knowledge as to the correct specification of the regression equation. In this case we would like to be able to *test* whether or not we have misspecified the regression equation. This is precisely how we approached the problem in connection with the assumptions about the regression disturbance in Chapter 8, where we described some of the tests for homoskedasticity and for nonautocorrelation. Here we consider some tests for specification errors involving omission of relevant explanatory variables; tests for linearity of the regression equation will be discussed in Section 11-3.

The problem of testing the hypothesis that no relevant explanatory variables have been omitted from the regression equation has been considered by Ramsey, who developed a test called RESET (for "Regression Specification Errors Test").[19] Let the true model be

$$\mathbf{y} = \mathbf{X}_1\boldsymbol{\beta}_1 + \mathbf{X}_2\boldsymbol{\beta}_2 + \boldsymbol{\varepsilon}, \tag{10.87}$$

where $\mathbf{X}_1 \rightarrow n \times K$ is nonstochastic and observable, $\mathbf{X}_2$ is unobservable, and $\boldsymbol{\varepsilon}$ satisfies all basic assumptions. The hypothesis to be tested is

$$H_0\colon \quad \boldsymbol{\beta}_2 = 0,$$
$$H_A\colon \quad \boldsymbol{\beta}_2 \neq 0.$$

The test procedure proposed by Ramsey is as follows. Since $\mathbf{X}_2$ is unobservable, $\mathbf{X}_2\boldsymbol{\beta}_2$ has to be approximated by $\mathbf{Z}\boldsymbol{\theta}$, where $\mathbf{Z} \rightarrow n \times P$ is a set of observable, nonstochastic test variables (to be specified shortly) and $\boldsymbol{\theta}$ is a $P \times 1$ vector of corresponding coefficients. The method of least squares is then applied to

$$\mathbf{y} = \mathbf{X}_1\boldsymbol{\beta}_1 + \mathbf{Z}\boldsymbol{\theta} + \mathbf{u}. \tag{10.88}$$

Using the formula in (10.17b), we obtain

$$\hat{\boldsymbol{\theta}} = (\mathbf{Z}'\mathbf{M}_1\mathbf{Z})^{-1}\mathbf{Z}'\mathbf{M}_1\mathbf{y},$$

[19] J. B. Ramsey, "Tests for Specification Errors in Classical Linear Least Squares Regression Analysis," *Journal of the Royal Statistical Society,* Series B, 31 (1969), pp. 350–371.

where $\mathbf{M}_1 = \mathbf{I} - \mathbf{X}_1(\mathbf{X}_1'\mathbf{X}_1)^{-1}\mathbf{X}_1'$. Therefore, using (10.87),

$$E(\hat{\boldsymbol{\theta}}) = (\mathbf{Z}'\mathbf{M}_1\mathbf{Z})^{-1}\mathbf{Z}'\mathbf{M}_1\mathbf{X}_2\boldsymbol{\beta}_2. \tag{10.89}$$

Thus, under H_0,

$$E(\hat{\boldsymbol{\theta}}) = \mathbf{0},$$

and, under H_A,

$$E(\hat{\boldsymbol{\theta}}) \neq \mathbf{0} \qquad \text{(unless } \mathbf{Z}'\mathbf{M}_1\mathbf{X}_2\boldsymbol{\beta}_2 = 0\text{)}.$$

This means that a *test of significance of* $\hat{\boldsymbol{\theta}}$, such as the F test presented in (10.46), would discriminate between the null and the alternative hypotheses as long as $\mathbf{Z}'\mathbf{M}_1\mathbf{X}_2\boldsymbol{\beta}_2 \neq \mathbf{0}$. This condition can be interpreted as follows. Let $\boldsymbol{\xi} = \mathbf{X}_2\boldsymbol{\beta}_2$ and consider

$$\boldsymbol{\xi} = \mathbf{X}_1\boldsymbol{\lambda}_1 + \mathbf{Z}\boldsymbol{\lambda}_2 + \mathbf{v}. \tag{10.90}$$

Then the least squares estimator of $\boldsymbol{\lambda}_2$ is

$$\begin{aligned}\hat{\boldsymbol{\lambda}}_2 &= (\mathbf{Z}'\mathbf{M}_1\mathbf{Z})^{-1}\mathbf{Z}'\mathbf{M}_1\boldsymbol{\xi} \\ &= (\mathbf{Z}'\mathbf{M}_1\mathbf{Z})^{-1}\mathbf{Z}'\mathbf{M}_1\mathbf{X}_2\boldsymbol{\beta}_2.\end{aligned}$$

Thus the condition that $\mathbf{Z}'\mathbf{M}_1\mathbf{X}_2\boldsymbol{\beta}_2 \neq 0$ is equivalent to the condition that $\hat{\boldsymbol{\lambda}}_2 \neq \mathbf{0}$, i.e., that $\mathbf{Z}$ and $\mathbf{X}_2$ are correlated (holding $\mathbf{X}_1$ constant). Thursby and Schmidt conducted an extensive Monte Carlo experiment to find suitable test variables, and the resulting suggestion is to use

$$\mathbf{Z} = [\mathbf{X}_1^2\ \mathbf{X}_1^3\ \mathbf{X}_1^4], \tag{10.91}$$

where $\mathbf{X}_1^r$ ($r = 2$, 3, and 4) is the same as $\mathbf{X}_1$ except that each element is raised to the rth power.[20] These test variables are likely to be correlated with $\mathbf{X}_2$; if they are not, the lack of correlation between the excluded variables and the powers of the included variables will tend to keep the bias down (see Figure 10-2). The appropriate

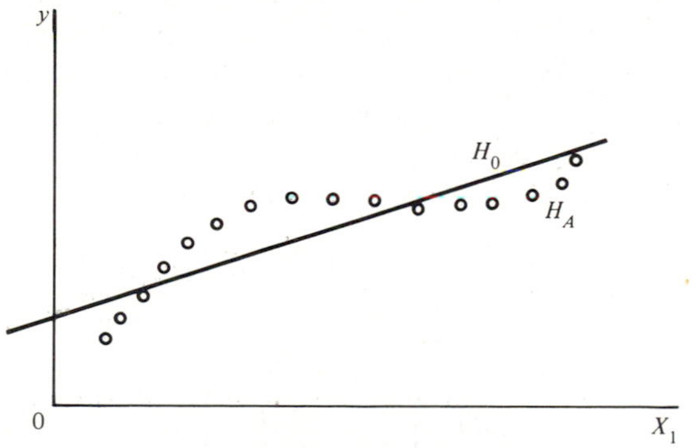

Figure 10-2

[20] J. G. Thursby and P. Schmidt, "Some Properties of Tests for Specification Error in a Linear Regression Model," *Journal of the American Statistical Association,* 72 (September 1977), pp. 635–641.

test to use is the F test for relevance of additional explanatory variables. The RESET test may be interpreted by noting that, under H_A, $E(\boldsymbol{\varepsilon})$ will be different from zero but is likely to follow a curve, as illustrated in Figure 10-2. The higher powers of $\mathbf{X}_1$ should capture the nonlinearity of $E(\boldsymbol{\varepsilon})$ if H_A is true.

A somewhat different approach to the problem of testing the hypothesis that no relevant explanatory variables have been omitted from the regression equation has been adopted by Utts, who developed the so-called "rainbow test."[21] For this test the specification of the regression equation and of the hypotheses is the same as in (10.87) above. The test is based on comparing two estimates of the variance of the regression disturbance, both of which are unbiased if the null hypothesis is true and both are biased when it is not. However, the bias will generally be larger for one than for the other. The test procedure involves two least squares regressions of $\mathbf{y}$ on $\mathbf{X}_1$, one based on all available n observations and one based on only the middle half of the observations (or, if $K > 2$, on the half of the observations whose "leverage"—as measured by h_{ii} in (10.55)—is relatively low). The idea of the test is illustrated in Figure 10-3. If the null hypothesis is correct, both estimated regression lines will fit

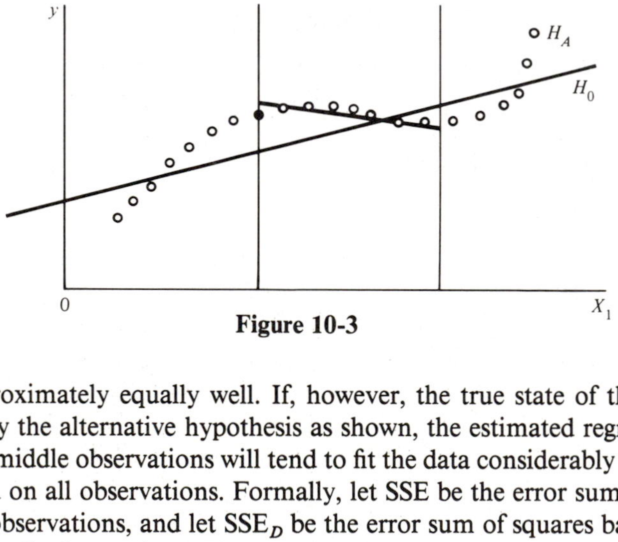

Figure 10-3

the data approximately equally well. If, however, the true state of the world is represented by the alternative hypothesis as shown, the estimated regression line based on the middle observations will tend to fit the data considerably better than the line based on all observations. Formally, let SSE be the error sum of squares based on all observations, and let SSE_D be the error sum of squares based on the middle m $(= n/2)$ observations. Then, under H_0 we have

$$E\left[\frac{\text{SSE}}{n-K}\right] = E\left[\frac{\text{SSE}_D}{m-K}\right] = \sigma^2,$$

whereas under H_A we have, at least in general,

$$E\left[\frac{\text{SSE}}{n-K}\right] > E\left[\frac{\text{SSE}_D}{m-K}\right] > \sigma^2.$$

[21] Jessica M. Utts, "The Rainbow Test for Lack of Fit in Regression," *Communications in Statistics—Theory and Methods,* 11 (1982), pp. 2801–2815.

Note that SSE can be viewed as a "restricted error sum of squares" because *all* observations are forced to fit a straight line, whereas SSE_D can be viewed as an "unrestricted error sum of squares" because only a *part* of the observations is forced to fit a straight line. In analogy with (7.51) the appropriate test statistic and its distribution then is

$$\frac{(SSE - SSE_D)/(n-m)}{SSE_D/(m-K)} \sim F_{n-m,\, m-K}. \qquad (10.92)$$

It can be shown that the rainbow test is a member of the RESET family of tests with the test variables Z being represented by a set of "dummy" variables corresponding to each of the observations not included in the middle part.[22]

From the preceding discussion, it is clear that the consequences of omitting relevant explanatory variables are the same as those of using an incorrect functional form. This means, therefore, that tests for linearity could also be interpreted as tests for nonomission of relevant explanatory variables. Several such tests are discussed in connection with nonlinear models in Section 11-4. Further, omitted relevant variables are also likely to affect the stability of the presumed regression coefficients so that tests for constancy of the regression coefficients may also not be distinguishable from tests for the nonomission of relevant variables. Such tests will be discussed in connection with varying parameter models, also in Section 11-7. Applying the battery of all these tests constitutes part of a "specification analysis," which is becoming increasingly more common among applied research workers in econometrics.[23]

EXERCISES

10-1. Consider the multiple regression equation

$$Y_i = \beta_1 + \beta_2 X_{i2} + \beta_3 X_{i3} + \cdots + \beta_K X_{iK} + \beta_{K+1} X_{i,K+1} + \cdots + \beta_Q X_{iQ} + \varepsilon_i.$$

Prove that

a. $SSR_Q \geq SSR_K$.

b. $R_Q^2 \geq R_K^2$.

10-2. Given the definitions of $\underline{\hat{\beta}}$, $\underline{\mathbf{X}}$, and $\underline{\mathbf{y}}$ as stated in connection with (10.15), prove that

a. $\underline{\hat{\beta}} = (\underline{\mathbf{X}}'\underline{\mathbf{X}})^{-1}(\underline{\mathbf{X}}'\underline{\mathbf{y}})$.

b. $\text{Var}(\underline{\hat{\beta}}) = \sigma^2(\underline{\mathbf{X}}'\underline{\mathbf{X}})^{-1}$.

c. $\underline{\mathbf{y}}'\underline{\mathbf{y}} = \mathbf{y}'\mathbf{y} - (\sum_t Y_t)^2/n$.

[22] P. Ochshorn, "Regression Specification Error Tests," unpublished, University of Michigan, December 1984.

[23] See, e.g., W. Krämer et al., "Diagnostic Checking in Practice," *Review of Economics and Statistics*, 67 (February 1985), pp. 118–123.

10-3. Given the least squares estimates

$$Y_t = 5 + \underset{(1)}{3}X_{t1} + \underset{(2)}{10}X_{t2} + e_t \qquad (n = 100),$$

and given that the sample coefficient of correlation between the two explanatory variables is 0.5, find the value of R^2.

10-4. Consider $\mathbf{y} = \mathbf{X}\boldsymbol{\beta} + \boldsymbol{\varepsilon}$ with K (the number of explanatory variables including the constant) equal to two. Show, by writing out all matrices in full, that the least squares formulas for the multiple regression model give the same answer as the formulas for the simple regression model developed in Section 7-3 without the use of matrix algebra.

10-5. It has been suggested that corporate investment behavior can be described by the relationship

$$I_t = \beta_1 + \beta_2 F_{t-1} + \beta_3 K_{t-1} + \varepsilon_t,$$

where I_t = current gross investment, F_{t-1} = end-of-period value of outstanding shares, and K_{t-1} = end-of-period capital stock. From the data for General Motors Corporation given in Table 10-2,

Table 10-2[a]

Year	I_t	F_{t-1}	K_{t-1}
1935	317.6	3078.5	2.8
1936	391.8	4661.7	52.6
1937	410.6	5387.1	156.9
1938	257.7	2792.2	209.2
1939	330.8	4313.2	203.4
1940	461.2	4643.9	207.2
1941	512.0	4551.2	255.2
1942	448.0	3244.1	303.7
1943	499.6	4053.7	264.1
1944	547.5	4379.3	201.6
1945	561.2	4840.9	265.0
1946	688.1	4900.9	402.2
1947	568.9	3526.5	761.5
1948	529.2	3254.7	922.4
1949	555.1	3700.2	1020.1
1950	642.9	3755.6	1099.0
1951	755.9	4833.0	1207.7
1952	891.2	4924.9	1430.5
1953	1304.4	6241.7	1777.3

Source: J. C. G. Boot and G. M. deWitt, "Investment Demand: An Empirical Contribution to the Aggregation Problem," *International Economic Review,* 1 (January 1960), pp. 3–30.

[a] All values (in millions of dollars) are deflated by appropriate price indexes.

a. Obtain least squares estimates of the regression coefficients and their estimated standard errors.

b. Calculate the value of R^2 and test for the existence of a relationship.

c. The values of F_{t-1} and K_{t-1} for the year 1954 are 5593.6 and 2226.3, respectively. What is the forecast value of I_{1954} and its 95% forecast interval? (The actual value of I_{1954} was 1486.7.)

10-6. Let E_i = total weekly planned expenditure of the ith household, X_{ig} = expenditure of the ith household on the gth commodity, and N_i = number of persons in the ith household. The variable N is nonstochastic. Consider the following model.

$$X_{ig} = \alpha_g + \beta_g E_i + \gamma_g N_i + u_{ig} \qquad (i = 1, 2, \ldots, n; \quad g = 1, 2, \ldots, G; \quad n > G).$$

Further,

$$E_i = \sum_{g=1}^{G} X_{ig} + v_i,$$

$$v_i = -\sum_{g=1}^{G} u_{ig}.$$

We assume that

$$E(u_{ig}) = 0,$$

$$E(\mathbf{u_g u_g'}) = \sigma_{gg}\mathbf{I_n},$$

$$E(\mathbf{u_g u_h'}) = \mathbf{0} \qquad (g \neq h),$$

where

$$\mathbf{u_g'} = [u_{1g} \quad u_{2g} \quad \ldots \quad u_{ng}].$$

Suppose we have obtained observations on E and X_g and have fitted the following equation by the ordinary least squares method:

$$X_{ig} = a_g + b_g E_i + e_{ig} \qquad (g = 1, 2, \ldots, G).$$

a. Under what conditions, if any, will b_g be an unbiased estimate of β_g?

b. Under what conditions, if any, will a_g be an unbiased estimate of α_g?

10-7. Using the model and the data of Example 10-5, test the hypothesis that no relevant explanatory variables have been omitted using the RESET and the "rainbow" test.

10-8. A production function for some industries is of the form

$$Y_i = a + \beta X_i + \varepsilon_i,$$

where Y = log output per worker, X = log capital per worker, and ε = stochastic disturbance, believed to satisfy all basic (classical) assumptions. Further, X and ε are independent. The data for industries A and B are as follows.

	Industry A	Industry B
n	20	20
$\bar{X}$	1	1
$\bar{Y}$	8	9
$\Sigma(X_i - \bar{X})^2$	12	10
$\Sigma(X_i - \bar{X})(Y_i - \bar{Y})$	10	12
$\Sigma(Y_i - \bar{Y})^2$	10	18

Treating the values of X as fixed, carry out the test of the hypothesis that both industries have the same production function (i.e., that the values of the intercept *and* of the slope are the same for A and B), assuming that $\text{Var}(\varepsilon_{it})$ is the same for both industries.

10-9. Consider the following model, for which all classical assumptions hold,

$$Y_t = \beta_1 + \beta_2 X_t + \beta_3 t + \varepsilon_t.$$

Prove that the LSE of β_2 in the above model is identical to the LSE of β_2 in the model

$$Y_t^* = \beta_1 + \beta_2 X_t^* + \varepsilon_t^*,$$

where Y^* = LS residuals from the regression of Y on t, and X^* = LS residuals from the regression of X on t.

10-10. A regression model is specified as

$$Y_i = \beta_1 + \beta_2 X_{i2} + \beta_3 X_{i3} + \varepsilon_i.$$

All classical assumptions hold except that $E(\varepsilon_i) = \gamma X_{i2}$. Let $\hat{\beta}_2$ and $\hat{\beta}_3$ be the usual LSEs of β_2 and β_3. Prove that $\hat{\beta}_2$ is biased but $\hat{\beta}_3$ is unbiased.

10-11. Suppose that in a classical linear regression model,

$$Y_t = \beta_1 + \beta_2 X_{t2} + \beta_3 X_{t3} + \varepsilon_t,$$

the sample values of X_3 represent an exact linear function of the values of X_2, i.e., $X_{t3} = a + bX_{t2}$ $(t = 1, 2, \ldots, T)$. The following methods for estimating β_2 have been suggested.

1. Regress Y_t on X_{t2} alone.
2. Regress $(Y_t - Y_{t-1})$ on $(X_{t2} - X_{t-1,2})$ and $(X_{t3} - X_{t-1,3})$.
3. Regress $(Y_t - \beta_3 X_{t3})$ on X_{t2} by scanning over different values of β_3 (suppose theory indicates that $0 \leq \beta_3 \leq 1$). Select that result which gives the minimum sum of squared residuals.

Comment on the feasibility of each method and explain why it is or is not feasible. If feasible, state the properties of the resulting estimator of β_2 and of the relevant t statistic.

10-12. Consider the following production function model.

$$Y_i = \beta_1 + \beta_2 X_{i2} + \beta_3 X_{i3} + \varepsilon_i,$$

where Y is log output, X_2 is log labor input, X_3 is log capital input, and the subscript i refers to the ith firm. All assumptions of the classical regression model are supposed to be satisfied. The information from a random sample of 23 firms is summarized as

$$(\underline{\mathbf{X}}'\underline{\mathbf{X}}) = \begin{bmatrix} 12 & 8 \\ 8 & 12 \end{bmatrix}, \qquad (\underline{\mathbf{X}}'\underline{\mathbf{y}}) = \begin{bmatrix} 10 \\ 8 \end{bmatrix}, \qquad (\underline{\mathbf{y}}'\underline{\mathbf{y}}) = [10].$$

Note that all measurements are in terms of deviations from sample means.

a. Find the least squares estimates of β_2 and β_3. Calculate the value of R^2.

b. Carry out a test for constant returns to scale, i.e., test the hypothesis

$$H_0: \quad \beta_2 + \beta_3 - 1 = 0$$

against the two-sided alternative.

c. Suppose that instead of testing for constant returns to scale you wish to assume constant returns a priori, i.e., you specify

$$\beta_3 = 1 - \beta_2.$$

Obtain the least squares estimate of β_2 under these circumstances.

d. Comment upon the difference (in terms of the desirable properties and the validity of the conventional t test) between the estimate of β_2 obtained *without* the assumption of constant returns to scale and the estimate of β_2 obtained *with* this assumption given that the assumption is (i) correct and (ii) incorrect.

10-13. Consider the regression model

$$Y_i = \beta_1 + \beta_2 X_{i2} + \beta_3 X_{i3} + \varepsilon_i,$$

for which all classical assumptions hold. The sample data are as those in Example 10-12.

a. Carry out a test of the hypothesis

$$H_0: \ \beta_2 = 1 \quad \textit{and} \quad \beta_3 = 0,$$

$$H_A: \ H_0 \text{ is not true.}$$

[NOTE: H_0 is a *joint* hypothesis about β_2 and β_3.]

b. Carry out a test of the hypothesis

$$H_0: \ \frac{\beta_2}{\beta_3} = \frac{5}{3},$$

$$H_A: \ \frac{\beta_2}{\beta_3} \neq \frac{5}{3}.$$

c. Suppose that *prior* to estimation you are told that $\beta_2/\beta_3 = 5/3$. Obtain efficient estimates of β_2 and β_3 given this (and the sample) information.

d. Calculate the estimated standard errors of the estimates of β_2 and β_3 obtained in (**c**) above.

11 Formulation and Estimation of Special Models

Multiple regression, because of its flexibility, is a suitable analytical tool for problems of statistical inference under conditions in which the imposition of prior knowledge about the regression equation leads to a departure from the standard linear regression model. In this chapter we consider several types of departures. Section 11-1 deals with the formulation and estimation of relationships that involve qualitative or binary explanatory variables. Included here are the well-known statistical techniques of "analysis of variance" and "analysis of covariance," both of which can be regarded as regression models with qualitative explanatory variables. In Section 11-2 we take up the problem of incorporating various prior restrictions on the coefficients of a linear relationship when carrying out the estimation. Section 11-3 contains description of some nonlinear models and deals with the problems of estimation and of testing for linearity. In Section 11-4 we examine models in which the response of the dependent variable to changes in the explanatory variables may be delayed. These models, which are known as *distributed lag models,* are common in applied economic research. Section 11-5 deals with models characterized by qualitative dependent variables that typically arise in connection with discrete choices and that are commonly represented as *logit* or *probit models.* In Section 11-6 we consider models with limited dependent variables that result from having censored or truncated samples and whose best known representation is the *Tobit model.* In Section 11-7 we describe several models that allow for variation in the regression coefficients. These models, which some researchers consider typical of many real-life situations, are known as *varying parameter models.* Section 11-8 involves models with unobservable variables represented by proxies or by a set of related variables. Section 11-9 deals with models pertaining to markets in disequilibrium. Finally, in Section 11-10 we consider various criteria for choosing among competing models. All topics discussed in this chapter are specialized and are treated at some length in the literature. We introduce these topics with the aim of giving the reader basic understanding of the problems involved and solutions proposed.

11-1 Models with Binary Regressors

Some phenomena that we observe cannot be measured but only counted. This is true of all qualitative characteristics of objects, people, time periods, etc. Our observation then consists of noting whether the given characteristic is or is not present. For instance, when the unit of observation is an adult man, we may note whether he is or is not a house owner, whether he has or has not a college degree, whether he does or does not smoke, or anything else that is relevant to the problem at hand. Since we can assign a value of 1 to the presence and 0 to the absence of the attribute in question, we may view it as a variable that is restricted to two values. (Of course, it is not necessary that the two values be 0 and 1. We may, if we wish, choose any other two values to represent the presence and the absence of the given attribute. For obvious reasons, 0 and 1 are chosen most commonly.) Such a variable is then called a "binary" or a "dummy" variable. We will discuss the problem of formulating and estimating models in which qualitative variables appear as explanatory variables of the regression equation, starting with simple models and progressing to more complex ones.

Single Qualitative Explanatory Variable

A simple regression model in which the explanatory variable is represented by a binary variable can be illustrated by the salaries offered to economics graduate students entering the academic labor market. Assume that these salaries are normally distributed with variance σ^2 and mean equal to μ_1 for candidates who have already received their Ph.D. and μ_0 for those who have not. This situation can be described by a regression model, with salary as the dependent variable and degree qualification as the explanatory variable. Formally,

$$Y_i = \alpha + \beta X_i + \varepsilon_i, \tag{11.1}$$

where Y_i is the salary of the ith candidate, and X_i is a binary variable such that

$$\begin{aligned} X_i &= 1 \quad \text{if the candidate has a Ph.D.,} \\ &= 0 \quad \text{otherwise.} \end{aligned}$$

The disturbance ε_i is a random variable that satisfies all the basic assumptions of the classical normal linear regression model. The mean values of Y_i corresponding to the two values of X_i are

$$E(Y_i|X_i = 0) = \alpha,$$

$$E(Y_i|X_i = 1) = \alpha + \beta.$$

Therefore,

$$\alpha = \mu_0,$$

and

$$\alpha + \beta = \mu_1,$$

or
$$\beta = \mu_1 - \mu_0.$$

This means that the intercept of the population regression line (11.1) measures the mean salary of a non-Ph.D., and the slope measures the difference between the mean salary of a Ph.D and that of a non-Ph.D. A test of the hypothesis that β is zero is then equivalent to the test that there is no difference between the mean salary of a Ph.D. and that of a non-Ph.D.

The coefficients of the regression equation (11.1) can be estimated by the method of the least squares. Under the assumptions of the classical normal linear regression model, the resulting estimates will have all the desirable properties. Recall that the formulas for the least squares estimators are

$$\hat{\beta} = \frac{\sum (X_i - \overline{X})(Y_i - \overline{Y})}{\sum (X_i - \overline{X})^2},$$
$$\hat{\alpha} = \overline{Y} - \hat{\beta}\overline{X}.$$

Let n_1 = number of candidates with a Ph.D. in the sample,

n_0 = number of candidates without a Ph.D. in the sample,

$\overline{Y}_1$ = sample mean salary of a candidate with a Ph.D.,

$\overline{Y}_0$ = sample mean salary of a candidate without a Ph.D.

Then

$$\sum_{i=1}^{n} X_i = n_1,$$
$$\sum_{i=1}^{n} X_i^2 = n_1,$$
$$\sum_{i=1}^{n} Y_i = n_1\overline{Y}_1 + n_0\overline{Y}_0,$$
$$\sum_{i=1}^{n} X_iY_i = n_1\overline{Y}_1.$$

Therefore,

$$\sum_i (X_i - \overline{X})(Y_i - \overline{Y}) = \sum_i X_iY_i - \frac{1}{n}\left(\sum_i X_i\right)\left(\sum_i Y_i\right)$$
$$= n_1\overline{Y}_1 - \frac{n_1}{n}(n_1\overline{Y}_1 + n_0\overline{Y}_0) = \frac{n_0n_1}{n}(\overline{Y}_1 - \overline{Y}_0)$$

and
$$\sum_i (X_i - \overline{X})^2 = \sum_i X_i^2 - \frac{1}{n}\left(\sum_i X_i\right)^2 = n_1 - \frac{n_1^2}{n} = \frac{n_0n_1}{n}.$$

This gives

$$\hat{\beta} = \frac{(n_0 n_1/n)(\overline{Y}_1 - \overline{Y}_0)}{n_0 n_1/n} = \overline{Y}_1 - \overline{Y}_0$$

and

$$\hat{\alpha} = \frac{1}{n}(n_1\overline{Y}_1 + n_0\overline{Y}_0) - (\overline{Y}_1 - \overline{Y}_0)\frac{n_1}{n} = \overline{Y}_0.$$

Thus the least squares estimator of the regression slope is equal to the difference between the sample mean salary of a Ph.D. and that of a non-Ph.D., and the least squares estimator of the regression intercept is equal to the sample mean salary of a non-Ph.D. The t test of the hypothesis that β is equal to zero described in (7.48) is in this case exactly the same as the t test of the hypothesis that two population means are equal. The latter is derived from (5.10).

In the preceding illustration the characteristic represented by the explanatory variable was dichotomous; i.e., only two possibilities were considered as relevant. But we can handle equally well models in which the explanatory characteristic is polytomous. The only consequence of this complication is that we need more than one binary variable to describe such a characteristic. For instance, suppose the starting salaries of the high school teachers of English are normally distributed with variance σ^2, the mean depending on whether the highest degree attained by the candidate is a B.A., an M.A., or a Ph.D. Let the mean starting salary for a B.A. be equal to μ_A; that for an M.A., μ_B; and that for a Ph.D., μ_C. The appropriate regression equation can be represented by

(11.2) $$Y_i = \beta_1 + \beta_2 X_{i2} + \beta_3 X_{i3} + \varepsilon_i,$$

where Y_i is the salary of the ith candidate, and

$$\begin{aligned} X_{i2} &= 1 \quad \text{if the highest degree of the candidate is a Ph.D.,} \\ &= 0 \quad \text{otherwise;} \\ X_{i3} &= 1 \quad \text{if the highest degree of the candidate is an M.A.,} \\ &= 0 \quad \text{otherwise.} \end{aligned}$$

Note that when $X_{i2} = 1$, X_{i3} must be equal to zero, and vice versa. The mean values of Y_i corresponding to different values of the regressors are

$$\begin{aligned} E(Y_i|X_{i2} = 1, X_{i3} = 0) &= \beta_1 + \beta_2, \\ E(Y_i|X_{i2} = 0, X_{i3} = 1) &= \beta_1 + \beta_3, \\ E(Y_i|X_{i2} = 0, X_{i3} = 0) &= \beta_1. \end{aligned}$$

It follows then that

$$\begin{aligned} \beta_1 &= \mu_A, \\ \beta_2 &= \mu_C - \mu_A, \\ \beta_3 &= \mu_B - \mu_A. \end{aligned}$$

This result is analogous to that obtained for the dichotomous classification of (11.1).

Note that the trichotomy in the preceding model is represented by *two* binary variables, each assuming a value of 0 or 1. It would be incorrect to use *one* variable with three values, say, 0 for a B.A., 1 for an M.A., and 2 for a Ph.D. If we did that and formed the regression model as

$$Y_i = \alpha + \beta W_i + \varepsilon_i,$$

where W_i is the explanatory variable with values 0, 1, and 2, we would have

$$E(Y_i | W_i = 0) = \alpha,$$

$$E(Y_i | W_i = 1) = \alpha + \beta,$$

$$E(Y_i | W_i = 2) = \alpha + 2\beta.$$

However, this implies that the difference between the mean salary of an M.A. and a B.A. is

$$(\alpha + \beta) - \alpha = \beta,$$

and the difference between the mean salary of a Ph.D. and an M.A. is

$$(\alpha + 2\beta) - (\alpha + \beta) = \beta.$$

That is, by using one variable with values 0, 1, and 2 (or any three equidistant values) we are, in fact, assuming that the difference between the salary of a Ph.D. and an M.A. is the same as that between the salary of an M.A. and a B.A. Unless we know a priori that this is the case, we are not justified in making such an assumption.

Note also that we cannot represent the trichotomy by three rather than by two binary variables (unless we drop the constant term in the regression equation). For if we did and formed the regression model as

$$Y_i = \beta_1 + \beta_2 X_{i2} + \beta_3 X_{i3} + \beta_4 X_{i4} + \varepsilon_i,$$

where X_{i2} and X_{i3} are defined as before and

$$\begin{aligned} X_{i4} &= 1 \quad \text{if the highest degree of the candidate is a B.A.,} \\ &= 0 \quad \text{otherwise,} \end{aligned}$$

the solution for $\hat{\beta}_1$, $\hat{\beta}_2$, $\hat{\beta}_3$, and $\hat{\beta}_4$ would be indeterminate. The reason is that

$$X_{i4} = 1 - X_{i2} - X_{i3},$$

and the least squares normal equations are not independent, or (what amounts to the same thing) $\mathbf{X'X}$ is a singular matrix. This holds quite generally: when the explanatory characteristic leads to a classification into G types, we use $(G - 1)$ binary variables for its representation. (Alternatively, we use G binary variables, but drop the constant term.)

Models with a single qualitative variable have been traditionally formulated in statistical texts as "one-way analysis of variance" models rather than as regression models with binary regressors. The two approaches are equivalent in the sense that they describe the same phenomenon and lead to the same test results about it. Consider a normally distributed random variable Y whose mean depends on a given polytomous characteristic that leads to a classification into G types. The variance of Y is constant, and the observations are assumed to be independent. By the "analysis of variance" approach we divide all of the observed values of Y into G groups according to the given characteristic, and formulate the model as

$$(11.3) \qquad Y_{ig} = \mu + \alpha_g + \varepsilon_{ig} \qquad (i = 1, 2, \ldots, n_g;\ g = 1, 2, \ldots, G).$$

Here Y_{ig} is the ith observation on Y in the gth group, μ is the "grand mean," α_g is the deviation of the mean of the gth group from μ, and ε_{ig} is a stochastic disturbance. Note that

$$\sum_{g=1}^{G} \alpha_g = 0.$$

Let us now compare the "analysis of variance" model with the corresponding regression model. The latter is given by

$$(11.4) \qquad X_{ig} = \beta_1 + \beta_2 X_{i2} + \beta_3 X_{i3} + \cdots + \beta_G X_{iG} + \varepsilon_{ig},$$

where $X_{ig} = 1$ if the observation belongs to the gth group,

$= 0$ otherwise $\quad (g = 2, 3, \ldots, G).$

To specify the coefficients of (11.4) in terms of the parameters of (11.3) and vice versa, we compare the two formulations for each group separately (Table 11-1).

Table 11-1

Group	Analysis of variance model	Regression model
1	$E(Y_{i1}) = \mu + \alpha_1$	$E(Y_{i1}) = \beta_1$
2	$E(Y_{i2}) = \mu + \alpha_2$	$E(Y_{i2}) = \beta_1 + \beta_2$
⋮	⋮	⋮
G	$E(Y_{iG}) = \mu + \alpha_G$	$E(Y_{iG}) = \beta_1 + \beta_G$

That is,

$$\mu + \alpha_1 = \beta_1,$$

$$\mu + \alpha_2 = \beta_1 + \beta_2,$$

$$\vdots$$

$$\mu + \alpha_G = \beta_1 + \beta_G,$$

or

$$\mu = \beta_1 + \frac{1}{G}(\beta_2 + \beta_3 + \cdots + \beta_G),$$

$$\alpha_1 = -\frac{1}{G}(\beta_2 + \beta_3 + \cdots + \beta_G),$$

$$\alpha_2 = \beta_2 - \frac{1}{G}(\beta_2 + \beta_3 + \cdots + \beta_G),$$

$$\vdots$$

$$\alpha_G = \beta_G - \frac{1}{G}(\beta_2 + \beta_3 + \cdots + \beta_G).$$

The hypothesis, tested with the help of the analysis of variance model, is that there is no difference between the group means; i.e.,

$$H_0: \quad \alpha_1 = \alpha_2 = \cdots = \alpha_G = 0,$$

$$H_A: \quad H_0 \text{ is not true.}$$

It is easy to see from the last column of Table 11-1 that this null hypothesis is exactly equivalent to the hypothesis that the slopes of the regression equation (11.4) are jointly equal to zero; that is,

$$H_0: \quad \beta_2 = \beta_3 = \cdots = \beta_G = 0,$$

$$H_A: \quad H_0 \text{ is not true.}$$

As we have shown earlier, to carry out a test of H_0 within the framework of the regression model, we use the F test described by (10.44). This is equivalent to the F test for the analysis of variance models that is traditionally given in the textbooks on statistics.[1] The regression model can also be used for testing the hypothesis that any one of the β coefficients is singly equal to zero, but the analysis of variance model is not readily suited for such a test.

Several Qualitative Explanatory Variables

Let us now extend the formulation of the regression models with qualitative explanatory variables to take into account more than one characteristic. Consider the following modification of the earlier example on the salaries of high school English teachers. Suppose the mean salary depends not only on the highest degree attained by the candidate, but also on whether the high school making the offer is public or private. The difference between the mean salaries in the public and the private school systems is presumed to be the same whatever the degree qualification. Again, we assume that salaries are normally distributed with variance σ^2 and that the observations are independent.

[1] See, e.g., J. E. Freund and R. E. Walpole, *Mathematical Statistics* 3rd ed. (Englewood Cliffs, NJ: Prentice-Hall, 1980), pp. 456–457.

Let μ_{A0} = mean salary for a B.A. in a private school;

μ_{A1} = mean salary for a B.A. in a public school;

μ_{B0} = mean salary for an M.A. in a private school;

μ_{B1} = mean salary for an M.A. in a public school;

μ_{C0} = mean salary for a Ph.D. in a private school;

μ_{C1} = mean salary for a Ph.D. in a public school.

Then a regression model can be formulated as

$$Y_i = \beta_1 + \beta_2 X_{i2} + \beta_3 X_{i3} + \gamma Z_i + \varepsilon_i, \tag{11.5}$$

where Y_i, X_{i2}, and X_{i3} are defined as in (11.2), and

$Z_i = 1$ if the school to which the ith candidate is applying is a public school,

$= 0$ otherwise.

Note again that when $X_{i2} = 1$, X_{i3} must be equal to zero. The mean values of Y_i corresponding to different values of the regressors are

$$\begin{aligned}
E(Y_i|X_{i2} = 1, X_{i3} = 0, Z_i = 1) &= \beta_1 + \beta_2 + \gamma,\\
E(Y_i|X_{i2} = 0, X_{i3} = 1, Z_i = 1) &= \beta_1 + \beta_3 + \gamma,\\
E(Y_i|X_{i2} = 0, X_{i3} = 0, Z_i = 1) &= \beta_1 + \gamma,\\
E(Y_i|X_{i2} = 1, X_{i3} = 0, Z_i = 0) &= \beta_1 + \beta_2,\\
E(Y_i|X_{i2} = 0, X_{i3} = 1, Z_i = 0) &= \beta_1 + \beta_3,\\
E(Y_i|X_{i2} = 0, X_{i3} = 0, Z_i = 0) &= \beta_1.
\end{aligned}$$

From this it follows that

$$\begin{aligned}
\beta_1 &= \mu_{A0},\\
\beta_2 &= \mu_{C0} - \mu_{A0} = \mu_{C1} - \mu_{A1},\\
\beta_3 &= \mu_{B0} - \mu_{A0} = \mu_{B1} - \mu_{A1},\\
\gamma &= \mu_{A1} - \mu_{A0} = \mu_{B1} - \mu_{B0} = \mu_{C1} - \mu_{C0}.
\end{aligned}$$

That is, β_1 measures the mean salary of a B.A. in a private high school, β_2 measures the difference between the mean salary of a Ph.D. and a B.A. (which is presumed to be the same in both school systems), β_3 measures the difference between the mean salary of an M.A. and a B.A. (also the same in both school systems), and γ represents the difference between the mean salaries in the public and the private schools.

The preceding regression model is represented in statistical texts as a "two-way analysis of variance" model. The two approaches are again equivalent.

Interaction Terms

The regression model with two, or more, explanatory characteristics can be generalized further by introducing "interaction terms." Consider the preceding example on the starting salaries of the high school English teachers. In this example we presume that the mean salary depends on the degree qualification of the candidate and on the type of high school, and that the difference between the mean salaries in the public and in the private school systems is the same for all degree qualifications. Suppose now that we do not wish to make the latter presumption. Then the regression model (11.5) can be modified as follows:

$$Y_i = \beta_1 + \beta_2 X_{i2} + \beta_3 X_{i3} + \gamma Z_i + \delta_2 X_{i2} Z_i + \delta_3 X_{i3} Z_i + \varepsilon_i, \tag{11.6}$$

where all the variables are defined as in (11.5). The mean values of Y_i corresponding to different values of the regressors are

$$E(Y_i|X_{i2}=1, X_{i3}=0, Z_i=1) = \beta_1 + \beta_2 + \gamma + \delta_2,$$
$$E(Y_i|X_{i2}=0, X_{i3}=1, Z_i=1) = \beta_1 + \beta_3 + \gamma + \delta_3,$$
$$E(Y_i|X_{i2}=0, X_{i3}=0, Z_i=1) = \beta_1 + \gamma,$$
$$E(Y_i|X_{i2}=1, X_{i3}=0, Z_i=0) = \beta_1 + \beta_2,$$
$$E(Y_i|X_{i2}=0, X_{i3}=1, Z_i=0) = \beta_1 + \beta_3,$$
$$E(Y_i|X_{i2}=0, X_{i3}=0, Z_i=0) = \beta_1.$$

This means that we can define the regression coefficients in terms of the mean salaries as

$$\beta_1 = \mu_{A0},$$
$$\beta_2 = \mu_{C0} - \mu_{A0},$$
$$\beta_3 = \mu_{B0} - \mu_{A0},$$
$$\gamma = \mu_{A1} - \mu_{A0},$$
$$\delta_2 = (\mu_{C1} - \mu_{C0}) - (\mu_{A1} - \mu_{A0}),$$
$$\delta_3 = (\mu_{B1} - \mu_{B0}) - (\mu_{A1} - \mu_{A0}).$$

The differences between the mean salaries in the public and the private systems are

$$\text{B.A.:} \quad \mu_{A1} - \mu_{A0} = \gamma,$$
$$\text{M.A.:} \quad \mu_{B1} - \mu_{B0} = \gamma + \delta_3,$$
$$\text{Ph.D.:} \quad \mu_{C1} - \mu_{C0} = \gamma + \delta_2.$$

The regression model (11.6) is equivalent to a model presented as a "two-way analysis of variance with interactions" in statistical literaure.

Qualitative and Quantitative Explanatory Variables

In the preceding models all of the included regressors were represented by binary variables. Such models are really not very frequent in economics. More frequently, we encounter models in which *some* regressors are binary and others are not. A traditional example is a consumption function estimated from time-series data that include a major war period. In this model the mean consumption is presumed to depend on income and on whether the period is one of peace or one of war. A simple way of representing this model is

$$C_t = \beta_1 + \beta_2 Y_t + \gamma Z_t + \varepsilon_t, \tag{11.7}$$

where C represents consumption, Y represents income, and Z is a binary variable such that

$$\begin{aligned} Z_t &= 1 \quad \text{if } t \text{ is a wartime period,} \\ &= 0 \quad \text{otherwise.} \end{aligned}$$

Then, we have

$$C_t = (\beta_1 + \gamma) + \beta_2 Y_t + \varepsilon_t \quad \text{(wartime),}$$

$$C_t = \beta_1 + \beta_2 Y_t + \varepsilon_t \qquad \text{(peacetime).}$$

Thus we are, in fact, postulating that in wartime the intercept of the consumption function changes from β_1 to $\beta_1 + \gamma$. A graphic illustration is given in Figure 11-1. If

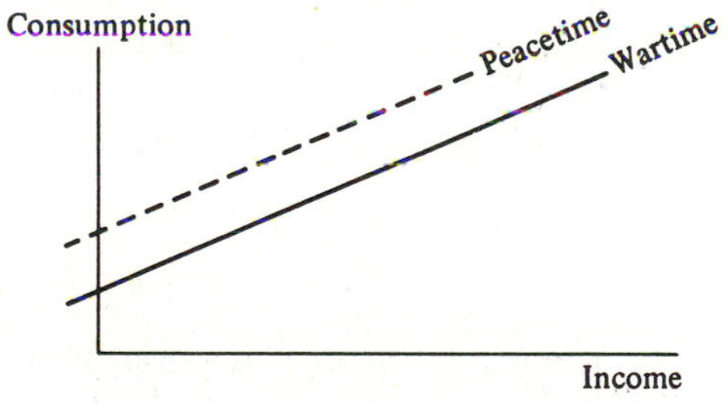

Figure 11-1

the intercept is viewed as representing the "subsistence level" of consumption, this model implies that the subsistence level changes during the war. Such a change is put forward as a hypothesis to be tested, i.e.,

$$H_0: \quad \gamma = 0,$$

$$H_A: \quad \gamma \neq 0.$$

Statistical texts show an equivalent formulation of models such as (11.7) under the name of "analysis of covariance."

The effect of war can be brought into the consumption function differently if we postulate that the war conditions affect the slope and not the intercept of the consumption function. According to this theoretical formulation, the regression model is

$$C_t = \beta_1 + \beta_2 Y_t + \delta Y_t Z_t + \varepsilon_t, \qquad (11.8)$$

where the variables are defined as before. In this case we have

$$C_t = \beta_1 + (\beta_2 + \delta)Y_t + \varepsilon_t \quad \text{(wartime)},$$
$$C_t = \beta_1 + \beta_2 Y_t + \varepsilon_t \quad \text{(peacetime)}.$$

Equation (11.8) implies that the effect of the war is to change the marginal propensity to consume as shown in Figure 11-2. This implication can be checked by testing the hypothesis that δ is zero.

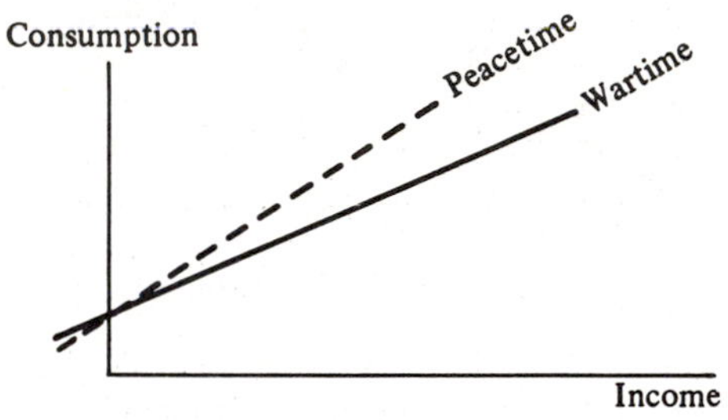

Figure 11-2

The third and final possibility of distinguishing between wartime and peacetime observations is to let *both* the intercept and the slope of the consumption function change in wartime. The regression equation would become

$$C_t = \beta_1 + \beta_2 Y_t + \gamma Z_t + \delta Y_t Z_t + \varepsilon_t. \qquad (11.9)$$

Then, we would have

$$C_t = (\beta_1 + \gamma) + (\beta_2 + \delta)Y_t + \varepsilon_t \quad \text{(wartime)},$$
$$C_t = \beta_1 + \beta_2 Y_t + \varepsilon_t \quad \text{(peacetime)}$$

These relations are illustrated in Figure 11-3. The interesting point about (11.9) is

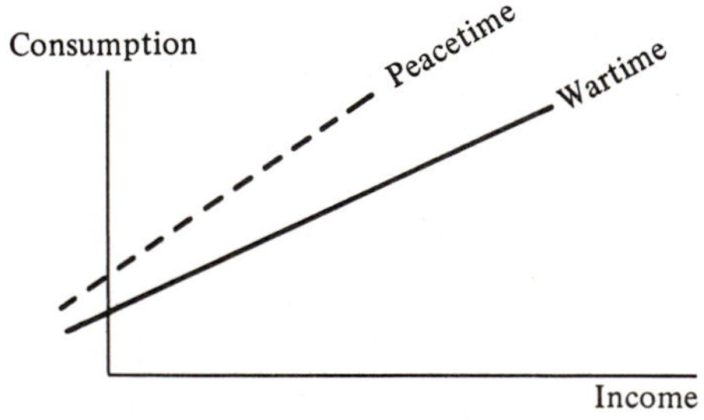

Figure 11-3

that the least squares estimators of the regression coefficients are exactly the same as those that would be obtained from two separate regressions of C_t on Y_t, one estimated from the peacetime observations and the other from the wartime observations. The proof is obtained by a straightforward application of the least squares formulas and will not be presented here. The only difference between the two approaches to estimation concerns σ^2. If, as we normally assume, the variance of ε_t is unchanged throughout the entire period, then its estimate from (11.9) based on *all* observations will be efficient, whereas the two estimates obtained from the two separate subsamples will not be. This is because the estimate of σ^2 based on either subsample does not utilize the information about σ^2 contained in the other subsample.

A restrictive feature of the preceding formulations concerning the difference between the peacetime and the wartime consumer behavior is the constancy of the shift—in intercept or in slope—throughout the entire wartime period. A more reasonable representation would perhaps be to let each of the war years to be characterized by its own intercept (or slope). This would involve introducing a separate dummy variable for each of the war years into the regression equation. If it is believed that the coefficients corresponding to the wartime dummy variables level off as the consumers get used to the wartime conditions, they could be restricted to lie on an appropriately specified curve. The way to implement such a restriction will be discussed in the following section.

Models with quantitative *and* qualitative explanatory variables are used most frequently in connection with regression models that include seasonal effects. These models are usually estimated from quarterly or monthly observations. For instance, consider the following simple regressions:

$$
\begin{aligned}
(11.10) \qquad & Y_t = \alpha_1 + \beta X_t + \varepsilon_t \qquad \text{(spring quarter)},\\
& Y_t = \alpha_2 + \beta X_t + \varepsilon_t \qquad \text{(summer quarter)},\\
& Y_t = \alpha_3 + \beta X_t + \varepsilon_t \qquad \text{(fall quarter)},\\
& Y_t = \alpha_4 + \beta X_t + \varepsilon_t \qquad \text{(winter quarter)}.
\end{aligned}
$$

Here the seasonal effects are presumed to shift the intercept of the regression function. The model can be described by a single regression equation extended by the introduction of binary regressors representing the seasonal factors,

$$(11.11) \qquad Y_t = \alpha + \beta X_t + \gamma_2 Q_{t2} + \gamma_3 Q_{t3} + \gamma_4 Q_{t4} + \varepsilon_t,$$

where

$$
\begin{aligned}
Q_{t2} &= 1 \quad \text{if } t \text{ is a summer quarter,}\\
&= 0 \quad \text{otherwise;}\\
Q_{t3} &= 1 \quad \text{if } t \text{ is a fall quarter,}\\
&= 0 \quad \text{otherwise;}\\
Q_{t4} &= 1 \quad \text{if } t \text{ is a winter quarter,}\\
&= 0 \quad \text{otherwise.}
\end{aligned}
$$

Note that the quarterly seasonal effects are represented by three, not four, binary regressors; otherwise, the least squares estimators of the regression coefficients would be indeterminate. A comparison of (11.11) and (11.10) reveals that

$$\alpha = \alpha_1,$$
$$\alpha + \gamma_2 = \alpha_2,$$
$$\alpha + \gamma_3 = \alpha_3,$$
$$\alpha + \gamma_4 = \alpha_4.$$

To examine the relevance of the seasonal effects in a regression model such as (11.11), we test the hypothesis that γ_2, γ_3, and γ_4 are jointly zero; that is,

$$H_0: \quad \gamma_2 = \gamma_3 = \gamma_4 = 0,$$
$$H_A: \quad H_0 \text{ is not true.}$$

The appropriate test then is the F test of (10.46).

The representation of seasonal effects in equation (11.11) involves only three seasonal dummy variables and makes the interpretation of the coefficients somewhat awkward. A more easily interpretable representation would be one with all four seasons explicitly accounted for and with the seasonal coefficients measuring seasonal deviations from the annual average, making their sum equal to zero. This can be accomplished by rewriting (11.11) as[2]

$$(11.12) \qquad Y_t = \alpha^* + \beta^* X_t + \gamma_1^* Q_{t1} + \gamma_2^* Q_{t2} + \gamma_3^* Q_{t3} + \gamma_4^* Q_{t4} + \varepsilon_t,$$

where

$$\alpha^* = \alpha + \frac{\gamma_2 + \gamma_3 + \gamma_4}{4},$$
$$\beta^* = \beta,$$
$$\gamma_1^* = -\frac{\gamma_2 + \gamma_3 + \gamma_4}{4},$$
$$\gamma_2^* = \gamma_2 - \frac{\gamma_2 + \gamma_3 + \gamma_4}{4},$$
$$\gamma_3^* = \gamma_3 - \frac{\gamma_2 + \gamma_3 + \gamma_4}{4},$$
$$\gamma_4^* = \gamma_4 - \frac{\gamma_2 + \gamma_3 + \gamma_4}{4},$$

and $Q_{t1} = 1$ if t is a spring quarter and 0 otherwise. The specification of the coefficients of (11.12) has been determined by choosing a constant k such that

$$(11.12a) \qquad \gamma_i^* = \gamma_i + k \quad (i = 1, 2, 3, \text{ and } 4)$$

[2] See D. B. Suits, "Dummy Variables: Mechanics V. Interpretation," *Review of Economics and Statistics,* 56 (February 1984), pp. 177–180.

where $$\gamma_1 = 0,$$

(11.12b) $$\sum_{i=1}^{4} \gamma_i^* = 0,$$

and requiring that α^* satisfies the condition

(11.12c) $$\alpha^* + \gamma_i^* = \alpha + \gamma_i, \quad (i = 1, 2, 3, \text{ and } 4),$$

in conformity with (11.11). This leads to

$$k = -\frac{\gamma_2 + \gamma_3 + \gamma_4}{4}$$

and $$\alpha^* = \alpha - k.$$

Estimates of the coefficients of (11.12) cannot be obtained by a direct application of the least squares method because the relevant least squares normal equations are not independent, but they can be easily calculated by using the least squares estimates of the coefficients of (11.11) to get

$$\hat{\alpha}^* = \hat{\alpha} + \frac{\hat{\gamma}_2 + \hat{\gamma}_3 + \hat{\gamma}_4}{4},$$

$$\hat{\beta}^* = \hat{\beta},$$

etc.

Since $\hat{\alpha}^*$ and each of the $\hat{\gamma}^*$s are linear combinations of the estimated coefficients of (11.11), their variances can be readily determined from the variance-covariance matrix of the estimated coefficients of (11.11). Thus

$$\text{Var}(\hat{\alpha}^*) = \text{Var}(\hat{\alpha}) + \sum_{i=2}^{4} \left[\frac{1}{16} \text{Var}(\hat{\gamma}_i) + \frac{2}{4} \text{Cov}(\hat{\alpha}, \hat{\gamma}_i) \right]$$
$$+ \frac{2}{16} \text{Cov}(\hat{\gamma}_2, \hat{\gamma}_3) + \frac{2}{16} \text{Cov}(\hat{\gamma}_2, \hat{\gamma}_4) + \frac{2}{16} \text{Cov}(\hat{\gamma}_3, \hat{\gamma}_4),$$

$$\text{Var}(\hat{\beta}^*) = \text{Var}(\hat{\beta}),$$

etc.

A Note on the Use of Deseasonalized Data

While we are on the subject of seasonal factors in regression equations, we may consider the implications of using "deseasonalized" time-series data in regression analysis. A common practice is to form the regression equation as

$$\tilde{Y}_t = \alpha + \beta \tilde{X}_t + \varepsilon_t,$$

where $\tilde{Y}$ and $\tilde{X}$ are the "deseasonalized" values of X and Y. "Deseasonalizing" means removing regular oscillatory movement of a one-year period from the original time series. This is done either by the statistical agency that makes the data available or by the econometrician. In our discussion we assume that the deseasonalizing has been successful in the sense that the seasonal elements have been completely removed from the series. These elements are usually considered to be additive or multiplicative. In the additive case, we can write

$$Y_t = \tilde{Y}_t + D_{tY},$$
$$X_t = \tilde{X}_t + D_{tX},$$

where D_{tY} and D_{tX} represent seasonal deviations contained in the respective series. Note that for, say, quarterly data,

$$D_{tY} = D_{t+4,\,Y},$$
$$D_{tX} = D_{t+4,\,X},$$

and

$$D_{tY} + D_{t+1,\,Y} + D_{t+2,\,Y} + D_{t+3,\,Y} = 0,$$
$$D_{tX} + D_{t+1,\,X} + D_{t+2,\,X} + D_{t+3,\,X} = 0,$$

for all t. If any series contains no seasonal elements, the corresponding D's would all be zero. The regression equation

$$\tilde{Y}_t = \alpha + \beta\tilde{X}_t + \varepsilon_t$$

then implies that

$$Y_t - D_{tY} = \alpha + \beta(X_t - D_{tX}) + \varepsilon_t \tag{11.13}$$

or

$$Y_t = (\alpha + D_{tY} - \beta D_{tX}) + \beta X_t + \varepsilon_t. \tag{11.13a}$$

That is, in this case the seasonal factors are assumed to operate by shifting the intercept of the regression function. This is equivalent to the formulation given by (11.10) or (11.11).

In the case of multiplicative seasonal elements, we can write

$$Y_t = \tilde{Y}_t S_{tY} \qquad \text{and} \qquad X_t = \tilde{X}_t S_{tX},$$

where S_{tY} and S_{tX} represent seasonal indexes pertaining to the respective series. Note that for, say, quarterly data,

$$S_{tY} = S_{t+4,\,Y} \qquad \text{and} \qquad S_{tX} = S_{t+4,\,X},$$

and

$$S_{tY} \times S_{t+1,\,Y} \times S_{t+2,\,Y} \times S_{t+3,\,Y} = 1,$$
$$S_{tX} \times S_{t+1,\,X} \times S_{t+2,\,X} \times S_{t+3,\,X} = 1,$$

for all t. If any series contains no seasonal elements, the corresponding Ss would all be equal to unity. The regression equation

$$\tilde{Y}_t = \alpha + \beta \tilde{X}_t + \varepsilon_t$$

in this case implies

$$\frac{Y_t}{S_{tY}} = \alpha + \beta \frac{X_t}{S_{tX}} + \varepsilon_t \tag{11.14}$$

or

$$Y_t = \alpha S_{tY} + \beta \frac{S_{tY}}{S_{tX}} X_t + \varepsilon_t^*, \tag{11.14a}$$

where $\varepsilon_t^* = S_{tY}\varepsilon_t$. Here it is assumed that the seasonal elements affect both the intercept and the slope of the regression equation and that the disturbance is heteroskedastic with variance equal to $\sigma^2 S_{tY}^2$. When a research worker is applying the least squares method to the deseasonalized data while making the usual basic assumptions about the disturbance as in (11.14), then he or she is implying *something* about the relationship between X and Y in the real, "nondeseasonalized" world. These implications are spelled out by (11.14a). If (11.14a) does not provide a true description of the relationship between X and Y, then the least squares estimators of α and β (based on deseasonalized data) do not, in general, possess the desirable properties that they would otherwise have.

It may be interesting to compare the least squares estimates of the regression coefficients of (11.11) with those based on seasonally adjusted data. Suppose a "deseasonalized" series is represented by the least squares residuals obtained by regressing the values of the series on the seasonal dummy variables. Let $\mathbf{y}$ by a $n \times 1$ vector of the values of the dependent variable, and let $\mathbf{D}$ be a $n \times 4$ matrix of the values of the seasonal dummy variables. Then an application of the least squares method—used purely as a "curve fitting" device—to

$$\mathbf{y} = \mathbf{D}\boldsymbol{\delta} + \text{error}$$

yields

$$\hat{\boldsymbol{\delta}} = (\mathbf{D}'\mathbf{D})^{-1}\mathbf{D}'\mathbf{y},$$

and the seasonally adjusted values of $\mathbf{y}$ are

$$\begin{aligned} \mathbf{y}^a &= \mathbf{y} - \mathbf{D}\hat{\boldsymbol{\delta}} \\ &= \mathbf{y} - \mathbf{D}(\mathbf{D}'\mathbf{D})^{-1}\mathbf{D}'\mathbf{y} \\ &= \mathbf{M}_D\mathbf{y}, \end{aligned}$$

where $\mathbf{M}_D$ is a symmetric and idempotent matrix. The same procedure can be applied to the explanatory variables X (of dimension $n \times K$) to give

$$\mathbf{X}^a = \mathbf{M}_D\mathbf{X}.$$

Let us now compare the least squares estimator of $\boldsymbol{\beta}_1$ in

$$\mathbf{y} = \mathbf{X}\boldsymbol{\beta}_1 + \mathbf{D}\boldsymbol{\delta} + \boldsymbol{\varepsilon}$$

with that of $\boldsymbol{\beta}_2$ in

$$\mathbf{y}^a = \mathbf{X}^a\boldsymbol{\beta}_2 + \mathbf{u}.$$

Now by (10.17a) we have

$$\hat{\boldsymbol{\beta}}_1 = (\mathbf{X}'\mathbf{M}_D\mathbf{X})^{-1}\mathbf{X}'\mathbf{M}_D\mathbf{y}.$$

For the "deseasonalized" model without the dummy variables, we have

$$\begin{aligned}\hat{\boldsymbol{\beta}}_2 &= (\mathbf{X}^{a\prime}\mathbf{X}^a)^{-1}\mathbf{X}^{a\prime}\mathbf{y}^a \\ &= (\mathbf{X}'\mathbf{M}_D'\mathbf{M}_D\mathbf{X})^{-1}\mathbf{X}'\mathbf{M}_D'\mathbf{M}_D\mathbf{y} \\ &= (\mathbf{X}'\mathbf{M}_D\mathbf{X})^{-1}\mathbf{X}'\mathbf{M}_D\mathbf{y},\end{aligned}$$

since $\mathbf{M}_D$ is idempotent. Thus, for this kind of "deseasonalization," using unadjusted variables and seasonal dummy variables is exactly equivalent to using seasonally adjusted variables without the seasonal dummy variables.[3] Of course, deseasonalizing a variable by regressing its values on a set of seasonal dummy variables is rather primitive since other systematic factors are disregarded. Deseasonalizing as currently practiced by government statisticians is based on various fairly sophisticated methods designed to approximate these "other systematic factors" without actually specifying a theoretically justified model. Since the success in removing seasonal elements from a series is rarely complete, deseasonalization introduces distortions whose seriousness is difficult to assess. Therefore it may be preferable to work with unadjusted data whenever possible and to include seasonal effects as part of the model.

11-2 Models with Restricted Coefficients

Here our problem is how to incorporate into our estimation procedure some prior information about a regression coefficient (or coefficients). Such information can be viewed as providing certain restrictions on one or more given regression coefficients. For instance, if we know a priori that the population regression line passes through the origin, then, if we use this prior knowledge, we are required to restrict the value of the intercept of the sample regression line to zero. The incorporation of this prior knowledge into the estimation procedure has two distinct aspects. First, we do not estimate the intercept, since its value is known; second, we estimate the slope of the regression line in such a way that the estimator has the

[3] See M. C. Lovell, "Seasonal Adjustment of Economic Time Series," *Journal of the American Statistical Association,* 58 (December 1963), pp. 993–1010. The result is known as the *Frisch–Waugh theorem.*

usual desirable properties *under the condition* that the intercept is zero. The second aspect is quite important because an estimator that has all the desirable properties under general conditions does not necessarily retain these properties when the conditions become special in some way. In our example, "general conditions" mean that the regression line can be anywhere in the plane. Once we specify that the regression line *must* pass through the origin, we impose a restriction that reduces the degree of generality.

In this section we consider several types of restrictions, some imposed by prior information about the *value* of the individual regression coefficients and others imposed by the *relations* among the individual regression coefficients.

Fixed-Value Restrictions

To illustrate the case where we have exact information about the value of one of the regression coefficients, we use a regression equation with two explanatory variables,

$$Y_i = \beta_1 + \beta_2 X_{i2} + \beta_3 X_{i3} + \varepsilon_i,$$

but the analysis applies, and can be easily extended, to equations with a larger number of explanatory variables. Suppose now that we know the value of the intercept a priori; in particular, suppose

$$\beta_1 = 0,$$

as is most commonly the case. Then, the regression equation becomes

$$Y_i = \beta_2 X_{i2} + \beta_3 X_{i3} + \varepsilon_i. \tag{11.15}$$

This specification of the regression equation now incorporates our prior knowledge about the value of the intercept as required. The least squares estimators of β_2 and β_3 can be obtained by minimizing the sum of squares S given by

$$S = \sum_i (Y_i - \beta_2 X_{i2} - \beta_3 X_{i3})^2.$$

The resulting estimators of β_2 and β_3 are

$$\hat{\beta}_2 = \frac{(\sum Y_i X_{i2})(\sum X_{i3}^2) - (\sum Y_i X_{i3})(\sum \mathrm{X}_{i2} X_{i3})}{(\sum X_{i2}^2)(\sum X_{i3}^2) - (\sum X_{i2} X_{i3})^2}, \tag{11.16}$$

$$\hat{\beta}_3 = \frac{(\sum Y_i X_{i3})(\sum X_{i2}^2) - (\sum Y_i X_{i2})(\sum X_{i2} X_{i3})}{(\sum X_{i2}^2)(X_{i3}^2) - (\sum X_{i2} X_{i3})^2}.$$

To derive the formulas for the variances of $\hat{\beta}_2$ and $\hat{\beta}_3$, we note that

$$\hat{\beta}_2 = \beta_2 + \frac{(\sum X_{i3}^2)(\sum X_{i2}\varepsilon_i) - (\sum X_{i2}X_{i3})(\sum X_{i3}\varepsilon_i)}{(\sum X_{i2}^2)(\sum X_{i3}^2) - (\sum X_{i2}X_{i3})^2},$$

$$\hat{\beta}_3 = \beta_3 + \frac{(\sum X_{i2}^2)(\sum X_{i3}\varepsilon_i) - (\sum X_{i2}X_{i3})(\sum X_{i2}\varepsilon_i)}{(\sum X_{i2}^2)(\sum X_{i3}^2) - (\sum X_{i2}X_{i3})^2}.$$

Therefore

$$\text{(11.17)} \quad \text{Var}(\hat{\beta}_2) = E(\hat{\beta}_2 - \beta_2)^2 = \frac{\sigma^2 \sum X_{i3}^2}{(\sum X_{i2}^2)(\sum X_{i3}^2) - (\sum X_{i2}X_{i3})^2},$$

$$\text{Var}(\hat{\beta}_3) = E(\hat{\beta}_3 - \beta_3)^2 = \frac{\sigma^2 \sum X_{i2}^2}{(\sum X_{i2}^2)(\sum X_{i3}^2) - (\sum X_{i2}X_{i3})^2},$$

$$\text{Cov}(\hat{\beta}_2, \hat{\beta}_3) = E(\hat{\beta}_2 - \beta_2)(\hat{\beta}_3 - \beta_3) = \frac{-\sigma^2 \sum X_{i2}X_{i3}}{(\sum X_{i2}^2)(\sum X_{i3}^2) - (\sum X_{i2}X_{i3})^2}.$$

It can be shown, by following the steps outlined in the first part of Section 10-1, that $\hat{\beta}_2$ and $\hat{\beta}_3$ have all the desirable properties. The variances of $\hat{\beta}_2$ and $\hat{\beta}_3$ can be estimated by references to (11.17), after we replace σ^2 by its unbiased estimator s^2 defined as

$$\text{(11.18)} \qquad s^2 = \frac{1}{n-2} \sum_i (Y_i - \hat{\beta}_2 X_{i2} - \hat{\beta}_3 X_{i3})^2.$$

Note that in (11.18) we divide the sum of the squares of residuals by $(n-2)$, since only two regression coefficients are unknown. All of these results can be easily generalized to apply to regression models with more than two explanatory variables.

The preceding case demonstrates the gain achieved by incorporating the prior knowledge about a regression coefficient in the estimation procedure. The gain is essentially twofold. First, we do not have to estimate β_1 since its value is known. Second, the restricted least squares estimators of β_2 and β_3, i.e., those estimators which incorporate the information that $\beta_1 = 0$, have a smaller variance than the ordinary unrestricted least squares estimators. The second type of gain represents a less obvious but very important feature of estimation with restrictions. For example, let $\hat{\beta}_2$ stand for the restricted estimator of β_2 as defined by (11.16), and let $\hat{\beta}_2^{ORD}$ represent the ordinary unrestricted least squares estimator of β_2 as defined by

(10.12). The ratio of the variances of the two estimators is

$$(11.19)\quad \frac{\mathrm{Var}(\hat{\beta}_2^{ORD})}{\mathrm{Var}(\hat{\beta}_2)} = \frac{\sigma^2 m_{33}/(m_{22}m_{33} - m_{23}^2)}{\sigma^2 \sum X_{i3}^2 /[(\sum X_{i2}^2)(\sum X_{i3}^2) - (\sum X_{i2}X_{i3})^2]}$$

$$= \frac{m_{33}[(m_{22} + n\overline{X}_2^2)(m_{33} + n\overline{X}_3^2) - (m_{23} + n\overline{X}_2\overline{X}_3)^2]}{(m_{33} + n\overline{X}_3^2)(m_{22}m_{33} - m_{23}^2)}$$

$$= 1 + \frac{n(\overline{X}_2 m_{33} - \overline{X}_3 m_{23})^2}{(m_{33} + n\overline{X}_3^2)(m_{22}m_{33} - m_{23}^2)},$$

which is clearly greater than, or at best equal to, one. Thus

$$\mathrm{Var}(\hat{\beta}_2^{ORD}) \geq \mathrm{Var}(\hat{\beta}_2).$$

A similar proof could be presented with respect to β_3. Note, however, that while the restricted estimators of β_2 and β_3 have smaller variances than their unrestricted counterparts, the value of R^2 is higher for the unrestricted sample regression line than for the restricted one. This is because the unrestricted least squares estimation leads to the maximum value of R^2 so that *any* departure from it must result in a decrease.

If the restriction that a given regression coefficient (or coefficients) is equal to a certain value (or values) is to be tested rather than assumed, we can estimate the regression model with and without the restrictions and use the standard test statistic

$$(11.20)\quad \frac{(\mathrm{SSE}_R - \mathrm{SSE}_U)/r}{\mathrm{SSE}_U/(n-K)} \sim F_{r,\, n-K},$$

as presented in (7.51). Note that r is the number of restrictions and K the number of unrestricted coefficients. For instance, if the model is given as

$$Y_i = \beta_1 + \beta_2 X_{i2} + \beta_3 X_{i3} + \varepsilon_i$$

and the restriction to be tested is that $\beta_2 = 0.9$, then the restricted error sum of squares (SSE_R) is obtained by applying the least squares method to

$$(Y_i - 0.9X_{i2}) = \beta_1 + \beta_3 X_{i3} + \varepsilon_i$$

or, equivalently, to

$$Y_i^* = \beta_1 + \beta_3 X_{i3} + \varepsilon_i$$

where $Y_i^* = Y_i - 0.9X_{i2}$. The unrestricted error sum of squares (SSE_U) is obtained by applying the least squares method to the unrestricted form of the model. When there is only *one* fixed restriction to be tested, the F test in (11.20) is equivalent to the standard t test.

Linear Restrictions

Frequently, the prior information available is not about the values of the individual regression coefficients, but about the relations among them. For instance, we may know a priori that one coefficient is equal to the sum of two other coefficients, or that certain coefficients form a geometric progression. These restrictions can be divided into two types, depending upon whether the relation between the coefficients is linear or nonlinear. We will discuss the *linear restrictions* first, because they are simpler. In either case, we find it convenient to compare the regression equation in which the restrictions are explicitly taken into account with the regression equation in which the restrictions are ignored. The parameters of the former will be called "restricted," and those of the latter "unrestricted." Such a juxtaposition will enable us to introduce the concept of "identification," which plays an important role in many econometric problems. Our discussion will be carried out in terms of examples that illustrate the type of problem and its solution and that can be easily modified to fit other cases.

Consider the problem of estimating a regression model with one explanatory variable and with additive seasonal effects. That is,

$$Y_t = \alpha_1 + \beta X_t + \varepsilon_t \quad \text{(spring quarter)},$$
$$Y_t = \alpha_2 + \beta X_t + \varepsilon_t \quad \text{(summer quarter)},$$
$$Y_t = \alpha_3 + \beta X_t + \varepsilon_t \quad \text{(fall quarter)},$$
$$Y_t = \alpha_4 + \beta X_t + \varepsilon_t \quad \text{(winter quarter)}.$$

By introducing binary variables for the last three quarters, we can rewrite the above compactly as

$$(11.21) \quad Y_t = \alpha_1 + \beta X_t + (\alpha_2 - \alpha_1)Q_{t2} + (\alpha_3 - \alpha_1)Q_{t3} + (\alpha_4 - \alpha_1)Q_{t4} + \varepsilon_t,$$

where

$$\begin{aligned} Q_{t2} &= 1 \quad \text{if } t \text{ is a summer quarter,} \\ &= 0 \quad \text{otherwise;} \\ Q_{t3} &= 1 \quad \text{if } t \text{ is a fall quarter,} \\ &= 0 \quad \text{otherwise;} \\ Q_{t4} &= 1 \quad \text{if } t \text{ is a winter quarter,} \\ &= 0 \quad \text{otherwise.} \end{aligned}$$

Here we have five restricted parameters: $\alpha_1, \alpha_2, \alpha_3, \alpha_4$, and β. The restrictions in this case are that α_2 must be equal to the coefficient of Q_{t2} *plus* the intercept, α_3 to the coefficient of Q_{t3} *plus* the intercept, and α_4 to the coefficient of Q_{t4} *plus* the intercept. The unrestricted form of (11.21) is

$$(11.21\text{a}) \qquad Y_t = \beta_1 + \beta_2 Q_{t2} + \beta_3 Q_{t3} + \beta_4 Q_{t4} + \beta_5 X_t + \varepsilon_t.$$

When we compare the unrestricted coefficients of (11.21a) with the restricted parameters of (11.21), we can see that

$$\beta_1 = \alpha_1,$$
$$\beta_2 = \alpha_2 - \alpha_1,$$
$$\beta_3 = \alpha_3 - \alpha_1,$$
$$\beta_4 = \alpha_4 - \alpha_1,$$
$$\beta_5 = \beta.$$

In this case there is a one-to-one correspondence between the unrestricted and the restricted parameters and a unique solution for the restricted parameters in terms of the unrestricted parameters. In particular,

$$\alpha_1 = \beta_1,$$
$$\alpha_2 = \beta_2 + \beta_1,$$
$$\alpha_3 = \beta_3 + \beta_1,$$
$$\alpha_4 = \beta_4 + \beta_1,$$
$$\beta = \beta_5.$$

A case like this is called *exact identification* to indicate the fact that the restricted parameters can be uniquely "identified" by reference to the unrestricted coefficients.

The practical importance of exact identification is that we can obtain least squares estimates of the unrestricted coefficients and use them to obtain estimates of the restricted parameters. Since the estimates of the restricted parameters are all linear functions of the estimates of the unrestricted coefficients, all of the desirable properties of the latter will be carried over to the former. The variances of the estimated restricted parameters can be determined from the variances and covariances of the estimated unrestricted coefficients. In particular,

$$\mathrm{Var}(\hat{\alpha}_1) = \mathrm{Var}(\hat{\beta}_1),$$
$$\mathrm{Var}(\hat{\alpha}_2) = \mathrm{Var}(\hat{\beta}_1) + \mathrm{Var}(\hat{\beta}_2) + 2\,\mathrm{Cov}(\hat{\beta}_1, \hat{\beta}_2),$$
$$\mathrm{Var}(\hat{\alpha}_3) = \mathrm{Var}(\hat{\beta}_1) + \mathrm{Var}(\hat{\beta}_3) + 2\,\mathrm{Cov}(\hat{\beta}_1, \hat{\beta}_3),$$
$$\mathrm{Var}(\hat{\alpha}_4) = \mathrm{Var}(\hat{\beta}_1) + \mathrm{Var}(\hat{\beta}_4) + 2\,\mathrm{Cov}(\hat{\beta}_1, \hat{\beta}_4),$$
$$\mathrm{Var}(\hat{\beta}) = \mathrm{Var}(\hat{\beta}_5).$$

The same relations hold between the respective estimates of the variances. Note that the same results for the estimates of the restricted parameters would be obtained by rewriting (11.21) as

$$Y_t = \alpha_1 Q_{t1} + \alpha_2 Q_{t2} + \alpha_3 Q_{t3} + \alpha_4 Q_{t4} + \beta X_t + \varepsilon_t, \tag{11.21b}$$

where $$Q_{t1} = 1 \quad \text{if } t \text{ is a spring quarter,}$$
$$= 0 \quad \text{otherwise.}$$

Equation (11.21b) is restricted to pass through the origin, and can be estimated by the method of least squares, as described at the outset of this section. The resulting estimates and their variances are precisely the same as those obtained from the unrestricted estimates of (11.21a).

Consider now a different case of linear restrictions, namely, one in which the sum of two or more of the regression coefficients is equal to a given number. A well-known example of such a restriction is the Cobb–Douglas production function characterized by constant returns to scale. Here we require that the sum of the regression slopes be equal to unity. Specifically,

(11.22) $$Y_t = \alpha_1 + \alpha_2 X_{i2} + (1 - \alpha_2)X_{i3} + \varepsilon_i,$$

where Y_i = log output, X_{i2} = log labor input, and X_{i3} = log capital input. We have two restricted parameters: α_1 and α_2. The unrestricted form of (11.22) is

(11.22a) $$Y_i = \beta_1 + \beta_2 X_{i2} + \beta_3 X_{i3} + \varepsilon_i.$$

The relationship between the unrestricted and the restricted parameters is

$$\beta_1 = \alpha_1,$$
$$\beta_2 = \alpha_2,$$
$$\beta_3 = 1 - \alpha_2.$$

In this case, the number of unrestricted coefficients exceeds the number of the restricted parameters, and there is no unique solution for α_2. In fact,

$$\alpha_1 = \beta_1,$$
$$\alpha_2 = \beta_2,$$

and $$\alpha_2 = 1 - \beta_3.$$

This case is called *overidentification,* alluding to the fact that there is more than one solution to "identify" the restricted parameter α_2.

Under the conditions of overidentification, we cannot proceed with estimation (as we can with exact identification) by estimating the unrestricted equation and then translating the results to obtain estimates of the restricted parameters. Rather, we must turn directly to the restricted equation (11.22). The least squares estimators of the restricted parameters can be obtained by minimizing

$$\sum_i [Y_i - \alpha_1 - \alpha_2 X_{i2} - (1 - \alpha_2)X_{i3}]^2$$

with respect to α_1 and α_2. It can be easily shown that the resulting estimates are exactly the same as those obtained by applying the least squares method to

(11.22b) $$Y_i^* = \alpha_1 + \alpha_2 X_{i2}^* + \varepsilon_i,$$

where Y_i^* is measured by $(Y_i - X_{i3})$ and X_{i2}^* by $(X_{i2} - X_{i3})$. Equation (11.22b) represents just another way of writing (11.22) by rearranging its terms. This possibility is always open whenever we have overidentification and whenever the restrictions are linear.

Another example of overidentifying restrictions relates to the difference in consumer behavior in peacetime and in wartime as discussed in Section 11-1. If the consumption function is such that each of the war years is characterized by its own intercept and if there are altogether m consecutive war years, then we have

$$C_t = \gamma_1 Z_{t1} + \gamma_2 Z_{t2} + \cdots + \gamma_m Z_{tm} + \beta Y_t + \varepsilon_t, \tag{11.23}$$

where
$$\begin{aligned} Z_{t1} &= 1 \quad \text{if } t \text{ is the first war year,} \\ &= 0 \quad \text{otherwise;} \\ Z_{t2} &= 1 \quad \text{if } t \text{ is the second war year,} \\ &= 0 \quad \text{otherwise;} \end{aligned}$$

etc. Suppose further that it is believed that the coefficients corresponding to the wartime dummy variables level off as consumers get used to the wartime conditions. A simple representation of this belief would be to restrict these coefficients to lie on a second-degree polynomial, i.e.,

$$\gamma_i = \lambda_0 + \lambda_1 i + \lambda_2 i^2 \qquad (i = 1, 2, \ldots, m). \tag{11.24}$$

This means that if $m > 3$, we can replace the m γ coefficients by the three λ coefficients. An appropriate substitution from (11.24) into (11.23) gives

$$\begin{aligned} C_t &= (\lambda_0 + \lambda_1 + \lambda_2)Z_{t1} + (\lambda_0 + 2\lambda_1 + 4\lambda_2)Z_{t2} \\ &\quad + \cdots + (\lambda_0 + m\lambda_1 + m^2\lambda_2)Z_{tm} + \beta Y_t + \varepsilon_t \\ &= \lambda_0 W_{t0} + \lambda_1 W_{t1} + \lambda_2 W_{t2} + \beta Y_t + \varepsilon_t, \end{aligned} \tag{11.25}$$

where
$$\begin{aligned} W_{t0} &= Z_{t1} + Z_{t2} + \cdots + Z_{tm} = 1, \\ W_{t1} &= Z_{t1} + 2Z_{t2} + \cdots + mZ_{tm}, \\ W_{t2} &= Z_{t1} + 4Z_{t2} + \cdots + m^2 Z_{tm}. \end{aligned}$$

As a third and final case of linear restrictions, we consider the case where the number of the restricted parameters is larger than the number of unrestricted coefficients. For example, suppose that family expenditure on fruit can be described by the regression equation

$$F_i = \alpha_F + \beta_F Y_i + \varepsilon_{iF},$$

where F = family expenditure on fruit, and Y = family income. Suppose further that family expenditure on vegetables can be described by

$$V_i = \alpha_V + \beta_V Y_i + \varepsilon_{iV},$$

where V = family expenditure on vegetables. Now if, as is commonly the case, the sample does not provide separate information on expenditure on fruit and on vegetables but only their total, we have to combine the foregoing regressions to get

$$G_i = (\alpha_F + \alpha_V) + (\beta_F + \beta_V)Y_i + \varepsilon_i, \tag{11.26}$$

where $G = F + V$, and $\varepsilon = \varepsilon_F + \varepsilon_V$. The unrestricted version of (11.26) is

$$G_i = \alpha + \beta Y_i + \varepsilon_i. \tag{11.26a}$$

When we compare the coefficients of the two equations, we get

$$\alpha = \alpha_F + \alpha_V \quad \text{and} \quad \beta = \beta_F + \beta_V.$$

Here we have four restricted parameters and only two unrestricted coefficients. Clearly, we cannot express the restricted parameters in terms of the unrestricted coefficients. This is known as the case of *underidentification,* in which the restricted parameters cannot be consistently estimated on the basis of the available sample information.

A common way of representing a set of m linear restrictions is to write

$$\mathbf{R}\boldsymbol{\beta} = \mathbf{r}, \tag{11.27}$$

where $\mathbf{R}$ is an $(m \times K)$ matrix of known constants, $\boldsymbol{\beta}$ a $(K \times 1)$ vector of the regression coefficients, and $\mathbf{r}$ an $(m \times 1)$ vector of known constants. For instance, when the prior information is of the form that the model is

$$Y_i = \beta_1 X_{i1} + \beta_2 X_{i2} + \beta_3 X_{i3} + \beta_4 X_{i4} + \varepsilon_i$$

and it is known that the first three regression coefficients are the same, i.e., that

$$\beta_1 = \beta_2 = \beta_3,$$

we have *two* (independent) constraints:

$$\beta_1 = \beta_2 \quad \text{and} \quad \beta_2 = \beta_3$$

and

$$\mathbf{R} = \begin{bmatrix} 1 & -1 & 0 & 0 \\ 0 & 1 & -1 & 0 \end{bmatrix}, \quad \mathbf{r} = \begin{bmatrix} 0 \\ 0 \end{bmatrix}.$$

In practice, estimation of the regression coefficients subject to linear restrictions can always be accomplished by substituting the restrictions into the regression equation prior to estimation. For instance, when the restrictions are that the first three regression coefficients are the same, we can rewrite the regression equation as

$$\begin{aligned} Y_i &= \beta_3(X_{i1} + X_{i2} + X_{i3}) + \beta_4 X_{i4} + \cdots + \beta_K X_{ik} + \varepsilon_i \\ &= \beta_3 X_{i3}^* + \beta_4 X_{i4} + \cdots + \beta_K X_{iK} + \varepsilon_i, \end{aligned}$$

where $X_{i3}^* = X_{i1} + X_{i2} + X_{i3}$. Estimates of $\beta_3, \beta_4, \ldots, \beta_K$ can be obtained by direct estimation, and those of β_1 and β_2 can be made equal to $\hat{\beta}_3$.

When the restrictions are to be tested for rather than assumed, we can again use the standard F test given in (11.20). Such a test can, of course, be carried out *only* if the restrictions are overidentifying, because in the case of an exact identification the restrictions are fulfilled by definition, and in the case of underidentification no consistent estimation is possible.

Nonlinear Restrictions

As our first case of nonlinear restrictions we consider *exact identification.* This can be illustrated by a simple version of the so-called "stock adjustment model." Suppose the volume of stock of a commodity that a firm "desires" to hold is equal to a given linear function of sales, i.e.,

$$Y_t^* = \alpha + \beta X_t,$$

where Y_t^* = desired level of stock at the end of period t, and X_t = sales during the period t. Y^* is, in general, not observable. Now suppose further that the adjustment on the part of each firm to the desired level in any one period is not complete, so that

$$Y_t - Y_{t-1} = \gamma(Y_t^* - Y_{t-1}) + \varepsilon_t,$$

where Y_t = actual level of stock at the end of period t. The parameter γ is called the "adjustment coefficient," and its value lies between 0 and 1. A value of γ close to zero indicates that only a small part of the gap between the desired and the actual level of stock is closed during any one period, while a value of γ close to unity indicates that a large part of the gap is closed. The disturbance ε_t is brought in to allow for random influences in carrying out the adjustment. Substituting for Y_t^* and rearranging terms, we obtain

$$Y_t = \alpha\gamma + \beta\gamma X_t + (1-\gamma)Y_{t-1} + \varepsilon_t. \tag{11.28}$$

This is an equation that explains investment in stock. All variables in this equation except ε_t are observable. In (11.28) we have three "restricted" parameters: α, β, and γ. The unrestricted counterpart of (11.28) is

$$Y_t = \beta_1 + \beta_2 X_t + \beta_3 Y_{t-1} + \varepsilon_t. \tag{11.28a}$$

The coefficients of (11.28a) are related to the parameters of (11.28) as follows:

$$\beta_1 = \alpha\gamma,$$

$$\beta_2 = \beta\gamma,$$

$$\beta_3 = 1 - \gamma.$$

In this case, we can obtain a unique solution for the restricted parameters in terms of the unrestricted coefficients; that is, we have *exact identification.* The solution is

$$\alpha = \frac{\beta_1}{1-\beta_3},$$

$$\beta = \frac{\beta_2}{1-\beta_3},$$

$$\gamma = 1 - \beta_3.$$

Note that α and β are *nonlinear* functions of the unrestricted β's.

To estimate the parameters of (11.28), we obtain least squares estimates of the unrestricted coefficients of (11.28a), and use the solution for α, β, and γ to obtain the corresponding estimates of these parameters. As for the desirable properties of the resulting estimators, we note that those estimators which are nonlinear functions of the unconstrained coefficients inherit the desirable asymptotic, but *not* small-sample, properties from the unconstrained estimators. The reason is that unbiasedness does not "carry over" *via* nonlinear functions (see Theorem 18 and the subsequent remarks in Section 6-1). In the present case, the unconstrained estimators themselves are not unbiased because of the presence of Y_{t-1} among the explanatory variables, so that *none* of the constrained estimators can be claimed to be unbiased. The variance of the restricted estimator of γ can be determined by reference to the variance of the unrestricted $\hat{\beta}_3$ if we note that

$$\text{Var}(\hat{\gamma}) = \text{Var}(\hat{\beta}_3).$$

The determination of the variances of $\hat{\alpha}$ and $\hat{\beta}$ is somewhat more troublesome because $\hat{\alpha}$ and $\hat{\beta}$ are not linear functions of the unrestricted estimators. However, there is an approximate formula that can be used in this case. The formula refers to the general case where an estimator, say, $\hat{\alpha}$, is a function of k other estimators such as, $\hat{\beta}_1, \hat{\beta}_2, \ldots, \hat{\beta}_k$; i.e.,

$$\hat{\alpha} = f(\hat{\beta}_1, \hat{\beta}_2, \ldots, \hat{\beta}_k).$$

Then the large-sample variance of $\hat{\alpha}$ can be approximated[4] as

$$\text{(11.29)} \quad \text{Var}(\hat{\alpha}) \approx \sum_k \left[\frac{\partial f}{\partial \beta_k}\right]^2 \text{Var}(\hat{\beta}_k) + 2 \sum_{j<k} \left[\frac{\partial f}{\partial \beta_j}\right]\left[\frac{\partial f}{\partial \beta_k}\right] \text{Cov}(\hat{\beta}_j, \hat{\beta}_k)$$

$$(j, k = 1, 2, \ldots, K; \quad j < k).$$

In matrix notation this can be written as

$$\text{(11.29a)} \qquad \text{Var}(\hat{\alpha}) \cong \left(\frac{\partial f}{\partial \boldsymbol{\beta}}\right)' E(\hat{\boldsymbol{\beta}} - \boldsymbol{\beta})(\hat{\boldsymbol{\beta}} - \boldsymbol{\beta})' \left(\frac{\partial f}{\partial \boldsymbol{\beta}}\right),$$

where

$$\left(\frac{\partial f}{\partial \boldsymbol{\beta}}\right)' = \left[\frac{\partial f}{\partial \beta_1}\; \frac{\partial f}{\partial \beta_2} \;\cdots\; \frac{\partial f}{\partial \beta_k}\right],$$

and

$$E(\hat{\boldsymbol{\beta}} - \boldsymbol{\beta})(\hat{\boldsymbol{\beta}} - \boldsymbol{\beta})' = \begin{bmatrix} \text{Var}(\hat{\beta}_1) & \text{Cov}(\hat{\beta}_1, \hat{\beta}_2) & \ldots & \text{Cov}(\hat{\beta}_1, \hat{\beta}_k) \\ \text{Cov}(\hat{\beta}_2, \hat{\beta}_1) & \text{Var}(\hat{\beta}_2) & \ldots & \text{Cov}(\hat{\beta}_2, \hat{\beta}_k) \\ \vdots & \vdots & & \vdots \\ \text{Cov}(\hat{\beta}_k, \hat{\beta}_1) & \text{Cov}(\hat{\beta}_k, \hat{\beta}_2) & \ldots & \text{Var}(\hat{\beta}_k) \end{bmatrix}.$$

(The approximation is obtained by using Taylor expansion for $f(\hat{\beta}_1, \hat{\beta}_2, \ldots, \hat{\beta}_k)$ around $\beta_1, \beta_2, \ldots, \beta_k$, dropping terms of the order of two or higher, and then

[4] See L. R. Klein, *A Textbook of Econometrics* (Evanston, Ill: Row, Peterson, 1953), p. 258. Strictly speaking, $\partial f/\partial \boldsymbol{\beta}$ is not mathematically defined. We use it to denote "$\partial f/\partial \hat{\boldsymbol{\beta}}$ evaluated at $\hat{\boldsymbol{\beta}} = \boldsymbol{\beta}$."

obtaining the variance by the usual formula.) For example, for

$$\hat{\alpha} = \frac{\hat{\beta}_1}{1 - \hat{\beta}_3},$$

we have

$$\text{Var}(\hat{\alpha}) \cong \left[\frac{1}{1-\beta_3}\right]^2 \text{Var}(\hat{\beta}_1) + \left[\frac{\beta_1}{(1-\beta_3)^2}\right]^2 \text{Var}(\hat{\beta}_3) + 2\left[\frac{1}{1-\beta_3}\right]\left[\frac{\beta_1}{(1-\beta_3)^2}\right] \text{Cov}(\hat{\beta}_1, \hat{\beta}_3).$$

This formula can be used to approximate the large-sample variance of $\hat{\alpha}$. Since the βs and their large-sample variances and covariances can be readily estimated by the application of the standard formulas, there is no problem in estimating the large-sample variances of the restricted estimators.

An alternative approach to estimating the parameters of (11.28) is to minimize the sum of squares S given by

$$S = \sum_{t=2}^{n} [Y_t - \alpha\gamma - \beta\gamma X_t - (1-\gamma)Y_{t-1}]^2$$

with respect to α, β, and γ. The resulting estimators of these parameters are called *nonlinear least squares estimators*. It can easily be shown that these estimators are exactly the same as those obtained from the estimated unconstrained coefficients of (11.28a). Further, since the logarithmic likelihood function for $Y_2, Y_3, \ldots, Y_n$ (conditional on Y_1) is

$$L = -\frac{n-1}{2}\log 2\pi\sigma^2 - \frac{1}{2\sigma^2}\sum_{t=2}^{n} [Y_t - \alpha\gamma - \beta\gamma X_t - (1-\gamma)Y_{t-1}]^2,$$

minimizing S with respect to α, β, and γ is equivalent to maximizing L with respect to the same parameters. Thus, if the regression disturbance is normally and independently distributed, nonlinear least squares estimators are the same as maximum likelihood estimators. Therefore, we can estimate their asymptotic variances by using the appropriate information matrix, which is equivalent to using (11.29).

EXAMPLE The case of nonlinear restrictions under conditions of exact identification is encountered in connection with one of the consumption function models considered by Zellner.[5] This model is not a "stock adjustment model" in the strict sense, but it has the same basic features. If we use a simple variant of the "permanent income hypothesis," we can postulate the consumption function as

$$C_t = \alpha + k(1-\lambda)Y_t + \lambda C_{t-1} + u_t$$

where C = real consumption, and Y = real income. The unrestricted counterpart of this

[5] The theoretical development is not given in Zellner's paper but can be found in A. Zellner, D. S. Huang, and L. C. Chau, "Further Analysis of the Short-Run Consumption Function with Emphasis on the Role of Liquid Assets," *Econometrica*, Vol. 33, July 1965, pp. 571–581.

equation is

$$C_t = \beta_1 + \beta_2 Y_t + \beta_3 C_{t-1} + u_t.$$

The disturbance term u_t was assumed to be nonautocorrelated. Zellner estimated the unrestricted function from 31 quarterly observations for the United States with the following result:

$$C_t = \underset{}{0.10} + \underset{(0.093)}{0.128} Y_t + \underset{(0.127)}{0.870} C_{t-1} + e_t, \quad \bar{R}^2 = 0.978.$$

Therefore, the estimates of the restricted parameters are

$$\hat{\alpha} = \hat{\beta}_1 = 0.10,$$

$$\hat{k} = \frac{\hat{\beta}_2}{1 - \hat{\beta}_3} = 0.985,$$

$$\hat{\lambda} = \hat{\beta}_3 = 0.870.$$

The estimate of the large-sample standard error of $\hat{\lambda}$ can be obtained directly from the unrestricted result. The estimated large-sample standard error of $\hat{k}$ can be found by using the approximation formula (11.29), i.e., by noting that

$$\text{Est. Var}(\hat{k}) = \left[\frac{1}{1 - \hat{\beta}_3}\right]^2 \text{Est. Var}(\hat{\beta}_2) + \left[\frac{\hat{\beta}_2}{(1 - \hat{\beta}_3)^2}\right]^2 \text{Est. Var}(\hat{\beta}_3)$$
$$+ 2\left[\frac{1}{1 - \hat{\beta}_3}\right]\left[\frac{\hat{\beta}_2}{(1 - \hat{\beta}_3)^2}\right] \text{Est. Cov}(\hat{\beta}_2, \hat{\beta}_3).$$

Estimates of $\text{Var}(\hat{\beta}_2)$ and $\text{Var}(\hat{\beta}_3)$ are directly available from Zellner's results. The estimate of $\text{Cov}(\hat{\beta}_2, \hat{\beta}_3)$ can be obtained by noting that

$$\text{Cov}(\hat{\beta}_2, \hat{\beta}_3) = \frac{-\sigma^2 m_{23}}{m_{22}m_{33} - m_{23}^2} = \frac{-\sigma^2 r_{23}\sqrt{m_{22}}\sqrt{m_{33}}}{m_{22}m_{33} - m_{23}^2} = -r_{23}\sqrt{\text{Var}(\hat{\beta}_2)}\sqrt{\text{Var}(\hat{\beta}_3)},$$

so that the only additional information needed is the value of r_{23}, the sample coefficient of correlation between Y_t and C_{t-1}. This value can be found from the relation between the F statistic and the two t statistics. First, since $\bar{R}^2 = 0.978$, it follows from (10.42) that

$$R^2 = 0.9795.$$

Therefore, by reference to (10.44),

$$F = \frac{R^2/(3-1)}{(1 - R^2)/(31 - 3)} = 669.$$

This enables us to utilize (10.45b):

$$669 = \frac{(0.128/0.093)^2 + (0.870/0.127)^2 + 2(0.128/0.093)(0.870/0.127)r_{23}}{2(1 - r_{23}^2)}.$$

This is a quadratic equation in r_{23} which has one positive and one negative root. We choose the positive root since the sample correlation between Y_t and C_{t-1} is clearly positive. This gives

$$r_{23} = 0.975,$$

and

$$\text{Est. Cov}(\hat{\beta}_2, \hat{\beta}_3) = -0.975 \times 0.093 \times 0.127 = -0.011515.$$

Therefore,

$$\text{Est. Var}(\hat{k}) = \left[\frac{1}{1-0.870}\right]^2 0.093^2 + \left[\frac{0.128}{(1-0.870)^2}\right]^2 0.127^2$$

$$+2\left[\frac{1}{1-0.870}\right]\left[\frac{0.128}{(1-0.870)^2}\right](-0.011515) = 0.095175.$$

Thus, the estimated large-sample standard errors of the restricted estimators are

$$s_{\hat{\lambda}} = 0.127 \qquad \text{and} \qquad s_{\hat{k}} = 0.308.$$

This means that both $\hat{\lambda}$ and $\hat{k}$ are highly significant.

To illustrate *overidentifying nonlinear restrictions,* we use a simple regression model in which the disturbance follows a first-order autoregressive scheme. In particular, suppose we have

$$Y_t = \alpha + \beta X_t + \varepsilon_t,$$

$$\varepsilon_t = \rho\varepsilon_{t-1} + u_t,$$

where $u_t \sim N(0, \sigma_u^2)$, and $E(u_t\varepsilon_{t-1}) = 0$. As mentioned in Section 8-3, the regression equation can be transformed in such a way that the autoregressive disturbance ε_t is eliminated. By lagging the regression equation by one period, multiplying it by ρ, and deducting the result from the original form of the regression equation, we obtain

$$Y_t - \rho Y_{t-1} = \alpha(1-\rho) + \beta(X_t - \rho X_{t-1}) + u_t.$$

This equation appears as (8.60) in Section 8-3. Alternatively,

$$(11.30) \qquad Y_t = \alpha(1-\rho) + \beta X_t - \beta\rho X_{t-1} + \rho Y_{t-1} + u_t,$$

which is a multiple regression equation with parameters α, β, and ρ. The unrestricted counterpart of (11.30) is

$$(11.30a) \qquad Y_t = \beta_1 + \beta_2 X_t + \beta_3 X_{t-1} + \beta_4 Y_{t-1} + u_t.$$

By comparing the two versions, we see that

$$\beta_1 = \alpha(1-\rho),$$

$$\beta_2 = \beta,$$

$$\beta_3 = -\beta\rho,$$

$$\beta_4 = \rho.$$

That is, we have four unrestricted coefficients and only three restricted parameters. Since there is no unique solution for any of the restricted parameters in terms of the unrestricted coefficients, we clearly have a case of *overidentification.* However, there is no great difficulty about estimating the restricted parameters by the maximum likelihood method as described in Section 8-3, where we also discuss several alternative estimation methods designed for this model. The maximum likelihood estimation method is available for any kind of overidentification; but in some cases the computations are highly complicated, and it is not always guaranteed that the maximum of the likelihood function is not a local one rather than a global one.

Finally, we consider *underidentification.* We shall illustrate this in the context of a model in which some parameters are overidentified and some are underidentified. Consider another consumption function model developed and estimated by Zellner, Huang, and Chau:[6]

$$C_t = (k - \alpha\eta)(1 - \lambda)Y_t + \alpha L_{t-1} - \alpha\lambda L_{t-2} + \lambda C_{t-1} + u_t, \tag{11.31}$$

where

$$u_t = \varepsilon_t - \lambda\varepsilon_{t-1},$$

and L = actual holdings of liquid assets at the end of the period. Thus we have four parameters—α, λ, k, and η—to estimate. The unrestricted version of (11.31) is

$$C_t = \beta_1 Y_t + \beta_2 L_{t-1} + \beta_3 L_{t-2} + \beta_4 C_{t-1} + u_t. \tag{11.31a}$$

There are then four unrestricted coefficients in (11.31a). The relation between the parameters of (11.31) and the coefficients of (11.31a) is

$$\beta_1 = (k - \alpha\eta)(1 - \lambda),$$

$$\beta_2 = \alpha,$$

$$\beta_3 = -\alpha\lambda,$$

$$\beta_4 = \lambda.$$

From this, we can see that

$$\alpha = \beta_2 \qquad \text{or} \qquad \alpha = -\frac{\beta_3}{\beta_4},$$

and

$$\lambda = \beta_4 \qquad \text{or} \qquad \lambda = -\frac{\beta_3}{\beta_2}.$$

Thus, α and λ are overidentified, but no solution exists for k and η. This means that k and η are underidentified. The implication of this is that α and λ can be estimated by the nonlinear least squares method, but no estimates of k and η are obtainable from the sample. All that can be done is to get an estimate of $(k - \alpha\eta)$.

EXAMPLE The estimates of the parameters of (11.31) have been obtained by Zellner, Huang, and Chau from quarterly data for the United States on the assumption that u_t is

[6] *Ibid.*

nonautoregressive. The result of the nonlinear least squares estimation is

$$\underset{}{C_t} = \underset{(0.085)}{0.475Y_t} + \underset{(0.045)}{0.226L_{t-1}} - 0.085L_{t-2} + \underset{(0.106)}{0.378C_{t-1}} + e_t.$$

Thus,

$$\hat{\alpha} = 0.226,$$

$$\hat{\lambda} = 0.378,$$

$$\hat{k} - 0.226\hat{\eta} = 0.763.$$

This equation was also estimated by the nonlinear least squares method with the addition of a constant term:

$$C_t = -12.470 + \underset{(0.080)}{0.538Y_t} + \underset{(0.050)}{0.376L_{t-1}} - 0.091L_{t-2} + \underset{(0.105)}{0.242C_{t-1}} + e_t.$$

The result of the unrestricted least squares estimation of the previous equation is

$$C_t = \underset{(3.606)}{-1.082} + \underset{(0.085)}{0.517Y_t} + \underset{(0.172)}{0.560L_{t-1}} - \underset{(0.181)}{0.296L_{t-2}} + \underset{(0.110)}{0.273C_{t-1}} + e_t.$$

Note that the unrestricted estimates are numerically different from the restricted estimates, but for some coefficients the differences are not overwhelming.

LR, LM, and W Tests

See also Greene (5th edition, p. 484)

If we wish to *test* the validity of nonlinear restrictions rather than assuming it a priori, we can use one of three asymptotically equivalent tests: the *likelihood ratio test* (LR), the *Wald test* (W), or the *Lagrange multiplier test* (LM). These tests are based on general principles and can be used for testing linear as well as nonlinear restrictions. They are, however, valid only asymptotically and thus are intended to be used in large samples. As in the case of linear restrictions, tests of nonlinear restrictions are possible only if the restrictions are *overidentifying.*

The *likelihood ratio test* is based on the idea that if the restrictions are true, the value of the likelihood function maximized with the restrictions imposed cannot differ too much from the value of the likelihood function maximized without the imposition of the restrictions. Formally, let $L(\tilde{\boldsymbol{\beta}}, \tilde{\sigma}^2)$ be the maximum of the log-likelihood function when the restrictions are imposed, and $L(\hat{\boldsymbol{\beta}}, \hat{\sigma}^2)$ be the maximum of the log-likelihood functions when the restrictions are not imposed. Then, asymptotically,

$$LR = -2[L(\tilde{\boldsymbol{\beta}}, \tilde{\sigma}^2) - L(\hat{\boldsymbol{\beta}}, \hat{\sigma}^2)] \sim \chi^2_m, \tag{11.32}$$

where m is the number of restrictions, which can always be determined easily by deducting the number of the restricted coefficients from the number of the unrestricted coefficients. As an illustration let us consider a simple regression model transformed to account for first-order autoregression of the disturbance. The restricted version of this model was presented in (11.30) and its unrestricted version was given in (11.30a). Let

$$\tilde{\sigma}^2 = \frac{1}{n}\sum \tilde{u}_t^2 \qquad \text{and} \qquad \hat{\sigma}^2 = \frac{1}{n}\sum \hat{u}_t^2,$$

where $\tilde{u}_t$ represents the residuals from the estimated restricted equation (11.30) and $\hat{u}_t$ represents the least squares residuals from the unrestricted equation (11.30a). Then we have

$$(11.33)\quad LR = -2\left[-\frac{n}{2}\log(2\pi\tilde{\sigma}^2) - \frac{1}{2\tilde{\sigma}^2}\sum \tilde{u}_t^2 + \frac{n}{2}\log(2\pi\hat{\sigma}^2) + \frac{1}{2\hat{\sigma}^2}\sum \hat{u}_t^2\right]$$

$$= n[\log \tilde{\sigma}^2 - \log \hat{\sigma}^2].$$

Since there are four unrestricted coefficients in (11.30a) and three restricted coefficients in (11.30), the number of restrictions is equal to one. (In terms of the coefficients of (11.30a), the restriction is that $\beta_2\beta_4 + \beta_3 = 0$.) Under the null hypothesis that the restrictions are correct, we have

$$n[\log \tilde{\sigma}^2 - \log \hat{\sigma}^2] \sim \chi^2_1.$$

A rejection of the null hypothesis in this case means that a longer lag—or a more complicated structure of lags—is appropriate, or that the regression equation has been misspecified.[7]

The *Wald test* is based on the extent to which the restrictions are violated when unrestricted rather than restricted estimates are used. A general expression for the restrictions on the regression coefficients and, therefore, of our null hypothesis is

$$(11.34)\qquad \mathbf{g}(\beta_1, \beta_2, \ldots, \beta_K) = 0.$$

If there are m restrictions, $\mathbf{g}(.)$ is an $(m \times 1)$ vector. Now if we substitute the restricted estimates $\tilde{\beta}_1, \tilde{\beta}_2, \ldots, \tilde{\beta}_K$ for $\beta_1, \beta_2, \ldots, \beta_K$ in (11.34), the equation still holds. If, however, we substitute the *unrestricted* estimates $\hat{\beta}_1, \hat{\beta}_2, \ldots, \hat{\beta}_K$, the equation no longer holds, at least in general. The Wald test is based on the extent to which $\mathbf{g}(\hat{\beta}_1, \hat{\beta}_2, \ldots, \hat{\beta}_K)$ departs from zero. The Wald test statistic and its asymptotic distribution is given as

$$(11.35)\qquad W = \hat{\mathbf{g}}'[\text{Est. Var-Cov}(\hat{\mathbf{g}})]^{-1}\,\hat{\mathbf{g}} \sim \chi^2_m,$$

where

$$\hat{\mathbf{g}}' = \mathbf{g}(\hat{\beta}_1, \hat{\beta}_2, \ldots, \hat{\beta}_K)',$$

and

[7] See J. D. Sargan, "Wages and Prices in the United Kingdom: A Study in Econometric Methodology," in D. F. Hendry and K. F. Wallis (eds.), *Econometrics and Quantitative Economics* (Oxford, England: Basil Blackwell, 1984), p. 279; also J. G. Thursby, "A Test Strategy for Discriminating between Autocorrelation and Misspecification in Regression Analysis," *Review of Economics and Statistics,* 63 (February 1981), pp. 118–119.

(11.36) $$\text{Est. Var-Cov}(\hat{\mathbf{g}}) = \left(\frac{\partial \hat{\mathbf{g}}}{\partial \hat{\boldsymbol{\beta}}}\right)' [\text{Est. Var-Cov}(\hat{\boldsymbol{\beta}})] \left(\frac{\partial \hat{\mathbf{g}}}{\partial \hat{\boldsymbol{\beta}}}\right),$$

$$\left(\frac{\partial \hat{\mathbf{g}}}{\partial \hat{\boldsymbol{\beta}}}\right)' = \begin{bmatrix} \frac{\partial \hat{g}_1}{\partial \hat{\beta}_1} & \frac{\partial \hat{g}_1}{\partial \hat{\beta}_2} & \cdots & \frac{\partial \hat{g}_1}{\partial \hat{\beta}_K} \\ \frac{\partial \hat{g}_2}{\partial \hat{\beta}_1} & \frac{\partial \hat{g}_2}{\partial \hat{\beta}_2} & \cdots & \frac{\partial \hat{g}_2}{\partial \hat{\beta}_K} \\ \vdots & \vdots & & \vdots \\ \frac{\partial \hat{g}_m}{\partial \hat{\beta}_1} & \frac{\partial \hat{g}_m}{\partial \hat{\beta}_2} & \cdots & \frac{\partial \hat{g}_m}{\partial \hat{\beta}_K} \end{bmatrix},$$

$$\text{Est. Var-Cov}(\hat{\boldsymbol{\beta}}) = \hat{\sigma}^2(\mathbf{X}'\mathbf{X})^{-1},$$

$$\hat{\sigma}^2 = (\mathbf{y} - \mathbf{X}\hat{\boldsymbol{\beta}})'(\mathbf{y} - \mathbf{X}\hat{\boldsymbol{\beta}})/n.$$

The subscript of $\hat{\mathbf{g}}$ identifies individual restrictions. If there is only one restriction, i.e., if $m = 1$, then the formula (11.36) is the same as (11.29a) presented earlier. As an illustration of the Wald test, let us consider again the autoregressive transformation (11.30) and its unrestricted version (11.30a). In this case there is only one restriction on the regression coefficients, which is $\beta_2\beta_4 = -\beta_3$, so that the function $\mathbf{g}(.)$ becomes

(11.37) $$\mathbf{g}(.) = \beta_2\beta_4 + \beta_3$$

Then

$$\left(\frac{\partial \hat{\mathbf{g}}}{\partial \hat{\boldsymbol{\beta}}}\right)' = [0 \quad \hat{\beta}_4 \quad 1 \quad \hat{\beta}_2],$$

so that

(11.38) $$\begin{aligned}\text{Est. Var}(\hat{\mathbf{g}}) = {} & \hat{\beta}_4^2 \,\text{Est. Var}(\hat{\beta}_2) + \text{Est. Var}(\hat{\beta}_3) \\ & + \hat{\beta}_2^2 \,\text{Est. Var}(\hat{\beta}_4) + 2\hat{\beta}_4 \,\text{Est. Cov}(\hat{\beta}_2, \hat{\beta}_3) \\ & + 2\hat{\beta}_2\hat{\beta}_4 \,\text{Est. Cov}(\hat{\beta}_2, \hat{\beta}_4) + 2\hat{\beta}_2 \,\text{Est. Cov}(\hat{\beta}_3, \hat{\beta}_4),\end{aligned}$$

and

(11.39) $$W = \frac{(\hat{\beta}_2\hat{\beta}_4 + \hat{\beta}_3)^2}{\text{Est. Var}(\hat{\mathbf{g}})}.$$

The last of the three asymptotic tests, the *Lagrange multiplier test* (sometimes also called the "score test"), is based on the extent to which the first-order conditions for maximizing the likelihood function are violated when the unrestricted estimates are replaced by the restricted ones. Let L denote the unrestricted log-likelihood function (i.e., the log-likelihood function written without the imposition of the restrictions) and let $\mathbf{S}(\boldsymbol{\beta})$—called "score"—denote $(\partial L/\partial \boldsymbol{\beta})$. Then if $\mathbf{S}(\boldsymbol{\beta})$ is evaluated at $\boldsymbol{\beta} = \hat{\boldsymbol{\beta}}$, it will be equal to zero. If, however, $\mathbf{S}(\boldsymbol{\beta})$ is evaluated at $\boldsymbol{\beta} = \tilde{\boldsymbol{\beta}}$, it will, in general, differ from zero. The LM test is based on the extent to which $\mathbf{S}(\boldsymbol{\beta})$ evaluated at $\boldsymbol{\beta} = \tilde{\boldsymbol{\beta}}$ departs from zero. The appropriate test statistic and its asymptotic distribution is

$$(11.40) \qquad LM = \mathbf{S}(\tilde{\boldsymbol{\beta}})'\mathbf{I}(\tilde{\boldsymbol{\beta}})^{-1}\mathbf{S}(\tilde{\boldsymbol{\beta}}) \sim \chi^2_m,$$

where
$$\mathbf{S}(\tilde{\boldsymbol{\beta}}) = \frac{\partial L}{\partial \boldsymbol{\beta}} \text{ evaluated at } \boldsymbol{\beta} = \tilde{\boldsymbol{\beta}},$$

$$\mathbf{I}(\tilde{\boldsymbol{\beta}})^{-1} = \left(-E\frac{\partial^2 L}{\partial \boldsymbol{\beta}^2}\right)^{-1} \text{ evaluated at } \boldsymbol{\beta} = \tilde{\boldsymbol{\beta}} \text{ and } \sigma^2 = \tilde{\sigma}^2,$$

$$= \tilde{\sigma}^2(\mathbf{X}'\mathbf{X})^{-1},$$

$$\tilde{\sigma}^2 = (\mathbf{y} - \mathbf{X}\tilde{\boldsymbol{\beta}})'(\mathbf{y} - \mathbf{X}\tilde{\boldsymbol{\beta}})/n.$$

Continuing again with the autoregressive transformation as an illustration, let us express the unrestricted version of the model given in (11.30a) in matrix notation as $\mathbf{y} = \mathbf{X}\boldsymbol{\beta} + \boldsymbol{\varepsilon}$ so that the log-likelihood function can be written as

$$L = -\frac{n}{2}\log(2\pi\sigma^2) - \frac{(\mathbf{y} - \mathbf{X}\boldsymbol{\beta})'(\mathbf{y} - \mathbf{X}\boldsymbol{\beta})}{2\sigma^2}$$

and
$$\frac{\partial L}{\partial \boldsymbol{\beta}} = -\frac{-2\mathbf{X}'\mathbf{y} + 2\mathbf{X}'\mathbf{X}\boldsymbol{\beta}}{2\sigma^2}.$$

Therefore

$$\mathbf{S}(\tilde{\boldsymbol{\beta}}) = \frac{\mathbf{X}'\mathbf{y} - \mathbf{X}'\mathbf{X}\tilde{\boldsymbol{\beta}}}{\tilde{\sigma}^2}$$

and

$$\mathbf{I}(\tilde{\boldsymbol{\beta}})^{-1} = \tilde{\sigma}^2(\mathbf{X}'\mathbf{X})^{-1}.$$

Thus the *LM* test statistic and its asymptotic distribution is given as

$$(11.41) \qquad LM = \frac{(\mathbf{X}'\mathbf{y} - \mathbf{X}'\mathbf{X}\tilde{\boldsymbol{\beta}})'[\tilde{\sigma}^2(\mathbf{X}'\mathbf{X})^{-1}](\mathbf{X}'\mathbf{y} - \mathbf{X}'\mathbf{X}\tilde{\boldsymbol{\beta}})}{\tilde{\sigma}^4} \sim \chi^2_m.$$

We may, if we wish, substitute $(\mathbf{X}'\mathbf{X})\hat{\boldsymbol{\beta}}$ for $\mathbf{X}'\mathbf{y}$ to get

$$(11.41\text{a}) \qquad LM = \frac{(\hat{\boldsymbol{\beta}} - \tilde{\boldsymbol{\beta}})'(\mathbf{X}'\mathbf{X})(\hat{\boldsymbol{\beta}} - \tilde{\boldsymbol{\beta}})}{\tilde{\sigma}^2} \sim \chi^2_m.$$

The different ideas underlying each of the three asymptotic tests described above are illustrated diagrammatically in Figure 11-4.[8] Note that here β is taken to be a scalar, $L(.)$ denotes the log-likelihood function, and $\tilde{\beta}$ and $\hat{\beta}$ refer to the restricted

[8] See A. Buse, "The Likelihood Ratio, Wald, and Lagrange Multiplier Test: An Expository Note," *The American Statistician,* 36 (August 1982), pp. 153–157.

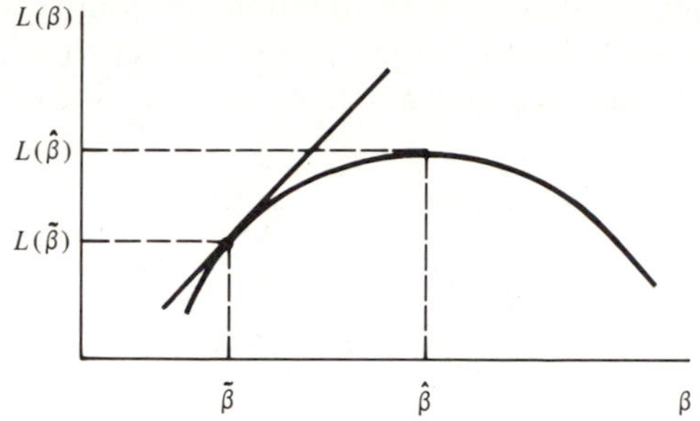

Figure 11-4

and unrestricted estimates of β, respectively, as before. The likelihood ratio test is based on the vertical distance between $L(\hat{\beta})$ and $L(\tilde{\beta})$, the W test is based on the horizontal distance between $\hat{\beta}$ and $\tilde{\beta}$, and the LM test is based on the slope of $L(\beta)$ at $\beta = \tilde{\beta}$. Asymptotically all three tests have the same asymptotic distribution and have the same power. The choice among them is typically based on convenience since W involves only unrestricted estimates, LM involves only restricted estimates, and LR involves both. In small samples the tests are likely to have different properties. In fact, if the restrictions are *linear*, then it can be shown that the values of the three test statistics are such that

$$LM < LR < W,$$

so that rejection of the null hypothesis can be favored by using LM, while acceptance of the null hypothesis can be favored by using W.[9] However, in the case of linear restrictions it is preferable to use the F-test presented in (11.20), which is valid in small samples as well. Asymptotically, the F-test is equivalent to the LR (or W or LM) test, anyway.[10]

Inequality Constraints

In many cases prior information about a regression coefficient is not given as a definite equality, but instead takes the form of an inequality. For instance, in the case of a linear consumption function, we know a priori that the coefficient attached to income (i.e., the marginal propensity to consume) lies between 0 and 1. In general, suppose the prior information about the regression coefficient β_k is

$$a \le \beta_k \le b,$$

where a and b are some known numbers, and $b > a$. Here we have the problem of estimating the coefficients of a regression equation subject to an inequality constraint on one of the regression coefficients. This kind of constraint is considerably

[9] E. R. Berndt and N. E. Savin, "Conflict Among Criteria for Testing Hypotheses in the Multivariate Regression Model," *Econometrica,* 45 (July 1977), pp. 1263–1278.

[10] See, e.g., P. Schmidt, *Econometrics* (New York: Marcel Dekker, 1976), pp. 25–26.

more awkward to incorporate into our estimation procedure than a definite equality. The simplest way is to obtain a least squares estimator of β_k by ignoring the inequality constraint altogether, and to define the constrained estimator of β_k, say, $\hat{\beta}_k$, as follows:

$$\begin{aligned} \hat{\beta}_k &= \hat{\beta}_k^{ORD} && \text{if } a \leq \hat{\beta}_k^{ORD} \leq b, \\ &= a && \text{if } \quad \hat{\beta}^{ORD} < a, \\ &= b && \text{if } \quad \hat{\beta}^{ORD} > b, \end{aligned} \tag{11.42}$$

where $\hat{\beta}_k^{ORD}$ is the ordinary, unrestricted estimator of β_k. Of course, since $\hat{\beta}_k$ is confined to a limited range, its distribution is no longer normal. However, if the prior information is correct, then as the sample size increases, the probability of getting the ordinary, unrestricted estimates outside the interval specified by the inequality becomes small, unless β_k is equal to either a or b. Thus, for large samples, we may regard the normal distribution as a reasonable approximation of the distribution of $\hat{\beta}_k$ of (11.42). Obviously, the closer the true value of β_k is to the center of the interval, the better the approximation will be. This approach to estimating the regression coefficients that are subject to inequality constraints has the disadvantage that the information about β_k is ignored in estimating the remaining regression coefficients. An alternative approach, which is free of this disadvantage, is to obtain estimators of the regression coefficient by maximizing the appropriate likelihood function subject to the inequality constaint (or constraints). This is a problem in quadratic programming, and its solution can be obtained by implementing the so-called Kuhn–Tucker conditions.[11] This solution is the same as that given in (11.42) except that if the constraint is binding (i.e., if $\hat{\beta}_k^{ORD} = a$ or b), the estimates of the regression coefficients *other than* β_k are obtained by the least squares method *after* the restriction that $\beta_k = a$ or b has been imposed. The resulting estimators are called *inequality constrained least squares* (ICLS) estimators. For example, in the regression equation

$$Y_i = \beta_1 + \beta_2 X_{i2} + \beta_3 X_{i3} + \varepsilon_i$$

with the prior restriction given as

$$a \leq \beta_2 \leq b,$$

the ICLS estimators become

$$\begin{aligned} &\tilde{\beta}_2 = \hat{\beta}_2^{ORD} && \text{and} && \tilde{\beta}_3 = \hat{\beta}_3^{ORD} && \text{if } a \leq \hat{\beta}_2^{ORD} \leq b, \\ &\tilde{\beta}_2 = a && \text{and} && \tilde{\beta}_3 = \frac{\sum (y_i' - a x_{i2}') x_{i3}'}{\sum x_{i3}'^2} && \text{if } \hat{\beta}_2^{ORD} < a, \\ &\tilde{\beta}_2 = b && \text{and} && \tilde{\beta}_3 = \frac{\sum (y_i' - b x_{i2}') x_{i3}'}{\sum x_{i3}'^2} && \text{if } \hat{\beta}_2^{ORD} > b. \end{aligned} \tag{11.43}$$

[11] See T. B. Fomby, R. C. Hill, and S. R. Johnson, *Advanced Econometric Methods* (New York: Springer-Verlag, 1984), pp. 102–106, or G. G. Judge et al., *The Theory and Practice of Econometrics,* 2nd ed. (New York: Wiley, 1985), pp. 62–69.

The sampling properties of the above ICLS estimators have recently been derived by a number of researchers.[12] In small samples the ICLS estimator is, in general, biased but has a smaller mean square error than the ordinary least squares (OLS) estimator. Asymptotically, if the true β_k lies *inside* the specified interval, then the asymptotic distribution of the ICLS estimator is the same as that of the OLS estimator. The reason for this is that if β_k lies inside the interval, then as sample size increases, more and more of the distribution of the ICLS estimator will lie inside the interval so that asymptotically the constraint becomes irrelevant. If, however, the true value of β_k is equal either to the lower or to the upper limit of the interval, the asymptotic distribution of the ICLS estimator is asymmetric and its mean square error is smaller than that of the OLS estimator. This occurs because no matter how large the sample size, there is a 50% probability that a value of the OLS estimator will fall outside the interval and, therefore, the same probability that a value of the ICLS estimator will be equal to the true value of β_k. Finally, if the inequality constraint is to be subjected to a test rather than being assumed a priori, we can use the likelihood ratio test presented in (11.32).[13]

Stochastic Restrictions

In some cases prior information takes the form of an inequality restriction that is not absolute but is subject to some uncertainty. Thus instead of asserting with certainty that

$$a \leq \beta_k \leq b,$$

we may want to declare only that this inequality is *very likely* to hold. Such a declaration, however, is a probability statement about β_k that in the context of classical statistics is rather problematic since β_k is a fixed parameter. In dealing with this type of prior information, Theil and Goldberger proposed to treat β_k *as if it were* a random variable and developed an estimation method for this case known as the *mixed estimation method.*[14] The method is based on the simplifying assumption that β_k can be viewed as a normally distributed variable with mean located at the center of the interval and with standard deviation such that the length of the interval is equal to four standard deviations. This means that we believe that the values of β_k near the middle of the interval are considerably more likely that those near the boundaries, and that the probability that β_k lies within the interval is equal to 0.9544. With these assumptions we can write

$$\text{(11.44)} \qquad \beta_k = \frac{a+b}{2} + u \qquad \text{and} \qquad (b-a) = 4\sqrt{\text{Var}(u)},$$

[12] See, e.g., M. Thomson, "Some Results on the Statistical Properties of an Inequality Constrained Least Squares Estimator in a Linear Model with Two Regressors," *Journal of Econometrics,* 19 (August 1982), pp. 215–231.

[13] For details and refinements see Judge et al., *op. cit.,* pp. 69–72.

[14] H. Theil and A. S. Goldberger, "On Pure and Mixed Statistical Estimation in Economics," *International Economic Review,* Vol. 2, January 1961, pp. 65–78.

where u has a normal distribution with mean

$$E(u) = 0$$

and variance

$$\text{Var}(u) = \frac{(b-a)^2}{16}.$$

The main idea behind the "mixed" estimation method is to combine the prior information about one or more of the regression coefficients with the information provided by the sample. This can be achieved by using the inequality restriction as if it were an additional observation, and then applying the least squares method to the "extended" sample. First, we can rewrite (11.44) as

$$\text{(11.44a)} \quad \frac{a+b}{2} = \beta_1 \times 0 + \beta_2 \times 0 + \cdots + \beta_k \times 1 + \cdots + \beta_K \times 0 + (-u),$$

which can be viewed as the $(n+1)$th observation on

$$Y_i = \beta_1 X_{i1} + \beta_2 X_{i2} + \cdots + \beta_k X_{ik} + \cdots + \beta_K X_{iK} + \varepsilon_i,$$

with $(-u)$ serving as the disturbance. However, since each ε has a variance equal to σ^2, while the variance of $(-u)$ is $(b-a)^2/16$, the $(n+1)$th observation as stated in (11.44a) would bring in heteroskedasticity. This can be easily remedied by multiplying both sides of (11.44a) by $\sigma\sqrt{16}/(b-a)$ to get

(11.44b)

$$\frac{(b+a)\sigma\sqrt{4}}{b-a} = \beta_1 \times 0 + \beta_2 \times 0 + \cdots + \beta_k \times \left[\frac{\sigma\sqrt{16}}{b-a}\right] + \cdots + \beta_K \times 0 + u^*,$$

where

$$u^* = \frac{-u\sigma\sqrt{16}}{b-a},$$

so that

$$\text{Var}(u^*) = \left[\frac{16\sigma^2}{(b-a)^2}\right] \text{Var}(u) = \sigma^2,$$

as desired. Then, the observations in the "extended" sample are

i	Y_i	X_{i1}	X_{i2}	$\cdots$	X_{ik}	$\cdots$	X_{iK}
1	Y_1	1	X_{12}	$\cdots$	X_{1k}	$\cdots$	X_{1K}
2	Y_2	1	X_{22}	$\cdots$	X_{2k}	$\cdots$	X_{2K}
$\vdots$	$\vdots$	$\vdots$	$\vdots$		$\vdots$		$\vdots$
n	Y_n	1	X_{n2}	$\cdots$	X_{nk}	$\cdots$	X_{nK}
$n+1$	$\frac{(b+a)\sigma\sqrt{4}}{b-a}$	0	0	$\cdots$	$\frac{\sigma\sqrt{16}}{b-a}$	$\cdots$	0

The value of the $(n + 1)$th observation on Y is not known because σ is not known. However, σ can be estimated by s [as defined by (10.36)] from the first n observations. As we have shown, s^2 is an unbiased, consistent, and asymptotically efficient estimator of σ^2.

In the case of two explanatory variables with the constraint

$$a \leq \beta_2 \leq b,$$

the "mixed" estimators are

(11.45)
$$\hat{\beta}_1 = \overline{Y} - \hat{\beta}_2\overline{X}_2 - \hat{\beta}_3\overline{X}_3,$$

$$\hat{\beta}_2 = \frac{m^*_{Y2}m^*_{33} - m^*_{23}\ {}_3}{m^*_{22}m^*_{33} - m^{*2}_{23}}.$$

$$\hat{\beta}_3 = \frac{m^*_{Y2}m^*_{22} - m^*_{Y2}m^*_{23}}{m^*_{22}m^*_{33} - m^{*2}_{23}}$$

where the m^*s refer to quantities based on the "extended" sample. Except for the obvious modifications, these formulas are the same as those for the ordinary, unrestricted least squares estimators given by (10.11) through (10.13). The variances of the "mixed" estimators can be estimated as follows:

(11.46)
$$\text{Est. Var}(\hat{\beta}_2) = \frac{s^2 m^*_{33}}{m^*_{22}m^*_{33} - m^{*2}_{23}}$$

$$\text{Est. Var}(\hat{\beta}_3) = \frac{s^2 m^*_{22}}{m^*_{22}m^*_{33} - m^{*2}_{23}}$$

These results have been obtained by analogy with (10.26) and (10.27). The "mixed" estimators as defined by (11.45) are consistent and asymptotically efficient under the given specification, but unbiasedness is difficult to prove because the formulas involve s^2 in a nonlinear way. Note that when the prior information is very vague, that is, when $(b - a) \rightarrow \infty$, the mixed estimators are indistinguishable from the ordinary least squares estimators. On the other hand, when the prior information is very sharp, that is, when $(b - a) \rightarrow 0$, the mixed estimator of β_2 will approach b and the mixed estimator of β_3 will be close to the ordinary least squares estimator of β_3 estimated under the restriction that $\beta_2 = b$.

The method of mixed estimation is somewhat controversial because of the ambiguity of treating β_k as a fixed parameter in the regression model and as a random variable in deriving the formula for the mixed estimator. The problem lies in the basis for the prior information. If, as noted by Theil and Goldberger, the probabilistic concept involved in (11.44) is of the "subjectivist" or "personalist" type,[15] then it is subject to the criticism that it represents "a model of introspection which is devoid of any theoretical basis."[16] Further difficulty arises in the presumption that

[15] *Ibid.*, p. 73.

[16] P. A. V. B. Swamy and J. S. Mehta, "Ridge Regression Estimation of the Rotterdam Model," *Journal of Econometrics*, Vol. 22, August 1983, p. 369.

the prior information is "unbiased" in the sense that the mean of β_k in (11.44) lies exactly in the center of the interval. It is, of course, possible to view the mixed estimator as a convenient approach that is not to be judged on the basis of its assumptions but solely on the results. The method of mixed estimation is noncontroversial when the prior information is an unbiased (and/or consistent) estimator of β_k obtained from a previous data-based statistical analysis. In this case we have

$$\hat{\beta}_k^* = \beta_k + u^*,$$

where $\hat{\beta}_k^*$ is the prior estimator obtained from an earlier sample and u^* is its sampling error whose estimated variance is also presumably available. Then, by reference to (11.44), $\hat{\beta}_k^*$ can be used in place of $(a+b)/2$, u^* in place of u, and the estimate of the variance of $\hat{\beta}_k^*$ in place of $(b-a)^2/16$.

EXAMPLE We may illustrate the method of "mixed" estimation by an example provided by Theil.[17] It is assumed that the consumption of textiles in the Netherlands can be represented as

$$y_t = \beta_1 + \beta_2 X_{t2} + \beta_3 X_{t3} + \varepsilon_t,$$

where y = log volume of textile consumption per capita, X_2 = log real income per capita, X_3 = log relative price of textiles, and t = time in years. All logarithms are common logarithms. The disturbance is assumed to satisfy all classical assumptions and to be uncorrelated with the explanatory variables. The data for the years 1923–1939 (17 observations) are given in Table 11-2. The results of ordinary least squares estimation are

$$\underset{}{y_t} = \underset{(0.306)}{1.374} + \underset{(0.156)}{1.143}\, X_{t2} - \underset{(0.036)}{0.829}\, X_{t3} + e_t.$$

The analyst presumably believes that in all likelihood the income elasticity of demand for textiles (β_2) is not outside the interval from 0.7 to 1.3, and that the price elasticity of demand for textiles (β_3) is not outside the interval from -1.0 to -0.4. In the language of mixed estimation these beliefs can be expressed as

$$\beta_2 \sim N(1.0; 0.15^2) \qquad \text{and} \qquad \beta_3 \sim N(-0.7; 0.15^2).$$

The original set of 17 observations is then extended by these two additional pieces of information so that now n = 19. The application of the mixed estimation procedure leads to the following revised results:

$$Y_t = \underset{(0.203)}{1.467} + \underset{(0.103)}{1.089}\, X_{t2} - \underset{(0.035)}{0.821}\, X_{t3} + e_t^*.$$

As can be seen, the incorporation of the prior information into the estimation procedure has resulted in bringing the estimated coefficients closer to the prior means.

The Effect of Restrictions on R^2 and on the Variance of the Forecast Error

In the case where the restricted parameters are exactly identified in terms of the unrestricted coefficients, the restricted estimates lead to the same sample regression

[17] H. Theil, *Principles of Econometrics* (New York: Wiley, 1971), pp. 102 and 347–350.

Table 11-2

Year	Volume of textile consumption per capita (1)	Real income per capita (2)	Relative price of textile (3)
	Index base 1925 = 100.		
1923	99.2	96.7	101.0
1924	99.0	98.1	100.1
1925	100.0	100.0	100.0
1926	111.6	104.9	90.6
1927	122.2	104.9	86.5
1928	117.6	109.5	89.7
1929	121.1	110.8	90.6
1930	136.0	112.3	82.8
1931	154.2	109.3	70.1
1932	153.6	105.3	65.4
1933	158.5	101.7	61.3
1934	140.6	95.4	62.5
1935	136.2	96.4	63.6
1936	168.0	97.6	52.6
1937	154.3	102.4	59.7
1938	149.0	101.6	59.5
1939	165.5	103.8	61.3

equation as the unrestricted estimates. This means that the value of R^2 and the forecast of the value of the dependent variable are the same for both sets of estimates. However, if the restricted estimation is carried out under conditions of overidentification or with inequality constraints, then the sample regression line based on the restricted estimates will be different from the sample regression line based on the unrestricted estimates. Since the unrestricted least squares estimates minimize the sum of squares of the residuals, they lead to the maximum attainable value of R^2. This necessarily implies that the value of R^2 for the restricted sample regression equation will be lower than, or equal to, the value of R^2 for the unrestricted sample regression equation. This fact has sometimes been used as an argument for supposing that a forecast of the value of the dependent variable based on the unrestricted estimates is better than one based on the restricted estimates. If we interpret the word "better" as meaning "having a smaller (or equal) variance of the forecast error," then the argument is fallacious. We shall prove this for the case of overidentification under linear restrictions, but the proof could be extended to nonlinear restrictions as well, at least asymptotically.

Consider, for instance, the regression equation (11.22), which we have used to illustrate overidentification with linear restrictions. The equation was presented as

$$Y_i = \alpha_1 + \alpha_2 X_{i2} + (1 - \alpha_2)X_{i3} + \varepsilon_i,$$

with the unrestricted version given by (11.22a) as

$$Y_i = \beta_1 + \beta_2 X_{i2} + \beta_3 X_{i3} + \varepsilon_i .$$

Suppose now that we wish to forecast the value of Y for some given values of the two explanatory variables, say X_{02} and X_{03}. Using the unrestricted regression equation, we would forecast the value of Y by, say, $\hat{Y}_0$, defined as

$$\hat{Y}_0 = \hat{\beta}_1 + \hat{\beta}_2 X_{02} + \hat{\beta}_3 X_{03},$$

where the $\hat{\beta}$s represent the unrestricted least squares estimates of the βs. Using the formula (10.58), we can determine the variance of the forecast error of $\hat{Y}_0$ as

$$(11.47)\quad E(\hat{Y}_0 - Y_0)^2 = \sigma^2 + \frac{\sigma^2}{n} + (X_{02} - \bar{X}_2)^2 \mathrm{Var}(\hat{\beta}_2) + (X_{03} - \bar{X})^2 \mathrm{Var}(\hat{\beta}_3)$$

$$+ 2(X_{02} - \bar{X}_2)(X_{03} - \bar{X}_3)\mathrm{Cov}(\hat{\beta}_2, \hat{\beta}_3)$$

$$= \sigma^2 \left[1 + \frac{1}{n} + \frac{(X_{02} - \bar{X}_2)^2 m_{33} + (X_{03} - \bar{X}_3)^2 m_{22}}{m_{22} m_{33} - m_{23}^2} - \frac{2(X_{02} - \bar{X}_2)(X_{03} - \bar{X}_3) m_{23}}{m_{22} m_{33} - m_{23}^2} \right].$$

On the other hand, if we use the restricted regression equation for forecasting the value of Y, we use $\tilde{Y}_0$ defined as

$$\tilde{Y}_0 = \hat{\alpha}_1 + \hat{\alpha}_2 X_{02} + (1 - \hat{\alpha}_2) X_{03},$$

where the $\hat{\alpha}$s represent the restricted least squares estimates of the αs. The variance of the forecast error in this case is

$$(11.48)\quad E(\tilde{Y}_0 - Y_0)^2 = E[(\tilde{Y}_0 - X_{03}) - (Y_0 - X_{03})]^2$$

$$= \sigma^2 + \frac{\sigma^2}{n} + [(X_{02} - X_{03}) - (\bar{X}_2 - \bar{X}_3)]^2 \mathrm{Var}(\hat{\alpha}_2)$$

$$= \sigma^2 \left[1 + \frac{1}{n} + \frac{(X_{02} - \bar{X}_2)^2 + (X_{03} - \bar{X}_3)^2}{m_{22} + m_{33} - 2m_{23}} - \frac{2(X_{02} - \bar{X}_2)(X_{03} - \bar{X}_3)}{m_{22} + m_{33} - 2m_{23}} \right].$$

Let us now compare (11.47) with (11.48). The difference between the two is

$$(11.49)\quad E(\hat{Y}_0 - Y_0)^2 - E(\tilde{Y}_0 - Y_0)^2$$

$$= \sigma^2 \left[\frac{(X_{02} - \bar{X}_2)^2 m_{33} + (X_{03} - \bar{X}_3)^2 m_{22} - 2(X_{02} - \bar{X}_2)(X_{03} - \bar{X}_3) m_{23}}{m_{22} m_{33} - m_{23}^2} - \frac{(X_{02} - \bar{X}_2)^2 + (X_{03} - \bar{X}_3)^2 - 2(X_{02} - \bar{X}_2)(X_{03} - \bar{X}_3)}{m_{22} + m_{33} - 2m_{23}} \right]$$

$$= \sigma^2 \left\{ \frac{[(X_{02} - \bar{X}_2)(m_{33} - m_{23}) + (X_{03} - \bar{X}_3)(m_{22} - m_{23})]^2}{(m_{22} m_{33} - m_{23}^2)(m_{22} + m_{33} - 2m_{23})} \right\}.$$

This expression is clearly positive (or zero), which indicates that the variance of the forecast error for the unrestricted predictor $\hat{Y}_0$ is larger than, or at best equal to, the variance of the forecast error for the restricted predictor $\tilde{Y}_0$. This means that the restricted regression equation leads to a better forecasting procedure than the unrestricted regression equation.

The Role of Prior Restrictions in Estimation

A useful way of ending this section may be by making a few remarks on the relevance of prior restrictions in estimation. Prior restrictions on the regression coefficients represent information about the population regression equation. If this information is correct, then we may increase the efficiency of our estimators by incorporating this information into our estimation procedure. The extent of this increase in efficiency depends on the type of information (i.e., how *specific* it is) and on the variances of the unconstrained estimators, assuming that these variances exist and that the unconstrained estimators are squared-error consistent. For instance, suppose the prior restriction is in the form of a statement that a given regression coefficient, say, β, is positive. Then, if the variance of the unconstrained estimator of β is small, we may get samples with a negative estimate of β only very rarely. Therefore, the restriction may not, for all practical purposes, be "restrictive" at all. In this case, the value of the prior information may be negligible. This brings up another aspect of prior information—namely, that its value diminishes with the size of the sample. This is because the variances of the unconstrained estimators will, in general, decrease as the sample size increases. This is true regardless of how specific the restrictions are. For example, even such a specific restriction as one that confines β to a given number is not of much value to us if, in fact, the estimates of β are highly concentrated in the near vicinity of the true value of the parameter. In the limit (i.e., when $n \to \infty$), prior information is of no more use. However, if the estimates tend to be highly concentrated around a value different from that specified by the restriction, then either our prior information is false, or the model is misspecified and the claim that the unconstrained estimator is consistent is not justified. Unfortunately, in economics our samples are typically small and generation of additional observations is severely limited, so that prior information is highly valuable. For this reason its use—frequently neglected in applied econometric work—ought to be strongly encouraged. If the restrictions are in doubt, though, and we carry out a *test* to check their validity, we have to worry about the subsequent inferential procedure because of the possible pretest bias.

11-3 Nonlinear Models

The models that we have considered so far have, with a few minor exceptions, all been characterized by linear regression equations. However, this is not as restrictive as it might at first appear for the following reasons. First, all the results for the linear regression models derived in the preceding chapters may apply within any modification to regression models that are nonlinear with respect to the variables but linear with respect to the parameters to be estimated. Second, regression models that are nonlinear with respect to the variables *as well as* with respect to the parameters to be estimated can be analyzed by using many of the basic principles and results derived in connection with purely linear models. Nonlinear regression models can thus be classified into two groups according to whether they are or are not linear with respect to the parameters to be estimated. We may call the first type "models that are intrinsically linear," and the second type "models that are intrinsically nonlinear." We shall discuss each type separately. In addition, we shall also consider the problem of how to test for linearity in the case where the functional form of the regression equation is in doubt.

Intrinsically Linear Models

A nonlinear model that is intrinsically linear is, as indicated, *nonlinear* with respect to the variables but *linear* with respect to the parameters to be estimated. The basic common characteristic of such models is that they can be converted into ordinary linear models by a suitable transformation of the variables. Frequently, such a transformation amounts to nothing more than relabeling one or more of the variables. We have already used some of these models without even having to pause over the fact that some of the variables entered the regression equation in a nonlinear way. Our present intention is to consider intrinsically linear models in a systematic way and with some attention to detail. As the first case, we take a model in which the regressors are represented by a *power series* in X_i:

$$Y_i = \beta_1 + \beta_2 X_i + \beta_3 X_i^2 + \cdots + \beta_K X_i^{K-1} + \varepsilon_i, \tag{11.50}$$

where X is nonstochastic and bounded, and ε satisfies all the assumptions of the classical normal linear regression model. For instance, the specification may call first for an increase and then for a decrease in $E(Y)$ in response to increases in X, as in the relationship between income and age of an individual. In this case, the power series would be given by a parabola

$$Y_i = \beta_1 + \beta_2 X_i + \beta_2 X_i^2 + \varepsilon_i,$$

as illustrated in Figure 11-5. But whatever the degree of the polynomial in (11.50), the equation can be rewritten as

$$Y_i = \beta_1 + \beta_2 Z_{i2} + \beta_3 Z_{i3} + \cdots + \beta_K Z_{iK} + \varepsilon_i, \tag{11.50a}$$

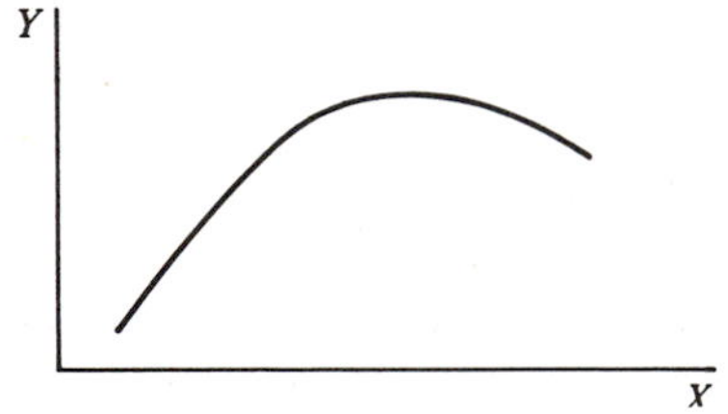

Figure 11-5

where $Z_2 = X, Z_3 = X^2, \ldots, Z_K = X^{K-1}$. Then, if the number of observations exceeds K, the ordinary least squares estimators of the regression coefficients of (11.50a) will have the desirable properties. However, the Zs will often be highly correlated, so that the variances of the estimated regression coefficients may be quite large. One nice feature of the power function (11.50) or its equivalent (11.50a) is that we can easily test the hypothesis that the degree of the polynomial is less than $(K-1)$. For example, we may wish to test the hypothesis that the regression equation is linear against the alternative hypothesis that the regression equation is represented by a polynomial of degree $(K-1)$. The formulation would be

$$H_0: \quad \beta_3 = \beta_4 = \cdots = \beta_K = 0,$$

$$H_A: \quad H_0 \text{ is not true.}$$

The relevant test procedure is described in Section 10-2, with the test statistic given by the formula (10.46).

The preceding discussion is of some relevance not only for the regression models in which the explanatory variable (or variables) enters in the form of a power function, but also for any nonlinear regression model in general. The reason is that any function $f(x)$ that is continuous and has a continuous pth derivative can be written as

$$f(x) = f(a) + (x-a)f'(a) + \frac{(x-a)^2}{2!}f''(a) + \frac{(x-a)^3}{3!}f'''(a) + \cdots + \frac{(x-a)^p}{p!}f^{(p)}(a) + R_{p+1}, \tag{11.51}$$

where a is any fixed number in the domain of X and

$$f(a) = f(x)\Big|_{x=a},$$

$$f'(a) = \frac{df(x)}{dx}\Big|_{x=a},$$

$$f''(a) = \frac{d^2f(x)}{dx}\Big|_{x=a},$$

$$\vdots$$

$$R_{p+1} = \text{remainder}.$$

The series given in (11.51) is called the *Taylor series expansion* of $f(x)$ around the point $x = a$. If p is sufficiently large, the remainder R_{p+1} will be small. Therefore, by disregarding R_{p+1} we obtain an approximation of $f(x)$, which we can make as close as we like by a suitable choice of p.

EXAMPLE 1 Let $f(x) = b_0 + b_1x + b_2x^2 + b_3x^3$, and let $p = 3$. Suppose we expand $f(x)$ around $x = 0$. Then we have

$$f(0) = b_0,$$

$$f'(0) = (b_1 + 2b_2x + 3b_3x^2)_{x=0} = b_1,$$

$$f''(0) = (2b_2 + 6b_3x)_{x=0} = 2b_2,$$

$$f'''(0) = 6b_3,$$

so that

$$f(x) = b_0 + (x-0)b_1 + \frac{(x-0)^2}{2}2b_2 + \frac{(x-0)^3}{6}6b_3$$

$$= b_0 + b_1x + b_2x^2 + b_3x^3,$$

which is exactly correct.

EXAMPLE 2 Let $f(x) = e^{bx}$, $p = 3$, and $a = 0$. Then we have

$$f(0) = 1,$$

$$f'(0) = (be^{bx})_{x=0} = b,$$

$$f''(0) = (b^2e^{bx})_{x=0} = b^2,$$

$$f'''(0) = (b^3e^{bx})_{x=0} = b^3,$$

so that
$$f(x) \approx 1 + bx + \left[\frac{b^2}{2}\right]x^2 + \left[\frac{b^3}{6}\right]x^3.$$

If, for instance, $b = 1$, then the approximate values of $f(x)$ for various values of x are

x	Exact $f(x)$	Approximate $f(x)$
0	1.0000	1.0000
0.5	1.6487	1.6458
1	2.7183	2.6667
2	7.3891	6.3333
3	20.0855	13.0000

As shown, the approximation becomes poorer as we move away from the value around which the series is being expanded.

The Taylor series expansion can be extended to apply to a function of more than one variable. In particular, the expansion for *two* variables is given by

$$(11.52)\quad f(x, z) = f(a, b) + f_x(a, b)(x-a) + f_z(a, b)(z-b)$$
$$+ \frac{1}{2!}[f_{xx}(a, b)(x-a)^2 + 2f_{xz}(a, b)(x-a)(z-b)$$
$$+ f_{zz}(a, b)(z-b)^2] + \cdots,$$

where
$$f_x(a, b) = \frac{\partial f(x, z)}{\partial x}\bigg|_{\substack{x=a\\z=b}},$$

$$f_z(a, b) = \frac{\partial f(x, z)}{\partial x}\bigg|_{\substack{x=a\\z=b}},$$

$$f_{xx}(a, b) = \frac{\partial^2 f(x, z)}{\partial x^2}\bigg|_{\substack{x=a\\z=b}},$$

$$f_{xz}(a, b) = \frac{\partial^2 f(x, z)}{\partial x \partial z}\bigg|_{\substack{x=a\\z=b}},$$

$$f_{zz}(a, b) = \frac{\partial^2 f(x, z)}{\partial z^2}\bigg|_{\substack{x=a\\z=b}},$$

etc.

The Taylor series expansion is often used to approximate a nonlinear function by a linear one. This is typically done by expanding the series around the sample mean of the explanatory variable (or variables) and dropping terms of order higher than one. In doing this, though, one has to be aware of the fact that the parameters estimated by the ordinary least squares method do not necessarily correspond to the parameters of the Taylor series expansion around the sample mean.[18] This is illustrated in Figure 11-6. The implication is that the "OLS estimates do not necessarily provide reliable information about the local properties (derivatives, elasticities) of unknown functions."[19]

Consider now a regression equation in which the change in $E(Y)$ corresponding to a unit change in X_j depends on the level of X_k. Formally, suppose the mean value of the dependent variable is some function of two nonstochastic explanatory variables X_2 and X_3,

$$E(Y_i) = f(X_{i2}, X_{i3}),$$

such that

$$\frac{\partial E(Y_i)}{\partial X_{i2}} = g(X_{i3})$$

and
$$\frac{\partial E(Y_i)}{\partial X_{i3}} = h(X_{i2}),$$

[18] See H. White, "Using Least Squares to Approximate Unknown Regression Functions," *International Economic Review,* 21 (February 1980), pp. 149–170.

[19] *Ibid.,* p. 152.

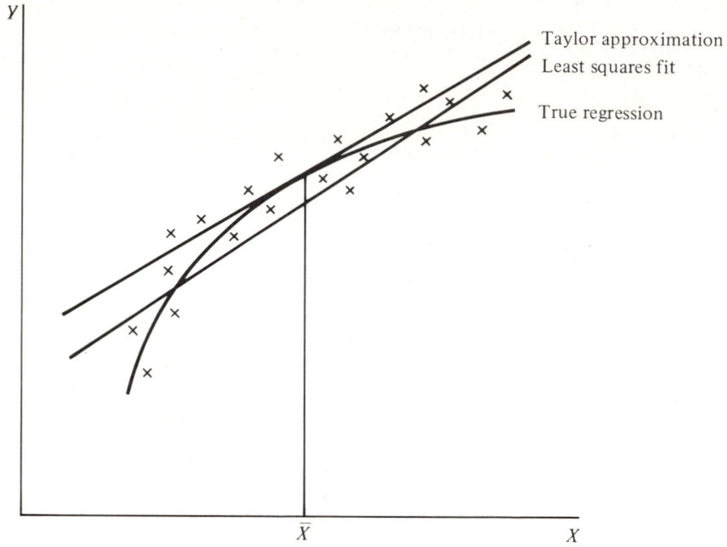

Figure 11-6

where $g(X_3)$ and $h(X_2)$ are some functions whose mathematical form is specified a priori. There are many situations in which such a model is appropriate. For example, in estimations of Engel curves from cross-section data, family expenditure on a given commodity is frequently considered to be dependent on family income and family size. It may be reasonable to expect that families of different sizes respond to a given change in income in a different way, and that families in different income brackets respond differently to a change in family size. The simplest formulation of such a model is obtained by introducing a so-called *interaction term,* defined as a multiple of the product of the two explanatory variables, into the linear regression equation:

(11.53) $$Y_i = \beta_1 + \beta_2 X_{i2} + \beta_3 X_{i3} + \beta_4 X_{i2} X_{i3} + \varepsilon_i .$$

In this model

$$\frac{\partial E(Y_i)}{\partial X_{i2}} = \beta_2 + \beta_4 X_{i3},$$

and

$$\frac{\partial E(Y_i)}{\partial X_{i3}} = \beta_3 + \beta_4 X_{i2}.$$

The functions $g(X_3)$ and $h(X_2)$ are both linear functions of the respective variables and have a common slope equal to β_4. Equation (11.53) is intrinsically linear because we can write $X_2 X_3 = X_4$.

The presence of the interaction terms in a regression equation has an important implication for the test of the hypothesis that a given explanatory variable is not relevant in the regression model in question, i.e., that it does not influence $E(Y)$.

When there are interaction terms in the equation, then any given explanatory variable may be represented by not one but several regressors. The hypothesis that this variable does not influence $E(Y)$ means that the coefficients of *all* regressors involving this variable are jointly zero. Therefore, the appropriate test of such a hypothesis is the F test described by (10.46). Usually we are also interested in testing the hypothesis that the change in $E(Y)$ corresponding to a unit increase in X_k is constant. This is equivalent to testing the hypothesis that the coefficients of the interaction "variables" are equal to zero.

EXAMPLE The use of the multiple regression model of Section 10-1 was illustrated by estimating the demand for oranges as a linear function of price and the amount spent on advertising. Let us now modify this example by specifying that the regression equation should also include the interaction term. That is, let

$$Y_i = \beta_1 + \beta_2 X_{i2} + \beta_3 X_{i3} + \beta_4 X_{i2} X_{i3} + \varepsilon_i,$$

where Y = quantity of oranges sold, X_2 = price, and X_3 = advertising expenditure. The details for the twelve available sample observations are given in Table 10-1. The results of the basic calculations are

$$\begin{aligned}
&m_{22} = 2250, \\
&m_{23} = -54, \qquad m_{33} = 4.8573, \\
&m_{24} = 10{,}237.5, \qquad m_{34} = 15.6854, \qquad m_{44} = 66{,}503.85, \\
&m_{Y2} = -3550, \qquad m_{Y3} = 125.2500, \qquad m_{Y4} = -13{,}542.50, \\
&m_{YY} = 6300.
\end{aligned}$$

(The subscript "4" denotes the interaction "variable" X_2X_3.) The estimated regression equation then is

$$\underset{}{Y_i = -93.140 + \underset{(0.832)}{1.508}X_{i2} + \underset{(9.803)}{43.990}X_{i3} - \underset{(0.131)}{0.446}X_{i2}X_{i3} + e_i,} \qquad R^2 = 0.984.$$

These results can be used for testing several interesting hypotheses. First, we shall test the hypothesis that X_2 does not influence $E(Y)$. Formally,

$$H_0: \quad \beta_2 = \beta_4 = 0,$$

$$H_A: \quad H_0 \text{ is not true.}$$

According to the test described in (10.46), the acceptance region for, say, the 5% level of significance, is

$$\frac{(\text{SSR}_Q - \text{SSR}_K)/(Q-K)}{\text{SSE}_Q/(n-Q)} \leq F_{Q-K,\, n-Q,\, 0.05}.$$

In this problem, we have $n = 12$, $Q = 4$, and $K = 2$, so that $F_{2,\,8,\,0.05} = 4.46$, as shown in the table of the F distribution. Now, from our sample we have

$$\text{SSR}_Q = 1.508 \times (-3550) + 43.990 \times 125.25 + (-0.446) \times (-13{,}542.5) = 6196.3,$$

$$\text{SSE}_Q = 6300 - 6196.3 = 103.7.$$

The value of SSR_K is to be obtained by regressing Y on X_3 alone, i.e., by applying the least squares estimation method to

$$Y_i = \beta_1^* + \beta_3^* X_{i3} + \varepsilon_i^*.$$

Then,

$$SSR_K = \hat{\beta}_3^* m_{Y3} = \left[\frac{m_{Y3}}{m_{33}}\right] m_{Y3} = \frac{125.25^2}{4.8573} = 3229.7.$$

Therefore,

$$\frac{(SSR_Q - SSR_K)/(Q-K)}{SSE_Q/(n-Q)} = \frac{(6196.3 - 3229.7)/(4-2)}{103.7/(12-4)} = 114.4,$$

which is considerably greater than the critical value 4.46. Therefore we reject the hypothesis that X_2 has no influence on $E(Y)$, and we do so even though the t ratio for the coefficient of X_2 is less than 2.0. Next, we shall test the same hypothesis with respect to X_3. The acceptance region is exactly the same as for the first test, and so are all the other calculations except for SSR_K. The value of SSR_K will be obtained by regressing Y on X_2, that is, by estimating the coefficients of

$$Y_i = \beta_1^{**} + \beta_2^{**} X_{i2} + \varepsilon_i^{**}.$$

Then, we have

$$SSR_K = \hat{\beta}_2^{**} m_{Y2} = \left[\frac{m_{Y2}}{m_{22}}\right] m_{Y2} = \frac{(-3550)^2}{2250} = 5601.1.$$

The value of the appropriate test statistic then becomes

$$\frac{(SSR_Q - SSR_K)/(Q-K)}{SSE_Q/(n-Q)} = \frac{(6196.3 - 5601.1)/(4-2)}{103.7/(12-4)} = 23.0,$$

which again is larger than the critical value, 4.46. Finally, we shall test the hypothesis that the coefficient attached to the interaction "variable" X_2X_3 is zero; i.e.,

$$H_0: \quad \beta_4 = 0,$$

$$H_A: \quad \beta_4 \neq 0.$$

The tabulated t value for a two-sided test at the 5% level of significance and with eight degrees of freedom is 2.306. Therefore, the 95% acceptance region is

$$-2.306 \leq \frac{\hat{\beta}_4}{s_{\hat{\beta}_4}} \leq 2.306.$$

Since in our case

$$\frac{\hat{\beta}_4}{s_{\hat{\beta}_4}} = \frac{-0.446}{0.131} = -3.405,$$

the null hypothesis has to be rejected.

Another intrinsically linear model involves a regression equation that is linear in terms of the logarithms of the variables. This is known as the *multiplicative model* and can be described as

$$Y_i = \alpha X_{i2}^{\beta_2} X_{i3}^{\beta_3} \cdots X_{iK}^{\beta_K} e^{\varepsilon_i}, \tag{11.54}$$

where $e = 2.718$. . . . A notable feature of this model is the fact that the elasticity of $E(Y)$ with respect to any of the explanatory variables is constant, i.e., that

$$\frac{\partial E(Y_i)}{\partial X_{ik}} \frac{X_{ik}}{E(Y_i)} = \beta_k \qquad (k = 2, 3, \ldots, K).$$

An example of such a model is the Cobb–Douglas production function. By taking logarithms (to base e) of both sides of (11.54), we obtain

$$\log Y_i = \log \alpha + \beta_2 \log X_{i2} + \beta_3 \log X_{i3} + \cdots + \beta_K \log X_{iK} + \varepsilon_i, \tag{11.54a}$$

which can be written as

$$Y_i^* = \alpha^* + \beta_2 X_{i2}^* + \beta_3 X_{i3}^* + \cdots + \beta_K X_{iK}^* + \varepsilon_i, \tag{11.54b}$$

where the starred symbols represent the logarithms of the unstarred counterparts.

Equation (11.54b) is clearly an ordinary linear multiple regression equation, and its estimation can proceed along the usual lines. Two points are worth mentioning, though. First, equation (11.54b) is linear with respect to α^* and the βs, but not with respect to α. Thus, if the assumptions of the classical normal linear regression model are satisfied, the ordinary least squares estimators of $\alpha^*, \beta_2, \beta_3, \ldots, \beta_K$ will have the desirable properties. Since

$$\alpha^* = \log \alpha,$$

the estimator of α will be given by

$$\hat{\alpha} = e^{\hat{\alpha}^*}.$$

While $\hat{\alpha}$ inherits all the desirable asymptotic properties from $\hat{\alpha}^*$, the small-sample properties of $\hat{\alpha}^*$, and in particular its unbiasedness, do not carry over to $\hat{\alpha}$. A closely related problem is that while the least squares predictor of log Y, say, $\widehat{\log Y}$, based on (11.54a) is unbiased, the derived predictor of Y,

$$\hat{Y} = e^{\widehat{\log Y}},$$

is biased. The prediction bias can be reduced by using $\tilde{Y}$ defined as

$$\tilde{Y} = e^{\widehat{\log Y} + s^2/2}, \tag{11.55}$$

where s^2 is an unbiased estimator of the variance of ε_i in (11.54a) or (11.54b).[20] Second, if we assume that ε_i is normally distributed with zero mean and variance σ^2, then we can write

$$Y_i = \alpha X_{i2}^{\beta_2} X_{i3}^{\beta_3} \cdots X_{iK}^{\beta_K} \eta_i$$

[20] See K. M. Dadkhah, "Confidence Interval for Predictions from a Logarithmic Model," *Review of Economics and Statistics,* 66 (August 1984), pp. 527–528.

where $\eta_i = e^{\varepsilon_i}$. Thus we are assuming that the *logarithm* of η_i is normally distributed with mean zero and variance σ^2. The distribution of η_i itself would be called *log-normal.* However, if the regression equation were specified as

$$Y_i = \alpha X_{i2}^{\beta_2} X_{i3}^{\beta_3} \cdots X_{iK}^{\beta_K} + \varepsilon_i,$$

no transformation of the variables could lead to a regression equation that would be linear in the βs, so the equation would have to be classified as intrinsically nonlinear.[21]

There exist many other nonlinear models that can be converted to linear models by a suitable transformation. In all of these models the problem of estimating the regression parameters is simplified by our ability to reduce the models to linearity. The only aspect of the transformation that deserves careful attention concerns the stochastic disturbance. In many cases the stochastic disturbance is introduced into the relationship in such a way that the linear transformation follows without any difficulty. However, the specification of the model—including the manner in which the disturbance is introduced—should not be dictated by mathematical or computational convenience. It is important to keep in mind that such a specification represents a commitment on our part concerning our prior knowledge and beliefs about the relationship that is being modeled. Since the stochastic disturbance determines the distribution of the dependent variable for any set of fixed values of the explanatory variables, its role in the regression model is quite crucial. Clearly, we need to be aware of the implications of the particular specification put forward. For instance, in the case of the Cobb–Douglas production function described by (11.54), the particular way in which the disturbance is introduced into the equation implies that the distribution of outputs for any given set of inputs is log-normal, i.e., skewed. This, then, must be our view of the world if we wish to insist on that given specification.

Intrinsically Nonlinear Models

Let us now turn to the *intrinsically nonlinear models,* i.e., models that are nonlinear with respect to the variables as well as with respect to the parameters. There is, of course, a great variety of these models; our discussion will be confined to a few interesting cases. Consider the relationship

$$Y_i = \alpha X_{i2}^{\beta_2} X_{i3}^{\beta_3} + \varepsilon_i, \qquad (11.56)$$

which is essentially the same as the multiplicative model (11.54) *except* that the disturbance enters as an additive rather than a multiplicative term. A relationship of this sort could, for instance, describe a demand function for some commodity,

[21] For a test to distinguish between these two kinds of specification of the disturbance term see D. Leech, "Testing the Error Specification in Nonlinear Regression," *Econometrica,* 43 (July 1975), pp. 719–725.

with Y standing for quantity demanded, X_2 for price, and X_3 for income. Since

$$\frac{\partial E(Y_i)}{\partial X_{i2}} \frac{X_{i2}}{E(Y_i)} = \beta_2$$

and

$$\frac{\partial E(Y_i)}{\partial X_{i3}} \frac{X_{i3}}{E(Y_i)} = \beta_3,$$

β_2 and β_3 would represent the price and the income elasticity, respectively. Now, as we pointed out earlier, there exists no transformation that would convert (11.56) into a linear relationship with respect to the parameters. However, if X_2 and X_3 are nonstochastic—or, if stochastic, independent of ε—and if ε satisfies all the assumptions of the classical normal regression model, we can use the maximum likelihood method of estimation. The likelihood function for a sample of size n is

$$(11.57) \qquad L = -\frac{n}{2} \log 2\pi - \frac{n}{2} \log \sigma^2 - \frac{1}{2\sigma^2} \sum_{i=1}^{n} (Y_i - \alpha X_{i2}^{\beta_2} X_{i3}^{\beta_3})^2.$$

The next step is to differentiate L with respect to α, β_2, β_3, and σ^2 and put the respective derivatives equal to zero. This leads to a system of four equations, which are nonlinear with respect to the four unknowns. An algebraic solution of this system is difficult, but there may be no difficulty about getting a solution using a computer, since programs for nonlinear estimation are available. These programs are essentially based on a systematic "trial-and-error" approach; i.e., the computer is asked to calculate the value of L for a number of different combinations of the parameter values until the maximum value of L is found. The values of the parameters corresponding to this maximum value of L are the desired maximum likelihood estimates and have the desirable asymptotic properties.

Another interesting intrinsically nonlinear model is the *logistic model,* represented as

$$(11.58) \qquad Y_i = \frac{\gamma}{1 + e^{\alpha + \beta X_i}} + \varepsilon_i \qquad (\gamma > 0, \quad \beta < 0).$$

In this case, the population regression line is given by a logistic "growth curve" as shown in Figure 11-7. Note that $E(Y)$ is confined to the values between 0 and γ. The

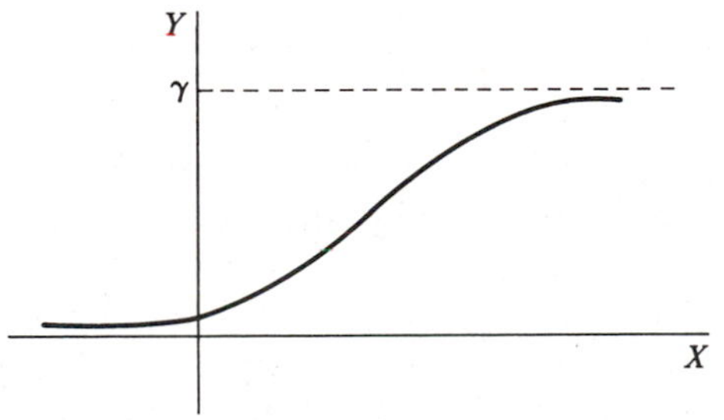

Figure 11-7

values of Y are, of course, not restricted. Again, we can obtain the maximum likelihood estimates of the parameters of (11.58) using a computer. The estimation problem becomes seemingly simplified if the specification of the logistic curve is

$$Y_i = \frac{\gamma}{1 + e^{\alpha + \beta X_i + \varepsilon_i}}, \tag{11.59}$$

since in this case we can write

$$\log\left(\frac{\gamma}{Y_i} - 1\right) = \alpha + \beta X_i + \varepsilon_i. \tag{11.59a}$$

The apparent simplification is because now only one parameter, γ, enters the regression equation in a nonlinear way. However, it should be noted that the model in (11.59) is markedly different from that given by (11.58). In particular, in (11.58) the values of Y for any given value of X can extend from $-\infty$ to $+\infty$, whereas in (11.59) the values of Y are confined to the interval from 0 to γ. This implies that, in (11.59), the dependent variable Y cannot have a normal distribution.

As a final illustration of an intrinsically nonlinear model, we consider the so-called CES (constant elasticity of substitution) production function represented as

$$Q_i = \gamma[\delta K_i^{-\rho} + (1 - \delta)L_i^{-\rho}]^{-\nu/\rho} e^{\varepsilon_i} \qquad (\gamma > 0;\ 1 > \delta > 0;\ \nu > 0;\ \rho \geq -1), \tag{11.60}$$

where Q = output, K = capital input, and L = labor input. The parameter γ is known as the "efficiency parameter," the parameter δ as the "distribution parameter," the parameter ν as the "returns-to-scale parameter," and the parameter ρ as the "substitution parameter." This type of production function has gained a great degree of popularity because it subsumes a number of other more specialized production functions. This degree of generality is achieved through the "substitution parameter" ρ, since the CES production function reduces to the Cobb–Douglas production function for $\rho = 0$, and to the "fixed-proportions" production function for $\rho \rightarrow \infty$. By taking logarithms (to base e) of both sides of (11.60), we obtain

$$\log Q_i = \log \gamma - \frac{\nu}{\rho} \log[\delta K_i^{-\rho} + (1 - \delta)L_i^{-\rho}] + \varepsilon_i. \tag{11.60a}$$

If K and L are nonstochastic—or, if stochastic, independent of ε—we can set up the likelihood function in the usual way and obtain the maximum likelihood estimates of γ, δ, ν, and ρ using a computer.

An alternative and a considerably more simple estimation of the parameters of the CES production function is possible if we replace (11.60a) by its approximation that is linear with respect to ρ. By using Taylor series formula (11.51), expanding log Q around $\rho = 0$, and dropping the terms involving powers of ρ higher than one, we obtain[22]

$$\text{(11.60b)} \qquad \log Q_i = \log \gamma + v\delta \log K_i + v(1-\delta)\log L_i - \tfrac{1}{2}\rho v\delta(1-\delta)[\log K_i - \log L_i]^2 + \varepsilon_i.$$

Note that the right-hand side of (11.60b) can be conveniently separated into two parts, one corresponding to the Cobb–Douglas production function and one representing a "correction" due to the departure of ρ from zero. The latter part, given by the term $-[\rho v\delta(1-\delta)/2][\log K_i - \log L_i]^2$, will disappear if $\rho = 0$. The estimation of the parameters of (11.60b) is the same as in the case of estimation with nonlinear restrictions under exact identification. The "unrestricted" version of (11.60b) is

$$\text{(11.60c)} \qquad \log Q_i = \beta_1 + \beta_2 \log K_i + \beta_3 \log L_i + \beta_4[\log K_i - \log L_i]^2 + \varepsilon_i,$$

which represents an intrinsically linear regression model. If the estimate of β_4 is not significantly different from zero, we would reject the CES model in favor of the Cobb–Douglas model. The parameters of (11.60b) are related to the coefficients of (11.60c) as follows:

$$\gamma = e^{\beta_1},$$

$$\delta = \frac{\beta_2}{\beta_2 + \beta_3},$$

$$v = \beta_2 + \beta_3,$$

$$\rho = \frac{-2\beta_4(\beta_2 + \beta_3)}{\beta_2\beta_3}.$$

Thus we can use ordinary least squares estimates of the βs to obtain estimates of the parameters of (11.60b). The estimated standard errors can be calculated by using the approximation formula (11.29). If (11.60b) is a reasonable approximation of (11.60a), and if the appropriate assumptions about K, L, and ε hold, the estimates of the production function parameters obtained in this way will be very nearly asymptotically efficient.

EXAMPLE To illustrate the estimation of the CES production function we use the data on inputs and output of 25 firms given in Table 11-3. The maximum likelihood method yields the following estimates of the production function parameters:

$$\log \hat{\gamma} = 1.0564,$$

$$\hat{\delta} = 0.4064,$$

$$\hat{v} = 0.8222,$$

$$\hat{\rho} = 0.6042.$$

[22] All logarithms are natural logarithms. If common logarithms were to be used, the term involving $[\log K_i - \log L_i]^2$ would have to be multiplied by 2.302585.

Table 11-3

Firm no.	K	L	Q
1	8	23	106.00
2	9	14	81.08
3	4	38	72.80
4	2	97	57.34
5	6	11	66.79
6	6	43	98.23
7	3	93	82.68
8	6	49	99.77
9	8	36	110.00
10	8	43	118.93
11	4	61	95.05
12	8	31	112.83
13	3	57	64.54
14	6	97	137.22
15	4	93	86.17
16	2	72	56.25
17	3	61	81.10
18	3	97	65.23
19	9	89	149.56
20	3	25	65.43
21	1	81	36.06
22	4	11	56.92
23	2	64	49.59
24	3	10	43.21
25	6	71	121.24

The estimates of the asymptotic standard errors of the maximum likelihood estimates were not calculated. Using the approximation of the CES production function given by (11.60b), we obtain

$$\log \tilde{\gamma} = 1.0696,$$

$$\underset{(0.0291)}{\tilde{\delta} = 0.4723,}$$

$$\underset{(0.0525)}{\tilde{\nu} = 0.8245,}$$

$$\underset{(0.1899)}{\tilde{\rho} = 0.4334.}$$

The figures in parentheses represent estimates of the asymptotic standard errors. The results show that the sample provides no strong evidence against the CES model.

The choice of the functional form of a regression equation should be made on theoretical or empirical grounds. Because such grounds are frequently difficult to establish, efforts have been made to solve the problem of choice in various ways. One approach has involved the use of a functional form that is flexible enough to approximate a variety of special forms. In the context of production functions the most prominent flexible form is the so-called *transcendental logarithmic* (or *translog*) *production function*. This is obtained from the approximation to the CES production function presented in (11.60c) by allowing the coefficients of $(\log K_i)^2$, $(\log L_i)^2$, and $-2(\log K_i)(\log L_i)$ to differ. Thus the translog production function for two inputs is

$$(11.61) \qquad \log Q_i = \alpha + \beta_K \log K_i + \beta_L \log L_i + \beta_{KK}(\log K_i)^2 + \beta_{LL}(\log L_i)^2 + \beta_{KL}(\log K_i)(\log L_i) + \varepsilon_i .$$

Another flexible form that is common in applied literature is the so-called *Box-Cox transformation* presented below in connection with tests for linearity. If even such flexible forms are considered to be too restrictive, one can—as a last resort—use a "dummy variable regression" explained in Section 9-2 and presented in equation (9.55). Such a formulation enables us only to test the relevance of an explanatory variable but not to estimate its effect on the dependent variable.

In general, the parameters of an intrinsically nonlinear model may be estimated by setting up the likelihood function and finding the maximum likelihood estimates. Under the classical assumptions concerning the stochastic disturbance and the explanatory variables, the resulting estimates will have all the desirable asymptotic properties. Of course, the application of the maximum likelihood method is contingent on the assumption that ε is normally distributed. If we do not wish to make this assumption, we can obtain our estimates by minimizing the sum of squared deviations of the observed values from the fitted values of Y, i.e., by the least squares method. Since the parameters to be estimated enter in a nonlinear way, this method is usually called the *nonlinear least squares method*. The principal difference between this and the ordinary (linear) least squares method is that in the linear case the estimates can be expressed as linear functions of the disturbances. This is not generally possible in the nonlinear case. The estimates obtained by the nonlinear least squares method are exactly the same as the maximum likelihood estimates whenever the maximization of the likelihood function is achieved by the minimization of the sum of squared deviations of the observed from the fitted values of Y. It can be shown that even without the assumption of normality the *asymptotic* distribution of the nonlinear least squares estimates is then normal and has the same mean and variance as the maximum likelihood estimates for the normal disturbance case.[23] Thus the assumption of normality of the stochastic disturbance is not always crucial.

Tests for Linearity

Our discussion, thus far, of estimating the parameters of a nonlinear model has presupposed that the functional form of the population regression equation is

[23] See Judge et al., *op. cit.*, pp. 195–203.

known, or assumed, a priori. If this is not the case, we may want to consider the specification of the functional form as a testable rather than a maintained hypothesis. In this context the most interesting hypothesis is that of linearity. That is, frequently we may wish to test the hypothesis that the population regression equation is linear with respect to the variables against some alternative hypothesis. The hypothesis of linearity can be tested in a number of ways, but unfortunately none of the tests is without drawbacks.

The simplest test of linearity is in the case in which the alternative hypothesis is that the regression equation involves a power function of a given degree. This test was already described in connection with (11.50) and (11.50a). Its disadvantage is that we have to commit ourselves to a power function of a specific degree as the alternative to the linear model. Note that the basic idea of this test rests on the fact that a linear function is a special case of a power function, namely, a power function of degree one. If the coefficients attached to the higher powers of the explanatory variable are all zero, the given power function reduces to a simple linear regression. This idea can be exploited by specifying other functional forms, which include linearity as a special case. Particularly suitable for this purpose is the *Box–Cox transformation*[24] specified as

$$\frac{Y_i^\lambda - 1}{\lambda} = \alpha + \beta\left(\frac{X_i^\lambda - 1}{\lambda}\right) + \varepsilon_i. \tag{11.62}$$

Let us examine this function for some selected values of λ. First, for $\lambda = 0$, the expressions $(Y^\lambda - 1)/\lambda$ and $(X^\lambda - 1)/\lambda$ appear to be indeterminate. However, we note that any finite positive number, say, Z, can be written as

$$Z = e^{\log Z},$$

where the base of the logarithm is e, and that $e^{\log Z}$ can be expanded as

$$e^{\log Z} = 1 + \log Z + \frac{1}{2!}(\log Z)^2 + \frac{1}{3!}(\log Z)^3 + \cdots.$$

Therefore, it follows that

$$\frac{Y_i^\lambda - 1}{\lambda} = \frac{1}{\lambda}\left[1 + \lambda \log Y_i + \frac{1}{2!}(\lambda \log Y_i)^2 + \cdots - 1\right]$$

$$= \log Y_i + \frac{\lambda}{2!}(\log Y_i)^2 + \frac{\lambda^2}{3!}(\log Y_i)^3 + \cdots.$$

For $\lambda = 0$,

$$\frac{Y_i^\lambda - 1}{\lambda} = \log Y_i,$$

[24] This specification was proposed in G. E. P. Box and D. R. Cox, "An Analysis of Transformations," *Journal of the Royal Statistical Society, Series B,* 26 (1964), pp. 211–243.

and, similarly,

$$\frac{X_i^\lambda - 1}{\lambda} = \log X_i.$$

This means that for $\lambda = 0$ (and for X and Y positive) the regression equation (11.62) reduces to

$$\log Y_i = \alpha + \beta \log X_i + \varepsilon_i.$$

Further, for $\lambda = 1$, we obtain

$$(Y_i - 1) = \alpha + \beta(X_i - 1) + \varepsilon_i$$

or

$$Y_i = \alpha^* + \beta X_i + \varepsilon_i,$$

where

$$\alpha^* = \alpha - \beta + 1,$$

which is a simple linear regression model.

In general, different values of λ in (11.62) lead to different functional specifications of the regression equation.[25] This allows us to test the linear hypothesis against the alternative hypothesis that the regression equation is some nonlinear function within the family of functions defined by (11.62). Formally,

$$H_0: \quad \lambda = 1,$$

$$H_A: \quad \lambda \neq 1.$$

To carry out the test, we need an estimate of λ and its standard error. Clearly, λ can be estimated along with the other parameters of (11.62) by the maximum likelihood method. In setting up the likelihood function for $Y_1, Y_2, \ldots, Y_n$, we have to derive the distribution of the Ys from the distribution of the ε s, which is assumed to be normal. By Theorem 19 of Section 7-3 (the "change-of-variable" theorem), we have

$$f(Y_i) = \left|\frac{d\varepsilon_i}{dY_i}\right| f(\varepsilon_i).$$

But

$$\varepsilon_i = \left(\frac{Y_i^\lambda - 1}{\lambda}\right) - \alpha - \beta\left(\frac{X_i^\lambda - 1}{\lambda}\right)$$

so that

$$\frac{d\varepsilon_i}{dY_i} = Y_i^{\lambda - 1}.$$

[25] Some attention has to be paid to the restrictions on the values of the dependent variable. Since, under the assumption of normality, the range of ε extends from $-\infty$ to $+\infty$, this should also be the range of $(Y^\lambda - 1)/\lambda$. However, for some values of λ (e.g., $\lambda = \frac{1}{2}$) this may not be possible, in which case only *approximate* normality can be required. This point was originally raised by J. B. Ramsey.

Therefore, the likelihood function for $Y_1, Y_2, \ldots, Y_n$ is

$$(11.63) \qquad L = (\lambda - 1) \sum_i \log Y_i - \frac{n}{2} \log (2\pi) - \frac{n}{2} \log \sigma^2 - \frac{1}{2\sigma^2} \sum_i \left[\left(\frac{Y_i^\lambda - 1}{\lambda} \right) - \alpha - \beta \left(\frac{X_i^\lambda - 1}{\lambda} \right) \right]^2.$$

The maximization of L with respect to the unknown parameters can be simplified by dividing the sample values of Y by the geometric mean of Y. If the values of Y scaled in this way are called Y^*, then $\Sigma \log Y_i^* = 0$ and the likelihood function will be free of the Jacobian term. Such a scaling leaves the parameter λ unaffected, but the intercept and the slope will now have a different interpretation.[26] The likelihood function can then be maximized by regressing $(Y^{*\lambda} - 1)/\lambda$ on $(X^\lambda - 1)/\lambda$ for a range of values of λ. The results corresponding to the minimum sum of squared residuals also yield the maximum value of L. Once the maximum likelihood estimates have been found, we can use the likelihood ratio test to test the linearity hypothesis that we are interested in. The test statistic—for a large sample test—is then given as

$$LR = -2[L(\lambda = 1) - L(\hat{\lambda})] \sim \chi_1^2$$

where $L(\lambda = 1)$ is equal to the maximum value of L for the *linear* regression model, and $L(\hat{\lambda})$ represents the maximum value of L when λ is set equal to its maximum likelihood value.

As mentioned earlier, the Box-Cox transformation is also used to represent flexible functional form when the functional form of the model is in doubt. For this purpose equation (11.62) may be generalized to allow for the transformation of the explanatory variable to be different from that of the dependent variable. Specifically, we write

$$(11.62a) \qquad \frac{Y_i^\lambda - 1}{\lambda} = \alpha + \beta \left(\frac{X_i^\mu - 1}{\mu} \right) + \varepsilon_i$$

where μ may be different from λ. This formulation covers a greater variety of specific functional forms than (11.62). For instance, when $\lambda = 1$ and $\mu = 0$, the equation represents a "semilogarithmic model"; when $\lambda = 1$ and $\mu = -1$, it represents a "reciprocal model"; etc. Maximum likelihood estimates of the unknown parameters can be obtained by searching over different values of λ and μ. Estimates of the standard error can be obtained by constructing the appropriate information matrix for *all* unknown parameters (including λ and μ), replacing all unknown parameters by their respective maximum likelihood estimates, and then inverting the matrix to obtain the desired estimated standard errors (by reference to the square roots of the diagonal terms). There is no difficulty in calculating the values of the estimated standard errors in this way, but analytical expressions are difficult to

[26] See J. J. Spitzer, "Variance Estimates in Models with the Box-Cox Transformation: Implications for Estimation and Hypothesis Testing," *Review of Economics and Statistics,* 66 (November 1984), pp. 645-652.

work out and are very complicated. It should be emphasized that if the estimated standard errors of the regression coefficients are obtained by treating λ and μ as *known,* they will be biased downward and the corresponding t values will be artificially inflated.[27]

At the end of our discussion of heteroskedasticity in Section 8-2 we emphasized the difficulty of distinguishing between heteroskedasticity and a nonlinear functional form of a regression equation. This problem is particularly acute in connection with the Box-Cox transformation function, which was originally intended to remove suspected heteroskedasticity but in econometrics has been mainly used for detecting nonlinear functional form. It has been pointed out that if the regression equation is linear but heteroskedastic, then the estimator of λ in the Box-Cox transformation function may be biased toward zero. Similarly misleading results may also be obtained when the regression equation is linear but the disturbance is autocorrelated. To deal with these problems it has been proposed to carry out a *joint* test (of the likelihood-ratio type) for linearity and homoskedasticity or for linearity and nonautocorrelation.[28]

Sometimes the only alternative to linear regression is *log-linear* regression so that the only relevant values of λ in the Box-Cox function (11.62) are $\lambda = 1$ and $\lambda = 0$. A simple large-sample test that is particularly suitable for this case is the so-called *PE test.*[29] Let

$$H_0: \quad Y_i = \alpha + \beta X_i + \varepsilon_{0i}, \tag{11.64a}$$

$$H_A: \quad \log Y_i = \gamma + \delta \log X_i + \varepsilon_{1i}, \tag{11.64b}$$

where the logarithms are natural logarithms. Combining (11.64a) and (11.64b), we can write

$$\pi(Y_i - \alpha - \beta X_i) + (1 - \pi)(\log Y_i - \gamma - \delta \log X_i) = \varepsilon_i, \tag{11.65}$$

where $\pi = 1$ when H_0 is true and $\pi = 0$ when H_A is true. Dividing both sides of (11.65) by π, substituting ε_{1i} for the corresponding expression from (11.64b), and

[27] *Ibid.* For application of the Box-Cox transformation as a flexible functional form see, e.g., J. Benus, J. Kmenta, and H. Shapiro, "The Dynamics of Household Budget Allocation to Food Expenditures," *Review of Economics and Statistics,* 68 (May 1976), pp. 129-138, or J. Heckman and S. Polachek, "Empirical Evidence on the Functional Form of the Earnings-Schooling Relationship,"*Journal of the American Statistical Association,* 69 (June 1974), pp. 350-354.

[28] For an elaboration and implementation of the tests see K. Lahiri and D. Egy, "Joint Estimation and Testing for Functional Form and Heteroskedasticity," *Journal of Econometrics,* 15 (February 1981), pp. 299-307; N. E. Savin and K. J. White, "Estimation and Testing for Functional Form and Autocorrelation: A Simultaneous Approach," *Journal of Econometrics,* 8 (August 1978), pp. 1-12; and T. G. Seaks and S. K. Layson, "Box-Cox Estimation with Standard Econometric Problems," *Review of Economics and Statistics,* 65 (February 1983), pp. 160-164.

[29] A general version of the PE test is presented in J. G. MacKinnon, H. White, and R. Davidson, "Tests for Model Specification in the Presence of Alternative Hypotheses: Some Further Results," *Journal of Econometrics,* 21 (January 1983), pp. 53-70. A specialized version of the test on which our discussion is based appeared in A. Bera and M. McAleer, "Further Results on Testing Linear and Log-Linear Regression Models," unpublished paper, Department of Statistics, Australian National University, 1982.

rearranging terms, we obtain

$$(11.66) \qquad Y_i = \alpha + \beta X_i + \theta_0 \varepsilon_{1i} + \varepsilon_i,$$

where $\theta_0 = (\pi - 1)/\pi$, which under H_0 is equal to zero. To carry out the test of H_0 against H_A we replace ϵ_{1i} by $\hat{\epsilon}_{1i}$, obtained by applying LSE to (11.64a) and (11.64b) and calculating $(\log \hat{Y}_i - \widehat{\log Y_i})$, and then use the standard t test to test the significance of the least squares estimate of θ_0. To allow for the possibility that *both* specifications may be wrong, we reverse the roles of H_0 and H_A and form

$$(11.67) \qquad \log Y_i = \gamma + \delta \log X_i + \theta_1 \varepsilon_{0i} + \varepsilon_i,$$

where $\theta_1 = -\pi/(1 - \pi)$, which under H_A is equal to zero. To implement the test we replace ϵ_{0i} by $\hat{\epsilon}_{0i}$, obtained by applying LSE to (11.64a) and (11.64b) and calculating $[\hat{Y}_i - \exp(\widehat{\log Y_i})]$, and then use the t test to test the significance of the least squares estimate of θ_1. If only one of $\hat{\theta}_0$ and $\hat{\theta}_1$ is significantly different from zero, the preferred model is clearly indicated. If both $\hat{\theta}_0$ and $\hat{\theta}_1$ are significantly different from zero, both model specifications are to be rejected. Finally, if neither $\hat{\theta}_0$ nor $\hat{\theta}_1$ is significantly different from zero, the tests offer no guidance in deciding between the linear and the log-linear form.

The hypothesis that the population regression equation is linear with respect to the variables can also be tested without specifying the alternative functional form or forms. This can be done by considering some of the implications of linearity in a more general way. The rather obvious implication of linearity is that the slope and the intercept of the regression equation must remain constant over *all* values of the explanatory variable. What we can do, then, is to divide the sample observations into a number of subsamples, each subsample corresponding to a different and nonoverlapping interval of values of the explanatory variable. We can estimate the slope and the intercept for each subsample and test whether there are any significant differences from one subsample to another. This is illustrated in Figure 11-8. To

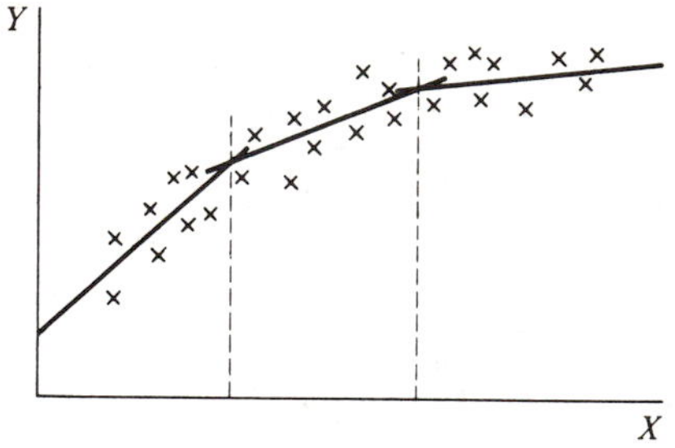

Figure 11-8

indicate how the test is carried out, we consider a sample of n observations, with the observations being arranged so that

$$X_1 \leq X_2 \leq X_3 \leq \cdots \leq X_n.$$

Suppose the sample is divided into three subsamples, with the values of the explanatory variable allocated as follows.

$$\text{Subsample 1:} \quad X_1, X_2, \ldots, X_k,$$

$$\text{Subsample 2:} \quad X_{k+1}, X_{k+2}, \ldots, X_m,$$

$$\text{Subsample 3:} \quad X_{m+1}, X_{m+2}, \ldots, X_n.$$

The regression model can be set up as

$$Y_i = \beta_1 + \beta_2 X_i + \gamma_1 Z_{i1} + \gamma_2 X_i Z_{i1} + \gamma_3 Z_{i2} + \gamma_4 X_i Z_{i2} + \varepsilon_i, \tag{11.68}$$

where

$$\begin{aligned} Z_{i1} &= 1 \quad \text{if } i \text{ belongs to subsample 1,} \\ &= 0 \quad \text{otherwise;} \\ Z_{i2} &= 1 \quad \text{if } i \text{ belongs to subsample 2,} \\ &= 0 \quad \text{otherwise.} \end{aligned}$$

The hypothesis of linearity can then be tested by testing

$$H_0: \quad \gamma_1 = \gamma_2 = \gamma_3 = \gamma_4 = 0,$$

$$H_A: \quad H_0 \text{ is not true.}$$

The appropriate F test, described in (10.46), has a disadvantage in that its result may depend on the way in which the sample is divided up. If the number of subsamples is too small, a departure from linearity may remain concealed, and if the number of subsamples is large, we lose many degrees of freedom and thus weaken the power of the test. As a compromise, it has been suggested that in practical applications three or four samples should be sufficient.[30]

Another test of linearity which does not rely on the specification of the alternative functional form is based on the scatter of the residuals around the sample regression line. The idea is to rely on the fact that, under the assumptions of the classical normal linear regression model, the disturbances are *randomly* scattered around the population regression line. If the population regression is *not* linear, the scatter of the disturbances around a straight line will no longer be random. In Figure 11-9

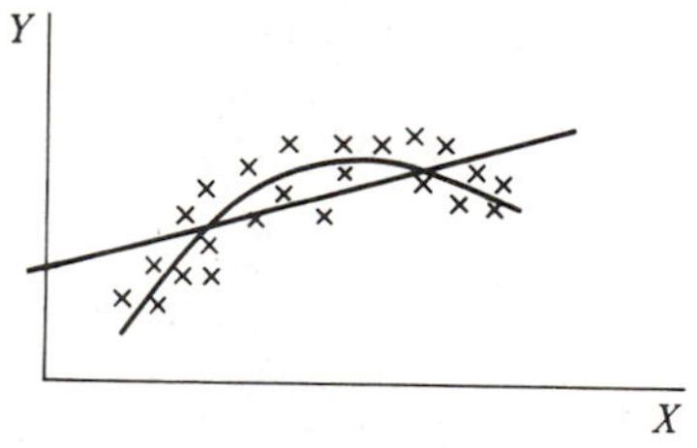

Figure 11-9

[30] This test is presented in R. L. Brown, J. Durbin, and J. M. Evans, "Techniques for Testing the Constancy of Regression Relationships over Time," *Journal of the Royal Statistical Society, Series B*, 37 (1975), pp. 149–163, as a "homogeneity test."

we can see how, because of the nonlinearity of the relation, the deviations from the straight line tend to be at first negative, then positive, and then negative again. This suggests that we can test linearity by determining whether the sequence of the deviations from the regression line is randomly arranged. This could be tested by the Durbin–Watson test described in Section 8-3, which was originally designed for testing the hypothesis that the disturbances are uncorrelated over time against the hypothesis that they follow a first-order autoregressive scheme. If the residuals are arranged according to increasing values of the explanatory variable rather than according to time, this test can be used to check whether the deviations from the population regression line are random. However, the Durbin–Watson test is not without disadvantages. If the ordering of the residuals according to time is similar to their ordering according to increasing values of the explanatory variable, we would be using very much the same test for linearity as for nonautoregression of the disturbances over time. This difficulty is due to the fact that, when the orderings are similar, both nonlinearity and autoregression in the disturbances tend to have the same implication with respect to the residuals.

Our ability to test the linearity hypothesis can be substantially enhanced in cases where we have *replicated* observations, that is, where there are several observations on the dependent variable for at least some values of the explanatory variable (or variables). This situation is illustrated in Figure 11-10. When replicated data of this

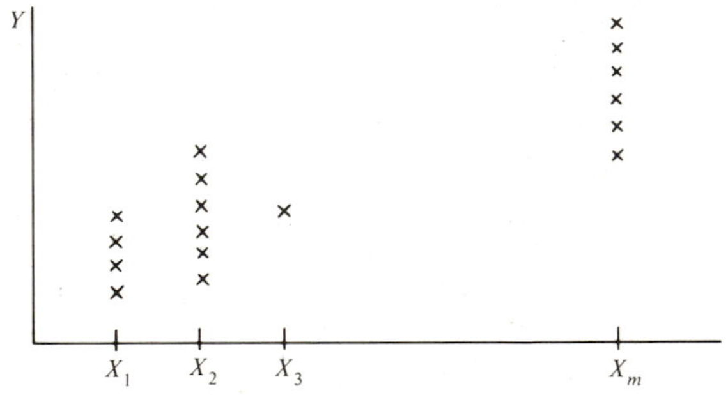

Figure 11-10

sort are available, we can test the linearity of a regression equation by using the so-called *lack-of-fit* (LOF) *test.* This test utilizes the additional information that comes from variation of Y within each group of observations. The linear regression model can in this case be written as

$$(11.69)\quad Y_{ij} = \alpha + \beta X_i + \varepsilon_{ij} \qquad (i = 1, 2, \ldots, m; j = 1, 2, \ldots, n_i; \sum n_i = n \quad (n > m)).$$

The null and the alternative hypotheses are

$$H_0:\quad E(Y_{ij}) = \alpha + \beta X_i,$$

$$H_A:\quad E(Y_{ij}) = \mu_i \qquad (\mu_i \neq \alpha + \beta X_i \text{ for at least one } i).$$

The idea of the test is based on the fact that with replicated data the variance of the disturbance can be estimated in two different ways, one related to the variation of Y_{ij} around μ_i and thus unrestricted by the specification of the linear regression model, and the other related to the variation of Y_{ij} around $(\alpha + \beta X_i)$ and thus restricted by the regression model. The *unrestricted* estimator of σ^2, say, s_U^2, is given as a weighted average of the m group variances of Y_{ij} around the respective group means, i.e.,

$$(11.70) \qquad s_U^2 = \frac{(n_1 - 1)s_1^2 + (n_2 - 1)s_2^2 + \cdots + (n_m - 1)s_m^2}{n - m}$$

$$= \frac{\text{SSP}}{n - m}$$

where $\quad s_i^2 = \frac{1}{n_i - 1}\sum_j (Y_{ij} - \bar{Y}_i)^2, \qquad \bar{Y}_i = \frac{1}{n_i}\sum_j Y_{ij},$

and SSP stands for "pure sum of squares." The *restricted* estimator of σ^2, say, s_R^2 is obtained from (11.69) following (7.35):

$$(11.71) \qquad s_R^2 = \frac{1}{n-2}\sum_i \sum_j e_{ij}^2$$

$$= \frac{\text{SSE}}{n-2},$$

where e_{ij} represents the least squares residuals from (11.69). If $\hat{Y}_i$ $(=\hat{\alpha} + \hat{\beta}X_i)$ denotes the fitted values of Y_{ij}, then we can write

$$(11.72) \qquad \sum_i \sum_j e_{ij}^2 = \sum_i \sum_j (Y_{ij} - \hat{Y}_i)^2$$

$$= \sum_i \sum_j [(Y_{ij} - \bar{Y}_i) - (\hat{Y}_i - \bar{Y}_i)]^2$$

$$= \sum_i \sum_j (Y_{ij} - \bar{Y}_i)^2 + \sum_i n_i(\hat{Y}_i - \bar{Y}_i)^2$$

$$= \text{SSP} + \text{SSL},$$

where SSL stands for "lack-of-fit sum of squares." Clearly, s_U^2 is unbiased under both H_0 and H_A, wheres s_R^2 is unbiased under H_0 but not under H_A. In fact, if H_A is true, $E(s_R^2) > \sigma^2$, because s_R^2 estimates the variation of Y_{ij} around a quantity other than its mean. The test is based on the observed differences between the two estimated variances. The appropriate test statistic is directly derived from the frequently used formula (7.51). Specifically, under H_0

$$(11.73) \qquad \frac{(\text{SSE} - \text{SSP})/(m - K)}{\text{SSP}/(n - m)} \sim F_{m-K,\, n-m},$$

where K represents the number of regressors, including the constant term. The number of restrictions is $(m - K)$ because $(n - K) - (n - m) = m - K$. A simple way of calculating SSP follows from the fact that SSP is equal to the error sum of squares from the least squares estimation of

$$Y_{ij} = \mu_1 D_{j1} + \mu_2 D_{j2} + \cdots + \mu_m D_{jm} + \varepsilon_{ij}, \tag{11.74}$$

where $D_{ij} = 1$ for each observation corresponding to X_i,

$= 0$ otherwise.

(Incidentally, the least squares estimation also yields $\hat{\mu}_i = \overline{Y}_i.$) This test is very clean and reasonably powerful, but it is limited by the availability of replicated data. When replicated data are not available, the "rainbow" test introduced in Section 10-4 is a reasonable alternative.

EXAMPLE Doran and Kmenta applied the LOF test to the standard model of individual earnings proposed by Jacob Mincer and frequently used in labor economics:[31]

$$\log W_{ij} = \beta_0 + \beta_1 X_i + \beta_2 X_i^2 + \beta_3 S_i + u_{ij},$$

where W_{ij} is the wage rate of the jth individual in the ith group; X_i is the "on job" work experience (common to all individuals in the ith group); S_i is the number of years of schooling (common to all individuals in the ith group); and u_{ij} is an independently distributed stochastic disturbance. The test was based on the data on 1958 married women taking part in the Fertility Survey carried out by the Norwegian Central Bureau of Statistics in 1977. Wages were measured in Kroner per hour and represented by the amount each woman was actually earning—or could be earning if she were to be employed at the time. Experience was measured by the number of years worked since completing the highest year of education, and education was measured by the number of years of schooling. The results were found to be

$$\log W_{ij} = \underset{(0.05)}{2.23} + \underset{(0.006)}{0.031}X_i - \underset{(0.00024)}{0.00068}X_i^2 + \underset{(0.004)}{0.078}S_i + e_{ij},$$

$n = 1958$, $m = 154$, $K = 4$, SSE $= 283.2$, and SSP $= 255.7$. The value of the LOF test statistic has turned out to be 1.29, which is highly significant. Thus the model as specified should be rejected in this case.

Our discussion of various tests of linearity may perhaps best be closed by emphasizing the similarity of the consequences of misspecification resulting from an incorrect functional form and those resulting from an omission of relevant explanatory variables. Without specified alternatives, the consequences of the two types of misspecification are observationally indistinguishable. In the absence of specified alternatives, tests for linearity may just as well be used for testing for a lack of omission of relevant explanatory variables, and vice versa. In particular, the LOF and the "rainbow" tests are very well suited for both purposes.

[31] H. Doran and J. Kmenta, "A Lack-of-Fit Test for Econometric Applications to Cross-Section Data," *Review of Economics and Statistics,* in press; J. Mincer, *Schooling, Experience and Earnings* (New York: Columbia University Press, 1974).

11-4 Distributed Lag Models

A simple regression equation designed to explain variations over time in the mean value of the dependent variable is given by

$$Y_t = \alpha + \beta X_t + \varepsilon_t,$$

where ε_t is a random variable with zero mean (conforming to other assumptions as specified), and X_t is either nonstochastic or, if stochastic, independent of ε_t. In setting up the regression equation in this way we are, in fact, assuming that the current value of Y may depend on the current value of X but *not* on any of the past values of X. A more general formulation, which would allow for the current as well as the past values of X to affect Y, would be written as

$$(11.75) \qquad Y_t = \alpha + \beta_0 X_t + \beta_1 X_{t-1} + \beta_2 X_{t-2} + \cdots + \beta_m X_{t-m} + \varepsilon_t.$$

This equation is the basis for the discussion of the present section. For simplicity we shall limit ourselves to the case of a nonstochastic X; a modification to allow for the case in which X is stochastic but independent of ε is quite straightforward.

The regression equation (11.75), extended by the relevant assumptions concerning the behavior of X and ε, is called a *distributed lag model* because the influence of the explanatory variable on $E(Y_t)$ is distributed over a number of lagged values of X. This number, m, may be either finite or infinite. However, we assume that the βs have a finite sum; i.e.,

$$\sum_{i=0}^{m} \beta_i < \infty.$$

This assumption is needed to eliminate the possibility of explosive values of $E(Y_t)$. We also define the *average lag* as the weighted mean of all the lags involved, with weights given by the relative size of the respective β coefficients. Formally,

$$\text{Average lag} = \frac{\sum i\beta_i}{\sum \beta_i},$$

where the summations run from $i = 0$ to $i = m$. Equation (11.75) could (at least in principle) be estimated by the least squares method, or by some other method which leads to estimates with some desirable properties under the given specifications about ε. Of course, if m is large, we may not have enough observations to estimate all the parameters. However, even if we do have enough observations, we are likely to encounter a high degree of multicollinearity, which would have a detrimental effect on the standard errors of the estimated coefficients. As a matter of fact, a distributed lag model has rarely been posited and estimated in as general a form as that specified in (11.75). Most frequently some restrictions are placed on the regression coefficients $\beta_0, \beta_1, \ldots, \beta_m$, so that the number of the regression parameters becomes substantially reduced. In practical applications these restrictions have been of two kinds—one resulting from the requirement that the βs should be declining in a geometric progression, and the other from the requirement that the βs should first be increasing and then decreasing.

Geometric Lag

By far the most popular form of a distributed lag is that of a *geometric lag distribution* characterized as

$$Y_t = \alpha + \beta_0(X_t + \lambda X_{t-1} + \lambda^2 X_{t-2} + \cdots) + \varepsilon_t, \tag{11.76}$$

where $0 \leq \lambda < 1$. Here the effect of X on $E(Y_t)$ extends indefinitely into the past (i.e., $m \rightarrow \infty$), but the coefficients decline in a fixed proportion so that the effect of the distant values of X eventually becomes negligible. This model has been rationalized in two different ways, each leading to the same description of the population regression equation, but each having a different implication for the behavior of the regression disturbance. The first rationalization is known as the *adaptive expectation model* and is based on the following reasoning. Suppose a simple regression model is modified so that $E(Y_t)$ is a linear function not of X_t but of the "expected" or "permanent" level of X at time $t+1$, say, X^*_{t+1}. One example would be a demand relationship in which the quantity demanded is a function of expected price, or a consumption function with "permanent income" as the explanatory variable. Then,

$$Y_t = \alpha + \beta X^*_{t+1} + \varepsilon_t, \tag{11.77}$$

where, as before, ε_t is a random variable with zero mean. Since X^*_{t+1} is not directly observable, we have to state how it is determined. Here, we postulate that

$$X^*_{t+1} - X^*_t = (1 - \lambda)(X_t - X^*_t), \tag{11.78}$$

or equivalently,

$$X^*_{t+1} = (1 - \lambda)X_t + \lambda X^*_t, \tag{11.78a}$$

where $0 \leq \lambda < 1$. This presupposes that the expected or permanent value of X for time $t+1$ is represented by a weighted average of the current value of X and the value of X expected in the current period. Such a formation of expectations is based on the idea that the current expectations are derived by modifying previous expectations in light of the current experience. Note that (11.78a) can also be written as

$$X^*_{t+1} = (1 - \lambda)(X_t + \lambda X_{t-1} + \lambda^2 X_{t-2} + \cdots). \tag{11.78b}$$

The substitution for X^*_{t+1} from (11.78b) into (11.77) gives

$$Y_t = \alpha + \beta(1 - \lambda)(X_t + \lambda X_{t-1} + \lambda^2 X_{t-2} + \cdots) + \varepsilon_t, \tag{11.79}$$

which represents the geometric lag model (11.76) with $\beta_0 = \beta(1 - \lambda)$. The size of the average lag in this case is

$$\frac{\beta(1-\lambda)(0 + \lambda + 2\lambda^2 + 3\lambda^3 + \cdots)}{\beta(1-\lambda)(1 + \lambda + \lambda^2 + \lambda^3 + \cdots)} = \frac{\beta(1-\lambda)[\lambda/(1-\lambda)^2]}{\beta(1-\lambda)[1/(1-\lambda)]} = \frac{\lambda}{1-\lambda}.$$

Equation (11.79) is clearly awkward from the point of view of estimation because of the infinite number of regressors. It can, however, be simplified by the application of the so-called Koyck transformation. By lagging (11.79) by one period, multiplying through by λ, and subtracting the result from (11.79), we obtain

(11.80) $$Y_t = \alpha(1-\lambda) + \beta(1-\lambda)X_t + \lambda Y_{t-1} + \eta_t,$$

where $$\eta_t = \varepsilon_t - \lambda\varepsilon_{t-1}.$$

The adaptive expectation model can be justified as a *rational expectation* model if it can be assumed that X is stochastic and its values are generated according to the scheme

(11.81) $$X_t = X_{t-1} + u_t - \lambda u_{t-1},$$

where u_t is a stochastic disturbance that satisfies all basic assumptions. Note that $(u_t - \lambda u_{t-1})$ represents a *moving average* process of first order. Since

$$u_{t-1} = X_{t-1} - X_{t-2} + \lambda u_{t-2},$$

we have, by substituting for u_{t-1} into (11.81),

$$\begin{aligned} X_t &= X_{t-1} + u_t - \lambda(X_{t-1} - X_{t-2} + \lambda u_{t-2}) \\ &= (1-\lambda)X_{t-1} + \lambda X_{t-2} + u_t - \lambda^2 u_{t-2}. \end{aligned}$$

By a successive substitution for u_{t-2}, u_{t-3}, etc., we obtain

$$X_t = (1-\lambda)(X_{t-1} + \lambda X_{t-2} + \lambda^2 X_{t-3} + \cdots) + u_t,$$

since $\lambda^\infty = 0$. The optimal (i.e., rational) predictor of X_{t+1} then is

$$X^*_{t+1} = (1-\lambda)(X_t + \lambda X_{t-1} + \lambda^2 X_{t-2} + \cdots),$$

since u_t has mean zero. By substituting for X^*_{t+1} into (11.77), we obtain (11.79). Thus adaptive expectations can be considered to be rational if the values of X are generated as specified in (11.81).

An alternative rationalization of the geometric lag is provided by the so-called *partial adjustment* or *habit persistence* model. Suppose the *desired* level of Y at time t, say, Y^*_t, is given by a linear function of some explanatory variable X_t as

(11.82) $$Y^*_t = \alpha + \beta X_t.$$

For instance, the mean desired level of inventory held by a firm may be a linear function of sales or the mean desired level of consumption may be a linear function of wealth. The values of Y^* are not directly observable, but we assume that an attempt is being made to bring the actual level of Y to its desired level, and that such an attempt is only partially successful during any one period. The reasons why a complete adjustment of Y to Y^* is not achieved in a single period may be varied; they may include technological constraints, institutional rigidities, persistence of habit, etc. The relationship between the actual and the desired level of Y may be specified as follows:

(11.83) $$(Y_t - Y_{t-1}) = (1-\gamma)(Y^*_t - Y_{t-1}) + \varepsilon_t,$$

where $0 \leq \gamma < 1$. The coefficient $(1-\gamma)$ is called the "adjustment coefficient" since it indicates the rate of adjustment of Y to Y^*. This coefficient enables us to determine the number of periods required to close a given proportion p of the gap between Y_t^* and Y_t. After one period, $(1-\gamma)$ is closed so that γ of the gap still remains. After two periods the extent of the closure is $(1-\gamma)+\gamma(1-\gamma)=1-\gamma^2$ and γ^2 remains. After n periods the proportion of the gap closed will be $1-\gamma^n$ so that we can write

$$1-\gamma^n = p.$$

The required number of periods to close p of the gap then is

$$n = \frac{\log(1-p)}{\log \gamma}.$$

Equation (11.83) can be solved for Y_t^* and the result substituted into (11.82). In this way we obtain

$$(11.84) \qquad Y_t = \alpha(1-\gamma) + \beta(1-\gamma)X_t + \gamma Y_{t-1} + \varepsilon_t.$$

Equation (11.84) is formally the same as the adaptive expectation model characterized by (11.80) *except* that the disturbance in (11.80), unlike that in (11.84), is generated by events of the preceding as well as the present period. Note also that (11.84) describes a geometric lag of the form

$$(11.84a) \qquad Y_t = \alpha + \beta(1-\gamma)(X_t + \gamma X_{t-1} + \gamma^2 X_{t-2} + \cdots) + \xi_t,$$

where

$$\xi_t = \varepsilon_t + \gamma\varepsilon_{t-1} + \gamma^2\varepsilon_{t-2} + \cdots.$$

An economic justification for the partial adjustment model can be provided when, for instance, Y represents a stock of capital and the cost associated with Y is

$$(11.85) \qquad C_t = a(Y_t - Y_t^*)^2 + b(Y_t - Y_{t-1})^2,$$

where the first term on the right-hand side represents the cost of being in disequilibrium and the second represents the cost of change. The cost minimizing rule then is

$$\frac{\partial C_t}{\partial Y_t} = 2a(Y_t - Y_t^*) + 2b(Y_t - Y_{t-1}) = 0.$$

This yields

$$Y_t - Y_{t-1} = \frac{a}{a+b}(Y_t^* - Y_{t-1}),$$

which, after letting $a/(a+b) = (1-\gamma)$ and after allowing for a stochastic disturbance in achieving cost minimization, is the same as (11.83).

Before turning our attention to the problem of estimating the regression coefficients of the geometric lag models, we should consider the formulation of models in which the distributed lag extends over more than one explanatory variable. In particular, let us take a model in which there are two explanatory variables, X and

Z, each exerting its effect on $E(Y_t)$ through its own geometrically distributed lag:

(11.86) $$Y_t = \alpha + \beta_0(X_t + \lambda X_{t-1} + \lambda^2 X_{t-2} + \cdots) + \delta_0(Z_t + \mu Z_{t-1} + \mu^2 Z_{t-2} + \cdots) + \varepsilon_t,$$

where $$0 \leq \lambda < 1 \quad \text{and} \quad 0 \leq \mu < 1.$$

For example, the demand for money may depend on "permanent" income and on an "expected" rate of interest. Equation (11.86) can be reduced to a more manageable form by applying the Koyck transformation twice in succession. First, we lag (11.86) by one period, multiply both sides by λ, and deduct the resulting equation from (11.86). This gives

(11.86a) $$Y_t = \alpha(1-\lambda) + \lambda Y_{t-1} + \delta_0[Z_t + (\mu - \lambda)Z_{t-1} + \mu(\mu - \lambda)Z_{t-2} + \mu^2(\mu - \lambda)Z_{t-3} + \cdots] + \beta_0 X_t + \varepsilon_t - \lambda\varepsilon_{t-1}.$$

Next, we lag (11.86a) by one period, multiply both sides by μ, and deduct the resulting equation from (11.86a). The result is

(11.86b) $$Y_t = \alpha(1-\lambda)(1-\mu) + (\lambda + \mu)Y_{t-1} - \lambda\mu Y_{t-2} + \beta_0 X_t - \beta_0\mu X_{t-1} + \delta_0 Z_t - \delta_0\lambda Z_{t-1} + \eta_t^*,$$

where $$\eta_t^* = \varepsilon_t - (\lambda + \mu)\varepsilon_{t-1} + \lambda\mu\varepsilon_{t-2},$$

which is a regression equation with six regressors (in addition to the constant term). It is clear that we could handle models with any number of distributed lags in a similar manner.

Let us now consider the problem of estimating the parameters of a geometrically distributed lag model,

$$Y_t = \alpha + \beta_0(X_t + \lambda X_{t-1} + \lambda^2 X_{t-2} + \cdots) + \varepsilon_t,$$

where ε_t is a random normal variable with mean zero and variance σ^2. Suppose further that the relation is generated by an *adaptive expectation* mechanism, as described by equations (11.77) and (11.78). Estimation of the parameters of this model depends on whether we assume the εs to be mutually independent or not. We shall start with the case where the εs are mutually independent; i.e., we assume that the disturbances are normally distributed and

(11.87) $$E(\varepsilon_t\varepsilon_s) = 0 \qquad (t \neq s).$$

The geometric lag model is clearly not suitable for estimation in its original form since it involves an infinite number of regressors. However, by applying the Koyck transformation, we can write

where $$Y_t = \alpha(1-\lambda) + \beta(1-\lambda)X_t + \lambda Y_{t-1} + \eta_t,$$

or $$Y_t = \alpha_0 + \beta_0 X_t + \lambda Y_{t-1} + \eta_t,$$

where $\alpha_0 = \alpha(1-\lambda)$, $\beta_0 = \beta(1-\lambda)$, and $\eta_t = \varepsilon_t - \lambda\varepsilon_{t-1}$.

This equation was presented earlier as (11.80). Its form is relatively simple, but this simplification has not been achieved without cost. The trouble with (11.80) is that the "new" disturbance η_t is correlated with Y_{t-1}, which is now one of the explanatory variables. In particular,

$$E(\eta_t Y_{t-1}) = E(\varepsilon_t - \lambda\varepsilon_{t-1})[\alpha + \beta(X_{t-1} + \lambda X_{t-2} + \cdots) + \varepsilon_{t-1}]$$
$$= -\lambda\sigma^2.$$

This means that the ordinary least squares estimates of the coefficients of (11.80) are *inconsistent* (see Section 8-4), and we have to resort to other estimation methods.

Consistent estimates of the coefficients of (11.80) under the assumption specified in (11.87) can be obtained in several ways. Perhaps the simplest is to use the *method of instrumental variables,* which we have described in connection with the "errors-in-variables" models in Section 9-1. Since equation (11.80) involves two explanatory variables, we have to find two instrumental variables, say, Z_1 and Z_2. These variables should satisfy the following conditions.

1. $\text{plim}\ \Sigma_t (Z_{1t} - \bar{Z}_1)\eta_t/n = 0$ and $\text{plim}\ \Sigma_t(Z_{2t} - \bar{Z}_2)\eta_t/n = 0.$
2. $\text{plim}\ \Sigma_t(Z_{1t} - \bar{Z}_1)X_t/n$ and $\text{plim}\ \Sigma_t(Z_{2t} - \bar{Z}_2)Y_{t-1}/n$ are both finite numbers different from zero.

An additional condition, which is not necessary for consistency but which helps to reduce the asymptotic variance of the instrumental variables estimator, is that the instrumental variables should be highly correlated with the respective regressors. It has been suggested that the following instrumental variables be used:

$$Z_{1t} = X_t \quad \text{and} \quad Z_{2t} = X_{t-1}.$$

That is, the instrumental variable for the first regressor, X_t, is to be X_t itself, and the instrumental variable for the second regressor, Y_{t-1}, is to be X_{t-1}. Clearly, since X_t is nonstochastic, it serves as an ideal instrumental varible for itself since it satisfies the necessary conditions and is "perfectly correlated" with X_t. The second instrumental variable also satisfies the necessary conditions and is likely to be correlated with Y_{t-1} by virtue of (11.76).

An alternative approach to estimating the coefficients of (11.79) is based on the *maximum likelihood* principle. The estimators can then be developed as follows.[32] Equation (11.79) can be rewritten as

$$\text{(11.88)} \qquad Y_t = \alpha + \beta(1-\lambda)(X_t + \lambda X_{t-1} + \lambda^2 X_{t-2} + \cdots + \lambda^{t-1}X_1)$$
$$+ \beta(1-\lambda)\lambda^t(X_0 + \lambda X_{-1} + \lambda^2 X_{-2} + \cdots) + \varepsilon_t.$$

[32] These estimators have been derived in the appendix of the paper by L. R. Klein, "The Estimation of Distributed Lags," *Econometrica,* 26 (October 1958), pp. 553–565, and operationally developed in P. J. Dhrymes, "Efficient Estimation of Distributed Lags with Autocorrelated Errors Terms," *International Economic Review,* 10 (February 1969), pp. 47–67, and in A. Zellner and M. S. Geisel, "Analysis of Distributed Lag Models with Application to Consumption Function Estimation," *Econometrica,* 38 (November 1970), pp. 865–888.

But since

$$E(Y_0) = \alpha + \beta(1-\lambda)(X_0 + \lambda X_{-1} + \lambda^2 X_{-2} + \cdots),$$

it follows that

$$\beta(1-\lambda)(X_0 + \lambda X_{-1} + \lambda^2 X_{-2} + \cdots) = E(Y_0) - \alpha.$$

Therefore (11.88) can be reformulated as

(11.88a) $$Y_t = \alpha + \beta_0 W_t^{(\lambda)} + (\theta_0 - \alpha)\lambda^t + \varepsilon_t,$$

where $$W_t^{(\lambda)} = X_t + \lambda X_{t-1} + \lambda^2 X_{t-2} + \cdots + \lambda^{t-1} X_1$$

and $$\theta_0 = E(Y_0).$$

The value of $E(Y_0)$ is the initial mean value of Y and can be regarded as a parameter. Note that if λ were known, equation (11.88a) would be a linear multiple regression equation with two explanatory variables, $W_t^{(\lambda)}$ and λ^t, and could be estimated by the ordinary least squares method. Of course, λ is generally not known and has to be estimated along with α, β_0, and θ_0. The logarithmic likelihood function for Y_1, $Y_2, \ldots, Y_n$ is

(11.89) $$L = -\frac{n}{2}\log(2\pi\sigma^2) - \frac{1}{2\sigma^2}\sum_{t=1}^{n}[Y_t - \alpha - \beta_0 W_t^{(\lambda)} - (\theta_0 - \alpha)\lambda^t]^2.$$

Maximizing L with respect to α, β_0, λ, and θ_0 is equivalent to minimizing

$$S^{(\lambda)} = \sum_{t=1}^{n}[Y_t - \alpha - \beta_0 W_t^{(\lambda)} - (\theta_0 - \alpha)\lambda^t]^2$$

with respect to the same parameters. Since we know that $0 \leq \lambda < 1$, we can easily calculate the minimizing values of α, β_0, and θ_0, and the corresponding value of $S^{(\lambda)}$, for different values of λ from 0 to 0.95 or 0.99. Then we select those values of α, β_0, θ_0, and λ that lead to the smallest value of $S^{(\lambda)}$. These values will be the maximum likelihood estimates of the respective parameters. If we have no information about X other than the sample values of $X_1, X_2, \ldots, X_n$, the maximum likelihood estimates of α, β_0, and λ obtained in this way will be asymptotically efficient. Their asymptotic variances can be estimated by using the appropriate information matrix.

EXAMPLE The preceding method has been applied to estimating the parameters of a consumption function model from United States quarterly observations 1947(I) to 1960(IV).[33] The consumption function is derived from an adaptive expectation model and

[33] See Zellner and Geisel, *op. cit.* The data on personal consumption expenditures and personal disposable income, both series price-deflated and seasonally adjusted, are presented in Z. Griliches et al., "Notes on Estimated Aggregate Quarterly Consumption Function," *Econometrica,* 30 (July 1962), pp. 491–500.

can be described as

$$C_t = \beta Y_t^* + \varepsilon_t,$$

$$Y_t^* - Y_{t-1}^* = (1-\lambda)(Y_t - Y_{t-1}^*),$$

where C = measured real consumption, Y^* = "normal" or "permanent" real income, and Y = measured real income. By combining the two equations and eliminating Y^*, we obtain

$$C_t = \beta(1-\lambda)Y_t + \lambda C_{t-1} + \varepsilon_t - \lambda\varepsilon_{t-1}.$$

The coefficients have been estimated from

$$C_t = \beta(1-\lambda)W_t^{(\lambda)} + \theta_0\lambda^t + \varepsilon_t,$$

where $$W_t^{(\lambda)} = Y_t + \lambda Y_{t-1} + \cdots + \lambda^{t-1}Y_1$$

and $$\theta_0 = E(C_0).$$

The sum of squared residuals (divided by the number of observations) has been calculated for different values of λ between 0 and 1; the results are shown in Figure 11-11. The curve has a

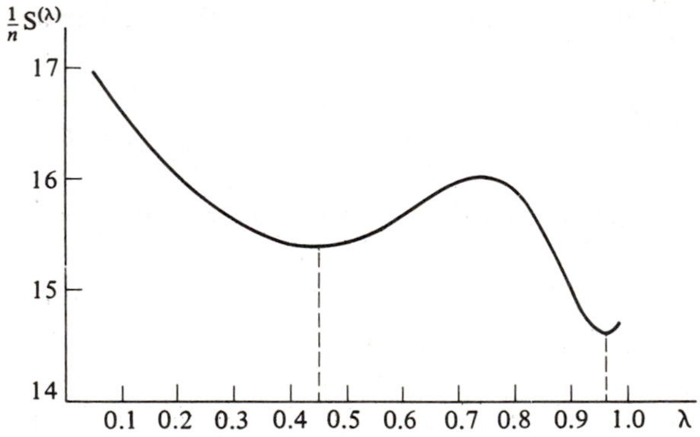

Figure 11-11

local minimum at $\lambda = 0.45$, and a global minimum at $\lambda = 0.963$. The latter is then the maximum likelihood estimate of λ. The corresponding estimates of β and θ_0 are

$$\hat{\beta} = 1.129 \qquad \text{and} \qquad \hat{\theta}_0 = 191.53.$$

Since β is supposed to measure the marginal propensity to consume out of "normal" income, a value larger than one is unreasonable a priori. Therefore, the results cannot be considered as acceptable. (Zellner and Geisel note that this result may be due to inadequacies of the particular model and/or data. If both the model and the data are thought to be adequate, then we should incorporate the restriction $0 < \beta < 1$ into our estimation procedure.)

A point to be noted about the maximum likelihood estimators obtained from (11.89) is that the term $(\theta_0 - \alpha)\lambda^t$ (called the "truncation remainder" term) approaches zero as t approaches infinity. Consequently, it makes no difference asymptotically whether this term is dropped or not. However, empirical evidence indicates that from the point of view of small sample efficiency it is better to retain the truncation remainder term than to drop it.[34]

Let us now change the specification of the adaptive expectation model by dropping the assumption of mutual independence of the εs as implied by (11.87), and replacing it by

(11.90) $$\varepsilon_t = \rho\varepsilon_{t-1} + u_t,$$

with $$E(\varepsilon_{t-1}u_t) = 0,$$

$$u_t \sim N(0, \sigma_u^2),$$

and $$\varepsilon_1 \sim N\left(0, \frac{\sigma_u^2}{1-\rho^2}\right).$$

To account for the autoregression of the disturbance, we subject (11.88a) to an autoregressive transformation as described in Section 8-3. Maximum likelihood estimates—either unconditional or conditional on Y_1—can then be obtained by searching over λ *and* ρ. These estimates will be asymptotically efficient; their asymptotic variances can be determined by reference to the appropriate information matrix.

EXAMPLE Zellner and Geisel[35] have applied the maximum likelihood method (conditional on Y_1) to the consumption model described in the preceding example, using the same set of observations. The results are

$$\hat{\beta} = \underset{(0.46)}{0.94},$$

$$\hat{\lambda} = \underset{(0.085)}{0.66},$$

$$\hat{\rho} = \underset{(0.076)}{0.69}.$$

The figures in parentheses are the estimated asymptotic standard errors. The results show that the estimate of λ is very close to that of ρ.

Let us now consider estimating the parameters of a geometrically distributed lag relation generated by a *partial adjustment* (or *habit persistence*) mechanism. Such a relation was represented by equation (11.84) as

$$Y_t = \alpha(1-\gamma) + \beta(1-\gamma)X_t + \gamma Y_{t-1} + \varepsilon_t,$$

where ε_t is a normally distributed random disturbance with mean zero and variance σ^2. The specification of the partial adjustment model does not lead to any further

[34] See, e.g., P. Schmidt, "The Small Sample Effect of Various Treatments of Truncation Remainders in the Estimation of Distributed Lag Models," *Review of Economics and Statistics,* 57 (August 1975), pp. 387–389.

[35] *Op. cit.*

restrictions on ε_t, which makes estimation much simpler than in the case of the adaptive expectation model. If it can be assumed that $E(\varepsilon_t \varepsilon_s) = 0$ for all $t \neq s$, then we can use the ordinary least squares method and obtain consistent and asymptotically efficient estimates of the parameters of (11.84). On the other hand, if ε_t follows a first-order autoregressive scheme, i.e., if

(11.91) $$\varepsilon_t = \rho\varepsilon_{t-1} + u_t,$$

where $$E(\varepsilon_{t-1}u_t) = 0,$$

$$u_t \sim N(0, \sigma_u^2),$$

and $$\varepsilon_1 \sim N\left(0, \frac{\sigma_u^2}{1-\rho^2}\right),$$

then the ordinary least squares method applied to (11.84) would lead to inconsistent estimates. In this case, we can use a transformation of (11.84) that eliminates ε_t. Maximum likelihood estimates of the unknown parameters can then be obtained by *searching* over ρ in the interval from -1 to $+1$. (It should be noted that the Cochrane-Orcutt iterative procedure does not work here because Y_{t-1} and ε_t are correlated and thus the initial estimate of ρ is inconsistent.[36] To test the hypothesis of no autoregression, we can use Durbin's h or m test discussed in Section 8-3.

Pascal Lag

In some instances, a distributed lag model with the weights declining geometrically from the current period into the past may not be altogether appropriate. For example, in a model relating current capital expenditures to current and past capital appropriations, it is much more reasonable to expect that the weights attached to capital appropriations at times $t, t-1, t-2, \ldots,$ would first rise and then decline instead of declining all the way. Such a distribution of weights may be called an *inverted V-lag distribution.* There are many ways in which such a lag distribution can be formulated. One possibility is to use the so-called *Pascal lag distribution.* This distribution can be described as follows. First rewrite (11.75) as

(11.75a) $$Y_t = \alpha + \beta(w_0X_t + w_1X_{t-1} + w_2X_{t-2} + \cdots) + \varepsilon_t,$$

where ε_t is a normally distributed disturbance with mean zero and variance σ^2. The weights corresponding to the Pascal lag model then are given as

$$w_i = \binom{i+r-1}{i}(1-\lambda)^r\lambda^i = \frac{(i+r-1)!}{i!(r-1)!}(1-\lambda)^r\lambda^i \qquad (i = 0, 1, 2, \ldots),$$

where r is some positive integer and λ a parameter to be estimated. The regression

[36] See R. Betancourt and H. Kelejian, "Lagged Endogenous Variables and the Cochrane-Orcutt Procedure," *Econometrica,* 49 (July 1981), pp. 1073-1078.

equation then becomes

$$(11.92)\quad Y_t = \alpha + \beta(1-\lambda)^r \left[X_t + r\lambda X_{t-1} + \frac{r(r+1)}{2!}\lambda^2 X_{t-2} + \cdots \right] + \varepsilon_t .$$

Note that when $r = 1$, we get $w_i = (1-\lambda)\lambda^i$, which means that the Pascal distribution reduces to a geometric lag distribution. For values of r greater than one, we may get inverted V-lag distributions. Figure 11-12 shows the distribution of weights for

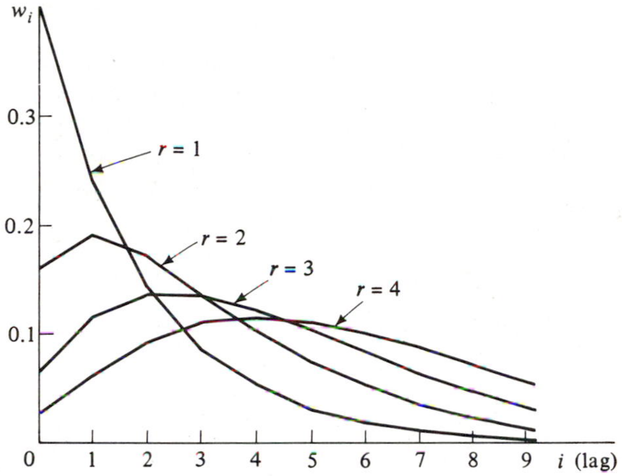

Figure 11-12

$\lambda = 0.6$ and for different values of r. A transformation analogous to the Koyck transformation used in connection with the adaptive expectation model can also be applied to the Pascal lag model. The resulting form is

(11.93)

$$Y_t + \binom{r}{1}(-\lambda)^1 Y_{t-1} + \binom{r}{2}(-\lambda)^2 Y_{t-2} + \cdots + \binom{r}{r}(-\lambda)^r Y_{t-r}$$

$$= \alpha(1-\lambda)^r + \beta(1-\lambda)^r X_t + \varepsilon_t + \binom{r}{1}(-\lambda)^1 \varepsilon_{t-1} + \cdots + \binom{r}{r}(-\lambda)^r \varepsilon_{t-r}.$$

The parameters of the Pascal lag model can be estimated by the maximum likelihood method by analogy with the maximum likelihood estimation of the adaptive expectation model.[37]

[37] See G. S. Maddala and A. S. Rao, "Maximum Likelihood Estimation of Solow's and Jorgenson's Distributed Lag Models," *Review of Economics and Statistics,* 53 (February 1971), pp. 80–88.

Rational Distributed Lag

In the transformed equation (11.93) of the Pascal lag model, the coefficients of the lagged Ys and εs are all constrained to be equal to specific functions of λ, and the coefficients of the lagged Xs are all set equal to zero. If we generalize (11.93) by removing these constraints, we obtain

(11.94)

$$Y_t + \delta_1 Y_{t-1} + \delta_2 Y_{t-2} + \cdots + \delta_r Y_{t-r}$$
$$= \alpha + \beta_0 X_t + \beta_1 X_{t-1} + \cdots + \beta_m X_{t-m} + \varepsilon_t + \delta_1 \varepsilon_{t-1} + \cdots + \delta_r \varepsilon_{t-r}.$$

Equation (11.94) describes the so-called *rational distributed lag model* introduced by Jorgenson.[38] Maximum likelihood estimation of the rational distributed lag model can be carried out in a way similar to that of the Pascal lag model.[39]

The presentation of the rational distributed lag model (and of other distributed lag models as well) can be facilitated by the use of the so-called *lag operator* notation. The lag operator L is defined as

$$Lx_t = x_{t-1}, \qquad L^2 x_t = x_{t-2}, \qquad \ldots, \qquad L^p x_t = x_{t-p},$$

and also $L^0 x_t = x_t$. Lag operators can be treated as ordinary algebraic symbols. For example,

$$L^p(L^q x_t) = L^p x_{t-q} = x_{t-q-p} = L^{p+q} x_t.$$

Further, a lag operator polynomial is defined as

$$f(L) = a_0 L^0 + a_1 L^1 + a_2 L^2 + \cdots + a_p L^p,$$

so that

$$f(L)x_t = a_0 x_t + a_1 x_{t-1} + \cdots + a_p x_{t-p}.$$

A general formulation of the rational distributed lag model in lag operator notation then is

$$f(L)Y_t = \alpha + g(L)X_t + f(L)\varepsilon_t$$

or

(11.94a) $$Y_t = \frac{\alpha}{f(L)} + \frac{g(L)}{f(L)} X_t + \varepsilon_t.$$

The adaptive expectation model, which is a special case of the rational distributed lag model, is given as

$$(1 - \lambda L)Y_t = \alpha(1 - \lambda) + \beta(1 - \lambda)X_t + (1 - \lambda L)\varepsilon_t$$

[38] D. W. Jorgenson, "Rational Distributed Lag Functions," *Econometrica*, 34 (January 1966), pp. 135–149.

[39] Maddala and Rao, *op. cit.*

or

$$(11.95)\qquad Y_t = \frac{\alpha(1-\lambda)}{1-\lambda L} + \frac{\beta(1-\lambda)}{1-\lambda L} X_t + \varepsilon_t.$$

The so-called *Box–Jenkins* (or ARMA) model, used in time-series analysis without recourse to economic theory, is of the form

$$f(L)Y_t = h(L)\varepsilon_t,$$

which is a simple modification of the rational distributed lag model.

Gamma Lag

Another type of lag distribution that can take on the form of an inverted V is the so-called *gamma distributed lag* introduced by Tsurumi, modified by Schmidt, and rationalized by Theil and Fiebig.[40] Here we present the modified version proposed by Schmidt. The weights in (11.75a) in the case of the gamma lag are given as

$$(11.96)\qquad w_i = (i+1)^{\delta/(1-\delta)}\lambda^i \qquad (i = 0, 1, 2, \ldots),$$

where $0 \leq \delta < 1$, and $0 \leq \lambda < 1$. For $\delta = 0$ the gamma lag reduces to the geometric lag. Maximum likelihood estimates of the unknown parameters can be obtained by searching over δ and λ.[41]

Polynomial Lag

A different formulation of the inverted V-lag model is possible in a situation in which we can assume that the weights w in

$$Y_t = \alpha + \beta(w_0 X_t + w_1 X_{t-1} + \cdots + w_m X_{t-m}) + \varepsilon_t$$

follow a polynomial of a given degree. Such models are called *polynomial lag models.* To formulate them we have to specify the appropriate degree of the polynomial and state the number of periods before the weights can be assumed to be zero. The estimation problem is quite straightforward. Suppose the degree of the polynomial is chosen to be four. Then to make each of the weights $w_0, w_1, \ldots, w_m$ lie along a fourth-degree polynomial curve, we specify

$$(11.97)\qquad w_i = \lambda_0 + \lambda_1 i + \lambda_2 i^2 + \lambda_3 i^3 + \lambda_4 i^4 \qquad (i = 0, 1, 2, \ldots, m).$$

[40] H. Tsurumi, "A Note on Gamma Distributed Lags," *International Economic Review,* 12 (June 1971), pp. 317–323; P. Schmidt, "An Argument for the Usefulness of the Gamma Distributed Lag Model," *International Economic Review,* 15 (February 1974), pp. 246–250; H. Theil and D. Fiebig, "A Maximum Entropy Approach to the Specification of Distributed Lags," *Economics Letters,* 7 (1981), pp. 339–342.

[41] See Schmidt, "An Argument . . . ," *op. cit.,* who also presents the information matrix for the calculation of the estimated standard errors.

Our polynomial lag model then becomes

$$(11.98)\quad Y_t = \alpha + \beta[\lambda_0 X_t + (\lambda_0 + \lambda_1 + \lambda_2 + \lambda_3 + \lambda_4)X_{t-1} + (\lambda_0 + 2\lambda_1 + 2^2\lambda_2 + 2^3\lambda_3 + 2^4\lambda_4)X_{t-2} + \cdots + (\lambda_0 + m\lambda_1 + m^2\lambda_2 + m^3\lambda_3 + m^4\lambda_4)X_{t-m}] + \varepsilon_t,$$

which can be concentrated as

$$(11.98a)\quad Y_t = \alpha + \beta\lambda_0 Z_{t0} + \beta\lambda_1 Z_{t1} + \cdots + \beta\lambda_4 Z_{t4} + \varepsilon_t,$$

where

$$Z_{t0} = X_t + X_{t-1} + \cdots + X_{t-m},$$
$$Z_{t1} = X_{t-1} + 2X_{t-2} + \cdots + mX_{t-m},$$
$$\vdots$$
$$Z_{t4} = X_{t-1} + 2^4 X_{t-2} + \cdots + m^4 X_{t-m}.$$

It is interesting to note that the imposition of the requirement that the weights lie along a fourth degree polynomial curve is equivalent to the imposition of $(m-4)$ restrictions of the form

$$(11.99)\quad w_i - 5w_{i-1} + 10w_{i-2} - 10w_{i-3} + 5w_{i-4} - w_{i-5} = 0$$

for $i = 5, 6, \ldots, m$. This can be easily confirmed by expressing the *w*s in terms of the λs using (11.97). In general, the requirement that the weights lie on a polynomial of degree p is equivalent to the imposition of $(m-p)$ restrictions of the form

$$(11.100)\quad w_i - \binom{p+1}{1} w_{i-1} + \binom{p+1}{2} w_{i-2} - \cdots + (-1)^p \binom{p+1}{p} w_{i-p} + (-1)^{p+1} w_{i-p-1} = 0$$

for $i = p+1, p+2, \ldots, m$. The imposition of the restrictions in (11.100) represents an alternative but equivalent way of forcing the weights to lie on a polynomial of a given degree. Some researchers add further additional restrictions that $w_{-1} = 0$ and $w_{m+1} = 0$. These restrictions are known as *end point restrictions.* Their use is, however, not recommended because the model involves only the weights w_0, $w_1, \ldots, w_m$ and gives no information on the behavior of the polynomial outside this range.[42]

Returning to equation (11.98a), we note that the equation involves seven parameters. However, the parameter β is clearly not identified; in practice its value is usually taken to be unity. The remaining parameters $\alpha, \lambda_0, \lambda_1, \ldots, \lambda_4$ can be estimated by ordinary least squares. If ε_t satisfies all the assumptions of the classical normal regression model, the resulting estimates will have all the desirable proper-

[42] See P. Schmidt and R. N. Waud, "The Almon Lag Technique and the Monetary versus Fiscal Policy Debate," *Journal of the American Statistical Association,* 68 (March 1973), pp. 11–19; also H. H. Kelejian and W. E. Oates, *Introduction to Econometrics* (New York: Harper & Row, 1981), p. 189.

ties. In case of autocorrelation, we can use one of the estimation methods described in Section 8-3. The estimated values of the λs can be substituted into (11.97) to obtain estimates of the weights $w_0, w_1, \ldots, w_m$. Since the resulting $\hat{w}$s are linear combinations of the $\hat{\lambda}$s, their estimated variances can be easily calculated from the estimated variances and covariances of the $\hat{\lambda}$s.

EXAMPLE The polynomial lag model was used by Almon[43] to estimate the relationship between current capital expenditures and current and past capital appropriations in the United States manufacturing industries. The degree of the polynomial in each case was 4, but the length of the lag was taken to be different for different industries. The data used for estimation were given by the quarterly observations for the years 1953–1961. The model was specified as

$$Y_t = \alpha_1 S_{t1} + \alpha_2 S_{t2} + \alpha_3 S_{t3} + \alpha_4 S_{t4} + w_0 X_t + w_1 X_{t-1} + \cdots + w_m X_{t-m} + \varepsilon_t,$$

where Y represents capital expenditures, the Ss represent seasonal dummy variables, and the Xs represent capital appropriations. The parameter α_4 was set equal to $(-\alpha_1 - \alpha_2 - \alpha_3)$. The weights were restricted by the conditions that $w_{-1} = 0$ and $w_{m+1} = 0$. The result for "all manufacturing industries" was

$$Y_t = -283S_{t1} + 12S_{t2} - 50S_{t3} + 320S_{t4} + \underset{(0.023)}{0.048}X_t + \underset{(0.016)}{0.099}X_{t-1} + \underset{(0.013)}{0.141}X_{t-2}$$

$$+ \underset{(0.023)}{0.165}X_{t-3} + \underset{(0.023)}{0.167}X_{t-4} + \underset{(0.013)}{0.146}X_{t-5} + \underset{(0.016)}{0.105}X_{t-6} + \underset{(0.024)}{0.053}X_{t-7} + e_t.$$

As can be seen, the chosen length of the lag in this case was 7 periods. The weights add up to 0.922; the difference between 0.922 and 1 can probably be accounted for by cancellations of past appropriations. The estimated weights are shown graphically in Figure 11-13.

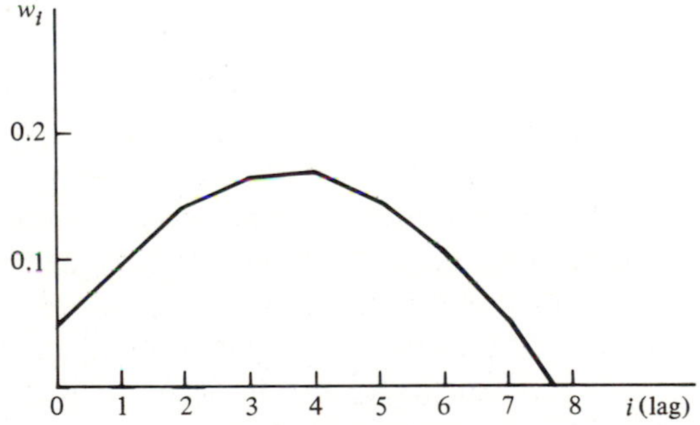

Figure 11-13

[43] S. Almon, "The Distributed Lag Between Capital Appropriations and Expenditures," *Econometrica,* 33 (January 1965), pp. 178–196. The parameters of the model are estimated with the help of the so-called "Lagrangian interpolation." However, this is an unnecessarily complicated and roundabout way of producing estimates that should be no different from those obtained by ordinary least squares as described by us. The only advantage of the Lagrangian interpolation procedure is that it is numerically more accurate with respect to round-off errors. See J. P. Cooper, "The Approaches to Polynomial Distributed Lag Estimation," *The American Statistician,* 26 (June 1972), pp. 32–35.

The polynomial lag model has veen very popular in applied work but it is not without problems. Perhaps the most serious of them is the usual uncertainty about the degree of the polynomial and the length of the lag. Most researchers tend to rely on some ad hoc criterion such as $\bar{R}^2$ when making their choice. The matter is relatively simple when the length of the lag (m) is known and only the degree of the polynomial (p) is uncertain. In this case we can follow a sequential testing procedure based on comparing restricted and unrestricted error sums of squares. We start by selecting the maximum polynomial degree that we think is possible, say, p^*—which could be equal to $(m-1)$—and test the hypothesis that the degree of the polynomial is (p^*-1), using the standard F test presented in (11.20) of Section 11-2. If the hypothesis is rejected, we stop and accept p^* as the appropriate degree. Otherwise we try one degree lower and test again. This is continued until the null hypothesis is rejected. The selected degree of the polynomial is then that corresponding to the last acceptable hypothesis. In following this procedure we have to be concerned about the true significance level of the test. The nominal significance level of the last test clearly understates the true probability of Error Type I, because it is conditional on the outcome of the tests that went on before (unless, of course, only one test is needed). According to Trivedi and Pagan,[44] the true level of significance of the qth test is given by

$$1-(1-\gamma_1)(1-\gamma_2)\cdots(1-\gamma_q),$$

where γ_j is the nominal level of significance of the jth individual test. Thus if, for instance, we use a 5% level of significance throughout and carry out three tests, the true level of significance of the third test will be 14.26%. If the finally chosen degree of the polynomial is larger than appropriate, the resulting estimates of the weights will be inefficient; if it is smaller, they will be biased and inconsistent.

If the length of the lag is not known—except for its possible maximum, say, m^*—we can carry out a sequence of tests of hypotheses

$$H_0^{(1)}:\quad w_{m^*}=0,\qquad H_0^{(2)}:\quad w_{m^*}=w_{m^*-1}=0,\quad \text{etc.},$$

using *unrestricted estimates* and employing the standard F test until we encounter a rejection. If the rejection occurs at the kth test, the selected length of the lag will be (m^*-k+1).[45] After the length of the lag has been determined, we can select the degree of the polynomial by the sequential testing procedure described above. The difficulty with selecting the length of the lag *and* the degree of the polynomial in this way is that the true level of significance is unknown.

[44] P. K. Trivedi and A. R. Pagan, "Polynomial Distributed Lags: A Unified Treatment," *Economic Studies Quarterly,* 30 (1979), pp. 37–49.

[45] See M. Pagano and M. J. Hartley, "On Fitting Distributed Lag Models Subject to Polynomial Restrictions," *Journal of Econometrics,* 16 (June 1981), pp. 171–198. When the length of the lag is understated—or if it is overstated by more than the degree of the polynomial—the resulting restricted estimates of the weights will be biased and inconsistent; see Schmidt and Waud, *op. cit.*

LaGuerre Lag

The finite length of the lag in a polynomial distributed lag model, in addition to being difficult to determine, may also be quite unrealistic at times. The influence of X on Y in many cases is likely to diminish gradually as time goes on rather than being cut off abruptly. Another possibly troublesome feature of the polynomial distributed lag is that the model does not allow for the case of *no lag* as a special case. Both of these shortcomings can be avoided with the use of a modified version of the polynomial lag model proposed by Schmidt and called the *LaGuerre lag model.*[46] In this model the weights are given by

(11.101) $$w_i = (\lambda_0 + \lambda_1 i + \cdots + \lambda_p i^p)\mu^i,$$

where $0 \leq \mu < 1$ and $i = 0, 1, 2, \ldots$. The LaGuerre lag model reduces to the geometric lag model when $\lambda_1 = \lambda_2 = \cdots = \lambda_p = 0$. The case of no lag occurs when $\mu = 0$ (on the presumption that $\mu^0 = 1$ even when $\mu = 0$). When i is large, the expression for w_i in (11.101) will be dominated by the term μ^i, so that the influence of X on Y decreases with the increase in i and eventually disappears as $i \to \infty$. For small values of i the polynomial term may be the dominating factor. The model can be estimated by the maximum likelihood method in a way similar to that of estimating the geometric, Pascal, and rational distributed lag models.[47] The small increase in complexity of this model compared to the polynomial distributed lag model seems well worth the effort in order to avoid some of the main shortcomings of the polynomial distributed lag.

Shiller Lag

Another modification of the polynomial lag model has been proposed by Shiller, who suggested that the equality restrictions in (11.100) be changed to *stochastic* restrictions.[48] The underlying idea is the presumption that prior information about the weights is likely to be that they should change in a "smooth" way (i.e., without substantial or abrupt jumps) rather than that they should lie *exactly* on a polynomial. Let us consider a polynomial of second degree for illustration. The implied restrictions on the weights in this case are

$$w_i - 3w_{i-1} + 3w_{i-2} - w_{i-3} = 0 \qquad (i = 3, 4, \ldots, m).$$

In contrast, the Shiller lag model is based on

(11.102) $$w_i - 3w_{i-1} + 3w_{i-2} - w_{i-3} = v_i,$$

[46] P. Schmidt, "A Modification of the Almon Distributed Lag," *Journal of the American Statistical Association,* 69 (September 1974), pp. 679–681.

[47] *Ibid.*

[48] R. J. Shiller, "A Distributed Lag Estimator Derived from Smoothness Priors," *Econometrica,* 41 (July 1973), pp. 775–788.

where v_i is to be viewed as a random variable with mean zero and variance σ_v^2. A convenient way of incorporating this restriction into the estimation process is by using the mixed estimation procedure described in Section 11-2. The quantity σ_v^2 is supposed to reflect the strength of our belief in the *exact* polynomial restrictions. When it is difficult to specify σ_v^2 a priori, Shiller proposes a "rule of thumb" formula for replacing σ_v^2 by s_v^2 defined as

$$s_v^2 = \frac{64(w_0 + w_1 + \cdots + w_m)^2}{m^4}. \tag{11.103}$$

The sum of the *w*s is to be specified a priori. (Frequently this may be unity.) Failing that, we may use ordinary unrestricted least squares estimates.

A Note on Rational Expectation Models

Rational expectation models, which have become very popular in economics, can often be represented in some form of a distributed lag model. The idea behind the rational expectation hypothesis is that economic agents do not waste information and that their expectations are basically the same as predictions based on economic theory.[49] We illustrate the rational expectation hypothesis by reference to a simple supply-demand model of a market for a farm product. Suppose we have

$$Q_t = \alpha_1 + \alpha_2 P_t + \alpha_3 X_t + \varepsilon_{1t} \qquad \text{(demand)},$$

$$Q_t = \beta_1 + \beta_2 P_t^* + \varepsilon_{2t} \qquad \text{(supply)},$$

where Q = quantity, P = actual price, X = income, P^* = anticipated price, and ε_{1t} and ε_{2t} are mutually independent random disturbances that have zero means, constant variances, and are nonautocorrelated. In equilibrium, supply equals demand, so that

$$\alpha_1 + \alpha_2 P_t + \alpha_3 X_t + \varepsilon_{1t} = \beta_1 + \beta_2 P_t^* + \varepsilon_{2t}$$

or

$$P_t = \frac{\beta_1 - \alpha_1}{\alpha_2} + \left(\frac{\beta_2}{\alpha_2}\right) P_t^* + \left(-\frac{\alpha_3}{\alpha_2}\right) X_t + \frac{\varepsilon_{2t} - \varepsilon_{1t}}{\alpha_2}. \tag{11.104}$$

Therefore, the optimal predictor of price based on economic theory—assuming that the parameters of the market are known—is $E(P_t)$. According to the rational expectation hypothesis, $E(P_t)$ should coincide with P_t^*, so that we have

$$P_t^* = \frac{\beta_1 - \alpha_1}{\alpha_2} + \left(\frac{\beta_2}{\alpha_2}\right) P_t^* + \left(-\frac{\alpha_3}{\alpha_2}\right) X_t^*, \tag{11.105}$$

where X_t^* is the anticipated value of X_t in the market, given all the knowledge

[49] For a lucid explanation of the rational expectation hypothesis see M. B. Stewart and K. F. Wallis, *Introductory Econometrics* (New York: Halsted Press, 1981), pp. 65-71, on which the main part of our discussion is based.

available to the economic agents at time $t-1$. Solving (11.105) for P_t^*, we obtain

(11.105a) $$P_t^* = \frac{\beta_1 - \alpha_1}{\alpha_2 - \beta_2} + \left(-\frac{\alpha_3}{\alpha_2 - \beta_2}\right) X_t^*.$$

In considering X_t^* we note that by deducting (11.105) from (11.104) we obtain

$$P_t - P_t^* = \left(-\frac{\alpha_3}{\alpha_2}\right)(X_t - X_t^*) + \frac{\varepsilon_{2t} - \varepsilon_{1t}}{\alpha_2}.$$

According to the rational expectation hypothesis, P_t^* is required to be an optimal predictor of P_t so that $P_t - P_t^*$ has to be "pure white noise," i.e., it has to be a nonautocorrelated random variable with mean zero and a constant variance. Now $(\varepsilon_{t2} - \varepsilon_{t1})/\alpha_2$ is pure white noise by definition, so $X_t - X_t^*$ *either* has to be equal to zero *or* it has to be pure white noise itself. Following are some possibilities:

1. X_t is nonstochastic and its exact value is known at time $t-1$.
2. The value of X_t is determined in another market and X_t^* is a rational predictor of X_t from that market. Thus $X_t - X_t^*$ is pure white noise.
3. The value of X_t is generated according to the scheme

   $$X_t = X_{t-1} + \varepsilon_t - \lambda\varepsilon_{t-1},$$

   where $0 \leq \lambda < 1$.
4. The value of X_t is generated according to the Box–Jenkins model, i.e.,

   $$X_t = \gamma_1 X_{t-1} + \gamma_2 X_{t-2} + \cdots + \gamma_p X_{t-p} + \varepsilon_t + \delta_1\varepsilon_{t-1} + \cdots + \delta_q\varepsilon_{t-q}$$

   and

   $$X_t^* = \gamma_1 X_{t-1} + \gamma_2 X_{t-2} + \cdots + \gamma_p X_{t-p} + \delta_1\varepsilon_{t-1} + \delta_2\varepsilon_{t-2} + \cdots + \delta_q\varepsilon_{t-q}.$$

In situation (1) X_t has the same role as the nonstochastic explanatory variable in a classical regression model. Unfortunately, in market models such as the one considered here, it is rather unlikely that the suppliers know the value of X_t at time $t-1$. Situation (2) is probably quite common but it has not drawn much attention in the literature, perhaps because of its complexity. It raises an interesting prospect of a chain determination of predictors since the market in which X_t is determined may, in turn, involve the prediction of another variable whose value is determined in yet another market, and so on. Situation (3) was discussed in connection with the adaptive expectation model and was presented in (11.81). It results in a geometric distributed lag model as demonstrated. Situation (4) is the one most commonly assumed in dealing with the rational expectation hypothesis. Unfortunately the specification of the Box–Jenkins model has no basis in economic or social theory. Further, the presumption that the parameters of the model are known—or can be very precisely represented by sample estimates—is questionable. The main reason for the popularity of the Box–Jenkins model is that in practice it seems to work well in the sense that it tends to be successful in making short-run predictions.

The determination of X_t^* leads to the determination of P_t. Substituting for P_t^* from (11.105a) into (11.104), we obtain

$$P_t = \gamma_1 + \gamma_2 X_t + \gamma_3 X_t^* + u_t, \tag{11.106}$$

where

$$\gamma_1 = \frac{\beta_1 - \alpha_1}{\alpha_2 - \beta_2}, \quad \gamma_2 = -\frac{\alpha_3}{\alpha_2}, \quad \gamma_3 = -\frac{\alpha_3 \beta_2}{\alpha_2(\alpha_2 - \beta_2)}, \quad \text{and} \quad u_t = \frac{\varepsilon_{2t} - \varepsilon_{1t}}{\alpha_2}.$$

Similarly, the equilibrium solution for Q_t becomes

$$Q_t = \delta_1 + \delta_2 X_t + \delta_3 X_t^* + v_t, \tag{11.107}$$

where the δs represent expressions in terms of the α s and β s, and $v_t = \varepsilon_{2t}$. The generation of X_t according to (3) or (4), for instance, leads to expressions for P_t and Q_t that take the form of a distributed lag model. Other schemes for generating X_t may also lead to distributed lags. A test of the rational expectation hypothesis could be based on testing the validity of the implied restrictions of the coefficients of (11.106) and (11.107).

Concluding Remarks

Distributed lags play an important role in applied economic research. Indeed, it has been stated that "a time series regression model arising in econometric research ought in nearly every case to be regarded as a distributed lag model until proven otherwise."[50] Certainly any econometric model involving lagged variables is—explicitly or implicitly—based on some sort of a distributed lag scheme. In order to make an appropriate evaluation of such a model, the mechanism leading to the introduction of the lagged variables should be explained and justified. Unfortunately, most of the empirical research involving lags in economic behavior is not soundly based on economic theory and relies largely on ad hoc specification. This is true even of the rational expectation models, which seem to fall back without much thought on the mechanistic formulations of the Box–Jenkins type.

Our discussion of distributed lag models has mainly consisted of enumeration and explanation of various distributed lag schemes that have been used in applied work. As such the discussion reflects the state of the art and is not very helpful in providing criteria for choice of any particular distributed lag model in any particular situation. If Nerlove's call for a "new" microeconomics based on econometrically relevant dynamic theory[51] is heeded, matters may improve.

[50] C. A. Sims, "Distributed Lags" in M. D. Intriligator and D. A. Kendrick (eds.), *Frontiers of Quantitative Economics,* Vol. II (Amsterdam: North-Holland, 1974), p. 289.

[51] M. Nerlove, "Lags in Economic Behavior," *Econometrica,* 40 (March 1972), pp. 221–251.

11-5 Models with Qualitative Dependent Variables

In many situations the dependent variable in a regression equation is not continuous but represents a discrete choice, such as participating or not participating in the labor force, purchasing or not purchasing a given appliance, or selecting a certain mode of transportation. Models involving dependent variables of this kind are called "discrete choice models," "qualitative response models," "categorical models," or "quantal models." The economic interpretation of these models is typically based on the principle of utility maximization leading to the choice of, say, A over B if the utility of A exceeds that of B. Alternatively, the observed occurrence of a given choice is considered to be an indicator of an underlying, unobservable continuous variable, which may be called "propensity to choose a given alternative." Such a variable is characterized by the existence of a threshold (or thresholds); crossing a threshold means switching from one alternative to another. For instance, a married woman's propensity to join the labor force may be directly related to the wage that she may receive in the market, which in turn may depend on her education and experience. Whether she actually joins the work force or not is likely to depend on whether her market wage does or does not exceed her threshold or "reservation" wage. This threshold or reservation wage, which is typically different for different women with the same education and experience, plays the role of a stochastic disturbance. Both approaches—utility maximization and the threshold approach—are, of course, closely related. In our discussion we follow the advice of Judge et al.[52] to bypass both approaches and deal directly with the determination of the probabilities of different choices as a function of the relevant explanatory variables.

The complexity of estimation and testing of models with qualitative dependent variables increases with the number of alternative choices. The simplest models are, of course, those with only two alternatives involving a binary or dichotomous dependent variable. By convenience and custom the dependent variable is given a value of 0 or 1. Thus, for example, a married woman in the labor force would be assigned $Y = 1$, whereas a married woman not in the labor force would be given $Y = 0$. Whether Y equals 0 or 1 depends on a set of explanatory variables and a stochastic disturbance. We will discuss models with dichotomous dependent variables first and then extend the discussion to models with polytomous dependent variables.

Throughout the discussion we will limit ourselves to models with only one explanatory variable (X) to simplify the notation; an extension to more than one explanatory variable is quite straightforward. In models with qualitative dependent variables, the relationship between X and Y need not necessarily be linear. In fact, the models used in applied work are mainly nonlinear; linear models are used mostly as quick and convenient approximations to nonlinear models. They are discussed here to provide a starting point for the commonly used nonlinear models.

[52] G. G. Judge et al., *op. cit.*, p. 756.

Linear Probability Model

Let us start with a model in which the binary dependent variable is a linear function of an explanatory variable, which is quantitative. As an example, consider a regression model designed to explain the ownership of a certain appliance—for instance, a dishwasher. Suppose the postulated regression equation is

$$Y_i = \alpha + \beta X_i + \varepsilon_i, \tag{11.108}$$

where X_i represents the income of the ith family, and Y_i is a binary variable such that

$$\begin{aligned} Y_i &= 1 \quad \text{if the } i\text{th family owns a dishwasher,} \\ &= 0 \quad \text{otherwise.} \end{aligned}$$

The explanatory variable X_i is assumed to be nonstochastic or, if stochastic, independent of ε_i. The disturbance ε_i is a random variable that has a zero mean and is independent of ε_j $(i \neq j)$. Since Y_i can only assume two different values, 0 and 1, we have, by the definition of mathematical expectation given by (3.25),

$$E(Y_i) = 1 \times f_i(1) + 0 \times f_i(0) = f_i(1),$$

where $f_i(1)$ is the probability that a family with income X_i has a dishwasher. Note that since from (11.108)

$$E(Y_i) = \alpha + \beta X_i,$$

the probability $f_i(1)$ is supposed to be different for different income levels. Thus $E(Y_i)$ can be interpreted as measuring the proportion of all families with income X_i who have a dishwasher. This implies that

$$0 \leq \alpha + \beta X_i \leq 1.$$

Let us now consider the disturbance ε_i. Since from (11.108)

$$\varepsilon_i = Y_i - \alpha - \beta X_i,$$

and since Y_i can only be equal to 0 or 1, it follows that for any given income X_i the disturbance can assume only two different values, $(-\alpha - \beta X_i)$ and $(1 - \alpha - \beta X_i)$. This means that ε_i is *not* normally distributed, but has a discrete distribution defined as

ε_i	$f(\varepsilon_i)$
$-\alpha - \beta X_i$	f_i
$1 - \alpha - \beta X_i$	$1 - f_i$
	1

The probabilities f_i and $(1 - f_i)$ can be determined by utilizing the assumption that $E(\varepsilon_i) = 0$. This means that

$$(-\alpha - \beta X_i)f_i + (1 - \alpha - \beta X_i)(1 - f_i) = 0,$$

which gives

$$f_i = 1 - \alpha - \beta X_i.$$

Therefore the variance of ε_i is

$$(11.109)\quad E(\varepsilon_i^2) = (-\alpha - \beta X_i)^2(1 - \alpha - \beta X_i) + (1 - \alpha - \beta X_i)^2(\alpha + \beta X_i)$$
$$= (\alpha + \beta X_i)(1 - \alpha - \beta X_i) = E(Y_i)[1 - E(Y_i)].$$

This means that ε_i is heteroskedastic since its variance depends on $E(Y_i)$.

Because of the special nature of the dependent variable in (11.108), there are some problems of estimation and prediction. The first problem is that of heteroskedasticity. This problem can be fairly easily overcome by using the weighted least squares formulas (8.13) and (8.14) of Section 8-2. The variance of ε_i can be consistently estimated by $\hat{\sigma}_i^2$ defined as

$$(11.110)\quad \hat{\sigma}_i^2 = \hat{Y}_i(1 - \hat{Y}_i),$$

where $\hat{Y}$ is the least squares fitted value of Y. The second problem concerns the least squares predictor $\hat{Y}$, which may be negative or may exceed 1 for some values of X. Since $\hat{Y}$ is an estimator of $E(Y)$, which is a probability, the values of $\hat{Y}$ should be confined to the interval [0, 1]. The third and the most serious problem is that the intercept and the slope of the assumed model are not constant for all values of X but change as follows.

1. For $X_i \leq -\alpha/\beta$, both the intercept and the slope are equal to zero.
2. For $-\alpha/\beta \leq X_i \leq (1 - \alpha)/\beta$, the intercept is equal to α, and the slope to β.
3. For $X_i \geq (1 - \alpha)/\beta$, the intercept is equal to one and the slope to zero.

These are illustrated in Figure 11-14. The least squares estimates of α and β based

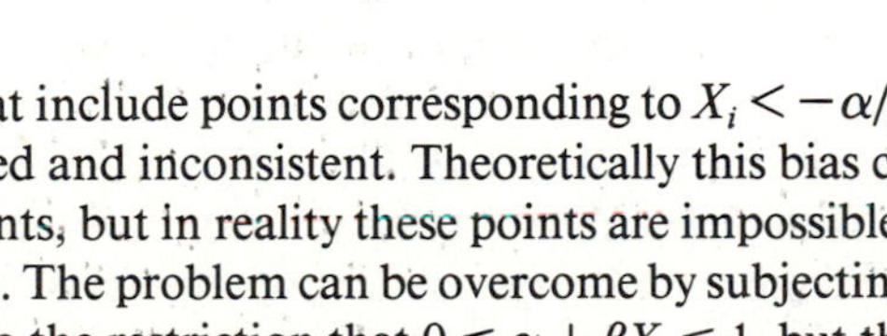

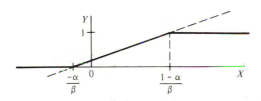

Figure 11-14

on observations that include points corresponding to $X_i < -\alpha/\beta$ or $X_i > (1 - \alpha)/\beta$ are, therefore, biased and inconsistent. Theoretically this bias could be avoided by excluding such points, but in reality these points are impossible to identify since α and β are unknown. The problem can be overcome by subjecting the weighted least squares estimates to the restriction that $0 \leq \alpha + \beta X_i \leq 1$, but this is messy and the sampling properties of the resulting estimator are not known.[53]

[53] Ibid., pp. 759–761.

Logit Model

The inadequacies of the linear probability model suggest that a nonlinear specification may be more appropriate. A natural candidate would be an S-shaped curve bounded in the interval (0, 1) and such that $E(Y_i) \rightarrow 0$ when $X_i \rightarrow -\infty$ and $E(Y_i) \rightarrow 1$ when $X_i \rightarrow +\infty$. One such curve is the *logistic curve* that corresponds to what is known as the *logit model.* This model is very popular in practical applications. Its specification is

$$E(Y_i) = \frac{1}{1 + e^{-\alpha - \beta X_i}} \tag{11.111}$$

$$= \frac{e^{\alpha + \beta X_i}}{1 + e^{\alpha + \beta X_i}},$$

where $E(Y_i) = P(Y_i = 1)$, as before. Denoting $E(Y_i) = \pi_i$ for simplicity and solving for $(\alpha + \beta X_i)$, we obtain

$$\log \frac{\pi_i}{1 - \pi_i} = \alpha + \beta X_i, \tag{11.112}$$

where all logarithms are *natural* logarithms. Note that $\pi_i/(1 - \pi_i)$ is the ratio of the odds of $Y_i = 1$ against $Y_i = 0$. The transformation in (11.112) is rather neat and has certainly helped the popularity of this model.

A couple of special features of the logit model may be worth noting. First, if we are interested in the effect of a change in X on the probability that $Y = 1$, we find that

$$\frac{\partial \pi_i}{\partial X_i} = \frac{\partial \pi_i}{\partial \log \pi_i(1 - \pi_i)} \times \frac{\partial \log \pi_i(1 - \pi_i)}{\partial X_i} \tag{11.113}$$

$$= \beta \pi_i(1 - \pi_i).$$

Second, if the logistic curve is viewed as a cumulative probability function of Z_i such that $P(Z_i \leq \alpha + \beta X_i) = 1/(1 + e^{-\alpha - \beta X_i})$, then the probability density of Z_i is

$$f(Z_i) = \frac{e^{Z_i}}{(1 + e^{Z_i})^2}.$$

This function is known as the *logistic distribution.*[54]

The estimation of the parameters of the logit model depends upon whether we have or do not have replicated observations on Y for each different value of X. When, as is more common, there are no (or only very few) replicated observations, the method to use is *maximum likelihood.* Since Y_i is a binomial variable which assumes a value of 1 with probability π_i and a value of 0 with probability $(1 - \pi_i)$, the log-likelihood function for n independent observations is

$$L = \sum_{i=1}^{n} [Y_i \log \pi_i + (1 - Y_i) \log(1 - \pi_i)]. \tag{11.114}$$

[54] If the *linear* probability model is viewed as a cumulative distribution function, then the corresponding density function is uniform.

This log-likelihood function is quite *general* and applies to *any* binomial distribution. For the *logit* model, in which the probabilities lie on a logistic curve, we substitute the expression for $E(Y_i)$ given in (11.111) for π_i. After some algebraic manipulation, this gives

$$L = \sum_i [Y_i(\alpha + \beta X_i) - \log(1 + e^{\alpha + \beta X_i})]. \tag{11.115}$$

The first-order conditions are

$$\frac{\partial L}{\partial \alpha} \equiv \sum_i (Y_i - \hat{\pi}_i) = 0, \tag{11.116}$$

$$\frac{\partial L}{\partial \beta} \equiv \sum_i (Y_i - \hat{\pi}_i)X_i = 0.$$

Since

$$\hat{\pi}_i = \frac{e^{\hat{\alpha} + \hat{\beta} X_i}}{1 + e^{\hat{\alpha} + \hat{\beta} X_i}},$$

the two equations in (11.116) can be solved for $\hat{\alpha}$ and $\hat{\beta}$. The asymptotic variances and covariances of $\hat{\alpha}$ and $\hat{\beta}$ can be obtained by reference to the information matrix.

When there are replicated observations, which could be the case when X is discrete or categorical, we replace Y_i by Y_{ij}, where $i = 1, 2, \ldots, m$ and $j = 1, 2, \ldots, n_i$. That means that when $X = X_i$, we have n_i observations on Y. Therefore, we can estimate π_i by p_i defined as

$$p_i = \frac{1}{n_i} \sum_{j=1}^{n_i} Y_{ij}. \tag{11.117}$$

Note that p_i is simply the sample proportion of "successes."

The availability of p_i, which is an unbiased and consistent estimator of π_i, enables us to adopt estimation strategies that are simpler than maximum likelihood estimation. Let

$$\varepsilon_i = p_i - \pi_i.$$

Then we can write

$$\begin{aligned}\log\left(\frac{p_i}{1 - p_i}\right) &= \log\left(\frac{\pi_i + \varepsilon_i}{1 - \pi_i - \varepsilon_i}\right)\\ &= \log\left(\frac{\pi_i}{1 - \pi_i}\right) \times \frac{1 + (\varepsilon_i/\pi_i)}{1 - \varepsilon_i/(1 - \pi_i)}\\ &= \log\left(\frac{\pi_i}{1 - \pi_i}\right) + \log\left(1 + \frac{\varepsilon_i}{\pi_i}\right) - \log\left(1 - \frac{\varepsilon_i}{1 - \pi_i}\right).\end{aligned}$$

Utilizing the expansion

$$\log(1 + a) = a - \frac{a^2}{2} + \frac{a^3}{3} - \cdots,$$

we have

$$\log\left(1+\frac{\varepsilon_i}{\pi_i}\right)=\frac{\varepsilon_i}{\pi_i}-\frac{(\varepsilon_i/\pi_i)^2}{2}+\cdots$$

and

$$\log\left(1-\frac{\varepsilon_i}{1-\pi_i}\right)=\frac{-\varepsilon_i}{1-\pi_i}-\frac{[-\varepsilon_i/(1-\pi_i)]^2}{2}+\cdots .$$

The terms of order higher than one can be dropped because they become very small when n_i is large. Thus we obtain the large-sample relation

(11.118) $$\log\left(\frac{p_i}{1-p_i}\right)=\alpha+\beta X_i+\frac{\varepsilon_i}{\pi_i}+\frac{\varepsilon_i}{1-\pi_i}$$

$$=\alpha+\beta X_i+\frac{\varepsilon_i}{\pi_i(1-\pi_i)}.$$

Note that

$$E\left[\frac{\varepsilon_i}{\pi_i(1-\pi_i)}\right]=0$$

and

(11.119) $$\operatorname{Var}\left[\frac{\varepsilon_i}{\pi_i(1-\pi_i)}\right]=\operatorname{Var}\left[\frac{p_i}{\pi_i(1-\pi_i)}\right]$$

$$=\frac{1}{[\pi_i(1-\pi_i)]^2}\times\frac{\pi_i(1-\pi_i)}{n_i}$$

$$=\frac{1}{n_i\,\pi_i(1-\pi_i)}.$$

A consistent estimator of $\operatorname{Var}[\varepsilon_i/\pi_i(1-\pi_i)]$, say, s_i^2, is given by

$$s_i^2=\frac{1}{n_ip_i(1-p_i)}.$$

Thus we can apply the least squares method to

(11.120) $$\frac{1}{s_i}\log\left(\frac{p_i}{1-p_i}\right)=\alpha\left(\frac{1}{s_i}\right)+\beta\left(\frac{X_i}{s_i}\right)+u_i.$$

The resulting estimates of α and β are known as *least squares estimates corrected for heteroskedasticity.*

An alternative estimation method to use when replicated observations are available is the so-called *minimum chi-square method.*[55] Since in large samples

$$p_i\sim N\left[\pi_i,\frac{\pi_i(1-\pi_i)}{n_i}\right],$$

[55] See, e.g., T. Amemiya, "The Maximum Likelihood, the Minimum Chi-Square and the Nonlinear Weighted Least Squares in the General Qualitative Response Model," *Journal of the American Statistical Association,* 71 (June 1976), pp. 347–351.

it follows that asymptotically

$$\frac{(p_i - \pi_i)\sqrt{n_i}}{\sqrt{\pi_i(1 - \pi_i)}} \sim N(0, 1)$$

and

$$\sum_{i=1}^{m} \frac{n_i(p_i - \pi_i)^2}{\pi_i(1 - \pi_i)} \sim \chi^2_m. \tag{11.121}$$

The expression (11.121) can then be minimized with respect to α and β. Since π_i is a nonlinear function of α and β, the minimum chi-square estimates can be viewed as weighted nonlinear least squares estimates. All three-methods — maximum likelihood, least squares corrected for heteroskedasticity, and minimum chi-square — lead to estimators that are asymptotically normal and have the same desirable asymptotic properties.

Probit Model

Another S-shaped curve that satisfies the requirements of a probability model is the *cumulative normal distribution function* corresponding to the so-called *probit model.* This model is usually derived as follows. Let us consider an unobservable variable Y_i^* given as

$$Y_i^* = \alpha + \beta X_i + \varepsilon_i,$$

where $\varepsilon_i \sim N(0, 1)$ and ε_i and $\varepsilon_j (i \neq j)$ are independent. The observable binary variable Y_i is related to Y_i^* in the following way.

$$\begin{aligned} Y_i &= 1 \quad \text{if } Y_i^* > 0, \\ &= 0 \quad \text{if } Y_i^* \leq 0. \end{aligned}$$

Then

$$\begin{aligned} E(Y_i) &= \pi_i = P(Y_i = 1) \\ &= P(Y_i^* > 0) = P(-\varepsilon_i < \alpha + \beta X_i) \\ &= F(\alpha + \beta X_i), \end{aligned} \tag{11.122}$$

where $F(\cdot)$ represents the cumulative distribution function of the standard normal distribution. That is,

$$F(\alpha + \beta X_i) = \int_{-\infty}^{\alpha + \beta X_i} f(z)dz,$$

where $f(z)$ represents the density function of $z \sim N(0, 1)$. Since $\pi_i = F(\alpha + \beta X_i)$, we can write

$$F^{-1}(\pi_i) = \alpha + \beta X_i, \tag{11.123}$$

where $F^{-1}(\pi_i)$ is the inverse of the standard normal cumulative distribution function.

The parameters α and β in (11.123) can be estimated by the maximum likelihood method using the log-likelihood function (11.114). Substituting for π_i from (11.122) into (11.114), we obtain

$$L = \sum \{Y_i \log F(\alpha + \beta X_i) + (1 - Y_i) \log[1 - F(\alpha + \beta X_i)]\}. \tag{11.124}$$

Maximizing L with respect to α and β and estimating the standard errors with the help of the information matrix is complicated, but computer programs for this purpose are readily available.

When we have replicated observations on Y for each different value of X, the problem of estimation becomes simpler. Let p_i be defined as in (11.117). Then we can write

$$F^{-1}(p_i) = F^{-1}(\pi_i + \varepsilon_i)$$

and, using the Taylor expansion around π_i, obtain

$$F^{-1}(p_i) = F^{-1}(\pi_i) + \frac{\partial F^{-1}(\pi_i)}{\partial \pi_i} \varepsilon_i + R_i,$$

where R_i represents terms of order higher than one, which can be dropped because they become very small when n_i is large. Further,

$$\begin{aligned}\frac{\partial F^{-1}(\pi_i)}{\partial \pi_i} &= \frac{\partial(\alpha + \beta X_i)}{\partial F(\alpha + \beta X_i)} \\ &= \frac{1}{\partial F(\alpha + \beta X_i)/\partial(\alpha + \beta X_i)} \\ &= \frac{1}{f(\alpha + \beta X_i)},\end{aligned}$$

where $f(\alpha + \beta X_i)$ is a standard normal density function evaluated at $\alpha + \beta X_i$. Therefore, we obtain the following large-sample relation.

$$F^{-1}(p_i) = \alpha + \beta X_i + \frac{\varepsilon_i}{f(\alpha + \beta X_i)}. \tag{11.125}$$

Note that

$$E\left[\frac{\varepsilon_i}{f(\alpha + \beta X_i)}\right] = 0,$$

$$\begin{aligned}\operatorname{Var}\left[\frac{\varepsilon_i}{f(\alpha + \beta X_i)}\right] &= \operatorname{Var}\left[\frac{p_i}{f(\alpha + \beta X_i)}\right] \\ &= \frac{\pi_i(1 - \pi_i)}{n_i[f(\alpha + \beta X_i)]^2}.\end{aligned} \tag{11.126}$$

The latter can be estimated consistently by replacing π_i by p_i and α and β by $\hat{\alpha}$ and $\hat{\beta}$, where $\hat{\alpha}$ and $\hat{\beta}$ are the ordinary least squares estimators of α and β in (11.125). After obtaining a consistent estimate of the variance of $\varepsilon_i/f(\alpha + \beta X_i)$, we can obtain least squares estimates corrected for heteroskedasticity as in the case of the logit model. Both estimators—maximum likelihood and least squares corrected for heteroskedasticity—are asymptotically normal and have all the desirable asymptotic properties.

Comparing the Logit and Probit Models

When dealing with binary dependent variables, a question naturally arises as to which of the two nonlinear models to choose. The best answer to that question would be based on theoretical grounds, but well-developed theory to determine the exact functional form appears to be lacking. Many authors, however, tend to agree on the following points.[56]

1. The logistic and cumulative normal functions are very close in the midrange, but the logistic function has slightly heavier tails than the cumulative normal (see Figure 11-15). Thus it does not matter much

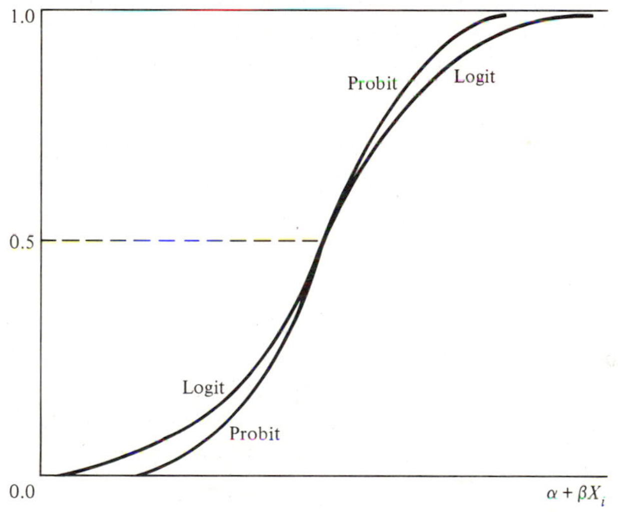

Figure 11-15

which function is used except in cases where the data are heavily concentrated in the tails.

2. The logistic function is used because it represents a close approximation to the cumulative normal and is simpler to work with. The close similarity between the logit and probit models is confined to dichotomous dependent variables. When the dependent variable is polytomous, there are major differences between the two models.

[56] Judge et al., *op. cit.*, p. 762; G. S. Maddala, *Limited Dependent and Qualitative Variables in Econometrics* (Cambridge, England: Cambridge University Press, 1983), p. 9; P. Schmidt and A. D. Witte, *An Economic Analysis of Crime and Justice* (Orlando, FL: Academic Press, 1984), p. 22.

Researchers are frequently interested in having a scalar measure of the "goodness of fit" of their model. In the standard regression model this role is taken by R^2 or $\bar{R}^2$; in the context of the logit or probit model a similar measure, called the *likelihood ratio index* (*LRI*), is given by

$$LRI = 1 - \frac{L(\hat{\Omega})}{L(\hat{\omega})}, \tag{11.127}$$

where $L(\hat{\Omega})$ is the maximum value of the log-likelihood function (11.114), and $L(\hat{\omega})$ is the maximum value of this function under the constraint that $\beta = 0$. Clearly, $0 \leq LRI \leq 1$ and the better the fit, the closer the value of *LRI* will be to one. The quantities $L(\hat{\Omega})$ and $L(\hat{\omega})$ can also be used to carry out a *likelihood ratio test* (described in Section 11-2) of the null hypothesis that X is irrelevant in the determination of $E(Y)$. The test statistic for the asymptotic test is

$$-2[L(\hat{\omega}) - L(\hat{\Omega})] \sim \chi_1^2.$$

Note that in general the number of the degrees of freedom of the chi-square variable is given by the number of the explanatory variables in the model.

In many applied studies the researchers use all three probability models that we have discussed—linear, logit, and probit—on the same data and compare the results. The distinctions among the three models can be summarized as follows:

Linear Probability Model: $\quad F(\alpha + \beta X_i) = \alpha + \beta X_i.$

Logit: $\quad F(\alpha + \beta X_i) = \dfrac{1}{1 + e^{-\alpha - \beta X_i}}.$

Probit: $\quad F(\alpha + \beta X_i) = \displaystyle\int_{-\infty}^{\alpha + \beta X_i} \frac{1}{\sqrt{2\pi}} e^{-z_i^2/2}\, dz_i,$

where $F(\cdot)$ represents a cumulative distribution function. It should be noted, though, that the values of the estimated coefficients are not comparable because the coefficients have a different interpretation in each model. To facilitate comparisons, Amemiya[57] suggested the following approximate scaling adjustments:

$$\hat{\alpha}_{\mathrm{LP}} \simeq 0.25\hat{\alpha}_{\mathrm{L}} + 0.5 \simeq 0.4\hat{\alpha}_{\mathrm{P}} + 0.5,$$

$$\hat{\beta}_{\mathrm{LP}} \simeq 0.25\hat{\beta}_{\mathrm{L}} \simeq 0.4\hat{\beta}_{\mathrm{P}},$$

where the subscript LP refers to the linear probability model, L to the logit model, and P to the probit model.

EXAMPLE Buse[58] estimated the relationship between a decision to purchase an automobile or a major household good and income, using data from the Survey of Consumer

[57] T. Amemiya, "Qualitative Response Models: A Survey," *Journal of Economic Literature,* 19 (December 1981), p. 1488.

[58] A. Buse, "A Technical Report on Binary Dependent Variables as Applied in the Social Sciences," mimeographed (Edmonton, Alberta: Alberta Human Resources Research Council, 1972).

Finances for 1952. The data were in the form of replicated observations, giving the proportion of households making a major purchase for different income groups in intervals of $1000. Each of the three models has been estimated by ordinary least squares (OLS), least squares corrected for heteroskedasticity, which Buse calls "generalized least squares" (GLS), and maximum likelihood (ML). The coefficients are in original units and have not been scaled. The results are presented in Table 11-4. The figures in parentheses are estimated standard errors. The value of R^2 represents a simple squared coefficient of correlation between the observed proportions (p_i) and the fitted proportions $(\hat{p}_i)$.

Table 11-4

		$\hat{\alpha}$	$\hat{\beta}$	R^2
Linear	OLS	.291	.034	.400
	GLS	.248	.055	.400
		(.032)	(.008)	
Logit	OLS	−.989	.159	.418
	GLS	−.959	.211	.408
		(.154)	(.037)	
	ML	−1.030	.226	.414
		(.145)	(.036)	
Probit	OLS	−.597	.097	.414
	GLS	−.624	.137	.409
		(.092)	(.022)	
	ML	−.639	.139	.408
		(.088)	(.022)	

Multinomial Logit Model

So far we have considered only those situations that involved only two possible outcomes so that the dependent variable was dichotomous. Let us now consider a set of three possible alternatives with no particular ordering. An example would be the choice of a mode of transportation such as car, bus, and bicycle. Let

$$\begin{aligned} Y_{ij} &= 1 \quad \text{if the } i\text{th individual chooses alternative } j \quad (j = 1, 2, \text{and } 3), \\ &= 0 \quad \text{otherwise,} \end{aligned}$$

and let $\pi_{ij} = P(Y_{ij} = 1)$. Clearly,

$$\pi_{i1} + \pi_{i2} + \pi_{i3} = 1.$$

The *multinomial logit model*[59] is then simply

$$\log\left(\frac{\pi_{i2}}{\pi_{i1}}\right) = \alpha_2 + \beta_2 X_i, \tag{11.128a}$$

[59] A similar model, called the *conditional logit model,* includes choice characteristics among the determinants of choice probabilities, whereas the multinomial logit model makes the choice probabilities dependent on individual characteristics only. See Maddala, *op. cit.,* p. 42.

(11.128b) $$\log\left(\frac{\pi_{i3}}{\pi_{i1}}\right) = \alpha_3 + \beta_3 X_i,$$

(11.128c) $$\pi_{i1} = 1 - \pi_{i2} - \pi_{i3}.$$

Therefore

$$\pi_{i1} = \frac{1}{1 + e^{\alpha_2 + \beta_2 X_i} + e^{\alpha_3 + \beta_3 X_i}},$$

$$\pi_{i2} = \frac{e^{\alpha_2 + \beta_2 X_i}}{1 + e^{\alpha_2 + \beta_2 X_i} + e^{\alpha_3 + \beta_3 X_i}},$$

$$\pi_{i3} = \frac{e^{\alpha_3 + \beta_3 X_i}}{1 + e^{\alpha_2 + \beta_2 X_i} + e^{\alpha_3 + \beta_3 X_i}}.$$

In general, for any J alternatives we have

(11.129) $$\pi_{ij} = \frac{e^{\alpha_j + \beta_j X_i}}{\sum_j e^{\alpha_j + \beta_j X_i}},$$

where $\alpha_1 = \beta_1 = 0$. The normalization, which is achieved by setting $\alpha_1 = \beta_1 = 0$ and using the first alternative as the benchmark for comparison, is sometimes referred to as "Theil normalization."[60] An alternative normalization would be one with $\Sigma_j \alpha_j = \Sigma_j \beta_j = 0$. The parameters of the multinomial logit model can be estimated by the maximum likelihood method based on the following log-likelihood function:

(11.130) $$L = \sum_{i=1}^{n} \sum_{j=1}^{J} Y_{ij} \log \pi_{ij}.$$

This log-likelihood function is globally concave so that its maximization is not too difficult unless there are many unknown parameters.

The multinomial logit model has a potential weakness inherent in the fact that choices between any two alternatives are assumed to be made independently of the remaining alternatives. This is known as "independence of irrelevant alternatives." How this may create problems is best illustrated by the following famous "red bus–blue bus" example. Suppose there are three modes of transportation for an individual to choose from: car, red bus, and a third alternative. Now according to the multinomial logit model, the odds of choosing the car rather than the red bus are specified the same way regardless of whether the third alternative is a train or a blue bus, which is clearly inappropriate. This problem arises whenever some of the available alternatives are close substitutes. It can be avoided by merging the substitutes, which is sometimes sensible. However, if the substitutes are not close enough to be comfortably merged yet are so close that their neglect might be suspect, the

[60] See Schmidt and Witte, *op. cit.*, p. 17. The name comes from H. Theil, "A Multinomial Extension of the Linear Logit Model," *International Economic Review*, 10 (June 1969), pp. 251–259.

multinomial logit model may not be appropriate. In such a situation a test of the "independence of irrelevant alternatives" hypothesis may be in order.[61]

Multinomial Probit Model

To avoid the problem arising from the assumption of independence of irrelevant alternatives, one may abandon the multinomial logit model in favor of the *multinomial probit model.* In this model the probabilities are generated from a multivariate normal distribution and are interdependent. Unfortunately, the model is very difficult—and expensive—to estimate.[62] The situation is much more manageable when the choice categories can be ordered as, for instance, in the case of attitudes to a proposition or an issue ("strongly approve," "approve," "indifferent," "disapprove," and "strongly disapprove"). The multinomial *ordered* probit model is based on the presumption of the existence of the relationship

$$Y_i^* = \alpha + \beta X_i + \varepsilon_i,$$

where Y_i^* is an unobservable variable, $\varepsilon_i \sim N(0, 1)$, and ε_i and ε_j $(i \neq j)$ are independent. It is assumed that Y_i^* is related to the observable alternative categories of choice as follows:

$$\begin{aligned} Y_i &= 1 \quad \text{if } Y_i^* < 0, \\ &= 2 \quad \text{if } 0 \leq Y_i^* < A_1, \\ &= 3 \quad \text{if } A_1 \leq Y_i^* < A_2, \\ &\ \ \vdots \\ &= M \quad \text{if } A_{M-2} \leq Y_i^*. \end{aligned}$$

Then we can specify the following probabilities:

$$\begin{aligned} P(Y_i = 1) &= F(-\alpha - \beta X_i), \\ P(Y_i = 2) &= F(A_1 - \alpha - \beta X_i) - F(-\alpha - \beta X_i), \\ P(Y_i = 3) &= F(A_2 - \alpha - \beta X_i) - F(A_1 - \alpha - \beta X_i), \\ &\ \ \vdots \\ P(Y_i = M) &= 1 - F(A_{M-2} - \alpha - \beta X_i), \end{aligned}$$

where $F(\cdot)$ is the cumulative distribution function of a standard normal variable. Maximum likelihood estimates of $\alpha, \beta, A_1, A_2, \ldots, A_{M-2}$ can be obtained from the appropriate log-likelihood function without much difficulty.

[61] See J. Hausman and D. McFadden, "Specification Tests for the Multinomial Logit Model," *Econometrica,* 52 (September 1984), pp. 1219–1240.

[62] See J. Hausman and D. A. Wise, "A Conditional Probit Model for Qualitative Choice: Discrete Decisions Recognizing Interdependence and Heterogeneous Preferences," *Econometrica,* 46 (March 1978), pp. 403–426.

Concluding Remarks

The models and methods discussed in this section are, for the most part, computationally quite complicated and would be impossible to implement without the help of modern computer technology. Even so, the cost and difficulty of some calculations (such as those involved in estimating the multinomial probit model) are still largely prohibitive. This will no doubt change as time goes on. In the meantime the interested researcher can make use of the available programs conveniently listed at the end of Amemiya's survey article.[63]

11-6 Models with Limited Dependent Variables

In this section we consider models involving dependent variables for which observations are limited to a certain range. An often-quoted example of such a situation originated in the pioneering work of Tobin, who analyzed household expenditure on durable goods as a function of income and other variables.[64] Tobin noted the distortion in the data resulting from the fact that a considerable number of households did not purchase a durable good during the year of the survey (see Figure 11-16). A possible explanation is that, since expenditure on durable goods is

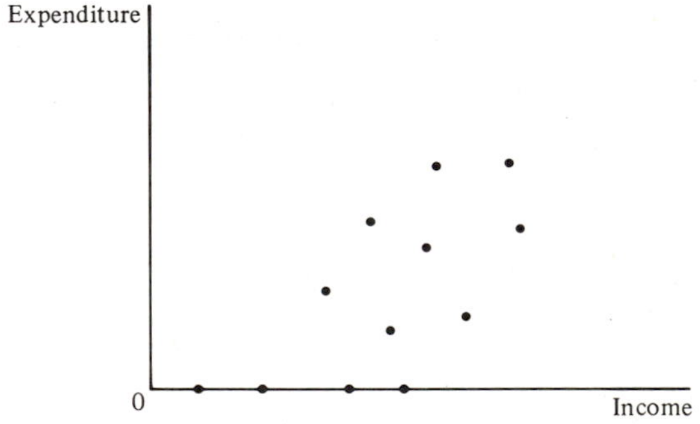

Figure 11-16

not continuous, purchases are not made until the "desire" to buy the good exceeds a certain level. However, we cannot observe desires, only expenditures, and those will be nonzero only if the good is actually purchased. "Negative" expenditures, corresponding to various levels of desire below the threshold level, cannot be observed, and all households with no purchases are recorded as showing zero expenditure. No distinction is made between households who were close to buying the good and those who had very little desire to do so.

[63] Amemiya, "Qualitative Response Models . . . ," *op. cit.*, p. 1532.

[64] J. Tobin, "Estimation of Relationships for Limited Dependent Variables," *Econometrica,* 26 (January 1958), pp. 24–36.

Another common example of a limited dependent variable relates to the wages of married women since wages are recorded only for women who are in the labor force. Wages of women whose "reservation wage" exceeds their market wage and who, therefore, stay at home are recorded as zero. No distinction is made between women whose reservation wage barely exceeds their market wage and those whose reservation wage is much higher than their market wage. Other examples of limited dependent variables can easily be found in the literature.

The restriction on the observable range of the dependent variable matters if the probability of falling below the cut-off point is not negligible. In terms of our examples, if only a very small proportion of the households in the population did not purchase a durable good, or if only a very small proportion of all women were not in the labor force, the limited nature of the dependent variable could be ignored. Thus there is no problem in dealing with household expenditure on food or clothing, or with recorded wages of adult males.

Let

$$Y_i^* = \alpha + \beta X_i + \varepsilon_i^* \qquad (i = 1, 2, \ldots, n) \tag{11.131}$$

be a regression equation for which *all* basic assumptions are satisfied. The dependent variable Y^* may, for instance, represent household expenditure on durable goods and X may represent income. For the households who purchased durable goods during the year of the survey, Y^* is equal to the actual expenditure; for those who did not, Y^* represents an index of the "desire" to purchase durable goods. For the households listed as not having purchased durable goods the value of Y^* is not observed and is recorded as zero. Thus instead of observing Y^*, we actually observe Y, which is defined as

$$\begin{aligned} Y_i &= Y_i^* \quad \text{if } Y_i^* > 0, \\ &= 0 \quad\ \ \text{if } Y_i^* \leq 0. \end{aligned} \tag{11.132}$$

Equation (11.131) then becomes

$$Y_i = \alpha + \beta X_i + \varepsilon_i, \tag{11.131a}$$

where Y_i is truncated at zero and ε_i is truncated at $-(\alpha + \beta X_i)$. This means that the lower tail of the distribution of Y_i—and of ε_i—is cut off and the probabilities are piled up at the cut-off point. The implication of this is that the mean of Y_i is different from that of Y_i^*, and the mean of ε_i is different from that of ε_i^*, which is zero. This is true whether the points for which $Y_i = 0$ are or are not included in the sample. Thus limiting the range of the values of the dependent variable leads to a nonzero mean of the disturbance and to biasedness and inconsistency of the least squares estimators.

In dealing with models with limited dependent variables, a distinction has to be made between *censored* and *truncated* samples. Censored samples occur when the only missing information are the values of the dependent variable in the unobservable range. Truncated samples refer to samples for which not only the values of Y are in the unobservable range but also the corresponding values of X are not observed *and* the number of missing values is unknown. Our discussion will be confined to the censored samples since these are considerably more common in econometrics.[65]

The formulation described by (11.131) and (11.132) is known as the *Tobit model.* It can be easily modified to accommodate a limiting value other than zero, such as γ_i. If γ_i is constant for all i, it can be absorbed into the regression constant. If γ_i is not constant but its values are known, equation (11.131a) would be changed to

$$Y_i + \gamma_i = \alpha + \beta X_i + \varepsilon_i,$$

and the analysis would remain unchanged. If, however, γ_i is *not* constant and *not* known—and the variables that determine it are also not known—the model cannot be consistently estimated. Further, if the values of the dependent variable are limited from above as well as from below and the limiting values are known, the analysis is only slightly more complicated. Finally, matters will be complicated even more—but can be managed—if the truncation point is related to a dependent variable of another relation (i.e., is stochastic). For instance, the wages of unionized workers can be observed only for workers in unionized firms, and whether a worker works or does not work in a unionized firm is determined by another relation.[66] The following discussion will be confined to the simple Tobit model, and to a single explanatory variable to simplify notation.

Maximum Likelihood Estimation

To construct the likelihood function for the Tobit model described by (11.131) and (11.132), we note that the entire sample consists of two different sets of observations. The first set contains the observations for which the value of Y is zero. For these observations we only know the values of X and the fact that $Y^* \leq 0$. The second set consists of all observations for which the values of both X and Y^* are known. The likelihood function then consists of two parts, each corresponding to the respective set of observations. In each set we make use of the assumption that $Y_i^* \sim N(\alpha + \beta X_i, \sigma^2)$ and that Y_i and Y_j $(i \neq j)$ are independent. For the first set we have

$$\begin{aligned} P(Y_i^* \leq 0) &= P\left(\frac{\varepsilon_i^*}{\sigma} \leq \frac{-\alpha - \beta X_i}{\sigma}\right) \\ &= F\left(\frac{-\alpha - \beta X_i}{\sigma}\right), \end{aligned}$$

where $F(\cdot)$ is a cumulative distribution function of a standard normal variable. For the second set of observations the likelihood function is conventional as in (7.26).

[65] For a discussion of truncated samples see, e.g., T. Amemiya, "Tobit Models: A Survey," *Journal of Econometrics* (January/February 1984), pp. 3–61; Maddala, *op. cit.;* or Schmidt and Witte, *op. cit.*

[66] See the references in the preceding footnote.

For all n observations the log-likelihood function is given as

$$L = \sum_{i=1}^{n} \left\{ (1 - Z_i) \log F\left(\frac{-\alpha - \beta X_i}{\sigma}\right) + Z_i \left[-\frac{1}{2}\log(2\pi\sigma^2) - \frac{1}{2\sigma^2}(Y_i - \alpha - \beta X_i)^2 \right] \right\}, \tag{11.133}$$

where

$$\begin{aligned} Z_i &= 1 \quad \text{if } Y_i > 0, \\ &= 0 \quad \text{if } Y_i = 0. \end{aligned}$$

Because of the special nature of the likelihood function for the Tobit model, the usual theorems about maximum likelihood estimators do not hold. However, Amemiya has proven that maximization of (11.133) with respect to the unknown parameters leads to estimators that are consistent and asymptotically normal, and that their variances can be derived from the information matrix based on (11.133).[67] The computation of the maximum likelihood estimates can be carried out by the application of the so-called EM algorithm, a computational method particularly suited for situations in which some observations are not directly observed.[68]

Two-Step Estimation

An ingenious way of approaching the problem of estimating the Tobit model has been proposed by Heckman.[69] Suppose that of all n observations there are m ($m < n$) observations for which $Y_i^* > 0$. The regression equation for these observations is

$$Y_i = \alpha + \beta X_i + \varepsilon_i \qquad (i = 1, 2, \ldots, m),$$

where Y_i and ε_i are truncated normal variables. The conditional expectation of Y_i given $Y_i^* > 0$ is

$$\begin{aligned} E(Y_i | Y_i^* > 0) &= \alpha + \beta X_i + E(\varepsilon_i | Y_i^* > 0) \\ &= \alpha + \beta X_i + E(\varepsilon_i | \varepsilon_i^* > -\alpha - \beta X_i) \end{aligned}$$

for $i = 1, 2, \ldots, m$. Given that $\varepsilon_i^* \sim N(0, \sigma^2)$, the mean of the corresponding truncated variable, ε_i, is[70]

$$E(\varepsilon_i | \varepsilon_i^* > -\alpha - \beta X_i) = \sigma\lambda_i, \tag{11.134}$$

[67] See T. Amemiya, "Regression Analysis When the Dependent Variable Is Truncated Normal," *Econometrica,* 41 (November 1973), pp. 997–1016. When the regression disturbance is *not* normally distributed, however, the maximum likelihood method based on the assumption of normality yields *inconsistent* estimates.

[68] See, e.g., G. C. Chow, *Econometrics* (New York: McGraw-Hill, 1983), pp. 268–271.

[69] J. J. Heckman, "Sample Selection Bias as a Specification Error," *Econometrica,* 47 (January 1979), pp. 153–161.

[70] See N. L. Johnson and S. Kotz, *Continuous Univariate Distributions—1* (Boston: Houghton Mifflin, 1970), pp. 81–83. The quantity λ_i is known as the "hazard rate," and its reciprocal is known as the "Mill's ratio."

where

$$\lambda_i = f\left(\frac{\alpha + \beta X_i}{\sigma}\right) \Big/ F\left(\frac{\alpha + \beta X_i}{\sigma}\right),$$

and $f(\cdot)$ represents the density and $F(\cdot)$ the cumulative distribution function of a standard normal variable. To allow for the nonzero mean of ε_i, the regression equation for the m observations for which $Y_i^* > 0$ can be written as

$$Y_i = \alpha + \beta X_i + \sigma\lambda_i + \varepsilon_i^* \qquad (i = 1, 2, \ldots, m). \tag{11.135}$$

If λ_i were observable, (11.135) would have a disturbance with zero mean and the least squares coefficients would be unbiased. Heckman's formulation of the Tobit model translates the problem of truncation into the problem of an omitted explanatory variable.

The quantity λ_i is not observable, but it can be consistently estimated by forming a likelihood function for the binary variable Z_i, defined in connection with (11.133) as

$$Z_i = 1 \quad \text{if } Y_i^* > 0,$$
$$= 0 \quad \text{if } Y_i^* \leq 0.$$

The log-likelihood function for the n observations on this variable is

$$\begin{aligned} L &= \sum_{i=1}^{n} [(1 - Z_i) \log P(Z_i = 0) + Z_i \log P(Z_i = 1)] \\ &= \sum_i [(1 - Z_i) \log(\varepsilon_i^* \leq -\alpha - \beta X_i) + Z_i \log(\varepsilon_i^* > -\alpha - \beta X_i)] \\ &= \sum_i \left[(1 - Z_i) \log F\left(\frac{-\alpha - \beta X_i}{\sigma}\right) + Z_i \log F\left(\frac{\alpha + \beta X_i}{\sigma}\right)\right]. \end{aligned} \tag{11.136}$$

The log-likelihood function (11.136) is, of course, the log-likelihood function for the *probit model* presented as equation (11.124) in Section 11-5. (Note, however, that in the probit model the disturbance is assumed to have variance 1, whereas in the Tobit model the variance is σ^2.) Its maximization, which is the first step of Heckman's two-step procedure, enables us to obtain consistent estimates of $(\alpha + \beta X_i)/\sigma$ and, therefore, of λ_i. The second step involves going back to (11.136), replacing λ_i by $\hat{\lambda}_i$, and applying the least squares method using the m observations for which $Y_i > 0$. The resulting estimators of α and β are consistent and asymptotically normal but the truncated nature of ε_i^*, leads to heteroskedasticity and, therefore, to biased and inconsistent calculated standard errors.[71] The additional disadvantage of the two-step estimator is that, according to the available evidence, it is inefficient compared to the maximum likelihood estimator.[72]

[71] See Amemiya, "Tobit Models . . . ," *op. cit.*, pp. 12–14, where the appropriate formulas for the asymptotic variances are given.

[72] See F. D. Nelson, "Efficiency of the Two-Step Estimator for Models with Endogenous Sample Selection," *Journal of Econometrics*, 24 (January/February 1984), pp. 181–196; H. J. Paarsch, "A Monte Carlo Comparison of Estimators for Censored Regression Models," *Journal of Econometrics*, 24 (January/February 1984), pp. 197–213.

Ordinary Least Squares Corrected for Asymptotic Bias

A simple moments method for consistent estimation of the Tobit model is available when both Y^* and X are normally distributed. The method was devised by Greene and proceeds as follows.[73] The joint normal distribution of Y^* and X can be written as

$$\begin{bmatrix} Y^* \\ X \end{bmatrix} \sim N\left\{\begin{bmatrix} \mu_{Y^*} \\ \mu_X \end{bmatrix}, \begin{bmatrix} \sigma_{Y^*Y^*} & \sigma_{Y^*X} \\ \sigma_{XY^*} & \sigma_{XX} \end{bmatrix}\right\}$$

where $\mu_{Y^*} = \alpha + \beta\mu_X$ and $\sigma_{XY^*} = \beta\sigma_{XX}$. Let us consider the ordinary least squares estimator of β, say, $\hat{\beta}$, based on all n sample observations. Using conditional variances and covariances, Greene shows that

$$\begin{aligned} \text{plim } \hat{\beta} &= \sigma_{XX}^{-1}\sigma_{XY^*}P(Y^* > 0) \\ &= \beta P(Y^* > 0). \end{aligned}$$

But given the bivariate normal distribution of Y^* and X, $P(Y^* > 0)$ is the marginal probability that Y^* exceeds zero, which is consistently estimated by the sample proportion of nonzero values of Y, i.e., by m/n. Thus a consistent estimator of β, say, $\tilde{\beta}$, is given as

$$\tilde{\beta} = \left(\frac{n}{m}\right)\hat{\beta}. \tag{11.137}$$

If the number of explanatory variables is greater than one, Greene suggests that each coefficient (other than the constant term) be adjusted by the same factor n/m.

EXAMPLE Greene[74] compares his method of ordinary least squares corrected for asymptotic bias with the maximum likelihood method by estimating a female labor supply equation in which the dependent variable is the number of hours worked. The data consist of a random sample of 2798 wives interviewed by the U.S. Bureau of the Census in 1967. The results are presented in Table 11-5. Figures in parentheses are the calculated standard errors. Explanatory variables denoted by an asterisk are dummy variables. The corrected least squares estimates for all coefficients except the constant term were obtained by multiplying the ordinary least squares coefficient by 2.1739, which corresponds to 46% nonzero responses. Although most explanatory variables are not normally distributed (eight of them are dummy variables), the corrected least squares estimates are quite close to the maximum likelihood estimates (which are consistent). Greene provides some Monte Carlo evidence that his method is fairly robust to nonnormality of the regressors unless the distributions are notably skewed.

[73] See W. H. Greene, "On the Asymptotic Bias of the Ordinary Least Squares Estimator of the Tobit Model," *Econometrica,* 49 (March 1981), pp. 505–513. Note that the expression (14) for σ_*^2, which is needed to obtain a consistent estimator of constant term, is incorrect. The correct formula is $\sigma_*^2 = S_{yy}/\{P - [f - m(1-P)][f + mP]\}$.

[74] *Ibid.*

Table 11-5 Female Labor Supply (hours)

Explanatory variable	Tobit estimates	
	MLE	Corrected OLS
X_1 (constant)	−2753.87(284.5)	−2824.74
X_2^* (small child)	−824.19(81.3)	−766.59
X_3^* (health)	−1009.85(110.4)	−894.89
X_4 (wage)	1026.62(10.33)	1211.30
X_5 (other income)	1.03(12.9)	1.59
X_6^* (south)	587.88(80.8)	598.17
X_7^* (farm)	−451.26(169.0)	−443.85
X_8^* (urban)	110.22(216.1)	104.67
X_9 (age)	19.32(4.8)	18.78
X_{10} (education)	22.59(11.5)	24.93
X_{11} (relative wage)	286.39(86.3)	269.46
X_{12}^* (second marriage)	25.33(61.8)	28.57
X_{13}^* (mean divorce probability)	481.02(85.03)	476.57
X_{14}^* (high divorce probability)	578.66(97.6)	530.80

Concluding Remarks

Models with limited dependent variables are applicable in a number of fields but are perhaps most extensively used in labor economics. Their estimation has been greatly facilitated by the development of new computational methods and programs.[75] An increasing number of specialists are engaged in research involving relaxation of assumptions on which the estimation methods are based (e.g., normality or homoskedasticity) and in the development and estimation of progressively more refined models.

11-7 Models with Varying Coefficients

One of the most important maintained hypotheses underlying a regression model is the constancy of the regression coefficients for all sample observations. Changes in the value of the dependent variable occur because of changes in the values of the explanatory variables and of the disturbance, but the regression coefficients are assumed to remain constant. Some authors, however, have considered this assumption to be too restrictive and proposed models that allow for variation in the regression coefficients. Some of these models are based on economic theory or other prior knowledge and, as a rule, involve nonstochastic, *systematic* coefficient variation. Examples are personal changes in behavior, or changes in production function coefficients caused by technical progress. In the context of macroeco-

[75] For an excellent overview see B. H. Hall, "Software for the Computation of Tobit Model Estimates," *Journal of Econometrics,* 24 (January/February 1984), pp. 215–222.

nomic relationships a belief in coefficient variation of this kind was given a boost by the so-called Lucas critique.[76] This critique rests on the claim that macroeconomic coefficients are determined by the expectations of economic agents concerning economic policy, and as policy changes, the expectations and the coefficients also change. There are also models that reflect the belief that regression models are misspecified in some undetermined way, and that such a misspecification can be substantially alleviated if not avoided altogether by allowing for stochastic variation of the coefficients. Our discussion will follow this distinction and will treat systematic and stochastic coefficient variation separately. The section concludes with a description of some tests for coefficient stability.

Systematic Coefficient Variation

Let us consider a simple regression model in which some variation of the coefficients is allowed for:

$$Y_i = \alpha_i + \beta_i X_i + \varepsilon_i \qquad (i = 1, 2, \ldots, n). \tag{11.138}$$

We have already discussed one such model when introducing the effect of seasonal factors in Section 11-1. The most common specification of seasonal effects is to allow the intercept—but not the slope—to vary from one season to another. In the case of quarterly observations this would be represented as

$$Y_t = \alpha_t + \beta X_t + \varepsilon_t \qquad (t = 1, 2, \ldots, n),$$

where

$$\alpha_t = \alpha_1 D_{t1} + \alpha_2 D_{t2} + \alpha_3 D_{t3} + \alpha_4 D_{t4},$$

and

$$\begin{aligned} D_{tj} &= 1 \quad \text{for the } j\text{th quarter} \qquad (j = 1, 2, 3, \text{ and } 4) \\ &= 0 \quad \text{otherwise.} \end{aligned}$$

This kind of coefficient variation may be called *season-dependent* variation. The presence of this type of variation can easily be detected by testing the significance of the coefficients attached to the seasonal dummy variables.

A similar type of coefficient variation, which may be called *trend-dependent* variation, was considered by Farley and Hinich.[77] A simplified version of their model is of the form

$$Y_t = \alpha + \beta_t X_t + \varepsilon_t \qquad (t = 1, 2, \ldots, n),$$

where $\beta_t = \beta + \gamma t$. The appropriate substitution then leads to

$$Y_t = \alpha + \beta X_t + \gamma t X_t + \varepsilon_t.$$

A test of the hypothesis that there is no trend in the regression slope is simply a test of the hypothesis that $\gamma = 0$. Sometimes the presence of a trend can be interpreted as

[76] R. E. Lucas, Jr., "Econometric Policy Evaluations: A Critique," in K. Brunner and A. H. Meltzer (eds.), *The Phillips Curve and Labor Markets* (Amsterdam: North-Holland, 1976).

[77] J. V. Farley and M. Hinich, "A Test for a Shifting Slope Coefficient in a Linear Model," *Journal of the American Statistical Association,* 65 (September 1970), pp. 1320–1329.

representing a certain definite factor or factors that influence the coefficients but are not measurable. For example, in the context of production functions the drift in the coefficients over time is thought to reflect technical progress. In fact, the term "trend" is always a camouflage for factors that change over time, and it would certainly be preferable if these factors could be identified and measured. Such factors may also arise in connection with cross-sectional observations. For instance, in models describing household behavior, the intercept and the slope in (11.138) may be different for different households because of differences in their socioeconomic status.[78] If Z_i represents a suitable measure of socioeconomic status, its influence on the regression coefficients may be represented as

$$\alpha_i = \alpha + \gamma Z_i,$$

$$\beta_i = \beta + \delta Z_i.$$

Coefficient variation of this sort may be called *factor-dependent.*

Switching Regressions

In certain situations the coefficients of a regression model remain constant for a period of time; then they change and remain constant at the new level. For instance, the coefficients of a wage equation may change after wage contract negotiations; the coefficients of a cost function may change because of a law concerning environmental protection; or the coefficients of a supply function may change because of an overseas cartel action. Situations of this kind are described by the *switching regression model,* and the periods within which the coefficients remain unchanged are called *regimes.* The switching regression model is represented as

$$(11.139) \qquad Y_t = \alpha_1 + \beta_1 X_t + \varepsilon_t \qquad (t = 1, 2, \ldots, t^*),$$

$$Y_t = \alpha_2 + \beta_2 X_t + \varepsilon_t \qquad (t = t^* + 1, t^* + 2, \ldots, n).$$

The disturbance ε_t is considered to satisfy all basic assumptions of a classical regression model. (If autocorrelation should occur, the equations are assumed to have been approximately transformed.) If the switching point t^* is known and the variance of the disturbance is the same in both regimes, the two equations (11.139) can be represented by one equation with a dummy variable for intercept and slope, i.e.,

$$(11.139a) \qquad Y_t = \alpha_1 + \beta_1 X_t + (\alpha_2 - \alpha_1)D_t + (\beta_2 - \beta_1)X_t D_t + \varepsilon_t,$$

where

$$D_t = 0 \quad \text{if } 1 \le t \le t^*,$$

$$= 1 \quad \text{if } t^* + 1 \le t \le n.$$

If t^* is known but the variances of the disturbances in the two regimes differ, we can estimate the two regression equations separately.

An interesting case arises when the switching point is not known. In this case the

[78] See, e.g., Benus, Kmenta, and Shapiro, *op. cit.,* pp. 129–138.

log-likelihood function

$$L = -\frac{n}{2}\log(2\pi) - \frac{1}{2\sigma_1^2}\sum_{t=1}^{t^*}(Y_t - \alpha_1 - \beta_1 X_t)^2$$
$$- \frac{1}{2\sigma_2^2}\sum_{t=t^*+1}^{n}(Y_t - \alpha_2 - \beta_2 X_t)^2$$

can be maximized with respect to $\alpha_1, \alpha_2, \beta_1, \beta_2, \sigma_1$, and σ_2 for different values of t^* from $t^* = 3$ to $t^* = n - 3$. The value of t^* that maximizes L is then the maximum likelihood estimate of t^*. The only difficulty with this procedure is that L is not continuous in t^* since t^* is an integer. This means that the second derivatives of L with respect to t^*, which are needed for the determination of the asymptotic variances, are inappropriate. However, the resulting distortions do not appear to be too serious.[79] To test for the presence of a switch, we can use the likelihood ratio test described in Section 11-2.

The switching regression model (11.139) has been extended to the situation in which switching is related to a given variable Z_i (which may or may not be equal to X_i). A switch occurs when the value of Z_i exceeds a certain unknown quantity. Another extension involves stochastic switching. In this situation it is assumed that nature chooses the allocation of observations to regimes 1 and 2 with unknown probabilities λ and $(1 - \lambda)$. And, of course, generalizations to more than one switching point have also been considered. These and other extensions of the basic switching model have been developed in a series of articles by Quandt and others.[80]

One of the major complaints against the switching model (11.139) is that the transition from one regime to another is abrupt. One way of mitigating this abruptness is by using *piecewise* (or *linear spline*) *regression.* The piecewise regression model requires that the two regression lines described by (11.139) meet at the switching point (known as a "knot"). If, as assumed, the switching point is at $t = t^*$, the requirement is that

$$\alpha_1 + \beta_1 X_{t^*} = \alpha_2 + \beta_2 X_{t^*}.$$

The imposition of this requirement leads to the following reformulation of (11.139a):

$$Y_t = \alpha_1 + \beta_1 X_t + (\beta_2 - \beta_1)(X_t - X_{t^*})D_t + \varepsilon_t, \tag{11.140}$$

where D_t is as in (11.139a). If the variance of the disturbance is the same in both regimes, (11.140) can be estimated by ordinary least squares; otherwise a correction for heteroskedasticity has to be made first. If t^* is not known, it can be estimated by the maximum likelihood method.

Joining the two straight lines according to (11.140) creates a broken line that,

[79] See S. M. Goldfeld and R. E. Quandt, *Nonlinear Methods in Econometrics* (Amsterdam: North-Holland, 1972), Chapter 9.

[80] For a convenient survey and references see S. M. Goldfeld and R. E. Quandt, "The Estimation of Structural Shifts by Switching Regressions," *Annals of Economic and Social Measurement,* 2 (October 1973), pp. 475–485.

according to some authors, is still fairly abrupt. For this reason Maddala[81] suggested replacing (11.139a) by

$$(11.141) \qquad Y_t = \alpha + \beta X_t + \gamma W_t + \delta W_t X_t + \varepsilon_t,$$

where
$$W_t = \frac{1}{1 + e^{\lambda + \mu Z_t}} \qquad (\mu < 0),$$

and Z_t is a specified variable that allocates observations to regimes. If $Z_t \to \infty$, $W_t \to 0$; if $Z_t \to -\infty$, $W_t \to 1$. The joining of the two regimes then occurs gradually unless the changes in Z_t are very substantial.

An alternative representation of a smooth transition from one regime to another is provided by the *cubic spline model* that is popular in engineering. This model consists of regression relationships that are polynomials of third degree:

$$(11.142) \qquad Y_t = \alpha_1 + \beta_1 X_t + \gamma_1 X_t^2 + \delta_1 X_t^3 + \varepsilon_t \qquad (t = 1, 2, \ldots, t^*),$$
$$Y_t = \alpha_2 + \beta_2 X_t + \gamma_2 X_t^2 + \delta_2 X_t^3 + \varepsilon_t \qquad (t = t^* + 1, t^* + 2, \ldots, n).$$

The requirement of a smooth transition implies not only that the two curves cross at the point $t = t^*$ but also that the first and the second derivatives of these curves are the same at this point. The implied restrictions, therefore, are

$$(11.143) \qquad \alpha_1 + \beta_1 X_{t^*} + \gamma_1 X_{t^*}^2 + \delta_1 X_{t^*}^3 = \alpha_2 + \beta_2 X_{t^*} + \gamma_2 X_{t^*}^2 + \delta_2 X_{t^*}^3,$$
$$\beta_1 + 2\gamma_1 X_{t^*} + 3\delta_1 X_{t^*}^2 = \beta_2 + 2\gamma_2 X_{t^*} + 3\delta_2 X_{t^*}^2,$$
$$2\gamma_1 + 6\delta_1 X_{t^*} = 2\gamma_2 + 6\delta_2 X_{t^*}.$$

The coefficients of (11.142) are to be estimated subject to these restrictions.

The weakness of all of the above models is that the smoothing process is quite ad hoc. What is really needed is a theory of optimizing behavior that would determine the transition from one regime to another in accordance with the costs and benefits of the move. The ad hoc formulations that we have described can at best serve only as approximations of unspecified adjustment behavior.

Stochastic Coefficient Variation

A number of authors have formulated variations in the regression coefficients in purely stochastic terms. We will present only a few of the proposed models because "the capacity of econometric theorists to 'invent' new varieties of models with continuous parameter variation tends to exceed the willingness and sometimes even the computational ability of researchers to apply them to real-world situations."[82]

Let us start with the so-called *adaptive regression model,* which we present in a

[81] G. S. Maddala, *Econometrics* (New York: McGraw-Hill, 1977), p. 396.

[82] J. Johnston, *Econometric Methods,* 3rd ed. (New York: McGraw-Hill, 1984), p. 410.

simplified form as

(11.144) $$Y_t = \alpha_t + \beta X_t + \varepsilon_t,$$
$$\alpha_t = \alpha_{t-1} + v_t,$$

where v_t is a normally and independently distributed random variable with mean zero and constant variance σ_v^2. Further, v_t is assumed to be independent of ε_t. The process by which the values of α_t are generated is known as a "random walk." Repeated substitution for $\alpha_t, \alpha_{t-1}, \ldots$, into the regression equation yields

(11.144a) $$Y_t = \alpha_0 + \beta X_t + \varepsilon_t^*,$$

where $$\varepsilon_t^* = \varepsilon_t + \sum_{i=1}^{t} v_i,$$

and α_0 is the initial value of the intercept. Then we have

$$E(\varepsilon_t^*) = 0,$$
$$\text{Var}(\varepsilon_t^*) = \sigma^2 + t\sigma_v^2,$$
$$\text{Cov}(\varepsilon_t^*, \varepsilon_{t-s}^*) = (t-s)\sigma_v^2 \qquad (0 < s < t).$$

This means that the disturbance in (11.144a) is heteroskedastic and autocorrelated. Further, $\text{Var}(\varepsilon_t^*) \to \infty$ as $t \to \infty$. Note that α_t can also be eliminated from (11.144) by substitution:

(11.144b) $$Y_t - Y_{t-1} = \alpha_t - \alpha_{t-1} + \beta(X_t - X_{t-1}) + \varepsilon_t - \varepsilon_{t-1}$$
$$= \beta(X_t - X_{t-1}) + v_t + \varepsilon_t - \varepsilon_{t-1}.$$

The parameters of the model can be estimated by the maximum likelihood method.[83]

A modification of the adaptive regression model is known as the *convergent parameter model.* Its simplified version can be specified as follows:

(11.145) $$Y_t = \alpha_t + \beta X_t + \varepsilon_t,$$
$$\alpha_t = (1-\lambda)\alpha + \lambda\alpha_{t-1} + v_t \qquad (0 \leq \lambda < 1),$$

where v_t is defined as in (11.144). The convergent parameter model would become the same as the adaptive regression model if $\lambda = 1$. The term $(1-\lambda)$ in (11.145) implements a tendency for α_t to converge toward a "normal" value of α. Repeated substitution for $\alpha_t, \alpha_{t-1}, \ldots$, into the regression equation leads to

(11.145a) $$Y_t = \alpha + \beta X_t + \varepsilon_t^*,$$

where $$\varepsilon_t^* = \varepsilon_t + v_t + \lambda v_{t-1} + \lambda^2 v_{t-2} + \cdots.$$

[83] The adaptive regression model was introduced in T. Cooley and E. C. Prescott, "An Adaptive Regression Model," *International Economic Review,* 14 (June 1973), pp. 364–371. Its maximum likelihood estimation is described in Judge et al., *op. cit.,* pp. 811–814.

Then we have

$$E(\varepsilon_t^*) = 0,$$

$$\text{Var}(\varepsilon_t^*) = \sigma^2 + \frac{\sigma_v^2}{1 - \lambda^2},$$

$$\text{Cov}(\varepsilon_t^*, \varepsilon_{t-s}^*) = \left(\frac{\lambda^s}{1-\lambda^2}\right)\sigma_v^2 \qquad (0 < s < t).$$

Thus the disturbance in (11.145a) is homoskedastic but autocorrelated. Here also α_t can be eliminated from (11.145) by substitution to give

$$\text{(11.145b)} \qquad Y_t - \lambda Y_{t-1} = \alpha_t - \lambda\alpha_{t-1} + \beta(X_t - \lambda X_{t-1}) + \varepsilon_t - \lambda\varepsilon_{t-1}$$
$$= (1-\lambda)\alpha + \beta(X_t - \lambda X_{t-1}) + w_t,$$

where
$$w_t = v_t + \varepsilon_t - \lambda\varepsilon_{t-1}.$$

Note that Y_{t-1} and w_t are correlated through ε_{t-1}. It can be shown that w_t is generated by a pure moving average process of first order. The model can be estimated by the maximum likelihood method.[84]

The preceding two models have been designed to explain observations made over time. In contrast, *the random coefficient model* (RCM) of Hildreth and Houck can be applied to either time-series or cross-sectional observations.[85] The model is based on the following reasoning. Since the standard regression model,

$$Y_i = \alpha + \beta X_i + \varepsilon_i,$$

can be written as

$$Y_i = \alpha_i + \beta X_i,$$

where $\alpha_i = \alpha + \varepsilon_i$, all stochastic variation is concentrated in the intercept. Hildreth and Houck sought to generalize this by allowing for stochastic variation in the slope as well. Their model is then specified as

$$\text{(11.146)} \qquad Y_i = \alpha_i + \beta_i X_i,$$

where
$$\alpha_i = \alpha + \varepsilon_i,$$
$$\beta_i = \beta + v_i,$$

and v_i is as defined in (11.144). Substitution for α_i and β_i into the regression equation leads to

$$\text{(11.146a)} \qquad Y_i = \alpha + \beta X_i + \varepsilon_i^*,$$

[84] The convergent parameter model was introduced in B. Rosenberg, "The Analysis of a Cross Section of Time Series by Stochastically Convergent Parameter Regression," *Annals of Economic and Social Measurement,* 2 (October 1973), pp. 399–428. The maximum likelihood estimation of the model is explained in detail in Rosenberg's article.

[85] C. Hildreth and J. Houck, "Some Estimators for a Linear Model with Random Coefficients," *Journal of the American Statistical Association,* 63 (June 1968), pp. 584–595.

where $$\varepsilon_i^* = \varepsilon_i + v_i X_i.$$

Then $$E(\varepsilon_i^*) = 0,$$

$$\text{Var}(\varepsilon_i^*) = \sigma^2 + \sigma_v^2 X_i^2,$$

$$\text{Cov}(\varepsilon_i^*, \varepsilon_j^*) = 0 \qquad (i \neq j).$$

Thus the disturbance in (11.146a) is heteroskedastic but not autocorrelated. The model can again be estimated by the maximum likelihood method.

EXAMPLE The random coefficient model of Hildreth and Houck was used in a study of the Phillips curve by Gordon and Hynes.[86] The specified relationship is

$$W_i = \beta_{1i} + \beta_{2i} U_i + \beta_{3i} M_i + \beta_{4i} P_i,$$

where W = percentage rate of change of money wages, U = rate of unemployment, M = percentage rate of change of the money stock, and P = percentage rate of change of labor productivity. The equation was estimated from annual data for 1930–1966 by ordinary least squares (based on the assumption of constant coefficients), and by the maximum likelihood method (assuming a random coefficient model). The results are presented in Table 11-6. Actual and predicted values of W for the years 1967–1972 are presented in Table 11-7. It appears that the wage changes in 1967–1972 are, on the whole, better predicted by the RC model than by the standard regression model.

Table 11-6

	Coefficients[a]			
Variable	OLS		RCM–MLE	
Constant term	.04033	(.01350)	.0537	(.0134)
Unemployment	−.00201	(.00111)	−.00264	(.00119)
Money	.3533	(.1103)	.2522	(.0603)
Productivity	.1284	(.0633)	.1689	(.0468)
$\bar{R}^2$	.70			
DW[b]	1.84			
n	37		37	

[a] Figures in parentheses are estimated standard errors.
[b] DW = the Durbin–Watson test statistic.

An interesting variation of Houck and Hildreth's random coefficient model has been considered by Swamy for modeling household behavior over time based on pooled cross-section and time-series observations.[87] Suppose we observe N house-

[86] D. F. Gordon and A. Hynes, "On the Theory of Price Dynamics," in E. Phelps (ed.), *Microeconomic Foundations of Employment and Inflation Theory* (New York: Norton, 1970), pp. 369–393. Our exposition follows that of B. Raj and A. Ullah, *Econometrics* (London: Croom Helm, 1981), pp. 111–116, from which we also quote the results.

[87] P. A. V. B. Swamy, *Statistical Inference in Random Coefficient Regression Models* (New York: Springer-Verlag, 1971).

Table 11-7[a]

	1967	1968	1969	1970	1971	1972
W	.04044	.06330	.05980	.05329	.05952	.07022
$\hat{W}$	.05219	.06584	.06203	.04090	.05428	.07128
$\tilde{W}$	.04431	.06279	.06034	.04481	.05594	.07150

[a] W = actual value; $\hat{W}$ = OLS prediction; $\tilde{W}$ = RCM–MLE prediction.

holds over T periods of time (usually years). Swamy's random coefficient model is then specified as

$$(11.147)\quad Y_{it} = \alpha_i + \beta_i X_{it} + \varepsilon_{it} \qquad (i = 1, 2, \ldots, N; \quad t = 1, 2, \ldots, T),$$

$$\alpha_i = \alpha + u_i,$$

$$\beta_i = \beta + v_i,$$

where u_i and v_i are normally distributed random variables with zero means. Thus Swamy considers it appropriate to view each household as being characterized by its own intercept and slope and to assume that the average intercept and slope of all households do not change over time. The model can be equivalently written as

$$(11.147a)\qquad Y_{it} = \alpha + \beta X_{it} + \varepsilon^*_{it},$$

where

$$\varepsilon^*_{it} = \varepsilon_{it} + u_i + v_i X_{it}.$$

Estimation of the model depends on the assumptions concerning ε, u, and v. In general, maximum likelihood estimation of this model is complicated but manageable.[88] A troublesome aspect of Swamy's model is the assumption that the "average" coefficients are constant over time. The composition of the households population changes as time goes on, and it is hard to believe that the newly entering households will exactly (or even approximately) offset the households that have been dissolved.

All of the preceding regression models with stochastically varying coefficients over time are related to a general formulation of stochastic coefficient variation known as the *Kalman filter state–space model.*[89] A simple version of this model was presented under the heading of "recursive estimation" in Section 10-2. The most common version of the Kalman filter model involves coefficients varying over time and may be represented as

$$(11.148a)\qquad Y_t = \alpha_t + \beta_t X_t + \varepsilon_t,$$

$$(11.148b)\qquad \alpha_t = \lambda_{11}\alpha_{t-1} + \lambda_{12}\beta_{t-1} + v_t,$$

$$(11.148c)\qquad \beta_t = \lambda_{21}\alpha_{t-1} + \lambda_{22}\beta_{t-1} + u_t,$$

[88] *Ibid.*

[89] For a detailed exposition see A. C. Harvey, "The Kalman Filter and Its Applications in Econometrics and Time-Series Analysis," *Methods of Operations Research,* 44 (1982), pp. 3–18.

where v_t and u_t are jointly distributed random errors with known variances and covariances. The λs and the initial values of α_t and β_t are also assumed to be known. Equation (11.148a) is known as the *measurement equation.* Equations (11.148b) and (11.148c) are known as *transition equations,* and α_t and β_t are called *state variables.* The Kalman filter model provides a flexible tool for modeling stochastic variation in the regression coefficients and is very popular in engineering. The requirement that the transition parameters, the variances and covariances of the transition error terms, and the initial values of the regression coefficients must be known represents a drawback, but users of the Kalman filter model manage to handle this in various ways. The main use of the Kalman filter model is for forecasting, for which the updating nature of the transition equations is particularly suited.

Models with stochastically varying regression coefficients have not been widely used in econometrics because of the ad hoc nature of their specification. As mentioned at the outset of this section, stochastic variation of the regression coefficients can be justified mainly as a way of accounting for a suspected misspecification of the regression equation. Without more information about the nature of the suspected misspecification, it is difficult to choose from the variety of models presented in the literature.

Testing the Stability of the Regression Coefficients

Since the stability of the regression coefficients is such an important part of the assumptions underlying the classical regression model, it may be advisable to regard it as a hypothesis to be tested. When the suspected variation of the regression coefficients is systematic, or when we are dealing with switching regressions, tests of the stability hypothesis are readily available and have been indicated in our discussion. In the case of stochastically varying coefficients, we found that a typical effect of coefficient variation is to make the regression disturbance heteroskedastic and possibly autocorrelated. This suggests the use of tests for homoskedasticity and nonautocorrelation discussed in Sections 8-2 and 8-3. In the case of the random coefficient model of Hildreth and Houck, some authors recommend the use of the Breusch–Pagan test.[90] Further, to the extent that stochastic coefficient variation is caused by misspecification due to omitted variables or nonlinearity, tests such as RESET or the "rainbow" test (discussed in Section 10-4) or the "lack-of-fit" test (discussed in Section 11-3) would be appropriate.

In addition to the tests that we have just mentioned, direct tests of coefficient stability—even without specifying the nature of the possible structural change—have also been developed. Let us assume that the sample observations have been appropriately ordered (for instance chronologically) and that the regression equation is given as

$$Y_t = \beta_{t1} + \beta_{t2}X_{t2} + \cdots + \beta_{tK}X_{tK} + \varepsilon_t. \tag{11.149}$$

[90] See Judge et al., *op. cit.*, p. 809. The test is described in Section 8-2.

Then the null hypothesis of coefficient stability and its alternative are

$$H_0: \quad \beta_{tj} = \beta_{sj} \qquad (t, s = 1, 2, \ldots, n; \quad j = 1, 2, \ldots, K),$$

$$H_A: \quad H_0 \text{ is not true.}$$

A natural way to test the null hypothesis is by prediction. If the observed value of Y falls outside the prediction interval, then the mechanism of the model is likely to have changed. The appropriate test for this purpose is "Chow's predictive test" presented in Section 10-2 and based on the F statistic given by (10.51). This test can be used sequentially as follows.[91] Divide the appropriately ordered observations into G mutually exclusive groups, with $m_1 (m_1 > K)$ observations in the first group, m_2 observations in the second group, etc. Note that $m_1 + m_2 + \cdots + m_G = n$. Further, let $n_g = m_1 + m_2 + \cdots + m_g$ for $g = 1, 2, \ldots, G$. Clearly, $n_G = n$. The *sequential F test* then involves the construction of $G - 1$ F statistics, each defined in accordance with (10.51) as

$$(11.150) \quad F_g = \frac{(\text{SSE}_g - \text{SSE}_{g-1})/m_g}{\text{SSE}_{g-1}/(n_{g-1} - K)} \sim F_{m_g, n_{g-1} - K} \quad (g = 2, 3, \ldots, G),$$

where SSE_g = least squares residual sum of squares based on the first n_g observations, and SSE_{g-1} = least squares residual sum of squares based on the first n_{g-1} observations. The F_gs are mutually independent, so the probability that none of the $G - 1$ test statistics rejects the null hypothesis is simply $(1 - \alpha_2)(1 - \alpha_3) \ldots (1 - \alpha_G)$, where $\alpha_g (g = 2, 3, \ldots, G)$ is the probability of Error Type I for the gth test.[92] How to determine the optimal number of groups of observations is unfortunately still an open question.

An alternative and frequently mentioned test is the *CUSUM (and CUSUM-square) test* of Brown, Durbin, and Evans.[93] Let the regression model under the null hypothesis be written as

$$\mathbf{y} = \mathbf{X}\boldsymbol{\beta} + \boldsymbol{\varepsilon},$$

where $\mathbf{y} \rightarrow n \times 1$, $\mathbf{X} \rightarrow n \times K$, $\boldsymbol{\beta} \rightarrow K \times 1$, and $\boldsymbol{\varepsilon} \rightarrow n \times 1$. Further, let y_t represent the tth element of $\mathbf{y}$, and $\mathbf{x}_t$ the tth row of $\mathbf{X}$. Define

$$\mathbf{X}_t = \begin{bmatrix} \mathbf{x}_1 \\ \mathbf{x}_2 \\ \vdots \\ \mathbf{x}_t \end{bmatrix} \quad \text{and} \quad \mathbf{Y}_t = \begin{bmatrix} y_1 \\ y_2 \\ \vdots \\ y_t \end{bmatrix}$$

[91] This procedure has been proposed in A. C. Harvey, "An Alternative Proof and Generalization of a Test for Structural Change," *The American Statistician,* 30 (August 1976), pp. 122–123. Harvey's proof is based on "recursive residuals," defined in (11.151).

[92] *Ibid.*

[93] R. L. Brown, J. Durbin, and J. M. Evans, "Techniques for Testing the Constancy of Regression Relationships over Time," *Journal of the Royal Statistical Society, Series B,* 37 (1975), pp. 149–192.

and

$$\hat{\boldsymbol{\beta}}_t = (\mathbf{X}_t'\mathbf{X}_t)^{-1}(\mathbf{X}_t'\mathbf{Y}_t).$$

The predictor of y_t based on observations $y_1, y_2, \ldots, y_{t-1}$ is given as

$$\tilde{y}_t = \mathbf{x}_t\hat{\boldsymbol{\beta}}_{t-1}.$$

The corresponding prediction error is $(y_t - \tilde{y}_t)$ and, under H_0,

$$E(y_t - \tilde{y}_t) = 0,$$

$$\text{Var}(y_t - \tilde{y}_t) = \sigma^2[1 + \mathbf{x}_t(\mathbf{X}_{t-1}'\mathbf{X}_{t-1})^{-1}\mathbf{x}_t'],$$

using (10.58) of Section 10-2. The CUSUM test is based on the *recursive residuals* defined as

$$w_t = \frac{y_t - \mathbf{x}_t\hat{\boldsymbol{\beta}}_{t-1}}{\sqrt{1 + \mathbf{x}_t(\mathbf{X}_{t-1}'\mathbf{X}_{t-1})^{-1}\mathbf{x}_t'}}. \tag{11.151}$$

Under H_0, $w_t \sim N(0, \sigma^2)$ and w_t and $w_s (t \neq s)$ are independent. The CUSUM test calls for plotting the quantity

$$W_t = \sum_{s=K+1}^{t} \frac{w_s}{\hat{\sigma}} \qquad (t = K+1, K+2, \ldots, n), \tag{11.152}$$

where

$$\hat{\sigma}^2 = \frac{1}{n-K-1} \sum_{s=K+1}^{n} (w_s - \overline{w})^2,$$

and

$$\overline{w} = \frac{1}{n-K} \sum_{s=1}^{n} w_s.$$

Under H_0, the approximate bounds for the path of W_t are given as follows. If we measure W on the vertical axis and t on the horizontal axis as in Figure 11-17, the

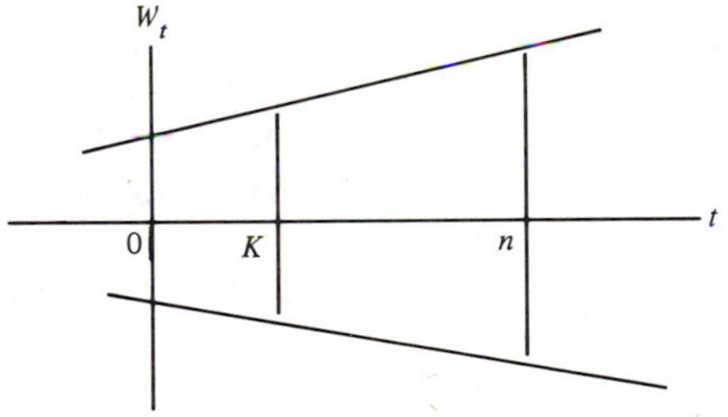

Figure 11-17

bounds are two straight lines passing through the points

t	W
K	$\pm a\sqrt{n-K}$
n	$\pm 3a\sqrt{n-K}$

where $a = 0.948$ for a significance level of 5%, and $a = 1.143$ for a significance level of 1%.[94] The null hypothesis is rejected if W_t crosses the boundary associated with the level of significance of the test for some t. If the coefficients are not constant, there may be a tendency for a disproportionate number of recursive residuals to have the same sign and to push W_t across the boundary. The CUSUM test is aimed mainly at detecting "systematic" movements in the coefficients. To detect "haphazard" rather than "systematic" types of movements of the coefficients, Brown and coauthors have proposed another test, called *CUSUM-square,* which involves plotting the quantity

$$S_t = \frac{\sum_{s=1}^{t} w_s^2}{\sum_{s=K+1}^{n} w_t^2} \qquad (t = K+1, K+2, \ldots, n). \tag{11.153}$$

Tables of critical values for various levels of significance are available.[95] Harvey and Collier have also proposed a test of the stability of the regression coefficients based on recursive residuals, called the *ψ test.*[96] The test statistic is

$$\psi = \frac{\bar{w}\sqrt{n-K}}{s_w}, \tag{11.154}$$

where $\bar{w}$ is defined as in (11.152) and

$$s_w^2 = \frac{1}{n-K-1} \sum_{t=K+1}^{n} (w_t - \bar{w})^2.$$

Under H_0, $\psi \sim t_{n-K-1}$. This test can be viewed as a check against systematic underprediction or overprediction.

Concluding Remarks

Models with varying coefficients have been praised by some researchers because they are realistic and do not impose such a rigid structure on the data as the standard regression model does. However, the use of varying coefficient models leaves one a bit uncomfortable because the models are not justified by theory. If regression coefficients vary, there must be a reason, and it is highly desirable to find out what that reason *is.* The search may not be easy, but it is worth trying. The use of varying coefficient models implies that we have given up trying to find the real causes of the variation.

[94] See A. C. Harvey, *The Econometric Analysis of Time Series* (New York: Halsted Press, 1981), p. 152.

[95] *Ibid.,* pp. 364–365.

[96] A. C. Harvey and P. Collier, "Testing for Functional Misspecification in Regression Analysis," *Journal of Econometrics,* 6 (July 1977), pp. 103–119.

11-8 Models with Unobservable Variables

In estimating econometric models or testing economic relationships, a researcher is sometimes faced with the problem of unobservable variables. In Section 9-1 we dealt with one type of unobservable variables, namely, those whose values were contaminated by errors of measurement. In this section we consider variables that are intrinsically unobservable, for instance, "education" or "intelligence." We will distinguish between unobservable variables that can be represented by *proxies,* and *latent variables* for which we have some determinants or indicators. An example of an unobservable variable represented by a proxy is "education," which is frequently approximated by years of schooling. Perhaps the most frequently used (and abused) proxy variable is the time trend, which is used to represent "technical progress," "tastes," "improvement in the labor force," and many other unobservable variables. An example of a latent variable is "intelligence," which is unobservable but for which there are available indicators such as results of IQ tests or performance on tests in econometrics.

Proxy Variables

Let us consider a simple regression model for which all classical assumptions hold:

(11.155) $$Y_i = \alpha + \beta X_i + \varepsilon_i .$$

Suppose X is not observable, but we observe a closely related variable X^*, which is determined as follows:

(11.156) $$X_i^* = \gamma + \delta X_i + u_i,$$

where u_i is a normally and independently distributed variable with mean zero and variance σ_u^2. Further, u_i and ε_j are independent for all $i, j = 1, 2, \ldots, n$. The variable X^* is called a proxy for X.[97] Solving (11.156) for X_i, we obtain

$$X_i = -\frac{\gamma}{\delta} + \frac{1}{\delta} X_i^* - \frac{u_i}{\delta}.$$

Substitution of this expression into (11.155) yields

(11.157) $$Y_i = \alpha^* + \beta^* X_i^* + \varepsilon_i^*,$$

where $\alpha^* = \alpha - (\beta\gamma/\delta)$, $\beta^* = \beta/\delta$, and $\varepsilon_i^* = \varepsilon_i - \beta(u_i/\delta)$. Since X_i^* and ε_i^* both depend on u_i, they are correlated, and the least squares estimator of β^* is inconsistent. If X^* were a perfect proxy for X, i.e., if u_i were equal to zero for all i, the least squares estimator of β^* would be a consistent estimator of β/δ, but we still would not have a

[97] A *proxy variable* is not to be confused with an *instrumental variable* defined in Section 9-1. Instrumental variables are used when X *is* observable but correlated with the regression disturbance.

consistent estimator of β. However, since the null hypothesis H_0: $\beta = 0$ is equivalent to H_0^*: $\beta^* = 0$, having a perfect proxy for X would enable us to test the relevance of X as an explanatory variable even though X is unobserved. Needless to say, perfect proxies are very rare.

An interesting situation arises when the model involves several explanatory variables of which one is not observable. Consider, for instance, the case when $K = 3$:

$$Y_i = \beta_1 + \beta_2 X_{i2} + \beta_3 X_{i3} + \varepsilon_i. \tag{11.158}$$

Suppose our interest is focussed on estimating β_2 when X_{i3} is not observable. Suppose further that we observe X_{i3}^*, which is related to X_{i3} as

$$X_{i3}^* = \gamma + \delta X_{i3} + u_i, \tag{11.159}$$

where u_i is defined as in (11.156). The least squares estimator of β_2, obtained by the formula (10.12) of Section 10-1, is

$$\hat{\beta}_2 = \frac{(\sum y_i' x_{i2}')(\sum x_{i3}^{*\prime 2}) - (\sum y_i' x_{i3}^{*\prime})(\sum x'_{i2} x_{i3}^{*\prime})}{(\sum x_{i2}'^2)(\sum x_{i3}^{*\prime 2}) - (\sum x_{i2}' x_{i3}^{*\prime})^2}, \tag{11.160}$$

where all variables are expressed in terms of deviations from their respective sample means. If we substitute for Y_i from (11.158) into (11.160) and take probability limits of both sides of the equation, we obtain

(11.160a)

$$\text{plim } \hat{\beta}_2 = \beta_2 + \beta_3 \text{ plim} \left[\frac{(\sum x_{i2}' x_{i3}'/n)(\sum x_{i3}^{*\prime 2}/n) - (\sum x_{i3}^{*\prime} x_{i3}'/n)(\sum x'_{i2} x_{i3}^{*\prime}/n)}{(\sum x_{i2}'^2/n)(\sum x_{i3}^{*\prime 2}/n) - (\sum x_{i2}' x^{*\prime}_{i3}/n)^2} \right].$$

Note that the expression in the square bracket in (11.160a) is the least squares estimator of the coefficient in the regression of X_3 on X_2 and X_3^*. If X_3^* were a perfect proxy for X_3, i.e., if u_i were equal to zero for all i, it would follow that plim $\hat{\beta}_2 = \beta_2$.

Since $\hat{\beta}_2$ defined by (11.160) is generally inconsistent, it is tempting to consider a simpler inconsistent estimator of β_2 obtained by dropping X_3 from (11.158). The resulting estimator, $\hat{\beta}_2^*$, is given as

$$\hat{\beta}_2^* = \frac{\sum y_i' x_{i2}'}{\sum x_{i2}'^2} \tag{11.161}$$

and

$$\text{plim } \hat{\beta}_2^* = \beta_2 + \beta_3 \text{ plim} \left[\frac{\sum x_{i2}' x_{i3}'/n}{\sum x_{i2}'^2/n} \right]. \tag{11.161a}$$

The choice between $\hat{\beta}_2$ and $\hat{\beta}_2^*$ represents a dilemma. If the criterion for the choice is the extent of asymptotic bias, then it can be shown that $\hat{\beta}_2$ is preferable.[98] This is true whether the explanatory variables are nonstochastic or stochastic. If, however, the criterion is the magnitude of the mean square error and the explanatory variables are stochastic, the choice is less certain but on the whole the use of a proxy is preferable.[99] The same appears to be true when the criterion is the asymptotic bias in the conventional tests of significance.[100] These conclusions are, of course, conditional on the assumptions concerning the proxy variables; they do not need to hold in general.[101]

The problem of proxy variables is closely related to the problem of errors of measurement. The distinction is that errors of measurement could, in principle, be eliminated by using better measuring instruments, whereas variables represented by proxies are basically unmeasurable.

Latent Variables

Theoretical derivations of regression models sometimes lead to formulations involving variables that are intrinsically not measurable but are related to measurable factors. We mentioned intelligence as one example of such a variable, but other examples are not difficult to find. Such variables are called *latent variables.* Perhaps the best known latent variable in economics is "permanent income," which is not measurable but is related to a number of measurable variables such as age, educational attainment, assets, etc. The simplest model involving a latent variable is a *multiple cause model,* which is specified as

$$Y_i = \beta X_i^* + \varepsilon_i, \qquad (11.162a)$$

$$X_i^* = \pi_i Z_{11} + \pi_2 Z_{i2} + \cdots + \pi_K Z_{iK}, \qquad (11.162b)$$

$$X_i = X_i^* + u_i, \qquad (11.162c)$$

where X^* is an unobservable latent variable, and Y, X, and $Z_1, Z_2, \ldots, Z_K$ are measurable. For example, X^* may be permanent income, Y may represent consumption, X may be measured income, and $Z_1, Z_2, \ldots, Z_K$ may stand for age, educational attainment, etc. The error terms are assumed to be mutually independent and to be normally and independently distributed with mean zero and var-

[98] See B. T. McCallum, "Relative Asymptotic Bias from Errors of Omission and Measurement," *Econometrica,* 40 (July 1972), pp. 757–758; M. R. Wickens, "A Note on the Use of Proxy Variables," *Econometrica,* 40 (July 1972), pp. 759–761.

[99] See D. J. Aigner, "MSE Dominance of Least Squares with Errors-of-Observation," *Journal of Econometrics,* 2 (December 1974), pp. 365–372; also T. Kinal and K. Lahiri, "Specification Error Analysis with Stochastic Regressors," *Econometrica,* 51 (July 1983), pp. 1209–1219.

[100] K. Ohtani, "A Note on the Use of a Proxy Variable in Testing Hypotheses," *Economics Letters,* 17 (1985), pp. 107–110.

[101] For a note of caution see P. A. Frost, "Proxy Variables and Specification Bias," *Review of Economics and Statistics,* 61 (May 1979), pp. 323–325.

iance σ^2 and σ_u^2, respectively. In matrix form the model becomes

(11.163a) $$\mathbf{y} = \mathbf{x}^*\beta + \boldsymbol{\varepsilon},$$

(11.163b) $$\mathbf{x}^* = \mathbf{Z}\boldsymbol{\pi},$$

(11.163c) $$\mathbf{x} = \mathbf{x}^* + \mathbf{u},$$

where $\mathbf{y} \rightarrow n \times 1$, $\mathbf{x}^* \rightarrow n \times 1$, $\beta \rightarrow 1 \times 1$, $\boldsymbol{\varepsilon} \rightarrow n \times 1$, $\mathbf{Z} \rightarrow n \times K$, $\boldsymbol{\pi} \rightarrow K \times 1$, $\mathbf{x} \rightarrow n \times 1$, and $\mathbf{u} \rightarrow n \times 1$. Substituting for $\mathbf{x}^*$ from (11.163b) into (11.163a) and (11.163c), we obtain

(11.164a) $$\mathbf{y} = \mathbf{Z}\boldsymbol{\pi}\beta + \boldsymbol{\varepsilon},$$

(11.164b) $$\mathbf{x} = \mathbf{Z}\boldsymbol{\pi} + \mathbf{u}.$$

Equations (11.164a) and (11.164b) are known as the *reduced form* of the model.

In the multiple cause model the main parameter of interest is β. Two methods have been proposed for its estimation: maximum likelihood and a two-stage method. The maximum likelihood method proposed by Goldberger[102] involves maximizing the following log-likelihood function,

(11.165) $$L = \text{constant} - \frac{n}{2}\log\sigma^2 - \frac{1}{2\sigma^2}(\mathbf{y} - \mathbf{Z}\boldsymbol{\pi}\beta)'(\mathbf{y} - \mathbf{Z}\boldsymbol{\pi}\beta)$$

$$-\frac{n}{2}\log\sigma_u^2 - \frac{1}{2\sigma_u^2}(\mathbf{x} - \mathbf{Z}\boldsymbol{\pi})'(\mathbf{x} - \mathbf{Z}\boldsymbol{\pi})$$

with respect to β, $\boldsymbol{\pi}$, σ^2, and σ_u^2. The two-stage method, proposed by Zellner,[103] involves rewriting (11.164a) and (11.164b) as

$$\mathbf{y} = \mathbf{Z}\boldsymbol{\gamma} + \boldsymbol{\varepsilon},$$

$$\mathbf{x} = \mathbf{Z}\boldsymbol{\pi} + \mathbf{u},$$

obtaining ordinary least squares estimates of $\boldsymbol{\gamma}$ and $\boldsymbol{\pi}$, and estimating σ^2 and σ_u^2 by s^2 and s_u^2, defined as follows:

(11.166a) $$s^2 = \frac{1}{n-K}(\mathbf{y} - \mathbf{Z}\hat{\boldsymbol{\gamma}})'(\mathbf{y} - \mathbf{Z}\hat{\boldsymbol{\gamma}}),$$

(11.166b) $$s_u^2 = \frac{1}{n-K}(\mathbf{x} - \mathbf{Z}\hat{\boldsymbol{\pi}})'(\mathbf{x} - \mathbf{Z}\hat{\boldsymbol{\pi}}).$$

The second stage then consists of minimizing

(11.167) $$S = \frac{1}{s^2}(\mathbf{y} - \mathbf{Z}\boldsymbol{\pi}\beta)'(\mathbf{y} - \mathbf{Z}\boldsymbol{\pi}\beta) + \frac{1}{s_u^2}(\mathbf{x} - \mathbf{Z}\boldsymbol{\pi})'(\mathbf{x} - \mathbf{Z}\boldsymbol{\pi})$$

[102] A. S. Goldberger, "Maximum Likelihood Estimation of Regressions Containing Unobservable Independent Variables," *International Economic Review,* 13 (February 1972), pp. 1–15.

[103] A. Zellner, "Estimation of Regression Relationships Containing Unobservable Independent Variables," *International Economic Review,* 11 (October 1970), pp. 441–454.

with respect to $\boldsymbol{\beta}$ and $\boldsymbol{\pi}$. The only difference between minimizing S in (11.167) and maximizing L in (11.165) is that in the case of S the variances of the disturbances are represented by their unrestricted estimates defined in (11.166a) and (11.166b), whereas in the case of L these variances are estimated along with $\boldsymbol{\beta}$ and $\boldsymbol{\pi}$. The two-stage estimators have the same asymptotic properties as the maximum likelihood estimators.[104] Further, Attfield[105] showed that misspecification of (11.164b) resulting from omission of relevant explanatory variables introduces inconsistency into the estimator of $\boldsymbol{\pi}$ but not of $\boldsymbol{\beta}$; the maximum likelihood and the two-stage estimator of $\boldsymbol{\beta}$ remain consistent.

Another well-known model involving latent variables is the *multiple-indicator multiple-cause model* (MIMIC). In this model the latent variable appears as an explanatory variable in several regression equations and is itself determined by a number of variables including a stochastic disturbance. The MIMIC model may be represented as

$$
\begin{aligned}
(11.168)\qquad Y_{i1} &= \beta_1 X_i^* + \varepsilon_{i1},\\
Y_{i2} &= \beta_2 X_i^* + \varepsilon_{i2},\\
&\ \vdots\\
Y_{ip} &= \beta_p X_i^* + \varepsilon_{ip},\\
X_i^* &= \pi_1 Z_{i1} + \pi_2 Z_{i2} + \cdots + \pi_K Z_{iK} + u_i,
\end{aligned}
$$

where the ε's are mutually independent and independent of u. Here the Y's are the *indicators* of X^* and the Z's are its *causes*. Maximum likelihood estimation of the model has been worked out by Jöreskog and Goldberger.[106]

EXAMPLE The MIMIC model was applied by Robins and West to the problem of estimation of home values.[107] The unobservable variable (X^*) is the true market value of the home, the indicators are the appraised value by a real estate firm (Y_1), the estimate of the value by the owner (Y_2), and the value appraised by county officials (Y_3). The causes of X^* are represented by twelve property characteristics such as age, lot size, number of rooms, etc. Each equation linking the Y's to X^* was specified to include a constant term. In the equation for Y_1 the

[104] A. Pagan, "Econometric Issues in the Analysis of Regressions with Generated Regressors," *International Economic Review,* 25 (February 1984), pp. 221–247.

[105] C. L. F. Attfield, "Consistent Estimation of Certain Parameters in the Unobservable Variable Model When There Is Specification Error," *Review of Economics and Statistics,* 65 (February 1983), pp. 164–167.

[106] K. G. Jöreskog and A. S. Goldberger, "Estimation of a Model with Multiple Indicators and Multiple Causes of a Single Latent Variable," *Journal of the American Statistical Association,* 70 (September 1975), pp. 631–639. A simplified computational procedure based on the EM algorithm is described in C.-F. Chen, "The EM Approach to the Multiple Indicators and Multiple Causes Model via the Estimation of the Latent Variable," *Journal of the American Statistical Association,* 76 (September 1981), pp. 704–708.

[107] P. K. Robins and R. W. West, "Measurement Errors in the Estimation of Home Values," *Journal of the American Statistical Association,* 72 (June 1977), pp. 290–294.

constant term was set equal to zero and the slope equal to one. The sample consisted of 138 houses owned by families in the Seattle Income Maintenance Experiment in 1971. The maximum likelihood estimates are presented in Table 11-8. The results indicate that home-

Table 11-8 Home Value Measurement Equations[a]

Source	Constant	Slope	$\hat{\sigma}$[b]
Appraised value	0	1.000	2.415
			(.158)
Owner estimate	1.257	.973	2.771
		(.119)	(.177)
Assessed value	−5.909	1.339	1.612
		(.120)	(.169)

[a] Figures in parentheses are estimated standard errors.
[b] $\hat{\sigma}$ = estimated standard deviation of ε.

owners tend to overvalue their homes by about $1260 but their estimates do not suffer from any multiplication bias (.973 is not significantly different from one). The standard deviation of the error term is about the same for the appraiser and the homeowner (2.415 vs. 2.771), indicating that, except for the additive bias, the appraiser and the homeowner determine their estimates of housing values with nearly the same degree of accuracy. The assessed value appears to suffer from bias.

The most complex model involving latent variables is the *covariance structure model,* popularly known as LISREL—the name of a computer program and an acronym for *li*near *s*tructural *rel*ations.[108] The model consists of a *structural relation* involving two types of latent variables, dependent (η) and independent (ξ), and of *measurement equations* linking the latent variables to their respective indicators. It is a simultaneous equation model with unobservable structural variables. (Simultaneous equation models with *observable* structural variables are discussed extensively in Chapter 13.) The complete specification of the model pertaining to a single observation is

$$\mathbf{B}\eta + \mathbf{\Gamma}\xi = \varepsilon, \tag{11.169a}$$

$$\mathbf{y} = \mathbf{\Lambda_y}\eta + \mathbf{u_y}, \tag{11.169b}$$

$$\mathbf{x} = \mathbf{\Lambda_x}\xi + \mathbf{u_x}, \tag{11.169c}$$

where $\eta \rightarrow G \times 1$, $\xi \rightarrow K \times 1$, $\mathbf{B} \rightarrow G \times G$, $\mathbf{\Gamma} \rightarrow G \times K$, $\varepsilon \rightarrow G \times 1$, $\mathbf{y} \rightarrow P \times 1$, $\mathbf{\Lambda_y} \rightarrow P \times G$, $\mathbf{u_y} \rightarrow P \times 1$, $\mathbf{x} \rightarrow Q \times 1$, $\mathbf{\Lambda_x} \rightarrow Q \times K$, and $\mathbf{u_x} \rightarrow G \times 1$. The following assumptions are made.

1. Expected values of all variables (latent and observed) are zero.
2. $E(\xi\varepsilon') = E(\xi\mathbf{u}_y') = E(\xi\mathbf{u}_x') = \mathbf{0}$, $E(\eta\mathbf{u}_y') = E(\eta\mathbf{u}_x') = \mathbf{0}$.

[108] LISREL is actually a registered trademark of the program. See K. G. Jöreskog and D. Sörbom, *LISREL V User's Guide* (Chicago: National Educational Resources, 1981).

3. $\boldsymbol{\varepsilon}$, $\mathbf{u_x}$, and $\mathbf{u_y}$ are mutually independent.
4. Observations are independent.

For maximum likelihood estimation it is also assumed that $\boldsymbol{\varepsilon}$, $\mathbf{u_x}$, and $\mathbf{u_y}$ each have a multivariate normal distribution.

The unknown parameters of the model are

$$\text{Structural parameters:} \quad \mathbf{B}, \boldsymbol{\Gamma}, \boldsymbol{\Lambda}_\mathbf{x}, \boldsymbol{\Lambda}_\mathbf{y}$$

$$\begin{aligned} \text{Variances and covariances:} \quad E(\boldsymbol{\xi}\boldsymbol{\xi}') &= \boldsymbol{\Phi}, \\ E(\boldsymbol{\varepsilon}\boldsymbol{\varepsilon}') &= \psi, \\ E(\mathbf{u_y}\mathbf{u_y}') &= \theta_{\mathbf{yy}}, \\ E(\mathbf{u_x}\mathbf{u_x}') &= \theta_{\mathbf{xx}}. \end{aligned}$$

Estimation of the model is based on two matrices, the matrix of the variances and covariances of the indicators ($\boldsymbol{\Sigma}$), and the matrix of the corresponding sample variances and covariances ($\mathbf{S}$). The dimension of both matrices is $(P+Q) \times (P+Q)$. The $\boldsymbol{\Sigma}$ matrix is defined as

$$\boldsymbol{\Sigma} = \begin{bmatrix} E(\mathbf{yy}') & E(\mathbf{yx}') \\ E(\mathbf{xy}') & E(\mathbf{xx}') \end{bmatrix}. \tag{11.170}$$

The elements of this matrix are expressions in terms of the unknown parameters. For the parameters to be identified, some restrictions (such as zero or equality restrictions) on the elements of $\boldsymbol{\Sigma}$ are necessary. The $\mathbf{S}$ matrix is defined as

$$\mathbf{S} = \begin{bmatrix} \mathbf{S}_{yy} & \mathbf{S}_{yx} \\ \mathbf{S}_{xy} & \mathbf{S}_{xx} \end{bmatrix}, \tag{11.171}$$

where

$$\mathbf{S}_{yy} = \begin{bmatrix} \frac{1}{n}\sum y_1^2 & \frac{1}{n}\sum y_1 y_2 & \cdots & \frac{1}{n}\sum y_1 y_P \\ \frac{1}{n}\sum y_2 y_1 & \frac{1}{n}\sum y_2^2 & \cdots & \frac{1}{n}\sum y_2 y_P \\ \vdots & & & \\ \frac{1}{n}\sum y_P y_1 & \frac{1}{n}\sum y_P y_2 & \cdots & \frac{1}{n}\sum y_P^2 \end{bmatrix},$$

$$\mathbf{S}_{yx} = \begin{bmatrix} \frac{1}{n}\sum y_1 x_1 & \frac{1}{n}\sum y_1 x_2 & \cdots & \frac{1}{n}\sum y_1 x_Q \\ \frac{1}{n}\sum y_2 x_1 & \frac{1}{n}\sum y_2 x_2 & \cdots & \frac{1}{n}\sum y_2 x_Q \\ \vdots & & & \\ \frac{1}{n}\sum y_P x_1 & \frac{1}{n}\sum y_P x_2 & \cdots & \frac{1}{n}\sum y_P x_Q \end{bmatrix},$$

$$\mathbf{S}_{xy} = \mathbf{S}'_{yx},$$

$$\mathbf{S}_{xx} = \begin{bmatrix} \frac{1}{n}\sum x_1^2 & \frac{1}{n}\sum x_1x_2 & \cdots & \frac{1}{n}\sum x_1x_Q \\ \frac{1}{n}\sum x_1x_2 & \frac{1}{n}\sum x_2^2 & \cdots & \frac{1}{n}\sum x_2x_Q \\ \vdots & & & \\ \frac{1}{n}\sum x_Qx_1 & \frac{1}{n}\sum x_Qx_2 & \cdots & \frac{1}{n}\sum x_Q^2 \end{bmatrix}.$$

The LISREL program provides for estimation based on different objective or "fitting" functions. The following choices are available.

1. Ordinary Least Squares: Minimize $\text{tr}(\mathbf{S} - \mathbf{\Sigma})^2$.
2. Generalized Least Squares: Minimize $\text{tr}(\mathbf{S} - \mathbf{\Sigma})^2\mathbf{S}^{-1}$.
3. Maximum Likelihood: Minimize $\log|\mathbf{\Sigma}| + \text{tr}(\mathbf{S\Sigma})^{-1}$.

Under the stated assumptions (including normality), the maximum likelihood estimators have all desirable asymptotic properties.[109]

EXAMPLE Jöreskog and Sörbom present an example of the use of the LISREL program by estimating a model of peer influences on students' ambitions proposed by Duncan et al.[110] The structural equations of the model are given as

$$\eta_1 = \beta_1\eta_2 + \gamma_1\xi_1 + \gamma_2\xi_2 + \gamma_3\xi_3 + \gamma_4\xi_4 + \varepsilon_1,$$

$$\eta_2 = \beta_2\eta_1 + \gamma_5\xi_3 + \gamma_6\xi_4 + \gamma_7\xi_5 + \gamma_8\xi_6 + \varepsilon_2,$$

where η_1 = respondent's ambitions, η_2 = respondent's friend's ambitions, ξ_1 = respondent's parents' aspirations for their child, ξ_2 = respondent's intelligence, ξ_3 = respondent's parents' socioeconomic status, ξ_4 = friend's parents' socioeconomic status, ξ_5 = friend's intelligence, and ξ_6 = friend's parents' aspirations for their child. The ηs and ξs are the latent variables of the system; the ηs are determined by the two structural equations and the ξs are exogenous. The measurement equations are

$$y_1 = \eta_1 + u_{y1},$$

$$y_2 = \lambda_2\eta_1 + u_{y2},$$

$$y_3 = \lambda_3\eta_2 + u_{y3},$$

$$y_4 = \eta_2 + u_{y4},$$

$$x_j = \xi_j \qquad (j = 1, 2, \ldots, 6),$$

[109] See D. J. Aigner et al., "Latent Variable Models in Econometrics," in Z. Griliches and M. D. Intriligator, *Handbook of Econometrics,* Vol. 2 (Amsterdam: North-Holland, 1984), pp. 1370–1371, for a careful discussion of the estimation aspects of the LISREL model.

[110] Jöreskog and Sörbom, *op. cit.,* pp. III.81–93; O.D. Duncan, A. O. Haller, and A. Portes, "Peer Influences on Aspirations: A Reinterpretation," *American Journal of Sociology,* 74 (January 1968), pp. 119–137.

where y_1 = respondent's occupational aspiration, y_2 = respondent's educational aspiration, y_3 = friend's educational aspiration, and y_4 = friend's occupational aspiration. The xs are defined by the ξs in this model; i.e., the ξs are assumed to be measurable. The description of the measurement of the variables involved is given in Duncan et al. Since there is no reason to expect that corresponding effects for the friend and the respondent will be different, the restriction that $\beta_1 = \beta_2$ was imposed.

The sample consisted of 329 Michigan high-school students paired with their best friends. Maximum likelihood estimates of the structural coefficients came out as

$$\underset{}{\eta_1} = \underset{(0.039)}{0.180\eta_2} + \underset{(0.039)}{0.164\xi_1} + \underset{(0.042)}{0.254\xi_2} + \underset{(0.042)}{0.221\xi_3} + \underset{(0.042)}{0.077\xi_4} + e_1,$$

$$\eta_2 = \underset{(0.039)}{0.180\eta_1} + \underset{(0.039)}{0.068\xi_3} + \underset{(0.040)}{0.218\xi_4} + \underset{(0.041)}{0.331\xi_5} + \underset{(0.036)}{0.152\xi_6} + e_2.$$

The results indicate that peer influence is significant, but that for both the respondents and their best friends the strongest influences on their ambitions are their own intelligence and socioeconomic status.

An alternative approach to the estimation of a covariance structure model known as *partial least squares* (PLS) has been proposed and developed by Wold.[111] The distinctive feature of the PLS method is the absence of *any* distributional assumptions. This method, which is based on an iterative procedure yielding successive approximations of the latent variables, has been extensively used in disciplines other than economics.

11-9 Disequilibrium Models

The standard assumption of most economic models is that markets get cleared because of the operation of the price mechanism, and that there is no excess supply or demand at existing prices. At the same time, observation of the markets indicates frequent and unintended changes in inventories and the existence of unfilled orders. Uncleared markets are particularly notable in the labor market, where unemployment as well as long lists of vacancies are common. These observations have led to the development of disequilibrium models designed to take into account the potential failure of the markets to clear. The field of disequilibrium economics and econometrics is fast growing and involves difficult conceptual and statistical problems. Our aim here is to provide only a very basic introduction to the main models considered in the literature.[112]

[111] H. Wold, "Model Construction and Evaluation When Theoretical Knowledge Is Scarce," in J. Kmenta and J. B. Ramsey, *Evaluation of Econometric Models* (New York: Academic Press, 1980), pp. 47–74.

[112] Two excellent recent surveys of disequilibrium models are available: Maddala, *Limited Dependent . . . , op. cit.,* Chapter 10; and R. E. Quandt, "Econometric Disequilibrium Models," *Econometric Reviews,* 1 (1982), pp. 1–63.

Basic Model

The basic model introduced by Quandt as a "switching regression model" can be represented as[113]

(11.172a) $$D_t = \alpha_1 + \beta_1 P_t + \gamma_1 X_{t1} + u_{t1},$$

(11.172b) $$S_t = \alpha_2 + \beta_2 P_t + \gamma_2 X_{t2} + u_{t2},$$

(11.172c) $$Q_t = Z_t(\alpha_1 + \beta_1 P_t + \gamma_1 X_{t1} + u_{t1}) + (1 - Z_t)(\alpha_2 + \beta_2 P_t + \gamma_2 X_{t2} + u_{t2}),$$

where D = demand, S = supply, Q = quantity traded, P = price, X_1 and X_2 are other explanatory variables, and Z is an exogenously determined dummy variable defined as

$$\begin{aligned} Z_t &= 1 \quad \text{if } D_t = Q_t, \\ &= 0 \quad \text{if } S_t = Q_t. \end{aligned}$$

The *us* are normally and independently distributed disturbances with zero means and constant variances. The three equations determine D, S, and Q; price is determined exogenously in some unspecified way. In equilibrium we would have $D_t = S_t = Q_t$, but the definition of Z_t precludes the possibility of an equilibrium situation in this model.

If we knew the values of Z_t, there would be no problem in separating the parameters of the demand and supply equations, but such a situation is rare. If Z_t is not known, the values of Z_t can, in principle, be regarded as a set of unknown parameters to be estimated along with the coefficients of the demand and supply equations. This can be done by using the maximum likelihood method for switching regressions with unknown switching points as described in Section 11-7. The situation here is complicated by the fact that there could be a lot of switching back and forth between supply and demand and, therefore, a possibly large number of switching points. This could result in an inordinate amount of computation. The computational burden may be one of the reasons why this model has not been very popular, but the main reason has probably been the fact that we usually have more prior information than the model presupposes.

Fair and Jaffee Model 1

This model, introduced by Fair and Jaffee,[114] consists of equations (11.172a) and (11.172b) from the basic model just discussed, but equation (11.172c) is replaced by

[113] R. E. Quandt, "The Estimation of the Parameters of a Linear Regression System Obeying Two Separate Regimes," *Journal of the American Statistical Association,* 53 (September 1958), pp. 873–880; see also Goldfeld and Quandt, "Nonlinear Methods . . . ," *op. cit.,* pp. 261–262.

[114] R. C. Fair and D. M. Jaffee, "Methods of Estimation for Markets in Disequilibrium," *Econometrica,* 40 (May 1972), pp. 497–514.

the condition that

$$Q_t = D_t \quad \text{if } D_t < S_t, \qquad (11.173)$$
$$Q_t = S_t \quad \text{if } D_t > S_t.$$

The values of D_t and S_t are, of course, unobservable. The presumption underlying this model is that the quantity traded in the market is always the *lower* of the two—quantity demanded and quantity supplied. This is illustrated in Figure 11-18

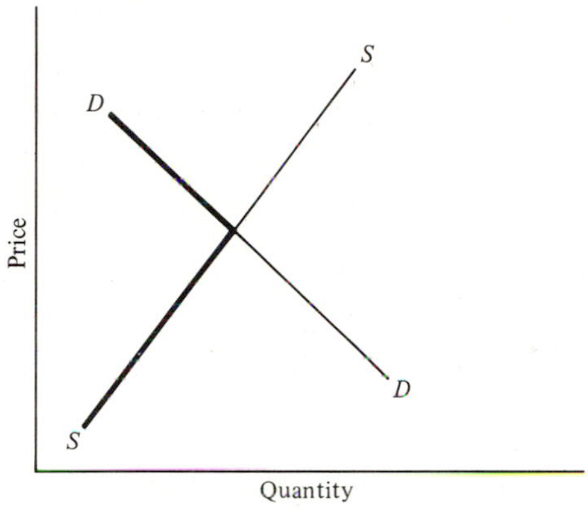

Figure 11-18

where the heavy line represents observed demand and supply quantities. In this model price is again determined exogenously in some unspecified way. Since D_t and S_t are not observable, the allocation of observations to the supply or demand regime is determined by the probability that $D_t \leq S_t$, which can be estimated.

Maximum likelihood estimation of this model has been worked out by Maddala and Nelson[115] and labeled "maximum likelihood estimation with unknown sample separation." Maddala[116] notes that there are two major problems with this model, one conceptual and one statistical. The conceptual problem is that the model does not contain enough prior information and too much is asked of the data, which leads to a loss of efficiency. If more thought were given to figuring out why disequilibrium exists, then probably more could be said about the separation of sample observations between supply and demand. The statistical problem, pointed out by Maddala and others, is that for some parameter values the likelihood function is unbounded and thus cannot be maximized.

[115] G. S. Maddala and F. Nelson, "Maximum Likelihood Methods for Markets in Disequilibrium," *Econometrica,* 42 (November 1974), pp. 1013–1030.

[116] Maddala, *Limited Dependent . . . , op. cit.,* p. 299.

Directional Model

This model was also first suggested by Fair and Jaffee.[117] It consists of equations (11.172a), (11.172b), (11.173) *and* the following.

(11.174)
$$P_t - P_{t-1} > 0 \quad \text{if } D_t > S_t,$$
$$P_t - P_{t-1} < 0 \quad \text{if } D_t < S_t.$$

This model is based on the principle that during the period of excess demand the price should be rising, and during the period of excess supply the price should be falling. Thus we can use the direction of the price change, which is observable, to give us information about the allocation of observations to supply and demand regimes. With the inclusion of (11.174), the determination of price is no longer completely unspecified, since the price change now depends on D_t and S_t.

Given the knowledge of how to separate sample observations between supply and demand according to the observed price behavior, one might be tempted to estimate the demand and supply equations separately on the basis of the respective observations. However, since P_t depends on D_t and S_t, it will be correlated with u_{t1} and u_{t2} and, therefore, separate least squares estimators of the coefficients will be inconsistent. Maximum likelihood estimation of the model is discussed by Maddala.[118]

Quantitative Model

One problem with the directional model is that the relationship between excess demand or supply and the price movement is too vague. In the *quantitative model* this relationship is spelled out exactly. The model consists of equations (11.172a), (11.172b), (11.173), *and*

(11.175)
$$P_t - P_{t-1} = \delta(D_t - S_t).$$

The parameters of this model can be estimated by maximum likelihood or by a two-stage procedure.[119]

It is interesting to note that the quantitative model has the *same observational implications* for price behavior as the "partial adjustment model" represented as

(11.176a)
$$D_t = \alpha_1 + \beta_1 P_t^* + \gamma_1 X_{t1} + u_{t1},$$

(11.176b)
$$S_t = \alpha_2 + \beta_2 P_t^* + \gamma_2 X_{t2} + u_{t2},$$

(11.176c)
$$D_t = S_t,$$

(11.176d)
$$P_t - P_{t-1} = (1 - \mu)(P_t^* - P_{t-1}),$$

[117] *Op. cit.*

[118] *Limited Dependent . . .*, *op. cit.*, pp. 305–306. A two-stage procedure is discussed on p. 308.

[119] *Ibid.*, pp. 306–309.

where P_t^* represents an equilibrium price that is not observable. Equation (11.176d) determines the adjustment toward equilibrium. Equating demand and supply according to (11.176c) and substituting for P_t^* from (11.176d) into (11.176a) and (11.176b), we obtain

$$P_t = \alpha^* + \beta^* P_{t-1} + \gamma_1^* X_{t1} + \gamma_2^* X_{t2} + u_{t1}^*, \tag{11.177}$$

where

$$\alpha^* = \frac{(\alpha_2 - \alpha_1)(1-\mu)}{\beta_1 - \beta_2},$$

$$\beta^* = \mu,$$

$$\gamma_1^* = -\gamma_1 \left(\frac{1-\mu}{\beta_1 - \beta_2}\right),$$

$$\gamma_2^* = \gamma_2 \left(\frac{1-\mu}{\beta_1 - \beta_2}\right),$$

and

$$u_t^* = \frac{(1-\mu)(u_{t1} - u_{t2})}{\beta_1 - \beta_2}.$$

Let us compare this with the corresponding equation implied by the quantitative model. Substitution from (11.172a) and (11.172b) into (11.175) leads to

$$P_t = \alpha^{**} + \beta^{**} P_{t-1} + \gamma_1^{**} X_{t1} + \gamma_2^{**} X_{t2} + u_t^{**}, \tag{11.178}$$

where

$$\alpha^{**} = \delta \left(\frac{\alpha_1 - \alpha_2}{1 - \beta_1\delta + \beta_2\delta}\right),$$

$$\beta^{**} = \frac{1}{1 - \beta_1\delta + \beta_2\delta},$$

$$\gamma_1^{**} = \gamma_1 \left(\frac{\delta}{1 - \beta_1\delta + \beta_2\delta}\right),$$

$$\gamma_2^{**} = -\gamma_2 \left(\frac{\delta}{1 - \beta_1\delta + \beta_2\delta}\right),$$

and

$$u_t^{**} = \frac{\delta(u_{t1} - u_{t2})}{1 - \beta_1\delta + \beta_2\delta}.$$

Clearly, (11.177) and (11.178) are observationally indistinguishable. However, according to Quandt, the difference between the two equations is that "the parameters of the demand and supply functions are generally identifiable in the disequilibrium model, but they are not necessarily identifiable in the partial adjustment model."[120]

A natural extension of the price adjustment equation (11.175) is to allow for the presence of a stochastic disturbance. The resulting model is called the *generalized quantitative model.* The addition of the disturbance in (11.175) means that D_t, S_t, and P_t are no longer in a deterministic relationship and that the change in price can no longer tell us precisely whether a given observation belongs to the supply or the demand regime. This complicates matters but maximum likelihood estimation is still possible, provided we make certain minor model modifications to assure identification.

EXAMPLE The directional and the quantitative models were used by Fair and Jaffee[121] to model the U.S. housing market. The demand and supply equations were specified as follows:

$$HS^D = \alpha_0 + \alpha_1 t + \alpha_2 \sum_{i=1}^{t-1} HS_i + \alpha_3 RM_{t-2} + u_t^D,$$

$$HS^S = \beta_0 + \beta_1 t + \beta_2 DF6_{t-1} + \beta_3 DHF3_{t-2} + \beta_4 RM_{t-1} + u_t^S,$$

where HS = housing starts, t = time, RM = mortgage rate, $DF6$ = six-month moving average of private savings deposits, and $DHF3$ = three-month moving average of borrowings by the savings and loan associations. The data were seasonally unadjusted monthly observations for the period June 1959 to November 1969. The authors used the directional and the quantitative models. The numerical results are too lengthy to present here, but the authors claim that they obtained "good results" for both models. They found that their coefficient estimates were not that much different from the estimates obtained on the assumption of full equilibrium.

Testing for Equilibrium

Since equilibrium and disequilibrium are two different states of the world, we may be able to test the claim that either state exists. The simplest and most desirable way of doing that would be by having one state of the world, such as the equilibrium state, as a special case of a general model that allows for equilibrium as well as disequilibrium. This would be possible if the source of potential disequilibrium could be identified and incorporated into the model. In this case the hypothesis of an equilibrium state would be a *nested hypothesis* and an appropriate test would be easy to design. With respect to the models discussed in this section, the nested hypothesis approach to testing is possible only with the quantitative model. In a state of equilibrium, any deviation of supply from demand or vice versa would be accompanied by a swift change in price. With reference to the price adjustment equation (11.175), this implies that the coefficient δ would have to be very large—strictly speaking, infinity. Thus a test of the hypothesis that $(1/\delta) = 0$ is an appropri-

[120] Quandt, "Econometric Disequilibrium Models," *op. cit.*, p. 6.

[121] *Op. cit.*

ate test of equilibrium. In the basic model, in the Fair and Jaffee Model 1, and in the directional model, the existence of disequilibrium is taken for granted. With respect to these models, the states of disequilibrium and equilibrium represent two nonnested hypotheses. Procedures for testing such hypotheses are discussed in the next section.

11-10 Model Choice

One of the most important problems in econometric research is to choose among competing models. This problem has recently received a great deal of attention, which it rightly deserves, but there are still many important questions to be answered. In this section we confine our attention to the situation where there are just two competing models and discuss some of the most commonly used criteria and tests. In the first part we consider the simpler problem of choosing among *nested models,* i.e., models specified so that one model is a special case of another model. In the second part we deal with the more difficult problem of choosing among *nonnested models,* i.e., models specified in such a way that neither model can be expressed as a special case of the other model. The section concludes with a discussion of some informal procedures of choosing models in practice.

Nested Models

Suppose two competing models are given as follows:

$$\text{Model I:} \qquad \mathbf{y} = \mathbf{X}_1\boldsymbol{\beta}_1 + \boldsymbol{\varepsilon},$$

$$\text{Model II:} \qquad \mathbf{y} = \mathbf{X}_1\boldsymbol{\beta}_1 + \mathbf{X}_2\boldsymbol{\beta}_2 + \boldsymbol{\varepsilon},$$

where $\mathbf{y} \rightarrow n \times 1$, $\mathbf{X}_1 \rightarrow n \times K_1$, $\boldsymbol{\beta}_1 \rightarrow K_1 \times 1$, $\mathbf{X}_2 \rightarrow n \times K_2$, $\boldsymbol{\beta}_2 \rightarrow K_2 \times 1$, and $\boldsymbol{\varepsilon} \rightarrow n \times 1$. The **X**s are taken to be nonstochastic and $\boldsymbol{\varepsilon}$ satisfies all classical assumptions. Model I is nested in Model II since it reduces to Model II when $\boldsymbol{\beta}_2 = 0$. The following criteria for making a choice have been proposed and used.

(a) Classical model selection. The simplest and the most straightforward method of choosing between Model I and Model II is to test the hypothesis H_0: $\boldsymbol{\beta}_2 = 0$ against H_A: $\boldsymbol{\beta}_2 \neq 0$. This leads to the well-known F test

$$\frac{(\text{SSE}_\text{I} - \text{SSE}_\text{II})/K_2}{\text{SSE}_\text{II}/(n - K_1 - K_2)} \sim F_{K_2,\, n-K_1-K_2}, \tag{11.179}$$

where SSE_I and SSE_II are the least squares error sum of squares from Models I and II, respectively. Rejection of the null hypothesis favors Model II, and nonrejection favors Model I. This test is not very powerful if X_1 and X_2 are highly collinear. (If the two models were nonlinear, we would use the likelihood ratio test.)

(b) Mean square error norm. An alternative criterion involves the comparison of mean square errors of the two models. Let

$$\hat{\beta}_1^* = \text{least squares estimator of } \beta_1 \text{ based on Model I,}$$

$$\hat{\beta}_1, \hat{\beta}_2 = \text{least squares estimators of } \beta_1 \text{ and } \beta_2 \text{ based on Model II.}$$

Define

$$\hat{\beta} = \begin{bmatrix} \hat{\beta}_1 \\ \hat{\beta}_2 \end{bmatrix}, \quad \hat{\beta}^* = \begin{bmatrix} \hat{\beta}_1^* \\ \mathbf{0} \end{bmatrix}, \quad \text{and} \quad \mathbf{X} = [\mathbf{X}_1 \ \mathbf{X}_2].$$

Model I is chosen if

$$E(\mathbf{X}\hat{\beta} - \mathbf{X}\beta)'(\mathbf{X}\hat{\beta} - \mathbf{X}\beta) - E(\mathbf{X}\hat{\beta}^* - \mathbf{X}\beta)'(\mathbf{X}\hat{\beta}^* - \mathbf{X}\beta) \geq 0; \tag{11.180}$$

otherwise the choice is Model II. Using some tedious but not difficult algebra, it can be shown that this criterion is equivalent to

$$\sigma^2 K_2 - \beta_2' \mathbf{X}_2' \mathbf{M}_1 \mathbf{X}_2 \beta_2 \geq 0 \tag{11.181}$$

or

$$K_2 \geq \frac{\beta_2' \mathbf{X}_2' \mathbf{M}_1 \mathbf{X}_2 \beta_2}{\sigma^2}. \tag{11.181a}$$

Note that this criterion would lead to the choice of Model I if β_2 were equal to zero, but Model I would be chosen even if β_2 were *not* equal to zero as long as its value does not make the right-hand side of the inequality (11.181a) exceed K_2.

The criterion (11.181)—or (11.181a)—is, of course, not operational because β^2 and σ^2 are not known. *If* we use the least squares estimators of β_2 and σ^2 defined as

$$\hat{\beta}_2 = (\mathbf{X}_2' \mathbf{M}_1 \mathbf{X}_2)^{-1} \mathbf{X}_2' \mathbf{M}_1 \mathbf{y}, \tag{11.182a}$$

$$s^2 = \frac{1}{n - K_1 - K_2} (\mathbf{y} - \mathbf{X}\hat{\beta})'(\mathbf{y} - \mathbf{X}\hat{\beta}), \tag{11.182b}$$

then the *operational* mean square error criterion becomes

$$\frac{(\text{SSE}_{\text{I}} - \text{SSE}_{\text{II}})/K_2}{\text{SSE}_{\text{II}}/(n - K_1 - K_2)} \leq 1. \tag{11.183}$$

Thus Model I would be chosen as long as the value of the F statistic in (11.179) does not exceed unity. This corresponds to a level of significance considerably greater than the conventional 5% or even 10%.

(c) $\bar{R}^2$ criterion. A frequent yardstick in choosing models is the *adjusted coefficient of determination* ($\bar{R}^2$) defined in Section 10-2. Define

$$\bar{R}_{\text{I}}^2 = 1 - \frac{\text{SSE}_{\text{I}}/(n - K_1)}{\text{SST}/(n - 1)}$$

and

$$\bar{R}^2_{\text{II}} = 1 - \frac{\text{SSE}_{\text{II}}/(n - K_1 - K_2),}{\text{SST}/(n-1)}$$

where $\text{SST} = \Sigma_i(Y_i - \bar{Y})^2$. The $\bar{R}^2$ *criterion* then leads to the choice of Model I if

(11.184) $$\bar{R}^2_{\text{I}} \geq \bar{R}^2_{\text{II}};$$

otherwise the choice is Model II.

To elaborate further, we note that $\bar{R}^2_{\text{I}} \geq \bar{R}^2_{\text{II}}$ is equivalent to

(11.185) $$\frac{\text{SSE}_{\text{II}}}{n - K_1 - K_2} \geq \frac{\text{SSE}_{\text{I}}}{n - K_1}$$

or

(11.185a) $$s^2 \geq s^2_{\text{I}},$$

where s^2 is defined as in (11.182b) and

$$s^2_{\text{I}} = \frac{(\mathbf{y} - \mathbf{X}\hat{\boldsymbol{\beta}}^*)'(\mathbf{y} - \mathbf{X}\hat{\boldsymbol{\beta}}^*)}{n - K_1}.$$

That means that Model I will be chosen if the estimated variance of the disturbance in Model I is less than that in Model II. Further, using (11.185) we have

$$0 \geq \frac{\text{SSE}_{\text{I}}}{n - K_1} - \frac{\text{SSE}_{\text{II}}}{n - K_1 - K_2}.$$

This can be written as

$$\frac{n - K_1}{n - K_1 - K_2} - 1 \geq \frac{\text{SSE}_{\text{I}} - \text{SSE}_{\text{II}}}{\text{SSE}_{\text{II}}}$$

or

$$1 \geq \frac{(\text{SSE}_{\text{I}} - \text{SSE}_{\text{II}})/K_2}{\text{SSE}_{\text{II}}/(n - K_1 - K_2)}.$$

This means that the $\bar{R}^2$ criterion is *exactly equivalent* to the operational mean square error criterion.

Nonnested Models

Let us now suppose that two competing models are nonnested as follows.

$$\text{Model I:} \qquad \mathbf{y} = \mathbf{X}_1\boldsymbol{\beta}_1 + \boldsymbol{\varepsilon},$$

$$\text{Model II:} \qquad \mathbf{y} = \mathbf{X}_2\boldsymbol{\beta}_2 + \boldsymbol{\varepsilon}.$$

The assumptions are the same as in the case of the nested models. In general, $\mathbf{X}_1$ and $\mathbf{X}_2$ may share some common variables. The choice between Model I and Model II can be considered as a testing problem. The hypotheses are

$$H_1: \quad E(\mathbf{y}) = \mathbf{X}_1\boldsymbol{\beta}_1,$$

$$H_2: \quad E(\mathbf{y}) = \mathbf{X}_2\boldsymbol{\beta}_2.$$

The problem of testing nonnested hypotheses was considered by Cox, who introduced the idea of modifying the likelihood ratio test for the nonnested case.[122] The idea behind Cox's approach to testing H_1 against H_2 is to consider to what extent Model I is capable of predicting the performance of Model II. The testing procedure of Cox, which is quite general, has spawned a number of variants for its application to nonnested regression models.[123] A particular virtue of the test is that it can be well adapted to nonlinear nonnested regressions.[124]

An alternative approach to testing H_1 against H_2 is based on *artificial nesting.* The simplest of the tests in this category is the F test based on the combined regression equation

$$\mathbf{y} = \mathbf{X}_1\boldsymbol{\beta}_1 + \overline{\mathbf{X}}_2\boldsymbol{\beta}_2 + \boldsymbol{\varepsilon}, \tag{11.186}$$

where $\overline{\mathbf{X}}_2$ is the same as $\mathbf{X}_2$ except that all variables common with $\mathbf{X}_1$ have been deleted. A test of H_1 is simply the standard F test of the hypothesis that $\boldsymbol{\beta}_2 = \mathbf{0}$.

An unsatisfactory aspect of the F test is that what H_1 is being tested against is *not* H_2 but a hybrid of H_1 and H_2 represented by (11.186). To get around this problem, Davidson and McKinnon[125] proposed the following nested regression equation:

$$\mathbf{y} = (1-\alpha)\mathbf{X}_1\boldsymbol{\beta}_1 + \alpha\mathbf{X}_2\boldsymbol{\beta}_2 + \boldsymbol{\varepsilon}, \tag{11.187}$$

where α is a parameter that sorts out (11.187) into H_1 and H_2. If $\alpha = 0$, (11.187) reduces to H_1; if $\alpha = 1$, (11.187) reduces to H_2. Thus testing H_1 is equivalent to testing the hypothesis that $\alpha = 0$. The complication is that α is not identified. To achieve identification Davidson and McKinnon propose to replace $\boldsymbol{\beta}_2$ by its simple least squares estimator $\hat{\boldsymbol{\beta}}_2$ defined as $\hat{\boldsymbol{\beta}}_2 = (\mathbf{X}_2'\mathbf{X}_2)^{-1}\mathbf{X}_2'\mathbf{y}$. The resulting test, called the *J test,* then involves applying the least squares method to

$$\mathbf{y} = (1-\alpha)\mathbf{X}_1\boldsymbol{\beta}_1 + \alpha\mathbf{X}_2\hat{\boldsymbol{\beta}}_2 + \boldsymbol{\varepsilon}^* \tag{11.187a}$$

and obtaining a least squares estimate of the coefficient α of $(\mathbf{X}_2\hat{\boldsymbol{\beta}}_2)$. When H_1 is true, the estimator of α divided by its conventionally estimated standard error is asymptotically distributed as $N(0, 1)$.

[122] D. R. Cox, "Tests of Separate Families of Hypotheses," in *Proceedings of the Fourth Berkeley Symposium on Mathematical Statistics and Probability* (Berkeley: University of California Press, 1961), pp. 239–253; see also Fomby et al., *op cit.,* pp. 418–423.

[123] See M. McAleer, "Specification Tests for Separate Models: A Survey," in M. L King and D. E. A. Giles (eds.), *Specification Analysis in the Linear Model* (London: Routledge and Kegan Paul, 1985).

[124] M. H. Pesaran and A. S. Deaton, "Testing Nonnested Nonlinear Regression Models," *Econometrica,* 46 (May 1978), pp. 677–694.

[125] R. Davidson and J. McKinnon, "Several Tests for Model Specification in the Presence of Alternative Hypotheses," *Econometrica,* 49 (May 1981), pp. 781–793.

A modification of the J test has been proposed by Fisher and McAleer who introduced an alternative test known as the *JA test.*[126] The authors point out that the asymptotic distribution of the estimator of α is determined under H_1, but under H_1

$$\begin{aligned} \text{plim } \hat{\boldsymbol{\beta}}_2 &= \text{plim} \left(\frac{\mathbf{X}_2'\mathbf{X}_2}{n}\right)^{-1} \frac{\mathbf{X}_2'\mathbf{y}}{n} \\ &= \text{plim} \frac{(\mathbf{X}_2'\mathbf{X}_2/n)^{-1}\mathbf{X}_2'(\mathbf{X}_1\boldsymbol{\beta}_1 + \boldsymbol{\varepsilon})}{n} \\ &= \text{plim } (\mathbf{X}_2'\mathbf{X}_2/n)^{-1}(\mathbf{X}_2'\mathbf{X}_1/n)\boldsymbol{\beta}_1 . \end{aligned}$$

Therefore Fisher and McAleer propose to replace $\hat{\boldsymbol{\beta}}_2$ by $\tilde{\boldsymbol{\beta}}_2$ defined as

$$\tilde{\boldsymbol{\beta}}_2 = (\mathbf{X}_2'\mathbf{X}_2)^{-1}\mathbf{X}_2'\mathbf{X}_1\hat{\boldsymbol{\beta}}_1,$$

where $\hat{\boldsymbol{\beta}}_1 = (\mathbf{X}_1'\mathbf{X}_1)^{-1}\mathbf{X}_1'\mathbf{y}$. The JA test then involves applying the least squares method to

$$\mathbf{y} = (1 - \alpha)\mathbf{X}_1\boldsymbol{\beta}_1 + \alpha\mathbf{X}_2\tilde{\boldsymbol{\beta}}_2 + \boldsymbol{\varepsilon}^{**} \tag{11.187b}$$

and obtaining a least squares estimate of the coefficient α of $(\mathbf{X}_2\tilde{\boldsymbol{\beta}}_2)$. The resulting estimator of α divided by its conventionally estimated standard error has a t distribution in small samples if $\mathbf{X}_1$ and $\mathbf{X}_2$ are nonstochastic. The J and JA tests are asymptotically equivalent.[127]

The small sample properties of the test statistics discussed above have been examined by means of Monte Carlo experiments.[128] The results indicate that the J test tends to reject the true hypothesis more frequently than it should and that the JA test has a relatively low power when $K_1 > K_2$. It is, therefore, suggested that the JA test is most useful when both models have about the same number of nonoverlapping explanatory variables.

One obvious difficulty with the tests of nonnested hypotheses is the asymmetry of H_1 and H_2. When we test H_1, we use H_2 as a way of challenging the validity of H_1. If H_1 is rejected, we do not conclude that H_2 is the true model, since H_1 may have been brought down by another challenger as well. To make a statement about the validity of H_2, we have to change the roles of H_1 and H_2 and go through the testing process again. Thus it is perfectly possible that both H_1 and H_2 are rejected, or that they both are accepted. If they are both rejected, neither model is useful in explaining the variation in the dependent variable. If they are both accepted, the data are apparently not rich enough to discriminate between the two hypotheses.

[126] G. R. Fisher and M. McAleer, "Alternative Procedures and Associated Tests of Significance for Nonnested Hypotheses," *Journal of Econometrics,* **16** (May 1981), pp. 103–119.

[127] A very lucid comparison of the tests with the help of Ballentine Venn diagrams is presented in P. Kennedy, *A Guide to Econometrics,* 2nd ed. (Cambridge, MA: MIT Press, 1985), pp. 85–86.

[128] L. G. Godfrey and M. H. Pesaran, "Tests of Nonnested Regression Models: Small Sample Adjustments and Monte Carlo Evidence," *Journal of Econometrics,* 21 (January 1983), pp. 133–154.

EXAMPLE McAleer, Fisher, and Volker[129] have applied the tests discussed above to various specifications of the demand for money functions. Three specifications were used. In Model I the explanatory variables were current and lagged permanent income, current and lagged short-term rate of interest, current and lagged price changes, and lagged money demand. Model II was the same as Model I except that the short-term rate of interest was replaced by the long-term rate of interest. Model III was the simple, traditional model with current permanent income, current long-term rate of interest, and lagged money demand as explantory variables. All models passed various specification tests for nonautoregression, homoskedasticity, structural stability, and noncorrelation between the explanatory variables and the disturbance. All possible pairs of models were subjected to the nonnested tests using annual data for the period 1904–1975. The somewhat surprising result was that each model was rejected against the other as being false.

The test procedures for nonnested models that we have discussed belong to classical statistics. From the Bayesian point of view an appropriate choice between two competing models can be made by considering the posterior probability of Model I relative to Model II, called *posterior odds ratio.*[130] The resulting measure involves a comparison of maximized likelihood functions for the two models and, therefore, is related to the Cox-type test statistics, but it also reflects prior odds.

Informal Model Selection

In current research practice, the availability of well-defined competing models is not that frequent. Economic theory can often indicate which explanatory variables should be included but does not give much guidance with respect to functional form, lags in behavior, inclusion of control variables (e.g., social or demographic), or measurement of variables. Typically a researcher is faced with a list of regressors of which some are clearly to be included in the equation but most are uncertain candidates. The researchers then resort to some ad hoc criteria that enable them to make a choice. Among such criteria belongs the $\bar{R}^2$ discussed in the early part of this section or, less frequently, various prediction or information criteria.[131]

A procedure sometimes used when the sample is large is to split the sample into two parts and use one part to help with model formulation, saving the other part for inference. Another procedure, called *cross-validation,* involves choosing that model which yields the smallest value of the cross-validation index defined as

$$P_j = (\mathbf{y}_1 - \mathbf{X}_{1j}\hat{\boldsymbol{\beta}}_{2j})'(\mathbf{y}_1 - \mathbf{X}_{1j}\hat{\boldsymbol{\beta}}_{2j}) + (\mathbf{y}_2 - \mathbf{X}_{2j}\hat{\boldsymbol{\beta}}_{1j})'(\mathbf{y}_2 - \mathbf{X}_{2j}\hat{\boldsymbol{\beta}}_{1j}),$$

[129] M. McAleer, G. Fisher, and P. Volker, "Separate Misspecified Regressions and the U.S. Long-Run Demand for Money Function," *Review of Economics and Statistics,* 64 (November 1982), pp. 572–583.

[130] A. Zellner, *An Introduction to Bayesian Inference in Econometrics* (New York: Wiley, 1971), Chapter 10.

[131] See, e.g., T. Amemiya, "Selection of Regressors," *International Economic Review,* 21 (June 1980), pp. 331–354.

where the subscripts 1 and 2 refer to the respective parts of the sample, the subscript j refers to the jth model, and $\hat{\boldsymbol{\beta}}_{ij} = (\mathbf{X}'_{ij}\mathbf{X}_{ij})^{-1}\mathbf{X}'_{ij}\mathbf{y}_i$ ($i = 1, 2$). Leamer[132] shows that minimizing the cross-validation index is equivalent to choosing a model on the basis of minimum estimated error variance *plus* a penalty for coefficient instability.

Probably the most common way of choosing a model in empirical research is by "data mining." A researcher confronted by a list of regressors tries various combinations of variables until satisfactory results (high R^2, "correct" signs of regression coefficients, a reasonable value of the Durbin–Watson test statistic, etc.) are obtained. This is known as "torturing the data until they confess." In an interesting experiment Freedman[133] constructed 100 rows (data points) and 51 columns (variables) of values drawn at random from a standard normal distribution. The first 50 columns were to represent 50 explanatory variables and the 51st column was to be the dependent variable. These data were analyzed in two successive multiple regressions. In the first pass, Y was run on all 50 Xs, and 21 variables that were significant at the 25% level were allowed to enter the equation on the second pass. The final result was an R^2 of 0.36, and six coefficients were found to be significant at the 5% level. Thus a definite relationship between the Y and the Xs was revealed, even though all variables were just "noise." Data mining is definitely unscientific and the results could be seriously misleading. At the very minimum, the researchers should follow the advice of Lovell and interpret the product of their exploratory data mining conservatively.[134] Lovell proposes a Rule of Thumb for deflating exaggerated claims of significance. For example, a data miner testing at a nominal 5% level of significance *after* picking the two best explanatory variables out of 5 candidates should claim only 12% significance, for 10 candidates the claimed level should be 22.6%, and for 20 candidates 40%.

A reasonable and commendable way of narrowing down the choice of models has been advocated by Hendry,[135] who developed a list of minimum conditions that econometric models should satisfy.

1. *Data coherency.* This involves conventional aspects such as homoskedasticity, absence of autocorrelation of the disturbances, goodness of fit, etc.
2. *Data admissibility.* It should be logically possible for the data to have been generated by the model in question.
3. *Theory consistency.*
4. *Parameter constancy.*

[132] E. E. Leamer, "Model Choice and Specification Analysis" in Z. Griliches and M. D. Intriligator (eds.), *Handbook of Econometrics,* Vol. 1 (Amsterdam: North-Holland, 1983), pp. 320–324.

[133] D. A. Freedman, "A Note on Screening Regression Equations," *The American Statistician,* 37 (May 1983), pp. 152–155.

[134] Michael C. Lovell, "Data Mining," *Review of Economics and Statistics,* 65 (February 1983), pp. 1–12.

[135] See, e.g., D. F. Hendry and J.-F. Richard, "On the Formulation of Empirical Models in Dynamic Econometrics," *Journal of Econometrics,* 20 (October 1982), pp. 3–33.

5. *Valid conditioning.* Explanatory variables, whose values are generated outside of the model, should not be correlated with the disturbance.
6. *Parsimonious parametrization* and *interpretable parameters of interest.*
7. *Encompassing.* The model should be able to explain the characteristics of all rival models.

While these conditions are clearly pragmatic, regarding them as principles to be followed would undoubtedly facilitate model choice and help us to progress toward purer empirical research.

EXERCISES

11-1. Three salesmen employed by a certain firm had the following weekly earnings in five consecutive days:

Salesman:	A	B	C
Weekly earnings ($):	928	924	793

An analysis-of-variance test of the null hypothesis that the mean earnings of the three salesmen are the same has been carried out, and the value of the F statistic found to be 5.00. Consider this problem as one of regression analysis, with the regression equation given by

$$Y_{ig} = \beta_1 + \beta_2 X_{i2} + \beta_3 X_{i3} + \varepsilon_i,$$

where

$$\begin{aligned} X_{i2} &= 1 \quad \text{if } i \text{ belongs to B,} \\ &= 0 \quad \text{otherwise;} \\ X_{i3} &= 1 \quad \text{if } i \text{ belongs to C,} \\ &= 0 \quad \text{otherwise;} \\ i &= 1, 2, \ldots, 5; \\ g &= 1, 2, 3. \end{aligned}$$

Find the least squares estimates of the regression coefficients and their estimated standard errors. Also, calculate the value of R^2.

11-2. The least squares estimates of a regression model are

$$Y_t = \underset{(1)}{10} + \underset{(\sqrt{0.5})}{5X_t} + e_t.$$

The explanatory variable X_t is a binary variable. Suppose that in checking the results it was found that the values of X_t were punched by mistake as 0 and 2 instead of 0 and 1. Make the appropriate corrections.

11-3. A regression equation explaining household expenditure on recreation as a function of income was estimated as

$$Y_t = \underset{(10)}{-25} + \underset{(16)}{35D_{t2}} + \underset{(15)}{40D_{t3}} - \underset{(8)}{15D_{t4}} + \underset{(0.02)}{0.05X_t} + e_t,$$

where Y = expenditure on recreation, X = income, and the Ds are quarterly dummies with the first quarter (January–March) left out. Determine the values of the estimated coefficients given that

a. The equation contains four seasonal dummies and no constant term.

b. The equation contains four seasonal dummies *and* the constant term, but the coefficients of the seasonal dummies represent deviations from the annual average and their sum is equal to zero.

11-4. A production function model is specified as

$$Y_i = \beta_1 + \beta_2 X_{i2} + \beta_3 X_{i3} + \varepsilon_i,$$

where Y = log output, X_2 = log labor input, and X_3 = log capital input. The subscript i refers to the ith firm. There are 23 observations in the sample, and the moment matrices (in terms of deviations from sample means) are

$$(\underline{\mathbf{X}}'\underline{\mathbf{X}}) = \begin{bmatrix} 12 & 8 \\ 8 & 12 \end{bmatrix}, \qquad (\underline{\mathbf{X}}'\underline{\mathbf{y}}) = \begin{bmatrix} 10 \\ 8 \end{bmatrix}, \qquad (\underline{\mathbf{y}}'\underline{\mathbf{y}}) = 10.$$

a. Find the least squares estimates of the regression coefficients β_2 and β_3 and their estimated standard errors. Calculate the value of R^2.

b. Carry out the test for constant returns to scale (i.e., test the hypothesis that $\beta_2 + \beta_3 = 1$) using (i) a t test; (ii) an F test; (iii) a likelihood ratio test; (iv) a Wald test; and (v) a Lagrange multiplier test.

c. Suppose now that you wish to impose the restriction that $\beta_2 + \beta_3 = 1$ a priori and to estimate the production function in that way. What, then, are the least squares estimate of β_2 and β_3 and their estimated standard errors? Also, what is the value of R^2 under this specification?

11-5. Consider the "stock adjustment" model

$$Y_t = \alpha\gamma + \beta\gamma X_t + (1 - \gamma)Y_{t-1} + \varepsilon_t.$$

Give the formula for the nonlinear least squares estimator of α, say, $\hat{\alpha}$. Derive the formula for the estimated variance of $\hat{\alpha}$ by using

a. The approximation formula (11.29).

b. The maximum likelihood information matrix.

11-6. Let $Y = Q/L$ and $X = K/L$, where Q = output, L = labor input, K = capital input, and the subscript i refers to the ith firm. Using the data presented in Table 11-3, estimate the following relationship.

$$\frac{Y_i^\lambda - 1}{\lambda} = \alpha + \beta\left(\frac{X_i^\lambda - 1}{\lambda}\right) + \varepsilon_i.$$

Test the hypothesis that $\lambda = 1$ against the hypothesis that $\lambda = 0$.

11-7. Using the model and the data of Exercise 10-5 of Chapter 10, carry out the following tests for linearity:

a. A segmented regression test (dividing the observations into three groups).

b. A rainbow test.

c. A RESET test.

11-8. Consider the following "rational distributed lag" model of Jorgenson:

$$Y_t + \delta_1 Y_{t-1} + \delta_2 Y_{t-2} = \alpha + \beta X_t + \varepsilon_t + \delta_1 \varepsilon_{t-1} + \delta_2 \varepsilon_{t-2}.$$

Using the Zellner-Geisel (or Dhrymes) approach, derive a computationally simple way of obtaining maximum likelihood estimates of the coefficients.

11-9. An aggregate consumption function is specified as

$$C_t = \beta_1 + \beta_2 L_t + w_0 Y_t + w_1 Y_{t-1} + \cdots + w_m Y_{t-m} + \varepsilon_t,$$

where C = consumption, L = liquid assets, and Y = income. The data are given in Table 11-9. Estimate this function using the following distributed lag formulations:

Table 11-9[a]

	C_t	Y_t	L_t
1955 I	248.7	263.0	207.6
II	253.7	271.5	209.4
III	259.9	276.5	211.1
IV	261.8	281.4	213.2
1956 I	263.2	282.0	214.1
II	263.7	286.2	216.5
III	263.4	287.7	217.3
IV	266.9	291.0	217.3
1957 I	268.9	291.1	218.2
II	270.4	294.6	218.5
III	273.4	296.1	219.8
IV	272.1	293.3	219.5
1958 I	268.9	291.3	220.5
II	270.9	292.6	222.7
III	274.4	299.9	225.0
IV	278.7	302.1	229.4
1959 I	283.8	305.9	232.2
II	289.7	312.5	235.2
III	290.8	311.3	237.2
IV	292.8	313.2	237.7
1960 I	295.4	315.4	238.0
II	299.5	320.3	238.4
III	298.6	321.0	240.1
IV	299.6	320.1	243.3
1961 I	297.0	318.4	246.1
II	301.6	324.8	250.0

Source: Z. Griliches et al. "Notes on Estimated Aggregate Quarterly Consumption Functions," *Econometrica,* Vol. 30, July 1962, p. 500.

[a] All values (in billions of dollars) are price deflated and seasonally adjusted.

a. Polynomial distributed lag.

b. LaGuerre lag.

c. Shiller lag.

11-10. In a trichotomous logit model the probabilities

$$\pi_{ij} = \frac{e^{\alpha_j + \beta_j X_i}}{\sum_j e^{\alpha_j + \beta_j X_i}},$$

$j = 1, 2, 3$; $i = 1, 2, \ldots, n$; and $\alpha_1 = \beta_1 = 0$ have been specified so that π_{i1} is treated as the residual probability. Suppose estimates of the αs and the βs have been obtained by the maximum likelihood method. At this stage you are asked to reparametrize the model so that the third rather than the first category is the reference category. How would you obtain the maximum likelihood estimates of the reparametrized model from the maximum likelihood estimates of the original model? Be specific.

11-11. A simple logit model is given as

$$\pi_i = \frac{1}{1 + e^{-\alpha - \beta X_i}},$$

where π_i = probability that the ith family owns a swimming pool, and X = family income. The null hypothesis is that income is an irrelevant variable. Test this hypothesis using the data for 12 Californian families given in Table 11-10. (The asterisk indicates families with a swimming pool.)

Table 11-10

Family no.	Income	Maintenance expenditure
1	80	
2	95*	76
3	105	
4	115	
5	125*	105
6	135*	113
7	145	
8	155	
9	165*	146
10	175*	135
11	185*	147
12	200*	155

11-12. Consider the model

$$Y_i^* = \alpha + \beta X_i + \varepsilon_i^*,$$

$$Y_i^* \sim N(\alpha + \beta X_i, \sigma^2),$$

where Y^* is not observed, but we observe

$$Y_i = Y_i^* \quad \text{when } \kappa_1 < Y_i^* < \kappa_2,$$
$$Y_i = \kappa_1 \quad \text{when } Y_i^* \leq \kappa_1,$$
$$Y_i = \kappa_2 \quad \text{when } Y_i^* \geq \kappa_2.$$

(The values of X are available for *all* observations.) Describe a way of obtaining consistent estimates of α and β in each of the following cases.

a. κ_1 is a known constant and $\kappa_2 \to \infty$.

b. κ_1 is an unknown constant and $\kappa_2 \to \infty$.

c. κ_1 and κ_2 are unknown constants.

11-13. Suppose $Y_i = \alpha + \beta X_i + \varepsilon_i$, where Y = expenditure on maintaining a swimming pool and X = income. The data on X and Y are given in Table 11-10. Obtain estimates of α and β based on the Tobit model specification.

11-14. Consider a simplified aggregate consumption function given as

$$C_t = \beta_1 + \beta_2 Y_t + \beta_3 L_t + \varepsilon_t.$$

Using the data in Table 11-9, test the hypothesis that the coefficients of this consumption function have remained constant throughout the period.

11-15. a. One version of the convergent parameter model is

$$Y_t = \alpha_t + \beta X_t$$
$$\alpha_t - \alpha = \lambda(\alpha_{t-1} - \alpha) + u_t \qquad (0 \leq \lambda < 1),$$

where u_t satisfies all classical assumptions. Show that this model is observationally indistinguishable from the following standard regression model with an AR(1) disturbance:

$$Y_t = \alpha + \beta X_t + \varepsilon_t,$$
$$\varepsilon_t = \rho\varepsilon_{t-1} + u_t \qquad (0 \leq \rho < 1).$$

b. Another version of the convergent parameter model is

$$Y_t = \alpha_t + \beta X_t + \varepsilon_t,$$
$$\alpha_t - \alpha = \lambda(\alpha_{t-1} - \alpha) + u_t.$$

Show that this model is observationally equivalent to the standard regression model with an MA(1) disturbance. (NOTE: Show that $u_t + \varepsilon_t - \lambda\varepsilon_{t-1} = w_t - \theta w_{t-1}$, where w_t is a disturbance that satisfies all classical assumptions and θ is a parameter that can be defined in terms of λ, σ_ε^2, and σ_u^2.)

11-16. Consider the following "single cause" model:

$$Y_i = \beta X_i^* + \varepsilon_i,$$
$$X_i^* = \pi_1 Z_{i1},$$
$$X_i = X_i^* + u_i,$$

where ε and u are mutually independent classical disturbances that are independent of Z_1.

a. Show that the two-stage estimator of β in this case is $\tilde{\beta} = \Sigma Y_i Z_{i1} / \Sigma X_i Z_{i1}$. Prove that $\tilde{\beta}$ is consistent and derive a consistent estimator of its variance.

b. Suppose that the model in **(a)** above has been misspecified and that the expression for X^* should have been

$$X_i^* = \pi_1 Z_{i1} + \pi_2 Z_{i2}.$$

Show that $\tilde{\beta}$ as defined in **(a)** above is *still* consistent.

11-17. A classical regression model is given as

$$Y_i = \beta_1 + \beta_2 X_{i2} + \beta_3 X_{i3} + \varepsilon_i.$$

Suppose that X_3 is not observable and that it is replaced by Z, which is related to X_3 by

$$Z_i = \gamma + \delta X_{i3} + u_i,$$

where u is a classical disturbance independent of ε. Two estimators of β_2 are being considered, one obtained by applying the least squares method to

$$Y_i = \beta_1 + \beta_2 X_{i2} + \beta_3^* Z_i + \varepsilon_i^*,$$

and the other by applying the least squares method to

$$Y_i = \beta_1 + \beta_2 X_{i2} + \varepsilon_i^{**}.$$

Compare the asymptotic biases of the two estimators.

11-18. Prove that the disequilibrium model

$$\begin{aligned} D_t &= \alpha_1 + \beta_1 P_t + \gamma_1 X_{t1} + u_{t1}, \\ S_t &= \alpha_2 + \beta_2 P_t + \gamma_2 X_{t2} + u_{t2}, \\ Q_t &= D_t \quad \text{if } D_t < S_t, \\ Q_t &= S_t \quad \text{if } D_t > S_t, \\ P_t - P_{t-1} &= \delta(D_t - S_t) \end{aligned}$$

is observationally equivalent to the "partial adjustment" model

$$\begin{aligned} D_t &= \alpha_1 + \beta_1 P_t^* + \gamma_1 X_{t1} + u_{t1}, \\ S_t &= \alpha_2 + \beta_2 P_t^* + \gamma_2 X_{t2} + u_{t2}, \\ D_t &= S_t \\ P_t - P_{t-1} &= (1 - \mu)(P_t^* - P_{t-1}). \end{aligned}$$

Examine Quandt's contention that the difference between the two models is that the parameters of the disequilibrium model are "generally identifiable," whereas the parameters of the partial adjustment model are not "necessarily identifiable."

11-19. The operational MSE criterion for choosing between two nested models,

Model I: $\quad \mathbf{y} = \mathbf{X}_1 \boldsymbol{\beta}_1 + \boldsymbol{\varepsilon},$

Model II: $\quad \mathbf{y} = \mathbf{X}_1 \boldsymbol{\beta}_1 + \mathbf{X}_2 \boldsymbol{\beta}_2 + \boldsymbol{\varepsilon},$

calls for choosing Model I if

$$K_2 \geq \frac{\hat{\beta}_2 X'_2 M_1 X_2 \hat{\beta}_2}{s^2}$$

as defined in the operational version of (11.181a) of the text. Prove that this is exactly equivalent to choosing Model I if

$$\frac{(\text{SSE}_\text{I} - \text{SSE}_\text{II})/K_2}{\text{SSE}_\text{II}/(n - K_1 - K_2)} \leq 1$$

as defined in (11.183) of the text.

11-20. Suppose we are considering a binary choice model with specified explanatory variables and we wish to estimate it on the basis of a given set of observations. Suggest a statistical testing procedure that would enable us to decide between a logit and a probit model. Describe and justify the proposed test procedure in detail.

12 Generalized Linear Regression Model and Its Applications

The classical regression model is based on rather restrictive assumptions concerning the behavior of the regression disturbance. An alternative model, known as the "generalized linear regression model," is considerably less restrictive in this respect. This model and its implications for estimating the regression coefficients are discussed in Section 12-1. An interesting application of this model to observations on a number of cross-sectional units over time is described in Section 12-2. Since such observations are now becoming more commonly available, the development of appropriate estimation procedures is very useful. Another and very ingenious application of the generalized linear regression model can be made when estimating a set of regression equations whose disturbances are correlated. The discussion of this application, which also provides a logical bridge between single-equation models and simultaneous equation models (to be discussed in Chapter 13), is presented in Section 12-3.

12-1 Generalized Linear Regression Model

The classical normal linear regression model is characterized by a number of assumptions concerning the stochastic disturbance in the regression equation, including homoskedasticity and nonautocorrelation. Specifically, the disturbance term ε_i in

$$Y_i = \beta_1 + \beta_2 X_{i2} + \beta_3 X_{i3} + \cdots + \beta_k X_{iK} + \varepsilon_i$$

is supposed to satisfy the following requirements:

$$E(\varepsilon_i^2) = \sigma^2 \qquad \text{for all } i,$$

$$E(\varepsilon_i \varepsilon_j) = 0 \qquad \text{for all } i \neq j.$$

These assumptions are given by (10.4) and (10.5); in the matrix notation they can be described, as in (10.4a–10.5a), by

$$E(\boldsymbol{\varepsilon}\boldsymbol{\varepsilon}') = \sigma^2 \mathbf{I}_n,$$

where

$$\boldsymbol{\varepsilon} = \begin{bmatrix} \varepsilon_1 \\ \varepsilon_2 \\ \vdots \\ \varepsilon_n \end{bmatrix},$$

and $\mathbf{I}_n$ is an identity matrix of order $(n \times n)$. If we do not make these two assumptions—but retain all the other assumptions of the classical normal linear regression model—we have the so-called *generalized linear regression model.* (Some authors also drop the assumption of normality of ε_i.) The full description of this model is

(12.1) $Y_i = \beta_1 + \beta_2 X_{i2} + \beta_3 X_{i3} + \cdots + \beta_K X_{iK} + \varepsilon_i$.

(12.2) The joint distribution of $\varepsilon_1, \varepsilon_2, \ldots, \varepsilon_n$ is multivariate normal.

(12.3) $E(\varepsilon_i) = 0 \qquad (i = 1, 2, \ldots, n)$.

(12.4) $E(\varepsilon_i \varepsilon_j) = \sigma_{ij} < \infty \qquad (i, j = 1, 2, \ldots, n)$.

(12.5) Each of the explanatory variables is nonstochastic and such that, for any sample size,

$$\frac{1}{n} \sum_{i=1}^{n} (X_{ik} - \bar{X}_k)^2$$

is a finite number different from zero for every $k = 2, 3, \ldots, K$.

(12.6) The number of observations exceeds the number of explanatory variables *plus* one, i.e., $n > K$.

(12.7) No exact linear relation exists between any of the explanatory variables.

Note that according to (12.3) and (12.4), σ_{ii} is the variance of ε_i, and σ_{ij} $(i \neq j)$ is the covariance of ε_i and ε_j. If we use matrix notation we can restate (12.1) as

(12.1a) $$\mathbf{y} = \mathbf{X}\boldsymbol{\beta} + \boldsymbol{\varepsilon},$$

where $\mathbf{y}$ is an $(n \times 1)$ vector of the sample values of Y, $\mathbf{X}$ is an $(n \times K)$ matrix of the sample values of $X_{i1}, X_{i2}, \ldots, X_{iK}$ (with $X_{i1} = 1$ for all i), $\boldsymbol{\beta}$ is a $(K \times 1)$ vector of the regression coefficients, and $\boldsymbol{\varepsilon}$ is an $(n \times 1)$ vector of the sample values of ε. The assumption (12.4) can be written as

$$E(\boldsymbol{\varepsilon}\boldsymbol{\varepsilon}') = \boldsymbol{\Omega}, \tag{12.4a}$$

where

$$\boldsymbol{\Omega} = \begin{bmatrix} \sigma_{11} & \sigma_{12} & \cdots & \sigma_{1n} \\ \sigma_{21} & \sigma_{22} & \cdots & \sigma_{2n} \\ \vdots & \vdots & & \vdots \\ \sigma_{n1} & \sigma_{n2} & \cdots & \sigma_{nn} \end{bmatrix}.$$

This model is called "generalized" because it includes other models as special cases. The classical normal linear regression model is one such special case, in which $\boldsymbol{\Omega}$ is a diagonal matrix with σ^2 in place of each of the diagonal elements. Another special case is the heteroskedastic model; here $\boldsymbol{\Omega}$ is again diagonal, but the diagonal elements are not necessarily all the same. For the model in which the disturbances follow a first-order autoregressive scheme, the matrix $\boldsymbol{\Omega}$ becomes

$$\boldsymbol{\Omega} = \sigma^2 \begin{bmatrix} 1 & \rho & \rho^2 & \cdots & \rho^{n-1} \\ \rho & 1 & \rho & \cdots & \rho^{n-2} \\ \vdots & \vdots & \vdots & & \vdots \\ \rho^{n-1} & \rho^{n-2} & \rho^{n-3} & \cdots & 1 \end{bmatrix}.$$

Let us now turn to the problem of estimating the parameters of the generalized linear regression model. We will assume for the present that the variances and covariances of the disturbances (i.e., the elements of the $\boldsymbol{\Omega}$ matrix) are known. First, we note that since the *ordinary least squares estimators* of the regression coefficients are obtained by minimizing

$$\sum_{i=1}^{n} (Y_i - \beta_1 - \beta_2 X_{i2} - \cdots - \beta_K X_{iK})^2,$$

they are exactly the same as the least squares estimators of the classical normal linear regression model; that is,

$$\hat{\boldsymbol{\beta}} = (\mathbf{X}'\mathbf{X})^{-1}(\mathbf{X}'\mathbf{Y}).$$

Note that

$$E(\hat{\boldsymbol{\beta}}) = E(\mathbf{X}'\mathbf{X})^{-1}\mathbf{X}'[\mathbf{X}\boldsymbol{\beta} + \boldsymbol{\varepsilon}] = \boldsymbol{\beta} + E(\mathbf{X}'\mathbf{X})^{-1}(\mathbf{X}'\boldsymbol{\varepsilon}) = \boldsymbol{\beta},$$

and

$$\text{plim } \hat{\boldsymbol{\beta}} = \boldsymbol{\beta} + \text{plim} \left[\frac{1}{n}\mathbf{X}'\mathbf{X}\right]^{-1}\left[\frac{1}{n}\mathbf{X}'\boldsymbol{\varepsilon}\right] = \boldsymbol{\beta}.$$

This shows that the ordinary least squares estimator of $\boldsymbol{\beta}$ of the generalized linear regression model is unbiased and consistent. Its variance-covariance matrix is

$$E(\hat{\beta}-\beta)(\hat{\beta}-\beta)' = E(\mathbf{X}'\mathbf{X})^{-1}\mathbf{X}'\boldsymbol{\varepsilon}\boldsymbol{\varepsilon}'\mathbf{X}(\mathbf{X}'\mathbf{X})^{-1} \tag{12.8}$$

$$= (\mathbf{X}'\mathbf{X})^{-1}\mathbf{X}'\boldsymbol{\Omega}\mathbf{X}(\mathbf{X}'\mathbf{X})^{-1}.$$

When $\boldsymbol{\Omega} = \sigma^2\mathbf{I}$, this reduces to the well-known formula $\sigma^2(\mathbf{X}'\mathbf{X})^{-1}$.

Next we derive the *best linear unbiased estimator* (BLUE) of the regression coefficients. The simplest way of doing this is to transform the original regression equation into an equivalent equation for which all classical assumptions hold. This is how we derived the BLU estimator in the case of heteroskedasticity in Section 8-2 and in the case of autoregressive disturbances in Section 8-3. In the general case with which we are dealing now, we premultiply the regression equation by a transformation matrix $\mathbf{P}$ of dimension $n \times n$ to get

$$\mathbf{Py} = \mathbf{PX}\boldsymbol{\beta} + \mathbf{P}\boldsymbol{\varepsilon}, \tag{12.9}$$

where $\mathbf{P}$ is such that

$$E(\mathbf{P}\boldsymbol{\varepsilon})(\mathbf{P}\boldsymbol{\varepsilon})' = \mathbf{I},$$

or, equivalently,

$$\mathbf{P}\boldsymbol{\Omega}\mathbf{P}' = \mathbf{I}.$$

(Of course, a transformation matrix for which $\mathbf{P}\boldsymbol{\Omega}\mathbf{P}' = k\mathbf{I}$, where k is some constant, would be equally acceptable.) We note that since

$$\mathbf{P}'(\mathbf{P}\boldsymbol{\Omega}\mathbf{P}')\mathbf{P} = \mathbf{P}'\mathbf{P},$$

it follows that

$$\mathbf{P}'\mathbf{P} = \boldsymbol{\Omega}^{-1}.$$

Further, given that $\boldsymbol{\Omega}$ is positive definite, there exists a *lower triangular* (or *diagonal*) matrix $\mathbf{P}$ such that $\mathbf{P}'\mathbf{P} = \boldsymbol{\Omega}^{-1}$.[1] In the special case of heteroskedasticity the transformation matrix implied by equation (8.11) of Section 8-2 is

$$\mathbf{P} = \begin{bmatrix} \frac{1}{\sigma_1} & 0 & \cdots & 0 \\ 0 & \frac{1}{\sigma_2} & \cdots & 0 \\ \vdots & \vdots & & \vdots \\ 0 & 0 & \cdots & \frac{1}{\sigma_n} \end{bmatrix},$$

and $\mathbf{P}'\mathbf{P} = \boldsymbol{\Omega}^{-1}$. In the case of first-order autoregression, the transformation matrix

[1] See P. J. Dhrymes, *Mathematics for Econometrics* (New York: Springer-Verlag, 1978), pp. 66-67.

implied by equation (8.61) of Section 8-3 is

$$\mathbf{P} = \begin{bmatrix} \sqrt{1-\rho^2} & 0 & 0 & \cdots & 0 & 0 \\ -\rho & 1 & 0 & \cdots & 0 & 0 \\ \vdots & \vdots & \vdots & & \vdots & \vdots \\ 0 & 0 & 0 & \cdots & -\rho & 1 \end{bmatrix},$$

and

$$\mathbf{P'P} = \begin{bmatrix} 1 & -\rho & 0 & \cdots & 0 & 0 \\ -\rho & 1+\rho^2 & -\rho & \cdots & 0 & 0 \\ \vdots & \vdots & \vdots & & \vdots & \vdots \\ 0 & 0 & 0 & \cdots & -\rho & 1 \end{bmatrix}.$$

Since

$$\mathbf{\Omega}^{-1} = \frac{1}{\sigma^2(1-\rho^2)} \begin{bmatrix} 1 & -\rho & 0 & \cdots & 0 & 0 \\ -\rho & 1+\rho^2 & -\rho & \cdots & 0 & 0 \\ \vdots & \vdots & \vdots & & \vdots & \vdots \\ 0 & 0 & 0 & \cdots & -\rho & 1 \end{bmatrix},$$

$\mathbf{P'P}$ is proportional to $\mathbf{\Omega}^{-1}$ and $\mathbf{P\Omega P'} = \sigma^2(1-\rho^2)\mathbf{I}$.

Since the transformed regression equation (12.9) satisfies all classical assumptions, the least squares estimator of $\boldsymbol{\beta}$ is BLUE. Denoting the BLUE of $\boldsymbol{\beta}$ by $\tilde{\boldsymbol{\beta}}$, we have

$$\begin{aligned} \tilde{\boldsymbol{\beta}} &= [(\mathbf{PX})'(\mathbf{PX})]^{-1}(\mathbf{PX})'(\mathbf{Py}) \\ &= (\mathbf{X'P'PX})^{-1}(\mathbf{X'P'Py}) \\ &= (\mathbf{X'\Omega^{-1}X})^{-1}(\mathbf{X'\Omega^{-1}y}). \end{aligned} \tag{12.10}$$

Further, since

$$\begin{aligned} \tilde{\boldsymbol{\beta}} &= (\mathbf{X'\Omega^{-1}X})^{-1}\mathbf{X'\Omega^{-1}}(\mathbf{X}\boldsymbol{\beta} + \boldsymbol{\varepsilon}) \\ &= \boldsymbol{\beta} + (\mathbf{X'\Omega^{-1}X})^{-1}\mathbf{X'\Omega^{-1}}\boldsymbol{\varepsilon}, \end{aligned}$$

the variance-covariance matrix of $\tilde{\boldsymbol{\beta}}$ is

$$\begin{aligned} E(\tilde{\boldsymbol{\beta}} - \boldsymbol{\beta})(\tilde{\boldsymbol{\beta}} - \boldsymbol{\beta})' &= E(\mathbf{X'\Omega^{-1}X})^{-1}\mathbf{X'\Omega^{-1}}\boldsymbol{\varepsilon\varepsilon}'\mathbf{\Omega^{-1}X}(\mathbf{X'\Omega^{-1}X})^{-1} \\ &= (\mathbf{X'\Omega^{-1}X})^{-1}. \end{aligned} \tag{12.11}$$

The estimator $\tilde{\boldsymbol{\beta}}$ is called the *generalized least squares* or *Aitken estimator.*[2]

[2] A. C. Aitken, "On Least Squares and Linear Combination of Observations," *Proceedings of the Royal Society of Edinburgh,* 55 (1934–35), pp. 42–48.

To measure the goodness of fit of a generalized least squares model, we can use the usual formula for R^2 defined as

$$R^2 = 1 - \frac{\text{SSE}}{\text{SST}},$$

where
$$\text{SSE} = (\mathbf{y} - \mathbf{X}\tilde{\boldsymbol{\beta}})'(\mathbf{y} - \mathbf{X}\tilde{\boldsymbol{\beta}}) = \tilde{\mathbf{e}}'\tilde{\mathbf{e}}$$

and

$$\text{SST} = \sum_i (Y_i - \bar{Y})^2 = \mathbf{y}'\left(\mathbf{I} - \frac{\boldsymbol{\iota}\boldsymbol{\iota}'}{n}\right)\mathbf{y},$$

where $\boldsymbol{\iota}' = [1\ 1\ \cdots\ 1]$. An alternative measure would be the squared coefficient of correlation between the fitted and the observed values of Y. Yet another alternative would be to use the formula for R^2 of the classical model and apply it to the transformed equation (12.9). The difficulty here is that the transformed matrix **PX** does not usually contain a constant term and consequently R^2 need not lie between 0 and 1. A way of overcoming this is to use *weighted* sums of squares (with weights given by the elements of $\boldsymbol{\Omega}^{-1}$) as follows:[3]

$$R^2 = 1 - \frac{\text{SSE}^*}{\text{SST}^*}, \tag{12.12}$$

where
$$\text{SSE}^* = \tilde{\mathbf{e}}'\boldsymbol{\Omega}^{-1}\tilde{\mathbf{e}}$$

and

$$\begin{aligned}\text{SST}^* &= (\mathbf{y} - \boldsymbol{\iota}\tilde{y})'\boldsymbol{\Omega}^{-1}(\mathbf{y} - \boldsymbol{\iota}\tilde{y}) \\ &= \mathbf{y}'\mathbf{P}'\left[\mathbf{I} - \frac{\mathbf{P}\boldsymbol{\iota}\boldsymbol{\iota}'\mathbf{P}'}{\boldsymbol{\iota}'\mathbf{P}'\mathbf{P}\boldsymbol{\iota}}\right]\mathbf{P}\mathbf{y},\end{aligned}$$

where
$$\tilde{y} = \frac{\boldsymbol{\iota}'\mathbf{P}'\mathbf{P}\mathbf{y}}{\boldsymbol{\iota}'\mathbf{P}'\mathbf{P}\boldsymbol{\iota}}.$$

In any case, since there are several different measures of R^2 for the generalized regression model, researchers—when presenting their results—should specify which measure is being used.

An interesting aspect of the generalized linear regression model is prediction. Suppose we wish to predict m future values of $\mathbf{y}$, to be denoted by $\mathbf{y}_0$, for a given set of values of $\mathbf{X}$, say, $\mathbf{X}_0$. The sample and the prediction periods can be represented as

$$\begin{aligned}\mathbf{y} &= \mathbf{X}\boldsymbol{\beta} + \boldsymbol{\varepsilon} && (n \text{ sample periods}), \\ \mathbf{y}_0 &= \mathbf{X}_0\boldsymbol{\beta} + \boldsymbol{\varepsilon}_0 && (m \text{ prediction periods}),\end{aligned} \tag{12.13}$$

[3] See G. G. Judge et al., *The Theory and Practice of Econometrics,* 2nd ed. (New York: Wiley, 1985), p. 32.

or, considered jointly, as

(12.13a) $$\mathbf{y}^* = \mathbf{X}^*\boldsymbol{\beta} + \boldsymbol{\varepsilon}^* \qquad (m + n \text{ periods}).$$

Then

$$\boldsymbol{\Omega}^* = E\begin{bmatrix} \boldsymbol{\varepsilon\varepsilon}' & \boldsymbol{\varepsilon\varepsilon}_0' \\ \boldsymbol{\varepsilon}_0\boldsymbol{\varepsilon}' & \boldsymbol{\varepsilon}_0\boldsymbol{\varepsilon}_0' \end{bmatrix} = \begin{bmatrix} \boldsymbol{\Omega}_{11} & \boldsymbol{\Omega}_{12} \\ \boldsymbol{\Omega}_{21} & \boldsymbol{\Omega}_{22} \end{bmatrix}.$$

Further, let the transformation matrix $\mathbf{P}$ be such that

(12.14) $$\mathbf{P}^*\boldsymbol{\Omega}^*\mathbf{P}^{*\prime} = \mathbf{I},$$

or

(12.14a) $$\mathbf{P}^{*\prime}\mathbf{P}^* = \boldsymbol{\Omega}^{*-1}.$$

Since $\mathbf{P}^*$ can be represented as a lower triangular matrix, it can be written as

$$\mathbf{P}^* = \begin{bmatrix} \mathbf{P}_{11} & \mathbf{0} \\ \mathbf{P}_{21} & \mathbf{P}_{22} \end{bmatrix},$$

where the dimensions of $\mathbf{P}_{11}$, $\mathbf{P}_{21}$, and $\mathbf{P}_{22}$ are the same as those of $\boldsymbol{\Omega}_{11}$, $\boldsymbol{\Omega}_{21}$, and $\boldsymbol{\Omega}_{22}$, respectively. Then the transformed version of equation (12.13a) becomes

(12.15) $$\begin{bmatrix} \mathbf{P}_{11} & \mathbf{0} \\ \mathbf{P}_{21} & \mathbf{P}_{22} \end{bmatrix}\begin{bmatrix} \mathbf{y} \\ \mathbf{y}_0 \end{bmatrix} = \begin{bmatrix} \mathbf{P}_{11} & \mathbf{0} \\ \mathbf{P}_{21} & \mathbf{P}_{22} \end{bmatrix}\begin{bmatrix} \mathbf{X} \\ \mathbf{X}_0 \end{bmatrix}\boldsymbol{\beta} + \begin{bmatrix} \mathbf{P}_{11} & \mathbf{0} \\ \mathbf{P}_{21} & \mathbf{P}_{22} \end{bmatrix}\begin{bmatrix} \boldsymbol{\varepsilon} \\ \boldsymbol{\varepsilon}_0 \end{bmatrix}.$$

This leads to

(12.15a) $$\mathbf{P}_{11}\mathbf{y} = \mathbf{P}_{11}\mathbf{X}\boldsymbol{\beta} + \mathbf{P}_{11}\boldsymbol{\varepsilon},$$

(12.15b) $$\mathbf{P}_{21}\mathbf{y} + \mathbf{P}_{22}\mathbf{y}_0 = (\mathbf{P}_{21}\mathbf{X} + \mathbf{P}_{22}\mathbf{X}_0)\boldsymbol{\beta} + (\mathbf{P}_{21}\boldsymbol{\varepsilon} + \mathbf{P}_{22}\boldsymbol{\varepsilon}_0).$$

To obtain best linear unbiased predictor (BLUP) of $\mathbf{y}_0$, say, $\tilde{\mathbf{y}}_0$, we replace $\boldsymbol{\beta}$ by $\tilde{\boldsymbol{\beta}}$, set the values of $\boldsymbol{\varepsilon}$ and $\boldsymbol{\varepsilon}_0$ equal to zero, and solve (12.15b) for $\tilde{\mathbf{y}}_0$. The result is

(12.16) $$\tilde{\mathbf{y}}_0 = \mathbf{X}_0\tilde{\boldsymbol{\beta}} - \mathbf{P}_{22}^{-1}\mathbf{P}_{21}(\mathbf{y} - \mathbf{X}\tilde{\boldsymbol{\beta}}).$$

Using (12.14) we can, after some tedious algebra, express the $\mathbf{P}$s in terms of the submatrices of $\boldsymbol{\Omega}^*$. Further, we note that $(\mathbf{y} - \mathbf{X}\tilde{\boldsymbol{\beta}})$ is an $(n \times 1)$ vector of generalized least squares residuals $\tilde{\mathbf{e}}$. Equation (12.16) can then be equivalently written as

(12.16a) $$\tilde{\mathbf{y}}_0 = \mathbf{X}_0\tilde{\boldsymbol{\beta}} + \boldsymbol{\Omega}_{21}\boldsymbol{\Omega}_{11}^{-1}\tilde{\mathbf{e}}.$$

To illustrate the use of equation (12.16a), let us consider the problem of predicting the value of y for the first out-of-sample observation (indexed $n + 1$) when the regression disturbance follows a first-order autoregressive process of the form

$\varepsilon_t = \rho\varepsilon_{t-1} + u_t$. In this case

$$\mathbf{P}^* = \left[\begin{array}{cccc|c} \sqrt{1-\rho^2} & 0 & \cdots & 0 & 0 \\ -\rho & 1 & \cdots & 0 & 0 \\ \vdots & \vdots & & & \vdots \\ 0 & 0 & \cdots & 1 & 0 \\ \hline 0 & 0 & \cdots & -\rho & 1 \end{array}\right],$$

so that

$$\text{(12.17)} \qquad \tilde{y}_{n+1} = \mathbf{X}_{n+1}\tilde{\boldsymbol{\beta}} - [0 \quad 0 \quad \cdots \quad 0 \quad -\rho] \begin{bmatrix} \tilde{\varepsilon}_1 \\ \tilde{\varepsilon}_2 \\ \vdots \\ \tilde{\varepsilon}_n \end{bmatrix}$$

$$= \mathbf{X}_{n+1}\tilde{\boldsymbol{\beta}} + \rho\tilde{\varepsilon}_n.$$

If we were to predict m future observations, the result would be

$$\text{(12.18)} \qquad \begin{bmatrix} \tilde{y}_{n+1} \\ \tilde{y}_{n+2} \\ \vdots \\ \tilde{y}_{n+m} \end{bmatrix} = \begin{bmatrix} \mathbf{X}_{n+1} \\ \mathbf{X}_{n+2} \\ \vdots \\ \mathbf{X}_{n+m} \end{bmatrix} \tilde{\boldsymbol{\beta}} + \begin{bmatrix} \rho\tilde{\varepsilon}_n \\ \rho^2\tilde{\varepsilon}_n \\ \vdots \\ \rho^m\tilde{\varepsilon}_n \end{bmatrix}.$$

The *maximum likelihood estimators* of the coefficients of the generalized regression model can be derived by noting that, under the assumptions of the model, the joint distribution of $\varepsilon_1, \varepsilon_2, \ldots, \varepsilon_n$ is given by[4]

$$f(\varepsilon_1, \varepsilon_2, \ldots, \varepsilon_n) = (2\pi)^{-(n/2)}|\boldsymbol{\Omega}|^{-(1/2)}e^{-(1/2)\boldsymbol{\varepsilon}'\boldsymbol{\Omega}^{-1}\boldsymbol{\varepsilon}},$$

where $|\boldsymbol{\Omega}|$ represents the determinant of the matrix $\boldsymbol{\Omega}$. The logarithmic likelihood function for $Y_1, Y_2, \ldots, Y_n$ is given by

$$\text{(12.19)} \qquad L = -\frac{n}{2}\log(2\pi) - \frac{1}{2}\log|\boldsymbol{\Omega}| - \frac{1}{2}(\mathbf{y} - \mathbf{X}\boldsymbol{\beta})'\boldsymbol{\Omega}^{-1}(\mathbf{y} - \mathbf{X}\boldsymbol{\beta})$$

$$= -\frac{n}{2}\log(2\pi) - \frac{1}{2}\log|\boldsymbol{\Omega}|$$

$$-\frac{1}{2}(\mathbf{y}'\boldsymbol{\Omega}^{-1}\mathbf{y} - 2\mathbf{y}'\boldsymbol{\Omega}^{-1}\mathbf{X}\boldsymbol{\beta} + \boldsymbol{\beta}'\mathbf{X}'\boldsymbol{\Omega}^{-1}\mathbf{X}\boldsymbol{\beta}).$$

[4] See A. S. Goldberger, *Econometric Theory* (New York: Wiley, 1964), p. 104. If the εs in the sample are *not* independent of any ε outside the sample, the joint distribution is conditional on the latter.

By differentiating L with respect on $\boldsymbol{\beta}$ and putting the result equal to zero, we obtain

$$-\tfrac{1}{2}(-2\mathbf{X}'\boldsymbol{\Omega}^{-1}\mathbf{y} + 2\mathbf{X}'\boldsymbol{\Omega}^{-1}\mathbf{X}\hat{\boldsymbol{\beta}}) = \mathbf{0},$$

where $\mathbf{0}$ is a $(K \times 1)$ vector of zeros. This gives

$$\hat{\boldsymbol{\beta}} = (\mathbf{X}'\boldsymbol{\Omega}^{-1}\mathbf{X})^{-1}(\mathbf{X}'\boldsymbol{\Omega}^{-1}\mathbf{y}),$$

which is exactly the same expression as that for the Aitken generalized least squares estimator of $\boldsymbol{\beta}$ given by (12.10). Since $\mathbf{P}\boldsymbol{\varepsilon}$ and $\mathbf{PX}$ satisfy all classical assumptions, $\hat{\boldsymbol{\beta}}$ has all desirable properties.

The preceding discussion has been carried out on the presumption that $\boldsymbol{\Omega}$, the variance-covariance matrix of the disturbances, is known. In many cases, of course, this is not the case and, therefore, the Aitken generalized least squares estimation procedure is not operational. However, suppose that we can find a *consistent estimator* of $\boldsymbol{\Omega}$, say, $\hat{\boldsymbol{\Omega}}$, and that we substitute $\hat{\boldsymbol{\Omega}}$ for $\boldsymbol{\Omega}$ in the Aitken formula to get a *feasible Aitken estimator* defined as

$$\tilde{\tilde{\boldsymbol{\beta}}} = (\mathbf{X}'\hat{\boldsymbol{\Omega}}^{-1}\mathbf{X})^{-1}(\mathbf{X}'\hat{\boldsymbol{\Omega}}^{-1}\mathbf{y}). \tag{12.20}$$

Under general conditions,[5] $\tilde{\tilde{\boldsymbol{\beta}}}$ has the same asymptotic properties as the pure Aitken estimator $\tilde{\boldsymbol{\beta}}$; i.e., it is consistent, asymptotically efficient, and asymptotically normal. The asymptotic variance-covariance matrix of $\tilde{\tilde{\boldsymbol{\beta}}}$ is given by

$$\text{Asympt. Var-Cov}(\tilde{\tilde{\boldsymbol{\beta}}}) = (\mathbf{X}'\boldsymbol{\Omega}^{-1}\mathbf{X})^{-1}. \tag{12.21}$$

A consistent estimator of the variance-covariance matrix of $\tilde{\tilde{\boldsymbol{\beta}}}$ is

$$\text{Est. Var-Cov}(\tilde{\tilde{\boldsymbol{\beta}}}) = (\mathbf{X}'\hat{\boldsymbol{\Omega}}^{-1}\mathbf{X})^{-1}. \tag{12.21a}$$

The small sample properties of $\tilde{\tilde{\boldsymbol{\beta}}}$ are generally difficult to establish. However, it has been shown that $\tilde{\tilde{\boldsymbol{\beta}}}$ is unbiased provided its expectation exists, and that a sufficient condition for the existence of $E(\tilde{\tilde{\boldsymbol{\beta}}})$ is the existence of $E[\text{tr}(\hat{\boldsymbol{\Omega}})\text{tr}(\hat{\boldsymbol{\Omega}}^{-1})]$.[6] For instance, if the disturbance follows a first-order autoregressive scheme, then

$$\begin{aligned}\text{tr}(\hat{\boldsymbol{\Omega}})\text{tr}(\hat{\boldsymbol{\Omega}}^{-1}) &= n\sigma^2\left(\frac{n + (n-2)\hat{\rho}^2}{\sigma^2(1-\hat{\rho}^2)}\right)\\ &= n\left(\frac{n+(n-2)\hat{\rho}^2}{1-\hat{\rho}^2}\right),\end{aligned}$$

where $\hat{\rho}$ is a consistent estimator of ρ. If for every sample $0 \leq \hat{\rho}^2 < 1$ and n is finite, then $\text{tr}(\hat{\boldsymbol{\Omega}})\text{tr}(\hat{\boldsymbol{\Omega}}^{-1})$ has a finite lower and a finite upper limit, so its expectation exists and $\tilde{\tilde{\boldsymbol{\beta}}}$ is unbiased.

[5] See P. Schmidt, *Econometrics* (New York: Marcel Dekker, 1976), pp. 70-71.

[6] The conditional unbiasedness of $\tilde{\tilde{\boldsymbol{\beta}}}$ has been proven by N. C. Kakwani, "The Unbiasedness of Zellner's Seemingly Unrelated Regression Equations Estimator," *Journal of the American Statistical Association,* 62 (March 1967), pp. 141-142; a sufficient condition for the existence of $E(\tilde{\tilde{\boldsymbol{\beta}}})$ is due to F. J. H. Don and J. R. Magnus, "On the Unbiasedness of Iterated GLS Estimator," *Communications in Statistics—Theory and Methods,* A9(5) (1980), pp. 519-527.

An obvious way of extending the two-stage Aitken estimator $\tilde{\tilde{\boldsymbol{\beta}}}$ is to use the second-stage residuals to form a new estimator of $\boldsymbol{\Omega}$, say, $\hat{\hat{\boldsymbol{\Omega}}}$, and to obtain a new estimator of $\boldsymbol{\beta}$, say, $\tilde{\tilde{\tilde{\boldsymbol{\beta}}}}$. This could be continued until convergence is reached. If $\boldsymbol{\varepsilon}$ is normally distributed and certain general conditions are satisfied, the resulting (iterative) estimators of $\boldsymbol{\beta}$ and $\boldsymbol{\Omega}$ are actually maximum likelihood estimators.[7] The iterative procedure is thus just a convenient way of calculating maximum likelihood estimates.

The main problem in feasible Aitken estimation is finding a consistent estimator of $\boldsymbol{\Omega}$. If there are no prior restrictions on any of its elements, the $\boldsymbol{\Omega}$ matrix involves $n(n+1)/2$ unknown parameters. It is clear that, with only n observations, estimation under these circumstances becomes impossible. Therefore, we can consider only those models for which we have at least some information—or are willing to make some assumptions—about the elements of $\boldsymbol{\Omega}$. One such type of models occurs in connection with heteroskedasticity (see Section 8-2), and another in connection with autocorrelated disturbances (see Section 8-3). We now discuss other restrictions on Ω that arise in other contexts.

12-2 Pooling of Cross-section and Time-Series Data

The question of the appropriate restrictions on $\boldsymbol{\Omega}$ is of special interest and significance in connection with *pooling cross-section and time-series observations,* as in the case of observations for a number of households (states, countries, etc.) over several periods of time. Here the behavior of the disturbances over the cross-sectional units (households, states, countries, etc.) is likely to be different from the behavior of the disturbances of a given cross-sectional unit over time. In particular, the relationship between the disturbances of two households at some specific time may differ from the relationship between the disturbances of a specific household at two different periods of time. Clearly, various kinds of prior specifications with respect to the disturbances will lead to various kinds of restrictions on $\boldsymbol{\Omega}$. In general, the regression equation for this type of data can be written as

$$Y_{it} = \beta_1 X_{it,1} + \beta_2 X_{it,2} + \cdots + \beta_K X_{it,K} + \varepsilon_{it} \qquad (i = 1, 2, \ldots, N;\ t = 1, 2, \ldots, T).$$

That is, the sample data are represented by observations on N cross sectional units over T periods of time. There are altogether $n = N \times T$ observations. The explanatory variables and the regression disturbance are presumed to satisfy the assumptions of the generalized linear regression model. In most (although not necessarily in all) cases, we will have $X_{it,1} = 1$ for all i and t. In matrix notation the regression

[7] See W. Oberhofer and J. Kmenta, "A General Procedure for Obtaining Maximum Likelihood Estimates in Generalized Regression Models," *Econometrica,* 42 (May 1974), pp. 579–590. The most important and in practice the most relevant conditions are that $\boldsymbol{\Omega}$ must not contain any elements of $\boldsymbol{\beta}$, and that the first-round estimate of $\boldsymbol{\Omega}$ is consistent.

equation can be written as

$$\mathbf{y} = \mathbf{X}\boldsymbol{\beta} + \boldsymbol{\varepsilon},$$

where

$$\mathbf{y} = \begin{bmatrix} Y_{11} \\ Y_{12} \\ \vdots \\ Y_{1T} \\ Y_{21} \\ Y_{22} \\ \vdots \\ Y_{NT} \end{bmatrix}, \qquad \mathbf{X} = \begin{bmatrix} X_{11,1} & X_{11,2} & \cdots & X_{11,K} \\ X_{12,1} & X_{12,2} & \cdots & X_{12,K} \\ \vdots & \vdots & & \vdots \\ X_{1T,1} & X_{1T,2} & \cdots & X_{1T,K} \\ X_{21,1} & X_{21,2} & \cdots & X_{21,K} \\ X_{22,1} & X_{22,2} & \cdots & X_{22,K} \\ \vdots & \vdots & & \vdots \\ X_{NT,1} & X_{NT,2} & \cdots & X_{NT,K} \end{bmatrix},$$

$$\boldsymbol{\varepsilon} = \begin{bmatrix} \varepsilon_{11} \\ \varepsilon_{12} \\ \vdots \\ \varepsilon_{1T} \\ \varepsilon_{21} \\ \varepsilon_{22} \\ \vdots \\ \varepsilon_{NT} \end{bmatrix}, \quad \text{and} \quad \boldsymbol{\beta} = \begin{bmatrix} \beta_1 \\ \beta_2 \\ \vdots \\ \beta_K \end{bmatrix}.$$

Therefore,

$$\boldsymbol{\Omega} =$$

$$\begin{bmatrix} E(\varepsilon_{11}^2) & E(\varepsilon_{11}\varepsilon_{12}) & \cdots & E(\varepsilon_{11}\varepsilon_{1T}) & E(\varepsilon_{11}\varepsilon_{21}) & E(\varepsilon_{11}\varepsilon_{22}) & \cdots & E(\varepsilon_{11}\varepsilon_{NT}) \\ E(\varepsilon_{12}\varepsilon_{11}) & E(\varepsilon_{12}^2) & \cdots & E(\varepsilon_{12}\varepsilon_{1T}) & E(\varepsilon_{12}\varepsilon_{21}) & E(\varepsilon_{12}\varepsilon_{22}) & \cdots & E(\varepsilon_{12}\varepsilon_{NT}) \\ \vdots & \vdots & & \vdots & \vdots & \vdots & & \vdots \\ E(\varepsilon_{1T}\varepsilon_{11}) & E(\varepsilon_{1T}\varepsilon_{12}) & \cdots & E(\varepsilon_{1T}^2) & E(\varepsilon_{1T}\varepsilon_{21}) & E(\varepsilon_{1T}\varepsilon_{22}) & \cdots & E(\varepsilon_{1T}\varepsilon_{NT}) \\ E(\varepsilon_{21}\varepsilon_{11}) & E(\varepsilon_{21}\varepsilon_{12}) & \cdots & E(\varepsilon_{21}\varepsilon_{1T}) & E(\varepsilon_{21}^2) & E(\varepsilon_{21}\varepsilon_{22}) & \cdots & E(\varepsilon_{21}\varepsilon_{NT}) \\ E(\varepsilon_{22}\varepsilon_{11}) & E(\varepsilon_{22}\varepsilon_{12}) & \cdots & E(\varepsilon_{22}\varepsilon_{1T}) & E(\varepsilon_{22}\varepsilon_{21}) & E(\varepsilon_{22}^2) & \cdots & E(\varepsilon_{22}\varepsilon_{NT}) \\ \vdots & \vdots & & \vdots & \vdots & \vdots & & \vdots \\ E(\varepsilon_{NT}\varepsilon_{11}) & E(\varepsilon_{NT}\varepsilon_{12}) & \cdots & E(\varepsilon_{NT}\varepsilon_{1T}) & E(\varepsilon_{NT}\varepsilon_{21}) & E(\varepsilon_{NT}\varepsilon_{22}) & \cdots & E(\varepsilon_{NT}^2) \end{bmatrix}.$$

This specification provides a general framework for the discussion of different models designed to deal with pooled cross-section and time-series data.

At this point we should note that the number of observations in the context of pooled cross-section and time-series data has two dimensions, N and T. All asymptotic properties of estimators are derived under the presumption that $N \to \infty$ and $T \to \infty$ and that N/T is different from zero or infinity for any N and T. Since frequently, though by no means always, N is large while T is small, some authors consider properties of estimators under the presumption that T is fixed while $N \to \infty$.[8] We do not follow this course because, in reality, the time goes on and T is *never* fixed. It is, however, true that some time series are rather short and that we are well advised to be concerned about the small sample properties of estimators whose asymptotic properties depend on $T \to \infty$.

A Cross-sectionally Heteroskedastic and Timewise Autoregressive Model

One approach to the specification of the behavior of the disturbances when we deal with cross-section and time-series data is to combine the assumptions that we frequently make about cross-sectional observations with those that are usually made when dealing with time series. As for the cross-sectional observations—for example, observations on individual households at a point (or period) of time—it is frequently assumed that the regression disturbances are mutually independent but heteroskedastic.[9] Concerning the time-series data, one usually suspects that the disturbances are autoregressive though not necessarily heteroskedastic. When dealing with pooled cross-section and time-series data, we may combine these assumptions and adopt a *cross-sectionally heteroskedastic and timewise autoregressive model.* The particular characterization of this model is

$$E(\varepsilon_{it}^2) = \sigma_i^2 \qquad \text{(heteroskedasticity)}, \tag{12.22}$$

$$E(\varepsilon_{it}\varepsilon_{jt}) = 0 \quad (i \neq j) \qquad \text{(cross-sectional independence)}, \tag{12.23}$$

$$\varepsilon_{it} = \rho_i \varepsilon_{i,t-1} + u_{it} \qquad \text{(autoregression)}, \tag{12.24}$$

where

$$u_{it} \sim N(0, \sigma_{ui}^2),$$

$$\varepsilon_{i1} \sim N\left(0, \frac{\sigma_{ui}^2}{1 - \rho_i^2}\right),$$

and

$$E(\varepsilon_{i,t-1} u_{jt}) = 0 \quad \text{for all } i, j.$$

Note that in this model we allow the value of the parameter ρ to vary from one cross-sectional unit to another. From these specifications we deduce

$$E(\varepsilon_{it}\varepsilon_{is}) = \rho^{t-s}\sigma_i^2 \qquad (t \geq s),$$

$$E(\varepsilon_{it}\varepsilon_{js}) = 0 \qquad (i \neq j).$$

[8] See, e.g., S. Nickell, "Biases in Dynamic Models with Fixed Effects," *Econometrica,* 49 (November 1981), pp. 1417–1426.

[9] See, e.g., S. J. Prais and H. S. Houthakker, *The Analysis of Family Budgets* (Cambridge, England: The University Press, 1955). The assumption of mutual independence of the cross-sectional units will be relaxed later.

By making the appropriate substitution, we find that for this model

$$\Omega = \begin{bmatrix} \sigma_1^2 \mathbf{V_1} & \mathbf{0} & \cdots & \mathbf{0} \\ \mathbf{0} & \sigma_2^2 \mathbf{V_2} & \cdots & \mathbf{0} \\ \vdots & \vdots & & \vdots \\ \mathbf{0} & \mathbf{0} & \cdots & \sigma_N^2 \mathbf{V_N} \end{bmatrix}, \tag{12.25}$$

where

$$\mathbf{V_i} = \begin{bmatrix} 1 & \rho_i & \rho_i^2 & \cdots & \rho_i^{T-1} \\ \rho_i & 1 & \rho_i & \cdots & \rho_i^{T-2} \\ \vdots & \vdots & \vdots & & \vdots \\ \rho_i^{T-1} & \rho_i^{T-2} & \rho_i^{T-3} & \cdots & 1 \end{bmatrix},$$

and each of the $\mathbf{0}$'s represents a $(T \times T)$ matrix of zeros.

To find consistent estimates of the elements of (12.25), we can proceed in the following way. First, we apply the ordinary least squares method to all $N \times T$ observations. The resulting estimates of the regression coefficients are unbiased and consistent, and can be used to calculate the regression residuals e_{it}. From these residuals, we can obtain consistent estimates of ρ_i, say, $\hat{\rho}_i$, by

$$\hat{\rho}_i = \frac{\sum e_{it} e_{i,t-1}}{\sum e_{i,t-1}^2} \qquad (t = 2, 3, \ldots, T). \tag{12.26}$$

When T is small, however, $\hat{\rho}_i$ may exceed one in absolute value. To avoid this possibility, we may estimate ρ_i by the sample coefficient of correlation between e_{it} and $e_{i,t-1}$, i.e., by

$$\hat{\rho}_i = \frac{\sum e_{it} e_{i,t-1}}{\sqrt{\sum e_{it}^2}\sqrt{\sum e_{i,t-1}^2}} \qquad (t = 2, 3, \ldots, T).$$

This is also a consistent estimator of ρ_i and its value is confined to the interval from -1 to $+1$ for *any* sample size.

Next, we use the $\hat{\rho}_i$'s to transform the observations in accordance with (8.61); that is, we form

$$Y_{it}^* = \beta_1 X_{it,1}^* + \beta_2 X_{it,2}^* + \cdots + \beta_K X_{it,K}^* + u_{it}^*, \tag{12.27}$$

where

$$Y_{it}^* = \sqrt{1 - \hat{\rho}_i^2}\, Y_{it} \qquad \text{for } t = 1,$$

$$Y_{it}^* = Y_{it} - \hat{\rho}_i Y_{i,t-1} \qquad \text{for } t = 2, 3, \ldots, T,$$

and

$$X_{it,k}^* = \sqrt{1 - \hat{\rho}_i^2}\, X_{it,k} \qquad \text{for } t = 1,$$

$$X_{it,k}^* = X_{it,k} - \hat{\rho}_i X_{i,t-1,k} \qquad t = 2, 3, \ldots, T,$$

$$k = 1, 2, \ldots, K,$$

$$i = 1, 2, \ldots, N.$$

The purpose here is to estimate σ_i^2 from observations that are, at least asymptotically, nonautoregressive since estimated variances based on autoregressive disturbances are, in general, biased. To this end, we can apply the ordinary least squares method to (12.27) for which we have NT observations. The resulting regression residuals, say, $\hat{u}_{it}^*$, can be used to estimate the variances of u_{it} (i.e., σ_{ui}^2) by

$$s_{ui}^2 = \frac{1}{T-K} \sum_{t=1}^{T} \hat{u}_{it}^{*2}. \tag{12.28}$$

Since $\sigma_{ui}^2 = \sigma_i^2(1-\rho_i^2)$, it follows that σ_i^2 can be estimated by

$$s_i^2 = \frac{s_{ui}^2}{1-\hat{\rho}_i^2}. \tag{12.29}$$

Since $\hat{\rho}_i$ is a consistent estimator of ρ_i and s_{ui}^2 is a consistent estimator of σ_{ui}^2, s_i^2 is a consistent estimator of σ_i^2.

Having obtained consistent estimators of ρ_i and σ_i^2, we have completed the task of deriving consistent estimators of the elements of $\mathbf{\Omega}$. By substituting for $\hat{\mathbf{\Omega}}$ in (12.20) and (12.21a), we obtain the desired estimates of the regression coefficients and of their variances. Iteration of this procedure until convergence is reached will lead to maximum likelihood estimates.

Since the evaluation of (12.20) and (12.21a) is quite burdensome computationally, we may subject the observations to a double transformation—one transformation designed to remove autoregression and the other to remove heteroskedasticity—and then use the ordinary least squares method on the transformed data. The autoregressive transformation is described by (12.27), so that we only have to worry about the transformation to remove heteroskedasticity. This transformation can be carried out by dividing both sides of (12.27) by s_{ui} obtained from (12.28), which leads to

$$Y_{it}^{**} = \beta_1 X_{it,1}^{**} + \beta_2 X_{it,2}^{**} + \cdots + \beta_K X_{it,K}^{**} + u_{it}^{**}, \tag{12.30}$$

where

$$Y_{it}^{**} = \frac{Y_{it}^*}{s_{ui}},$$

$$X_{it,k}^{**} = \frac{X_{it,k}^*}{s_{ui}} \qquad (k = 1, 2, \ldots, K),$$

$$u_{it}^{**} = \frac{u_{it}^*}{s_{ui}},$$

$$t = 1, 2, \ldots, T,$$

$$i = 1, 2, \ldots, N.$$

The disturbance u_{it}^{**} is asymptotically nonautoregressive and homoskedastic. The equation (12.30) can then be estimated by the ordinary least squares method, utilizing all of the NT pooled observations. The resulting estimates will be the same as those obtained by the two-stage formulas (12.20) and (12.21a).

A somewhat different version of the cross-sectionally heteroskedastic and timewise autoregressive model is obtained when we assume that the parameter ρ has the same value for all cross-sectional units; i.e., when

$$\rho_i = \rho_j = \rho \qquad \text{for all } i, j = 1, 2, \ldots, N.$$

In this case, the matrix $\mathbf{\Omega}$ becomes

$$\mathbf{\Omega} = \begin{bmatrix} \sigma_1^2\mathbf{V} & \mathbf{0} & \cdots & \mathbf{0} \\ \mathbf{0} & \sigma_2^2\mathbf{V} & \cdots & \mathbf{0} \\ \vdots & \vdots & & \vdots \\ \mathbf{0} & \mathbf{0} & \cdots & \sigma_N^2\mathbf{V} \end{bmatrix}, \tag{12.31}$$

where

$$\mathbf{V} = \begin{bmatrix} 1 & \rho & \rho^2 & \cdots & \rho^{T-1} \\ \rho & 1 & \rho & \cdots & \rho^{T-2} \\ \vdots & \vdots & \vdots & & \vdots \\ \rho^{T-1} & \rho^{T-2} & \rho^{T-3} & \cdots & 1 \end{bmatrix}.$$

The estimation of the regression coefficients can proceed in exactly the same way as in the previous case, except that formula (12.26) for $\hat{\rho}_i$ is replaced by

$$\hat{\rho} = \frac{\sum_i \sum_t e_{it}e_{i,t-1}}{\sum_i \sum_t e_{i,t-1}^2} \qquad (i = 1, 2, \ldots, N;\ t = 2, 3, \ldots, T), \tag{12.32}$$

and the variables in (12.27) are transformed by using $\hat{\rho}$ instead of $\hat{\rho}_i$. (To avoid the possibility of obtaining a value of $|\hat{\rho}|$ greater than one, it may be advisable to estimate ρ by the coefficient of correlation between e_{it} and $e_{i,t-1}$.) The remaining steps in the estimation procedure are unchanged.

The preceding analysis has been carried out on the assumption that the explanatory variables are nonstochastic. If, however, the explanatory variables should contain a lagged dependent variable—perhaps as a result of a partial adjustment process discussed in Section 11-4—then there would be a correlation between the lagged dependent variable and the disturbance. In this case the proposed estimator of ρ_i would be inconsistent. A consistent estimator can be obtained by using (12.27) and searching over various values of ρ_i in the interval between -1 and $+1$. Alternatively, an instrumental variable method (with the lagged value of one of the Xs serving as an instrument for the lagged dependent variable) can be used in the first stage of estimation.

EXAMPLE The preceding model was utilized by R. C. Fair to estimate the effects of changes in relative prices on the country shares in international trade.[10] The data used were quarterly observations on 47 countries for the period 1971–1979. The dependent variable

[10] R. C. Fair, "Estimated Effects of Relative Prices on Trade Shares," Cowles Foundation Discussion Paper No. 597, Yale University, June 1981.

was relative change in the share of country i's total merchandise imports imported from country j, and the explanatory variable was relative change in the export price index of country j. No constant term was included and the first observation for each country was dropped to simplify the transformation. An iterative (rather than a two-stage) procedure was used. The results were very good. For only three countries (Yugoslavia, Mexico, and China) was the sign of the regression coefficient positive, contrary to expectation. Of the remaining countries approximately 80% had t statistics greater than or equal to 2.0 in absolute value, and only five countries had t statistics less than 1.0 in absolute value.

A Cross-sectionally Correlated and Timewise Autoregressive Model

In many circumstances the most questionable assumption of the preceding model is that the cross-sectional units are mutually independent. For instance, when the cross-sectional units are geographical regions with arbitrarily drawn boundaries—such as the states of the United States—we would not expect this assumption to be well satisfied. If we then generalize the preceding model by dropping the assumption of mutual independence, we have what may be termed a *cross-sectionally correlated and time-wise autoregressive model.* The specification of the behavior of the disturbances in this model is as follows.

(12.33) $$E(\varepsilon_{it}^2) = \sigma_{ii} \qquad \text{(heteroskedasticity)},$$

(12.34) $$E(\varepsilon_{it}\varepsilon_{jt}) = \sigma_{ij} \qquad \text{(mutual correlation)},$$

(12.35) $$\varepsilon_{it} = \rho_i \varepsilon_{i,t-1} + u_{it} \qquad \text{(autoregression)},$$

where
$$u_{it} \sim N(0, \phi_{ii}),$$
$$E(\varepsilon_{i,t-1}u_{jt}) = 0,$$
$$E(u_{it}u_{jt}) = \phi_{ij},$$
$$E(u_{it}u_{js}) = 0 \qquad (t \neq s),$$
$$\sigma_{ii} = \frac{\phi_{ii}}{1-\rho_i^2},$$
$$\sigma_{ij} = \frac{\phi_{ij}}{1-\rho_i\rho_j},$$
$$i, j = 1, 2, \ldots, N,$$
$$t = 1, 2, \ldots, T.$$

The initial value of ε is assumed to have these properties:

$$\varepsilon_{i1} \sim N\left(0, \frac{\phi_{ii}}{1-\rho_i^2}\right),$$

$$E(\varepsilon_{i1}\varepsilon_{j1}) = \frac{\phi_{ij}}{1-\rho_i\rho_j}.$$

Note that the variances of the us have now been denoted by the symbol ϕ rather than by σ_u^2, as in the preceding, simpler model. The matrix $\mathbf{\Omega}$ for the present model is

$$(12.36) \qquad \mathbf{\Omega} = \begin{bmatrix} \sigma_{11}\mathbf{V_{11}} & \sigma_{12}\mathbf{V_{12}} & \cdots & \sigma_{1N}\mathbf{V_{1N}} \\ \sigma_{21}\mathbf{V_{21}} & \sigma_{22}\mathbf{V_{22}} & \cdots & \sigma_{2N}\mathbf{V_{2N}} \\ \vdots & \vdots & & \vdots \\ \sigma_{N1}\mathbf{V_{N1}} & \sigma_{N2}\mathbf{V_{N2}} & \cdots & \sigma_{NN}\mathbf{V_{NN}} \end{bmatrix},$$

where
$$\mathbf{V_{ij}} = \begin{bmatrix} 1 & \rho_j & \rho_j^2 & \cdots & \rho_j^{T-1} \\ \rho_i & 1 & \rho_j & \cdots & \rho_j^{T-2} \\ \rho_i^2 & \rho_i & 1 & \cdots & \rho_j^{T-2} \\ \vdots & \vdots & \vdots & & \vdots \\ \rho_i^{T-1} & \rho_i^{T-2} & \rho_i^{T-3} & \cdots & 1 \end{bmatrix}.$$

To obtain consistent estimates of the elements of $\mathbf{\Omega}$, we first apply the ordinary least squares method to all of the pooled observations, and calculate the corresponding residuals e_{it}. These residuals are used for obtaining $\hat{\rho}_i$ by application of the formula (12.26). With the help of $\hat{\rho}_i$, we transform the variables and form (12.27). To this equation we again apply the ordinary least squares method and calculate the residuals $\hat{u}_{it}^*$. The variances and covariances of the εs (i.e., σ_{ij}) can then be estimated by

$$(12.37) \qquad s_{ij} = \frac{\hat{\phi}_{ij}}{1 - \hat{\rho}_i\hat{\rho}_j},$$

where
$$\hat{\phi}_{ij} = \frac{1}{T-K} \sum_{t=1}^{T} \hat{u}_{it}^* \hat{u}_{jt}^*.$$

In this way we obtain consistent estimates of ρ_i and σ_{ij} and, therefore, of $\mathbf{\Omega}$. This enables us to use the formulas (12.20) and (12.21a), and thus to obtain asymptotically efficient estimates of the regression coefficients and of their variances.

This procedure can be simplified by applying the feasible Aitken estimation formulas (12.20) and (12.21a) to the *transformed* variables, that is, by using an estimator of $\boldsymbol{\beta}$

$$(12.38) \qquad \tilde{\tilde{\tilde{\boldsymbol{\beta}}}} = (\mathbf{X}^{*\prime}\hat{\mathbf{\Phi}}^{-1}\mathbf{X}^*)^{-1}(\mathbf{X}^{*\prime}\hat{\mathbf{\Phi}}^{-1}\mathbf{y}^*)$$

with

$$(12.39) \qquad \text{Asympt. Var-Cov}(\tilde{\tilde{\tilde{\boldsymbol{\beta}}}}) = (\mathbf{X}^{*\prime}\hat{\mathbf{\Phi}}^{-1}\mathbf{X}^*)^{-1},$$

where the elements of $\mathbf{y}^*$ and $\mathbf{X}^*$ are defined as in (12.27). The matrix $\hat{\mathbf{\Phi}}$ is the estimated variance–covariance matrix of the us, and it is of the order $NT \times NT$. Its full description is

$$(12.40)\qquad \hat{\boldsymbol{\Phi}} = \begin{bmatrix} \hat{\phi}_{11}\mathbf{I_T} & \hat{\phi}_{12}\mathbf{I_T} & \cdots & \hat{\phi}_{1N}\mathbf{I_T} \\ \hat{\phi}_{21}\mathbf{I_T} & \hat{\phi}_{22}\mathbf{I_T} & \cdots & \hat{\phi}_{2N}\mathbf{I_T} \\ \vdots & \vdots & & \vdots \\ \hat{\phi}_{N1}\mathbf{I_T} & \hat{\phi}_{N2}\mathbf{I_T} & \cdots & \hat{\phi}_{NN}\mathbf{I_T} \end{bmatrix},$$

where the $\hat{\phi}_{ij}$s are as defined in (12.37), and $\mathbf{I_T}$ is an identity matrix of order $T \times T$.

There is a slight problem with the preceding transformation. From (12.36) we have

$$(12.41)\qquad \mathbf{V_{ij}^{-1}} = \frac{1}{1-\rho_i\rho_j}\begin{bmatrix} 1 & -\rho_j & 0 & \cdots & 0 & 0 \\ -\rho_i & 1+\rho_i\rho_j & -\rho_j & \cdots & 0 & 0 \\ 0 & -\rho_i & 1+\rho_i\rho_j & \cdots & 0 & 0 \\ \vdots & \vdots & \vdots & & \vdots & \vdots \\ 0 & 0 & 0 & \cdots & -\rho_i & 1 \end{bmatrix}.$$

If the transformation to remove autoregression is to be successful, then $\mathbf{V_{ij}^{-1}}$ should—except for a factor of proportionality—be equal to $(\mathbf{P_i'P_j})'$, just as $\mathbf{V_{ii}^{-1}}$ equals $\mathbf{P_i'P_i}/(1-\rho_i^2)$. In fact, however,

$$(12.42)\qquad (\mathbf{P_i'P_j})' = \begin{bmatrix} \sqrt{1-\rho_j^2} & -\rho_j & \cdots & 0 \\ 0 & 1 & \cdots & 0 \\ 0 & 0 & \cdots & 0 \\ \vdots & \vdots & & \vdots \\ 0 & 0 & \cdots & -\rho_j \\ 0 & 0 & \cdots & 0 \end{bmatrix} \begin{bmatrix} \sqrt{1-\rho_i^2} & 0 & 0 & \cdots & 0 & 0 \\ -\rho_i & 1 & 0 & \cdots & 0 & 0 \\ \vdots & \vdots & \vdots & & \vdots & \vdots \\ 0 & 0 & 0 & \cdots & -\rho_i & 1 \end{bmatrix}$$

$$= \begin{bmatrix} \sqrt{1-\rho_i^2}\sqrt{1-\rho_j^2}+\rho_i\rho_j & -\rho_j & 0 & \cdots & 0 & 0 \\ -\rho_i & 1+\rho_i\rho_j & -\rho_j & \cdots & 0 & 0 \\ 0 & -\rho_i & 1+\rho_i\rho_j & \cdots & 0 & 0 \\ \vdots & \vdots & \vdots & & \vdots & \vdots \\ 0 & 0 & 0 & \cdots & -\rho_i & 1 \end{bmatrix}.$$

Thus, apart from the factor of proportionality, the two matrices differ in the first element of the first row. This problem does not arise for $\mathbf{P_i'P_j}$ in which the first element of the first row equals to one. There are several ways of dealing with this problem. First, we could use transformation matrices with the first row completely omitted; that is, we could use the Cochrane–Orcutt rather than the Prais–Winsten transformation. Second, we could ignore the problem, since—unless ρ_i and ρ_j are considerably different—the discrepancy is likely to be small and, in any case, it is asymptotically irrelevant.

The question of whether or not to use a cross-sectionally correlated model can be decided on a priori grounds or by means of a statistical test. If the cross-sectional units are randomly selected households or firms, then a cross-sectional independence is an appropriate assumption. If, on the other hand, cross-sectional units are the states of the United States, then cross-sectional independence is less likely. When there is doubt, one can use a likelihood ratio test since cross-sectional independence is a special case of cross-sectional correlation.

An Error Component Model

A different approach to the specification of the behavior of the disturbances when combining cross-section and time-series data has been adopted by the proponents of the so-called *error component model.* The basic assumption here is that the regression disturbance is composed of three independent components—one component associated with time, another associated with the cross-sectional units, and the third varying in both dimensions. Specifically,

$$\varepsilon_{it} = u_i + v_t + w_{it} \qquad (i = 1, 2, \ldots, N;\ t = 1, 2, \ldots, T), \tag{12.43}$$

where

$$u_i \sim N(0, \sigma_u^2),$$
$$v_t \sim N(0, \sigma_v^2),$$
$$w_{it} \sim N(0, \sigma_w^2),$$

and the components u_i, v_t, and w_{it} satisfy the following conditions:

$$E(u_i v_t) = E(u_t w_{it}) = E(v_t w_{it}) = 0,$$
$$E(u_i u_j) = 0 \qquad (i \neq j),$$
$$E(v_t v_s) = 0 \qquad (t \neq s),$$
$$E(w_{it} w_{is}) = E(w_{it} w_{jt}) = E(w_{it} w_{js}) = 0 \qquad (i \neq j;\ t \neq s).$$

Note that this implies that ε_{it} is *homoskedastic* with variance given by

$$\text{Var}(\varepsilon_{it}) = \sigma^2 = \sigma_u^2 + \sigma_v^2 + \sigma_w^2.$$

The coefficient of correlation between ε_{it} and ε_{jt} $(i \neq j)$—i.e., between the disturbances of two different cross-sectional units at a given point of time—is

$$\frac{\text{Cov}(\varepsilon_{it}, \varepsilon_{jt})}{\sqrt{\text{Var}(\varepsilon_{it})\text{Var}(\varepsilon_{jt})}} = \frac{\sigma_v^2}{\sigma_u^2 + \sigma_v^2 + \sigma_w^2} \qquad (i \neq j).$$

The coefficient of correlation between ε_{it} and ε_{is} $(t \neq s)$—i.e., between the disturbances of a given cross-sectional unit at two different point of time—is

$$\frac{\mathrm{Cov}(\varepsilon_{it}, \varepsilon_{is})}{\sqrt{\mathrm{Var}(\varepsilon_{it})\mathrm{Var}(\varepsilon_{is})}} = \frac{\sigma_u^2}{\sigma_u^2 + \sigma_v^2 + \sigma_w^2} \qquad (t \neq s).$$

This last feature of the error component model means that, for each cross-sectional unit, the correlation of the disturbances over time remains *unchanged* no matter how far apart in time the disturbances are. This contrasts sharply with the usual assumption of first-order autoregression, which implies that the degree of correlation declines geometrically with the time distance involved. Finally, the coefficient of correlation between ε_{it} and ε_{js} is

$$\frac{\mathrm{Cov}(\varepsilon_{it}, \varepsilon_{js})}{\sqrt{\mathrm{Var}(\varepsilon_{it})\mathrm{Var}(\varepsilon_{js})}} = 0 \qquad (i \neq j;\, t \neq s).$$

By using these results we find that the matrix $\mathbf{\Omega}$ for the error component model is

$$\mathbf{\Omega} = \begin{bmatrix} \sigma_u^2\mathbf{A_T} & \sigma_v^2\mathbf{I_T} & \cdots & \sigma_v^2\mathbf{I_T} \\ \sigma_v^2\mathbf{I_T} & \sigma_u^2\mathbf{A_T} & \cdots & \sigma_v^2\mathbf{I_T} \\ \vdots & \vdots & & \vdots \\ \sigma_v^2\mathbf{I_T} & \sigma_v^2\mathbf{I_T} & \cdots & \sigma_u^2\mathbf{A_T} \end{bmatrix}, \tag{12.44}$$

where $\mathbf{A_T}$ is a $(T \times T)$ matrix defined as

$$\mathbf{A_T} = \begin{bmatrix} \dfrac{\sigma^2}{\sigma_u^2} & 1 & \cdots & 1 \\ 1 & \dfrac{\sigma^2}{\sigma_u^2} & \cdots & 1 \\ \vdots & \vdots & & \vdots \\ 1 & 1 & \cdots & \dfrac{\sigma^2}{\sigma_u^2} \end{bmatrix}$$

and $\mathbf{I_T}$ is an identity matrix of order $T \times T$. The elements of the $\mathbf{\Omega}$ matrix can be consistently estimated in a number of ways.[11] Under the assumption of normality of ε_{it}, iteration of the estimation procedure until convergence is reached will lead to maximum likelihood estimates. A transformation of the regression equation to yield a disturbance that satisfies all classical assumptions is also available.[12]

The preceding three-component model, introduced to econometrics by Balestra

[11] Formulas for unbiased estimation of σ_u^2, σ_v^2, and σ_w^2 are derived in W. A. Fuller and G. E. Battese, "Estimation of Linear Models with Crossed-Error Structure," *Journal of Econometrics,* 2 (May 1974), pp. 67–78. A computer program for calculation of these estimates is available as a part of the Statistical Analysis System (SAS), Department of Statistics, North Carolina State University, Raleigh, NC 27607. (See *Journal of Econometrics,* 3 (May 1975), p. 203.)

[12] See, e.g., T. B. Fomby, R. C. Hill, and S. R. Johnson, *Advanced Econometric Methods* (New York: Springer-Verlag, 1984), pp. 334–336.

and Nerlove in 1966,[13] has not been used very much in applied work. Balestra and Nerlove themselves have, in actual application, used a two-component model of the form

(12.45) $$\varepsilon_{it} = u_i + w_{it},$$

where all assumptions are as in (12.43). The two-component model has been widely used for illustration of the error component modeling approach and in applications. For this model the matrix $\mathbf{\Omega}$ becomes

(12.46) $$\mathbf{\Omega} = \begin{bmatrix} \sigma_u^2 \mathbf{A_T} & 0 & \cdots & 0 \\ 0 & \sigma_u^2 \mathbf{A_T} & \cdots & 0 \\ \vdots & \vdots & & \vdots \\ 0 & 0 & \cdots & \sigma_u^2 \mathbf{A_T} \end{bmatrix},$$

where $\mathbf{A_T}$ is defined as in (12.44). The transformation matrix in this case is relatively simple:[14]

(12.47) $$\mathbf{P} = \begin{bmatrix} \mathbf{P_i} & 0 & \cdots & 0 \\ 0 & \mathbf{P_i} & \cdots & 0 \\ \vdots & \vdots & & \vdots \\ 0 & 0 & \cdots & \mathbf{P_i} \end{bmatrix},$$

where

$$\mathbf{P_i} = \mathbf{I_T} - \alpha \frac{\boldsymbol{\iota}\boldsymbol{\iota}'}{T},$$

$$\alpha = 1 - \frac{\sigma_w}{\sqrt{T\sigma_u^2 + \sigma_w^2}},$$

and $\boldsymbol{\iota}' = [1 \;\; 1 \;\; \cdots \;\; 1]$ with T elements. The transformed regression equation then becomes

(12.48) $$(Y_{it} - \alpha \overline{Y}_i) = \beta_1(1-\alpha) + \beta_2(X_{it2} - \alpha \overline{X}_{i2}) + \cdots + \beta_K(X_{itK} - \alpha \overline{X}_{iK}) + w_{it}^*,$$

where

$$\overline{Y}_i = \frac{1}{T}\sum_{t=1}^{T} Y_{it}, \qquad \overline{X}_{i2} = \frac{1}{T}\sum_{T=1}^{T} X_{it2}, \qquad \text{etc.}$$

If α were known, least squares estimation of (12.48) would lead to generalized least squares estimates of the original regression equation. Feasible Aitken estimation is possible since consistent estimators of σ_u^2 and σ_w^2 are available.[15]

[13] P. Balestra and M. Nerlove, "Pooling Cross-Section and Time-Series Data in the Estimation of a Dynamic Model: The Demand for Natural Gas," *Econometrica,* 34 (July 1966), pp. 585–612.

[14] See Fomby, Hill, and Johnson, *op. cit.,* p. 333.

[15] *Ibid.,* pp. 333–334.

The generalized least squares estimator of the two-component model can be expressed as a weighted average of two ordinary least squares estimators, one based on cross-sectional variation of averages over time called a "between" estimator, and the other based on variation over time around cross-sectional averages called a "within" estimator.[16] This can be best illustrated by means of a simple regression model without a constant term,

$$Y_{it} = \beta X_{it} + \varepsilon_{it}.$$

The "between" estimator ($\hat{\beta}_B$) is then the least squares estimator of β_B in the regression equation

$$\bar{Y}_i = \beta_B \bar{X}_i + \bar{\varepsilon}_i,$$

whereas the "within" estimator ($\hat{\beta}_W$) is the least squares estimator of β_W in the regression equation

$$(Y_{it} - \bar{Y}_i) = \beta_W (X_{it} - \bar{X}_i) + (w_{it} - \bar{w}_i).$$

The same estimator of β_W could also be obtained by applying the least squares method to the so-called *covariance* model or *least squares dummy variables* model (LSDV) discussed below.

The generalized least squares estimator of β turns out to be

$$\tilde{\beta} = \frac{\hat{\beta}_W W_{xx} + \hat{\beta}_B \theta B_{xx}}{W_{xx} + \theta B_{xx}}, \tag{12.49}$$

where

$$W_{xx} = \sum_i \sum_t (X_{it} - \bar{X}_i)^2,$$

$$B_{xx} = T \sum_i \bar{X}_i^2,$$

and

$$\theta = \frac{\sigma_w^2}{\sigma_w^2 + T\sigma_u^2}.$$

From (12.49) it is possible to determine which of the two kinds of variation has more influence on $\hat{\beta}$. When T is large, or when σ_u^2 is large relative to σ_w^2, θ will be very small and the generalized least squares estimator will be very similar to the "between" (or LSDV) estimator.

When the explanatory variables include a lagged dependent variable and the error variances are known, the generalized least squares estimator retains its desirable asymptotic properties. If, however, the error variances are not known—as is usually the case—the feasible Aitken estimator derived for nonstochastic explanatory variables is biased and inconsistent. To obtain consistent estimates of the unknown parameters, we can use the maximum likelihood method. (If, instead of the search method, we wish to use an iterative procedure, we have to start with consistent estimates of the error variances, such as those based on instrumental

[16] See, e.g., G. S. Maddala, *Econometrics* (New York: McGraw-Hill, 1977), pp. 326–331.

variable residuals.) An alternative, two-stage procedure proposed by Nerlove and labeled 2RC appears to have good small sample properties.[17]

The error component model is based on the presumption of the presence of specific cross-sectional and time-related effects (or of cross-sectional effects only if we assume a two-component model). A test for the presence of these effects has been devised by Breusch and Pagan.[18] For the three-component model, the null and the alternative hypotheses are

$$H_0: \quad \sigma_u^2 = \sigma_v^2 = 0,$$
$$H_A: \quad H_0 \text{ is not true.}$$

The test is a Lagrange multiplier test described in general terms in Section 11-3. The test statistic is

$$\text{(12.50)} \quad \text{LM} = \frac{NT}{2}\left\{\frac{1}{T-1}\left[\frac{\sum_i(\sum_t \hat{u}_{it})^2}{\sum_i\sum_t \hat{u}_{it}^2} - 1\right]^2 + \frac{1}{N-1}\left[\frac{\sum_t(\sum_i \hat{u}_{it})^2}{\sum_i\sum_t \hat{u}_{it}^2} - 1\right]^2\right\} \sim \chi_2^2,$$

where the $\hat{u}$s are the ordinary least squares residuals. For the two-component model we have

$$H_0: \quad \sigma_u^2 = 0,$$
$$H_A: \quad \sigma_u^2 \neq 0,$$

and

$$\text{(12.51)} \qquad \text{LM} = \frac{NT}{2(T-1)}\left[\frac{\sum_i(\sum_t \hat{u}_{it})^2}{\sum_i\sum_t \hat{u}_{it}^2} - 1\right]^2 \sim \chi_1^2.$$

EXAMPLE The two-component model was used by Baltagi and Griffin in their study of the demand for gasoline.[19] In the basic model the dependent variable was gas consumption

[17] M. Nerlove, "Further Evidence on the Estimation of Dynamic Economic Relations from a Time Series of Cross Sections," *Econometrica,* 39 (March 1971), pp. 359–382.

[18] T. S. Breusch and A. R. Pagan, "The Lagrange Multiplier Test and Its Applications to Model Specification in Econometrics," *Review of Economic Studies,* 47 (1980), pp. 239–254.

[19] B. H. Baltagi and J. M. Griffin, "Gasoline Demand in the OECD: An Application of Pooling and Testing Procedures," *European Economic Review,* 27 (July 1983), pp. 117–137.

per car, and the explanatory variables were per capita income, price of gasoline, and stock of cars per capita. All variables were measured in logarithms. The data consisted of a pooled sample for 18 OECD countries and covered the years 1960 to 1978. The authors found that the gain in efficiency from pooling was large, particularly with respect to the income and price effects. The income elasticity estimates ranged from 0.54 to 0.60, and the price elasticity estimates ranged from −0.47 to −0.36, depending upon the particular feasible Aitken estimation method used.

A Covariance Model

Another model that is commonly used when dealing with pooled cross-section and time-series observations is the so-called *covariance model.* We mention this as a postscript to the present section because the covariance model is generally treated within the framework of the classical regression model rather than as a generalized regression model. The idea behind the covariance model is the supposition that each cross-sectional unit and each time period are characterized by their own special intercept. This feature is incorporated into the regression equation by the introduction of binary variables. The regression equation then becomes

$$\text{(12.52)} \quad Y_{it} = \beta_1 + \beta_2 X_{it,2} + \cdots + \beta_K X_{it,K} + \gamma_2 Z_{it,2} + \gamma_3 Z_{it,3} + \cdots + \gamma_N Z_{it,N} + \delta_2 W_{it,2} + \delta_3 W_{it,3} + \cdots + \delta_T W_{it,T} + \varepsilon_{it},$$

where

$$\begin{aligned} Z_{it,i} &= 1 \quad \text{for the } i\text{th cross-sectional unit,} \\ &= 0 \quad \text{otherwise} \qquad (i = 2, 3, \ldots, N); \\ W_{it,t} &= 1 \quad \text{for the } t\text{th time period,} \\ &= 0 \quad \text{otherwise} \qquad (t = 2, 3, \ldots, T). \end{aligned}$$

The disturbance ε_{it} is supposed to satisfy the assumptions of the classical normal linear regression model. (We could, of course, allow ε_{it} to be autoregressive or heteroskedastic and then choose an appropriate estimation method.) Note that with the foregoing specification of the regression equation, we have

$$\begin{aligned} Y_{11} &= \beta_1 + \beta_2 X_{11,2} + \cdots + \beta_K X_{11,K} + \varepsilon_{11}, \\ Y_{12} &= (\beta_1 + \delta_2) + \beta_2 X_{12,2} + \cdots + \beta_K X_{12,K} + \varepsilon_{12}, \\ &\vdots \\ Y_{1T} &= (\beta_1 + \delta_T) + \beta_2 X_{1T,2} + \cdots + \beta_K X_{1T,K} + \varepsilon_{1T}, \\ Y_{21} &= (\beta_1 + \gamma_2) + \beta_2 X_{21,2} + \cdots + \beta_K X_{21,K} + \varepsilon_{21}, \\ Y_{22} &= (\beta_1 + \gamma_2 + \delta_2) + \beta_2 X_{22,2} + \cdots + \beta_K X_{22,K} + \varepsilon_{22}, \\ &\vdots \\ Y_{NT} &= (\beta_1 + \gamma_N + \delta_T) + \beta_2 X_{NT,2} + \cdots + \beta_K X_{NT,K} + \varepsilon_{NT}. \end{aligned}$$

Equation (12.52) contains $K + (N - 1) + (T - 1)$ regression coefficients to be estimated from $N \times T$ observations. If the model is correctly specified and the classical assumptions are satisfied, the ordinary least squares estimates of the regression coefficients will be unbiased and efficient.

The covariance model presented in (12.52) has not been used much in practice. A more common model has been one in which the time binary variables do not appear at all and the constant term is replaced by a binary variable for the first cross-sectional unit. The representation of this model then is

$$(12.53) \qquad Y_{it} = \beta_2 X_{it,2} + \beta_3 X_{it,3} + \cdots + \beta_K X_{it,k} + \lambda_1 Z_{it,1} + \lambda_2 Z_{it,2} + \cdots + \lambda_N Z_{it,N} + \varepsilon_{it}.$$

This model is frequently called the *least squares dummy variables* (LSDV) model, indicating the appropriateness of the least squares estimation method. In matrix notation the model can be written as

$$(12.53a) \qquad \mathbf{y} = \mathbf{X}\boldsymbol{\beta} + \mathbf{Z}\boldsymbol{\lambda} + \boldsymbol{\varepsilon},$$

where $\mathbf{y} \rightarrow NT \times 1$, $\mathbf{X} \rightarrow NT \times (K-1)$, $\boldsymbol{\beta} \rightarrow (K-1) \times 1$, $\mathbf{Z} \rightarrow NT \times N$, $\boldsymbol{\lambda} \rightarrow N \times 1$, and $\boldsymbol{\varepsilon} \rightarrow NT \times 1$. Of course, as N approaches infinity, the number of coefficients also approaches infinity, so that consistent estimation of $\boldsymbol{\lambda}$ is not possible. However, the least squares estimator of $\boldsymbol{\beta}$ *is* consistent.[20]

Since N is frequently very large, a standard application of the least squares estimation formulas may not be feasible. It would then pay to use the partitioned least squares estimation formulas (10.17a) and (10.17b) of Chapter 10, and to take advantage of the special structure of the matrix $\mathbf{Z}$. The results are

$$(12.54a) \qquad \hat{\boldsymbol{\beta}} = (\mathbf{X}'\mathbf{M_Z}\mathbf{X})^{-1}\mathbf{X}'\mathbf{M_Z}\mathbf{y},$$

where $$\mathbf{M_Z} = \mathbf{I} - \mathbf{Z}(\mathbf{Z}'\mathbf{Z})^{-1}\mathbf{Z}',$$

$$\mathbf{X}'\mathbf{M_Z}\mathbf{X} = \begin{bmatrix} \sum_i \sum_t X_{it,2}^2 - T\sum_i \bar{X}_{i,2}^2 & \cdots & \sum_i \sum_t X_{it,2}X_{it,K} - T\sum_i \bar{X}_{i,2}\bar{X}_{i,K} \\ \sum_i \sum_t X_{it,2}X_{it,3} - T\sum_i \bar{X}_{i,2}\bar{X}_{i,3} & \cdots & \sum_i \sum_t X_{it,3}X_{it,K} - T\sum_i \bar{X}_{i,3}\bar{X}_{i,K} \\ \vdots & & \vdots \\ \sum_i \sum_t X_{it,2}X_{it,K} - T\sum_i \bar{X}_{i,2}\bar{X}_{i,K} & \cdots & \sum_i \sum_t X_{it,K}^2 - T\sum_i \bar{X}_{i,K}^2 \end{bmatrix},$$

[20] See C. Cornwell and P. Schmidt, "Panel Data with Cross-Sectional Variation in Slopes as Well as in Intercept," Econometrics Workshop Paper No. 8404, Michigan State University, September 1984.

and

$$\mathbf{X}'\mathbf{M_Z y} = \begin{bmatrix} \sum_i \sum_t X_{it,2}Y_{it} - T\sum_i \bar{X}_{i,2}\bar{Y}_i \\ \sum_i \sum_t X_{it,3}Y_{it} - T\sum_i \bar{X}_{i,3}\bar{Y}_i \\ \vdots \\ \sum_i \sum_t X_{it,K}Y_{it} - T\sum_i \bar{X}_{i,K}\bar{Y}_i \end{bmatrix},$$

given that

$$\bar{X}_{i,2} = \frac{1}{T}\sum_t X_{it,2}, \qquad \bar{X}_{i,3} = \frac{1}{T}\sum_t X_{it,3}, \qquad \text{etc.}$$

Further,

(12.54b) $$\hat{\lambda} = (\mathbf{Z}'\mathbf{M_x Z})^{-1}\mathbf{Z}'\mathbf{M_x y},$$

where $\mathbf{M_x} = \mathbf{I} - \mathbf{X}(\mathbf{X}'\mathbf{X})^{-1}\mathbf{X}'$, so that

$$\begin{bmatrix} \hat{\lambda}_1 \\ \hat{\lambda}_2 \\ \vdots \\ \hat{\lambda}_N \end{bmatrix} = \begin{bmatrix} \bar{Y}_1 \\ \bar{Y}_2 \\ \vdots \\ \bar{Y}_N \end{bmatrix} - \begin{bmatrix} \bar{X}_{1,2} & \bar{X}_{1,3} & \cdots & \bar{X}_{1,K} \\ \bar{X}_{2,2} & \bar{X}_{2,3} & \cdots & \bar{X}_{2,K} \\ \vdots & \vdots & & \vdots \\ \bar{X}_{N,2} & \bar{X}_{N,3} & \cdots & \bar{X}_{N,K} \end{bmatrix} \begin{bmatrix} \hat{\beta}_2 \\ \hat{\beta}_3 \\ \vdots \\ \hat{\beta}_K \end{bmatrix}$$

The constant term and the estimated γ's of (12.52)—with the W's dropped—can be recovered as follows:

$$\hat{\beta}_1 = \hat{\lambda}_1, \qquad \hat{\gamma}_2 = \hat{\lambda}_2 - \hat{\lambda}_1, \qquad \ldots, \qquad \hat{\gamma}_N = \hat{\lambda}_N - \hat{\lambda}_1.$$

Further,

$$\begin{aligned} \text{SSR} = {} & \hat{\beta}_2 \sum_i \sum_t \left(X_{it,2} - \frac{1}{NT}\sum_i \sum_t X_{it,2}\right)\left(Y_{it} - \frac{1}{NT}\sum_i \sum_t Y_{it}\right) \\ & + \hat{\beta}_3 \sum_i \sum_t \left(X_{it,3} - \frac{1}{NT}\sum_i \sum_t X_{it,3}\right)\left(Y_{it} - \frac{1}{NT}\sum_i \sum_t Y_{it}\right) + \cdots \\ & + \hat{\beta}_K \sum_i \sum_t \left(X_{it,K} - \frac{1}{NT}\sum_i \sum_t X_{it,K}\right)\left(Y_{it} - \frac{1}{NT}\sum_i \sum_t Y_{it}\right) \\ & + \hat{\gamma}_2 \sum_i \sum_t \left(Z_{it,2} - \frac{1}{N}\right)\left(Y_{it} - \frac{1}{NT}\sum_i \sum_t Y_{it}\right) \\ & + \hat{\gamma}_3 \sum_i \sum_t \left(Z_{it,3} - \frac{1}{N}\right)\left(Y_{it} - \frac{1}{NT}\sum_i \sum_t Y_{it}\right) + \cdots \\ & + \hat{\gamma}_N \sum_i \sum_t \left(Z_{it,N} - \frac{1}{N}\right)\left(Y_{it} - \frac{1}{NT}\sum_i \sum_t Y_{it}\right). \end{aligned}$$

Then

$$s^2 = \frac{\text{SST} - \text{SSR}}{NT - K - N},$$

where
$$\text{SST} = \sum_i \sum_t \left(Y_{it} - \frac{1}{NT} \sum_i \sum_t Y_{it} \right)^2.$$

Finally,

(12.55a) $$\text{Est. Var-Cov}(\hat{\boldsymbol{\beta}}) = s^2(\mathbf{X}'\mathbf{M_Z X})^{-1}$$

(12.55b) $$\text{Est. Var-Cov}(\hat{\boldsymbol{\lambda}}) = s^2(\mathbf{Z}'\mathbf{M_X Z})^{-1}.$$

If our interest is confined to the estimation of $\boldsymbol{\beta}$, the result provided by (12.54a) can also be obtained by "differencing out" the dummy variables from (12.53) and applying the least squares method to

(12.53b) $$Y_{it} - \overline{Y}_i = \beta_2(X_{it,2} - \overline{X}_{i,2}) + \beta_3(X_{it,3} - \overline{X}_{i,3}) + \cdots + \beta_K(X_{it,K} - \overline{X}_{i,K}) + \varepsilon_{it}^*$$

where $\overline{X}_{i,2}, \overline{X}_{i,3}, \ldots, \overline{X}_{i,K}$ are defined as above; $\overline{Y}_i = (1/T)\,\Sigma_t Y_{it}$; and $\varepsilon_{it}^* = \varepsilon_{it} - \overline{\varepsilon}_i$. Using these results can save us a considerable amount of computational effort, particularly when N is very large.

An obvious question in connection with the covariance model is whether the inclusion of the dummy variables—and the consequent loss of the number of degrees of freedom—is really necessary. The reasoning underlying the covariance model is that in specifying the regression model we have failed to include relevant explanatory variables that do not change over time (and possibly others that do change over time but have the same value for all cross-sectional units), and that the inclusion of dummy variables is a cover-up of our ignorance. If in doubt, the need for the inclusion of the dummy variables can easily be tested by means of an F test. All we have to do is to estimate the regression equation with and without the dummy variables and compare the resulting error sums of squares by means of an F test. On the other hand, we may be concerned about the presumption that all cross-sectional units have the same slopes and wonder whether pooling of observations is actually justified or not. In this case we can estimate the regression coefficients for each cross-sectional unit separately and compare the resulting total error sum of squares with that obtained from the application of the LSDV model, again by means of an F test. If we proceed in accordance with the result of the test, we have to be concerned about a pretest bias, though.

There is an obvious similarity between the error component model discussed earlier and the covariance model just introduced. The comparison is particularly pertinent in the case of a two-component model and an LSDV model, both of which are widely used in practice. In the case of the error component model the specific characteristic of a cross-sectional unit is a normally distributed random variable, whereas in the case of the covariance model the specific characteristic of a cross-sectional unit is a parameter. In the statistical literature the error component model is known as a *random effect* model, whereas the covariance model is referred to as a *fixed effect* model. A good explanation of the relation between the two models has been provided by Mundlak who suggested that the cross-sectional effects can always be considered random (since the effects cannot be known or estimated until *after* the sample has been drawn), but that in a covariance model the inference is *conditional* on the particular sample values drawn.[21] In the case of an error component model, unconditional inference is possible by virtue of the specific assumption about the distribution of the cross-sectional effects. No such assumption is made when a covariance model is used.

As an example, consider the problem of estimating an agricultural production function for wheat from the data on a sample of farms observed over a number of years. The dependent variable is the production of wheat, and the explanatory variables are the relevant inputs. In addition, however, a relevant explanatory variable is also the quality of soil, which varies over farms but remains constant over time. Inference concerning the coefficients of various inputs can then be unconditional with respect to the quality of soil, or it could be conditional on the quality of soil of the particular farms included in the sample. The advantage of using the error component model is that we save a number of degrees of freedom (since the only unknown parameter involved is the variance of the cross-sectional characteristic) and thus obtain more efficient estimates of the regression parameters. The disadvantage is that if the cross-sectional characteristic is correlated with the included explanatory variables, the estimated regression coefficients are biased and inconsistent. The advantage of the covariance model is that it protects us against a specification error caused by such a correlation, but its disadvantage is a loss of efficiency because of the increased number of parameters to be estimated. Thus the crucial factor to consider is the possibility of a correlation between the cross-sectional characteristic and the included explanatory variables. In our example concerning a farm production function, the quality of soil is most likely to be correlated with agricultural inputs since farmers whose soils is poor are likely to compensate by using more fertilizer and possibly other inputs, and vice versa. An interesting point noted in connection with the generalized least squares formula (12.49) for the two-component model is that as $T \rightarrow \infty$, the generalized least squares estimator of the regression coefficients becomes the same as the least squares estimator of the LSDV model, so that the two models are asymptotically equivalent.

If there is doubt about the correlation between the cross-sectional characteristic and the included explanatory variables, we may carry out a test of the null hypothesis that no such correlation exists against the alternative hypothesis that there is a correlation. For this purpose we can use the test derived by Hausman and already used in connection with errors of measurement in Section 9-1.[22] Here we present the test in two different forms. Under the null hypothesis that $E(\mathbf{X}'\boldsymbol{\varepsilon}) = \mathbf{0}$, the GLS

[21] Y. Mundlak, "On the Pooling of Time-Series and Cross-Section Data," *Econometrica,* 46 (January 1978), pp. 69–85.

[22] J. A. Hausman, "Specification Tests in Econometrics", *Econometrica,* 46 (November 1978), pp. 1251–1271.

estimator of β of the error component (random effect) model should not be very different from the least squares estimator of β of the covariance (fixed effect) model. Provided no other classical assumption is violated, a statistically significant difference between these two estimators indicates that $E(\mathbf{X}'\boldsymbol{\varepsilon})$ is different from zero. If $\hat{\boldsymbol{\beta}}$ denotes the least squares covariance estimator and $\tilde{\boldsymbol{\beta}}$ the generalized least squares error component estimator, then we can take $\hat{\boldsymbol{\beta}} - \tilde{\boldsymbol{\beta}}$, denoted by Hausman as $\hat{\mathbf{q}}$, as the basis for the relevant test statistic. The estimator $\hat{\boldsymbol{\beta}}$ is consistent under both H_0 and H_A, but not efficient when H_0 is true. On the other hand, $\tilde{\boldsymbol{\beta}}$ is consistent *and* efficient under H_0, but not consistent when H_0 is not true. Further, it can be shown that the covariance between $\hat{\mathbf{q}}$ and $\tilde{\boldsymbol{\beta}}$ is zero, so that $\text{Var}(\hat{\mathbf{q}}) = \text{Var}(\hat{\boldsymbol{\beta}}) - \text{Var}(\tilde{\boldsymbol{\beta}})$. If $\hat{\boldsymbol{\beta}}$ and $\tilde{\boldsymbol{\beta}}$ were scalars, then, asymptotically and under H_0, $\hat{\mathbf{q}}/[\text{Var}(\hat{\mathbf{q}})]^{1/2}$ would be a standard normal variable. When, as usual, $\hat{\boldsymbol{\beta}}$ and $\tilde{\boldsymbol{\beta}}$ are vectors, the test statistic and its asymptotic distribution become

$$\hat{\mathbf{q}}'[\text{Var-Cov}(\hat{\mathbf{q}})]^{-1}\hat{\mathbf{q}} \sim \chi^2_{K-1}, \tag{12.56}$$

where K is the number of explanatory variables (including a constant term) as before. When $\tilde{\boldsymbol{\beta}}$ is replaced by a feasible Aitken estimator $\tilde{\tilde{\boldsymbol{\beta}}}$ and the $\text{Var}(\tilde{\boldsymbol{\beta}})$ by a consistent estimator of $\text{Var}(\tilde{\tilde{\boldsymbol{\beta}}})$, the asymptotic distribution of $\hat{\mathbf{q}}$ is unchanged.

An alternative and asymptotically equivalent test involves a modified version of the transformed equation of the error component model presented in (12.48) and written in matrix form as

$$\mathbf{y}^* = \mathbf{X}^*\boldsymbol{\beta} + \mathbf{w}^*,$$

where $\mathbf{y}^*$ and $\mathbf{X}^*$ refer to the transformed variables defined as in (12.48). Hausman's test, asymptotically equivalent to (12.56), involves the application of the least squares method to

$$\mathbf{y}^* = \mathbf{X}^*\boldsymbol{\beta} + \hat{\mathbf{X}}\boldsymbol{\gamma} + \mathbf{w}^*, \tag{12.57}$$

where $\hat{\mathbf{X}}$ is a matrix of the explanatory variables expressed in terms of deviations from the respective cross-sectional means. A typical element of $\hat{\mathbf{X}}$ then is $X_{it,k} - (1/T)\,\Sigma_t X_{it,k}$ $(k = 2, 3, \ldots, K)$. The test of the null hypothesis is a test of significance of $\hat{\boldsymbol{\gamma}}$, which is a standard F test. This version of Hausman's test was already presented as (9.35b) in connection with errors of measurement in Section 9-1.

12-3 Seemingly Unrelated Regressions

Under the assumptions of the classical normal linear regression model, the least squares estimators of the regression coefficients were found to be unbiased and efficient. This result was derived on the understanding that the specification of the model represents *all* there is to know about the regression equation and the variables involved. If there exists some other piece of information that has not been taken into account, then the result concerning the properties of the least squares estimators can no longer be considered established. One such additional piece of information would be the knowledge that the disturbance in the regression equation under consideration could be correlated with the disturbance in some other regression equation. In the present section we shall consider such a situation and examine the implications for estimation of the regression coefficients.

Suppose we are concerned with the problem of estimating the coefficients of any one or all of the following M regression equations.

$$\begin{aligned} Y_{1t} &= \beta_{11}X_{1t,1} + \beta_{12}X_{1t,2} + \cdots + \beta_{1K_1}X_{1t,K_1} + \varepsilon_{1t}, \\ Y_{2t} &= \beta_{21}X_{2t,1} + \beta_{22}X_{2t,2} + \ldots + \beta_{2K_2}X_{2t,K_2} + \varepsilon_{2t}, \\ &\vdots \\ Y_{Mt} &= \beta_{M1}X_{Mt,1} + \beta_{M2}X_{Mt,2} + \cdots + \beta_{MK_M}X_{Mt,K_M} + \varepsilon_{Mt}, \\ t &= 1, 2, \ldots, T. \end{aligned} \tag{12.58}$$

Using matrix notation, we can write

$$\begin{aligned} \mathbf{y_1} &= \mathbf{X_1}\boldsymbol{\beta}_1 + \boldsymbol{\varepsilon}_1, \\ \mathbf{y_2} &= \mathbf{X_2}\boldsymbol{\beta}_2 + \boldsymbol{\varepsilon}_2, \\ &\vdots \\ \mathbf{y_M} &= \mathbf{X_M}\boldsymbol{\beta}_\mathbf{M} + \boldsymbol{\varepsilon}_\mathbf{M}, \end{aligned} \tag{12.58a}$$

or

$$\mathbf{y_m} = \mathbf{X_m}\boldsymbol{\beta}_\mathbf{m} + \boldsymbol{\varepsilon}_\mathbf{m} \qquad (m = 1, 2, \ldots, M), \tag{12.58b}$$

where $\mathbf{y_m}$ is a $(T \times 1)$ vector of the sample values of the dependent variable, $\mathbf{X_m}$ is a $(T \times K_m)$ matrix of the sample values of the explanatory variables, $\boldsymbol{\beta}_\mathbf{m}$ is a $(K_m \times 1)$ vector of the regression coefficients, and $\boldsymbol{\varepsilon}_\mathbf{m}$ is a $(T \times 1)$ vector of the sample values of the disturbances. We assume that $\boldsymbol{\varepsilon}_\mathbf{m}$ is normally distributed with mean

$$E(\varepsilon_{mt}) = 0 \qquad (t = 1, 2, \ldots, T) \tag{12.59}$$

and that its variance-covariance matrix is given by

$$E(\boldsymbol{\varepsilon}_\mathbf{m}\boldsymbol{\varepsilon}'_\mathbf{m}) = \sigma_{mm}\mathbf{I_T}, \tag{12.60}$$

where $\mathbf{I_T}$ is an identity matrix of order $(T \times T)$. The explanatory variables are taken to be nonstochastic and such that $(\mathbf{X'_m X_m})/T$ is nonsingular and its limit (for $T \to \infty$) exists. This means that each of the equations is expected to satisfy the assumptions of the classical normal linear regression model. Now, suppose further that we cannot rule out the possibility that the regression disturbances in different equations are *mutually correlated*. In this case we have

$$E(\boldsymbol{\varepsilon}_\mathbf{m}\boldsymbol{\varepsilon}'_\mathbf{p}) = \sigma_{mp}\mathbf{I_T} \qquad (m, p = 1, 2, \ldots, M). \tag{12.61}$$

Thus σ_{mp} is the covariance of the disturbances of the mth and the pth equation, which is assumed to be constant over all observations. This covariance represents the *only* link between the mth and the pth equation. Because this link is rather subtle, the system of M equations is called a system of *seemingly unrelated regres-*

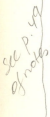

sion equations. Examples of such regressions would be demand functions for various commodities or production functions for different industries, with observations made over time (or over some cross-sectional units). The disturbance in the demand equation for commodity A is likely to be correlated with the disturbance in the demand equations for commodities B, C, etc. Similarly, the disturbance in the production function for one industry may be correlated with the disturbances in the production functions for other industries. Note that if the regression equations (12.58) are such that the regression coefficients in each equation are the *same* as the regression coefficients in any other equation, the whole system would reduce to a single equation, and the observations would represent pooled cross-section and time-series data.

Estimation When the Variance–Covariance Matrix Is Known

Let us now turn to the problem of estimating the coefficients of the seemingly unrelated regression equations. One possible approach is to apply the ordinary least squares method to each equation separately. This would give

$$\hat{\boldsymbol{\beta}}_{\mathbf{m}} = (\mathbf{X}'_{\mathbf{m}}\mathbf{X}_{\mathbf{m}})^{-1}(\mathbf{X}'_{\mathbf{m}}\mathbf{y}_{\mathbf{m}})$$

and
$$E(\hat{\boldsymbol{\beta}}_{\mathbf{m}} - \boldsymbol{\beta}_{\mathbf{m}})(\hat{\boldsymbol{\beta}}_{\mathbf{m}} - \boldsymbol{\beta}_{\mathbf{m}})' = \sigma_{mm}(\mathbf{X}'_{\mathbf{m}}\mathbf{X}_{\mathbf{m}})^{-1}.$$

Note that

$$E(\hat{\boldsymbol{\beta}}_{\mathbf{m}}) = \boldsymbol{\beta}_{\mathbf{m}} + E(\mathbf{X}'_{\mathbf{m}}\mathbf{X}_{\mathbf{m}})^{-1}(\mathbf{X}'_{\mathbf{m}}\boldsymbol{\varepsilon}_{\mathbf{m}}) = \boldsymbol{\beta}_{\mathbf{m}}$$

and
$$\text{plim}\ \hat{\boldsymbol{\beta}}_{\mathbf{m}} = \boldsymbol{\beta}_{\mathbf{m}} + \text{plim}\left[\frac{1}{T}\mathbf{X}'_{\mathbf{m}}\mathbf{X}_{\mathbf{m}}\right]^{-1}\left[\frac{1}{T}\mathbf{X}'_{\mathbf{m}}\boldsymbol{\varepsilon}_{\mathbf{m}}\right] = \boldsymbol{\beta}_{\mathbf{m}},$$

which means that the ordinary least squares estimators of the regression coefficients are unbiased and consistent. Thus the major question is that of efficiency. By estimating each equation separately and independently, we are disregarding the information about the mutual correlation of the disturbances, and the efficiency of the estimators becomes questionable.

To take into account the correlation of the disturbances across equations, we compress (12.58) into one big equation:

$$\begin{bmatrix} \mathbf{y}_1 \\ \mathbf{y}_2 \\ \vdots \\ \mathbf{y}_M \end{bmatrix} = \begin{bmatrix} \mathbf{X}_1 & \mathbf{0} & \cdots & \mathbf{0} \\ \mathbf{0} & \mathbf{X}_2 & \cdots & \mathbf{0} \\ \vdots & \vdots & & \vdots \\ \mathbf{0} & \mathbf{0} & \cdots & \mathbf{X}_M \end{bmatrix} \begin{bmatrix} \boldsymbol{\beta}_1 \\ \boldsymbol{\beta}_2 \\ \vdots \\ \boldsymbol{\beta}_M \end{bmatrix} + \begin{bmatrix} \boldsymbol{\varepsilon}_1 \\ \boldsymbol{\varepsilon}_2 \\ \vdots \\ \boldsymbol{\varepsilon}_M \end{bmatrix}. \tag{12.62a}$$

This can be written more compactly as

$$\mathbf{y} = \mathbf{X}\boldsymbol{\beta} + \boldsymbol{\varepsilon}, \tag{12.62b}$$

where $\mathbf{y}$ is a $(MT \times 1)$ vector, $\mathbf{X}$ is a $(MT \times \Sigma_{m=1}^{M} K_m)$ matrix, $\boldsymbol{\beta}$ is a $(\Sigma_{m=1}^{M} K_m \times 1)$ matrix, and the dimension of $\boldsymbol{\varepsilon}$ is $(MT \times 1)$. Note that, by the assumptions (12.59) through (12.61), the variance-covariance matrix of $\boldsymbol{\varepsilon}$ is

(12.63)

$$\boldsymbol{\Omega} = E(\boldsymbol{\varepsilon\varepsilon}')$$

$$= \begin{bmatrix} E(\boldsymbol{\varepsilon}_1\boldsymbol{\varepsilon}_1') & E(\boldsymbol{\varepsilon}_1\boldsymbol{\varepsilon}_2') & \cdots & E(\boldsymbol{\varepsilon}_1\boldsymbol{\varepsilon}_{\mathbf{M}}') \\ E(\boldsymbol{\varepsilon}_2\boldsymbol{\varepsilon}_1') & E(\boldsymbol{\varepsilon}_2\boldsymbol{\varepsilon}_2') & \cdots & E(\boldsymbol{\varepsilon}_2\boldsymbol{\varepsilon}_{\mathbf{M}}') \\ \vdots & \vdots & & \vdots \\ E(\boldsymbol{\varepsilon}_{\mathbf{M}}\boldsymbol{\varepsilon}_1') & E(\boldsymbol{\varepsilon}_{\mathbf{M}}\boldsymbol{\varepsilon}_2') & \cdots & E(\boldsymbol{\varepsilon}_{\mathbf{M}}\boldsymbol{\varepsilon}_{\mathbf{M}}') \end{bmatrix} \begin{bmatrix} \sigma_{11}\mathbf{I_T} & \sigma_{12}\mathbf{I_T} & \cdots & \sigma_{1M}\mathbf{I_T} \\ \sigma_{21}\mathbf{I_T} & \sigma_{22}\mathbf{I_T} & \cdots & \sigma_{2M}\mathbf{I_T} \\ \vdots & \vdots & & \vdots \\ \sigma_{M1}\mathbf{I_T} & \sigma_{M2}\mathbf{I_T} & \cdots & \sigma_{MM}\mathbf{I_T} \end{bmatrix},$$

where, as before, $\mathbf{I_T}$ is an identity matrix of order $(T \times T)$. The information about the correlation of the disturbances across equations is then contained in the description of the $\boldsymbol{\Omega}$ matrix, and it can be taken into account in that form.

The equation (12.62b), together with the assumptions about $\mathbf{X}$ and $\boldsymbol{\varepsilon}$, can be viewed as a generalized linear regression model (discussed in Section 12-1). The best linear unbiased estimator of $\boldsymbol{\beta}$ for this model is given by the generalized least squares formula as

$$\tilde{\boldsymbol{\beta}} = (\mathbf{X}'\boldsymbol{\Omega}^{-1}\mathbf{X})^{-1}(\mathbf{X}'\boldsymbol{\Omega}^{-1}\mathbf{y}). \tag{12.64}$$

In the context of the seemingly unrelated regressions, this becomes

(12.64a)

$$\tilde{\boldsymbol{\beta}} = \begin{bmatrix} \sigma^{11}(\mathbf{X}_1'\mathbf{X}_1) & \sigma^{12}(\mathbf{X}_1'\mathbf{X}_2) & \cdots & \sigma^{1M}(\mathbf{X}_1'\mathbf{X}_{\mathbf{M}}) \\ \sigma^{21}(\mathbf{X}_2'\mathbf{X}_1) & \sigma^{22}(\mathbf{X}_2'\mathbf{X}_2) & \cdots & \sigma^{2M}(\mathbf{X}_2'\mathbf{X}_{\mathbf{M}}) \\ \vdots & \vdots & \cdots & \vdots \\ \sigma^{M1}(\mathbf{X}_{\mathbf{M}}'\mathbf{X}_1) & \sigma^{M2}(\mathbf{X}_{\mathbf{M}}'\mathbf{X}_2) & \cdots & \sigma^{MM}(\mathbf{X}_{\mathbf{M}}'\mathbf{X}_{\mathbf{M}}) \end{bmatrix}^{-1} \begin{bmatrix} \sum_{m=1}^{M} \sigma^{1m}(\mathbf{X}_1'\mathbf{y}_{\mathbf{m}}) \\ \sum_{m=1}^{M} \sigma^{2m}(\mathbf{X}_2'\mathbf{y}_{\mathbf{m}}) \\ \vdots \\ \sum_{m=1}^{M} \sigma^{Mm}(\mathbf{X}_{\mathbf{m}}'\mathbf{y}_{\mathbf{m}}) \end{bmatrix}$$

where σ^{mp} represents the element that appears in the mth row and pth column of the inverse of the matrix

$$\begin{bmatrix} \sigma_{11} & \sigma_{12} & \cdots & \sigma_{1M} \\ \sigma_{21} & \sigma_{22} & \cdots & \sigma_{2M} \\ \vdots & \vdots & & \vdots \\ \sigma_{M1} & \sigma_{M2} & \cdots & \sigma_{MM} \end{bmatrix}.$$

Further, the variance-covariance matrix of $\tilde{\boldsymbol{\beta}}$ is given by

$$E(\tilde{\boldsymbol{\beta}} - \boldsymbol{\beta})(\tilde{\boldsymbol{\beta}} - \boldsymbol{\beta})' = (\mathbf{X}'\boldsymbol{\Omega}^{-1}\mathbf{X})^{-1}. \tag{12.65}$$

Under the assumption of normality, $\tilde{\boldsymbol{\beta}}$ also represents the maximum likelihood estimator of $\boldsymbol{\beta}$. Since the ordinary least squares estimator of $\boldsymbol{\beta}$ is

$$\hat{\boldsymbol{\beta}} = (\mathbf{X}'\mathbf{X})^{-1}(\mathbf{X}'\mathbf{y}),$$

which is, in general, different from $\tilde{\boldsymbol{\beta}}$, ordinary least squares estimation of the seemingly unrelated regressions is *not efficient.*

An interesting question concerning the application of the generalized least squares estimator to seemingly unrelated regressions relates to the special conditions under which this estimator is, in fact, equivalent to the ordinary least squares estimator. One such obvious case exists when the equations are not seemingly but *actually* unrelated; i.e., when $\sigma_{mp} = 0$ for all $m \neq p$. In this case $\tilde{\boldsymbol{\beta}}$ becomes

$$\tilde{\boldsymbol{\beta}} = \begin{bmatrix} \sigma^{11}(\mathbf{X}_1'\mathbf{X}_1) & 0 & \cdots & 0 \\ 0 & \sigma^{22}(\mathbf{X}_2'\mathbf{X}_2) & \cdots & 0 \\ \vdots & \vdots & & \vdots \\ 0 & 0 & \cdots & \sigma^{MM}(\mathbf{X}_M'\mathbf{X}_M) \end{bmatrix}^{-1} \begin{bmatrix} \sigma^{11}(\mathbf{X}_1'\mathbf{y}_1) \\ \sigma^{22}(\mathbf{X}_2'\mathbf{y}_2) \\ \vdots \\ \sigma^{MM}(\mathbf{X}_M'\mathbf{y}_M) \end{bmatrix}$$
$$= (\mathbf{X}'\mathbf{X})^{-1}(\mathbf{X}'\mathbf{y}),$$

which is the formula for the least squares estimator. The two estimators are also equivalent when each of the seemingly unrelated regressions involves exactly the *same* values of the same explanatory variables; i.e., when $\mathbf{X}_m = \mathbf{X}_p$ for all m and p. We shall prove the equivalence of the generalized and ordinary least squares formulas in this case for a set of two equations, but the proof can be extended to any number of equations. (The proof could also be extended to where $\mathbf{X}_m$ and $\mathbf{X}_p$ are not exactly the same but $\mathbf{X}_m$ is a linear combination of $\mathbf{X}_p$.) Now, for $M = 2$ and $\mathbf{X}_1 = \mathbf{X}_2$, the generalized estimator is

$$\begin{bmatrix} \tilde{\boldsymbol{\beta}}_1 \\ \tilde{\boldsymbol{\beta}}_2 \end{bmatrix} = \begin{bmatrix} \sigma^{11}(\mathbf{X}_1'\mathbf{X}_1) & \sigma^{12}(\mathbf{X}_1'\mathbf{X}_1) \\ \sigma^{21}(\mathbf{X}_1'\mathbf{X}_1) & \sigma^{22}(\mathbf{X}_1'\mathbf{X}_1) \end{bmatrix}^{-1} \begin{bmatrix} \sigma^{11}(\mathbf{X}_1'\mathbf{y}_1) + \sigma^{12}(\mathbf{X}_1'\mathbf{y}_2) \\ \sigma^{21}(\mathbf{X}_1'\mathbf{y}_1) + \sigma^{22}(\mathbf{X}_1'\mathbf{y}_2) \end{bmatrix},$$

or

$$\begin{bmatrix} \sigma^{11}(\mathbf{X}_1'\mathbf{X}_1)\tilde{\boldsymbol{\beta}}_1 + \sigma^{12}(\mathbf{X}_1'\mathbf{X}_1)\tilde{\boldsymbol{\beta}}_2 \\ \sigma^{21}(\mathbf{X}_1'\mathbf{X}_1)\tilde{\boldsymbol{\beta}}_1 + \sigma^{22}(\mathbf{X}_1'\mathbf{X}_1)\tilde{\boldsymbol{\beta}}_2 \end{bmatrix} = \begin{bmatrix} \sigma^{11}(\mathbf{X}_1'\mathbf{y}_1) + \sigma^{12}(\mathbf{X}_1'\mathbf{y}_2) \\ \sigma^{21}(\mathbf{X}_1'\mathbf{y}_1) + \sigma^{22}(\mathbf{X}_1'\mathbf{y}_2) \end{bmatrix}.$$

But

$$\begin{bmatrix} \sigma^{11} & \sigma^{12} \\ \sigma^{21} & \sigma^{22} \end{bmatrix} = \begin{bmatrix} \sigma_{11} & \sigma_{12} \\ \sigma_{12} & \sigma_{22} \end{bmatrix}^{-1} = \frac{1}{\sigma_{11}\sigma_{22} - \sigma_{12}^2} \begin{bmatrix} \sigma_{22} & -\sigma_{12} \\ -\sigma_{12} & \sigma_{11} \end{bmatrix},$$

so that we have

$$\sigma_{22}(\mathbf{X}_1'\mathbf{X}_1)\tilde{\boldsymbol{\beta}}_1 - \sigma_{12}(\mathbf{X}_1'\mathbf{X}_1)\tilde{\boldsymbol{\beta}}_2 = \sigma_{22}(\mathbf{X}_1'\mathbf{y}_1) - \sigma_{12}(\mathbf{X}_1'\mathbf{y}_2),$$
$$-\sigma_{12}(\mathbf{X}_1'\mathbf{X}_1)\tilde{\boldsymbol{\beta}}_1 + \sigma_{11}(\mathbf{X}_1'\mathbf{X}_1)\tilde{\boldsymbol{\beta}}_2 = -\sigma_{12}(\mathbf{X}_1'\mathbf{y}_1) + \sigma_{11}(\mathbf{X}_1'\mathbf{y}_2).$$

The solution for $\tilde{\boldsymbol{\beta}}_1$ and $\tilde{\boldsymbol{\beta}}_2$ is then

$$\tilde{\boldsymbol{\beta}}_1 = (\mathbf{X}_1'\mathbf{X}_1)^{-1}(\mathbf{X}_1'\mathbf{y}_1) \qquad \text{and} \qquad \tilde{\boldsymbol{\beta}}_2 = (\mathbf{X}_1'\mathbf{X}_1)^{-1}(\mathbf{X}_1'\mathbf{y}_2),$$

which is the same as the ordinary least squares results. Finally, when in a system of two equations the $\mathbf{X}_2$ matrix of the second equation is a submatrix of the $\mathbf{X}_1$ matrix of the first equation, i.e., when $\mathbf{X}_1 = [\mathbf{X}_2\mathbf{X}_1^*]$, then the generalized least squares estimator of $\boldsymbol{\beta}_2$ is equal to the ordinary least squares estimator. (The generalized least squares estimator of $\boldsymbol{\beta}_1$, however, is different from the ordinary least squares estimator.)[23]

In deriving the BLUE of the generalized linear regression model in Section 12-1, we transformed the regression equation to obtain a disturbance that would satisfy all classical assumptions. Specific transformation matrices were determined for the heteroskedastic and the autoregressive disturbances in Section 12-1, and transformations appropriate for various models involving pooled cross-section and time-series data were discussed in Section 12-2. A suitable transformation can also be found for seemingly unrelated regressions.[24] Let us consider two seemingly unrelated regressions transformed as follows.

$$(12.66)\qquad \begin{bmatrix} \mathbf{I} & \mathbf{0} \\ a_1\mathbf{I} & a_2\mathbf{I} \end{bmatrix} \begin{bmatrix} \mathbf{y}_1 \\ \mathbf{y}_2 \end{bmatrix} = \begin{bmatrix} \mathbf{I} & \mathbf{0} \\ a_1\mathbf{I} & a_2\mathbf{I} \end{bmatrix} \begin{bmatrix} \mathbf{X}_1 & \mathbf{0} \\ \mathbf{0} & \mathbf{X}_2 \end{bmatrix} \begin{bmatrix} \boldsymbol{\beta}_1 \\ \boldsymbol{\beta}_2 \end{bmatrix} + \begin{bmatrix} \mathbf{I} & \mathbf{0} \\ a_1\mathbf{I} & a_2\mathbf{I} \end{bmatrix} \begin{bmatrix} \boldsymbol{\varepsilon}_1 \\ \boldsymbol{\varepsilon}_2 \end{bmatrix}$$

where a_1 and a_2 are constants (scalars) to be determined. For the transformation to yield the desired result we require that

$$\begin{bmatrix} 1 & 0 \\ a_1 & a_2 \end{bmatrix} \begin{bmatrix} \varepsilon_{1t} \\ \varepsilon_{2t} \end{bmatrix} = \begin{bmatrix} v_{1t} \\ v_{2t} \end{bmatrix},$$

where

1. $E(v_{1t}) = E(v_{2t}) = 0$,
2. $\text{Var}(v_{1t}) = \text{Var}(v_{2t}) = \sigma_{11}$,
3. $\text{Cov}(v_{1t}, v_{2t}) = 0$.

Condition (1) is automatically fulfilled by virtue of the assumptions concerning $\boldsymbol{\varepsilon}$. Condition (2) leads to

$$\text{Var}(\varepsilon_{1t}) = \sigma_{11},$$

$$a_1^2\text{Var}(\varepsilon_{1t}) + a_2^2\text{Var}(\varepsilon_{2t}) + 2a_1a_2\text{Cov}(\varepsilon_{1t}, \varepsilon_{2t}) = \text{Var}(v_{1t}),$$

or

$$(12.67a)\qquad a_1^2\sigma_{11} + a_2^2\sigma_{22} + 2a_1a_2\sigma_{12} = \sigma_{11}.$$

Condition (3) yields

$$\text{Cov}(\varepsilon_{1t}, a_1\varepsilon_{1t} + a_2\varepsilon_{2t}) = 0$$

[23] N. S. Revankar, "Some Finite Sample Results in the Context of Two Seemingly Unrelated Regression Equations", *Journal of the American Statistical Association,* 69 (March 1974), pp. 183–188.

[24] R. W. Bacon, "A Simplified Exposition of Seemingly Unrelated Regressions and the Three Stage Least Squares", *Oxford Bulletin of Economics and Statistics,* 36 (August 1974), pp. 229–233.

or

(12.67b) $$a_1\sigma_{11} + a_2\sigma_{12} = 0.$$

Solving (12.67a) and (12.67b) for a_1 and a_2, we obtain

(12.68) $$a_1 = \pm\sqrt{\frac{\rho^2}{1-\rho^2}}, \quad \text{and} \quad a_2 = \mp\sqrt{\frac{\sigma_{11}}{\sigma_{22}(1-\rho^2)}},$$

where $\rho = \sigma_{12}/\sqrt{\sigma_{11}\sigma_{22}}$. The transformed system then becomes

(12.69) $$\begin{bmatrix} \mathbf{y}_1 \\ a_1\mathbf{y}_1 + a_2\mathbf{y}_2 \end{bmatrix} = \begin{bmatrix} \mathbf{X}_1 & \mathbf{0} \\ a_1\mathbf{X}_1 & a_2\mathbf{X}_2 \end{bmatrix}\begin{bmatrix} \boldsymbol{\beta}_1 \\ \boldsymbol{\beta}_2 \end{bmatrix} + \begin{bmatrix} \mathbf{v}_1 \\ \mathbf{v}_2 \end{bmatrix}.$$

If a_1 and a_2 were known, an application of ordinary least squares to (12.69) would yield generalized least squares estimates. The transformation could be extended to more than two equations in a straightforward manner.

Because the generalized least squares estimator is BLUE, its variance is smaller than, or at best equal to, the variance of the ordinary least squares estimator. It is appropriate then to ask what the difference between variances is and on what it depends. We shall answer by reference to the simple system of two seemingly unrelated regressions given as

(12.70) $$Y_{1t} = \beta_{11} + \beta_{12}X_{1t} + \varepsilon_{1t},$$
$$Y_{2t} = \beta_{21} + \beta_{22}X_{2t} + \varepsilon_{2t},$$

Note that the variance-covariance matrix of the generalized least squares estimators of β_{12} and β_{22} is

$$E(\underline{\tilde{\beta}} - \underline{\beta})(\underline{\tilde{\beta}} - \underline{\beta}) = (\underline{\mathbf{X}}'\boldsymbol{\Omega}^{-1}\underline{\mathbf{X}})^{-1}.$$

In this case

$$(\underline{\tilde{\beta}} - \underline{\beta}) = \begin{bmatrix} \tilde{\beta}_{12} - \beta_{12} \\ \tilde{\beta}_{22} - \beta_{22} \end{bmatrix} \quad \text{and} \quad \underline{\mathbf{X}} = \begin{bmatrix} (X_{11} - \bar{X}_1) & 0 \\ (X_{12} - \bar{X}_1) & 0 \\ \vdots & \vdots \\ (X_{1T} - \bar{X}_1) & 0 \\ 0 & (X_{21} - \bar{X}_2) \\ 0 & (X_{22} - \bar{X}_2) \\ \vdots & \vdots \\ 0 & (X_{2T} - \bar{X}_2) \end{bmatrix}.$$

This means that

$$\begin{bmatrix} \mathrm{Var}(\tilde{\beta}_{12}) & \mathrm{Cov}(\tilde{\beta}_{12}, \tilde{\beta}_{22}) \\ \mathrm{Cov}(\tilde{\beta}_{12}, \tilde{\beta}_{22}) & \mathrm{Var}(\tilde{\beta}_{22}) \end{bmatrix} = (\sigma_{11}\sigma_{22} - \sigma_{12}^2)\begin{bmatrix} \sigma_{22}m_{X_1X_1} & -\sigma_{12}m_{X_1X_2} \\ -\sigma_{12}m_{X_1X_2} & \sigma_{11}m_{X_2X_2} \end{bmatrix}^{-1}.$$

In particular, the variance of the generalized least squares estimator of β_{12} is

$$\text{(12.71)} \qquad \mathrm{Var}(\tilde{\beta}_{12}) = \frac{(\sigma_{11}\sigma_{22} - \sigma_{12}^2)\sigma_{11} m_{X_2X_2}}{\sigma_{11}\sigma_{22} m_{X_1X_1} m_{X_2X_2} - \sigma_{12}^2 m_{X_1X_2}^2}.$$

If we let

$$\rho_{12} = \frac{\sigma_{12}}{\sqrt{\sigma_{11}\sigma_{22}}}$$

represent the coefficient of correlation between ε_{1t} and ε_{2t}, and if we let

$$r_{12} = \frac{m_{X_1X_2}}{\sqrt{m_{X_1X_1} m_{X_2X_2}}}$$

represent the sample coefficient of correlation between X_{1t} and X_{2t}, then we can write

$$\mathrm{Var}(\tilde{\beta}_{12}) = \frac{\sigma_{11}\sigma_{22}(1 - \rho_{12}^2)\sigma_{11} m_{X_2X_2}}{\sigma_{11}\sigma_{22}(1 - \rho_{12}^2 r_{12}^2) m_{X_1X_1} m_{X_2X_2}} = \frac{\sigma_{11}}{m_{X_1X_1}}\left(\frac{1 - \rho_{12}^2}{1 - \rho_{12}^2 r_{12}^2}\right).$$

On the other hand, the variance of the ordinary least squares estimator of β_{12}, say, $\hat{\beta}_{12}$, is

$$\mathrm{Var}(\hat{\beta}_{12}) = \frac{\sigma_{11}}{m_{X_1X_1}}.$$

Therefore, the ratio of the two variances is

$$\text{(12.72)} \qquad \frac{\mathrm{Var}(\tilde{\beta}_{12})}{\mathrm{Var}(\hat{\beta}_{12})} = \frac{1 - \rho_{12}^2}{1 - \rho_{12}^2 r_{12}^2} \leq 1.$$

This ratio is a decreasing function of ρ_{12}^2 and an increasing function of r_{12}^2. This means that the gain in efficiency of the generalized least squares estimator over the ordinary squares estimator is greatest when the disturbances in the two equations are highly correlated and, at the same time, the explanatory variables are uncorrelated. Table 12-1 gives the values of the ratio $\mathrm{Var}(\tilde{\beta}_{12})/\mathrm{Var}(\hat{\beta}_{12})$ for different

Table 12-1

	ρ_{12}^2					
r_{12}^2	0	0.1	0.3	0.5	0.7	0.9
0	1.000	0.900	0.700	0.500	0.300	0.100
0.1	1.000	0.909	0.722	0.526	0.323	0.110
0.3	1.000	0.928	0.769	0.588	0.380	0.137
0.5	1.000	0.947	0.823	0.667	0.461	0.182
0.7	1.000	0.967	0.886	0.769	0.588	0.270
0.9	1.000	0.989	0.959	0.909	0.811	0.526
1.0	1.000	1.000	1.000	1.000	1.000	1.000

values of ρ_{12}^2 and r_{12}^2. Clearly, the gain in efficiency is in many cases very substantial. These results could be extended to a more complex system of seemingly unrelated regressions as well.

Estimation When the Variance-Covariance Matrix Is Unknown

In the preceding discussion we assumed that the elements of the $\mathbf{\Omega}$ matrix (i.e., the variances and covariances of the regression disturbances) are known. However, if they are not known, as is generally the case, we can replace $\mathbf{\Omega}$ by a consistent estimator of $\mathbf{\Omega}$. As pointed out in Section 12-1, the resulting estimator of $\boldsymbol{\beta}$ has—under general conditions—the same asymptotic properties as the generalized least squares estimator. Our problem, then, is to find consistent estimators of the variances and covariances of the regression disturbances. One possibility is to estimate these variances and covariances from ordinary least squares residuals (which we call e_{mt}) as suggested by Zellner in his path-breaking paper.[25] For this, we may use

$$\hat{\mathbf{\Omega}} = \begin{bmatrix} s_{11}\mathbf{I_T} & s_{12}\mathbf{I_T} & \cdots & s_{1M}\mathbf{I_T} \\ s_{21}\mathbf{I_T} & s_{22}\mathbf{I_T} & \cdots & s_{2M}\mathbf{I_T} \\ \vdots & \vdots & & \vdots \\ s_{M1}\mathbf{I_T} & s_{M2}\mathbf{I_T} & \cdots & s_{MM}\mathbf{I_T} \end{bmatrix}, \tag{12.73}$$

where

$$s_{mp} = \frac{1}{T-K_m}\sum_{t=1}^{T} e_{mt}e_{pt},$$
$$K_m \geq K_p,$$
$$m, p = 1, 2, \ldots, M.$$

It is well known that s_{mm} is an unbiased and consistent estimator of σ_{mm}, and it can be shown that s_{mp} $(m \neq p)$ is a consistent estimator of σ_{mp}. [Since we are only concerned with consistency, we could use T instead of $(T - K_m)$ in calculating the estimates of σ_{mp} without affecting the asymptotic properties of the estimator of $\boldsymbol{\beta}$. Many computer programs give users a choice of division by T or by $(T - K)$.] The resulting estimator of $\boldsymbol{\beta}$ is

$$\tilde{\tilde{\boldsymbol{\beta}}} = (\mathbf{X}'\hat{\mathbf{\Omega}}^{-1}\mathbf{X})^{-1}(\mathbf{X}'\hat{\mathbf{\Omega}}^{-1}\mathbf{y}) \tag{12.74}$$

and

$$\text{Asympt. Var-Cov}(\tilde{\tilde{\boldsymbol{\beta}}}) = (\mathbf{X}'\mathbf{\Omega}^{-1}\mathbf{X})^{-1}. \tag{12.75}$$

The two-stage Aitken estimator of $\boldsymbol{\beta}$ is asymptotically equivalent to the generalized

[25] A. Zellner, "An Efficient Method of Estimating Seemingly Unrelated Regressions and Tests for Aggregation Bias," *Journal of the American Statistical Association,* 57 (June 1962), pp. 348–368.

least squares estimator and, therefore, to the maximum likelihood estimator of $\boldsymbol{\beta}$. Thus this estimator is asymptotically efficient and its asymptotic distribution is normal. With respect to the small sample properties of the two-stage Aitken estimator, we have some theoretical and some experimental results indicating that this estimator is unbiased and efficient relative to the ordinary least squares estimator.[26]

An alternative approach to the problem of estimating the elements of $\boldsymbol{\Omega}$ is to use the maximum likelihood method. In accordance with (12.19), the log likelihood function for $\mathbf{y}$ in the context of seemingly unrelated regressions is

$$(12.76) \qquad L = -\frac{MT}{2}\log(2\pi) - \tfrac{1}{2}\log|\boldsymbol{\Omega}| - \tfrac{1}{2}(\mathbf{y} - \mathbf{X}\boldsymbol{\beta})'\boldsymbol{\Omega}^{-1}(\mathbf{y} - \mathbf{X}\boldsymbol{\beta}).$$

We can differentiate L with respect to the elements of $\boldsymbol{\beta}$ *and* $\boldsymbol{\Omega}$, set the resulting derivatives equal to zero, and then solve for the values of the unknown parameters. The maximum likelihood estimators of $\boldsymbol{\beta}$ and $\boldsymbol{\Omega}$ then are

$$(12.77) \qquad \hat{\boldsymbol{\beta}} = (\mathbf{X}'\hat{\boldsymbol{\Omega}}^{-1}\mathbf{X})^{-1}(\mathbf{X}'\hat{\boldsymbol{\Omega}}^{-1}\mathbf{y}),$$

$$\hat{\boldsymbol{\Omega}} = \begin{bmatrix} \hat{\sigma}_{11}\mathbf{I}_T & \hat{\sigma}_{12}\mathbf{I}_T & \cdots & \hat{\sigma}_{1M}\mathbf{I}_T \\ \hat{\sigma}_{21}\mathbf{I}_T & \hat{\sigma}_{22}\mathbf{I}_T & \cdots & \hat{\sigma}_{2M}\mathbf{I}_T \\ \vdots & \vdots & & \vdots \\ \hat{\sigma}_{M1}\mathbf{I}_T & \hat{\sigma}_{M2}\mathbf{I}_T & \cdots & \hat{\sigma}_{MM}\mathbf{I}_T \end{bmatrix},$$

where

$$\hat{\sigma}_{mp} = \frac{1}{T}(\mathbf{y_m} - \mathbf{X_m}\hat{\boldsymbol{\beta}}_\mathbf{m})'(\mathbf{y_p} - \mathbf{X_p}\hat{\boldsymbol{\beta}}_\mathbf{p}),$$

$$m, p = 1, 2, \ldots, M.$$

The analytical solution of (12.77) is quite complicated since the equations are nonlinear in the unknowns, but it can be obtained by starting with the two-stage Aitken estimator and iterating until convergence is reached.[27]

The maximum likelihood estimator can also be used for the purpose of testing the hypothesis that $\boldsymbol{\Omega}$ is a diagonal matrix, i.e., that the regression equations are *actually*—and not just seemingly—unrelated. A suitable test would be a likelihood ratio test discussed in Section 11-2. The application of this test would involve a comparison of the values of the likelihood functions when the regression coefficients are estimated by ordinary least squares and when they are estimated by $\hat{\boldsymbol{\beta}}$ of (12.77).

[26] See A. Zellner, "Estimators of Seemingly Unrelated Regressions: Some Exact Finite Sample Results," *Journal of the American Statistical Association,* 58 (December 1963), pp. 977–992; N. C. Kakwani, *op. cit.;* J. Kmenta and R. F. Gilbert, "Small Sample Properties of Alternative Estimators of Seemingly Unrelated Regressions," *Journal of the American Statistical Association,* 63 (December 1968), pp. 1180–1200.; N. S. Revankar, "Use of Restricted Residuals in SUR Systems: Some Finite Sample Results," *Journal of the American Statistical Association,* 71 (March 1976), pp. 183–188.

[27] Kmenta and Gilbert, *op. cit.* Another estimator that gives exactly the same results as MLE for *all* sample sizes is the estimator proposed by L. G. Telser, "Iterative Estimation of a Set of Linear Regression Equations," *Journal of the American Statistical Association,* 59 (Sept. 1964), pp. 845–862.

EXAMPLE As an example of seemingly unrelated regressions, consider the following set of investment functions for individual firms:

$$I_t = \beta_{m1} + \beta_{m2}C_{t-1} + \beta_{m3}F_{t-1} + \varepsilon_{mt},$$

where I = gross investment, C = end-of-period capital stock, and F = end-of-period value of outstanding shares. Estimates for General Electric and Westinghouse were based on annual data for 1935–1954.[28]

General Electric

OLS: $$I_t = \underset{(31.3742)}{-9.9563} + \underset{(0.0257)}{0.1517}C_{t-1} + \underset{(0.0156)}{0.0266}F_{t-1} + e_t,$$

2-S Aitken: $$I_t = \underset{(29.3212)}{-27.7193} + \underset{(0.0250)}{0.1390}C_{t-1} + \underset{(0.0145)}{0.0383}F_{t-1} + e_t,$$

ML: $$I_t = \underset{(29.6608)}{-30.7485} + \underset{(0.0255)}{0.1359}C_{t-1} + \underset{(0.0145)}{0.0405}F_{t-1} + e_t;$$

Westinghouse

OLS: $$I_t = \underset{(8.0153)}{-0.5094} + \underset{(0.0561)}{0.0924}C_{t-1} + \underset{(0.0157)}{0.0529}F_{t-1} + e_t,$$

2-S Aitken: $$I_t = \underset{(7.5452)}{-1.2520} + \underset{(0.0530)}{0.0640}C_{t-1} + \underset{(0.0145)}{0.0576}F_{t-1} + e_t,$$

ML: $$I_t = \underset{(7.5149)}{-1.7016} + \underset{(0.0529)}{0.0593}C_{t-1} + \underset{(0.0144)}{0.0557}F_{t-1} + e_t.$$

As can be seen, there appears to be some—though by no means a great—gain in efficiency by going from ordinary least squares to two-stage Aitken or maximum likelihood estimation. The reason for this relatively low gain in efficiency is, at least in part, the high degree of correlation between the explanatory variables in the two equations.

A measure of the goodness of fit for seemingly unrelated regressions, devised by McElroy, is denoted by R_z^2 and given as[29]

$$R_z^2 = 1 - \frac{\tilde{\boldsymbol{\varepsilon}}'\hat{\boldsymbol{\Omega}}^{-1}\tilde{\boldsymbol{\varepsilon}}}{\mathbf{y}'\hat{\boldsymbol{\Delta}}^{-1}\mathbf{y}}$$

where $\tilde{\boldsymbol{\varepsilon}}$ is an $(MT \times 1)$ vector of two-stage Aitken residuals, $\hat{\boldsymbol{\Omega}}$ is as defined in (12.73), and $\hat{\Delta}^{-1}$ is the same as $\hat{\Omega}^{-1}$ except that each $\mathbf{I_T}$ gets replaced by $\mathbf{A_T}$, where $\mathbf{A_T} = \mathbf{I_T} - (\iota\iota'/\mathrm{T})$. This measure is confined to the interval from 0 to 1 and is related to the (asymptotic) F test statistic by

$$F_z = \frac{R_z^2}{1 - R_z^2}\left(\frac{MT - K}{K - M}\right)$$

where $K = \Sigma_m K_m$. (For the preceding example $R_z^2 = 0.632$ and $F_{z(4,\,34)} = 14.62$.)

[28] The results are based on the data given in J. C. G. Boot and G. M. deWitt, "Investment Demand: An Empirical Contribution to the Aggregation Problem," *International Economic Review,* 1 (January 1960), pp. 3–30. The estimated standard errors are adjusted for the number of degrees of freedom.

[29] M. B. McElroy, "Goodness of Fit for Seemingly Unrelated Regressions," *Journal of Econometrics,* 6 (November 1977), pp. 381–387.

In the preceding discussion we have only considered the situation in which the number of observations (T) is the same for every equation. However, no great complication arises when the numbers of observations for different equations are not the same.[30] Let us consider a set of two seemingly uncorrelated regression equations with T observations on both equations for the initial period, and T^* additional observations on the second equation for the subsequent period. The $\mathbf{\Omega}$ matrix can then be presented as

$$\mathbf{\Omega} = \begin{bmatrix} \sigma_{11}\mathbf{I_T} & \sigma_{12}\mathbf{I_T} & \mathbf{0} \\ \sigma_{21}\mathbf{I_T} & \sigma_{22}\mathbf{I_T} & \mathbf{0} \\ \mathbf{0} & \mathbf{0} & \sigma_{22}\mathbf{I_{T^*}} \end{bmatrix}. \tag{12.78}$$

The parameters σ_{11} and σ_{12} can be estimated in the usual way using the T available observations, but the question is how to estimate σ_{22}. When T^* is not very large, the simplest way would be to estimate σ_{22} using only the T common observations, since using all $T + T^*$ observations might lead to $\hat{\mathbf{\Omega}}$ that is not positive definite. When T^* is large, then maximum likelihood might be the best solution.

Estimation of Seemingly Unrelated Regressions with Autoregressive Disturbances

As another point connected with the problem of estimating seemingly unrelated regressions, we consider the case where the disturbances in each equation are not independent *over time,* but follow a first-order autoregressive scheme as described in Section 8-3. In this case the assumptions (12.60) and (12.61) stated at the outset of the present section are replaced by

$$E(\boldsymbol{\varepsilon}_\mathbf{m}\boldsymbol{\varepsilon}_\mathbf{m}') = \sigma_{mm} \begin{bmatrix} 1 & \rho_m & \cdots & \rho_m^{T-1} \\ \rho_m & 1 & \cdots & \rho_m^{T-2} \\ \vdots & \vdots & & \vdots \\ \rho_m^{T-1} & \rho_m^{T-2} & \cdots & 1 \end{bmatrix}, \tag{12.79}$$

$$E(\boldsymbol{\varepsilon}_\mathbf{m}\boldsymbol{\varepsilon}_\mathbf{p}') = \sigma_{mp} \begin{bmatrix} 1 & \rho_p & \cdots & \rho_p^{T-1} \\ \rho_m & 1 & \cdots & \rho_p^{T-2} \\ \vdots & \vdots & & \vdots \\ \rho_m^{T-1} & \rho_m^{T-2} & \cdots & 1 \end{bmatrix}, \tag{12.80}$$

$$m, p = 1, 2, \ldots, M,$$

where ρ_m is the coefficient of autocorrelation in the mth equation. Here, we can estimate ρ_m separately for each equation, using one of the consistent methods

[30] P. Schmidt, "Estimation of Seemingly Unrelated Regressions with Unequal Numbers of Observations", *Journal of Econometrics,* 5 (May 1977), pp. 365–377.

described in Section 8-3. Suppose the resulting estimates are called $\hat{\rho}_m$. They can be used to transform the original observations so that the system of seemingly unrelated regressions now becomes

(12.81) $$Y^*_{mt} = \beta_{m1}X^*_{mt,1} + \beta_{m2}X^*_{mt,2} + \cdots + \beta_{mK_m}X^*_{mt,K_m} + u_{mt},$$

where
$$\begin{aligned} Y^*_{mt} &= Y_{mt}\sqrt{1-\hat{\rho}^2_m} && \text{for } t = 1,\\ &= Y_{mt} - \hat{\rho}_m Y_{m,t-1} && \text{for } t = 2, 3, \ldots, T,\\ X^*_{mt,k} &= X_{mt,k}\sqrt{1-\hat{\rho}^2_m} && \text{for } t = 1,\\ &= X_{mt,k} - \hat{\rho}_m X_{m,t-1,k} && \text{for } t = 2, 3, \ldots, T,\\ k &= 1, 2, \ldots, K_m,\\ m &= 1, 2, \ldots, M. \end{aligned}$$

The regressions in (12.81) can be estimated by the two-stage Aitken method in the usual way. The resulting estimates of the regression coefficients have the same asymptotic properties as Aitken's generalized least squares estimates.[31]

A generalization of the preceding model to allow for the so-called *vector autoregressive disturbances* has been proposed by Guilkey and Schmidt.[32] The generalization consists of postulating that the disturbance in each equation depends not only on its *own* lagged value, but also on the lagged values of the disturbances appearing in other equations of the system. For $M = 2$ this would give

(12.82) $$\begin{aligned} \varepsilon_{1t} &= \rho_{11}\varepsilon_{1,t-1} + \rho_{12}\varepsilon_{2,t-1} + u_{1t},\\ \varepsilon_{2t} &= \rho_{21}\varepsilon_{1,t-1} + \rho_{22}\varepsilon_{2,t-1} + u_{2t}. \end{aligned}$$

The specification of autoregression of this form leads to a more complicated Ω matrix than in the case of a simple first-order autoregression, but since the ρs can easily be estimated from the least squares residuals, there is no problem in obtaining two-stage Aitken estimates.

Estimation of Seemingly Unrelated Regressions with Lagged Dependent Variables

So far we have assumed that the *X*s are nonstochastic. This assumption would be violated if the explanatory variables included lagged dependent variables in some or all of the regression equations. If the disturbances in each equation satisfy the classical assumptions, the presence of lagged dependent variables creates no prob-

[31] See R. W. Parks, "Efficient Estimation of a System of Regression Equations when Disturbances are Both Serially and Contemporaneously Correlated,' *Journal of the American Statistical Association,* 62 (June 1967), pp. 500–509; J. Kmenta and R. F. Gilbert, "Estimation of Seemingly Unrelated Regressions with Autoregressive Disturbances," *Journal of the American Statistical Association,* 65 (March 1970), pp. 186–197.

[32] D. K. Guilkey and P. Schmidt, "Estimation of Seemingly Unrelated Regressions with Vector Autoregressive Errors," *Journal of the American Statistical Association,* 68 (September 1973), pp. 642–647.

lem since in this case the asymptotic properties of the two-stage Aitken estimator are not affected. If, however, the disturbances are autoregressive or vector autoregressive, the presence of lagged dependent variables leads to inconsistent least squares estimates, so that the use of least squares residuals results in an inconsistent estimator of $\mathbf{\Omega}$. In this case we may start with instrumental variable residuals (or with residuals based on nonlinear least squares estimates of transformed regression equations) and iterate to obtain maximum likelihood estimates, which are consistent and asymptotically efficient.[33]

EXERCISES

12-1. Consider a regression equation to be estimated from observations on N households for 2 consecutive periods of time. Assume that the regression disturbances are cross-sectionally uncorrelated but timewise autoregressive with $\rho_i = \rho_j$ for all i, j.

a. Determine the elements of $\mathbf{\Omega}$ (the variance-covariance matrix of the regression disturbances).

b. Devise an estimation procedure that would lead to a consistent estimator of $\mathbf{\Omega}$.

c. Devise a transformation of the observations that would enable us to use the ordinary least squares method to get asymptotically efficient estimates of the regression coefficients.

12-2. A regression model to be estimated from pooled cross-section and time-series data is given by

$$Y_{it} = \beta X_{it} + \varepsilon_{it} \qquad (t = 1, 2, \ldots, 21; i = 1, 2).$$

Alternatively, we may write

$$\begin{bmatrix} \mathbf{y}_1 \\ \mathbf{y}_2 \end{bmatrix} = \begin{bmatrix} \mathbf{X}_1 \\ \mathbf{X}_2 \end{bmatrix} \beta + \begin{bmatrix} \boldsymbol{\varepsilon}_1 \\ \boldsymbol{\varepsilon}_2 \end{bmatrix},$$

where $\mathbf{y}_i \rightarrow (21 \times 1)$, $\mathbf{X}_i \rightarrow (21 \times 1)$, $\boldsymbol{\varepsilon}_i \rightarrow (21 \times 1)$, and β is a scalar. Assume that the Xs are nonstochastic and bounded and that

$$E(\varepsilon_{it}) = 0,$$

$$E(\varepsilon_{it}\varepsilon_{is}) = 0 \qquad (t \neq s),$$

$$E(\varepsilon_{it}\varepsilon_{jt}) = \sigma_{ij}.$$

The sample data are given as follows.

$$\mathbf{X}_1'\mathbf{X}_1 = 10, \qquad \mathbf{X}_1'\mathbf{y}_1 = 10, \qquad \mathbf{y}_1'\mathbf{y}_1 = 13.90,$$

$$\mathbf{X}_1'\mathbf{X}_2 = 8, \qquad \mathbf{X}_1'\mathbf{y}_2 = 8, \qquad \mathbf{y}_1'\mathbf{y}_2 = 11.92,$$

$$\mathbf{X}_2'\mathbf{X}_2 = 10, \qquad \mathbf{X}_2'\mathbf{y}_1 = 8, \qquad \mathbf{y}_2'\mathbf{y}_2 = 12.30.$$

$$\mathbf{X}_2'\mathbf{y}_2 = 8,$$

Obtain an asymptotically efficient estimate of β and its estimated standard error.

[33] A. C. Harvey, *The Econometric Analysis of Time Series* (New York: Halsted Press, 1981), pp. 296–298.

12-3. Consider the following two regression equations.

$$\begin{aligned} Y_{1t} &= \beta_1 X_{1t} + \varepsilon_{1t} \\ Y_{2t} &= \beta_2 X_{2t} + \varepsilon_{2t} \end{aligned} \qquad (t = 1, 2, \ldots, 21).$$

Assume that the Xs are nonstochastic and bounded, and that

$$\begin{aligned} \varepsilon_{it} &\sim N(0, \sigma_{ii}) && (i = 1, 2), \\ E(\varepsilon_{it}\varepsilon_{is}) &= 0 && (t \neq s), \\ E(\varepsilon_{it}\varepsilon_{jt}) &= \sigma_{ij} && (i, j = 1, 2). \end{aligned}$$

The sample results are

$$\begin{aligned} &\sum X_{1t}^2 = 10, && \sum X_{1t}Y_{1t} = 10, && \sum Y_{1t}^2 = 12.0, \\ &\sum X_{2t}^2 = 10, && \sum X_{1t}Y_{2t} = 8, && \sum Y_{2t}^2 = 12.4, \\ &\sum X_{1t}X_{2t} = 8, && \sum X_{2t}Y_{1t} = 8, && \sum Y_{1t}Y_{2t} = 10.0. \\ & && \sum X_{2t}Y_{2t} = 8, && \end{aligned}$$

Find asymptotically efficient estimates of the regression coefficients and their estimated standard errors by using

a. Zellner's two-stage Aitken method.

b. The maximum likelihood method.

12-4. A set of three seemingly unrelated regression equations is specified as

$$\begin{aligned} Y_{i1} &= \alpha_1 + \beta_1 X_{i1} + \varepsilon_{i1}, \\ Y_{i2} &= \alpha_2 + \beta_2 X_{i2} + \varepsilon_{i2}, \\ Y_{i3} &= \alpha_3 + \beta_3 X_{i3} + \varepsilon_{i3}, \end{aligned}$$

The variance–covariance matrix of the disturbances is assumed to be known. Consider two estimators of β_1, the first obtained by applying the Aitken generalized least squares estimation to all three equations, and the second by applying this method only to the first two equations. Examine the efficiency of the first estimator relative to the second.

12-5. Consider the following set of demand equations for different commodities to be estimated from time-series data.

$$V_{it} = \alpha_i + \beta_i P_{it} + \gamma_i V_t + \varepsilon_{it},$$

where V_{it} = expenditure on the ith commodity, P_{it} = price of the ith commodity, and V_t = total expenditure on all commodities. Since $\Sigma_i V_{it} = V_t$, the following restrictions are in effect.

$$\sum_i \alpha_i = 0, \qquad \sum_i \beta_i p_{it} = 0, \quad \sum_i \gamma_i = 1, \qquad \sum_i \varepsilon_{it} = 0.$$

Describe an estimation procedure that would yield asymptotically efficient estimates of the regression coefficients.

12-6. A two-equation seemingly unrelated regression model,

$$\mathbf{Y}_1 = \mathbf{X}\boldsymbol{\beta}_1 + \boldsymbol{\varepsilon}_1,$$

$$\mathbf{Y}_2 = \mathbf{X}\boldsymbol{\beta}_2 + \boldsymbol{\varepsilon}_2,$$

is characterized by vector-autoregressive disturbances of the form

$$\varepsilon_1(t) = \rho_{11}\varepsilon_1(t-1) + \rho_{12}\varepsilon_2(t-1) + v_1(t),$$

$$\varepsilon_2(t) = \rho_{21}\varepsilon_1(t-1) + \rho_{22}\varepsilon_2(t-1) + v_2(t),$$

where the vs represent "pure white noise," and the terms in parentheses refer to time periods.

a. Show that the current values of the εs can be expressed in the form

$$\varepsilon_1(t) = \alpha_{11}\varepsilon_1(t-1) + \alpha_{12}\varepsilon_1(t-2) + \zeta_1(t),$$

$$\varepsilon_2(t) = \alpha_{21}\varepsilon_2(t-1) + \alpha_{22}\varepsilon_2(t-2) + \zeta_2(t),$$

where the αs are constants and the ζs are functions of the vs only. Present each α and each ζ in terms of the original expressions involved in the vector-autoregressive representation.

b. Determine the elements of the $\boldsymbol{\Omega}$ matrix (of dimension $2T \times 2T$).

12-7. **(a).** Consider a set of three seemingly unrelated regressions, written jointly as $\mathbf{y} = \mathbf{X}\boldsymbol{\beta} + \boldsymbol{\varepsilon}$, where $\mathbf{y} \to 3T \times 1$, etc. Find a transformation matrix $\mathbf{P}$ such that the application of the least squares method to the transformed equations will yield the (pure) Aitken estimator.

b. Consider a set of two seemingly unrelated regressions,

$$\mathbf{y}_1 = \mathbf{X}_1\boldsymbol{\beta}_1 + \varepsilon_1,$$

$$\mathbf{y}_2 = \mathbf{X}_2\boldsymbol{\beta}_2 + \varepsilon_2,$$

where $\mathbf{X}_1 = [\mathbf{X}_2\ \mathbf{Z}]$, i.e., $\mathbf{X}_2$ is a subset of $\mathbf{X}_1$. Compare the Aitken estimator of the second equation with that of ordinary least squares estimator.

c. Consider the following set of two seemingly unrelated regressions.

$$y_{1t} = \beta_1 x_{1t} + \varepsilon_{1t} \qquad (t = 1, 2, \ldots, 20),$$

$$y_{2t} = \beta_2 x_{2t} + \varepsilon_{2t}.$$

The sample variances and covariances are as follows.

	y_1	y_2	x_1	x_2
y_1	100	20	4	1
y_2	20	150	0	0
x_1	4	0	10	−2
x_2	1	0	−2	5

Test the hypothesis that $\beta_1 = \beta_2$ against $\beta_1 \neq \beta_2$.

13 Simultaneous Equation Systems

Economic models frequently involve a *set* of relationships designed to explain the behavior of certain variables. For instance, a simple model of the market for a given commodity may involve a supply and a demand function, and may explain the equilibrium price and quantity of the commodity exchanged in the market. Similarly, a model of aggregate income may explain the determination of various income components by means of appropriately specified relationships. In such models the problem of estimating the parameters has special features that are not present when a model involves only a single relation. In particular, when a relation is a part of a system, some regressors are typically stochastic and correlated with the regression disturbance. In this case the ordinary least squares estimators of the regression coefficients are inconsistent and other methods must be devised to provide consistent estimates.

This chapter is concerned with the problem of estimating equations that belong to a system of relations, and with the analysis and interpretation of such systems. Section 13-1 contains a general description of simultaneous equation systems and introduces some basic concepts. Section 13-2 deals with the problem of identification, which is crucially important for estimation. The discussion represents a logical extension of the identification problem from the single-equation models of Section 11-2 to the multiequation models of this chapter. In Section 13-3 we describe several methods of estimating a single equation that is embedded in a simultaneous equation system, while the methods presented in Section 13-4 are designed to provide estimates for *all* equations of the system. In Section 13-5 we consider a simultaneous equation system in which the disturbances in individual equations are heteroskedastic and/or autocorrelated. Section 13-6 is concerned with comparing different methods of estimation and also deals with certain special topics. Finally, Section 13-7 provides an analysis and interpretation of dynamic economic systems.

13-1 Description of Simultaneous Equation Systems

The basic requirement an economic model must satisfy is that the number of the variables whose values are to be explained must be equal to the number of independent relationships in the model, otherwise the values of these variables would not be determinate. In addition to the variables whose values are to be explained a model may, and usually does, contain variables whose values are not immediately affected by the mechanism described by the model. The relevance of these variables lies in their role as explanatory factors. This leads to a distinction between those variables whose values are to be explained by the model and those that contribute to providing such an explanation; the former are called *endogenous* and the latter *predetermined.* Predetermined variables can be subdivided into *exogenous* and *lagged endogenous* variables. The values of the exogenous variables are completely determined outside the system under consideration, whereas the values of the lagged endogenous variables are represented by the past values of the endogenous variables of the model. Models having no lagged endogenous variables are not uncommon, but models without any predetermined variables are rather rare. For example, a model of the market for given commodity may involve a supply and a demand relation, with current equilibrium price and quantity exchanged as the endogenous variables, and the factors that account for systematic shifts of the supply and the demand functions as the predetermined variables. *A model is said to constitute a system of simultaneous equations if all of the relationships involved are needed for determining the value of at least one of the endogenous variables included in the model.* This implies that at least one of the relationships includes more than one endogenous variable.

The classification of variables as endogenous and predetermined is very important as far as economic theory is concerned since a necessary condition for the completeness of theory is that the number of endogenous variables is equal to the number of independent equations in the system. The classification of variables is also crucially important for estimation because the main distinguishing feature of predetermined variables is that they are contemporaneously uncorrelated with the disturbances of the equations in which they appear. There is no problem in recognizing *lagged* variables as predetermined, but the determination of *exogeneity* of a variable is sometimes unclear. A concern with this problem has led to a discussion of the concept of *causality* in econometrics. Although the concepts of causality and exogeneity are not identical, it is nevertheless possible to conclude that if a variable Y is—in some sense—caused by a variable X, Y cannot be considered to be exogenous in a system in which X also appears. A widely discussed definition of causality has been proposed by Granger.[1] In the context of two variables, X and Y, the claim that X is *not* caused by Y is to be rejected, according to Granger, if the current values of X can be better explained by the current value of Y and the past

[1] For a survey of the literature on causality see, e.g., G. G. Judge et al., *The Theory and Practice of Econometrics,* 2nd ed. (New York: Wiley, 1985), pp. 667–669. For a critical discussion see R. K. Conway et al., "The Impossibility of Causality Testing," *Agricultural Economics Research,* 36 (Summer 1984), pp. 1–19.

values of X and Y than by the past values of X alone. This definition—or, for that matter, any other definition—of causality is not without problems. Econometricians as a rule avoid the concept of causality altogether and determine the classification of variables by considerations based on economic theory or on common sense. For instance, in a set of equations describing the aggregate demand and supply of food, the price of food and the quantity of food sold are determined in the market and thus are clearly endogenous, if equilibrium conditions prevail. The aggregate income of consumers, on the other hand, affects the demand for food but is largely unaffected by the price and quantity of food sold, which makes it exogenous.

The definition of a simultaneous equation system can be given a rigorous interpretation when an economic model has been specifically formulated as a set of well-defined stochastic relationships, that is, when it has been turned into what is generally called an *econometric model.* Typically, economic theory tells us which relations make up the model, which variables are to be included in each of the relations, and what is the sign of some of the partial derivatives. As a rule, economic theory has very little to say about the functional form of the relations, the time lags involved, and the values of the parameters. Also, the relations are deterministic, so that no allowance is made for the presence of stochastic disturbances. In order to put an economic model into the form of a testable proposition, it is necessary to specify the functional form of the relations, the timing of the variables, and the stochastic characterization of the system. The end result is an econometric model that is ready for estimation or testing. This model represents a summary of the prior knowledge of the investigator concerning the phenomenon in question. Given the current state of economics, this prior knowledge is derived in part from economic theory, and in part from ad hoc reasoning or guessing. For example, consider the following simplified supply–demand model for a commodity:

$$Q = f_1(P, Y) \qquad \text{(demand)},$$

$$Q = f_2(P) \qquad \text{(supply)},$$

$$\frac{\partial f_1}{\partial P} \leq 0, \qquad \frac{\partial f_1}{\partial Y} \geq 0, \qquad \frac{\partial f_2}{\partial P} \geq 0,$$

where Q = equilibrium quantity exchanged on the market, P = equilibrium price, and Y = income of the consumers. The variables Q and P are endogenous, and Y is exogenous. Note that both relations are needed for determining the values of the two endogenous variables, so that the system is one of simultaneous equations. An econometric model representing these relations might look as follows:

$$(13.1) \qquad Q_t = \alpha_1 + \alpha_2 P_t + \alpha_3 Y_t + u_{1t} \qquad \text{(demand)},$$

$$Q_t = \beta_1 + \beta_2 P_t + u_{2t} \qquad \text{(supply)},$$

$$\alpha_2 \leq 0, \qquad \alpha_3 \geq 0, \qquad \beta_2 \geq 0,$$

where αs and βs are parameters, us are random disturbances, and t represents a specific period of time. Each disturbance is characterized by the assumptions of the classical normal linear regression model. The variances and the covariance of the disturbances are

$$E(u_{1t}^2) = \sigma_{11},$$
$$E(u_{2t}^2) = \sigma_{22},$$
$$E(u_{1t}u_{2t}) = \sigma_{12}.$$

Equations (13.1) are called the *structural form* of the model under study. This form is derived from economic theory. The structural equations can be solved for the endogenous variables to give

$$(13.2) \qquad Q_t = \left(\frac{\alpha_2\beta_1 - \alpha_1\beta_2}{\alpha_2 - \beta_2}\right) - \left(\frac{\alpha_3\beta_2}{\alpha_2 - \beta_2}\right)Y_t + \left(\frac{-\beta_2 u_{1t} + \alpha_2 u_{2t}}{\alpha_2 - \beta_2}\right),$$

$$P_t = \left(\frac{-\alpha_1 + \beta_1}{\alpha_2 - \beta_2}\right) - \left(\frac{\alpha_3}{\alpha_2 - \beta_2}\right)Y_t + \left(\frac{-u_{1t} + u_{2t}}{\alpha_2 - \beta_2}\right).$$

The solution given by (13.2) is called the *reduced form* of the model. The reduced form equations show explicitly how the endogenous variables are *jointly dependent* on the predetermined variables and the disturbances of the system. In the case of (13.2), we can see that the values of Q_t and P_t are fully determined by Y_t, u_{1t}, and u_{2t}. The value of Y_t, on the other hand, is believed to be determined outside of the market in question and to be in no way influenced by P_t or Q_t. If Y_t is random, it is assumed to be distributed independently of u_{1t} and u_{2t}.

It may be interesting to note the composition of the effect of Y_t on Q_t in (13.2). The coefficient of Y_t in the reduced form equation for Q_t represents a *total* effect of Y_t on Q_t. This effect consists of a *direct* effect of Y_t on Q_t, given by the coefficient α_3 of the demand equation in (13.1), and of an *indirect* effect of Y_t on Q_t through P_t, defined as

$$\frac{-\alpha_3\beta_2}{\alpha_2 - \beta_2} - \alpha_3 = \frac{-\alpha_2\alpha_3}{\alpha_2 - \beta_2}.$$

The two effects add up to a positive total effect.

From the point of view of statistical inference, the single relevant characteristic of the simultaneous equation systems—and one that requires special consideration—is the appearance of endogenous variables among the explanatory variables of at least some of the structural equations. This leads to problems because the endogenous variables are, in general, correlated with the disturbance of the equation in which they appear. Consider the supply-demand model of (13.1). In both equations the endogenous P_t appears as an explanatory variable. But from (13.2) we can see that

$$E(P_t u_{1t}) = \frac{-\sigma_{11} + \sigma_{12}}{\alpha_2 - \beta_2}$$

and

$$E(P_t u_{2t}) = \frac{-\sigma_{12} + \sigma_{22}}{\alpha_2 - \beta_2},$$

which shows that P_t is correlated with both disturbances. As pointed out in Section

8-4, the existence of correlation between an explanatory variable and the disturbance leads to inconsistency of the ordinary least squares estimator of the regression coefficients.[2] It appears, then, that the crucial aspect of the predetermined variables in a system is that they are not contemporaneously correlated with the disturbances.

In general, the structural form of a simultaneous equation system can be described by

$$\begin{aligned}(13.3)\quad & \beta_{11}y_{1t} + \beta_{12}y_{2t} + \cdots + \beta_{1G}y_{Gt} + \gamma_{11}x_{1t} + \gamma_{12}x_{2t} + \cdots + \gamma_{1K}x_{Kt} = u_{1t},\\ & \beta_{21}y_{1t} + \beta_{22}y_{2t} + \cdots + \beta_{2G}y_{Gt} + \gamma_{21}x_{1t} + \gamma_{22}x_{2t} + \cdots + \gamma_{2K}x_{Kt} = u_{2t},\\ & \vdots \\ & \beta_{G1}y_{1t} + \beta_{G2}y_{2t} + \cdots + \beta_{GG}y_{Gt} + \gamma_{G1}x_{1t} + \gamma_{G2}x_{2t} + \cdots + \gamma_{GK}x_{K1} = u_{Gt},\end{aligned}$$

where the ys are endogenous variables, the xs are predetermined variables, the us are stochastic disturbances, and $t = 1, 2, \ldots, T$. The βs and the γs are known as the structural coefficients. There are G endogenous and K predetermined variables in the system. Generally, of course, not all endogenous and predetermined variables will appear in every equation since some of the βs and γs will be known to be zero. Further, in each equation one of the βs is taken to be unity, thus indicating that one of the endogenous variables serves as the "dependent" variable when the equation is written out as a standard regression equation. It should also be noted that some of the equations may actually be identities, which means that all their coefficients are known and that they contain no stochastic disturbances. The whole system of equations may be written in matrix form as

$$(13.3a)\qquad \mathbf{B}\mathbf{y}_t + \mathbf{\Gamma}\mathbf{x}_t = \mathbf{u}_t,$$

where

$$\underset{(G\times 1)}{\mathbf{y}_t = \begin{bmatrix} y_{1t} \\ y_{2t} \\ \vdots \\ y_{Gt} \end{bmatrix}}, \quad \underset{(K\times 1)}{\mathbf{x}_t = \begin{bmatrix} x_{1t} \\ x_{2t} \\ \vdots \\ x_{Kt} \end{bmatrix}}, \quad \underset{(G\times 1)}{\mathbf{u}_t = \begin{bmatrix} u_{1t} \\ u_{2t} \\ \vdots \\ u_{Gt} \end{bmatrix}},$$

$$\underset{(G\times G)}{\mathbf{B} = \begin{bmatrix} \beta_{11} & \beta_{12} & \cdots & \beta_{1G} \\ \beta_{21} & \beta_{22} & \cdots & \beta_{2G} \\ \vdots & \vdots & & \vdots \\ \beta_{G1} & \beta_{G2} & \cdots & \beta_{GG} \end{bmatrix}}, \quad \underset{(G\times K)}{\mathbf{\Gamma} = \begin{bmatrix} \gamma_{11} & \gamma_{12} & \cdots & \gamma_{1K} \\ \gamma_{21} & \gamma_{22} & \cdots & \gamma_{2K} \\ \vdots & \vdots & & \vdots \\ \gamma_{G1} & \gamma_{G2} & \cdots & \gamma_{GK} \end{bmatrix}}.$$

[2] This statement is based on the standard presumption that the sample variance of Y is finite as $n \to \infty$. If the sample variance of Y grows without limit—as would be the case if the values of Y were to follow an upward trend with no bounds—the least squares estimator of β_2 in (13.1) is consistent. See W. Krämer, "On the Consequences of Trend for Simultaneous Equation Estimation," *Economics Letters,* 14 (1984), pp. 23–30.

If there are constant terms in any of the equations, one of the x's will be equal to unity for all $t = 1, 2, \ldots, T$. A matrix representation of all T observations can be given as

$$\mathbf{YB}' + \mathbf{X\Gamma}' = \mathbf{U}, \tag{13.3b}$$

where $\mathbf{Y}$ is a $T \times G$ matrix of observations on the G endogenous variables, $\mathbf{X}$ is a $T \times K$ matrix of observations on the K predetermined variables, and $\mathbf{U}$ is a $T \times G$ matrix of the values of the G disturbances.

With respect to the stochastic disturbances, we stipulate that each disturbance satisfies the assumptions of the classical normal linear regression model, i.e., that

$$u_{gt} \sim N(0, \sigma_{gg}), \qquad g = 1, 2, \ldots, G;$$

$$E(u_{gt}u_{gs}) = 0, \qquad t, s = 1, 2, \ldots, T; \quad t \neq s.$$

However, we do not rule out the possibility that the disturbances are correlated across equations, i.e., that

$$E(u_{gt}u_{ht}) = \sigma_{gh} \qquad (g, h = 1, 2, \ldots, G).$$

In matrix notation these assumptions become

$$\mathbf{u}_t = N(\mathbf{0}, \mathbf{\Phi}), \tag{13.4}$$

$$E(\mathbf{u}_t\mathbf{u}_s') = \mathbf{0}, \tag{13.5}$$

where

$$\mathbf{\Phi} = \underset{(G \times G)}{\begin{bmatrix} \sigma_{11} & \sigma_{12} & \cdots & \sigma_{1G} \\ \sigma_{21} & \sigma_{22} & \cdots & \sigma_{2G} \\ \vdots & \vdots & & \vdots \\ \sigma_{G1} & \sigma_{G2} & \cdots & \sigma_{GG} \end{bmatrix}}.$$

The matrix $\mathbf{\Phi}$ is known as the variance–covariance matrix of the structural disturbances. If there are any identities present, $\mathbf{\Phi}$ refers only to the equations that are not identities, and its dimension is appropriately reduced.

The reduced form of the system is obtained by solving the structural form equations for the values of the endogenous variables, that is, by expressing the y's in terms of the x's and the u's. The result may be written as

$$\begin{aligned} y_{1t} &= \pi_{11}x_{1t} + \pi_{12}x_{2t} + \cdots + \pi_{1K}x_{Kt} + v_{1t}, \\ y_{2t} &= \pi_{21}x_{1t} + \pi_{22}x_{2t} + \cdots + \pi_{2K}x_{Kt} + v_{2t}, \\ &\vdots \\ y_{Gt} &= \pi_{G1}x_{1t} + \pi_{G2}x_{2t} + \cdots + \pi_{GK}x_{Kt} + v_{Gt}. \end{aligned} \tag{13.6}$$

The π's represent the reduced form coefficients and the v's the reduced form disturbances. In general, each reduced form disturbance is a linear function of *all* structural disturbances. Using matrix notation, we may write (13.6) as

(13.6a) $$\mathbf{y}_t = \mathbf{\Pi}\mathbf{x}_t + \mathbf{v}_t,$$

where $$\mathbf{\Pi} = \underset{(G \times K)}{\begin{bmatrix} \pi_{11} & \pi_{12} & \cdots & \pi_{1K} \\ \pi_{21} & \pi_{22} & \cdots & \pi_{2K} \\ \vdots & \vdots & & \vdots \\ \pi_{G1} & \pi_{G2} & \cdots & \pi_{GK} \end{bmatrix}}, \qquad \mathbf{v}_t = \underset{(G \times 1)}{\begin{bmatrix} v_{1t} \\ v_{2t} \\ \vdots \\ v_{Gt} \end{bmatrix}}.$$

The relation between the structural form and the reduced form can be derived explicitly by solving (13.3a) for $\mathbf{y}_t$. This gives

(13.6b) $$\mathbf{y}_t = -\mathbf{B}^{-1}\mathbf{\Gamma}\mathbf{x}_t + \mathbf{B}^{-1}\mathbf{u}_t.$$

Comparing this result with the reduced form (13.6a), we can see that

(13.7) $$\mathbf{\Pi} = -\mathbf{B}^{-1}\mathbf{\Gamma}$$

and

(13.8) $$\mathbf{v}_t = \mathbf{B}^{-1}\mathbf{u}_t.$$

The variance–covariance matrix of the reduced form disturbances, $\mathbf{\Psi}$, is

(13.9) $$\mathbf{\Psi} = E(\mathbf{v}_t\mathbf{v}_t') = E[\mathbf{B}^{-1}\mathbf{u}_t\mathbf{u}_t'(\mathbf{B}^{-1})'] = \mathbf{B}^{-1}\mathbf{\Phi}(\mathbf{B}^{-1})'.$$

EXAMPLE 1 The supply–demand model described by (13.1) is

$$Q_t - \alpha_1 - \alpha_2 P_t - \alpha_3 Y_t = u_{1t},$$
$$Q_t - \beta_1 - \beta_2 P_t \qquad\qquad = u_{2t}.$$

This can be written in the pattern of (13.3a) as

$$\begin{bmatrix} 1 & -\alpha_2 \\ 1 & -\beta_2 \end{bmatrix}\begin{bmatrix} Q_t \\ P_t \end{bmatrix} + \begin{bmatrix} -\alpha_1 & -\alpha_3 \\ -\beta_1 & 0 \end{bmatrix}\begin{bmatrix} 1 \\ Y_t \end{bmatrix} = \begin{bmatrix} u_{1t} \\ u_{2t} \end{bmatrix}.$$

The reduced form of the system is

$$\begin{bmatrix} Q_t \\ P_t \end{bmatrix} = \begin{bmatrix} \pi_{11} & \pi_{12} \\ \pi_{21} & \pi_{22} \end{bmatrix}\begin{bmatrix} 1 \\ Y_t \end{bmatrix} + \begin{bmatrix} v_{1t} \\ v_{2t} \end{bmatrix},$$

where

$$\begin{bmatrix} \pi_{11} & \pi_{12} \\ \pi_{21} & \pi_{22} \end{bmatrix} = -\mathbf{B}^{-1}\mathbf{\Gamma} = -\begin{bmatrix} 1 & -\alpha_2 \\ 1 & -\beta_2 \end{bmatrix}^{-1}\begin{bmatrix} -\alpha_1 & -\alpha_3 \\ -\beta_1 & 0 \end{bmatrix}$$
$$= -\left[\frac{1}{\alpha_2 - \beta_2}\right]\begin{bmatrix} -\beta_2 & \alpha_2 \\ -1 & 1 \end{bmatrix}\begin{bmatrix} -\alpha_1 & -\alpha_3 \\ -\beta_1 & 0 \end{bmatrix}$$
$$= -\left[\frac{1}{\alpha_2 - \beta_2}\right]\begin{bmatrix} (\alpha_1\beta_2 - \alpha_2\beta_1) & \alpha_3\beta_2 \\ (\alpha_1 - \beta_1) & \alpha_3 \end{bmatrix}$$

and

$$\begin{bmatrix} v_{1t} \\ v_{2t} \end{bmatrix} = \mathbf{B}^{-1}\begin{bmatrix} u_{1t} \\ u_{2t} \end{bmatrix} = \begin{bmatrix} \dfrac{1}{\alpha_2 - \beta_2} \end{bmatrix}\begin{bmatrix} -\beta_2 & \alpha_2 \\ -1 & 1 \end{bmatrix}\begin{bmatrix} u_{1t} \\ u_{2t} \end{bmatrix} = \begin{bmatrix} \dfrac{1}{\alpha_2 - \beta_2} \end{bmatrix}\begin{bmatrix} -\beta_2 u_{1t} + \alpha_2 u_{2t} \\ -u_{1t} + u_{2t} \end{bmatrix}.$$

Of course, these results are the same as those given by (13.2).

EXAMPLE 2 The following represents a highly simplified model of the economy.

$$\begin{aligned}
C_t &= \alpha_0 + \alpha_1 Y_t + \alpha_2 C_{t-1} + u_{1t} && \text{(consumption)},\\
I_t &= \beta_0 + \beta_1 r_t + \beta_2 I_{t-1} + u_{2t} && \text{(investment)},\\
r_t &= \gamma_0 + \gamma_1 Y_t + \gamma_2 M_t + u_{3t} && \text{(money market)},\\
Y_t &= C_t + I_t + G_t && \text{(income identity)},
\end{aligned}$$

where C = consumption, Y = income, I = investment, r = rate of interest, M = money supply, and G = government expenditure. The variables C_t, I_t, Y_t, and r_t are endogenous; the remaining variables are predetermined. We can describe the model as

$$\begin{bmatrix} 1 & 0 & -\alpha_1 & 0 \\ 0 & 1 & 0 & -\beta_1 \\ 0 & 0 & -\gamma_1 & 1 \\ -1 & -1 & 1 & 0 \end{bmatrix}\begin{bmatrix} C_t \\ I_t \\ Y_t \\ r_t \end{bmatrix} + \begin{bmatrix} -\alpha_0 & -\alpha_2 & 0 & 0 & 0 \\ -\beta_0 & 0 & -\beta_2 & 0 & 0 \\ -\gamma_0 & 0 & 0 & -\gamma_2 & 0 \\ 0 & 0 & 0 & 0 & -1 \end{bmatrix}\begin{bmatrix} 1 \\ C_{t-1} \\ I_{t-1} \\ M_t \\ G_t \end{bmatrix} = \begin{bmatrix} u_{1t} \\ u_{2t} \\ u_{3t} \\ 0 \end{bmatrix}.$$

The reduced form of this system is

$$\begin{bmatrix} C_t \\ I_t \\ Y_t \\ r_t \end{bmatrix} = \frac{1}{\Delta}\begin{bmatrix} \alpha_0(1-\beta_1\gamma_1) + \alpha_1(\beta_0 + \beta_1\gamma_0) & \alpha_2(1-\beta_1\gamma_1) & \alpha_1\beta_2 & \alpha_1\beta_1\gamma_2 & \alpha_1 \\ \alpha_0\beta_1\gamma_1 + (1-\alpha_1)(\beta_0 + \beta_1\gamma_0) & \alpha_2\beta_1\gamma_1 & (1-\alpha_1)\beta_2 & (1-\alpha_1)\beta_1\gamma_2 & \beta_1\gamma_1 \\ \alpha_0 + \beta_0 + \beta_1\gamma_0 & \alpha_2 & \beta_2 & \beta_1\gamma_2 & 1 \\ (\alpha_0 + \beta_0)\gamma_1 + (1-\alpha_1)\gamma_0 & \alpha_2\gamma_1 & \beta_2\gamma_1 & (1-\alpha_1)\gamma_2 & \gamma_1 \end{bmatrix}$$

$$\times \begin{bmatrix} 1 \\ C_{t-1} \\ I_{t-1} \\ M_t \\ G_t \end{bmatrix} + \frac{1}{\Delta}\begin{bmatrix} 1-\beta_1\gamma_1 & \alpha_1 & \alpha_1\beta_1 \\ \beta_1\gamma_1 & 1-\alpha_1 & (1-\alpha_1)\beta_1 \\ 1 & 1 & \beta_1 \\ \gamma_1 & \gamma_1 & 1-\alpha_1 \end{bmatrix}\begin{bmatrix} u_{1t} \\ u_{2t} \\ u_{3t} \end{bmatrix},$$

where $\Delta = 1 - \alpha_1 - \beta_1\gamma_1$.

Types of Structural Models

The position of the zero elements in the **B** matrix indicates which endogenous variables do not appear in different structural equations. This is used as a criterion for distinguishing between various types of structures.

(a) If **B** is *diagonal*, i.e., if

$$\mathbf{B} = \begin{bmatrix} \beta_{11} & 0 & \cdots & 0 \\ 0 & \beta_{22} & \cdots & 0 \\ \vdots & \vdots & & \vdots \\ 0 & 0 & \cdots & \beta_{GG} \end{bmatrix},$$

only one endogenous variable appears in each equation. This means that the equations are not simultaneous but *seemingly unrelated*. This case has been discussed in Section 12-3.

(b) If **B** is *block-diagonal*, i.e., if

$$\mathbf{B} = \begin{bmatrix} \mathbf{B}_1 & \mathbf{0} & \cdots & \mathbf{0} \\ \mathbf{0} & \mathbf{B}_2 & \cdots & \mathbf{0} \\ \vdots & \vdots & & \vdots \\ \mathbf{0} & \mathbf{0} & \cdots & \mathbf{B}_R \end{bmatrix},$$

where $\mathbf{B}_1, \mathbf{B}_2, \ldots, \mathbf{B}_R$ are square matrices and the **0**'s represent zero matrices of appropriate dimensions, then each block contains its own set of endogenous variables. In this case we have not one but R systems of simultaneous equations. Each block constitutes a separate system since, in the derivation of the reduced form solutions, we utilize only the structural equations of the same block. This can be clearly seen if we partition the structural equations in the following way:

$$\begin{bmatrix} \mathbf{B}_1 & \mathbf{0} & \cdots & \mathbf{0} \\ \mathbf{0} & \mathbf{B}_2 & \cdots & \mathbf{0} \\ \vdots & \vdots & & \vdots \\ \mathbf{0} & \mathbf{0} & \cdots & \mathbf{B}_R \end{bmatrix} \begin{bmatrix} \mathbf{y}_t^{(1)} \\ \mathbf{y}_t^{(2)} \\ \vdots \\ \mathbf{y}_t^{(R)} \end{bmatrix} + \begin{bmatrix} \mathbf{\Gamma}_1 \\ \mathbf{\Gamma}_2 \\ \vdots \\ \mathbf{\Gamma}_R \end{bmatrix} \mathbf{x}_t = \begin{bmatrix} \mathbf{u}_t^{(1)} \\ \mathbf{u}_t^{(2)} \\ \vdots \\ \mathbf{u}_t^{(R)} \end{bmatrix},$$

where $\mathbf{y}_t^{(r)}$ is a $(G_r \times 1)$ vector of the endogenous variables appearing in the rth block, $\mathbf{u}_t^{(r)}$ is a $(G_r \times 1)$ vector of the corresponding structural disturbances, and $\mathbf{\Gamma}_r$ is a $(G_r \times K)$ matrix of the γ coefficients in the structural equations of the rth block $(r = 1, 2, \ldots, R)$. The reduced form solution for $\mathbf{y}_t^{(r)}$ is

$$\mathbf{y}_t^{(r)} = -\mathbf{B}_r^{-1}\mathbf{\Gamma}_r\mathbf{x}_t + \mathbf{B}_r^{-1}\mathbf{u}_t^{(r)} \qquad (r = 1, 2, \ldots, R).$$

In this result there is no reference to any equation outside of the rth block. When the **B** matrix is block-diagonal, we speak of a *nonintegrated structure*. If the variance–covariance matrix of the structural disturbances is also block-diagonal in the same way as the **B** matrix, then each block can be treated as a separate system when it comes to estimation. However, if the variance–covariance matrix of the structural disturbances is not block-diagonal, then the blocks are only "seemingly" unrelated. We may add that there is also another, stricter kind of nonintegration known as *dynamic nonintegration.* This condition prevails when the structural equations in any one block do not involve current *as well as* lagged endogenous variables from any other block. This kind of nonintegration implies that not only the current value but also the path through time of an endogenous variable are determined entirely by reference to the equations of the block in which the variable in question appears. We shall comment further on this in Section 13-7.

(c) If **B** is triangular, i.e., if

$$\mathbf{B} = \begin{bmatrix} \beta_{11} & 0 & \cdots & 0 \\ \beta_{21} & \beta_{22} & \cdots & 0 \\ \vdots & & & \vdots \\ \beta_{G1} & \beta_{G2} & \cdots & \beta_{GG} \end{bmatrix},$$

the system is known as *triangular.* In this case the solution for the *g*th endogenous variable involves only the first *g* structural equations. This means that all *G* structural equations are needed for the solution only in the case of the last endogenous variable y_{Gt}. The first structural equation involves only one endogenous variable so that it coincides with the first reduced form equation. (If *B* is triangular *and* $E(u_t u_t')$ is diagonal, the system is called *recursive.*)

(d) If **B** is block-triangular, i.e., if

$$\mathbf{B} = \begin{bmatrix} \mathbf{B}_{11} & \mathbf{0} & \cdots & \mathbf{0} \\ \mathbf{B}_{21} & \mathbf{B}_{22} & \cdots & \mathbf{0} \\ \vdots & \vdots & & \vdots \\ \mathbf{B}_{R1} & \mathbf{B}_{R2} & \cdots & \mathbf{B}_{RR} \end{bmatrix},$$

where the **Bs** are matrices of given dimensions, the system is called *block-triangular.* This system has the same characteristics as the triangular system just described, except that reference is made to blocks of equations rather than to individual equations themselves.

(e) If **B** is neither diagonal nor triangular (block or otherwise), we speak of an *integrated structure.* Such structures have commanded the greatest attention of econometricians and provide the main subject for our discussion of simultaneous equation systems. A system of equations characterized by an integrated structure is sometimes called a *general interdependent system.*

13-2 The Identification Problem

Because there are endogenous variables among the explanatory variables in simultaneous equations, ordinary least squares estimators of the structural coefficients are not consistent, at least in general. However, in the reduced form equations the explanatory variables are represented by the predetermined variables of the system, so that ordinary least squares estimators of the reduced form coefficients are consistent. This suggests that we may try to estimate the structural coefficients via the reduced form. The question then is whether we can derive estimates of the structural coefficients from the consistent estimates of the reduced form coefficients. Obviously, we can do this providing we can express the structural coefficients—the βs and the γs—in terms of the reduced form coefficients—the πs. Thus the problem is one of *identification,* as was discussed in the context of a single equation model in Section 11-2. At present we face the same problem with a system of equations. The reduced form equations described by (13.6a) as

$$\mathbf{y}_t = \mathbf{\Pi x}_t + \mathbf{v}_t$$

represent the unrestricted version of these equations, while the form (13.6b) given by

$$\mathbf{y}_t = -\mathbf{B}^{-1}\mathbf{\Gamma x}_t + \mathbf{B}^{-1}\mathbf{u}_t$$

represents the restricted version. As with a single equation model, when there is a one-to-one correspondence between the restricted and the unrestricted parameters (in the sense that there is a unique solution for the restricted parameters in terms of the unrestricted coefficients) we have *exact identification.* On the other hand, when the number of the unrestricted coefficients exceeds the number of the restricted parameters and there is no unique solution, we have *overidentification.* Finally, if the number of unrestricted coefficients is insufficient for the solution, we have *underidentification.* An equation is said to be identified if it is either exactly identified or overidentified.

We may illustrate the identification problem by reference to the supply-demand model (13.1),

$$Q_t = \alpha_1 + \alpha_2 P_t + \alpha_3 Y_t + u_{1t} \qquad \text{(demand)},$$
$$Q_t = \beta_1 + \beta_2 P_t + u_{2t} \qquad \text{(supply)},$$

and its reduced form (13.2),

$$Q_t = \pi_{11} + \pi_{12} Y_t + v_{1t},$$
$$P_t = \pi_{21} + \pi_{22} Y_t + v_{2t}.$$

The simplest way of finding out whether it is possible to express the α's and the β's in terms of the π's is to substitute for Q_t and P_t from the reduced form (13.2) into the structural form (13.1). This gives

$$(\pi_{11} + \pi_{12} Y_t + v_{1t}) = \alpha_1 + \alpha_2(\pi_{21} + \pi_{22} Y_t + v_{2t}) + \alpha_3 Y_t + u_{1t} \qquad \text{(demand)},$$
$$(\pi_{11} + \pi_{12} Y_t + v_{1t}) = \beta_1 + \beta_2(\pi_{21} + \pi_{22} Y_t + v_{2t}) + u_{2t} \qquad \text{(supply)}.$$

In light of the definition of v_{1t} and v_{2t} given earlier, the stochastic disturbances in each equation cancel out, and we are left with

$$\pi_{11} + \pi_{12}Y_t = (\alpha_1 + \alpha_2\pi_{21}) + (\alpha_2\pi_{22} + \alpha_3)Y_t \qquad \text{(demand)},$$

$$\pi_{11} + \pi_{12}Y_t = (\beta_1 + \beta_2\pi_{21}) + \beta_2\pi_{22}Y_t \qquad \text{(supply)}.$$

The equalities implied by the demand equation are

$$\pi_{11} = \alpha_1 + \alpha_2\pi_{21} \qquad \text{and} \qquad \pi_{12} = \alpha_2\pi_{22} + \alpha_3.$$

Since there are only two equalities, we cannot solve for the three unknowns represented by α_1, α_2, and α_3. The equalities for the supply equation are

$$\pi_{11} = \beta_1 + \beta_2\pi_{21} \qquad \text{and} \qquad \pi_{12} = \beta_2\pi_{22}.$$

This leads to

$$\beta_1 = \pi_{11} - \frac{\pi_{12}\pi_{21}}{\pi_{22}},$$

$$\beta_2 = \frac{\pi_{12}}{\pi_{22}}.$$

Thus the demand equation is underidentified, and the supply equation is exactly identified.

Clearly, it would be desirable to have some general rule for determining the identification status of any given structural equation. Such a rule can be derived in the following way. The structural equations are

$$\mathbf{B}\mathbf{y}_t + \mathbf{\Gamma}\mathbf{x}_t = \mathbf{u}_t,$$

while the reduced form equations are

$$\mathbf{y}_t = \mathbf{\Pi}\mathbf{x}_t + \mathbf{v}_t.$$

By substituting for $\mathbf{y}_t$ from the reduced form expression into the structural form, we obtain

$$\mathbf{B}\mathbf{\Pi}\mathbf{x}_t + \mathbf{B}\mathbf{v}_t + \mathbf{\Gamma}\mathbf{x}_t = \mathbf{u}_t.$$

But since

$$\mathbf{v}_t = \mathbf{B}^{-1}\mathbf{u}_t,$$

we can write

$$\mathbf{B}\mathbf{\Pi}\mathbf{x}_t = -\mathbf{\Gamma}\mathbf{x}_t$$

or

$$\mathbf{B}\mathbf{\Pi} = -\mathbf{\Gamma}.$$

This is the relation used in determining the identification status of the demand and the supply equations. We shall now try to use this relation for deriving a general identification criterion for each structural equation. Writing out the matrices in full, we have

$$\begin{bmatrix} \beta_{11} & \beta_{12} & \cdots & \beta_{1G} \\ \beta_{21} & \beta_{22} & \cdots & \beta_{2G} \\ \vdots & \vdots & & \vdots \\ \beta_{G1} & \beta_{G2} & \cdots & \beta_{GG} \end{bmatrix} \begin{bmatrix} \pi_{11} & \pi_{12} & \cdots & \pi_{1K} \\ \pi_{21} & \pi_{22} & \cdots & \pi_{2K} \\ \vdots & \vdots & & \vdots \\ \pi_{G1} & \pi_{G2} & \cdots & \pi_{GK} \end{bmatrix} = - \begin{bmatrix} \gamma_{11} & \gamma_{12} & \cdots & \gamma_{1K} \\ \gamma_{21} & \gamma_{22} & \cdots & \gamma_{2K} \\ \vdots & \vdots & & \vdots \\ \gamma_{G1} & \gamma_{G2} & \cdots & \gamma_{GK} \end{bmatrix}.$$

For a single equation of the system, say, the gth, this becomes

$$(13.10) \quad [\beta_{g1} \quad \beta_{g2} \quad \cdots \quad \beta_{gG}] \begin{bmatrix} \pi_{11} & \pi_{12} & \cdots & \pi_{1K} \\ \pi_{21} & \pi_{22} & \cdots & \pi_{2K} \\ \vdots & \vdots & & \vdots \\ \pi_{G1} & \pi_{G2} & \cdots & \pi_{GK} \end{bmatrix} = -[\gamma_{g1} \quad \gamma_{g2} \quad \cdots \quad \gamma_{gK}]$$

or

$$(13.10a) \qquad \boldsymbol{\beta}_g \boldsymbol{\Pi} = -\boldsymbol{\gamma}_g,$$

where

$$\boldsymbol{\beta}_g = [\beta_{g1} \quad \beta_{g2} \quad \cdots \quad \beta_{gG}],$$

$$\boldsymbol{\gamma}_g = [\gamma_{g1} \quad \gamma_{g2} \quad \cdots \quad \gamma_{gK}].$$

If all of the endogenous and the predetermined variables of the system do not appear in the gth equation, some of the βs and some of the γs will be equal to zero.

Let G^{Δ} = number of endogenous variables that appear in the gth equation (i.e., number of the nonzero elements in $\boldsymbol{\beta}_g$);

$G^{\Delta\Delta} = G - G^{\Delta}$;

K^* = number of predetermined variables that appear in the gth equation (i.e., number of the nonzero elements in $\boldsymbol{\gamma}_g$);

$K^{**} = K - K^*$.

Without a loss of generality, we assume that the elements of $\boldsymbol{\beta}_g$ and $\boldsymbol{\gamma}_g$ are arranged in such a way that the nonzero elements appear first, being followed by the zero elements. Then we can partition $\boldsymbol{\beta}_g$ and $\boldsymbol{\gamma}_g$ as

$$(13.11) \qquad \boldsymbol{\beta}_g = [\boldsymbol{\beta}_{\Delta} \quad \mathbf{0}_{\Delta\Delta}],$$

$$\boldsymbol{\gamma}_g = [\boldsymbol{\gamma}_{*} \quad \mathbf{0}_{**}],$$

where

$$\boldsymbol{\beta}_{\Delta} = [\beta_{g1} \quad \beta_{g2} \quad \cdots \quad \beta_{gG^{\Delta}}] \rightarrow 1 \times G^{\Delta},$$

$$\mathbf{0}_{\Delta\Delta} = [0 \quad 0 \quad \cdots \quad 0] \rightarrow 1 \times G^{\Delta\Delta},$$

$$\boldsymbol{\gamma}_{*} = [\gamma_{g1} \quad \gamma_{g2} \quad \cdots \quad \gamma_{gK^*}] \rightarrow 1 \times K^*,$$

$$\mathbf{0}_{**} = [0 \quad 0 \quad \cdots \quad 0] \rightarrow 1 \times K^{**}.$$

The matrix $\mathbf{\Pi}$ can be partitioned in a corresponding way as

$$\mathbf{\Pi} = \begin{bmatrix} \mathbf{\Pi}_{\Delta *} & \mathbf{\Pi}_{\Delta **} \\ \mathbf{\Pi}_{\Delta\Delta *} & \mathbf{\Pi}_{\Delta\Delta **} \end{bmatrix}, \tag{13.12}$$

where

$$\mathbf{\Pi}_{\Delta *} \rightarrow (G^{\Delta} \times K^*),$$

$$\mathbf{\Pi}_{\Delta **} \rightarrow (G^{\Delta} \times K^{**}),$$

$$\mathbf{\Pi}_{\Delta\Delta *} \rightarrow (G^{\Delta\Delta} \times K^*),$$

$$\mathbf{\Pi}_{\Delta\Delta **} \rightarrow (G^{\Delta\Delta} \times K^{**}).$$

By using (13.11) and (13.12), we can rewrite (13.10a) as

$$[\boldsymbol{\beta}_{\Delta} \quad \mathbf{0}_{\Delta\Delta}] \begin{bmatrix} \mathbf{\Pi}_{\Delta *} & \mathbf{\Pi}_{\Delta **} \\ \mathbf{\Pi}_{\Delta\Delta *} & \mathbf{\Pi}_{\Delta\Delta **} \end{bmatrix} = -[\boldsymbol{\gamma}_{*} \quad \mathbf{0}_{**}]. \tag{13.13}$$

This leads to the following equalities:

$$\underset{(1 \times G^{\Delta})(G^{\Delta} \times K^*)}{\boldsymbol{\beta}_{\Delta}\mathbf{\Pi}_{\Delta *}} = \underset{(1 \times K^*)}{-\boldsymbol{\gamma}_{*}}, \tag{13.14}$$

$$\underset{(1 \times G^{\Delta})(G^{\Delta} \times K^{**})}{\boldsymbol{\beta}_{\Delta}\mathbf{\Pi}_{\Delta **}} = \underset{(1 \times K^{**})}{\mathbf{0}_{**}}. \tag{13.15}$$

Since one of the βs in each structural equation equals unity, the equalities (13.14) and (13.15) involve $(G^{\Delta} - 1)$ unknown β's and K^* unknown γs. The equality (13.15) is particularly important since it does not involve any γs. If we can solve (13.15) for $\boldsymbol{\beta}_{\Delta}$, we can solve for $\boldsymbol{\gamma}_{*}$ easily from (13.14). Now, equality (13.15) contains altogether K^{**} equations, one for each element of the $(1 \times K^{**})$ vector. Clearly, if we want to obtain a solution for the $(G^{\Delta} - 1)$ unknown elements of $\boldsymbol{\beta}_{\Delta}$, we need at least $(G^{\Delta} - 1)$ equations. That means that we require that

$$K^{**} \geq G^{\Delta} - 1. \tag{13.16}$$

This is known as the *order condition* for identifiability. This condition, in fact, states that a necessary condition for identification of a given structural equation is that the number of predetermined variables excluded from the given equation is at least as large as the number of endogenous variables included in the equation less one. Note that this is only a *necessary* and not a sufficient condition for identification since the K^{**} equations in (13.15) may not be independent. That is, it may happen that the equations in (13.15) contain fewer than $G^{\Delta} - 1$ different pieces of information about the relation between the βs and the πs. Thus a necessary *and* sufficient condition for identification is that the number of independent equations in (13.15) is $G^{\Delta} - 1$. This will be the case if and only if the order of the largest nonzero determinant that can be formed from all square submatrices of $\mathbf{\Pi}_{\Delta **}$ is $G^{\Delta} - 1$, i.e., if and only if

$$\text{rank}(\mathbf{\Pi}_{\Delta **}) = G^{\Delta} - 1. \tag{13.17}$$

This is known as the *rank condition* for identifiability.

A convenient way of determining the rank of $\mathbf{\Pi}_{\Delta**}$ involves partitioning the matrices of the structural coefficients as follows:

$$\mathbf{B} = \begin{bmatrix} \boldsymbol{\beta}_\Delta & \mathbf{0}_{\Delta\Delta} \\ \mathbf{B}_\Delta & \mathbf{B}_{\Delta\Delta} \end{bmatrix}, \qquad \mathbf{\Gamma} = \begin{bmatrix} \boldsymbol{\gamma}_* & \mathbf{0}_{**} \\ \mathbf{\Gamma}_* & \mathbf{\Gamma}_{**} \end{bmatrix},$$

where $\boldsymbol{\beta}_\Delta$, $\boldsymbol{\gamma}_*$, $\mathbf{0}_{\Delta\Delta}$, and $\mathbf{0}_{**}$ are row vectors defined as in (13.11), and

$$\mathbf{B}_\Delta \rightarrow (G-1) \times G^\Delta,$$

$$\mathbf{B}_{\Delta\Delta} \rightarrow (G-1) \times G^{\Delta\Delta},$$

$$\mathbf{\Gamma}_* \rightarrow (G-1) \times K^*,$$

$$\mathbf{\Gamma}_{**} \rightarrow (G-1) \times K^{**}.$$

Note that $\mathbf{B}_{\Delta\Delta}$ and $\mathbf{\Gamma}_{**}$ are matrices of the structural coefficients for the variables omitted from the gth equation but included in other structural equations. If we now form a new matrix $\mathbf{\Delta}$ defined as

$$\mathbf{\Delta} = [\mathbf{B}_{\Delta\Delta} \quad \mathbf{\Gamma}_{**}],$$

then

(13.17a) $$\text{rank}(\mathbf{\Pi}_{\Delta**}) = \text{rank}(\mathbf{\Delta}) - G^{\Delta\Delta}.$$

This can be proved as follows. Let $\mathbf{\Delta}_*$ be defined as

$$\mathbf{\Delta}_* = \begin{bmatrix} \mathbf{0}_{**} & \mathbf{0}_{\Delta\Delta} \\ \mathbf{\Gamma}_{**} & \mathbf{B}_{\Delta\Delta} \end{bmatrix}.$$

Clearly, the rank of $\mathbf{\Delta}_*$ is the same as that of $\mathbf{\Delta}$ since the rank of a matrix is not affected by enlarging the matrix by a row of zeros, or by switching any columns. Now, $\mathbf{\Delta}_*$ can be written as

$$\mathbf{\Delta}_* = \begin{bmatrix} \boldsymbol{\beta}_\Delta & \mathbf{0}_{\Delta\Delta} \\ \mathbf{B}_\Delta & \mathbf{B}_{\Delta\Delta} \end{bmatrix} \begin{bmatrix} -\mathbf{\Pi}_{\Delta**} & \mathbf{0}_{\Delta,\Delta\Delta} \\ -\mathbf{\Pi}_{\Delta\Delta**} & \mathbf{I}_{\Delta\Delta} \end{bmatrix},$$

where $\mathbf{0}_{\Delta,\Delta\Delta}$ is $G^\Delta \times G^{\Delta\Delta}$ matrix of zeros, and $\mathbf{I}_{\Delta\Delta}$ is an identity matrix of order $G^{\Delta\Delta} \times G^{\Delta\Delta}$. To see that, we carry out the multiplication indicated in the above equality to obtain.

$$\mathbf{\Delta}_* = \begin{bmatrix} -\boldsymbol{\beta}_\Delta \mathbf{\Pi}_{\Delta**} & \mathbf{0}_{\Delta\Delta} \\ (-\mathbf{B}_\Delta \mathbf{\Pi}_{\Delta**} - \mathbf{B}_{\Delta\Delta}\mathbf{\Pi}_{\Delta\Delta**}) & \mathbf{B}_{\Delta\Delta} \end{bmatrix}.$$

But, by (13.15),

$$-\boldsymbol{\beta}_\Delta \mathbf{\Pi}_{\Delta**} = \mathbf{0}_{**},$$

and, from the equality $\mathbf{B\Pi} = -\mathbf{\Gamma}$, it follows that

$$-\mathbf{B}_\Delta \mathbf{\Pi}_{\Delta**} - \mathbf{B}_{\Delta\Delta}\mathbf{\Pi}_{\Delta\Delta**} = \mathbf{\Gamma}_{**}.$$

Utilizing the theorem that if a matrix $\mathbf{A}$ is multiplied by a nonsingular matrix the product has the same rank as **A**, we can write

$$\begin{aligned}
\text{rank}(\mathbf{\Delta}_*) &= \text{rank}(\mathbf{B}^{-1}\mathbf{\Delta}_*) \\
&= \text{rank}\begin{bmatrix} -\mathbf{\Pi}_{\Delta **} & \mathbf{0}_{\Delta,\Delta\Delta} \\ -\mathbf{\Pi}_{\Delta\Delta **} & \mathbf{I}_{\Delta\Delta} \end{bmatrix} \\
&= \text{rank}\begin{bmatrix} -\mathbf{\Pi}_{\Delta **} & \mathbf{0}_{\Delta,\Delta\Delta} \\ -\mathbf{\Pi}_{\Delta\Delta **} & \mathbf{I}_{\Delta\Delta} \end{bmatrix}\begin{bmatrix} \mathbf{I}_{**} & \mathbf{0}_{**,\Delta\Delta} \\ \mathbf{\Pi}_{\Delta\Delta **} & \mathbf{I}_{\Delta\Delta} \end{bmatrix} \\
&= \text{rank}\begin{bmatrix} -\mathbf{\Pi}_{\Delta **} & \mathbf{0}_{\Delta,\Delta\Delta} \\ \mathbf{0}_{\Delta\Delta,**} & \mathbf{I}_{\Delta\Delta} \end{bmatrix} \\
&= \text{rank}(\mathbf{\Pi}_{\Delta **}) + G^{\Delta\Delta},
\end{aligned}$$

where $\mathbf{0}_{**,\Delta\Delta}$ and $\mathbf{0}_{\Delta\Delta,**}$ are zero matrices of order $K^{**} \times G^{\Delta\Delta}$ and $G^{\Delta\Delta} \times K^{**}$, respectively, and $\mathbf{I}_{**}$ is an identity matrix of order $K^{**} \times K^{**}$. This completes the proof of (13.17a). It is clearly much easier to determine the rank of $\mathbf{\Pi}_{\Delta **}$ from (13.17a) than from the direct solution for $\mathbf{\Pi}_{\Delta **}$ in terms of the structural coefficients.

The order and rank conditions enable us to set up the following general rules for determining the identification status of a structural equation.

1. If $K^{**} > G^{\Delta} - 1$ and $\text{rank}(\mathbf{\Pi}_{\Delta **}) = G^{\Delta} - 1$, we have overidentification.
2. If $K^{**} = G^{\Delta} - 1$ and $\text{rank}(\mathbf{\Pi}_{\Delta **}) = G^{\Delta} - 1$, we have exact identification.
3. If $K^{**} \geq G^{\Delta} - 1$ and $\text{rank}(\mathbf{\Pi}_{\Delta **}) < G^{\Delta} - 1$, the structural equation is underidentified.
4. If $K^{**} < G^{\Delta} - 1$, the structural equation is underidentified.

EXAMPLE 1 The supply–demand model described by (13.1) is

$$Q_t = \alpha_1 + \alpha_2 P_t + \alpha_3 Y_t + u_{1t} \qquad \text{(demand)},$$

$$Q_t = \beta_1 + \beta_2 P_t + u_{2t} \qquad \text{(supply)},$$

Consider the identification status of the demand equation first. There are two included endogenous variables, Q_t and P_t, so that

$$G^{\Delta} - 1 = 1.$$

Since no predetermined variables of the system are excluded from the demand equation, we have

$$K^{**} = 0.$$

Therefore,

$$K^{**} < G^{\Delta} - 1,$$

which means that the order condition is not satisfied and, therefore, the demand equation is *underidentified.*

Turning now to the supply equation, we note that there are again two included endogenous variables, Q_t and P_t, i.e., that

$$G^{\Delta} - 1 = 1,$$

but there is now one predetermined variable, Y_t, which appears in the system but not in the supply equation. Thus, in this case we have

$$K^{**} = 1,$$

so that the order condition is satisfied. With respect to the rank condition, we have

$$\text{rank}(\mathbf{\Delta}) = \text{rank}[-\alpha_3] = 1.$$

Then, by (13.17a),

$$\text{rank}(\mathbf{\Pi}_{\Delta **}) = 1 - 0 = 1,$$

and the rank condition is also satisfied. Note that equality (13.15) for the supply equation of our model is

$$[1 \quad -\beta_2] \begin{bmatrix} \pi_{QY} \\ \pi_{PY} \end{bmatrix} = 0,$$

which involves one equation and one unknown; i.e., the supply function is *exactly* identified.

EXAMPLE 2 An aggregate model of the economy has been given as follows:

$$C_t = \alpha_0 + \alpha_1 Y_t + \alpha_2 C_{t-1} + u_t \qquad \text{(consumption)},$$
$$I_t = \beta_0 + \beta_1 r_t + \beta_2 I_{t-1} + u_{2t} \qquad \text{(investment)},$$
$$r_t = \gamma_0 + \gamma_1 Y_t + \gamma_2 M_t + u_{3t} \qquad \text{(money market)},$$
$$Y_t = C_t + I_t + G_t \qquad \text{(income identity)}.$$

For each of the first three structural equations, we have

$$G^{\Delta} - 1 = 1,$$
$$K^{**} = 3,$$

so that the order condition is satisfied in every case. As for the rank condition, the rank of $\mathbf{\Delta}$ for the *consumption function* is

$$\text{rank}(\mathbf{\Delta}) = \text{rank} \begin{bmatrix} 1 & -\beta_1 & -\beta_2 & 0 & 0 \\ 0 & 1 & 0 & -\gamma_2 & 0 \\ -1 & 0 & 0 & 0 & -1 \end{bmatrix} = 3.$$

Therefore,

$$\text{rank}(\mathbf{\Pi}_{\Delta **}) = 3 - 2 = 1,$$

so that the rank condition is satisfied. This means that the consumption function is *identified.* Note that the equality (13.15) in the case of our consumption function becomes

$$[1 \quad -\alpha_1] \begin{bmatrix} \pi_{CI_{-1}} & \pi_{CM} & \pi_{CG} \\ \pi_{YI_{-1}} & \pi_{YM} & \pi_{YG} \end{bmatrix} = [0 \quad 0 \quad 0].$$

That is, there are three equations to determine one unknown; i.e., the consumption function is *overidentified.* The derivation of the rank condition for the remaining two structural equations would follow along the same lines.

The determination of the identification status of an equation of a simultaneous equation system can become rather complicated when the available information about the parameters involved is in a form other than a simple exclusion of variables. The order and rank conditions of identification are of no help if, for instance, the information about the parameters involves coefficient restrictions across equations or restrictions on the variance–covariance matrix of the disturbances. A relatively simple though inelegant way of finding out whether parameters are identified or not is by determining the existence—or the lack of existence—of a solution of the first-order conditions for maximizing the appropriate likelihood function. If, as assumed, the conditions for consistency (and asymptotic efficiency) of the maximum likelihood estimates are satisfied, then their existence implies identifiability of the parameters involved.[3] Since an analytical solution of the first-order conditions is likely to be hard to get, one may take advantage of the available computer programs for maximum likelihood estimation of simultaneous equation systems and try to obtain numerical estimates. Existence of such estimates is, under the appropriate assumptions (and given a sufficiently high degree of numerical precision), an indication of identifiability.

Identification Through Restrictions on the Disturbance Variance–Covariance Matrix

The preceding examination of the identifiability conditions has shown that a structural equation can be identified by specifying that some of the variables appearing in the system are omitted from the equation in question. Since omitting a variable from a linear equation is equivalent to specifying that the corresponding β or γ coefficient is equal to zero, it can be said that identification of an equation is achieved by *zero restrictions* on some of the coefficients. (Of course, identification could also be achieved by *nonzero* restrictions on the structural coefficients, e.g., by specifying that some coefficients are equal to given numbers that are not necessarily zero, or by specifying the ratio or ratios between coefficients in a linear equation.) But if this is the case, it should also be possible to achieve identification by prior restrictions on some of the elements of the variance–covariance matrix of the regression disturbances. We shall illustrate this by reference to the supply–demand model (13.1). In examining the identification status of the structural equations we concluded that, given the zero restrictions on the structural coefficients, the demand equation is underidentified while the supply equation is exactly identified. Let us now add a further restriction by specifying that the disturbances in the two

[3] See E. Greenberg and C. E. Webster, *Advanced Econometrics* (New York: Wiley, 1983), p. 223, or A. Gabrielsen, "Consistency and Identifiability," *Journal of Econometrics,* 8 (October 1978), pp. 261–263.

equations are mutually independent, i.e., that

$$E(u_{1t}u_{2t}) = 0$$

for all t. Our previous results, obtained by utilizing the zero restrictions on the structural coefficients, have led to the following relations between the structural and the reduced form coefficients:

$$\pi_{11} = \alpha_1 + \alpha_2\pi_{21}, \qquad \pi_{11} = \beta_1 + \beta_2\pi_{21},$$

$$\pi_{12} = \alpha_2\pi_{22} + \alpha_3, \qquad \pi_{12} = \beta_2\pi_{22}.$$

As noted earlier, we can solve these equations for the βs but not for the αs. However, now we may add another relation that follows from the zero restriction on the covariance of the two disturbances. First, we note that the reduced form disturbances are given by

$$v_{1t} = \frac{-\beta_2 u_{1t} + \alpha_2 u_{2t}}{\alpha_2 - \beta_2},$$

$$v_{2t} = \frac{-u_{1t} + u_{2t}}{\alpha_2 - \beta_2}.$$

Therefore we can write

$$u_{1t} = v_{1t} - \alpha_2 v_{2t},$$

$$u_{2t} = v_{1t} - \beta_2 v_{2t}.$$

Thus the restriction

$$E(u_{1t}u_{2t}) = 0$$

implies that

$$E(v_{1t} - \alpha_2 v_{2t})(v_{1t} - \beta_2 v_{2t}) = 0$$

or

(13.18) $$\psi_{11} - \alpha_2\psi_{12} - \beta_2\psi_{12} + \alpha_2\beta_2\psi_{22} = 0,$$

where the ψs represent the elements of the variance-covariance matrix of the reduced form disturbances. Since we know that

$$\beta_2 = \frac{\pi_{12}}{\pi_{22}},$$

we can solve (13.18) for α_2 to obtain

$$\alpha_2 = \frac{\pi_{12}\psi_{12} - \pi_{22}\psi_{11}}{\pi_{12}\psi_{22} - \pi_{22}\psi_{12}}.$$

Also, since

$$\alpha_1 = \pi_{11} - \alpha_2\pi_{21}$$

and $$\alpha_3 = \pi_{12} - \alpha_2\pi_{22},$$

we can solve for α_1 and α_3. Thus, with the added restriction on the covariance of the structural disturbances, the previously underidentified demand equation becomes identified.

Underidentification

The question of identification is important because of its implications for estimation and hypothesis testing. If a structural equation is identified, we can obtain consistent estimators of its coefficients. In the case of underidentification, however, it is not possible to derive consistent estimators of the structural coefficients. Of course, we can estimate the coefficients of an underidentified structural equation by the method of ordinary least squares, but the resulting estimates are inconsistent. The fact that consistent estimation of the coefficients of an underidentified structural equation breaks down can be illustrated by reference to the supply–demand model (13.1). We found that—in the absence of any prior information about the variance–covariance matrix of the disturbances—the demand equation of the system is underidentified. This equation was given as

$$Q_t = \alpha_1 + \alpha_2 P_t + \alpha_3 Y_t + u_{1t}.$$

Suppose we try to estimate the coefficients of this equation by the method of *instrumental variables,* which leads to consistent estimates. This method was described in connection with estimating regression models with errors in variables in Section 9-1, and in connection with distributed lag models in Section 11-4. It involves pairing each explanatory variable of the equation to be estimated with an instrumental variable. The latter is supposed to be uncorrelated with the regression disturbance, but correlated with the explanatory variable with which it is paired. In the case of our demand equation, the explanatory variables are Y_t and P_t. Since Y_t is uncorrelated with u_{1t} by assumption, it can serve as its own instrumental variable, so that we need only to find an instrumental variable for P_t. Let this variable be called Z_t. Then the "instrumental variable normal equations" are

$$\sum_t Q_t = \alpha_1^\dagger T + \alpha_2^\dagger \sum_t P_t + \alpha_3^\dagger \sum_t Y_t,$$

$$\sum_t Q_t Z_t = \alpha_1^\dagger \sum_t Z_t + \alpha_2^\dagger \sum_t P_t Z_t + \alpha_3^\dagger \sum_t Y_t Z_t,$$

$$\sum_t Q_t Y_t = \alpha_1^\dagger \sum_t Y_t + \alpha_2^\dagger \sum_t P_t Y_t + \alpha_3^\dagger \sum_t Y_t^2,$$

where $\alpha_1^\dagger$, $\alpha_2^\dagger$, and $\alpha_3^\dagger$ are the instrumental variable estimators of the respective coefficients. The solution for, say, $\alpha_2^\dagger$, is

$$\alpha_2^\dagger = \frac{m_{QZ} m_{YY} - m_{QY} m_{YZ}}{m_{PZ} m_{YY} - m_{PY} m_{YZ}},$$

where

$$m_{QZ} = \sum_t (Q_t - \overline{Q})(Z_t - \overline{Z}),$$

$$m_{YY} = \sum_t (Y_t - \overline{Y})^2,$$

etc. Since from the reduced form solution we have

$$(Q_t - \bar{Q}) = \left(\frac{-\alpha_3\beta_2}{\alpha_2 - \beta_2}\right)(Y_t - \bar{Y}) + (v_{1t} - \bar{v}_1),$$

$$(P_t - \bar{P}) = \left(\frac{-\alpha_3}{\alpha_2 - \beta_2}\right)(Y_t - \bar{Y}) + (v_{2t} - \bar{v}_2),$$

it follows that

$$\text{plim}\ \frac{1}{T} m_{QZ} = \left(\frac{-\alpha_3\beta_2}{\alpha_2 - \beta_2}\right) \text{plim}\ \frac{1}{T} m_{YZ},$$

$$\text{plim}\ \frac{1}{T} m_{QY} = \left(\frac{-\alpha_3\beta_2}{\alpha_2 - \beta_2}\right) \text{plim}\ \frac{1}{T} m_{YY},$$

$$\text{plim}\ \frac{1}{T} m_{PZ} = \left(\frac{-\alpha_3}{\alpha_2 - \beta_2}\right) \text{plim}\ \frac{1}{T} m_{YZ},$$

$$\text{plim}\ \frac{1}{T} m_{PY} = \left(\frac{-\alpha_3}{\alpha_2 - \beta_2}\right) \text{plim}\ \frac{1}{T} m_{YY}.$$

Therefore,

$$\text{plim}\ \alpha_2^\dagger = \frac{\left(\frac{-\alpha_3\beta_2}{\alpha_2 - \beta_2}\right) \text{plim}\ \frac{m_{YZ}}{T} \cdot \text{plim}\ \frac{m_{YY}}{T} - \left(\frac{-\alpha_3\beta_2}{\alpha_2 - \beta_2}\right) \text{plim}\ \frac{m_{YY}}{T} \cdot \text{plim}\ \frac{m_{YZ}}{T}}{\left(\frac{-\alpha_3}{\alpha_2 - \beta_2}\right) \text{plim}\ \frac{m_{YZ}}{T} \cdot \text{plim}\ \frac{m_{YY}}{T} - \left(\frac{-\alpha_3}{\alpha_2 - \beta_2}\right) \text{plim}\ \frac{m_{YY}}{T} \cdot \text{plim}\ \frac{m_{YZ}}{T}}$$

$$= \frac{0}{0},$$

i.e., plim $\alpha_2^\dagger$ is indeterminate. Similar results can be obtained for $\alpha_1^\dagger$ and $\alpha_3^\dagger$. Thus the instrumental variable method breaks down as claimed.

Our inability to obtain consistent estimates of the structural coefficients of an underidentified equation can also be explained in a more intuitive way. In the supply-demand model (13.1), we note that the identification of the supply equation is due to the presence of the exogenous income variable in the demand function. If this variable did not appear in the demand function, both equations of the model would be underidentified. In that case all observations on price and quantity would be scattered around the single point of intersection of the mean price and the mean quantity. An increase in the number of observations in the sample would only increase the denseness of the points without providing any more information about the two lines to be estimated. With the income variable present, however, the demand function shifts with changes in income and, in this way, we observe points that are scattered around the supply function. The more points we observe, the more accurate are the estimates of the coefficients of the supply function. Since there is no exogenous variable in the supply equation, we cannot trace out the demand function in a similar way. However, if the disturbances of the two functions are mutually independent, their covariance is zero, and this additional information enables us to identify the parameters of the demand function as well. Note that since the parameters of underidentified equations cannot be consistently estimated, the hypotheses about their values cannot be refuted by sample observations. This means that the underlying theory is, from scientific viewpoint, incomplete.

13-3 Single-Equation Methods of Estimation

In Section 13-1 we emphasized that the ordinary least squares method of estimation applied to the structural equations of a simultaneous equation system in general leads to inconsistent estimates. Therefore we have to develop other methods to obtain consistent estimates of the structural coefficients. As stated, this is not possible when a structural equation is underidentified.

Our concern here is with structural equations that are identified and for which consistent methods of estimation are available. We have two categories of methods of estimating structural equations: (1) methods designed to estimate a single structural equation with only a limited reference to the rest of the system and (2) methods by which all equations of the system are estimated simultaneously. This section deals with methods belonging to the first category.

Estimation of an Exactly Identified Equation

Consider the problem of estimating an *exactly identified* structural equation belonging to a general interdependent system of simultaneous equations with no restrictions on the variance-covariance matrix of the disturbances. In this case there exists a unique solution for the structural coefficients in terms of the reduced form coefficients. The reduced form equations are given by (13.6a) as

$$\mathbf{y}_t = \mathbf{\Pi x}_t + \mathbf{v}_t,$$

where $\mathbf{y}_t$ is a $(G \times 1)$ vector of the endogenous variables, $\mathbf{\Pi}$ is a $(G \times K)$ matrix of the reduced form coefficients, $\mathbf{x}_t$ is a $(K \times 1)$ vector of the predetermined variables, and $\mathbf{v}_t$ is a $(G \times 1)$ vector of the reduced form disturbances. Since the reduced form disturbances are represented by linear combinations of the structural disturbances, they satisfy all the assumptions of the classical normal linear regression model. The predetermined variables, which serve as explanatory variables in the reduced form equations, are either nonstochastic or, if stochastic, independent of the current disturbances. We shall also assume that they have finite variances and covariances as $T \rightarrow \infty$, and that there exists no exact linear relation between them. If the predetermined variables include lagged endogenous variables, we assume that the initial values of these variables are fixed. Under these assumptions, the application of the ordinary (unrestricted) least squares method to each reduced form equation leads to consistent estimates of the π's. If *all* structural equations are exactly identified, these estimates will be equivalent to the maximum likelihood estimates and will, in addition to consistency, also possess the properties of asymptotic efficiency and asymptotic normality. The ordinary least squares estimates of the reduced form coefficients can be used to determine the corresponding estimates of the structural coefficients as specified by (13.14) and (13.15). The latter are called *indirect least squares* (ILS) *estimates.* They are, in general, given as nonlinear functions of the reduced form estimates and inherit all their asymptotic properties.

EXAMPLE To illustrate the use of the indirect least squares method, we use the supply–demand model described by (13.1) as

$$Q_t = \alpha_1 + \alpha_2 P_t + \alpha_3 Y_t + u_{1t} \qquad \text{(demand)},$$

$$Q_t = \beta_1 + \beta_2 P_t + u_{2t} \qquad \text{(supply)},$$

where Q_t and P_t are endogenous and Y_t is exogenous. Without any restrictions on the variance–covariance matrix of the disturbances, the demand equation is underidentified, but the supply equation is exactly identified. The reduced form equations are

$$Q_t = \pi_{11} + \pi_{12} Y_t + v_{1t},$$

$$P_t = \pi_{21} + \pi_{22} Y_t + v_{2t}.$$

Substituting the reduced form expression for Q_t and P_t into the supply equation, we obtain

$$\pi_{11} + \pi_{12} Y_t + v_{1t} = \beta_1 + \beta_2(\pi_{21} + \pi_{22} Y_t + v_{2t}) + u_{2t}.$$

Therefore,

$$\pi_{11} = \beta_1 + \beta_2 \pi_{21},$$

$$\pi_{12} = \beta_2 \pi_{22},$$

or

$$\beta_2 = \frac{\pi_{12}}{\pi_{22}},$$

$$\beta_1 = \pi_{11} - \frac{\pi_{12}\pi_{21}}{\pi_{22}}.$$

Now the ordinary least squares estimators of the reduced form coefficients are

$$\hat{\pi}_{12} = \frac{m_{QY}}{m_{YY}},$$

$$\hat{\pi}_{11} = \overline{Q} - \left(\frac{m_{QY}}{m_{YY}}\right) \overline{Y},$$

$$\hat{\pi}_{22} = \frac{m_{PY}}{m_{YY}},$$

$$\hat{\pi}_{21} = \overline{P} - \left(\frac{m_{PY}}{m_{YY}}\right) \overline{Y},$$

where

$$m_{QY} = \sum_t (Q_t - \overline{Q})(Y_t - \overline{Y}),$$

$$m_{PY} = \sum_t (P_t - \overline{P})(Y_t - \overline{Y}),$$

$$m_{YY} = \sum_t (Y_t - \overline{Y})^2.$$

Hence the indirect least squares estimators of β_1 and β_2 are

$$\tilde{\beta}_2 = \frac{m_{QY}}{m_{PY}},$$

$$\tilde{\beta}_1 = \overline{Q} - \left(\frac{m_{QY}}{m_{PY}}\right)\overline{P}.$$

The problem of estimating the coefficients of a structural equation can also be approached by resorting to the *instrumental variable* (IV) *method.* Suppose the structural equation that we wish to estimate is the first equation of the system, i.e.,

$$(13.19)\quad \beta_{11}y_{1t} + \beta_{12}y_{2t} + \cdots + \beta_{1G}y_{Gt} + \gamma_{11}x_{1t} + \gamma_{12}x_{2t} + \cdots + \gamma_{1K}x_{Kt} = u_{1t}.$$

This involves no loss of generality since the structural equations can be written in any order we like. Let us suppose further that β_{11} is equal to unity, and that the included endogenous and predetermined variables are $y_{1t}, y_{2t}, \ldots, y_{G^\Delta t}, x_{1t}, x_{2t}, \ldots, x_{K^*t}$. Then (13.19) can be written as

$$(13.19a)\quad y_{1t} = -\beta_{12}y_{2t} - \beta_{13}y_{3t} - \cdots - \beta_{1G^\Delta}y_{G^\Delta t} - \gamma_{11}x_{1t} - \gamma_{12}x_{2t} - \cdots - \gamma_{1K^*}x_{K^*t} + u_{1t}.$$

In matrix notation, equation (13.19a) can be expressed as

$$(13.20)\quad \mathbf{y}_1 = \mathbf{Y}_1\boldsymbol{\beta}_1 + \mathbf{X}_1\boldsymbol{\gamma}_1 + \mathbf{u}_1,$$

where

$$\underset{(T\times 1)}{\mathbf{y}_1 = \begin{bmatrix} y_{11} \\ y_{12} \\ \vdots \\ y_{1T} \end{bmatrix}},\quad \underset{(T\times \overline{G^\Delta - 1})}{\mathbf{Y}_1 = \begin{bmatrix} y_{21} & y_{31} & \cdots & y_{G^\Delta 1} \\ y_{22} & y_{32} & \cdots & y_{G^\Delta 2} \\ \vdots & \vdots & & \vdots \\ y_{2T} & y_{3T} & \cdots & y_{G^\Delta T} \end{bmatrix}},\quad \underset{(T\times K^*)}{\mathbf{X}_1 = \begin{bmatrix} x_{11} & x_{21} & \cdots & x_{K^*1} \\ x_{12} & x_{22} & \cdots & x_{K^*2} \\ \vdots & \vdots & & \vdots \\ x_{1T} & x_{2T} & \cdots & x_{K^*T} \end{bmatrix}},$$

$$\underset{(\overline{G^\Delta - 1}\times 1)}{\boldsymbol{\beta}_1 = \begin{bmatrix} -\beta_{12} \\ -\beta_{13} \\ \vdots \\ -\beta_{1G^\Delta} \end{bmatrix}},\quad \underset{(K^*\times 1)}{\boldsymbol{\gamma}_1 = \begin{bmatrix} -\gamma_{11} \\ -\gamma_{12} \\ \vdots \\ -\gamma_{1K^*} \end{bmatrix}}.$$

An alternative way of writing (13.20) is

$$(13.20a)\quad \mathbf{y}_1 = \mathbf{Z}_1\boldsymbol{\alpha}_1 + \mathbf{u}_1,$$

where

$$\mathbf{Z}_1 = [\mathbf{Y}_1 \quad \mathbf{X}_1] \quad \text{and} \quad \boldsymbol{\alpha}_1 = \begin{bmatrix} \boldsymbol{\beta}_1 \\ \boldsymbol{\gamma}_1 \end{bmatrix}.$$

An instrumental variable estimator of the structural coefficients is

$$\alpha^{\dagger} = (\mathbf{W}_1'\mathbf{Z}_1)^{-1}(\mathbf{W}_1'\mathbf{y}_1), \tag{13.21}$$

and its estimated variance-covariance matrix is

$$\text{Est. Var-Cov}(\alpha^{\dagger}) = s_{11}(\mathbf{W}_1'\mathbf{Z}_1)^{-1}(\mathbf{W}_1'\mathbf{W}_1)(\mathbf{Z}_1'\mathbf{W}_1)^{-1}, \tag{13.22}$$

where $\mathbf{W}_1$ is a $T \times (G^{\Delta} - 1 + K^*)$ matrix of the observed values of the chosen instrumental variables.[4] The estimator s_{11} can be obtained by the formula

$$s_{11} = \frac{(\mathbf{y}_1 - \mathbf{Z}_1\alpha_1^{\dagger})'(\mathbf{y}_1 - \mathbf{Z}_1\alpha_1^{\dagger})}{(T - G^{\Delta} + 1 - K^*)}. \tag{13.23}$$

(The consistency of the estimator will not be changed if we use any denominator D in place of $(T - G^{\Delta} + 1 - K^*)$ *providing* plim $(D/T) = 1$.) As for the choice of appropriate instrumental variables, the problem is confined to the $(G^{\Delta} - 1)$ included endogenous variables, since the predetermined variables included in the equation can serve as their own instrumental variables. Natural candidates for the "outside" instrumental variables would be the predetermined variables that appear in the system but not in the equation to be estimated. The number of these is K^{**}, which, in the case of an *exactly identified* structural equation, is just equal to $(G^{\Delta} - 1)$. Let $\underline{\mathbf{X}}_1$ be the matrix of the observed values of the excluded predetermined variables, i.e., let

$$\underline{\mathbf{X}}_1 = \begin{bmatrix} x_{K^*+1,1} & x_{K^*+2,1} & \cdots & x_{K1} \\ x_{K^*+1,2} & x_{K^*+2,2} & \cdots & x_{K2} \\ \vdots & \vdots & & \vdots \\ x_{K^*+1,T} & x_{K^*+2,T} & \cdots & x_{KT} \end{bmatrix}. \tag{13.24}$$

The order in which these variables are arranged is immaterial. Then the instrumental variables for our structural equation can be taken as

$$\mathbf{W}_1 = [\underline{\mathbf{X}}_1 \quad \mathbf{X}_1] \tag{13.25}$$

Therefore,

$$\mathbf{W}_1'\mathbf{Z}_1 = \begin{bmatrix} \underline{\mathbf{X}}_1' \\ \mathbf{X}_1' \end{bmatrix} [\mathbf{Y}_1 \quad \mathbf{X}_1] = \begin{bmatrix} \underline{\mathbf{X}}_1'\mathbf{Y}_1 & \underline{\mathbf{X}}_1'\mathbf{X}_1 \\ \mathbf{X}_1'\mathbf{Y}_1 & \mathbf{X}_1'\mathbf{X}_1 \end{bmatrix},$$

and

$$\mathbf{W}_1'\mathbf{y}_1 = \begin{bmatrix} \underline{\mathbf{X}}_1'\mathbf{y}_1 \\ \mathbf{X}_1'\mathbf{y}_1 \end{bmatrix}.$$

Hence the instrumental variable estimator of the structural coefficients in the exactly identified case is

$$\alpha_1^{\dagger} = \begin{bmatrix} \beta_1^{\dagger} \\ \gamma_1^{\dagger} \end{bmatrix} = \begin{bmatrix} \underline{\mathbf{X}}_1'\mathbf{Y}_1 & \underline{\mathbf{X}}_1'\mathbf{X}_1 \\ \mathbf{X}_1'\mathbf{Y}_1 & \mathbf{X}_1'\mathbf{X}_1 \end{bmatrix}^{-1} \begin{bmatrix} \underline{\mathbf{X}}_1'\mathbf{y}_1 \\ \mathbf{X}_1'\mathbf{y}_1 \end{bmatrix}. \tag{13.26}$$

[4] See Judge et al., *op. cit.*, pp. 167-169.

Further, following (13.22) and (13.23) we define a consistent estimator of the variance–covariance matrix of $\boldsymbol{\alpha}^{\dagger}$ as

(13.27)

$$\text{Est. Var–Cov}(\boldsymbol{\alpha}^{\dagger}) = s_{11} \begin{bmatrix} \underline{\mathbf{X}}_1'\mathbf{Y}_1 & \underline{\mathbf{X}}_1'\mathbf{X}_1 \\ \mathbf{X}_1'\mathbf{Y}_1 & \mathbf{X}_1'\mathbf{X}_1 \end{bmatrix}^{-1} \begin{bmatrix} \underline{\mathbf{X}}_1'\underline{\mathbf{X}}_1 & \underline{\mathbf{X}}_1'\mathbf{X}_1 \\ \mathbf{X}_1'\underline{\mathbf{X}}_1 & \mathbf{X}_1'\mathbf{X}_1 \end{bmatrix} \begin{bmatrix} \mathbf{Y}_1'\underline{\mathbf{X}}_1 & \mathbf{Y}_1'\mathbf{X}_1 \\ \mathbf{X}_1'\underline{\mathbf{X}}_1 & \mathbf{X}_1'\mathbf{X}_1 \end{bmatrix}^{-1},$$

where s_{11} is determined as in (13.23).

The instrumental variable estimator (13.26) is, in fact, *exactly the same* as the indirect least squares estimator described earlier. We shall not give a general proof of this proposition, but we will demonstrate its validity with reference to the supply equation of the supply–demand model (13.1). This equation,

$$Q_t = \beta_1 + \beta_2 P_t + u_{2t},$$

is exactly identified, with Y_t being the excluded predetermined variable. In terms of the notation used for instrumental variable estimation, we have

$$\mathbf{Z}_1 = [\mathbf{P} \quad \boldsymbol{\iota}],$$
$$\mathbf{W}_1 = [\mathbf{Y} \quad \boldsymbol{\iota}],$$
$$\mathbf{y}_1 = [\mathbf{Q}],$$

where

$$\underset{(T\times 1)}{\mathbf{Q} = \begin{bmatrix} Q_1 \\ Q_2 \\ \vdots \\ Q_T \end{bmatrix}}, \quad \underset{(T\times 1)}{\mathbf{P} = \begin{bmatrix} P_1 \\ P_2 \\ \vdots \\ P_T \end{bmatrix}}, \quad \underset{(T\times 1)}{\mathbf{Y} = \begin{bmatrix} Y_1 \\ Y_2 \\ \vdots \\ Y_T \end{bmatrix}}, \quad \underset{(T\times 1)}{\boldsymbol{\iota} = \begin{bmatrix} 1 \\ 1 \\ \vdots \\ 1 \end{bmatrix}}.$$

Then

$$\mathbf{W}_1'\mathbf{Z}_1 = \begin{bmatrix} \mathbf{Y}' \\ \boldsymbol{\iota}' \end{bmatrix} [\mathbf{P} \quad \boldsymbol{\iota}] = \begin{bmatrix} \sum_t P_t Y_t & \sum_t Y_t \\ \sum_t P_t & T \end{bmatrix},$$

and

$$\mathbf{W}_1'\mathbf{y}_1 = \begin{bmatrix} \mathbf{Y}' \\ \boldsymbol{\iota}' \end{bmatrix} [\mathbf{Q}] = \begin{bmatrix} \sum_t Q_t Y_t \\ \sum_t Q_t \end{bmatrix}.$$

Therefore, by (13.21) we have

(13.28)

$$\begin{bmatrix} \beta_2^\dagger \\ \beta_1^\dagger \end{bmatrix} = \frac{1}{T\sum P_tY_t - (\sum P_t)(\sum Y_t)} \begin{bmatrix} T & -\sum_t Y_t \\ -\sum_t P_t & \sum_t P_tY_t \end{bmatrix} \begin{bmatrix} \sum_t Q_tY_t \\ \sum_t Q_t \end{bmatrix}$$

$$= \begin{bmatrix} \dfrac{m_{QY}}{m_{PY}} \\ \bar{Q} - \left(\dfrac{m_{QY}}{m_{PY}}\right)\bar{P} \end{bmatrix}.$$

Clearly, these formulas are exactly the same as the indirect least squares formulas.

The equivalence of the indirect least squares and the instrumental variable estimator enables us to use the instrumental variable formula for the asymptotic variance-covariance matrix of the estimated coefficients. This is very useful since the derivation of the asymptotic variance-covariance matrix of the indirect least squares estimator is otherwise awkward. For example, consider estimating the variance-covariance matrix of the estimated coefficients of the supply equation discussed in (13.1). By appropriate substitution into (13.27) we obtain

(13.29) Est. Var-Cov $\begin{bmatrix} \beta_2^\dagger \\ \beta_1^\dagger \end{bmatrix}$

$$= s_{22} \begin{bmatrix} \sum_t P_tY_t & \sum_t Y_t \\ \sum_t P_t & T \end{bmatrix}^{-1} \begin{bmatrix} \sum_t Y_t^2 & \sum_t Y_t \\ \sum_t Y_t & T \end{bmatrix} \begin{bmatrix} \sum_t P_tY_t & \sum_t P_t \\ \sum_t Y_t & T \end{bmatrix}^{-1}$$

$$= \frac{s_{22}}{(Tm_{PY})^2} \begin{bmatrix} T^2 m_{YY} & -T(\sum P_t)\, m_{YY} \\ -T(\sum P_t)\, m_{YY} & (\sum P_t)^2 m_{YY} + Tm_{PY}^2 \end{bmatrix}$$

$$= s_{22} \begin{bmatrix} \left(\dfrac{m_{YY}}{m_{PY}^2}\right) & \left(\dfrac{-\bar{P}m_{YY}}{m_{PY}^2}\right) \\ \left(\dfrac{-\bar{P}m_{YY}}{m_{PY}^2}\right) & \left(\dfrac{\bar{P}^2 m_{YY}}{m_{PY}^2} + \dfrac{1}{T}\right) \end{bmatrix},$$

where

$$(13.30) \qquad s_{22} = \frac{1}{T-2} \sum_t (Q_t - \beta_1^\dagger - \beta_2^\dagger P_t)^2$$

$$= \frac{1}{T-2} \left(\frac{m_{QQ}m_{PY}^2 - 2m_{QY}m_{QP}m_{PY} + m_{PP}m_{QY}^2}{m_{PY}^2} \right).$$

EXAMPLE The supply equation in (13.1) can be estimated from the annual data on the American meat market for the period 1919–1941.[5]

Q_t = per capita consumption of meat (pounds),

P_t = retail prices of meat (index, 1935–39 = 100),

Y_t = per capita disposable real income (dollars).

The sample means of these variables are

$$\bar{Q} = 166.1913,$$

$$\bar{P} = 92.3391,$$

$$\bar{Y} = 495.5652;$$

the sums of squares and cross-products of the deviations from sample means are

$$m_{QQ} = 1{,}369.53826, \qquad m_{PP} = 1{,}581.49478,$$

$$m_{QP} = -352.55217, \qquad m_{PY} = 8{,}354.59130,$$

$$m_{QY} = 3{,}671.91304, \qquad m_{YY} = 83{,}433.65217.$$

The indirect least squares estimates of the structural coefficients of the supply equation are

$$\tilde{\beta}_2 = \frac{3{,}671.91304}{8{,}354.59130} = 0.43951,$$

$$\tilde{\beta}_1 = 166.1913 - 0.43951 \times 92.3391 = 125.60749.$$

The estimate of the variance of the structural disturbance, calculated according to (13.30), is

$$s_{22} = \frac{1{,}984.9311}{21} = 94.5205.$$

The estimated variances of the indirect least squares estimates are then obtained from (13.29) as follows:

$$\text{Est. Var}(\tilde{\beta}_2) = 94.5205 \left(\frac{83{,}433.65217}{8{,}354.59130^2} \right) = 0.11298318,$$

$$\text{Est. Var}(\tilde{\beta}_1) = 94.5205 \left(\frac{92.3391^2 \times 83{,}433.65217}{8{,}354.59130^2} + \frac{1}{23} \right) = 10.23547072.$$

[5] From G. Tintner, *Econometrics* (New York: Wiley, 1965), p. 169.

Thus the final result of indirect least squares estimation is

$$Q_t = \underset{(3.19929)}{125.60749)} + \underset{(0.33613)}{0.43951}P_t + \hat{u}_{2t}.$$

For comparison we also present the (inconsistent) ordinary least squares estimates of the supply equation:

$$Q_t = 145.60676 - 0.22292P_t + e_{2t}.$$

The estimation of an *exactly identified* structural equation when identification is achieved by *restrictions on the variance-covariance matrix* of the structural disturbances can also be examined in the context of the supply-demand model (13.1). The demand equation

$$Q_t = \alpha_1 + \alpha_2 P_t + \alpha_3 Y_t + u_{1t}$$

—which, in the case of no restrictions on the variance-covariance matrix of the disturbances, is underidentified—becomes exactly identified if we assume that u_{1t} and u_{2t} are uncorrelated, as discussed in Section 13-2. The identifying relations between the structural coefficients and the reduced form parameters are as follows. First, by substituting the reduced form expressions for Q_t and P_t into the demand equation, we obtain

(13.31) $$\pi_{11} = \alpha_1 + \alpha_2\pi_{21},$$

(13.32) $$\pi_{12} = \alpha_2\pi_{22} + \alpha_3.$$

Next, from (13.18) we know that

$$\psi_{11} - \alpha_2\psi_{12} - \beta_2\psi_{12} + \alpha_2\beta_2\psi_{22} = 0,$$

where the ψs are the elements of the variance-covariance matrix of the reduced form disturbances and β_2 is a structural coefficient of the supply equation. Since from the results for the supply equation we get

$$\beta_2 = \frac{\pi_{12}}{\pi_{22}},$$

we can write

(13.33) $$\alpha_2 = \frac{\pi_{12}\psi_{12} - \pi_{21}\psi_{11}}{\pi_{12}\psi_{22} - \pi_{22}\psi_{12}}.$$

Equations (13.31), (13.32), and (13.33) enable us to express the structural coefficients α_1, α_2, and α_3 in terms of the πs and ψs of the reduced form equations. The reduced form parameters can be estimated by application of the ordinary least squares formulas. From the estimates of the reduced form parameters we can determine the corresponding estimates of the αs. Since both equations are now exactly identified, these estimates are maximum likelihood estimates, and their asymptotic variance-covariance matrix can be determined by reference to the information matrix for the appropriate likelihood function. Note that the likelihood function for the sample observations on Q_t and P_t of our supply–demand model is

$$L = -T\log(2\pi) - \frac{T}{2}\log(\sigma_{11}\sigma_{22}) + T\log|\alpha_2 - \beta_2|$$

$$-\frac{1}{2\sigma_{11}}\sum_t (Q_t - \alpha_1 - \alpha_2 P_t - \alpha_3 Y_t)^2 - \frac{1}{2\sigma_{22}}\sum_t (Q_t - \beta_1 - \beta_2 P_t)^2.$$

EXAMPLE We will estimate the demand equation of (13.1) on the assumption of zero covariance between u_{1t} and u_{2t} from the data on the American meat market given in the preceding example. First, note that the ordinary least squares estimators of the reduced form coefficients are

$$\hat{\pi}_{12} = \frac{m_{QY}}{m_{YY}},$$

$$\hat{\pi}_{11} = \bar{Q} - \hat{\pi}_{12}\bar{Y},$$

$$\hat{\pi}_{22} = \frac{m_{PY}}{m_{YY}},$$

$$\hat{\pi}_{21} = \bar{P} - \hat{\pi}_{22}\bar{Y}.$$

The variances and the covariance of the reduced form disturbances are estimated as follows.

$$\hat{\psi}_{11} = \frac{m_{QQ} - \hat{\pi}_{12}m_{QY}}{T} = \frac{m_{QQ}m_{YY} - m_{QY}^2}{Tm_{YY}},$$

$$\hat{\psi}_{22} = \frac{m_{PP} - \hat{\pi}_{22}m_{PY}}{T} = \frac{m_{PP}m_{YY} - m_{PY}^2}{Tm_{YY}},$$

$$\hat{\psi}_{12} = \frac{m_{QP} - \hat{\pi}_{12}m_{PY} - \hat{\pi}_{22}m_{QY} + \hat{\pi}_{12}\hat{\pi}_{22}m_{YY}}{T} = \frac{m_{QP}m_{YY} - m_{QY}m_{PY}}{Tm_{YY}}.$$

By substituting these results into (13.33) we find, after some simplifications,

$$\tilde{\alpha}_2 = \frac{m_{QY}m_{QP} - m_{QQ}m_{PY}}{m_{QY}m_{PP} - m_{QP}m_{PY}}$$

$$= \frac{3{,}671.91304 \times (-352.55217) - 1{,}369.53826 \times 8{,}354.59130}{3{,}671.91304 \times 1{,}581.49478 - (-352.55217) \times 8{,}354.59130} = -1.4551.$$

Further, from (13.31), we have

$$\tilde{\alpha}_1 = \hat{\pi}_{11} - \tilde{\alpha}_2\hat{\pi}_{21} = 206.5374,$$

and from (13.32),

$$\tilde{\alpha}_3 = \hat{\pi}_{12} - \tilde{\alpha}_2\hat{\pi}_{22} = 0.1897.$$

Therefore, the estimated demand equation is

$$Q_t = 206.5374 - 1.4551P_t + 0.1897Y_t + \hat{u}_{1t}.$$

Under the assumptions of the model, these estimates are consistent and asymptotically efficient. For comparison we also present the ordinary least squares estimates, which are not consistent:

$$Q_t = 185.8452 - 0.9739P_t + 0.1418Y_t + e_{1t}.$$

Two-Stage Least Squares Estimation

In estimating an *overidentified* structural equation belonging to a general interdependent system of equations, there are several methods leading to consistent estimation that can be used. Probably the best-known single equation method is that of *two-stage least squares* (2SLS). Suppose the overidentified structural equation is the first equation of the system

$$\mathbf{y}_1 = \mathbf{Y}_1\boldsymbol{\beta}_1 + \mathbf{X}_1\boldsymbol{\gamma}_1 + \mathbf{u}_1, \tag{13.34}$$

where $\mathbf{y}_1$ is a $(T \times 1)$ vector of the endogenous variable whose coefficient in the first equation is one, $\mathbf{Y}_1$ is a $T \times (G^\Delta - 1)$ matrix of the remaining endogenous variables in the first equation, $\mathbf{X}_1$ is a $(T \times K^*)$ matrix of the predetermined variables in the first equation, and $\mathbf{u}_1$ is a $(T \times 1)$ vector of the disturbances in this equation. An alternative way of writing (13.34) is

$$\mathbf{y}_1 = \mathbf{Z}_1\boldsymbol{\alpha}_1 + \mathbf{u}_1, \tag{13.34a}$$

where $\quad \mathbf{Z}_1 = [\mathbf{Y}_1 \quad \mathbf{X}_1] \quad$ and $\quad \boldsymbol{\alpha}_1 = \begin{bmatrix} \boldsymbol{\beta}_1 \\ \boldsymbol{\gamma}_1 \end{bmatrix}.$

The matrix $\mathbf{Y}_1$ can be partitioned to give

$$\mathbf{Y}_1 = [\mathbf{y}_2 \quad \mathbf{y}_3 \quad \cdots \quad \mathbf{y}_{G^\Delta}],$$

where each of the **y**s is a vector of order $T \times 1$. The reduced form equations for these variables are

$$\begin{aligned} \mathbf{y}_2 &= \mathbf{X}\boldsymbol{\pi}_2 + \mathbf{v}_2, \\ \mathbf{y}_3 &= \mathbf{X}\boldsymbol{\pi}_3 + \mathbf{v}_3, \\ &\vdots \\ \mathbf{y}_{G^\Delta} &= \mathbf{X}\boldsymbol{\pi}_{G^\Delta} + \mathbf{v}_{G^\Delta}, \end{aligned}$$

where **X** is a $(T \times K)$ matrix of *all* predetermined variables in the system, each of the $\boldsymbol{\pi}$s represents a $(K \times 1)$ vector of the corresponding reduced form coefficients, and each of the **v**s is a $(T \times 1)$ vector of the corresponding reduced form disturbances. Let

$$\mathbf{V}_1 = [\mathbf{v}_2 \quad \mathbf{v}_3 \quad \cdots \quad \mathbf{v}_{G^\Delta}]$$

and

$$\mathbf{Y}_1 - \mathbf{V}_1 = [\mathbf{X}\boldsymbol{\pi}_2 \quad \mathbf{X}\boldsymbol{\pi}_3 \quad \cdots \quad \mathbf{X}\boldsymbol{\pi}_{G^\Delta}].$$

Therefore (13.34) can be written as

(13.35) $$\mathbf{y}_1 = (\mathbf{Y}_1 - \mathbf{V}_1)\beta_1 + \mathbf{X}_1\gamma_1 + (\mathbf{u}_1 + \mathbf{V}_1\beta_1).$$

Since $(\mathbf{Y}_1 - \mathbf{V}_1)$ depends only on $\mathbf{X}$ and does not involve any disturbance, it is uncorrelated with $(\mathbf{u}_1 + \mathbf{V}_1\beta_1)$. Thus applying the ordinary least squares method to (13.35) would lead to consistent estimates of β_1 and γ_1. The difficulty is that $\mathbf{V}_1$—and therefore $(\mathbf{Y}_1 - \mathbf{V}_1)$—is not observable. However, we can replace $\mathbf{V}_1$ by the corresponding reduced form least squares residuals and use

$$\mathbf{Y}_1 - \hat{\mathbf{V}}_1 = \hat{\mathbf{Y}}_1 = [\mathbf{X}\hat{\pi}_2 \quad \mathbf{X}\hat{\pi}_3 \quad \cdots \quad \mathbf{X}\hat{\pi}_{G\Delta}].$$

Clearly,

$$\text{plim}(\mathbf{Y}_1 - \hat{\mathbf{V}}_1) = [\mathbf{X}\pi_2 \quad \mathbf{X}\pi_3 \quad \cdots \quad \mathbf{X}\pi_{G\Delta}] = \mathbf{Y}_1 - \mathbf{V}_1,$$

so that $(\mathbf{Y}_1 - \hat{\mathbf{V}}_1)$ and $(\mathbf{u}_1 + \hat{\mathbf{V}}_1\beta_1)$ are *asymptotically uncorrelated.* Therefore, if we apply the ordinary least squares method to

(13.36) $$\mathbf{y}_1 = \hat{\mathbf{Y}}_1\beta_1 + \mathbf{X}_1\gamma_1 + \mathbf{u}_1^*,$$

where $$\mathbf{u}_1^* = \mathbf{u}_1 + \hat{\mathbf{V}}_1\beta_1,$$

we obtain consistent estimates of β_1 and γ_1. These estimates are called "two-stage least squares" because the estimation process may be viewed as consisting of two successive applications of the ordinary least squares method. In the first stage we estimate the reduced form equations for $\mathbf{y}_2, \mathbf{y}_3, \ldots, \mathbf{y}_{G\Delta}$ and calculate the fitted values of these variables. In the second stage we apply the least squares method to (13.36) where the fitted values of $\mathbf{y}_2, \mathbf{y}_3, \ldots, \mathbf{y}_{G\Delta}$ are used as explanatory variables.

By analogy with (13.34a), equation (13.36) could also be written as

(13.36a) $$\mathbf{y}_1 = \hat{\mathbf{Z}}_1\alpha_1 + \mathbf{u}_1^*,$$

where $$\hat{\mathbf{Z}}_1 = [\hat{\mathbf{Y}}_1 \quad \mathbf{X}_1].$$

The application of the least squares method to (13.36a) leads to

(13.37) $$\tilde{\tilde{\alpha}}_1 = \begin{bmatrix} \tilde{\tilde{\beta}}_1 \\ \tilde{\tilde{\gamma}}_1 \end{bmatrix} = (\hat{\mathbf{Z}}'\hat{\mathbf{Z}})^{-1}(\hat{\mathbf{Z}}\mathbf{y}_1) = \begin{bmatrix} \hat{\mathbf{Y}}_1'\hat{\mathbf{Y}}_1 & \hat{\mathbf{Y}}_1'\mathbf{X}_1 \\ \mathbf{X}_1'\hat{\mathbf{Y}}_1 & \mathbf{X}_1'\mathbf{X}_1 \end{bmatrix}^{-1} \begin{bmatrix} \hat{\mathbf{Y}}_1'\mathbf{y}_1 \\ \mathbf{X}_1'\mathbf{y}_1 \end{bmatrix}$$

or, since

$$\hat{\mathbf{Y}}_1 = \mathbf{X}\hat{\pi}_1 = \mathbf{X}(\mathbf{X}'\mathbf{X})^{-1}\mathbf{X}'\mathbf{Y}_1$$

and

$$\hat{\mathbf{Y}}_1'\mathbf{X}_1 = (\mathbf{Y}_1 - \hat{\mathbf{V}}_1)'\mathbf{X}_1 = \mathbf{Y}_1'\mathbf{X}_1,$$

(13.37a) $$\tilde{\tilde{\alpha}}_1 = \begin{bmatrix} \mathbf{Y}_1'\mathbf{X}(\mathbf{X}'\mathbf{X})^{-1}\mathbf{X}'\mathbf{Y}_1 & \mathbf{Y}_1'\mathbf{X}_1 \\ \mathbf{X}_1'\mathbf{Y}_1 & \mathbf{X}_1'\mathbf{X}_1 \end{bmatrix}^{-1} \begin{bmatrix} \mathbf{Y}_1'\mathbf{X}(\mathbf{X}'\mathbf{X})^{-1}\mathbf{X}'\mathbf{y}_1 \\ \mathbf{X}_1'\mathbf{y}_1 \end{bmatrix}.$$

Further, since $\hat{\mathbf{V}}_1'\hat{\mathbf{Y}}_1 = 0$ and $\hat{\mathbf{Y}}_1'\hat{\mathbf{Y}}_1 = (\mathbf{Y}_1 - \hat{\mathbf{V}}_1)'(\mathbf{Y}_1 - \hat{\mathbf{V}}_1) = \mathbf{Y}_1'\mathbf{Y}_1 - \hat{\mathbf{V}}_1'\hat{\mathbf{V}}_1$, equation (13.37) can be written as

$$(13.38)\qquad \tilde{\tilde{\alpha}}_1 = \begin{bmatrix} \tilde{\tilde{\beta}}_1 \\ \tilde{\tilde{\gamma}}_1 \end{bmatrix} = \begin{bmatrix} \mathbf{Y}_1'\mathbf{Y}_1 - \hat{\mathbf{V}}_1'\hat{\mathbf{V}}_1 & \mathbf{Y}_1'\mathbf{X}_1 \\ \mathbf{X}_1'\mathbf{Y}_1 & \mathbf{X}_1'\mathbf{X}_1 \end{bmatrix}^{-1} \begin{bmatrix} \mathbf{Y}_1'\mathbf{y}_1 - \hat{\mathbf{V}}_1'\mathbf{y}_1 \\ \mathbf{X}_1'\mathbf{y}_1 \end{bmatrix}.$$

This is the form in which the formula for the two-stage least squares estimator is usually presented because it shows clearly how this estimator differs from the (inconsistent) ordinary least squares estimator, which is given as

$$(13.39)\qquad \hat{\alpha}_1 = \begin{bmatrix} \hat{\beta}_1 \\ \tilde{\gamma}_1 \end{bmatrix} = \begin{bmatrix} \mathbf{Y}_1'\mathbf{Y}_1 & \mathbf{Y}_1'\mathbf{X}_1 \\ \mathbf{X}_1'\mathbf{Y}_1 & \mathbf{X}_1'\mathbf{X}_1 \end{bmatrix}^{-1} \begin{bmatrix} \mathbf{Y}_1'\mathbf{y}_1 \\ \mathbf{X}_1'\mathbf{y}_1 \end{bmatrix}.$$

The two-stage least squares estimator can also be presented as an *instrumental variable estimator,* with $\hat{\mathbf{Y}}_1$ serving as an instrument for $\mathbf{Y}_1$ and $\mathbf{X}_1$ serving as its own instrument. This can be shown as follows. According to (13.21), an instrumental variable estimator of the coefficients of the first structural equation is

$$\alpha_1^\dagger = (\mathbf{W}_1'\mathbf{Z}_1)^{-1}(\mathbf{W}_1'\mathbf{y}_1),$$

where $\mathbf{W}_1$ is a matrix of the instrumental variables. By putting

$$\mathbf{W}_1 = [\hat{\mathbf{Y}}_1 \quad \mathbf{X}_1],$$

we obtain

$$\mathbf{W}_1'\mathbf{Z}_1 = \begin{bmatrix} \hat{\mathbf{Y}}_1' \\ \mathbf{X}_1' \end{bmatrix} [\mathbf{Y}_1 \quad \mathbf{X}_1] = \begin{bmatrix} \hat{\mathbf{Y}}_1'\mathbf{Y}_1 & \hat{\mathbf{Y}}_1'\mathbf{X}_1 \\ \mathbf{X}_1'\mathbf{Y}_1 & \mathbf{X}_1'\mathbf{X}_1 \end{bmatrix},$$

and

$$\mathbf{W}_1'\mathbf{y}_1 = \begin{bmatrix} \hat{\mathbf{Y}}_1'\mathbf{y}_1 \\ \mathbf{X}_1'\mathbf{y}_1 \end{bmatrix}.$$

But

$$\hat{\mathbf{Y}}'\mathbf{Y}_1 = (\mathbf{Y}_1 - \hat{\mathbf{V}}_1)'\mathbf{Y}_1 = \mathbf{Y}_1'\mathbf{Y}_1 - \hat{\mathbf{V}}_1'(\hat{\mathbf{Y}}_1 + \hat{\mathbf{V}}_1) = \mathbf{Y}_1'\mathbf{Y}_1 - \hat{\mathbf{V}}_1'\hat{\mathbf{V}}_1,$$

and, from previous results,

$$\hat{\mathbf{Y}}_1'\mathbf{X}_1 = \mathbf{Y}_1'\mathbf{X}_1,$$
$$\hat{\mathbf{Y}}_1'\mathbf{y}_1 = \mathbf{Y}_1'\mathbf{y}_1 - \hat{\mathbf{V}}_1'\mathbf{y}_1.$$

Therefore,

$$(13.40)\qquad \alpha_1^\dagger = \begin{bmatrix} \mathbf{Y}_1'\mathbf{Y}_1 - \hat{\mathbf{V}}_1'\hat{\mathbf{V}}_1 & \mathbf{Y}_1'\mathbf{X}_1 \\ \mathbf{X}_1'\mathbf{Y}_1 & \mathbf{X}_1'\mathbf{X}_1 \end{bmatrix}^{-1} \begin{bmatrix} \mathbf{Y}_1'\mathbf{y}_1 - \hat{\mathbf{V}}_1'\mathbf{y}_1 \\ \mathbf{X}_1'\mathbf{y}_1 \end{bmatrix},$$

which is precisely the same formula as that for $\tilde{\tilde{\alpha}}_1$ given by (13.38). Because of the equivalence of $\alpha_1^\dagger$ and $\tilde{\tilde{\alpha}}_1$, we can use formula (13.22) to estimate the asymptotic variance-covariance matrix of the two-stage least squares estimator. This gives

$$\text{(13.41)} \quad \text{Est. Var-Cov}(\tilde{\tilde{\alpha}}_1) = s_{11}(\mathbf{W}_1'\mathbf{Z}_1)^{-1}(\mathbf{W}_1'\mathbf{W}_1)(\mathbf{Z}_1'\mathbf{W}_1)^{-1} = s_{11}(\mathbf{W}_1'\mathbf{Z}_1)^{-1}$$

$$= s_{11}\begin{bmatrix} \mathbf{Y}_1'\mathbf{Y}_1 - \hat{\mathbf{V}}_1'\hat{\mathbf{V}}_1 & \mathbf{Y}_1'\mathbf{X}_1 \\ \mathbf{X}_1'\mathbf{Y}_1 & \mathbf{X}_1'\mathbf{X}_1 \end{bmatrix}^{-1}.$$

Since $\sigma_{11} = \text{Var}(u_{1t})$, a consistent estimator of σ_{11} is, according to (13.23),

$$\text{(13.42)} \quad s_{11} = \frac{(\mathbf{y}_1 - \mathbf{Y}_1\tilde{\tilde{\boldsymbol{\beta}}}_1 - \mathbf{X}_1\tilde{\tilde{\boldsymbol{\gamma}}}_1)'(\mathbf{y}_1 - \mathbf{Y}_1\tilde{\tilde{\boldsymbol{\beta}}}_1 - \mathbf{X}_1\tilde{\tilde{\boldsymbol{\gamma}}}_1)}{T - G^{\Delta} + 1 - K^*}.$$

Note that the application of the ordinary least squares method to (13.36) or (13.36a) leads to two-stage least squares estimates of the structural coefficients, but the corresponding sum of squared residuals—based on replacing $\mathbf{Y}_1$ by $\hat{\mathbf{Y}}_1$—is *not* the appropriate quantity for estimating σ_{11}. To estimate σ_{11} we have to go back to the first-stage equation (13.34) or (13.34a) involving $\mathbf{Y}_1$ and *not* $\hat{\mathbf{Y}}_1$.

The two-stage least squares estimator, although consistent, is in general not asymptotically efficient because it does not take into account the correlation of the structural disturbances across equations. However, its construction does not require a complete knowledge of the whole system; all that is needed is a listing of all predetermined variables and their sample values. Further, no other instrumental variable estimator based on instruments that are linear combinations of the predetermined variables has a smaller asymptotic variance than the two-stage least squares estimator.[6]

When the two-stage least squares method is applied to an exactly identified equation, the resulting estimates are the same as those obtained by the indirect least squares method described earlier. We shall not give a general proof of this proposition, but we will demonstrate its validity with reference to the supply equation of the supply-demand model (13.1). This equation,

$$Q_t = \beta_1 + \beta_2 P_t + \varepsilon_{2t},$$

is exactly identified, with Y_t (income) being the excluded predetermined variable. The indirect least squares estimators of β_1 and β_2 were found to be

$$\text{(13.43)} \quad \tilde{\beta}_2 = \frac{m_{QY}}{m_{PY}},$$

$$\tilde{\beta}_1 = \bar{Q} - \left(\frac{m_{QY}}{m_{PY}}\right)\bar{P}.$$

The two-stage least squares estimators of β_1 and β_2 are obtained by applying the ordinary least squares method to the supply equation *after* replacing P_t by $\hat{P}_t$, where $\hat{P}_t$ is defined as

$$\hat{P}_t = \hat{\pi}_{21} + \hat{\pi}_{22} Y_t$$

[6] See P. Schmidt, *Econometrics* (New York: Marcel Dekker, 1976), pp. 164-165.

Here $\hat{\pi}_{21}$ and $\hat{\pi}_{22}$ represent the ordinary least squares estimators of the respective coefficients. The two-stage least squares estimators of β_1 and β_2 then are

$$\tilde{\tilde{\beta}}_2 = \frac{m_{Q\hat{P}}}{m_{\hat{P}\hat{P}}}, \tag{13.44}$$

$$\tilde{\tilde{\beta}}_1 = \overline{Q} - \left(\frac{m_{Q\hat{P}}}{m_{\hat{P}\hat{P}}}\right)\overline{P},$$

since $\overline{\hat{P}} = \overline{P}$. Further,

$$\begin{aligned} m_{Q\hat{P}} &= \sum (Q_t - \overline{Q})(\hat{P}_t - \overline{P}) \\ &= \hat{\pi}_{22} \sum (Q_t - \overline{Q})(Y_t - \overline{Y}) \\ &= \hat{\pi}_{22} m_{QY} \end{aligned}$$

and

$$\begin{aligned} m_{\hat{P}\hat{P}} &= \sum (\hat{P}_t - \overline{P})^2 \\ &= \hat{\pi}_{22}^2 \sum (Y_t - \overline{Y})^2 \\ &= \hat{\pi}_{22} \left(\frac{m_{PY}}{m_{YY}}\right) m_{YY} \\ &= \hat{\pi}_{22} m_{PY}. \end{aligned}$$

Therefore

$$\frac{m_{Q\hat{P}}}{m_{\hat{P}\hat{P}}} = \frac{m_{QY}}{m_{PY}}$$

and the right-hand side of (13.44) is exactly the same as that of (13.43).

EXAMPLE Following is a simplified model designed to explain variations in the consumption and prices of food.

$$\begin{aligned} Q_t &= \alpha_1 + \alpha_2 P_t + \alpha_3 D_t + u_{1t} \qquad \text{(demand)}, \\ Q_t &= \beta_1 + \beta_2 P_t + \beta_3 F_t + \beta_4 A_t + u_{2t} \qquad \text{(supply)}. \end{aligned} \tag{13.45}$$

Here Q_t = food consumption per head, P_t = ratio of food prices to general consumer prices, D_t = disposable income in constant prices, F_t = ratio of preceding year's prices received by farmers for products to general consumer prices, and A_t = time in years. The variables Q_t and P_t are endogenous, while D_t, F_t, and A_t are predetermined. The demand equation is overidentified; the supply equation is exactly identified. Instead of estimating this model from actual data, we will *simulate* the sample observations on prices and quantities by presetting the values of the parameters, specifying the sample values of the predetermined variables, and drawing the values of the disturbances at random from a normal population. Using such an artificial sample, we may try various methods to compare the estimates of the parameters with their true values. Specifically, let the true model be

$$\text{(13.45a)} \qquad Q_t = 96.5 - 0.25P_t + 0.30D_t + u_{1t} \qquad \text{(demand)},$$

$$Q_t = 62.5 + 0.15P_t + 0.20F_t + 0.36A_t + u_{2t} \qquad \text{(supply)},$$

The true reduced form for this model is

$$\text{(13.46)} \qquad Q_t = 75.25 + 0.1125D_t + 0.125F_t + 0.225A_t + v_{1t},$$

$$P_t = 85.00 + 0.75D_t - 0.50F_t - 0.90A_t + v_{2t}.$$

Suppose now that we draw at random two sets of 20 values of $N(0, 1)$ deviates. Let us call the values belonging to the first set ε_{1t} and those belonging to the second set ε_{2t} ($t = 1, 2, \ldots, 20$). The values of the reduced form disturbances are then constructed as

$$v_{1t} = 2\varepsilon_{1t},$$

$$v_{2t} = -0.5\, v_{1t} + \varepsilon_{2t}.$$

This implies the following variance-covariance matrix of the reduced form disturbances:

$$\mathbf{\Psi} = \begin{bmatrix} 4 & -2 \\ -2 & 2 \end{bmatrix}.$$

Since for our model

$$u_{1t} = v_{1t} + 0.25v_{2t},$$

$$u_{2t} = v_{1t} - 0.15v_{2t},$$

the variance-covariance matrix of the structural disturbances is

$$\mathbf{\Phi} = \begin{bmatrix} 3.125 & 3.725 \\ 3.725 & 4.645 \end{bmatrix}.$$

The choice of the values of the elements of $\mathbf{\Psi}$ is, of course, arbitrary. The sample values of D_t and F_t are taken from a paper by Girschick and Haavelmo.[7] They represent actual values for the United States economy for the years 1922-1941, expressed in terms of index numbers with the average for 1935-39 = 100. The values of Q_t and P_t are calculated according to (13.46). The resulting sample data are given in Table 13-1. The ordinary least squares estimates of the reduced form equations are

$$Q_t = 71.2035 + 0.1592D_t + 0.1383F_t + 0.0760A_t + \hat{v}_{1t}, \qquad R^2 = 0.7232,$$

$$P_t = 90.2678 + 0.6632D_t - 0.4884F_t - 0.7370A_t + \hat{v}_{2t}, \qquad R^2 = 0.9434.$$

These may be compared with the true reduced form equations given by (13.46). Applying the two-stage least squares method to the structural equations in (13.45), we obtain

$$\underset{(7.9208)}{Q_t = 94.6333} - \underset{(0.0965)}{0.2436P_t} + \underset{(0.0469)}{0.3140D_t} + \tilde{\tilde{u}}_{1t} \qquad \text{(demand)},$$

$$\underset{(12.0105)}{Q_t = 49.5324} + \underset{(0.0999)}{0.2401P_t} + \underset{(0.0472)}{0.2556F_t} + \underset{(0.0996)}{0.2529A_t} + \tilde{\tilde{u}}_{2t} \qquad \text{(supply)}.$$

[7] M. A. Girschick and T. Haavelmo, "Statistical Analysis of the Demand for Food: Examples of Simultaneous Estimation of Structural Equations," *Econometrica*, 15 (April 1947), pp. 79-110; reprinted in W. C. Hood and T. C. Koopmans (eds.), *Studies in Econometric Method* (New York: Wiley, 1953).

Table 13-1

Q_t	P_t	D_t	F_t	A_t
98.485	100.323	87.4	98.0	1
99.187	104.264	97.6	99.1	2
102.163	103.435	96.7	99.1	3
101.504	104.506	98.2	98.1	4
104.240	98.001	99.8	110.8	5
103.243	99.456	100.5	108.2	6
103.993	101.066	103.2	105.6	7
99.900	104.763	107.8	109.8	8
100.350	96.446	96.6	108.7	9
102.820	91.228	88.9	100.6	10
95.435	93.085	75.1	81.0	11
92.424	98.801	76.9	68.6	12
94.535	102.908	84.6	70.9	13
98.757	98.756	90.6	81.4	14
105.797	95.119	103.1	102.3	15
100.225	98.451	105.1	105.0	16
103.522	86.498	96.4	110.5	17
99.929	104.016	104.4	92.5	18
105.223	105.769	110.7	89.3	19
106.232	113.490	127.1	93.0	20

The figures in parentheses are the estimated standard errors. These results may be compared with the true structural equations (13.45a). It is also interesting to show the (inconsistent) ordinary least squares estimates of the two structural equations:

$$Q_t = 99.8954 - 0.3163P_t + 0.3346D_t + \hat{u}_{1t}, \qquad R^2 = 0.7638 \qquad \text{(demand)},$$

$$Q_t = 58.2754 + 0.1604P_t + 0.2481F_t + 0.2483A_t + \hat{u}_{2t}, \qquad R^2 = 0.6548 \qquad \text{(supply)}.$$

The two-stage least squares results can be used to test hypotheses about the coefficients of the model. The standard practice is to rely on the asymptotic properties of the two-stage least squares estimators and to use the usual t tests and F tests of regression analysis. In particular, in large samples we can make use of the standard formula

$$\frac{(\text{SSE}_R - \text{SSE}_U)/r}{\text{SSE}_U/(T - G^{\Delta} + 1 - K^*)} \sim F_{r,\, T-G^{\Delta}+1-K^*},$$

where SSE_R and SSE_U are the restricted and unrestricted two-stage least squares residuals, and r is the number of restrictions imposed by the null hypothesis.[8]

[8] R. Startz, "Computation of Linear Hypothesis Tests for Two-Stage Least Squares," *Economics Letters*, 11 (1983), pp. 129–131.

k Class Estimators

The formula for the two-stage least squares estimator as given by (13.38) can be generalized to cover a whole class of different estimators. These estimators, known as *k class estimators,* are defined as

$$(13.47) \qquad \tilde{\boldsymbol{\alpha}}_1^{(k)} = \begin{bmatrix} \tilde{\boldsymbol{\beta}}_1^{(k)} \\ \tilde{\boldsymbol{\gamma}}_1^{(k)} \end{bmatrix} = \begin{bmatrix} \mathbf{Y}_1'\mathbf{Y}_1 - k\hat{\mathbf{V}}_1'\hat{\mathbf{V}}_1 & \mathbf{Y}_1'\mathbf{X}_1 \\ \mathbf{X}_1'\mathbf{Y}_1 & \mathbf{X}_1'\mathbf{X}_1 \end{bmatrix}^{-1} \begin{bmatrix} \mathbf{Y}_1'\mathbf{y}_1 - k\hat{\mathbf{V}}_1'\mathbf{y}_1 \\ \mathbf{X}_1'\mathbf{y}_1 \end{bmatrix}.$$

This formula differs from (13.38) only because $\hat{\mathbf{V}}_1'\hat{\mathbf{V}}_1$ and $\hat{\mathbf{V}}_1'\mathbf{y}_1$ are multiplied by a scalar k. This scalar can be set a priori to be equal to some number, or its value can be determined from the sample observations according to some rule. We have already encountered two k class estimators; namely the two-stage least squares estimator for which $k = 1$, and the ordinary least squares estimator [given by (13.39)] for which $k = 0$. The fact that the ordinary least squares estimator belongs to the k class indicates that not all k class estimators are consistent. To find which values of k lead to consistent estimates, we first note that (13.47) can be formally expressed as a formula for an *instrumental variable estimator.* This can be shown as follows. An instrumental variable estimator of the first structural equation is, according to (13.21), defined as

$$\boldsymbol{\alpha}_1^{\dagger} = (\mathbf{W}_1'\mathbf{Z}_1)^{-1}(\mathbf{W}_1'\mathbf{y}_1),$$

where

$$\mathbf{Z}_1 = [\mathbf{Y}_1 \quad \mathbf{X}_1],$$

as before. By choosing the instrumental variables as

$$\mathbf{W}_1 = [(\mathbf{Y}_1 - k\hat{\mathbf{V}}_1) \quad \mathbf{X}_1],$$

we have

$$\boldsymbol{\alpha}_1^{\dagger} = \begin{bmatrix} (\mathbf{Y}_1 - k\hat{\mathbf{V}}_1)'\mathbf{Y}_1 & (\mathbf{Y}_1 - k\hat{\mathbf{V}}_1)'\mathbf{X}_1 \\ \mathbf{X}_1'\mathbf{Y}_1 & \mathbf{X}_1'\mathbf{X}_1 \end{bmatrix}^{-1} \begin{bmatrix} (\mathbf{Y}_1 - k\hat{\mathbf{V}}_1)'\mathbf{y}_1 \\ \mathbf{X}_1'\mathbf{y}_1 \end{bmatrix}.$$

However,

$$(\mathbf{Y}_1 - k\hat{\mathbf{V}}_1)'\mathbf{Y}_1 = \mathbf{Y}_1'\mathbf{Y}_1 - k\hat{\mathbf{V}}_1'(\hat{\mathbf{Y}}_1 + \hat{\mathbf{V}}_1) = \mathbf{Y}_1'\mathbf{Y}_1 - k\hat{\mathbf{V}}_1'\hat{\mathbf{V}}_1,$$

$$(\mathbf{Y}_1 - k\hat{\mathbf{V}}_1)'\mathbf{X}_1 = \mathbf{Y}_1'\mathbf{X}_1 - k\hat{\mathbf{V}}_1'\mathbf{X}_1 = \mathbf{Y}_1'\mathbf{X}_1,$$

$$(\mathbf{Y}_1 - k\hat{\mathbf{V}}_1)'\mathbf{y}_1 = \mathbf{Y}_1'\mathbf{y}_1 - k\hat{\mathbf{V}}_1'\mathbf{y}_1;$$

therefore,

$$(13.48) \qquad \boldsymbol{\alpha}_1^{\dagger} = \begin{bmatrix} \mathbf{Y}_1'\mathbf{Y}_1 - k\hat{\mathbf{V}}_1'\hat{\mathbf{V}}_1 & \mathbf{Y}_1'\mathbf{X}_1 \\ \mathbf{X}_1'\mathbf{Y}_1 & \mathbf{X}_1'\mathbf{X}_1 \end{bmatrix}^{-1} \begin{bmatrix} \mathbf{Y}_1'\mathbf{y}_1 - k\hat{\mathbf{V}}_1'\mathbf{y}_1 \\ \mathbf{X}_1'\mathbf{y}_1 \end{bmatrix},$$

which is precisely the same as $\tilde{\boldsymbol{\alpha}}^{(k)}$ in (13.47). However, $\mathbf{W}_1$ does not qualify as a set of instrumental variables *unless* these variables are asymptotically uncorrelated with the structural disturbance $\mathbf{u}_1$, i.e., unless

$$\text{plim}\ \frac{1}{T}\mathbf{W}_1'\mathbf{u}_1 = \mathbf{0}.$$

That is, we require

(13.49) $$\text{plim}\,\frac{1}{T}(\mathbf{Y}_1 - k\hat{\mathbf{V}}_1)'\mathbf{u}_1 = \mathbf{0},$$

(13.50) $$\text{plim}\,\frac{1}{T}\mathbf{X}_1'\mathbf{u}_1 = \mathbf{0}.$$

Now (13.50) is always satisfied, since all predetermined variables are uncorrelated with the structural disturbances by definition. As for (13.49), we have

(13.49a) $$\begin{aligned}\text{plim}\,\frac{1}{T}(\mathbf{Y}_1 - k\hat{\mathbf{V}}_1)'\mathbf{u}_1 &= \text{plim}\,\frac{1}{T}\mathbf{Y}_1'\mathbf{u}_1 - \text{plim}\,k\cdot\text{plim}\,\frac{1}{T}\hat{\mathbf{V}}_1'\mathbf{u}_1\\ &= \text{plim}\,\frac{1}{T}(\hat{\mathbf{Y}}_1 + \hat{\mathbf{V}}_1)'\mathbf{u}_1 - \text{plim}\,k\cdot\text{plim}\,\frac{1}{T}\hat{\mathbf{V}}_1'\mathbf{u}_1\\ &= \text{plim}\,\frac{1}{T}\hat{\mathbf{V}}_1'\mathbf{u}_1 - \text{plim}\,k\cdot\text{plim}\,\frac{1}{T}\hat{\mathbf{V}}_1'\mathbf{u}_1.\end{aligned}$$

Since $\text{plim}(\hat{\mathbf{V}}_1'\mathbf{u}_1)/T$ is a finite number different from zero, it follows that

$$\text{plim}\,\frac{1}{T}(\mathbf{Y}_1 - k\hat{\mathbf{V}}_1)'\mathbf{u}_1 = 0,$$

if and only if

(13.51) $$\text{plim}\,k = 1.$$

This condition is automatically fulfilled in the case of two-stage least squares estimation in which k is *always* equal to one. Further, it can be shown that the asymptotic variance-covariance matrix of all k class estimators for which

(13.52) $$\text{plim}\,\sqrt{T}(k-1) = 0$$

reduces to (13.41).[9] This means that all of these estimators must have the same asymptotic variance-covariance matrix as the two-stage least squares estimator. This matrix is usually estimated as follows:

(13.53) $$\text{Est. Var-Cov}(\tilde{\alpha}^{(k)}) = s_{11}\begin{bmatrix}\mathbf{Y}_1'\mathbf{Y}_1 - k\hat{\mathbf{V}}_1'\hat{\mathbf{V}}_1 & \mathbf{Y}_1'\mathbf{X}_1\\ \mathbf{X}_1'\mathbf{Y}_1 & \mathbf{X}_1'\mathbf{X}_1\end{bmatrix}^{-1}$$

where

(13.54) $$s_{11} = \frac{(\mathbf{y}_1 - \mathbf{Z}_1\tilde{\alpha}_1^{(k)})'(\mathbf{y}_1 - \mathbf{Z}_1\tilde{\alpha}_1^{(k)})}{T - G^{\Delta} + 1 - K^*}.$$

This, of course, is asymptotically equivalent to (13.41).

[9] Schmidt, *op. cit.*, pp. 167–169.

Limited Information Maximum Likelihood Estimation

Another single equation estimator, which is known as the *limited information maximum likelihood* (LIML) *estimator,* also belongs to the k class family and is consistent. It is derived by maximizing the likelihood function for the observations on the endogenous variables included in the equation to be estimated. The phrase "limited information" means that, in setting up the likelihood function, we limit ourselves to those endogenous variables that appear in the equation under investigation and disregard the overidentifying restrictions on the other structural equations. Suppose the equation we wish to estimate is the first one of the system as described by (13.34). The part of the system that is relevant for the limited information maximum likelihood estimation then is

$$\mathbf{y}_1 = \mathbf{Y}_1\boldsymbol{\beta}_1 + \mathbf{X}_1\boldsymbol{\gamma}_1 + \mathbf{u}_1, \tag{13.55a}$$

$$\mathbf{Y}_1 = \mathbf{X}\boldsymbol{\pi}_1 + \mathbf{V}_1, \tag{13.55b}$$

where $\mathbf{Y}_1 = [\mathbf{y}_2 \quad \mathbf{y}_3 \quad \cdots \quad \mathbf{y}_{G\Delta}]$, $\mathbf{V}_1 = [\mathbf{v}_2 \quad \mathbf{v}_3 \quad \cdots \quad \mathbf{v}_{G\Delta}]$, and $\boldsymbol{\pi}_1 = [\boldsymbol{\pi}_2 \quad \boldsymbol{\pi}_3 \quad \cdots \quad \boldsymbol{\pi}_{G\Delta}]$. Equivalently, we may write

$$\mathbf{y}_1 = (\mathbf{X}\boldsymbol{\pi}_1)\boldsymbol{\beta}_1 + \mathbf{X}_1\boldsymbol{\gamma}_1 + \mathbf{v}_1, \tag{13.56a}$$

$$\mathbf{Y}_1 = \mathbf{X}\boldsymbol{\pi}_1 + \mathbf{V}_1, \tag{13.56b}$$

where $\mathbf{v}_1 = \mathbf{u}_1 + \mathbf{V}_1\boldsymbol{\beta}_1$ in accordance with (13.8).

The limited information maximum likelihood estimates are then obtained by maximizing the likelihood function for $\mathbf{y}_1$ and $\mathbf{Y}_1$ with respect to $\boldsymbol{\beta}_1, \boldsymbol{\gamma}_1, \boldsymbol{\pi}_1$, and the variances and covariances of the $\mathbf{v}$s. A simple way of calculating the limited information maximum likelihood estimates is by treating equations (13.55a) and (13.55b) as a system of seemingly unrelated regression equations (disregarding the correlation between $\mathbf{Y}_1$ and $\mathbf{u}_1$) and applying the iterative Aitken method.[10]

The representation (13.56a) and (13.56b) of the equations for limited information maximum likelihood estimation is the same as that for the "multiple cause" model discussed in connection with unobservable variables in Section 11-8. In (13.56a) the unobservable variable is $E(\mathbf{Y}_1) = \mathbf{X}\boldsymbol{\pi}_1$. This representation brings out clearly the distinction between the two-stage least squares and the limited information maximum likelihood estimation. The two-stage least squares method is based on estimating (13.56b) first, substituting $\hat{\boldsymbol{\pi}}_1$ for $\boldsymbol{\pi}_1$ in (13.56a), and then estimating $\boldsymbol{\beta}_1$ and $\boldsymbol{\gamma}_1$. The limited information maximum likelihood method, on the other hand, is based on estimating $\boldsymbol{\pi}_1, \boldsymbol{\beta}_1$, and $\boldsymbol{\gamma}_1$ *simultaneously.* Asymptotically there is, of course, no difference.

The results obtained by maximizing the likelihood function for $\mathbf{y}_1$ and $\mathbf{Y}_1$ can also be obtained by utilizing the so-called *least variance ratio principle.* The equivalence of the two approaches is well known.[11] The least variance ratio estimates are derived

[10] See A. Pagan, "Some Consequences of Viewing LIML as an Iterated Aitken Estimator," *Economics Letters,* 3 (1979), pp. 369–372. See also page 644.

[11] Schmidt, *op. cit.,* pp. 170–177.

as follows. The first structural equation

$$\mathbf{y}_1 = \mathbf{Y}_1\boldsymbol{\beta}_1 + \mathbf{X}_1\boldsymbol{\gamma}_1 + \mathbf{u}_1$$

can be written as

$$\tilde{\mathbf{y}}_1 = \mathbf{X}_1\boldsymbol{\gamma}_1 + \mathbf{u}_1, \tag{13.57}$$

where

$$\tilde{\mathbf{y}}_1 = \mathbf{y}_1 - \mathbf{Y}_1\boldsymbol{\beta}_1.$$

The "composite" variable $\tilde{\mathbf{y}}_1$ represents a linear combination of the endogenous variables included in the first structural equation. If its values could be observed, we could estimate γ_1 by the ordinary least squares method. This would lead to

$$\hat{\boldsymbol{\gamma}}_1 = (\mathbf{X}_1'\mathbf{X}_1)^{-1}\mathbf{X}_1'\tilde{\mathbf{y}}_1,$$

and the sum of the squared residuals would be

$$\mathrm{SSE}_1 = (\tilde{\mathbf{y}}_1 - \mathbf{X}_1\hat{\boldsymbol{\gamma}}_1)'(\tilde{\mathbf{y}}_1 - \mathbf{X}_1\hat{\boldsymbol{\gamma}}_1) = \tilde{\mathbf{y}}_1'\tilde{\mathbf{y}}_1 - \tilde{\mathbf{y}}_1'\mathbf{X}_1(\mathbf{X}_1'\mathbf{X}_1)^{-1}\mathbf{X}_1'\tilde{\mathbf{y}}_1.$$

Note that in (13.57) the explanatory variables consist of the predetermined variables included in the first structural equation. If this set were extended to include *all* the predetermined variables of the system, we would have

$$\tilde{\mathbf{y}}_1 = \mathbf{X}\boldsymbol{\gamma} + \mathbf{u}_1, \tag{13.58}$$

where $\mathbf{X}$ is a $(T \times K)$ matrix of all predetermined variables and

$$\underset{(K\times 1)}{\boldsymbol{\gamma}} = \begin{bmatrix} \boldsymbol{\gamma}_1 \\ \mathbf{0}_{**} \end{bmatrix}.$$

If we applied the ordinary least squares method to (13.58)—ignoring the fact that the true value of some of the γ coefficients is zero—we would get

$$\hat{\boldsymbol{\gamma}} = (\mathbf{X}'\mathbf{X})^{-1}(\mathbf{X}'\tilde{\mathbf{y}}_1),$$

and the sum of the squared residuals would be

$$\mathrm{SSE} = (\tilde{\mathbf{y}}_1 - \mathbf{X}\boldsymbol{\gamma})'(\tilde{\mathbf{y}}_1 - \mathbf{X}\boldsymbol{\gamma}) = \tilde{\mathbf{y}}_1'\tilde{\mathbf{y}}_1 - \tilde{\mathbf{y}}_1'\mathbf{X}(\mathbf{X}'\mathbf{X})^{-1}\mathbf{X}'\tilde{\mathbf{y}}_1.$$

Since the addition of further explanatory variables can never increase the residual sum of squares, the ratio

$$l = \frac{\mathrm{SSE}_1}{\mathrm{SSE}} = \frac{\tilde{\mathbf{y}}_1'\tilde{\mathbf{y}}_1 - \tilde{\mathbf{y}}_1'\mathbf{X}_1(\mathbf{X}_1'\mathbf{X}_1)^{-1}\mathbf{X}_1'\tilde{\mathbf{y}}_1}{\tilde{\mathbf{y}}_1'\tilde{\mathbf{y}}_1 - \tilde{\mathbf{y}}_1'\mathbf{X}(\mathbf{X}'\mathbf{X})^{-1}\mathbf{X}'\tilde{\mathbf{y}}_1} \tag{13.59}$$

can never be smaller than unity.

The problem now is to estimate the elements of $\boldsymbol{\beta}_1$. Let us write

$$\tilde{\mathbf{y}}_1 = \mathbf{Y}_{1\Delta}\boldsymbol{\beta}_{1\Delta}, \tag{13.60}$$

where

$$\mathbf{Y}_{1\Delta} = [\mathbf{y}_1 \quad \mathbf{y}_2 \quad \cdots \quad \mathbf{y}_{G^\Delta}] \quad \text{and} \quad \boldsymbol{\beta}_{1\Delta} = \begin{bmatrix} 1 \\ \beta_{12} \\ \vdots \\ \beta_{1G^\Delta} \end{bmatrix} = \begin{bmatrix} 1 \\ -\boldsymbol{\beta}_1 \end{bmatrix}.$$

Therefore, (13.59) can be written as

$$l = \frac{\boldsymbol{\beta}'_{1\Delta}\mathbf{W}_{1*}\boldsymbol{\beta}_{1\Delta}}{\boldsymbol{\beta}'_{1\Delta}\mathbf{W}_1\boldsymbol{\beta}_{1\Delta}}, \tag{13.59a}$$

where

$$\mathbf{W}_{1*} = \mathbf{Y}'_{1\Delta}\mathbf{Y}_{1\Delta} - (\mathbf{Y}'_{1\Delta}\mathbf{X}_1)(\mathbf{X}'_1\mathbf{X}_1)^{-1}\mathbf{X}'_1\mathbf{Y}_{1\Delta},$$

$$\mathbf{W}_1 = \mathbf{Y}'_{1\Delta}\mathbf{Y}_{1\Delta} - (\mathbf{Y}'_{1\Delta}\mathbf{X})(\mathbf{X}'\mathbf{X})^{-1}\mathbf{X}'\mathbf{Y}_{1\Delta}.$$

The least variance ratio estimator of $\boldsymbol{\beta}_{1\Delta}$ is given by those values of the β coefficients that lead to the smallest value of l. Thus we have to minimize l with respect to $\boldsymbol{\beta}_{1\Delta}$. Taking the first derivative of l, we get

$$\frac{\partial l}{\partial \boldsymbol{\beta}_{1\Delta}} = \frac{2(\mathbf{W}_{1*}\boldsymbol{\beta}_{1\Delta})(\boldsymbol{\beta}'_{1\Delta}\mathbf{W}_1\boldsymbol{\beta}_{1\Delta}) - 2(\boldsymbol{\beta}'_{1\Delta}\mathbf{W}_{1*}\boldsymbol{\beta}_{1\Delta})(\mathbf{W}_1\boldsymbol{\beta}_{1\Delta})}{(\boldsymbol{\beta}'_{1\Delta}\mathbf{W}_1\boldsymbol{\beta}_{1\Delta})^2}. \tag{13.61}$$

By setting this equal to zero, we obtain

$$\mathbf{W}_{1*}\tilde{\boldsymbol{\beta}}_{1\Delta} - \left[\frac{\tilde{\boldsymbol{\beta}}'_{1\Delta}\mathbf{W}_{1*}\tilde{\boldsymbol{\beta}}_{1\Delta}}{\tilde{\boldsymbol{\beta}}'_{1\Delta}\mathbf{W}_1\tilde{\boldsymbol{\beta}}_{1\Delta}}\right]\mathbf{W}_1\tilde{\boldsymbol{\beta}}_{1\Delta} = \mathbf{0} \tag{13.62}$$

or

$$(\mathbf{W}_{1*} - l\mathbf{W}_1)\tilde{\boldsymbol{\beta}}_{1\Delta} = \mathbf{0}. \tag{13.62a}$$

Now, for $\tilde{\boldsymbol{\beta}}_{1\Delta} \neq \mathbf{0}$ we must have

$$\text{Det}(\mathbf{W}_{1*} - l\mathbf{W}_1) = 0; \tag{13.63}$$

that is, the determinant of the matrix $(\mathbf{W}_{1*} - l\mathbf{W}_1)$—whose dimension is $(G^\Delta \times G^\Delta)$—must equal zero. Since all elements of $\mathbf{W}_{1*}$ and $\mathbf{W}_1$ can be determined from the sample observations, equation (13.63) becomes a polynomial of G^Δ degree in l. As noted, we want l to be as close to unity as possible, and thus the appropriate root of (13.63) is the smallest one, say, l_1. By using l_1 in place of l in (13.62a), we can obtain a solution for the $(G^\Delta - 1)$ unknown elements of $\tilde{\boldsymbol{\beta}}_{1\Delta}$. The elements of $\boldsymbol{\gamma}_1$ are then estimated by

$$\tilde{\boldsymbol{\gamma}}_1 = (\mathbf{X}'_1\mathbf{X}_1)^{-1}(\mathbf{X}'_1\tilde{\mathbf{y}}_1) = (\mathbf{X}'_1\mathbf{X}_1)^{-1}(\mathbf{X}'_1\mathbf{Y}_{1\Delta})\tilde{\boldsymbol{\beta}}_{1\Delta}. \tag{13.64}$$

These are the limited information maximum likelihood estimates.

When the limited information maximum likelihood estimator was introduced, we mentioned that it belongs to the k class family. We can now elaborate by stating that, for this estimator,

$$k = l_1$$

and that

$$\text{plim } l_1 = 1,$$

$$\text{plim } \sqrt{T}(l_1 - 1) = 0.$$

The proof of these propositions can be found elsewhere.[12] Their implications are that the limited information maximum likelihood estimator is consistent and that it has the same asymptotic variance–covariance matrix as the two-stage least squares estimator. One difference between these two estimators is that the limited information maximum likelihood estimator is *invariant* with respect to the choice of the endogenous variable whose structural coefficient is to be equal to one, whereas the two-stage least squares estimator is not invariant in this respect. Consider the first structural equation written as

$$\beta_{11}y_{1t} + \beta_{12}y_{2t} + \cdots + \beta_{1G^\Delta}y_{G^\Delta t} + \gamma_{11}x_{1t} + \cdots + \gamma_{1K^{**}}x_{K^{**}t} = u_{1t}.$$

In deriving the two-stage least squares estimator and the limited information maximum likelihood estimator, we have taken the value of β_{11} to be equal to one. This means that the structural equation may be written as

$$y_{1t} = -\beta_{12}y_{2t} - \cdots - \beta_{1G^\Delta}y_{G^\Delta t} - \gamma_{11}x_{1t} - \cdots - \gamma_{1K^{**}}x_{K^{**}t} + u_{1t}.$$

In our notation the two-stage least squares estimate of β_{12} is $\tilde{\tilde{\beta}}_{12}$ and the limited information maximum likelihood estimate is $\tilde{\beta}_{12}$. Now suppose we change our specification and take β_{12}, rather than β_{11}, to be equal to one. Then the structural equation would be written as

$$y_{2t} = -\beta_{11}y_{1t} - \cdots - \beta_{1G^\Delta}y_{G^\Delta t} - \gamma_{11}x_{1t} - \cdots - \gamma_{1K^{**}}x_{K^{**}t} + u_{1t}.$$

The two-stage least squares estimate of β_{11} is $\tilde{\tilde{\beta}}_{11}$, and the limited information maximum likelihood estimate is $\tilde{\beta}_{11}$. Then, in general,

$$\tilde{\tilde{\beta}}_{11} \neq \frac{1}{\tilde{\tilde{\beta}}_{12}},$$

but

$$\tilde{\beta}_{11} = \frac{1}{\tilde{\beta}_{12}}.$$

This is what is meant by "invariance" of the limited information maximum likelihood estimator. In this respect it is unique among all members of the k class family.[13] Invariance may be useful whenever economic theory offers no guidance concerning the choice of endogenous variable for which the structural coefficient is to be unity. Finally, it may be noted that when the structural equation is exactly identified, the limited information maximum likelihood method leads to the same result as the indirect least squares method and the two-stage least squares method.

[12] *Ibid.*

[13] See A. S. Goldberger, "An Instrumental Variable Interpretation of k-Class Estimation," *Indian Economic Journal,* 13, No. 3 (1965), pp. 424–431.

EXAMPLE We can illustrate the construction of the limited information maximum likelihood estimates by reference to the food market model (13.45). The two-equation model given by (13.45) is

$$Q_t = \alpha_1 + \alpha_2 P_t + \alpha_3 D_t + u_{1t} \qquad \text{(demand)},$$

$$Q_t = \beta_1 + \beta_2 P_t + \beta_3 F_t + \beta_4 A_t + u_{2t} \qquad \text{(supply)}.$$

The sample observations ($T = 20$) are given in Table 13-1. For the demand equation, which is overidentified, we have

$$\mathbf{Y}_{1\Delta} = \begin{bmatrix} Q_1 & P_1 \\ Q_2 & P_2 \\ \vdots & \vdots \\ Q_{20} & P_{20} \end{bmatrix}, \quad \mathbf{X}_1 = \begin{bmatrix} 1 & D_1 \\ 1 & D_2 \\ \vdots & \vdots \\ 1 & D_{20} \end{bmatrix}, \quad \mathbf{X} = \begin{bmatrix} 1 & D_1 & F_1 & A_1 \\ 1 & D_2 & F_2 & A_2 \\ \vdots & \vdots & \vdots & \vdots \\ 1 & D_{20} & F_{20} & A_{20} \end{bmatrix},$$

$$\boldsymbol{\beta}_{1\Delta} = \begin{bmatrix} 1 \\ -\alpha_2 \end{bmatrix}, \quad \boldsymbol{\gamma}_1 = \begin{bmatrix} \alpha_1 \\ \alpha_3 \end{bmatrix}.$$

Then,

$$\mathbf{W}_{1*} = \begin{bmatrix} \Sigma Q_t^2 & \Sigma Q_t P_t \\ \Sigma Q_t P_t & \Sigma P_t^2 \end{bmatrix} - \begin{bmatrix} \Sigma Q_t & \Sigma Q_t D_t \\ \Sigma P_t & \Sigma P_t D_t \end{bmatrix} \begin{bmatrix} T & \Sigma D_t \\ \Sigma D_t & \Sigma D_t^2 \end{bmatrix}^{-1} \begin{bmatrix} \Sigma Q_t & \Sigma P_t \\ \Sigma Q_t D_t & \Sigma P_t D_t \end{bmatrix},$$

and

$$\mathbf{W}_1 = \begin{bmatrix} \Sigma Q_t^2 & \Sigma Q_t P_t \\ \Sigma Q_t P_t & \Sigma P_t^2 \end{bmatrix} - \begin{bmatrix} \Sigma Q_t & \Sigma Q_t D_t & \Sigma Q_t F_t & \Sigma Q_t A_t \\ \Sigma P_t & \Sigma P_t D_t & \Sigma P_t F_t & \Sigma P_t A_t \end{bmatrix}$$

$$\times \begin{bmatrix} T & \Sigma D_t & \Sigma F_t & \Sigma A_t \\ \Sigma D_t & \Sigma D_t^2 & \Sigma D_t F_t & \Sigma D_t A_t \\ \Sigma F_t & \Sigma F_t D_t & \Sigma F_t^2 & \Sigma F_t A_t \\ \Sigma A_t & \Sigma A_t D_t & \Sigma A_t F_t & \Sigma A_t^2 \end{bmatrix}^{-1} \begin{bmatrix} \Sigma Q_t & \Sigma P_t \\ \Sigma Q_t D_t & \Sigma P_t D_t \\ \Sigma Q_t F_t & \Sigma P_t F_t \\ \Sigma Q_t A_t & \Sigma P_t A_t \end{bmatrix}.$$

Thus the determinant of $(\mathbf{W}_{1*} - l\mathbf{W}_1)$ is a second-degree polynomial in l. Its two roots are

$$l_1 = 1.1739 \qquad \text{and} \qquad l_2 = 24.8535.$$

Therefore, (13.62a) becomes

$$[\mathbf{W}_{1*} - 1.1739\, \mathbf{W}_1] \begin{bmatrix} 1 \\ -\tilde{\tilde{\alpha}}_2 \end{bmatrix} = \begin{bmatrix} 0 \\ 0 \end{bmatrix}. \tag{13.65}$$

The two equations in (13.65) lead to the same value of $\tilde{\alpha}_2$.

$$\tilde{\alpha}_2 = -0.2295.$$

The solution for $\tilde{\gamma}_1$ is obtained from (13.64) as

$$\tilde{\boldsymbol{\gamma}}_1 = \begin{bmatrix} \tilde{\alpha}_1 \\ \tilde{\alpha}_3 \end{bmatrix} = \begin{bmatrix} T & \Sigma D_t \\ \Sigma D_t & \Sigma D_t^2 \end{bmatrix}^{-1} \begin{bmatrix} \Sigma Q_t & \Sigma P_t \\ \Sigma Q_t D_t & \Sigma P_t D_t \end{bmatrix} \begin{bmatrix} 1 \\ 0.2295 \end{bmatrix} = \begin{bmatrix} 93.6192 \\ 0.3100 \end{bmatrix}.$$

The estimated standard errors of these estimates are calculated in accordance with (13.53) and (13.54). The results for both equations of the model are

$$\underset{}{Q_t} = \underset{(8.0312)}{93.6192} - \underset{(0.0980)}{0.2295P_t} + \underset{(0.0474)}{0.3100D_t} + \tilde{u}_{1t} \qquad \text{(demand)},$$

$$\underset{}{Q_t} = \underset{(12.0105)}{49.5324} + \underset{(0.0999)}{0.2401P_t} + \underset{(0.0472)}{0.2556F_t} + \underset{(0.0996)}{0.2529A_t} + \tilde{u}_{2t} \qquad \text{(supply)}.$$

The estimated demand equation may be compared with the true demand equation in (13.45a) as well as with the result obtained for the two-stage least squares method in the preceding example. The results for the supply equation—which is exactly identified—are precisely the same as those obtained by the two-stage least squares method.

13-4 System Methods of Estimation

The single equation estimation methods lead to estimates that are consistent but, in general, not asymptotically efficient. The reason for the lack of asymptotic efficiency is the disregard of the correlation of the disturbances across equations. (An alternative explanation for the lack of asymptotic efficiency is that single equation estimators do not take into account prior restrictions on other equations in the model.) This parallels the situation in which a regression equation belonging to a set of seemingly unrelated regressions is estimated by the ordinary least squares method (see Section 12-3). If we do not take into account the correlation between the disturbances of different structural equations, we are not using all the available information about each equation and, therefore, do not attain asymptotic efficiency. This deficiency can be overcome—as in the case of seemingly unrelated regressions—by estimating all equations of the system simultaneously. For this purpose we can use one of the so-called *system methods* described in this section.

Three-Stage Least Squares Estimation

The simplest system method is that of *three-stage least squares* (3SLS), which involves a straightforward application of the Aitken generalized estimation to the system of structural equations. The system can be written, in accordance with (13.36), as

$$\begin{aligned} \mathbf{y}_1 &= \hat{\mathbf{Y}}_1\boldsymbol{\beta}_1 + \mathbf{X}_1\boldsymbol{\gamma}_1 + \mathbf{u}_1^*, \\ \mathbf{y}_2 &= \hat{\mathbf{Y}}_2\boldsymbol{\beta}_2 + \mathbf{X}_2\boldsymbol{\gamma}_2 + \mathbf{u}_2^*, \\ &\vdots \\ \mathbf{y}_G &= \hat{\mathbf{Y}}_G\boldsymbol{\beta}_G + \mathbf{X}_G\boldsymbol{\gamma}_G + \mathbf{u}_G^*, \end{aligned} \tag{13.66}$$

where
$$\mathbf{y}_g \rightarrow T \times 1,$$
$$\hat{\mathbf{Y}}_g \rightarrow T \times (G_g^{\Delta} - 1),$$
$$\mathbf{X}_g \rightarrow T \times K_g^*,$$
$$\boldsymbol{\beta}_g \rightarrow (G_g^{\Delta} - 1) \times 1,$$
$$\boldsymbol{\gamma}_g \rightarrow K_g^* \times 1,$$
$$\mathbf{u}_g^* \rightarrow T \times 1.$$

Note that G_g^{Δ} = number of endogenous variables included in the gth equation,

K_g^* = number of predetermined variables included in the gth equation,

$g = 1, 2, \ldots, G.$

If there are any identities in the system, they are simply omitted from (13.66). Alternatively, we may describe the system as

(13.66a)
$$\begin{aligned}
\mathbf{y}_1 &= \hat{\mathbf{Z}}_1\boldsymbol{\alpha}_1 + \mathbf{u}_1^*,\\
\mathbf{y}_2 &= \hat{\mathbf{Z}}_2\boldsymbol{\alpha}_2 + \mathbf{u}_2^*,\\
&\vdots\\
\mathbf{y}_G &= \hat{\mathbf{Z}}_G\boldsymbol{\alpha}_G + \mathbf{u}_G^*,
\end{aligned}$$

where
$$\hat{\mathbf{Z}}_g = [\hat{\mathbf{Y}}_g \quad \mathbf{X}_g],$$
$$\boldsymbol{\alpha}_g = \begin{bmatrix} \boldsymbol{\beta}_g \\ \boldsymbol{\gamma}_g \end{bmatrix}.$$

A compact way of writing (13.66a) is

(13.66b)
$$\begin{bmatrix} \mathbf{y}_1 \\ \mathbf{y}_2 \\ \vdots \\ \mathbf{y}_G \end{bmatrix} = \begin{bmatrix} \hat{\mathbf{Z}}_1 & \mathbf{0} & \cdots & \mathbf{0} \\ \mathbf{0} & \hat{\mathbf{Z}}_2 & \cdots & \mathbf{0} \\ \vdots & \vdots & & \vdots \\ \mathbf{0} & \mathbf{0} & \cdots & \hat{\mathbf{Z}}_G \end{bmatrix} \begin{bmatrix} \boldsymbol{\alpha}_1 \\ \boldsymbol{\alpha}_2 \\ \vdots \\ \boldsymbol{\alpha}_G \end{bmatrix} + \begin{bmatrix} \mathbf{u}_1^* \\ \mathbf{u}_2^* \\ \vdots \\ \mathbf{u}_G^* \end{bmatrix},$$

or

(13.66c)
$$\mathbf{y} = \hat{\mathbf{Z}}\boldsymbol{\alpha} + \mathbf{u}^*,$$

where
$$\mathbf{y} \rightarrow GT \times 1,$$
$$\hat{\mathbf{Z}} \rightarrow GT \times \sum_{g=1}^{G} (G_g^{\Delta} - 1 + K_g^*),$$
$$\boldsymbol{\alpha} \rightarrow \sum_{g=1}^{G} (G_g^{\Delta} - 1 + K_g^*) \times 1,$$
$$\mathbf{u}^* \rightarrow GT \times 1.$$

Describing the system of equations in the form (13.66c) enables us to apply the two-stage Aitken estimation formula (12.74). This leads to

$$\hat{\tilde{\tilde{\alpha}}} = (\hat{\mathbf{Z}}'\hat{\mathbf{\Omega}}^{-1}\hat{\mathbf{Z}})^{-1}(\hat{\mathbf{Z}}'\hat{\mathbf{\Omega}}^{-1}\mathbf{y}), \tag{13.67}$$

where

$$\hat{\mathbf{\Omega}} = \begin{bmatrix} \tilde{\psi}_{11}\mathbf{I}_T & \tilde{\psi}_{12}\mathbf{I}_T & \cdots & \tilde{\psi}_{1G}\mathbf{I}_T \\ \tilde{\psi}_{21}\mathbf{I}_T & \tilde{\psi}_{22}\mathbf{I}_T & \cdots & \tilde{\psi}_{2G}\mathbf{I}_T \\ \vdots & \vdots & & \vdots \\ \tilde{\psi}_{G1}\mathbf{I}_T & \tilde{\psi}_{G2}\mathbf{I}_T & \cdots & \tilde{\psi}_{GG}\mathbf{I}_T \end{bmatrix}, \tag{13.68}$$

and

$$\tilde{\psi}_{gh} = \frac{(\mathbf{y}_g - \hat{\mathbf{Y}}_g\tilde{\boldsymbol{\beta}}_g - \mathbf{X}_g\tilde{\boldsymbol{\gamma}}_g)'(\mathbf{y}_h - \hat{\mathbf{Y}}_h\tilde{\boldsymbol{\beta}}_h - \mathbf{X}_h\tilde{\boldsymbol{\gamma}}_h)}{(T - G_g + 1 - K_g)}, \tag{13.69}$$

$$G_g^{\Delta} + K_g^{*} \geq G_h^{\Delta} + K_h^{*},$$

$$g, h = 1, 2, \ldots, G,$$

and $\tilde{\boldsymbol{\beta}}$ and $\tilde{\boldsymbol{\gamma}}$ represent the two-stage least squares estimates of the respective coefficients. (Some authors prefer using T instead of $(T - G_g + 1 - K_g)$ in the denominator of $\tilde{\psi}_{gh}$; this makes no difference to the asymptotic properties of the three-stage least squares estimator. Note, however, that $\hat{\mathbf{\Omega}}$ will be singular if the number of equations exceeds the number of observations.) The three-stage least squares estimator of the structural coefficients then is

$$\hat{\tilde{\tilde{\alpha}}} = (\hat{\mathbf{Z}}'\hat{\mathbf{\Omega}}^{-1}\hat{\mathbf{Z}})^{-1}(\hat{\mathbf{Z}}'\hat{\mathbf{\Omega}}^{-1}\mathbf{y}) \tag{13.70}$$

$$= \begin{bmatrix} \tilde{\psi}^{11}(\hat{\mathbf{Z}}_1'\hat{\mathbf{Z}}_1) & \tilde{\psi}^{12}(\hat{\mathbf{Z}}_1'\hat{\mathbf{Z}}_2) & \cdots & \tilde{\psi}^{1G}(\hat{\mathbf{Z}}_1'\hat{\mathbf{Z}}_G) \\ \tilde{\psi}^{21}(\hat{\mathbf{Z}}_2'\hat{\mathbf{Z}}_1) & \tilde{\psi}^{22}(\hat{\mathbf{Z}}_2'\hat{\mathbf{Z}}_2) & \cdots & \hat{\psi}^{2G}(\hat{\mathbf{Z}}_2'\hat{\mathbf{Z}}_G) \\ \vdots & \vdots & & \vdots \\ \tilde{\psi}^{G1}(\hat{\mathbf{Z}}_G'\hat{\mathbf{Z}}_1) & \tilde{\psi}^{G2}(\hat{\mathbf{Z}}_G'\hat{\mathbf{Z}}_2) & \cdots & \tilde{\psi}^{GG}(\hat{\mathbf{Z}}_G'\hat{\mathbf{Z}}_G) \end{bmatrix}^{-1} \begin{bmatrix} \sum_g \hat{\psi}^{1g}(\hat{\mathbf{Z}}_1'\mathbf{y}_g) \\ \sum_g \tilde{\psi}^{2g}(\hat{\mathbf{Z}}_2'\mathbf{y}_g) \\ \vdots \\ \sum_g \tilde{\psi}^{Gg}(\hat{\mathbf{Z}}_G'\mathbf{y}_g) \end{bmatrix},$$

where $\hat{\psi}^{gh}$ represents the corresponding element of the *inverse* of $\hat{\mathbf{\Omega}}$. As in the two-stage Aitken estimator of Section 12-3, the variance–covariance matrix of the three-stage least squares estimator can be estimated by

$$\text{Est. Var–Cov}(\hat{\tilde{\tilde{\alpha}}}) = (\hat{\mathbf{Z}}'\hat{\mathbf{\Omega}}^{-1}\hat{\mathbf{Z}})^{-1}. \tag{13.71}$$

The preceding way of deriving the three-stage least squares estimator shows clearly that the underlying idea is to take into account the correlation of the disturbances across equations by treating (13.66) as a set of seemingly unrelated equations. An alternative and common—but less intuitive—way of deriving the three stage estimator can also be presented. The structural equations of the system can be written as

$$\text{(13.72)} \qquad \begin{aligned} \mathbf{y}_1 &= \mathbf{Z}_1\boldsymbol{\alpha}_1 + \mathbf{u}_1, \\ \mathbf{y}_2 &= \mathbf{Z}_2\boldsymbol{\alpha}_2 + \mathbf{u}_2, \\ &\vdots \\ \mathbf{y}_G &= \mathbf{Z}_G\boldsymbol{\alpha}_G + \mathbf{u}_G, \end{aligned}$$

where

$$\mathbf{Z}_g = [\mathbf{Y}_g \ \mathbf{X}_g],$$

$$\boldsymbol{\alpha}_g = \begin{bmatrix} \boldsymbol{\beta}_g \\ \boldsymbol{\gamma}_g \end{bmatrix}.$$

Premultiplying each equation of (13.72) by $\mathbf{X}'$ gives

$$\text{(13.73)} \qquad \begin{aligned} \mathbf{X}'\mathbf{y}_1 &= \mathbf{X}'\mathbf{Z}_1\boldsymbol{\alpha}_1 + \mathbf{X}'\mathbf{u}_1, \\ \mathbf{X}'\mathbf{y}_2 &= \mathbf{X}'\mathbf{Z}_2\boldsymbol{\alpha}_2 + \mathbf{X}'\mathbf{u}_2, \\ &\vdots \\ \mathbf{X}'\mathbf{y}_G &= \mathbf{X}'\mathbf{Z}_G\boldsymbol{\alpha}_G + \mathbf{X}'\mathbf{u}_G. \end{aligned}$$

This can be written as

$$\text{(13.73a)} \qquad \begin{bmatrix} \mathbf{X}'\mathbf{y}_1 \\ \mathbf{X}'\mathbf{y}_2 \\ \vdots \\ \mathbf{X}'\mathbf{y}_G \end{bmatrix} = \begin{bmatrix} \mathbf{X}'\mathbf{Z}_1 & \mathbf{0} & \cdots & \mathbf{0} \\ \mathbf{0} & \mathbf{X}'\mathbf{Z}_2 & \cdots & \mathbf{0} \\ \vdots & \vdots & & \vdots \\ \mathbf{0} & \mathbf{0} & \cdots & \mathbf{X}'\mathbf{Z}_G \end{bmatrix} \begin{bmatrix} \boldsymbol{\alpha}_1 \\ \boldsymbol{\alpha}_2 \\ \vdots \\ \boldsymbol{\alpha}_G \end{bmatrix} + \begin{bmatrix} \mathbf{X}'\mathbf{u}_1 \\ \mathbf{X}'\mathbf{u}_2 \\ \vdots \\ \mathbf{X}'\mathbf{u}_G \end{bmatrix},$$

or

$$\text{(13.73b)} \qquad \bar{\bar{\mathbf{y}}} = \bar{\bar{\mathbf{Z}}}\boldsymbol{\alpha} + \bar{\bar{\mathbf{u}}},$$

where

$$\begin{aligned} \bar{\bar{\mathbf{y}}} &\to KG \times 1, \\ \bar{\bar{\mathbf{Z}}} &\to KG \times \sum_{g=1}^{G} (G_g^{\Delta} - 1 + K_g^*), \\ \boldsymbol{\alpha} &\to \sum_{g=1}^{G} (G_g^{\Delta} - 1 + K_g^*) \times 1, \\ \bar{\bar{\mathbf{u}}} &\to KG \times 1. \end{aligned}$$

We note that

$$E(\bar{\bar{\mathbf{u}}}\bar{\bar{\mathbf{u}}}') = \begin{bmatrix} \sigma_{11}(\mathbf{X}'\mathbf{X}) & \sigma_{12}(\mathbf{X}'\mathbf{X}) & \cdots & \sigma_{1G}(\mathbf{X}'\mathbf{X}) \\ \sigma_{21}(\mathbf{X}'\mathbf{X}) & \sigma_{22}(\mathbf{X}'\mathbf{X}) & \cdots & \sigma_{2G}(\mathbf{X}'\mathbf{X}) \\ \vdots & \vdots & & \vdots \\ \sigma_{G1}(\mathbf{X}'\mathbf{X}) & \sigma_{G2}(\mathbf{X}'\mathbf{X}) & \cdots & \sigma_{GG}(\mathbf{X}'\mathbf{X}) \end{bmatrix},$$

where the σs represent variances and covariances of the structural disturbances. Application of the Aitken generalized least squares formula to (13.73b) leads to

$$\bar{\bar{\alpha}} = (\bar{\bar{\mathbf{Z}}}'\Theta^{-1}\bar{\bar{\mathbf{Z}}})^{-1}(\bar{\bar{\mathbf{Z}}}'\Theta^{-1}\bar{\bar{\mathbf{y}}}), \tag{13.74}$$

where

$$\Theta = E(\bar{\bar{\mathbf{u}}}\bar{\bar{\mathbf{u}}}').$$

Consistent estimates of the variances and covariances of the structural disturbances can be obtained by using the two-stage least squares residuals. That is, we can obtain consistent estimates of σ_{gh} by utilizing

$$s_{gh} = \frac{(\mathbf{y}_g - \mathbf{Y}_g\tilde{\beta}_g - \mathbf{X}_g\tilde{\gamma}_g)'(\mathbf{y}_h - \mathbf{Y}_h\tilde{\beta}_h - \mathbf{X}_h\tilde{\gamma}_h)}{(T - G_g^\Delta + 1 - K_g^*)}, \tag{13.75}$$

$$G_g^\Delta + K_g^* \geq G_h^\Delta + K_h^*,$$

$$g, h = 1, 2, \ldots, G.$$

Then $\boldsymbol{\alpha}$ can be estimated by

(13.76)

$$\hat{\hat{\alpha}} = (\bar{\bar{\mathbf{Z}}}'\hat{\Theta}^{-1}\bar{\bar{\mathbf{Z}}})^{-1}(\bar{\bar{\mathbf{Z}}}'\hat{\Theta}^{-1}\bar{\bar{\mathbf{y}}})$$

$$= \begin{bmatrix} s^{11}\mathbf{Z}_1'\mathbf{X}(\mathbf{X}'\mathbf{X})^{-1}\mathbf{X}'\mathbf{Z}_1 & s^{12}\mathbf{Z}_1'\mathbf{X}(\mathbf{X}'\mathbf{X})^{-1}\mathbf{X}'\mathbf{Z}_2 & \cdots & s^{1G}\mathbf{Z}_1'\mathbf{X}(\mathbf{X}'\mathbf{X})^{-1}\mathbf{X}'\mathbf{Z}_G \\ s^{21}\mathbf{Z}_2'\mathbf{X}(\mathbf{X}'\mathbf{X})^{-1}\mathbf{X}'\mathbf{Z}_1 & s^{22}\mathbf{Z}_2'\mathbf{X}(\mathbf{X}'\mathbf{X})^{-1}\mathbf{X}'\mathbf{Z}_2 & \cdots & s^{2G}\mathbf{Z}_2'\mathbf{X}(\mathbf{X}'\mathbf{X})^{-1}\mathbf{X}'\mathbf{Z}_G \\ \vdots & \vdots & & \vdots \\ s^{G1}\mathbf{Z}_G'\mathbf{X}(\mathbf{X}'\mathbf{X})^{-1}\mathbf{X}'\mathbf{Z}_1 & s^{G2}\mathbf{Z}_G'\mathbf{X}(\mathbf{X}'\mathbf{X})^{-1}\mathbf{X}'\mathbf{Z}_1 & \cdots & s^{GG}\mathbf{Z}_G'\mathbf{X}(\mathbf{X}'\mathbf{X})^{-1}\mathbf{X}'\mathbf{Z}_G \end{bmatrix}^{-1}$$

$$\times \begin{bmatrix} \sum_g s^{1g}\mathbf{Z}_1'\mathbf{X}(\mathbf{X}'\mathbf{X})^{-1}\mathbf{X}'\mathbf{y}_g \\ \sum_g s^{2g}\mathbf{Z}_2'\mathbf{X}(\mathbf{X}'\mathbf{X})^{-1}\mathbf{X}'\mathbf{y}_g \\ \vdots \\ \sum_g s^{Gg}\mathbf{Z}_G'\mathbf{X}(\mathbf{X}'\mathbf{X})^{-1}\mathbf{X}'\mathbf{y}_g \end{bmatrix},$$

where s^{gh} represents the corresponding element of the *inverse* of $\hat{\Theta}$. The expression (13.76) is equivalent to (13.70). Further,

$$\text{Est. Var-Cov}(\hat{\hat{\alpha}}) = (\bar{\bar{\mathbf{Z}}}'\hat{\Theta}^{-1}\bar{\bar{\mathbf{Z}}})^{-1}, \tag{13.77}$$

which is equivalent to (13.71).[14] Under the assumptions stated at the outset of this chapter, the three-stage least squares estimates of the structural coefficients are consistent and asymptotically efficient. (If the predetermined variables in the sys-

[14] For a proof see A. Maravall, "A Note on Three-Stage Least Squares Estimation," *Journal of Econometrics,* 4 (November 1976), pp. 325–330.

tem include lagged endogenous variables, their initial values are assumed to be fixed.) In models in which it can be assumed that the structural disturbances are uncorrelated across equations, $\mathbf{\Theta}$ will be diagonal, and the three-stage least squares estimates will be the same as the two-stage least squares estimates. We also note that the three-stage least squares estimator, like the two-stage estimator, is *not invariant* with respect to the choice of the endogenous variable whose structural coefficient is to be unity. A final point worth mentioning is that in applying the three-stage least squares method, the omission of exactly identified equations will not affect the three-stage least squares estimates of the coefficients of the remaining equations.[15] This means that exactly identified equations add no information that is relevant for estimation of the overidentified equations of the system. The reverse, however, is not true.

EXAMPLE Continuing with the food market example, we use the results from the application of the two-stage least squares method to estimate the variance–covariance matrix of the structural disturbances. By (13.75) this is

$$\tilde{\mathbf{\Phi}} = \begin{bmatrix} s_{11} & s_{12} \\ s_{21} & s_{22} \end{bmatrix} = \begin{bmatrix} 3.8664 & 4.3574 \\ 4.3574 & 6.0396 \end{bmatrix}.$$

The three-stage least squares estimates of the structural coefficients then are

$$\underset{(7.9208)}{Q_t = 94.6333} - \underset{(0.0965)}{0.2436P_t} + \underset{(0.0469)}{0.3140D_t} + \tilde{\tilde{\tilde{u}}}_{1t} \qquad \text{(demand)},$$

$$\underset{(11.8934)}{Q_t = 52.1972} + \underset{(0.0997)}{0.2286P_t} + \underset{(0.0440)}{0.2282F_t} + \underset{(0.0729)}{0.3611A_t} + \tilde{\tilde{\tilde{u}}}_{2t} \qquad \text{(supply)}.$$

The supply equation is exactly identified and, therefore, adds no information for estimating the overidentified demand equation. Thus the three-stage least squares estimates of the demand equation are the same as those obtained by the two-stage least squares method. However, the three-stage least squares results for the supply equation are different from those obtained by the two-stage least squares method.

It may be noted that the residuals from the estimated three-stage least squares equations can be used to obtain new estimates of the variances and covariances of the structural disturbances. These can then replace the previous estimates in the three-stage least squares formula, thus leading to new estimates of the structural coefficients. The process could be repeated until there is no change in the estimated structural coefficients. The resulting estimates, known as *iterative three-stage least squares* (I3SLS) *estimates,* have the same asymptotic properties as the ordinary three-stage least squares estimates.[16] For our food market example, the estimated

[15] See A. Zellner and H. Theil, "Three-Stage Least Squares: Simultaneous Estimation of Simultaneous Equations," *Econometrica,* 30 (January 1962), pp. 63–68. If *all* equations in the system are exactly identified, the three-stage least squares estimator will be the same as the two-stage least squares estimator.

[16] See A. Madansky, "On the Efficiency of Three-Stage Least Squares Estimation," *Econometrica,* 32 (January–April 1964), p. 55.

coefficients converged at the tenth decimal place after nine iterations. The final estimates of the variance-covariance matrix of the structural disturbances are

$$\overset{\approx}{\boldsymbol{\Phi}} = \begin{bmatrix} 3.8664 & 5.0907 \\ 5.0907 & 6.9564 \end{bmatrix}.$$

As a result, the converged iterative three-stage least squares are

$$\underset{}{Q_t} = \underset{(7.9208)}{94.6333} - \underset{(0.0965)}{0.2436}P_t + \underset{(0.0469)}{0.3140}D_t + \overset{\equiv}{u}_{1t} \qquad \text{(demand)},$$

$$Q_t = \underset{(12.8051)}{52.6618} + \underset{(0.1075)}{0.2266}P_t + \underset{(0.0468)}{0.2234}F_t + \underset{(0.0720)}{0.3800}A_t + \overset{\equiv}{u}_{2t} \qquad \text{(supply)}.$$

Full Information Maximum Likelihood Estimation

Another system method designed for estimating the structural coefficients of a simultaneous equation system is the *full information maximum likelihood* (FIML) *method.* It involves the usual application of the maximum likelihood principle to all stochastic equations of the system simultaneously. Consider the complete system

$$\mathbf{B}\mathbf{y}_t + \boldsymbol{\Gamma}\mathbf{x}_t = \mathbf{u}_t$$

specified in (13.3a), and the corresponding variance-covariance matrix of the disturbances

$$\boldsymbol{\Phi} = E(\mathbf{u}_t\mathbf{u}_t').$$

On the assumptions previously specified, the joint distribution of the elements of $\mathbf{u}_t$ is

$$f(\mathbf{u}_t) = (2\pi)^{-(G/2)}|\boldsymbol{\Phi}|^{-(1/2)}e^{-(\mathbf{u}_t'\boldsymbol{\Phi}^{-1}\mathbf{u}_t)/2}.$$

The probability transformation from the unobservable $\mathbf{u}_t$ to the observable $\mathbf{y}_t$ is

$$f(\mathbf{y}_t|\mathbf{x}_t) = f(\mathbf{u}_t)\left|\frac{\partial \mathbf{u}_t}{\partial \mathbf{y}_t}\right| = f(\mathbf{u}_t)\left|\frac{\partial(\mathbf{B}\mathbf{y}_t + \boldsymbol{\Gamma}\mathbf{x}_t)}{\partial \mathbf{y}_t}\right| = f(\mathbf{u}_t)|\mathbf{B}|,$$

where $|\mathbf{B}|$ is the Jacobian, given by the absolute value of the determinant of the matrix $\mathbf{B}$. Then the logarithmic likelihood function for the T observations on $\mathbf{y}_t$ conditional on the values of $\mathbf{x}_t$ is

$$L = -\frac{GT}{2}\log(2\pi) - \frac{G}{2}\log|\boldsymbol{\Phi}| + T\log|\mathbf{B}| - \frac{1}{2}\sum_{t=1}^{T}(\mathbf{B}\mathbf{y}_t + \boldsymbol{\Gamma}\mathbf{x}_t)'\boldsymbol{\Phi}^{-1}(\mathbf{B}\mathbf{y}_t + \boldsymbol{\Gamma}\mathbf{x}_t). \tag{13.78}$$

The maximum likelihood estimators of $\mathbf{B}$, $\boldsymbol{\Gamma}$, and $\boldsymbol{\Phi}$ are then obtained by maximizing (13.78) with respect to these parameters. These estimators are consistent, asymptotically efficient, and their asymptotic distribution is normal. This means that they have the same asymptotic properties—and the same asymptotic variance-covariance matrix—as the three-stage least squares estimators. The asymptotic variance-covariance matrix of the full information maximum likelihood estimators can be estimated in the usual way by reference to the appropriate information matrix.

EXAMPLE To illustrate the construction of the logarithmic likelihood function (13.78), we use the food market model (13.45), given as

$$Q_t = \alpha_1 + \alpha_2 P_t + \alpha_3 D_t + u_{1t} \qquad \text{(demand)},$$
$$Q_t = \beta_1 + \beta_2 P_t + \beta_3 F_t + \beta_4 A_t + u_{2t} \qquad \text{(supply)}.$$

Here,

$$\mathbf{y}_t' = [Q_t \quad P_t], \qquad \mathbf{x}_t' = [1 \quad D_t \quad F_t \quad A_t]$$

and

$$\mathbf{B} = \begin{bmatrix} 1 & -\alpha_2 \\ 1 & -\beta_2 \end{bmatrix}, \qquad \mathbf{\Gamma} = \begin{bmatrix} -\alpha_1 & -\alpha_3 & 0 & 0 \\ -\beta_1 & 0 & -\beta_3 & -\beta_4 \end{bmatrix}, \qquad \mathbf{\Phi} = \begin{bmatrix} \sigma_{11} & \sigma_{12} \\ \sigma_{12} & \sigma_{22} \end{bmatrix}.$$

Then

$$|\mathbf{\Phi}| = |\sigma_{11}\sigma_{22} - \sigma_{12}^2|,$$
$$|\mathbf{B}| = |-\beta_2 + \alpha_2|,$$

and

$$(\mathbf{B}\mathbf{y}_t + \mathbf{\Gamma}\mathbf{x}_t)'\mathbf{\Phi}^{-1}(\mathbf{B}\mathbf{y}_t + \mathbf{\Gamma}\mathbf{x}_t)$$

$$= [u_{1t} \quad u_{2t}]\frac{1}{|\mathbf{\Phi}|}\begin{bmatrix} \sigma_{22} & -\sigma_{12} \\ -\sigma_{12} & \sigma_{11} \end{bmatrix}\begin{bmatrix} u_{1t} \\ u_{2t} \end{bmatrix} = \frac{1}{|\mathbf{\Phi}|}(\sigma_{22}u_{1t}^2 + \sigma_{11}u_{2t}^2 - 2\sigma_{12}u_{1t}u_{2t}),$$

where

$$u_{1t} = Q_t - \alpha_1 - \alpha_2 P_t - \alpha_3 D_t,$$
$$u_{2t} = Q_t - \beta_1 - \beta_2 P_t - \beta_3 F_t - \beta_4 A_t.$$

Therefore, the logarithmic likelihood function (13.78) becomes

$$(13.79) \quad L = -\frac{GT}{2}\log(2\pi) - \frac{T}{2}\log(\sigma_{11}\sigma_{22} - \sigma_{12}^2) + T\log|\alpha_2 - \beta_2|$$
$$- \frac{1}{2(\sigma_{11}\sigma_{22} - \sigma_{12}^2)}\left\{\sigma_{22}\sum_{t=1}^{T}(Q_t - \alpha_1 - \alpha_2 P_t - \alpha_3 D_t)^2\right.$$
$$+ \sigma_{11}\sum_{t=1}^{T}(Q_t - \beta_1 - \beta_2 P_t - \beta_3 F_t - \beta_4 A_t)^2$$
$$\left. - 2\sigma_{12}\sum_{t=1}^{T}(Q_t - \alpha_1 - \alpha_2 P_t - \alpha_3 D_t)(Q_t - \beta_1 - \beta_2 P_t - \beta_3 F_t - \beta_4 A_t)\right\},$$

where $|\alpha_2 - \beta_2|$ stands for the absolute value of $(\alpha_2 - \beta_2)$.

In the preceding exposition we did not consider the possibility that the system might include identities as well as stochastic equations. If that is the case, the variance-covariance matrix of the structural disturbances will be singular so that its inverse will not exist. One way of dealing with this problem is to eliminate all identities (and the corresponding endogenous variables) by substitution before setting up the likelihood function. For instance, consider the model

$$C_t = \alpha_0 + \alpha_1 Y_t + \alpha_2 C_{t-1} + u_{1t} \qquad \text{(consumption)},$$

$$I_t = \beta_0 + \beta_1 r_t + \beta_2 I_{t-1} + u_{2t} \qquad \text{(investment)},$$

$$r_t = \gamma_0 + \gamma_1 Y_t + \gamma_2 M_t + u_{3t} \qquad \text{(money market)},$$

$$Y_t = C_t + I_t + G_t \qquad \text{(income identity)},$$

where C = consumption, Y = income, I = investment, r = rate of interest, M = money supply, and G = government expenditure. The variables C_t, Y_t, I_t, and r_t are endogenous; the remaining variables are predetermined. The income identity can be eliminated by substituting for Y_t into the rest of the system. The system then becomes

$$C_t = \left(\frac{\alpha_0}{1-\alpha_1}\right) + \left(\frac{\alpha_1}{1-\alpha_1}\right) I_t + \left(\frac{\alpha_1}{1-\alpha_1}\right) G_t + \left(\frac{\alpha_2}{1-\alpha_1}\right) C_{t-1} + \left(\frac{1}{1-\alpha_1}\right) u_{1t},$$

$$I_t = \beta_0 + \beta_1 r_t + \beta_2 I_{t-1} + u_{2t},$$

$$r_t = \gamma_0 + \gamma_1 C_t + \gamma_1 I_t + \gamma_1 G_t + \gamma_2 M_t + u_{3t},$$

which involves only stochastic equations.

EXAMPLE The full information maximum likelihod estimates of the structural equations of the food market model are

$$\underset{}{Q_t} = \underset{(8.0312)}{93.6192} - \underset{(0.0980)}{0.2295}P_t + \underset{(0.0474)}{0.3100}D_t + \hat{u}_{1t} \qquad \text{(demand)},$$

$$Q_t = \underset{(12.7460)}{51.9445} + \underset{(0.1078)}{0.2373}P_t + \underset{(0.0457)}{0.2208}F_t + \underset{(0.0765)}{0.3697}A_t + \hat{u}_{2t} \qquad \text{(supply)}.$$

We note that the estimates of the coefficients of the demand equation are identical with the limited information maximum likelihod estimates given earlier. Again, this is the result of the fact that the supply equation is exactly identified and, therefore, provides no information about the demand equation.

An ingenious way of interpreting the full information maximum likelihood estimates as instrumental variable estimates—and of providing a convenient iterative procedure for their calculation—has been developed by Hausman.[17] By extension

[17] J. A. Hausman, "Full Information Instrumental Variable Estimation of Simultaneous Equation Models," *Annals of Economic and Social Measurement,* 3 (October 1974), pp. 641–652; also J. A. Hausman, "An Instrumental Variable Approach to Full-Information Estimators for Linear and Certain Nonlinear Econometric Models," *Econometrica,* 43 (July 1975), pp. 727–738.

of (13.34), we can present the system of equations as

$$(13.80)\qquad \begin{bmatrix} \mathbf{y}_1 \\ \mathbf{y}_2 \\ \vdots \\ \mathbf{y}_G \end{bmatrix} = \begin{bmatrix} \mathbf{Z}_1 & \mathbf{0} & \cdots & \mathbf{0} \\ \mathbf{0} & \mathbf{Z}_2 & \cdots & \mathbf{0} \\ \vdots & \vdots & & \vdots \\ \mathbf{0} & \mathbf{0} & \cdots & \mathbf{Z}_G \end{bmatrix} \begin{bmatrix} \boldsymbol{\alpha}_1 \\ \boldsymbol{\alpha}_2 \\ \vdots \\ \boldsymbol{\alpha}_G \end{bmatrix} + \begin{bmatrix} \mathbf{u}_1 \\ \mathbf{u}_2 \\ \vdots \\ \mathbf{u}_G \end{bmatrix}$$

or, in compact notation,

$$(13.80\text{a})\qquad \mathbf{y} = \mathbf{Z}\boldsymbol{\alpha} + \mathbf{u}.$$

Further, let us define

$$(13.81)\qquad \overline{\mathbf{W}}' = \begin{bmatrix} \hat{\mathbf{Z}}_1' & \mathbf{0} & \cdots & \mathbf{0} \\ \mathbf{0} & \hat{\mathbf{Z}}_2' & \cdots & \mathbf{0} \\ \vdots & \vdots & & \vdots \\ \mathbf{0} & \mathbf{0} & \cdots & \hat{\mathbf{Z}}_G' \end{bmatrix} \begin{bmatrix} \hat{\sigma}_{11}\mathbf{I} & \hat{\sigma}_{12}\mathbf{I} & \cdots & \hat{\sigma}_{1G}\mathbf{I} \\ \hat{\sigma}_{21}\mathbf{I} & \hat{\sigma}_{22}\mathbf{I} & \cdots & \hat{\sigma}_{2G}\mathbf{I} \\ \vdots & \vdots & & \vdots \\ \hat{\sigma}_{G1}\mathbf{I} & \hat{\sigma}_{G2}\mathbf{I} & \cdots & \hat{\sigma}_{GG}\mathbf{I} \end{bmatrix}^{-1}$$

where

$$\hat{\mathbf{Z}}_g = [\mathbf{X}\hat{\boldsymbol{\pi}}_g \quad \mathbf{X}_g],$$

$$\hat{\sigma}_{gh} = \frac{(\mathbf{y}_g - \mathbf{Z}_g\hat{\boldsymbol{\alpha}}_g)'(\mathbf{y}_h - \mathbf{Z}_h\hat{\boldsymbol{\alpha}}_h)}{T},$$

and $\hat{\boldsymbol{\pi}}_g$ is the gth column of $-\hat{\boldsymbol{\Gamma}}(\hat{\mathbf{B}}^{-1})'$, $g, h = 1, 2, \ldots, G$. Then the full information maximum likelihood estimator of $\boldsymbol{\alpha}$ can be expressed as

$$(13.82)\qquad \hat{\boldsymbol{\alpha}} = (\overline{\mathbf{W}}'\mathbf{Z})^{-1}\overline{\mathbf{W}}'\mathbf{y}.$$

Of course, the values of $\hat{\boldsymbol{\alpha}}$ cannot be directly calculated since $\overline{\mathbf{W}}$ involves $\hat{\boldsymbol{\alpha}}$. However, we may start by evaluating $\overline{\mathbf{W}}$ using a two-stage least squares—or any other consistent—estimate of $\boldsymbol{\alpha}$, calculate the corresponding value of $\hat{\boldsymbol{\alpha}}$, and iterate until convergence is achieved.

13-5 Estimation of Models with Nonspherical Disturbances

In the preceding sections of this chapter we have worked on the assumption that the structural disturbances are homoskedastic and nonautocorrelated. However, when the observations are made over time, the disturbances are likely to be autocorrelated. When the observations are cross-sectional, the assumption of homoskedasticity is frequently implausible. Disturbances that violate either or both of these assumptions are called *nonspherical*. In this section we consider the problem of estimating simultaneous equation models with such disturbances.[18]

[18] This section relies heavily on K. Bollen and J. Kmenta, "Estimation of Simultaneous Equation Models with Autoregressive or Heteroskedastic Disturbances," paper presented at the World Congress of the Econometric Society in Cambridge, MA, August 17–24, 1985.

Weighted Two-Stage Least Squares and Three-Stage Least Squares Estimation

Let the first structural equation be, as in (13.34),

$$\mathbf{y}_1 = \mathbf{Y}_1\boldsymbol{\beta}_1 + \mathbf{X}_1\boldsymbol{\gamma}_1 + \mathbf{u}_1$$

or

$$\mathbf{y}_1 = \mathbf{Z}_1\boldsymbol{\alpha}_1 + \mathbf{u}_1.$$

With respect to $\mathbf{u}_1$, we assume

(13.83) $$E(\mathbf{u}_1) = \mathbf{0} \qquad \text{and} \qquad E(\mathbf{u}_1\mathbf{u}_1') = \sigma_{11}\boldsymbol{\Omega}_1.$$

This means that $\mathbf{u}_1$ could be autocorrelated or heteroskedastic or both. For the time being we also assume that the system does not contain any lagged endogenous variables. In this case the ordinary least squares estimates of the reduced form coefficients are consistent. Therefore, the straightforward application of the two-stage least squares method leads to consistent estimates of the structural coefficients, but the asymptotic variances are larger than they would be if the autoregressive or heteroskedastic nature of the disturbances were taken into account. Further, the estimated variances of the coefficients are inconsistent, so the standard tests of significance and confidence intervals are not valid. An improved estimation method, which we call *weighted two-stage least squares* (W2SLS), can be devised as follows. The reduced form equations for $\mathbf{Y}$ are

(13.84) $$\mathbf{Y}_1 = \mathbf{X}\boldsymbol{\Pi}_1 + \mathbf{V}_1$$

as in (13.55). Assuming for the time being that $\boldsymbol{\Omega}_1$ is known, we estimate $\boldsymbol{\Pi}_1$ as

(13.85) $$\tilde{\boldsymbol{\Pi}}_1 = (\mathbf{X}'\boldsymbol{\Omega}_1^{-1}\mathbf{X})^{-1}\mathbf{X}'\boldsymbol{\Omega}_1^{-1}\mathbf{Y}_1.$$

Note that we deliberately used $\boldsymbol{\Omega}_1^{-1}$ as the weighting matrix although it is *not the variance-covariance matrix of* $\mathbf{V}_1$. The predicted values of $\mathbf{Y}_1$ are

(13.86) $$\tilde{\mathbf{Y}}_1 = \mathbf{X}\tilde{\boldsymbol{\Pi}}_1.$$

Defining $\tilde{\mathbf{V}}_1 = \mathbf{Y}_1 - \tilde{\mathbf{Y}}_1$, we note that

(13.87) $$\begin{aligned}\mathbf{X}'\boldsymbol{\Omega}_1^{-1}\tilde{\mathbf{V}}_1 &= \mathbf{X}'\boldsymbol{\Omega}_1^{-1}\mathbf{Y}_1 - \mathbf{X}'\boldsymbol{\Omega}_1^{-1}\mathbf{X}\tilde{\boldsymbol{\Pi}}_1 \\ &= \mathbf{0}.\end{aligned}$$

Replacing $\mathbf{Y}_1$ by $\tilde{\mathbf{Y}}_1$ in the structural equation under consideration, we obtain

(13.88) $$\mathbf{y}_1 = \tilde{\mathbf{Y}}_1\boldsymbol{\beta}_1 + \mathbf{X}_1\boldsymbol{\gamma}_1 + (\tilde{\mathbf{V}}_1\boldsymbol{\beta}_1 + \mathbf{u}_1)$$

or

(13.89) $$\mathbf{y}_1 = \tilde{\mathbf{Z}}_1\boldsymbol{\alpha}_1 + (\tilde{\mathbf{V}}_1\boldsymbol{\beta}_1 + \mathbf{u}_1),$$

where $\tilde{\mathbf{Z}}_1 = [\tilde{\mathbf{Y}}_1 \quad \mathbf{X}_1]$. The W2SLS estimator of $\boldsymbol{\alpha}_1$ then is

(13.90) $$\tilde{\alpha}_1 = (\tilde{\mathbf{Z}}_1'\boldsymbol{\Omega}_1^{-1}\tilde{\mathbf{Z}}_1)^{-1}\tilde{\mathbf{Z}}_1'\boldsymbol{\Omega}_1^{-1}\mathbf{y}_1.$$

The asymptotic properties of $\tilde{\alpha}_1$ can be derived as follows. First we note that

(13.91) $$\tilde{\alpha}_1 = (\tilde{\mathbf{Z}}_1\mathbf{\Omega}_1^{-1}\tilde{\mathbf{Z}}_1)^{-1}\tilde{\mathbf{Z}}_1'\mathbf{\Omega}^{-1}(\tilde{\mathbf{Z}}_1\alpha_1 + \tilde{\mathbf{V}}_1\beta_1 + \mathbf{u}_1).$$

But

(13.92) $$\begin{aligned}\tilde{\mathbf{Z}}_1'\mathbf{\Omega}_1^{-1}\tilde{\mathbf{V}}_1\beta_1 &= \begin{bmatrix}\tilde{\mathbf{Y}}_1' \\ \mathbf{X}_1'\end{bmatrix}\mathbf{\Omega}_1^{-1}\tilde{\mathbf{V}}_1\beta_1 \\ &= \begin{bmatrix}\tilde{\mathbf{\Pi}}_1'\mathbf{X}'\mathbf{\Omega}_1^{-1}\tilde{\mathbf{V}}_1\beta_1 \\ \mathbf{X}_1'\mathbf{\Omega}_1^{-1}\tilde{\mathbf{V}}_1\beta_1\end{bmatrix} \\ &= \mathbf{0}.\end{aligned}$$

Therefore we obtain the following simplification:

(13.93) $$\tilde{\alpha}_1 = \alpha_1 + (\tilde{\mathbf{Z}}_1'\mathbf{\Omega}_1^{-1}\tilde{\mathbf{Z}}_1)^{-1}\tilde{\mathbf{Z}}_1'\mathbf{\Omega}_1^{-1}\mathbf{u}_1$$

and

(13.94) $$\begin{aligned}\text{plim } \tilde{\alpha}_1 &= \alpha_1 + \text{plim}(\tilde{\mathbf{Z}}_1'\mathbf{\Omega}_1^{-1}\tilde{\mathbf{Z}}_1/\mathrm{T})^{-1}(\tilde{\mathbf{Z}}_1'\mathbf{\Omega}_1^{-1}\mathbf{u}_1/\mathrm{T}) \\ &= \alpha_1.\end{aligned}$$

Further

(13.95) $$\begin{aligned}&\text{Asymp. Var } \sqrt{T}\,(\tilde{\alpha}_1 - \alpha_1) \\ &= \text{plim}[T(\tilde{\mathbf{Z}}_1'\mathbf{\Omega}_1^{-1}\tilde{\mathbf{Z}}_1)^{-1}\tilde{\mathbf{Z}}_1'\mathbf{\Omega}_1^{-1}\mathbf{u}_1\mathbf{u}_1'\mathbf{\Omega}_1^{-1}\tilde{\mathbf{Z}}_1(\tilde{\mathbf{Z}}_1'\mathbf{\Omega}_1^{-1}\tilde{\mathbf{Z}})^{-1}] \\ &= \text{plim}\left[\left(\frac{\tilde{\mathbf{Z}}_1'\mathbf{\Omega}_1^{-1}\tilde{\mathbf{Z}}_1}{T}\right)^{-1}\left(\frac{\tilde{\mathbf{Z}}_1'\mathbf{\Omega}_1^{-1}\mathbf{u}_1\mathbf{u}_1'\mathbf{\Omega}_1^{-1}\tilde{\mathbf{Z}}_1}{T}\right)\left(\frac{\tilde{\mathbf{Z}}_1'\mathbf{\Omega}_1^{-1}\tilde{\mathbf{Z}}_1}{T}\right)\right]^{-1} \\ &= \sigma_{11}\text{plim}\left(\frac{\tilde{\mathbf{Z}}_1'\mathbf{\Omega}_1^{-1}\tilde{\mathbf{Z}}_1}{T}\right)^{-1}.\end{aligned}$$

Thus a consistent estimator of the variance–covariance matrix of $\tilde{\alpha}_1$ is

(13.96) $$\text{Est. Var–Cov}(\tilde{\alpha}_1) = s_{11}(\tilde{\mathbf{Z}}_1'\mathbf{\Omega}_1^{-1}\tilde{\mathbf{Z}})^{-1},$$

where

(13.97) $$s_{11} = \frac{(\mathbf{y}_1 - \mathbf{Z}_1\tilde{\alpha}_1)'\mathbf{\Omega}_1^{-1}(\mathbf{y}_1 - \mathbf{Z}_1\tilde{\alpha}_1)}{T - G_1 + 1 - K_1}.$$

The W2SLS can be extended to yield asymptotically efficient *weighted three-stage least squares* (W3SLS) estimates. This can be accomplished by first noting that the W2SLS estimator of α_1 in (13.90) could also have been obtained by applying the OLS method to

(13.98) $$\mathbf{P}_1\mathbf{y}_1 = \mathbf{P}_1\tilde{\mathbf{Z}}_1\alpha_1 + \mathbf{u}_1^*,$$

where $\mathbf{P}_1$ is a $T \times T$ matrix such that $\mathbf{P}_1'\mathbf{P}_1 = \mathbf{\Omega}_1^{-1}$ and $\mathbf{u}_1^* = \mathbf{P}_1(\mathbf{u}_1 + \tilde{\mathbf{V}}_1\beta_1)$. If we now consider all G equations of the system, we have

$$
\begin{aligned}
(13.99) \qquad \mathbf{P}_1\mathbf{y}_1 &= \mathbf{P}_1\tilde{\mathbf{Z}}_1\boldsymbol{\alpha}_1 + \mathbf{u}_1^*, \\
\mathbf{P}_2\mathbf{y}_2 &= \mathbf{P}_2\tilde{\mathbf{Z}}_2\boldsymbol{\alpha}_2 + \mathbf{u}_2^*, \\
&\vdots \\
\mathbf{P}_G\mathbf{y}_G &= \mathbf{P}_G\tilde{\mathbf{Z}}_G\boldsymbol{\alpha}_G + \mathbf{u}_G^*.
\end{aligned}
$$

These equations can be estimated simultaneously by the two-stage Aitken method, using the W2SLS residuals to estimate the variances and covariances of the disturbances.

Estimation with Unknown Ωs: The Case of Heteroskedasticity and Autoregression

In practice the elements of the $\mathbf{\Omega}_1$ matrix will rarely be known and have to be estimated, and $\mathbf{\Omega}_1$ in (13.90), (13.96), and (13.97) will have to be replaced by its estimate $\hat{\mathbf{\Omega}}_1$. The estimation does, of course, depend on the structure of $\mathbf{\Omega}_1$. When the disturbances are *heteroskedastic,* then $\mathbf{\Omega}_1$ is diagonal. If the variance of the disturbance is proportional to the square of one of the explanatory exogenous variables, say, the kth one, i.e., if

$$(13.100) \qquad \sigma_{11i} = \sigma_{11}X_{ik}^2 \qquad (i = 1, 2, \ldots, T),$$

then the ith diagonal element of $\mathbf{\Omega}_1^{-1}$ is simply $1/X_{ik}^2$. If, however, the heteroskedasticity is of the type

$$(13.101) \qquad \sigma_{11i} = \sigma_{11}X_{ik}^{\lambda_1},$$

where λ_1 is an unknown parameter, then λ_1 has to be estimated along with $\boldsymbol{\alpha}_1$. This can be accomplished by calculating the value of s_{11} in (13.97) for different assumed values of λ_1 within some interval (typically 0.00–3.00) and choosing a combination of values of λ_1 and $\boldsymbol{\alpha}_1$ that corresponds to the minimum value of s_{11}.

When the disturbance is autoregressive of first order, i.e., when

$$(13.102) \qquad u_{1t} = \rho_1 u_{1,t-1} + \varepsilon_{1t},$$

where ε_{1t} is a classical disturbance that is independent of $u_{1,t-1}$, then

$$(13.103) \qquad \mathbf{\Omega}_1 = \begin{bmatrix} 1 & \rho_1 & \cdots & \rho_1^{T-1} \\ \rho_1 & 1 & \cdots & \rho_1^{T-2} \\ \vdots & \vdots & & \vdots \\ \rho_1^{T-1} & \rho_1^{T-2} & \cdots & 1 \end{bmatrix}.$$

Given the absence of lagged endogenous variables, the unknown ρ_1 can be estimated from the ordinary two-stage least squares residuals. That is, we first calculate

$$\hat{\mathbf{Y}}_1 = \mathbf{X}\hat{\Pi}_1 = \mathbf{X}(\mathbf{X}'\mathbf{X})^{-1}\mathbf{X}'\mathbf{Y}_1, \tag{13.104}$$

and then apply the ordinary least squares method to

$$\mathbf{y}_1 = \hat{\mathbf{Y}}_1\boldsymbol{\beta}_1 + \mathbf{X}_1\boldsymbol{\gamma}_1 + \mathbf{u}_1^{**} \tag{13.105}$$

and get $\hat{\boldsymbol{\beta}}_1$ and $\hat{\boldsymbol{\gamma}}_1$. The calculated residuals

$$\hat{\mathbf{u}}_1 = \mathbf{y}_1 - \mathbf{Y}_1\hat{\boldsymbol{\beta}}_1 - \mathbf{X}_1\hat{\boldsymbol{\gamma}}_1 \tag{13.106}$$

are then used to estimate ρ_1 by

$$\hat{\rho}_1 = \frac{\sum_t \hat{u}_{1t}\hat{u}_{1,t-1}}{\sqrt{\sum \hat{u}_{1t}^2}\sqrt{\sum \hat{u}_{1,t-1}^2}} \qquad (t = 2, 3, \ldots, T). \tag{13.107}$$

To extend the procedure to 3SLS, we note that in the case of heteroskedasticity $\mathbf{P}_1$ is a diagonal matrix with $1/\sqrt{\sigma_{11i}}$ as the ith diagonal element, whereas in the case of first-order autoregression $\mathbf{P}_1$ is defined as

$$\mathbf{P}_1 = \begin{bmatrix} \sqrt{1-\rho_1^2} & 0 & \cdots & 0 & 0 \\ -\rho_1 & 1 & \cdots & 0 & 0 \\ \vdots & \vdots & & \vdots & \vdots \\ 0 & 0 & \cdots & -\rho_1 & 1 \end{bmatrix}. \tag{13.108}$$

An analogous transformation matrix can be determined for each of the G equations of the system. The unknown elements of the transformation matrices can be estimated by using the procedure developed for the first structural equation described above. The transformed equations can then be estimated *simultaneously* by the two-stage Aitken method, using W2SLS residuals to estimate the variances and covariances of the transformed disturbances, as follows:

$$s_{gh} = \frac{(\hat{\mathbf{P}}_g\mathbf{y}_g - \hat{\mathbf{P}}_g\mathbf{Z}_g\tilde{\boldsymbol{\alpha}}_g)'(\hat{\mathbf{P}}_h\mathbf{y}_h - \hat{\mathbf{P}}_h\mathbf{Z}_h\tilde{\boldsymbol{\alpha}}_h)}{T - G_g^{\Delta} + 1 - K_g^*} \tag{13.109}$$

$$(G_g^{\Delta} + K_g^* \geq G_h^{\Delta} + K_h^*;\ g, h = 1, 2, \ldots, G),$$

where $\hat{\mathbf{P}}_g$ is such that $\hat{\mathbf{P}}_g'\hat{\mathbf{P}}_g = \hat{\boldsymbol{\Omega}}_g^{-1}$.

Estimation of Models with Lagged Endogenous Variables

Let us now consider a simultaneous equation *model with lagged endogenous variables*. As far as the treatment of heteroskedasticity is concerned, the presence of lagged endogenous variables among the predetermined variables of the system makes no difference since the estimates of the usual reduced form equations are consistent. Thus in the case of heteroskedasticity we can still proceed with estimation as outlined above. When, however, the disturbances are autoregressive, the lagged endogenous variables are correlated with the reduced form disturbances and the least squares estimates (weighted or unweighted) of the reduced form coefficients are biased and inconsistent. Therefore the estimation strategy described above has to be modified.[19]

To account for the presence of lagged endogenous variables, we write the first structural equation in the form

$$\begin{aligned} \mathbf{y}_1 &= \mathbf{Y}_1\boldsymbol{\beta}_1 + \mathbf{Y}_{-1,1}\gamma_{11} + \mathbf{X}_1\boldsymbol{\gamma}_1 + \mathbf{u}_1 \\ &= \mathbf{Z}_1\boldsymbol{\alpha}_1 + \mathbf{u}_1, \end{aligned} \tag{13.110}$$

where $\mathbf{Y}_{-1,1}$ is a matrix of lagged endogenous variables (which may include a column of lagged values of $\mathbf{y}_1$), and $\mathbf{X}_1$ is a matrix of purely exogenous variables. Instead of the standard reduced form presented in (13.84), we treat $\mathbf{Y}_{-1,1}$ *as if it were* endogenous and form

$$\begin{aligned} \mathbf{Y}_1 &= \mathbf{X}\boldsymbol{\Pi}_{11} + \mathbf{X}_{-1}\boldsymbol{\Pi}_{12} + \mathbf{W}_1 \\ &= \mathbf{X}^*\boldsymbol{\Pi}_1^* + \mathbf{W}_1, \\ \mathbf{Y}_{-1,1} &= \mathbf{X}\boldsymbol{\Pi}_{21} + \mathbf{X}_{-1}\boldsymbol{\Pi}_{22} + \mathbf{W}_2 \\ &= \mathbf{X}^*\boldsymbol{\Pi}_2^* + \mathbf{W}_2, \end{aligned} \tag{13.111}$$

where $\mathbf{X}$ is a matrix of all purely exogenous variables in the system, $\mathbf{X}_{-1}$ is a matrix of the lagged values of $\mathbf{X}$, and $\mathbf{W}_1$ and $\mathbf{W}_2$ are the error terms.

By analogy with (13.85), we estimate $\boldsymbol{\Pi}_1^*$ and $\boldsymbol{\Pi}_2^*$ as

$$\begin{aligned} \tilde{\boldsymbol{\Pi}}_1^* &= (\mathbf{X}^{*\prime}\boldsymbol{\Omega}_1^{-1}\mathbf{X}^*)^{-1}\mathbf{X}^{*\prime}\boldsymbol{\Omega}_1^{-1}\mathbf{Y}_1, \\ \tilde{\boldsymbol{\Pi}}_2^* &= (\mathbf{X}^{*\prime}\boldsymbol{\Omega}_1^{-1}\mathbf{X}^*)^{-1}\mathbf{X}^{*\prime}\boldsymbol{\Omega}_1^{-1}\mathbf{Y}_{-1,1}. \end{aligned} \tag{13.112}$$

The corresponding "predictions" of $\mathbf{Y}_1$ and $\mathbf{Y}_{-1,1}$ then become

$$\begin{aligned} \tilde{\mathbf{Y}}_1 &= \mathbf{X}^*\tilde{\boldsymbol{\Pi}}_1^*, \\ \tilde{\mathbf{Y}}_{-1,1} &= \mathbf{X}^*\tilde{\boldsymbol{\Pi}}_2^*. \end{aligned} \tag{13.113}$$

By replacing $\mathbf{Y}_1$ by $\tilde{\mathbf{Y}}_1$ and $\mathbf{Y}_{-1,1}$ by $\tilde{\mathbf{Y}}_{-1,1}$ in (13.110) we obtain

$$\mathbf{y}_1 = \tilde{\mathbf{Z}}_1\boldsymbol{\alpha}_1 + (\tilde{\mathbf{W}}_1\boldsymbol{\beta}_1 + \tilde{\mathbf{W}}_2\gamma_{11} + \mathbf{u}_1), \tag{13.114}$$

where $\tilde{\mathbf{Z}}_1 = [\tilde{\mathbf{Y}}_1 \quad \tilde{\mathbf{Y}}_{-1,1} \quad \mathbf{X}_1]$, $\tilde{\mathbf{W}}_1 = \mathbf{Y}_1 - \tilde{\mathbf{Y}}_1$, and $\tilde{\mathbf{W}}_2 = \tilde{\mathbf{Y}}_{-1,1} - \tilde{\mathbf{Y}}_{-1,1}$. The resulting estimator of $\boldsymbol{\alpha}_1$, to be called *autoregressive two-stage least squares* (A2SLS) estimator, is given as

$$\tilde{\boldsymbol{\alpha}}_1 = (\tilde{\mathbf{Z}}_1'\boldsymbol{\Omega}_1^{-1}\tilde{\mathbf{Z}}_1)^{-1}\tilde{\mathbf{Z}}_1'\boldsymbol{\Omega}_1^{-1}\mathbf{y}_1. \tag{13.115}$$

[19] In our analysis involving autoregressive disturbances we adopt the strategy of treating lagged endogenous variables as current endogenous variables, following, among others, M. B. Stewart and K. F. Wallis, *Introductory Econometrics*, 2nd ed. (New York: Halsted Press, 1981); or H. Kelejian and W. E. Oates, *Introduction to Econometrics*, 2nd ed. (New York: Harper and Row, 1981).

Since, as can easily be shown, $\tilde{\mathbf{Z}}_1'\boldsymbol{\Omega}_1^{-1}\tilde{\mathbf{W}}_1 = \tilde{\mathbf{Z}}_1'\boldsymbol{\Omega}_1^{-1}\tilde{\mathbf{W}}_2 = 0$, we have

(13.116) $$\tilde{\boldsymbol{\alpha}}_1 = \boldsymbol{\alpha}_1 + (\tilde{\mathbf{Z}}_1'\boldsymbol{\Omega}_1^{-1}\tilde{\mathbf{Z}}_1)^{-1}\tilde{\mathbf{Z}}_1'\boldsymbol{\Omega}_1^{-1}\mathbf{u}_1,$$

and it follows that—with $\boldsymbol{\Omega}_1$ known—the asymptotic properties of $\tilde{\boldsymbol{\alpha}}_1$ are the same as those derived in (13.94) and (13.95). For estimating ρ_1 in (13.103) we use unweighted 2SLS residuals obtained by applying the OLS method to

(13.117) $$\mathbf{y}_1 = \hat{\mathbf{Y}}_1\boldsymbol{\beta}_1 + \hat{\mathbf{Y}}_{-1,1}\gamma_{11} + \mathbf{X}_1\boldsymbol{\gamma}_1 + \mathbf{u}_1^*,$$

where $$\hat{\mathbf{Y}}_1 = \mathbf{X}^*\hat{\boldsymbol{\Pi}}_1^* = \mathbf{X}^*(\mathbf{X}^{*\prime}\mathbf{X}^*)^{-1}\mathbf{X}^{*\prime}\mathbf{Y}_1$$

and

$$\hat{\mathbf{Y}}_{-1,1} = \mathbf{X}^*\hat{\boldsymbol{\Pi}}_2 = \mathbf{X}^*(\mathbf{X}^{*\prime}\mathbf{X}^*)^{-1}\mathbf{X}^{*\prime}\mathbf{Y}_{-1,1}.$$

If the resulting unweighted 2SLS estimates are called $\hat{\hat{\boldsymbol{\alpha}}}_1$, then the corresponding residuals are defined as

(13.118) $$\hat{\hat{\mathbf{u}}}_1 = \mathbf{y}_1 - \mathbf{Z}_1\hat{\hat{\boldsymbol{\alpha}}}_1.$$

The estimator of ρ_1 is, in analogy with (13.107),

(13.119) $$\hat{\rho}_1 = \frac{\sum_t \hat{\hat{u}}_{1t}\hat{\hat{u}}_{1,t-1}}{\sqrt{\sum_t \hat{\hat{u}}_{1t}^2}\sqrt{\sum_t \hat{\hat{u}}_{1,t-1}^2}} \qquad (t = 2, 3, \ldots, T).$$

This leads to the desired estimator of $\boldsymbol{\alpha}_1$. The iterative procedure, which is recommended, involves using this estimator of ρ_1 for constructing a new set of residuals, yielding a new estimator of ρ_1, and so on until convergence.[20] The *autoregressive three-stage least squares* (A3SLS) procedure can be developed as in the case of no lagged endogenous variables.

The preceding treatment of structural disturbances that follow a first-order autoregressive scheme can easily be extended to the case where the disturbances are *vector autoregressive,* i.e., where

(13.120)
$$u_{gt} = \rho_{g1}u_{1,t-1} + \rho_{g2}u_{2,t-1} + \cdots + \rho_{gG}u_{G,t-1} + \varepsilon_t \qquad (g = 1, 2, \ldots, G).$$

In this case the matrix $\boldsymbol{\Omega}_g$ is somewhat more complicated, but the approach to estimation as outlined above is basically unchanged. The ρs of (13.120) can be estimated by the ordinary least squares method after replacing the us by some appropriate residuals (based on consistent first-round estimates of the structural coefficients).

Throughout this section we have considered only two-stage or three-stage estimation because of the relative simplicity of these methods. It is, of course, possible to use the full information maximum likelihood approach and construct and maximize the relevant likelihood function with respect to *all* unknown parameters,

[20] See, e.g., Stewart and Wallis, *op. cit.*

including those appearing in the $\mathbf{\Omega}$ matrices. This is conceptually simple, but the procedure may be difficult to implement, particularly if the system is large.[21]

In some situations we may wish to consider the existence of nonspherical disturbances as a testable rather than a maintained hypothesis and carry out a test of the null hypothesis that the structural disturbances are homoskedastic and nonautocorrelated against an alternative hypothesis specified according to the modeling situation at hand. The most straightforward approach to such a testing problem is to use the likelihood ratio test described in Section 11-2. This test involves maximum likelihood estimation of the unknown parameters of the system with and without the constraints imposed by the null hypothesis, and a comparison of the values of the respective maximized likelihood function. When the maximum likelihood estimates are difficult to obtain, we can evaluate the likelihood functions using three-stage (or iterative three-stage) least squares estimates in place of the full information maximum likelihood estimates. Since the likelihood ratio test is an asymptotic test and the two types of estimators have the same asymptotic distribution, the suggested modification of the likelihood ratio test should leave its asymptotic validity unaffected.

13-6 Comparison of Alternative Methods of Estimation and Special Topics

In discussing the methods of estimating structural equations of a general interdependent system with classical (spherical) disturbances, we have been using the food market model for which the true values of the parameters are known. Therefore, it might be interesting to compare the results obtained for this model by the different estimation methods. In making the comparison, however, we should keep in mind that we have only one sample on which to base the comparisons. In this case comparing various estimators is like comparing different guns on the basis of one shot from each. The summary of the results is shown in Table 13-2, which also includes the OLS estimates. The latter are inconsistent, but they are nevertheless sometimes used in applied work, mainly because they are simple to compute. In our particular example, their performance in estimating the supply equation compares quite well with that of the 2SLS and LIML estimators. With respect to the consistent methods, we can distinguish between the results for the overidentified demand equation and those for the exactly identified supply equation. In the case of the *demand equation,* we obtain identical results for 2SLS, 3SLS, and I3SLS, on one hand, and for LIML and FIML on the other. The reasons for this were given in the text. (However, note that, if the model contained — in addition to the exactly identified equation — *more than one* overidentified equation, the results for the

[21] An illuminating description of the full information maximum likelihood estimation of a simultaneous equation model with first-order autoregressive disturbances (and an application of the procedure) can be found in R. C. Fair, *Specification, Estimation, and Analysis of Macroeconometric Models* (Cambridge, MA: Harvard University Press, 1984).

Table 13-2

	Demand			Supply			
Method[a]	Constant	P_t	D_t	Constant	P_t	F_t	A_t
True values of coefficients	96.5	−0.25	0.30	62.5	0.15	0.20	0.36
			ESTIMATES				
OLS	99.8954	−0.3163	0.3346	58.2754	0.1604	0.2481	0.2483
	(7.5194)	(0.0907)	(0.0454)	(11.4629)	(0.0949)	(0.0462)	(0.0975)
2SLS	94.6333	−0.2436	0.3140	49.5324	0.2401	0.2556	0.2529
	(7.9208)	(0.0965)	(0.0469)	(12.0105)	(0.0999)	(0.0472)	(0.0996)
LIML	93.6192	−0.2295	0.3100	49.5324	0.2401	0.2556	0.2529
	(8.0312)	(0.0980)	(0.0474)	(12.0105)	(0.0999)	(0.0472)	(0.0996)
3SLS	94.6333	−0.2436	0.3140	52.1972	0.2286	0.2282	0.3611
	(7.9208)	(0.0965)	(0.0469)	(11.8934)	(0.0997)	(0.0440)	(0.0729)
I3SLS	94.6333	−0.2436	0.3140	52.6618	0.2266	0.2234	0.3800
	(7.9208)	(0.0965)	(0.0469)	(12.8051)	(0.1075)	(0.0468)	(0.0720)
FIML	93.6192	−0.2295	0.3100	51.9445	0.2373	0.2208	0.3697
	(8.0312)	(0.0980)	(0.0474)	(12.7460)	(0.1078)	(0.0457)	(0.0765)
			SAMPLING ERRORS				
OLS	3.3954	−0.0663	0.0346	−4.2246	0.0104	0.0481	−0.1117
2SLS	−1.8667	0.0064	0.0140	−12.9676	0.0901	0.0556	−0.1071
LIML	−2.8808	0.0205	0.0100	−12.9676	0.0901	0.0556	−0.1071
3SLS	−1.8667	0.0064	0.0140	−10.3028	0.0786	0.0282	0.0011
I3SLS	−1.8667	0.0064	0.0140	−9.8382	0.0766	0.0234	0.0200
FIML	−2.8808	0.0205	0.0100	−10.5555	0.0873	0.0208	0.0097

[a] OLS ordinary least squares
2SLS two-stage least squares
LIML limited information maximum likelihood
3SLS three-stage least squares
I3SLS iterative three-stage least squares
FIML full information maximum likelihood

system methods would differ from those for the single equation methods.) In the present case there is therefore no gain in going from the single equation methods (2SLS or LIML) to the system methods (3SLS, I3SLS, or FIML). Furthermore, the results for 2SLS and LIML do not appear to be markedly different. As for the *supply equation,* we obtain identical results for the 2SLS and LIML methods. Comparing the system methods with the single equation methods, we see that the former clearly performed better than the latter. There is, however, no clear-cut answer to the question as to *which* of the system methods performed best. On the grounds of computational effort the 3SLS is, of course, the one to be preferred. In assessing the general performance of the consistent methods, we note that *in each case* the true values of the coefficients are covered by the conventionally calculated 95% confidence intervals. This result would be expected for a large sample, since the estimated standard errors are justified on asymptotic grounds, but it is gratifying to see it happen also in a sample of only 20 observations.

All simultaneous equation estimation methods discussed in this section have some desirable asymptotic properties. These properties become effective in large samples, but since our samples are mostly small, we would be more interested in knowing the *small sample properties* of these estimators. Unfortunately, our knowledge in this respect is far from complete. The results from the food market example presented in Table 13-2 relate to a single set of values of the various estimators, but they give no information about the characteristics of their sampling distributions. Ideally, we would like to know the mathematical description of the distributions of each of the estimators. Such knowledge is available only for a small number of special cases.[22] From this we can conclude that the small sample distribution of the 2SLS estimator of an overidentified equation has a finite mean, but that its variance is, at least in some cases, infinite. The shape of the distribution appears to be similar to that of the normal distribution, but its peak is taller and its tails thicker than in the case of the normal distribution. Most of the evidence on the small sample properties of the simultaneous equation estimators comes from sampling (or Monte Carlo) experiments similar to those described in Chapter 2 and in the concluding part of Section 8-3 (our food example, for instance, could serve as the first sample of a Monte Carlo experiment). Since a survey of these experiments can be found elsewhere,[23] only the main results will be reported here. For the most part, the experimenters have presented some of the basic characteristics of the sampling distributions rather than their full description. Typically, these characteristics were the mean, the variance, and the mean square error. Of course, when an estimator has no finite variance, the value of the variance or of the mean square error of an experimental sampling distribution has no meaning, since it tends to increase without limit as the number of samples increases. Nevertheless, these values may serve as a basis for comparison of alternative estimators in relation to the same samples whose number is fixed. While the results of different experiments do not appear to be in complete agreement in all respects, some common features have been confirmed repeatedly. In particular, the OLS estimator tends to have a larger bias but a smaller variance than 2SLS or LIML. If the mean square error is used as a criterion in comparing the single equation estimators, the results are somewhat mixed. In some cases the OLS estimator performs better than 2SLS or

[22] Convenient surveys of the analytical results and their evaluation can be found in R. L. Basmann, "Exact Finite Sample Distribution for Some Econometric Estimators and Test Statistics," in M. D. Intriligator and D. A. Kendrick (eds.), *Frontiers of Quantitative Econometrics,* Vol. 2 (Amsterdam: North-Holland, 1974); P. C. B. Phillips, "Exact Small Sample Theory in the Simultaneous Equation Model," in Z. Griliches and M. D. Intriligator (eds.), *Handbook of Econometrics,* Vol. I (Amsterdam: North-Holland, 1983); and W. E. Taylor, "On the Relevance of Finite Sample Distribution Theory," *Econometric Reviews,* 2 (1983), pp. 1–139.

[23] See, e.g., Judge et al., *op. cit.,* pp. 609–613. For an annotated bibliography of Monte Carlo studies see E. R. Sowey, "A Classified Bibliography of Monte Carlo Studies in Econometrics," *Journal of Econometrics,* 1 (December 1973), pp. 377–395.

LIML, in others worse, and sometimes about the same. When 2SLS is compared with LIML, it appears that the former usually leads to smaller mean square errors than the latter, particularly when the exogenous variables are highly intercorrelated. As for the system estimators, from the available evidence it appears that the asymptotic advantage of the system methods over the single equation methods persists also in small samples, although not in an equally pronounced way. However, the FIML method appears to be more sensitive to errors of specification (such as omitting a relevant explanatory variable) than 2SLS.

In assessing various estimation methods, we are frequently concerned not only with the properties of the estimators, but also with the performance of the methods when it comes to *hypothesis testing.* In this context the most important quantity is the ratio of the estimated coefficient to its estimated standard error. This test statistic is frequently referred to as the "t ratio" in spite of the fact that the t distribution is not necessarily appropriate. When consistent simultaneous equation estimation methods are used, the asymptotic distribution of this statistic is normal. In small samples the desired acceptance regions or confidence intervals are usually determined by reference to the tabulated t distribution. This procedure is clearly not exactly valid, since the test statistic does *not* have a t distribution. The question, then, is whether the t distribution can serve as a tolerable approximation of the true distribution so that the results of the tests and of interval estimation are not seriously distorted. The available Monte Carlo evidence suggests that the distortion is usually (although not always) reasonably small. For instance, Cragg, who has conducted a large number of experiments, concludes on this point as follows.

> Usually use of the standard errors of the consistent methods would lead to reliable inferences, but this was not always the case. The standard errors of DLS were not useful for making inference about the true values of the coefficients.[24]

A very similar conclusion was reached by Summers.[25] This suggests that, at least from the point of view of hypothesis testing or interval estimation, the OLS method is inferior to the consistent methods of estimation.

As far as econometric practice is concerned, the preceding discussion about simultaneous equation estimators and their properties is still to a large extent academic. In a survey of the characteristics of recent U.S. macroeconometric models, Theil and Clements found that of ten major models examined, five were estimated by OLS, three by OLS and 2SLS, one by 2SLS, and one by 2SLS and LIML.[26] Clearly, OLS still appears to be the most common estimation method, and system methods of estimation are not much in use. In light of the available results, this is rather unfortunate.

[24] J. G. Cragg, "On the Relative Small-Sample Properties of Several Structural-Equation Estimators," *Econometrica,* 35 (January 1967), p. 109. The term "DLS" refers to the OLS estimator.

[25] R. M. Summers, "A Capital Intensive Approach to the Small Sample Properties of Various Simultaneous Equation Estimators," *Econometrica,* 33 (January 1965), pp. 1–41.

[26] H. Theil and K. W. Clements, "Recent Methodologial Advances in Economic Equation Systems," *American Behavioral Scientist,* 23 (July/August 1980), pp. 789–809.

Forecasting

Another relevant criterion for judging various estimators is their ability to *forecast.* In simultaneous equations the values of the endogenous variables can be predicted by reference to the reduced form equations. Suppose the $(K \times 1)$ vector of the values of the predetermined variables for the period of the forecast is $\mathbf{x}_0$. Then the forecast values of the G endogenous variables are

$$\hat{\mathbf{y}}_0 = \hat{\mathbf{\Pi}}\mathbf{x}_0,$$

Where $\hat{\mathbf{\Pi}}$ is a $(G \times K)$ matrix of the reduced form coefficients estimated from the sample observations. Now, consistent estimates of $\mathbf{\Pi}$ can be obtained either by a direct application of the OLS method to the reduced form equations, or by using consistent estimates of the structural coefficients, say, $\tilde{\mathbf{B}}$ and $\tilde{\mathbf{\Gamma}}$, and setting

$$\tilde{\mathbf{\Pi}} = -\tilde{\mathbf{B}}^{-1}\tilde{\mathbf{\Gamma}} \tag{13.121}$$

in accordance with (13.7). If the estimated reduced form coefficients are obtained by a direct application of OLS, they are called "unrestricted"; otherwise, they are called "restricted" or "derived." Unless all structural equations are exactly identified, the unrestricted and the derived reduced form coefficients will not coincide. Since the unrestricted least squares estimator of $\mathbf{\Pi}$ does not, in general, incorporate the prior restrictions imposed by the relation

$$\mathbf{\Pi} = -\mathbf{B}^{-1}\mathbf{\Gamma},$$

it is tempting to conclude that it will be asymptotically less efficient than the derived estimator. However, this turns out to be the case *only* when $\mathbf{B}$ and $\mathbf{\Gamma}$ are estimated by one of the asymptotically efficient methods such as 3SLS or FIML. When $\mathbf{B}$ and $\mathbf{\Gamma}$ are estimated by 2SLS, the derived reduced form estimator is not necessarily more asymptotically efficient than the unrestricted estimator.[27] The reason for this is presumably that

> there are two types of information in this context: *sample* information and *a priori* information. Ordinary least squares uses all the sample information and none of the a priori information, while the two-stage least squares derived reduced form estimator uses all a priori information on the structural parameters but, typically, only some of the relevant sample information, unless all of the equations in the system are just identified. Therefore the relative efficiency is, in general, undeterminable. Since the three-stage least squares derived reduced form estimates use all the available sample and a priori information, they are superior to either the ordinary least squares or two-stage least squares derived reduced form estimates.[28]

On the basis of Monte Carlo experiments there is some evidence that these results tend to hold in small samples as well.[29]

[27] P. Dhrymes, "Restricted and Unrestricted Reduced Forms: Asymptotic Distribution and Relative Efficiency," *Econometrica,* 41 (January 1973), pp. 119–134.

[28] T. B. Fomby, R. C. Hill, and S. R. Johnson, *Advanced Econometric Methods* (New York: Springer Verlag, 1984), p. 518.

[29] Summers, *op. cit.,* pp. 31–32.

From the preceding discussion we conclude that a forecast based on 3SLS (or FIML) derived reduced form estimates is optimal on asymptotic grounds. Of course, if the structural disturbances are autoregressive or vector autoregressive, a forecast based on a feasible Aitken predictor will have a smaller asymptotic variance than a forecast that does not utilize the information contained in the current disturbances.

Sometimes a forecast based on an econometric model can be supplemented by a forecast from another source. For instance, forecasts may be available from sample surveys of intentions or plans, or preliminary values may be obtainable from a government agency. Forecasts from different sources can be pooled and the overall forecast error can be reduced. The mechanism for doing this is provided by the *Kalman filter* method.[30] Let $\hat{\mathbf{y}}_1$ be a vector of the predicted values of $\mathbf{y}$ obtained from an econometric model, and let $\hat{\mathbf{y}}_2$ be a vector of the predicted values of $\mathbf{y}$ obtained from another source. Assume that both types of predictions are unbiased, and that the prediction errors are given as

$$\mathbf{e}_1 = \mathbf{y} - \hat{\mathbf{y}}_1,$$

$$\mathbf{e}_2 = \mathbf{y} - \hat{\mathbf{y}}_2,$$

where $\mathbf{e}_1 \sim N(\mathbf{0}, \mathbf{\Sigma}_{11})$, $\mathbf{e}_2 \sim N(\mathbf{0}, \mathbf{\Sigma}_{22})$, and $E(\mathbf{e}_1\mathbf{e}_2') = \mathbf{\Sigma}_{12}$. Further, let the pooled predictor of $\mathbf{y}$, say, $\bar{\mathbf{y}}$, be given by

$$\text{(13.122)} \qquad \begin{aligned} \bar{\mathbf{y}} &= (\mathbf{I} - \mathbf{K})\hat{\mathbf{y}}_1 + \mathbf{K}\hat{\mathbf{y}}_2 \\ &= \hat{\mathbf{y}}_1 + \mathbf{K}(\hat{\mathbf{y}}_2 - \hat{\mathbf{y}}_1), \end{aligned}$$

where $\mathbf{K}$ is a weighting matrix whose elements are to be determined. The pooled prediction error then is

$$\text{(13.123)} \qquad \begin{aligned} \mathbf{y} - \bar{\mathbf{y}} &= \mathbf{y} - [(\mathbf{I} - \mathbf{K})(\mathbf{y} - \mathbf{e}_1) + \mathbf{K}(\mathbf{y} - \mathbf{e}_2)] \\ &= (\mathbf{I} - \mathbf{K})\mathbf{e}_1 + \mathbf{K}\mathbf{e}_2, \end{aligned}$$

and its variance-covariance matrix is

$$\text{(13.124)} \qquad E(\mathbf{y} - \bar{\mathbf{y}})(\mathbf{y} - \bar{\mathbf{y}})' = (\mathbf{I} - \mathbf{K})^2\mathbf{\Sigma}_{11} + 2\mathbf{K}(\mathbf{I} - \mathbf{K})\mathbf{\Sigma}_{12} + \mathbf{K}^2\mathbf{\Sigma}_{22}.$$

Minimizing the variance-covariance matrix of the pooled prediction error with respect to $\mathbf{K}$, we obtain

$$\text{(13.125)} \qquad \mathbf{K} = (\mathbf{\Sigma}_{11} - \mathbf{\Sigma}_{12})(\mathbf{\Sigma}_{11} + \mathbf{\Sigma}_{22} - 2\mathbf{\Sigma}_{12})^{-1}.$$

Note that if the two prediction errors are independent (i.e., if $\mathbf{\Sigma}_{12} = \mathbf{0}$), the errors are weighted in inverse relation to their respective variances.

When a forecast based on an econometric model is made before the values of the exogenous variables are known, it is called an ex ante forecast. In this type of forecast the values of the exogenous variables are typically represented by intelligent guesses. An ex ante forecast error is composed of four separate parts.

[30] See M. Athans, "The Importance of Kalman Filtering for Economic Systems," *Annals of Economic and Social Measurement,* 3 (January 1974), pp. 49–64.

1. Error due to the presence of stochastic disturbances.
2. Error in estimating the coefficients of the model.
3. Error in predicting the values of the exogenous variables.
4. Error due to model misspecification.

Under certain assumptions it is possible to isolate—at least approximately—the four sources of forecast error and attempt to make improvements where they are most needed.[31]

Forecasting performance is frequently used for comparing different econometric models. The three most commonly used measures of predictive accuracy are

Root Mean Square Error: $$\text{RMSE} = \sqrt{\sum (y_i - \hat{y}_i)^2/M}$$

Mean Absolute Error: $$\text{MAE} = \sum |y_i - \hat{y}_i|/M$$

Theil's Inequality Coefficient: $$U = \frac{\sqrt{(\Delta y_i - \Delta\hat{y}_i)^2/M}}{\sqrt{\sum (\Delta y_i)^2/M}}$$

$$(i = T+1, T+2, \ldots, T+M),$$

where y and $\hat{y}$ are the actual and the predicted values of y, respectively, and Δ represents either absolute or percentage change. The RMSE penalizes models with large prediction errors more than MAE does. Further, $U = 1$ indicates a forecast just as accurate as one of "no change" ($\Delta y_i = 0$), and a value of U greater than one means that the prediction is less accurate than the simple prediction of no change.[32]

Specification Error Tests

The correct specification of simultaneous equation models is of much concern to the model builders and to econometricians involved in the development of statistical test procedures. The earliest test developed for simultaneous equation models is the *test of overidentifying restrictions,* designed to test the null hypothesis that the overidentifying restrictions (i.e., the restrictions leading to the exclusion of some variables from some equations) are correct against the alternative hypothesis that they are improper. The test is based on the idea that if the null hypothesis is true, the unrestricted estimates of the reduced form coefficients should not be very different from the estimates restricted by (13.7). The implementation of the test involves a straightforward application of the likelihood ratio principle.[33]

A test of the specification of exogeneity of the variables designated as exogenous involves testing the null hypothesis of no correlation between these variables and the structural disturbances. To test this hypothesis we can use the test proposed by

[31] See Fair, *Specification . . . , op. cit.,* Ch. 8.

[32] *Ibid.*

[33] See, e.g., Judge et al., *op. cit.,* pp. 614–616.

Hausman[34] that was discussed in connection with errors of measurement in Section 9-1 and in connection with the error component model in Section 12-2. As explained earlier, the idea of Hausman's test is to utilize two estimators of the parameters involved, one that is consistent and asymptotically efficient under H_0 but inconsistent under H_A, and one that is consistent under both H_0 and H_A but asymptotically inefficient under H_0. A comparison of the two estimators leads to a test presented in (12.56) of Section 12-2. In the context of simultaneous equation models, the asymptotically efficient (under H_0) estimator considered by Hausman is 3SLS and the asymptotically inefficient estimator is 2SLS, which is consistent as long as any correlation between an "exogenous" variable and a disturbance occurs in another equation of the system. A variant of the test involving just one equation of the model was proposed by Spencer and Berk.[35] The test is based on the fact that the 2SLS estimator is asymptotically efficient among all instrumental variable estimators represented by a linear combination of the predetermined variables of the system. In adapting Hausman's test to a single equation, Spencer and Berk use 2SLS in place of 3SLS, and use an instrumental variable estimator (*other* than 2SLS) that is consistent under both H_0 and H_A.

A simple version of the test proposed by Spencer and Berk proceeds as follows. Let the gth structural equation be written as

$$\mathbf{y}_g = \mathbf{Z}_g\boldsymbol{\alpha}_g + \mathbf{u}_g \qquad (g = 1, 2, \ldots, G),$$

where $\mathbf{Z}_g = [\mathbf{Y}_g \quad \mathbf{X}_{1g} \quad \mathbf{X}_{2g}]$, $\mathbf{Y}_g$ represents the right-hand side endogenous variables, $\mathbf{X}_{1g}$ represents the included predetermined variables that are known to be uncorrelated with $\mathbf{u}_g$, and $\mathbf{X}_{2g}$ represents the included variables that may be correlated with $\mathbf{u}_g$. The null hypothesis is that $\mathbf{X}_{2g}$ and $\mathbf{u}_g$ are uncorrelated. The test involves two sets of instrumental variables for $\mathbf{Z}_g$, one defined as $\hat{\mathbf{Z}}_g = [\hat{\mathbf{Y}}_g \quad \mathbf{X}_{1g} \quad \mathbf{X}_{2g}]$, where $\hat{\mathbf{Y}}_g$ is the least squares predictor of $\mathbf{Y}_g$ based on *all* predetermined variables in the system (including $\mathbf{X}_{1g}$ and $\mathbf{X}_{2g}$), and the other defined as $\tilde{\mathbf{Z}}_g = [\tilde{\mathbf{Y}}_g \quad \mathbf{X}_{1g} \quad \tilde{\mathbf{X}}_{2g}]$, where $\tilde{\mathbf{Y}}_g$ and $\tilde{\mathbf{X}}_{2g}$ are the least squares predictors of $\mathbf{Y}_g$ and $\mathbf{X}_{2g}$, respectively, that are based on all predetermined variables in the system *except* $\mathbf{X}_{2g}$. The use of $\hat{\mathbf{Z}}_g$ as an instrument for $\mathbf{Z}_g$ leads to the usual 2SLS estimator, which is not consistent under the alternative hypothesis, whereas the use of $\tilde{\mathbf{Z}}_g$ leads to an estimator that is consistent under both H_0 and H_A but inefficient relative to 2SLS when H_0 is true. The test—by analogy with (12.57)—consists of testing the significance of the least squares coefficient of $\tilde{\mathbf{Z}}_g^*$ in

$$\mathbf{y}_g = \hat{\mathbf{Z}}_g\boldsymbol{\alpha}_g + \tilde{\mathbf{Z}}_g^*\boldsymbol{\delta}_g + \mathbf{u}_g^*,$$

where $\tilde{\mathbf{Z}}_g^* = [\tilde{\mathbf{Y}}_g \quad \tilde{\mathbf{X}}_{2g}]$, since otherwise the presence of $\mathbf{X}_{1g}$ in both $\hat{\mathbf{Z}}_g$ and $\tilde{\mathbf{Z}}_g$ would

[34] J. A. Hausman, "Specification Tests in Econometrics," *Econometrica,* 46 (November 1978), pp. 1251–1271; see also A. Nakamura and M. Nakamura, "On the Relationships Among Several Specification Error Tests Presented by Durbin, Wu, and Hausman," *Econometrica,* 49 (November 1981), pp. 1583–1588.

[35] D. E. Spencer and K. N. Berk, "A Limited Information Specification Test," *Econometrica,* 49 (July 1981), pp. 1079–1085.

lead to perfect multicollinearity. This test is more useful for practical purposes than the original Hausman's test, which involves the whole system of equations.

A concern of some importance in specifying simultaneous equation models is the stability of the structural coefficients. In the context of a single-equation regression model the most common test of the stability of the regression coefficients is the CUSUM (or CUSUMSQ) test of Brown, Durbin, and Evans presented in (11.152) and (11.153) of Section 11-7. A straightforward adaptation of this test to a structural equation of an equation system was developed by Giles.[36] If we wish to test the stability of the coefficients of

$$\mathbf{y}_1 = \mathbf{Y}_1\boldsymbol{\beta}_1 + \mathbf{X}_1\boldsymbol{\gamma}_1 + \mathbf{u}_1,$$

we define

$$\mathbf{y}_1^* = \mathbf{y}_1 - \mathbf{Y}_1\tilde{\tilde{\boldsymbol{\beta}}}_1,$$

where $\tilde{\tilde{\boldsymbol{\beta}}}_1$ is a 2SLS estimator of $\boldsymbol{\beta}_1$, and write

$$\mathbf{y}_1^* = \mathbf{X}_1\boldsymbol{\gamma}_1 + \mathbf{u}_1^*. \tag{13.126}$$

Equation (13.126) can be used for the construction of the recursive residuals and of the CUSUM and CUSUMSQ test statistics as described by (11.151), (11.152), and (11.153) of Section 11-7.

Finally, a question may arise concerning the possibility of omitting some relevant predetermined variables from the system altogether. To test the hypothesis that no relevant predetermined variables have been left out, we can apply the tests discussed in connection with the standard regression model to (13.126), or to the reduced form equations of the system. Appropriate tests for this purpose would be the RESET and the "rainbow" test of Section 10-4, and the tests for linearity described in Section 11-3.

Triangular and Recursive Systems

We have dealt so far with the estimation problem for a general interdependent system of equations. We shall now briefly consider the estimation problem in the case where the system is *triangular.* As stated in Section 13-1, a system

$$\mathbf{B}\mathbf{y}_t + \boldsymbol{\Gamma}\mathbf{x}_t = \mathbf{u}_t$$

with *no* restrictions on the variance–covariance matrix of $\mathbf{u}_t$ is called triangular if the matrix $\mathbf{B}$ is triangular. A well-known example of a triangular system is the so-called "cobweb model," which may be represented as

$$(13.127) \qquad \begin{aligned} Q_t &= \alpha_1 + \alpha_2 P_{t-1} + u_{1t} \qquad &\text{(supply)},\\ P_t &= \beta_1 + \beta_2 Q_t + \beta_3 Y_t + u_{2t} \qquad &\text{(demand)}, \end{aligned}$$

[36] D. E. A. Giles, "Testing for Parameter Stability in Structural Econometric Relationships," *Economics Letters,* 7 (1981), pp. 323–326.

where Q = equilibrium quantity, P = equilibrium price, and Y = income (exogenous). Here

$$\mathbf{B} = \begin{bmatrix} 1 & 0 \\ -\beta_2 & 1 \end{bmatrix} \quad \text{and} \quad \mathbf{\Gamma} = \begin{bmatrix} -\alpha_1 & -\alpha_2 & 0 \\ -\beta_1 & 0 & -\beta_3 \end{bmatrix}.$$

Note that the supply equation involves only one endogenous variable—the dependent variable—and, therefore, using ordinary least squares would lead to consistent estimates. These estimates would not be asymptotically efficient, though, because they disregard the implied correlation between the disturbances of the two equations. The demand equation could be consistently estimated by ILS. Alternatively, both equations could be estimated by one of the system methods, in which case the estimates would be not only consistent but also asymptotically efficient. A simple way of calculating FIML estimates of a system in which the matrix **B** is triangular is by making use of the result of Lahiri and Schmidt, who found that treating such a system as a set of seemingly unrelated regressions (disregarding the correlation between $\mathbf{y}_t$ and $\mathbf{u}_t$) and applying the Aitken iterative method to it will produce FIML estimates.[37]

If the system

$$\mathbf{B}\mathbf{y}_t + \mathbf{\Gamma}\mathbf{x}_t = \mathbf{u}_t$$

is *recursive*—that is, if **B** is triangular and the variance-covariance matrix of the structural disturbances, $\mathbf{\Phi}$, is diagonal—the estimation problem becomes really simple. The reason is that the endogenous variables, which serve as explanatory factors in the structural equations, are *not* correlated with the disturbance of the equation in which they appear. For instance, in the demand equation of (13.127) the explanatory variables include the endogenous variable Q_t. However, if u_{1t} and u_{2t} are independent and nonautoregressive, then

$$E(Q_t u_{2t}) = E[(\alpha_1 + \alpha_2 P_{t-1} + u_{1t})u_{2t}] = 0.$$

This means that *the application of the OLS method to each of the structural equations leads to consistent and asymptotically efficient estimates.* (In the absence of lagged endogenous variables, the OLS estimates are also *unbiased.*) It should be emphasized that this is true only if the system is *recursive,* not otherwise. Finally, we note that if **B** is block-triangular and the $\mathbf{\Phi}$ matrix is correspondingly block-diagonal, then the equations corresponding to each diagonal block of $\mathbf{\Phi}$ can be treated as belonging to separate systems. Of course, this also simplifies estimation considerably.

Miscellaneous Topics

The entire discussion in this chapter has been limited to linear equations. In practice many models involve nonlinearities, and the estimation methods devel-

[37] K. Lahiri and P. Schmidt, "On the Estimation of Triangular Structural Systems," *Econometrica,* 46 (September 1978), pp. 1217–1221. This model is frequently discussed in sociology under the heading of a "path analysis method."

oped for linear models have to be modified. Conceptually the simplest case is when all endogenous variables (and all structural disturbances) enter the model linearly and the nonlinearities are confined to the parameters. (This, for instance, might be the case in models with rational expectations since rational expectations frequently lead to nonlinear restrictions on the coefficients.) In this case it is relatively simple to construct the appropriate likelihood function, but its maximization might be computationally difficult. Models that are nonlinear in the variables are better handled by a modified 2SLS or 3SLS procedure.[38] Another complication arises when a simultaneous equation model involves variables that contain measurement errors or are latent. Such models may, under certain circumstances, be estimated best with the help of the LISREL program discussed in connection with unobservable variables in Section 11-8.

An interesting problem frequently encountered with large econometric models is the case of *undersized samples.* This problem arises when the number of predetermined variables in the model exceeds the number of observations. In this case it is impossible to estimate the coefficients of the reduced form by the least squares method. To get out of this predicament, Brundy and Jorgenson suggested replacing the unrestricted reduced form estimates — normally used for 2SLS and 3SLS — by restricted reduced form estimates.[39] The latter are obtained by estimating the structural equations of the system by an instrumental variable method. The choice of instruments from among the predetermined variables is not very important. One possibility is to choose as instruments those predetermined variables that are most closely related to the structural equation to be estimated. After obtaining the restricted reduced form estimates, we proceed with the two-stage least squares method as usual. The *new* structural estimates are then used for *new* restricted reduced form estimates, and so on until convergence. This method is called the *limited information instrumental variable* (LIVE) *method.* When — as in iterative three-stage least squares (I3SLS) — it is extended to *all* equations of the system (utilizing the correlation of the structural disturbances across equations), it is called the *full information instrumental variable* (FIVE) *method.*

The specification of simultaneous equation models designed to explain the changes in economic variables over time involves adjustment processes that lead to dynamic relationships and lags in variables. Unfortunately, dynamic economic theory is not developed enough to provide a reliable guide for the coefficient restrictions typically imposed by econometric model builders. This has led some econometricians to a search for alternatives to standard simultaneous equations modeling procedures. Probably the best known alternative was introduced by Sims and is known as a *vector autoregressive* (VAR) *model.*[40] A general representation of a

[38] For an extremely clear discussion of simultaneous equation models that are nonlinear see Kelejian and Oates, *op. cit.,* Ch. 8; see also H. H. Kelejian, "Two-Stage Least Squares and Econometric Models Linear in the Parameters But Nonlinear in the Endogenous Variables," *Journal of the American Statistical Association,* 66 (June 1971), pp. 373–374.

[39] J. M. Brundy and D. W. Jorgenson, "Efficient Estimation of Simultaneous Equations by Instrumental Variables," *Review of Economics and Statistics,* 53 (August 1971), pp. 207–224.

[40] C. A. Sims, "Macroeconomics and Reality," *Econometrica,* 48 (January 1980), pp. 1–48.

VAR model takes the form

(13.128) $$\mathbf{y}_t = \mathbf{a}_0 + \mathbf{A}_1\mathbf{y}_{t-1} + \mathbf{A}_2\mathbf{y}_{t-2} + \cdots + \mathbf{A}_m\mathbf{y}_{t-m} + \mathbf{u}_t,$$

where $\mathbf{y}_t$ is a $G \times 1$ vector defined as in (13.3a), $\mathbf{y}_{t-1}, \mathbf{y}_{t-2}, \ldots, \mathbf{y}_{t-m}$ are lagged values of $\mathbf{y}_t$, $\mathbf{a}_0$ is a $G \times 1$ vector of constants, and the **A**s are $G \times G$ matrices of vector autoregressive coefficients. The disturbance $\mathbf{u}_t$ is presumed to obey all classical assumptions. Since there are no current endogenous variables on the right-hand side of (13.128) and all equations have the same regressors, OLS estimation is appropriate. The VAR model is definitely not a simultaneous equation interdependent model and avoids the need for making sometimes controversial distinctions between endogenous and exogenous variables. For quarterly data the number of lags (m) is usually chosen to be 6 or 8 quarters and is assumed to be the same for all variables. The model is simple but suffers from the problem of involving a large number of parameters, even when the number of variables is not large. Even if a long series of observations on each variable were available, the constancy of the parameters over a long period of time is doubtful.

Criticism of simultaneous equation models similar to that of Sims has also been raised by time-series analysts. In their book *Forecasting Economic Time Series,* Granger and Newbold formulate their criticism as follows.

> The reader may well already have gathered that any skepticism we feel with regard to the worth of econometric models, as generaly constructed, as forecasting tools is based not on doubts as to their ability to represent adequately the structure of economic relationships in a functional sense, but rather on their frequently cursory and invariably insufficiently general treatment of the specification of lag and error structure.[41]

This criticism is well directed and undoubtedly justified. Econometric model builders, on the other hand, are doubtful about the ability of time-series analysts to forecast economic variables without making any use of the knowledge provided by economic theory. An economist finds it unbelievable that, for instance, a forecast of sales of a product can be made without any reference to price and to supply and demand analysis. Attempts at reconciling the econometric approach to model building with the standard time-series analysis of observations usually proceed as follows. A dynamic econometric model is represented in terms of the lag operator notation introduced in Section 11-4 as

(13.129) $$\mathbf{A}(L)\mathbf{y}_t + \mathbf{B}(L)\mathbf{x}_t = \mathbf{C}(L)\mathbf{u}_t,$$

where $\mathbf{A}(L)$, $\mathbf{B}(L)$, and $\mathbf{C}(L)$ are matrices of polynomials in powers of L, and $\mathbf{y}_t$, $\mathbf{x}_t$, and $\mathbf{u}_t$ are defined as in (13.3a). Time-series analysts then supplement this specification by *assuming* that the values of the exogenous variables are generated by an autoregressive process of the form

(13.130) $$\mathbf{D}(L)\mathbf{x}_t = \mathbf{E}(L)\mathbf{v}_t,$$

[41] C. W. J. Granger and P. Newbold, *Forecasting Economic Times Series* (New York: Academic Press, 1977), p. 202.

where $\mathbf{D}(L)$ and $\mathbf{E}(L)$ are different matrices of polynomials in powers of L, and $\mathbf{v}_t$ is a classical disturbance vector. Substitution for $\mathbf{x}_t$ from (13.130) into (13.129) enables us to express $\mathbf{y}_t$ as a multivariate autoregressive-moving average process (ARMA) of time-series analysis.

The trouble with the preceding reconciliation is the completely ad hoc assumption about the generation of the values of the exogenous variables. Since by definition there is no theory explaining the determination of the values of exogenous variables, the assumption of an autoregressive scheme is not theoretically justified and is not to be trusted. Without theory, its justification on empirical grounds cannot be considered reliable.

13-7 Analysis of Dynamic Econometric Models

A simultaneous equation model represents a set of relations between the endogenous and the predetermined variables of a system. If the predetermined variables are all purely exogenous, then the model specifies how the exogenous variables, together with the stochastic disturbances, generate the values of the endogenous variables at a given point (or period) of time. This was illustrated in detail in the food market example of Section 13-2. However, if the predetermined variables also include lagged endogenous variables, then the model specifies not only how the predetermined variables (together with the disturbances) generate the current values of the endogenous variables, but also how the time paths of the exogenous variables and the disturbances determine the time paths of the endogenous variables. This is implicit in the structure of the model, but it is of some interest to have such a dynamic dependence formulated explicitly. Further questions of interest concern the stability of the system, and the influence of the past values of the exogenous variables on the current values of the endogenous variables. The purpose of this section is to examine these questions, since providing the answers represents a natural and important part of the work of an econometrician. Our approach will be to illustrate the problems and their solution by reference to a specific model; in this way the special concepts of dynamic analysis will acquire a concrete meaning. However, the basic procedures can easily be adapted to other models as well.

Consider the following simple model of the economy:

$$
\begin{aligned}
C_t &= \alpha_0 + \alpha_1 Y_t + \alpha_2 C_{t-1} + u_{1t} && \text{(consumption)},\\
I_t &= \beta_0 + \beta_1 r_t + \beta_2 I_{t-1} + u_{2t} && \text{(investment)},\\
r_t &= \gamma_0 + \gamma_1 Y_t + \gamma_2 M_t + u_{3t} && \text{(money market)}\\
Y_t &= C_t + I_t + G_t && \text{(income identity)},
\end{aligned}
\tag{13.131}
$$

where C = consumption, Y = income, I = investment, r = rate of interest, M = money supply, and G = government expenditure, C, Y, I, and r are endogenous; M and G are exogenous. The latter may be viewed as policy variables that can be, and have been, manipulated at will by the policymakers. The reduced form of this system is

$$C_t = \pi_{11} + \pi_{12}C_{t-1} + \pi_{13}I_{t-1} + \pi_{14}M_t + \pi_{15}G_t + v_{1t}, \tag{13.132}$$

$$I_t = \pi_{21} + \pi_{22}C_{t-1} + \pi_{23}I_{t-1} + \pi_{24}M_t + \pi_{25}G_t + v_{2t}, \tag{13.133}$$

$$Y_t = \pi_{31} + \pi_{32}C_{t-1} + \pi_{33}I_{t-1} + \pi_{34}M_t + \pi_{35}G_t + v_{3t}, \tag{13.134}$$

$$r_t = \pi_{41} + \pi_{42}C_{t-1} + \pi_{43}I_{t-1} + \pi_{44}M_t + \pi_{45}G_t + v_{4t}. \tag{13.135}$$

The reduced form coefficients can, of course, be expressed in terms of the structural coefficients. In the language of dynamic analysis, the reduced form coefficients are called *impact multipliers,* since they measure the immediate response of the endogenous variables to changes in the predetermined variables. For instance, π_{15} measures the change in the mean value of current consumption due to a unit change in current government expenditure, given the current value of the money supply and given the level of consumption and investment in the preceding period.

The reduced form equations are useful mainly for short-term forecasting. We can forecast the next period's values of the endogenous variables on the basis of our knowledge of the current values of I and C and of the forthcoming values of the policy variables. However, we cannot use the reduced form equations to determine how the system operates under continuous impact of the exogenous variables. For instance, the reduced form equation for consumption shows that the current value of consumption depends not only on the current values of G and M but also on the previous values of consumption and investment. This is not greatly illuminating because it pushes part of the responsibility for explaining the current level of consumption onto its own immediate history. To understand the mechanism of the determination of consumption and of other endogenous variables, we need a solution that would determine the level of these variables *without* reference to their immediate past. Such a solution can be obtained by manipulating the reduced form equations so that all lagged endogenous variables are eliminated. This elimination can proceed in two steps. First we reformulate the reduced form equations so that each equation contains only one endogenous variable, whether current or lagged. Then we remove the lagged endogenous variables as intended.

Let us take the reduced form equation for consumption. Here the only "foreign" lagged endogenous variable is I_{t-1}. Now, from (13.133) we have

$$I_t - \pi_{23}I_{t-1} = \pi_{21} + \pi_{22}C_{t-1} + \pi_{24}M_t + \pi_{25}G_t + v_{2t} \tag{13.136}$$

or

$$I_{t-1} - \pi_{23}I_{t-2} = \pi_{21} + \pi_{22}C_{t-2} + \pi_{24}M_{t-1} + \pi_{25}G_{t-1} + v_{2,t-1}. \tag{13.136a}$$

Further, lagging (13.132) by one period and multiplying by $-\pi_{23}$ gives

$$-\pi_{23}C_{t-1} = -\pi_{11}\pi_{23} - \pi_{12}\pi_{23}C_{t-2} - \pi_{13}\pi_{23}I_{t-2} - \pi_{14}\pi_{23}M_{t-1} - \pi_{15}\pi_{23}G_{t-1} - \pi_{23}v_{1,t-1}. \tag{13.137}$$

By adding (13.132) and (13.137), we obtain

$$(13.138)\qquad \begin{aligned} C_t = {} & \pi_{11}(1-\pi_{23}) + (\pi_{12}+\pi_{23})C_{t-1} - \pi_{12}\pi_{23}C_{t-2} \\ & + \pi_{13}(I_{t-1} - \pi_{23}I_{t-2}) + \pi_{14}M_t - \pi_{14}\pi_{23}M_{t-1} \\ & + \pi_{15}G_t - \pi_{15}\pi_{23}G_{t-1} + v_{1t} - \pi_{23}v_{1,t-1}. \end{aligned}$$

Substitution for $(I_{t-1} - \pi_{23}I_{t-2})$ from (13.136a) into (13.138) then leads to

$$(13.139)\qquad \begin{aligned} C_t = {} & [\pi_{11}(1-\pi_{23}) + \pi_{13}\pi_{21}] \\ & + (\pi_{12}+\pi_{23})C_{t-1} + (\pi_{13}\pi_{22} - \pi_{12}\pi_{23})C_{t-2} \\ & + \pi_{14}M_t + (\pi_{13}\pi_{24} - \pi_{14}\pi_{23})M_{t-1} \\ & + \pi_{15}G_t + (\pi_{13}\pi_{25} - \pi_{15}\pi_{23})G_{t-1} \\ & + v_{1t} - \pi_{23}v_{1,t-1} + \pi_{13}v_{2,t-1}, \end{aligned}$$

or, in obvious notation,

$$(13.139a)\qquad C_t = \delta + \mu_1 C_{t-1} + \mu_2 C_{t-2} + \kappa_0 M_t + \kappa_1 M_{t-1} + \nu_0 G_t + \nu_1 G_{t-1} + \varepsilon_t.$$

Equation (13.139), or its equivalent (13.139a), is called the *fundamental dynamic equation* for the consumption variable. Similar equations could be derived for the remaining endogenous variables of the system. Since it can be shown that in a general interdependent linear system each variable satisfies the same final autoregressive equation,[42] we will refer to consumption alone. The fundamental dynamic equation has special importance in determining the stability of the system, and we shall return to it. Our present aim is to express current consumption in terms of current and past values of the exogenous variables and disturbances, which can be done by a series of successive substitutions. First, note that by (13.139a) the expression for C_t at $t = 1$ is

$$(13.140)\qquad C_1 = \delta + \mu_1 C_0 + \mu_2 C_{-1} + \kappa_0 M_1 + \kappa_1 M_0 + \nu_0 G_1 + \nu_1 G_0 + \varepsilon_1.$$

The values of C_0 and C_{-1} have been determined prior to the beginning of the series and are called the *initial conditions*. For the purpose of dynamic analysis we shall assume them to be given. The values of M_0 and G_0 are of no special interest to us and can be merged with the constant term, so that (13.140) can be written as

$$(13.140a)\qquad C_1 = \eta + \mu_1 C_0 + \mu_2 C_{-1} + \kappa_0 M_1 + \nu_0 G_1 + \varepsilon_1.$$

Next, the expression for C_t at $t = 2$ is

$$(13.141)\qquad C_2 = \delta + \mu_1 C_1 + \mu_2 C_0 + \kappa_0 M_2 + \kappa_1 M_1 + \nu_0 G_2 + \nu_1 G_1 + \varepsilon_2.$$

Since C_0 is taken as given, we have only to eliminate C_1 from (13.141), by substitut-

[42] See A. S. Goldberger, *Impact Multipliers and Dynamic Properties of the Klein–Goldberger Model* (Amsterdam: North-Holland Publishing Company, 1959), pp. 106–108.

ing from (13.140a), which gives

(13.142)
$$C_2 = (\delta + \mu_1\eta) + (\mu_1^2 + \mu_2)C_0 + \mu_1\mu_2 C_{-1} + \kappa_0 M_2 + (\kappa_1 + \kappa_0\mu_1)M_1 + \nu_0 G_2 + (\nu_1 + \nu_0\mu_1)G_1 + \varepsilon_2 + \mu_1\varepsilon_1 .$$

In a similar way we can obtain a solution for C_3, C_4, etc. The outcome is a general expression for C_t, which is

(13.143)
$$C_t = \eta_t + \eta_1 C_0 + \eta_2 C_{-1} + \zeta_0 M_t + \zeta_1 M_{t-1} + \cdots + \zeta_{t-1} M_1 + \xi_0 G_t + \xi_1 G_{t-1} + \cdots + \xi_{t-1} G_1 + \varepsilon_t + \theta_1 \varepsilon_{t-1} + \cdots + \theta_{t-1}\varepsilon_1 .$$

Thus C_t is—for a set of given initial conditions—expressed purely in terms of current and lagged exogenous variables and disturbances. (If the system is stable, η_t becomes a constant for large t.) Similar expressions could be derived for the other endogenous variables. These equations are called the *final form* of the equation system. They show how the time paths of the exogenous variables determine the time path of each endogenous variable. The coefficients attached to the exogenous variables are here called the *dynamic multipliers.* Note that equations such as (13.143) can also be used to answer questions concerning the influence of some past policy action on the current level of the endogenous variables, or the extent of corrective measures necessary to bring about some desired changes in the endogenous variables over any number of future periods.

Stability Conditions and Dynamic Analysis

Let us now turn to the question of the stability of a system. In general, we say that a system is stable if, in a situation where the values of the exogenous variables are held constant through time, the mean values of the endogenous variable settle down to some constant levels. (The actual values of the endogenous variables will, of course, fluctuate because of the effect of the stochastic disturbances. We will consider only cases where the probability is very small that an otherwise stable system could turn unstable because of random disturbances.) This means that a system is considered unstable if, for constant values of the exogenous variables, the mean values of the endogenous variables either explode or display a regular oscillatory movement. One way of determining whether a system is stable or not is to refer to the final form equations. Clearly, if the system is to settle down when the levels of the exogenous variables are unchanged, the sums of each set of dynamic multipliers must be finite. That is, the requirement for stability is that the sums

$$\sum_{i=0}^{\infty} \zeta_i \quad \text{and} \quad \sum_{i=0}^{\infty} \xi_i$$

are finite. These sums represent the *long-run* or *equilibrium multipliers* for consumption with respect to money supply and to government expenditure. Another way of finding out whether a system is stable or not is to examine the fundamental dynamic equation. If the exogenous variables are held constant (and the disturbances are disregarded), this equation becomes an ordinary linear nonhomogeneous difference equation and can be solved as such. In our case we have from (13.139a)

(13.144) $$C_t - \mu_1 C_{t-1} - \mu_2 C_{t-2} = \text{constant}.$$

The characteristic equation for (13.144) is

(13.145) $$\lambda^2 - \mu_1 \lambda - \mu_2 = 0$$

with roots

$$\lambda_{1,2} = \frac{\mu_1 \pm \sqrt{\mu_1^2 + 4\mu_2}}{2}.$$

The system is stable if and only if the absolute value of the largest root (or modulus) of (13.145) is smaller than one. If this is the case, we can determine the equilibrium mean value of consumption from (13.139a) as

(13.146) $$C_E = \frac{\delta + \kappa_0 M_t + \kappa_1 M_{t-1} + \nu_0 G_t + \nu_1 G_{t-1}}{1 - \mu_1 - \mu_2}.$$

The stability condition is clearly important from the economic point of view. It should also be realized that the existence of stability (or, at worst, of a regular oscillatory pattern) is, in fact, assumed in the process of estimation. The assumption that the predetermined variables of the system have finite variances as $t \to \infty$ applies also to the lagged endogenous variables, and this assumption would be violated if the endogenous variables were to grow or decline without limit. If this assumption were not made, there would be difficulties in proving the asymptotic properties of estimators.

The final form equation can be derived in general terms as follows. Making an explicit allowance for lagged endogenous variables in the reduced form, we can write

(13.147) $$\mathbf{y}_t = \boldsymbol{\pi}_1 \mathbf{y}_{t-1} + \boldsymbol{\pi}_2 \mathbf{x}_t + \mathbf{v}_t.$$

Successive substitution for $\mathbf{y}_{t-1}$, $\mathbf{y}_{t-2}$, etc., leads to

(13.148) $$\mathbf{y}_t = \sum_{j=1}^{\infty} \boldsymbol{\pi}_1^j \boldsymbol{\pi}_2 \mathbf{x}_{t-j} + \mathbf{v}_t^*.$$

Then we have the following.

Impact multipliers: $\boldsymbol{\pi}_2$

jth dynamic multiplier: $\boldsymbol{\pi}_1^j \boldsymbol{\pi}_2$

Equilibrium multiplier: $\sum_{j=1}^{\infty} \boldsymbol{\pi}_1^j \boldsymbol{\pi}_2 = (\mathbf{I} - \boldsymbol{\pi}_1)^{-1} \boldsymbol{\pi}_2$

The dynamic solution given by the final form equations answers questions concerning the influence of hypothetical changes in the exogenous variables of the system. If we are interested in the effect of changes in the values of exogenous variables that actually did take place during the period under observation, we may trace these more conveniently by using first differences. In our model we have, by reference to (13.143),

$$(13.149) \quad C_t - C_{t-1} = (\eta_t - \eta_{t-1}) + \zeta_0(M_t - M_{t-1}) + \zeta_1(M_{t-1} - M_{t-2}) + \cdots + \zeta_{t-2}(M_2 - M_1) + \zeta_{t-1}M_1 + \xi_0(G_t - G_{t-1}) + \xi_1(G_{t-1} - G_{t-2}) + \cdots + \xi_{t-2}(G_2 - G_1) + \xi_{t-1}G_1 + \omega_t.$$

The first term on the right-hand side indicates the influence of the initial conditions and of the dynamics of the system operating in absence of any changes in the exogenous variables. For systems that are stable the value of this term will diminish as the system moves from the initial position, and will eventually approach zero. The terms $\zeta_{t-1}M_1$ and $\xi_{t-1}G_1$ measure the influence of the starting levels of the exogenous variables. The term ω_t summarizes the influence of the random disturbances. By substituting the actual values of the exogenous variables for the period under investigation into (13.149), we can determine the part that any policy measure played in affecting the observed change in the level of consumption.

The preceding discussion has been carried out in terms of the population parameters which are, of course, not known and must be replaced by sample estimates. Therefore, it would be desirable to accompany each estimate with its standard error. Formulas for estimating the standard errors are available for the impact multipliers of the reduced form equations, and also for the dynamic multipliers of the final form equations.[43] As for the characteristic roots that are crucial for the determination of the stability condition of a system, a formula for the asymptotic variance of the largest root has been derived by Theil and Boot and by Oberhofer and Kmenta.[44]

EXAMPLE A model of the United States economy for the period 1921–1941, known as Klein Model I, has been estimated as follows:[45]

[43] P. Schmidt, "The Asymptotic Distribution of Dynamic Multipliers," *Econometrica,* 41 (January 1973), pp. 161–164.

[44] H. Theil and J. C. G. Boot, "The Final Form of Econometric Equation Systems," *Review of the International Statistical Institute,* 30 (1962), pp. 136–152; W. Oberhofer and J. Kmenta, "Estimation of Standard Errors of the Characteristic Roots of a Dynamic Econometric Model," *Econometrica,* 41 (January 1973), pp. 171–177. See also P. Schmidt, "The Algebraic Equivalence of the Oberhofer–Kmenta and Theil–Boot Formulae for the Asymptotic Variance of a Characteristic Root of a Dynamic Econometric Model," *Econometrica,* 42 (May 1974), pp. 591–592.

[45] The model is presented in L. R. Klein, *Economic Fluctuations in the United States 1921–1941* (New York: Wiley, 1950), pp. 65–68. The estimates of the coefficients are two-stage least squares estimates given in A. S. Goldberger, *Econometric Theory* (New York: Wiley, 1964), p. 365.

Consumption: $C_t = 16.555 + 0.017P_t + 0.216P_{t-1} + 0.810W_t + \tilde{\tilde{u}}_{1t};$

Investment: $I_t = 20.278 + 0.150P_t + 0.616P_{t-1} - 0.158K_{t-1} + \tilde{\tilde{u}}_{2t};$

Private wages: $W_t^* = 1.500 + 0.439E_t + 0.147E_{t-1} + 0.130A_t + \tilde{\tilde{u}}_{3t};$

Product: $Y_t + T_t = C_t + I_t + G_t;$

Income: $Y_t = P_t + W_t;$

Capital: $K_t = K_{t-1} + I_t;$

Wages: $W_t = W_t^* + W_t^{**};$

Private product: $E_t = Y_t + T_t - W_t^{**}.$

Endogenous variables

C	consumption	Y	national income
I	investment	K	end-of-year capital stock
W^*	private wage bill	W	total wage bill
P	profits	E	private product

Table 13-3
Dynamic Multipliers of G on $(Y + T)$

Lag	Multiplier
0	1.773
1	1.567
2	0.881
3	0.232
4	−0.219
5	−0.456
6	−0.519
7	−0.466
8	−0.355
9	−0.227
10	−0.112
11	−0.025
12	0.031
13	0.058
14	0.064
15	0.057
16	0.042
17	0.027
18	0.013
19	0.002
20	−0.004
Total	2.071

Exogenous variables	G	government expenditure
	W^{**}	government wage bill
	T	indirect taxes
	A	time in years (1931 = 1)

All variables except time are measured in billions of constant (1934) dollars. We are especially interested in the income variable. The estimated fundamental dynamic equation for this variable is

$$\begin{aligned} Y_t - 1.726Y_{t-1} + 1.029Y_{t-2} - 0.183Y_{t-3} &\\ = 4.880 + 1.773G_t - 1.493G_{t-1} + 0.154A_t - 0.294A_{t-1} + 0.162A_{t-2} &\\ - 1.254T_t + 0.673T_{t-1} + 0.213T_{t-2} + 0.183T_{t-3} + 0.663W_t^{**} &\\ - 1.443W_{t-1}^{**} + 1.029W_{t-2}^{**} - 0.183W_{t-3}^{**} + \tilde{\omega}_t. \end{aligned}$$

The characteristic equation

$$\lambda^3 - 1.726\,\lambda^2 + 1.029\,\lambda - 0.183 = 0$$

has as its roots

$$\lambda_1 = 0.310 \quad \text{and} \quad \lambda_{2,3} = 0.708 \pm 0.298i.$$

Table 13-4 Changes in $(Y + T)$ Accounted by Past and Current Changes in G

Year	$\Delta(Y + T)$	Due to changes in G
1922	4.7	−0.9
1923	7.1	−1.4
1924	0.1	0.5
1925	4.0	0.8
1926	3.1	0.8
1927	0.7	2.4
1928	0.2	2.4
1929	2.8	1.8
1930	−5.6	3.0
1931	−7.2	4.2
1932	−8.6	1.6
1933	1.1	−1.8
1934	5.0	−1.4
1935	4.8	−0.5
1936	9.6	−0.8
1937	1.6	0.4
1938	−3.1	3.9
1939	8.7	5.7
1940	6.4	5.6
1941	13.2	15.2

The modulus of the complex roots is $\sqrt{0.708^2 + 0.298^2} = 0.768$, which is smaller than unity. Thus, according to our estimates, the system appears stable. Table 13-3 shows the dynamic multipliers of government expenditure on income (Y) or net national product ($Y + T$). Finally, we are interested in how government expenditure affected the changes in the net national product during the period 1921–1941. Table 13-4 shows the actual changes in $(Y + T)$ as well as those estimated to be due to current and past changes in government expenditure. The latter were calculated in accordance with (13.149) as

$$\xi_0(G_t - G_{t-1}) + \xi_1(G_{t-1} - G_{t-2}) + \cdots + \xi_{t-2}(G_2 - G_1).$$

Table 13-4 may be used to examine the extent of anticyclical fiscal policy effects during the period.

EXERCISES

13-1. A highly simplified Keynesian model of the economy is

$$C_t = \alpha + \beta Y_t + \varepsilon_t,$$
$$Y_t = C_t + I_t,$$

where Y = income, C = consumption, and I = exogenous investment. Show that the ILS, 2SLS, LIML, and FIML methods of estimation lead to identical results.

13-2. Consider the simultaneous equation model

$$Y_{1t} = \beta_{12} Y_{2t} + \gamma_{11} + u_{1t},$$
$$Y_{2t} = \gamma_{21} + \gamma_{22} X_t + u_{2t},$$

where X is a nonstochastic exogenous variable. The disturbances are assumed to have zero means and constant variances, and to be nonautocorrelated over time. Further, u_{1t} and u_{2t} are mutually independent. Compare the variances of the ordinary least squares and the indirect least squares estimator of β_{12}.

13-3. Tintner's model of the American meat market is

$$Y_{1t} = a_0 + a_1 Y_{2t} + a_2 X_{1t} + u_{1t} \qquad \text{(demand)},$$
$$Y_{1t} = b_0 + b_1 Y_{2t} + b_2 X_{2t} + b_3 X_{3t} + u_{2t} \qquad \text{(supply)},$$

where u_{1t} and u_{2t} are disturbance terms, Y_{1t} and Y_{2t} are endogenous variables, and X_{1t}, X_{2t}, and X_{3t} are predetermined variables. These variables are defined as follows.

Y_1 per capita meat consumption,

Y_2 index of meat prices,

X_1 per capita disposable income,

X_2 index of meat processing costs,

X_3 index of agricultural production costs.

The $T \times 1$ disturbance vectors, $\mathbf{u}_1$ and $\mathbf{u}_2$, are assumed to have the following variance–

covariance matrix:

$$E\begin{bmatrix}\mathbf{u}_1\\ \mathbf{u}_2\end{bmatrix}[\mathbf{u}_1' \quad \mathbf{u}_2'] = \begin{bmatrix}\sigma_{11}\mathbf{I}_T & \sigma_{12}\mathbf{I}_T\\ \sigma_{12}\mathbf{I}_T & \sigma_{22}\mathbf{I}_T\end{bmatrix}.$$

a. Discuss the identification of the two equations.

b. Suppose that it is known a priori that $b_2/b_3 = K$, where K is a known number. Discuss the identification properties of the model after adding this specification.

c. Suppose instead that the term a_3X_{4t} is added to the demand equation, where X_4 is an index of prices of nonanimal proteins and fats. How does this alter the identification of the model?

13-4. Assume the following aggregate model for the economy:

$$C_t = \alpha_1 + \alpha_2 D_t + u_{1t},$$

$$I_t = \beta_1 + \beta_2 Y_t + \beta_3 Y_{t-1} + u_{2t},$$

$$Y_t = D_t + T_t,$$

$$Y_t = C_t + I_t + G_t,$$

Table 13-5[a]

1920	C	D	Y	I
1920	—	—	47.1	—
1921	41.9	40.6	48.3	−0.2
1922	45.0	49.1	53.0	1.9
1923	49.2	55.4	60.1	5.2
1924	50.6	56.4	60.2	3.0
1925	52.6	58.7	64.2	5.1
1926	55.1	60.3	67.3	5.6
1927	56.2	61.3	68.0	4.2
1928	57.3	64.0	68.2	3.0
1929	57.8	67.0	71.0	5.1
1930	55.0	57.7	65.4	1.0
1931	50.9	50.7	58.2	−3.4
1932	45.6	41.3	49.6	−6.2
1933	46.5	45.3	50.7	−5.1
1934	48.7	48.9	55.7	−3.0
1935	51.3	53.3	60.5	−1.3
1936	57.7	61.8	70.1	2.1
1937	58.7	65.0	71.7	2.0
1938	57.5	61.2	68.6	−1.9
1939	61.6	68.4	77.3	1.3
1940	65.0	74.1	83.7	3.3
1941	69.7	85.3	96.9	4.9

Source: L. R. Klein, *Economic Fluctuations in the United States 1921–1941* (New York: Wiley, 1950), p. 135.

[a] All variables measured in billions of 1934 dollars.

where C = consumption, D = net national income, I = investment, Y = net national product, T = indirect taxes, and G = government expenditures. The variables C, D, I, and Y are endogenous; T and G are exogenous.

a. Examine the conditions of identification of the first two equations of the model.

b. Obtain consistent estimates of the consumption and investment equations using data in Table 13-5 for the United States economy, 1921–1941.

13-5. Using the results from Exercise 13-4,

a. Derive the fundamental dynamic equation and use it to determine whether the system is stable or not.

b. Calculate the dynamic multipliers of Y with respect to G.

c. Find the value of the long-run (equilibrium) multiplier of Y with respect to G.

13-6. Consider the following dynamic model of the market for a certain commodity:

$$S_t = \alpha_0 + \alpha_1 P_t + u_{1t},$$

$$D_t = \beta_0 + \beta_1 P_t + u_{2t},$$

$$P_t - P_{t-1} = m(Q_{t-1} - Q_{t-2}) + u_{3t},$$

$$S_t - D_t = Q_t - Q_{t-1},$$

where S_t = production, D_t = sales, P_t = price, and Q_t = end-of-period level of stock. Note that

$$\alpha_1 > 0,$$

$$\beta_1 < 0,$$

$$\alpha_0 < \beta_0,$$

$$m < 0.$$

a. Determine the identification status of the first three equations.

b. Show that the time path of Q_t is determined by a second-order homogeneous difference equation, and that the time path of P_t is determined by a first-order nonhomogeneous difference equation.

c. Derive the conditions for the existence of stability in this market.

d. Disregarding the stochastic disturbances, find the value of m for which the time path of P_t is one of regular oscillations.

Appendix

A. Algebra of Summations

Expressions involving sums are widely used in statistics. They are usually abbreviated with the help of the so-called "Σ notation." The basic definition relating to this notation states that if m and n are integers and $m \leq n$, then

$$\sum_{i=m}^{n} x_i = x_m + x_{m+1} + x_{m+2} + \cdots + x_n.$$

This notation is used most frequently with sums of observations on a given variable or variables, with the subscript designating the numbering of the observations. When this notation is used, the following rules are useful:

(A.1) $$\sum_{i=1}^{n} kx_i = k \sum_{i=1}^{n} x_i.$$

Proof:

$$\sum_{i=1}^{n} kx_i = kx_1 + kx_2 + \cdots + kx_n = k(x_1 + x_2 + \cdots + x_n) = k \sum_{i=1}^{n} x_i.$$

(A.2) $$\sum_{i=1}^{n} k = nk.$$

Proof:

$$\sum_{i=1}^{n} k = k + k + \cdots + k = nk.$$

(A.3) $$\sum_{i=1}^{n} (x_i + y_i) = \sum_{i=1}^{n} x_i + \sum_{i=1}^{n} y_i.$$

Proof:

$$\sum_{i=1}^{n}(x_i+y_i)=(x_1+y_1)+(x_2+y_2)+\cdots+(x_n+y_n)$$

$$=(x_1+x_2+\cdots+x_n)+(y_1+y_2+\cdots+y_n)=\sum_{i=1}^{n}x_i+\sum_{i=1}^{n}y_i.$$

Useful formulas are established by considering the sum of the first n positive integers and the sums of their powers. The results, given without proof, are

(A.4) $$\sum_{i=1}^{n} i=1+2+\cdots+n=\tfrac{1}{2}[n(n+1)]=\tfrac{1}{2}[(n+1)^2-(n+1)],$$

(A.5) $$\sum_{i=1}^{n} i^2=1^2+2^2+\cdots+n^2=\tfrac{1}{6}[n(n+1)(2n+1)]$$

$$=\tfrac{1}{3}[(n+1)^3-\tfrac{3}{2}(n+1)^2+\tfrac{1}{2}(n+1)],$$

(A.6) $$\sum_{i=1}^{n} i^3=1^3+2^3+\cdots+n^3=\tfrac{1}{4}[n^2(n+1)^2]$$

$$=\tfrac{1}{4}[(n+1)^4-2(n+1)^3+(n+1)^2],$$

(A.7) $$\sum_{i=1}^{n} i^4=1^4+2^4+\cdots+n^4=\tfrac{1}{30}[n(n+1)(2n+1)(3n^2+3n-1)]$$

$$=\tfrac{1}{5}[(n+1)^5-\tfrac{5}{2}(n+1)^4+\tfrac{5}{3}(n+1)^3-\tfrac{1}{6}(n+1)].$$

The Σ notation can also be extended to multiple sums. For instance, a double summation is defined as

$$\sum_{i=1}^{n}\sum_{j=1}^{m}x_{ij}=\sum_{i=1}^{n}(x_{i1}+x_{i2}+\cdots+x_{im})$$

$$=(x_{11}+x_{21}+\cdots+x_{n1})+(x_{12}+x_{22}+\cdots+x_{n2})$$

$$+\cdots+(x_{1m}+x_{2m}+\cdots+x_{nm}).$$

The following double-summation rules are of special interest.

(A.8) $$\sum_{i=1}^{n}\sum_{j=1}^{m}(x_{ij}+y_{ij})=\sum_{i=1}^{n}\sum_{j=1}^{m}x_{ij}+\sum_{i=1}^{n}\sum_{j=1}^{m}y_{ij}.$$

Proof:

$$\sum_{i=1}^{n}\sum_{j=1}^{m}(x_{ij}+y_{ij})=\sum_{j=1}^{m}(x_{1j}+y_{1j})+\sum_{j=1}^{m}(x_{2j}+y_{2j})+\cdots+\sum_{j=1}^{m}(x_{nj}+y_{nj})$$

$$=\sum_{j=1}^{m}(x_{1j}+x_{2j}+\cdots+x_{nj})+\sum_{j=1}^{m}(y_{1j}+y_{2j}+\cdots+y_{nj})$$

$$=\sum_{i=1}^{n}\sum_{j=1}^{m}x_{ij}+\sum_{i=1}^{n}\sum_{j=1}^{m}y_{ij}.$$

(A.9)
$$\sum_{i=1}^{n}\sum_{j=1}^{m} x_i = m\sum_{i=1}^{n} x_i.$$

Proof:

$$\sum_{i=1}^{n}\sum_{j=1}^{m} x_i = \sum_{j=1}^{m}\left[\sum_{i=1}^{n} x_i\right] = m\sum_{i=1}^{n} x_i.$$

(A.10)
$$\sum_{i=1}^{n}\sum_{j=1}^{m} x_i y_j = \left[\sum_{i=1}^{n} x_i\right]\left[\sum_{j=1}^{m} y_j\right].$$

Proof:

$$\sum_{i=1}^{n}\sum_{j=1}^{m} x_i y_j = \sum_{i=1}^{n} (x_i y_1 + x_i y_2 + \cdots + x_i y_m)$$
$$= y_1\sum_{i=1}^{n} x_i + y_2\sum_{i=1}^{n} x_i + \cdots + y_m\sum_{i=1}^{n} x_i = \left[\sum_{i=1}^{n} x_i\right]\left[\sum_{j=1}^{m} y_j\right].$$

(A.11)
$$\sum_{i=1}^{n}\sum_{j=1}^{m} x_i y_{ij} = \sum_{i=1}^{n} x_i \sum_{j=1}^{m} y_{ij}.$$

Proof:

$$\sum_{i=1}^{n}\sum_{j=1}^{m} x_i y_{ij} = \sum_{i=1}^{n} (x_i y_{i1} + x_i y_{i2} + \cdots + x_i y_{im}) = \sum_{i=1}^{n} x_i(y_{i1} + y_{i2} + \cdots + y_{im})$$
$$= \sum_{i=1}^{n} x_i \sum_{j=1}^{m} y_{ij}.$$

(A.12)
$$\left[\sum_{i=1}^{n} x_i\right]^2 = \sum_{i=1}^{n} x_i^2 + 2\sum_{i=1}^{n-1}\sum_{j=i+1}^{n} x_i x_j = \sum_{i=1}^{n} x_i^2 + 2\sum_{i<j} x_i x_j.$$

Proof:

$$\left[\sum_{i=1}^{n} x_i\right]^2 = (x_1 + x_2 + \cdots + x_n)^2$$
$$= x_1^2 + x_2^2 + \cdots + x_n^2 + 2(x_1x_2 + x_1x_3 + \cdots + x_1x_n$$
$$+ x_2x_3 + x_2x_4 + \cdots + x_{n-1}x_n) = \sum_{i=1}^{n} x_i^2 + 2\sum_{i<j} x_i x_j.$$

A special case of (A.12) is

(A.13)
$$\sum_{i=1}^{n} (x_i - \bar{x})^2 = -2\sum_{i<j} (x_i - \bar{x})(x_j - \bar{x}).$$

Proof: Since

$$\sum_{i=1}^{n} (x_i - \bar{x}) = 0,$$

we have

$$\left[\sum_{i=1}^{n}(x_i-\bar{x})\right]^2=\sum_{i=1}^{n}(x_i-\bar{x})^2+2\sum_{i<j}(x_i-\bar{x})(x_j-\bar{x})=0,$$

or

$$\sum_{i=1}^{n}(x_i-\bar{x})^2=-2\sum_{i<j}(x_i-\bar{x})(x_j-\bar{x}).$$

B. Elements of Matrix Algebra

Definitions

An $(M \times N)$ matrix is defined as a rectangular array of real numbers arranged in M rows and N columns as in

$$\mathbf{A}=\begin{bmatrix} a_{11} & a_{12} & \cdots & a_{1N} \\ a_{21} & a_{22} & \cdots & a_{2N} \\ \vdots & \vdots & & \vdots \\ a_{M1} & a_{M2} & \cdots & a_{MN} \end{bmatrix}. \tag{B.1}$$

The numbers a_{ij} ($i = 1, 2, \ldots, M$; $j = 1, 2, \ldots, N$) are the *elements of* **A**; the term a_{ij} itself is frequently used to designate a typical element of **A**. The number of rows and columns—in the case of (B.1) given as $M \times N$—is referred to as the *order* or the *dimension* of the matrix. A matrix of order 1×1 is a *scalar,* a matrix of order $M \times 1$ is called a *column vector,* and a matrix of order $1 \times N$ is called a *row vector.* A matrix with an equal number of rows and columns is a *square matrix.* The sum of the diagonal elements of a square matrix is called the *trace* of the matrix. A *diagonal matrix* is a square matrix such that each element that does not lie along the principal diagonal is equal to zero; i.e.,

$$\mathbf{A}=\begin{bmatrix} a_{11} & 0 & \cdots & 0 \\ 0 & a_{22} & \cdots & 0 \\ \vdots & \vdots & & \vdots \\ 0 & 0 & \cdots & a_{MM} \end{bmatrix}.$$

An *identity* or a *unit matrix* is a diagonal matrix whose diagonal elements are all equal to one; i.e.,

$$\mathbf{I}=\begin{bmatrix} 1 & 0 & \cdots & 0 \\ 0 & 1 & \cdots & 0 \\ \vdots & \vdots & & \vdots \\ 0 & 0 & \cdots & 1 \end{bmatrix}.$$

Sometimes we use a subscript to indicate the order of the identity matrix in question, e.g., $\mathbf{I_M}$. Finally, a *zero matrix* is any matrix whose elements are all zero.

Basic Operations with Matrices

(B.2) **Equality of matrices:** $\mathbf{A} = \mathbf{B}$ *if and only if* $\mathbf{A}$ *and* $\mathbf{B}$ *are of the same order and* $a_{ij} = b_{ij}$ *for all i, j.*

(B.3) **Addition of matrices:** $\mathbf{A} + \mathbf{B} = \mathbf{C}$ *if and only if* $\mathbf{A}$, $\mathbf{B}$, *and* $\mathbf{C}$ *are of the same order and* $a_{ij} + b_{ij} = c_{ij}$ *for all i, j.*

EXAMPLE

$$\begin{bmatrix} 5 & 0 \\ 2 & -4 \end{bmatrix} + \begin{bmatrix} -1 & 3 \\ 3 & 5 \end{bmatrix} = \begin{bmatrix} 4 & 3 \\ 5 & 1 \end{bmatrix}.$$

(B.4) **Scalar multiplication:** *If k is a scalar, then* $k\mathbf{A} = [ka_{ij}]$.

This means that if we want to multiply a matrix $\mathbf{A}$ by a scalar, we have to multiply each element of $\mathbf{A}$.

(B.5) **Matrix multiplication:** *If* $\mathbf{A}$ *is of order* $M \times N$ *and* $\mathbf{B}$ *is of order* $N \times P$, *then the product of the two matrices is given as*

$$\mathbf{AB} = \mathbf{C},$$

where $\mathbf{C}$ *is a matrix of order* $M \times P$ *whose element in the ith row and the jth column is given by*

$$c_{ij} = \sum_{k=1}^{N} a_{ik} b_{kj}.$$

That is, the element c_{11} is obtained by multiplying the elements of the first row of $\mathbf{A}$ by the elements of the first column of $\mathbf{B}$ and then summing over all terms; the element c_{12} is obtained by performing the same operation with the elements of the first row of $\mathbf{A}$ and the second column of $\mathbf{B}$, and so on.

EXAMPLE 1

$$\begin{bmatrix} a_{11} & a_{12} \\ a_{21} & a_{22} \\ a_{31} & a_{32} \end{bmatrix} \begin{bmatrix} b_{11} & b_{12} \\ b_{21} & b_{22} \end{bmatrix} = \begin{bmatrix} (a_{11}b_{11} + a_{12}b_{21}) & (a_{11}b_{12} + a_{12}b_{22}) \\ (a_{21}b_{11} + a_{22}b_{21}) & (a_{21}b_{12} + a_{22}b_{22}) \\ (a_{31}b_{11} + a_{32}b_{21}) & (a_{31}b_{12} + a_{32}b_{22}) \end{bmatrix}$$

EXAMPLE 2

$$\begin{bmatrix} 1 & 2 & 3 \\ 4 & 5 & 6 \end{bmatrix}\begin{bmatrix} 7 & 10 \\ 8 & 11 \\ 9 & 12 \end{bmatrix} = \begin{bmatrix} (1\times 7+2\times 8+3\times 9) & (1\times 10+2\times 11+3\times 12) \\ (4\times 7+5\times 8+6\times 9) & (4\times 10+5\times 11+6\times 12) \end{bmatrix}$$

$$= \begin{bmatrix} 50 & 68 \\ 122 & 167 \end{bmatrix}.$$

Note that, in general,

$$\mathbf{AB} \neq \mathbf{BA}.$$

This inequality implies that we must distinguish between pre- and postmultiplication by a matrix.

Transposition

(B.6) *If* $\mathbf{A}$ *is an* $(M \times N)$ *matrix, then the* transpose *of* $\mathbf{A}$, *denoted by* $\mathbf{A}'$, *is an* $(N \times M)$ *matrix obtained by interchanging the rows with the columns in* $\mathbf{A}$; *i.e.,*

$$\mathbf{A}' = \begin{bmatrix} a_{11} & a_{21} & \cdots & a_{M1} \\ a_{12} & a_{22} & \cdots & a_{M2} \\ \vdots & \vdots & & \vdots \\ a_{1N} & a_{2N} & \cdots & a_{MN} \end{bmatrix}.$$

EXAMPLE

$$\mathbf{A} = \begin{bmatrix} 2 & 5 \\ 3 & 6 \\ 4 & 7 \end{bmatrix}, \qquad \mathbf{A}' = \begin{bmatrix} 2 & 3 & 4 \\ 5 & 6 & 7 \end{bmatrix}.$$

The following theorems apply to transposed matrices:

(B.7) $$(\mathbf{A}')' = \mathbf{A},$$

(B.8) $$(\mathbf{A} + \mathbf{B})' = \mathbf{A}' + \mathbf{B}',$$

(B.9) $$(\mathbf{AB})' = \mathbf{B}'\mathbf{A}'.$$

The proofs follow directly from the definition of matrix operations.

(B.10) *If* $\mathbf{A}$ *is a square matrix and* $\mathbf{A} = \mathbf{A}'$, *then* $\mathbf{A}$ *is symmetric.*

A well-known expression involving a transpose of a vector is known as *quadratic form*. Suppose $\mathbf{x}$ is an $(M \times 1)$ nonzero vector and $\mathbf{A}$ is a square and symmetric matrix of order $M \times M$. Then the quadratic form of $\mathbf{x}$ is a scalar defined as

(B.11)
$$\mathbf{x}'\mathbf{A}\mathbf{x} = \sum_{i=1}^{M} \sum_{j=1}^{M} a_{ij} x_i x_j.$$

EXAMPLE If

$$\mathbf{x} = \begin{bmatrix} x_1 \\ x_2 \end{bmatrix} \quad \text{and} \quad \mathbf{A} = \begin{bmatrix} a_{11} & a_{12} \\ a_{21} & a_{22} \end{bmatrix},$$

then

$$\mathbf{x}'\mathbf{A}\mathbf{x} = [x_1 \quad x_2] \begin{bmatrix} a_{11} & a_{12} \\ a_{21} & a_{22} \end{bmatrix} \begin{bmatrix} x_1 \\ x_2 \end{bmatrix} = [x_1 \quad x_2] \begin{bmatrix} a_{11}x_1 + a_{12}x_2 \\ a_{21}x_1 + a_{22}x_2 \end{bmatrix}$$
$$= a_{11}x_1^2 + a_{12}x_1x_2 + a_{21}x_1x_2 + a_{22}x_2^2 = a_{11}x_1^2 + 2a_{12}x_1x_2 + a_{22}x_2^2.$$

A symmetric matrix $\mathbf{A}$ is called *positive definite* if $\mathbf{x}'\mathbf{A}\mathbf{x} > 0$,and *positive semidefinite* if $\mathbf{x}'\mathbf{A}\mathbf{x} \geq 0$. Similarly, $\mathbf{A}$ is *negative definite* if $\mathbf{x}'\mathbf{A}\mathbf{x} < 0$, and *negative semidefinite* if $\mathbf{x}'\mathbf{A}\mathbf{x} \leq 0$. Note that all variance–covariance matrices are positive definite.

Partitioned Matrices

Frequently it is convenient to *partition* a matrix into submatrices. In this case the submatrices are treated as scalar elements except that care has to be taken to insure that the rules of matrix multiplication are preserved. In particular, if

$$\mathbf{A} = \begin{bmatrix} \mathbf{P}_{11} & \mathbf{P}_{12} \\ \mathbf{P}_{21} & \mathbf{P}_{22} \end{bmatrix} \quad \text{and} \quad \mathbf{B} = \begin{bmatrix} \mathbf{Q}_{11} & \mathbf{Q}_{12} \\ \mathbf{Q}_{21} & \mathbf{Q}_{22} \end{bmatrix},$$

where the dimensions of the submatrices are

$$\mathbf{P}_{11} \rightarrow (M_1 \times N_1), \qquad \mathbf{Q}_{11} \rightarrow (N_1 \times R_1),$$
$$\mathbf{P}_{12} \rightarrow (M_1 \times N_2), \qquad \mathbf{Q}_{12} \rightarrow (N_1 \times R_2),$$
$$\mathbf{P}_{21} \rightarrow (M_2 \times N_1), \qquad \mathbf{Q}_{21} \rightarrow (N_2 \times R_1),$$
$$\mathbf{P}_{22} \rightarrow (M_2 \times N_2), \qquad \mathbf{Q}_{22} \rightarrow (N_2 \times R_2),$$

then

(B.12)
$$\mathbf{A}' = \begin{bmatrix} \mathbf{P}'_{11} & \mathbf{P}'_{21} \\ \mathbf{P}'_{12} & \mathbf{P}'_{22} \end{bmatrix}$$

and

$$\text{(B.13)} \qquad \mathbf{AB} = \begin{bmatrix} \mathbf{P}_{11}\mathbf{Q}_{11} + \mathbf{P}_{12}\mathbf{Q}_{21} & \mathbf{P}_{11}\mathbf{Q}_{12} + \mathbf{P}_{12}\mathbf{Q}_{22} \\ \mathbf{P}_{21}\mathbf{Q}_{11} + \mathbf{P}_{22}\mathbf{Q}_{21} & \mathbf{P}_{21}\mathbf{Q}_{12} + \mathbf{P}_{22}\mathbf{Q}_{22} \end{bmatrix}.$$

Determinants

A determinant is a scalar whose value is calculated by a certain rule from a square matrix. The determinant of matrix $\mathbf{A}$ is denoted by det $\mathbf{A}$ or $|\mathbf{A}|$. The rules for calculating determinants are as follows. For a (2×2) matrix

$$\mathbf{A} = \begin{bmatrix} a_{11} & a_{12} \\ a_{21} & a_{22} \end{bmatrix},$$

the determinant is given by

$$\text{(B.14)} \qquad \det \mathbf{A} = a_{11}a_{22} - a_{12}a_{21}.$$

Note that the value of det $\mathbf{A}$ has been obtained by multiplying certain elements of $\mathbf{A}$ by certain other elements, and then by assigning a positive or a negative sign to the resulting product. If we use solid lines to designate products with a positive sign, and dashed lines to designate products with a negative sign, then the rule for calculating the determinant of a (2×2) matrix can be represented schematically as in Figure B-1(a).

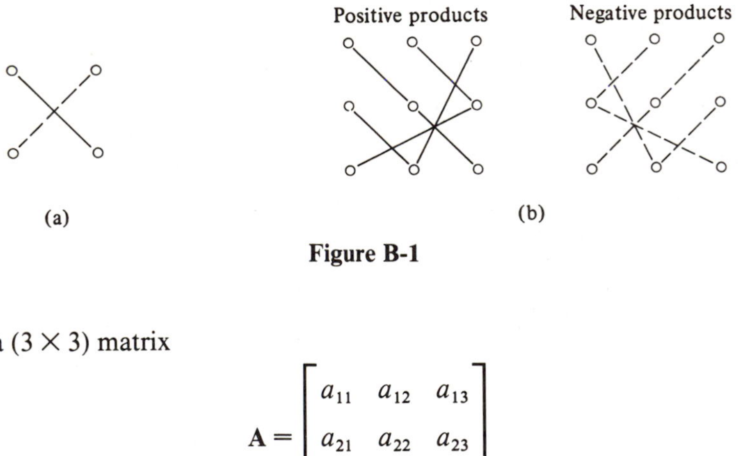

Figure B-1

For a (3×3) matrix

$$\mathbf{A} = \begin{bmatrix} a_{11} & a_{12} & a_{13} \\ a_{21} & a_{22} & a_{23} \\ a_{31} & a_{32} & a_{33} \end{bmatrix}$$

the determinant is

$$\text{(B.15)} \qquad \det \mathbf{A} = a_{11}a_{22}a_{33} + a_{12}a_{23}a_{31} + a_{13}a_{32}a_{21} - a_{13}a_{22}a_{31} - a_{23}a_{32}a_{11} - a_{33}a_{21}a_{12},$$

and the schematic representation is shown in Figure B-1(b).

For square matrices of higher order, the schematic rules for calculating determinants become messy and are rarely used. Instead we use a general rule for calculating determinants of matrices of *any* order. This rule involves the use of *minors* and *cofactors.* Suppose we take a matrix **A** of order $M \times M$ and eliminate the ith row and the jth column, i.e., eliminate the row and the column corresponding to the element a_{ij}. Then the determinant of the resulting $(M-1) \times (M-1)$ matrix is called a *minor* of a_{ij}. A *cofactor* of a_{ij} is simply the minor of a_{ij} multiplied by $(-1)^{i+j}$. A common term to designate a cofactor of a_{ij} is $\mathbf{A_{ij}}$. The general rule for evaluating the determinant of **A** is to take *any* row or *any* column of **A**, multiply each element by the corresponding cofactor, and then add the results. Thus the determinant of an $(M \times M)$ matrix **A** can be calculated as

$$\text{(B.16)} \qquad \det \mathbf{A} = a_{11}\mathbf{A_{11}} + a_{12}\mathbf{A_{12}} + \cdots + a_{1M}\mathbf{A_{1M}}.$$

In formula (B.16) we use the first row as the basis for calculations, but any other row, or any column, would do equally well. The importance of the "cofactor formula" (B.16) is that it enables us to reduce a determinant of any order to a linear combination of determinants of lower order. Of course, this formula also applies to the cases of $M = 2$ and $M = 3$, for which we gave special formulas in (B.14) and (B.15). For $M = 2$ we have

$$\mathbf{A} = \begin{bmatrix} a_{11} & a_{12} \\ a_{21} & a_{22} \end{bmatrix},$$

$$\mathbf{A_{11}} = a_{22},$$

$$\mathbf{A_{12}} = -a_{21},$$

so that, by (B.16),

$$\det \mathbf{A} = a_{11}(a_{22}) + a_{12}(-a_{21}) = a_{11}a_{22} - a_{12}a_{21},$$

which is the same answer as that in (B.14). Further, for $M = 3$ we have

$$\mathbf{A} = \begin{bmatrix} a_{11} & a_{12} & a_{13} \\ a_{21} & a_{22} & a_{23} \\ a_{31} & a_{32} & a_{33} \end{bmatrix},$$

$$\mathbf{A_{11}} = \det \begin{bmatrix} a_{22} & a_{23} \\ a_{32} & a_{33} \end{bmatrix} = a_{22}a_{33} - a_{23}a_{32},$$

$$\mathbf{A_{12}} = -\det \begin{bmatrix} a_{21} & a_{23} \\ a_{31} & a_{33} \end{bmatrix} = -a_{21}a_{33} + a_{23}a_{31},$$

$$\mathbf{A_{13}} = \det \begin{bmatrix} a_{21} & a_{22} \\ a_{31} & a_{32} \end{bmatrix} = a_{21}a_{32} - a_{22}a_{31},$$

so that, by (B.16),

$$\det \mathbf{A} = a_{11}(a_{22}a_{33} - a_{23}a_{32}) + a_{12}(-a_{21}a_{33} + a_{23}a_{31}) + a_{13}(a_{21}a_{32} - a_{22}a_{31})$$
$$= a_{11}a_{22}a_{33} - a_{11}a_{23}a_{32} - a_{12}a_{21}a_{33} + a_{12}a_{23}a_{31} + a_{13}a_{21}a_{32} - a_{13}a_{22}a_{31},$$

which is the same expression as that in (B.15).

Some interesting and useful properties of determinants are

(B.17) Interchanging any two rows or any two columns of **A** changes the sign of det **A**.

(B.18) If every element of a row, or of a column, of **A** is multiplied by a scalar, then det **A** is multiplied by the same scalar.

(B.19) If any row (column) of **A** is extended by the addition of a multiple of any other row (column), the value of det **A** is unaltered.

(B.20) The value of the determinant of a matrix in which two rows (or two columns) are identical is zero.

(B.21) $\det \mathbf{A} = \det \mathbf{A}'$.

(B.22) $\det \mathbf{AB} = (\det \mathbf{A})(\det \mathbf{B})$.

Determinants are also used to describe certain properties of matrices. In particular, if $\det \mathbf{A} = 0$, then **A** is called *singular,* and if $\det \mathbf{A} \neq 0$, then **A** is called *nonsingular.* Further, the order of the largest nonzero determinant contained in an $(M \times N)$ matrix is called the *rank* of the matrix.

EXAMPLE 1 If

$$\mathbf{A} = \begin{bmatrix} 1 & 2 & 3 \\ 4 & 5 & 6 \\ 7 & 8 & 10 \end{bmatrix},$$

then

$$\det \mathbf{A} = 1 \times 5 \times 10 + 2 \times 6 \times 7 + 3 \times 8 \times 4 - 3 \times 5 \times 7 - 6 \times 8 \times 1 - 10 \times 4 \times 2 = -3.$$

The same result could have been obtained by the "cofactor formula" (B.16):

$$\det \mathbf{A} = 1 \times \det \begin{bmatrix} 5 & 6 \\ 8 & 10 \end{bmatrix} + 2 \times (-1) \det \begin{bmatrix} 4 & 6 \\ 7 & 10 \end{bmatrix} + 3 \times \det \begin{bmatrix} 4 & 5 \\ 7 & 8 \end{bmatrix}$$
$$= 1 \times 2 + 2 \times 2 + 3 \times (-3) = -3.$$

Note also that

$$\mathbf{A}' = \begin{bmatrix} 1 & 4 & 7 \\ 2 & 5 & 8 \\ 3 & 6 & 10 \end{bmatrix} \quad \text{and} \quad \det \mathbf{A}' = -3.$$

Suppose we change **A** by (a) multiplying the first row by 4 and deducting the result from the second row, and (b) multiplying the first row by 7 and deducting the result from the third row. The resulting matrix, say, **A***, is

$$\mathbf{A}^* = \begin{bmatrix} 1 & 2 & 3 \\ (4-4) & (5-8) & (6-12) \\ (7-7) & (8-14) & (10-21) \end{bmatrix} = \begin{bmatrix} 1 & 2 & 3 \\ 0 & -3 & -6 \\ 0 & -6 & -11 \end{bmatrix}$$

and

$$\det \mathbf{A}^* = 1 \det \begin{bmatrix} -3 & -6 \\ -6 & -11 \end{bmatrix} = -3 = \det \mathbf{A}.$$

EXAMPLE 2 Let

$$\mathbf{A} = \begin{bmatrix} 1 & 2 \\ 3 & 4 \end{bmatrix} \quad \text{and} \quad \mathbf{B} = \begin{bmatrix} 5 & 6 \\ 7 & 8 \end{bmatrix}.$$

Then

$$\det \mathbf{A} = 1 \times 4 - 2 \times 3 = -2,$$

$$\det \mathbf{B} = 5 \times 8 - 6 \times 7 = -2.$$

Now, define

$$\mathbf{C} = \mathbf{AB} = \begin{bmatrix} 1 & 2 \\ 3 & 4 \end{bmatrix} \begin{bmatrix} 5 & 6 \\ 7 & 8 \end{bmatrix} = \begin{bmatrix} 19 & 22 \\ 43 & 50 \end{bmatrix}$$

and note that

$$\det \mathbf{C} = 950 - 946 = 4 = (\det \mathbf{A})(\det \mathbf{B})$$

Matrix Inversion

The *inverse* of a square matrix **A** is a matrix that, when premultiplied or postmultiplied by **A**, yields the identity matrix. The inverse of **A** is denoted by $\mathbf{A}^{-1}$. Thus we define

(B.23) $\mathbf{B} = \mathbf{A}^{-1}$ *if and only if* $\mathbf{BA} = \mathbf{AB} = \mathbf{I}$.

Not all matrices have an inverse. The following theorem establishes the conditions under which an inverse exists.

(B.24) *The matrix* **A** *has an inverse if and only if* $\det \mathbf{A} \neq 0$, *that is, if and only if* **A** *is a nonsingular matrix.*

The calculation of an inverse involves the formation of the so-called *adjoint*. The adjoint of a square matrix **A** is defined as a matrix that is formed from **A** by replacing each element of **A** by the corresponding cofactor, and by transposing the result. If we denote the adjoint of **A** by adj **A**, then we have

(B.25)
$$\text{adj}\,\mathbf{A} = \begin{bmatrix} \mathbf{A}_{11} & \mathbf{A}_{12} & \cdots & \mathbf{A}_{1M} \\ \mathbf{A}_{21} & \mathbf{A}_{22} & \cdots & \mathbf{A}_{2M} \\ \vdots & \vdots & & \vdots \\ \mathbf{A}_{M1} & \mathbf{A}_{M2} & \cdots & \mathbf{A}_{MM} \end{bmatrix}' = \begin{bmatrix} \mathbf{A}_{11} & \mathbf{A}_{21} & \cdots & \mathbf{A}_{M1} \\ \mathbf{A}_{12} & \mathbf{A}_{22} & \cdots & \mathbf{A}_{M2} \\ \vdots & \vdots & & \vdots \\ \mathbf{A}_{1M} & \mathbf{A}_{2M} & \cdots & \mathbf{A}_{MM} \end{bmatrix}.$$

The inverse of **A** is then obtained as follows:

(B.26)
$$\mathbf{A}^{-1} = \frac{1}{\det \mathbf{A}}\,\text{adj}\,\mathbf{A}.$$

It can be shown[1] that

(B.27)
$$(\mathbf{AB})^{-1} = \mathbf{B}^{-1}\mathbf{A}^{-1},$$

(B.28)
$$(\mathbf{A}^{-1})' = (\mathbf{A}')^{-1}.$$

Note that the result in (B.28) implies that if **A** is symmetric (and nonsingular), then $\mathbf{A}^{-1}$ is also symmetric.

EXAMPLE 1 If

$$\mathbf{A} = \begin{bmatrix} a_{11} & a_{12} \\ a_{21} & a_{22} \end{bmatrix},$$

then

$$\mathbf{A}_{11} = a_{22},$$
$$\mathbf{A}_{12} = -a_{21},$$
$$\mathbf{A}_{21} = -a_{12},$$
$$\mathbf{A}_{22} = a_{11},$$

and

$$\text{adj}\,\mathbf{A} = \begin{bmatrix} a_{22} & -a_{21} \\ -a_{12} & a_{11} \end{bmatrix}' = \begin{bmatrix} a_{22} & -a_{12} \\ -a_{21} & a_{11} \end{bmatrix}.$$

Therefore,

$$\mathbf{A}^{-1} = \frac{1}{a_{11}a_{22} - a_{12}a_{21}} \begin{bmatrix} a_{22} & -a_{12} \\ -a_{21} & a_{11} \end{bmatrix}.$$

EXAMPLE 2 If

$$\mathbf{A} = \begin{bmatrix} 1 & 2 & 3 \\ 4 & 5 & 6 \\ 7 & 8 & 10 \end{bmatrix},$$

[1] See, e.g., J. Johnston, *Econometric Methods,* 3rd ed. (New York: McGraw-Hill, 1984), p. 133.

then $\mathbf{A}_{11} = 2, \quad \mathbf{A}_{21} = 4, \quad \mathbf{A}_{31} = -3,$

$\mathbf{A}_{12} = 2, \quad \mathbf{A}_{22} = -11, \quad \mathbf{A}_{32} = 6,$

$\mathbf{A}_{13} = -3, \quad \mathbf{A}_{23} = 6, \quad \mathbf{A}_{33} = -3,$

and $\det \mathbf{A} = -3.$

Therefore,

$$\operatorname{adj}\mathbf{A} = \begin{bmatrix} 2 & 2 & -3 \\ 4 & -11 & 6 \\ -3 & 6 & -3 \end{bmatrix}' = \begin{bmatrix} 2 & 4 & -3 \\ 2 & -11 & 6 \\ -3 & 6 & -3 \end{bmatrix},$$

and

$$\mathbf{A}^{-1} = \frac{1}{-3}\begin{bmatrix} 2 & 4 & -3 \\ 2 & -11 & 6 \\ -3 & 6 & -3 \end{bmatrix} = \begin{bmatrix} -\frac{2}{3} & -\frac{4}{3} & 1 \\ -\frac{2}{3} & \frac{11}{3} & -2 \\ 1 & -2 & 1 \end{bmatrix}.$$

To check this result we multiply

$$\mathbf{A}^{-1}\mathbf{A} = \begin{bmatrix} -\frac{2}{3} & -\frac{4}{3} & 1 \\ -\frac{2}{3} & \frac{11}{3} & -2 \\ 1 & -2 & 1 \end{bmatrix}\begin{bmatrix} 1 & 2 & 3 \\ 4 & 5 & 6 \\ 7 & 8 & 10 \end{bmatrix}$$

$$= \begin{bmatrix} (-\frac{2}{3} - \frac{16}{3} + 7) & (-\frac{4}{3} - \frac{20}{3} + 8) & (-\frac{6}{3} - \frac{24}{3} + 10) \\ (-\frac{2}{3} + \frac{44}{3} - 14) & (-\frac{4}{3} + \frac{55}{3} - 16) & (-\frac{6}{3} + \frac{66}{3} - 20) \\ (1 - 8 + 7) & (2 - 10 + 8) & (3 - 12 + 10) \end{bmatrix} = \begin{bmatrix} 1 & 0 & 0 \\ 0 & 1 & 0 \\ 0 & 0 & 1 \end{bmatrix}.$$

Partitioned Inversion

Sometimes we may be interested in obtaining the inverse of a matrix in partitioned form. Suppose $\mathbf{A}$ is partitioned as

$$\mathbf{A} = \begin{bmatrix} \mathbf{P}_{11} & \mathbf{P}_{12} \\ \mathbf{P}_{21} & \mathbf{P}_{22} \end{bmatrix},$$

where the dimensions of the submatrices are

$$\mathbf{P}_{11} \rightarrow M_1 \times M_1,$$
$$\mathbf{P}_{12} \rightarrow M_1 \times M_2,$$
$$\mathbf{P}_{21} \rightarrow M_2 \times M_1,$$
$$\mathbf{P}_{22} \rightarrow M_2 \times M_2.$$

Then

$$\mathbf{A}^{-1} = \begin{bmatrix} \mathbf{Q}_{11}^{-1} & -\mathbf{P}_{11}^{-1}\mathbf{P}_{12}\mathbf{Q}_{22}^{-1} \\ -\mathbf{Q}_{22}^{-1}\mathbf{P}_{21}\mathbf{P}_{11}^{-1} & \mathbf{Q}_{22}^{-1} \end{bmatrix},$$

where
$$\mathbf{Q}_{11} = \mathbf{P}_{11} - \mathbf{P}_{12}\mathbf{P}_{22}^{-1}\mathbf{P}_{21},$$
$$\mathbf{Q}_{22} = \mathbf{P}_{22} - \mathbf{P}_{21}\mathbf{P}_{11}^{-1}\mathbf{P}_{12}.$$

Note that the inverse of a block-diagonal matrix is also block-diagonal. Specifically,

(B.29)
$$\text{If } \mathbf{A} = \begin{bmatrix} \mathbf{P}_{11} & \mathbf{0} \\ \mathbf{0} & \mathbf{P}_{22} \end{bmatrix}, \quad \text{then } \mathbf{A}^{-1} = \begin{bmatrix} \mathbf{P}_{11}^{-1} & \mathbf{0} \\ \mathbf{0} & \mathbf{P}_{22}^{-1} \end{bmatrix}.$$

Further,
$$|\mathbf{A}| = |\mathbf{P}_{11} - \mathbf{P}_{12}\mathbf{P}_{22}^{-1}\mathbf{P}_{21}| \cdot |\mathbf{P}_{22}|$$
$$= |\mathbf{P}_{22} - \mathbf{P}_{21}\mathbf{P}_{11}^{-1}\mathbf{P}_{12}| \cdot |\mathbf{P}_{11}|$$

or
$$|\mathbf{A}| = |\mathbf{P}_{11}| \cdot |\mathbf{Q}_{22}|.$$

Differentiation in Matrix Notation

Let $y = f(x_1, x_2, \ldots, x_M)$ be a scalar, and let $\mathbf{x}$ be a column vector defined as
$$\mathbf{x} = \begin{bmatrix} x_1 \\ x_2 \\ \vdots \\ x_M \end{bmatrix}.$$

Then, the first partial derivative of y with respect to each element of $\mathbf{x}$ is defined as

(B.30)
$$\frac{\partial y}{\partial \mathbf{x}} = \begin{bmatrix} \dfrac{\partial y}{\partial x_1} \\ \dfrac{\partial y}{\partial x_2} \\ \vdots \\ \dfrac{\partial y}{\partial x_M} \end{bmatrix},$$

and the second partial derivative as

(B.31)
$$\frac{\partial^2 y}{\partial \mathbf{x}^2} = \begin{bmatrix} \dfrac{\partial^2 y}{\partial x_1^2} & \dfrac{\partial^2 y}{\partial x_1 \partial x_2} & \cdots & \dfrac{\partial^2 y}{\partial x_1 \partial x_M} \\ \dfrac{\partial^2 y}{\partial x_2 \partial x_1} & \dfrac{\partial^2 y}{\partial x_2^2} & \cdots & \dfrac{\partial^2 y}{\partial x_2 \partial x_M} \\ \vdots & \vdots & & \vdots \\ \dfrac{\partial^2 y}{\partial x_M \partial x_1} & \dfrac{\partial^2 y}{\partial x_M \partial x_2} & \cdots & \dfrac{\partial^2 y}{\partial x_M^2} \end{bmatrix}.$$

These basic rules can be applied to some frequently encountered cases. First, if

$$\mathbf{a} = \begin{bmatrix} a_1 \\ a_2 \\ \vdots \\ a_M \end{bmatrix}$$

where a_i $(i = 1, 2, \ldots, M)$ are constants, then

$$\text{(B.32)} \qquad \frac{\partial(\mathbf{a}'\mathbf{x})}{\partial \mathbf{x}} = \mathbf{a}.$$

This can be easily demonstrated by noting that

$$\mathbf{a}'\mathbf{x} = \sum_{i=1}^{M} a_i x_i,$$

and by using the rule (B.30). Second, if $\mathbf{A}$ is a symmetric matrix of order $M \times M$ whose typical element is a constant a_{ij}, then

$$\text{(B.33)} \qquad \frac{\partial(\mathbf{x}'\mathbf{A}\mathbf{x})}{\partial \mathbf{x}} = 2\mathbf{A}\mathbf{x}.$$

This follows from the fact that

$$\mathbf{x}'\mathbf{A}\mathbf{x} = \sum_{i=1}^{M} \sum_{j=1}^{M} a_{ij} x_i x_j,$$

and from the application of the rule of differentiation in (B.30). Finally, if $\mathbf{A}$ and $\mathbf{B}$ are two symmetric matrices whose elements are constants and whose order is $M \times M$, then

$$\text{(B.34)} \qquad \frac{\partial\left(\dfrac{\mathbf{x}'\mathbf{A}\mathbf{x}}{\mathbf{x}'\mathbf{B}\mathbf{x}}\right)}{\partial \mathbf{x}} = \frac{2(\mathbf{A}\mathbf{x})(\mathbf{x}'\mathbf{B}\mathbf{x}) - 2(\mathbf{x}'\mathbf{A}\mathbf{x})(\mathbf{B}\mathbf{x})}{(\mathbf{x}'\mathbf{B}\mathbf{x})^2}.$$

This can be proved in the same way as (B.33).

C. Asymptotic Distributions in Regression Models with Stochastic Explanatory Variables[2]

Regression models with stochastic explanatory variables are frequently encountered in econometrics. It is commonly assumed that when least squares is applied to such models it produces estimators that are asymptotically normal. The proofs of such results are not readily available in the econometrics literature, however, and

[2] This appendix section was written by E. Philip Howrey and Saul H. Hymans, Professors of Economics and Statistics, The University of Michigan.

many of the proofs that are cited or sketched apply only to special cases such as full independence of the regressors and the random disturbance. In this appendix we present a set of fairly general conditions which guarantee that the least squares estimator of the slope coefficient in a linear regression model will be normally distributed asymptotically. These conditions can accommodate a wide variety of assumptions about the stochastic nature of the explanatory variable and do not require normality of the disturbance term. We then verify that these conditions are satisfied in a number of common econometric applications.

Consider the linear regression model

$$Y_t = \alpha + \beta X_t + \varepsilon_t$$

where, for $t = 1, 2, \ldots, T$, ε_t and X_t satisfy the following assumptions.

1. The disturbances ε_t are drawn independently from a common distribution with mean zero and variance σ^2.
2. The explanatory variable X_t can be represented by the equation

   $$X_t = \mu + \sum_{j=0}^{\infty} \theta_j v_{t-j}$$

   where (a) the parameters θ_j satisfy the inequality

   $$0 < \sum_{j=0}^{\infty} |\theta_j| < \infty,$$

   (b) the random variables v_t are drawn independently from a common distribution with mean zero and variance δ^2, and (c) the sample variance of X, $\Sigma(X_t - \bar{X})^2/T$, is a consistent estimator of the population variance of X.[3]
3. The random variables ε_t and v_{t-j} are independent for all values of $j \geq 0$ and for all values of $j < J$ where J is a negative integer; that is, the current value of ε is independent of current and past values of v and values of v more than $|J|$ periods in the future.

Assumption (1) is standard and requires no comment other than to emphasize that we do *not* assume that ε is drawn from a normal distribution. Assumption (2) implies that the expected value of X_t is μ and the variance of X_t is $\sigma_X^2 = \delta^2 \sum_{j=0}^{\infty} \theta_j^2$, a finite positive number. The representation of $X_t - \mu$ as a weighted average of current and past values of the random variable v is very general since it can produce nearly any pattern of correlation between X_t and X_{t+s} that would be relevant for economic data. Assumptions (2) and (3) permit us to relax the usual assumption of independence of X and ε in ways that are of importance for econometric applications. The importance of assumption (3) itself will become clear when we prove our theorem and apply it to particular econometric models.

[3] A sufficient condition for the sample variance of X_t to be consistent for the population variance is that the v_t defined in assumption (2) has a finite fourth moment. For proof, see Wayne A. Fuller, *Introduction to Statistical Time Series* (New York: Wiley, 1976), pp. 239–240.

The Basic Central Limit Theorem

Our central limit theorem is concerned with the limiting distribution of $\sqrt{T}(\hat{\beta} - \beta)$ where $\hat{\beta}$ is the least squares estimator of β.

Theorem *Assumptions (1)–(3) imply that* $\sqrt{T}\,(\hat{\beta} - \beta)$ *is asymptotically normally distributed with mean 0 and variance* σ^2/σ_X^2.

Before proving the theorem we provide a rigorous definition of the concept of convergence in distribution that is used throughout.

> **Definition.** Let X be a random variable with a known distribution, and let X_T be a random variable whose distribution can change as T changes. The statements "X_T converges in distribution to X" and "X_T is asymptotically distributed as X" mean that for all values of a and b for which $a < b$,
>
> $$\lim_{T \to \infty} P(a < X_T < b) = P(a < X < b).$$

Convergence in distribution of X_T to X means that as T increases the probability distribution of X_T becomes more like that of X. We will often use the notation "$X_T \xrightarrow{D} X$" or "$X_T \xrightarrow{D} N(0, \sigma^2)$" to indicate that X_T converges in distribution to X or X_T converges in distribution to a normal random variable with mean zero and variance σ^2.

We now turn to the proof of our basic theorem. The least squares estimator of β is written in the usual form

$$\hat{\beta} = \frac{\sum x_t' Y_t}{\sum x_t'^2} = \beta + \frac{\sum x_t' \varepsilon_t}{\sum x_t'^2}$$

where $x_t' = X_t - \overline{X}$, and we seek to establish the asymptotic distribution of

$$\sqrt{T}(\hat{\beta} - \beta) = \sqrt{T}\frac{\sum x_t'\varepsilon_t}{\sum x_t'^2} = \frac{\sqrt{T}\left[\sum x_t'\varepsilon_t/T\right]}{\sum x_t'^2/T}$$

as $T \to \infty$. We have already assumed that $\Sigma x_t'^2/T$ converges in probability to σ_X^2. Thus, the random variable $\sqrt{T}(\hat{\beta} - \beta)$ is a ratio whose denominator converges in probability to a finite nonzero constant. This implies that $\sqrt{T}(\hat{\beta} - \beta)$ will itself have an asymptotic distribution if its numerator has an asymptotic distribution. Further, if the numerator $\sqrt{T}[\Sigma x_t'\varepsilon_t/T] \xrightarrow{D} N(0,\ \sigma^2\sigma_X^2)$, it follows that $\sqrt{T}(\hat{\beta} - \beta) \xrightarrow{D} N(0,\ \sigma^2/\sigma_X^2)$.[4] What remains, therefore, is to establish that $\sqrt{T}[\Sigma x_t'\varepsilon_t/T] \xrightarrow{D} N(0,\ \sigma^2\sigma_X^2)$.

[4] This result is an application of what is frequently referred to as "Cramér's theorem," which states that if X_T is a product of the random variables u_T and V_T and u_T converges in probability to a nonzero constant u, while $V_T \xrightarrow{D} V$, then $X_T = u_T V_T \xrightarrow{D} uV$. For proof, see Harold Cramér, *Mathematical Methods of Statistics* (Princeton, NJ: Princeton University Press, 1946), pp. 254–255.

The expression $\sqrt{T}[\Sigma x_t'\varepsilon_t/T]$ can be rewritten as

$$\sqrt{T}\left[\sum x_t'\varepsilon_t/T\right] = \sqrt{T}\left[\sum (X_t - \bar{X})\varepsilon_t/T\right]$$

$$= \sqrt{T}\left[\sum \{(X_t - \mu) - (\bar{X} - \mu)\}\varepsilon_t/T\right]$$

$$= \sqrt{T}\left[\sum (X_t - \mu)\varepsilon_t/T\right] - \sqrt{T}\left[\sum (\bar{X} - \mu)\varepsilon_t/T\right]$$

$$= \sqrt{T}\left[\sum (X_t - \mu)\varepsilon_t/T\right] - (\bar{X} - \mu)\sqrt{T}(\bar{\varepsilon}).$$

Since the probability limit of $(\bar{X} - \mu)\sqrt{T}(\bar{\varepsilon})$ is zero,[5] $\sqrt{T}[\Sigma x_t'\varepsilon_t/T]$ and $\sqrt{T}[\Sigma(X_t - \mu)\varepsilon_t/T]$ will have the same limiting distribution, and we need only examine $\sqrt{T}[\Sigma(X_t - \mu)\varepsilon_t/T]$.[6]

We now make use of assumption (2) to rewrite $\sqrt{T}[\Sigma(X_t - \mu)\varepsilon_t/T]$ as follows. Since

$$X_t - \mu = \sum_{j=0}^{\infty} \theta_j v_{t-j},$$

it follows that for any positive interger k, $X_t - \mu$ can be written as

$$X_t - \mu = \sum_{0}^{k} \theta_j v_{t-j} + \sum_{k+1}^{\infty} \theta_j v_{t-j},$$

$$= X_{kt}^{*} + X_{kt}^{**}$$

where $$X_{kt}^{*} = \sum_{0}^{k} \theta_j v_{t-j} \quad \text{and} \quad X_{kt}^{**} = \sum_{k+1}^{\infty} \theta_j v_{t-j}.$$

Consequently

$$\sqrt{T}\left[\sum (X_t - \mu)\varepsilon_t/T\right] = \sqrt{T}\left[\sum X_{kt}^{*}\varepsilon_t/T\right] + \sqrt{T}\left[\sum X_{kt}^{**}\varepsilon_t/T\right].$$

We now establish the following two results, which will be used to complete the proof.

(i) For any value of T, $\text{plim}_{k\to\infty}(\sqrt{T}[\Sigma X_{kt}^{**}\varepsilon_t/T]) = 0$.
(ii) For any value of k, $\sqrt{T}[\Sigma X_{kt}^{*}\varepsilon_t/T] \xrightarrow{D} N(0, \sigma^2\delta^2 \Sigma_{j=0}^{k} \theta_j^2)$ as $T \to \infty$.

Proof of (i): The expected value of $\sqrt{T}[\Sigma X_{kt}^{**}\varepsilon_t/T]$ is

$$E\left(\sqrt{T}\left[\sum X_{kt}^{**}\varepsilon_t/T\right]\right) = \sum[E(X_{kt}^{**}\varepsilon_t)/\sqrt{T}].$$

[5] The standard (Lindeberg–Levy) Central Limit Theorem implies that $\sqrt{T}(\bar{\varepsilon})$ converges in distribution to a normal random variable. Assumption (2) guarantees that $\bar{X}$ is a consistent estimator of μ so that $\text{plim}(\bar{X} - \mu) = 0$. It follows that $(\bar{X} - \mu)\sqrt{T}(\bar{\varepsilon})$ has a zero probability limit. See, e.g., Henri Theil, *Principles of Econometrics* (New York: Wiley, 1971), p. 371.

[6] Here we make use of the result that if X_T converges in distribution to X and plim $Y_T = 0$, it follows that $X_T + Y_T$ converges in distribution to X. See, e.g., *ibid.*

Since X_{kt}^{**} depends on $v_{t-k-1}, v_{t-k-2}, \ldots$, it follows from assumption (3) that X_{kt}^{**} and ε_t are independent. Consequently,

$$E(X_{kt}^{**}\varepsilon_t) = E(X_{kt}^{**})E(\varepsilon_t) = 0,$$

and we have $E(\sqrt{T}[\Sigma X_{kt}^{**}\varepsilon_t/T]) = 0$.

Given the definition of X_{kt}^{**}, the independence of X_{kt}^{**} and ε_t, and the fact that $E(X_{kt}^{**}) = E(\varepsilon_t) = 0$, it follows that

$$\begin{aligned} \operatorname{Var}(X_{kt}^{**}\varepsilon_t) &= E[(X_{kt}^{**}\varepsilon_t)^2] \\ &= \operatorname{Var}(X_{kt}^{**}) \operatorname{Var}(\varepsilon_t) \\ &= \sigma^2\delta^2 \sum_{k+1}^{\infty} \theta_j^2. \end{aligned}$$

Further

$$\begin{aligned} \operatorname{Cov}(X_{kt}^{**}\varepsilon_t, X_{k,t-1}^{**}\varepsilon_{t-1}) &= E(X_{kt}^{**}\varepsilon_t X_{k,t-1}^{**}\varepsilon_{t-1}) \\ &= E(\varepsilon_t)E(X_{kt}^{**}X_{k,t-1}^{**}\varepsilon_{t-1}) \\ &= 0, \end{aligned}$$

since ε_t is independent of ε_{t-1}, X_{kt}^{**}, and $X_{k,t-1}^{**}$. Consequently,

$$\begin{aligned} \operatorname{Var}\left(\sqrt{T}\left[\sum X_{kt}^{**}\varepsilon_t/T\right]\right) &= \sum \operatorname{Var}(X_{kt}^{**}\varepsilon_t/\sqrt{T}) \\ &= \sum \left(\sigma^2\delta^2 \sum_{k+1}^{\infty} \theta_j^2\right)\Big/ T \\ &= \sigma^2\delta^2 \sum_{k+1}^{\infty} \theta_j^2 \\ &= \sigma^2\delta^2 \left(\sum_{j=0}^{\infty} \theta_j^2 - \sum_{j=0}^{k} \theta_j^2\right). \end{aligned}$$

It is clear from this that

$$\lim_{k\to\infty} \operatorname{Var}\left(\sqrt{T}\left[\sum X_{kt}^{**}\varepsilon_t/T\right]\right) = 0,$$

so that, regardless of the value of T, $\sqrt{T}[\Sigma X_{kt}^{**}\varepsilon_t/T]$ converges in mean square and hence in probability to zero as $k \to \infty$.

Proof of (ii): The standard central limit theorem states that if $Z_1, Z_2, \ldots, Z_T$ is a set of independent random variables drawn from the same distribution with mean zero and variance σ^2, then $\sqrt{T}(\bar{Z}) \xrightarrow{D} N(0, \sigma^2)$. A more powerful result is needed to establish the limiting distribution of $\sqrt{T}[\Sigma X_{kt}^{*}\varepsilon t/T]$, however, since $X_{kt}^{*}\varepsilon_t$ and $X_{ks}^{*}\varepsilon_s$ are uncorrelated but not independent for all $t \neq s$. The more general result that we need is that if $Z_1, Z_2, \ldots, Z_T$ is a set of uncorrelated random variables with $E(Z_t) = 0$, $\operatorname{Var}(Z_t) = \sigma^2$, and Z_t and Z_s are independent if they are separated by at least m observations where m is some positive integer, then, again, $\sqrt{T}(\bar{Z}) \xrightarrow{D} N(0, \sigma^2)$.[7]

An argument similar to that used in the proof of (i) establishes that

$$E(X^*_{kt}\varepsilon_t) = 0,$$

$$\text{Var}(X^*_{kt}\varepsilon_t) = \sigma^2\delta^2 \sum_{j=0}^{k} \theta_j^2,$$

and, for $t \neq s$,

$$\text{Cov}(X^*_{kt}\varepsilon_t, X^*_{ks}\varepsilon_s) = 0.$$

Now consider any two elements separated by m observations:

$$X^*_{kt}\varepsilon_t = \sum_{j=0}^{k} \theta_j v_{t-j}\varepsilon_t$$

$$X^*_{k,t+m}\varepsilon_{t+m} = \sum_{j=0}^{k} \theta_j v_{t+m-j}\,\varepsilon_{t+m}.$$

The vs contained in $X^*_{k,t+m}\varepsilon_{t+m}$ are $v_{t+m}, v_{t+m-1}, \ldots, v_{t+m-k}$. If we take $m = k + |J| + 1$, the vs in question become

$$v_{t+k+|J|+1}, v_{t+k+|J|}, \ldots, v_{t+|J|+1},$$

and, by assumption (3), ε_t is independent of each of these vs. This establishes the fact that $X^*_{kt}\varepsilon_t$ and $X^*_{ks}\varepsilon_s$ are independent for $|t-s| \geq k + |J| + 1$ and we conclude that $\sqrt{T}[\Sigma X^*_{kt}\varepsilon_t/T] \xrightarrow{D} N(0, \sigma^2\delta^2 \Sigma_{j=0}^{k} \theta_j^2)$.

Returning to the expression of interest,

$$\sqrt{T}\left[\sum (X_t - \mu)\varepsilon_t/T\right] = \sqrt{T}\left[\sum X^*_{kt}\varepsilon_t/T\right] + \sqrt{T}\left[\sum X^{**}_{kt}\varepsilon_t/T\right],$$

we have shown that for k sufficiently large $\sqrt{T}[\Sigma X^{**}_{kt}\varepsilon_t/T]$ is negligible, and that as T increases $\sqrt{T}[\Sigma X^*_{kt}\varepsilon_t/T] \xrightarrow{D} N(0, \sigma^2\delta^2\Sigma_{j=0}^{k}\theta_j^2)$. Under these conditions, the asymptotic distribution of $\sqrt{T}[\Sigma(X_t - \mu)\varepsilon_t/T]$ is the same as that of $\sqrt{T}[\Sigma X^*_{kt}\varepsilon_t/T]$, which in turn is obtained by letting first T and then k increase.[8] We therefore conclude that $\sqrt{T}[\Sigma(X_t - \mu)\varepsilon_t/T]$ converges in distribution to a normal random variable with

[7] See, e.g., T. W. Anderson, *The Statistical Analysis of Time Series* (New York: Wiley, 1971), pp. 427–428, for the proof of a theorem which establishes this result.

[8] The justification for this "sequential argument" is provided by a result given in Anderson (*ibid.*, p. 425), which states that if the random variable U_T can be written as

$$U_T = V_{kT} + W_{kT}$$

for $k = 1, 2, \ldots$, where V_{kT} and W_{kT} satisfy (a) $\text{plim}_{k\to\infty} W_{kT} = 0$ without regard to the value of T, (b) for any fixed value of k, $V_{kT} \xrightarrow{D} V_k$ as $T \to \infty$, and (c) $V_k \xrightarrow{D} V$ as $k \to \infty$, then $U_T \xrightarrow{D} V$ as $T \to \infty$.

mean zero and variance equal to

$$\lim_{k\to\infty} \sigma^2\delta^2 \sum_{j=0}^{k} \theta_j^2 = \sigma^2\delta^2 \sum_{j=0}^{\infty} \theta_j^2 = \sigma^2\sigma_X^2,$$

which completes the proof of the theorem.

Applications

The central limit theorem of the preceding section is directly applicable to a number of specific types of stochastic regressors that are commonly encountered in econometrics. We discuss the following special cases: (1) $X_1, X_2, \ldots, X_T$ is a random sample fully independent of ε; (2) X_t is generated by an autoregressive process and is fully independent of ε; (3) X_t is generated by a moving average process and is fully independent of ε; (4) X_t is a lagged dependent variable; (5) X_t is an endogenous variable in a diagonally recursive system; and (6) X_t is an exogenous variable to be used as an instrument in a simultaneous equations model.

Case 1. Random sample X independent of ε. In this case $X_t = \mu + v_t$ so that $\theta_0 = 1$ and $\theta_j = 0$ for all $j > 0$, and the assumptions of the theorem are satisfied. It follows from our central limit theorem that $\sqrt{T}(\hat{\beta} - \beta) \xrightarrow{D} N(0, \sigma^2/\delta^2)$.

Recall that if the disturbances are independent *normal* random variables with mean zero and variance σ^2 and the explanatory variable X_t is nonstochastic, $\hat{\beta}$ is normal with mean β and variance $\sigma^2/\Sigma x_t'^2$, so that $\sqrt{T}(\hat{\beta} - \beta)$ is normal with mean zero and variance $\sigma^2/(\Sigma x_t'^2/T)$. Our results show that in the corresponding limiting distribution of $\sqrt{T}(\hat{\beta} - \beta)$ with random sample X, $\Sigma x_t'^2/T$ is replaced by δ^2, the population variance of X.

Case 2. Autoregressive X independent of ε. If X_t satisfies the first-order equation

$$X_t - \mu = \rho(X_{t-1} - \mu) + v_t$$

with $|\rho| < 1$, it follows, by repeated substitution, that

$$X_t = \mu + \sum_{j=0}^{\infty} \rho^j v_{t-j},$$

so that $\theta_j = \rho^j$. Since $|\rho| < 1$, $\Sigma|\theta_j|$ is finite and $\Sigma\theta_j^2 = 1/(1 - \rho^2)$. Thus the assumptions of the theorem are satisfied, and we conclude that $\sqrt{T}(\hat{\beta} - \beta) \xrightarrow{D} N(0, \sigma^2(1 - \rho^2)/\delta^2)$. We merely note that a similar result holds if X_t is generated by a stable autoregressive process of any finite order.

Case 3. Moving average X independent of ε. If X_t is a moving average of the form

$$X_t = \mu + \sum_{j=0}^{q} \theta_j v_{t-j},$$

which satisfies the conditions of assumption (2), the Central Limit Theorem implies that $\sqrt{T}(\hat{\beta} - \beta) \xrightarrow{D} N[0, \sigma^2/(\delta^2\Sigma_0^q\theta_j^2)]$.

Case 4. $X_t = Y_{t-1}$. In the lagged dependent variable case, the model is

$$\begin{aligned} Y_t &= \alpha + \beta Y_{t-1} + \varepsilon_t \\ &= \alpha + \beta X_t + \varepsilon_t \qquad (|\beta| < 1), \end{aligned}$$

with

$$X_t = Y_{t-1} = \mu + \sum_{j=1}^{\infty} \beta^{j-1}\varepsilon_{t-j} = \mu + \sum_{j=0}^{\infty} \beta^j v_{t-j},$$

where $\mu = \alpha/(1-\beta)$ and $v_t = \varepsilon_{t-1}$. It is clear from the definition of v_t that ε_t and v_{t-j} are independent for all $j \geq 0$ and $j < J = -1$. Under the restriction that $|\beta| < 1$, it follows that Var $X_t = \sigma^2/(1-\beta^2)$. This case is thus similar to case 2, and we conclude that $\sqrt{T}(\hat{\beta} - \beta) \xrightarrow{D} N[0, (1-\beta^2)]$. Note that the model $Y_t = \alpha + \beta Y_{t-k} + \varepsilon_t$ $(k > 1)$ can be handled in exactly the same fashion.

Case 5. Diagonally recursive system. Suppose that X_t is an endogenous variable in the recursive system

$$\begin{aligned} X_t &= \gamma + \delta Z_t + \eta_t \\ Y_t &= \alpha + \beta X_t + \varepsilon_t \end{aligned}$$

where (a) the Z_t are drawn independently from a common distribution with mean zero and variance σ_z^2; (b) the η_t are drawn independently from a common distribution with mean zero and variance σ_η^2 and η_t and Z_s are independent for all t and s; and (c) the ε_t satisfy assumption (1) and are independent of both η_s and Z_s for all t and s. It follows that X_t can be written as $X_t = \gamma + v_t$ where $v_t = \delta Z_t + \eta_t$. Thus, v_1, v_2, . . . , v_T is a set of independent random variables drawn from a common distribution with mean zero and variance $\delta^2\sigma_z^2 + \sigma_\eta^2$ and ε_t is independent of v_s for all t and s. This case is therefore equivalent to case 1 above, and we conclude that $\sqrt{T}(\hat{\beta} - \beta) \xrightarrow{D} N[0, \sigma^2/(\delta^2\sigma_z^2 + \sigma_\eta^2)]$.

Case 6. Simultaneous equations model. Consider a single equation,

$$y_t = \alpha + \beta Y_t + \varepsilon_t,$$

embedded in a simultaneous system where Y_t is also an endogenous variable. If X_t is an exogenous variable in some other equation in the model, an instrumental variable estimator of β is

$$\hat{\beta} = \frac{\sum x_t' y_t}{\sum x_t' Y_t} = \beta + \frac{\sum x_t' \varepsilon_t}{\sum x_t' Y_t},$$

and

$$\sqrt{T}(\hat{\beta} - \beta) = \frac{\sqrt{T}\left[\sum x_t'\varepsilon_t/T\right]}{\sum x_t' Y_t/T}.$$

If the ε_t satisfy assumption (1) and X_t is (a) a random sample, (b) autoregressive, or (c) a moving average, the assumptions of the central limit theorem will be satisfied so that $\sqrt{T}[\Sigma x_t'\varepsilon_t/T]$ will converge in distribution to a normal random variable with mean 0 and variance $\sigma^2\text{Var}(X_t)$. Provided that $\Sigma x_t'Y_t/T$ converges in probability to a finite nonzero constant, say, Q, we conclude that $\sqrt{T}(\hat{\beta} - \beta) \xrightarrow{D} N[0, \sigma^2\text{Var}(X_t)/Q^2]$.

The proof of the basic central limit theorem can also be used to establish the asymptotic normality of the generalized least squares estimator of β when the ε_t disturbances are generated by an autoregressive process with known parameters as in Howrey and Hymans.[9] Further, the procedures that we have employed can be extended to show that $\sqrt{T}(\hat{\alpha} - \alpha) \xrightarrow{D} N[0, \sigma^2(\sigma_X^2 + \mu^2)/\sigma_X^2]$, where $\hat{\alpha}$ is the least squares estimator of the intercept in the stochastic regressor model, and that in fact $\sqrt{T}(\hat{\alpha} - \alpha)$ and $\sqrt{T}(\hat{\beta} - \beta)$ are asymptotically bivariate normal with zero means, the variances already indicated, and covariance $-\mu\sigma^2/\sigma_X^2$. Finally, the basic theorem can be extended to cover the case of a multiple linear regression with stochastic regressors and thereby establish the asymptotic multivariate normality of the least squares estimator of the β vector when the regressors are any mixture of autoregressive, moving average, or lagged dependent variables satisfying conditions that are generalizations of assumptions (2) and (3) as in Howrey and Hymans.[9]

[9] E. Philip Howrey and Saul H. Hymans, "A Central Limit Theorem with Applications to Econometrics." Discussion paper R-110.83, Research Seminar in Quantitative Economics, The University of Michigan, 1983.

D. Statistical Tables

Table D-1 Areas Under the Normal Distribution

z	.00	.01	.02	.03	.04	.05	.06	.07	.08	.09
0.0	.0000	.0040	.0080	.0120	.0160	.0199	.0239	.0279	.0319	.0359
0.1	.0398	.0438	.0478	.0517	.0557	.0596	.0636	.0675	.0714	.0753
0.2	.0793	.0832	.0871	.0910	.0948	.0987	.1026	.1064	.1103	.1141
0.3	.1179	.1217	.1255	.1293	.1331	.1368	.1406	.1443	.1480	.1517
0.4	.1554	.1591	.1628	.1664	.1700	.1736	.1772	.1808	.1844	.1879
0.5	.1915	.1950	.1985	.2019	.2054	.2088	.2123	.2157	.2190	.2224
0.6	.2257	.2291	.2324	.2357	.2389	.2422	.2454	.2486	.2517	.2549
0.7	.2580	.2611	.2642	.2673	.2704	.2734	.2764	.2794	.2823	.2852
0.8	.2881	.2910	.2939	.2967	.2995	.3023	.3051	.3078	.3106	.3133
0.9	.3159	.3186	.3212	.3238	.3264	.3289	.3315	.3340	.3365	.3389
1.0	.3413	.3438	.3461	.3485	.3508	.3531	.3554	.3577	.3599	.3621
1.1	.3643	.3665	.3686	.3708	.3729	.3749	.3770	.3790	.3810	.3830
1.2	.3849	.3869	.3888	.3907	.3925	.3944	.3962	.3980	.3997	.4015
1.3	.4032	.4049	.4066	.4082	.4099	.4115	.4131	.4147	.4162	.4177
1.4	.4192	.4207	.4222	.4236	.4251	.4265	.4279	.4292	.4306	.4319
1.5	.4332	.4345	.4357	.4370	.4382	.4394	.4406	.4418	.4429	.4441
1.6	.4452	.4463	.4474	.4484	.4495	.4505	.4515	.4525	.4535	.4545
1.7	.4554	.4564	.4573	.4582	.4591	.4599	.4608	.4616	.4625	.4633
1.8	.4641	.4649	.4656	.4664	.4671	.4678	.4686	.4693	.4699	.4706
1.9	.4713	.4719	.4726	.4732	.4738	.4744	.4750	.4756	.4761	.4767
2.0	.4772	.4778	.4783	.4788	.4793	.4798	.4803	.4808	.4812	.4817
2.1	.4821	.4826	.4830	.4834	.4838	.4842	.4846	.4850	.4854	.4857
2.2	.4861	.4864	.4868	.4871	.4875	.4878	.4881	.4884	.4887	.4890
2.3	.4893	.4896	.4898	.4901	.4904	.4906	.4909	.4911	.4913	.4916
2.4	.4918	.4920	.4922	.4925	.4927	.4929	.4831	.4932	.4934	.4936
2.5	.4938	.4940	.4941	.4943	.4945	.4946	.4948	.4949	.4951	.4952
2.6	.4953	.4955	.4956	.4957	.4959	.4960	.4961	.4962	.4963	.4964
2.7	.4965	.4966	.4967	.4968	.4969	.4970	.4971	.4972	.4973	.4974
2.8	.4974	.4975	.4976	.4977	.4977	.4978	.4979	.4979	.4980	.4981
2.9	.4981	.4982	.4983	.4984	.4984	.4985	.4985	.4986	.4986	.4986
3.0	.4987	.4987	.4987	.4988	.4988	.4989	.4989	.4989	.4990	.4990

Table D-2 Values of $t_{\alpha,\nu}$

ν	$\alpha=0.10$	$\alpha=0.05$	$\alpha=0.025$	$\alpha=0.01$	$\alpha=0.005$	ν
1	3.078	6.314	12.706	31.821	63.657	1
2	1.886	2.920	4.303	6.965	9.925	2
3	1.638	2.353	3.182	4.541	5.841	3
4	1.533	2.132	2.776	3.747	4.604	4
5	1.476	2.015	2.571	3.365	4.032	5
6	1.440	1.943	2.447	3.143	3.707	6
7	1.415	1.895	2.365	2.998	3.499	7
8	1.397	1.860	2.306	2.896	3.355	8
9	1.383	1.833	2.262	2.821	3.250	9
10	1.372	1.812	2.228	2.764	3.169	10
11	1.363	1.796	2.201	2.718	3.106	11
12	1.356	1.782	2.179	2.681	3.055	12
13	1.350	1.771	2.160	2.650	3.012	13
14	1.345	1.761	2.145	2.624	2.977	14
15	1.341	1.753	2.131	2.602	2.947	15
16	1.337	1.746	2.120	2.583	2.921	16
17	1.333	1.740	2.110	2.567	2.898	17
18	1.330	1.734	2.101	2.552	2.878	18
19	1.328	1.729	2.093	2.539	2.861	19
20	1.325	1.725	2.086	2.528	2.845	20
21	1.323	1.721	2.080	2.518	2.831	21
22	1.321	1.717	2.074	2.508	2.819	22
23	1.319	1.714	2.069	2.500	2.807	23
24	1.318	1.711	2.064	2.492	2.797	24
25	1.316	1.708	2.060	2.485	2.787	25
26	1.315	1.706	2.056	2.479	2.779	26
27	1.314	1.703	2.052	2.473	2.771	27
28	1.313	1.701	2.048	2.467	2.763	28
29	1.311	1.699	2.045	2.462	2.756	29
inf.	1.282	1.645	1.960	2.326	2.576	inf.

This table is abridged from Table IV of R. A. Fisher, *Statistical Methods for Research Workers,* published by Oliver and Boyd Ltd., Edinburgh, by permission of the author and publishers.

Table D-3 Values of $\chi^2_{\alpha,\nu}$

ν	$\alpha = 0.995$	$\alpha = 0.99$	$\alpha = 0.975$	$\alpha = 0.95$	$\alpha = 0.05$	$\alpha = 0.025$	$\alpha = 0.01$	$\alpha = 0.005$	ν
1	0.0000393	0.000157	0.000982	0.00393	3.841	5.024	6.635	7.879	1
2	0.0100	0.0201	0.0506	0.103	5.991	7.378	9.210	10.597	2
3	0.0717	0.115	0.216	0.352	7.815	9.348	11.345	12.838	3
4	0.207	0.297	0.484	0.711	9.488	11.143	13.277	14.860	4
5	0.412	0.554	0.831	1.145	11.070	12.832	15.086	16.750	5
6	0.676	0.872	1.237	1.635	12.592	14.449	16.812	18.548	6
7	0.989	1.239	1.690	2.167	14.067	16.013	18.475	20.278	7
8	1.344	1.646	2.180	2.733	15.507	17.535	20.090	21.955	8
9	1.735	2.088	2.700	3.325	16.919	19.023	21.666	23.589	9
10	2.156	2.558	3.247	3.940	18.307	20.483	23.209	25.188	10
11	2.603	3.053	3.816	4.575	19.675	21.920	24.725	26.757	11
12	3.074	3.571	4.404	5.226	21.026	23.337	26.217	28.300	12
13	3.565	4.107	5.009	5.892	22.362	24.736	27.688	29.819	13
14	4.075	4.660	5.629	6.571	23.685	26.119	29.141	31.319	14
15	4.601	5.229	6.262	7.261	24.996	27.488	30.578	32.801	15
16	5.142	5.812	6.908	7.962	26.296	28.845	32.000	34.267	16
17	5.697	6.408	7.564	8.672	27.587	30.191	33.409	35.718	17
18	6.265	7.015	8.231	9.390	28.869	31.526	34.805	37.156	18
19	6.844	7.633	8.907	10.117	30.144	32.852	36.191	38.582	19
20	7.434	8.260	9.591	10.851	31.410	34.170	37.566	39.997	20
21	8.034	8.897	10.283	11.591	32.671	35.479	38.932	41.401	21
22	8.643	9.542	10.982	12.338	33.924	36.781	40.289	42.796	22
23	9.260	10.196	11.689	13.091	35.172	38.076	41.638	44.181	23
24	9.886	10.856	12.401	13.848	36.415	39.364	42.980	45.558	24
25	10.520	11.524	13.120	14.611	37.652	40.646	44.314	46.928	25
26	11.160	12.198	13.844	15.379	38.885	41.923	45.642	48.290	26
27	11.808	12.879	14.573	16.151	40.113	43.194	46.963	49.645	27
28	12.461	13.565	15.308	16.928	41.337	44.461	48.278	50.993	28
29	13.121	14.256	16.047	17.708	42.557	45.722	49.588	52.336	29
30	13.787	14.953	16.791	18.493	43.773	46.979	50.892	53.672	30

Based on Table 8 of *Biometrika Tables for Statisticians, Volume I.* By permission of the *Biometrika* trustees.

Table D-4A Values of $F_{0.05, \nu_1, \nu_2}$

ν_2 = degrees of freedom for denominator	ν_1 = degrees of freedom for numerator: 1	2	3	4	5	6	7	8	9	10	12	15	20	24	30	40	60	120	∞
1	161	200	216	225	230	234	237	239	241	242	244	246	248	249	250	251	252	253	254
2	18.5	19.0	19.2	19.2	19.3	19.3	19.4	19.4	19.4	19.4	19.4	19.4	19.4	19.5	19.5	19.5	19.5	19.5	19.5
3	10.1	9.55	9.28	9.12	9.01	8.94	8.89	8.85	8.81	8.79	8.74	8.70	8.66	8.64	8.62	8.59	8.57	8.55	8.53
4	7.71	6.94	6.59	6.39	6.26	6.16	6.09	6.04	6.00	5.96	5.91	5.86	5.80	5.77	5.75	5.72	5.69	5.66	5.63
5	6.61	5.79	5.41	5.19	5.05	4.95	4.88	4.82	4.77	4.74	4.68	4.62	4.56	4.53	4.50	4.46	4.43	4.40	4.37
6	5.99	5.14	4.76	4.53	4.39	4.28	4.21	4.15	4.10	4.06	4.00	3.94	3.87	3.84	3.81	3.77	3.74	3.70	3.67
7	5.59	4.74	4.35	4.12	3.97	3.87	3.79	3.73	3.68	3.64	3.57	3.51	3.44	3.41	3.38	3.34	3.30	3.27	3.23
8	5.32	4.46	4.07	3.84	3.69	3.58	3.50	3.44	3.39	3.35	3.28	3.22	3.15	3.12	3.08	3.04	3.01	2.97	2.93
9	5.12	4.26	3.86	3.63	3.48	3.37	3.29	3.23	3.18	3.14	3.07	3.01	2.94	2.90	2.86	2.83	2.79	2.75	2.71
10	4.96	4.10	3.71	3.48	3.33	3.22	3.14	3.07	3.02	2.98	2.91	2.85	2.77	2.74	2.70	2.66	2.62	2.58	2.54
11	4.84	3.98	3.59	3.36	3.20	3.09	3.01	2.95	2.90	2.85	2.79	2.72	2.65	2.61	2.57	2.53	2.49	2.45	2.40
12	4.75	3.89	3.49	3.26	3.11	3.00	2.91	2.85	2.80	2.75	2.69	2.62	2.54	2.51	2.47	2.43	2.38	2.34	2.30
13	4.67	3.81	3.41	3.18	3.03	2.92	2.83	2.77	2.71	2.67	2.60	2.53	2.46	2.42	2.38	2.34	2.30	2.25	2.21
14	4.60	3.74	3.34	3.11	2.96	2.85	2.76	2.70	2.65	2.60	2.53	2.46	2.39	2.35	2.31	2.27	2.22	2.18	2.13
15	4.54	3.68	3.29	3.06	2.90	2.79	2.71	2.64	2.59	2.54	2.48	2.40	2.33	2.29	2.25	2.20	2.16	2.11	2.07
16	4.49	3.63	3.24	3.01	2.85	2.74	2.66	2.59	2.54	2.49	2.42	2.35	2.28	2.24	2.19	2.15	2.11	2.06	2.01
17	4.45	3.59	3.20	2.96	2.81	2.70	2.61	2.55	2.49	2.45	2.38	2.31	2.23	2.19	2.15	2.10	2.06	2.01	1.96
18	4.41	3.55	3.16	2.93	2.77	2.66	2.58	2.51	2.46	2.41	2.34	2.27	2.19	2.15	2.11	2.06	2.02	1.97	1.92
19	4.38	3.52	3.13	2.90	2.74	2.63	2.54	2.48	2.42	2.38	2.31	2.23	2.16	2.11	2.07	2.03	1.98	1.93	1.88
20	4.35	3.49	3.10	2.87	2.71	2.60	2.51	2.45	2.39	2.35	2.28	2.20	2.12	2.08	2.04	1.99	1.95	1.90	1.84
21	4.32	3.47	3.07	2.84	2.68	2.57	2.49	2.42	2.37	2.32	2.25	2.18	2.10	2.05	2.01	1.96	1.92	1.87	1.81
22	4.30	3.44	3.05	2.82	2.66	2.55	2.46	2.40	2.34	2.30	2.23	2.15	2.07	2.03	1.98	1.94	1.89	1.84	1.78
23	4.28	3.42	3.03	2.80	2.64	2.53	2.44	2.37	2.32	2.27	2.20	2.13	2.05	2.01	1.96	1.91	1.86	1.81	1.76
24	4.26	3.40	3.01	2.78	2.62	2.51	2.42	2.36	2.30	2.25	2.18	2.11	2.03	1.98	1.94	1.89	1.84	1.79	1.73
25	4.24	3.39	2.99	2.76	2.60	2.49	2.40	2.34	2.28	2.24	2.16	2.09	2.01	1.96	1.92	1.87	1.82	1.77	1.71
30	4.17	3.32	2.92	2.69	2.53	2.42	2.33	2.27	2.21	2.16	2.09	2.01	1.93	1.89	1.84	1.79	1.74	1.68	1.62
40	4.08	3.23	2.84	2.61	2.45	2.34	2.25	2.18	2.12	2.08	2.00	1.92	1.84	1.79	1.74	1.69	1.64	1.58	1.51
60	4.00	3.15	2.76	2.53	2.37	2.25	2.17	2.10	2.04	1.99	1.92	1.84	1.75	1.70	1.65	1.59	1.53	1.47	1.39
120	3.92	3.07	2.68	2.45	2.29	2.18	2.09	2.02	1.96	1.91	1.83	1.75	1.66	1.61	1.55	1.50	1.43	1.35	1.25
∞	3.84	3.00	2.60	2.37	2.21	2.10	2.01	1.94	1.88	1.83	1.75	1.67	1.57	1.52	1.46	1.39	1.32	1.22	1.00

Abridged from M. Merrington and C. M. Thompson, "Tables of percentage points of the inverted beta (*F*) distribution," *Biometrika,* 33 (1943), p. 73. By permission of the *Biometrika* trustees.

Table D-4B Values of $F_{0.01, \nu_1, \nu_2}$

ν_2 = degrees of freedom for denominator	ν_1 = degrees of freedom for numerator: 1	2	3	4	5	6	7	8	9	10	12	15	20	24	30	40	60	120	∞
1	4052	5000	5403	5625	5764	5859	5928	5982	6023	6056	6106	6157	6209	6235	6261	6287	6313	6339	6366
2	98.5	99.0	99.2	99.2	99.3	99.3	99.4	99.4	99.4	99.4	99.4	99.4	99.4	99.5	99.5	99.5	99.5	99.5	99.5
3	34.1	30.8	29.5	28.7	28.2	27.9	27.7	27.5	27.3	27.2	27.1	26.9	26.7	26.6	26.5	26.4	26.3	26.2	26.1
4	21.2	18.0	16.7	16.0	15.5	15.2	15.0	14.8	14.7	14.5	14.4	14.2	14.0	13.9	13.8	13.7	13.7	13.6	13.5
5	16.3	13.3	12.1	11.4	11.0	10.7	10.5	10.3	10.2	10.1	9.89	9.72	9.55	9.47	9.38	9.29	9.20	9.11	9.02
6	13.7	10.9	9.78	9.15	8.75	8.47	8.26	8.10	7.98	7.87	7.72	7.56	7.40	7.31	7.23	7.14	7.06	6.97	6.88
7	12.2	9.55	8.45	7.85	7.46	7.19	6.99	6.84	6.72	6.62	6.47	6.31	6.16	6.07	5.99	5.91	5.82	5.74	5.65
8	11.3	8.65	7.59	7.01	6.63	6.37	6.18	6.03	5.91	5.81	5.67	5.52	5.36	5.28	5.20	5.12	5.03	4.95	4.86
9	10.6	8.02	6.99	6.42	6.06	5.80	5.61	5.47	5.35	5.26	5.11	4.96	4.81	4.73	4.65	4.57	4.48	4.40	4.31
10	10.0	7.56	6.55	5.99	5.64	5.39	5.20	5.06	4.94	4.85	4.71	4.56	4.41	4.33	4.25	4.17	4.08	4.00	3.91
11	9.65	7.21	6.22	5.67	5.32	5.07	4.89	4.74	4.63	4.54	4.40	4.25	4.10	4.02	3.94	3.86	3.78	3.69	3.60
12	9.33	6.93	5.95	5.41	5.06	4.82	4.64	4.50	4.39	4.30	4.16	4.01	3.86	3.78	3.70	3.62	3.54	3.45	3.36
13	9.07	6.70	5.74	5.21	4.86	4.62	4.44	4.30	4.19	4.10	3.96	3.82	3.66	3.59	3.51	3.43	3.34	3.25	3.17
14	8.86	6.51	5.56	5.04	4.70	4.46	4.28	4.14	4.03	3.94	3.80	3.66	3.51	3.43	3.35	3.27	3.18	3.09	3.00
15	8.68	6.36	5.42	4.89	4.56	4.32	4.14	4.00	3.89	3.80	3.67	3.52	3.37	3.29	3.21	3.13	3.05	2.96	2.87
16	8.53	6.23	5.29	4.77	4.44	4.20	4.03	3.89	3.78	3.69	3.55	3.41	3.26	3.18	3.10	3.02	2.93	2.84	2.75
17	8.40	6.11	5.19	4.67	4.34	4.10	3.93	3.79	3.68	3.59	3.46	3.31	3.16	3.08	3.00	2.92	2.83	2.75	2.65
18	8.29	6.01	5.09	4.58	4.25	4.01	3.84	3.71	3.60	3.51	3.37	3.23	3.08	3.00	2.92	2.84	2.75	2.66	2.57
19	8.19	5.93	5.01	4.50	4.17	3.94	3.77	3.63	3.52	3.43	3.30	3.15	3.00	2.92	2.84	2.76	2.67	2.58	2.49
20	8.10	5.85	4.94	4.43	4.10	3.87	3.70	3.56	3.46	3.37	3.23	3.09	2.94	2.86	2.78	2.69	2.61	2.52	2.42
21	8.02	5.78	4.87	4.37	4.04	3.81	3.64	3.51	3.40	3.31	3.17	3.03	2.88	2.80	2.72	2.64	2.55	2.46	2.36
22	7.95	5.72	4.82	4.31	3.99	3.76	3.59	3.45	3.35	3.26	3.12	2.98	2.83	2.75	2.67	2.58	2.50	2.40	2.31
23	7.88	5.66	4.76	4.26	3.94	3.71	3.54	3.41	3.30	3.21	3.07	2.93	2.78	2.70	2.62	2.54	2.45	2.35	2.26
24	7.82	5.61	4.72	4.22	3.90	3.67	3.50	3.36	3.26	3.17	3.03	2.89	2.74	2.66	2.58	2.49	2.40	2.31	2.21
25	7.77	5.57	4.68	4.18	3.86	3.63	3.46	3.32	3.22	3.13	2.99	2.85	2.70	2.62	2.53	2.45	2.36	2.27	2.17
30	7.56	5.39	4.51	4.02	3.70	3.47	3.30	3.17	3.07	2.98	2.84	2.70	2.55	2.47	2.39	2.30	2.21	2.11	2.01
40	7.31	5.18	4.31	3.83	3.51	3.29	3.12	2.99	2.89	2.80	2.66	2.52	2.37	2.29	2.20	2.11	2.02	1.92	1.80
60	7.08	4.98	4.13	3.65	3.34	3.12	2.95	2.82	2.72	2.63	2.50	2.35	2.20	2.12	2.03	1.94	1.84	1.73	1.60
120	6.85	4.79	3.95	3.48	3.17	2.96	2.79	2.66	2.56	2.47	2.34	2.19	2.03	1.95	1.86	1.76	1.66	1.53	1.38
∞	6.63	4.61	3.78	3.32	3.02	2.80	2.64	2.51	2.41	2.32	2.18	2.04	1.88	1.79	1.70	1.59	1.47	1.32	1.00

Abridged from M. Merrington and C. M. Thompson, "Tables of percentage points of the inverted beta (*F*) distribution," *Biometrika,* 33 (1943), p. 73. By permission of the *Biometrika* trustees.

Table D-5A
Durbin–Watson Statistic:
5% Significance Points of
d_L and d_U

k' is the number of regressors excluding the intercept.

	$k'=1$		$k'=2$		$k'=3$		$k'=4$		$k'=5$		$k'=6$		$k'=7$		$k'=8$		$k'=9$		$k'=10$	
n	d_L	d_U	d_L	d_U	d_L	d_U	d_L	d_U	d_L	d_U	d_L	d_U	d_L	d_U	d_L	d_U	d_L	d_U	d_L	d_U
6	0.610	1.400	—	—	—	—	—	—	—	—	—	—	—	—	—	—	—	—	—	—
7	0.700	1.356	0.467	1.896	—	—	—	—	—	—	—	—	—	—	—	—	—	—	—	—
8	0.763	1.332	0.559	1.777	0.368	2.287	—	—	—	—	—	—	—	—	—	—	—	—	—	—
9	0.824	1.320	0.629	1.699	0.455	2.128	0.296	2.588	—	—	—	—	—	—	—	—	—	—	—	—
10	0.879	1.320	0.697	1.641	0.525	2.016	0.376	2.414	0.243	2.822	—	—	—	—	—	—	—	—	—	—
11	0.927	1.324	0.758	1.604	0.595	1.928	0.444	2.283	0.316	2.645	0.203	3.005	—	—	—	—	—	—	—	—
12	0.971	1.331	0.812	1.579	0.658	1.864	0.512	2.177	0.379	2.506	0.268	2.832	0.171	3.149	—	—	—	—	—	—
13	1.010	1.340	0.861	1.562	0.715	1.816	0.574	2.094	0.445	2.390	0.328	2.692	0.230	2.985	0.147	3.266	—	—	—	—
14	1.045	1.350	0.905	1.551	0.767	1.779	0.632	2.030	0.505	2.296	0.389	2.572	0.286	2.848	0.200	3.111	0.127	3.360	—	—
15	1.077	1.361	0.945	1.543	0.814	1.750	0.685	1.977	0.562	2.220	0.447	2.472	0.343	2.727	0.251	2.979	0.175	3.216	0.111	3.438
16	1.106	1.371	0.982	1.539	0.857	1.728	0.734	1.935	0.615	2.157	0.502	2.388	0.398	2.624	0.304	2.860	0.222	3.090	0.155	3.304
17	1.133	1.381	1.015	1.536	0.897	1.710	0.779	1.900	0.664	2.104	0.554	2.318	0.451	2.537	0.356	2.757	0.272	2.975	0.198	3.184
18	1.158	1.391	1.046	1.535	0.933	1.696	0.820	1.872	0.710	2.060	0.603	2.257	0.502	2.461	0.407	2.667	0.321	2.873	0.244	3.073
19	1.180	1.401	1.074	1.536	0.967	1.685	0.859	1.848	0.752	2.023	0.649	2.206	0.549	2.396	0.456	2.589	0.369	2.783	0.290	2.974
20	1.201	1.411	1.100	1.537	0.998	1.676	0.894	1.828	0.792	1.991	0.692	2.162	0.595	2.339	0.502	2.521	0.416	2.704	0.336	2.885
21	1.221	1.420	1.125	1.538	1.026	1.669	0.927	1.812	0.829	1.964	0.732	2.124	0.637	2.290	0.547	2.460	0.461	2.633	0.380	2.806
22	1.239	1.429	1.147	1.541	1.053	1.664	0.958	1.797	0.863	1.940	0.769	2.090	0.677	2.246	0.588	2.407	0.504	2.571	0.424	2.734
23	1.257	1.437	1.168	1.543	1.078	1.660	0.986	1.785	0.895	1.920	0.804	2.061	0.715	2.208	0.628	2.360	0.545	2.514	0.465	2.670
24	1.273	1.446	1.188	1.546	1.101	1.656	1.013	1.775	0.925	1.902	0.837	2.035	0.751	2.174	0.666	2.318	0.584	2.464	0.506	2.613
25	1.288	1.454	1.206	1.550	1.123	1.654	1.038	1.767	0.953	1.886	0.868	2.012	0.784	2.144	0.702	2.280	0.621	2.419	0.544	2.560
26	1.302	1.461	1.224	1.553	1.143	1.652	1.062	1.759	0.979	1.873	0.897	1.992	0.816	2.117	0.735	2.246	0.657	2.379	0.581	2.513
27	1.316	1.469	1.240	1.556	1.162	1.651	1.084	1.753	1.004	1.861	0.925	1.974	0.845	2.093	0.767	2.216	0.691	2.342	0.616	2.470
28	1.328	1.476	1.255	1.560	1.181	1.650	1.104	1.747	1.028	1.850	0.951	1.958	0.874	2.071	0.798	2.188	0.723	2.309	0.650	2.431
29	1.341	1.483	1.270	1.563	1.198	1.650	1.124	1.743	1.050	1.841	0.975	1.944	0.900	2.052	0.826	2.164	0.753	2.278	0.682	2.396
30	1.352	1.489	1.284	1.567	1.214	1.650	1.143	1.739	1.071	1.833	0.998	1.931	0.926	2.034	0.854	2.141	0.782	2.251	0.712	2.363
31	1.363	1.496	1.297	1.570	1.229	1.650	1.160	1.735	1.090	1.825	1.020	1.920	0.950	2.018	0.879	2.120	0.810	2.226	0.741	2.333
32	1.373	1.502	1.309	1.574	1.244	1.650	1.177	1.732	1.109	1.819	1.041	1.909	0.972	2.004	0.904	2.102	0.836	2.203	0.769	2.306
33	1.383	1.508	1.321	1.577	1.258	1.651	1.193	1.730	1.127	1.813	1.061	1.900	0.994	1.991	0.927	2.085	0.861	2.181	0.795	2.281
34	1.393	1.514	1.333	1.580	1.271	1.652	1.208	1.728	1.144	1.808	1.080	1.891	1.015	1.979	0.950	2.069	0.885	2.162	0.821	2.257
35	1.402	1.519	1.343	1.584	1.283	1.653	1.222	1.726	1.160	1.803	1.097	1.884	1.034	1.967	0.971	2.054	0.908	2.144	0.845	2.236
36	1.411	1.525	1.354	1.587	1.295	1.654	1.236	1.724	1.175	1.799	1.114	1.877	1.053	1.957	0.991	2.041	0.930	2.127	0.868	2.216
37	1.419	1.530	1.364	1.590	1.307	1.655	1.249	1.723	1.190	1.795	1.131	1.870	1.071	1.948	1.011	2.029	0.951	2.112	0.891	2.198
38	1.427	1.535	1.373	1.594	1.318	1.656	1.261	1.722	1.204	1.792	1.146	1.864	1.088	1.939	1.029	2.017	0.970	2.098	0.912	2.180
39	1.435	1.540	1.382	1.597	1.328	1.658	1.273	1.722	1.218	1.789	1.161	1.859	1.104	1.932	1.047	2.007	0.990	2.085	0.932	2.164
40	1.442	1.544	1.391	1.600	1.338	1.659	1.285	1.721	1.230	1.786	1.175	1.854	1.120	1.924	1.064	1.997	1.008	2.072	0.952	2.149
45	1.475	1.566	1.430	1.615	1.383	1.666	1.336	1.720	1.287	1.776	1.238	1.835	1.189	1.895	1.139	1.958	1.089	2.022	1.038	2.088
50	1.503	1.585	1.462	1.628	1.421	1.674	1.378	1.721	1.335	1.771	1.291	1.822	1.246	1.875	1.201	1.930	1.156	1.986	1.110	2.044
55	1.528	1.601	1.490	1.641	1.452	1.681	1.414	1.724	1.374	1.768	1.334	1.814	1.294	1.861	1.253	1.909	1.212	1.959	1.170	2.010
60	1.549	1.616	1.514	1.652	1.480	1.689	1.444	1.727	1.408	1.767	1.372	1.808	1.335	1.850	1.298	1.894	1.260	1.939	1.222	1.984
65	1.567	1.629	1.536	1.662	1.503	1.696	1.471	1.731	1.438	1.767	1.404	1.805	1.370	1.843	1.336	1.882	1.301	1.923	1.266	1.964
70	1.583	1.641	1.554	1.672	1.525	1.703	1.494	1.735	1.464	1.768	1.433	1.802	1.401	1.837	1.369	1.873	1.337	1.910	1.305	1.948
75	1.598	1.652	1.571	1.680	1.543	1.709	1.515	1.739	1.487	1.770	1.458	1.801	1.428	1.834	1.399	1.867	1.369	1.901	1.339	1.935
80	1.611	1.662	1.586	1.688	1.560	1.715	1.534	1.743	1.507	1.772	1.480	1.801	1.453	1.831	1.425	1.861	1.397	1.893	1.369	1.925
85	1.624	1.671	1.600	1.696	1.575	1.721	1.550	1.747	1.525	1.774	1.500	1.801	1.474	1.829	1.448	1.857	1.422	1.886	1.396	1.916
90	1.635	1.679	1.612	1.703	1.589	1.726	1.566	1.751	1.542	1.776	1.518	1.801	1.494	1.827	1.469	1.854	1.445	1.881	1.420	1.909
95	1.645	1.687	1.623	1.709	1.602	1.732	1.579	1.755	1.557	1.778	1.535	1.802	1.512	1.827	1.489	1.852	1.465	1.877	1.442	1.903
100	1.654	1.694	1.634	1.715	1.613	1.736	1.592	1.758	1.571	1.780	1.550	1.803	1.528	1.826	1.506	1.850	1.484	1.874	1.462	1.898
150	1.720	1.746	1.706	1.760	1.693	1.774	1.679	1.788	1.665	1.802	1.651	1.817	1.637	1.832	1.622	1.847	1.608	1.862	1.594	1.877
200	1.758	1.778	1.748	1.789	1.738	1.799	1.728	1.810	1.718	1.820	1.707	1.831	1.697	1.841	1.686	1.852	1.675	1.863	1.665	1.874

Table D-5A *(cont.)*
Durbin–Watson Statistic:
5% Significance Points of
d_L and d_U

k' is the number of regressors excluding the intercept.

	$k'=11$		$k'=12$		$k'=13$		$k'=14$		$k'=15$		$k'=16$		$k'=17$		$k'=18$		$k'=19$		$k'=20$	
n	d_L	d_U	d_L	d_U	d_L	d_U	d_L	d_U	d_L	d_U	d_L	d_U	d_L	d_U	d_L	d_U	d_L	d_U	d_L	d_U
16	0.098	3.503	—	—	—	—	—	—	—	—	—	—	—	—	—	—	—	—	—	—
17	0.138	3.378	0.087	3.557	—	—	—	—	—	—	—	—	—	—	—	—	—	—	—	—
18	0.177	3.265	0.123	3.441	0.078	3.603	—	—	—	—	—	—	—	—	—	—	—	—	—	—
19	0.220	3.159	0.160	3.335	0.111	3.496	0.070	3.642	—	—	—	—	—	—	—	—	—	—	—	—
20	0.263	3.063	0.200	3.234	0.145	3.395	0.100	3.542	0.063	3.676	—	—	—	—	—	—	—	—	—	—
21	0.307	2.976	0.240	3.141	0.182	3.300	0.132	3.448	0.091	3.583	0.058	3.705	—	—	—	—	—	—	—	—
22	0.349	2.897	0.281	3.057	0.220	3.211	0.166	3.358	0.120	3.495	0.083	3.619	0.052	3.731	—	—	—	—	—	—
23	0.391	2.826	0.322	2.979	0.259	3.128	0.202	3.272	0.153	3.409	0.110	3.535	0.076	3.650	0.048	3.753	—	—	—	—
24	0.431	2.761	0.362	2.908	0.297	3.053	0.239	3.193	0.186	3.327	0.141	3.454	0.101	3.572	0.070	3.678	0.044	3.773	—	—
25	0.470	2.702	0.400	2.844	0.335	2.983	0.275	3.119	0.221	3.251	0.172	3.376	0.130	3.494	0.094	3.604	0.065	3.702	0.041	3.790
26	0.508	2.649	0.438	2.784	0.373	2.919	0.312	3.051	0.256	3.179	0.205	3.303	0.160	3.420	0.120	3.531	0.087	3.632	0.060	3.724
27	0.544	2.600	0.475	2.730	0.409	2.859	0.348	2.987	0.291	3.112	0.238	3.233	0.191	3.349	0.149	3.460	0.112	3.563	0.081	3.658
28	0.578	2.555	0.510	2.680	0.445	2.805	0.383	2.928	0.325	3.050	0.271	3.168	0.222	3.283	0.178	3.392	0.138	3.495	0.104	3.592
29	0.612	2.515	0.544	2.634	0.479	2.755	0.418	2.874	0.359	2.992	0.305	3.107	0.254	3.219	0.208	3.327	0.166	3.431	0.129	3.528
30	0.643	2.477	0.577	2.592	0.512	2.708	0.451	2.823	0.392	2.937	0.337	3.050	0.286	3.160	0.238	3.266	0.195	3.368	0.156	3.465
31	0.674	2.443	0.608	2.553	0.545	2.665	0.484	2.776	0.425	2.887	0.370	2.996	0.317	3.103	0.269	3.208	0.224	3.309	0.183	3.406
32	0.703	2.411	0.638	2.517	0.576	2.625	0.515	2.733	0.457	2.840	0.401	2.946	0.349	3.050	0.299	3.153	0.253	3.252	0.211	3.348
33	0.731	2.382	0.668	2.484	0.606	2.588	0.546	2.692	0.488	2.796	0.432	2.899	0.379	3.000	0.329	3.100	0.283	3.198	0.239	3.293
34	0.758	2.355	0.695	2.454	0.634	2.554	0.575	2.654	0.518	2.754	0.462	2.854	0.409	2.954	0.359	3.051	0.312	3.147	0.267	3.240
35	0.783	2.330	0.722	2.425	0.662	2.521	0.604	2.619	0.547	2.716	0.492	2.813	0.439	2.910	0.388	3.005	0.340	3.099	0.295	3.190
36	0.808	2.306	0.748	2.398	0.689	2.492	0.631	2.586	0.575	2.680	0.520	2.774	0.467	2.868	0.417	2.961	0.369	3.053	0.323	3.142
37	0.831	2.285	0.772	2.374	0.714	2.464	0.657	2.555	0.602	2.646	0.548	2.738	0.495	2.829	0.445	2.920	0.397	3.009	0.351	3.097
38	0.854	2.265	0.796	2.351	0.739	2.438	0.683	2.526	0.628	2.614	0.575	2.703	0.522	2.792	0.472	2.880	0.424	2.968	0.378	3.054
39	0.875	2.246	0.819	2.329	0.763	2.413	0.707	2.499	0.653	2.585	0.600	2.671	0.549	2.757	0.499	2.843	0.451	2.929	0.404	3.013
40	0.896	2.228	0.840	2.309	0.785	2.391	0.731	2.473	0.678	2.557	0.626	2.641	0.575	2.724	0.525	2.808	0.477	2.892	0.430	2.974
45	0.988	2.156	0.938	2.225	0.887	2.296	0.838	2.367	0.788	2.439	0.740	2.512	0.692	2.586	0.644	2.659	0.598	2.733	0.553	2.807
50	1.064	2.103	1.019	2.163	0.973	2.225	0.927	2.287	0.882	2.350	0.836	2.414	0.792	2.479	0.747	2.544	0.703	2.610	0.660	2.675
55	1.129	2.062	1.087	2.116	1.045	2.170	1.003	2.225	0.961	2.281	0.919	2.338	0.877	2.396	0.836	2.454	0.795	2.512	0.754	2.571
60	1.184	2.031	1.145	2.079	1.106	2.127	1.068	2.177	1.029	2.227	0.990	2.278	0.951	2.330	0.913	2.382	0.874	2.434	0.836	2.487
65	1.231	2.006	1.195	2.049	1.160	2.093	1.124	2.138	1.088	2.183	1.052	2.229	1.016	2.276	0.980	2.323	0.944	2.371	0.908	2.419
70	1.272	1.986	1.239	2.026	1.206	2.066	1.172	2.106	1.139	2.148	1.105	2.189	1.072	2.232	1.038	2.275	1.005	2.318	0.971	2.362
75	1.308	1.970	1.277	2.006	1.247	2.043	1.215	2.080	1.184	2.118	1.153	2.156	1.121	2.195	1.090	2.235	1.058	2.275	1.027	2.315
80	1.340	1.957	1.311	1.991	1.283	2.024	1.253	2.059	1.224	2.093	1.195	2.129	1.165	2.165	1.136	2.201	1.106	2.238	1.076	2.275
85	1.369	1.946	1.342	1.977	1.315	2.009	1.287	2.040	1.260	2.073	1.232	2.105	1.205	2.139	1.177	2.172	1.149	2.206	1.121	2.241
90	1.395	1.937	1.369	1.966	1.344	1.995	1.318	2.025	1.292	2.055	1.266	2.085	1.240	2.116	1.213	2.148	1.187	2.179	1.160	2.211
95	1.418	1.929	1.394	1.956	1.370	1.984	1.345	2.012	1.321	2.040	1.296	2.068	1.271	2.097	1.247	2.126	1.222	2.156	1.197	2.186
100	1.439	1.923	1.416	1.948	1.393	1.974	1.371	2.000	1.347	2.026	1.324	2.053	1.301	2.080	1.277	2.108	1.253	2.135	1.229	2.164
150	1.579	1.892	1.564	1.908	1.550	1.924	1.535	1.940	1.519	1.956	1.504	1.972	1.489	1.989	1.474	2.006	1.458	2.023	1.443	2.040
200	1.654	1.885	1.643	1.896	1.632	1.908	1.621	1.919	1.610	1.931	1.599	1.943	1.588	1.955	1.576	1.967	1.565	1.979	1.554	1.991

From N. E. Savin and K. J. White, "The Durbin–Watson Test for Serial Correlation with Extreme Sample Sizes or Many Regressors," *Econometrica*, 45 (November 1977), pp. 1989–1996. Corrections: R. W. Farebrother, *Econometrica*, 48 (September 1980), p. 1554. Reprinted by permission of The Econometric Society.

Table D-5B
Durbin–Watson Statistic: 2.5% Significance Points of d_L and d_U

k' is the number of regressors excluding the intercept.

	$k'=1$		$k'=2$		$k'=3$		$k'=4$		$k'=5$		$k'=6$		$k'=7$		$k'=8$		$k'=9$		$k'=10$	
n	d_L	d_U	d_L	d_U	d_L	d_U	d_L	d_U	d_L	d_U	d_L	d_U	d_L	d_U	d_L	d_U	d_L	d_U	d_L	d_U
6	0.489	1.258	—	—	—	—	—	—	—	—	—	—	—	—	—	—	—	—	—	—
7	0.564	1.191	0.372	1.775	—	—	—	—	—	—	—	—	—	—	—	—	—	—	—	—
8	0.633	1.172	0.450	1.628	0.291	2.184	—	—	—	—	—	—	—	—	—	—	—	—	—	—
9	0.690	1.163	0.520	1.547	0.365	1.997	0.234	2.502	—	—	—	—	—	—	—	—	—	—	—	—
10	0.744	1.165	0.582	1.493	0.433	1.877	0.302	2.300	0.192	2.749	—	—	—	—	—	—	—	—	—	—
11	0.793	1.172	0.640	1.456	0.495	1.791	0.366	2.158	0.253	2.545	0.160	2.943	—	—	—	—	—	—	—	—
12	0.838	1.183	0.693	1.433	0.555	1.725	0.426	2.051	0.312	2.394	0.215	2.745	0.135	3.096	—	—	—	—	—	—
13	0.878	1.196	0.742	1.418	0.609	1.677	0.484	1.966	0.369	2.276	0.269	2.592	0.185	2.909	0.115	3.219	—	—	—	—
14	0.915	1.209	0.786	1.409	0.659	1.641	0.538	1.900	0.425	2.178	0.323	2.468	0.234	2.759	0.160	3.044	0.100	3.320	—	—
15	0.949	1.222	0.827	1.405	0.706	1.614	0.589	1.848	0.478	2.099	0.376	2.363	0.284	2.633	0.206	2.899	0.141	3.156	0.087	3.403
16	0.980	1.235	0.864	1.403	0.749	1.594	0.636	1.806	0.528	2.035	0.427	2.276	0.334	2.525	0.252	2.775	0.182	3.018	0.124	3.251
17	1.009	1.249	0.898	1.403	0.788	1.578	0.680	1.773	0.575	1.983	0.475	2.204	0.383	2.434	0.299	2.666	0.225	2.897	0.162	3.119
18	1.035	1.261	0.930	1.405	0.825	1.567	0.720	1.746	0.619	1.939	0.521	2.143	0.430	2.356	0.345	2.572	0.269	2.790	0.202	3.003
19	1.060	1.274	0.960	1.407	0.859	1.558	0.758	1.723	0.660	1.902	0.565	2.092	0.475	2.289	0.390	2.491	0.313	2.695	0.243	2.898
20	1.083	1.286	0.987	1.411	0.890	1.551	0.794	1.705	0.699	1.871	0.606	2.047	0.517	2.231	0.434	2.420	0.356	2.612	0.285	2.804
21	1.104	1.297	1.013	1.415	0.920	1.546	0.827	1.690	0.735	1.845	0.645	2.009	0.558	2.181	0.475	2.359	0.397	2.539	0.325	2.721
22	1.124	1.308	1.036	1.419	0.947	1.543	0.858	1.678	0.769	1.823	0.681	1.977	0.597	2.138	0.515	2.304	0.438	2.475	0.365	2.647
23	1.143	1.319	1.059	1.424	0.973	1.541	0.887	1.668	0.801	1.804	0.716	1.948	0.633	2.100	0.553	2.257	0.477	2.417	0.404	2.580
24	1.161	1.329	1.080	1.429	0.997	1.539	0.914	1.659	0.831	1.788	0.748	1.924	0.668	2.066	0.589	2.215	0.514	2.366	0.442	2.521
25	1.178	1.339	1.099	1.434	1.020	1.539	0.939	1.652	0.859	1.773	0.779	1.902	0.701	2.037	0.624	2.177	0.550	2.321	0.479	2.468
26	1.193	1.349	1.118	1.439	1.041	1.539	0.963	1.646	0.886	1.761	0.808	1.883	0.732	2.011	0.657	2.143	0.584	2.280	0.514	2.420
27	1.208	1.358	1.135	1.445	1.061	1.539	0.986	1.641	0.911	1.751	0.836	1.866	0.761	1.988	0.688	2.113	0.616	2.243	0.547	2.376
28	1.223	1.367	1.152	1.450	1.080	1.540	1.008	1.638	0.935	1.742	0.862	1.851	0.789	1.967	0.718	2.087	0.648	2.210	0.580	2.337
29	1.236	1.375	1.168	1.455	1.098	1.541	1.028	1.634	0.957	1.734	0.886	1.838	0.816	1.948	0.746	2.062	0.677	2.180	0.610	2.301
30	1.249	1.383	1.183	1.460	1.116	1.543	1.047	1.632	0.979	1.727	0.910	1.827	0.841	1.931	0.773	2.040	0.706	2.153	0.640	2.269
31	1.261	1.391	1.197	1.465	1.132	1.544	1.066	1.630	0.999	1.721	0.932	1.816	0.865	1.916	0.799	2.021	0.733	2.128	0.669	2.239
32	1.273	1.399	1.211	1.470	1.147	1.546	1.083	1.628	1.018	1.715	0.953	1.807	0.888	1.903	0.823	2.003	0.759	2.106	0.696	2.212
33	1.284	1.406	1.224	1.474	1.162	1.548	1.100	1.627	1.037	1.711	0.973	1.799	0.910	1.891	0.846	1.986	0.784	2.085	0.722	2.187
34	1.295	1.413	1.236	1.479	1.176	1.550	1.116	1.626	1.054	1.707	0.992	1.791	0.931	1.880	0.869	1.971	0.807	2.066	0.747	2.164
35	1.305	1.420	1.248	1.484	1.190	1.553	1.131	1.626	1.071	1.703	1.011	1.784	0.950	1.870	0.890	1.958	0.830	2.049	0.771	2.143
36	1.315	1.426	1.259	1.488	1.203	1.555	1.145	1.625	1.087	1.700	1.028	1.778	0.969	1.860	0.911	1.945	0.852	2.033	0.794	2.124
37	1.324	1.433	1.270	1.493	1.215	1.557	1.159	1.625	1.102	1.697	1.045	1.773	0.988	1.852	0.930	1.934	0.873	2.019	0.816	2.106
38	1.333	1.439	1.280	1.497	1.227	1.560	1.172	1.626	1.117	1.695	1.061	1.768	1.005	1.844	0.949	1.923	0.893	2.005	0.837	2.089
39	1.342	1.445	1.290	1.502	1.238	1.562	1.185	1.626	1.131	1.693	1.076	1.764	1.022	1.837	0.967	1.914	0.912	1.993	0.857	2.074
40	1.350	1.451	1.300	1.506	1.249	1.564	1.197	1.626	1.145	1.692	1.091	1.760	1.038	1.831	0.984	1.905	0.930	1.981	0.877	2.060
45	1.388	1.477	1.343	1.525	1.298	1.577	1.251	1.630	1.205	1.687	1.157	1.745	1.109	1.806	1.061	1.870	1.013	1.935	0.964	2.002
50	1.420	1.500	1.380	1.543	1.339	1.588	1.297	1.636	1.255	1.685	1.212	1.737	1.168	1.790	1.125	1.845	1.081	1.902	1.037	1.960
55	1.447	1.520	1.411	1.559	1.373	1.600	1.335	1.642	1.297	1.686	1.258	1.732	1.219	1.779	1.179	1.828	1.139	1.878	1.099	1.930
60	1.471	1.538	1.438	1.573	1.404	1.610	1.369	1.649	1.334	1.688	1.298	1.730	1.262	1.772	1.225	1.816	1.189	1.861	1.152	1.907
65	1.492	1.554	1.461	1.587	1.430	1.620	1.398	1.655	1.365	1.692	1.333	1.729	1.299	1.767	1.266	1.807	1.232	1.847	1.198	1.889
70	1.511	1.569	1.482	1.599	1.453	1.630	1.424	1.662	1.393	1.695	1.363	1.729	1.332	1.764	1.301	1.800	1.269	1.837	1.238	1.875
75	1.528	1.582	1.501	1.610	1.474	1.638	1.446	1.668	1.418	1.699	1.390	1.730	1.361	1.763	1.332	1.796	1.303	1.830	1.273	1.865
80	1.544	1.594	1.518	1.620	1.493	1.647	1.467	1.674	1.441	1.703	1.414	1.732	1.387	1.762	1.360	1.793	1.332	1.824	1.305	1.856
85	1.558	1.605	1.534	1.629	1.510	1.654	1.485	1.680	1.461	1.707	1.436	1.734	1.410	1.762	1.385	1.791	1.359	1.820	1.333	1.849
90	1.570	1.615	1.548	1.638	1.525	1.662	1.502	1.686	1.479	1.711	1.455	1.736	1.432	1.762	1.407	1.789	1.383	1.816	1.358	1.844
95	1.582	1.624	1.561	1.646	1.539	1.668	1.518	1.691	1.495	1.715	1.473	1.739	1.451	1.763	1.428	1.788	1.405	1.814	1.382	1.840
100	1.593	1.633	1.573	1.654	1.552	1.675	1.532	1.696	1.511	1.719	1.490	1.741	1.468	1.764	1.447	1.788	1.425	1.812	1.403	1.837
150	1.669	1.696	1.656	1.710	1.642	1.724	1.629	1.738	1.615	1.752	1.601	1.766	1.587	1.780	1.572	1.796	1.559	1.811	1.544	1.826
200	1.715	1.735	1.704	1.745	1.694	1.755	1.684	1.765	1.674	1.776	1.664	1.787	1.653	1.797	1.643	1.808	1.632	1.819	1.622	1.830

Table D-5B *(cont.)*
Durbin–Watson Statistic: 2.5% Significance Points of d_L and d_U

k' is the number of regressors excluding the intercept.

	$k'=11$		$k'=12$		$k'=13$		$k'=14$		$k'=15$		$k'=16$		$k'=17$		$k'=18$		$k'=19$		$k'=20$	
n	d_L	d_U	d_L	d_U	d_L	d_U	d_L	d_U	d_L	d_U	d_L	d_U	d_L	d_U	d_L	d_U	d_L	d_U	d_L	d_U
16	0.077	3.471	—	—	—	—	—	—	—	—	—	—	—	—	—	—	—	—	—	—
17	0.110	3.330	0.068	3.529	—	—	—	—	—	—	—	—	—	—	—	—	—	—	—	—
18	0.145	3.206	0.099	3.399	0.061	3.578	—	—	—	—	—	—	—	—	—	—	—	—	—	—
19	0.182	3.095	0.131	3.281	0.089	3.457	0.055	3.620	—	—	—	—	—	—	—	—	—	—	—	—
20	0.221	2.993	0.165	3.175	0.118	3.347	0.080	3.507	0.050	3.656	—	—	—	—	—	—	—	—	—	—
21	0.260	2.901	0.201	3.076	0.150	3.245	0.108	3.404	0.073	3.551	0.045	3.686	—	—	—	—	—	—	—	—
22	0.299	2.818	0.238	2.987	0.184	3.151	0.138	3.307	0.098	3.453	0.067	3.589	0.041	3.714	—	—	—	—	—	—
23	0.337	2.743	0.275	2.905	0.219	3.064	0.169	3.217	0.126	3.362	0.090	3.498	0.061	3.623	0.038	3.737	—	—	—	—
24	0.375	2.676	0.312	2.831	0.254	2.984	0.202	3.132	0.156	3.275	0.116	3.411	0.083	3.537	0.056	3.653	0.035	3.758	—	—
25	0.411	2.616	0.348	2.764	0.289	2.911	0.235	3.054	0.187	3.194	0.144	3.328	0.107	3.454	0.077	3.571	0.052	3.679	0.032	3.777
26	0.447	2.561	0.383	2.703	0.324	2.844	0.269	2.983	0.219	3.118	0.174	3.250	0.134	3.375	0.100	3.493	0.071	3.602	0.048	3.703
27	0.481	2.511	0.417	2.647	0.358	2.782	0.302	2.916	0.250	3.048	0.203	3.177	0.161	3.300	0.124	3.418	0.092	3.528	0.066	3.630
28	0.514	2.466	0.451	2.595	0.391	2.726	0.335	2.855	0.282	2.983	0.234	3.108	0.190	3.229	0.150	3.345	0.116	3.456	0.086	3.560
29	0.546	2.424	0.483	2.549	0.423	2.674	0.367	2.799	0.314	2.922	0.264	3.044	0.219	3.162	0.178	3.277	0.141	3.387	0.108	3.491
30	0.576	2.387	0.514	2.506	0.455	2.626	0.398	2.747	0.345	2.866	0.295	2.984	0.248	3.100	0.205	3.212	0.166	3.321	0.132	3.425
31	0.605	2.352	0.544	2.467	0.485	2.582	0.429	2.698	0.375	2.814	0.325	2.928	0.277	3.041	0.233	3.151	0.193	3.258	0.156	3.361
32	0.634	2.320	0.574	2.430	0.515	2.542	0.459	2.653	0.405	2.765	0.354	2.876	0.306	2.986	0.261	3.094	0.220	3.198	0.181	3.300
33	0.661	2.291	0.602	2.397	0.544	2.504	0.488	2.612	0.434	2.720	0.383	2.828	0.335	2.934	0.289	3.039	0.247	3.142	0.207	3.242
34	0.687	2.264	0.629	2.366	0.572	2.469	0.516	2.573	0.463	2.678	0.412	2.782	0.363	2.886	0.317	2.988	0.273	3.089	0.233	3.187
35	0.712	2.239	0.655	2.338	0.598	2.437	0.544	2.538	0.491	2.639	0.439	2.740	0.391	2.840	0.344	2.940	0.300	3.038	0.259	3.134
36	0.736	2.217	0.680	2.311	0.624	2.407	0.570	2.504	0.517	2.602	0.467	2.700	0.418	2.798	0.371	2.895	0.327	2.991	0.285	3.085
37	0.759	2.195	0.704	2.287	0.649	2.379	0.596	2.473	0.544	2.568	0.493	2.663	0.444	2.758	0.398	2.852	0.353	2.946	0.311	3.038
38	0.782	2.176	0.727	2.264	0.673	2.353	0.620	2.444	0.569	2.536	0.519	2.628	0.470	2.720	0.424	2.812	0.379	2.903	0.336	2.993
39	0.803	2.157	0.749	2.243	0.696	2.329	0.644	2.417	0.594	2.506	0.544	2.595	0.496	2.684	0.449	2.774	0.404	2.863	0.361	2.951
40	0.824	2.140	0.771	2.223	0.719	2.307	0.668	2.392	0.617	2.478	0.568	2.564	0.520	2.651	0.474	2.738	0.429	2.825	0.386	2.911
45	0.916	2.071	0.868	2.141	0.820	2.213	0.772	2.286	0.725	2.360	0.679	2.435	0.634	2.511	0.589	2.587	0.545	2.663	0.503	2.739
50	0.993	2.020	0.949	2.082	0.905	2.144	0.861	2.208	0.817	2.273	0.774	2.338	0.732	2.405	0.689	2.471	0.648	2.539	0.607	2.606
55	1.058	1.983	1.018	2.037	0.977	2.092	0.937	2.148	0.897	2.205	0.856	2.263	0.817	2.322	0.777	2.382	0.738	2.441	0.699	2.502
60	1.115	1.954	1.077	2.002	1.040	2.051	1.002	2.102	0.965	2.153	0.927	2.205	0.890	2.257	0.853	2.310	0.816	2.364	0.780	2.418
65	1.163	1.932	1.129	1.975	1.094	2.020	1.059	2.065	1.024	2.111	0.989	2.158	0.955	2.205	0.920	2.253	0.885	2.302	0.851	2.351
70	1.206	1.914	1.174	1.954	1.141	1.994	1.109	2.035	1.076	2.077	1.044	2.120	1.011	2.163	0.979	2.206	0.946	2.250	0.914	2.295
75	1.243	1.900	1.213	1.936	1.183	1.974	1.153	2.011	1.122	2.049	1.092	2.088	1.061	2.128	1.031	2.168	1.000	2.208	0.970	2.249
80	1.277	1.889	1.249	1.922	1.220	1.957	1.192	1.991	1.163	2.026	1.135	2.062	1.106	2.098	1.077	2.135	1.048	2.172	1.019	2.210
85	1.307	1.880	1.280	1.911	1.254	1.943	1.227	1.975	1.200	2.007	1.173	2.040	1.146	2.074	1.119	2.108	1.092	2.142	1.064	2.177
90	1.334	1.873	1.309	1.901	1.284	1.931	1.259	1.961	1.233	1.991	1.208	2.022	1.182	2.053	1.156	2.085	1.131	2.117	1.105	2.149
95	1.358	1.866	1.335	1.894	1.311	1.921	1.287	1.949	1.263	1.977	1.239	2.006	1.215	2.035	1.190	2.065	1.166	2.094	1.141	2.125
100	1.381	1.861	1.358	1.887	1.335	1.913	1.313	1.939	1.290	1.965	1.267	1.992	1.244	2.020	1.221	2.047	1.198	2.075	1.175	2.104
150	1.529	1.842	1.515	1.857	1.500	1.873	1.485	1.889	1.470	1.905	1.456	1.922	1.440	1.939	1.425	1.955	1.410	1.972	1.395	1.989
200	1.611	1.841	1.600	1.852	1.589	1.864	1.578	1.875	1.567	1.887	1.556	1.899	1.545	1.911	1.534	1.922	1.523	1.934	1.511	1.947

From Savin and White, *op. cit.*, by permission of The Econometric Society.

Table D-5C
Durbin–Watson Statistic:
1% Significance Points of
d_L and d_U

k' is the number of regressors excluding the intercept.

	$k'=1$		$k'=2$		$k'=3$		$k'=4$		$k'=5$		$k'=6$		$k'=7$		$k'=8$		$k'=9$		$k'=10$	
n	d_L	d_U	d_L	d_U	d_L	d_U	d_L	d_U	d_L	d_U	d_L	d_U	d_L	d_U	d_L	d_U	d_L	d_U	d_L	d_U
6	0.390	1.142	—	—	—	—	—	—	—	—	—	—	—	—	—	—	—	—	—	—
7	0.435	1.036	0.294	1.676	—	—	—	—	—	—	—	—	—	—	—	—	—	—	—	—
8	0.497	1.003	0.345	1.489	0.229	2.102	—	—	—	—	—	—	—	—	—	—	—	—	—	—
9	0.554	0.998	0.408	1.389	0.279	1.875	0.183	2.433	—	—	—	—	—	—	—	—	—	—	—	—
10	0.604	1.001	0.466	1.333	0.340	1.733	0.230	2.193	0.150	2.690	—	—	—	—	—	—	—	—	—	—
11	0.653	1.010	0.519	1.297	0.396	1.640	0.286	2.030	0.193	2.453	0.124	2.892	—	—	—	—	—	—	—	—
12	0.697	1.023	0.569	1.274	0.449	1.575	0.339	1.913	0.244	2.280	0.164	2.665	0.105	3.053	—	—	—	—	—	—
13	0.738	1.038	0.616	1.261	0.499	1.526	0.391	1.826	0.294	2.150	0.211	2.490	0.140	2.838	0.090	3.182	—	—	—	—
14	0.776	1.054	0.660	1.254	0.547	1.490	0.441	1.757	0.343	2.049	0.257	2.354	0.183	2.667	0.122	2.981	0.078	3.287	—	—
15	0.811	1.070	0.700	1.252	0.591	1.464	0.488	1.704	0.391	1.967	0.303	2.244	0.226	2.530	0.161	2.817	0.107	3.101	0.068	3.374
16	0.844	1.086	0.737	1.252	0.633	1.446	0.532	1.663	0.437	1.900	0.349	2.153	0.269	2.416	0.200	2.681	0.142	2.944	0.094	3.201
17	0.874	1.102	0.772	1.255	0.672	1.432	0.574	1.630	0.480	1.847	0.393	2.078	0.313	2.319	0.241	2.566	0.179	2.811	0.127	3.053
18	0.902	1.118	0.805	1.259	0.708	1.422	0.613	1.604	0.522	1.803	0.435	2.015	0.355	2.238	0.282	2.467	0.216	2.697	0.160	2.925
19	0.928	1.132	0.835	1.265	0.742	1.415	0.650	1.584	0.561	1.767	0.476	1.963	0.396	2.169	0.322	2.381	0.255	2.597	0.196	2.813
20	0.952	1.147	0.863	1.271	0.773	1.411	0.685	1.567	0.598	1.737	0.515	1.918	0.436	2.110	0.362	2.308	0.294	2.510	0.232	2.714
21	0.975	1.161	0.890	1.277	0.803	1.408	0.718	1.554	0.633	1.712	0.552	1.881	0.474	2.059	0.400	2.244	0.331	2.434	0.268	2.625
22	0.997	1.174	0.914	1.284	0.831	1.407	0.748	1.543	0.667	1.691	0.587	1.849	0.510	2.015	0.437	2.188	0.368	2.367	0.304	2.548
23	1.018	1.187	0.938	1.291	0.858	1.407	0.777	1.534	0.698	1.673	0.620	1.821	0.545	1.977	0.473	2.140	0.404	2.308	0.340	2.479
24	1.037	1.199	0.960	1.298	0.882	1.407	0.805	1.528	0.728	1.658	0.652	1.797	0.578	1.944	0.507	2.097	0.439	2.255	0.375	2.417
25	1.055	1.211	0.981	1.305	0.906	1.409	0.831	1.523	0.756	1.645	0.682	1.776	0.610	1.915	0.540	2.059	0.473	2.209	0.409	2.362
26	1.072	1.222	1.001	1.312	0.928	1.411	0.855	1.518	0.783	1.635	0.711	1.759	0.640	1.889	0.572	2.026	0.505	2.168	0.441	2.313
27	1.089	1.233	1.019	1.319	0.949	1.413	0.878	1.515	0.808	1.626	0.738	1.743	0.669	1.867	0.602	1.997	0.536	2.131	0.473	2.269
28	1.104	1.244	1.037	1.325	0.969	1.415	0.900	1.513	0.832	1.618	0.764	1.729	0.696	1.847	0.630	1.970	0.566	2.098	0.504	2.229
29	1.119	1.254	1.054	1.332	0.988	1.418	0.921	1.512	0.855	1.611	0.788	1.718	0.723	1.830	0.658	1.947	0.595	2.068	0.533	2.193
30	1.133	1.263	1.070	1.339	1.006	1.421	0.941	1.511	0.877	1.606	0.812	1.707	0.748	1.814	0.684	1.925	0.622	2.041	0.562	2.160
31	1.147	1.273	1.085	1.345	1.023	1.425	0.960	1.510	0.897	1.601	0.834	1.698	0.772	1.800	0.710	1.906	0.649	2.017	0.589	2.131
32	1.160	1.282	1.100	1.352	1.040	1.428	0.979	1.510	0.917	1.597	0.856	1.690	0.794	1.788	0.734	1.889	0.674	1.995	0.615	2.104
33	1.172	1.291	1.114	1.358	1.055	1.432	0.996	1.510	0.936	1.594	0.876	1.683	0.816	1.776	0.757	1.874	0.698	1.975	0.641	2.080
34	1.184	1.299	1.128	1.364	1.070	1.435	1.012	1.511	0.954	1.591	0.896	1.677	0.837	1.766	0.779	1.860	0.722	1.957	0.665	2.057
35	1.195	1.307	1.140	1.370	1.085	1.439	1.028	1.512	0.971	1.589	0.914	1.671	0.857	1.757	0.800	1.847	0.744	1.940	0.689	2.037
36	1.206	1.315	1.153	1.376	1.098	1.442	1.043	1.513	0.988	1.588	0.932	1.666	0.877	1.749	0.821	1.836	0.766	1.925	0.711	2.018
37	1.217	1.323	1.165	1.382	1.112	1.446	1.058	1.514	1.004	1.586	0.950	1.662	0.895	1.742	0.841	1.825	0.787	1.911	0.733	2.001
38	1.227	1.330	1.176	1.388	1.124	1.449	1.072	1.515	1.019	1.585	0.966	1.658	0.913	1.735	0.860	1.816	0.807	1.899	0.754	1.985
39	1.237	1.337	1.187	1.393	1.137	1.453	1.085	1.517	1.034	1.584	0.982	1.655	0.930	1.729	0.878	1.807	0.826	1.887	0.774	1.970
40	1.246	1.344	1.198	1.398	1.148	1.457	1.098	1.518	1.048	1.584	0.997	1.652	0.946	1.724	0.895	1.799	0.844	1.876	0.749	1.956
45	1.288	1.376	1.245	1.423	1.201	1.474	1.156	1.528	1.111	1.584	1.065	1.643	1.019	1.704	0.974	1.768	0.927	1.834	0.881	1.902
50	1.324	1.403	1.285	1.446	1.245	1.491	1.205	1.538	1.164	1.587	1.123	1.639	1.081	1.692	1.039	1.748	0.997	1.805	0.955	1.864
55	1.356	1.427	1.320	1.466	1.284	1.506	1.247	1.548	1.209	1.592	1.172	1.638	1.134	1.685	1.095	1.734	1.057	1.785	1.018	1.837
60	1.383	1.449	1.350	1.484	1.317	1.520	1.283	1.558	1.249	1.598	1.214	1.639	1.179	1.682	1.144	1.726	1.108	1.771	1.072	1.817
65	1.407	1.468	1.377	1.500	1.346	1.534	1.315	1.568	1.283	1.604	1.251	1.642	1.218	1.680	1.186	1.720	1.153	1.761	1.120	1.802
70	1.429	1.485	1.400	1.515	1.372	1.546	1.343	1.578	1.313	1.611	1.283	1.645	1.253	1.680	1.223	1.716	1.192	1.754	1.162	1.792
75	1.448	1.501	1.422	1.529	1.395	1.557	1.368	1.587	1.340	1.617	1.313	1.649	1.284	1.682	1.256	1.714	1.227	1.748	1.199	1.783
80	1.466	1.515	1.441	1.541	1.416	1.568	1.390	1.595	1.364	1.624	1.338	1.653	1.312	1.683	1.285	1.714	1.259	1.745	1.232	1.777
85	1.482	1.528	1.458	1.553	1.435	1.578	1.411	1.603	1.386	1.630	1.362	1.657	1.337	1.685	1.312	1.714	1.287	1.743	1.262	1.773
90	1.496	1.540	1.474	1.563	1.452	1.587	1.429	1.611	1.406	1.636	1.383	1.661	1.360	1.687	1.336	1.714	1.312	1.741	1.288	1.769
95	1.510	1.552	1.489	1.573	1.468	1.596	1.446	1.618	1.425	1.642	1.403	1.666	1.381	1.690	1.358	1.715	1.336	1.741	1.313	1.767
100	1.522	1.562	1.503	1.583	1.482	1.604	1.462	1.625	1.441	1.647	1.421	1.670	1.400	1.693	1.378	1.717	1.357	1.741	1.335	1.765
150	1.611	1.637	1.598	1.651	1.584	1.665	1.571	1.679	1.557	1.693	1.543	1.708	1.530	1.722	1.515	1.737	1.501	1.752	1.486	1.767
200	1.664	1.684	1.653	1.693	1.643	1.704	1.633	1.715	1.623	1.725	1.613	1.735	1.603	1.746	1.592	1.757	1.582	1.768	1.571	1.779

Table D-5C *(cont.)*
Durbin–Watson Statistic:
1% Significance Points of
d_L and d_U

k' is the number of regressors excluding the intercept.

	$k'=11$		$k'=12$		$k'=13$		$k'=14$		$k'=15$		$k'=16$		$k'=17$		$k'=18$		$k'=19$		$k'=20$	
n	d_L	d_U	d_L	d_U	d_L	d_U	d_L	d_U	d_L	d_U	d_L	d_U	d_L	d_U	d_L	d_U	d_L	d_U	d_L	d_U
16	0.060	3.446	—	—	—	—	—	—	—	—	—	—	—	—	—	—	—	—	—	—
17	0.084	3.286	0.053	3.506	—	—	—	—	—	—	—	—	—	—	—	—	—	—	—	—
18	0.113	3.146	0.075	3.358	0.047	3.557	—	—	—	—	—	—	—	—	—	—	—	—	—	—
19	0.145	3.023	0.102	3.227	0.067	3.420	0.043	3.601	—	—	—	—	—	—	—	—	—	—	—	—
20	0.178	2.914	0.131	3.109	0.092	3.297	0.061	3.474	0.038	3.639	—	—	—	—	—	—	—	—	—	—
21	0.212	2.817	0.162	3.004	0.119	3.185	0.084	3.358	0.055	3.521	0.035	3.671	—	—	—	—	—	—	—	—
22	0.246	2.729	0.194	2.909	0.148	3.084	0.109	3.252	0.077	3.412	0.050	3.562	0.032	3.700	—	—	—	—	—	—
23	0.281	2.651	0.227	2.822	0.178	2.991	0.136	3.155	0.100	3.311	0.070	3.459	0.046	3.597	0.029	3.725	—	—	—	—
24	0.315	2.580	0.260	2.744	0.209	2.906	0.165	3.065	0.125	3.218	0.092	3.363	0.065	3.501	0.043	3.629	0.027	3.747	—	—
25	0.348	2.517	0.292	2.674	0.240	2.829	0.194	2.982	0.152	3.131	0.116	3.274	0.085	3.410	0.060	3.538	0.039	3.657	0.025	3.766
26	0.381	2.460	0.324	2.610	0.272	2.758	0.224	2.906	0.180	3.050	0.141	3.191	0.107	3.325	0.079	3.452	0.055	3.572	0.036	3.682
27	0.413	2.409	0.356	2.552	0.303	2.694	0.253	2.836	0.208	2.976	0.167	3.113	0.131	3.245	0.100	3.371	0.073	3.490	0.051	3.602
28	0.444	2.363	0.387	2.499	0.333	2.635	0.283	2.772	0.237	2.907	0.194	3.040	0.156	3.169	0.122	3.294	0.093	3.412	0.068	3.524
29	0.474	2.321	0.417	2.451	0.363	2.582	0.313	2.713	0.266	2.843	0.222	2.972	0.182	3.098	0.146	3.220	0.114	3.338	0.087	3.450
30	0.503	2.283	0.447	2.407	0.393	2.533	0.342	2.659	0.294	2.785	0.249	2.909	0.208	3.032	0.171	3.152	0.137	3.267	0.107	3.379
31	0.531	2.248	0.475	2.367	0.422	2.487	0.371	2.609	0.322	2.730	0.277	2.851	0.234	2.970	0.196	3.087	0.160	3.201	0.128	3.311
32	0.558	2.216	0.503	2.330	0.450	2.446	0.399	2.563	0.350	2.680	0.304	2.797	0.261	2.912	0.221	3.026	0.184	3.137	0.151	3.246
33	0.585	2.187	0.530	2.296	0.477	2.408	0.426	2.520	0.377	2.633	0.331	2.746	0.287	2.858	0.246	2.969	0.209	3.078	0.174	3.184
34	0.610	2.160	0.556	2.266	0.503	2.373	0.452	2.481	0.404	2.590	0.357	2.699	0.313	2.808	0.272	2.915	0.233	3.022	0.197	3.126
35	0.634	2.136	0.581	2.237	0.529	2.340	0.478	2.444	0.430	2.550	0.383	2.655	0.339	2.761	0.297	2.865	0.257	2.969	0.221	3.071
36	0.658	2.113	0.605	2.210	0.554	2.310	0.504	2.410	0.455	2.512	0.409	2.614	0.364	2.717	0.322	2.818	0.282	2.919	0.244	3.019
37	0.680	2.092	0.628	2.186	0.578	2.282	0.528	2.379	0.480	2.477	0.434	2.576	0.389	2.675	0.347	2.774	0.306	2.872	0.268	2.969
38	0.702	2.073	0.651	2.164	0.601	2.256	0.552	2.350	0.504	2.445	0.458	2.540	0.414	2.637	0.371	2.733	0.330	2.828	0.291	2.923
39	0.723	2.055	0.673	2.143	0.623	2.232	0.575	2.323	0.528	2.414	0.482	2.507	0.438	2.600	0.395	2.694	0.354	2.787	0.315	2.879
40	0.744	2.039	0.694	2.123	0.645	2.210	0.597	2.297	0.551	2.386	0.505	2.476	0.461	2.566	0.418	2.657	0.377	2.748	0.338	2.838
45	0.835	1.972	0.790	2.044	0.744	2.118	0.700	2.193	0.655	2.269	0.612	2.346	0.570	2.424	0.528	2.503	0.488	2.582	0.448	2.661
50	0.913	1.925	0.871	1.987	0.829	2.051	0.787	2.116	0.746	2.182	0.705	2.250	0.665	2.318	0.625	2.387	0.586	2.456	0.548	2.526
55	0.979	1.891	0.940	1.945	0.902	2.002	0.863	2.059	0.825	2.117	0.786	2.176	0.748	2.237	0.711	2.298	0.674	2.359	0.637	2.421
60	1.037	1.865	1.001	1.914	0.965	1.964	0.929	2.015	0.893	2.067	0.857	2.120	0.822	2.173	0.786	2.227	0.751	2.283	0.716	2.338
65	1.087	1.845	1.053	1.889	1.020	1.934	0.986	1.980	0.953	2.027	0.919	2.075	0.886	2.123	0.852	2.172	0.819	2.221	0.786	2.272
70	1.131	1.831	1.099	1.870	1.068	1.911	1.037	1.953	1.005	1.995	0.974	2.038	0.943	2.082	0.911	2.127	0.880	2.172	0.849	2.217
75	1.170	1.819	1.141	1.856	1.111	1.893	1.082	1.931	1.052	1.970	1.023	2.009	0.993	2.049	0.964	2.090	0.934	2.131	0.905	2.172
80	1.205	1.810	1.177	1.844	1.150	1.878	1.122	1.913	1.094	1.949	1.066	1.984	1.039	2.022	1.011	2.059	0.983	2.097	0.955	2.135
85	1.236	1.803	1.210	1.834	1.184	1.866	1.158	1.898	1.132	1.931	1.106	1.965	1.080	1.999	1.053	2.033	1.027	2.068	1.000	2.104
90	1.264	1.798	1.240	1.827	1.215	1.856	1.191	1.886	1.166	1.917	1.141	1.948	1.116	1.979	1.091	2.012	1.066	2.044	1.041	2.077
95	1.290	1.793	1.267	1.821	1.244	1.848	1.221	1.876	1.197	1.905	1.174	1.934	1.150	1.963	1.126	1.993	1.102	2.023	1.079	2.054
100	1.314	1.790	1.292	1.816	1.270	1.841	1.248	1.868	1.225	1.895	1.203	1.922	1.181	1.949	1.158	1.977	1.136	2.006	1.113	2.034
150	1.473	1.783	1.458	1.799	1.444	1.814	1.429	1.830	1.414	1.847	1.400	1.863	1.385	1.880	1.370	1.897	1.355	1.913	1.340	1.931
200	1.561	1.791	1.550	1.801	1.539	1.813	1.528	1.824	1.518	1.836	1.507	1.847	1.495	1.860	1.484	1.871	1.474	1.883	1.462	1.896

From Savin and White, *op. cit.*, by permission of The Econometric Society.

Table D-5D Durbin–Watson Statistic for Fourth-Order Autoregression (Wallis Test): 5% Significance Points of $d_{4,L}$ and $d_{4,U}$

For regressions without quarterly dummy variables ($k = k' + 1$)

	$k'=1$		$k'=2$		$k'=3$		$k'=4$		$k'=5$	
n	$d_{4,L}$	$d_{4,U}$	$d_{4,L}$	$d_{4,U}$	$d_{4,L}$	$d_{4,U}$	$d_{4,L}$	$d_{4,U}$	$d_{4,L}$	$d_{4,U}$
16	0.774	0.982	0.662	1.109	0.549	1.275	0.435	1.381	0.350	1.532
20	0.924	1.102	0.827	1.203	0.728	1.327	0.626	1.428	0.544	1.556
24	1.036	1.189	0.953	1.273	0.867	1.371	0.779	1.459	0.702	1.565
28	1.123	1.257	1.050	1.328	0.975	1.410	0.898	1.487	0.828	1.576
32	1.192	1.311	1.127	1.373	1.061	1.443	0.993	1.511	0.929	1.587
36	1.248	1.355	1.191	1.410	1.131	1.471	1.070	1.532	1.013	1.598
40	1.295	1.392	1.243	1.442	1.190	1.496	1.135	1.550	1.082	1.609
44	1.335	1.423	1.288	1.469	1.239	1.518	1.189	1.567	1.141	1.620
48	1.369	1.451	1.326	1.493	1.281	1.537	1.236	1.582	1.191	1.630
52	1.399	1.475	1.359	1.513	1.318	1.554	1.276	1.595	1.235	1.639
56	1.426	1.496	1.389	1.532	1.351	1.569	1.312	1.608	1.273	1.648
60	1.449	1.515	1.415	1.548	1.379	1.583	1.343	1.619	1.307	1.656
64	1.470	1.532	1.438	1.563	1.405	1.596	1.371	1.629	1.337	1.664
68	1.489	1.548	1.459	1.577	1.427	1.608	1.396	1.639	1.364	1.671
72	1.507	1.562	1.478	1.589	1.448	1.618	1.418	1.648	1.388	1.678
76	1.522	1.574	1.495	1.601	1.467	1.628	1.439	1.656	1.411	1.685
80	1.537	1.586	1.511	1.611	1.484	1.637	1.457	1.663	1.431	1.691
84	1.550	1.597	1.525	1.621	1.500	1.646	1.475	1.671	1.449	1.696
88	1.562	1.607	1.539	1.630	1.515	1.654	1.490	1.677	1.466	1.702
92	1.574	1.617	1.551	1.639	1.528	1.661	1.505	1.684	1.482	1.707
96	1.584	1.626	1.563	1.647	1.541	1.668	1.519	1.690	1.496	1.712
100	1.594	1.634	1.573	1.654	1.552	1.674	1.531	1.695	1.510	1.717

For regressions including a constant term and quarterly dummy variables ($k = k'' + 4$)

	$k''=1$		$k''=2$		$k''=3$		$k''=4$		$k''=5$	
n	$d_{4,L}$	$d_{4,U}$	$d_{4,L}$	$d_{4,U}$	$d_{4,L}$	$d_{4,U}$	$d_{4,L}$	$d_{4,U}$	$d_{4,L}$	$d_{4,U}$
16	1.156	1.381	1.031	1.532	0.902	1.776	0.777	2.191	0.693	2.238
20	1.228	1.428	1.123	1.556	1.013	1.726	0.899	1.954	0.806	2.042
24	1.287	1.459	1.199	1.565	1.107	1.694	1.011	1.856	0.928	1.949
28	1.337	1.487	1.261	1.576	1.181	1.679	1.099	1.803	1.025	1.889
32	1.379	1.511	1.312	1.587	1.243	1.673	1.171	1.773	1.104	1.850
36	1.414	1.532	1.355	1.598	1.293	1.672	1.230	1.755	1.170	1.824
40	1.445	1.550	1.391	1.609	1.336	1.674	1.279	1.745	1.225	1.807
44	1.471	1.567	1.422	1.620	1.373	1.677	1.321	1.739	1.272	1.795
48	1.494	1.582	1.450	1.630	1.404	1.681	1.357	1.737	1.312	1.788
52	1.514	1.595	1.474	1.639	1.432	1.686	1.389	1.736	1.347	1.782
56	1.533	1.608	1.495	1.648	1.456	1.691	1.416	1.736	1.377	1.779
60	1.549	1.619	1.514	1.656	1.478	1.696	1.441	1.737	1.404	1.777
64	1.564	1.629	1.531	1.664	1.497	1.700	1.463	1.739	1.429	1.776
68	1.577	1.639	1.546	1.671	1.515	1.705	1.482	1.741	1.450	1.775
72	1.590	1.648	1.560	1.678	1.531	1.710	1.500	1.743	1.470	1.776
76	1.601	1.656	1.573	1.685	1.545	1.714	1.517	1.746	1.488	1.776
80	1.611	1.663	1.585	1.691	1.559	1.719	1.531	1.748	1.504	1.777
84	1.621	1.671	1.596	1.696	1.571	1.723	1.545	1.751	1.519	1.778
88	1.630	1.677	1.607	1.702	1.582	1.727	1.558	1.753	1.533	1.779
92	1.639	1.684	1.616	1.707	1.593	1.731	1.570	1.756	1.546	1.781
96	1.647	1.690	1.625	1.712	1.603	1.735	1.580	1.759	1.558	1.782
100	1.654	1.695	1.633	1.717	1.612	1.739	1.591	1.761	1.569	1.784

From K. F. Wallis, "Testing for Fourth-Order Correlation in Quarterly Regression Equations," *Econometrica,* 40 (July 1972), pp. 623–624. Reprinted by permission of The Econometric Society.

Table D-5E Durbin–Watson Statistic for Fourth-Order Autoregression (Wallis Test): 1% Significance Points of $d_{4,L}$ and $d_{4,U}$

For regressions with an intercept but without quarterly dummy variables ($k = k' + 1$).

	$k' = 1$		$k' = 2$		$k' = 3$		$k' = 4$		$k' = 5$	
n	$d_{4,L}$	$d_{4,U}$	$d_{4,L}$	$d_{4,U}$	$d_{4,L}$	$d_{4,U}$	$d_{4,L}$	$d_{4,U}$	$d_{4,L}$	$d_{4,U}$
16	0558	0.737	0.465	0.857	0.373	1.032	0.283	1.107	0.216	1.218
20	0.706	0.862	0.623	0.957	0.540	1.079	0.458	1.165	0.390	1.280
24	0.822	0.960	0.748	1.039	0.674	1.135	0.599	1.216	0.533	1.316
28	0.915	1.038	0.849	1.106	0.782	1.185	0.715	1.257	0.653	1.343
32	0.990	1.101	0.932	1.160	0.872	1.228	0.811	1.293	0.754	1.367
36	1.053	1.153	1.000	1.207	0.946	1.266	0.891	1.324	0.838	1.389
40	1.107	1.198	1.058	1.246	1.009	1.299	0.958	1.351	0.910	1.409
44	1.153	1.237	1.108	1.281	1.063	1.328	1.017	1.376	0.972	1.428
48	1.193	1.270	1.152	1.311	1.110	1.354	1.067	1.398	1.026	1.445
52	1.228	1.300	1.190	1.337	1.151	1.377	1.112	1.417	1.073	1.461
56	1.259	1.327	1.224	1.361	1.188	1.398	1.151	1.435	1.115	1.475
60	1.287	1.351	1.254	1.383	1.220	1.417	1.186	1.452	1.152	1.489
64	1.312	1.372	1.281	1.402	1.249	1.434	1.217	1.467	1.185	1.501
68	1.335	1.392	1.306	1.420	1.276	1.450	1.245	1.481	1.215	1.513
72	1.356	1.410	1.328	1.437	1.300	1.465	1.271	1.494	1.243	1.524
76	1.375	1.426	1.349	1.452	1.322	1.479	1.295	1.506	1.268	1.534
80	1.393	1.441	1.368	1.466	1.342	1.491	1.316	1.517	1.291	1.544
84	1.409	1.455	1.385	1.479	1.361	1.503	1.336	1.527	1.312	1.553
88	1.424	1.468	1.401	1.491	1.378	1.514	1.355	1.537	1.331	1.561
92	1.438	1.481	1.416	1.502	1.394	1.524	1.372	1.546	1.349	1.570
96	1.451	1.492	1.431	1.513	1.409	1.534	1.388	1.555	1.366	1.577
100	1.464	1.503	1.444	1.522	1.423	1.543	1.402	1.563	1.382	1.584

For regressions with an intercept and quarterly dummy variables ($k = k'' + 4$).

	$k'' = 1$		$k'' = 2$		$k'' = 3$		$k'' = 4$		$k'' = 5$	
n	$d_{4,L}$	$d_{4,U}$	$d_{4,L}$	$d_{4,U}$	$d_{4,L}$	$d_{4,U}$	$d_{4,L}$	$d_{4,U}$	$d_{4,L}$	$d_{4,U}$
16	0.934	1.107	0.837	1.218	0.747	1.413	0.669	2.083	0.622	2.105
20	0.991	1.165	0.900	1.280	0.808	1.454	0.716	1.752	0.640	1.815
24	1.059	1.216	0.979	1.316	0.898	1.448	0.815	1.633	0.742	1.711
28	1.118	1.257	1.048	1.343	0.977	1.448	0.904	1.583	0.837	1.661
32	1.168	1.293	1.107	1.367	1.043	1.454	0.978	1.559	0.918	1.633
36	1.212	1.324	1.157	1.389	1.100	1.463	1.042	1.550	0.987	1.616
40	1.250	1.351	1.200	1.409	1.149	1.474	1.096	1.547	1.046	1.608
44	1.284	1.376	1.238	1.428	1.191	1.485	1.143	1.548	1.097	1.604
48	1.313	1.398	1.271	1.445	1.228	1.496	1.184	1.552	1.141	1.603
52	1.339	1.417	1.300	1.461	1.261	1.507	1.220	1.557	1.180	1.604
56	1.363	1.435	1.327	1.475	1.290	1.518	1.252	1.563	1.215	1.606
60	1.384	1.452	1.350	1.489	1.316	1.528	1.281	1.570	1.246	1.609
64	1.403	1.467	1.372	1.501	1.339	1.538	1.306	1.576	1.274	1.613
68	1.421	1.481	1.391	1.513	1.361	1.547	1.330	1.582	1.299	1.617
72	1.437	1.494	1.409	1.524	1.380	1.556	1.351	1.589	1.322	1.621
76	1.452	1.506	1.425	1.534	1.398	1.564	1.371	1.595	1.343	1.625
80	1.466	1.517	1.441	1.544	1.415	1.572	1.389	1.601	1.362	1.630
84	1.479	1.527	1.455	1.553	1.430	1.579	1.405	1.607	1.380	1.634
88	1.491	1.537	1.468	1.561	1.444	1.587	1.421	1.613	1.397	1.639
92	1.502	1.546	1.480	1.570	1.458	1.593	1.435	1.618	1.412	1.643
96	1.513	1.555	1.492	1.577	1.470	1.600	1.448	1.624	1.427	1.647
100	1.523	1.563	1.502	1.584	1.482	1.606	1.461	1.629	1.440	1.651

From D. E. A. Giles and M. L. King, "Fourth-Order Autocorrelation: Further Significance Points for the Wallis Test," *Journal of Econometrics* 8 (October 1978), p. 257.

E. The Greek Alphabet

THE GREEK ALPHABET

A	α	alpha	N	ν	nu
B	β	beta	Ξ	ξ	xi
Γ	γ	gamma	O	o	omicron
Δ	δ	delta	Π	π	pi
E	ε	epsilon	P	ρ	rho
Z	ζ	zeta	Σ	σ	sigma
H	η	eta	T	τ	tau
Θ	θ	theta	Υ	υ	upsilon
I	ι	iota	Φ	ϕ	phi
K	κ	kappa	X	χ	chi
Λ	λ	lambda	Ψ	ψ	psi
M	μ	mu	Ω	ω	omega

Index